Able to Travel

True Stories by and for People with Disabilities

A ROUGH GUIDE SPECIAL

Other available Rough Guides

Amsterdam • Australia • Barcelona • Berlin • Brazil
Brittany & Normandy • Bulgaria • California & West Coast USA • Crete
Cyprus • Czech & Slovak Republics • Egypt • Europe • Florida • France
Germany • Greece • Guatemala & Belize • Holland, Belgium & Luxembourg
Hong Kong • Hungary • Ireland • Italy • Kenya • Mediterranean Wildlife
Mexico • Morocco • Nepal • New York • Paris • Peru • Poland • Portugal
Prague • Provence • Pyrenees • St Petersburg • San Francisco
Scandinavia • Sicily • Spain • Thailand • Tunisia • Turkey
Tuscany & Umbria • USA • Venice • West Africa
Women Travel • Zimbabwe & Botswana

Forthcoming
Corsica • England • Scotland • Wales

W9-ATW-375

Able to Travel Credits

Text editor:	John Fisher
Series editor:	Mark Ellingham
Editorial:	Martin Dunford, Jonathan Buckley, Greg Ward, Jules Brown, Graham Parker
Production:	Susanne Hillen, Andy Hilliard, Gail Jammy, Vivien Antwi, Melissa Flack, Alan Spicer
Publicity:	Richard Trillo
Finance:	Celia Crowley

Published 1994 by Rough Guides Ltd, 1 Mercer Street, London WC2H 9QJ.

Distributed by the Penguin Group:

Penguin Books Ltd, 27 Wrights Lane, London W8 5TZ
Penguin Books USA Inc., 375 Hudson Street, New York 10014, USA
Penguin Books Australia Ltd, 487 Maroondah Highway, PO Box 257, Ringwood, Victoria 3134, Australia
Penguin Books Canada Ltd, 10 Alcorn Avenue, Toronto, Ontario, Canada M4V 1E4
Penguin Books (NZ) Ltd, 182–190 Wairau Road, Auckland 10, New Zealand

Originally published in the United States and Canada as *The Real Guide: Able to Travel*.

Typeset in Linotron Univers and Century Old Style to an original design by Andrew Oliver.
Printed in the United Kingdom by Cox and Wyman Ltd (Reading).

Map artwork and Illustrations by Sally Davies.

624pp.
Includes index

A catalogue record for this book is available from the British Library.

ISBN 1-85828-110-5

Able to Travel

True Stories by and for People with Disabilities

A ROUGH GUIDE SPECIAL

Edited by
Alison Walsh

Associate editors
Jodi Abbott and Margaret (Peg) L. Smith

THE ROUGH GUIDES

Acknowledgements

Initial inspiration for the format of this book came from another Rough Guide Special, **Women Travel**, edited by Natania Jansz and Miranda Davies: thanks to them, and to Mark Ellingham, who helped shape the original idea.

Thanks to the hundreds of **contributors** for their accounts, information, anecdotes, and know-how. Those whose accounts are included have been acknowledged in the text—their hard graft produced the core of the book. Those who submitted material for the *Travel Notes* are also acknowledged in the text; thanks to them for taking time to put thoughts on paper. And to the many whose accounts were not included, thank you for making the effort and for your patience when decisions seemed to take forever. Special thanks to Bjo Ashwill, Norris Blackburn, Mary Allgire, Tracy Schmitt, Cathy O'Reilly, David Robbins, Thomas and Grace Tucker, Lloyd Tucker, Robert Alonzo, Dorothy Kitchen, Christine Warburton, Ro Impey, Malby Goodman, Jeanette Huber, Polly Higgins, and the family of Stephen Hunt.

The thorough research work, dedication, and good humour of **Peg Smith** in the US and **Jodi Abbott** in Canada were vital and much appreciated; thanks also to Dayna Hiemstra and Debbie Reynolds for their contributions, and to Michael Abbott for his help and hospitality. Peg Smith would like to say a sincere thank you to family and friends who supported her.

For valuable facts, figures, opinions, and encouragement, I am indebted to an army of knowledgeable people, including Ade Dobler, Susan Sygall, Sharon Riechers, Jackie West, Dina Maeckelberghe, Erin Haag, Leif Forsberg, Sonja Lindh, Sheena Taylor, Michelle Hill, Louise Hendriksen, Helen McAuley, Cathy Smart, Marc Langlois, Ed Harrison, the Duke family, Irene Shanefield, Nancy Thompson, Joanne St-Onge, Edward Antczak, Peter Shea, Steven Deitemeyer, Glenys Snow, Jeanette Resella, Barbara Shaw, Valerie Saunders, Maundy Todd, Sue Harrington, MaryEllen Collins, Gordon Couch, John Stanford, Roland Earl, Lawrence Poole, Evangeline Méthot, and Julie Plamondon. Thanks also to those involved in the travel industry who answered our pleas for information: there are too many to list, but Jane Whigham, Annalise McKean Marcus, Susan D. Harrington, Sandy Murphy, Leslie McNair, Terri Mather, Erin Mouré, Leslie D. Young, Karen Rodgers O'Neil, Beth A. Shannon, Joyce M. Hyde, Susan Morris and Anne-Marie Mooney deserve special mention.

At *Rough Guides*, I thank John Fisher for his calming influence and expert overall control of the editing and production of this book; and the rest of the team for their skill and patience.

I am grateful to Monica, Todd, and Charlein Garrett for overwhelming hospitality in BC; to Steve and Linda and their families for keeping my spirits up; to my grandparents for encouragement and the Panafax UF-311; and to my parents for constant support.

Finally, my thanks to Adam and Eva Gordon, Monte Carlo, and all at Deer Leap swimming pool—couldn't have done it without you.

Help Us Update

Able to Travel aims to give disabled travelers space to share their experiences and air their opinions. If this one works there will be a **second edition**, for which we will need new accounts and updated information for the *Practicalities* and *Travel Notes*. Anyone wishing to write, or contribute in any way, should contact Alison Walsh, c/o The Rough Guides, 1 Mercer Street, London WC2H 9QJ. Please send a brief letter first, stating where you intend to travel or what you'd like to write about.

Contents

Foreword

Introduction

555 PRACTICALITIES

For Stephen Hunt, who died in spring 1992, before writing up his last journey, from London, England to the US by plane and then overland from Los Angeles to Belize, via Mexico and Guatemala, in a used car. A gifted writer, he was addicted to travel, and his views and style exerted a strong influence during the editing of this book.

Foreword

S omeone once said that the more you travel away from home the more you learn about it, and that when you travel you learn not only about another culture but also more about who you are. For me, travel is a way to feel the intensity of life, to learn, to explore, and to see everyday life from a new perspective. Traveling around the world in my wheelchair has had its difficulties and rewards, but for those of us who have travel in our blood it's an experience we want to share with others—those with or without disabilities. I believe that those of us with disabilities need to share our stories, the information that we learned, the difficulties and the exhilarations, so that we may clear a path for others.

Travel means many things to many people. For some it's a luxurious cruise, for others it's volunteering on a community project in Central America, for some it's participating in an organized tour of Europe, but for me it's hanging a backpack from my wheelchair, having no set plans, and letting life weave its adventure for me.

Yet, it must be stated that people with disabilities are still faced with obstacles and discrimination wherever they go—from not being able to use the bathroom on a plane to encountering ignorant attitudes and people saying "you can't do this" and "you can't do that". In the US, the Americans with Disabilities Act will begin to remedy some of this discrimination by laws that will force some transportation, communications, and accommodation to become more accessible to people of all disabilities. But this will only make a small impact on travelers with disabilities who want to explore other countries.

When all of us who travel refuse to accept limitations imposed on us and demand the same rights to travel as our non-disabled peers, we begin to pave the way for others. People with disabilities need to meet each other; we need to share our stories, our lives, our experiences. When I traveled in Thailand I saw a young boy who could not walk begging in the street. Our eyes met for an instant, and for a brief moment we understood each other. Though our lives are vastly different, we still share a common experience.

This book is a way for all of us to share our stories, not only with other potential travelers with disabilities, but also with *all* travelers who love meeting new people, discovering new cultures, and tasting new foods. Perhaps it will encourage those who have only dreamed of travel, perhaps it will allow us to plan new adventures, and perhaps it will educate everyone that people with disabilities have a *right* to travel, to experience the unknown, the joys and disappointments, and the feeling that we are all part of a single planet that needs to bring its family closer together.

I hope this book will make you want to curl up with a hot chocolate on a cold day, or an ice tea on a hot day, and relive the adventures of the travelers—and perhaps look out your window and ask, "So where next?".

Susan Sygall, *Mobility International USA*

Able to Travel

A s a celebration of travel for its own sake, as a demonstration of the desire to "get away from it all" and to travel widely, freely, and independently, these stories speak for themselves. In addition, they are a source of reference, a pool of experiences, advice, opinions, recommendations, and criticisms that will not only be valuable to other travelers with disabilities, but also provide food for thought for all those involved in the travel industry—worldwide.

The division of the book into **sections** has been based on the nature and numbers of accounts received as much as on geographical boundaries or political definitions. For example, the Commonwealth of Independent States (CIS; the former Soviet Union) is included in the Northern Europe section because the account that covers travel there relates to western parts of the CIS, close to Europe. The last collection of accounts—**Travel, Tours, and Cruises**—covers a mixed bag of countries, and describes cruises, expeditions, work-related travel, and overland tours, as well as a few of the high and low points in the careers of some seasoned travelers.

The **Introduction** to each section summarizes the findings of the accounts that follow and gives an overview of the picture for travelers with disabilities in the countries covered. It picks out the problems and may offer some suggestions for change. It highlights the good points and describes the new initiatives.

The **Travel Notes** expand on points mentioned in the accounts, with additional information included where available and relevant to the contributors' stories. There may be mention of tour operators recommended by other contributors; perhaps discussion of different means of transport or types of accommodation; some addresses, contacts, and books for further research; some general points on access and facilities.

The *Travel Notes* are not standardized because every country has a different approach to providing facilities and information for visitors with disabilities (indeed, many have an indifferent approach, making this section very brief). Sometimes the notes for a number of countries are grouped in one section. The Scandinavian countries are covered this way because accounts of travel in Denmark and Finland were not received but some information and comments were submitted. In Asia the *Travel Notes* have been gathered into two sections, in Africa into one, and in The Caribbean and Latin America into one, largely because there is very little information available on these parts of the world (this does not mean they are inaccessible, but a wheelchair symbol is definitely a rare sight in the tourist literature).

The **Practicalities** section comes after the accounts and is the place to find a mixture of hard facts, comment, and criticism concerning every aspect of preparing for and enjoying a trip. There are sections on travel by air, land, and sea; a discussion of the pros and cons of group travel and of independent travel; advice on obtaining adequate travel insurance, and what equipment and medicines to take; some tips on finding suitable accommodation; guidelines explaining how to get the best out of your travel agent and how to travel successfully using mainstream operators (there's also a list of agents and tour companies that specialize in organizing travel for people with disabilities); there are scores of addresses, a list of useful books, magazines, and newsletters—and more.

All who work for the agencies that disseminate information for travelers with disabilities know that the gathering of accurate information, and committing it to print, is a nightmare task, not least because of the speed with which changes in facilities and services are being introduced. It's hard to keep up, and this book is no different to any other in that apologies must be made in advance for information which will be out of date before publication.

There have been other problems. Many in the **travel industry** have been reluctant or unable to supply information, either ignoring letters and phone calls or answering with bland generalizations that do not stand up to detailed questioning. There are clearly some operators who simply do not want to be approached by clients with disabilities, usually because they fear extra costs, extra problems, or extra work. On the whole the stories in this book show that these fears are completely unfounded.

Those members of the travel industry who *do* make efforts to accommodate people with disabilities—and their numbers are increasing—very often do not adequately **advertise their facilities** or services; they do not define them, they do not ensure that all company employees know of them, they do not get their message across. It's then a chicken-and-egg situation: people are not aware of the facilities, so do not use them, and the operator concludes that they are not needed, and ceases to offer them.

Another cause of failure is the mistaken belief that people with disabilities want **"special services"** laid on for them. In general, we do not: we want only to be accommodated within the existing framework of travel and tourism operations. In the experience of many travelers, "special" treatment often means transfer to the slow lane; it may also mean separation from traveling companions who are not disabled; and it frequently involves loss of independence—removal of barriers is preferable to provision of an alternative route that avoids the barriers but can only be negotiated with the help of someone else, particularly if assistance must come from a member of staff who already has a busy schedule.

Another familiar scenario is the blaze of publicity surrounding the introduction of a new facility or "special service", followed by a failure to incorporate this information into the **standard brochures** and tour guides—this is where travelers with disabilities wish to read about accessible facilities, not in specialist access guides which may be out of date or not comprehensive because the organizations producing them are struggling to keep afloat financially. Tour operators, tourist boards, travel agents, and accommodation and transportation operators all publish brochures—often expensively produced, and always regularly updated. If they are really serious about attracting travelers with disabilities, they must address these potential clients via these publications, and produce them on cassette and in large-print format on request.

The travel industry is slowly waking up to the disabled section of the market, however, and a number of companies and individuals are working steadily and conscientiously to accommodate travelers with disabilities. These efforts must be encouraged, and wherever we have heard good reports of services or facilities we have tried to give them adequate space in this book. Any operators who feel that they have been overlooked or misrepresented should contact the Editor and send a full description of their facilities; perhaps more important, they should ask a disabled customer who has used their facilities to write to us with their comments.

Many operators are still unwilling to ensure full provision for people with *all* types of disability. Their excuses—that improvements in accessibility are too expensive or that it is impossible to provide facilities that suit all disabled people—do not stand up. Many modifications can be made easily and cheaply, and consultation with people who have disabilities saves both time and money. Every traveler has different tastes and styles of traveling, different budgets, different requirements, and different expectations of their travels: no expense has been spared in researching the needs of able-bodied tourists; it is no less commercially sound, particularly in the light of recent downturns in some parts of the business, to explore thoroughly another section of the market.

There is plenty of help available for this research—organizations of disabled people as well as individuals with disabilities. In the US, many organizations try to encourage and direct change, including *Access for Travel*, *Paralysis Society of America*, *The Opening Door, Inc*, and *Travel Industry and Disabled Exchange* (*TIDE*). In Canada, *Kéroul* is a long-established and effective organization working in this area. In Australia there is *ACROD*, in New Zealand the *Disabled Persons Assembly* and the *New Zealand CCS*. In the UK, *Tourism for All* is a joint venture involving the national and regional tourist boards and the *Holiday Care Service*. All of these are discussed in the relevant *Travel Notes*.

A common claim is that treating a person with a disability like any other traveler is physically impossible: tour companies dismiss their programs as unsuitable or inaccessible ("why not try a specialist operator for disabled people?"); escorted bus tour operators say their trips are run to tight schedules and there's no time to load or unload a person in a wheelchair via hydraulic lift—to name but two examples. These are dubious claims, and the writers of this book make a good case for attempting the impossible, but in the meantime it is surely not too much to ask that procedures for customers with disabilities are kept **simple**, avoiding segregation; developed in **consultation** with disabled people; **made known** in honest, regularly updated, crystal-clear format, easy to obtain and preferably part of the mainstream customer literature; and constantly **reviewed** and improved.

Perhaps most important of all, these procedures must be **flexible**. The root cause of an enormous number of problems experienced by disabled travelers is the rigidity of officialdom—employees who insist that this is the way they have to do it and if it's inconvenient or uncomfortable, too bad. Two air travelers in wheelchairs are told they cannot sit in the same row on the plane because this contravenes safety regulations. A railway traveler is *told* where to sit, instead of being asked where he or she would be most comfortable. A wheelchair user is assigned a "handicap suite" on the ninth floor of a luxury hotel, leaving him to ponder his chances in the event of fire or a broken-down elevator.

Since all travelers are different, the only way to treat them is to ask how each one wishes to play it. Too often, assumptions are made and disabled travelers are bundled off to distant recesses of vehicles or stations, just because that's company policy. By asking first if the person with a disability needs any help, an opening is made; the traveler can state where he or she wants to go, and how, and the operator—who is, after all, providing a service—can make the arrangements.

This philosophy must extend beyond accommodation to include accessible public buildings, tourist attractions, transport, countryside, and information. With the passing of the **Americans with Disabilities Act** there is in the US a chance of enforcing full access, along with non-discrimination and integration—what in the past has tended to be seen as a "nice thing to do" has been enshrined in law as a right, though there remain some problems in ensuring full implementation of the Act and some powerful bodies are opposing some of its regulations. In Canada there is no legislation specifically addressing members of the travel industry, and there are problems with enforcement of the non-discrimination and human rights aspects of the Constitution, but the **National Strategy for the Integration of Persons with Disabilities** has made funds available to make transportation, housing, employment, education, and recreation more accessible.

These are signs of a move toward more coherent policy and more acceptable procedures, with the ultimate aim of **total integration** of everyone, whatever their disability, into the general marketplace of vacations and travel. There are still many parts of the world where this aim is low on the list of priorities, sometimes because ailing economies, natural disasters, wars, or famines make more pressing demands on meagre government finances. But there are also many richer nations that have yet to recognize the importance of this goal.

The achievement of true integration of people with disabilities into the travel scene will be cause for some celebration. It will entail travelers with disabilities freely choosing their vacations and traveling anywhere in the world, unrestricted by their environment. Then this book will be redundant as a source of reference—no information necessary because travelers will set off in the knowledge that they will reach their destinations in comfort, find suitable accommodation, enter all the museums, shops, restaurants, and art galleries on their itineraries, be able to use the public rest rooms and the public transportation networks, and explore the local countryside. *Able to Travel* will be nothing more than entertainment, a collection of travelers' tales, indistinguishable from those of travelers without disabilities.

Until we reach that happy state, we continue to travel, sometimes to impossible places. With or without the aid of the travel industry, often with help from passers-by and fellow travelers, we have probably visited every country in the world. We share our experiences and information in order to make travel easier for others, and we work to persuade governments and travel industries to remove the barriers. To this end, input from *anyone* with an interest in travel must be useful: every disabled traveler first and foremost, but also every companion or member of the family who travels with a person with a disability, every tour operator and travel agent, every transport operator and accommodation owner—all have a contribution to make. This book airs some of those contributions, albeit mainly from the consumer's viewpoint. It is a collection of opinions, facts, and experiences to throw into the melting pot.

A Note on Language

Each contributor has the freedom to express him/herself using whatever terms he or she is comfortable with. There is some difference of opinion over exactly which words and terms are acceptable and which are not, even within this small sample of around 100 writers. The debate concerning the use of "mental disability" versus "learning difficulties", and "handicap" versus "disability" continues, and there are differences in emphasis among people with disabilities in Britain and those in the USA and Canada, so it has been difficult to single out a system that will be acceptable to all.

We have tried to steer a middle course, to use words that portray people with disabilities in a positive and appropriate manner, drawing on the advice of our contributors, while at the same time keeping the text concise and allowing the narrative to flow. We've chosen to use "disabled" instead of "handicapped", and to avoid certain terms including "confined to a wheelchair" (unless contributors describe themselves in this way), and "physically challenged" (still favored by many specialist tour operators arranging travel for people with disabilities, although most organizations of people with disabilities support the view that a disability is a fact of life, not a challenge, and this term is merely a euphemism which avoids reality).

PART ONE

NORTH
AMERICA

Introduction

Until the passing of the **Americans with Disabilities Act** 1990 (ADA) each state in the USA was responsible for its own arrangements for provision of access and facilities, so legislation, standards of facilities, and information about them varied widely. Some states have more to do than others in order to meet ADA standards of accessibility, and there will be variations from state to state for several years to come. Nonetheless, the ADA is the envy of people with disabilities the world over. While many countries still grapple with achieving basic physical access, America has forged ahead with legislation which demands that designers, planners, operators, and employers think farther than a couple of grab bars and a few ramps—the ADA definition of disability covers everything from arthritis to tuberculosis. For travelers visiting the States from less accessible parts of the world, the ADA will spread the icing on the cake—our contributors already find much to praise on their travels.

In **Canada**, too, the general impressions are good. The Canadian Constitution's clause preventing discrimination on the basis of physical or mental disability may not carry the same weight as the detailed specifics of the ADA, but the *Independence 92 International Congress and Exposition on Disability*, held in Vancouver, was billed as the beginning of a "Decade of Action," and this sums up the mood in Canada. The Canadian government is in the process of implementing a five-year **National Strategy for the Integration of Persons with Disabilities**, which should help to remove some of the remaining barriers. It lacks a legislative timetable and is not as far-reaching as it could be, but there's plenty of activity at a local level, and Canadians with disabilities can be as forceful as their American counterparts, so there are grounds for optimism.

There is still much to be done—to remove attitudinal barriers; to dispel a lingering desire in the travel industry to segregate disabled travelers from the mainstream; to encourage transport operators currently dragging their feet over costs; to ensure effective promotion of accessible facilities. These and other familiar problems remain, and the new legislation will be most effective for newly constructed facilities; some operators of existing facilities can argue that alterations are not "readily achievable" or impossible "without undue burden or expense." And there is not enough attention paid to the provision of reliable access information concerning existing facilities.

Some reference to disabled visitors is made in an increasing number of **state or provincial tourist brochures**, and this may reflect a general trend away from providing separate access guides. But there is no evidence of a real move toward the gathering of reliable information and its incorporation into all mainstream tourist literature. If this were encouraged, information for disabled visitors would be much easier to come by. In the meantime, you'll often have a four- to six-week wait for brochures that don't tell you very much. Tourism office staff are usually highly efficient in person, and other sources, such as the *Canadian Paraplegic Association* or *Mobility International*, are very helpful. But extracting information in advance may be a slow process.

Perhaps the theory is that visitors do not need to **research**; they can simply assume that access is good wherever they are likely to go. The following accounts offer much supporting evidence for this, but many travelers appreciate and use guidebooks for disabled visitors, and there is much to be gained from good planning based on easy and quick access to such guides. As contributors point out, the USA and Canada are vast, and with a limited vacation and tight funds it's important to have at least some idea of what you want to visit, what transport to use, where to stay, and what's accessible.

Air travel is probably the most efficient way to get around, and most airlines offering domestic flights are happy to accommodate people with any form of disability, although seat pre-assignment may be problematic. For travelers who like the independence of personal transport, **adapted rental cars** are also available, but there is only one national rental company (*Hertz*) that goes out of its way to attract drivers with disabilities. If you have a bulky wheelchair to stow, or you prefer not to transfer, your best bet is an adapted van and these are not too difficult to find.

Facilities are good on the newer urban **trains**, as noted particularly in the accounts of Washington DC, San Francisco, and Vancouver. *Amtrak* scores highly for its efforts on the US national network, as does Canada's *VIA Rail*. Access is not perfect but *Amtrak* and *VIA* are ahead of many European networks. Travel on **buses** is not such an easy option. Although some cities operate accessible bus services, these are not always successful, and inter-city bus companies have so far failed to provide facilities for boarding wheelchair users on their vehicles—a recurring theme throughout this book. *Greyhound* offers a discount which allows a disabled person to travel with a companion for the price of one ticket, but will have no lift-equipped buses for several years.

There are no problems reported with using **taxis**, apart from Christine Panton's unfortunate experience (p.28), which had nothing to do with disability. Wheelchair-accessible cabs are tested in Vancouver (p.75), and on Oahu, Hawaii (p.37).

Many **boat** trips are described in these accounts, and wheelchair users managed them all. Special boarding procedures, well-designed vessels, and willing crew members make possible a ride on the famous *Maid of the Mist* under Niagara Falls, shooting rapids on the St. Lawrence, a wildlife cruise in Alaska, a dinner sunset cruise in Hawaii, and a whale-watching trip off Nova Scotia.

According to our contributors, good **access to public buildings and tourist attractions** is the norm. Carolyn Lucas found that even the caves in Frijoles Canyon, near Santa Fe, had ramped access. Visitors with disabilities can enjoy all the museums and galleries of the Smithsonian Institution in Washington DC, the casinos of Las Vegas, the scent of pine in the Canadian Rockies . . . the list is endless.

Although the praise far outweighs the criticism, however, it's not all roses. Carolyn Lucas comments on the bad road and sidewalk surfaces, high curbs, and patchy provision of ramps in New York City. Nic Fleming found that New York's accessible buses were unwilling to stop for wheelchair users. The majority of rides in Walt Disney World, Florida, are accessible to disabled people, but facilities are not so good at the original Disneyland, in California. Stephen Fuller (p.38) describes the difficulties of ascertaining exact access details from hotels before arriving.

The **rest room and bathroom facilities** in the States come under scrutiny from Arthur Goldthorpe, whose involvement with UK access committees enables him to compare designs of facilities on each side of the Atlantic.

Suitable **accommodation** seems easy to find, whatever your budget, partly thanks to the large scale of buildings. Arthur Goldthorpe and Shirley Lihou quickly located self-catering or motel accommodation once at their destinations. Those who booked ahead generally found good facilities in hotels and motels. The widespread availability of accessible accommodation is probably partly the result of the constant flow of meetings and conferences, often held at hotels, organized by the numerous **associations of disabled people**. Vigorous lobbying has forced progress in many areas, including access, housing, transport, employment, training, and education. But perhaps equally important has been the thorough exploration of both the US and Canada by their own disabled citizens, educating those in the travel industry simply by traveling—that, in the end, is what will change attitudes.

USA

Drama on the East Coast

In June 1989, after months of preparation, Carolyn Lucas started a four-month trip to the USA, funded by the Winston Churchill Memorial Trust, to undertake a study entitled "The Training and Employment of Professional Actors with Disabilities in the USA." Her husband took a sabbatical to accompany her and pursue courses of his own. This is the first of three accounts written on their return to Great Britain. Carolyn uses a wheelchair—she is capable of walking, but finds it too painful.

We were ambitious, perhaps overambitious. The plan was to spend June on the East Coast, visiting Washington DC, Boston, and New York, passing through nine states and fitting in sightseeing as well as working on the project. We had a tough start, with an eleven-hour journey to Washington via New York, changing planes and negotiating customs and immigration at the frenetic JFK airport. (A tip here: avoid flying via JFK—it's a huge airport, the staff are overworked, and the heat in summer is a killer.) One-third of the aircraft's baggage, including our own, was accidentally left there.

Once in Washington, it took us two hours, in a rented Buick, in the dark, to find our hosts' address—we had directions from the wrong airport. We had reserved our car in advance from the UK, ordering the smallest possible model, but in both Washington and Boston, when they saw me and the wheelchair plus four months' worth of luggage, they offered us a larger car. So we found ourselves cruising around in a limousine at no extra charge.

Washington DC was our base for most of the month, and the *Very Special Arts Festival* provided a focus for our stay. One of the Kennedy family started the *Very Special Arts* organization and it now runs projects all over the world. It is based at the Kennedy Center, a prestigious flat-roofed structure by the Potomac river. Why flat-roofed? According to one commentary, presidents who die of natural causes are commemorated by domes and needles; those cut down in their prime, like Kennedy and Lincoln, are awarded flat roofs.

Dancers, artists, actors, and musicians with disabilities come from countries all over the world to display their skills in this week-long festival, which also includes seminars, workshops, and exhibitions. It's a huge enterprise with funds to match, and it introduced me to new contacts as well as affording me the opportunity to meet many of the people I would come across later in my travels.

A group of sight-impaired children from London represented the UK with a choreographed circus routine. *Access Theater*, from Santa Barbara, California, performed *Storm Readings*, by a severely disabled writer appearing with his brother and a signing actress. This play was presented in the Ford Theater, where Abraham Lincoln was assassinated—the box in which he was shot is still draped in flags. One of the highlights of the festival was the perfor-mance of a play by a young writer based on her own experiences of living with muscular dystrophy. Produced by a well-known director, it was a very creditable first script which won the Henry Fonda Award.

Our first full day was the hottest June 1st ever recorded in Washington—98°F with 100 percent humidity. We had our first experience of getting hopelessly lost in Washington's obsessively over-planned road system, something we repeated several times daily for the remainder of our stay. Traffic lights by the thousand, every traffic circle quite different in design from all the others, with a forest of speed and parking signs but no directions until you have overshot your junction—once in the wrong lane and swept across the Potomac river into Virginia, you can say goodbye to Washington for the next hour or two!

So, instead of driving in Washington, check out the marvelous Metrorail system—clean and efficient—and do the rest on foot (or wheel). My appointments tended to be at opposite ends of the city and, as the Metrorail network is not extensive, my use of it was limited. But you should have no problem in seeing the main sights if you use a combination of Metrorail and the accessible buses. It was very heartening to see two guys in wheelchairs on their way to work by Metrorail—unimaginable on the London Underground.

Of all the Washington monuments, the most affecting was the Vietnam War Memorial, a black marble wall engraved with the names of the 50,000 men who died in that terrible war. Set into a grass bank in a tapering V-shape, it begins with one name and rises to hundreds in each column. Relatives were "rubbing" the engraved names, and posies and tributes littered the base. The crowds were silent as they walked away.

"You are almost guaranteed access in every building you are likely to visit"

One thing I discovered early in my visit is that federal funding to any organization is contingent on the provi-sion of full access for disabled persons to their premises. This has had such an impact on public consciousness that you are almost guaranteed access in every building you are likely to visit. Parking for disabled motorists is usually available, too, with heavy penal-ties for those who abuse it. This commitment, enshrined in legislation, has been crucial in the fight for civil rights for disabled people.

My study took me to Gallaudet Model Secondary School for the Deaf, which has an extensive theater program and sets some of its students off on a career in the performing arts. The course at Gallaudet is notable for the quality of the teaching. Well-known directors and teachers in the theater are invited to conduct workshops. On my visit a mixed group of Russian and American deaf students were taking a movement class with a member of the *Merce Cunningham Dance Company* from New York. The Russians were accompanied by their director and his wife, and were taking part in the summer school. I was told with great excitement that plans were in motion to set up a theater for the deaf in Moscow in a building recently donated by the government.

The deaf community in the USA seemed to me to be the best integrated and most successful and active in the disabled arts movement. Highly "vocal," and fighting their corner for the past twenty years, they have attained a high degree of respect in the theater world, which in turn has had its effect on public consciousness and acceptance. American Sign Language lends itself to dramatic presentation: it is expressive and lyrical, and can create a kind of poetry in movement that would be hard to achieve with the more blunt and utilitarian British Sign Language.

"It was hard not to be shocked at the evidence of human degradation as we ran the gauntlet on 42nd Street"

Reasonably priced accommodation in **New York** is difficult to come by, but we were offered rooms at a center for new playwrights, in a converted church on 44th Street, close to the theater district on Broadway. At $30 a night, as opposed to $100 in a hotel, our two small, shabby rooms were much appreciated, even if it meant hobbling up two flights of stairs.

We discovered later that the area in which we were staying, around Times Square and the bus station, is known locally as "Hell's Kitchen"—not the most salubrious in Manhattan. The first afternoon we decided to orient ourselves and walked in the immediate vicinity, taking in Grand Central Station, the Empire State and Chrysler buildings, and the Rockefeller Center. Loud, fast, brash, and steamy, New York is everything that I was ever told and, for those who live in it and love it, vital and exhilarating.

But it was hard not to be shocked at the evidence of human degradation as we ran the gauntlet on 42nd Street—junkies openly snorting coke, the homeless huddled in doorways, disturbed people of all ages turned out of mental institutions to survive on the streets. The destitute scavenge in trash cans, filling up bags and carts with empty cans and bottles, to be redeemed for cash at supermarkets.

On my arrival in New York, I was invited to a meeting of a *People with Disabilities Committee*, formed by the three entertainment unions. The meeting took place in a splendid 44th-floor suite in Times Square, overlooking the Hudson river. Everyone was very welcoming and many were anxious to tell me their own experiences of being a performer with a disability.

I was impressed by the businesslike manner in which the meeting was conducted and by the dedication of the union executives who had initiated the committee. Annual auditions are set up, open to all actors with disabilities, and casting agents and directors are invited. Screen Actors Guild, Equity, and the American Federation of Television and Radio Artistes have appointed Affirmative Action officers, who work full-time at promoting the notion of minority groups—including the disabled—participating fully in TV work, advertising, and the performing arts. The Screen Actors Guild officer, Elaine Brody, was very generous with her time and described to me how she traveled all over the States, convincing advertising agents and their clients of the need to represent *all* sections of society in their promotional material.

Our plans to take a car into Manhattan had been greeted as madness by everyone. We were told that the traffic is horrific and parking impossible. I suppose it depends on what you are used to; in our case it is central London, so the driving styles were familiar enough and the density of traffic was certainly no worse than at home. In fact, once you have worked out the one-way streets, the grid system makes it much easier to find your way than in London. Parking can be a problem, but armed with a temporary disabled parking permit, organized in advance, it is by no means impossible. Prepare to pay a lot for overnight parking, though—cars have to be off the streets for street cleaning.

Taxis are an alternative means of transport, if you can manage them, and since they comprise at least fifty percent of the traffic in Manhattan there's no shortage. But you will need nerves of steel: the driving is unpredictable and the road surfaces comparable to a lunar landscape. New York taxi drivers—short on knowledge of the city, I was told, and many of them unable to speak English—use their horns constantly as a means of communication.

In between appointments, we found time for short bursts of sightseeing: to the Statue of Liberty, taking in the view of the Manhattan skyline, to the World Trade Center's 107th-floor observation deck, and to the smart shops on Madison Avenue. The Trump Tower, with its expensive boutiques, is a masterpiece of vulgarity in salmon-pink marble, with glossy brass trimmings, and plants cascading into an atrium fountain.

A Jesuit, Brother Ricky Curry, runs the *National Theater Workshop of the Handicapped*, the only training establishment exclusively for disabled people in the country. The criteria for securing a place here are not physical ones, but students must have stamina, creativity, and intelligence. Brother Curry is an ebullient and persuasive character who founded the center in 1977. He has a disability himself and is aware, through personal experience, of the difficulties that talented people face in the performing arts. But he insists that, with professional training and high motivation, his students can achieve a successful career as actor, director, or playwright.

"The city is all its reputation claims for it and more—manic, sweltering in summer, deafening, and sometimes threatening"

New York can be daunting if you are not accustomed to inner city life—disabled or not. You'll need a tough helper if you use a wheelchair: curbs are high, the provision of ramps is random and the roads are like rollercoasters and full of potholes. Prepare for your visit by deciding on your method of transport and contacting the appropriate organization for advice (see *Travel Notes*). Access to buildings is nearly always provided.

The city is all its reputation claims for it and more—manic, sweltering in summer, deafening, and sometimes threatening. But being disabled sometimes helps—I was wished well by junkies on occasion! Try to find somewhere to stay where you can get some sleep (the university campuses let rooms during the vacations). Garbage trucks, taxi horns, sirens, burglar alarms, and general all-night mayhem conspire to prevent sleep—and you'll need every minute you can grab. New York is not for the faint-hearted, but visit it if you can, just for the experience.

Boston had a familiarity about it. British and Irish origins are immediately apparent in its architecture and layout—narrow streets, churches, and a market square which claims more eating places per square yard than anywhere else in the nation. The skyline of towering skyscrapers, seen from a harbor cruiser, is now not so different from that of New York and, astonishingly, has only developed in the last ten years.

The trains on the Rapid Transport System, known as the "T," just miss out on being accessible. There are elevators at most stations, but the two steps onto the trains are steep and we did have to negotiate a turnstile once. The buses are accessible, I'm told, although I didn't use them. Parking and finding our way about presented the usual city problems. Some of the terrain was hilly, so take a strong companion, and ramps are only patchily supplied.

Boston is trying to revive its cultural center—five new theaters are to open soon. As part of this revitalization, we saw a production of a version of *The Bacchae* on Boston Common, with a chorus of lissom, sequinned, leotard-clad girls and young men, singing rock songs between the dramatic episodes. At least it was free.

Visits to the National Theater of the Deaf and to Yale University took us out of Boston, far into the Connecticut countryside. Chester, a small village tucked away into wooded hills halfway between Boston and New York, seemed an unlikely location for a professional company of deaf actors. Yale University, far from the rolling green campus I'd imagined, was disappointingly set in the drab port of New Haven, and we suffered in the extreme heat there.

But Connecticut was redeemed for us by the town of Mystic, which provided a superb "experience" of seventeenth-century life. The site has been set up with restored buildings, complete with working shipyard, forge, and a rope factory in a shed a quarter of a mile long. With the sun setting over the Mystic river, we could really have gone back in time.

Making our way along the coast, we drove across Conanicut Island into our ninth state, Rhode Island. Newport is best known as a yachting center and has a rather over-restored, touristy wharf. It also boasts the oldest (and very handsome) Episcopalian church in the USA. Out on the headland, Palladian mansions, on the grandest scale, sit alongside French châteaux and German Baroque castles. Many are open to the public.

Boston marked the end of the first part of our travels. Next stop, Los Angeles, a very different world and a blissfully relaxing one for those with mobility problems—and the weather is perfect, too!

Another America

From Los Angeles, on the second leg of her four-month tour of the USA, Carolyn Lucas traveled into New Mexico. As a wheelchair user, she found surprisingly few obstacles, even in the desert.

The journey to Santa Fe by train is probably the nearest I will ever get to feeling like an intrepid traveler, and was one of the highlights of our American trip. We had wanted to visit a different part of America, and decided on New Mexico. Flying would have

meant missing the landscape; it was too far to drive, but *Amtrak*—usually an expensive way to travel—was offering a reduction on twenty percent of the tickets, to $94 for the 2000-mile round trip.

Relaxing in the comfort of an *Amtrak* car is the way to survey the majesty and scale of the American landscape. Passing through the mountains from Los Angeles to the Mojave Desert, through Arizona and into the high desert of New Mexico, gives some idea of what the continent has to offer.

We pulled out of the Art Deco, Spanish-style Grand Union Station in Los Angeles at 8:30pm, pulled by the vast, silver *Southwest Chief* locomotive.

We could not but feel a thrill of anticipation for the seventeen-hour overnight journey (four days for those carrying on to New York), 1000 miles and one third of the way across America.

Collected from the station by truck—for the halt, lame, blind, and infirm—we and our luggage had been deposited in the "handicapped only" compartment, and settled in the spacious car for only twelve people. Stretching out on the reclining seats, with pillow and footrest, we were welcomed by our attendant and told that we would be well looked after and our meals brought to us. One gentleman even plugged in his respirator.

"A parched landscape of red sandstone, dried-up stream beds, and jagged, black lava fields—home to countless rattlesnakes"

By the time we rolled out of the station, it was dark. The train trundled slowly and soundlessly, except for the distinctive American loco hooting, through the Los Angeles suburbs of Pasadena and Pomona. The lights of the city were left behind at San Bernardino; we climbed through the mountains and down into the Mojave Desert.

Dark, distant mounds were silhouetted in the moonlight, sage brush and scrub lined the track and there was the occasional trail of head- and tail-lights as trucks headed across the desert in the darkness, or lined up in convoys to sleep the night away beside the road. We stopped at Barstow and Needles—ghost stations in the dead of night.

After a brief sleep, we woke to dawn breaking over the Coconino Plateau in Arizona. The sun cast long shadows over the ponderosa pines, mesquite bushes and meadows of tall, yellow daisies. The conductor arrived with our breakfast, selected from an extensive menu, as we crossed the flat lands of the Navajo Reservation, with distant views of the buttes and mesas of the Painted Desert. The blood red of the Little Colorado river trickled beside the track.

At Gallup, "American Indian Capital of the World" (the usual hamburger bars and tourist-trap craft shops), a guide from the Laguna tribe boarded and gave us a commentary on the landscape and local people living in the ancient pueblos that we could see from the train. Traditional adobe houses sat alongside mobile homes; the more isolated dwellings had a truck rusting in the yard and maybe a horse. Sacred sites were pointed out to us, and the uranium mines owned and administered by the tribes.

Crossing into New Mexico, the terrain had changed into a parched landscape of red sandstone, dried-up stream beds, and jagged, black lava fields—home to countless rattlesnakes.

Across the Continental Divide, mountain ranges appeared in the distance and we came to the valley of the Rio Grande. Not very grand here, but a pastoral and domestic picture of trees and green fields on the approach to Albuquerque. The train stopped for cleaning and servicing and we were invited to stretch our legs and look at the traditional craftwork on display.

The legendary Santa Fe Railroad actually bypasses Santa Fe. Either the terrain was too difficult, or the locals were reluctant to find the cash to take the railroad into the town. Our rental car met us at Lamy, the nearest station, 15 miles away in the desert.

This is high desert. Santa Fe is at 2100m elevation and you can often see at least 50 miles in every direction—to ochre and red sandstone cliffs, rock faces, mountains and mesas. One million years ago, a volcanic eruption in the Jemez Mountains spewed lava over a 400-square-mile area, a thousand feet thick in places. The lava has eroded away into spectacular rock and cliff formations, leaving a labyrinth of canyons.

In Frijoles Canyon, part of the Bandelier National Monument, the Anasazi ancestors of the indigenous people exploited the natural features of the soft rock and scoured out the Swiss-cheese holes to make homes for themselves, high on the canyon walls. They then added adobe extensions to enlarge their living quarters. The remains of the circular adobe village lie at the foot of the canyon. A steep ramp made even the caves wheelchair accessible, and there was very little that I could not get to in the area. The views are stunning, and plenty of picnic places are provided, with accessible rest rooms in all public places.

We drove up the 10,000-foot Sangre de Cristo mountains to sit, joined by chipmunks, among the aspens. We listened to La Traviata under the stars at the Santa Fe Opera, 10 miles into the desert, wheelchair space provided.

Taos, an old town and native American pueblo, is the mecca for tourists, and we headed there along the mountain road. The famous multistoried pueblo and massive, walled adobe church of St Francis are a focus for all the artists of the area.

Until recently, the tiny Indian or Spanish villages were almost cut off, and they retain a remote and primitive air. Truchas church is like a Welsh hilltop chapel, albeit with vibrantly colored, painted reredos, lace curtains at the window, and an ancient stove in the nave. Chimayo has the only healing shrine in the States, and a little room, stifling with heat from votive candles, is crammed with testimonies, the crutches of the healed and offerings of all sorts. Next door, an even smaller room contains the red healing dust in a hole in the floor, to be applied or dissolved in water and drunk. As we left, a party of Mexican women arrived, covering their heads and chanting as they entered the church.

Santa Fe has an interesting range of architecture, mostly wheelchair accessible, ranging from old and new adobe structures (including the local Safeway supermarket and parking lot!) to Spanish-inspired buildings and "Wild West" wooden arcades. It is an "arty" place—galleries abound and indigenous art proliferates, produced by native American artists or white Americans jumping on the bandwagon. Craftsmen and women, selling pots and silver and turquoise jewelry, sat under the arcades of the Palace of the Governors, which housed Spanish viceroys, then Pueblo People, and finally US government officials.

Antique Navajo rugs, Hopi *katchinas*, and Pueblo pots could be found in the galleries along the narrow, sun-soaked Canyon Road. It was a pleasant place to spend a bonus two hours, as our train, coming from Chicago, had been delayed by flash floods.

Our journey back was comfortable. Tourists from the Grand Canyon, loaded with rucksacks and bleary-eyed with sleep, boarded the train at Flagstaff, Arizona, in the early hours. Dawn came up over the Mojave Desert, silhouetting the Joshua trees and the shacks littering the sides of the track. The train hauled itself through the mountains and back into Los Angeles around 9am. The contrast between the open vistas of desert and mountains in New Mexico and the urban sprawl and glistening skyscrapers of downtown Los Angeles could not have been greater. We had certainly achieved our aim of catching a glimpse of another America.

Drama on the West Coast

After the East Coast cities of Washington DC, New York and Boston, then Los Angeles and New Mexico (described in the previous two accounts), Carolyn Lucas finished off her working vacation with a month in San Francisco.

When the early navigators, including Sir Francis Drake in 1579, passed down the Californian coast, they missed the gap at the Golden Gate. The existence of the inland sea of San Francisco Bay was not discovered for another two hundred years.

Probably the most spectacularly situated city in the world, San Francisco is certainly America's most beautiful. This stretch of Northern California has much to offer—a dramatic coastline, redwood forests, historic Spanish missions, the Sierra Nevada mountain range, the wine country of the Napa Valley and Mendocino and Sonoma counties, and of course the city itself. San Francisco is tucked into the bay, joined to the other cities which ring the water by the Bay Bridge, and to Marin County by the Golden Gate Bridge.

Our base for the final month of our trip was Sausalito, a short drive over the Golden Gate Bridge from San Francisco. One of our first expeditions was with an ex-forester who knew and loved the city and wanted to show it off to his English visitors. We must have looked a strange sight, with myself in a wheelchair, my husband, and a tall, elderly gentleman in stetson and cowboy boots. However, most things go in San Francisco!

The ferry from Sausalito took us across the bay (chair lift for wheelchair users on the boat, of course) and we wandered down Market Street and through the Embarcadero complex of homes, shops, and offices, to the Bank of America. Not many tourists know about the cocktail bar in the Bank of America, the tallest building in San Francisco, towering above even the famous "Pyramid." The bar, on the 52nd floor, is open to all visitors, commanding panoramic views over the city, the bay, the docks, Alcatraz, and other islands.

Angel Island, which we overlooked from our bedroom, is a popular weekend picnic spot, reached by boat from the city or from Tiburon. It is a nature reserve with an five-mile, paved perimeter trail. Cloaked in mist when we went, the island is usually a good spot for lovely views of the bay.

San Francisco is built on forty hills, many of them practically vertical—residents negotiating them every day soon develop a distinct list! But a virtue of the city is that it is compact enough to get around on foot or wheel, without the use of a car, by using buses (*MUNI*—the *San Francisco Municipal Railroad* operates the transport system in the city), trains (*MUNI* or *BART*—the *Bay Area Rapid Transit* rail system, which runs into the city from the East Bay and outer suburbs), and the occasional cab. All public transit is accessible, and helpful information for disabled people is available. But it is hilly, so you need a strong pusher.

> *"She did not give anyone the opportunity to deny her the right to follow her chosen vocation"*

We took an exciting trip on a cable car (folding the chair). At one point, halfway up one of the hills, a car pulled out in front of us, necessitating an abrupt halt. It seemed that we were prevented from rolling back into the bay by nothing more than the brute force of the conductors hauling on the brakes. Accompanied by much bellowing and clanging of bells, we endured a hair-raising lurch back to the nearest level junction, before cranking up for a new charge up the hill.

Other attractions of San Francisco include the Japanese Tea Garden, complete with tea-house, pagodas, and landscaped gardens, and several art museums in the Golden Gate Park. The Mexican Museum at Fort Mason has a shop crammed with enticing, inexpensive, and colorful gifts. The Ghirardelli complex, on the site of the old chocolate factory, is a fun place to walk around, with shops and restaurants; Pier Nine with its vast range of seafood is nearby. San Francisco is a gourmet's delight—food of every nationality is available, and there is no finer Chinese food outside China.

"The disability movement in America really had its beginnings on the campus at Berkeley"

When you have exhausted the city, take the ferry across to Sausalito and visit the scale-model of San Francisco Bay. Though open to tourists, the model was constructed by the Army Corps of Engineers and is used primarily to study the impact of natural and artificial changes in the bay, tidal movements, salinity, and the shifting of silt. I met a wheelchair-bound guide here, who had previously worked on Mount Tamalpais in Marin County. When I asked her if she had come across any resistance to her becoming a ranger, she replied that she did not give anyone the opportunity to deny her the right to follow her chosen vocation.

The Pacific coastline of Marin County, all of it National Park, is surprisingly varied. It ranges from precipitous cliffs to the calm, coastal marshes of Point Reyes, with its earthquake trail at the site of the epicenter of the devastating 1906 earthquake. A fence with a staggered twenty-foot gap has been retained to show how far the earth moved. This trail and others are accessible. Tomales Bay lies along the San Andreas Fault, protected from the coastal cloud, and has lovely silver sands like those of Hearts Desire

Beach. We called in for lunch at Bolinas, a quirky, creekside village of "alternative," Sixties-type inhabitants who regularly cut down all the signs to the place.

Mount Tamalpais is the highest mountain in Marin. A long, twisty drive took us to the top where we could see, from the accessible trail at the summit, the tops of the San Francisco skyscrapers emerging above the plume of cloud pouring in through the Golden Gate. The views are extensive—to the end of the fifty-mile bay, south to the Big Sur mountains, and to the Farallon Islands out to sea. Sometimes, they claim, even the snow-crested Sierra Nevada peaks, some two hundred miles away, can be seen.

Climatic conditions here are extraordinary. A pall of cloud often hangs over the coast and it finds escape routes through gaps in the mountains. Low cloud pours through the canyons at tremendous speed, like dry ice on a stage, disappearing into thin air when it reaches the brilliant sun and cloudless skies of San Francisco Bay.

The disability movement in America really had its beginnings on the University of California campus at Berkeley, in the East Bay area, where the first Center for Independent Living was founded, so I took the opportunity to find out about it. I met Judy Heumann, of the World Institute on Disability, who told me about the Americans with Disabilities Act, which was passed by Congress during my stay. This federal act is seen as part of the civil rights legislation, outlawing discrimination of any sort toward disabled people with regard to employment, transport, and accessibility. It is parallel to the legislation already adopted by most states in America, but acknowledges the rights of disabled people in Federal law.

I was invited to see the latest production of *Theater Unlimited*. The play, performed mostly by talented, mentally disabled youngsters, was based on research that uncovered the use and abuse of developmentally disabled conscripts in World War II. What was striking was that the material—evolved through improvization by the group, with a professional writer to hand—in no way talked down to either performers or audience. It was a competent script and could have held its own on a professional stage.

A visit to a production company making educational films took us to Sacramento, California's capital. It is a pleasant, green city, despite its location in the heat of the San Joaquin Valley. The old town, down by the Sacramento river, has been lovingly restored in typical "Western" style: there are saloons, hotels, and stores with flat-fronted, wooden arcades or decorated, plastered balustrades and raised boardwalks.

The Pacific Railroad ran through Sacramento on its way to San Francisco. The town is now the site of an excellent railroad museum which includes a simulated, moving Pullman coach, as well as massive locos that carried the early settlers across the forbidding Sierras.

"The offending vehicle was unceremoniously hauled away. If only that would happen at my local supermarket"

One of the joys of driving in the States is the availability of parking spaces. You rarely find an able-bodied person in a space reserved for the disabled: the penalties of being cited or towed might have something to do with it. The only parking transgression I witnessed was at a motor-racing circuit where we arrived to find the disabled spaces full. The tough lady in charge pointed to a sleek, red Firebird and said, "If they're disabled, I'm Queen Elizabeth!" She called a tow-truck and the offending vehicle was unceremoniously hauled away. If only that would happen at my local supermarket.

The Sierra Nevadas contain one of the most dramatic valleys in the world, at Yosemite. During the Ice Age, glaciers filled the valley formed by the Merced river. As they moved, they gouged out a great trough, deepening into a valley until eventually a lake formed. As the river slowly deposited silt, the lake vanished but streams continued to pour from the mountains into the valley, producing the legendary waterfalls.

Yosemite's popularity ensures that the campgrounds, cabins, and hotel are full most of the year, and numbers of visitors are strictly limited. We had booked some weeks ahead and were lucky enough to be reserved a cabin with ramp and bathroom (not all have this facility). Disabled guests can also be accommodated at the *Ahwahnee Hotel*. Facilities for disabled people are excellent and, apart from one restaurant, all are accessible. Perhaps the nicest surprise is the number of paved trails, some steepish, but still manageable in a wheelchair.

The waterfalls are mostly dry in the fall, but Bridal Veil, although wispy and blown around by the wind, sported a rainbow halfway down. My husband climbed high to see another fall, while I spent a magical morning sketching in a meadow ringed by pines and surrounded by mountains. Climbers on El Capitan, over half a mile high, on one of the sheerest rock faces in the world, were mere specks, even with binoculars. Their sleeping hammocks hung from hooks on the cliff like seaweed pods. We walked to Mirror Lake, now mostly dry and turning into meadow, and sat in the trees by the emerald pools of the river rimmed with golden sand.

A long drive took us to Glacier Point, high above our cabin, to see the magnificent views down the Yosemite Valley and over the High Sierras. We watched Half Dome turn red as the sun went down, and the moon rising, moving imperceptibly as if being pulled by a string from behind the distant peaks.

It's another lengthy drive to Mariposa Grove, home of the giant sequoias or redwoods. A truck tours the grove, stopping at the 2700-year-old Grizzly Giant—295 feet high and nearly 30 feet in girth—and the tree through which a bus can be driven.

When the Spanish controlled California, Father Junipero Serra, a Franciscan missionary in Mexico, took on the task of founding a series of missions up the Californian coast. From San Diego in the south to Sonoma in the north there are 21 missions, built in the Spanish style and restored after their secularization in the middle of the nineteenth century. Carmel, south of Monterey, is one of the most beautiful—"the jewel of the missions." Set back from the ocean, in the Carmel Valley, the white walls are ablaze with bougainvillaea and hibiscus, and the gardens burgeon with shrubs, flowers, and cacti. Inside, church and living quarters are brightly painted with Mexican designs.

"Four wines at a time are offered at each winery, and you really have to visit several to compare"

John Steinbeck lived in the Monterey area and made it the setting for much of his work, including *Cannery Row* and *Tortilla Flat*. Its main claim to fame these days, though, is the Monterey Bay Aquarium. As if they are not rich enough, the residents of Pebble Beach charge tourists for the "Seventeen Mile Drive" along the coastal road. But it's worth paying the few dollars to drive through the pine trees lining the golf course to watch the Pacific breaking over the boulder-strewn beaches.

South of Carmel, the mountains of Big Sur plunge thousands of feet into the Pacific Ocean. The Pacific Coastal Highway clings perilously to the edge, and viewpoints are provided at regular intervals to survey the majestic coastline. At one such point, we could hear the honking of sea-lions, visible only through binoculars, basking on the rocks below.

In the 1860s it was discovered that the climate of Northern California is ideally suited to the cultivation of grapes. European immigrants soon set up wineries in the Napa Valley and on the slopes of Sonoma and Mendocino counties. The wineries are all very hospitable and open their vineyards for tours and wine tasting. In retrospect, it might have been wiser to take a tour, rather than drive. Four wines at a time are offered at each winery, and you really have to visit several to compare.

With visits to Calistoga (an early mining town, with hot springs and a spa), nearby Old Faithful (the geyser which spouts every forty minutes, on the dot) and the settlements along the Russian river in Sonoma County, we had come to the end of our four months of travel—not before time, as it happens. Two weeks after our departure, the 1989 earthquake struck. I had asked a few San Franciscans how it was that they were able to live with the prospect of a major disaster under their feet. The response was always the same: "Well, we've lived in Ohio (or Kansas or Iowa) and we suffered truly terrifying hurricanes regularly. San Francisco is such a beautiful place to live, we'll chance it!" I could see their point.

One of the Crowd

In Washington DC, Frances Hill found that wheelchair access to public buildings and public transit is no longer a dream but a reality. It is a city which has taken the needs of the disabled into account.

"The Nation's Capital," as they say on TV, is the home of the US government, the National Archives, and the FBI. If you are lucky enough to fly in on one of the frequent clear days, the vast green areas and multitude of white buildings will leave a lasting impression.

We stayed at the *Days Inn Downtown*, which has several rooms adapted for disabled people. These are very comfortable; in some an extra inch or two would have been welcome in the doorways, but it was possible to maneuver. Some rooms have queen-size beds, others two singles (plus sofa bed). Fold-up cots are available for a small extra charge. Being senior citizens, my husband and I obtained a special rate.

Having rested, unpacked, and "settled" to some extent, we sallied forth to explore. Washington is a well-designed city, divided into four quadrants, the northwest containing most of the places you'll want to visit. All the sidewalks have "curb cuts"—areas at corners flush with the road: no jolting (good news for wheelchair riders who have pain); no struggle to lift the chair (good news for companions); no taking a run at it—just smooth sailing from sidewalk to road and back again. There are tactile markers for the visually impaired.

It wasn't long before we noticed box-like structures resembling bus shelters at regular intervals along the sidewalks. Further investigation revealed that these contained elevators descending to the Metrorail, to the level where tickets are purchased. The fare system is simplicity itself—a single charge regardless of distance. We each bought a magnetic strip ticket from a machine and found that the remaining balance was automatically printed each time we inserted the ticket at the barrier. When it was near used up, the remaining credit was recorded and added to our new ticket. All so easy—no lengthy lines for tickets before each journey.

Passing through the barrier, we came to the stairs, travelators and an elevator with the wheelchair sign displayed (elderly people and mothers with strollers are also free to use it). Thus we descended to the level of our choice and boarded the train, the floor of which was flush with the platform (again, the edges were well marked for visually impaired travelers). Spaces were provided on the train for safe and convenient positioning of my chair, and before arrival at each station the name was announced quite distinctly, giving passengers time to prepare for exit. The stations are wide, with many seats, high vaulted roofs and excellent lighting and ventilation—not a bit of litter or graffiti in sight (sadly, not so in the street elevators).

"I was utterly thrilled to be just like any other passenger"

I saw several disabled passengers using the trains—alone, well dressed, carrying briefcases, obviously business people, as well as students on their way to school or college, chattering eagerly and "one of the crowd." I was utterly thrilled to be just like any other passenger and would have happily spent all day exercising my new-found freedom and independence. Of course, there was too much to do to spend hours on the subway, but we did use the trains every day and saw many parts of the city that we would never have found by car (Washington, like any big city, has its parking problems).

My main objective was to visit the National Gallery and as much of the

Smithsonian Institution as possible. Since childhood I've loved the Impressionist painters and have seen many works in London, but "Woman with a Parasol" only in books and on postcards. To see the original close-up was a wonderful experience. I sat in front of it and gazed and gazed, feeling like a teenager meeting her pop star idol.

"While glad of any form of admission, I am always pleased not to be part of the 'Deliveries'"

The gallery has much to offer besides the pictures. There are many visual pleasures, including the architecture and layout of the display halls, and a lovely large restaurant and garden, with moderately priced service and cafeteria sections, the whole facing a glassed-in "waterfall wall" which is beautifully relaxing. The elevators, rest rooms, restaurant, and gallery are all accessible.

Indeed, all the buildings of the Smithsonian are accessible. It is an amazing collection of museums and galleries, tastefully incorporated into their surroundings, with many parks and garden backgrounds, and an absolute minimum of litter (it is rare to see any around the city). The complex was the inspiration of James Smithson, an English scientist who in 1846 bequeathed half a million dollars to "found an establishment for the increase and diffusion of knowledge among men." It is now administered as a private foundation, funded mainly by Congress but also by a succession of large legacies over the years.

All buildings have front-door entrances for the disabled; while glad of any form of admission, I am always pleased not to be part of the "Deliveries." There is so much to see that on a short stay you have to be selective. To name just a few of the options: the National History Museum; the African, Near Eastern, and Asian Museum; the Botanical Gardens; the Freer Art Gallery, which was formerly a private collection containing the famous Whistler Blue Room (the guard who unlocked and showed us this was as pleased and proud as if he had painted it himself); the Hirshorn Museum and Garden of Sculpture; the Famous Explorers' Exhibition at the offices of the National Geographic magazine. Admission is free to everything except the J.F. Kennedy Center for Performing Arts.

We spent half a day touring the National Air and Space Museum, a must for my husband, who served in the RAF during World War II. The sight of V1s and V2s brought back some vivid memories. The museum charts the history of powered flight from the days of the Wright brothers' flimsy craft to the giants of space exploration. The static exhibits are wonderfully augmented by audiovisual information. We were particularly intrigued to enter a space module containing figures depicting life aboard the craft. We would have stayed longer but had to leave when a bomb scare closed the building!

For a change of pace we visited the National Zoological Gardens (easily reached on the subway) which are well laid out in undulating grounds with a clearly marked wheelchair route. I was pleased to see that the animals had plenty of room in which to live and roam. The big attraction was a disappointment—giant pandas are far less endearing than their toy counterparts. Surprisingly, we found access to the restaurant very difficult, eventually settling for entrance via the exit—there are plenty of food stands throughout the grounds but most had long lines.

Apart from the Smithsonian, which deserves a vacation all to itself (don't be put off by so many museums—several have modern themes and there is something to suit everyone), there are the other tourist attractions of Washington: the White House, Capitol, Jefferson

Memorial, Arlington Cemetery, the Lincoln Memorial—the latter is awe-inspiring when floodlit at night.

At the White House there are free tours, but you have to wait in line for tickets on a time and day of issue basis; be prepared to wait or even return on another day should the quota be filled. There are seats at frequent intervals along the route.

Viewing is somewhat limited for wheelchair users: the first floor only is accessible, but the staircase is lovely and you can sit and let your imagination run riot as you wait for the return of your group. We learned some interesting details about the history of this fine building, and at least I can say "I've been there!"

A car is unnecessary in Washington, but we did use one to drive south to the 80,000-hectare Shenandoah Valley National Park, which is best seen in early to mid-October when the colors of the fall leaves are truly spectacular. (September to October tends to be off-season for visiting Washington; April to May is the time to see the War Commemorative cherry trees in bloom.) The "tourist route" to Shenandoah is along the 100-mile Skyline Drive, which provides breath-taking views of the valley itself and the Appalachian Mountains. The many well-equipped parking areas allowed us to stop and take in the scenery at our leisure.

Also worth a visit—and essential if you are a history buff—is Gettysburg, up north in Pennsylvania, which has exhibits depicting scenes from the Civil War. There are many other battle-grounds nearby, a stark reminder to the carefree vacationer that not much more than a hundred years ago this young country almost tore itself apart in bloody battles which claimed over a million lives.

Bargain Breaks in Southern California

Arthur Goldthorpe makes regular visits to his son and daughter-in-law in California, accompanied by his wife, Nina, and his youngest son, David. Although in a wheelchair permanently, Arthur also wears braces which enable him to stagger a few paces with support.

All our visits have been made around Easter for two reasons: to coincide with David's school or college vacations, and to take advantage of the low-season rates and special package deals. In 1989, we booked with *American Airlines*, at the low-season rate, from Manchester to San Diego via Chicago. This necessitated a change of plane at Chicago; judging by our previous experiences of flight delays, time taken boarding and leaving aircraft, customs and immigration, and finding a wheel-chair-accessible rest room, the hour allotted in the schedule for the transfer seemed pretty short—but we decided to risk it.

I rely on being able to "walk," with the aid of my braces, down the aisle of the aircraft to a toilet at least once during a transatlantic crossing, using the backs of the seats for support. We had as usual reserved seats close to the toilets, but realized that my customary laborious excursion would be impossible because the seats and other hand-holds ran out before reaching the cubicle.

Necessity being the mother of invention (if you have to go, you have to go!), I summoned the chief cabin attendant and asked if I could use one of the food carts as a mobile support to bridge the gap. With her help edging the cart forward, I was able to complete the journey to the rest room. On this aircraft the cubicle had a sloping roof, and the usual lack of handholds made standing up even more difficult than I had anticipated. It is not surprising that I was nearly exhausted when I finally fell back into my seat.

My heroics apparently did not go unnoticed. As we were waiting in the aircraft for ground staff to bring the narrow transit chair needed for my disembarkation, the chief cabin attendant approached and graciously presented me with a splendid box of *American Airlines* chocolates, adding, "Please accept these with our compliments, and thank you for traveling with *American Airlines*." David assures me that she added under her breath, "Have you thought of traveling back with *United*?" but I cannot confirm this!

> **"It was only by hanging on grimly that I was able to prevent the transit chair from rolling around the cabin"**

Our flight itinerary suggested that we would land at O'Hare airport in Chicago and leave from the same terminal. In reality, we landed at a subsidiary terminal, and passengers had to transfer by bus to the main *American Airlines* terminal for customs and immigration. I remained on the aircraft, waiting for the paramedics to bring the transit chair, getting more fidgety as time passed.

By the time help arrived, my own wheelchair had been whisked off with the rest of the luggage, so that I had to remain strapped into the narrow lifting chair when transferred to the very dilapidated transit vehicle. It was only by hanging on grimly to the sides of

the vehicle that I was able to prevent the transit chair from rolling around the cabin during the short drive to join the rest of my family. If I had not been strong enough to do this, it would have been a dangerous journey.

To offload its passengers the vehicle had a tail-lift, which successfully unloaded the one other disabled passenger and was then returned to allow me to disembark. As the operator pressed the "down" control, the button fell off and we lost more precious minutes as a solution to the problem was sought. Just as a sharp piece of plastic was found to activate the circuit when pushed into the broken switch, Nina and David arrived with my own chair, having rescued it from the luggage carousel, cleared customs and immigration, and located the boarding gate for our next flight.

Then followed a mad rush down seemingly endless corridors, without any mechanical assistance from travelators—this in one of America's busiest airports. Stopping only for a toilet call, we raced straight to the boarding gate for immediate transfer into the waiting plane.

Whatever the frustrations and anxieties of the change-over, the flight itself soon made up for them. It was a perfect, cloudless sky as we left the Great Lakes and cruised over miles of completely flat terrain, divided into huge, neat farms by grids of roads. The land became gradually more undulating, the roads and farms more varied, as we approached the foothills of the southern end of the Rockies.

Flying westwards in the late afternoon in March, with long shadows cast by the dying sun, we could easily appreciate the contours of the ground below. Soon we were passing over mile after mile of snowcapped peaks of the Rockies. On the west side of the mountains the landscape became arid, a barren wilderness of deserts and mountain ridges.

"Sometimes extraordinary efforts are made to allow disabled people to enjoy leisure facilities"

The most moving experience, however, was flying over the Grand Canyon, marveling at the scale and beauty of this gash in the earth's surface, as it lay bathed in evening light. This flight from Chicago to San Diego intensified one of the feelings aroused by my visits to California—humble admiration for the early pioneers who crossed this enormous, inhospitable wilderness in the center of America, with primitive, ox-drawn wagons, to reach the fertile west coast.

San Diego is a beautiful city, built around a large bay, naturally protected by the Point Loma peninsula, and home to the United States South Pacific fleet. The smaller Mission Bay is devoted to aquatic sports and has miles of beaches which make it an ideal vacation spot. The city claims to have the most equitable climate in the USA. Among its attractions are an exciting and extensive Sea World, the magnificent Balboa Park with its museums, the world-famous San Diego Zoo, and a well-preserved Old Town on the site of the first European settlement in California.

The first few days of our three-week vacation were spent living out of suitcases in my son Christopher's small apartment in the hills overlooking Mission Bay. This gave us time to look for suitable wheelchair-accessible accommodation. A visit to the *International Visitor Information Center* secured the last copy of an access guide to San Diego—very modest by UK standards—and a much more useful accommodation directory, which indicated which hotels or self-catering units had an "HR," or handicapped room. Imagine our delight when we found from the directory that *Beach Cottages*, in a prime position on the promenade next to the beach, had an HR on the second floor with elevator access, at a reasonable price within our budget.

We knew from our previous trips to America that although all new buildings have to provide facilities for disabled people, the standards vary considerably from those in the UK. Access into and around premises (including beaches) is generally very good; indeed sometimes extraordinary efforts are made to allow disabled people to enjoy leisure facilities; but suitable bathroom and toilet facilities for more severely disabled people can sometimes be hard to find.

The bathroom in our suite at *Beach Cottages* was typical of others that I have come across in the USA. There was plenty of circulation space, with good access to the sink, and a bath with shower unit inside. Unfortunately, two sliding glass panels, running along the edge of the bath as splash guards, meant that only half of the bath could be exposed at any one time, thus making it very difficult for anyone disabled to use either bath or shower.

The toilet in this room was adjacent to the bath, so that there was no support rail on that side; instead, there was a wall-mounted rail behind the toilet and a fixed "L" rail from wall to floor at what we would consider the transfer side. I found it possible to position my chair obliquely across the front of the bowl and transfer from there, but this may not suit everyone. The message is—wherever possible—check out the bathroom before booking any accommodation.

In spite of the differences in design of facilities, it is still possible to tour the USA without detailed planning and pre-booking because there is so much accommodation readily available in all price brackets. Very reasonable accommodation can be booked either on a room-per-night basis (irrespective of the number of occupants) or as "efficiencies." The latter have a small kitchen area which I have found useful for a quick wash if the bathroom required a heroic effort to enter. On several occasions, when my difficulties had been explained to the manager, we were offered an efficiency at the lower, room-per-night, rate, on condition that we did not use the cooking facilities.

"A one-legged roller-skater propelling himself along at incredible speed with two elbow crutches"

The complex of *Beach Cottages* and the block containing our apartment led straight out to the boardwalk, a fairly narrow walkway which runs several miles up and down the foreshore. It seemed to be permanently frequented by a mobile mass of young, elegant Californians, ostentatiously keeping fit and displaying their charms in skimpy beachwear. Unlike our English resorts, which bristle with a profusion of "thou shalt not" signs in an attempt to keep footpaths for pedestrians, the board-walk in San Diego offered a good-humored challenge to dodge the cyclists, skateboarders, roller-skaters, and joggers speeding in both directions. Other vehicles included manual and powered wheelchairs, a motorcycle, a huge, custom-built tricycle, and a one-legged roller-skater propelling himself along at incredible speed with two elbow crutches.

A major bonus of being in the center of a vacation area is the profusion of restaurants and takeouts. Because of the competition there were many cost-saving inducements at various establishments. These discounts made substantial savings in our vacation budget and were freely advertised with the necessary vouchers in the local weekend papers. At one restaurant, as senior citizens, my wife and I could order allegedly smaller portions of the standard meals at a reduced cost, and still stagger from the table grossly overfed. Two meals for the price of one were widely available at slack times, and many takeout (or home-delivery) establishments gave discounts on future purchases, or a free giant Coke

with each order. For anyone really hungry, an omelette restaurant offered free meals to any person who could finish their 32-egg special!

Useful savings were also obtained in other ways—many of the larger hotel chains, for example, give a ten-percent discount to senior citizens, but this has to be arranged when checking in. With senior citizen discounts for Nina and myself, and a bargain saver for David, the cost of a boat trip around the harbor in San Diego was reduced from $11 per person to $7. To board the boat it was necessary to descend a horrendously steep ramp, but before we could ask for help two burly sailors appeared and manhandled me down the slope to the lower level of the vessel. As I was unable to get on the upper deck to take photographs, I was positioned in my wheelchair with an open window to my right and within reaching distance of the small bar on my left.

The cruise covered most parts of the enormous natural harbor, with good views of the naval vessels, an airforce base, and the downtown skyline of San Diego accompanied by a detailed commentary. A most impressive feature of the bay is the high-level Coronado Bridge linking mainland San Diego with the upscale coastal suburb of Coronado. The white-clapboard, red-roofed and turreted *Hotel del Coronado* has been used for location shots in many films, the most famous being *Some Like it Hot*.

Another bargain was a "Gamblers' Break," which enabled us to fly to Las Vegas and have two nights at a first-rate hotel at very modest cost. This included a package of incentives, ranging from free shrimp cocktails with a meal to reduced admission to shows, used to lure us into various casinos. The color, bustle, and vitality of "the Strip" at night is unique, and you need spend no money to enjoy wandering through the casinos, which are all freely open to the public and invariably wheelchair accessible.

As one moves eastward from the densely populated coastal strip of California, the hills become ranges of mountains and between them the flat plains become progressively more arid. Grass gives way to scrub and then desert, on a scale which only becomes apparent when driving through or flying over the states of California, Arizona, Utah, and Nevada. Few people fail to be fascinated by the way in which different desert plants have adapted to their climate. This is typified by the symbiosis between the tall saguaro of the Arizona landscape and the foothill or yellow paloverde.

The seeds of the saguaro need the shade of a bush to become established, and usually germinate beneath a paloverde tree which, with its very deep root system, survives on the moisture which has seeped far into the ground. The saguaro, with its expansive root system just below the surface, does not compete with the host tree; it can quickly absorb water from any sudden rainstorms and is capable of storing up to six tons in its expandable trunk.

"It became clear that driving here was only for the brave or foolhardy"

If you are fortunate enough to be in the desert in the few weeks in spring when the flowering season breaks, you will see this usually barren country briefly transformed into a breathtaking, gigantic rock garden, with a profusion of flowering shrubs, small cacti, and other ground plants in yellow, white, red, and pink.

San Diego is only eight miles from the Mexican border, and we spent a memorable day in Tijuana, where the gloss put on for the tourists cannot hide the poverty evident only a block or so away from the colorful main shopping streets. Since the insurance rates for American cars crossing into Mexico are astronomical—a true reflection of the risks, as we discovered later—we left our car in a parking lot by the border, and crossed through customs with little formality.

On entering Mexico we were immediately besieged by hordes of small boys, drumming up business for taxis to go the mile or so into the center of Tijuana. Without meaning to, we found ourselves being guided to one of the mass of large, yellow "Tijuana taxis," parked haphazardly in the loading area. Our vehicle was a veteran classic "gas-guzzler," able to accommodate the four other members of the family comfortably across the back seat. This left me to transfer into the front seat over an "L"-shaped tear in the leather upholstery.

My wheelchair was tossed into the trunk by our driver, whose build was in proportion to his taxi, and with a screech of tyres we shot off toward Tijuana. The car bounced over rough patches, scraping the exhaust pipe noisily on the ground. As we plunged into an undisciplined traffic jam across a road junction, where each inch of ground had to be stolen by nerve or guile, it became clear that driving here was only for the brave or foolhardy.

The main shopping street of Tijuana (Avenida Revolución) is a mixture of bazaar-type stores—full of colorful Mexican pottery, hats, and other souvenirs—and very expensive shops containing exquisite leather goods, glassware, and jewelry. On the sidewalks, every few paces would bring forth an invitation to purchase cheap beads and other goods from Mexican children; at intervals, sadly, poor families huddled together, begging with a plastic bowl. Being unsure of the standard of hygiene or the strength of the chilli, we took a safe option and went to *Woolworths de Mexico* where, but for the pricing of the goods, we could almost have been in a main street store anywhere in the UK.

Our 1989 vacation was blessed by a freak spring heatwave, with temperatures touching 96°F one April day. This is quite rare for San Diego, even in summer, and it enhanced the image of "Sunny California," making us count the months, on our return, until our next visit to this beautiful part of America.

It's OK to Scream in Orlando

In April 1987, Stephen Latham and five friends spent two weeks in Orlando, Florida. The group consisted of three quadraplegics (Stephen, Stuart, and Dave) and two paraplegics (Bob and Ian), with an able-bodied friend (Austin) as nurse and escort.

As it was to be something of a working vacation for Austin, the remaining group members decided that it was only right that we should pay for his flight and accommodation—we drew the line at his bar bill! Austin deserves special mention as we could not have managed the vacation without him.

We chose Orlando as our destination for several reasons: I had been there before, and I recommended it; the weather is good; there are countless attractions, and, most important, *everywhere* is accessible. We picked April as the best time to go because it would be easier to get around—easier for pushing the wheelchairs, as the weather is not unbearably hot (although temperatures reached the high eighties while we were there) and there are not the huge crowds that are found in the summer, especially at the major attractions.

We booked our vacation with *Jetsave* through our local travel agent, but we ensured that they were well acquainted with our requirements, particularly with regard to our hotel rooms. The choice of hotel and room can make or break a vacation for a disabled person—this point needs to be stressed to all who work in the travel business. We chose a *Holiday Inn* hotel because it has rooms for disabled guests, is well situated, with numerous bars, shops, and eating places close at hand, and, again, I could recommend it.

The airline staff (*British Caledonian*, now *British Airways*) were helpful—no better, no worse than other airlines I've used. The *Jetsave* package was good value for money but we did land at Bangor, Maine, for refueling. All passengers had to disembark here for customs but we were allowed to stay on the aircraft. I have since flown with *British Airways*, and although the flight was more expensive we still landed at Bangor.

"We were ready to hit the town, or, in our tired condition, at least to slap it gently"

For the transfer from Orlando airport to the hotel, a bus was laid on. However, as this entailed being lifted onto the bus, and we had only one escort, we arranged with the tour rep to use taxis. We arrived at the hotel, found our rooms, and were ready to hit the town, or, in our tired condition, at least to slap it gently.

The major attractions of Orlando are well known—Disney World, Epcot, Sea World, Kennedy Space Center, Wet 'n Wild, Boardwalk and Baseball, to name a few—and we were determined to visit as many as possible. The tour operators run trips to the main attractions but as these involved the use of buses we decided to rent a car.

We had tried (through our travel agent in England) to rent a car with hand controls, but as a result of problems with the rental company (*Avis*) we had to take a car without them. (*Avis* also tried to overcharge us for several hundred miles which we had not covered, and this issue was not resolved until we were back in England.) We rented a large station wagon (rather like the *QE2* on wheels) which would accommodate us all, although it was rather cramped. Luckily we all had lightweight, folding wheelchairs with removable wheels, which could be stored in the back, leaving the inside of the car resembling a giant construction kit. An advantage of having the car was that we could make our own timetables, visiting what we liked, when we liked, and staying as long as we wished. The only problem we experienced was in having one driver and five "backseat drivers," all issuing instructions at the same time.

We used the car for one week, while the second, more leisurely week was spent around the hotel and at local attractions, to which we could push. It is best to space your activities out, visiting an attraction or two for a few days, then having a rest day. Attempting to visit something every day is extremely tiring—not only for disabled people. On one of our quiet days we went on a helicopter trip over Disney World, Epcot, and Sea World. Although expensive, it was a good experience and well worth it. As with the buses, you have to be lifted aboard the helicopter, so able-bodied friends are invaluable.

A three-day pass for Disney World and Epcot enabled us to spend a day in each attraction, finishing on the third morning with Disney World and traveling by monorail (only a five- to ten-minute trip) across to Epcot for the remainder of the day. Some of the high-

lights for us were a four-hour "quick visit" to the *Rose and Crown* English pub in Epcot, and watching some of the group attempting to board one of the rides while it was still moving (this was one of the few which could not be completely stopped for boarding).

All the shows and rides are good, but those which should not be missed include the Country Bear Jamboree, the Pirates of the Caribbean, and the Haunted Mansion (all in Disney World), as well as the Living Seas in Epcot, and the Sea-Lion and Otter Show at Sea World.

"It is not that they don't want to help, but their insurance laws, and the fear of litigation if anything goes wrong, deter them"

There is so much to see and do in the theme parks that it is a good idea to pick up the guidebooks or leaflets at the entrance and follow the route which takes you around the attractions that appeal most. There are special vantage points and viewing sections for the disabled at the shows, and often priority access is given in the theme parks. Able-bodied people do not abuse this system, and it is efficiently supervised by the park's employees. At the Kennedy Space Center, special arrangements for disabled people are made for tours of the base.

One note of warning should be sounded concerning the theme-park rides. The majority of the rides are fine for disabled people, but the "white-knuckle" rides are a different matter. If you decide to go on one of these rides, you *must* have an able-bodied person with you, if only to cover your legs with theirs to keep yours in place. However, on this vacation I was persuaded to go on one of these rides alone—the general idea was that you spun round and round and finished the ride upside down. Thinking that gravity would hold my legs in place, I decided to ride in the car on my own.

Not recommended! My brain must have been back at the hotel when I made that decision. No sooner had the ride started than I realized that this was *not* my idea of a fun day out. While I was hanging on for grim death to keep my backside on the seat, my legs were doing a breakdancing exhibition, twirling above my head. Questions such as "have I written my will?" flashed through my mind, but I was too busy screaming to think of much else.

"The only drawback to Florida is that it can spoil other vacation destinations for you"

One of my friends noticed the trouble and managed to attract the ride operator's attention. She stopped the ride, there was no harm done, and we all had a good laugh. When I joined the ride, I had jokingly asked the girl if it was OK to scream . . . .

Although the people of Florida are generally very friendly, they are not likely to help with lifting either disabled person or chair. This particularly applies to theme-park employees and bus or taxi drivers. It is not that they don't want to help, but their insurance laws, and the fear of litigation if anything goes wrong, deter them. If they injure you, they are afraid that you'll "sue the pants off them."

Nightlife is well catered for. We visited numerous bars and eating places (Chinese, seafood, Italian, Japanese, fast-food, you name it), all close to the hotel. It was great to be pushing around at midnight, wearing only T-shirts and trousers, and it was strange to come out of cool, air-conditioned bars and restaurants into the warm air outside.

To reach the nightspots, we did our "chicken run," which entailed waiting for a break in the traffic and then pushing across a four-lane highway. Drivers usually let us cross, but it was hair-raising at times. On several evenings, entertainment was provided by the locals (mostly youngsters), cruising up and down the main street by our hotel. We simply sat on the sidewalk, drinking cans of beer, laughing and joking with them as they passed by.

Even the best laid plans can go wrong, and things went wrong for us, but the incidents made us laugh and provided entertaining stories when we got home. On one trip, to a shopping mall, we made a bad choice of route and ended up having to push five miles back to our hotel, most of the way along a busy main road against the traffic (there was no sidewalk).

At the end of our night out at a local German *Bier Keller*, Austin followed us, after a couple of minutes, out of the bar and found a scene of pure chaos. I had unwittingly tried to push open a locked door with my footplates, been thrown off balance and was attempting to get back into the vertical position. Two of the group were definitely "under the influence" and one was being supported by the fourth member. The fifth man, having laughed so much at what was happening, had accidentally rolled backwards off a high step and fallen out of his wheelchair.

". . . If you sit at home forever pondering the pros and cons you'll never get to shake hands with Mickey Mouse, will you?"

I wholeheartedly recommend Florida to disabled people. Most of our party have been back to Orlando, this time in a larger group of fourteen people (five disabled, five able-bodied wives or relatives, and four children), and again had a great time. The only drawback to Florida is that it can spoil other vacation destinations for you— they don't have the same appeal any more! Everyone needs a vacation now and again, and if you sit at home forever pondering the pros and cons you'll never get to shake hands with Mickey Mouse, will you?

Corinne's Choice

Shirley Lihou's daughter, Corinne, has Down's syndrome and at the age of 28 is literate and numerate to the level of a ten-year-old. When asked where she would like to go on vacation, Corinne replied, "Disney World—to see my friends."

After much saving, we were whirring over the Atlantic on a *Monarch Airlines* Boeing 757, on a family vacation to Florida. It was the fall of 1988—hurricane season—and we caught the slipstream of Hurricane Gilbert.

We had not pre-booked any accommodation, but after picking up a rented *Alamo* car (booked by our travel agent in England) we quickly came across a suitable motel. We were followed by an English couple whom we had met in the car rental offices. They had visited the area before and were very interested in Corinne. We discovered that the wife had been a geriatric nurse; it is often the case that those who have had contact with disabled people are able to approach Corinne without appearing awkward or embarrassed. By traveling around with Corinne we hope that the public will learn to accept "different" people more easily. We have always found people on vacation very ready to chat, and pleasantly curious about our daughter, who is also keen to exchange words.

To keep the cost down we mostly used travel lodges or motels. As we were visiting in the off-peak season, we (three) had the use of a six-berth family apartment for the first four nights whilst we were visiting Disney World. The cost did not include utensils, so we had to venture forth to the local supermarket to stock up. We bought articles that we could take home, such as a handleless, dual-purpose, stainless-steel pan—one in which we could boil eggs there, and later use as drinking bowl for our dog back home!

We had been advised to allow four whole days in Disney World, which covers a huge area, but we were not convinced. We wished to see more than Disney World for our money. Equipped with flat shoes, picnic basket, and the book, *What not to see in Disney World* (in other words, how to do the resort justice when time is short), we set off early every morning with a pre-arranged schedule. We did not admit to being tired until we returned to our motel!

Corinne's favorite rides were Jungle Cruise, 20,000 Leagues under the Sea, and "flying" aboard a pirate galleon with Peter Pan through the skies over London to Never-Never Land. Her visit to Mission Control, followed by "blast off" on moving seats for a journey to Mars, scored another hit—Corinne believed she was actually going there! The All-America parade, held every afternoon in Main Street in "The Land of Make-Believe—The Magic Kingdom" was another highlight. To be photographed with Pluto was sheer bliss, and as for those masks of Pluto, Mickey and Donald, even Mommy wore one—she was really in the spirit.

Of course, you can stay at the conveniently located accommodation within the Walt Disney World Resort, so that you can return to the attractions in the evening after a rest in your hotel. Unless you want a really upscale vacation spent entirely in the Disney World village, however, it's an unecessary expense, especially if you have fortitude like us.

Moving on to another major attraction in the resort, Epcot, we found something which Corinne deemed "even better than The Magic Kingdom." At the Magic Eye Theater we viewed a three-dimensional "musical motion picture space adventure film," starring Michael Jackson. There was never a dull moment in Epcot, and we returned to the car full of chatter about what we liked best.

The enormous, gleaming geosphere called Spaceship Earth, 185 feet high and dominating the whole of Epcot, is two worlds in one—Future World and World Showcase. The time machine took us from the distant past to a possible future, a fantastic experience. The process of loading and unloading visitors on and off the rail cars was very slick and the waiting time minimal.

If needed, a limited number of wheelchairs and motorized trikes are available at the stroller and wheelchair rental station at the base of the spaceship. Complimentary tape cassettes and portable recorders, intended to assist sight-impaired guests, can be obtained from the information center (Earth Station). To encourage the use of dining facilities in Epcot, food and drink are not allowed into the center, but we were ignorant of this fact beforehand and no-one seemed to notice. Food and drinks were rather expensive inside.

Corinne was fascinated by The Living Seas, another Epcot attraction. We watched dolphins, sharks, and groupers swimming lazily around us in gigantic tanks. The never-ending stream of visitors had no time to notice my daughter and me kneeling on the carpet with our noses glued to the sides of these tanks—we were hypnotized.

"A version of The Wizard of Oz, performed by 'Sea-Lions of the Silver Screen'"

Sea World, a major attraction situated off Interstate 4 and International Drive, is home to the four-ton killer whale, Shamu, and Baby Shamu who was born in captivity. Corinne's face was a picture when Shamu surged from the depths of the tank and dramatically swept a wet-suited lady about twenty feet into the air. How she applauded! At the Sea-Lion and Otter Stadium we witnessed a version of The Wizard of Oz, performed by "Sea-Lions of the Silver Screen." During the intervals a brilliant mime artist entertained the audience; Corinne was captivated and giggled throughout all his antics.

After the hectic pace in Orlando, we were glad to find a more peaceful resort for the remainder of our vacation. We weren't aware that Florida is so low-lying—only a couple of feet above sea level in most places. As we drove west through Tampa we were surprised to discover the main highway flooded. We were diverted down to the Gulf of Mexico and, wishing to be near the sea but not to the tourist-weary towns of St. Petersburg or Clearwater, we drove a little farther south, opposite Sarasota and in manatee (sea-cow) country.

The journey was uneventful but the weather was sultry and we passed several "Evacuation Point" signs, which we later realized were to assist the population when the storms came and a hasty escape was necessary. We could appreciate their importance when Hurricane Gilbert hovered in the distance, turning the skies to shades of deep purple, blue, and black, churning up the sea and whipping through the palms. We wondered, as we sipped our wine on the porch at the *Silver Beach Resort*, Longboat Key, where the porpoises and pelicans would take shelter from the relentless blast. Corinne was excited, not foreseeing the outcome if the hurricane turned its fearsome head inland. Thankfully, it did not, veering instead toward Texas, but I contemplated how quickly I could pack if the need arose.

We followed up a recommendation and visited *Moore's Stone Crab*, a restaurant founded in 1927 by Jack Moore who walked the flats in the bays, collecting stone crabs by hand. As his business grew, he started rowing a boat up and down the coast, sleeping on the beach at night. All traps used today are built by hand and crabs are brought in daily. The claws are carefully removed and the live crabs are returned to the waters to regenerate their claws. The Florida lobster (crawfish) is also trapped, and all other seafood is local, coming from the fishing village of Cortez or from the Florida Keys.

Corinne was determined to fish, so we purchased a small rod and reel from the Cortez harbor shop. She managed to bring in a flounder and a sheepshead along the estuary, but unhooking them was left to her father! I found a disused crab-pot in which to keep them for a while and photograph them; we later set them free.

Another must for Corinne was a "live" American football game. On the recommendation of a waiter serving in a nearby restaurant, her father took her to see a local high school game. They set off one evening to the Balvanz stadium to see the Bayshore High School team (The Bruins) play the Tampa Bay Vo-Tech "Fighting Vulcans," complete with cheerleaders and a marching band called The Honeybears. Corinne and her father returned at midnight. "It was brill!" exclaimed Corinne.

We satisfied our daughter's last request—to visit Spaceport USA—on the day before our departure from Orlando airport. A modern, air-conditioned, double-decker bus took us around the campus on a two-hour tour with taped commentary. There were many stopping points along the route.

The 56,656-hectare Kennedy Space Center reservation protects more endangered species of birds, mammals, and reptiles than any other area of the USA. Sanctuaries were set up in 1963 and 1975, and alligators and herons can be viewed on the primitive Barrier Beach.

"Corinne still recalls the spectacular film, 'The Dream is Alive,' which was shot by NASA astronauts on their missions"

The terrain covered by the Kennedy Space Center was first mapped by Spanish explorers over four centuries ago. Cape Canaveral was selected as the launch site for testing long-range guided missiles after World War II. In 1964, NASA (National Aeronautics and Space Administration) was relocated to Merritt Island, which was chosen for the gigantic Apollo rocket, around which we were able to walk.

Corinne took many photographs, including one alongside Saturn 5, which dwarfed her. During the tour we saw a recreation of the first lunar landing. Corinne still recalls the spectacular film, "The Dream is Alive," which was shot by NASA astronauts on their missions. Watching the space shuttle lift off on the massive, five-story screen is a thrilling experience—from countdown to touchdown we could believe we were there!

Our daughter's bedroom is bedecked with posters of her American experience and she still has a taste for burgers. We had to get used to a few cultural differences, but wherever we traveled we were *all* made to feel welcome, and at no time did we encounter prejudice. We would repeat the adventure without hesitation.

Whirlwind USA

At the age of 63 and after a 20-year remission, Christine Panton had cancer again and required radiotherapy on a daily basis. Three months after she had finished the treatment she was weak and couldn't walk far without getting out of breath. She had been advised to eat a good protein meal at least three times a day; this caused her to put on 35 pounds, which exacerbated her arthritis in feet and hips. Christine's husband, Jim, is diabetic and needs insulin twice a day, but as long as he keeps his drugs cold and eats at regular intervals, the world is his oyster.

I felt frail and depressed, but the promise of a six-week vacation was as a carrot to a donkey. I just *had* to be well enough to go. First, I checked with my specialist (I'm afraid I didn't confess how extensively we were going to travel). Jim ordered an adequate supply of insulin and ensured that the details in his Medic-Alert bracelet were clear and correct. We consulted our travel agent regarding insurance, stating our medical problems, and obtained cover for all eventualities.

The next step was pure excitement. Every relevant brochure was studied and discussed. The American tourist office in London sent us information on temperatures, advice on clothing and eating out, even free tickets to tourist attractions. Many tour operators offer tailor-made packages to the States, but *American Express* seemed the most flexible; it is available to non cardholders and can be booked through most travel agents.

America is an enormous place, each state like a separate country, and we wanted to see it all. Gradually, we sorted our priorities, and the finished package was everything we could have hoped for. It cost about $3500 per

person in 1988, including the flights (seven in all), hotel rooms (not food), two-week bus tour, and villa rental in Florida. All our accommodation was excellent and my request for vegetarian meals on all flights was honored, although not by very appetizing ones. Our outward and return flights were with *British Airways*, our internal flights with *Continental Airlines*—all gave the usual civil service, cramped seating, and mediocre meals.

First stop—JFK airport, New York. The courtesy bus took us through slum areas, miles of filth and graffiti, and deposited us outside beautiful Grand Central Station. Here we were tricked by a bogus taxi driver, who pocketed our fare and melted into the landscape. After this we caught a yellow cab and the driver, a huge man, gave us a lesson on survival in New York: "Never trust anyone, and hang on to your money." Then he restored our faith in human nature by refusing any payment.

I shall never forget my first glimpse of the amazing Manhattan skyline—it was thrilling. But we were glad to reach our air-conditioned room, away from the 99 percent humidity outside. We were 21 floors up but could still hear the constant traffic noise and wailing of police and paramedic sirens. There was a rock concert on at Madison Square Gardens, exactly opposite our hotel. The road was filled with mounted police and excited fans. We watched from the hotel foyer and marveled at this bustling, terrifying city.

"By the time I realized I'd been tricked, our other bag had gone"

Next day was spent walking the streets to Times Square, which was disappointingly seedy, awash with garbage and pathetic human derelicts. Later, we enjoyed a spectacular river trip to the Statue of Liberty, then returned to visit *Macy's*, which I found bewildering and too big for comfort.

On the following day we waited at the hotel for the bus to Newark airport. I guarded the luggage in the lobby while Jim kept watch in the street. Two swarthy men approached me: "Your bus is in and your fellow wants you." I picked up the nearest bag and staggered outside; by the time I realized I'd been tricked, our other bag had gone.

It's a common trick—a lookout man notes the position of a possible victim and telephones from the lobby to his waiting accomplices. We were fortunate that the bag I grabbed contained all our drugs and medication, together with money and passports. Wicked, dirty old New York—I wouldn't have missed you for the world.

After the robbery we were shocked and therefore negligent about eating properly. I arrived in Los Angeles exhausted, and Jim was totally confused, unable to find his baggage tickets or remember our destination. Once aware of our problems, the chap on the gate was instantly helpful, waiving the baggage-ticket check and showing me the way to phone for the hotel shuttle bus. A few sugar lumps and a candy bar later, Jim was his old self again! A comfortable night in the *Mayfair Hotel* gave us time to regain our equilibrium and we were up bright and early to meet our friends from Cherry Valley.

The next five days were spent in a whirl of wonder. We visited Universal Studios and Disneyland. We watched tumbleweeds blowing in the pretty streets of Palm Springs and sailed around a hotel lounge on a pleasure boat. Huge glass walls rose at our approach and we sailed majestically out of the hotel and around the golf course. We were only visitors to the hotel, and we only ordered iced tea, but we were made to feel as welcome as the most affluent guest.

We had intended to visit the *Spruce Goose* (flying boat) and the *Queen Mary*, both at Long Beach, but first we drove to a campground 50 miles away and 8000 feet up Big Bear Mountain. Here I fell in love with the cheeky blue jays and the peaceful pine forests where they live. Seeing my rapture, our long-suffering friends offered to fetch their trailer-home, so that we might camp there for two nights. This could only happen in America, I thought, as we sped 50 miles down the mountain, stocked up at a shopping mall and struggled back just in time to go to bed.

"The pace of the trip is quite fast—we were required to rise at 6am on most mornings—and there is little time for relaxation"

The forest was a magical place by day, but breathtaking when a huge moon shone through the trees and the heat of the day gave way to the perishing cold of the night. The campground was perfect, complete with fire-pit, barbecue, and picnic table. We spent the next day in nearby Big Bear City, where an Octoberfest was in full swing. Everyone gave us a great welcome and there was singing, dancing, and drinking, which ended in much hilarity and a rather hair-raising drive back to camp.

Saying a reluctant farewell to Pat and Leo, we returned to our hotel in Los Angeles and the following morning met the *Greyhound* bus which was to take us on "The West Coast Wonderland Tour." This is offered as an escorted bus tour or an independent tour by self-drive car. The price includes several excursions, accommodation, and a few (very good) meals. The pace of the trip is quite fast—we were required to rise at 6am on most mornings—and there is little time for relaxation if you take advantage of the extra excursions, which in my opinion were worth every cent.

The steps of the bus were steep but willing hands were always there to help. The bus was comfortable, air-conditioned, and equipped with a toilet which we were asked not to use unless we were desperate. Normally, cold drinks are available on board, but it was late in the season (September) and we had to fend for ourselves. We stopped at least once each morning and afternoon for about half an hour, as well as stops for sightseeing and lunch.

We soon learned to stock up on canned drinks for the journey. It was difficult to find pure fruit juice—most drinks were of the sickly sweet, cola variety. To a diabetic person regular food is a necessity, so we were careful both to allow time to eat before embarking on the day's program, and to carry sufficient snacks and drinks on the bus to cover the gaps between meals.

At the start of the bus trip I confided my medical problem to our courier and whenever we stopped I had the opportunity to choose between joining the others, or leaving my husband to explore while I sat inside the coach (where the air conditioning was left on for me) or outside where the courier often found me a seat or recommended a café.

We joined the tour on the fourth day—the rest of the group had been sightseeing in LA for three days. Our first stop was Sea World, where I marveled at the rapport between the sea creatures, including dolphins and whales, and the humans with whom they performed. On to San Diego, where I purchased a large Mexican hat—how glad I was to have it during the following scorching ten days.

"We sat at candle-lit tables beneath the stars, listening to 'cowboys' singing"

A spectacular drive through the desert came next, and a pause to photograph giant cacti. I wandered happily in open-toed sandals until warned of rattlesnakes, black widow spiders, and tarantulas. Thank goodness we saw nothing but a lizard. The scenery unfolded in never-ending grandeur, until we reached Rawhide where we sat at candle-lit tables beneath the stars, listening to "cowboys" singing. Smoke curled high from the barbecue where 1600 giant steaks are cooked each night. I don't eat steak but chicken was happily substituted.

The highlight of the tour was a helicopter trip over the Grand Canyon—I am desperately afraid of heights but I knew I *must* go. Flying low over the treetops, the pilot warned us to "prepare for a sudden drop beneath us." Nothing could have prepared me for the enormity of the void which suddenly replaced the land below. The canyon is, in places, over 25 miles wide, and stretches for some 5000 feet down to the tiny river glimmering in the distance. I clutched my husband as we flew between mountain ridges and deep clefts, wheeling and soaring among multicolored rocks that are millions of years old. During the half-hour trip, the theme music to *Chariots of Fire* was softly played into our earphones. It was one of the few times when I have welcomed background music—it fitted the occasion exactly and each time I hear it I relive that awe-inspiring experience.

Ironically, this ride also gave me my worst moment of the vacation—trying to get into the helicopter. My husband had already been strapped in, and I just hadn't the strength to pull myself up. I suppose to the ground crew it was a hilarious sight—a fat lady dangling precariously and needing an undignified push. To me it was humiliating and exhausting. If I had asked for help in advance there would have been no problem, but once on the launching pad with all that noise it was impossible to make anyone understand. Nevertheless, I would do it again, dangle and all.

From brash Las Vegas, where we stayed at the opulent *Golden Nugget* and visited the incredible *Caesar's Palace*, we traveled on to Yosemite National Park. I sat in an amphitheater while a ranger gave a talk on bears and forest fires, and cicadas "sang" in the pine trees. Yosemite is a rugged wilderness and we felt rather cheated that we were only given a few hours to enjoy it, when the itinerary had stated two days. These changes may be made if the driver or courier deem it necessary, perhaps because of weather conditions or other factors outside their control.

"We watched the sun go down with such a flourish that as it slipped over the rim of the world everyone stood up and clapped"

We fell in love with San Francisco, however, where we rode on a cable car and took a trip around the bay amidst noisy sea-lions and seals, then strolled around Fisherman's Wharf and sampled clam chowder. We traveled the Pacific Coast Drive on our last day, pausing for lunch at Carmel, where the pedestrian has right of way and cars stop whenever you cross the pretty, tree-lined streets.

Back in LA we parted from our tour companions, spent one more night, and took a 5am flight to New Orleans. We had chosen to stay in the French Quarter, which is the oldest part. Although some areas appear neglected and seedy, there are many beautiful buildings, their delicate, wrought-iron balconies hung with flowering baskets. Our hotel (*The Royal Sonesta*) was luxurious, built around a garden courtyard with heated swimming pool—much enjoyed in the early evenings—and large patio (with bar).

The days were hot and humid, but it is in the warm evenings and after dark that New Orleans comes to life. Jazz music spills out from every doorway and the streets are thronged with pedestrians wandering from bar to bar, enjoying the live bands and foot-tapping the night away. There are also many sex shops and girlie shows, invitations to orgies and other dubious delights— we stuck to the jazz.

Five heady days later we flew to Orlando where my old school friend of fifty years ago was there to meet us, having driven for eleven hours from North Carolina. We were to entertain Iris and her husband, Bill, in a rented villa about thirty miles north of Tampa airport, with easy access to Highway 19, in Port Richey on the west coast of Florida.

The comfortable, well-equipped bungalow on the edge of a lake had its own swimming pool (unheated) and came with a free car. There were three double bedrooms, two bathrooms, a large living room-dining room, and a superb kitchen, all spotless. The patio furniture included sunbeds, table, and chairs. The surrounding properties were all different, many in Spanish style and with delightful cactus gardens. The weather here, as in most places we visited, can be extremely hot and it is essential to check with your travel agent when you choose your dates.

Our problem with the heat was keeping the insulin cool! In Europe we have always found a refrigerated mini-bar in our room; we expected to find the same in America—not so. However, the *New York Penta Hotel* provided us with one as soon as we explained our predicament. A couple of the smaller hotels agreed to keep the insulin overnight in their kitchen fridge. Our greatest discovery was the ice machine—to be found on each floor of most large hotels. We only had to fill the plastic ice-bucket (provided in each room) and the drugs stayed cool in our air-conditioned rooms despite the heat and humidity outside. Jim also took a small "cool pack" which was frozen overnight and then kept, with his insulin, in a waterproof shaving kit for daytime travel—this proved invaluable.

We thought the highways and scenery of Florida were rather bill-boarded and commercial. In Tarpon Springs, a sponge-diving center almost entirely inhabited by Greeks, we took a boat trip and watched a sponge diver at work. Surprisingly, sponges are black and slimy when harvested—they don't look fit to go in the tub. The Greeks run many good restaurants and gift shops selling sponges, shells, lovely junk jewelry, summer clothes, and other such tourist treasures.

Due to our late arrival the owner of the villa allowed us to stay an extra day—typical of the generosity and desire to please which we experienced all over the States. Our last evening was spent in an outdoor restaurant overlooking the Gulf of Mexico. Here we watched the sun go down with such a flourish that as it slipped over the rim of the world everyone stood up and clapped.

The four of us drove in leisurely fashion up the East Coast for ten more days with Iris and Bill in North Carolina. They had previously lived on the beach but, finding the hurricanes too lively, bought a bit of pine forest inland and had their home transported on the back of a truck to its new site. Two men had to sit on the roof to push the overhead wires out of the way of the chimney, but Iris didn't even have to pack her china.

The house had been mounted high among the trees, with utility rooms and garages beneath. It was like living with the birds and quite delightful except for the water bugs—black, shiny creatures, inclined to scuttle across bathroom floors just as I was about to have a shower.

"Our greatest problem was that our disabilities didn't show. To the world, we looked like a man with a lazy, fat wife"

The natives of North Carolina have the most charming accent and everyone was friendly and hospitable. The countryside is almost English, and full of interesting sights. Many of the old plantations are now clubs and golf courses; the roadside cafés have rest rooms for "Men folk" and "Wimmin folk," and play background revivalist music.

It was in one of these cafés, with its red gingham tablecloths and jam-jar glasses, that I asked what "hush puppies" were. A passing waitress heard and, within minutes, brought a basket full of little cornbread rolls for me to try, and a pile of pretty paper place mats which had southern recipes printed on them. "Take them home to England," she said, "to remember us by." As if I needed anything to remind me of these warmhearted people.

We viewed the pretty town of Wilmington from a horse-drawn buggy, and chugged up the river in a beautiful paddle-steamer. The US battleship *North Carolina* is at anchor here; it is a fascinating museum, surrounded by notices saying, "Don't feed the crocodiles."

I attended the local church where, after a happy service and some wonderful singing from an all-female choir, I was surrounded by kind folks wishing me well. The local people hugged and kissed me on meeting, and when our stay ended, five of them turned out to wave, bearing gifts, and posies to pin on my suit.

From Wilmington airport, Jim and I flew to Raleigh, where we changed flights for the last leg of our trip, to Washington DC. The flight from Wilmington was in a small aircraft which held about twenty people sitting in bucket seats each side of a narrow aisle. There were wonderful views, as it did not fly very high. The baggage check at Wilmington is very slow because it is only a small airport, so allow plenty of time; transfer between planes was directly across the runway.

Washington looked from the air like a multicolored carpet—it was the fall and the trees were a riot of autumn hues. On the ground, our overall impression was of beauty and poverty, side by side—clean, white buildings and men wrapped in sacks on park benches. Our last day was spent in the Smithsonian Institute, where I walked through a space rocket and performed a simulated landing on the moon!

Back to earth with a vengeance for our overnight return journey to dear old England. It was good to be home, but what a vacation. In retrospect, our greatest problem was that our disabilities didn't show. To the world, we looked like a man with a lazy, fat wife who both needed constant feeding! This only goes to show that you should never judge a sausage by its skin—I hated being fat, was sick to death of eating, and would have been delighted to walk around with the others.

If you are similarly placed, my advice is to notify in advance any needs you may have, whether it be on the plane, bus, or at the hotel, and not be afraid to ask for help. You'll get it and served with a smile. Our overwhelming memory of America is the friendliness of its people and their willingness to please. "Enjoy" is a much-used word over there, and that's what we did.

Alaska Tour

Bob Huskey was injured in a diving accident in 1956 and is C-5,6 quadriplegic, unable to walk at all. He and his wife, Bea, have traveled extensively on their own and with their three children all over the USA over the last 33 years. In June 1991 they traveled to Alaska with Alaska Heritage Tours.

Bob had wanted to visit the 49th state since reading adventure stories as a child. Much of Alaska is north of the Arctic Circle and largely undeveloped; a good deal of the development, including the Alaska Highway (only recently paved), came during World War II because of the strategic military location of the area.

As we sat on the patio of the Clarion Hotel in Anchorage, the roar of the seaplanes—about one every minute—made me realize that almost everyone in Alaska travels by small plane. Later, when we were eating, it was interesting to hear pilots talking about where they had been, where they were off to, swapping stories—we had read about the bush pilots and their adventures but this was the real McCoy! We were told that the lake on which the hotel is situated is adjacent to the busiest seaplane airport in the world, and there is a ten-year wait for a mooring spot. Although we were assured that we could take a flight, time would not allow it, and we experienced feelings that recurred many times in the next ten days—too much to see and not enough time.

We arrived on Wednesday evening and were met at the airport by Glenn Williams and his accessible van; Glenn was to be our tour guide for one week, later in the trip. We rented a car at an agency just across the street from the Clarion. They did not have hand controls, so Bea drove. This is unusual for us—we like to rent a car with hand controls so that Bob can do his share of the driving. We spent the next four days sightseeing on our own.

Driving south out of Anchorage we began to see the wildlife as soon as we left the city: moose, eagles, and Dall sheep. We didn't stop at the accessible swamp—yes, a boardwalk through a marshland—although Bob wanted to (wife driving). The drive was spectacular: Cook's inlet lay to our right and snow-capped mountains rose on our left. Our destinaton was Seward, where we had reservations for a boat tour and a hotel for one night.

The Kenai Fjords boat tour was certainly one of the highlights for us. We got into Seward about noon and took the afternoon tour. The boat tour operators were expecting the wheelchair and were very helpful. We could sit inside the cabin or be outside on the deck, and Bob was free to move around as he wanted. The Kenai Fjords are like fingers reaching into the mainland—each one a total surprise and each surpassing the last with its beauty. One of the surprises amidst the gorgeous scenery was a breathtaking home built on a rock—totally separate from the sheer cliffs of the mainland; the residents had their plane and boat moored at the base of the rock.

Everyone on the tour boat stood at the rail looking at the vast array of birds and other wildlife. The captain needed only a signal that some form of wildlife was off one side and he would turn the boat so that everyone could get a view or a picture. The variety and beauty of the birds was particularly stunning, perhaps because we were there at nesting time. On a large rock we saw sea lions basking in the sun. On another rocky ridge jutting high out of the water we saw mountain goat families stepping lightly on what looked to us like vertical cliffs. We saw how the great earthquake of 1964 had changed the shoreline of the fjords.

We spent the night at the New Seward Best Western Hotel (we think the "Old" was damaged in the earthquake) which was accessible. Our breakfast was ordered through room service from a restaurant across the street from the hotel (standard procedure—not because of the wheelchair). Seward is a very small town but everyone was friendly and extremely helpful. The tourist season is short and they make the most of it!

Friday morning we loaded our car and headed for Homer, which is located on the lower Kenai Peninsula. As we drove out of Seward we turned down a dirt road to see Exit Glacier

National Park. There are so many glaciers in Alaska that they almost becoming boring. But we were at the park early, and in the morning sun the ice was breathtaking. Paved walkways led us almost all the way to the edge of the glacier, and we could feel the cold air coming off the ice. The rangers, who were obliging and informative, told us that the paths around the glacier often have to be closed because of bears coming into the area—the bears always have right of way!

"Moose have become something of a nuisance to the locals as they wander into people's yards and help themselves to shrubs or flowers for lunch"

Homer has been accessible by car only since the early 1950s. A paved road now strings together the coastal towns of Kenai, Soldotna, and Ninilchik. The last is an old Russian village dominated by the onion dome of the church which stands on a cliff overlooking the village and Cook's inlet. Like many of the "towns" we stopped in, Ninilchik is really just a tiny village with a store and a post office, where the villagers try to preserve some of their heritage, but it is unique and well worth a stop.

As we drove into Homer, we encountered a mother moose and her twins walking down the highway. Moose have become something of a nuisance to the locals as they wander into people's yards and help themselves to shrubs or flowers for lunch. Across Cook's inlet there is a magnificent view of two volcanoes—Mt. Iliamna, rising 10,000 feet above the sea, and Mt. Redoubt, which became active again in 1989.

Homer is one of the main fishing hubs in Alaska. Here you can rent a boat or simply fish along the water's edge. We saved the fishing trip for next time. There are many rules and regulations for fishing in Alaska and it is advisable to head out with a guide who knows all the ins and outs.

In Homer we stayed at the *Bidarka Inn*, where our room was accessible but the restaurant was not. The next morning we stopped at a restaurant in a resort on what is called Homer Spit—a small "tail" of land jutting into the bay. The parking lot was a real challenge—large rocks embedded in dirt—but since we never allow this sort of obstacle to stand in our way we made it with minimal difficulty. The restaurant was accessible by a long wooden ramp and we ate looking out at the bay, watching the boats and the sun glistening on the water. We then made our way back to Anchorage by the same road: Alaska has two main highways and they both run north–south from Fairbanks to Homer or Fairbanks to Valdez, with a connecting arm north of Anchorage and one from Mt. McKinley.

We saw so much beautiful scenery: the mountains were all still snow-capped; the wild flowers were in bloom, and the land was criss-crossed by small streams running fast and clear. We saw an eagle sitting on a rock one morning, fishing for his first meal of the day. We had experienced so much in the first four days, on our own driving tour, that we were already overwhelmed by the dimensions and grandeur of Alaska. Although we doubted that the trip could improve, we had yet to meet Glenn Williams and discover his plans for us.

Back in Anchorage, we were ready to take off with Glenn and his accessible van, a modified Ford sixteen-seater, with a portable ramp for loading wheelchairs. For those who wish to stay in their wheelchairs there is a tie-down; others can transfer to a regular captain's chair seat. Glenn can accommodate both wheelchair users and able-bodied passengers on the same tour, and many of his tours are made up of mixed groups. We were very surprised to learn that we would be the only two on this tour—how lucky can you get!

We drove south out of Anchorage and after several stops (Bob was told we could stop as often as he liked) Glenn drove the van onto a flatbed train car. The train transports people and their cars to Whittier for the ferry ride to Valdez. Everyone in Whittier lives in the same barracks—one address for all! After boarding the ferry, Bob transferred to a stair climber—his first experience of one—and went up to the main deck, where he settled back into his own chair. Once on-board he could move freely out on deck or remain in the cabin. We had come dressed to stay on deck (long underwear, winter coats and hats) which we did most of the trip, except when eating our evening meal. During the trip across Prince William Sound we saw otters swimming on their backs, seals lounging on ice floes, birds of all kinds, and of course the magnificent Columbia Glacier spilling ice floes into the water.

Valdez is the end of the Alaskan Pipe Line. Later we saw the oil lines which travel the length of Alaska both above and below ground, from their starting point at Prudhoe Bay in the Arctic Ocean to their termination at Valdez, a distance of about 900 miles. It was 10:30 at night when we arrived in Valdez, but it was still light and we were able to walk around a bit. We stayed at the Westmark Valdez.

"Even today many people use dog sleds for everyday transportation during the winter months"

Valdez is an attractive town which was rebuilt higher up the mountainside after being wiped out by the tidal waves that followed the 1964 earthquake. It is hard to describe the feeling of isolation there. One road heads north, passing through spectacular mountains, waterfalls, and glaciers, but the going is slow and the surface rough as a result of the freezing and thawing during the severe winters, and it's an all-day drive to Fairbanks. There are very few cars on the highway, even in the tourist season. Access to an airplane is almost essential for residents of Valdez.

Glenn kept his promise and pulled off the road frequently to let us gawk; Bob was able to get out of the van as often as he wanted. One of the most awe-inspiring sights was the Elias-Wrangell mountain range on the Canada–USA border. This area has been placed by each country on the World Heritage list of striking natural areas. It is North America's largest grouping of glaciers and greatest concentration of peaks reaching over 16,000 feet. We were lucky enough to see them across the Copper river valley on a clear, crisp day.

Fairbanks was wonderful, but we were glad it was summer—they had had twelve feet of snow the previous winter! The University of Alaska sits on a hill at the edge of town and it is said that the student dormitories there have the most beautiful view of any campus in the world. Fairbanks was as far north as we went, but we hope to return and take a trip above the Arctic Circle. We took a boat trip and stopped at a recreated native American village where we saw a dog sled demonstration and got to pet the dogs; we were amazed at how small they were. Later on, we stopped at the museum of the Iditorad Dog Sled Race and saw the curator's dog. Even today many people use dog sleds for everyday transportation during the winter months. When we returned to the Regency Hotel in Fairbanks at about 11pm we took pictures outside just as if it were daytime.

No trip to Alaska would be complete without a stop at the highest peak in North America (20,320 feet)—Mt. McKinley, or "Denali," as the natives call it. A helicopter tour of the area was perhaps the highlight of our trip; certainly for Bob it was the most exciting. Glenn had made all the arrangements, so we were expected and Bob was lifted into the helicopter. We saw our only bear of the tour, along with mountain goats and a different perspec-

tive of the glaciers. The actual mountain peak is best viewed from a distance and is not always visible because of weather conditions. A mountain that high creates its own weather system: just because you fly close to the mountain does not mean you will see the peak. We caught a glimpse of it from several miles south, looking back towards the mountain.

On the drive to Anchorage from Fairbanks, the last leg of our tour, we visited a musk ox farm, where they comb the underfur from the animals to make yarn for the locals to knit unbelievably soft hats, scarves, and gloves. We passed through the Matanuska Valley where the growing season is short but the long daylight hours allow the growth of record-size vegetables. We stopped in Nenana, where villagers lay bets on when the Tanana river will thaw.

Alaska is a wonderful place to visit. The people are friendly and keen to show off the natural wonders of their state and to tell how they survive the long winters: some leave for Hawaii (or "out," as they say) come October, but most stay and relish the cold and snow, the fishing and hunting. On our next trip dog-sledding will be a must, along with a raft ride, a plane ride, fishing, and a trip to Point Barrow.

One thing to remember when traveling in Alaska: there are not many hotels outside of Anchorage so you must plan ahead. Glenn made all of our arrangements, including the hotel reservations for the time we spent on our own. He is very knowledgeable about the needs of a wheelchair user, and is both helpful and accommodating. We flew *TWA* from St. Louis, Missouri, to Seattle, Washington, then *Alaska Airlines* to Anchorage. On the trip home we had a lot of help from the folks at *Alaska Airlines*; otherwise, we would not have made the connection. Our luggage arrived the next day! But nothing could spoil our memories of Alaska, and we both recommend this trip to everyone.

Hawaii: a paradise for the SCI

Stephen Fuller has a spinal cord injury as a result of a diving accident over twenty years ago, and is paralyzed from the shoulders down. He has lived in Stockton, California, all his life and, until being hit by a car about six years ago, had never been much farther than San Francisco. Stephen had been trying to obtain a new electric wheelchair from Medi-Cal but they kept refusing it until his was demolished in the car accident. He also received compensation—enough money to put down on a new van and go to Hawaii.

Every time I visit Hawaii I go to Honolulu, on the island of Oahu, not because I don't want to see any of the other islands but because of the transportation situation. Oahu is the only one that has public transportation from the airport to the hotels as well as to other parts of the island, unless you can transfer into a car—and if you are in an electric chair you still have to find a way to transport your chair to the hotel. I know some quads don't mind using a manual chair, but when I go to Hawaii I prefer not to depend on anyone to get around, and the transfers back and forth from chair to car would cause me a lot of pain.

Of the two transportation systems available, I prefer Handi-Van, run by the City and County of Honolulu, although neither this nor the alternative, Handi-Cab, is perfect. Handi-Vans are lift-equipped minibuses and you must obtain a transit pass before you can use them; you can do this in person or by calling the office before your trip and sending a doctor's letter to verify your disability. Officially they won't carry luggage, so they are no good for airport transfers, but you can try—I've got away with it a couple of times. You

have to give advance notice and be prepared not to be picked up exactly on time and to pick up other riders along the way. If you don't mind seeing parts of the island that you hadn't planned to go through, Handi-Van is a useful service.

Handi-Cab is a privately owned company that uses standard vans with six-inch raised roofs and fold-up ramps instead of lifts. The advantage is that when you book a van you are the only passenger they pick up and they take you directly to your destination. The company charges only for the client in a wheelchair, so friends or family go free. It's useful for point-to-point transportation, such as shopping trips or restaurant outings, but not cheap—$9 for pickup and $2.25 per mile. The charge for the one-way airport transfer to Waikiki is $35. There are also tours, charged per person—a day-long tour of the island will cost around $100. When I used them a couple of years ago for an airport transfer they left me stranded and I spent four hours at the airport trying to find a way to my hotel, but they may have improved since then.

> **"You should be prepared for the fact that Hawaii is very close to the equator so the sun tends to burn unprotected skin quickly"**

There are a few car rental places that rent passenger vans, and if you ask they will usually be happy to take a seat out so that with the aid of a ramp you can board without transferring from your wheelchair. On my last trip I talked to Aloha Car Rental and they were charging full-size vans for $60 per day or around $300 per week. It's advisable to call around a few companies when you arrive in Hawaii. Wheelchair ramps can be rented from Abbey Foster (☎808/845-5000) for around $50 a week. This medical equipment company is highly recommended and can help with wheelchair repair as well as rental of supplies and equipment. If you need anything in your hotel room, such as a Hoyer lift, you can call and put the rental on your charge card, giving time of arrival and departure, and they will have it waiting for you at the hotel.

I've been to Hawaii in summer, winter, spring, and fall, and found the climate fairly constant, the only difference being that the summer months are about five degrees warmer and a little more humid. A lot of SCI people have a problem with heat, but I've found that there is always a trade wind—if I get overheated in the sun I sit in the shade under some palm trees for a while and cool off real quick. All the same, you should be prepared for the fact that Hawaii is very close to the equator so the sun tends to burn unprotected skin quickly; I suggest a visit to an Island Tan store—there's one in Royal Hawaiian Shopping Center.

The travel agent I use—Janice McCarthy of *Great Adventure Travel Agency* in Lodi, California—goes to Hawaii often and visits a few hotels every time to find out if they are accessible for a wheelchair. Since she is not in a chair she doesn't know what I need in a room so she tells me which hotels are accessible and gives me the phone numbers; then I can call and ask the appropriate questions. I've learned by experience to ask more than general questions: in 1988 I went to the *Waikiki Gateway*, unfortunately one of the hotels my travel agent hadn't checked out, and when I called to discuss accessibility I was assured the bathroom door was wide enough, although they didn't have the measurements, because a wheelchair user lived in the hotel and had no problems; in fact, the door was 18 to 20 inches wide, the seat on my chair is 20 inches and the wheelbase wider than that. Now I always ask for the exact measurement.

The next thing I check is the airline policy on batteries, and I also ask the airline if they will pre-assign me a bulkhead seat next to the door where passengers get on and off the plane—

this enables me to transfer directly from my wheelchair to my seat. Otherwise, there are two transfers involved—first to an aisle chair, then, after being wheeled down the plane, from aisle chair to the aircraft seat—and this is painful for many wheelchair users, especially quads.

On my trips the most accommodating airline—and usually the one offering the best prices—has been *American Trans Air*, a charter airline used by different tour companies, including *Suntrips*, an operator I've used a couple of times and like a lot. *America Trans Air* will pre-assign a bulkhead seat, and their staff are friendly and helpful. *Suntrips'* only requirement is that you disconnect the battery cables from the battery (if it's a wet cell battery). Make sure you mark cables and terminals so that the airline maintenance people reconnect the battery correctly, especially if it's a 24V system. On my most recent trip I flew on *Northwest Airlines* and thought their service was real good. They made me disconnect the batteries and managed to get them hooked up properly; they also pre-assigned us bulkhead seats.

"I haven't discovered anywhere on the island with wheelchair access to the ocean"

I've stayed at several hotels and condos. We rented the *Waikiki Lanai*, a two-bedroom apartment, for $100 a day, and a one-bedroom condo at the *Waikiki Banyan* cost the same amount. It sounds expensive but split four ways the price wasn't so bad—with the exception of my last trip I've never paid over $450 for my hotel and round-trip air fare. The bathrooms at both these apartments would be difficult for most people in wheelchairs, but the arrangement suited me because I have a hard time transferring to shower or tub, and only use the sink to back up to and wash my hair. I've recently stayed at two other hotels with inaccessible bathrooms—the *Colony Surf Hotel* (from $150 a night), about a mile from Waikiki center and on the beach, and the *Outrigger Reef Towers* (about $100 a night), in the middle of the action; both had large bedrooms and adjoining kitchenette.

The *Sheraton Moana Surfrider*, the *Outrigger Malia*, and the *Hyatt Regency Waikiki* are all completely wheelchair-accessible. The bathrooms are very large and equipped with grab-bars around tub and toilet. None had roll-in showers when I stayed but I was told in 1989 that the *Sheraton* planned to install one in the near future. The *Halekulani* is the only hotel I am aware of that has roll-in showers (in four of its fourteen accessible rooms), and I reckon it's the best hotel in Waikiki, but rates are over $250 a day. Of the three hotels I stayed in, the *Sheraton Moana Surfrider* was most comfortable, and real plush; it was also the most expensive, at $170 a day. The hotel is on the beach but it was impossible for me to get to the ocean—I haven't discovered anywhere on the island with wheelchair access to the ocean, but the *Surfrider* had plans to put a walkway from the back of the hotel and across the beach so that people in chairs can get into the water.

The *Hawaii Prince Hotel Waikiki* (rooms start at about $195 per night) is reported by the ADA Commissioner to meet ninety-five percent of the ADA regulations for hotel accessibility. If you have a problem finding a hotel that is accessible you can call the *Commission on Persons with Disabilities* (☎808/548-7606, voice or TDD) and they will be able to tell you which hotels have been recently renovated and which they have assessed. They also have a brochure on tourist attractions that they have assessed for accessibility.

There are all kinds of accessible things to do as well as some activities that require a little help. Paradise Park, in the rainforest about twenty minutes from Waikiki, is the wettest part of

Oahu. There are paved paths throughout, and bird shows, cultural shows, and a dazzling array of flowers and plant life to see. Wiamea Falls Park, on North Shore, is similar but worth checking out for the cliff diving, dinner shows, and other entertainment. Neither park is expensive to visit.

"I saw thirty-foot waves hitting the beaches at Sunset and Wiamea, one of the most spectacular sights I've ever seen"

Next to the accessible Honolulu Zoo, in Waikiki, is the Kodak Hula Show, which lasts about an hour, is a lot of fun, and teaches something about the Hawaiian culture. Another big draw for many visitors is a *luau*, or "traditional feast," and the best one I've found, costing around $20, is *Germains*, also recommended for both access and food by other wheelchair users who are resident on the island. It's on the beach, which makes a great setting for the show, and there is plenty of good Hawaiian food. In spite of the sand it's possible to get to some areas without too much trouble, and if you have problems the staff are real helpful. I suggest you mention if you're in a wheelchair when you call to make reservations.

Another fun thing to do is a sunset dinner cruise. I've been on two different boats, the *Aikana* and the *Ilikai*, which are both accessible. Of the two I preferred the *Ilikai* because it's bigger and has better food. All of the cruises include dinner, Hawaiian show, dancing, open bar, and a spectacular view, and the cost is about $30.

For nightclubbers there are several spots offering everything from rock to country. I've been told by other people in chairs that *Scruples* is accessible—it's a smart dance club on Kuhio Avenue. The *Wave Waikiki* is my favorite accessible club: they play heavy rock music, live until 2am and recorded until 4am, enhanced by an excellent sound and light system. It can get crowded, but you meet a lot of new people that way. The Wave is on Kalakaua on the Diamond Head side of the Ala Wai canal and there's a $4 cover charge but sometimes the guy on the door lets a chair in free.

The *Jazz Cellar* is a heavy metal club on the ocean side of Lewers Street. It's not the easiest place to get into but worth the effort if you like heavy metal. If you talk to the bouncer at the front door they will open the back door, where there's a steep ramp, after which only a couple of steps to negotiate and you're in. I managed it with just my friend Michelle's help, so most people will be able to manage.

Of the accessible restaurants that I've tried, I recommend the *New Orleans Bistro*, on Kuhio—they serve outstanding Cajun food and it's one of my favorite places to eat. The *Shorebirds* restaurant at the beachside *Outrigger Reef* hotel (some accessible rooms, $120) is another favorite, where the waitress brings your meat uncooked and you have to cook it on a thirty-foot barbecue. I make it a point to eat at the *Hard Rock Café* at least a couple of times when I visit Hawaii—they serve good food and great Long Island ice teas, play good music and charge reasonable prices. Finally, for atmosphere and the views (the food is also tasty), try the revolving restaurant, *Windows of Hawaii*. There are restaurants to fit anyone's budget, but if none of them suit you there are fast food outlets all over Waikiki and ethnic kitchens serving snacks at the Makai Market and the International Food Court.

For those who want to burn off the calories, there are opportunities for more active pastimes. Some places will take disabled people scuba diving or snorkeling, and you can find these in the Yellow Pages. I like to go up in a sail plane and I recommend a private airport over on North Shore, called Dillingham Field. Flights cost about $45 for half an hour but it's money well spent. You can see some of Hawaii's most famous beaches from the air— Sunset Beach, Banzai Pipeline, and Wiamea. In November 1991 I saw thirty-foot waves hitting the beaches at Sunset and Wiamea, one of the most spectacular sights I've ever seen. The people at Dillingham Field will also take a disabled person sky diving (attached to an able-bodied jumper), and I'm planning to give that a try.

Hawaii is as close to perfect as I have found. I've met a few people in chairs who moved to the islands after spending their vacations there, and they all tell me that it's an ideal place for those of us in wheelchairs. I understand that there are nearly 50,000 people in wheelchairs living on Oahu alone—there have to be good reasons for that, and I think I've discovered some of them.

Hang Loose in Hawaii

Jackie Runge has a number of conditions, including bronchiectasis, chronic sinusitis' and arthritis, and, in her words, is not a writer. Her traveling companion, Peg Smith, is a photo-journalist and the Pennsylvania Field Editor and Travel Editor for Disabled Outdoors Magazine. Both live in Oil City, Pennsylvania.

Our trip started quietly with a ten-mile drive to Franklin Airport where we caught a commuter flight to Pittsburgh International, and spent the night at the

Hampton Inn. Early the next morning we boarded our *United Airlines* flight. It was delayed in taking off because the flight crew hadn't arrived due to foggy weather. We arrived at the huge O'Hare airport in Chicago and were surprised to find that although we were connecting with another *United* flight the terminals seemed to be miles apart. Even using the "people walker" did not help to shorten the distance, and I advise anyone landing at this airport to allow lots of extra time to make connections. After a very long hike we boarded for the next leg of our journey—onward to Los Angeles.

That's when the adventure started! I was taking photos out the window at 37,000 feet, it was so clear. As we flew over the Midwest, I felt like Gulliver viewing a Lilliputian landscape checkered with farms. Jackie had to go to the bathroom. A short time passed, and while I was glued to the window a flight attendant tapped me on the shoulder and said quietly, "Your companion is in the back of the plane, passed out cold." My heart stopped. I threw my camera onto the seat, jumped up and rushed to her aid.

With the help of an oxygen mask, Jackie became more alert. Thank goodness she is a registered nurse as she was the only medically trained person on the plane! As her head cleared, she was able to tell me what to do. It appeared that the abrupt take-off had caused extreme pressure changes which aggravated her sinus condition. To make a long story short, we traveled to Los Angeles on the floor of the plane.

The *United Airlines* crew were sincerely concerned and bent over backward to assist. Even after we departed the airplane in Los Angeles, one of the flight attendants sat with us for a time in the terminal. She told us that although airlines carry a medical bag the crew are not allowed to open it—only a physician can gain access, if one happens to be aboard. This is hard to believe, and we feel that at least one crew member on each flight should be a certified EMT (emergency medical technician), paramedic, or at least trained in CPR (cardiac pulmonary resuscitation).

"The fish swam all around us and the water was unreal, warm as bath water and clear as glass"

A major decision had to be made: should we continue our vacation plans, or try to return home? As California is about as close to Hawaii as it is to Pennsylvania, and the medication Jackie had taken seemed to have helped, she decided to continue. So we caught our breath, and then took off for Hawaii on a United Airlines DC10.

We arrived in Hawaii exhausted, it is such a long flight across the Pacific. Jackie was stiff and sore, but did not experience another "attack." The *Your Main Tour* guide, "Cousin Steve," greeted us at the airport with a warm "Aloha!," flowered leis, and kisses— what a country! We collected our luggage (yes, it was all there—we hadn't seen it since Franklin), and were shuttled by bus to the *Ocean Resort Hotel* in Waikiki Beach which would be our home for the next five days.

This was the first tour package either of us had ever tried, and our group consisted mainly of retired couples. We had figured that it would be at a slower pace, and the price of the trip was so reasonable—how could we pass it up? However, the tour itself involved bus excursions, and Jackie could not deal with the fumes or the "jostling around," so we rented a car and did our own thing. We joined the official tour at the various airports, stayed with them until we arrived at the next hotel, and took off on our own again. We drove our companions crazy—they couldn't figure out if we were members of the tour group or not.

On the island of Oahu we snorkeled in Hanauma Bay, an underwater State and National Park. The fish swam all around us and the water was unreal, warm as bath water and clear as glass. The beach is picture-postcard white and immaculate. We loved it here and came back several times. Most coral reefs and snorkeling opportunities are far from the shore and this is one of the few places on the island where it is possible to reach them via tram down the steep cliffs.

Thanks to the rental car we were able to enjoy our vacation at leisurely pace, and everything—from the Bonzai Pipeline where the world's surfers test their skills to dinner at several Hawaiian shows—was accessible. We drove on every road on the island, passing vast pineapple and sugar cane fields, and following spectacular coastlines. We took pictures of Diamond Head, an extinct volcano and Waikiki's most famous landmark, from every possible angle. We toured the Punchbowl National Memorial Cemetery of the Pacific, where the dead of all the US Pacific wars, including Vietnam, are buried, and we saw the *USS Arizona* Memorial and Pearl Harbor. We visited a shirt factory, where about forty seamstresses were hunched over sewing machines creating Hawaiian shirts and muu muus—brightly colored, loose-fitting dresses, and we joined a catamaran sunset cruise.

We made one big mistake, a day trip with the tour group to the Polynesian Cultural Center. Jackie got a 24-hour 'flu bug and spent the day in a daze with fever and chills. As we had gone with the group, we were trapped, and couldn't return to the hotel. To make matters worse, I had to find long pants and sweat shirt—in Hawaii!—for Jackie, who was shivering. It was not easy, but I found some warm clothing—bizarre, and costing a small fortune, but Jackie appreciated the effort.

The next few days we took it easy and went to the IMAX theater, explored the International Market Place, visited Iolani Palace (built for King David Kalakaua in 1882) and the State Capitol building, ate in a restaurant while viewing fish in a three-story aquarium, watched long boat racing (the state sport), fell in love with teriyakiburgers and banana splits, watched fire dancers and even tried hula dancing (I'm convinced the native Hawaiians are all double-jointed).

"I made the fatal mistake of turning my back on the ocean for a split second, and—pow!—a wave hit the kayak like thunder and I was caught between the boat and the shoreline"

We decided to rent a sea kayak, put down a deposit of $700, requested life jackets (they don't automatically offer them), and were told the craft would be delivered "to the beach." But the rental company's man dropped it off next to the parking lot and the beach was on the other side of a sand dune! It was at this point we discovered how heavy a double kayak is. Two young people took pity on us and carried it to the shoreline for us; we were given a brief lesson, some information on where not to go, and set free.

We moved from the shore, across coral reefs filled with rainbow-colored fish, and out into the Pacific Ocean. After several hours, when we had paddled quite a way out, an uncontrollable coughing fit hit Jackie, probably triggered by the warm, moist air. The only thing I could do was keep us upright and try to get us back to shore as quickly as possible. The tide had come in while we were out, so we were forced to get quite close to the shoreline and jump off together on the land side of the breakers. I made the fatal mistake of turning my back on the ocean for a split second, and—pow!—a wave hit the kayak like thunder and I was caught between the boat and the shoreline. When I surfaced and stood up, my knee was bleeding and throbbing—we made quite a sight, I'm sure, but we survived and both hope to try kayaking again someday.

Our vacation continued on to the other major islands, but if I were to advise on accessibility I would have to say that Oahu has more options than the other isles. One of the highlights of our trip was the ease of access to shops, banks, restaurants, etc. Most are open-air, with direct access from the street and no heavy doors. The existence of Handi-cabs, accessible transport requiring just 24 hours' notice, is another bonus for the wheelchair traveler.

One of the problems encountered in visiting other islands was traveling on the inter-island airplanes, which are small and boarded via long stairways—these proved difficult for the part-time wheelchair user in our group. Once on the islands, I saw no special services provided for seeing or hearing impaired visitors. The wheelchair user in our group had difficulty at times but passers by or others in the group were always willing to assist. At the peak of the tourist season (15 December to 15 April), of course, crowds hamper access to anything. The bathroom at our Oahu hotel would have been almost impossible to access in a wheelchair, and accessibility at hotels in the islands varies widely. **TIDE** (*Travel Industry and Disabled Exchange*) inspected over forty hotels on five Hawaiian islands in the fall of 1991, a survey commissioned by *Classic Hawaii Reservations*, a travel wholesaler in San Jose, California (☎800/221-3949). Their services must be booked through a travel agent. Whoever you travel with, I would advise consulting everyone—airlines, hotels, car rental companies, tour operators—personally before signing on with any tour; it is unwise to assume that your needs will be met.

USA: TRAVEL NOTES

Sources of information

There's a bewildering number of places you *could* go to for information on traveling around the States, but unfortunately none that is likely to be able to answer all your questions straight away. As ever, out-of-date and partial information is much too common. Still, the situation here is better than in most parts of the world, and with patience and perseverance, a great deal of advance planning is possible.

STATE TOURISM OFFICES

The first stop for information should be the **State tourism offices**, whose addresses are listed on the next page. They are usually slow to respond to brochure requests and endless patience is required to get through on the phone, particularly on the 800 numbers. If you can take things as they come and prefer to avoid too much preplanning, go in person to the city, county, or state tourism offices; if you must plan ahead, to be sure of obtaining copies of the brochures you need, write at least a month in advance of departure to the states you think you'd like to visit; some states charge a fee to cover mailing of accommodation guides.

Provision of access information is often inadequate—incompletely explained, indicated by barely visible symbols, and unverified—and several states ignore the issue altogether. About two thirds of states include a mention of facilities for disabled visitors in one or more of their general brochures—in the tour guides, accommodation guides, and/or other brochures, such as calendars of events; those states that have achieved most in terms of integration of access information—however basic—into the major publications include Alabama, Alaska, Illi-

USA: TRAVEL NOTES

nois, Kentucky, Maryland, Mississippi (one glaring omission—the "Outdoors" brochure), Missouri, Vermont, Washington DC, and Wisconsin. Too many states seem to assume that disabled visitors only want to know about accessibility of accommodation and museums—it may surprise them that disabled people, no less than able-bodied tourists, like to take boat rides, try their hand at canoeing, go up in hot air balloons, and get out into the wilderness; it's time to include some wheelchair symbols in these sections of the brochures, too—Alaska has taken the lead here.

Some states (including Hawaii, Maine, Minnesota, North Carolina, Oregon, Vermont, Virginia, West Virginia, Washington DC, Washington State, and Wyoming) produce specific access guides, booklets, or fact sheets, only a few of which are both comprehensive and current—**North Carolina and Virginia** stand out.

North Carolina Department of Economic and Community Development, Travel and Tourism Division, 430 North Salisbury Street, Raleigh, NC 27611; ☎919/733-4171 or 800/VISIT NC. A 380-page, looseleaf guide, *ACCESS North Carolina*, has been produced by the *Division of Vocational Rehabilitation Services* of the NC Department of Human Resources (☎919/733-3364), and is distributed free by the *Travel and Tourism Division*. The guide is beautifully produced, with large color photographs acting as dividers between sections, and access details (for those with mobility, sensory, or mental disabilities) are clearly explained for hundreds of visitor attractions, from waterfalls to lighthouses, beach parks to wineries. Data used in the production of this guide were gathered by trained researchers through June 1990. There is nothing on transport, and accommodations are not included but those with facilities for disabled guests are indicated in the main North Carolina tour guide.

Virginia Division of Tourism, 1021 East Cary Street, Richmond, VA 23219; ☎804/786-2051. A comprehensive handbook, *The Virginia Travel Guide for the Disabled* (1989), was published by William A. Duke Jr. and his wife Cheryl T. Duke who saw the need for such a guide as a result of their traveling experiences with their son, Paul, who has muscular dystrophy. The 300-page guide is a mine of clear, detailed information—on accommodation, transport, attractions, services for disabled people, dialysis centers and more—and is useful to those with mobility, visual, or hearing disabilities. For a copy of the 1989 edition, send a check for $5 to *The Opening Door, Inc.*, Route 2, Box 1805, Woodford, VA 22580; ☎804/633 6752. The *Virginia Division of Tourism* had plans in March 1992 to launch a campaign to support another edition; if successful there will be large quantities available for free distribution in 1993.

Other states covered by our contributors offer the following information.

Alaska Division of Tourism, Department 901, PO Box 110801, Juneau, AK 99811-0801; ☎907/465-2010. "Handicap access" is indicated via wheelchair symbol throughout the *Official State Guide Vacation Planner*, covering accommodations, restaurants, activities, attractions, charter boat operators, travel agents, and tour operators. It's good to see total integration of at least some information for disabled tourists into all subject areas of the main tour guide; inclusion of an outline of facilities offered should be the next step.

Operators who advertise that they can accommodate disabled clients in Alaska include the following: *America and Pacific Tours* (customized tours anywhere in Alaska; ☎907/272-9401), *Affordable Alaska* (four to eleven days from $398; ☎907/225-9415 or 800/678-6986), *Glacier Bay Tours and Cruises* (round trip by air to Glacier Bay National Park, glacier wildlife cruises or sportfishing charters; ☎800/622-2042), *Point South RV Tours* (escorted RV tours; ☎714/247-1222), *Sound Water Adventures* (wildlife cruises on wheelchair-accessible 12-passenger boat; ☎907/472-2455), *Alaska Rainforest Tours* ("handicap accommodations by prior arrangement"; ☎907/463-3466).

Peg Smith recommends Pat Niven of the *Alaska Northwest Travel Service* (130 Second Avenue South, Edmonds, Wa 98020; ☎206/775-4504 or 800/533-7381), not a specialist in travel for disabled clients but gives a highly professional service to everyone. Peg also recom-

USA: TRAVEL NOTES

mends traveling on the **state-run ferry system** to explore Alaska's Inside Passage—it's cheap and fairly accessible, although cabins are small, and cars can be transported. Contact *Alaska Marine Highway* (☎800/642-0066) for schedule or reservations. A two-year "Handicapped Person Pass" is available for a $10 fee from *Alaska Marine Highway* (Attn: Pass Desk), PO Box R, Juneau, Alaska 99811-2505; applications take up to six weeks to process.

California Office of Tourism, Department CTPG 92, PO Box 189, Sacramento, CA 95812. California is one of the states that did not respond to our inquiries, but the 1992 edition of the free, 200-page *California Travel Planning Guide*, available from this address, is reported to list "handicap facilities" at accommodations and attractions. According to *SATH* (see below), a bold capital **H** would have been easier to pick out than mentions in the text. Another complaint from *SATH* is that many attractions which do have facilities for disabled visitors, such as San Diego Zoo, are not listed as accessible. Again according to *SATH*, the *Hotel and Motel Association* puts out a state-wide guide which notes wheelchair-accessible properties, and the *San Francisco Lodging Guide* (free from the *San Francisco Convention & Visitors Bureau*, PO Box 6977, San Francisco, CA 94101) lists many "wheelchair accessible" properties—hotels, motels, apartments, B&Bs, hostels, RV parks—in the city and surrounding counties; as always, travelers should call to confirm details.

Hawaii Visitors Bureau, Waikiki Business Plaza, 2270 Kalakaua Avenue, Honolulu, HI 96815; ☎808/923-1811. A booklet has been prepared by the *Commission on Persons with Disabilities* (5 Waterfront Plaza, Suite 210, Honolulu, HI 96813; 808/548-7606, voice or TDD; or offices on Maui, Kauai, and Big Island). The *Aloha Guide to Accessibility for persons with mobility impairments in the State of Hawaii* is published (1990) in two parts: Part I deals with transport, tours, parking, medical and equipment, and support services; Part II covers hotels, visitor attractions, beaches and parks, theaters, shopping centers, and government buildings; both parts include facilities on Oahu, Maui, Kauai, and Big Island.

Washington DC Convention and Visitors Association, 1212 New York Avenue, NW, Washington DC 20005; ☎202/789-7000. Distributes a useful fact sheet and six-page "Feature Release" which should enable any visitor with a disability to make the most of the attractions of the city. Useful publications are listed, including *Access Washington: A Guide to Metropolitan Washington for the Physically Disabled*, which outlines wheelchair access at hotels, motels, restaurants, sightseeing attractions, shopping malls, theaters, and libraries, and includes information on accessible transport; the guide can be obtained, price $6, from the *Information, Protection and Advocacy Center for Handicapped Individuals* (*IPACHI*), 300 Eye Street, NE, Suite 202, Washington DC 20002; ☎202/547-8081 voice, ☎202/547-6556 TDD. *Smithsonian: A Guide for Disabled Visitors* can be obtained (in print or Braille) by writing to the *Visitor Information Associates Reception Center* (Smithsonian Institution, Washington DC 20560) or phoning ☎202/357 2700 (voice) or ☎202/357 1729 (TDD).

State of New York, 1 Commerce Plaza, Albany, NY 12245; ☎518/474-4116 or 800/225-5697. The main travel guide lists accessible campgrounds and uses a clearly explained access code for tourist attractions covering parking, steps at entrance, elevators, and grab bars in rest rooms; information is updated with the assistance of the NY State Easter Seal Society (845 Central Avenue, Albany, NY 12206; ☎518/438-8785). *Opening the Outdoors to People with Disabilities* is a pamphlet listing accessible facilities at recreational areas including campgrounds and fishing sites. *Guide to New York State Operated Parks, Historic Sites and their Programs* indicates those facilities that are "handicapped accessible" in state parks.

New Mexico Tourism and Travel Division, 1100 St. Francis Drive, Santa Fe, NM 87503; ☎505/827-0291 or 800/545-2040; Disabled Determinant Services ☎505/841-2200. The wheelchair symbol is used only on their state map. Scant mention in the guides does not necessarily mean scant attention to provision of facilities for disabled people, though—Carolyn Lucas experienced few problems.

USA: TRAVEL NOTES

Massachusetts Office of Travel and Tourism, 100 Cambridge Street, Boston, MA 02202; ☎617/727-3205 or 800/447-6277. Another non-responder in our survey. You might get a better response from Boston's *Information Center for Individuals with Disabilities* (27–43 Wormwood Street, Boston, MA 02210-1606; ☎617/727-5540 or 1-800/462-5015, voice and TDD); there is a fact sheet of resources for disabled travelers, and staff will answer requests for information by phone or mail, or in person (the center is open Mon–Fri 9am–5pm).

The other state tourism offices are:

Alabama Bureau of Tourism & Travel, 401 Adams Ave., PO Box 4309, Montgomery AL 36103 (☎205/242-4169 ☎1-800/ALABAMA) TDD ☎205/240-3150

Arizona Office of Tourism, 1100 W Washington St., Phoenix AZ 85007 (☎602/542-8687)

Arkansas Department of Parks & Tourism, One Capitol Mall, Little Rock AR 72201 (☎501/682-7777, ☎1-800/828-8974)

Colorado Tourism Board, 1625 Broadway, Suite 1700, Denver CO 80202 (☎303/ 592-5510, ☎1-800/COLORADO)

Connecticut Tourism Division, CT Dept. of Economic Development, 865 Brook St, Rocky Hill, CT 06067-3402 (☎1-800/CT BOUND)

Delaware State Tourism Office, 99 Kings Hwy., Box 1401, Dover DE 19903 (☎302/736-4271, ☎1-800/441-8846)

Florida Division of Tourism, 126 Van Buren St., Tallahassee FL 32301 (☎904/487-1462)

Georgia Tourist Division, 285 Peachtree Center Ave., Suite 1000, Atlanta GA 30303, (☎706/656-3553, ☎800/VISIT-GA)

Idaho Travel Council, 7000 W State St., Rm. 108, State Capitol Building, Boise ID 83720 (☎208/334-2470, ☎1-800/635-7820)

Illinois Bureau of Tourism, 620 E. Adams St., Springfield IL 62701 (☎217/782-7500, ☎800/ABE-0121)

Indiana Division of Tourism, 1 N. Capitol Ave. #700, Indianapolis IN 46204 (☎317/232-8860, ☎1-800/782-3775)

Iowa Division of Tourism, 200 E. Grand Ave., Des Moines IA 50309 (☎515/242-4705)

Kansas Department of Economic Development, Travel & Tourism Division, 400 SW Eighth St., Topeka KS 66603 (☎913/296-2009, ☎800/252-6727)

Kentucky Department of Travel Development, PO Box 2011, Frankfort KY 40602 (☎502/564-4930, ☎1-800/225-8747)

Louisiana Office of Tourism, Box 94291, Baton Rouge LA 70804-9291 (☎504/342-8119, ☎1-800/334-8626)

Maine Publicity Bureau, 97 Winthrop St., Hallowell ME 04347 (☎207/582-9300)

Maryland Office of Tourism Development, 217 E Redwood St., Baltimore MD 21202 (☎410/333-6611)

Michigan Travel Bureau, 333 S Capitol Ave., PO Box 30226, Lansing MI 48909 (☎517/373-0670, ☎1-800/543-2937) TDD ☎800/722-8191 (MI only)

Minnesota Office of Tourism, 250 Skyway Level, 375 Jackson St., St. Paul MN 55101 (☎612/296-5029, U.S ☎1-800/657-3700, Can. ☎800/766-8687)

Mississippi Department of Economic Development–Tourism Division, PO Box 22825, Jackson MS 39205 (☎601/359-3297, ☎1-800/647-2290)

Missouri Division of Tourism, PO Box 1055, Jefferson City, Missouri MO 65102 (☎341/751-4133)

Montana Department of Commerce, 1424 Ninth Ave., Helena MT 59620-0401 (☎800/444-2654 in MT, ☎1-800/541-1447 outside MT)

Nebraska Division of Tourism & Travel, PO Box 94666, Lincoln NE 68509 (☎402/471-OK, ☎1-800/228-4307)

Nevada Commission on Tourism, 5151 S Carson St., Carson City NV 89710 (☎702/687-4322, ☎800/237-0774)

New Hampshire Office of Vacation Travel, 105 Loudon Rd., PO Box 856, Concord NH 03302-0856 (☎603/271-2666)

New Jersey Division of Travel & Tourism, 20 West State St., CN 826, Trenton NJ 08525-0826 (☎609/292-2470, ☎800/537-7397)

USA: TRAVEL NOTES

New York City CVB, Two Columbus Circle, New York NY 10019 (☎212/397-8222)

North Dakota Tourism Division, Liberty Memorial Building, 604 East Blvd, Bismarck ND 58505 (☎800/435-5663)

Ohio Office of Travel & Tourism, Box 1001, Columbus OH 4326-0001 (☎614/466-8844, ☎800/BUCKEYE)

Oklahoma Tourism & Recreation, Box 60788, Oklahoma City OK 73146-0789 (☎405/521-3981, ☎800/652-6552, brochures)

Oregon Tourism Division, 775 Summer St. NE, Salem OR 97310 (☎503/373-1270, ☎800/547-7842 outside OR)

Pennsylvania Bureau of Travel Development, 433 Forum Building, Harrisburg PA 17120 (☎717/787-5453, ☎800/237-4363 outside OR)

Rhode Island Tourism Dept., 7 Jackson Walkway, Providence RI 02903 (☎401/277-2601, ☎800/556-2484)

South Carolina Department of Parks, Recreation & Tourism, 1205 Pendleton St., #522, Columbia SC 29201 (☎803/734-0135)

South Dakota Department of Tourism, 711 Wells Ave., Pierre SD 57501 (☎605/773-3301, ☎1-800/952-3625)

Tennessee Department of Tourism Development, PO Box 23170, Nashville TN 37202 (☎615/741-2158)

Texas Department of Commerce, Tourism Division, Box 12728, Austin TX 78711 (☎512/462-9191)

Utah Travel Council, Council Hall, Capitol Hill, Salt Lake City UT 84114 (☎801/538-1030)

Vermont Travel Division, 134 State St., Montpelier VT 05602 (☎802/828-3236)

Washington State Tourism Development Division, Department of Trade & Economic Development, 101 General Administration Building, Olympia WA 98504-0613 (☎206/586-3024)

West Virginia Travel West Virginia, State Capitol Complex, 2101 Washington St., E Charleston WV 25305 (☎ 304/348-2286, ☎1-800/CALL-WVA)

Wisconsin Tourism Development, 123 W. Washington Ave., PO Box 7970, Madison WI 53707 (☎608/266-7621, ☎1-800/432-TRIP travel literature, ☎1-800/372-2737 travel information)

Wyoming Division of Tourism, I-25 at College Dr., Cheyenne WY 82002 (☎307/777-7777, ☎1-800/225-5996)

SPECIALIST NATIONAL ORGANIZATIONS

When state tourism offices fail to deliver, or you want answers to specific questions, or simply some advice from people with solid experience, there are two **national organizations that are specialists in travel**, and will give the perspective of the traveler with a disability rather than that of the travel industry:

Mobility International USA, PO Box 3551, Eugene, Oregon 97403; ☎503/343-1248. The US office of London-based *Mobility International* (see p.544), MIUSA is a national, not-for-profit organization whose purpose is to promote and facilitate opportunities for people with disabilities to participate in international educational exchange and travel. The organization is included here because information on travel within the USA is also available, via their well-produced, highly readable, and reasonably priced publications, and through their travel information and referral service. The office is staffed by friendly, knowledgeable people, always busy but helpful and efficient.

Travelin' Talk, PO Box 3534, Clarksville, TN 37043-3534; ☎615/552-6670. The brainchild of Rick Crowder, energetic Disabled American of the Year 1991, *Travelin' Talk* is an information network providing assistance to travelers with disabilities, working from the same principle as the one on which this book is founded—the most reliable information and advice comes from another disabled person. Members all over North America (and some in other countries) join up and contribute whatever feel able, for example access information about their own area, or hospitality to travelers passing through. A resource directory of members—both individuals and organizations—willing to assist disabled travelers has been published, and extensive listings of services for travelers with

USA: TRAVEL NOTES

disabilities have been compiled. The quarterly newsletter (also available in large print, Braille, or on cassette) keeps members up to date with the expanding network, activities, and travel experiences of members, and developments on the travel scene.

TRAVEL INDUSTRY CONTACTS

Organizations that set out to promote **better understanding between the travel industry and travelers with disabilities** include:

Access for Travel, 1429 10th Street West, Kirkland, WA 980033; ☎206/828-4220 or 488-8297. Formed as an outgrowth of Wheelchair Journeys (see *Directory*, p.600). Carol Lee Power and Norma Nickols provide training for persons in the travel industry to help them accommodate the increasing senior market as well as travelers with disabilities.

Society for the Advancement of Travel for the Handicapped (**SATH**), 347 Fifth Avenue, Suite 610, New York, NY 10016; ☎212/447-7284. A non-profit travel industry organization whose members include travel agents, tour operators, hotel and airline management (perhaps explaining the continued use of the term "the handicapped" in all their literature—and even their name), as well as disabled people. *SATH* is "dedicated to the creation of barrier-free acccess and to the widest possible circulation of information concerning travel opportunities for all handicapped people." The regular one-year subscription ($45) entitles members to receipt of the quarterly newsletter, *SATH NEWS*, which contains travel information from the USA and all over the world. The publication of *Reprints from SATH NEWS 1987–1992*, in which items are gathered together by subject, makes a useful reference guide for travelers (cost: $10 members, $15 non-members), but the omission of publication date of each entry is infuriating—this information constantly changes, and something originally printed in 1987 is likely to be in need of double checking.

The Opening Door, Inc. (see Virginia travel guide, above). The Duke family work as a team to promote access awareness and are active consultants, most recently working with *Embassy Suites* (see *Accommodation*).

Travel Industry and Disabled Exchange (*TIDE*), 5435 Donna Avenue, Tarzana, CA 91356; ☎818/343-6339. This organization was formed with the aim of promoting understanding of the needs of both groups—people with disabilities, and people involved in the travel industry. By disseminating information and literature to the general public, travelers with disabilities, travel agents, and other members of the travel industry, it is hoped that travel by people with disabilities will be facilitated. Their quarterly newsletter, *TIDE'S IN*, contains articles covering worldwide travel as well as developments in the USA. Yearly membership is $15.

LOCAL RESOURCES

There are also sources of information at a more **local level**—branches of national organizations of people with your own disability, resource centers for disabled people, Centers for Independent Living. Many of these can help and will be listed in the Yellow Pages. If you have travel inquiries specific to your disabilities you should make use of the disability organizations: the *Arthritis Foundation*, for example, publishes a series of pamphlets, available from local chapters, one of which is called *Travel and Arthritis*; the *Eastern Paralyzed Veterans Association* (75-20 Astoria Boulevard Jackson Heights, NY 11370-1178; ☎718/803-EPVA) offers a variety of services, directories, books, pamphlets—free but donations are gratefully accepted and tax-deductible.

Tour operators

Making **independent travel arrangements** in the USA is pretty straightforward and the preferred method for many disabled travelers, but often savings can be made by booking a **package**, or it may be that your special interest or activity vacation needs to be organized by a tour company that specializes in that area. There are thousands of US **tour companies and travel agencies** (most people book a tour company package through a travel agent), and whatever your desires there will almost certainly be one offering a suitable program.

Having selected your dream vacation, the next thing to discover is whether or not the tour company can accommodate your own disability-

USA: TRAVEL NOTES

related requirements. Many companies will be able to, or at least will do their best to arrange a troublefree trip, but an alarming number (despite the ADA rulings—see below) still prefer to see disabled clients directed toward those tour operators and travel agencies which have set themselves up as experts in planning travel for disabled people. There are certainly plenty of these, and some provide an excellent service *and* charge reasonable rates, but the cost of this special treatment is often steep—too steep for many disabled travelers. (This is partly down to the insurance companies—according to Jack Huffman of *Evergreen Travel Service*, "There is no known statistical data to show that disabled people pose a greater risk than others, yet disabled tour operators are consistently hit with sky-high premiums, thus causing higher prices to the consumer.")

For a selection of companies that **specialize in travel for disabled people**, and a few that combine expertise in this area with general travel operations, see *Directory*, p.597. Included are those that responded to our inquiries or were recommended by disabled people; many offer international travel arrangements as well as tours in North America. See also *Tours and Cruises* for cruise specialists. For more ideas consult *A World of Options for the 90s* and *The Complete Directory for People with Disabilities* (see *Books*, p.61).

The *Directory of Travel Agents for the Disabled* (1991, Twin Peaks Press) supplies a more extensive (worldwide) but less informative listing; it is more or less a collection of addresses and phone numbers, with no indication of what each company has to offer, and not always completely up to date.

The *National Tour Association* (☎606/253-1036) publishes a list of nearly forty tour companies that "can accommodate the disabled on their escorted tours" but, again, this is a list of addresses with no indication of facilities or services offered, and only five companies (*California Tour Consultants, Domenico Tours, Organizers Etc, Hospitality Tours,* and *Sundial Special Vacations*) provided us with further information: the first three are non-specialists—*Domenico* makes no mention of disabled clients in their brochure, *California*

Tour Consultants (☎714/362-2908 or 800/227-4276) says their ability to provide services is evaluated on an individual group basis, depending on the group's requirements, and *Organizers Etc* (☎303/771-1178 or 800/283-2754) can accommodate disabled clients (individuals or groups) on some of their active sports and cruise packages; the two specialists are listed on p.598 and p.599.

It's depressing that although the section of the **ADA** applicable to travel agents came into force in January 1992, *TIDE* (see above) held a seminar on the new law in that month and found that most agents had never heard of the legislation. Existing travel agency offices must be made accessible "if readily achievable," but this does not deal with the most difficult barrier, which is that of communicating with and serving all disabled clients as efficiently as able-bodied clients. The ADA stipulates that travel agents cannot deny service to any client with a disability or—and there is some controversy over this—refer such a person to an agency with more experience in this area. While the arguments and the tendency to steer disabled clients toward programs offered by specialists in travel for disabled people continue, there is little hope of dispelling ignorance, improving awareness among travel agents and tour operators, and achieving true integration.

Segregation of disabled travelers from the mainstream should not be encouraged, particularly in the wake of the ADA. In one of the world's most accessible countries it should not be necessary to enlist "specialists" in order to enjoy a vacation. And it should not be necessary for a travel agent to be disabled, like Janice Perkins of *Hinsdale Travel Service*, in order to communicate effectively between client and travel operators; there are plenty of resources available to help those in the travel industry (from organizations such as *SATH* and *TIDE* as well as from the industry itself, through *ASTA*), and the more experience travel agents have of disabled clients the better they will serve. Probably the best advice is to **find a local travel agent** who is conscientious and willing both to search out any additional information you need and to use mainstream tour operators, and stick with this agent for all your travels.

USA: TRAVEL NOTES

Transport

It's probably true to say that the success of the ADA hinges on the elimination of inaccessible links in the transport chain. The situation varies widely across the country, and there is still a long way to go, but the accessible links are slowly being introduced so that people with disabilities can undertake more and more journeys—perhaps involving plane, train, and bus—knowing that there is no point at which they will be left stranded.

AIR TRAVEL

Facilities and physical access at the major **airports** are generally good, and the required ramps, curb cuts, accessible rest rooms, shops, and eating or drinking facilities are mostly provided. There are an increasing number of lift-equipped shuttle services between terminals and parking lots, and the ADA will require some shuttle companies to purchase lift-equipped vehicles. But there have been some reports of difficulties in covering the sometimes long distances between terminals when making connections—both Arthur Goldthorpe and Peg Smith experienced some problems at Chicago; there is a need for more accessible intra-terminal transport systems. There is also scope for action to remove communication barriers for travelers with visual, hearing, or speech disabilities; some recent improvements have been the installation of an audio loop at Boston's Logan International and a paging system for hearing-impaired travelers at Baltimore–Washington International. The most up-to-date and comprehensive survey of airport facilities worldwide is **Access Travel: Airports** (sixth edition, August 1991); for a free copy write Consumer Information Center, Pueblo, CO 81009. Many airports publish access guides—call in advance to obtain a copy—and *SATH NEWS* (see *Sources of information*, above) is a good source of updates on airport facilities.

Pressure to improve access at airports has been reasonably effective but the recent enforcement of the **Air Carrier Access Act** 1986 (ACAA) and ADA should break down the final barriers. Existing facilities owned, leased, or operated by US airlines are subject to the regulations of the ACAA. The main features of the new act are summarised below, but briefly, by March 1993, all carrier facilities must include one accessible route from an airport entrance to ticket counters, boarding locations and baggage handling areas; terminals must be designed so that the routes minimize any extra distance that wheelchair users must travel compared to other passengers. Public airports are also affected by Title II of the ADA, private airports by Title III; new facilities designed and constructed for first occupancy later than 26 January 1993, and any alterations to existing buildings, must be architecturally and communicatively accessible. Denver International Airport, scheduled to open in October 1993, should be one of the first to benefit from the ADA requirements.

The major issues to be resolved with the **airlines** include provision of accessible lavatories on narrow-bodied aircraft, access to small commuter planes, and airline employee training to improve standards of assistance, communication with disabled passengers, and handling of mobility aids—including safe stowage of wheelchairs in the hold, and proper reassembly of chairs, and hooking up of batteries, on arrival. The policy for pre-assigning seats varies among airlines and is not always satisfactory; this should be queried in advance, before making a reservation. Airlines that can probably be relied on to pre-assign bulkhead seats if required, according to our contributors, include *Delta*, *Northwest*, and *United*, and the charter airline *American Trans Air*.

At the time of writing, the *Air Transport Association* had called for a review of the ACAA and ADA, crying "too expensive," so the facilities described in the box may yet be stalled. That said, air travel is still probably the best way for disabled travelers to cover long distances in the US, and facilities and accessibility are second to none on the world's airways. If you have never flown before, a quick run through the basics of the ACAA should reassure you that most procedures are in place to ensure a smooth journey on domestic flights; you'll also know what to expect and when to make a fuss if airlines appear to be avoiding their obligations.

USA: TRAVEL NOTES

Although potentially presenting more difficulties, **small planes** do not have to be out of bounds for wheelchair users, if the airline is prepared to make the effort. We have received this report from a traveler who took her disabled son on a day tour of the Grand Canyon with *Scenic Airlines*, who "did not blink at carrying a wheelchair and were kind and helpful throughout."

"The flight over the canyon was unbelievable, all orange, pink, and mauve rocks and deep green trees and bushes. An excellent lunch was included in the price and we had time for a walk along the rim, taking in some spectacular views. All facilities were wheelchair accessible, bar one tiny old house.

"The temperature was very high, well over 100 degrees. This posed problems on the return flight as the aircraft was not pressurized. Our son fainted and we had trouble getting him to regain consciousness. I asked the pilot for oxygen but he did not carry any. The pilot immediately took the aircraft down to treetop height and made an emergency landing at Las Vegas.

"Christopher had come round by this time, but the police, paramedics, and two ambulances were waiting at the airport—all very dramatic. *Scenic Airlines* staff were most concerned and ready to assist in any way they could. It is important to check carefully before booking if you think an unpressurized aircraft or lack of oxygen may endanger your health; there are other aircraft available."

Scenic Airlines (241 Reno Avenue, Las Vegas, NV 89119; ☎702/739-8065, voice; ☎702/597-2208, TDD) carries many passengers who use wheelchairs—both on their motorcoach ground tours and their air tours of the Canyon; although their planes and coaches are not accessible their staff assist competently with all transfers.

To keep up with all the latest information on air access issues, equipment, and regulations, it's a good idea to subscribe to **Access to the Skies Newsletter** (there are four issues published a year) by sending a check for $12 to *Paralysis Society of America*/ATTS Program, 801 Eighteenth Street, NW, Washington DC 20006.

THE AIR CARRIER ACCESS ACT

The major ACAA regulations (described more fully in the Department of Transportation booklet, *New Horizons for the Air Traveler with a Disability*, December 1991, provided to passengers on request by *Delta*) state:

1. Travelers with disabilities must be provided **information** upon request concerning facilities and services available to them. If general information or reservations are provided via the phone, a TDD or TT (text telephone) service must be available. Passengers should be aware that for a number of years facilities described may not be available on all planes (see 10–12), and aircraft may be changed without warning. (In our investigations the airlines that were most willing to put their commitment to serving passengers with disabilities down on paper, and to explain their procedures, were *Delta*— first by a long chalk—then *Northwest*, *Continental*, *United*, and *America West*. No response could be obtained, by letter or phone, from *American*, *TWA*, or *USAir*.)

2. Each airline must have a **Complaints Resolution Officer** (CRO) and a copy of the ACAA available at each airport.

3. Carriers may require up to 48 hours **advance notice** and one hour advance check-in from a person who wishes to receive (a) transportation for an electric wheelchair on an aircraft with fewer than 60 seats, (b) provision by the carrier of hazardous materials packaging for a battery or other device, (c) accommodations for ten or more disabled passengers traveling as a group, or (d) provision of an on-board wheelchair on an aircraft with an inaccessible lavatory (see 13).

4. A disability is not sufficient grounds for a carrier to request a **medical certificate**. A certificate may only be required if the person traveling (a) is on a stretcher or in an incubator, (b) needs medical oxygen during the flight, (c) has a medical condition which causes the carrier to have reasonable doubt that the individual can complete the flight safely without medical assistance, or (d) has a communicable disease.

5. A carrier may only require a passenger to be **accompanied** under certain circumstances: if the person is traveling on a stretcher or in an

USA: TRAVEL NOTES

incubator; if the person is unable to comprehend or respond appropriately to safety instructions; if the person's mobility impairment is such that he or she is unable to assist in his or her own evacuation of the aircraft; or if the person has severe hearing and vision disabilities that prevent him or her from acting on instructions in an emergency. If this is contrary to the passenger's assurances that he or she can travel alone, the carrier cannot charge for the transportation of the attendant, though the carrier may designate an individual to act as the attendant.

6. Boarding and deplaning assistance (from properly trained service personnel) must be available to the disabled passenger. For large and medium-sized aircraft, hand carriage is not appropriate, and level boarding ramps, mobile lounges, or lifting devices (other than those used for freight) should be used. On **connecting flights** the delivering carrier is responsible for assisting the passenger with a disability to reach the next flight.

7. Battery-powered wheelchairs must be accepted, except where cargo compartment size or aircraft airworthiness considerations do not permit. When it is possible to load, store, secure, and unload with the wheelchair always in an upright position, and the battery is securely attached to the chair, the carrier may not remove a spillable battery from the chair. It is never necessary to remove an unspillable battery. Carriers may not charge for packaging of spillable batteries. Wheelchairs and other assistive devices must be given priority over cargo and baggage when stowed in the cargo compartment, and must be among the first items unloaded.

8. The air carrier *may* offer the opportunity to **preboard**; the passenger may accept or decline. (In practice, most airlines offer this facility, and it's usually a good idea to accept.)

9. Carriers can present a special **safety briefing** to an individual whose disability precludes him or her from understanding the general briefing at any time before take-off; most choose to do this before the other passengers board, if the disabled passsenger has chosen to preboard. Briefings on video will have an open caption or sign language insert as old videos are replaced, unless this would be too small to be seen or would interfere with the video.

10. Carriers must permit **guide dogs** or other service animals with appropriate identification to accompany an individual with a disability. Identification may include cards, written documentation, presence of harness, or the credible verbal assurance of the passenger using the animal. Carriers must permit an animal to accompany a disabled traveler to any chosen seat unless the animal obstructs the aisle or other area that must remain clear.

11. New aircraft delivered after April 1992 with more than 30 passenger seats will have **movable armrests** on at least half of the aisle seats.

12. New aircraft delivered after April 1992 with 100 or more passenger seats must provide **priority space in the cabin** for stowage of at least one passenger-owned folding wheelchair (this also applies to smaller aircraft if there is a closet large enough to accommodate a folding wheelchair. *United* advises that sixty percent of their aircraft have closets large enough for stowage of one folding chair.)

13. New wide-bodied (dual-aisled) aircraft ordered after April 5, 1990 or delivered after April 5, 1992 must have at least one **accessible lavatory**, equipped with door locks, call buttons, grab bars, and lever faucets, and with sufficient space to allow a passenger to enter using the on-board wheelchair, maneuver, and use the facilities with the same degree of privacy as other passengers. For both 10 and 11, aircraft undergoing refurbishment must meet the accessibility requirements for the affected features.

14. As of April 5, 1992, *all aircraft with 60 or more passenger seats* must carry an **on-board wheelchair** if there is an accessible lavatory, *or* if a passenger gives advance notice that he or she can use an inaccessible lavatory but needs an on-board chair to reach it, even if the aircraft predated the rule and has not been refurbished. Two aircraft have already been exempted from this rule—the Aerospatiale/Aeritalia ATR-72 and the British Aerospace ATP, both of which are used by several commuter airlines.

USA: TRAVEL NOTES

15. Carriers must provide **training for all personnel** who deal with the traveling public, to familiarize them with the relevant Department of Transport regulations, the carrier's procedures for providing travel to persons with disabilities, including safe operation of any equipment used to accommodate such persons, and how to respond appropriately to travelers with different disabilities.

RAIL TRAVEL

America's **rail network** is not comprehensive, and it tends to be a relatively expensive way to travel, but facilities for disabled passengers are good and, as with air travel, there are some special discounts to look out for. As well as regular train journeys, *Amtrak* (*National Railroad Passenger Corporation*, 60 Massachusetts Avenue, NE, Washington DC 20002; ☎202/906-3000) offer several tour options, including destination vacations/hotel packages, national parks vacations, air-rail travel plan, rail/sail vacations, and day sightseers. When you make reservations, give 24 hours' notice and either use a travel agent or call (toll free) ☎1-800 and ask for USA-RAIL, the Special Services Desk. Assistance can then be arranged according to your requirements. Hearing-impaired passengers should call ☎1-800/523-6590 (TDD) or ☎202/523-6591 (voice) for information and reservations. Guide animals can accompany passengers in the car, at no extra charge.

All *Amtrak* major city **stations** and most other staffed stations are accessible to passengers with disabilities; personal assistance will be offered in boarding and detraining (including wheelchair lifts) when advance notice is given. The lower level of all Superliner (western long-distance) trains is accessible via portable ramp. The ADA requires that all existing Amtrak stations must be accessible by 26 July 2010, and new stations must be accessible.

On **trains**, the ADA rules are that existing stock must have one accessible car per train by 26 July 1995, and new rail cars ordered after 26 August 1990 must be accessible. Currently, specially equipped cars have a maximum aisle and door width of 30 inches; wheelchairs over 26 inches wide cannot be carried. Standard-size battery-powered wheelchairs may be transported in at least one passenger car on all trains. *Amtrak* short-distance and corridor trains include one or more food service cars with accessible coach seating. The bi-level Superliner trains offer wheelchair-accessible lower-level coach seating. Many eastern overnight services include accessible seating and rest rooms and, when available, sleeping cars with accommodation specially designed for use by disabled passengers, including accessible rest rooms. Included in the brochure, *Discover America—Amtrak's America*, there is a detailed listing of sleeping accommodations in their Superliner and Heritage (eastern long-distance) trains. This includes location in car; size of room, lower berth, and upper berth; access to upper berth; toilet or sink in room; luggage storage capacity; and notes to indicate ease of access to different bedrooms.

Oxygen systems can be carried subject to certain restrictions—they must not be dependent on train-generated power, and there are weight limitations; call ☎800/USA-RAIL for advice. Some special diet requests can be accommodated: vegetarian food is available in long-distance dining cars; 72 hours' notice is required for other diets such as low fat and kosher. Medication should be carried in hand luggage, just as on aircraft; checked baggage is not accessible.

BUS TRAVEL

Greyhound **buses** (*Greyhound Lines, Inc.*, Tour and Travel Department, PO Box 660362, Dallas, TX 75266-0362; ☎214/715-7067 or 800/528-0447) form an extensive intercity network, a cheap means of touring the country, and operate a *Travel Assistance* program for passengers with disabilities. Although not likely to be equipped with lifts for some time (*Greyhound* successfully lobbied for a seven-year extension on their ADA obligation to start buying accessible buses), the vehicles are not out of bounds to wheelchair users—staff will assist with boarding and alighting from the bus—and on tours *Greyhound* will help with selecting hotels that are accessible to passengers with "special needs." Drivers or other staff will assist passengers who need help with stowage or retrieval of

USA: TRAVEL NOTES

mobility aids; devices that cannot be stored in the passenger compartment will be placed in the baggage compartment. A companion or guide dog may travel at no additional charge with passengers who need assistance when traveling. Passengers who travel alone and will require assistance, and those who require a battery box, should call ☎800/752-4841 at least 48 hours prior to departure and supply itinerary and details of their needs; *Greyhound* will call the origin, transfer points, and destination to inform personnel at those locations of the needs of the passenger and date/time of travel.

Other bus operators and people who run tours by bus will generally use similar vehicles and offer a similar level of service. The West Coast alternative operator *Green Tortoise*, based in San Francisco (☎510/821-0803 or ☎800/227-4766), for example, has been reported to be helpful, though it offers no special facilities. The buses run between the major cities—Los Angeles, San Francisco, and Seattle—and they also run low-priced tours.

DRIVING AND CAR RENTAL

A handful of **car rental** companies offer cars with hand controls, given sufficient notice. *Hertz* is way ahead of the others: hand controls are available, at no additional charge ($25 deposit required on non-credit-card rentals), at all of the 900 *Hertz* corporate rental locations in the US, on any vehicle in the rental location's fleet; reservations for hand-controlled cars (left or right) should be made two days in advance (☎800/654-3131, voice; ☎800/654-2280, TDD, Mon–Fri 7am–7pm, Central Standard Time); one-way rentals of vehicles equipped with hand controls are allowed (*Hertz* is the only company to offer this option) and there are no additional charges to the disabled traveler for this service. *Hertz* has designated accessible parking at car-return areas at all corporate locations. Disabled renters are provided with special "handicapped parking placards" which permit them to park in spaces reserved for disabled drivers; renters should bring their "handicapped permit" to the rental counter. Finally, the rule that a renter must have both credit card and valid driver's license has been waived for blind and visually impaired clients who can now rent using their own credit card and their driver's accompanying drivier's license.

Avis would put nothing in writing, but persistent calls revealed that at least 48 hours' notice is required (☎800/331-1212, voice; ☎800/331-2323, TDD) for hand controls (left or right) which are available at all locations, and no deposit is required. Stephen Latham had trouble with this company.

Budget was also reluctant to discuss its facilities, and told us they have only a few vehicles available with hand controls (☎800/527-0700, voice only).

National (☎800/328-4567, voice; ☎800/328-6323, TDD) can supply vehicles with hand controls in some locations—call at least two days in advance to check availability—but only on Class F, full-size cars; there is no extra charge and no deposit required.

Although you should be safe with *Hertz*, Arthur Goldthorpe suggests taking a car without hand controls, rented more cheaply from a local company, if you are traveling with an able-bodied companion. His decision was colored by meeting two young disabled Americans in Florida who had ordered a car with hand controls to be available at Miami airport when they arrived. On landing they were told that the car was not ready as the fittings had only arrived that day. They had to travel fifty miles to Fort Lauderdale and return next day for their car.

By shopping around, using the Yellow Pages, it's possible to find good deals with local companies, including a fair rate for Collision Damage Waiver (which you must have). Many firms will bring the vehicle to your door and then allow you to drop it off in the airport parking lot when you leave.

It's also worth doing your arithmetic when considering a fly-drive deal, remembering that each person in a party will be paying an extra supplement for the use of a single car—if there is an able-bodied driver in the party it will be cheaper to rent a car from a local firm.

A comfortable alternative for those who find transferring to a car difficult or painful is to rent a **van** with adaptations for disabled drivers or passengers. There are a few major operators, with franchises in different locations across the US, including:

USA: TRAVEL NOTES

Wheelchair Getaways (5105 Route 33/34, (Wall) Farmingdale, NJ 07727; ☎908/938-4050 or 800/221-0034) offers rental, leasing, or purchase of late-model, fully air-conditioned vans with automated wheelchair lifts. Rental rates (1992, excluding fuel) are: daily, $85; weekend, 4pm Fri to 10am Mon, $180; week, $510; month, $1900. Qualified drivers are available on request.

Wheelers Accessible Van Rental, Inc. (6614 West Sweetwater, Glendale, AZ 85304; ☎602/878-3540 or 800/456-1371) offers Chrysler mini-vans with lowered floors and manually operated ramps; hand controls are available; rental can be on a daily ($89), weekly ($475) or monthly ($1595) basis. *Wheelers* vans are available in Florida, California, Arizona, Colorado, and Maui, Hawaii (see *Over the Rainbow*, p.599); they can also deliver to Nevada and New Mexico.

There are also several local operators, which can be found in the Yellow Pages. For example, *CEH* (Consulting and Engineering for the Handicapped) *Inc.* (4457 63rd Circle North, Pinellas Park, FL 34665; ☎813/522-0364 or 800/677-0364) has the following vans for rental: 1985 Chevy hi-top, with auto-lift, hand controls, six-way power seat, wheelchair lock-downs, and power steering; 1982 Ford drop floor, with automatic swing lift, hand controls, quick-change driver's seat, and chair locks; 1981 Ford drop floor, with auto-lift and passenger wheelchair lock-downs; 1977 Dodge, with hand controls, automatic swing lift, and lock-downs. Rates are $50 per day, $325 per week, and $1200 per month, all plus seven percent sales tax; 250 miles per week free, additional mileage at 15 cents per mile. Vans can be delivered to major airports in Florida.

Consult the *Directory of Accessible Van Rentals*, by Helen Hecker (1992, Twin Peaks Press, $5 plus $2 postage; ☎206/694-2462 or 800/637-2256) for more ideas.

The *American Automobile Association* (*AAA*, 1000 AAA Drive, Heathrow, FL 32746-5063; ☎407/444-7000) produces information for disabled drivers in the form of *The Handicapped Driver's Mobility Guide*, (sixth edition, 1991, $5.95); other services include individual state guidebooks, trip planning, reservations, monthly magazine, and vehicle repair.

There are no longer differences in state **parking regulations for disabled motorists**; the Department of Transportation has decreed that all state licenses issued to disabled persons must carry a three-inch square international access symbol, and each state must provide placards bearing this symbol, to be hung from the rear-view mirror—the placards are blue for permanent disabilities, red for temporary (maximum of six months). More information can be obtained from your state motor vehicle office.

As in other parts of the world, the rise of the **self-service gas station** is unwelcome for many disabled drivers. The state of California has addressed this by changing its laws so that most service stations are required to provide full service to disabled drivers at self-service prices. In Colorado, *Conoco* is offering full service at self-service prices between 7am and 2pm daily at more than seventy *Conoco* stations, with the intention of expanding the program around the country.

CITY TRANSPORTATION

Cabs are generally plentiful and large enough to accommodate a folded wheelchair in the trunk, but for those who prefer not to transfer there is a need for many more accessible vans operating as a taxi service. A couple that have been reported to us are *SuperShuttle* (☎800/554-3146), which can provide transfers in a lift-equipped van, with 24 hours' notice, at Los Angeles (☎213/338-1111), San Francisco (☎510/558-8500), Phoenix (☎602/244-9000), and Dallas (☎817/329-2000) airports, and *Handicabs of the Pacific, Inc.* (PO Box 22428, Honolulu, HI 96822; ☎808/524-3866; see p.37), which offers taxi and tour services in vans with ramps and lock-downs.

There are accessible **urban bus networks** in several towns and cities, although in many cases only major routes are served by accessible vehicles and there are wide variations across the country. In Las Vegas, for example, Arthur Goldthorpe found that every other bus running up and down "the Strip" had a lift (accessible buses being identified by a blue wheelchair symbol on the front, and a hoist next to the side door), while in San Diego very

USA: TRAVEL NOTES

few routes had accessible buses. The ADA aims to address this issue. The rulings are that new bus stations must be accessible, new public transit buses ordered after August 26, 1990 must be accessible, and transit authorities must provide comparable paratransit or other special transportation services to individuals with disabilities who cannot use fixed bus route services, "unless undue burden would result."

Carolyn Lucas reports accessible buses in San Francisco, Boston, and New York. By the end of 1990 some 75 percent of New York buses were fitted with hydraulic lifts and wheelchair spaces. Visitors can apply for "handicapped ID card," enabling them to take advantage of the "Reduced-Fare Program for Disabled Persons." Card holders obtain roughly half-price travel on local buses, some longer journeys, and on the subway. Write to the *New York City Department of Transportation*, Reduced-Fare Program for Disabled Persons, 253 Broadway, 5th Floor, New York, NY 10007 (☎212/240-4131). In 1990 Nic Fleming had this to say of New York buses: "The lifts hardly ever work, and the drivers hate having to stop and get the seldom-used machinery into action. They usually refuse to stop for wheelchair passengers." It is hoped that the ADA will see an end to that attitude. The *Eastern Paralyzed Veterans Association* (see *Sources of information*, p.48) has published a free booklet, *1991 Guide to Riding Wheelchair Accessible Buses in New York City*.

Key stations in **rapid, light, and commuter rail systems** must be made accessible by July 26, 1993, with extensions up to twenty years for commuter rail, thirty years for rapid and light rail. Existing systems must change gradually, but several are relatively new and have been built accessible—for example, Atlanta, San Francisco, Washington DC. In Washington DC each Metrorail station is equipped with an elevator (with Braille number plates) to all platforms from street level. The driver makes station and on-board announcements of train destinations and stops. Hearing-impaired passengers are warned of an approaching train by pulsating lights along the platform edge.

Accommodation

Thanks to the activities of the numerous organizations of disabled people in the USA, including regular meetings all over the country, many involved in the US **hotel and motel** trade are aware of the needs of guests with disabilities. The passing of the ADA will force those who have not yet acted to remove physical barriers in existing facilities, "if readily achievable"—if not, alternative methods of providing the service must be offered, again "if readily achievable." In addition, all new construction and alterations of facilities must be accessible, and auxiliary aids and services (such as assistive listening devices, sign language interpreters, or Braille material) must be provided, at no cost, to individuals with vision or hearing disabilities, "unless an undue burden would result." There is clearly room for maneuver here for those who can make a case that alterations to improve access would impose an undue financial burden. But overall the ADA is good news for disabled travelers in the States, who will mostly be able to find accessible accommodation in all price brackets, although it's wise to check the bathroom layout before booking.

The big hotel and motel **chains** have accessible rooms in many of their properties and often use the access symbol in their directories, although the facilities the symbol represents are usually unclear. *Best Western, Days Inns of America, Holiday Inns, Howard Johnson, Sheraton,* and *Vagabond* are all recommended by contributors.

However, it's worth investigating the **smaller establishments**, in particular the huge array of self-catering units, if only to escape the "sameness" of the chains. Unless you are traveling to a very popular spot in the height of the season, you should not feel obliged to book. With some help from the local visitor information center you are very unlikely to find yourself without a roof over your head and more than likely to save yourself a few bucks.

Christine Panton recommends the *Mayfair Hotel* (1256 W. 7th Street, Los Angeles, CA 90017; ☎310/484 9624), *Golden Nugget Hotel* (129 E. Fremont, Las Vegas, NV 89125; ☎702/

USA: TRAVEL NOTES

385 7111), *Sir Francis Drake Hotel* (Powell and Sutter Streets, San Francisco, CA 94101; ☎510/392 7755), *Carmel Mission Inn* (Highway 1 at Rio Road, Carmel, CA 93922; ☎408/624 1841) and *The Royal Sonesta Hotel* (Bourbon Street, New Orleans, LA; ☎504/586 0300).

All **Walt Disney World** resort hotels (Central Reservations, ☎407/934-7639) are accessible by wheelchair. The *Polynesian Village* is most convenient for visitors in wheelchairs and is comprised of longhouses named after Pacific islands: the Moorea and Oahu (elevators have Braille characters) have several first-floor rooms with wider automatic entrance doors and specially equipped bathrooms; the monorail stops here, allowing convenient acess to the Magic Kingdom. There are also numerous hotels and motels outside of the park which offer facilities for guests with disabilities: write the *Orlando/Orange County Convention and Visitors Bureau* (PO Box 948570, Maitland, FL 32794-8570) for a copy of Orlando—Official Visitors Guide. If planning a trip to Walt Disney World, arm yourself also with a copy of their comprehensive *Guidebook for Disabled Guests* (write Walt Disney World Company, PO Box 10000, Lake Buena Vista, FL 32830-1000).

NATIONAL MOTEL AND HOTEL CHAINS

The big motel and hotel chains are often your safest bet for accessible accommodation: there are plenty of excellent local alternatives, of course, but with a chain at least you'll know what to expect. For "economy lodging" prices go for *La Quinta, Red Roof Inns*; other reasonably priced accommodation can be found at *Days Inns, Howard Johnson*, and *Travelodge*. The facilities offered everywhere should in theory increase and improve as a result of the ADA, but this is the situation as of mid-1992:

Best Western, PO Box 10203, Phoenix, AZ 85064-0203; ☎602/957-4200 or 800/528-1234; for hearing-impaired customers in contiguous 48-states only, ☎800/528-2222, TDD and answering machine. Wheelchair symbol used to indicate "barrier-free facilities for handicapped." Clients can be put in direct contact with the hotel via the central computerized reservations service.

Comfort Inns, 10750 Columbia Pike, Silver Springs, MD 20901-4439; ☎301/593-5600 or 800/228-5150. Some rooms are said to be "designed for handicapped accessibility;" availability can be checked on the computer.

Days Inns of America, Inc., 2751 Buford Highway, NE, Atlanta, GA 30324-3276; ☎706/325-4000 or 800/325-2525, voice; ☎800/222-3297, TDD. Some rooms are marked in the directory as designed for accessibility.

Doubletree Hotels (*Canadian Pacific*), New York National Sales, 555 Madison Avenue, Suite 815, New York, NY 10022; ☎212/754-7800 or 800/528-0444. Nothing in the directory but most hotels do have rooms with features such as bathrooms with wide doorways, and grab bars; facilities vary at each hotel and can be confirmed on reservation.

Embassy Suites, Inc., 850 Ridgelake Boulevard, Suite 400, Memphis, TN 38120; ☎901/680-7200 or 800/362-2779, voice; ☎800/458-4708, TDD. Beginning in 1990, this chain has been working with the Duke family (who produced the Virginia access guide; see p.44) to implement new standards of access which meet and exceed ADA requirements, involving both new construction and retrofitting of all existing 100 hotels. Facilities that go beyond the requirements for barrier-free accommodations will include roll-in showers with flip-down seats, beds on frames with no obstruction, graphic-identified, barrier-free paths of access to all public areas, and specially equipped guest suites. Extraordinary services to be made available on request include amplified room phones, talking or vibrating alarm clocks, low-vision alarm clocks and radios, and tel-ease telephone pads. A unique "disability etiquette training program," developed by the Dukes, called Opening Doors, will be taught to all 6000 *Embassy Suites* employees by year-end 1992. (The cost of a suite at an *Embassy* hotel is comparable to the price of a single room at a traditional upscale hotel, and includes two separate rooms, work areas, and mini-kitchens, and free, cooked-to-order breakfast.)

Hilton Hotels, PO Box 5567, Beverly Hills, CA 90209; ☎310/205-4545 or 800/445-8667, voice; ☎800/368-1133, TDD. Nothing in the directory,

USA: TRAVEL NOTES

and no overall description of facilities for disabled guests available at the time of writing.

Holiday Inns, Corporate Headquarters, Three Ravinia Drive, Suite 2000, Atlanta, GA 30346-2149; ☎706/604-2000 or 800/465-4329 (☎800/HOLIDAY), voice; ☎800/238-5544, TDD. Wheelchair symbol used to indicate "rooms equipped to accommodate wheelchairs"; a symbol is also used to indicate those hotels which have the "Visual Art System" for hearing-impaired guests.

Howard Johnson, Corporate Headquarters, 339 Jefferson Road, PO Box 278, Parsippany, NJ 07054-0728; ☎201/428-9700 or 800/446-4656 (☎800/I-GO-HOJO), voice; ☎800/654-8442, TDD. Wheelchair symbol is used in the directory to indicate hotels with facilities including wide doors to bedroom and bathroom, grab bars for tub and toilet, ramp-type curb from parking lot to sidewalk, and to the hotel entrance. Many locations have these facilities. The brochure states that "Guide dogs are always welcome".

Hyatt International Corporation, 200 West Madison Street, Chicago, IL 60606; ☎312/750-1234 or 800/233-1234. It was the President of *Hyatt*, Darryl Hartley-Leonard, who summed up the hotel industry's initial reaction to the ADA: "the end of the world as we know it." But *Hyatt* has bitten the bullet and rented Barrier-Free Environments, Inc., North Carolina, an architectural and product design firm specializing in building design for persons with disabilities, with a commitment to become "as barrier-free as possible" by 1995; their program includes nationwide recruitment of persons with disabilities, and sensitivity programs for employees. Improvements to accessibility include strobe light smoke detectors that are both audible and visual, lights that blink with a knock on the door, and Braille signs for elevators, as well as the usual grab bars, lever handles, and wide doors. Contact central reservations for advice on exact facilities available at each property.

La Quinta Motor Inns, Inc., PO Box 790064, San Antonio, TX 78279-0064; ☎512/366-6000 or 800/531-5900, voice; ☎800/426-3101. Directory states that there are a limited number of rooms with full accessibility for physically disabled guests (bath area railing, accessible closet and vanity, low-pile carpeting, hand-held shower unit, and remote control TV) at each property.

Ramada, 2111 Wilson Boulevard, Arlington, VA 22201 (☎703/525-0879); 1850 Parkway Place, Marietta, GA 30067 (☎404/423-7773); PO Box 278, Parsippany, NJ 07054-0278 (☎201/428-9700); ☎800/2-RAMADA, voice; ☎800/228-3232, TDD. Locations displaying the wheelchair symbol in the directory have one or more of the following facilities: wheelchair-accessible guest rooms, special bathroom fixtures, public areas with easy-access ramps and wide doors.

Red Roof Inns, Inc., 4355 Davidson Road, Hilliard, OH 43026-2491; ☎614/876-3200 or 800/843-7663 (800/THE-ROOF). The largest privately owned and operated (no franchises) economy lodging chain in the US. Most of their 209 motels have rooms equipped with grab bars and space for wheelchair maneuverability; these are indicated in the directory. A chainwide ADA survey, conducted in 1991, evaluated facilities, access, personnel, and employment.

Sheraton, 60 State Street, Boston, MA 02109; ☎617/367-3600 or 800/325-3535, voice; ☎800/325-1717, TDD. Hotels with facilities for disabled guests are indicated in the directory, but details should be obtained from individual hotels.

Travelodge, Forte Hotels, Inc., 35 East 64th Street, Suite 3B, New York, NY 10021; ☎212/249-5300 or 800/255-3050, voice; ☎800/255-9523. Nothing in the directory, but reservations clerks assure that there are facilities at every hotel, and each hotel will endeavor to meet the needs of any client with a disability, according to individual requirements.

Super 8 Motels, Inc., 1910 8th Ave, NE, Aberdeen, SD 57401-3207; ☎605/225-2272 or 800/843-1991. The directory uses a symbol to indicate motels equipped with disabled facilities (most motels are so marked).

Susse Chalet, Chalet Susse International, Inc., Chalet Drive, Wilton, NH 03086-0657; ☎800/524-2538 (☎800/5-CHALET). Budget chain of about 35 properties in the northeast and mid-Atlantic states. Wheelchair-accessible rooms at most locations, indicated in the directory.

USA: TRAVEL NOTES

Vagabond Hotels, Inc., 6170 Cornerstone Court East, Suite 100, San Diego, CA 92121-3767; ☎619/455-1800 or 800/522-1555 (from US), 800/468-2251 (from Canada). Directory uses the wheelchair symbol to indicate accessible rooms at around 50 percent of locations. Most are in California, a few in Arizona and Nevada. Rates range around $50.

The Great Outdoors

For visitors to **National Parks** there is an outstanding resource, the *Access America Guide: An Atlas and Guide for Visitors with Disabilities*, which covers 37 Eastern, Southwestern, Rocky Mountain, and Western National Parks. It costs $72.45 to individuals and non-profit organizations, from Northern Cartographic (PO Box 133, Burlington, VT 05402; ☎802/860-2886; orders by Visa or Mastercard, ☎802/655-4321; also available in four separate volumes, $10.95 each plus $2 postage, from the Disability Bookshop, ☎206/694-2462 or ☎800/637-2256), but a significant amount of information contained in the complete volume is not included in these regional guides. The *Access America Guide* contains useful information for visitors with mobility impairments, hearing, visual, or developmental disabilities; there are more than 250 detailed, full-color maps, graphics, and drawings, and the guide is spiral-bound for ease of handling, with large-print text. Access evaluations are based on national and federal standards and cover campgrounds, lodging, transportation, visitor centers, and adventure tours. Some accounts by visitors with disabilities are also included.

Yosemite National Park (PO Box 577, CA 95389; ☎209/372-0515, voice; ☎209/372-4726, TDD) can supply general information direct, but an invaluable guide is *Access Yosemite National Park* ($7.95), a one-park excerpt from its parent publication, above. Reservations for hotels or lodges can be made up to one year in advance by contacting *Yosemite Reservations* (541 East Home Ave, Fresno, CA 93727; ☎209/372-1000, voice; ☎209/255-8345, TDD) or writing *Ticketron*, Department R, 401 Hackensack Avenue, Hackensack, NJ 07601. Carolyn Lucas recommends a disabled unit among the "rustic tent cabins" in Curry Village. Reservations are required for campgrounds in Yosemite Valley during the spring, summer, and fall, and must be made in advance through *Ticketron*.

Accessible **campgrounds** are reasonably widespread in the US, but information on facilities is hard to find in the guidebooks. The *KOA* (Kampgrounds of America; ☎800/347-8880) directories include no access details; they suggest calling campgrounds direct to check accessibility. *Woodall's Campground Directory* indicates accessible rest room facilities only, but plans are under way to inspect all locations (over 8500 private campgrounds and RV parks) for wider accessibility criteria, with the intention of introducing the "handicap symbol" in their next editions. The North American Edition ($16.95), Eastern Edition ($11.60), and Western Edition ($11.40) are all available from Woodall Publishing Co., 28167 North Keith Drive, PO Box 5000, Lake Forest, IL 60045-5000; ☎708/362-6700 or 800/323-9076.

The US Department of Agriculture **Forest Service** (201 14th Street, SW, PO Box 96090, Washington DC 20090-6090; ☎202/205-1760), is also in the process of developing a listing of accessible sites but it will take several years as there are thousands of sites to evaluate; in the meantime, visitors are encouraged to contact the forests they plan to visit in advance, using the addresses from the pamphlet, *A Guide to your National Forests*.

The Forest Service in Highlands Ranger District (Flat Mountain Road, Route 1, Box 247, Highlands, NC 28741) has developed accessible facilities at Balsam Lake Lodge and Recreation Area, where there are accessible accommodations ($12 per night) and nature trails, as well as accessible facilities for boating and fishing. **Pathways for the Future** (PO Box 2114, Sylva, NC 28779; ☎704/586-2471) is involved with the management and development of Balsam Lake and is a non-profit membership (individuals, $12 yearly) organization that works to promote barrier-free outdoor recreational programs and activities.

The **National Audubon Society** (Audubon Ecology Camps and Workshops, 613 Riversville Road, Greenwich, CT 06831; ☎203/869-2017), the **Nantahala Outdoor Center** (US 19W, Box 41, Bryson City, NC 28713; ☎704/488-2175),

USA: TRAVEL NOTES

and **Outward Bound** (384 Field Point Road, Greenwich, CT 06830; ☎203/661-0797 or 800/243-8520) are all reported to be able and willing to accommodate people with disabilities on some of their programs.

The **Disabled Outdoors Foundation** (2052 West 23rd Street, Chicago, IL 60608; ☎312/927-6834) was founded in 1988 as a clearing house for information for the disabled person looking for recreational facilities and adaptive recreational gear. The *Disabled Outdoors Magazine* is the Foundation's quarterly magazine covering outdoor activities for sportspersons with disabilities (US $10, Can $16 yearly).

Citizens or permanent residents of the US who have been "medically determined to be blind or permanently disabled" can obtain the **Golden Access Passport**, a free lifetime entrance pass to those federally operated parks, monuments, historic sites, recreation areas, and wildlife refuges which charge entrance fees. The pass must be picked up in person, from the areas described, and it also provides a 50 percent discount on fees charged for facilities such as camping, boat launching, and parking.

Access and Facilities

The message in these accounts, almost all written before the ADA was passed, is clear: **access to buildings, sporting activities, and tourist attractions**, including national parks, beaches, forests, mountains, or desert, is good—in the eyes of most visitors from Europe it is excellent. **Access to the arts** gives further cause for admiration. Carolyn Lucas describes the work of some gifted groups of disabled actors in the States; facilities for disabled theater-goers are equally impressive. At the John F. Kennedy Center for the Performing Arts in Washington DC, it goes without saying that all theaters are accessible to wheelchair users but in addition there are infrared listening systems in three of the six main theaters. With a set of headphones a hearing-impaired patron may "sit anywhere in the house, adjust the volume and enjoy!" For blind patrons there are recordings of scripts with detailed descriptions of sets and costumes in shows performed in the Opera House, Eisenhower and Terrace theaters.

Many theaters in major cities offer discounts to handicapped patrons for some performances. The National Theater, also in Washington DC, offers a limited number of half-priced tickets on Tuesday, Wednesday, and Thursday evenings and Sunday afternoons. The National is unique in the USA in providing a permanent booth for a narrator to describe the performance scene by scene; this narration is available twice a month, transmitted by headphone to visually handicapped members of the audience.

Arthur Goldthorpe sounds a cautionary note regarding **rest room facilities**: although most places have cubicles ostensibly for disabled people, the layout often fails to allow sufficient space for lateral transfer. A design frequently encountered in older buildings is an extended cubicle three feet wide with handrails attached each side. If you cannot transfer in these circumstances you may have to rely on rest rooms in the fast-food restaurants; on the West Coast, it seems, *McDonald's* provides better facilities than *Burger King*!

Cubicles for disabled people do not have integral sinks, so that you may have to grapple with awkward faucets and towels or hand-driers that are difficult to reach. The unisex rest room—necessary for those who rely on help from a spouse or companion of the opposite sex—is relatively rare in the USA; in over four months of traveling Arthur Goldthorpe found only one rest room clearly marked as "Unisex." Anyone requiring this facility might be lucky in smaller shops and restaurants, where a single, unisex washroom often provides the space needed for a wheelchair.

For more information on the ADA contact ADA, Civil Rights Division of the Department of Justice, PO Box 6618, Washington DC 20035-6118; ☎202/514-0301, voice; ☎202/514-0381/0383, TDD.

Health

A word of warning about the climate of the East Coast, from Carolyn Lucas: "It can be extreme in summer and winter; the best time to go is spring or fall. The humidity can be so enervating that you quickly run out of energy, especially if you or your companion are lugging a wheelchair around. Out of town, insects can be vicious and

USA: TRAVEL NOTES

a doctor should see to their bites. My husband was affected and had to take a course of antibiotics as a precaution against possible development of rheumatoid arthritis."

A range of services—covering pretty much every eventuality—are listed in the **Yellow Pages**, usually under the headings, Human Services, Health Services, or Disabled Services.

Repair, sale, and rental of **wheelchairs** are handled by medical supply companies, which can be found via the Yellow Pages. For tire repair, try a bike shop.

If you need information regarding sale or repair of **hearing aids**, and sale or rental of TDD, contact *The National Association of the Deaf* (814 Thayer Avenue, Silver Springs, MD 20910; ☎301/587-1788). Hearing-aid dealers are listed in the Yellow Pages; they require a prescription from an audiologist in order to sell or repair hearing aids.

The *National Information Center on Deafness* (Gallaudet University, 800 Florida Avenue NE, Washington DC 20002; ☎202/651-5051, voice; ☎202/651-5052, TDD; ☎800/332-1124, tele-consumer hotline, voice and TDD) has information on TDDs and a booklet listing resources for hearing-impaired travelers, T*ravel Resources for Deaf and Hard of Hearing People*.

The *National Federation of the Blind* (1800 Johnson Street, Baltimore, MD 21230; ☎410/659-9314) can send white **canes** and other specialized equipment anywhere in the States, and will also issue identification cards certifying blindness—these may have to be produced for discounts on bus or train tickets.

Books

A World of Options for the 90s: A Guide to International Educational Exchange, Community Service, and Travel for Persons with Disabilities, by Susan Sygall and Cindy Lewis (1990, *Mobility International USA*; $16 non-members, $14 members). Fine writing by people who know all the angles. Covers the world but contains useful sections relevant to journeys within the US—on travel by air, train, bus, and car; listings of specialized tour and travel agents, organizations that assist travelers with disabilities, resource materials, hotels; and some entertaining personal travel experiences.

The Wheelchair Traveler, by Douglass Annand (1990; US $20, Can $22, from Ball Hill Road, Milford, NH 03055; ☎603/673-4539). Listings of hotels, motels, restaurants, and sightseeing attractions, using a rating system to describe accessibility. No rating is guaranteed, but the author is a well-traveled wheelchair user and all listings are said to be from knowledgeable sources—other travelers with disabilities, and organizations.

The Complete Directory for People with Disabilities, edited by Leslie Mackenzie (1991, $69.95; Grey House Publishing, Pocket Knife Square, Lakeville, CT 06039; ☎203/435-0868). Nearly 600 pages, paperbound, containing 6000 entries divided into: Institutions, Media, Products, and Programs. Not worth buying for the Travel and Transportation section alone, which certainly isn't "complete," but a useful general reference work.

Resource Directory for the Disabled, by Richard Neil Shrout (1991, $45; Facts on File, Inc., 460 Park Avenue South, New York, NY 10016). Nearly 400 pages, hardbound, divided into four sections—General Resources, and Resources for Mobility Impaired, Visually Impaired, and Hearing Impaired. Each lists Travel Helps; Appliances, Devices, and Aids; Recreation, Sports, and Social Opportunities; Organizations; Associations and Support Groups; Employment/Training Opportunities; Education; Publications. Fewer entries than the *Complete Directory*, but more information and a sensible layout make it easier to use, and it's cheaper. Again, not worth buying for the travel information alone: the Travel Helps sections for mobility impaired and visually impaired people are very brief, although there is a bigger entry for those with hearing disabilities.

Canada

Satisfied Customers

Traveling across North America by Greyhound, spending days and nights on board, might seem a little crazy and impractical for a full-time wheelchair user. But Dee Hopkins did it, in 1983, accompanied by her husband, Gerry.

Whatever the time of day or night, no matter how long or short the journey, traveling by *Greyhound* is exciting. Thundering along the highways we had conflicting feelings—not wanting the journey to end, yet looking forward to reaching our destination, where we could begin a new adventure. The drivers made it even more enjoyable; they were friendly and helpful, and pointed out places of interest, especially to us, occupying the front seats which gave us splendid views of the passing countryside. Our fellow passengers seemed to feel the same sense of excitement, almost trepidation, as they boarded, and it didn't take long for a special kind of camaraderie to develop among us. We exchanged vacation experiences, discussed our plans, and took advice about our proposed destinations.

No one seemed to mind that we had to take our time getting on, or that we had to take the front seats. The only way I could get up the steps was to sit and push up with my arms until I reached the top, where Gerry lifted me and put me on the seat. Trousers are the most dignified clothing for this operation. The unusual method of ascent didn't worry me, especially since

twice a day the passengers are asked to leave the bus and it is taken away for a thorough cleaning, inside and out.

When booking, I had supplied a doctor's certificate, stating that I need help, so that we were able to take advantage of the scheme (Travel Assistance), whereby I bought a ticket and my companion traveled free. This was very important because money was our main problem; we had to work on a very tight budget because Gerry gave up work to look after me. The most difficult decision was choosing where to go; in the end, after a trip to our local library to look up the *Greyhound* timetables (we Xeroxed the appropriate pages), we booked a ten-day trip, leaving midweek from Portsmouth, New Hampshire, and traveling through the Rockies, across Canada.

Traveling light was essential; trying to push a wheelchair overloaded with luggage as well as me would be almost impossible. So we restricted ourselves to a small suitcase of lightweight clothes which rested either on the arms of the wheelchair in front of me or on the footplates, between my knees. A flight-bag was hung from the handles at the back, and Gerry carried a holdall over his shoulder.

Thanks to the kind invitation of my penpal in Maine, we were able to spend our first night with friends, who saw us on our way with plenty of provisions—meat in small tins and jars for sandwiches, coffee and dried milk, soft drinks in cartons, cheese and crackers, nuts and raisins, puddings in easy-to-open cartons, and many other items which saved us having to shop. We did treat ourselves to one hot meal a day, mainly takeouts which were so huge that we usually needed only one for both of us.

The first bus was to take us to Boston, Massachusetts, where we would change buses and carry on into Canada, via Syracuse, Albany, Buffalo, and Niagara Falls. We said farewell to our friends, who were a little worried about us—they gave us an envelope with some dollars in, to use in emergencies, but we were determined not to use it, and we returned it unopened when we finished our journey.

We slept on the bus that first night, partly to save money and partly because we wanted to arrive at Niagara Falls first thing in the morning. Sleeping on the buses is easy, especially if (as recommended) you take a small travel pillow, or have a shoulder to rest on—I had both. I also took a small blanket, as the air conditioning can be a little too efficient at night. However, I don't recommend sleeping consecutive nights on the bus; had money not been such an important consideration we would have spent every night in a motel.

The first thing we did on arrival at Niagara Falls was to find a much-needed hot breakfast, with coffee. After that we made our way across the small town to the Tourist Information Office, where they supplied us with the name and address of an inexpensive motel, and with all the information we needed about the area, including the times of a

sightseeing tour, due to start later that morning.

We found the motel clean and comfortable, with color TV and two queen-size beds, which we collapsed onto for a couple of hours. Later we climbed aboard Bessie bus for a very interesting tour, which we found surprisingly inexpensive—and it certainly saved us a lot of energy. We passed the falls and then followed the river. The fact that impressed me was that the falls started way downriver, thousands of years ago, and since then have gradually cut back into the rock to reach their current position. The river was slowed down in recent years by a very long barrier which can control the flow; it is hoped that this will slow down the process of erosion.

We were taken down the cliffs to the rapids; the others had to climb down many stairs but I was able to descend in a small elevator. My most vivid memory of the falls is the color of the water—deep, deep green, almost like crème-de-menthe—and the ferocity of it, cascading down with a deafening roar, so close to the road and only separated from us by a slim iron railing.

"The job of the front-seat occupants was to watch out for stray moose"

The next day we were back on the *Greyhound*, heading this time for Toronto. There we had a few hours to spare, so we left our bags in a locker and made our way out of the bus station, trying to remember our route for the journey back. The shopping area was fantastic, my favorite being the photographic shop, where customers could change into old-fashioned clothes and be photographed, the finished product developed in authentic sepia tones.

As usual, I had to find a rest room, and in 1983 the facilities for disabled people were nowhere near the level provided now in Canada and the USA; the awareness of disabled people's needs was not as high. Back at the bus station, I was getting desperate, so we sought out one of the many security guards who patrol the bus stations at night. We explained our predicament, and the fact that we had another hour to wait before catching our bus, and he escorted us to the Ladies. He stopped everyone going in, and when the last woman came out he waved my husband and me inside—now that is what I call service! What surprised us was that no one seemed to mind, and Toronto bus station is a very busy place, even at night.

"We proved we could do it on a shoestring and still have a good time"

At 1am we boarded the bus and headed out of the city. Our driver informed us that we were on Moose Patrol; we thought he was joking, but he told us that the job of the front-seat occupants was to watch out for stray moose that happen to roam onto the highway. If hit the moose can cause a serious accident, not to mention the damage to themselves.

It was still dark when we reached Lake Superior; we followed the lake for miles before we came to a smaller lake and beside it the little town of Wawa, originally an Ajibwa settlement, named after the cry of the Canada geese that call there during migration. At this time, the lake is covered with them. As the sun rose we left Wawa, after our rest stop, and we were able to see beautiful Lake Superior shimmering orange in the morning rays.

Our next stop was Thunder Bay, a compact and attractive town, renowned for its amethyst mines. As we traveled toward it we saw the purple seams in the rocks where the engineers had blasted through to build the highway. We had planned to stay one night before traveling on through the Rockies to Vancouver, but my legs had become so swollen that we decided to

abandon our plans to see the Rockies, and stayed put for three days.

We climbed off the bus, collected our bits together and made for the Tourist Information Office where, once again, we obtained a comprehensive list of motels, their facilities, and prices. We found a cheap one with cooking facilities, color TV, telephone, and the regulation queen-size beds. The only problem we encountered at all in our accommodation was the showers—I couldn't stand up in them. We sorted this out by putting a towel on the floor under the shower; I then sat on the towel and showered, after which my husband lifted me onto my chair. All our motel rooms were very spacious, so I had no trouble maneuvering the wheelchair once inside.

We enjoyed our stay in Thunder Bay. The weather was very hot, but not humid, and we walked everywhere (or my husband did). The streets were all straight, as if laid out on a grid, and very wide. The locals seemed amused to see us plodding along the streets— they all use cars. We found the people rather reserved and, although helpful, not very receptive to strangers. Perhaps this is because it is not really a tourist town, more a small industrial center, with ships coming and going at the docks. There are few places of interest for the tourist, apart from the amethyst mines, where guided tours can be made (but not by wheelchair users), and the jewelry shops in town.

Late in the afternoon on the third day, we boarded the bus for our journey home. After a long ride in the darkness, we experienced another beautiful Canadian sunrise. The driver showed us where a tornado had passed, leaving a trail of destruction a couple of miles wide. We passed through the nickel-mining town of Sudbury, then arrived in Toronto. We had planned to spend the night in the city but as there was a big exhibition on, we couldn't find a room, so we had to head back to the bus.

At 12:30am the bus heaved its way tentatively onto the still-busy streets, back to the border and into the USA. A couple from our bus were held up at the border by customs officials, leaving us way behind schedule. We were worried about our connections at Buffalo and Boston, and several other passengers were affected, so the driver contacted Buffalo and asked them to hold up the bus for us. That driver in turn contacted Boston and we were able to continue to Portsmouth, and our friends.

No sooner had we arrived home than we were planning another trip. We don't know if we'll ever get to go again, but it will certainly be fun planning. There are a few things we would change, such as not sleeping so much on the bus, but shortage of money and time (we were only given seven days on our Canadian visas) gave us little choice on this trip. We proved we could do it on a shoe-string and still have a good time, and at the end of our journey, despite a tinge of regret that we didn't reach the Rockies, our greatest emotion was satisfaction.

Canada: Second to None

Although confined to a wheelchair for the past 26 years with muscular dystrophy, Christine Swan is a fairly "active" disabled person, able to work full time, to drive, and to lead a very full life. In September 1983 she and a companion carried out an all-expenses-paid research trip on behalf of a tour company (Travelmarrs) to assess the facilities for the disabled traveler in Canada*. They covered some 2000 miles across the country from east to west, starting in Toronto and finishing in Vancouver.

We arrived in Toronto in brilliant, mid-afternoon sunshine with temperatures in the upper eighties. Our first few days were full of interesting sights, including

Black Creek Settlers' Village and the CN Tower. Because of the nature of the village—early settlers' houses (many with steps), unpaved roads—it would be difficult, without spoiling its authenticity, to make it entirely accessible to disabled visitors, and it was impossible to view many of the buildings internally. We gained access to the lower viewing area in the CN Tower by elevator, but a wide heating-system grille around the revolving area prohibited wheelchair-bound visitors from fully appreciating the view.

But the highlight of our stay in Toronto has to be our visit to Niagara. After lunching—on scallops in champagne; veal in cheese and tomato sauce with vegetables; fudge cake with hot chocolate sauce; ice cream and heavy cream; coffee and hazelnut liqueur—in the Skylon Tower revolving restaurant, I was able to don the regulation hooded oilskin and sail in the *Maid of the Mist* to the foot of the falls, where our senses were overwhelmed by the mighty rush of water and the spray which engulfs the excited passengers.

We stayed in Toronto at the *Inn on the Park*, where breakfasts were taken

---

*The project that sponsored this trip was sunsequently abandoned due to "lack of support and interest", and the company is no longer involved in holidays for disabled people.

beside the open-air swimming pool, served by attractive waitresses in skimpy shorts. Ramps were provided at intervals over three or four steps leading to the dining room and to the pool area but these, particularly the internal ramps, were very steep and I needed three attendants to negotiate them in my chair. In addition, my wheelchair, which is fairly narrow (21.5in), would only just go through the bathroom doorway. The brochure did state that any bathroom door could be removed on request but this is not ideal when sharing a room. In all other respects, however, the hotel was very satisfactory.

"In the winter, this freezes over and thousands of office workers skate to work on it"

After four days, it was off by train on a seven-hour journey to the beautiful capital, Ottawa. Canada's national railroad company, *VIA Rail*, is to be commended on the thought and planning which it devotes to facilities for disabled passengers, and on the advice it gives to intending disabled travelers. The service and willingness of *VIA* personnel on our journey was first class.

In Ottawa we were treated to a performance of *The Gondoliers* at the Arts Center, which has level access and helpful staff. The restaurant is accessible and the theater has a gently sloping walkway in three sections to the upper-floor auditorium. The Ottawa Art Gallery also has level access and good facilities.

The following day we viewed Government House, the embassy buildings, each set in magnificent grounds, the Prime Minister's house, overlooking the Ottawa river, and the Training School for Mounties. We had a guided tour of the Senate buildings (special entrance for disabled visitors) which were completely accessible. There is virtually no industry in Ottawa—the majority of the residents are employed by the government—so it's a clean city, architecturally beautiful, with lovely parks in the center. The Rideau Canal also runs through the center; in the winter, this freezes over and thousands of office workers skate to work on it.

After Ottawa, we traveled back to Toronto for a three-hour flight to Saskatoon, Saskatchewan, where we flew into rain and cooler weather. One of the trips we enjoyed here was a visit to the Western Development Museum, a complete indoor village with sidewalks, and shops stocked as they were a hundred years ago. There are carriages and cars in the road, and a train station with sound effects. We had no access problems apart from the double doors at the entrance, which were set too close together, allowing insufficient room to get the wheelchair through into the space before opening the inner doors.

We stayed at the *Holiday Inn*, where access to the dining room was level but, in common with most other hotels, the bathroom was too small for maneuvering. Upon leaving, we were advised that this hotel did have a special room for disabled guests, but we had not been booked into it. We visited the *Saskatoon Inn*, a hotel and restaurant, very new at the time, designed with sloped walkways throughout from first to second floor. It was a real showpiece, with indoor swimming pool and gardens.

From Saskatoon, we drove about 250 miles across the vast wheatfields of the Prairies to Regina, where our first port of call was the Royal Canadian Mounted Police Museum and Chapel. The museum is accessible; the guide advised us that a ramp was shortly to be provided for the three steps at the entrance to the chapel. The *Regina Inn* supplied our accommodation, and the facilities in both bedroom and bathroom were convenient; the dining room had level access.

Another flight took us 500 miles to Calgary—not, as I'd imagined, a small "cowboy town," but a large city with many skyscrapers where, like New York, the sidewalks downtown rarely see the sun. The only view I had of the Calgary Stampede Showground was from the revolving restaurant in the Calgary Tower (good access by elevator) where we had breakfast one morning—sausage, bacon, pancakes and maple syrup; the works!

There were several steps at the front entrance of *The Palliser Hotel*, but we obtained access through the rear entrance via the elevator from the parking lot. The toilet was situated behind the bathroom door and we were unable to maneuver my wheelchair around. We were transferred to another room which was better. There was flat access to the dining rooms in this hotel and in the *Chateau Airport*, where we were booked into a suite for disabled guests. Here there was room to maneuver in the bathroom, a useful handrail on the wall next to the toilet and lever faucet on the sink, but the sink was set too high—another common problem in the hotels we inspected. The bedroom was fine.

> *"There are pine-log cottages, each specially designed for the disabled, and paved trails through the forests"*

From Calgary we took a two-day, 500-mile trip into the Rocky Mountains. Those were bright and sunny days; never have I been anywhere so beautiful. The lakes at the foot of the mountains are a rich, sapphire blue; there are perfectly shaped pine trees growing on the sides of the snowcapped mountains; the air is crystal clear; the silence is both calming and awe-inspiring. At every bend in the road we were presented with a view more lovely than the last, not just for a few miles but for hundreds upon hundreds of miles.

While in the Rockies we visited the *William Watson Lodge*, Kananaskis Country, which has been provided by the Canadian government for handicapped residents of the Province of Alberta. There are pine-log cottages, each specially designed for the disabled, and paved trails through the forests which lead to viewing areas overlooking the mountains and lakes. At each junction in the trails, the texture of the ground changes, so that a blind person can tell where the turns are. We were shown around by Ross, who is blind but knew his way instinctively and was able to describe the breathtaking views to us. It was a real pleasure for me to go through the forests with the scent of pines heavy in the air—this is something that we wheelchair-bound folk are not often able to do.

On the first night of our Rockies trip we had a balcony room overlooking the lake at *Chateau Lake Louise*. It was dark when we arrived but it was a good start to the following day to wake up to the sun shining on snowcapped peaks and the blue lake just below our window. The bedroom and bathroom were adequate but again I had difficulty moving around the bathroom. We had to negotiate five or six steps to the dining room where we feasted on reindeer steaks, but there is another dining room with level access—it was closed on the day of our visit.

We would have given anything to sit all day and take in the beauty of the surroundings at *Chateau Lake Louise*, but we had to move on, another 250 miles or so, to Jasper. Here we were booked into a suite for disabled guests in a superb hotel, *Chateau Jasper*, where the proprietor had obviously given much thought to the facilities. This was the only hotel with space next to the toilet for sideways transfer, although it was too close to the wall on the other side for my needs. There was a handrail beside the toilet, lever door handles and a sloping mirror toward the sink. However, the sink was set much too high and the modern, pull-out faucet was difficult.

We took a cable car to the top of Whistler's Mountain which was concealed by cloud. There was no problem with boarding or leaving the cable car but the sides of the car were a little too high to enable seated passengers to take in the view. The viewing area at the peak was accessible—we sat and shivered in driving snow!

The next day we drove back to Calgary and flew on to our final city, Vancouver. It's easy to understand why so many people settle here: the harbors are lovely, and Stanley Park (with totem poles, peaceful lakes, and accessible aquarium) beautiful; the winters on this side of Canada are mild, with perhaps only one or two falls of snow; Glenmore (the revitalized dockside area) is interesting and attractive, as well as easily accessible. Both the city and the island are places which I should like to visit again and spend more time in.

"With careful planning and a sense of humor it is possible to achieve the impossible"

We stayed at the *Hyatt Regency*, which offered excellent facilities and well-planned rooms. The ferry to Vancouver Island was accessible, although the route to and from the ferry by elevator for disabled passengers could have been better marked, and there was a long walk to board the ferry from the departure lounge.

Of course, we were privileged on our trip. We were transported by car, driven in each province by a guide provided by the tourist boards, and we received VIP treatment, with visits to the mayors of several cities, press interviews, and TV appearances. But none of this detracts from the fact that we

met many kind and helpful people during our stay, and it was clear that facilities for the disabled are kept very much in mind. There are dropped curbs in every city, ramps where there is even just one step, and accessible elevators everywhere. I was also very impressed by the fleets of Handy-Dart and Wheel-Trans buses, which transport disabled people on any trip that they wish to make.

It is very difficult to ensure that *every* hotel room is suitable for *every* disabled person, or for every type of handicap. The two main problems which I encountered were the limited space around the toilet and the height of the sink: it is not necessary for the wheelchair to go under the sink, only up to it. Our bedrooms were generally satisfactory, with plenty of room to maneuver, but all the hotels we used were first class—I doubt that the facilities at the cheaper hotels would be so good.

The most trying part of traveling abroad, especially on long trips, remains the flights, where one's wheelchair is whisked away at the airport and loaded into the hold, to be produced again (if you're lucky) at the destination. More training should be given to airline staff regarding the correct method of lifting, and they should always be prepared to listen to the disabled person's requests and advice on this. The aircraft seats are particularly restricting and, of course, one is expected to be superman (or woman) as far as visiting the rest room is concerned.

Even so, with careful planning and a sense of humor, it is possible to achieve the impossible. I have spent many other happy vacations, before and after my trip to Canada, but few that approach the high standard of hotels or scenery, and none that surpass it.

Large Marge Steals the Show

When he traveled to Canada in 1989, Steve Veness was 29 years old and had been a paraplegic for ten years.

"Yes, of course we'll come over and see you," my wife Judy and I had somewhat rashly promised when we heard that our friends were to be posted to Canada for three years.

After eighteen months, a large dose of guilt at our unfulfilled promise, coupled with a dash of adventurous spirit, saw us wandering aimlessly through London's Heathrow airport, trying to look as though we knew where we were going. Well, we did know that—Nova Scotia, Toronto, Niagara, and the Rockies were all firmly on our itinerary; the big unknown was how we would fare en route.

We had booked our *Air Canada* flights through *Thomas Cook* who, they assured me, had told the airline that I would need full assistance with boarding and deplaning. Sure enough, *Air Canada* oozed confidence, and with an air of polite matter-of-factness swept me (and Judy) straight onto the 767 ahead of the crowds.

Although we didn't know it at the time, we were already gaining the first of several advantages that we were to enjoy on our vacation as a result of my disability. This only dawned on us later, when we flew from Toronto to Calgary and had to rough it in economy class—on all the other flights we were given business-class seats, although we had paid for economy throughout our trip.

At Halifax airport, after a smooth, civilized (business-class) journey, we were brought down to earth by our first flight of stairs, by a rental car with no hand controls, and by the rain! The stairs, to be fair, did have a (very slow) stair-lift, and the rain we were used to, but the lack of hand controls meant that Judy would have to drive the 75 miles across Nova Scotia to our hotel in the Annapolis Valley (she was not amused!). My admiration for the fact that *Hertz* was prepared to fit hand controls to each car we rented for no extra charge soon evaporated, to be replaced by tired cynicism amid the flurry of apologies. Two days later, with hand controls fitted (to a larger car at no extra cost) and charges for the first two days waived, admiration returned and was to remain throughout three weeks of trouble-free driving in four different cars.

Nova Scotia is a curious mixture of easy-going, rural provincialism and brash American influence. It is not a materially rich area, but it is dotted with small farming towns, the inhabitants of which seem to enjoy a quality of life that cannot be measured in pounds or dollars. Despite severe winters, the long, warm summers allow the province to grow large quantities of apples, peaches, blueberries, wheat, corn, and other vegetables. We were able to enjoy a wide range of fresh produce by visiting the inexpensive pick-your-own farms.

Religion is clearly important to the people of Nova Scotia: each town has several fine wooden churches, usually in pristine condition with a recent coat of white paint. Most of the churches had ramped access (uncommon in the UK); indeed, access to buildings throughout Nova Scotia—and the rest of Canada—was very good.

In contrast to the peaceful grace of Nova Scotia's churches, eating out was an American fast-food affair, with "Donut" shops and burger-bars very much in evidence. One favorable aspect of the fast-food restaurants is that many have rest rooms which are accessible to wheelchairs—no bad thing given the Canadian habit of never allowing you to empty your coffee cup. Another point in their favor (in my eyes) is that they serve enormous helpings. One could easily manage on two meals a day—so I'm told.

Our flight to Toronto was another smooth one and this time a hand-controlled car was waiting for us at the airport, which was just as well, since we hit Toronto at 5pm on a Friday afternoon in a thunderstorm—Judy was definitely *not* going to drive! For anyone considering renting a car with hand controls, they seem to be fitted on the left of the steering wheel in Canada—this takes a little getting used to if you are accustomed to controls on the right.

> *"We were able to see many species of wildlife, including mountain goats, bighorn sheep, mule deer, elk, and coyote"*

Toronto is a very clean city which exudes an air of confidence in the future. A large number of modern buildings were under construction or had just been completed. As well as the ubiquitous office buildings and shopping malls, recent buildings include the Skydome—a vast sports stadium which is home to the Toronto Blue Jays baseball team—and the CN Tower, which at over 1700ft is the world's largest free-standing construction. These two are sited close to one another and I strongly advise against trying to visit either on a day when the Blue Jays are playing at home!

We booked the *Bond Place Hotel* in Toronto through *Thomas Cook*, who indicated that it was suitable for wheelchairs. It was, provided you didn't want to go to the toilet—our room had an *en suite* bathroom with a door width of no more than 21 inches (53cm). Fortunately, I was able to transfer via a chair onto the toilet, and as we were only staying for two nights we made do.

For us, the real reason for stopping off at Toronto was to visit Niagara Falls, which appear on the map to be very close to Toronto. In fact, we drove about 125 miles from our hotel in the city center to the falls—the size of the country was one aspect of Canada we found difficult to come to terms with. Having arrived before 9am to beat the Labor Day weekend crowds, we thought we would be able to head back to the hotel by early afternoon.

Things didn't go quite according to plan: we did everything, bar the barrel-ride, and we had to drag ourselves away at 10:30pm! Half expecting the falls to be an anticlimax, we soon realized that none of the guidebooks do them justice. Two factors were particularly pleasing: access to all the main tourist attractions was excellent (and we bypassed the long lines to the falls tunnels and to the truly exhilarating *Maid of the Mist* boat trip); in addition, we were pleasantly surprised not to be stung with exorbitant prices or poor quality in any of the attractions, including the excellent *Terrace Restaurant* where we had lunch.

After Toronto and Niagara, we headed west to the heart of the Rockies, in search of "the great outdoors." The area centered around Banff and Lake Louise presents a heady mixture of massive, snowcapped peaks, clear mountain air, tumbling rivers, snow, ice, and plentiful wildlife. Although cross-country hikes are clearly out of the question for us, many of the most famous spots in the region are accessible by road or by short, well-laid paths from the road.

Not to be missed are Lake Louise (including brunch at *Chateau Lake Louise*, overlooking the lake), Moraine Lake, and Takkakaw Falls (1250 feet high and spectacular in a very different way to Niagara). As well as giving its name to a ski village nearby, Lake Louise is a very popular tourist attraction. The green waters of the lake, hemmed in by lofty mountains on three sides, attract visitors by the hundred each day. To see it at its best, go there at sunrise, before the crowds arrive, and watch the pink mountains mirrored in the surface of the lake.

Also worthwhile is the drive along the Icefields Parkway to the Athabasca Glacier, stopping at the Peyto Lake viewpoint on the way. On that drive, and also on the way to Radium Hot Springs, we were able to see many species of wildlife, including mountain goats, bighorn sheep, mule deer, moose, and coyote. In case this sounds like too much wilderness, the region does have centers of civilization in the form of fine restaurants, such as that at the *Post Hotel* in the village of Lake Louise, and good shopping, especially in the center of Banff.

We had an excellent (but expensive) meal at the *Post Hotel*; the staff was very friendly, access was good, and the hotel had an aura of unpretentious luxury. If we ever get the chance to go to the Rockies again I hope we can afford to stay (and eat!) at the *Post Hotel*. In Banff, *Melissa's* is *the* place for breakfast—a six-ounce sirloin steak with eggs is one of the more popular offerings on the menu.

"Five magnificent humpback whales and many porpoises"

After our time in the Rockies we had planned a two-night stop back in Nova Scotia, to say goodbye to our friends before flying back to the UK. In the event, our last full day in Canada was a day which will live in our memories for a long time to come. While we were "out West," our friends had booked a whale-watching trip from Brier Island on the westernmost tip of the Nova Scotia peninsula.

Rising early, and feeling slightly jet-lagged, we drove 200 miles down the peninsula, across two drive-on ferries, to arrive at the tiny fishing port just in time for the trip. My slight anxieties about how I was going to get onto the boat disappeared as four strong men easily lifted me—somewhat heavier after three weeks in Canada—together with wheelchair, on board. (In fact, I was not the only person in a wheelchair on that trip.)

Once we had left the harbor we motored out into the Bay of Fundy on a flat-calm sea. We were soon lucky enough to see the first of five magnificent humpback whales and many porpoises. The people running these trips are scientists engaged in whale research; they were therefore able to give an informed and enthusiastic commentary on the whales' behavior. The scientists can recognize individual whales from their markings, and they were pleased when we sighted "Large Marge" together with her eight-month-old calf—a mere baby at 23ft in length.

The whales did not seem to mind the boat and at times swam alongside and underneath (one actually went to sleep beside us!), but the calf was very inquisitive, not having seen the boat before. The organizers sight whales on 97 percent of the trips (and refund ticket money if none are seen) but we were especially lucky to see so many, and such a wide variety of behaviors, including breaching (jumping clear of the sea), feeding—and sleeping! In every sense it proved a fitting climax for our vacation.

Canada is not a country we would have visited unprompted, but it left us with some lasting memories—of homey farming communities, busy city streets, awesome natural grandeur, and vast open spaces untouched by human influence. When we think of Canada we think of Lake Louise at sunrise, Niagara Falls seen from *Maid of the Mist*, and a mother and calf swimming in unison. We also think of the people we met—friendly, generous, and proud of their country—for whom my wheelchair never seemed to be a problem. Our trip not only gave us a feel for their land, but also made us realize how easy and worthwhile long-distance travel can be.

Proud to be a Montréaler

Dorothea Boulton is confined to a wheelchair. When in August 1988 her daughter, Jane, took up a research post at McGill University, Montréal, it seemed the ideal opportunity for Dorothea and her husband, Paul, to visit Canada.

We started planning our visit when Jane suggested that May or June were suitable months to consider; during the winter months it is extremely cold, with a lot of snow, while in July and August it is very hot and humid. We decided on May and, as our departure date drew closer, the weather in Montréal was cool and wet, presenting us with a packing dilemma—we knew that it would soon become quite warm. Indeed, we were to see for ourselves that spring comes quickly in Canada, and just as quickly turns to summer.

Jane collected as much information as she could and brought home various guidebooks at Christmas. In addition, we obtained advice and information on flights, fares, and packages from *Wardair*, *British Airways*, and *Air Canada*. We eventually selected four city-center hotels which seemed to offer the special facilities that we needed (accessible entrance, rooms with an adapted bathroom, elevators large enough, and doorways wide enough to accommodate a wheelchair). On her return to Montréal, Jane visited all four hotels and inspected them.

We chose to stay at the *Holiday Inn Crowne Plaza* in central (downtown) Montréal, although the facilities offered there were similar to those at the other three hotels, and indeed many other hotels outside the downtown area. Our room was large, and the well-adapted bathroom provided sufficient turning space for my wheelchair. There were bars around both bath and toilet; the sink was at a comfortable height; the only disadvantage was the lack of walk-in shower.

After we had booked our flights with *Air Canada* I had to complete a complicated medical form before the airline would confirm my ticket (not a problem we had experienced on our previous travels with *British Airways*). On arrival at Heathrow, the arrangements made on booking worked well and *Air Canada* staff met us at all the relevant places, finally lifting me to my seat on the plane.

We were settled in by the cabin staff and took off on time. The flight went smoothly and we even coped with emptying my catheter bag. (We carry a urine bottle in a suitable plastic bag which we use at the seat—easier and less embarrassing if side seats near the toilet are pre-booked, and most airlines will arrange this.)

After seven hours we landed on schedule during a downpour. Again, all the arrangements worked perfectly and we were soon in a taxi with Jane, enjoying the hour-long drive into the city. We had been warned about the standards of driving in Montréal but it still came as a shock when our taxi driver, realizing that he was not allowed to turn right at a set of traffic lights, promptly turned left, stopped, then reversed the five hundred yards to our hotel against three lanes of traffic.

The facilities offered by the *Holiday Inn* were excellent and, after a good night's sleep to recover from the jet lag, we were ready to start exploring. Jane was working during the day, so we were on our own. We had decided not to rent a car, but to use taxis, which are reasonably cheap. Jane supplied us with city guides, including a very good one for the disabled visitor, *Montréal—Useful Information for the Handicapped*, which gave us some idea of what to see.

The weather started cool and showery, but after only two days the sun came out and it rapidly became hotter, resulting in temperatures in the nineties. As I have difficulty coping with heat we soon appreciated the air conditioning in the hotel and the shopping malls.

Modern Montréal is famous for its underground city, reached via one of the many fabulous shopping malls. I have never seen so many good quality clothes shops, but then the Montréalers are extremely chic and fashion conscious. Each mall has two or three levels above and below ground; on the lowest level there is always a large, open square filled with tables and chairs. At lunchtime these areas come alive as the small takeout stands around the perimeter open and offer food of almost every nationality.

It is said that eating out is the Montréaler's favorite hobby. At the end of their day's work, the city's inhabitants crowd into the hundreds of small restaurants which line many of the streets and small squares. During our ten days in the city we ate at many restaurants offering different cuisines at very fair prices. There is entertainment in the form of street theater, there are craft stalls to browse among, and the atmosphere is wonderful.

"The beauty of the stained glass windows, the color, and the carvings took our breath away"

The main shopping street, with yet more boutiques, department stores, and restaurants, is St. Catherine Street, which forms the backbone of the downtown commercial center. Leading off it is Crescent Street, restored to its nineteenth-century elegance and housing more stylish boutiques and art galleries. In the evenings the bars, restaurants, and trendy nightclubs come into their own.

The larger part of Montréal is situated on an island, in the center of which is Mont Royal, a beautiful natural park known locally as the Mountain. We spent a lovely day exploring it, although Paul needed a long sleep in

the sun to recover after pushing me to the top. About a third of the way up the Mountain is Beaver Lake, which in winter months is an outdoor skating rink. Also in winter the Mountain is crisscrossed by ski trails, and on the steeper slopes there are downhill ski runs. When we visited, the Montréalers were enjoying the first hot weather of the year by picnicking and strolling along the many paths.

Most of the city center is very modern, with numerous skyscrapers, but in close proximity there is the old town to be explored. In 1960, Old Montréal (the original city) was a deserted collection of old buildings. During the first half of the twentieth century the population gradually moved away from the river and the port, toward the new commercial center of the city. But in the early Sixties Old Montréal was declared an area of historic interest, and commercial activity slowly returned.

Much of the area has been restored and has become a major tourist attraction which one can tour by horse-drawn *calèche* (carriage)—I'm afraid this was one of those things which we didn't attempt. The center of Old Montréal is place Jacques Cartier—a lovely square surrounded by outdoor cafés, restaurants, and craft shops.

There are many historic buildings and museums to visit in the old town but, for us, the most outstanding was the Notre Dame Basilica, in the place d'Armes, the center of religious and economic activity during the nineteenth century. The basilica is not an attractive church from the outside but, as we entered, the beauty of the stained glass windows, the color, and the carvings took our breath away. We spent a long time quietly absorbing the artistic and architectural treasures in this church.

The entrance to the Vieux Port (old port) is from place Jacques Cartier. Montréal is one of the world's largest inland ports, situated on the St. Lawrence river but almost a thousand miles from the Atlantic Ocean. Pleasure cruises can be joined from the Vieux Port, and the great river is the scene of much summertime activity.

"The panoramic view from the top, over Montréal, the surrounding region, and the St. Lawrence River, was worth the agony"

As it was very hot (even for May), Jane suggested that we might like to take a cruise, but my husband had other plans! He had noticed in the guidebook an entry with the wheelchair symbol next to it—"Shooting the Lachine rapids in a jet boat"—and duly made inquiries. Yes, they could manage a disabled person as long as I could "hold on" (I can—just). We were told to bring a change of clothing as we may "get a little wet."

We arrived at the wharf 45 minutes before noon. "Help!," I thought when I saw the boat, "What am I doing? I don't even like little boats." The shallow-draft jet boat could seat twenty people, and in it we were to mount and descend the rapids where the St. Lawrence drops some 42 feet in a series of steps.

Our party gathered—French Canadians, Mexicans, and ourselves—and we were given our instructions and our protective clothing. Two men dressed me in a thick, woollen sweater, waterproof jacket, life jacket, waterproof trousers, and rubber boots. We were all given a waterproof poncho to put on when we arrived at the rapids.

When everyone was suitably dressed, my wheelchair was bounced down twelve steps onto the floating jetty alongside the boat, and I was lifted in. I sat in the center of the boat and at this point one of the crew kindly took a photograph of us! The trip upriver to the rapids took about forty minutes and provided fine views of the city. I knew we had arrived when everyone else stood up and became very excited.

Then started one of the most exhilarating experiences of my life as the boat was driven up and down the rapids six times. We encountered whirlpools and giant waves, and endured soaking after soaking—from head to foot. It was marvelous! Not once did I feel apprehensive, only a sense of loss when we set off back to the port.

We were all convinced that we were soaked through to the skin, but when we shed our protective clothing there was not a damp patch to be found. My sense of achievement was made all the greater when my husband said, "I'm proud of you—I really didn't think you'd make it when you first saw the boat." But I did, and it was one of the highlights of our trip.

In 1976 Montréal hosted the Olympic Games; a visit to the Olympic Park, and to the Botanical Gardens which are situated nearby, makes a pleasant change to museums and shopping malls. The park is vast and includes the main stadium, the swimming pools, the velodrome, and all the facilities of a major sports center. Towering above the stadium is the world's tallest inclined tower, rising to more than 500ft above the ground, a height which is equivalent to a fifty-story building. In the upper front section the angle of inclination is 45 degrees, which perhaps should be compared with that of the Leaning Tower of Pisa—only five degrees.

The top three stories of the tower form observation decks which are reached by way of an exterior cable car, the only one of its kind in the world. It travels up the backbone of the tower and has two level cabins which can accommodate ninety people. As I have difficulty with glass-fronted elevators, the thought of the cable car was daunting. Although I made it to the observation deck, I must admit that my eyes were tightly shut on both journeys. However, the panoramic view from the top, over Montréal, the surrounding region, and the St. Lawrence river, was worth the agony.

A shuttle train runs from the Olympic Park to the Botanical Gardens, on the other side of a busy highway. The gardens are the third largest in the world and we spent a pleasant day exploring the different layouts and the greenhouses. The latest addition is a Japanese Garden, still in the process of construction but already providing a beautiful and peaceful oasis away from the crowds.

This was our first vacation spent entirely in a city and we were pleasantly surprised. Montréal provided us with a wealth of things to do and see. Inevitably there is much that we missed, so the city is well up on our list of places to be revisited. Perhaps next time we will be able to visit during the colder months and see the winter sports, both in Montréal and in the nearby Laurentian mountains, as well as enjoy the many cultural events staged in the city.

Although Montréal is French-speaking, with a different accent to that of European French, most people speak English and there are few communication difficulties. We enjoyed meeting the Canadian people, finding them charming and very helpful. Montréalers are justly proud of their city and we were made welcome throughout our stay.

Transportation Issues in Vancouver

In July 1986, The Fourth International Conference on Mobility and Transport for Elderly and Disabled Persons was held in Vancouver as one of the "theme periods" of Expo 86. Rod Semple, a severely disabled (multiple sclerosis) English immigrant in Canada and a leading light in the fight for the improvement of conditions for people with disabilities, attended the conference with his wife, Janet.

We arrived at Toronto's Lester B. Pearson airport in good time and, baggage and other formalities attended to, we were assisted aboard the *Air Canada* L10-11. Arriving at Vancouver airport four and a half hours later, we noticed a couple of Handy-Dart vans—the Vancouver equivalent of Toronto's Wheel-Trans. On learning that these vans wouldn't be able to take us (we hadn't made an application for a temporary pass), Janet and I decided to try out one of the wheelchair-accessible cabs run by *Vancouver Taxi*.

We were to use this fleet of Checker Taxis and Chrysler "Magic Vans," which have raised roofs and portable ramps, quite extensively during our week in Vancouver; although too expensive for everyday use, a small fleet of them could probably operate quite profitably in Toronto (they also carry able-bodied passengers and, occasionally, small pieces of furniture!).

Our accommodation turned out to be something of a disappointment, the bathroom being not too accessible and the furniture old and chipped. We were very fortunate in that after a couple of days we were able to move to the *Georgian Court Hotel*, which is adjacent to Expo and is in the downtown area. It has two "handicapped suites" and we highly recommend it.

BC Transit had recently opened its computer-operated SkyTrain rapid transit system, which runs between the Vancouver Waterfront station and New Westminster. The entire system is wheelchair accessible; the stations have elevators and the trains have space for wheelchairs in the cars. We often used the SkyTrain system to travel to and from New Westminster.

We also rode the wheelchair-accessible SeaBus ferry, which sails from the Waterfront station across Burrard Inlet to Lonsdale Quay in North Vancouver. The views from the ferry are spectacular—the Vancouver skyline, the North Shore mountains, and the shipping in the inlet. This stretch of water is busy with yachts, smaller boats, and floating gas stations for the convenience of boats and seaplanes. There are landing strips for the seaplanes, with walkways to the shore for the island commuters. The planes fly in time after time in the morning, unloading the workers, then collect them all for the homeward journey from 4:30pm onward. Many hotels look out over this scene, with the North Shore and Grouse Mountain (wrap up well—there's snow most of the year on the mountain, but a very pleasant restaurant at the top) in the background.

Following a "getting acquainted" reception at the University of British Columbia (UBC) on Sunday night, the conference started in earnest on Monday morning. The delegates (approximately five hundred people from around the world) took part in the opening ceremonies and the first debate—Compulsory versus Voluntary Compliance with Legislation—dealing with issues involved in setting up transportation systems for the disabled. After the opening session the delegates split up to attend the symposia of their choice.

As North York (Ontario) member of the *TTC Wheel Trans Community Committee*, and Chairman of the *North York Transportation Committee for the Physically Disabled*, I chose to attend the symposium on Municipal Specialized Transportation Services. We discussed the organization of parallel transit systems for the disabled in the Canadian Western Provinces and London, England, as well as a subsidized taxi service in Québec.

Other lectures I attended on Monday dealt with inter-city bus transportation (my own particular "bag"), using the Newfoundland Roadcruiser as an example of what can be done. One of the exhibits at the outdoor display at the conference was *Transport Canada*'s Accessobus, a new MCI 102A3 highway bus fitted with a centrally mounted elevator which can lift a person in a wheelchair to one of two tie-down locations on the bus.

The day's formal activities wound up with the showing of the *British Rail* film "Just like the rest of us," which showed the efforts that *BR* is making to provide access to its rail network. In the evening we headed over to a scenic spot behind the Museum of Anthropology, overlooking the ocean, for a salmon barbecue with native American entertainment. We watched the sun set behind the mountains.

> *"It is my fervent hope that inter-city bus companies will abandon their traditional apathy toward those of us who cannot climb the bus steps"*

A trip to the Expo 86 site was scheduled for Tuesday afternoon as part of the conference events. I was lucky enough to be one of the two people in wheelchairs who rode the Accessobus from UBC to Expo—it was great! After Expo the bus was to be loaned to inter-city bus carriers across Canada for evaluation. It is my fervent hope that inter-city bus companies will abandon their traditional apathy towards those of us who cannot climb the bus steps. Is there any good reason why we should be denied access to what is supposed to be a public transportation system?

On arrival at Expo we were met by members of the A (for Access) Team, a group of young people who assisted the delegates in wheelchairs throughout the conference period and whose services were very much appreciated. With the help of Thomas, Janet and I spent the rest of the day looking at Expo, using the wheelchair-accessible monorail to visit parts of the site.

People in wheelchairs were given priority at most of the pavilions, which helped considerably since long lines seemed to be the norm. We visited the British, German, Italian, and Ontario pavilions, took the SkyTrain shuttle to the Canada pavilion and returned to the main site by *Transport Canada* wheelchair-van. After a late supper in the Romanian pavilion it was time to head back to the hotel.

After the final and most interesting (as far as I was concerned) seminar, on coordination and privatization of transit systems, the official closing ceremonies took place, and I then joined an optional tour of *BC Transit*'s handyDART (DART stands for Dial-A-Ride Transportation) offices in New Westminster. The evening found us in Gastown, enjoying supper at *The Old Spaghetti Factory*.

Most restaurants in Vancouver are accessible and there is a wide variety of cuisines to choose from. Canadian-Chinese food is excellent and very reasonably priced. China Town is fun to explore, not as oriental or as captivating as its namesake in San Francisco, but certainly worth a visit.

On Thursday we took the SkyTrain to New Westminster to visit a temporary exhibition, Transporama 86, on the river front. It was an interesting collection of old cars, trucks, a street car, trolley bus, and several old train cars. After spending some time there we traveled back to Main Street station in Vancouver, where we took a look at the *VIA Rail* pavilion. A combination of large displays, mime artists, and movies are used to show the story of train travel in Canada. Also featured is a train of old, restored *Canadian Pacific Railroad* passenger cars, billed as "The Millionaires' Train." I could only see

this from the outside but I understand that the interior is quite impressive.

Our final full day in the Vancouver area started with some uncertainty. We wanted to visit Victoria, on Vancouver Island, but were not sure how to get there with me in a wheelchair. In the end, we were able to set up a ride on handyDART over 75 percent of the trip on land, *Vancouver Taxi* handling the rest. *BC Ferries* managed the waterborne section.

"Victoria has the reputation of being more British than the Brits themselves"

The cruise through the mountainous Gulf Islands was very pleasant if rather windy. To be fair, it's not always windy, and the views—landward to Vancouver and the north coast of British Columbia, or seaward to Vancouver Island and the other islands—are difficult to describe without sounding "over the top"; it's an experience which should not be missed and is easily within reach of any wheelchair user.

Traveling on a ship with elevators was a first for me, and we made good use of them. We met one young chap on the ferry who was making the journey from Vancouver to Seattle unaccompanied in an electric wheelchair. He was using a combination of para-transit systems and ferry boats, and he told us that he'd made the trip several times.

Victoria is a pretty seaside town with very attractive landscaped areas along the main roads, and a beautiful shoreline. It has the reputation of being more British than the Brits themselves. There is an interesting Marineland, built out into the sea. Visitors descend in a sort of glass elevator to the sea bed where they can observe marine life where it should be observed. I wondered . . . do the fish gather daily to see what's new in the human tank?

HandyDART dropped us outside the famous *Empress Hotel* in Victoria. After the traditional English high tea we boarded a double-decker bus for a tour of Victoria—one can sometimes do surprising things in a wheelchair! We had time to do just a little shopping before taking the handyDART back to the ferry at Swartz Bay, stopping en route at Butchart Gardens.

Originally a disused quarry and an ugly blot on the countryside, the owner's wife undertook to turn Butchart into a paradise for horticultural types and flower lovers. Hillside and valley paths wander among rare trees and gorgeous blooms, both common and exotic. Because of the sheltered location and the care lavished upon the gardens, all plants flourish in healthy profusion. One well-traveled man said that they were the loveliest gardens he'd seen—praise indeed from an English gardener!

Our flight back to Toronto went fine except for a pig-headed *Air Canada* passenger rep who didn't feel inclined to exert his strapping, six-foot frame to assist another employee in transferring me to my own wheelchair at Toronto airport. He preferred instead to kick suitcases off the conveyor belt and stroll around trying to look important. After some thirty minutes the transfer was accomplished with someone else's more willing assistance. Too bad, *Air Canada*, up to this point you did well, but please improve your food! (Subsequently, *Air Canada* sent me a letter of apology and a check to cover the cost of the unsatisfactory food.)

It was a fascinating conference and a wonderful trip. Conference aside, Vancouver for the vacationer offers a great deal: good access, good food, wheelchair-friendly transport, and masses to do. Scenically, it lacks for nothing. From almost all vantage points the views are incredible, from UBC across to the North Shore, from North Shore back over the city, from Grouse Mountain over everything. The best time to go is March to June, or September after Labor Day.

CANADA: TRAVEL NOTES

Sources of Information

Although many of Canada's provincial tourism brochures contain some reference to disabled visitors, and an indication of accommodations that are said to be accessible, too often there are no details of the facilities and services available, and access to transport and to local tour programs is ignored. In general the tourism authorities duck the issue by relying on **disability organizations**. For more detailed information and advice visitors are usually referred to the provincial offices of the *Canadian Paraplegic Association* or, in Québec, *Kéroul*.

Canadian Paraplegic Association (*CPA*), #201, 1500 Don Mills Road, Don Mills, Ontario M3B 3K4; ☎416/391-0203. Through a combination of counseling and rehabilitation, information and referral, advocacy, and other services, the *CPA* assists people with a spinal cord injury to become—as far as possible—independent in the community. The *CPA* has divisional offices throughout Canada in each province, and for the traveler these can provide information on the accessibility of local hotels, tourist attractions, and transportation, as well as assistance in finding a travel companion if required. Each province sets its own membership fees, usually about $10; a quarterly magazine, *Caliper*, keeps members in touch, and provincial divisions also publish their own newsletters. Provincial addresses are given below, after each provincial tourism office.

CANADA: TRAVEL NOTES

Kéroul (*Tourisme pour Personnes à Capacité Physique Restreinte*), 4545 avenue Pierre-de-Coubertin, CP 1000, succursale M, Montréal, Québec H1V 3R2; ☎514/252-3104. *Kéroul* aims to make tourist infrastructures accessible and hospitable, so that disabled people can travel whenever and however they wish. Consultation services for individual members ($10 yearly subscription) and member organizations ($40 yearly) include preparation of itineraries, and reference to an information bank on the accessibility of tourist facilities. *Kéroul* is involved in researching accessible tourist attractions and services, and designing methods for classification of accessibility. Information on Québec, Canada, and other countries is updated periodically in the Documentation Center. Publications include a bilingual quarterly information magazine, *Le Baladeur*, and a special insert, *Le Québec accessible* (1991), which is a bilingual guide to accessible accommodations, restaurants, and tourist attractions in Montréal and Québec City; *Accès Tourisme* (1989) is a bilingual guide containing information and addresses for disabled travelers. Discounts available to members include 20 percent on publications, 10 percent on Desjardin travel insurance, and reduced rates on car rentals from *Hertz*. *Kéroul* also organizes seminars, training workshops, and conferences for people involved in tourism.

Canadian Rehabilitation Council for the Disabled (*CRCD*), 45 Sheppard Avenue, Suite 801, Toronto, Ontario M2N 5W9; ☎416/250-7490. The *CRCD* publishes two magazines—*Access* (bimonthly) and *Rehabilitation Digest* (quarterly)—both of which contain travel items from time to time, and a useful book, *Handi-Travel: A Resource Book for Disabled and Elderly Travelers* (most recent edition 1987, but supplement containing updated contacts and addresses published in the fall of 1992). *Handi-Travel* can be obtained by sending a check or money order for $12.95 plus $2.50 shipping to Abilities, Box 527, Station P, Toronto, ON M5S 2T1. The *CRCD* usually refers specific inquiries to the *CPA* or *Kéroul*, or to the travel and information service at the **Jewish Rehabilitation Hospital**, Health Sciences Information Center, 3205 Place Alton Goldbloom, Chomedey, Laval, Québec H7V 1R2; ☎514/688-9550. The Center has a collection of travel guides for people with disabilities covering 500 cities all over the world.

PROVINCIAL TOURISM OFFICES

Alberta Tourism, Box 2500, Edmonton T5J 2Z4; in Alberta, ☎800/222-6501 (in Edmonton, ☎427-4321); outside Alberta and from the US, ☎800/661-8888. As well as an information sheet for disabled visitors, all the major brochures give a basic indication of wheelchair accessibility, but no details of facilities. The main tour guide notes wheelchair access at some tourist attractions. The campground guide uses the wheelchair symbol. The accommodation guide indicates those properties that have wheelchair-accessible rooms and/or accessible public areas, and provides separate lists of hotels that have rooms designed for guests in wheelchairs, those that have standard rooms with accessible bathrooms, and those that have wheelchair-accessible public rest room and/or restaurant areas. *Free Wheelin': A Guide to Wheelchair Accessibility in Banff* contains information on access to restaurant and accommodation facilities, collected in April 1991; copies can be obtained from the Parks Information Office (☎403/762-4256), the Chamber of Commerce (☎403/762-3777), or the Banff National Park Health Unit (☎403/762-2990). *CPA* (Alberta) Head Office is at #305, 11010-101 Street, Edmonton T5H 4B9; ☎403/424-6312.

Tourism British Columbia, Parliament Buildings, Victoria V8V 1X4 or Box C-34971, Seattle, WA 98124-1971; ☎604/387-1642 or 800/663-6000. The accommodation guide uses three symbols to indicate wheelchair accessible, partly accessible (includes level entrance and parking), or aids for hearing-impaired guests at hotels, resorts, motels, B&Bs, lodges, cabins, guest ranches, and campgrounds. The main tour guide lists a few addresses for "the physically challenged," and the road map indicates provincial parks with some access for wheelchair users (no details of facilities). *CPA* (British Columbia) Head Office is at 780 SW Marine Drive, Vancouver V6P 5Y7; ☎604/324-3611.

CANADA: TRAVEL NOTES

Travel Manitoba, 7th Floor, 155 Carlton Street, Winnipeg R3C 3H8; ☎204/945-3777. The only mention of facilities for visitors with disabilities is in a listing of "Campgrounds and Waysides" in which wheelchair access is indicated at some sites. The *CPA* can supply a copy of *Easy Wheeling Manitoba*, but this is no longer current (information gathered in 1983). *CPA* (Manitoba) Head Office is at 825 Sherbrook Street, Winnipeg R3A 1M5; ☎204/786-4753.

New Brunswick Economic Development and Tourism, PO Box 12345, Fredericton E3B 5C3; from within New Brunswick, ☎800/442 4442; from Canada and the US, ☎800/561-0123. The main tour guide includes accommodation listings that are marked with a comprehensive system of clearly explained access codes—three levels of wheelchair access, two levels of access for hearing disabled guests (facilities include flashing light smoke alarm, TDD, and interpretation service), and two levels of access for visually disabled guests (facilities include elevators with Braille or bell signals to identify floors; bright lighting and color contrast wall/carpet at reception, stairways, and hallways; raised identification symbols at eye level on wall to right of doors on public bathrooms, conference rooms, recreation areas, and bedrooms; large print or Braille menus; tactile warning strips on stairways and at entrance to all public rooms). The campgrounds listing also indicates those that are accessible to wheelchairs. There's a separate information sheet listing historical sites and attractions with facilities for disabled visitors, plus accessible restaurants in Moncton. Finally, the *Prince Edward Island Visitors Guide* uses the wheelchair symbol to indicate accessible accommodations.

CPA (New Brunswick) is at 65 Brunswick Street, Fredericton E3B 1G5; ☎506/455-9607. Another useful source is the *Premier's Council on the Status of Disabled Persons*, 6th Floor, Suite 648, Kings Place, Fredericton E3B 5H8; ☎800/442-4412.

Newfoundland and Labrador Department of Development, Tourism and Promotions Branch, PO Box 8730, St John's, NF A1B 4K2; ☎709/729-2830 or 800/563-6353. Wheelchair accessibility at some accommodations is mentioned in the main tour guide; ability to accommodate disabled clients is also noted in the local tour operators listing.

Northwest Territories Economic Development and Tourism, Yellowknife X1A 2L9; ☎403/920-6322. There is a small paragraph in the main brochure directing travelers with disabilities to the *NWT Council for Disabled Persons*, Box 1387, Yellowknife X1A 2P1; ☎403/873-8230, voice; ☎403/920-2674, TDD.

Tourism Nova Scotia, PO Box 456, Halifax B3J 2R5; *Check In* computerized reservation and travel information system, ☎800/565-0000 (in Halifax or Dartmouth ☎425-5781); from the US, ☎800/341-6096 (Maine only, ☎800/492-0643). The main tour guide indicates hotels and motels that provide certain minimum levels of access for guests with mobility, visual, or hearing impairment. The symbols used in each case are clearly explained. In addition, wheelchair access at campgrounds and sightseeing attractions is noted. Readers are referred to the *Nova Scotia League for Equal Opportunities* (Box 8204, Halifax B3K 5L9; ☎902/422-4768) for details of transport services and access to recreational facilities, and to the *CPA* (#150, 1310 Hollis Street, Halifax B3J 3D3; ☎902/423-1277) for further information or assistance.

Ontario Travel, Ministry of Tourism and Recreation, 77 Bloor Street West, Toronto M7A 2R9; ☎416/965-4008 or 800/ONTARIO (800/268-3736 in French), voice; ☎416/314-6557 (or call collect), TDD. From Toronto calling area, 416/314-0944, or 416/314-0956 in French. In 1990/1991, the Ministry masterminded an impressive operation which aimed to improve the quality of service and information available to disabled travelers. *Project Challenge*, later known as the "*Open for Business* Accessibility Program," worked on four fronts: standardizing accessibility criteria; educating the tourism and recreation industry about the market and needs of disabled clients; improving the methods of collection of accessibility information from the industry; and improving dissemination of information to disabled customers.

Phase 2 of the project was launched in March 1991 and entailed encouraging operators

CANADA: TRAVEL NOTES

to make use of an education pack containing a training video, accessibility workbook, access survey, tape measure, and pencil. Phase 3—the integration of the results of access surveys of tourist establishments into ministry tourism information services (including a new database) and publications—began in May 1992.

At the time of writing, while most publications do not include accessibility information, the new database does. Travelers who would like detailed information are asked to send an inquiry outlining approximate dates of travel, area(s) to be visited, type(s) of accommodation and mode of transportation desired, and degree of accessibility required. Travel counselors then research the inquiry using the database, a reference library, and ministry publications, and send a detailed response. They call this "one-stop shopping."

The Ministry (along with The Office for Disabled Persons) provided funds for the publication of a new edition of the comprehensive accessibility guide, *Toronto With Ease*, which can be obtained free of cost by mail from Ontario March of Dimes, Information Services, 60 Overlea Blvd, Toronto ON M4H 1B6; send $3.75 to cover postage and handling. Copies can also be obtained in person from a number of sources; call ☎485-4308 for details.

CPA (Ontario) is at the same address as the National Office.

Tourisme Québec, PO Box 20,000, Québec G1K 7X2; from Montréal area, ☎873-2015; from elsewhere in Canada, and the USA, ☎800/363-7777; or visit Maison du Tourisme de Québec, 12 rue Sainte-Anne, or Maison du Tourisme de Montréal, Centre Infotouriste, 1001 rue du Square-Dorchester. The main tour guides contain no information for disabled people. The standard *Montréal Tourist Guide* lists accessible hotels, gives an indication of accessibility of attractions, and supplies a few useful addresses. If that is not enough, *Montréal—Useful Information for the Handicapped*, is free from the *Greater Montréal Convention and Visitors Bureau* (1555 Peel Street, Suite 600, Montréal H3A 1X6; ☎514/871-1595). Québec's version of the *CPA*, the *Association des Paraplégiques du Québec*, tends to pass on travel inquiries to *Kéroul*. The

tourist board also refers inquiries from disabled people to the *Association Régionale pour le Loisir de Personne Handicapé de l'Ile de Montréal*, 525 Dominion Street, Montréal H3J 2B7; ☎514/933-2739.

Tourism Saskatchewan, 1919 Saskatchewan Drive, Regina S4P 3V7; in Saskatchewan, ☎800/667-7538 (in Regina, ☎787-2300); outside Saskatchewan and from the US, ☎800/667-7191. None of the brochures contain information for visitors with disabilities. *CPA* (Saskatchewan) is at #3, 3012 Louise Street, Saskatoon S7J 3L8; ☎306/652-9644.

Tour Operators

As in the US, it should not be necessary to use a travel agent or tour operator who specializes in serving clients with disabilities to tour Canada, although of course there are some who prefer to travel this way and can afford the generally higher prices charged by the specialist operator. There are a few Canadian travel agencies and tour operators that specialize in tours and individual travel for people with disabilities. These are listed, along with the US-based companies, in *Directory*, p.597.

Travel industry personnel have no excuse for ignorance of the concerns of travelers with disabilities, nor of the current rules, regulations, and policies relevant to travel for disabled people, since the publication of a new edition (1991) of ***The Disabled Traveler: A Guide for Travel Counselors***. Published by the *Canadian Institute of Travel Counselors of Ontario*, this manual was written by Cinnie Noble, a founding member of *SATH* (see USA *Travel Notes*), with help from Shirley Shelby, who owns the travel agency *Travel Helpers*, Toronto, and provides arrangements for athletes and recreational travelers who are disabled. If it achieves just one of its aims—to demystify and simplify the process involved in arranging travel for disabled people—the guide will have made a valuable contribution. Although most of the text concentrates on travel for people with mobility, visual, or hearing impairment, there are tips on making travel arrangements for clients who have

CANADA: TRAVEL NOTES

epilepsy, developmental disabilities, respiratory ailments, speech impairments, and diabetes. It includes advice on booking travel by air, cruise ship, train, tourbus, rental car, and ferry; there is chapter on booking accommodations, and a suggested letter of inquiry to send out to hotels when confirming access details. There is a section on booking tour packages and—travel counselors take note—it describes briefly what specialists have to offer but adds the following sensible advice:

"Tours that are 'specialized' are not for everyone. Keep in mind that not all people who are disabled necessarily want to be on a tour with other people who are disabled. Some may not wish to even be on a group tour. Tours of this nature are an option for many who do not want to have to contend with barriers."

Transport

Unless you have all the time in the world, long distances in Canada should be covered **by air**. In fact, even short hops are often easier in a plane than by train or bus.

AIR TRAVEL

The main differences between Canadian and American **air travel** are that in Canada travelers with disabilities are more likely to be asked to fill in forms—certainly to indicate handling and medical advice—and in some instances this will lead to a request for clearance from a physician. More generally, there appear to be no rigid timescales for carriers to achieve objectives such as those outlined in the US Air Carrier Access Act. *Transport Canada's* 14-point plan in the National Strategy for the Integration of Persons with Disabilities does not include any measures concerning accessible features on aircraft. However, the department's goal is "to ensure that people with disabilities can travel anywhere in Canada without encountering either physical or attitudinal barriers" so presumably this will include provision of accessible aircraft rest rooms and 100 percent availability of on-board wheelchairs at some point in the future.

On the plus side, seat pre-assignment seems to work well on Canadian carriers (with *Air Canada* at time of reservation; on *Canadian Airlines* only within 24 hours of departure), and both *Air Canada* and *Canadian* offer fifty percent discounts on fares for the companions of non-self-reliant passengers—with *Air Canada* this applies for travel within North America, for *Canadian* it applies for travel within Canada and to or from the US (including Hawaii). *Air Canada* requires the traveler's doctor to call and verify that an assistant is required; *Canadian* use the INCAD/MEDIF form (see *Practicalities*, p.570) to obtain doctor's confirmation.

Most *Air Canada* aircraft (except the DC-9, Boeing 747 Combi, and all commuter planes) carry on-board wheelchairs but these should be requested at the time of reservation; the chairs can be used on the narrow-aisle aircraft that are operated by *Air Canada's* five regional "connector" airlines. On larger aircraft, such as the Boeing 767, 747, and Airbus 320, the on-board wheelchair can squeeze into at least one rest room—it's cramped, as ever, but privacy curtains can be used and the door left open to extend the available space somewhat. Steve Veness (p.69) received outstanding service from *Air Canada*, and this airline has a good reputation amongst travelers with disabilities, although Dorothea Boulton (p.72) found their medical form rather off-putting.

Canadian Airlines (formerly *Wardair*) is praised by several contributors, not least for the high quality of their food! Staff is reported helpful and friendly. On-board wheelchairs are carried on B747, B767, and A320 aircraft. Rest rooms will not admit the on-board wheelchair, but those on the left-hand side of the main passenger cabin have features such as grab bars and privacy curtains that are supposed to compensate by allowing transfer from the chair with the door left open.

Facilities at **airports** are generally good and some airports publish leaflets detailing the accessible features of their terminals (see also *Access Travel: Airports*, a free booklet available from Consumer Information Center, Pueblo, CO 81009, USA). There are still areas that need attention and even with newly built terminals there are design oversights and simple errors that occur in spite of consultation with advisory

CANADA: TRAVEL NOTES

groups of disabled people. Judith O'Leary reports (*Rehabilitation Digest*, Spring 1991) that one member of such a group inspected the finished facilities at Terminal 3, Toronto's Pearson International airport, and rated them nine out of ten for accessibility. However, there was room for improvement in four areas: access from the parking garage is difficult because of manually operated doors at the top of an incline; there are no markings or changes in texture on the floor of the Grand Hall; the signage throughout the terminal is inadequate; and there should be more moving walkways in a terminal of this size.

So barriers remain, for travelers with mobility as well as sensory disabilities, but overall most airports are usable by most people even if some have to allow a little more time to find their way around. Both *Air Canada* and *Canadian* allow passengers to remain in their own wheelchairs until they board the plane; at most airports *Air Canada* offers the option of using a self-propelled Manten wheelchair within the terminal and to give direct access to the aircraft seat. Boarding of the large and medium-size planes is usually by air-bridge or, rarely, by lifting vehicle.

John Bignell experienced some difficulties when flying between Toronto and Pittsburgh in 1988. On the outward journey, at Toronto airport, he had to transfer to a small Jetstream which was parked away from the ramp. Even in its lowest position, the ramp ended in mid-air, with a service stair down to the runway and an internal flight of stairs for passengers. Fortunately, John can manage a few steps, but there was a solid rail on the right and a lethal rope on the left, the exact opposite of what he requires, which is to hold his stick in his right hand and something solid in his left. John's comment: "I did not enjoy my ascent! Please can we have something solid on both sides."

This experience should soon be a thing of the past. As part of its role in the five-year National Strategy, *Transport Canada* will contribute funds to airline companies to improve boarding on small commuter aircraft. In February 1992 the department announced in-service demonstrations with *Air Canada* at airports in Winnipeg and Ottawa to show the merits of two new small-aircraft boarding systems—the Connector (Just Mobility Products) and the PAL-651 (Hobart Airport Systems).

Transport Canada also plans to encourage better access to **ground transportation at airports**. It has made funds available to operators of airport shuttle buses and taxis so that they can purchase accessible vehicles and improve access to existing fleets. In addition, for onward travel from airports, the goal is to make 10 percent of all rental cars acessible within five years, by providing financial support to car rental companies for purchase and retrofitting of vehicles with hand controls.

RAIL TRAVEL

If you have a little more time to spare there is no doubt that travel **by train** can be one of the highlights of a trip—some of the routes covered by Canada's national rail network, *VIA Rail*, are through spectacular scenery. Over the last twelve years or so, *VIA Rail* has improved access to its stations and trains for passengers in wheelchairs. A helpful booklet, *Services for Passengers with Special Needs*, is available from any *VIA Rail* station or from the Customer Relations Department, VIA Rail Canada Inc., PO Box 8116, Station A, Montréal, Québec H3C 3N3; area phone numbers for reservations, information, or tickets by mail are listed in this booklet.

A wheelchair tie-down, storage box containing narrow wheelchair (25 inches wide), tie-down straps and reducer tool (to reduce width of manual chairs), and accessible rest room with grab bars, transfer seat, and sliding door (35 inches wide), are available in **LRC** ("light, rapid, and comfortable") first-class cars (VIA 1) traveling the Québec–Windsor Corridor (major stops include Montréal, Ottawa, Kingston, Toronto, and London); it is necessary to reserve wheelchair accommodation on the LRC. **Conventional trains** now being renovated will be equipped with wheelchair tie-downs, narrow wheelchairs, tools to reduce the width of manual chairs, and grab bars in rest rooms that will be accessible by means of the narrow wheelchair (door width 22.5 inches on RDC cars, 24 inches on Dayniter cars, 21 inches on café coaches). By summer 1992 all trains on

CANADA: TRAVEL NOTES

the Western Transcontinental routes had been refurbished and equipped with a tie-down in-coach service as well as an accessible rest room. Facilities in the East continued to lag behind, although refurbishment of the train to Gaspé, Québec, was scheduled for completion in August 1992. On older, unrestored equipment passengers must transfer from their wheelchairs to coach seat or sleeping car accommodation; a special narrow chair is available for use in the sleeping car aisles but not in the coach aisles.

VIA accepts manual **wheelchairs**, not exceeding 32 inches (81cm) in width and 72 inches (182cm) in all other dimensions, as checked baggage, and electric wheelchairs weighing no more than 250 pounds (114kg), provided that the departure and destination stations have the facilities to load and unload them. This can be checked when booking. For example, major stations in the West (Vancouver, Edmonton, Jasper, Saskatoon, Winnipeg) have station-based wheelchair lifts; at smaller stations staff and those traveling with the wheelchair user must manually lift the person and chair into the train. Transport Canada aims to assist here, by making funds available to VIA to acquire boarding devices that make trains more accessible.

Those with speech or hearing impairment can obtain information and make reservations in Canada by telephone: in Toronto, ☎416/368-6406; elsewhere in Canada, ☎1-800/268-9503.

VIA requires a minimum of **48 hours' notice** of any special requests, in order to deploy staff effectively or make other arrangements; if you give more notice than this it is advisable to confirm any requests within 48 hours of travel. Your ticket will show that a Special Service Request (SSR) has been issued.

The **services that are available** with this advance notice include the following: boarding assistance at many stations; pre-boarding if you arrive an hour before departure; voltage regulators on certain trains for the use of respirators; non-allergenic pillows for passengers with allergies; stretcher service; meals served in sleeping compartments to passengers unable to use the restaurant facilities; special meals; a roomette at no extra charge, subject to availability, for blind passengers who have reserved an upper berth and are traveling with a guide dog (dogs accompanying blind or deaf passengers may travel in any class); free travel for an escort if a passenger is unable to provide for his or her personal needs (eating, medical care, or personal hygiene, or lifting on and off trains where VIA does not provide this service)—a medical certificate, or an identification card issued by an association recognized by VIA, must be produced.

The National Timetable indicates **accessible stations** (with parking, accessible rest rooms, and ramps) and stations where trains can be boarded from the platform by wheelchair lift or with assistance from VIA personnel. If you have any questions that your travel agent cannot answer, write to Customer Relations (address above).

BUS TRAVEL

Despite the access limitations, Greyhound **intercity bus travel** is a viable option for a wheelchair user with a strong companion who can travel free on the Travel Assistance program, or for other travelers who are unable to make the trip alone. It will be several years before Greyhound buses are equipped with wheelchair lifts but in the meantime staff will give assistance with boarding and disembarking (see USA Travel Notes for more information).

In general, intercity bus services are inaccessible to wheelchair users without assistance. There is hope for change, however, as another initiative from Transport Canada, part of its five-year strategy, is the allocation of federal funds to Canadian intercity bus operators for the purchase or installation of lifts and other devices to make buses more accessible. Funds have also been made available for developing, testing, and demonstrating a new accessible **charter bus**. A wheelchair-accessible charter bus with hydraulic lift and on-board accessible rest room, plus TV, video, and stereo, can currently be rented for groups (up to 15 passengers in wheelchairs, with tie-downs) from National Motor Coach Systems, Box 3220, Station B, Calgary, Alberta T2M 4L7; ☎403/240-1992.

CANADA: TRAVEL NOTES

DRIVING

Car rental with *Hertz* began badly for Steve Veness (p.69) but turned out well in the end. *Hertz* (☎800/263-0600) offers cars with hand controls at all corporate locations in Canada, with five days' notice (see USA *Travel Notes* for more on this rental company's approach to clients with disabilities). *Avis* (☎800/879-2847) offers cars with hand controls at nearly forty cities, with up to four days' notice. *Tilden Rent A Car* (☎800/387-4747) can supply adapted vehicles in all major cities, with a minimum of five day's notice. *Thrifty Car Rental* (☎416/612-1881) had no cars with hand controls available at the time of writing but were piloting a few across the country.

A 24-foot **motorhome with hydraulic lift** can be rented by the week or longer from *Motorhome Vacations Canada* (12563 Highway 50, Bolton, Ontario L7E 5R9; ☎416/857-2253).

Each province makes its own arrangements for disabled drivers' **parking**. Permits issued by any other North American licensing jurisdiction will generally be recognized everywhere, but parking attendants may not be familiar with stickers from outside their province so it's a good idea to make sure the wheelchair symbol is visible from both front and rear of the car, and to display your permit clearly.

CITY TRANSPORTATION

If you use a manual chair and can transfer to and from a car seat, you should have no need of adapted transport, but *CPA* offices should be able to supply a list of companies providing accessible **taxis**, as well as details of the local special transit services for disabled travelers. In Edmonton, for example, physically disabled visitors can use the *DATS* (*Disabled Adult Transportation System*; ☎403/468-6025); in Vancouver *BC Transit*'s handyDART (☎604/264-5000); and in Toronto Wheel-Trans (☎416/393-4111): for all of these you must apply for a temporary registration number. These services are economical to use but have the disadvantage of all "dial-a-ride" systems—rides are shared, and often call at several stops along the way, and they must be booked one or two days in advance. Such alternative transit systems for people with disabilities provide a useful service in the absence of fully accessible public transportation but they are not the complete answer.

BC Transit (1200 West 73rd Avenue, Vancouver, BC V6P 6M2; ☎604/264-5000; route information, ☎261-5100), one of Canada's most enlightened transit agencies, appears to recognize this and is working hard to develop full-service accessible public transportation alongside the handyDART custom transit system. A province-wide planning program for fully accessible transit systems has been announced, with Greater Vancouver leading the way. The Vancouver Regional Transit System is already equipped with more than 200 wheelchair-accessible vehicles. By the end of 1991, accessible service (for wheelchairs and scooters) was offered on 46 of 161 bus routes, although not all buses on these routes are lift-equipped—look for the letter "L" in the timetable, indicating the times when lift-equipped buses are scheduled to stop at accessible stops. There is space for two wheelchairs, with full tie-down facilities, on each lift-equipped bus.

Both SeaBus (p.76) and SkyTrain (p.75) are accessible, and SeaBus connects with SkyTrain and two lift-equipped bus routes at Waterfront Station in downtown Vancouver. All 17 SkyTrain stations have elevators except Granville; travelers who are unable to use an escalator can exit at Burrard and call *Vancouver Taxi* (☎255-5111) for transportation to Granville—this service is free for HandyPass holders. Anyone with a disability may register for a HandyPass, which entitles the holder to concession fares throughout the transit system; one passenger accompanying each registered HandyPass holder is entitled to travel free; call ☎264-5000 for an application form, processing takes a few days.

BC Transit has also addressed the problem of providing the opportunity for spontaneous door-to-door travel by devising a scheme to offer affordable accessible taxis. *Vancouver Taxi*'s thirty wheelchair-accessible vehicles can be rented like any other taxi, but are rather expensive for everyday use, so *BC Transit* has recently introduced a "Taxi Saver Program," with 22 taxi companies participating, twelve of

CANADA: TRAVEL NOTES

which have some wheelchair-accessible vehicles available. Anyone who is eligible to use handyDART and has obtained a HandyPass may purchase a book of Taxi Saver coupons with a face value of $40 for the price of $20, then call the taxi company of their choice and book direct.

The large-print booklet, *Rider's Guide to Accessible Transit*, includes information on buses, SkyTrain, SeaBus, handyDART, and HandyPass, as well as route maps.

FERRIES

Still in the Vancouver area, there are facilities for wheelchair users on several ships operated by **BC Ferries** (information and reservations, ☎604/669-1211, Vancouver; ☎604/386-3431, Victoria)—accessible rest rooms on 14 vessels and elevators on 15 (indicated in the information leaflet, *Welcome Aboard BC Ferries*), although the elevators may not serve all decks. There are accessible cabins on some vessels, for example on the *Queen of the North*, the Inside Passage ferryliner which sails year-round between Port Hardy on Vancouver Island and Prince Rupert to the north. Reduced fares are available to disabled passengers who are unable to travel alone: apply for an Identification Card to 1112 Fort Street, Victoria V8V 4V2 (☎604/381-1401), enclosing written confirmation of permanent disability from a doctor, to obtain fifty percent reductions on regular fares and the same for a traveling companion. Drivers who wish to be parked next to the elevators on board the ferries are issued with windshield cards to alert the loading crew.

For information on ferry services on the East Coast contact **Marine Atlantic**, Box 250, North Sydney, Nova Scotia B2A 3M3; ☎902/794-500. In general the newer terminals and ships are built to accommodate passengers with disabilities, and adaptations have been made to existing facilities so that most vessels and terminals are suitably equipped.

Accommodation

Finding suitable **accommodation** should not be too difficult for wheelchair users, but as ever, to be really sure, you'll need to check with the hotel before booking, and base your plans on information supplied by the tourism office or the *CPA* rather than a travel agent.

It is rare for the provincial accommodation guides to mention hotel **facilities for people with disabilities other than restricted mobility**. These travelers may find help from associations of people with their disability, such as the *Canadian Hearing Society* (Information Services Department, 271 Spadina Road, Toronto, ON M5R 2V3; ☎416/964-9595, voice; ☎416/964-0023, TDD) or the *Canadian National Institute for the Blind* (320 MacLeod Street, Ottawa, ON K2P 1A3; ☎613/563-4021), but in general the best bet is to contact accommodation operators direct, particularly if taking along a guide animal.

Many **hotel and motel chains** have properties that cater to some degree for disabled guests, including (see also USA *Travel Notes*): *Best Western* (☎800/528-1234), *Canadian Pacific* (1 University Ave, Suite 400, Toronto, ON M5J 2P1; ☎416/367-7197; reservations, ☎800/268-9411), *Days Inns* (☎800/325-2525), *Hilton* (☎416/362-3771 or 800/268-9275), *Holiday Inns* (☎800/465-4329 or, in Toronto, ☎486-6400), *Howard Johnson* (☎800/446-4656), *Novotel* (☎800/221-4542), *Quality Inns* (☎800/544-4444), *Ramada* (☎800/268-8998), *Relax Inns* (☎403/259-9800 or 800/66-RELAX), *Sheraton* (☎800/325-3535), *Travelodge* (☎800/255-3050).

Relatively few hotels offer facilities for guests with visual or hearing disabilities, and those that offer the full range of facilities for wheelchair users—parking, level entrances, ramps, spacious rooms for handicapped guests, access to all public rooms, wide doorways, large elevators, and accessible public rest rooms—tend to be in the higher price brackets. But you may not need the complete range, and there is so much accommodation to choose from that you are sure to find something to suit both your budget and your access requirements, or that is manageable and comfortable with minor adaptations or furniture rearrangement.

As in the States, it's worth trying the independent establishments and smaller chains

CANADA: TRAVEL NOTES

of inns and motels—the tourism authorities provide ample accommodation lists that at least make a good starting point for vacation planning, and many travelers successfully look for accessible accommodation along the way, finding this less troublesome than trying to ascertain access details in advance. The motels and smaller hotels are often cheaper and more likely to provide a room on the first floor; one contributor found himself in a "handicapped suite" on the ninth floor of the Pittsburgh *Hilton*—not ideal in the event of a fire.

A number of hotels are recommended by our contributors. Dorothea Boulton stayed at the *Holiday Inn Crowne Plaza* (420 rue Sherbrooke Ouest, Montréal H3A 1B4; ☎514/842-6111), one of many accessible hotels in downtown Montréal. Her daughter inspected three other properties (addresses in the *Montréal* accommodation guide) and found similar facilities at *Delta Montréal* (the guide now lists this as accessible only to an escorted wheelchair user), *Hotel des Gouverneurs-Le Grand*, and *Le Méridien Montréal*.

Steve Veness made his choice from the Nova Scotia, Alberta, and British Columbia accommodation guides. *Mid Valley Motel* (Middleton, Nova Scotia; ☎902/825-3433) is an inexpensive, cheerful, and accessible motel. *Mountaineer Lodge* (Box 150, Lake Louise, AL T0L 1E0; ☎403/522-3844) is much smarter, ideally placed for touring the Rockies, easily accessible but quite expensive. *Sunset Motel* (Box 86, Radium Hot Springs, BC V0A 1M0; ☎604/347-9863) is not so well placed for touring the Rockies but has spotless, good-value self-catering units (one to three bedrooms), good accessibility, and very friendly, helpful owners. Steve also suggests that, if you can afford it, you stay at the *Post Hotel* (Box 69, Lake Louise, AL T0L 1E0; ☎403/522-3989).

Christine Swan recommends *Chateau Jasper* (Box 1418, Jasper, AL T0E 1E0; ☎403/852-5644) and the *Hyatt Regency* (655 Burrard Street, Vancouver V6C 2R7; ☎604/687-6543). Also in Vancouver, Rod Semple was very pleased with *The Georgian Court Hotel* (773 Beatty Street, V6B 2M4; ☎604/682-5555).

Access and Facilities

Standards are high at the majority of Canada's tourist attractions, from Niagara Falls to Montréal's shopping malls; from a cruise around Vancouver's Gulf Islands to a performance at the Ottawa Arts Center. Reports of assistance from Canadians, willingly and cheerfully given, are plentiful. Making your own travel arrangements is easy, and travel without an escort, even for someone more than slightly disabled, is certainly possible—on planes, many trains and boats, and of course by car; problems remain on buses, although the situation is improving slowly. Nonetheless, spontaneous travel is still only a dream for too many disabled people.

In a country with such a wealth of natural beauty and tremendous opportunity to enjoy outdoor pursuits, there is surprisingly little reference to the accessibility of these attractions in the tourist brochures. However, the *CPA* is under contract to assist the *Canadian Parks Service* in developing accessibility guidelines and implementation timetables, and assessing new technology for National Parks, Historic Canals, and Historic Sites. Divisions of the *CPA* with offices nearest to the parks are most heavily involved in this work. Progress is being made in making outdoor facilities accessible to visitors with disabilities.

In British Columbia, there has been considerable activity over the past few years to improve access to parks, starting with a survey carried out in 1987 by the **Columbia Society of Interdependent Living** (SOIL). The survey included 13 communities in Upper Columbia Valley, adjoining BC provincial parks, and three national parks; results were submitted to Parks Canada and to BC Parks, and a directory was prepared, called *Let's Get Around the Upper Columbia Valley*. The parks responded well to *Columbia SOIL*'s recommendations and lobbying: for example, at Kootenay National Park there is now front-door access by ramp, accessible changing rooms, a water-submersible wheelchair for access to the mineral pools, ramps for the hot pools, and access to the cooler swimming pool. Olive Lake, in Kootenay Dominion Park, will be totally accessible by 1993, and camping facilities at Redstreak

CANADA: TRAVEL NOTES

Campground are being retrofitted and upgraded to ensure full accessibility.

Columbia SOIL is also involved in creating a barrier-free destination property in southeastern BC, using some 30 acres of the old township center in Spillimacheen, between Yoho and Kootenay National Parks. On this site they plan to offer accessible offices, cabins, and camping, trails, gardens, and horticultural programs, cottage/craft industries, workshops, educational facilities, and a recycling depot. In the surrounding area there are opportunities for all kinds of activities, including white water rafting, swimming, boat tours, kayaking, skiing, horse riding, hiking, helicopter rides, and wildlife sanctuaries. Funds are limited, so the project moves slowly, but it's good to see such energy and enthusiasm going into making the wilderness accessible—too many disabled people are denied this experience.

Columbia SOIL is a non-profit society and the only one in Canada to register as incorporating both environmental and disability issues, aiming to actively improve and conserve the natural environment and to improve the quality of life for persons with disabilities—whether physical, mental, psychological, social, or cultural. For more information, and to learn how you can contribute to the development of Spillimacheen, contact Glenys Snow, Columbia SOIL, Box 19, Spillimacheen, BC V0A 1P0; ☎604/346-3257 or 3276.

An account of the activities of *Columbia SOIL* is just one of many reports in "Canada's lifestyle magazine for people with disabilities"—***Abilities***—a glossy, wide-ranging, substantial quarterly ($12 one year, $18 two years; check or money order to Abilities, PO Box 527, Station P, Toronto, ON M5S 2T1) that keeps readers with disabilities up to date with developments and opportunities on the travel, sport, and recreational scenes, as well as many other issues such as health, education, employment, housing, and technology.

Abilities also keeps up a running commentary on progress toward a society in which people with disabilities are fully integrated and barriers to their free movement and employment are removed. Although both the Canadian Charter of Rights and Freedoms, and the Canadian Human Rights Act confirm the right to equal access to services, programs, and facilities from the federal government and from employers under federal jurisdiction, the *Canadian Human Rights Commission* reported in *Abilities* Spring 1992 issue that much remains to be done to achieve this, in particular for those with disabilities other than mobility impairment.

In general, there appear to be a lot of fine words in federal charters and acts, prohibiting discrimination against people with physical or developmental disabilities, and even some considerable sums of money being earmarked for certain projects. But without timetables for change, or rigidly enforced specific requirements that, for example, all new aircraft, trains, buses, and ferries are fully accessible, improvements will be piecemeal and inadequate, no matter how much government money is made available. The *Canadian Disability Rights Council*, founded in 1988, is calling for legislated timetables, among other measures, to give teeth to the fine words. For the moment, however, the government has not responded. As in the US, any successes in increasing awareness and forcing change to remove barriers to people with disabilities will in large part be due to disabled people themselves.

PART TWO

THE CARIBBEAN & LATIN AMERICA

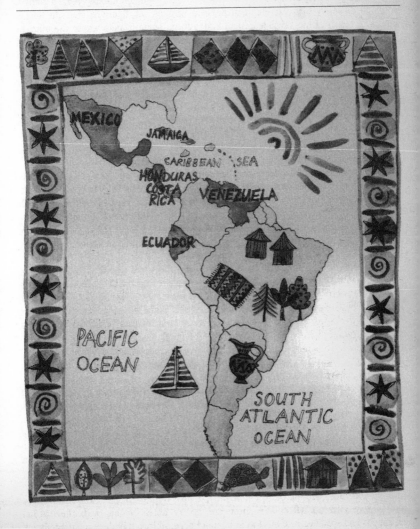

Introduction

It's hard to imagine a greater contrast in terms of access and facilities for disabled people than that between North and South—or Central—America. Many Latin American governments are unable to provide adequate living conditions for the majority of their peoples; they have not even begun to think of building an accessible environment. Neither precarious democracies nor harsh dictatorships create a climate in which disability organizations and pressure groups can flourish. The situation is similar in much of the Caribbean, and although on some islands where the tourism industry is well advanced a growing number of hotels can accommodate disabled guests, getting around remains difficult owing to the terrain—rough surfaces on roads and sidewalks, high curbs, pot-holes, and sand.

As far as the traveler is concerned, however, these countries are rich in terms of **attractions**: the awe-inspiring mountains and rainforest; spectacular wildlife and exotic plant species; perfect beaches and glorious seas—Caribbean, Pacific, or South Atlantic; fascinating temples and other relics of ancient civilizations; beautiful colonial architecture and smart boutiques in the modern cities. Whether to enjoy these, the many brands of Latin American and Caribbean music and cooking, or to browse among the handicrafts, tourists are visiting the continent in growing numbers.

Naturally enough, Latin Americans are keen to promote their assets and attract as many tourists (and their wallets) as possible. On the Venezuelan island of Margarita the rapid recent development of the main town, Porlamar, has included ramps at all entrances, and provision of first-class hotels with good access to all amenities. Maybe—just maybe—this is a result of the fact that a significant proportion of visitors come from the States, and wherever the North American tourist has been the chances of finding a mobile ramp or a grab bar are increased.

But Margarita is very much the exception, and the sheer **physical difficulties** of travel in Latin America or the Caribbean may explain why relatively few accounts of travel here were received in the first place; even stay-put vacations, such as that described by Greg Baker, are likely to entail some obstacles. Meanwhile, the task of educating the governments, planners, designers, and tourism operators has barely started. Removal of basic physical obstacles—on public transportation, in accommodation and public buildings, at tourist attractions—is often an inexpensive and simple matter but for now, in most Latin American and Caribbean countries, it is not even considered, and action may still be years away.

At least two forms of **transport**—aircraft and taxis—are no less accessible than in many other parts of the world, and most disabled travelers will be able to use both. There are no special facilities on trains or at stations, but with assistance train travel is possible. Perhaps most tricky are the many different types of boat: accessible gangways, lifts, widened doorways, and adapted rest rooms are rare sights, and some acrobatics and several pairs of hands may be required when boarding and moving about on board.

Reliable information on **accessible accommodation** will be virtually impossible to find, so your best bet will be to follow the example of Lawrence Poole or Sue Kelley and simply turn up. Of course there are luxury hotels which, with their grand entrances and spacious rooms, tend to be more accessible, but budget accommodation often throws up all the usual obstacles. Doorways in city hotels may be too small for wheelchairs; jungle lodges are often raised on stilts. However, villas and small inns, cabins or beach huts are often manageable. It's necessary to compromise, adapt, and sometimes ask for help. Although accommodations are rarely fully accessible, few are really impossible.

The nature of many of the most spectacular tourist attractions makes exploration by wheelchair hard work, and **removal of barriers** here is hard—and can entail reshaping the landscape. Trekking through rainforest, following the Inca Trail to Machu Picchu, or watching wildlife among the craggy Galapagos islands present formidable problems. It can be done, but not without strong companions, and travelers should always be ready to call a halt when conditions become too tricky; as Lawrence Poole discovered in Costa Rica, there are times when discretion is the better part of valor.

The attitude and helpfulness of the ordinary citizens cannot be faulted: only good reports, of friendly assistance, often from people with no concern for their own comfort or safety, have been received; one wheelchair user found her progress along a busy sidewalk in Buenos Aires easier than in many European cities, pedestrians moving aside without fuss or hesitation, like the Red Sea in front of Moses; Lawrence Poole was rescued from the Costa Rican jungle by a friendly local when his previously accessible path turned to sludge in a downpour; Greg Baker gained access to the ocean with a little help from the "beach guys" in Jamaica.

The people of Latin America and the Caribbean, and a few enlightened tour operators, make possible some fairly **adventurous travel**, including bird-watching from a dugout in the Ecuadorean rainforest and hiking across lava formations to spot flightless cormorants in the Galapagos islands. Flights in light aircraft above the Angel Falls and over the Andes, jeep rides, and jungle walks—those who really want to can participate in most activities. And, as more disabled travelers take the plunge and consider Central and South America and the Caribbean islands as viable destinations, the authorities will see that provision of facilities for them makes sound commercial sense.

A few accessible rooms and ramps in the luxury hotels are not enough, however, either for the tourists who wish to venture outside their resorts or for the people with disabilities who live in these countries. Massive improvements in the infrastructure and in basic public services are required, and will only be possible if the battles against national debt, inflation, and inhuman regimes can be won; the ensuing stability may then allow the introduction of proper **financial support** for the changes needed to enable disabled people to achieve equal rights and greater independence.

Meanwhile, there is no shortage of energy among disabled people themselves. *Mobility International USA* (see USA *Travel Notes*) has been instrumental in promoting an exchange of ideas and encouraging disabled Central Americans to channel this energy into effective action. Fernando Perez started *Mobility International Mexico* after talking to *MIUSA* president, Susan Sygall, and during an exchange visit to Oregon in 1991 he said, "More than seven percent of the Mexican population, about five million people, have some sort of disability. These people do not have any adaptations to mainstream into society, so they are kept on the sidelines. We want to change that." As in other parts of the world, change will come slowly, through hard work and persistent lobbying, but when it does, conditions for disabled travelers, too, will improve dramatically.

In this section the *Travel Notes* are gathered together after the accounts.

Jamaica

The Ultimate Restorative Vacation

Apart from a stay at the Half Moon Club outside of Montego Bay, which was "wonderful, accessible, and tres cher," Greg Baker's time in Jamaica has been almost entirely spent in villas in a small development west of Ocho Rios called Mammee Bay, where he and his companion Gail have rented ten times since 1980. Greg was injured in an auto accident in Greece in 1968, and is an SCI quad with good hand and arm movement.

It's 7am—it could be any morning—on the terrace of *Villa Terra Nova*. A ketch beats into the gentle easterly trade wind past a tiny fishing boat just off the point at the tip of Mammee Bay. Glancing past the *Sandals* resort a mile down the beach, past the inlet where some of the filming of the first James Bond movie, *Dr. No*, took place, across the scalloped bay to the east, it seems that Ocho Rios, some ten miles distant, has vanished in the early morning haze and only the sea and the blue-green hills of Jamaica stretch away to the horizon. At this moment Columbus and his fleet could come flying down the trade looking for safe harbor, as they did in May 1494 on the Second Voyage. They sailed past this point where I'm sitting and anchored a few miles west of here at what is now called Discovery Bay. In his log Columbus described this island as "the fairest that eyes have

beheld." Five hundred years of tumultuous history later, it is still possible to concur with these words.

Starting twelve years ago, our early trips were motivated by our fascination with Jamaica's history and our curiosity about the culture which has resulted from it. Now, on our tenth visit, it is the beauty of this particular spot, the kindness of the people associated with it, and, to be honest, the ease of travel from home that makes Jamaica the ultimate in a restorative vacation.

The three-and-a-half-hour charter flight (nonstop from Chicago) went smoothly; the Havana air traffic controllers didn't force us to detour around Cuba as they sometimes have done. Deplaning at Montego Bay, though, provides one of those quintessential moments when the traveler is aware of having left the familiar and entered a very different realm. As the two Jamaican "assistance personnel" (baggage handlers, really) prepared to cart me down the boarding steps in the battered and footrest-less aisle chair, the flight attendant protests mightily that I am not strapped in, a gross breach of regulations. With a knowing smile, the lead fellow, never pausing in his progress out and down, shouts over the airport roar, "Yah mon, no problem ya see." I just inhale the shock of heat and humidity, saying to myself, "We made it again."

And, indeed, it is like a homecoming. After meeting our driver as arranged and enjoying the 90-minute "re-entry" drive along the north shore to *Terra Nova*, we're greeted with hugs at the door by Elsie, Valencia, Rhona, and Denzel.

Why a villa rather than a hotel? Here are a few good reasons. We've come to know our hosts and admire them for their warmth, their perseverance in coping with Jamaica's difficult economy and the odd hurricane, and their many skills, including Elsie's cooking and Denzel's gardening. Beside this personal touch, which is simply not part of a hotel vacation, this villa in particular (but also the others we've stayed in) is more comfortable than any hotel. *Terra Nova* has four large bedrooms—three of which have ocean views—around an airy central living-dining room. The pool sparkles in the tropical sun and the view from the adjoining deck is magnificent at any time of day or night. To this last we can attest, having spent varying portions of four nights in 1986 tracking Halley's comet through the southern skies—a truly unforgettable sight.

The canopy of three palms that used to provide the deck with a speckled dancing shade is gone but new baby palms there and plantings around the villa are thriving. Why new? The landscape, indeed the villa itself, was largely destroyed by Hurricane Gilbert in 1988. As Denzel puts it, "Gilbert, him walk on de sea, den him walk on de land, yah mon. Him verra cruel, verra hard." We had seen just how hard when we visited in the spring of 1989 and Elsie took us to see *Terra Nova*.

The rebuilding of the roof had begun but the devastation was still overwhelming. The house stood open and ransacked by the sea. My wheelchair could not negotiate the debris and rubble, but Gail picked her way around to the sea side of the house and reported that the front yard and pool looked as if the ocean floor had been dumped there. Now that the place has been beautifully restored, it's hard to imagine the chaos Nature was able to wreak. Denzel's green thumb is responsible for nursing the plantings along, and Gail, an avid gardener, delights in plumbing his remarkable knowledge of the local flora.

"A Creole homestyle cuisine, full of the surprises of local ingredients"

Another aspect of the villa's comfort is the fact that it is, for the most part, accessible to a wheelchair. Once the step from the driveway into the house is negotiated, everything (except one bedroom) is on one level. The lawn growing between the concrete stepping stones to the pool provides a few bumps but nothing insurmountable. Our bedroom is large, with a roll-in closet, twin sinks in the vanity, and a separate bathroom containing toilet (but no grab bars or special equipment), tub, and shower stall with a tile threshold a couple of inches high. This last can be dealt with by transferring to one's traveling shower chair or by having a villa-mate yank one's wheelchair over the threshold.

Not only do the accommodations beat any hotel's, but the food is superior to all but some of the most luxurious and expensive resorts. Can I just tell you about breakfast? Freshly squeezed orange juice; a platter of fruit sections including pineapple, papaya, mango, and watermelon, surrounded by wedges of lime; then, any of a number of possibilities—Elsie's corn muffins (which are, as they say in California, to die for), banana fritters, pancakes, cinnamony French toast, poached eggs on callaloo (a delicious spinach-like green), bacon and ackee (a fruit that when cooked resembles scrambled eggs). Enough. Suffice it to say that lunch and dinner are equally wonderful. Elsie presents a Creole homestyle cuisine, full of the surprises of local ingredients and reflecting Jamaica's Arawak, African, Chinese, and Indian, as well as British, roots.

"Would we like to buy a couple of lobsters from the two young entrepreneurs with spearguns?"

One of the happy obligations of any trip to *Terra Nova* is the settling of the grocery bill. Elsie will take care of this if you like, but the trip into the quaint, largely unspoiled St. Ann's Bay should not be missed for a taste of Jamaica away from the all-inclusive resorts or the tourist welter of Ocho Rios or Montego Bay. Established as Sevilla Nueva in 1509, the first Spanish capital of Jamaica, and later as a port and trading center for the many sugar plantations on the north coast, St. Ann's Bay seethes with history under its modest appearance. A motley cluster of tin-roofed houses, their pastel clapboard partially hidden by a riot of bougainvilaea, climb the hill behind the main street. Most of the stone warehouses from the colonial days are overgrown and empty, but the marketplace in the square teems with smells and colors: cassava, yams, allspice berries, curry, tomatoes, okra, bananas. Down the street is the statue commemorating the birthplace of Jamaican hero Marcus Garvey. A change of currency at the bank, perhaps, and the purchase of a few essentials: a bottle of Appleton Estate Special rum, for example—at $4 this is a purchasing decision one need not agonize over—and then back to the villa, where we are presented with another food choice. Would we like to buy a couple of lobsters from the two young entrepreneurs with spearguns?

With visions of Elsie's lobster salad urging us on, we give thumbs up to this offer and prepare for the main event—the beach.

We have a healthy respect for the tropical sun as it approaches midday and would rather not be likened to the mad dogs and Englishmen of Noel Coward, a long-time resident of Jamaica (his house, Firefly, is an hour's drive east of here). We therefore make the five-minute trip to the beach as soon after breakfast as we can manage. The first obstacle lies in wait before we even get to the road. To prevent cattle from wandering off the grazing lands of the former plantation to the west and munching the villas' shrubbery and lawn, each residence has a cattle guard installed at the end of the driveway. This contraption, which consists of steel tubes set several inches apart over a shallow pit, not only does a good job against bucolic invaders, but also provides quite a challenge to wheelchairs and their pushers. The back wheels can jolt over the rails without danger, as long as the chair remains tilted back and the pusher (or puller) can find sure footing and not twist an ankle in one of the cracks. Denzel often offers help at this juncture.

"I'm transported over the last few feet of sand and plunked down in the clear, warm sea"

The second test is the road itself, now shimmering in the heat since the villas block the cool ocean breeze. I can remember years ago pushing much of the way to the beach on my own; time and the hurricanes have taken their toll on the sidewalk, however, making for a rough, pitted surface with lots of loose stones. Now the easiest method is for Gail to push me in the tilted-back, two-wheel position, which is why we usually refer to this as her warm-up exercise—very warm. At the beach driveway we cross another cattle guard, this one somewhat less precarious due to a narrow margin of concrete on one side of the bars. Gail can get sure footing and one of my tires on this ledge, which could presumably give beach access to an exceedingly skinny cow. As we cross, a "Halloo" from the foliage above calls our attention to Hendrick, one of the beach employees who is now perched in the branches. He offers us a fresh mango from the several ripe ones he has just gathered while we wonder how we could have passed by this anonymous tree all these years without realizing its true identity.

Up the driveway, a quick burst over thirty feet of sand, up two steps, and we're being cooled by the breeze under the shade of the beach pavilion, a sturdy structure some twenty feet square where one can find shade, snacks, and cold bottles of two old Jamaican friends—Ting, a marvelous grapefruity soft drink, and Red Stripe beer. But the point here is the Caribbean, the glorious sweep of sea and sky, and, in the low season, the absolutely empty beach. Gail usually reads and suns herself for a bit on the beach chair while I read in the pavilion, but it's not long before the Topsiders and shirt come off, the mask and snorkel go on, and I give the high sign to Hendrick or one of the other beach guys. Held in a "fireman's carry" between two of them, I'm transported over the last few feet of sand and plunked down in the clear, warm sea. At last!

Protected by an ancient sunken pier just thirty feet from shore, Mammee Bay is an ideal beach. The gentle waves, fine white sand, and gently sloping bottom make it congenial for waders, splashers, swimmers, talkers, and snorkelers of all ages. For years, lack of imagination and sheer indolent bliss kept me puttering back and forth, buoyant in this sunny wetness, and content with floating, experimenting with strokes remembered from my days of competitive swimming. Lately, though, both of us have become more interested in the world beneath the

surface, venturing first around to the ocean side of the pier, which has really become a living coral reef, and then the 200 or so yards out to the second reef, the "real" one. This latter trip requires that there be very little wind (lest we be blown west on to the rocks in front of *Terra Nova*) and some teamwork since the second reef is quite a distance for an arms-only swimmer. For "teamwork," read "Gail's fins"; next year I plan to try a pair of the webbed gloves that my swimmers use during workouts. This is a totally exhilarating and new experience for us, and we look forward to learning more about diving and tropical reefs.

"A cold Red Stripe washes away the salt taste while we blow dry in the breeze"

Despite the temptation to stay longer, we stick to the Noel Coward rule, aided in our resolve by the several slabs of formerly pale, now painfully red—or is that purple?—skin lying on the sand. Another quick carry accomplishes my hasty retreat to the pavilion, where a cold Red Stripe washes away the salt taste while we blow dry in the breeze. We settle our account—say a total of $4 for beach chair, tips for my carriers, and beer—and head back to the villa via the now even more infernal road. Hendrick sometimes takes over the pushing chores, filling us in on the latest local auto accidents and robberies; he seems to revel in being the bearer of bad tidings. Return is celebrated with a plunge into the pool (for Gail), a hot shower, perhaps a short gin and tonic with a wedge of incomparable Jamaican lime. Lunch, anyone?

An afternoon out of the sun, napping and especially reading allows our brains to keep pace with our bodies in the rejuvenation process. This year, we add a new wrinkle by signing up with Winsome, a trained masseuse who plies her trade among the villas. There is nothing quite like being pummeled, kneaded, and stretched in the shade of the verandah while gazing out at the blue Caribbean. For newer visitors to Jamaica, a rental car—right-hand drive only (a British legacy), available at Montego Bay and Ocho Rios—opens up all kinds of more active afternoon possibilities: short trips to Dunn's River Falls, the market and jerk pork center in Ocho Rios, Shaw Park gardens, or Fern Gully; and longer excursions to Rose Hall, a colonial English manor house made famous by the murderous "White Witch," a banana plantation, or the Bob Marley memorial at his birthplace in the tiny hill village of Nine Miles.

Later, after dinner concludes with a wee piece of lime meringue pie, we repair to the pool deck as the lights wink on up in Chalky Hill and across the bay in Ocho Rios. Our evenings are generally early ones here, but we can enjoy tracing a few constellations and awaiting moonrise, calmed by the gentle rhythm of the dark surf and thankful that this "fairest isle" has welcomed us again.

Costa Rica

A Month in Paradise

In August 1977, when Lawrence Poole had the accident that put him in a wheelchair, he was National Sales Manager for a large company and as such traveled continuously. After six weeks in intensive care, he spent eleven months in hospital rooms where he would often escape into the travel posters that papered his walls. In the following account, Lawrence describes his experiences in Costa Rica.

Paralyzed from the T4 vertebra, with a broken arm, sternum, and clavicle, I was most frustrated by needing help to get from my wheelchair to my bed. I longed for the day when I could transfer myself and regain my independence. One day I was introduced to a roommate who was a veteran paraplegic with seven years' experience. We chatted amiably about the "tricks of the trade"; then he called for an orderly to help put him to bed. I was stunned and in a flash saw myself a prisoner of my dependence on others for the rest of my life. After he was tucked in, I casually asked how come he still needed help with basic transfers and he answered that at home he had a trapeze bar over his bed and he just swung in or out, but without his equipment he didn't feel he had the equilibrium to transfer safely. I took a mental memo that I'd learn to do without any form of bar or rail or anything else. From now on, the chair,

hand controls for my car, and total freedom.

My first trip after leaving the hospital—driving some 900 miles to Nova Scotia—taught me about relative accessibility and how a sturdy pair of jeans would allow me to "bum" up any number of stairs, dragging my chair behind me. Accessibility hasn't been a consideration since. I also learned that wheelchairs and sandy beaches could be tricky, that salt water corrodes metal and that paraplegics don't automatically float. Most importantly, I learned that "if there's a will there's a way."

In 1992, Suzy and I decided to discover "paradise on earth." Suzy is my life partner and our proposed Eden was the tiny country of Costa Rica, Central America. About the size of Nova Scotia, it has eight temperate zones, each with its own biodiversity, touches both the Caribbean and the Pacific oceans, and is sprinkled with volcanos, jungles, savannas, mangroves, and beaches. Having abolished its army in 1948, Costa Rica is populated by one of the friendliest peoples in the world. The central valley is home to about half the country's two and a half million people, most in and around San Jose or Atajuela, and they must cross the mountains to reach either coast. This valley is called the "eternal spring," boasting a year-round temperature of 71°F, while the coasts average about 86°F (humid on the Caribbean side and more arid and breezy on the Pacific). Costa Rica has a dry and a wet season, and because its sun shines throughout Canada's icy winter it is fast becoming a favorite escape for frigid Québecers.

"Suzy and I began to unwind from the year's accumulated stress"

We landed at the Juan Santamaria International airport in San Jose and waited for the special aisle chair in order to deplane. In Montréal we had boarded the L1011 from the door at the center of the cabin and I easily transferred from my wheelchair to a seat, but here the plane aligned itself with its front doorway at the terminal and I was a long way back. The special chair arrived, I was strapped in like a sausage and pushed to the front of the plane where my wheelchair was waiting, ready for adventure.

The airport is totally accessible, with gentle slopes, ramps, and elevators. Having cleared immigration and customs we claimed our luggage, rented a car, and were off. Our first stop was the *Hotel Irazu*, which is relatively accessible (the main features—front desk, restaurant, room, and bathroom—pose no major barriers for a wheelchair).

We had left Montréal at 4am and hadn't slept at all, so an afternoon nap by the pool was called for, after which we wheeled over to Marisquos, an outdoor seafood restaurant where we could have a couple of beers and indulge in some people-watching. We finally dispelled the memory of Canada's cold and snow by tackling the paella, which was deliciously loaded with every shellfish imaginable—we almost finished it!

After a good night's sleep we dragged out maps and guidebooks before heading up to Turrialba. It's a two-hour drive (with several stops for directions) and a 2200-foot vertical climb to the *Albergue Mirador Pochotel*, which nestles in the clouds and offers a spectacular view of coffee farms, the town, the Rio Reventazon (winter training grounds for whitewater rafters and canoers), and the Guayabo National Monument (an ancient Olmec ceremonial center which is being excavated).

The Pochotel is not perfectly accessible, but manageable. Our room was large and comfortable. Once I squeezed through the narrow doorway to the bathroom, I could remove the footrests and negotiate a turn toward the toilet and shower. I asked Suzy to hand me a wooden chair which was in the bedroom, and positioned it in the shower—a simple transfer and I was in business. The Pochotel has four cabins facing a near-vertical drop and a breathtaking view of the valley below, and two rooms at the very edge of the cliff. Avoiding the stairs which link the cabins with the restaurant area, I wheeled out to the road and up the mountain a hundred feet. After a good look round, Suzy and I began to unwind from the year's accumulated stress—vacation was officially starting.

Over the next two nights, wearing sweaters to ward off the mountain breezes, and slowly sipping rum, we loosely planned our month in paradise. We slept soundly in the clean, cool air, and rose to find the valley filled with thick clouds; refreshed and swathed in cotton batting by Mother Gaia herself, the town slowly greeted the day, beckoning the sun which already warmed us above, where we ate *gallo pinto* and eggs with our locally grown coffee.

We descended from our eyrie to explore, enjoying CATIE, the immense tropico-agriculture research station, sharing local color and activities, and experiencing no problems with access until we decided to investigate the Olmec excavations. At the entrance to Guayabo National Park we were told that we needed a guide because of the 57 varieties of venomous snakes which populate the jungle. We were also told that the descent into the valley was precarious for a wheelchair but that our guide would help with "mucho gusto" (a great pleasure)—this is how Costa Ricans (or Ticos, as they call themselves) always describe their efforts to assist a tourist. I decided the safest way to proceed was backward in a sort of fall which I could control. Down we slid, the guide and I, struggling and falling farther into the murk.

"A little acrobatic squeezing around the beds and into the bathroom was required"

While Suzy and the guide never lost their good humor, I began to wonder just how far down is down. Stopping to rest, I asked Suzy to scout ahead and she came back with the report that the path was getting steeper, narrower, wetter, and more precarious. I decided that discretion really is the better part of valor, and suggested that she should continue, taking all kinds of photos, and that I could view them in our living room, surrounded by our fifty tropical plants. Up we climbed, back into the sunshine. As I meandered about, admiring flora and fauna, Suzy explored the ruins. The slides she took confirmed that I really didn't miss too much.

The next day we left Turrialba for the Caribbean coast and the port city of Limón. We would visit the city on our way back, but now I was anxious to see some of the outstandingly lush greenery and we headed for the Cahuita National Park, a rainforest on a beach which is considered a surfers' mecca. After driving through banana plantations, we found a community dotted with tiny cabins and a few small hotels at the entrance to the park, and checked into Cabinas Palmar. Here a little acrobatic squeezing around the beds and into the bathroom was required, but we weren't in the tropics to stay indoors so the tiny room did not dissuade.

Leaving our luggage, we set off to explore the jungle. I was stunned to see the wheelchair symbol nailed to a tree, and wondered what universal access meant in the jungle. Crossing a small bridge into the park, I immediately encountered the bane of wheelchairs everywhere—deep, soft sand—but a park ranger ran over, and he pulled, pushed, and steered the chair toward a trail of harder packed sand which was easy to ride on and which led into the jungle. We entered the forest and, with the exception of a couple of soft spots which required a struggle, I wheeled merrily along, exploring, being explored, and feeling awed by the beauty that is tropical jungle.

Some 45 minutes along the trail, the sky opened, and I experienced the true meaning of the term "rainforest." The water was warm, soothing, and coming down a lot harder than most hotel showers. Within seconds we were drenched to the skin (which felt great) and within minutes our hard trail was reduced to mush (which didn't). And 45 minutes is a long way into the jungle. I started to wonder how I could possibly maneuver when a very physically fit young Tico jogged toward us, surveyed the challenge and offered to help. Suzy, he, and I battled our way back to civilization. Parked at a table at the local watering hole, we spent time with our new friend, discussed everything and nothing (Suzy is fluent in Spanish), and were told wonderful things about Puerto Viejo, near the Panama border.

That night we dined in a fully accessible restaurant (meaning street level), watched the crabs race across the street, listened to the breeze whisper through the palms, and slept like sweaty babies in our tiny cabina. In the morning we went out for a trip farther down the coast. In Puerto Viejo we checked into a beautiful resort called *Punta Cocles*, at the edge of the Talamanca rainforest reserve. Here, well-appointed cabins were linked to the main building by concrete paths covered by a thatched roof system, perfect for wheelchair jockeys.

"We sipped rum punch, enjoying the patio, the pool, and the wall of jungle surrounding us"

Our room was spacious and air-conditioned, and the bathroom offered fairly easy access (the only challenge was the transfer from my chair to toilet seat to a plastic garden chair in the shower). The resort has a nice swimming pool which we used as soon as we'd unpacked—bliss. As we sipped rum punch, enjoying the patio, the pool, and the wall of jungle surrounding us, I noticed four stairs to the dining area, but was informed that I could be helped up the stairs or could have a waiter serve us on the patio (on different days we did both).

Puerto Viejo is a tiny and charming hamlet with an absolutely black beach of volcanic sand. We enjoyed Earl Brown's oceanfront restaurant (a palm frond shack) which offers typical Costa Rican fare—grilled fish, rice and beans, fried plantain, and salad. We ate, drank cold beer, and traded stories with Earl, some American surfers, international volunteers working on an ecology project, and local fishermen. After a few days of "pure vida," we headed back up the coast to Limón, staying at the *Matama Hotel* on the road to Moin. The *Matama* is relatively accessible (one small step to our air-conditioned room, easy bathroom access, two steps to the restaurant, a swimming pool) and sits amid spectacular gardens.

We visited Limón and while having ice cream by the marketplace met a Tico who proposed a three-and-a-half-hour ride up jungle canals by pirogue (giant dug-out canoe) to the Tortuguero National Park, which is at the other end of the coast, near Nicaragua. He assured us that access for wheelchairs was no problem and that we would be helped—with "mucho gusto"—where we needed it. He sold us on the idea and we left the next morning for an exhilarating, Bogie-style trip into the jungle where we saw an incredible diversity of colors, every shade of green imaginable, and monkeys, alligators, tapirs, peccaries, sloths, and birds of every description. The pirogue was comfortable and we motored along nature's highway, seemingly into the depths of nowhere. Here, nowhere, the frame of my wheelchair cracked in half. A pipe forming the base support had rusted out (too many beaches) and I was now doomed.

We only briefly enjoyed Tortuguero before the calamity, and then had to get back in the boat and return to civilization. I was a bit stressed by the alternatives I faced, and the boat ride seemed longer coming out than going in. I had the phone number of a paraplegic in San Jose who fixes wheelchairs; I could call Montréal and have my spare chair put on a plane; I could find a local mechanic or welder; I could go home and ruin my holiday—this last alternative was quickly dismissed as folly.

"For the next few days I experienced freedom of movement like I hadn't in a long time"

We got back to the Matama at 4:55pm (it was Friday afternoon) and as luck (or good living) would have it my contact in San Jose was just leaving his office for the weekend but assured me that he would meet us the next day at his shop and all would be well again. We sat around the hotel, ate, drank, and enjoyed Caribbean music for the rest of the evening. In the morning we drove back to the capital.

Saturday afternoon we met Edgar Montoya, who operates "Edmont" (see *Travel Notes*) with a mission to provide all kinds of services to the Costa Rican disabled community and to disabled travelers. This most charismatic Tico greeted us with two mechanics who took my chair apart and had it fixed within a couple of hours. Edgar and his friends refused any kind of compensation and seduced us into visiting Edgar's place on the Pacific coast. We made plans to meet at Estrillos Este, at an inn called the *Pelican*. After a leisurely Sunday morning drive, we found the *Pelican* to be relatively accessible (certain rooms, restaurant and swimming pool at ground level; the bathroom has two steps but I could transfer directly from my chair to the raised and spotless tiled floor and bum along easily) and we decided to spend a few days there.

We met our new friends and discovered why Edgar has a house here: even the beach is accessible, being of hard-packed sand. Edgar lent me his all-terrain vehicle (the ultimate para toy) and for the next few days I experienced freedom of movement like I hadn't in a long time. The Pelican and the region surrounding Estrillos Este typify tropical living, languishingly hot and humid, with flora and fauna to suit, and food and drink appropriate to conditions of enforced idleness. We did little and enjoyed it all. After a few days we made plans to meet our friends again later in our voyage and headed up into the mountains where the weather was cooler and the pace a little more lively. We visited the Poas Volcano (accessible administration building and trails), coffee-growing regions, and then headed for the Monteverde Cloud Forest Reserve.

You have to earn Monteverde. The last 24 miles of dirt road spiral up into the clouds for nearly three hours. At each turn I could not believe that the road could get worse (but it did) and could not imagine that the view could get more spectacular (and it did). At the entrance to the reserve we checked into *Hotel de la Montaña* and were pleased to find it totally accessible (rooms, bathrooms, and restaurant all on one floor). Our room was on a mirador which faced the Pacific and we could see the Gulf of Nicoya laid out below us.

"A place called 'paradise' in the midst of paradise was worth investigating"

Monteverde is a real cloud forest: on a clear day, with sun shining, you are stalked, enveloped, and sprayed by a mist of cool mountain cloud which then drifts off, allowing the sun to erase its handiwork. That night, after dining commune-style with other adventurers, we sat and stared at stars which seemed larger than my closed fist and barely beyond reach. The next morning, Suzy went deep into the forest with a guide while I hovered at the entranceway with hundreds of hummingbirds. The trails are not wheelchair friendly but I had plenty to still my mind right where I was.

After another magical evening we headed back down, having decided to visit the Guanacaste Province and its dry tropical climate. We were drawn to a place called Paraíso on the map—a place called "paradise" in the midst of paradise was worth investigating. In Paraíso we were directed to a hotel called Iguanazul and found beautiful little villas surrounding a large swimming pool, overlooking a Pacific white-sand beach. The rooms were large and totally accessible (two steps, but management built a wooden ramp before I finished my first beer; they even placed a plastic chair in the shower before we had a chance to ask). Iguanazul is gorgeous, and when we were told that the fourth night is free if you stay three, the deal was done.

We met great people and learned about the rich diversity of the dry tropical forest. Here, in marked contrast to the lush tropics, there isn't much green during the dry season. The predominant color is sepia brown, with startling bursts of green, red, pink, or mauve supplied by flowering trees and bushes; the region reminded me more of Texas than exotic Central America. As a finishing touch, *Iguanazul* has the greatest floorshow on earth—every evening, at 6pm sharp, the sun dips into the sea and splashes the sky with every color in the spectrum.

"We hung around the town square like locals, soaking up the atmosphere"

After enjoying our free night we headed farther north and spent a few days on Playa Potrera at a lovely inn called *Bahia Flamingo*, which was totally accessible (large rooms, restaurant, and swimming; Rufus, the manager, put a deckchair in the shower and I had to transfer from my chair to toilet seat to shower, but this was the only hitch). Rufus even decided to lay boards down on the beach to provide access, but this proved impractical as they tended to slip out from under my wheels. The pool was adequate for keeping the heat off and the gazebos overlooking the sea provided all the beach I needed.

While we were there the temperature hovered at 95°F, so Suzy and I fell into an energetic pattern that saw us move less than 300 yards per day, between room, pool, food, margaritas, and sea breezes. After a few days of this we decided to head

back toward the eternal spring and drove inland, around Lake Arenal and the living, breathing Arenal volcano and its hot springs, over mountains where clouds shut out both highway and scenery.

We finally saw the late afternoon blue sky and found a room at a hotel called *El Lugar*, in Tilarán. This smalltown hotel was comfortable and easily accessed (large rooms, bathrooms, restaurant; the only minor problem was an inaccessible link to the restaurant from the inside, solved by wheeling out into the street and around the corner to enter the restaurant via the main door). We stopped in Tilarán simply to cut the day's drive, but discovered a lovely little town, typical of regional Costa Rica. That night we hung around the town square like locals, soaking up the atmosphere.

The next morning we drove into San Jose, met our friend Edgar, and spent the last days of our trip talking about the possibilities that exist in paradise. Costa Ricans tend to have that pleasant "can do" attitude, which probably results from managing over 5000 co-operatives and countless family enterprises in a thriving democracy. We formed a partnership, incorporated, met with architects and lawyers, and are now all involved in realizing a wonderful project: we are building a ten-room inn on the beach at Estrillos Este. Called *Su Lugar del Pacífico* ("Your Place on the Pacific"), it will, of course, be designed with universal access features at every stage. As we settled into our seats for the return flight, Suzy and I had none of the usual post-trip blues; this time we were only commuting between home and home.

Honduras

Mayan Mysteries

From the age of six Lawrence Poole has been enthralled by Mayan culture: an aunt lived in Bogotà, Colombia, and on a Christmas trip home brought him a silver ring adorned with a Mayan mask. Since that time he's been aware of the mysterious "forests of kings," which were highly civilized long before the Europeans conquered American shores, and for years he's read the myths and legends that linked the native peoples of America. Recently, when a friend, Gerard, moved to Honduras for three years to become part of a Canadian International Development Agency forestry project, Lawrence and his partner Suzy decided to visit.

We were aware that Honduras has no tourist infrastructure to speak of (even less so for the disabled traveler) and thus we surrendered to the unknown by surrounding it with the known: we would stay in Costa Rica for a week before and after our Mayan adventure. This allowed us to fly an inexpensive charter from Montréal to Costa Rica and our host would have Honduras tickets waiting for us there. Gerard was living in the coastal town of La Ceiba, so we flew from San Jose to the Honduran capital of Tegucigalpa and transferred to a local airline for the flight to the coast.

Tegucigalpa apparently has one of the shortest runways in the world and it is totally surrounded by mountains.

Our pilot safely applied full brakes as soon as our landing gear touched solid, and we scraped ourselves off the back of the seats in front of us. Being the last to deplane we sat patiently for a while and then were informed that the airport really didn't have the facilities to help a wheelchair. The airport had no narrow aisle chair and no way of lowering me to the ground. While they worked out the details, an elderly baggage handler picked me up (at 6 feet 4 inches tall and weighing some 200 pounds, no easy feat), carried me to my chair and then had a forklift brought to the doorway. I wheeled onto a pallet used for loading luggage and, with the lift fully extended some 30 feet in the air, we rushed across the ground to board our waiting connection. At one point I noticed that the elderly gentleman and Suzy, who was sharing the pallet with me, were holding onto my chair for support and I reminded them that I wasn't secured to anything!

Loaded onto our connecting flight, we took off and veered right as soon as the undercarriage left the runway. Sitting by the window I was convinced the wingtip would touch ground (brother, I thought, you wanted adventure) but a moment later we were safely aloft and I relaxed. I gazed down at the hills and the mountains that cradle the capital and I was saddened by the look of the place. The city really seemed dirty and the surrounding land was just so much red dirt. I couldn't notice any trees—anywhere.

Landing in La Ceiba, I instructed the baggage handlers (making use of Suzy's fluent Spanish) on how best to help a wheelchair down the plane's steps and, when I finally came to rest on the ground, I resisted an urge to kiss the concrete. Wheeling toward the terminal building, I spotted a lovely set of five or six stairs and the large crowd beyond it. Peering into the crowd I saw Gerard and Mark (who was also visiting and would soon become a friend). I stopped at the foot of the stairs, recognized that they could not come out to help me (immigration, customs) and, as I shifted my focus around, noticed how dismal the buildings and equipment looked, and wondered about the armed soldiers who were everywhere. Welcome to Honduras. I was later told that there have been over 300 internal coups, rebellions, and wars in this country—during this century.

Baggage handlers rushed over to help me and we made it up the stairs more by good-natured enthusiasm than wheelchair-handling skills. Through the bureaucracy and out the other side of the building—here only a couple of steps and Gerard and Mark to help. I stopped the parade in order to take a good look at the country and was gratified by expanses of green—trees, bushes, shrubs, and grasses—great, I thought, there's still some jungle left.

La Ceiba is the country's biggest port, exporting bananas and pineapples from the north coast. Hopping into Gerard's four-wheel drive Land Rover, we drove to and through town, and toured along the way. I inquired about an accessible hotel and was told that there probably wasn't one but that either way we would stay with Gerard. Reaching his home I was pleased to find a very modern town house in a nice quiet neighborhood. We unloaded the jeep and were given a lovely room at the top of fifteen stairs. Gerard and Mark insisted that running me up and down would be no hardship, but after the first try they grudgingly agreed when I commented that they might not find this so amusing after a while. However, this was a temporary arrangement as we would be off to visit the area of Copán and the Mayan ruins within a couple of days.

"I met a snake-oil salesman"

While in La Ceiba I found that accessibility is relatively easy when most buildings are single-story, and I had no trouble with restaurants or markets and such. I met a snake-oil salesman. This guy had a microphone and an air-raid speaker hooked to a car battery and he gathered a crowd. There, in the street, using deadly snakes as his shill, he sold snake oil—and did well at it. We visited the beautiful but unkempt beaches at La Barre and Miramar, and found no real tourists or tourist structures (this would have been the height of the season if they had one).

We drove into the Nombre de Dios mountain range, where Gerard was working on reforestation, and I really started to appreciate the beauty of this land which is at once blessedly rich in its biodiversity and wretchedly poor in its standards of living. The next day we headed toward the Pico Bonito National Park which is being developed with the help of the American Peace Corps. Later we had supper with Canadian and American aid workers and I learned that not only was this second largest of the Central American countries affected by years of political strife, but also the social structures were based on whatever international aid projects were in vogue and on the needs of the CIA during their forays into the neighboring areas. Not quite a vision of wise planning.

Finally we set out for Las Ruinas de Copán, an ancient Mayan city where 30,000 people suddenly stepped off the face of the world. Copán straddles the Guatemalan border in the western corner of the country. As we drove I waved to the *campesinos* (peasant farmers), time and again seeing weary, strained faces spring to life, smile, and wave back. Passing through San Pedro Sula, a modern-looking town, and avoiding the *Pizza Hut*, *Chicken Shack*, and *Lucky's Chinese Food*, we found a typical restaurant called *Meson Español*, which was easily accessed and offered good food and great atmosphere. We saw a hotel called *Bolivar,* consisting of cabins at ground level surrounding a pool, but we did not stay, driving on to the village of Copán Ruinas, near the site of the ruins. During our journey we crossed three army checkpoints and I wondered about the dreams and wishes of heavily armed 14- and 15-year-olds. At last we spotted an ancient Mayan stele on a hill and below it a lush valley partially obscured by low-level clouds.

Copán Ruinas is a very pleasant village of cobblestone streets spoked out from the town square. It is a short distance from the old Mayan city of the same name. We stayed at the *Hotel Marina* on the plaza; after being helped over two giant steps I entered an old mansion with a small center courtyard, surrounded by rooms and a small restaurant. The place had an eerie feel. Our room was spacious with large Spanish pieces of darkwood furnishings on ruby linoleum which reflected a stern indigo-gray on the yellowing white walls. Although comfortable, it was a bit strange. A corner was sealed off by a partial divider which was tiled with black and white ceramic squares.

A large blue plastic shower curtain almost hid a toilet, sink, and shower. These were one step up from the main red floor, and while I could pop a wheelie to access the antique lino platform, I had to place a long bench between the toilet and shower in order to slide into the narrow stall. No problem. Off we went to explore the town.

Wheeling about the cobblestones was challenging, and in the plaza I attracted a parade of children who slowly followed and shyly watched. Later, Suzy translated as they figured that the Señor must be very rich in order not to have to walk, and I realized that not many wheelchairs had been there before. We found our way to a restaurant called La Llama del Bosque, up a couple of very steep steps (everything is constructed to avoid the water runoff during the rainy season) and I was glad that Gerard and Mark were such genial travelmates, sparing Suzy the work which is often hers. The restaurant oozed atmosphere and we ate here during the couple of days we stayed (I noted that I shouldn't get stuck here with a need of the rest room, which was out back and down some stairs).

"A lost city of tens of thousands is an awesome sight"

We discovered *Salva Vida* (*Lifesaver*, which has to be one of the better beers I've ever sipped) and ordered *pollo arroz* (chicken with rice) which is a typical dish. We chatted with archaeologists and a team of Americans from Doctors Without Borders who were giving up vacation time to come and serve. Mark fell in love with our waitress, María—really a challenge when they didn't speak a common language, but Suzy was able to lie for both of them. Late into the night (it was about 8:45pm but the entire town was closed) we headed back to our hotel and found it bolted shut. We had to awaken the owner who, still wearing his nightcap, let us in and we retired (I wasn't all done but there was nothing else to do).

The next morning, awakened by roosters, dogs, traffic on the cobblestones, and people greeting each other ever so loudly, I found out why everyone went to sleep so early—4am is normal rise and shine. Plunging into the day, the shower offered considerably less than a trickle and by 7am we set off to find the ruins. I was impressed. A lost city of tens of thousands is an awesome sight. The administration building, museum, cafeteria, and dig are easily accessible, even while Copán is being reclaimed from a ravenous jungle. We took on a guide who proved to be a most charming man. He was born and raised in the area and worked with the scientists from the Carnegie Foundation when they dug and searched. He spent the entire day with us, explaining the ancient culture.

"At the rate that ruins were being uncovered, there was another 200 years of work"

Our guide demystified the inner workings of the old empire, the layout of the town of Copán, the stelae, the pyramids, and the mystical doings of the Mayan priest-kings. He spoke of the Mayan view that integrated science and religion, how their system of mathematics was based on the spiral and its link with the center of our galaxy. He told us how ancient practices like the spiral dance were still used by shamans in remote areas to contact the spirit world, and how the Mayans knew of the existence of black holes and other phenomena millennia before our modern physicists. Then he told us the ancients had land routes to Asia and their legends talked of a lost continent in the Pacific rim. He described a sport that made soccer seem tame, and the ceremonial blood lettings that provoked altered states of consciousness.

We discussed world views on gods and personal power. He wanted to show me his home, higher in the mountains, and explained how both he and his father-in-law meditated under a pyramid they had constructed. After discussing the route, some distance up narrow trails, we came off the spiritual plane and agreed that a visit in a wheelchair might not be too easy. We wandered about the site and I could feel the presence of the past. Toward the end of the day he explained how, at the rate that ruins were being uncovered, there was another 200 years of work before a complete story of this region could be surmised.

After returning to our hotel before nightfall (on these roads it is absolute) we ate at the restaurant and left early enough to make curfew. Early sleep, early rise, and we were back at the ruins for solitary wanderings and wonderings. At certain points, when I could suspend disbelief, I felt the ancient Maya and knew why they had called me for so long. Theirs was a world of spiritual power and my link with that power had given me strength in all my times of trial. I wheeled by the ballcourt, over to a stele which was dedicated to 18 Rabbit, one of the great kings, and sat silently. I thanked him for sharing the power of the spirit with me.

We returned to our hotel after a couple of hours, packed up the Land Rover, and headed home, stopping off so that Mark and María could bill and coo their sad promises. On the highway back to La Ceiba, somewhere, I suddenly asked Gerard where a small cutoff road might lead. He suggested that as it aimed toward the Caribbean, it might lead to a Garifuna village. The Garifuna are English-speaking, black Carib descendants of natives who were exiled from the island of St. Vincent when it was British colonial policy simply to exile people when they wished to appropriate land. Some way along, the small road forked and I asked Gerard to turn right.

We had to slip into four-wheel drive in order to negotiate our way through a very deep bog. Crossing to the other side we found a tiny village of cane and driftwood huts with palm-frond roofs, on one of the most beautiful beaches I've ever seen. We saw tables on the front lawn of the prettiest spot on the shore, and knew we'd found somewhere to eat.

"Life here was still, by and large, as it was when they arrived centuries ago"

We poured out of the Land Rover and were besieged by attractive, laughing children who greeted us with a torrent of questions about the wheelchair. Gerard negotiated a meal after the lady in charge welcomed us saying that the lazy man hadn't gone fishing that morning, and she had little to offer. Gerard came out of the house holding a monster lobster and said, "Bad luck, all they've got is four of these." We laughed and ordered *Salva Vida* while our hostess prepared a feast.

Chatting with the older kids, I gathered that life here was still, by and large, as it was when they arrived centuries ago. The children are raised by all the villagers, who share certain tasks. The house where we sat had the task of greeting visitors and preparing food for them; men fished or worked outside the village; women worked the gardens and did most everything else. For entertainment, the younger boys raced up majestic palm trees or played drums on oil cans, and the girls danced; older kids tended the younger ones and the eldest ones made love, starting the cycle anew. We ate, drank, were entertained, sunned where the winds kissed the sands, swam, and thought that this might be the most wonderful place on earth.

Venezuela

Success in South America

Sue Kelley, a wheelchair user, and her husband Tony spent the first half of July 1990 on the island of Margarita, off the north coast of Venezuela. They found excellent facilities for disabled people.

The name Margarita means "pearl" in Greek, and it was the lure of the pearl which led to the first Spanish settlement of this part of South America. Spanish is the native tongue of the islanders and the natural pearls found today are recovered by fishermen and sold to local jewelers.

The journey from London to Margarita with Venezuela's national airline, *Viasa*, was long, some fourteen hours in all, but service on board was good and we had ample legroom. We landed in Paris to take on more passengers, then took off for Caracas where we were taken by bus to another airport across town. There we boarded a smaller plane which flew first to Barcelona (in Venezuela), then on to Porlamar airport, Margarita.

The tour company reps were waiting to greet us, once immigration formalities had been completed and we had retrieved our baggage. Only momentarily surprised and certainly not put off their stride when they spotted my wheelchair, they took us on another bus to our hotel, the *Margarita Concorde*. We were so tired that we just rolled into bed.

Once refreshed we took stock of our surroundings. The hotel had excellent facilities for someone in a wheelchair: it was ramped throughout, to all its amenities, including the pool and the beach. Situated on the beach was a large, wooden platform with a thatched roof and bar at one end; it was only a couple of feet from the water and was a good place to park myself and enjoy the sights and sounds of the sea, with its large population of pelicans.

We were taken on a bus tour on the first day, to get us acquainted with the eastern side of the island; visits to the western side should be made only in a four-wheel drive vehicle. Jeeps can be rented at very reasonable rates, or one can participate in an organized jeep safari. We took the former option, and discovered that Margarita could be mistaken for two islands.

The larger, eastern half is the more densely populated, with many villages of Spanish colonial-style buildings scattered along the coastline. Palm trees are predominant, along with an abundance of tropical flowers and fauna the like of which we only see in hothouses.

Between the coast and its green, hilly backdrop lie valleys full of banana, mango, avocado, melon, and pineapple plantations.

The western side is a largely uninhabited desert wilderness, with few roads and only the occasional fishing village. It looks like Arizona, with its bare cliffs and heavy concentration of cacti, some round like soccer balls, sprouting pink flowers, others as tall as trees. My most vivid memory is of the incongruous meeting-point of desert landscape and ocean, with the dramatic colors of a sunset lighting up the sky.

On the north coast of the island, approximately midway between west and east, lies La Restinga lagoon, a network of waterways surrounded by mangrove trees. We rented a boat and its driver at a cost of about 350 *bolivars* (about $9; gas was very cheap, around 25 cents a gallon, but inflation was running at 100 percent). While wandering through the channels of La Restinga, we were shown the beds of oysters growing among the roots of the mangroves. The pearls cultivated from these oysters are sold mainly to Japanese buyers—many find their way onto necklaces made by Mikimoto.

Margarita has many splendid beaches, and an efficient bus service to and from the hotel is provided for guests who wish to explore those farther afield. The most tranquil waters are found on the southern shores, but working northward along the east coast the waves become stronger and beaches here are popular with surfers. Since taxis are so cheap on the island, I didn't even try the bus service, but a couple of strong helpers would be necessary to negotiate the steps at the entrance. I have on past vacations gone up the steps of buses on my bottom—a little undignified but it works.

The main town of Margarita is Porlamar. We were surprised to find a well-planned town with a wide selection of designer shops. As a tax-free shopping zone, Porlamar sells many goods, from clothes and jewelry to alcohol and perfume. In the main streets are the designer shops but up the side streets one can browse in shops selling local crafts and handmade items. The center of the town is quite modern, with sidewalks ramped at intervals. There are traffic lights to assist pedestrians crossing the busy four-lane roads, and we found the majority of drivers most courteous and patient, allowing us to cross at our leisure. While wandering around the town we stopped to watch a game of basketball—a favorite sport, taken very seriously by the locals. There are many places to eat in Porlamar and we found the dishes on offer—not only in the town but also on the beaches and in the hotel—varied, well presented, and very reasonably priced. A three-course meal for two cost the equivalent of around $7.

A statue of Simon Bolivar stands in the town center. He is credited with winning Venezuela's independence from the Spanish, and many roads, as well as the currency, are named after him.

"We flew inland to the savannah, dotted with herds of cattle and a few horses, and crisscrossed by rivers"

A short taxi ride to the outskirts took us to a large textile market which required several hours to walk around. Traditional handicrafts made from local materials can be found all over the island. Each town has its own specialty: hammocks and furniture in Santa Anna; handbags or *mapires* from broom and hemp cord in Pedro Gonzalez; traditional and modern ceramics in El Cercado, to name but a few.

The Venezuelan government has not been slow to realize the potential financial rewards to be gained from tourism. It is funding the development of Porlamar's center, with new hotels planned and a shopping mall which is expected to generate some $14 million in additional business each year. A special dock is also planned for the many cruise ships that take millions of tourists annually to other ports in the Caribbean. These plans, added to the fact that Porlamar is only a short drive along excellent roads from the airport, mean that the town is destined to become a thriving tourist center.

"Scarlet macaws, parakeets, and toucans fly in and out of the trees"

It is my guess that the Venezuelans' strong commercial sense has played a part in persuading the architects of the facilities on Margarita to make the majority of amenities accessible to *all* tourists; we found ramps at entrances almost everywhere, making life easier not only for disabled visitors, but also for mothers pushing babies in strollers.

Evenings are not my best time, but for those who like a bit of nightlife, the hotel had a number of spots: a vocal group in the lobby bar, a dance band in one of the restaurants, and a disco on the top floor. There were also occasional barbecues by the pool, with steel bands providing the music. The younger members of our party often went to the discos in town and enjoyed them. At weekends many girls from the Venezuelan mainland joined the disco crowd—there are said to be four girls to one boy in Caracas!

Flights from Porlamar to Caracas left every hour and cost $10 round trip. Several tours were also offered and we decided to participate in one which included a flight over the Angel Falls— the tallest waterfall in the world. The Twin Otter would take three hours to reach the falls, stopping midway for refueling.

From the ragged coastline, where streams rush through lush vegetation toward the sea, we flew inland to the savannah, dotted with herds of cattle and a few horses, and crisscrossed by rivers, the largest of which is the Orinoco. Sir Walter Raleigh traveled up the Orinoco in his bid to find the lost city of El Dorado, over a century after Christopher Columbus had penetrated this hinterland and thought he'd found the Garden of Eden.

The pale green of the prairies started to roll into foothills, and we could pick out roads and the occasional mine (Venezuela is rich in minerals, oil, gold, and diamonds). As the foothills were succeeded by mountains and dense jungle, we spotted many rivers, dropping sharply from one level to another as we neared Angel Falls.

Some fifteen times higher than Niagara Falls, but with a smaller volume of water, Angel Falls cascade down from the Auyantepuy mesa, whose flat top is 45 miles in diameter. There seem to be hundreds of these sheer-sided, flat-topped mountains, and the isolated environments on top, in which unique plants flourish, are said to have inspired Conan Doyle's "Lost World." We flew around the falls four times in all before landing at an airstrip in the jungle called Kavac. Here Tony and I separated from the rest of the party, which was to proceed on a trek through the jungle, under waterfalls and upriver in a dugout canoe.

The two of us were taken by jeep to the Indian village of Canaima, situated on a lagoon into which three waterfalls plunge. There is a small beach, with a few sunbeds, and visitors can swim in the waters of the lagoon which are stained the color of Coca-Cola by minerals; the Indians believe that the waters have healing properties. The village is neatly laid out and spotlessly clean. We were provided with a lunch of beef, vegetables, and a corn-like potato, followed by fresh fruit. While enjoying our lunch, sitting beside the lagoon under trees laden with ripe mangoes, we were able to watch the scarlet macaws, parakeets, and toucans fly in and out of the trees, picking up food that had been left for them. It was wonderfully relaxing and we sat there until evening started to draw in.

We were taken back to the airstrip to join our now exhausted but happy party for the return flight. When we stopped for refueling at Angosturi we were able to look over the plane which Jimmy Angel was flying when he discovered Angel Falls in the late 1930s.

Energetic visitors can also take a trek up the Amazon by horse and canoe, or an expedition from Kavac through the jungle, over rivers and chasms, Indiana Jones style. The village of Canaima is also used as a base for trekking into the jungle, one possibility—only for good swimmers and the very fit—being a three-day trek following the river to the base of Angel Falls. Other activities include micro-light flying, fishing trips, water-skiing, scuba diving, and snorkeling.

This was a very successful vacation for us, and involved no long-term planning—we didn't even inquire about accessible accommodation when booking. The tour company reps, Grant and Toni, were not only friendly but also very helpful, full of energy, information, and enthusiasm. In the first year that Margarita has been actively promoted to British tourists, we found that nothing had been forgotten as far as the provision of facilities is concerned.

Ecuador

A Golden Wedding Anniversary

Hugh Chetwynd-Talbot is paralyzed from the hips down, and wears weight-bearing braces on both legs. He was 76 years old in July 1985 when he and his wife, Cynthia, celebrated their golden wedding anniversary in a lodge in the upper Amazon jungle.

When I spotted a picture of the *Orellana Flotel* in a glossy travel brochure, we agreed that floating up or down the Amazon would be a pleasant way to spend our anniversary, and that our old friends Peter and Maria could probably have us to stay for a day or two in Quito, the capital of Ecuador.

"While you are about it," they wrote, "you might as well do the cruise around the Galapagos Islands." They made it all sound so easy.

I have found that, apart from giving the travel agent a clear idea of my disability, it is useless to ask whether particular hazards are likely to be insurmountable. Having committed myself, I feel that I must go through with it. Had I foreseen the hazards which lay ahead on this trip, I doubt that I should have undertaken it. Jane, our travel agent, entered wholeheartedly into the adventure and took great trouble over details and planning. To our joy, she arranged for us to link up with a *World Wildlife Fund* package tour in Quito. Our flight was with *Air France* via Paris and Guyana to Quito, taking some seventeen hours.

We flew over the rainforests of Guyana and then over the snow-covered peaks of the Andes as dawn was breaking. Quito is 9350 feet above sea level, in a valley between high Andean ranges which, with their many active volcanoes, rise in places to 18,700 feet. The landing at Quito is dramatic: after weaving his way down a winding, narrow valley, the pilot appears to put the enormous plane down in a street—the runway is in the middle of the city.

In spite of the early hour, Peter was there to meet us and whisked us away to his bungalow a few miles outside Quito, approached up an avenue of avocados. Central Ecuador lies in a wide valley between two massive ridges of the Andes, each of them boasting snow-covered volcanoes, seven in all. Cotopaxi (19,600 ft) is the highest volcano in the world. The sun setting on the white peaks is a very lovely sight. Covering the valley as we did in Peter's Land Rover, over appallingly rough roads, I encountered no difficulties at all and became more and more confident.

Being on the Equator, there are no seasons as we know them, and the climate at about 4000 feet is very pleasant; the countryside is not unlike parts of northern England. Quito itself is delightful, too, but it has been ravaged so often by earthquakes that it is noticeably lacking in really old buildings. Nevertheless, the Spanish influence is much in evidence; Ecuador did not achieve independence from Spain until 1835.

About twenty percent of the population is of Spanish or European descent; eighty percent are impoverished but proudly independent Indians. The local village markets display their embroidery, silver and gold work, woodcarving, and fascinating *objets d'art* carved out of bread which is specially treated for the purpose. The Indian villagers object most strongly to being photographed, and one of our party had his camera broken.

"The Ecuadorean guide surveyed me and my sticks with some gloom"

At the end of the week we left Peter and Maria and joined the *World Wildlife* party of twelve, with whom we were to fly down to the Amazon basin and board the *Orellana*. Doctor Derrick Green, the group leader, and Maurice, the Ecuadorean guide, surveyed me and my sticks with, I thought, some gloom. They had never had to cope with a disabled person before. I assured them that I should be quite happy to sit on deck with my powerful binoculars.

"You're not traveling five thousand miles just to do that," said Derrick.

A superb, if precarious, flight, past two of the snow-clad volcano peaks—Reventador and Cayambe—and down into the steamy heat of the rainforest,

brought us to a tiny airstrip. Children playing on it scattered as we circled to land; a rickety bus took us to the river bank and the first difficult hurdle—a two-foot gap, between the shore and the "flotel," in which I could see fast-flowing, muddy water.

"An anaconda had been caught underneath it a few minutes before we arrived"

A scramble over that on all fours brought the second hurdle into view—nearly vertical ladders only eighteen inches wide led from deck to deck; food was on the lower one, our cabin (and bathroom) on the middle one, and the bar and observation deck were on the top. I need width in order to obtain a good handhold, so the narrow ladder looked insurmountable for me. However, with much help from my gallant wife, who took care of my feet, we managed the ladder, not only on that occasion but on several others.

The next day, our wedding anniversary, we took to dugout canoes—most exciting affairs, fashioned out of single cedar trees. Powered by two 30-kilowatt outboard motors, the canoes travel at about 30 miles per hour and require skilled operation by the steersman and a man sitting in the prow, as the river—about 1000 yards wide—is littered with uprooted trees, stuck on hidden sandbanks.

After an hour or so, and a visit to a missionary station, we turned off into a narrow creek where the dense jungle pressed down low over the banks, and there were wonderful creepers hanging from trees about 250 feet high. Some three miles up the creek we pulled into the bank.

"This is where we land to get to the jungle lodge," said Derrick. I looked aghast at the muddy bank and the rough, steep track beyond it.

"There's a tractor and trailer at the top," said Derrick, encouragingly.

"Can't be done," I said, half fearing, half hoping that I might be asked to return alone to the *Orellana*.

"You'll have to hump him," said Cynthia, and she showed Derrick and Maurice how to make a fireman's lift by linking their hands under my behind. Away we went, Cynthia leading the way with one of my heavy, brace-weighted legs under each arm. The temperature was a very moist 102 degrees. As we walked down the aisle fifty years earlier, we could scarcely have foreseen such a way of celebrating its anniversary.

Limoncocha Jungle Lodge is a primitive affair of bamboo, built on stilts as a precaution against creepy-crawlies. An anaconda had been caught underneath it a few minutes before we arrived. Divided into four-berth cubicles, the lodge had a dining area with a bar in one corner.

After lunch, Derrick announced a bird-watching cruise in a flat-bottomed boat on the large lake which we could see through a gap in the jungle. It was about a mile away and down 150 rather slippery wooden steps. Undaunted by their efforts during the approach to the lodge, the carrying team went into action again. The last few feet were particularly exciting for me as I could look down from my perch—past the narrow duckboard on which Derrick, Maurice, and Cynthia were somehow keeping their feet—to where some shoals of fish were swimming in the clear, shallow water of the lake. "Piranha," said Maurice.

As we coasted around the lake, we had an excellent view of the virgin jungle surrounding it. Experts making this circuit have counted 463 species of birds and predators; we can name but one or two. There were brightly colored macaws and members of the parrot family, as well as a very curious, large game bird called a hoatzin. Butterflies were everywhere, some of them the size of teacups. There were no signs of monkeys, and Derrick told

us that the natives have almost eradicated them with their blowpipes which can kill at a range of 140 yards.

It was too early for the *caymans* (alligators), although we did see one as it emerged from the high grass to enter the water. The rest of the party returned after dark to photograph them by flashlight, including a baby which Derrick pulled into the boat for them to examine.

We returned to the lodge in time for dinner, but I was slower than the rest in cleaning myself up. By the time Cynthia and I reached the bar, the whisky had run out and we had to salute each other in fizzy lemonade. At the end of the dinner, Derrick produced an iced cake, which he had somehow nursed all the way from Quito, a charming gesture to bring a happy anniversary to an end. Derrick told us that we had scored a double first: the first disabled person to reach the lodge, and the first couple to use it for a golden wedding anniversary celebration.

"There is complete trust between the animal world and human beings"

Jungle walks followed, then a further night in the "flotel" and a hair-raising flight back over the Andes, in thick cloud with one engine hiccupping. We had been up at 5:30am most mornings, but in the luxury of a hotel in Quito we enjoyed a brief two days of doing virtually nothing before flying 600 miles over the Pacific to the Galapagos islands.

Our plane landed on a bleak, windswept, little island on which a wooden shed and some rest rooms were the only buildings; the latter were firmly padlocked and we were told that had they been open we should not have enjoyed using them. A bus, even more rickety than the one at the Amazon airstrip, took us a couple of miles to a jetty where a *panga* (gig) awaited us.

Maurice had been replaced by Mongo, who quickly adopted the "humping" technique for carrying me. He had to perform some quite remarkable and at times dangerous acrobatics, with me clinging desperately around his neck.

Mongo and Derrick manhandled me into the *panga*, then out of it at the foot of the gangway of the yacht, the *Santa Cruz*, which was to be our home for the next eight days. Ships of that size are fairly easy for me to negotiate, as good handholds are available in most places. The main hazards are the substantial storm-sills, about six inches high in main doorways.

The routine was for the *Santa Cruz* to move from one island to another during the night. A shore visit would leave the ship at 9:30am and return about noon, when we would "up anchor" and move on again to another island. There followed another shore visit during the afternoon, getting back on board about 6:30pm. Dinner at 7:30pm and a briefing at 9:30pm (about the flora and fauna to be seen the next day) left one ready for an early bed.

In this way the main points of interest in most of the islands were covered and were amplified by Derrick and Mongo, whose knowledge was profound. Derrick had spent seven years in the islands, studying the giant tortoises for his university thesis, and he referred to the archipelago as "my islands." His delight in them made me, I suspect, even more determined than myself that I should see all that I possibly could.

The sea was far from flat and the *Santa Cruz* was unable to get close inshore, so the daily disembarkation and boarding were often hazardous. It was comparatively easy to stand behind Mongo on the gangway and clasp him about the neck, ready for him to pick the right moment to jump into the *panga*. It was far more difficult for us to be propped upright in the bobbing *panga* and for Mongo then to jump out of the boat and onto the gangway. The *panga* was often moving up and down

by ten feet or more in relation to the foot of the gangway.

Having gotten me ashore, my helpers used the humping technique in order to take me to the most inaccessible places so that I could see items of special interest. Much of the flora and fauna are unique, not only to the Galapagos but also to an individual island. Everywhere, there is complete trust between the animal world and human beings: sea-lion colonies had to be invited to stop playing "I'm the king of the castle" while we landed on their rocks; a frigate bird sat, unmoved, on a nest with a chick under her while I took a photograph at a range of about six feet.

"The evening lights threw purple shadows over the volcanoes and the clouds seemed to reflect the rippling lava below"

The government of Ecuador exercises some control of the archipelago; in theory, only 25,000 people may visit the islands in any one year (though in fact the real figure may be twice that) and the rules for visitors are very strict. Five Ecuadoreans, who broke one of the rules by bringing shells back to the yacht, were not allowed to go ashore for the next two days.

It is difficult to single out any particular landing out of about fifteen which Mongo and Derrick did with me, but our last one stands out in my memory. It was on Fernandina, by far the largest island in the archipelago, on which there are five active volcanoes. One of them erupted as recently as 1984 and we could see clearly how the lava, pouring down and cooling as it went, left great black ribs several feet high, with deep crevasses between them—rough going indeed for my intrepid team, but they never faltered.

They had to carry me for about 550 yards before we reached sand and they could pause for a rest. As we pressed on to the far end of the island we saw the unique flightless cormorants, found only on Fernandina. These birds are so free from predators that the energy for flying would be wasted and their wings have become rudimentary, useful only for balancing on land; they swim beautifully.

I had already made acquaintance with land iguanas; on Fernandina I met—at very close quarters indeed—their cousins, the marine iguanas. They live during the day in the sea, absorbing plankton. When they come ashore in the late afternoon, they lie on the rocks in a close mass, expelling a constant spray of salt water out of their system. It hangs over them like mist and can be seen from quite a distance. Both land and marine iguanas might be the inspiration for pictures of dragons, but they are quite harmless and I had them crawling over my feet as I watched them.

No account of the Galapagos islands would be complete without mention of the ubiquitous frigate birds, with their extraordinary, scarlet-chested display—the biggest chest wins the bride. We saw blue, red, and masked boobies with strikingly colored feet; charming penguins; and a rather solitary pair of pelicans, each of which had lost an eye. Pelicans pair for life, and Derrick said they must have paired in sympathy for one another!

As we left Fernandina for the *Santa Cruz*, the evening lights threw purple shadows over the volcanoes and the clouds seemed to reflect the rippling lava below. As the ship headed for Baltra Island and our rendezvous the next morning with a Boeing 727, the sunset was the most beautiful of our entire trip, putting the finishing touch to our mid-Pacific idyll.

I learned a lesson from the Galapagos experience, which had never occurred to me before. Neither Mongo nor I could wear life jackets during our antics, and with my iron-clad legs I would have sunk like a stone, probably taking Mongo with me, if he had lost his footing. In my eagerness to get ashore I allowed Mongo to risk his life in helping me. On reflection I believe that we should be very careful regarding what we allow others to do for us. I have never encountered the least prejudice, and always received an almost embarrassing degree of generosity, kindness, and understanding, on the part of both officials and fellow travelers—it would be wrong to abuse this.

LATIN AMERICA: TRAVEL NOTES

Sources of Information

No Caribbean or Latin American **tourist information offices** seem to have much information to send disabled visitors; the best way to learn anything about these countries before departure is to do plenty of reading—guidebooks, travelogs, and novels—and pick the brains of an experienced tour operator. For the Caribbean, where tourism is more developed, there are a few useful specialist organizations.
Embassy of Jamaica, 1850 "K" Street, NW, #353, Washington DC 20006; ☎202/452-0660.

Instituto Costarricense de Turismo, Plaza de la Cultura, Calle 5/Ave Central, San Jose, Costa Rica; ☎506/22-10-90.

Costa Rica National Tourist Bureau, 110 Brickell Avenue, BIV Tower #801, Miami, FL 33131, USA; ☎305/358-2150 or 800/327-7033.

Honduras Tourism Institute, Ministry of Tourism, PO Box 154-C, Tegucigalpa, Honduras; ☎504/22-4002.

Honduras Information Service, 501 Fifth Avenue, Suite 1611, New York, NY 10017; ☎212/490-0766.

Corporación de Turismo de Venezuela, Parque Central, Torre Oeste, piso 37, Caracas 1010, Venezuela; ☎2/5078815.

Consulate General of Venezuela, 2 Carlton Street, Suite 703, Toronto, ON, M5B 1J3; ☎416/477-680.

Ecuador Tourist Information, 7270 NW 12th Street, #400, PO Box 52-6532, Miami, FL 33152-6532; ☎305/477-0041 or 800/553-6673.

Caribbean Tourism Organization, 20 East 46th Street, New York, NY 10017-2417; ☎212/682-0435. Produces a list of hotels that have facilities (not defined) for guests with disabilities. The list covers over twenty Caribbean islands, including Anguilla, Aruba, the Bahamas, Barbados, Dominican Republic, Jamaica, St. Lucia, St. Martin, Trinidad and Tobago, and the US Virgin Islands. In addition, a few tourist boards can give some guidance to travelers looking for accessible accommodation, either in the form of a separate list (eg the Bahamas, Barbados, Jamaica) or by indicating appropriate hotels in a standard accommodations list (eg Puerto Rico).

Cayman Islands Department of Tourism (420 Lexington Avenue, Suite 2733, New York, NY 10170; ☎212/682-5582; offices in several other US cities, and in Canada at 234 Eglington Avenue East, Suite 306, Toronto, ON M4P 1K5; ☎416/485-1550) publishes a *Rate Sheet and Fact Folder* which indicates several "handicap accessible" hotels, and a couple of diving schools that offer this facility.

Tour Operators

There are numerous **mainstream tour operators** offering everything from sun and sea to trekking in the Andes; for the traveler with a disability it is simply a question of finding an operator with a positive and flexible attitude, and this is often made easier with the help of a sympathetic travel agent, as both Lawrence Poole and Hugh Chetwynd-Talbot confirm.

Hugh worked with a conscientious UK travel agent and linked up with a **World Wildlife Fund** tour group in Quito; he was delighted with the practical assistance given by group leader and guides. For more information on the WWF vacation program contact them at 1250 24th Street, NW, Washington DC 20037; ☎202/293-4800.

Lawrence speaks highly of Janine Fafard, a "wonderfully organized and knowledgeable resource person who can organize any sort of Costa Rican vacation and has an affinity for the accessibility needs of the disabled traveler." Janine is trilingual and will happily make reservations anywhere in the country; she "visits every nook and cranny she recommends." Based in San Jose, Janine's tourist booking service is called **Rainbow Connections** (☎506/40-73-25, voice or fax) but she also works with *Panorama Tours* (☎506/33-02-33), a big Canadian operator.

Cambio C.A. can help you plan Honduran eco-adventures, including exploration trips to Copán, canoeing, hiking, or biking trips, and treks into rain and cloud forests. This operator is located in the *Gran Hotel Sula*, San Pedro Sula; ☎504/44-40-44; fax 504/44-40-45.

Expediciones Manu (Procuradores 50, PO Box 606, Cusco, Peru; ☎84/22-66-71 or 23-99-74; fax 84/23-67-06) offers several tours of the

CARIBBEAN: TRAVEL NOTES

Manu National Park in southeastern Peru, varying in length from five to nine days, some of which are said to be accessible to people with disabilities—they have little actual experience of disabled travelers, but a positive and flexible attitude and are keen not to exclude anyone. Trips into the rainforest are led by experienced guides (main working languages English, Spanish, and German). The tour programs make mouthwatering reading for anyone with an interest in the wildlife and flora of the region.

People with **specific medical requirements**, including those who require continuous oxygen or hemodialysis treatments on an ambulatory basis, and those who have chronic heart conditions or are convalescing from heart surgery, may wish to investigate the range of package vacations offered by *TLC* (*Tomorrow's Level of Care*; see *Directory*, p.599), a network of health professionals providing assistance to travelers visiting **Barbados**.

For anyone wanting to spend their vacations doing something a little different, there are a few organizations offering some interesting possibilities. Those who'd like to take part in **Mobility International USA**'s exchange program with Central American countries such as Costa Rica and Mexico should contact *MIUSA* at their headquarters in Oregon (see p.544).

Earthwatch (see Travel, Tours, and Cruises *Travel Notes*, p.547) has a good record of accepting volunteers with disabilities on their field research projects, and offers some fairly demanding expeditions involving scientific research work and conservation; projects in this part of the world have included helping to save leatherback turtles in the Caribbean, studying coral reefs in Belize, and working in the rainforests of Brazil and Costa Rica.

Operation Raleigh conservation, community, and adventure projects (see Australia and New Zealand, p.472) are open to anyone aged 17 to 25 who can swim and speak some English. Examples of projects in Latin America include setting up a four-year study of seismic acitivity and environmental change in southern Chile, and community work in Panama and Chile involving the building of 17 clinics, 20 schools, and 34 bridges.

Getting There

Greg Baker took a charter flight from Chicago to Montego Bay, **Jamaica**; the fare for spring 1992 was $367. *Air Jamaica* and *American Airlines* fly from Miami to Kingston and Montego Bay, *Northwest* from Tampa, Florida, to Montego Bay, and *Air Canada* direct to Kingston and Montego Bay from Toronto. The **Caribbean** is generally well served by inexpensive charters as well as by the major Canadian and US airlines, and flying times, especially from the Eastern seaboard, are short enough for most travelers to survive cramped seating and inaccessible rest rooms. Facilities at airports are variable, with some fairly rough and ready arrangements for boarding and deplaning. **Cruising** can also be a relaxing, if expensive, way to discover the Caribbean islands; there are several reasonably accessible vessels sailing these waters (see "Travel, Tours, and Cruises").

Lawrence Poole advises that there are two charter companies (*AirTransat* during the high season and *Nationair* year round) flying out of Montréal to San Jose, **Costa Rica**. Many Canadian carriers and US airlines offer connections through Miami or New Orleans. Other possibilities include *Delta* from Dallas Fort Worth, and *Northwest* from Detroit and Minneapolis. Juan Santamaria airport in San Jose is totally accessible.

For **Honduras** most connections are through Miami, from where *TAM* and *Taca* fly daily to Tegucigalpa. *Lacsa* and *American Airlines* fly several times a week from New York and *Continental* from Houston. There are no facilities for wheelchair users at Honduran airports.

Sue Kelley was pleased with service and legroom aboard her *Viasa* flight to Caracas, **Venezuela**; this airline will seat disabled passengers near the rest rooms but does not carry aisle chairs. *Viasa* flies to Caracas out of Toronto, New York, Miami, and Houston. *United* flies direct to Caracas out of New York and Miami; *American* flies out of Miami. A wheelchair service is available at Caracas airport.

The national airline of **Ecuador**, *Ecuatoriana*, flies to Quito and Guayaquil from New York, Miami, Los Angeles, and Chicago. Several other South American airlines fly out of

LATIN AMERICA: TRAVEL NOTES

Miami to Guayaquil; *SAETA* also flies to Quito. *Continental* flies to Guayaquil from Houston via Panama City. *American* flies from Miami into Quito. Facilities at airports are basic.

Transport

Domestic **flights** are probably the smoothest way to cover any sort of distance; facilities at airports usually consist of no more than a manual lifting service for boarding and exiting the plane, but at least there is plenty of help available, and the flight might be slightly more comfortable, quicker, and safer than traveling along rough and dusty roads. In Costa Rica, *Sansa* (the domestic airline) flies to every corner of the country for between $10 and $20, one way. An "AirTaxi" can be hired for about $150, to fly you just about anywhere; since the country is very mountainous, a 20-minute flight often replaces a 4- or 5-hour drive along rough roads. In Honduras five domestic airlines fly from Tegucigalpa, San Pedro Sula, and La Ceiba to many smaller communities and to the Bay Islands; don't expect any wheelchair facilities. In Venezuela the state capitals and other major cities, as well as the Caribbean isles, are served by *Aeropostal* and *Avensa*. Domestic flights in Ecuador are handled by *TAME*, *SAETA*, and *SAN* (also to the Galapagos).

Cross-continent, self-drive travel is not for the faint-hearted or the non-Spanish/Portuguese speaker: mountains, rainforest, swamps, grasslands, or parched plains offer a formidable choice of terrain. But **car or jeep rental** is good for exploring the more populated regions, as Sue Kelley discovered in the Venezuelan island of Margarita. Lawrence Poole reports that road travel is safe in Costa Rica, and car or jeep rentals are readily available (from $300 per week); traffic in the main cities and towns is easy to negotiate. Cars can be rented from most major centers in Honduras for similar prices, but be warned that Honduran police prey on rental drivers and will be very sticky over any infraction—such as having your wheels over the white line at a stop sign—in order to extract some sort of fine.

Traffic congestion in many Latin American cities is legendary, and it's often wise to switch to **taxis** for getting around. Wheelchairs are easily stowed in the trunk, and rates are low. In Costa Rica taxi fares average about $4 per hour ($10 from the airport to most hotels). In Honduras rates of between $0.50 and $2 per person can be negotiated to take you from one end of most towns to the other; for longer distances, rates should be about $1.50 to $2 per hour.

Buses are often used for airport transfers or organized tours; hydraulic lifts and tie-downs are unheard of, and most people with limited mobility will need assistance. Long-distance buses will almost invariably be crowded and uncomfortable, with few concessions to those who can't battle their way to a seat: but if you can manage them, they're very much part of the Latin American experience. In general they run just about everywhere, are extremely cheap, and assistance can easily be negotiated

Train travel is also possible with help, and there are some spectacular rides through fabulous scenery, but it's not the easiest or most reliable way to get around. That said, we've had a few reports of successful journeys—a large group of youngsters with disabilities traveled by Peruvian train from Machu Picchu to Cuzco, followed by a 12-hour journey to Juliaca in 1988, and a Swedish wheelchair user reports no problems with boarding the train in her chair and traveling from Argentina to Paraguay. It's a possibility for the more adventurous traveler, but guard your belongings on the trains: in Peru especially they're notorious for robberies.

Many forms of **waterborne transport** are available, from dugouts to sleek hydrofoils. Again there are no concessions to disabled passengers: muddy banks to scramble down, steep flights of stairs between decks, and delicate balancing acts required for boarding and disembarking are just a few of the hazards, but strong companions and willing crew members seem to make up for the deficiencies in accessibility.

Accommodation

The general lack of information for disabled travelers, combined with the difficulties of attempting to make independent reservations—let alone inquiries about steps and door widths—at any but the big international

CARIBBEAN: TRAVEL NOTES

hotels, suggests that it might be best to adopt Nic Fleming's approach to finding accessible accommodation (see p.550): assume that all problems can be solved on the spot, and simply turn up armed with a positive attitude.

This certainly worked for Sue Kelley in **Venezuela**; Sue stayed at the *Hotel Margarita Concorde* (Avenida Raúl Leoni, Bahía El Morro, Porlamar, Nueva Esparta, Isla de Margarita; ☎95/613333), where all amenities, including the beach, were fully accessible.

In contrast, although nothing defeated him, Hugh Chetwynd-Talbot's accommodation in **Ecuador** was far from ideal: food, cabin, and bar each on separate decks on the *Orellana Flotel*, linked by nearly vertical ladders, and no gangway for boarding; *Limoncocha Jungle Lodge* built on stilts; six-inch storm-sills in the doorways on board the *Santa Cruz*.

Lawrence Poole searched out accommodation as he went along and stayed at the following hotels in **Costa Rica** (room rates quoted in US dollars, double occupancy): *Hotel Irazu*, San Jose (☎32-48-11; $50–60); *Albergue Mirador Pochotel*, Turrialba (☎56-01-11; $20–25); *Cabinas Palmar*, Cahuita (☎58-15-15 ext. 243; $12–20); *Hotel Punta Cocles*, Puerto Viejo (☎34-03-06; $50–60); *Hotel Matama*, Limón (☎58-11-23 or 58-19-19; $50–60); *Auberge Pelican*, Estrillos Este (contact via fax in Parrita: 77-91-08; $25–30); *Hotel de la Montaña*, Monteverde (☎61-18-46; $50 per person, three meals included); *Hotel Iguanazul*, Playa Junquillal (☎32-14-23; $50–60); *Bahia Flamingo Hotel*, Playa Potrera, Bahia Flamingo (☎68-09-76; $40–50); *Hotel El Lugar*, Tilarán (☎69-57-11; $25–30). Lawrence suggests that these accommodations make a good beginning if you're planning a trip, but there are hundreds more—little inns and out-of-the-way cabins, as well as a few major hotels; tourism is now the second major industry and rooms abound. While Lawrence has never encountered anything specifically accessible, he's rarely met anything that was absolutely impossible. One piece of advice regarding booking: Costa Ricans enjoy 17 legal holidays per year (aside from annual vacations) and love to travel within their own country so if planning a visit between Christmas and New Year, or during Semana

Santa (the week before Easter) reserve well in advance.

Tourism is less well developed in **Honduras**. Major hotels include the *Honduras Maya* (☎504/32-31-91) in Tegucigalpa; the *Partenon Beach* (☎504/43-04-04) in La Ceiba; the *Gran Hotel Sula* (☎504/52-99-99) in San Pedro Sula; and *Anthony's Key Resort* (☎504/45-11-40) in Roatán (Bay Islands).

If you want to be sure of a reasonably accessible room, or at least to have a couple of definite reservations around which to work a more casual itinerary, the *Best Western*, *Hilton*, *Holiday Inn*, *Inter-Continental*, and *Ramada* **hotel chains** have some properties in Latin America and the Caribbean, and a pretty good record on accessibility. The *Best Western*, *Holiday Inn*, and *Ramada* directories use the wheelchair symbol to indicate availability of rooms with facilities for guests with disabilities. The *Hyatt* chain is reported to be carrying out necessary alterations to make its Caribbean properties (Puerto Rico, Cayman Islands, Aruba, and St. John, US Virgin Islands) accessible as well as its US hotels.

A good **travel agent** should have access to the *Caribbean Hotel Association*'s "Gold Book," which covers Central America as well as uses the bold "**H**" symbol to indicate hotels that have wheelchair-accessible facilities. The agent should also be prepared to inquire in more detail, and obtain specific information from individual hotels as necessary.

It's worth considering **villa accommodation** for a stay-put vacation, for the reasons outlined by Greg Baker. Greg stayed at *Villa Terra Nova*, where rates run from $1500 to $3000 depending on the season and number of people in the party. It is customary to leave a gratuity for the house staff—between $4 and $10 per guest per day, depending on the number of people in the party. For specific information on *Terra Nova* and more general information on Mammee Bay villas, contact Naomi Gallatin, 11 Sturges Common, Westport, CT 06880; ☎203/255-1997.

Access and Facilities

Briefly, access to public transportation, government buildings and offices, major museums,

LATIN AMERICA: TRAVEL NOTES

churches or cathedrals, and many tourist attractions, is poor and there are no special facilities for disabled people. The terrain poses more problems, everywhere from busy street to idyllic beach—there are no easy answers to soft sand, and roads and sidewalks in the region suffer from the effects of devastating hurricanes and earthquakes as well as simple lack of maintenance. A blind traveler, Mary Allgire describes getting around San Jose, Costa Rica: "Negotiating the streets of San Jose with its three-foot curbs and tumultuous traffic certainly was a challenge! My fears were not alleviated significantly when I was informed that if somebody becomes disabled because of an injury sustained in a car accident the driver of the car is held responsible for all of your needs for the rest of your life!"

Latin America and the Caribbean cover a vast area, though, and it is inaccurate to dismiss all of every country as inaccessible. In Jamaica Greg Baker managed to gain access to the essentials of life—beach, ocean, beach pavilion, and villa—with a companion and a friendly local or two. The facilities encountered by Sue Kelley at her Venezuelan hotel and by Lawrence Poole at most of his accommodations were perfectly adequate, and Lawrence even encountered the international access symbol in the rainforest! He also points out that the climate lends itself to outdoor living, so that access to attractions, restaurants, bars, etc, is often relatively easy. Of course there are some formidable obstacles, and these are not always negotiable, but all our contributors had memorable and successful vacations, lending weight to the view that anything is possible, given the right attitude, and plenty of help from passersby.

The fact remains that many of these countries are in the "developing world" and political priorities have not yet included physical access. There is generally little interest, at government level or among the tourist authorities, in providing access to all amenities, rest rooms for disabled people, parking for disabled drivers—or in compiling information on the subject. However, if Sue Kelley's theory is correct, and the Venezuelan authorities have recognized the economic sense of attracting *all* tourists to Porlamar's center, then there may be hope for the rest of Latin America, and the Caribbean, particularly in countries that are struggling with crippling national debts and high inflation, where tourism promises prosperity.

The aims must be to allow people with disabilities greater independence, and to provide easy access not only to the shopping malls and city centers, but also to the wild places. For disabled travelers this is the responsibility of US and Canadian tour companies as well as the governments of the countries they are visiting: while the difficulties may be pointed out so that they are appreciated by intending travelers, it is discriminatory and defeatist to suggest that all travelers with disabilities should choose an easier, more accessible destination. It would be good to see the infectious enthusiasm of our contributors picked up by a few more mainstream travel agents and tour companies.

Health and Insurance

The health worries in Latin America seem to be predominantly the effects of high altitude and the weird and wonderful insect life—as well, of course, as Montezuma's Revenge. But a bit of common sense, advice from Richard Dawood (see *Books*), and a good guidebook should dispel the myths and ensure adequate preparation. Carry insect repellent and anti-diarrhea treatment as well as your usual drugs. Off the beaten track and in countries where hospitals are few and far between (in Honduras, for example, they are only to be found in larger towns) it's wise to carry a first aid kit (see *Practicalities*, p..569)

Anti-malaria pills are recommended in Central America and parts of South America, but with the rise of resistant malarial parasites in Latin America precautions such as avoiding stagnant water, regular application of insect repellent, use of mosquito nets in certain areas such as the coastal region of Honduras, and vigilance around dusk when mosquitoes like to bite, are sensible. However, the risks of contracting malaria should not be overstated—they are much less for visitors to Latin America than for travelers in other parts of the world, such as tropical Africa.

CARIBBEAN: TRAVEL NOTES

If visiting **high-altitude locations** pregnant women and those with very high blood pressure, or with heart or respiratory problems, should consult their doctors. For everyone else the best precaution is to ascend slowly, spending a few days at each level before moving on. At high altitudes you'll need suntan lotion, hat, and effective sunglasses during the day and warm clothes at night.

It's advisable to stick to **bottled water** in many parts of Latin America. Water is safe to drink from any faucet in Costa Rica, but bottled water is recommended on the Caribbean side due to the disruption of services after the 1991 earthquake. Drink bottled water in Honduras. Running water is safe in Quito, Guayaquil, and Cuenca, but elsewhere in Ecuador you should drink bottled water. In general, take local advice, and if in doubt, don't drink it: hotels should always supply drinking water.

There are well-trained, English-speaking doctors in most countries of Latin America and the Caribbean, and good pharmacists in all big cities. Costa Rica holds first place in Latin America for their medical services, and good clinics and hospitals are available everywhere. Medical care facilities are widely available in the more developed areas of the Caribbean such as Barbados, Bahamas, and Jamaica.

Useful Contacts

In **Costa Rica**, "Edmont" and Edgar Montoya can supply disabled travelers with anything they need, including hand controls installed on a rental car (even a four-wheel, standard drive). Edgar speaks fluent English and can be reached on his cellular phone, ☎29-26-32 (wait for beep and dial 292 on a touch-tone phone).

Books

Travelers' Health, by Richard Dawood (Oxford University Press), has a section on the effects of altitude as well as many other useful chapters covering every possible eventuality.

In the Realms of Gold (Michael Joseph) is written by wheelchair traveler and food critic, Quentin Crewe.

The Real Guides to Mexico, Guatemala and Belize, Brazil, and Peru are excellent general guides: try also the *Central American Handbook*, *South American Handbook*, and *Caribbean Handbook*.

Greg Baker recommends *Traditional Jamaican Cookery*, by Norma Benghiat (Penguin); *Marcus Garvey and the Vision of Africa*, by John Henrik Clark (Random House); and *Catch a Fire: The Life of Bob Marley* (Holt, Rinehart, Winston).

Lawrence Poole recommends *The New Key to Costa Rica*, by Beatrice Blake (Publications in English, distributed by Bookpeople in the US, Ulysse in Canada); *The Tico Times*, a weekly English newspaper in Costa Rica (☎506/22-00-40); and *Backpacking in Mexico and Central America*, by Hilary Bradt (Bradt Enterprises, Cambridge, MA).

TELEPHONE CODES:

From the US and Canada dial 011 (international code) and then 1809 for Jamaica, 506 for Costa Rica, 504 for Honduras, 58 for Venezuela, and 593 for Ecuador.

PART THREE

NORTHERN EUROPE

Introduction

T he whole of northern Europe is covered in this section, along with one account of a trip to the western edge of the Commonwealth of Independent States (formerly the Soviet Union). Although the differences may soon start to fade, there is still a huge gulf between Eastern and Western Europe as far as facilities for disabled travelers go, and conditions for many disabled Eastern Europeans are grim.

Many of our contributors find that **independent travel**, with its advantages of flexibility and freedom to set the pace and to choose accommodation and routes, is the only way to go (see *Practicalities*, p.562), and it's certainly feasible in Europe. But the idea of a **package deal** shouldn't be completely dismissed, particularly for first-time visitors or for anyone with a very tight budget. If you're new to a country you might find that spending the first week letting someone else do the organizing gives you confidence to explore on your own for the rest of the vacation; and tour operators and airlines can often negotiate more competitive rates than individual travelers. This is particularly true of car rental, which is expensive in Europe but much cheaper when booked in advance—if you need hand controls you'll have to give advance warning in any case.

Disabled travelers should in theory be able to choose any of the hundreds of operators offering vacations in Europe—the options are too numerous to list, so only those used or recommended by contributors are mentioned in the *Travel Notes*. The potential pitfalls of booking with an operator who doesn't specialize in travel for disabled people can be minimized by following the guidelines given in the *Practicalities* (p.559).

Air travelers from North America to Europe are spoiled for choice: dozens of airlines fly to the major European cities, although there are fewer options for Eastern Europe. A **transatlantic flight** for the passenger with a disability is the same as any long-haul flight—a question of surviving uncomfortable seating and cramped, and to some people inaccessible, rest room facilities (see *Practicalities*, p.572). Choosing an airline usually entails finding one that allows the best level of comfort given your own particular requirements, at the lowest possible price.

Check Sunday newspaper travel sections or—perhaps the safest option—consult a good, preferably tried and tested, travel agent to find the best deals; you can also try discount flight specialists, travel clubs, or consolidators—see *Directory*, p.595. The **cheapest flights** generally leave from the airline's "hub" cities—New York, Atlanta, Dallas, Chicago, Los Angeles, San Francisco, Seattle, Vancouver, Toronto, and Montréal are the main ones—and these tend to be nonstop, which avoids the hassle of plane changes. London, Paris, and Amsterdam, followed closely by Frankfurt, Milan, and Rome, are the cheapest "gateway" cities into Europe.

Reports of **domestic air travel** in northern Europe have been generally optimistic. But there are some gripes, in the main resulting from airport officials who insist on channeling every disabled passenger through exactly the same "special" handling procedure. Boarding and disembarking may have to be performed without lifting vehicles or air-bridges because of the size of the aircraft and lack of facilities at regional airports. If the human lifting service is well trained and prepared to adopt the carrying technique that best suits each passenger, this need not cause problems, but for those who cannot maintain their posture it can be an unpleasant experience.

There's more **money** in northern and western Europe than in the eastern and Mediterranean countries, and therefore the changes required to improve access should be affordable, but awareness of the requirements of disabled people, and willingness to respond, remain low in the travel industry all over Europe, and change comes slowly and almost grudgingly. In some areas, such as **access to public buildings**, **tourist attractions**, **and transport**, Europe has a long way to go to catch up with North America.

In Europe the age of the building often works against attempts to make it accessible to wheelchair users. It is perhaps unfair to compare the totally accessible Metrorail in Washington DC with the London Underground. But improving access, even in old buildings and antiquated transport systems, does not have to involve unsightly alterations or be prohibitively expensive. The barriers to change on London's buses, as Stephen Hunt explains (p.168), usually have more to do with attitude than finance. In Sweden, Gripsholm Castle in Mariefred, which dates back to the sixteenth century, has been made fully accessible by the purchase of a stair-climbing wheelchair—much cheaper than an elevator and causing no damage to the fabric of the building.

There *are* accessible **metro systems** in northern Europe, but many partially accessible systems are spoiled by fiercely sprung gates, long distances to cover at interchanges, difficult door handles on trains, no textured surfaces for blind passengers, no visible monitors for those with hearing disabilities. There is still much to be done. The cheapest form of transport in cities—the **bus**—remains largely inaccessible. On the **trains**, it's not good enough to plan new rolling stock for the Nineties that makes only partial provision for some disabled passengers; wheelchair users should be given the choice to remain in their chairs or transfer to a seat, and they must be given independent access to the train and to on-board toilets. Specialist taxi or van services for disabled people cannot be a substitute for a totally accessible public transit system unless they provide a full, scheduled service covering the entire network.

The **ferry companies** operating routes between continental Europe and Britain, Ireland, or Scandinavia have incorporated facilities for disabled passengers on their newer ships. *Sealink Stena Line*, *P&O*, and *Brittany Ferries* are singled out for praise. Many people make the crossings with their cars or camper vans (RVs), but the generous fare reductions available to members of British disabled drivers' motoring organizations are not applicable to those traveling in rented vehicles.

Driving conditions in the north of Europe are reasonable and main roads generally well maintained, but availability of rental cars with hand controls is poor. There are no official reciprocal parking arrangements for holders of disabled drivers' parking permits, but it's always worth carrying your permit as local police may make some concessions, and it will almost always be recognized in privately owned parking lots. The number of highway service stations with accessible facilities is on the increase; several countries supply lists of them, making route planning easier. On minor roads, however, it is often difficult to find any rest rooms, let alone wheelchair-accessible ones.

Accommodation, more often than not, is far from totally accessible, but the situation is not impossible and it's getting better. We received many accounts from people who traveled through Europe without pre-booking (see also *Practicalities*, "Sleeping"). However, there is much confusion over the use of the wheelchair symbol in hotel lists or guidebooks, and a rather cavalier over-use of the phrase "clients must check details of accessibility with the hotel before booking," or words to that effect.

The amount of **information** which is out of date is also disturbing—material published in the early Eighties is still sent out by tourist boards. It's almost as though the International Year of the Disabled (1981) spurred a few energetic groups into action and they've now lost enthusiasm—or their source of finance. This is a pity because outdated information can be worse than no information.

Ireland

Looking for Literary Ireland

Greg Baker teaches high school English at The Latin School of Chicago. He is an SCI quad, independent, with good hand and arm movement, and he travels with an able-bodied companion.

"May the road rise up to greet you . . ." This Irish line flashes through my mind as I stare at the sidewalk a few inches from my eyes. I'm still in my wheelchair but just barely, my precipitous flight toward an even closer greeting from the road checked by my outflung arms. I balance precariously until Gail is able to get the brakes on, grab my backpack, and pull me back to a sitting position. A close call but nothing extraordinary: my front caster had caught a crack in the sidewalk while I was noting the charms of the Georgian houses around Merrion Square in Dublin. We start on our way again, but it takes only a couple of bumpy inches to announce the fact that this was no ordinary brush with the dangers of forward momentum. The rubber on the suspect front wheel has declared a hasty divorce from the wheelrim.

My unruly mood harmonizes not at all with the pleasant cool of the Dublin evening. Well, thinks I, just another unexpected moment in a day full of more or less unpleasant surprises. But by then we should have known that in Ireland the unsought is what you're most apt to find.

We had gone to seek the literary Ireland of Joyce and Yeats by enrolling in a seminar on Joyce's *Ulysses*. This was one of the offerings of a Massachusetts-based outfit, *The Humanities Institute*, which runs summer programs in Oxford, Edinburgh, Dublin, and, more recently, Athens. The three-week course at Trinity College was a natural for me as a teacher of *Ulysses*, and for Gail as a Gaelic descendant, no doubt, of Queen Maeve.

Our search had begun a week before the seminar started when we drove from the Shannon airport up to Galway. We hunted down the haunts of Nora Barnacle, Joyce's future wife, looked for the cemetery at Oughterard, where Michael Furey is buried in *The Dead*, explored the beautiful coast and rugged mountains of Connemara, and visited Lady Gregory's Coole Park and Yeats' tower at Thor Ballylee before driving into Dublin.

Our lodging in town was an accessible room (although the ramp to the front door was too steep) in an eighteenth-century dormitory at Trinity that is reputed to have been the domicile of the young Jonathan Swift. The class met Monday through Thursday mornings, leaving us the afternoons free to search out pub music, the best Guinness, sidewalk produce markets, hallowed spots of Irish history, and the settings of *Ulysses*. Joyce once claimed that if Dublin were destroyed, it could be recreated to the smallest detail from his writings. Nelson's Pillar, of course, was blown up by the IRA in 1966 and urban renewal has altered parts of the city, but we found Joyce's "dear dirty Dublin" still recognizable from his writings—so much that we had anticipated and visualized, but each day was punctuated by one surprise after another.

"Two young British soldiers in camouflage, automatic weapons in hands"

Most of our Dublin wanderings were done, and comfortably so, on foot/wheel, but on the two weekends we loaded the rental car and headed for different corners of the island. The first one we spent touring the southeast: the Wicklow mountains; the valley of Glendalough; Norman castles; and Waterford. The next Thursday we traveled to the northwest, to Donegal and Yeats country: his grave at the little church in Drumcliff under brooding Ben Bulben; a mural on the side of a building in Sligo depicting ten freshly painted crosses (for the martyrs of the Easter Rising) and the motto "We remember 1916"; the lake at Inisfree; and Queen Maeve's cairn, a huge stone barrow atop a major prominence from which the druids must have thought

they could see the whole world; the mysterious lavender gloom giving up its last ghostly twilight from the mirrored surface of the Bay of Donegal at midnight.

"None of our classmates had believed our border tales, which admittedly were taking on mythic proportions"

A Celtic idyll? Well, yes—except for the inevitable Irish surprises: the thumpa-thumpa of a band shaking our room with the merriment of wedding receptions well into *both* nights in our Donegal hotel; or finding ourselves in a line of halted autos in the one-street village of Glencolmkille, stopped by the Garda before the church in deference to a funeral procession which wasn't due to start for a half hour; or the more serious surprise as we motored back to Dublin through Northern Ireland.

Near the border south of Enniskillen, the road dipped and swept around a blind curve to reveal two young British soldiers in camouflage, automatic weapons in hands at a well-fortified checkpoint. Scanning our papers and listening to Gail's composed but tense explanation of our stay in Dublin, the young fellow sipped his soup out of a canteen and relaxed his grip on the gun a bit, turning it away from us (but I could see he was covered by a rifle barrel and a pair of eyes within the bunker). He looked at us pointedly and said, "At least they aren't shooting at you down there," and waved us on.

So, thinks I to myself, thinks I in Merrion Square, as I stare at the naked wheelrim beneath me, perhaps our weekend in the wild northwest is the cause of our rocky, and last, Monday in Dublin. That morning none of our classmates had believed our border tales, which admittedly were taking on mythic proportions. Later, none of the sweaters fit me at the Dublin Woollen Company. Finally, our trip to

Mulligan's on Poolbeg Street, a famous traditional pub, for the "best pint of Guinness in Dublin," had started promisingly enough despite the raised eyebrows when we entered—raised less at the sight of my wheelchair than at the presence of a woman in the pub proper (there is a connected room next door for "mixed company"). But the stout was fine, and the bare wood floors and aged booths quietly urged us to do some journal writing.

"The iron rule of Irish etiquette is that you always stand your round"

Suddenly I felt my chair dragged backward, brakes on, coming to rest next to the great hulk of the man who had pulled me there without rising from his small table. This sloshed old fellow with bulbous red nose and slurred speech revealed to us his worship of our compatriot, golfing great Jack Nicklaus, even pulling out a well-worn photo of him and a young Jack at an Irish tournament in the mid-1960s. He then began worrying that Gail, who had been studiously ignoring this encounter by continuing to write in her journal, was copying down his speech, which had become a barely intelligible stream of thick brogue. As it circled repetitiously around the mysteries of the sports world, I could think only of the "queer old josser" who accosts the young narrator in Joyce's story, *An Encounter*. Tennis was his next topic, and Gail had become "Virginia Wade." As I wondered if we were about to be shown another smudged photograph, I glanced around the room and, seeing a few knowing smiles watching us, decided that we were surely not his first victims.

When I turned back to the table, four new pints had magically appeared. A dilemma: we had to leave in order to eat dinner and make it to the theater by eight; but the iron rule of Irish etiquette is that you always stand your round. How could we drink the pints before us,

then reciprocate the gesture and still make the performance (or even find our way back to Trinity)? And why were there four glasses? Had the old josser bought them? Was one of the pub regulars showing us true Irish hospitality, or exercising some sly humor at the expense of the tourists? Feeling like Odysseus confronting the twin dangers of Scylla and Charybdis, we unheroically considered the fact that we were to leave Dublin in three days, then prudently put away our journals, left a careless number of pound notes scattered on the table amid the four proud pints, and slunk guiltily out the door.

So really, my bruised palms and wrecked caster are all of a thematic piece on this "Moansday," as Joyce would've called it. How appropriate that the night's play is Samuel Beckett's masterpiece of existential despair, *Waiting for Godot*. Before I can be consumed by my angst, however, Gail grabs the wayward tire and wrestles it back onto the rim, and we race the last couple of blocks to the Focus Theatre, located on an alley off of Pembroke Street.

"I'll have to be picked up out of my chair, carried up the short flight of stairs, and plunked into a seat"

Our ill luck continues at this tiny spot, where we find that there isn't a glimmer of hope of getting a wheelchair into the cramped space. I'll have to be picked up out of my chair, carried up the short flight of stairs, and plunked into a seat. A fellow in the box office wearing a red leather tie and a thin, intense man with receding fair hair are all-too-optimistic, it seems to me; they won't hear of us not seeing the play. Destiny seems quite sure of herself here so I go with the flow. The interior of the theater is unprepossessing: four rows of fifteen seats each; a bare stage but for the solitary scrawny tree from which Estragon will soon propose hanging himself. Not very promising; a sidelight to the literary wonders we have already experienced.

"Peter seems inordinately pleased that a Yank could possess this piece of trivia and insists on buying us pints apiece at O'Hourihan's on Leeson Street"

But we're in for a surprise, the most rewarding one of the trip. The production is a revelation, far removed from the ponderous, self-conscious versions of the play we're familiar with. The actors are skilled vaudevillians, their physical movements hilariously reflecting dreams dashed and hopes restored. Their lines, unmoving on the page, fall into the natural rhythms of Beckett's native Dublin; the playwright, instead of being one among many in an anthology of European theater (he originally wrote the play in French), becomes unmistakably a writer with a sense of Irish place and tradition. Indeed, many lines suddenly echo in stark outline central scenes from *Ulysses*, both comedically and politically. The latter theme is underlined in the character of the whip-wielding Pozzo, here played as an English gentleman in riding boots. Exciting, funny, moving—an extraordinary and unexpected evening of theater.

After the house empties and I'm lugged out to my chair in the alley, the intense fellow with the resonant north Dublin accent introduces himself as Peter Sheridan, director of this wonderful production. We excitedly try to communicate our enthusiasm for the performance and the epiphanies into Beckett—about whom I know little— it has just provided. My ransacked memory, however, does yield one scholarly tidbit: Beckett translated the play from French into English himself. Peter seems inordinately pleased that a Yank could possess this piece of trivia and insists on buying us pints apiece at O'Hourihan's on Leeson Street.

We go, we drink, we talk. He stands the first round and tells us about living in Chicago and going to Wrigley Field in 1972, about chance encounters with Blackfoot Indians. We tell him about our border experience, was that yesterday? He tells us about the months he spent living in the North, fasting and writing his play, *Diary of a Hunger Striker*. We stand our round and tell him about our wheelchair experiences in Dublin. He tells us about his paralyzed childhood neighbor, author Christy Brown, whose autobiographical works, *Down All the Days* and *My Left Foot*, recount his amazing life in working-class Dublin. (Peter's brother Jim made the latter book into an award-winning film in 1989.)

Stories and tales galore. All of us lose track of rounds. We bemoan the fact that we're leaving the city on Thursday and Ireland the following Monday. He invites us to dinner on Wednesday with his wife, Sheila. The publican calls, "Time, gentlemen," despite the fact that at least half the pub's customers are female. Hearing this traditional last call and having learned our lesson earlier in the day, we square things by ordering one more, at this point superfluous, round. Peter and I trade Joyce's voices from the Cyclops episode:

"Could you make a hole in another pint, Terry?"

"Can a swim duck?"

Gail and I made it back safely to Trinity that evening. Two nights later Peter introduced us to Sheila— gracious, warm, funny, and like her husband thoroughly generous and without pretension. Our hours together that night were just as fascinating and wonderful as our first meeting with Peter, when Irish literature in the unanticipated form of Samuel Beckett had brought us together somehow. And when we took off from Shannon a few days later we knew we had done a good job of finding Joyce and Yeats just as we had hoped, but our friendship with the Sheridans, which endures to this day, was the Irish surprise we value most.

Sidetracked in Ireland

As a result of a combination of achondroplasia and restricted growth syndrome, Annie Delin is not much more than three feet tall. The practical effects of this are that she cannot walk very far or stand for long. Although she doesn't use a wheelchair ordinarily she takes a child's stroller when she travels, and a companion to push it. In August 1989 she went with three friends to Ireland.

When I told people my summer vacation was to be in Ireland, a particular tone of caressing warmth came into the voices of those who'd already been. "Oh, you'll love it," they all said.

Nevertheless, we went away with a certain set of ideas in our heads. Ireland would be beautiful and green. The west coast would have cliffs and wildlife—it would be a little like Wales or the wild parts of Scotland. Only at the last minute did we remember to take our passports. This was, after all, a foreign country. Until we disembarked at Dun Laoghaire, it hadn't entered our heads how foreign somewhere as close as Ireland might be. It's almost England, isn't it? They speak the same language, share our history, have the same climate.

By the end of a week, we found that we were fundamentally wrong on all those counts. No English person could use the language in such an unashamedly poetic way—we could only guess that the Gaelic language, spoken for preference in most of the places we visited, must be as beautiful. Our history is shared only because we rode roughshod over their own history to impose ours onto it, but the countryside speaks of a different past, of traditions and people.

And the climate is the most surprising part. It rains, which makes Ireland green, and in the mountains the mists are ever present, but the warmth of the air on wet and dry days encourages yucca trees to reach a height of thirty feet in gardens all over the country. On the Dingle Peninsula the hedgerows are of shocking pink fuschia flowers, and the heather and gorse on the moors form a startling carpet of purple and gold. If rain alone does this, why does it only happen in Ireland?

Four of us traveled together, jammed into one car with luggage and two tents, a box of foodstuffs and a portable gas stove. My concessions to essential comfort (to reduce the risks of stiff joints and rheumatism) were an air-bed, which attracted universal contempt because the foot pump was slow and had to be operated by everyone except me, a stool to sit on, and a quantity of warm clothes, even though it was August.

We thought of taking my wheelchair in case we needed to cover distances that I couldn't walk, but I decided against it for reasons of space and self-image. We could always use the car, even if only for short hops around towns, from one parking space to another. Traveling with three girlfriends who knew me well, I didn't need to feel worried about stating my requirements forcefully if I was too tired or stiff to walk.

"We went into Kelly's Bar and tried Irish Guinness. Everything they say is true"

Camping isn't the ideal style of accommodation if sitting in the damp, constantly bending down, or wriggling around trying to get dressed in a two-person tent are likely to aggravate your physical problems. On the other hand, how can you beat sitting on a cliff top, swaddled in sleeping bags and sweaters, drinking the contents of a three-liter wine-box and then simply rolling into the tent? The sea air blows in and the waves still whisper as you fall into drunken sleep. You couldn't do it in a warm, dry Bed & Breakfast.

The cliff top was our first night's camp, near the tiny town of Wicklow. We had crossed from Holyhead on a ferry which arrived at 6:30am (for cheaper tickets). The amazingly Mediterranean look of Dun Laoghaire woke us up for a bit, but we still needed to sleep. Fortune made us drive farther than we intended, ignoring a large and impersonal campground, until we came to Silver Strand.

We found, on waking up, that we had a private beach of clean, soft sand with a gentle slope into the sea. The steps leading down the cliff became steeper as we descended but there was a hand-rail, and the way back up was a lot easier because my friends carried me!

We booked for two nights, thus giving ourselves time to spend the next day in Dublin. The National Gallery there had a wheelchair to lend us, giving me the chance to absorb Irish Art without a backache. The poet W.B. Yeats had a brother called Jack, we discovered, whose paintings hold the same magic as the poetry. We bought far too many books and pictures, and transformed our tarpaulin dining area into an open-air reading room when we got back to camp.

Wicklow itself doesn't seem big enough to have named a whole county, but its quiet ways and quaint appear-ances charmed us. Every storefront had been hand-painted in a style which was not quite as professional as sign-writing, making it attractive in an idio-syncratic way. In the evening we went into Kelly's Bar and tried Irish Guinness. Everything they say is true.

Since our intention had been to spend the week in County Kerry, we set off the next day. Nothing had prepared us for the fact that Ireland has no major highways. By the time we reached Limerick—which didn't live up to the poetic implications of its name—we were tired and fed up with traveling behind slow vehicles on two-lane roads.

The drivers do tend to pull over to allow you to pass, but they cannot do much if the road winds or is overloaded with oncoming traffic.

The result of our arduous journey was that we camped at Killarney, fifty miles short of our intended destination (the Dingle Peninsula). The camp-ground was not as enchanting as the first, and much busier; we had by then discovered that campers are a strange breed in Ireland, where Bed and Breakfasts in what seems like half the nation's houses cater to the tourist trade.

"You're as welcome as the flowers in May"

Camping at Killarney did mean that the following day we were tempted to stop and look at Muckross Abbey, within a mile of the town. It was then that we noticed what a delightful place Killarney is, nestled in a valley against the Ring of Kerry mountains, its church spire rising from the town.

Muckross, a fourteenth-century abbey destroyed by Cromwell in the seventeenth, is set in a huge expanse of lakes, holy islands, and wild parkland. It is closed to vehicles, which makes for a tranquil setting but leaves only two options for getting there—walking or taking one of the horse-drawn gigs for which Killarney is apparently famed. These are sold hard by men who have scant regard for charity, and feel that your inability to walk is not their prob-lem. Not allowing myself to feel annoyed, I paid £5 (Irish) for one mile to the abbey, and reasoned that this was the whole point of Mobility Allowance—to spend it on getting places.

Fortunately, it was a place worth getting to. We spent a good part of the day around the lakes and ended up driving only about twenty miles to our third and final camp—down a dirt road in the heart of the Ring of Kerry. Here was another advantage of camping. There wasn't a B&B for miles and we were camping in country silence, mist-shrouded mountains all around us, and the sheep kept out of the camp only by ditches. These, incidentally, were not enough to keep the cows out at night—as we found when we woke to a cowpat so close to the tent flap we wondered why we hadn't been trampled in our sleep.

The Ring of Kerry campground catered for the real traveler. A communal games and dining room offered two electric stoves operated by coin meters, and this was clearly a luxury for the cyclists we encountered—from Germany, France, even New Zealand—who were "doing" Ireland by bike.

In this camp, as in the others, the showers would have been impossible for me to use alone. Their six-foot-high coin meters and ludicrously small compartments were almost made up for by the therapeutic effect of streams of very hot water, but I had to do most of my dressing in the open because I couldn't sit down in the cubicles.

Our nearest town was Kenmare, where we decided to treat ourselves to a meal out. The previous night we had drunk Guinness and listened to Irish music in Killarney. This time, in the Ivy Leaf, we ate a combination of traditional Irish and modern French cuisine—wild Irish salmon marinaded in honey and dill, yam pie and pistachio ice cream with raspberry sauce, and a selection of Irish cheeses with a fiercely pungent odor.

When we'd eaten, the chef came to tell us that Ireland's finest folk musician was playing across the road in the hotel where the Kenmare Folk Club meets. Noel Hill was on his way to Tralee, where the Rose of Tralee festival started the next day. There he played to support Van Morrison and tickets cost £16. We saw him in an upstairs room in Kenmare for £4 and had a rousing good time.

There was just a day left to reach Dingle—which we'd expected to be our vacation base. We made it in a day trip

and glimpsed spectacular cliff-top views through the shifting mists. When the sun burst out it lit the sea around the islands in an ultramarine glow. The islands, inhabited for centuries, were abandoned less than forty years ago and are now populated by birds and seals. In the evening we got caught in the traffic and ribaldry of Tralee as the festival started. Perhaps more time would have allowed us to enjoy it; as it was, we couldn't wait to leave it behind.

"My reception there was almost unblemished by prejudice or short-sightedness"

Knowing that the next day we'd be speeding back to the east coast—glancing at Cork, bypassing Blarney Castle, talking through Waterford—we all felt that we'd done Ireland an injustice. A week was more of a whirlwind tour than a vacation. On our last night we stayed again at Wicklow, with a few hours in the blazing sunshine on the silver beach, and our first ocean swim of the trip—we hadn't had time elsewhere.

Waiting in the morning for the ferry to start loading, we spent our last Irish pennies on tea from a dockside stand. When my friend thanked the stand-holder, he replied, "You're as welcome as the flowers in May." We felt Ireland had been glad to have us.

When I go back to Ireland, as I surely will, there are several things I will know. My reception there was almost unblemished by prejudice or short-sightedness—partly, I believe, because the Irish are kind and welcoming whatever the circumstances. The only difficulty came at Dublin Castle, where an attendant wouldn't let us park in the inner area under the castle "because we had English number plates."

If I travel by car I know I'll be sidetracked by sights and views and opportunities at every turn. To travel west it would be better—for those who can afford it—to fly to Shannon and rent a car, allowing as much time in the west as originally planned. Perhaps, taking the sensible option, I'd also decide to use B&Bs next time—for the comfort of a warm, dry bed and a hot bath. At least I will know that wherever I go there will most definitely be accommodation available.

There hasn't been space to mention the ancient forests, the stone "beehive" huts built by Christian hermits, the famed dolphin at Dingle, and the way people inquired with genuine interest what we thought of Ireland at every chance encounter. Ireland deserves plenty of time from every traveler, both to get to know the country and to enjoy its many charms.

Abandoning Ship in Galway

Although born in Ireland, Helena O'Keefe had not been back since spending many months in hospital and taking early retirement as a result of disabilities caused by rheumatoid arthritis.

My sister said that sailing up the west coast was the perfect way to appreciate the miles of bays, cliffs, and mountains, but she thought the wheelchair would be a problem. So did I. We considered renting a cottage but did not want to be confined to one area. Mom, who is in her seventies, still had a trailer and awning—would a touring vacation be appropriate?

There are a set of problems when I am away from home: how high is the bed, how far is the toilet, are there steps or stairs, can I choose when to rest or eat, and—just as important—will the wheelchair pusher enjoy the vacation too? My brother was able to take time off in September and offered to help with arrangements and the hard work. As I weigh less than 110 lb he is able to lift me about and is skilled at getting me, in the chair, down flights of stairs, to the astonishment of passers-by. By towing the family trailer we were

able to take special equipment, including an adapted Porta-potti, all of which took the strain out of traveling. The wheelchair is standard issue; it folds quite easily but takes up most of the trunk. The spares kit wasn't needed, but I wouldn't travel without it—and a pump.

"When planning what to do and see once there we made good use of the tourist information offices"

We used the Irish Tourist Board information to plan our route, going first to County Waterford, visiting relatives and seeing how much it had altered. From there it was the N24 to Limerick, N18 to Galway and the Atlantic coast, and on up the N59 to Westport to explore County Mayo. When planning what to do and see once there we made good use of the tourist information offices in the larger towns; these are always well marked, they supply plenty of free information, and they recommend accommodation and make reservations.

Although the Fishguard to Rosslare crossing is only three and a half hours, the total journey time from southern England is much longer. The M4 highway gives way to local roads, and the Welsh hills go on and on. It helps to check in early and be settled before the majority of passengers arrive.

We made our reservations through the *Disabled Drivers' Motor Club* and wrote to *Sealink* explaining that we'd need access to the elevator. At Fishguard we repeated this to everyone who checked our tickets and we were given a distinctive windshield sticker. I have found all the ferry operators cooperative as long as they are fully informed. We were directed to a parking place by the service elevator and escorted to the main deck along with cases of duty free goods. Some of the smaller, older ferries do not have passenger elevators, so it's important to arrange for help back to the car deck later—this avoids competing with the kitchen garbage at the end of the voyage.

"It seemed that the wheelchair was rather a novelty"

We booked a cabin, so that we had space to relax, but the high sills made the rest room difficult to use. All the women's rooms on board seemed very tricky for wheelchairs, but the bar, restaurant, and cafeteria were accessible.

Customs formalities were brief and we did not need passports. Finding our way out of Rosslare harbor, into Wexford and onto the N25 was not so easy. Distances did not look odd once we realized that they were in kilometers on the newer signs; the place names were in Irish and English. The main routes (N roads) were well marked and partly four-lane. The maximum speed limit was 55mph (88kph) and in the countryside there was very little traffic.

As we approached Waterford a car began flashing at us. Mom said, "I think it's all right. I bet it's Eamon Cusack come out to meet us." She was right. When we stopped, our cousin explained that he had been waiting to escort us through the city and along the narrow, unlit country lanes to the campground on the cliffs at Dunmore.

There were special problems as Maeve Binchy's book, *Echoes,* was being filmed for TV, and most of Dunmore had been blocked off or altered to the style of the 1950s.

During our visit we looked at about a dozen campgrounds, none of them really suitable for wheelchairs. Washing and toilet facilities were basic, with few adapted rest rooms or shower cubicles. When shopping we often encountered surprise at seeing a wheelchair and, although we were always welcomed, access would have been a real problem without my brother and sister to push. Anyone using a manual chair on their own would need to be very fit to cope. The tourist board leaflet, *Accommodation for the Disabled,* listed accommodation suitable for disabled people, but we were unable to find specific information on access to the sights or to public buildings.

The newer visitor attractions are well adapted for wheelchairs. In County Clare, Aillwee Caves, where prehistoric bears had wintered with the stalactites and stalagmites, are accessible throughout, as is the Burren Display Center. The Burren is a limestone area, startlingly beautiful with many rare alpine and arctic plants and, surprisingly, Mediterranean species growing alongside. Spectacular when viewed from a car, this would make fascinating back-packing country. The upland limestone pavements must be eerie by moonlight—even at noon they felt inhabited, although they were quite empty and silent, not a tree for miles.

Also in County Clare, the visitors' center, rest rooms, and café at the Cliffs of Moher (650 feet high) are accessible with help, but parking is difficult. There is a very long, gravel path from the parking lot to the cliff top, where protective walls obstruct the views. Visitors require agility to enjoy this place, and to escape the crowds—it was the only place on our tour that was overrun with tourists.

Farther along the coast we stopped at Galway, the busiest town we visited and the only one with any nightlife apart from pubs and restaurants. Many of the streets and sidewalks were narrow, but the harbor area and tourist information office were accessible. Most of the shops were quite small but happy to accommodate a wheelchair. Many were craft or gift shops, selling Irish linen, pottery, alcohol, Donegal tweed, Aran knitwear, and Waterford glass. We were welcomed in cafés and pubs, even when tables or chairs had to be moved to make space. It seemed that the wheelchair was rather a novelty, which perhaps explains the special attention we received.

Our second campsite was at Spittal on Galway Bay. It was flat and exposed, giving clear views across the bay to the Burren. We parked beside 3-foot-high boulders marking the edge of the strand and wondered why no one else had chosen to enjoy such views. The answer came during the night: the wind kept rising, the sea roared, the van shook, and spray covered the windows. We slept badly and woke feeling damp. After arranging to leave the trailer in a safer spot we phoned a little place Mom remembered in Dugort, Achill Island, to see if they could put us up.

"As we traveled through the Connemara mountains the twentieth century faded"

Driving along the edge of Lough Corrig below a bare granite ridge, we stopped to photograph a donkey cart loaded with turf. (Remember to take plenty of film—it's very expensive and can be difficult to find.) The cart-driver said he was the only one left—the rest of the turf was moved by truck. The lough was dotted with row boats, each holding two fishermen; it's a good area for fishing.

There were few cars or houses. As we drew closer to the mountains the small fields gave way to bogs, then scrub and stones, and finally bare rock. We learned to fill up whenever we saw a gas station; they close after tea and on Sundays and, like human habitation, are scarce in the west. Obtaining cash was also a hit and miss affair, and we often had to accept unfavorable exchange rates.

"The few houses are small and huddle together, their backs to the Atlantic gales"

As we traveled through the Connemara mountains the twentieth century faded. Apart from the road and telegraph poles, everything we saw had existed for thousands of years. The silver streak on top of a high peak near the coast puzzled me at first. It turned out to be St. Patrick's chapel on top of Croagh Patrick (2475 feet), reached by a thousand-year-old track winding up the mountain.

We drove for miles along the edge of Clew Bay, passing huge areas of bog and the occasional ruined stone cottage. From the dock at Newport the goods for Achill Island used to be loaded onto boats, until the bridge was built twenty miles up the coast. The once busy town has shrunk, and a four-story warehouse that used to store wool from the island's sheep is now the convent home of a small group of nuns. We were attracted to it by a large mural of Mary the Queen of the Sea above the door, and by a sign saying "TEAS, SWEETS, GIFTS." Inside the massive stone walls we found a small shop with locally made toys and knitwear, and a spotlessly clean tearoom and rest rooms. The Filippini Sisters provided sustaining, home-made food and everything was accessible. As we went back outside, into the sunshine, the convent suddenly became busy as local people hurried in for a religious service.

On the approach to the bridge connecting Achill Island with the rest of County Mayo, the patches of grass and heather were so sparse that even the sheep had lost interest. There must have been trees once—we saw stumps and broken trunks in parts of the bog where turf had been cut and stacked.

My grandparents had come to Achill Island eighty years ago to manage the post office; it must have seemed the farthest outpost of civilization. The few houses are small and huddle together, their backs to the Atlantic gales. In sheltered spots trees have rooted and the narrow valleys are packed with rhododendrons; flowers dot the hedges of wild fuschia like specks of blood. With its seal caves, wild cliffs, and amethyst-bearing mountains, the island is a retreat for lovers of solitary pursuits or walking.

The hotel (*Grays*) is really a row of converted cottages. Luckily there is a first-floor room with a rest room beside it. The dining room is on the same level. We found it comfortable and hospitable, but I wouldn't recommend it for unaccompanied wheelchair users.

We took the coast road back to Galway, staying at Clifden, a popular town in summer and the center for west-coast sailing. It lies in a sheltered estuary surrounded by tree-covered hills which rise gradually to the mountains. The little harbor is always busy and there are lots of places to stay and to eat. We found the same holiday atmosphere all along the Connemara coast, all without busloads of tourists.

My sister left us to return to work. She said later that the journey by bus and train was difficult, with poor connections and delays. We made our way back to the caravan at Spittal and dried everything out. When the rain started again we hitched up and drove about 185 miles across the country. Most of it was flat. It kept raining. At Rosslare we found a place to eat but it was all rather dull and cheerless after the west coast.

Back in Wales it was still raining. By the time we reached England it had stopped. I'd advise anyone going to Ireland to take waterproofs and an umbrella!

Sibling Rivalry

Nancy Bower-Meale gave up work because of rheumatoid arthritis in 1966. In 1977 she made the trip to Belfast alone (plus wheelchair) and since then has been back many times.

A phone call from my sister set the ball rolling. With her husband she was planning a week away in the Cotswolds. They would travel over by ferry with their car, and on their way home would collect me for a much needed vacation, she told me. It was a large, comfortable car and I could have a cabin on the boat from Liverpool to Belfast. She was obvi-ously very pleased with her offer. After all, for over three years my only expeditions had been a weekly trip to church and I could no longer get into our garden. It was, she considered, an offer not to be refused, especially since I'd have two able-bodied traveling companions.

But refused it was. I reacted with horror and dread, not only to the idea of the sea crossing (I only have to stand on a pier to feel seasick), but also to the thought of moving out of my cosy little orbit and having to cope in an entirely new situation. How would I manage washing, or the rest room? Would the chairs be right? What about the Ulster bombs and shootings? How would I face getting out of bed in a strange house to start a different kind of day? I firmly declined the offer with thanks.

My sister replied that it was a great opportunity—perhaps the only one I'd get—to see her and my nieces and nephew in their own home, and she was surprised that I was chickening out! Stung into reaction, I retorted that I'd travel by air, making my own arrangements. There was no going back after that affirmation, and the following days were spent in wondering exactly *how* I was going to travel solo by air.

"I realized that being able to communicate is far more important than mobility"

I eventually phoned the local travel agent and discovered that *British Airways* really would "take good care" of me. I arranged for the Red Cross to take me by car (at minimal cost) to London's Heathrow airport and meet me on my return. Since then I've used the local cab firm for such trips, always explaining my circumstances, and have found their drivers to be consistently helpful and courteous. This mode of transport gives a great boost to the desire for independence and is, after all, what the Mobility Allowance is for.

Arriving at Heathrow I found that *BA* has a special check-in desk for wheelchair-bound travelers, where I waited for a porter to wheel me through security checks to the departure lounge. I was the first passenger aboard, in a roomy bulkhead seat. Then one of the cabin crew gave me my first shock—we would be delayed for anything up to two hours. But would I like a pot of tea and some cookies? I felt like royalty, although I did think about the problem of access to the toilet should I indulge in an extra cuppa. As if reading my mind, the cabin atendant added that I should press the nearby button or just call out for help if I required it.

Before long the seat next to me was taken by a young girl. I was pleased to have someone to talk to, hoping to keep panic at bay, but to my opening remarks she replied, "Je suis Française," and for the rest of the flight, which mercifully started sooner than anticipated, my mind was fully taken up in practising the French conversation I'd been studying at home on cassettes. This worked like magic—I realized that being able to communicate is far more important than mobility. By touchdown at Belfast's Aldergrove airport I was elated with a new-found confidence.

The day after my arrival we drove along the shore road of Strangford Lough to do some bird-watching. Named by the Vikings "Strong Ford" because of the strong currents, the area attracts many species of migrating birds and at low tide presents a fascinating scene of bird activity. For those, like myself, who have a problem handling weighty binoculars, I recommend the use of small opera-glasses. Like the proverbial half loaf, they are better than none at all, and I find mine adequate for a distance of about 100 feet.

"Northern Ireland, more than most places, learned to provide good wheelchair access, through the tragedy of 'The Troubles'"

Moving southeast to Downpatrick we viewed the reputed burial place of St. Patrick. We were the only visitors and were able to enjoy a few moments of quiet reflection on the life of this fifth-century saint. Born somewhere along the west coast of Britain, the story goes that at the age of sixteen he was carried off by raiders to become a slave in Ireland. He managed to escape to mainland Europe, where he underwent religious training, but was then called in a dream to return to Ireland to preach the gospel of Christ. He arrived in Ireland as a missionary priest in about 432 AD, and through his preaching and ministry overcame all pagan opposition to establish Christianity throughout the island.

In County Antrim, north and west of Belfast, I saw the distinctive Slemish Mountain, with its flat top, where (legend has it) the enslaved Patrick was a herdsman and grazed his master's sheep. The sheep were our only companions as we toured the quiet hills of Antrim; the only sounds when we stopped came from the sheep nibbling at the grass or from the clear waters of a stream running over stones. Everywhere we went in Northern Ireland the road traffic was minimal compared to what I was used to, and we often stopped beside the sea or halfway up a hill to enjoy the view with no worries about obstructing the road.

We made a memorable trip along the scenic Antrim coast road, with the sea often just a few yards away and good views over the Irish Sea to Scotland's mountains. Rounding Torr Head in the north we glimpsed Rathlin Island and, beyond it, the Atlantic Ocean stretching away to the Arctic and the North Pole. Our homeward journey took us through some of the Nine Glens of Antrim, wild country where Flora Macdonald is said to have brought Bonnie Prince Charlie to her kinsfolk after their flight from Scotland. Fairy thorns were pointed out to me, bringing to mind the opening lines of the very first poem I'd had to learn at school. My sister and I chanted in unison:

Up the airy mountain
Down the rushey glen,
We daren't go a-hunting
For fear of little men.
(William Allingham: "The Fairies")

Cut down or mutilate a fairy thorn, it was believed in years gone by, and you'd bring down the wrath of the wee folk on your head and your family. Much to my disappointment, I didn't spot any "little men"—perhaps I should have taken the opera-glasses.

The social history of Northern Ireland is encapsulated in the Ulster Folk and Transport Museum at Cultra, east of Belfast, where a typical village has been reconstructed using original buildings. The low thatched cottages are genuine, down to the pots and pans and intricately patterned patchwork quilts, and a peat fire burning in the hearth completes the authentic atmosphere.

"I realized that in some respects air travel for the unaccompanied wheelchair user is more relaxing than for the average traveler"

Belfast provides a contrast to these rural scenes, but it's not the city of violence depicted on our TV screens. As with the violence and mugging in any city, "The Troubles" are for the most part restricted to a tiny minority in particular areas, which are easily avoided. There are streets where a car cannot be parked unattended, but I have only once seen armed soldiers, on the outskirts of Belfast. Ringed by hills, the capital of Northern Ireland seems dominated by the large number of church spires and towers, as well as the old mill chimneys, reminders of the linen that brought Belfast its nineteenth-century prosperity. Samson and Goliath, the huge gantries in the Harland & Wolff shipyard, stand guard over the Lagan river as it widens into Belfast Lough; from here the *Titanic* sailed on her disastrous maiden voyage.

My day in Belfast would not have been possible without my wheelchair and the Orange Badge which allowed us to park (a pleasant change from London's West End, where the Orange Badge is not officially recognized). Of course, I was fortunate to be with my sister and brother-in-law who knew the city, but I was impressed by the friendliness and courtesy shown by members of the RUC concerning parking and by the hotel waitress who expertly accommodated my wheelchair and me at the table. Access to the *Europa Hotel* (Great Victoria Street) for lunch was good, and I was thrilled to recognize one of the well known Irish folk groups, The Chieftains. I was delighted with the ease of access to Crane's Bookshop in Rosemary Street, where rows of bookcases are widely spaced and no shelf is out of the wheelchair occupant's range of vision. Since my first visit three new accessible bookshops have opened in Royal Avenue.

Northern Ireland, more than most places, learned to provide good wheelchair access, through the tragedy of "The Troubles" which have not only killed but also maimed. A great deal of new building has taken place relatively recently—at a time when the importance of access, for the able-bodied as well as disabled, had been recognized. For example, the new shopping complex in Royal Avenue has been built with an adjacent parking lot.

Perhaps access seemed simpler in Northern Ireland because geographically it is small and people seem very aware of their neighbors and their needs. They show a great warmth and kindness, and give a tremendous welcome to visitors, so that any obstacles for the wheelchair traveler are quickly overcome. At my brother-in-law's golf club one evening three strong young men volunteered to carry me in my wheelchair up a flight of steps to the restaurant so that the visitor from "across the water" could appreciate the magnificent view over the Ards Peninsula and Strangford Lough.

My flight to Heathrow on the way home was uneventful, and I realized that in some respects air travel for the unaccompanied wheelchair user is more relaxing than for the average traveler. No baggage to carry and no long walk from check-in desk to aircraft, also a reserved seat close to the rest room!

Back in my own home I felt the richer for having gained a new interest in Irish history and literature, and an awareness that I could again read the travel pages, knowing that with a little homework beforehand I could once more indulge in the luxury of a vacation—the next time with my husband.

Since that first trip I've returned to Northern Ireland several times and my sister and brother-in-law have retired to County Antrim. If speed turns you on there's some lovely driving to be had on the new, relatively uncrowded highways. But one of the features which I find most attractive remains—I can still enjoy leisurely drives down quiet lanes, stopping to admire the view or to sit by a hedgerow scented with honeysuckle and bright with wild fuschia.

IRELAND: TRAVEL NOTES

Sources of information

Irish Tourist Board (Bord Fáilte), 757 Third Avenue, New York, NY 10017 (☎212/418-0800); 160 Bloor Street East, Suite 934, Toronto, Ontario M4W 1B9 (☎416/929-2777). Will always make an effort to answer specific queries, referring inquiries to the *National Rehabilitation Board* (see below) if necessary. The main accommodation guide includes a list of accommodation deemed suitable for disabled people.

National Rehabilitation Board (write to the Access Officer, 25 Clyde Road, Ballsbridge, Dublin 4, Ireland; ☎1/684181; fax 1/685029). Two free guides, *Accommodation for Disabled Persons* (1989) and *Dublin: A Guide for Disabled Persons* (1990), are designed to be read together with tourist board publications,

IRELAND: TRAVEL NOTES

and the information they contain is somewhat limited. The *NRB* is in the process of gathering information on all areas of interest to tourists with disabilities, aiming to publish a series of fact sheets during 1992–1993.

Northern Ireland Tourist Board, 276 Fifth Avenue, Suite 500, New York, NY 10001-4509 (☎212/686-6250); *British Tourist Authority*, 94 Cumberland Street, Suite 600, Toronto, Ontario M5R 3N3 (☎416/925-6326). The wheelchair symbol is used in their accommodation guide, *Where to Stay: Northern Ireland*. They plan to replace *The Disabled Tourist in Northern Ireland—Things to See, Places to Stay* (1985) with a new guide, prepared by **Disability Action** (2 Annadale Avenue, Belfast BT7 3JR, Northern Ireland; ☎0232/491011), but there has been some wrangling over funding. Meanwhile, *Disability Action* will send what printed information they have on receipt of an International Reply Coupon, and help with accommodation queries where possible.

Northern Ireland is also included, of course, in many of the publications that cover the whole of Britain: see the England and Wales *Travel Notes*.

Tour Operators

In the last decade Northern Ireland has come a few steps closer to making life easier for disabled people, and much of this breakthrough is thanks to County Down travel agent, **Philip Wright**, a wheelchair user whose personal crusade has resulted in many hotels and guesthouses throughout Northern Ireland now registering access a priority. As well as the very successful *Threshold Travel*, specializing in accessible fly-drive or cruise vacations for British and Irish tourists to the USA, Philip is responsible for *Wright Lines* (The Old Mill, Ballydown, Banbridge, Co Down, BT32 4JB, Northern Ireland; ☎08206/62126; fax 08206/62026), a travel agency with fully computerized database offering "the best accommodation in Ireland"—guesthouse, self-catering, or hotel—from the Fermanagh Lake District to Tralee.

Greg Baker's trip (p.126) was with **The Humanities Institute, Inc.** (Martha Mueller, Director), PO Box 18, Belmont, MA 02178, USA.

Getting There

The national **airline** of Ireland, *Aer Lingus*, flies direct from Boston, New York, and Chicago to Shannon and Dublin. Several major airlines operate from the USA and Canada to Belfast International via London Heathrow, Glasgow, and Manchester. There are also direct charter flights from New York, Florida, and Toronto.

Travel to Ireland from Britain is relatively expensive but all the airlines offer APEX and budget round-trip fares. *Aer Lingus* and *British Airways* are well known for their smooth treatment of disabled passengers, and there are frequent flights from London Heathrow, Glasgow, and Manchester, connecting with transatlantic flights. Other possibilities from Britain include *Air UK* (☎0345/666777), *British Midland* (☎071/589 5599), *Britannia Airways* (☎0582/405737), *Capital Airlines* (☎0345/800777), *Dan Air* (☎0345/100200), and *Ryan Air* (☎071/435 7101).

The shortest **ferry** crossing from Britain is from Stranraer or Cairnryan in Scotland to Larne, Northern Ireland (2hr 20min), operated by *P&O* (Cairnryan, Stranraer, Dumfries DG9 8RF, UK; ☎05812/276) and *Sealink Stena Line* (Charter House, Park Street, Ashford, Kent TN24 8EX, UK; ☎0233/647047).

B&I Line (Reliance House, Water Street, Liverpool L2 8TP, UK; ☎051/227 3131; or in Dublin, ☎1/788077) sails from Wales to Ireland (Pembroke–Rosslare and Holyhead–Dublin) and its ships are equipped with a service elevator and accessible rest room, as well as some cabins with wide doors.

On the Cairnryan–Larne route *P&O's Ionic Ferry* is better suited for disabled passengers than the *Europic Ferry*: it has accessible rest rooms, elevators to main passenger areas, and wide entrances to bar, restaurant, and lounges.

Sealink Stena Line covers routes from Wales to Ireland (Holyhead–Dun Laoghaire and Fishguard–Rosslare) and Scotland to Northern Ireland (Stranraer–Larne). The *Stena Felicity* (Fishguard–Rosslare) is equipped with adapted cabins and rest rooms. The *Stena Hibernia* (Stranraer–Larne and Holyhead–Dun Laoghaire) has elevators but access to some parts of the ship is via stairs.

IRELAND: TRAVEL NOTES

The three ferry companies offer substantial fare concessions to members of the *Disabled Drivers' Association* (*DDA*, Ashwellthorpe Hall, Norwich NR16 1EX, UK; ☎050841/449) or the *Disabled Drivers' Motor Club* (*DDMC*, Cottingham Way, Thrapston, Northants NN14 4PL, UK; ☎0832/734724); these apply to overseas members, too, but some quirk of bureaucracy makes the concessions only available to those who are traveling in their own vehicles—fine for anyone traveling Australian-style, buying a camper van in England, touring Europe and selling it at the end of their trip, but not much good to anyone else. Annual membership fees are small, and there is a £4 handling fee for each ferry booking. It's advisable to give at least six weeks' notice of intention to travel by ferry if you can take advantage of these concessions—full details of the booking procedures for each ferry company can be obtained from the *DDA* and *DDMC*.

All these ports are reasonably accessible, but Rosslare's new terminal stands out, with smooth walkways, excellent signs, both audio and visual announcements, adapted rest rooms, and wheelchair-friendly cafeteria. The design, layout, and ambience here greatly impressed judges in the 1990 *European Year of Tourism* competition for best facilities for disabled tourists in Europe.

Transport

Dublin **airport** is fully accessible and boarding or disembarking is usually by airbridge. At Shannon there are accessible rest rooms and boarding is by airbridge. Access is also good at Belfast International, where disabled passengers are usually boarded/disembarked by "nose-loader" (a movable corridor which extends from the passenger lounge into the aircraft), sometimes (on some *British Airways* flights) by high-lift ambulance, and occasionally by carry-chair. There is an accessible Airbus service, which runs every half-hour, hourly on Sundays, connecting the airport with the city of Belfast. The bus is equipped with a side-loading wheelchair lift and wheelchair space can be booked in advance (☎0232/320011 ext. 419). Facilities at other airports vary and you are

likely to require some sort of assistance; consult the Aer Rianta Duty Officer at the airport you wish to use.

On the Irish **railroads**, accessible rest rooms and mobile rails for boarding wheelchairs are available at most mainline stations, but the aisles in the cars are too narrow for wheelchairs, and passengers who wish to remain in their chairs must sit in the vestibule (which is at least air conditioned). Refreshments can be obtained from the traveling food cart.

Dublin's suburban rail system (*DART*) is for the most part accessible, but at stations situated on a bend there may be a wide gap between train and platform, and assistance may be required. Gates have to be locked at some stations for security reasons (a special key can be obtained from the *National Rehabilitation Board*) and this may make access difficult for passengers in wheelchairs.

Irish **buses** are generally inaccessible to wheelchair users. In Dublin, new vehicles added to the *Bus Átha Cliath* (*Dublin Bus*) fleet from 1990 onward have improved identification; a public address system; easily reached bell pushes; more hand-rails; and less mountainous steps which are better illuminated and with clearly defined edges, at entrance and exit—but no hydraulic lift and no wheelchair spaces.

Driving is an attractive and easy alternative here. Cars with hand controls can be rented from *Hertz* in Northern Ireland only, seven days' advance notice required. You could also rent a lift-equipped van from *Wheelchair Travel* (see England and Wales *Travel Notes*), and take it across to Ireland on the ferry, but remember that there are no fare concessions to drivers of rented vehicles and these are expensive crossings. Parking on single or double yellow lines is not allowed in Dublin and parking during business hours is tricky. In other towns consult local police before attempting any unorthodox parking, but in general there shouldn't be too many problems in country areas.

Along the way you'll find a fair number of accessible rest rooms, although some require a special key. This can be obtained from the *National Rehabilitation Board* or the *Irish Wheelchair Association* (Blackheath Drive, Clontarf, Dublin 3, Ireland; ☎1/338241).

IRELAND: TRAVEL NOTES

Accommodation

Several useful publications have been listed under *Sources of Information*, although one contributor who used *Accommodation for Disabled Persons* stopped consulting it after the second day of her trip because "almost every B&B we stopped at was wheelchair accessible as long as someone was there to help—and we never ran short of people more than willing to lend a hand."

For accompanied wheelchair users, Helena O'Keefe (p.133) liked *Grays Guesthouse* (Dugort, Achill Island, County Mayo, Ireland; ☎98/43244).

In Northern Ireland, the *Share Center* (Smiths Strand, Lisnaskea, County Fermanagh BT92 0EQ, Northern Ireland; ☎03657/22122 or 21892; fax 03657/21893) enables both able-bodied and disabled people to take a very reasonable vacation on the shores of Lough Erne, where they can sail, canoe, or learn traditional crafts, as well as enjoying the social life and exploring the surrounding countryside. In addition to the central guesthouse, there is a campsite, all designed for use by disabled people. Funds to build this residential activity center were raised by small groups and schools throughout Northern Ireland and it was opened in 1981.

Few campgrounds in Ireland have any special facilities, but contributors did manage.

Books

Ireland is included in the *RADAR* guide, *Holidays in the British Isles*, published annually (see England and Wales *Travel Notes*).
The Real Guide to Ireland. Comprehensive guide to Ireland, North and South.

TELEPHONE CODES:

From the US and Canada dial 011 (international code) and then 353 for the Republic of Ireland, 44 for Northern Ireland.

Scotland

High Expectations North of the Border

Paul Cox is a quadriplegic, the son of a Yorkshire miner. His paternal grandfather was Scottish, a professional soccer player whose career brought him to England. In September 1989 Paul chose Scotland for a vacation in the hope of discovering not only something of his grandfather's life, but also some signs of the centuries-old struggle between Scotland and England.

Apart from all that, I'd just bought a new car and was dying to try it out on a long run. The north of Scotland was said to be a driver's dream in comparison with the rest of Britain.

My vacation north of the border almost didn't get the chance to fulfil these expectations. After making detailed inquiries of its facilities, I'd reserved a self-catering chalet in Aviemore with a girlfriend. This, the car, and the aids I could pack into it would, I felt, minimize the inconveniences of "making do" with other transport, hotels, and their facilities. But between planning and departure the girlfriend had gone and I was stuck for someone to accompany me.

RADAR had already sent me a list of addresses matching the type of vacation I wanted; next they suggested a number of care attendant agencies. Some of these are voluntary and require notice; some ask for full payment but can often supply help

immediately. Circumstances dictated the latter option in my case. The risk in using such agencies is that you're not going to get on with your helper. But it's a small risk: people attracted to this type of work, whether volunteers or professionals, are almost by definition not unpleasant. My helper was competent with the basics, nice and interested, and we got on.

She was also Scottish, which meant that she knew what wasn't worth seeing—helpful, since it was soon apparent that I'd underestimated the size of the country. Perhaps it only felt big because of the relative lack of people in the parts we touched; the bulk of the population is crammed into the neck of land between the Glasgow and Edinburgh conurbations. We were based in the Highlands, well north of this, where there was room to move. And what a place to move in! Such variety of landscapes: elemental, geological landscapes—peaks and plateaux, hard rock and soft glens, peat and pine—in which people and buildings appear as afterthoughts. Here the earth dominates, with its look, its feel, and its smells.

Aviemore is a touristy ski center with the spartan feel of a pioneer town. It's in the heart of the Cairngorm mountains, car-stopping in themselves, but chosen principally as a strategically placed starting point—this was always going to be a driving vacation. I'm glad the roads *were* as good as they said, because we covered an awful lot of them: 2300 miles in a week. Whether long and straight, winding sharply or softly, flat or hilly, they were superbly maintained. North of Pitlochry I don't recall a pothole, and we glided from place to place, above the road surface rather than on it, chewing gum, listening to Ry Cooder and the wind whistling through the sun-roof, feeling like stars in a road movie.

"The spectacularly glacial northwest coastline, hewn and heaved high out of the sea"

Map book and *Good Food Guide* in hand, we set off each morning with the day half planned, half left to chance. Often we were pleasantly surprised, much less often disappointed. What remains clearest is the drive through Glencoe Pass. I was vaguely aware of the English-instigated massacre there in 1692 of 38 MacDonalds by the Campbell clan. I was also aware that the Scottish tourist industry has cashed in on the legend grown from this event and positively promotes the place as one cloaked in perpetual gloom. Undoubtedly the closed-in mountain formation lends itself to overcast conditions at certain points on most days. But we happened on particularly fine weather and although I did feel a

"Wuthering Heights" gloom when high on desolate Rannoch Moor, the descent from there into the broad valley of a rolling, tumbling River Coe was a descent into relief.

It's hard to turn around anywhere in northern Scotland and not be struck by the physical geography. One day stands out in this respect, a day spent traveling along and around the Caledonian Canal. When completed in 1847, this sixty-mile chain of lochs and canals joined the Irish Sea to the North Sea and cut the northwest Highlands from the rest of Scotland. It's a prime example of the Scots adding to Nature, making her work better for them. The artificial 23 miles of canal finished off what the Great Glen Fault almost achieved, and enabled vessels to avoid the dangerous northern route via the Hebrides and Pentland Firth. Fishing boats and pleasure craft can now float in safety from a western coastline deeply indented by fjords, or sea lochs, and fragmented by islands and peninsulas, to a lower, straighter eastern coastline characterized by several great drowned inlets, or firths. These boats pass Lochs Linnhe, Lochy, Oich, and Ness; particularly impressive is Loch Ness, forbidding in its size and cold bronze feel. It's easy to see why the legend sticks.

High up on the west coast is the unspoiled fishing village of Ullapool. Although there is the odd souvenir and trinket shop, the folksy heart of the place seems self-contained. From Ullapool we drove down the spectacularly glacial northwest coastline, hewn and heaved high out of the sea. We caught sight of the Isle of Skye and stopped for coffee at a fine little folk museum in Gairloch; we stayed for two hours, fascinated as it bared Scotland's soul from the time of the aboriginal Picts and the immigrant tribe of Scots (who were actually Irish), through myriad bloody clan feuds, right up to the almost-as-primitive early twentieth century.

After that it was back to the visual drama of the coastline (or coast-zigzag)—a dream of a drive, jarred awake by the US military; I knew that the Clyde Firth was infested with defense establishments, but to come across an armed-to-the-teeth super-power this far north was not just chilling, it was incongruous. It's easy to forget such things—too easy I fear—when the next day you discover a place of such simple, peaceful beauty as the hunting lodge we found on Loch Tummel. I wanted to take the place home with me. It was perfect, down to the unreal stillness of the silver-surfaced loch and, inside, where we ate earthy smoked salmon, the slightly eccentric, not-quite-of-this-century maître d'.

"Because we saw and did and felt so much, I can offer only my impressions"

Because we saw and did and felt so much, I can offer only my impressions: the lack of trash and graffiti; the clearness of the air (I saw a rainbow the colors of which were so distinct it looked artificial); the unobtrusive hydroelectric works, tucked neatly away in hillfolds or amid trees, keeping environmental disturbance to a minimum; superb food almost everywhere we stopped (usually recommended by the *Good Food Guide*, which is good on wheelchair access); the people no more or less friendly, the streets and buildings no more or less accessible than in my home area.

John O'Groats—famous as the most northerly point—was disappointing, not so much because of the busloads of tourists lining up to be photographed under the sign to Land's End at the southern extremity of Britain, but because after the seeming endlessness of the A9 up there I could see land out north: I wanted to have arrived at the end of the world. The sheep—laid out in the road, cool as nightclub bouncers,

chewing grass and staring us out—were the nearest thing to wildlife we saw, which was a shame. Also missing was the sound of the bagpipes, one of the few things that can give me goose-pimples and make me shiver. That would have been nice, so too the sight of a stag.

I didn't sit in the middle of that field on Culloden Moor, where the Duke of Cumberland's army slaughtered one thousand Jacobite rebels—in forty minutes!—in 1746. Seeing the name on a sign was enough to make me think about it, and that's all one can do now. Believing that an extended stationary stare would bring me no nearer to the past than a glance from the car, I sped homeward on the M9 past the Bannockburn Monument near Sterling, scene of Robert Bruce's routing of a huge English army in 1314. For the same reason we didn't stop at other battle sites: Dunbar (1650, Cromwell, aftermath of the English Civil War); Flodden (1513, James IV, an attempt to assuage his own Scottish barons); Killiecrankie (1689, another Jacobite revolt). If any of these events *are* relevant to an understanding of my history—any more relevant than, say, the Highland clearances or the countless unmarked border feuds—this vacation did not clarify how.

But perhaps I expected too much. I chose the Highlands not to find the "real" Scotland but to escape people and cities. In doing so I was avoiding history in the making, for it is people who make history. If I'd gone to the cities I'd have come across a different Scotland, one that would evoke different feelings in me, probably more immediately meaningful feelings given that where most of the people are is where most of the coalfields were. No, despite all my talk of the atavistic pull of Scotland, a vacation for me is ultimately a "getting away." It was a wonderful escape, and I'll be going back.

First Trip to Scotland

Charlotte Billington has cerebral palsy and has written two accounts of organized group vacations. On p.243 she describes a Project Phoenix Trust Study Tour in Sweden. Here she writes about her vacation with the Disaway Trust in June 1989. Her group was based at Crieff, near Perth, on the edge of the Highlands.

We traveled to Scotland by Tourbus from Victoria, London (I picked it up in Newport Pagnell). The journey took nearly fifteen hours, mainly because of the number of stops on the way, and we arrived at our hotel at 11pm feeling absolutely exhausted. The hotel had expected us three hours earlier, so the salad with which we were presented was a bit on the dry side!

After playing with a couple of lettuce leaves, our only desire was to hit the sack as soon as possible. Once we'd sorted out which suitcase belonged to whom, and returned missing jackets to their rightful owners, we all piled into the two elevators and headed upstairs for our rooms.

But not for us a quick collapse into our beds! Many of the wheelchairs could not fit through the bathroom doorways, and this resulted in most of us changing rooms, including my helper and myself. What the other residents thought of all the noise is not recorded—probably just as well—but by 2am peace had descended and we at last got some sleep.

The first thing on the agenda in the morning was to have a carpenter take the bathroom doors off their hinges for the duration of our stay. The hotel staff did make a genuine effort to be helpful toward disabled guests. Apart from two elevators which went to all floors, there was a specially equipped bathroom on the first floor, with all necessary attach- ments to enable us to have a bath or shower in comfort, as well as a raised toilet for those who have difficulty in getting up from a low seat.

All sports facilities were accessible for a wheelchair user, and there was a choice of table tennis, snooker, tennis, golf, and swimming in a heated pool. To gain access to the pool it was necessary to inform the staff, who placed two planks over the six steps leading into the pool and were very willing to help with wheelchairs. The sauna could be booked in advance.

The hotel grounds offer an interesting if rather hilly stroll through a wide selection of flowers, shrubs, and trees—enough to keep keen gardeners talking for weeks! As the hotel stands on a hill above Crieff, it commands a superb view over Strathearn to the Ochil hills, and west to the Grampians. It is also a stone's throw from *Gleneagles* and its famous golf courses.

The food was very good: buffet-style breakfast, lunch from the sandwich and salad bar, and five-course dinner with wine. Vegetarians and those on special diets were catered for if advance notice was given. Men were expected to wear a tie for dinner as well as on the dance floor. Regular dances took place in the hotel ballroom (but mainly for the over 60s), and other leisure facilities included the TV and cinema room, the drawing room and loggia, the Winter Garden and library.

"The gradients were such that each wheelchair would have needed a team of packhorses"

Our first visit of the week was to Scone Palace in Perth. Known as the Crowning Place of the Kings of the Scots on the Stone of Scone, the palace is also the home of Lord Mansfield and is famous for its 400-year-old collection of rare porcelain, clocks, needlework, and furniture. Only the first floor is open to the public and is accessible to wheelchairs apart from half a dozen steps leading into the main entrance hall. Our driver overcame this problem by maneuvering the bus so that the tail-lift came to rest on the top step and we could wheel straight in. We were met by the tartan-clad guides who conduct the tourist groups around the house, delivering a well-practiced history of its treasures.

After the tour we emerged onto the beautifully manicured lawns, admiring the peacocks in all their finery. We wandered around the magnificent grounds, then disappeared around the back of the palace, through a courtyard to a small teashop. Once the staff had gotten over the shock of seeing eight-een of us in wheelchairs plus our help-ers, they were very amenable, moving tables and chairs aside so that we could settle down to tea, cakes, and sand-wiches. Next door was a souvenir shop, also a rest room for disabled visitors—since most of us wanted to use it, this was a long stop.

We headed back to the hotel via Perth, which is an unremarkable town sitting at the mouth of the River Tay. The squat, austere, granite buildings nestle cheek by jowl with the earlier architectural pomposity of the Victorian era, but the beauty of the surrounding hills provides a redeeming feature. The town itself is also very hilly, making it difficult for wheelchairs.

For the same reason, an exploration of Crieff was abandoned. The gradients were such that each wheelchair would have needed a team of packhorses to pull it. Visits to the Weaver's House and to the Highland Tryst Museum were cancelled as both places had very difficult access and room for only one wheelchair inside (heat and tiredness also dampened our enthusiasm). We again had access problems at the Glen Turret distillery—Scotland's oldest—but we were able to see an interesting video of the distilling process, as well as taste a wee dram of the golden liquid.

A trip to the Stuart Crystal Factory, just outside Crieff, was more successful in terms of access. We watched the fascinating process, stage by stage; it was also displayed on video in case we missed anything. In the shop where the crystal is sold the prices ranged from £5 to £500—something for all tastes and pockets.

"Most of us decided to take a spin in our wheelchairs on the dance floor"

Across the road, at the Crieff Visitors' Centre, we watched the crea-tion of Britain's premier *millefiori* and lampwork paperweights, and toured the famous Thistle Factory, center for production of hand-painted pottery. The center is equipped with a good café and a disabled persons' rest room.

We took advantage of the facilities and then drove to the Scottish Deer Centre at Cupar, in Fife. The farm is situated in fifty acres of beautiful park-land in the Howe of Fife. The visitors' center is housed in an early nineteenth-century courtyard made fully accessi-ble for wheelchairs. We were allowed to go down into the pens, where the red deer clambered about over bales of hay, showing off, it seemed, for the benefit of the human onlookers. They were so tame and friendly that we were able to pat and stroke them, after which we watched a video explaining the deer's life cycle, and the activities of the local conservationists who are working to preserve the species.

The day was rounded off with a production of Agatha Christie's *Witness for the Prosecution*, performed at the Pitlochry Festival Theatre. It was an excellent evening's entertainment. The theater is relatively new—it was opened by Prince Charles in 1979—and combines modern architecture with good facilities which are accessible to all members of the community.

Our day trip to Edinburgh took in a guided tour of Holyrood House, including some of the magnificent state rooms and apartments used by the royal family when visiting Scotland. We had a picnic in the grounds of the house before boarding the bus for a quick trip to the shops on Princes Street. The Royal Mile would have been impossible to negotiate in a wheelchair (the gradient is one in two) but we did at least drive along it.

That evening we returned to the hotel to discover that a dance had been arranged. Most of the younger females in our party, including myself, thought that this would be an opportunity to meet some of the local "talent." We couldn't have been more wrong. I'm not sure whether our hotel made a point of catering to old people, or the population of Scotland really is severely lacking in younger folk, but it wasn't the first time on this vacation that we'd noticed a preponderance of senior citizens around us. However, after swallowing our disappointment, most of us decided to take a spin in our wheelchairs on the dance floor and we ended up hugely enjoying ourselves.

A bright, hot, and sunny Thursday was perfect for a cruise on Loch Katrine. The ride to the Trossachs took about two hours and we arrived at a pretty little bay which was also functional, providing accessible tea shop, souvenir shop, and rest room. The *SS Sir Walter Scott* was fully accessible and there was a choice of remaining in our wheelchairs or transferring to one of the wooden benches placed at strategic vantage points all around the deck. The captain pointed out the parts of the dramatic landscape around us which featured in the history and literature of Scotland, particularly in the novels of Sir Walter Scott. This was a fascinating and inexpensive trip, well worth the two-hour journey from Crieff.

Our last full day was spent in Pitlochry, where mountains, lochs, and rivers make a spectacular setting for the town. Pitlochry was still attractive when we visited but is fast losing its charm in the race to woo the tourists. The High Street is full of souvenir shops selling tacky Scottish memorabilia, and large numbers of cafés and teashops, most of which are reasonably accessible. The only accessible rest room is in the parking lot at the back of the town.

"You need to make sure that your wheelchair is in good condition if you want to go exploring in those wild landscapes"

The Strathearn regional hydroelectric plant is based in Pitlochry, and the visitors' center offers an exhibition using maps and diagrams to explain how electricity is generated and distributed to different parts of the region. The exhibition is free and accessible for those in wheelchairs but two strong helpers are needed for the steps in the entrance hall. We were also able to see the Fish Ladder and watch the salmon leaping.

The last evening was hot: some people went for a swim, some grabbed a last-minute sunbathe, others went to their rooms to contemplate the gaping mouth of an open suitcase. Sunday saw us wend our way back to London. Scotland had scored highly with all of us. To say that the scenery is spectacular is an understatement; the shapes and colors defy the most skilled photographer, and you need to make sure that your wheelchair is in good condition if you want to go exploring in those wild landscapes. I cannot say that I got to know the Scots people, but it takes more than one visit to do that, and I'm sure to go back.

SCOTLAND: TRAVEL NOTES

Sources of Information

Scottish Tourist Board, 23 Ravelston Terrace, Edinburgh EH4 3EU; ☎031/332 2433; fax 031/343 1513. Contact them in advance (address your request to the Information Department; they will send material overseas) for a free booklet, *Practical Information (3) for Visitors with Disabilities to Scotland* (information contained is correct at June 1992), which lists accessible accommodation (inspected by the tourist board), attractions and events, sports and activities, and useful addresses and publications. It also gives valuable transport advice and information, including details of ferry services to the islands. Full details of the grading scheme used for assessing accommodation can be obtained from the tourist board. The booklet is also available from tourist information centers throughout Scotland. The main tourist information office, the *Edinburgh and Scotland Tourist Information Centre*, above the Waverley Market (3 Princes Street, Edinburgh EH2 2QP; ☎031/557 1700), is fully accessible.

A scheme for assessing access at tourist attractions has yet to be worked out, but local access guides can be consulted. The tourist board's Central Information Department holds reference guides for visitors with disabilities, including *Arts and Disability Checklist* (Arts Council), *Access to the Arts* (City of Glasgow), and *Orkney Isles Access and Information Guide* (Voluntary Services, Orkney). The *BP ACCESS Guide: Access to Scotland's Performing Arts Venues* was launched in 1992 and describes availability of sign language interpretation and audio descriptions as well as wheelchair access.

Access in Lothian (published 1991, update scheduled for early 1993; available from the tourist board or from Fiona Bonar, Editor, *Access in Lothian*, 13 Johnston Terrace, Edinburgh; ☎031/220 6855, voice or Minicom) was compiled by the Lothian Voluntary Committee on Disability Services and Lothian Coalition of Disabled People. It is a collection of pamphlets covering everything tourists are likely to visit: Public Rest Rooms; Pubs and Bars; Parks and Gardens; Restaurants and Cafés; Indoor Sports Centres; Movie Theatres, Concert Halls, and Theatres; Public Libraries; Places of Interest; Hotels and Guesthouses. The introductory leaflet advises that the **Edinburgh International Festival** (office at 21 Market Street, Edinburgh; ☎031/226 4001) and the **Edinburgh Festival Fringe Society** (office at 180 High Street, Edinburgh; ☎031/226 5257) produce brochures with brief access details to all their performance sites. Both offices are accessible to wheelchair users.

Disability Scotland (formerly *Scottish Council on Disability*), Information Service, Princes House, 5 Shandwick Place, Edinburgh EH2 4RG; ☎031/229 8632; fax 031/229 5168. This organization works closely with the tourist board, and the Information Department offers the most comprehensive service in Scotland on aids, equipment, services, and facilities connected with disability. There are over twenty information lists, regularly updated, some of which (Holidays, Transport, Wheelchairs, Sport, and Physical Recreation) would be useful to prospective vacationers in Scotland. The holidays database includes information on hotels, guesthouses, bed and breakfast (B&B), camping, sports and leisure facilities.

Forestry Commission, 231 Corstorphine Road, Edinburgh EH12 7AT; ☎031/334 0303. Provides useful information on its accessible forest trails, campgrounds, and picnic areas.

The National Trust for Scotland, 5 Charlotte Square, Edinburgh EH2 4DU; ☎031/226 5922. Charity that controls many beautiful houses and gardens: contact for leaflet, *Information about Trust Properties for Disabled Visitors* (send International Reply Coupon, or pick up from any *NT* property).

Transport and Accommodation

On the whole the situation with accommodation and transport (as well as general access and facilities) in Scotland is the same as for the whole of Britain, so see the England and Wales *Travel Notes*. But also consult *Disability Scotland* (above) and the *Scottish Tourist Board Practical Information (3)* booklet on the subjects of transport and accommodation, access and facilities.

SCOTLAND: TRAVEL NOTES

Wheelchair user Stephen Hunt has this to say about finding accessible B&B accommodation: "Where are all these disabled vacationers who can afford to stay in the kind of guesthouse and hotel that fill every disabled vacation guide? According to all the guidebooks, Scotland is no place for me. I can't pay the cost of a wheelchair-logo hotel, and I won't pay the price of losing my independence to an organized group tour. Never one to resist an impulse, I rented a car and, before the month was out, was heading, with a friend at the wheel, towards Scotland and the Great British bed and breakfast."

Stephen traveled in 1991 and found manageable accommodation wherever he stopped, although sometimes the bathrooms required "some acrobatics." Their cheapest B&B was £13 (about $22) and they never paid more than £22 ($41). At Loch Ness, after several unsuccessful stops, a landlady phoned her daughter, who arrived five minutes later and conveyed them to her bungalow B&B where Stephen had the full run of the house and a low-level bath which allowed him his first bath of the week. In Edinburgh the *Tourist Accommodation Bureau* directed them to the university dorms where Stephen was given his own room and bathroom, pre-adapted for a disabled student, complete with emergency panic button; there was a bar, a lounge, and a bowl of real Scottish porridge for breakfast—five-star arrangements for the one-star price of £22.

TELEPHONE CODE:

From the US and Canada dial 011 (international code) and then 44 for Scotland.

England & Wales

Wild Eric and the Devil's Chair

Isobel Williams has multiple sclerosis. In the summer of 1987 she took her three-wheeler on vacation to Wales and Shropshire.

I've never felt the urge to sunbathe on some foreign beach or to sample the delights of Blackpool's Golden Mile. I like peace and quiet, and so does my husband. For some twenty years we found it for two weeks every summer with old friends, the Johnsons, who had moved to a dairy farm in rural Wales.

We traveled by car, taking our four terriers, stopping en route in the county of Shropshire. I had suffered from what I thought was back trouble for years, but in 1981 multiple sclerosis was diagnosed. Although I still drive, I can manage only short distances; my husband doesn't drive so Wales seemed out of reach.

In 1987 Mrs Johnson had been recently widowed and I was anxious to see her. To increase my mobility I had purchased a battery-operated trike and I read that *British Rail* could accommodate passengers in wheelchairs. Why not go to Wales by train? I knew that my husband wouldn't leave his garden or his dogs (not to mention his rabbits and canaries), so I resolved to go alone.

The first step was to buy a *Disabled Person's Railcard*, which makes the fare much cheaper. The procedure then is to phone the station of departure the

day before the journey commences. I arranged to be met at the other end, and a friend took me to the station in her car. The trike is easily dismantled to stow in the car and was soon reassembled at the station. There was sloping access to the station, and when the train arrived a small portable ramp was placed at the entrance to the baggage car and I was asked to enter. I was a bit taken aback at this but was assured that there was a window, so I rode the trike up the ramp into the car. Several parcels were loaded, the ramp was removed and we were on our way.

It was surprisingly comfortable, with a good view out of the window. No fighting for the best seat, I could sit at whatever angle I chose, and there were no other passengers to bother me. But it would have been far too cold in winter.

I had to make two changes, first at Birmingham New Street, then at Shrewsbury. The conductor seemed to know all about my journey so I didn't worry about missing the connections. As far as Birmingham the train followed much the same route as the road I knew so well. When we arrived at Birmingham someone was there to meet me, as promised. He carried my suitcase, taking me up in the luggage elevator to the platform for the Shrewsbury train. It was a busy station, the largest junction in Europe, I was told. Thank goodness *BR* treated me as a parcel—let loose on my own I would have been hopelessly lost!

When the Shrewsbury train pulled in, another ramp was put in place, and with a bit of pushing I was in my second, much bigger baggage car. I had a box of day-old chicks for company, cheeping and chattering all the way to Shrewsbury. There I was met as before and transferred to a dear little local train. As there was no baggage car they somehow squeezed me into the passenger car. This line was a single track and the engine hooted mournfully at every bend.

As we drew into Aberystwyth station I could see my friend's son, Jim, waiting for me. The journey had taken about five hours and I had expected to feel exhausted, but I was in quite good shape. Only about twenty miles to go, this time by road.

At Cilrhyg the farmyard slopes steeply down from the road. The farmhouse is old and square, built of stone with a slate roof. About 200m below there is a shallow river, which the cows cross twice a day in summer as they come in to be milked. Over the road the ground rises steeply to the wooded *vron* (sloping field). In winter, water rushes down through the yard to the river.

The 31-hectare farm stands alone, a couple of miles from the tiny village— two shops, a pub, and a post office. There is no sound except from a passing car or tractor and, of course, the birds. There are red kites about—once or twice I've spotted one. The land at the side of the lanes is not sprayed and is full of wild flowers never seen by the roadside at home—foxgloves, meadowsweet, flag irises, and wild strawberries.

> *"The unfenced road winds through the mountains, where a few long-tailed sheep snatch a living from those barren pastures"*

Mrs. Johnson didn't go out but there weren't many days that passed without a visitor. Everything came to the door—I even bought a pair of pants while I was there! A neighboring farmer brought the daily paper together with any local news that he'd heard. The butcher brought the meat and put it away in the fridge; there was a baker, a mobile grocer, and a man with fresh mackerel. We were very slow to answer the door; Susie the springer spaniel beat us to it every time. She would stand on her hind legs, turn the doorknob with her paw and step back, opening the door—rather disconcerting for strangers!

I spent much of my time at Cilrhyg in the sunroom on the south side of the house. It was full of plants and always warm, even on a dull day. Mrs. Johnson and I sat there talking endlessly. If it was a fine day I sat outside on my trike but the yard was too steep for me to go far.

In Wales the land is so hilly that any flat land is highly prized. At Cilrhyg the pasture bordering the river is completely flat, about 300 feet above sea level. Jim's brother David and his wife live on a much hillier farm, higher up. David took me to see it one afternoon, after a struggle to get me into the Land Rover. They keep some horses, milking cows, and sheep, and were having a go at strawberry growing.

Our mealtimes were arranged to suit Jim's milking. He worked alone, and cows have to be milked twice a day, every day of the year. He came in for his breakfast at about 10am and we would sit at the table for hours, unless he wanted to get away to the market.

Any work about the farm had to be done between milkings.

Jim didn't have much time to spare from his Guernsey cows, but he did find time to take me to Aberystwyth, a fine seaside town twenty miles west of Cilrhyg, at the center of the gentle curve of Cardigan Bay. We drove to the seafront and watched the large ships passing on the horizon. The tall, narrow hotels on the esplanade give a rather dignified air to the seafront. There is a pier and a sandy beach, but there weren't many bathers that day, despite the June sunshine.

My week at Cilrhyg was soon over. I was to spend the second week with Mrs. Johnson's daughter, Rachel, in Shropshire. Rachel and I are old friends (we were bridesmaids at each other's weddings) and she drove down to the farm to fetch me.

The drive from Cilrhyg to Bishop's Castle is most enjoyable, first passing Tregaron bog, said to be the largest in Europe and surely one of the last really wild places left in the British Isles. Then the unfenced road winds through the mountains, where a few long-tailed sheep snatch a living from those barren pastures. Hill farmers cultivate impossible slopes and little streams rush downhill.

There are vast, gloomy forest plantations, the trees in straight lines like so many soldiers, the fire brooms stacked ready, just in case. On past little Welsh houses, paint gleaming in colors we'd never think of using. Then on to the main road, through Devil's Bridge with its tourists and ice-cream stands, and through Newtown into Shropshire with its prosperous farms and half-timbered houses.

Rachel's home is approached along narrow lanes with high banks. The old farmhouse was built of local stone and the beautiful garden created by Rachel. It stands on level ground surrounded by hills, the largest being the Long Mynd, much of which is owned by the National Trust. There is good access to

viewpoints on the Long Mynd and to the information center, shop, and café at Carding Mill Valley.

Cyril manages the 400-hectare farm, growing grain and fodder on the lower portion. The rest is hillside and moor, where heather and windberries grow and the sheep and cattle graze in the summer. There are several milking cows, hens, and sometimes geese being fattened for Christmas. A shepherd and a tractor driver work with Cyril, and Rachel does the books and anything else that needs doing.

There is a large concrete farmyard, ideal for my trike, and I was even able to go up the road. I also sat outside listening to the curlews and watching the clouds scudding over the Long Mynd. Rachel's capuchin pigeons strutted importantly on the lawn and if I sat still enough one would fly onto my lap.

"On December 22 all the ghosts in Shropshire are said to meet on the Stiperstones"

This part of Shropshire is full of legends of witches and ghosts. Rachel took me up to the Stiperstones hills, a wild and lonely place. On December 22 all the ghosts in Shropshire are said to meet on the Stiperstones. Wild Eric is there with his wife Godda, his men, and a pack of yellow-eyed hounds. Should Wild Eric be seen at any other time, soldiers will perish far away. The last time he was seen was three days before the Falklands War. Nearby is a rock formation known as the Devil's Chair; when cloud covers the Stiperstones, the Devil is said to be in his chair!

The second week of the Wimbledon tennis tournament was in full swing and I found it difficult to tear myself away from the TV, but we visited the butterfly farm at Country World, Yockleton, near Shrewsbury. There were plenty of benches so I managed quite well without my trike (I can still walk a little); wheelchair users will find the farm quite accessible. The butterflies live in a huge greenhouse amidst many exotic plants, including a twenty-foot-high abutilon—I have one about three feet high, so I thought that was big! I'd like to have watched the butterflies for longer but I couldn't stand the heat in the greenhouse.

After a farewell barbecue it was time to go home. I phoned Shrewsbury station and the journey went smoothly as before; *BR* certainly looked after me well. It was good to get home and see my husband and the dogs. It's grand to go away but even better to come home.

It Rains in the Lakes

Self-catering in the Lake District might seem an improbable choice of vacation for a severely disabled couple. Caryl and Pete Lloyd managed it in 1989 with a great deal of careful planning and two very willing helpers.

My husband and I live in our own small apartment in a large residential center run by *The Spastics Society*. We are as independent as our disabilities allow, and fully responsible for organizing our vacations. This means writing lots of letters and finding suitable helpers, which can be very difficult but is not impossible.

We are fortunate as far as transport is concerned because we own a small van which has been adapted to take our chairs and all the other necessities for a comfortable vacation. But we do have to find helpers who are willing to drive it as well as give us complete daily living care.

In past years we have been abroad with organizations such as *The Across Trust* but this meant that we had to go with a group and share helpers. We much prefer to take vacations as a couple with our own escorts, mainly because of the circumstances in which we live—we have independence at home, so we like to enjoy it as far as possible when we travel.

I wrote to the *Disabled Living Foundation* asking for information on suitable self-catering accommodation for two severely disabled people in wheelchairs plus at least two helpers. From their information we discovered that the *John Grooms Association* owns, among other properties, a bungalow in Ambleside, on the north shore of Lake Windermere. I'd never been to the Lakes, so this was the one we chose.

We didn't have to find helpers on this trip because our friends Jo and Jane, whom we met in 1988, had already offered to help us again. We found Jo and Jane through an organization called *Holiday Helpers*, which matches up able-bodied helpers with disabled vacationers. You meet up before the vacation and if you don't get on you have to try again—it's important not to give up at this stage.

When you need as much help as we do, it's vital to state your requirements clearly. If possible, spend at least 24 hours with the helpers, so that you can decide whether or not they can cope. Don't make things too easy for them on this first meeting—remember that when you are on vacation you will be in strange surroundings and even simple tasks will be more difficult. And a piece of advice for both helper and disabled person: don't be afraid to say no! This will save both parties from a potentially disastrous vacation—and I speak from experience.

That's most of the hard work done, apart from saving the money. Unless you are traveling with family, friend, or an organized group, you have to pay for your helper's vacation, including food and in some cases spending money. This must be sorted out before you set off. Going on vacation is a costly business, but we think it's well worth it as long as you go through the preparations realistically and with care.

Jo and Jane joined us on the evening before our departure to help with the packing. For a self-catering trip this is no small task and involves clothes, food, kitchen utensils, and bedding, to name but a few. Finally everything was ready, and as we had over 250 miles to travel we set off early the next morning.

We made good time, although it was a Saturday morning in the height of the vacation season. We stopped twice at motorway service stations and the only difficulty was the usual one of not being able to get our wheelchairs close to the tables because all the seats are fixed to the floor. So we had to sit at the end and this meant that we were in the way, but most people were understanding.

"We had only ourselves to please"

Thanks to clear instructions from *John Grooms*, we had no problems finding "Nationwide," which was to be our home for the next two weeks. When I first saw the bungalow, all kinds of thoughts were spinning around in my head: would we be able to get on the toilet, would Jane like the kitchen, would the bedroom be big enough? But the bathroom was huge, there was plenty of room for us to move around in our chairs, and there was a color TV which worked!

It didn't take us long to sort ourselves out and find things in the kitchen. I could hardly believe that for a whole two weeks this lovely bungalow was ours! We could lie in bed, have a drink whenever we wished, have a hot bath every morning—absolute bliss. No waiting around for someone to come and put you on the toilet. We

had only ourselves to please. It was peaceful and the views from most of the windows were beautiful.

"We rarely get a chance to be right out in the wilds"

The summer of 1989 was dry and sunny but, let me tell you, it rains in the Lakes! This didn't stop us having a good time—far from it. Because it was mid-August the traffic was extremely heavy, so we stayed around Ambleside over both weekends. But we weren't confined to the bungalow: Jo and Jane were quite happy to push us to the town, although with steps and crowds to negotiate we had to sit outside nearly all the shops. We were able to get down to the lakeside and we had a very enjoyable boat trip on Lake Windermere. There was plenty of room for people in wheelchairs on board the pleasure boat, and the crew was very helpful.

In the bungalow we found much information on the local sights, and in the lakeside paperstore we bought *A Guide to the Lakes and Surrounding Areas for the Disabled Tourist*, a useful booklet. From this we found out about footpaths for wheelchairs just outside Ambleside and managed to locate the shorter one. It was a bit rough and therefore hard work for our pushers, but exciting for us as we rarely get a chance to be right out in the wilds.

With our own van we could go out whenever we wished. There is a tail-lift at the back and the only tricky part is clamping the chairs down to the floor, but Jo soon mastered it. He also liked driving, so we planned circular routes, often involving two or three hours on the road.

One day we went to the Scottish border and stopped at the first house in Scotland. After refreshments Jo and Jane pushed us to Gretna Green's famous smithy. We were able to get in through the back way and didn't have to pay. The other tourists were very friendly and did not mind making space for us. That interesting visit and the journey there through beautiful scenery made a lovely day out—I felt good to be alive!

We made a tour of the lakes, starting with a drive around the north end of Lake Windermere and continuing north past Grassmere and Thirlmere. The weather restricted our views to some extent—it was very misty and rained heavily at times—but we were able to appreciate the beauty of the thick woods surrounding the lakes, and the mountains rising from beyond the tree line.

> **"Cream all over my face and a grin from ear to ear—this is my idea of having fun!"**

We climbed into the hills, past Bassenthwaite and Ullswater, with sheep grazing on the higher ground. Skirting Derwentwater we drove up through a rough pass with the crags disappearing into the clouds. Then we crept down a winding, steep road from the rocky scree and boulders to the gentler slopes, all shades of green, and the trees around Lake Buttermere. We ended up at Cockermouth, where we explored the town until the heavens opened and we hurried back to the van. The rain kept up all the way back to Ambleside and our cosy home.

Toward the end of our vacation we decided to spend a day at the seaside. So off we went to Morecambe, but the sea was nowhere in sight—just miles of rather dirty brown sand. There was a brisk wind blowing onshore and the sun was in and out all day. Much to our surprise there were no crowds there, so we had plenty of room to be wheeled along the seafront. We found a pleasant, quiet snack bar on the front; everyone was friendly and helped to hold the doors open. In the indoor shopping area I spotted my favorite cake. I bought one and ate it there and then, whipped cream all over my face and a grin from ear to ear—this is my idea of having fun. I did see the sea in the end, as it was high tide by the time we left, which made my day.

In order to allow our helpers to recover their strength, we usually went for a long drive one day and then stayed close to Ambleside the next. We spent most evenings watching TV or playing Scrabble, enjoying a very strong nightcap. This may sound rather boring but for us it was fun and we could all drink knowing that we didn't have far to go to bed.

We did go out for one meal but it was not a good area for eating out, unless you count the hotels which were a bit costly for us. Jane and I went to the local movie theater in spite of a flight of steps at the front entrance—there was a back entrance on the level. The staff said they'd move a seat for me but I am able to transfer from my wheelchair. We stopped off after the movie to collect some fries to take to the men of our party who stayed home at "Nationwide."

Our memories of our vacation in the Lakes are the marvelous company of Jo and Jane, the wild and dramatic scenery, and the delightful freedom of being able to do just what we wanted when we wanted. None of it would have been possible without our wonderful helpers, who had to do everything for us apart from think. It is hard work helping people 24 hours a day for two weeks, but with give and take on both sides it can be rewarding for everyone.

English Country Holiday

Vivienne Adcock's disabilities arise from a condition which she contracted at the age of two. She was hospitalized for five years with TB of the hip and spine, during which time an accident occurred when a nurse was taking a full-length plaster cast off Vivienne's right leg. The nurse cut through tendons from hip to knee, and as a result Vivienne has a considerably shorter leg, stiff hip, permanently bent knee, and curvature of the spine. But she and her husband love to travel: here she enjoys life on a Wiltshire farm, which they visited in 1988.

At the very edge of a little village called Kington St. Michael, near Chippenham, lies Priory Farm, and on it a converted granary, purpose built for persons with disabilities, where there are no hazardous steps or any other obstacles to overcome. The granary sleeps two in separate beds of the "three bears" variety, both as comfy as Goldilocks' Mamma Bear's bed. It is tastefully decorated and furnished with antiques. There is an intercom to the farmhouse, and a spacious and thoughtfully equipped bathroom, plus a small kitchen area where you can make drinks and prepare picnics. This is bed and breakfast accommodation, with evening meals by arrangement. A car is necessary for exploration of the surrounding area and can be parked almost directly outside the granary.

Priscilla and Colin Labouchere, who own the farm, are out to provide very special vacations. They keep Belted Galloway cattle and Friesland sheep, and opposite the granary is a landscaped pond, which is the home of ornamental wildfowl. Another resident is Totty, a pony previously owned by a rag merchant. These days she responds to a quieter voice, with dignity and a sense of humor. "Tell her a joke and she'll laugh," urges Cilla—and she does! Totty will gladly pull you along in her cart which is adapted for wheelchairs. Cilla wins hearts with her endless tales of animal adventures, and—usually before breakfast—she carves ducks. These wooden replicas are so realistic that my husband couldn't resist constantly fingering them to assure himself that they weren't covered with real feathers.

There is a limited number of beds available at *Priory Cottage*, should your extended family or friends be coming with you, and the farmhouse is only a few yards from the granary, with easy access to the dining area and living room. Also available is an electric scooter which allows you to go where the mood takes you, up and down the lanes or over the fields to the brook.

As we spent so many happy hours seated around the pond we were interested to learn how it had materialized. Cilla patented an invention—a structure for taking the backache out of attending to sheep—and with the proceeds financed the building and stocking of the pond. The entire family gave a hand with the digging, using the farm tractor, and finally introducing their precious new family of a dozen pairs of waterfowl, including rare breeds. We never tired of watching the antics of these ducks, sharing our picnics with them and listening to duck anecdotes from our hostess.

Apart from the area around the farm there are many interesting and pretty places to visit within a fifteen-mile radius. We traveled as far as about thirty miles, covering a good bit of the Cotswolds. The River Windrush flows through the village of Bourton-on-the-Water under picturesque low stone bridges. There is a riverside path which leads to some quiet corners, and beyond the green you can enjoy secluded lanes with cottages of golden Cotswold stone.

But if you need a change from the quiet life, Bourton-on-the-Water is a bustling place with lots to see and do. I enjoyed a visit to the model village of Bourton, which even includes a model of the model! Although it is suffering from the ravages of time, I was enchanted by the attention to detail in miniature trees, shrubs, and flower-beds. Go there half an hour before closing time, when you can hear strains of music from the church on one side and the chapel on the other. Sadly, the paths are too narrow to take wheelchairs.

"We stayed all afternoon, painting and watching the occasional horse passing over the bridge"

Also worth visiting is Birdland, in the grounds of a Tudor manor, where you can see and speak to brightly colored parrots and macaws, their plumage flashing as they fly among the trees. There are penguins swimming in a glass-sided pool, toucans in the aviary and hummingbirds in the tropical houses. Wheelchairs are available here.

For contrast in the Cotswolds we recommend lunch at the ancient Mill Inn, in the small village of Withington. The building is of great historical interest and the atmosphere and menu are a rare treat. We had one of their home-made steak, kidney, bacon, and mushroom deep pies—every mouthful a joy. On a warm day you can eat in the garden with its miniature low bridge over a stream. We stayed all afternoon, painting and watching the occasional horse passing over the bridge.

Slimbridge Wildfowl and Wetlands Centre is another good place to make for, with every concession to the disabled visitor, including a taped guided tour (free of charge) for blind or partially sighted people. We spent about six hours there watching the largest and most varied collection of wildfowl in the world. We had lunch outdoors beside the beautifully landscaped lake, home to six species of flamingo. Hundreds of geese and ducks wander the grounds, ever hopeful of sharing the visitors' picnics; seed can be purchased for feeding them. There is a visitor center with fine exhibitions of paintings, a movie theater, gift shop, and restaurant, and an observatory.

My first visit to Slimbridge was with my husband soon after we were married. It was a bus ride from where we were staying and having missed the one bus of the day we were rescued by the local milkman. He took us all the way perched on the back of his truck, with legs swinging in time with the clanking bottles. The center was very new then and quite different; the path surfaces were of rough gravel which spoiled the visit for me, but the memory makes me thankful for the improved access today, at Slimbridge and at many other places of interest.

Stourhead garden, laid out in the eighteenth century with lakes, temples, and rare botanic specimens, is rated among our favorite National Trust properties and we've been there three times. The path around the edge of the main lake is about a mile long, wide enough for wheelchairs, and has a good smooth surface. We stopped at the tearoom before starting on our walk and arranged a cold lunch for our return—it gets very busy, especially on weekends. Wheelchairs are available at the Stourton village entrance to the garden and inside the house; there are thirteen steps up to the first floor of the house.

Back at the farm there is a large folder of information and many written comments and suggestions from previous disabled visitors, with stress on easy access and adapted rest rooms. It's a delightful area, with far too much to fit into a week.

Bird-watching in Nottingham

In this passage, Vivienne Adcock describes a bird-watching vacation based at a Winged Fellowship center in Nottingham, in 1989.

Perhaps Nottingham, an industrial city in the English Midlands, seems an unlikely spot for bird-watching, but John Wyatt, organizer and leader on behalf of the RSPB, knows better. In 1989 he had been running this sort of vacation for two years, and we were impressed by his careful planning and efficient organization.

Following a warm welcome over a pot of tea on our arrival at *Skylarks Holiday Centre*, any physical help that would be needed during our stay was discussed. The center is modern with bright decor and plenty of space. Most of the bedrooms overlook beautiful lawns and a well-kept, secluded garden with seats tucked away in patios and in nooks and crannies near a small pond. We saw quite a bit of wildlife here with minimal effort.

The center adjoins the National Water Sports Centre and Nature Reserve at Holme Pierrepoint, which was created out of an area of worked-out gravel pits. The reserve is managed by the Nottinghamshire Trust for Nature Conservation and all the different types of habitat on the reserve can be seen from the nature trail.

"We had what I would call an 'action-packed vacation'"

The trail paths are excellent both for wheelchair users and for those with walking difficulties. There are several places for a sit and the first time I visited I managed almost the whole circuit with the aid of elbow crutches. The habitats for wildlife include two lakes, reed beds, dense areas of willow (a haven for warblers), and carpets of orchids in the summer, with clearings attractive to butterflies. Three hides allow close-up views of birds; from one of them we watched activity at the tern table and—a special treat for us—the courtship dance of the great crested grebe.

On our second visit to the reserve I went by wheelchair and was able to see tiny frogs. The bonus of the day was that the Wildlife Management team had rigged up netting the previous evening in order to catch a few species for ringing. We were able to touch and hold—as well as see at close quarters—reed warbler, reed bunting, willow warbler, and song thrush.

We had what I would call an "action-packed vacation." By 10am each day we set off in a specially adapted *Winged Fellowship* van, returning in time to freshen up before the evening meal. In the evenings the bird-watching group (which in this instance was small—five disabled visitors and five helpers) met in a separate room for slide shows of what we were hoping to see the next day, then what we had seen, and checklists of the day's sightings.

Not all of the bird-watching was done in Nottingham. On our first venture to Leicestershire's Rutland Waters the rain tipped down unmercifully, but once inside the Egleton Interpretive Centre at the southernmost point of the village we were welcomed with steaming hot drinks. We looked at slides of the reserve and were given a potted history of the huge area (1214ha) of open water. Since it was constructed in 1975 it has become one of the most important wildfowl sanctuaries in Britain, with its purpose-built islands, shingle banks, and three lagoons. We later had time to look at the displays of information at the center, and an attractive shop.

John and company had come fully equipped for all eventualities, and when we returned to our bus we were handed extra waterproofs. I hit the record by wearing fourteen items of clothing! But we arrived at the hide to find it surprisingly comfortable, with molded plastic chairs and two telescopes rigged up for our use. Before long the rain lessened and we made some unexpected and unusual sightings. About an hour later the picnic was distributed—attractively arranged salads, pies, chips, fruit, cookies, cake, and as many hot drinks as we could wish for. The reserve wardens joined us and it was one big party. I have since discovered that many bird lovers take their lunch into the hides and stay for several hours. I didn't imagine it could be so exciting.

"78 species were spotted at these sites, out of which I claim to have seen 66"

The next day we drove to Welbeck Park and Clumber Park, hoping to see honey buzzards at the first site. We were disappointed but carried on to Clumber Park where I had my first experience of being pushed through woods in a wheelchair. I am usually very limited as regards rough ground and distances, walking slowly with elbow crutches, and most of my time is spent looking down rather than up. My particular delight in the woods was being able to look up at the cathedral-like canopies of spring leaves while listening to the symphony of woodland birds.

In Derbyshire, on another outing, we made first for Swallow Moss, a reserve which is not open to the public except down one track. We picnicked at one end of this moorland in the hope of seeing red and black grouse. Unexpected entertainment, similarly colored, arrived in the shape of a company of cadets with blackened faces, whose leader, distinguished by his red beret, crouched, stalked and beckoned them on until they took cover by our bus. We tried hard to contain our amusement as many of the cadets looked self-conscious and somewhat sheepish. At the other end of the track we were rewarded with sightings of grouse and wheatear.

At Wetton Mill we walked along an old railroad track by the Manifold river. This is a good hard track for wheelchairs, with no traffic passing. The scenery is beautiful and the track has a slight incline, leaving the fast flowing river just below to the right, and steep banks on the left, eventually ending in dramatic cave mouths, marking an ancient level of the river. The area is rich in wild flowers and birds, and we learned to look to the higher slopes for goldfinch, linnet, and whinchat, while lower down we sighted tree pipits, spotted flycatcher, whitethroat, and blackcap. On our return we scanned the river from the bridge in vain for the promised kingfisher, but were consoled with a long study of the habits of the dipper.

During our five-day stay 78 species were spotted at these sites, out of which I claim to have seen 66—not bad for a beginner, although whether or not I'd recognize them again is questionable! Our leader and helpers were with us throughout each day, including mealtimes, and their patience seemed limitless. Those of us who were slower or didn't know very much about the subject were embraced as equal with the "old hands," and we had a lot of fun together.

Leicestershire Bells

Jane Nyman, who has Parkinson's disease, has spent many vacations in convents (she writes about the English Convent in Bruges on p.228), but she was rather nonplussed when it was suggested that she try a vacation in a Trappist monastery in deepest Leicestershire.

I knew very little about Trappist monasteries, except that this order was originally French and that the monks spent the greater part of their days in silence. As far as I could gather, they led a very frugal existence shut away from the world.

I then encountered a Trappist monk in Belgium and he turned out to be a dapper little man from Zaire with an elegant short beard, impeccably dressed in a pin-striped suit. He was studying at the University of Brussels and, somehow, he did not fit the image. He questioned me minutely about aspects of the Anglican faith, and either I did not know or had forgotten the answers. Panic-stricken, my French failed me, and I decided that in future I would avoid Trappist monks.

"There was a lovely pub . . . in case I could not stand the Trappist regime and needed to decamp at short notice!"

As for taking a vacation in a Trappist monastery, I had visions of a great many church services, a cold stone cell, and bread and cheese meals, so I arranged for a friend to take me over for a sneak preview of the monastery before I committed myself. It was a cold spring day, with a piercing wind, and despite directions from the Guest Master, who had assured me that we could not miss it, we had some difficulty in locating the monastery and its large bell tower.

However, I was delighted to find that there was a lovely pub, not a hundred yards from the gate. Since this is "Quorn country," famous for its fox-hunting, the bar was filled with hunting horns (genuine) and hunting prints. It was warm and welcoming; the food was excellent and reasonably priced. I made a note of their weekly terms and their phone number, in case I could not stand the Trappist regime and needed to decamp at short notice!

The monastery was built in the 1930s but the solidity of its walls suggested a far earlier tradition. The monks derive their income from a number of enterprises on the premises, thus ensuring that they spend a maximum amount of time in prayer, while at the same time being self-sufficient. There is a farm, a guesthouse, and a shop which is open for about three hours a day. The monks also run a pottery and a printing press, although these are out of bounds to guests.

The shop sells a marvelous mixture of items, ranging from Catholic bric-à-brac to postcards and home-made honey. There's a good selection of pottery at very fair prices, and some nicely carved Nativity scenes in the Austrian tradition. They also sell printed stationery and a wide range of religious books. As the monks who run the shop are relaxed and possessed of a good sense of humor, I found myself returning again and again. The silence rules certainly did not apply there. I still do not know whether or not they were pulling my leg when they assured me that they sold teapots with three spouts, but were temporarily out of stock.

The monastery caters to people who are on retreat, or for people who simply need a vacation. I met Catholics as well as non-Catholics, and some who did not seem to belong to any persuasion but simply liked the atmosphere. I met two elderly sisters who had been going there for years, as it was a convenient place for them to meet, geographically about halfway between their two homes.

I discovered that the single men and married couples were housed in the monastery itself, and the single ladies slept in a building about a hundred yards away, down the drive. While it is the Guest Master who books you in and answers any queries that you may have, there is also a warden for the women's guesthouse, who gives you a warm welcome.

The Guest Master, who I discovered had been a keen cricketer in the past, produced a list of regulations for me to read. I found that very helpful: if you decide to come here for a vacation, you cannot inadvertently break the rules. He checked that I was not on any special diet, and I asked if I could be put in a room near the bathrooms. It was also explained that I would need to be able to climb one flight of stairs. Having settled the details, I felt quite happy to reserve a five-day stay.

Although there are some rules, attendance at church is not one of them. The main rules are that there is silence after the last office (about 7:30pm) until breakfast time, although this was not strictly observed in the ladies' guesthouse, and that the main gates are locked at this time. In practice, I did not find it difficult to observe this rule, as my day tended to start very early and by 7:30pm I was glad to be in bed.

I arrived in the middle of a heatwave in May. My room was tiny but adequate, and only three of us had to share the bathroom. I heaved a sigh of relief when I unpacked and found a hot-water bottle in the drawers. There was a radiator in my room but I assumed (wrongly, as it turned out) that it would not be turned on if we had a couple of chilly days. There was a small living room downstairs, containing one of those weird and wonderful machines for making tea and coffee with ten variations. The first night I was there I learned the reason for the embargo on nightlife. The monks begin their devo-

tions at 3:30am and guests are welcome to join them. You do not have to worry about an alarm clock, as a huge bell tolls at 3:30am and again at 4am. From where I slept I could look out over rolling farmland and see the bell tower looming out of the morning mist. Soon, when my body had adjusted to the different routine, I enjoyed being woken so early.

"Despite their old-fashioned way of life and clothing, the monks went in for modern technology in a big way"

After meals, the guests join in the washing-up and this is quite a good way of getting to know your fellow guests. Indeed, the rules positively encourage guests to talk to each other. Although most of the monastery is out of bounds to guests, the monks came flocking across to greet and have tea or coffee with their particular friends.

At first it sounded a little odd to listen to these elderly monks in their traditional white habits with enormously long sleeves (two feet longer than their arms) discussing the merits of various computers. But I soon discovered that despite their old-fashioned way of life and clothing, the monks went in for modern technology in a big way. While the Guest Master was welcoming me, his bleep went off and this happened again when I was talking to a saintly 84-year-old monk who was quite happy to discuss the merits of abortion with me. These men might seem to lead a life cut off from the modern world, but they are as up to date in their thinking as anyone outside the monastery. As the monastery is enormous, the bleep system made perfect sense; it was just that I had never linked saintliness and modern technology in my mind.

The church is huge and the monks sing their office at one end, like an invisible choir. As I am the nosy sort, I found this disappointing, but at Mass the monks and guests make a large circle and you can gawk to your heart's content.

In addition to a bedroom, each guest is allocated a private; living room, so that if you wish to be alone to read or write, or to talk to a monk, you have complete privacy. Although guests who are on retreat are expected to get on with it by themselves, if you have any sort of problem there is always someone available for a chat.

I sometimes needed help with cutting up food, but this was always done without fuss. Occasionally, I needed help to walk to my seat in church, but again help was immediately given. The atmosphere was very peaceful and I felt myself gradually unwind. The monastery provides three cooked meals a day, as well as tea and coffee, which is too much for me. It was so hot that at lunchtime I nipped off to my devotions in the pub, for a cooling drink.

I got up early and went to church, after which I was glad of my "English" breakfast. I read, lounged about in the lovely garden on comfortable wooden benches, did embroidery, and periodically went for a drive in the car in the very beautiful countryside. There is a village about three miles away, with a train station and a selection of shops. Loughborough is only about ten miles away, if you hanker for a town, but most people had come to escape "civilization" and were content with the quiet life.

One night, we had a tremendous thunderstorm while we were in church. The lights went out half a dozen times but the emergency lighting functioned well. The problem was, how to get back to supper, in the torrential rain, without getting soaked to the skin . . .. I drove back to find the Guest Master assembling a collection of large, black brollies, and monks with towels at the ready, to dry our hair. When I returned to my room after supper, my windows had been closed and the radiator was warm.

Although I normally use a wheelchair outside, I found that I did not need one and instead used my car to move between the women's guesthouse, the monastery, and the church. The accommodation would not be suitable for an indoor wheelchair user. If you are disabled you need a car to get out and about.

If you don't like being woken early, take some earplugs or just close the window to prevent the bell from waking you. If you are a "single" and you cannot face a vacation on your own, this offers a way of meeting people in a relaxed way. My fellow guests were a very mixed bunch, ranging from a lad who had been out of work for several years, to an amateur weatherforecaster, who worried when we had a storm that he was not at home to take the rain readings. There was also an ex-nun, with a delightful sense of humor, who wore glamorous clothes, a few deacons and parish priests, as well as others who were difficult to fit into any category.

If you have very little money, you make a donation to the monastery and you do not receive a bill. It is tactfully indicated how much your stay costs the monks (in 1989 it was £10 a day) and you may give more or less according to your circumstances. For total board, I thought it excellent value for money. If *haute cuisine* and a lively nightlife are what you require, this vacation is not for you, but as a restful break in lovely countryside it is ideal.

Cornish Adventure Holiday

In May 1989 Veronica Smith, herself a wheelchair user, was one of eight members of staff who took a group of children to the specially adapted Churchtown Farm Field Studies Centre at Lanlivery in Cornwall.

We met outside the school in Cambridge at 8:30am: sixteen children between the ages of eleven and sixteen (ten wheelchair disabled, two ambulant disabled, four able-bodied) and eight members of staff (six able-bodied and two wheelchair disabled). To transport all of us and our luggage we had rented a tourbus with a lift. Getting us all safely aboard was a work of art; some children transferred to seats, but those in electric chairs stayed put and their chairs were clamped to the floor of the bus. Extra space had to be found for spare wheelchairs and for two hoists.

"It was curious to see a boy in an electric wheelchair with a pitchfork or broom wedged down the side, mucking out a dirty stall!"

We set off only a few minutes later than intended and, initially, apart from Linda's chair coming unclamped, the journey was uneventful. After an hour or so, we became aware of an unpleasant smell—the bus was belching out clouds of pungent, black fumes. Next the engine began to stall—something was definitely wrong! We stopped at a service area, unloaded everyone, and headed for food and much needed coffee, leaving the driver to phone for advice. He managed to make temporary repairs and we continued on our way, arriving at the center in time to unpack before the evening meal.

The center is superbly equipped for disabled people and has a large number of staff, including a resident night nurse, who was able to turn the boys with muscular dystrophy, thus enabling the staff to have an uninterrupted night's rest.

For daytime activities we split up into two groups, each with eight children, four of our staff and between two and four staff from the center, depending on the nature of the day's activities. On our first full day my group was based at the center's own farm. The children were able to participate in many new activities, including bottle-feeding the lambs, feeding the pigs, collecting eggs, grooming ponies, and mucking out cows and horses. It was curious to see a boy in an electric wheelchair with a pitchfork or broom wedged down the side, mucking out a dirty stall! We had a chance to inspect and handle the small animals kept at the farm, including snakes. All of the children were happy to hold a snake or have it draped around their necks; some of the staff were not so keen!

Our group then had to plan our evening meal, cooking their own food in the open, over a campfire. The wood-collecting expedition was successful and we soon had a suitably large pile, at which point ominous black clouds began to gather and we returned briefly to the center to don warm clothes and waterproofs. On the way back to the field, Jeremy managed to slide off the bumpy grass track and tip his electric wheelchair over, landing underneath it. But he was quickly righted and no damage sustained, by Jeremy or his chair.

"Abseiling and rock climbing were our activities for the next day"

When we arrived back at the field it was pouring down, so the children cooked their food on camping stoves in the shelter of an open-sided barn. By the time we'd finished our meal the rain had stopped and we were able to light the fire, have a somewhat tuneless sing-song, and play silly games.

Abseiling and rock climbing were our activities for the next day. We set off in two minivans across Bodmin Moor to a disused quarry. There we unloaded and played a hectic wheelchair chase game on the quarry floor, which involved much laughter and hitting members of the opposing team with rolled-up newspapers. This worked up an appetite for the picnic lunch, after which the serious business of the day began.

Rock climbing was first on the agenda. Robert, who has cerebral palsy but is ambulant, decided to accept the instructor's invitation to climb up the almost sheer rockface of the quarry. He was kitted out with a safety helmet and connected securely to a rope; looking slightly less confident, he set off with the instructor amid shouts of encouragement from the others. All went well until Robert had reached the halfway point, when he seemed to realize the enormity of what he was doing and "froze." After considerable help and cajoling, he completed the climb, feeling justifiably pleased with himself but leaving me with a few more gray hairs!

"The quarry walls were too steep for wheelchair abseiling"

Meanwhile, David had gotten out of his chair and; with some help, was scrambling delightedly over the boulders and rocks of the quarry floor. Neil was driving around in his electric chair, whizzing through puddles, hitting the water with sticks, and generally getting into a very pleasurable mess.

Next came the abseiling, in which all the group took part. The quarry walls were too steep for wheelchair abseiling but there was a very steep grassy hill which proved ideal. It was a complicated business roping up chairs and children safely, but well worth the effort. Even those who were apprehensive to start with enjoyed the experience; most had more than one go, and everyone learned to control their own descent, with varying degrees of assistance.

After supper that evening the children tried one of two craft activities—pottery or making a collage. This was relaxing after an energetic day and provided a good opportunity for boasting of their achievements.

The center has its own specially adapted cruiser moored in the small, picturesque port of Fowey. The boat is flat bottomed and the bow lets down to allow loading of wheelchairs. We headed out of the harbor toward the open sea. It was a fresh day and the wind was strong, creating sizable waves. The noise, the splashing and bouncing across the waves were all greatly enjoyed, and once back inside the harbor the children were each able to have a turn at controlling the boat—at times we must have resembled a wildly tacking yacht!

After lunch it was time for canoeing. Some of the center staff had paddled out to join us in two canoes. We cruised up a quiet creek and began loading them up. This involved hauling each canoe up the partially lowered bow and into the boat; transfer of children into the canoes was then safe and relatively easy. All of the children except Linda were able to take part; Linda and I stayed on the motor boat, enjoying a quiet coffee, while the others paddled off, in high spirits, up the creek to explore.

The canoeists were tired when they returned and we all headed back to the center. After supper, those with enough energy left made good use of the indoor swimming pool.

We had one "day off" during our stay, when we could choose our own activity. Our two groups joined together and after much debate we decided to drive to Flambard's Theme Park, near Helston. The park has a range of attractions, including funfair rides, remote controlled model vehicles, and various indoor theme exhibitions—an excellent one portrays life in the Blitz. Everything is fully accessible, so that the children were able to go off without needing a member of staff with them. There is a large gift shop, a highly popular "clotted cream by post" center, and a great deal of junk food on sale, all of which was relished by the children—the food provided at *Churchtown Farm* was very good but, for the children, did not have the same appeal as ice cream or french fries!

Toward the end of our week we had the help of four naval ratings from a nearby training ship: their assistance was welcomed by us all, but particularly by some of the older girls! We decided to make good use of the extra muscle power and spend part of the day at a local cove. Great strength was certainly needed when dragging the wheelchairs across the sand to a pleasantly sheltered picnic spot. After lunch most of the children got out of their chairs and sat chatting, played in the sand or went for a wade. David and Neil did not want to transfer from their chairs but did want to wade, so they parked at the edge of the sea with feet and wheels just in the water. Later in the afternoon we left the beach, drove to a bluebell wood, and went for a delightful scent-filled walk; the entire wood was a mass of blue.

On our last day we set off once more for Fowey and the motor cruiser, but this time we towed two sail boats behind us. These boats had been cleverly adapted so that even the most severely disabled children could control them independently. Each boat held six people and could be powered by sails or motor.

There was a strong breeze and the boats cut through the water at exhilarating speed. To begin with the sails were used, with the children working the ropes and at the tiller. Later the engines were put to use and the most severely disabled were able to sit strapped securely into a specially constructed seat in the stern of each boat. From here they took charge of the boats, controlling speed and direction by using a joystick in the same way as for maneuvering their electric chairs. This was an enormous success and quite made the children's vacation.

ENGLAND & WALES: TRAVEL NOTES

Sources of Information

Wales Tourist Board, *British Tourist Authority*, 40 West 57th Street, New York, NY 10019-4001; ☎212/581-470. A guide for visitors with disabilities, *Accessible Wales*, was published in 1991 by the *Wales Council for the Disabled* (Llys Ifor, Crescent Road, Caerphilly, Mid-Glamorgan CFB 1XL; ☎0222/887325) in association with the tourist board. The guide is available in British bookstores (price £2) and it covers accommodation (three grades of accessibility), transport, tourist attractions, sporting activities, places to eat and drink, public rest room facilities, emergency contacts, wheelchair repair agents. It also lists local access guides and where to obtain them.

Welsh Water (Dwr Cymru): Land and Leisure (Tir a Hamdden Ltd.), Cambrian Way, Brecon, Powys LD3 7HP; ☎0874/3181. Information on access to sailing, fishing, birdwatching, and nature trails on and around the Welsh reservoirs is contained in a free booklet, *Reservoir Recreation with Special Interest to the Disabled*.

ENGLAND & WALES TRAVEL NOTES

English Tourist Board, *British Tourist Authority*, 40 West 57th Street, New York, NY 10019-4001 (212/581-4700); 94 Cumberland Street, Suite 600, Toronto, Ontario M5R 3N3 (416/925-6326). Both the level of information provision by the regional and county tourist boards and the general disability awareness among tourism operators have improved in recent years. A significant factor in this change for the better has been *Tourism for All*, a joint study (report published September 1989) carried out by the *English Tourist Board* and the *Holiday Care Service* (see *Useful Contacts*, below), involving representatives from voluntary organizations, national tourist boards, and the tourism industry.

An important outcome of this study will be the introduction of a national scheme to identify accommodation that is accessible to three categories of guests: (1) independent wheelchair users; (2) wheelchair users with assistance; (3) wheelchair users who are able to walk a few paces and up a maximum of three steps. The new symbols will be awarded as a result of the *ETB's* own inspection, rather than relying on hotel managers to supply information. Unfortunately this will take some time to incorporate into the tourist board publications, and the 1993 editions of the **Where To Stay** guides (a series of four substantial guides, available in UK bookstores: *Hotels and Guesthouses in England; B&Bs, Farmhouses, Inns and Hostels in England; Self-Catering Holiday Homes in England; Camping and Caravan Parks in Britain*) will contain no symbols. It is hoped that the 1994 editions will carry the results of the survey.

In the meantime, the **Holiday Care Service** (see *Useful Contacts*) has published a series of *Accessible Accommodation* leaflets, covering each of the twelve regions in England plus one for Cornwall (there is also one each for Scotland and Wales). These are available from the *Holiday Care Service* or the tourist boards. Although useful, the leaflets make depressing reading, as very few places receive the Category 1 description. Clearly, there is a long way to go before the accommodation sector of the tourist industry can prove that it has taken the philosophy of *Tourism for All* to heart.

Of the English county tourist boards, it is perhaps worth singling out Kent, where the *Holiday Care Service* has been contracted to advise and work on a program that will help disabled visitors enjoy the county. Objectives include: the improvement of the accessibility of accommodation, attractions, and transport; disability awareness training for providers of Kent vacations; inspection of accommodation listed in future editions of *Kent for Disabled People*.

Tour Operators

Can Be Done Ltd (7–11 Kensington High Street, London W8 5NP; ☎081/907 2400; fax 081/909 1854) is managed by Jackie Scott who is a wheelchair user and, wherever possible, she inspects hotels to check facilities before recommending them to clients. *Can Be Done* handles tours, events, and days out for individuals or groups, accompanied by qualified guides; all vehicles are fully adapted and lift-equipped; days start at a civilized hour, and tours are suitable for anyone wanting to travel at a leisurely pace. Clients can discuss their own itineraries but, to give an idea of prices, a six-day North of England tour, starting from London and taking in Haworth, Castle Howard, Harrogate, the Peak District, Manchester, and the Yorkshire Moors, costs £360 (about $670) per person.

Getting There

London is usually one of the cheapest "gateway" cities in Europe. From eastern and central USA the best deals are out of New York and Chicago to London; of the major carriers—*American, British Airways, United*, and *Virgin Atlantic*—we have received many good reports of the last three from disabled passengers; *Virgin* probably offers best value for money. From the West Coast, the major airlines fly frequently from LA, San Francisco, and Seattle; *British Airways* flights are plentiful and competitive, fares starting at $700 to London. From Canada, the big airlines fly to London from Montréal and Toronto at least once daily; *Air Canada* and *Canadian* have a good reputation.

ENGLAND & WALES TRAVEL NOTES

Transport

Public transit bodies have been notoriously slow to respond to the needs of disabled passengers, and the view that disabled passengers must be shunted into separate services (parallel transit systems) is deeply entrenched. This is illustrated by an account of a British wheelchair user's "discovery" of accessible public transit in Los Angeles back in 1988, and the comparison he draws with public transportation in London. It still holds true some five years later:

"The day after we arrived on vacation in California I was out eagerly looking for a bus. The first stop we came to displayed the wheelchair logo. Not only that but the route went direct to Venice, cradle of the beat generation and on my list of sightseeing 'musts.' Still slightly incredulous I stuck out my hand as the bus approached. It stopped, at a flick of the driver's switch the exit steps unfolded into a hydraulic platform and I was on board and slotted into a wheelchair space that conveniently doubled as standing room for commuters. As we pulled away I couldn't help wondering where the catch was.

On returning to London it was back to good old *Dial-a-Ride* and the one trip a month syndrome. Three weeks before I'd gone along with it, and all the agonizing and hand-wringing by the powers that be about accessible public transportation and the insuperable problems of finance and logistics. Then I'd seen how simple it actually was—the reasonable cost (quite feasible for a fair percentage of *London Transport* buses), the ease of operation and, what it really comes down to, the fact that everyone had taken me for granted, just another passenger. In London, on the other hand, all I can expect is to shuttle backward and forward to Heathrow airport or slowly circulate mainline train stations in a vehicle emblazoned with the caption "Carelink" to show how different I am from other people. That is the gulf of attitudes." (From an article by Stephen Hunt, writing as David Hunt, first published in *Go By Bus*, June 1988.)

While several companies offer accessible **tourbuses** for rent—see *Getting Around by Bus and Coach* (available from the *Bus & Coach Council*, Sardinia House, 52 Lincoln Fields, London WC2A 3LZ; ☎071/831 7546) and the *RADAR* holiday guide (see *Books*)—it's access to ordinary scheduled intercity and inner city services that's needed, with hydraulic lifts installed as standard on *all* public buses.

LONDON TRANSPORT

In 1990 a petition with 38,000 signatures was presented to Parliament by the *London Dial-a-Ride Users' Association*, pressing for legislation that would require all new buses and tourbuses purchased from 1992 by UK operators to be accessible to people with disabilities, including wheelchair users. By mid-1992 there was no sign of action.

For full-time wheelchair users, Carelink and Airbus (see *Air Travel*, below) remain the only fully accessible **bus services** in central London, although there is an expanding network of lift-equipped single-deck "Mobility Buses" (there's that special labeling again) operating in the suburbs. It is true that Airbus was the world's first fully accessible airport bus link, and that the Carelink buses now carry anyone who wants to use them, disabled or not, but who would want to travel from Paddington to Victoria via Euston, St. Pancras, King's Cross, Liverpool Street, and Waterloo? A slow clockwise circular route round the mainline train stations is not the solution to London's accessible transport problems.

For those who have some degree of mobility, special features are now specified for all new buses and are being retrospectively fitted to 2500 existing double-deckers. On new vehicles these include lower entrance and exit steps, and on new and newly fitted buses there are color-contrasted and nonslip handrails, "Bus Stopping" signs that illuminate when the bell is rung, palm-operated bells and high-visibility step edging—some two thirds of London's buses are scheduled to have these features by spring 1993. A large-print central London bus map is available from the **Unit for Disabled Passengers** (London Transport, 55 Broadway, London SW1H 0BD; ☎071/222 5600, or Minicom 071/918 3015; for free information pack on the Unit, write, or phone ☎071/918 3312, voice or Minicom).

ENGLAND & WALES TRAVEL NOTES

As well as London Buses, the *London Transport (LT) Group* has two other operating businesses—London Underground and the Docklands Light Railroad. Much of the **Underground** network is inaccessible to wheelchairs. A 120-page book, *Access to the Underground* (70p over the counter at *LT* Travel Information Centres at King's Cross, Euston, Oxford Circus, Piccadilly Circus, Victoria, and Heathrow Central; next update scheduled February 1993), gives full details, and a free leaflet, *Access to Central London Underground Stations*, gives an at-a-glance list of stations in the central area, showing whether access is by stairs, escalator, or elevator. Also available free from the *Unit for Disabled Passengers* are a large-print Underground map, a tactile Central London Underground map, "Helping Hand" notepads, and two cassette tapes, "A talking map of the London Underground" and "A talking Underground station guide." The Travel Information Service (☎071/222 1234), operating 24 hours a day, has a Minicom number, ☎071/918 3015. The Jubilee Line extension (Green Park to Stratford) will be fully accessible (scheduled completion mid-1990s), and new trains built for the Central Line will have audible door buzzers and automated digital-speech announcements of station names; similar features are in place on renovated trains operating on other lines.

The **Docklands Light Railway** is accessible, with same-level access from platform to train, and elevators from street to platform, but check facilities at interchanges with Underground or *British Rail* stations. The upgrading program, still in progress in mid-1992, involved the closure of the railroad at evenings and weekends, but the replacement bus service could be supplemented by a wheelchair-accessible Mobility Bus at two hours' notice. For up-to-date information on the service, phone the Dockland Travel Hotline (☎071/918 4000).

TRAIN TRAVEL

British Rail has made significant progress in improvement of access and facilities for disabled passengers on trains and at stations. However, some conflicting reports of *BR*'s service have been received, in spite of the fact that staff members receive instruction from a detailed training video which explains how to meet the differing needs of all disabled customers. Disabled passengers may still be left stranded when they have carefully followed instructions to give advance notice of requests for assistance. There are still too many stations that are simply inaccessible to wheelchairs. Provision of wheelchair-accessible rest rooms on trains are poor, and wheelchair users are still forced to travel in the baggage compartment on Network Southeast (Kent and Sussex), although this is rare elsewhere in the country. *BR*'s reliance on audible announcements, without information monitors inside the trains as well as on platforms, means that many deaf travelers find train journeys more of a trial than air travel.

All regular Intercity services offer a space, 26 inches (67cm) wide, for a wheelchair in the passenger car. Wide doors, automatic interior doors, and grab-rails are standard facilities. There is a wheelchair-accessible toilet on London–Glasgow services, and all new mainline stock will have one adapted toilet per train. There are no plans to introduce larger compartments on Intercity Sleepers to allow disabled passengers to transfer comfortably from wheelchair to bed.

Modern Sprinter and Pacer trains are in service on most regional routes, replacing stock of 1950s vintage. Trains on long-distance routes are equipped with a wheelchair-accessible toilet. Full-time wheelchair users either travel in the vestibule or in the passenger car seating area—the latter should be the norm if we are to believe *BR*'s stated aim: "to enable wheelchair users, if they so wish, to travel in their wheelchairs throughout their journey within the public saloon alongside other passengers and not in guards' vans or special compartments."

Network Southeast is served by some older trains, which *BR* claims have up to fifteen years' life in them; restructuring to accommodate wheelchairs is deemed uneconomical, and as a stop-gap solution baggage cars are being "upgraded" to provide a more comfortable environment—heat, light, wheelchair restraints, and a tip-up seat for a companion. Accessible, sliding-door stock is being introduced on inner

ENGLAND & WALES TRAVEL NOTES

and outer suburban routes. On long-distance routes, trains have Intercity-type facilities.

BR has equipped more than 130 principal stations with facilities for four main categories of disabled rail travelers: ambulant disabled, wheelchair users, sight impaired, and hearing impaired. Further stations are being upgraded to full accessibility. Facilities include conveniently sited parking spaces, signing to indicate easiest routes and call-for-assistance facilities, adapted rest rooms (fitted with National Key System locks; see *Driving*, below), passenger elevators, induction loops at ticket office windows and travel centers, inductive couplers fitted to public phones, access to catering facilities, medium-level phones, white markings on platform edges and stairs, and portable ramps for access to trains.

There are fare reductions for a wheelchair user or visually impaired person and one companion, but for foreign visitors these only apply on full-fare tickets; thus it is usually better to buy one of the ordinary range of cheap tickets such as Saver, Cheap Day Return, and AwayBreak. Only British residents can apply for a *Disabled Persons Railcard* which costs £14 and gives concessions on all tickets.

Careful planning and advance warning is necessary if you are traveling alone and require assistance on your journey, and the assumption seems to be that disabled people never need to travel at short notice and are expert at preplanning. Travelers from North America should contact the Manager of their nearest mainline station on arrival in Britain (phone numbers supplied in the passenger care leaflet *British Rail and Disabled Travelers*, available at any station). *British Rail International*—offices at 1500 Broadway, New York, NY 10036 (☎212/575-2667), or 94 Cumberland Street, Toronto, ON M5R 1A3 (☎416/929-3333)—have copies of *A Guide to British Rail for Disabled People* (see *Books*, below) but they won't make any special arrangements for you.

AIR TRAVEL

Probably the best means of public transportation for the disabled person—**air travel**—is unfortunately the most expensive way to get around Britain, and there are no fare conces-

sions for disabled passengers. Facilities at the major airports are generally accessible, with provision of ramps, curb cuts, automatic doors, elevators, and adapted rest rooms being taken seriously, although niggling design faults and omissions remain and even feature in newly built terminals. At Stansted, for example, opened in March 1991, the glare from the glass roof makes monitors difficult to read; the floor is a joy for wheelchair users but slippery for ambulant disabled people and lacking in textured surfaces for those with visual disabilities; the doors on the accessible rest rooms are heavy—and these blunders occurred in spite of consultation with disability groups during the design of the airport buildings.

There are induction loop audio points at Birmingham, Gatwick, Heathrow, and Stansted, but only delays are announced at Gatwick. At Stansted there are two signing members of staff on the information desk and two in Security. The Mincom Supertel (☎0293/513179) at Gatwick can be used not only to phone in to the airport for flight information but also by a passenger wishing to contact a deaf person who has the link in their home. Telephones that can be amplified are installed at several airports, including Aberdeen, Belfast, Gatwick, Heathrow, Manchester, and Stansted. There is a touch map for blind passengers at Birmingham.

Boarding and disembarking at Heathrow and Gatwick is nearly always direct from or to the terminal, with no need for lifting equipment. At Stansted international flights are boarded/disembarked from satellites through covered air-bridges; the satellites are reached via wheelchair-accessible "automated track transit link" (trains without drivers). At Cardiff-Wales boarding/disembarking is either by airbridge or manual lifting. Lifting vehicles are available at many regional airports, including Birmingham, Bristol, East Midlands, Leeds/Bradford, Luton, Manchester, Newcastle, and the Scottish airports; their use may depend on the size of the aircraft.

Public transit links from the nearest city to airport are most accessible at Belfast (see *Ireland Travel Notes*), Heathrow, and Gatwick. Anyone can use *London Transport*'s wheel-

ENGLAND & WALES TRAVEL NOTES

chair-accessible Carelink bus service (hourly, every day; first bus 8:30am from Victoria Station, last bus 7:15pm Waterloo to Paddington only), which connects London's mainline train stations with Airbus 1 at Victoria and Airbus 2 at Euston. Each Airbus can carry two wheelchairs and shuttles between central London and the four **Heathrow** terminals; Airbuses run between 6:40am and 9:20pm daily on Route A1 from Victoria, and between 6:30am and 8:30pm daily on Route A2 from Euston. *British Rail*'s **Gatwick** Express (departures every 15 minutes during the day, hourly at night) is wheelchair-accessible (no advance warning necessary) and operates between Victoria Station and Gatwick's South Terminal, where there are elevators from the platforms.

For advice on transport to and from airports contact TRIPSCOPE (see *Useful Contacts*).

DRIVING

Driving is a popular method of vacation transport, and **cars with hand controls** can be rented from *Hertz* (seven days' notice required) at corporate locations throughout the UK. *Hertz* was the only international car rental company to respond to our requests for information for disabled travelers and to show real commitment to extending their services to meet the requirements of disabled drivers.

Self-drive, wheelchair-adapted vans (a choice of four models, two with automatic transmission, two stick-shift) are available from *Wheelchair Travel*, 1 Johnston Green, Guildford, Surrey GU2 6XS; ☎0483/233640; fax 0483/39661. We have received several glowing reports of this service from satisfied US and Canadian customers. From March to end of September (1992) rates vary from £640 to £835 for two weeks (about $1200–1500; minumum period 4 days, discounts for more than 2 weeks), depending on the model rented, and include delivery to and collection from London Heathrow or Gatwick, unlimited milage, *RAC* breakdown recovery service, and a National Key Scheme key (see below). The vans are equipped with hydraulic tail-lift capable of lifting 550 pounds, tracking system with adjustable locking wheelchair clamps, and safety harness for wheelchair occupants.

Although primarily a self-drive service, *Wheelchair Travel* can provide a driver to escort passengers from airport to hotel as well as for conducted tours. An expert registered guide (wheelchair user, William Forrester) is also offered for self-drive tours in London and day trips out of London. Any group of two to eight people, of which at least one is a full-time wheelchair user, can rent the vans. Extra services include free use of a lightweight manual wheelchair for a second person of limited mobility, and a voltage adaptor/convertor is available to recharge wheelchair batteries.

To book a van, first contact *Wheelchair Travel* to ascertain availability, at least six weeks in advance of your trip; they—or their agents (*Evergreen Travel Service Inc.*, 4114-198th SW, Lynwood, WA 98036, ☎800/435-2286; *Travel Helpers Limited*, 156 Duncan Mill Road, Suite 5, Don Mills, ON M3B 2N2, ☎416/443-0583)—will forward a booking form, to be completed and returned to the UK. *Wheelchair Travel* will issue booking confirmation with details of vehicle choice, seat plan, deposit, and balance due. Arrangements can be made for those wishing to take their van across to the European Continent, or to Ireland, but plenty of advance notice is required to allow time to obtain the necessary documentation and continental breakdown service, and there will be an extra charge to cover additional wear and tear on the vehicle; perhaps more important, fare concessions on the ferries do not apply to drivers of rented vehicles.

Finding accessible rest rooms should not be too difficult in Britain. Apply to *RADAR* (see *Useful Contacts*) for the key to about 3000 accessible public rest rooms covered by the National Key Scheme. The key costs £3 and the *National Key Scheme Guide* another £3 if you pick them up from the *RADAR* office. If you order by mail in advance you must send £9.11 to cover postage to North America, but transatlantic mailing can be avoided by asking that the key and guide be sent to your first accommodation address for collection on your arrival. The *AA Guide for the Disabled Traveler* (see *Books*) includes a survey of the facilities at motorway service areas. *Shell UK Oil* (Shell-Mex House,

ENGLAND & WALES TRAVEL NOTES

The Strand, London WC2R 0DX; ☎071/257 3045) produces a free directory of facilities available at *Shell* garages, *Easier Motoring for Disabled Drivers*.

The **Orange Badge Scheme**, effective everywhere except parts of London (parking in London is difficult but not impossible—be prepared to cruise around for a while, looking for an empty meter), does not extend to holders of North American disabled drivers' parking permits. However, if you need to park in a restricted zone (on yellow lines) during your stay in one area, stop at the local police station and try to obtain permission—it's worth a try. It's also advisable to carry your US or Canadian permit for off-road parking (eg supermarkets, multistory parking lots, tourist attractions) where there are designated spaces for disabled drivers. Most owners of these will recognize the international wheelchair symbol. Be warned that abuse of designated spaces by able-bodied drivers is a fairly common phenomenon in Britain.

For more information and ideas on transport, the *RADAR* holiday guide (see *Books*) covers all eventualities: air, sea, and train travel; car and bus rental; escort, taxi, and private ambulance services; trailers for adaptation. The *Holiday Care Service* and *TRIPSCOPE* (see *Useful Contacts*) can also assist.

Accommodation

The range of accessible accommodation in Britain is limited, particularly at the cheaper end of the scale. This is an acute problem in London, where hotel rates are astronomical. That said, the Great British Bed and Breakfast should not be dismissed as inaccessible: there are no B&B access guides, but some of the tourist board publications use the wheelchair symbol, and several of our contributors have used them successfully in England, Wales, Scotland, and Ireland—with minor adaptations, and compromise on both sides, many B&Bs can accommodate disabled guests, and owners will often refer travelers on to a more accessible property if their own is unsuitable.

The introduction of the *Tourism for All Accessible* symbol is a step in the right direction, with properties being inspected and awarded the symbol on the basis of specific accessibility criteria: a public entrance to the building must be accessible to disabled people from a letting-off point or car-parking place; where an establishment has a parking lot, a space should be reserved for a disabled guest on request; disabled people must have access to public areas in the building, including reception, dining room, living room and bar; and a minimum of one first-floor bedroom (per twenty rooms) with bath or shower and toilet facilities suitable for wheelchair use must be provided.

Managers of accommodation wishing to display the symbol must apply to the *Holiday Care Service*, the *Hotel and Holiday Consortium*, or the relevant national tourist board. The first four awards of the symbol went to *The London Tara Hotel* (Scarsdale Place, Kensington, London W8 5SR; ☎071/937 7211), *Hospitality Inn,* Irvine, Scotland (46 Annick Road, Irvine, Ayrshire KA11 4LD; ☎0294/74272), *Gorslwyd Farm* (Tan-y-Groes, Cardigan, Dyfed SA43 2HZ, Wales; ☎0239/810593), and the *Trusthouse Forte Travelodges*, details of which can be obtained from the *RADAR* guide.

Consort Hotels (Selective Hotel Reservations, 9 Boston Street, Suite 10, Lynn, MA 01904; ☎617/581-0844 or 800/223-6764), has adopted the *Tourism for All* "Model Policy Statement," setting out the intention to provide facilities for disabled people, and their brochure, *UK Holidays & Short Breaks: Nice 'n Easy*, lists forty accessible hotels—in England, Scotland, and Wales.

The National Trust (36 Queen Anne's Gate, London SW1H 9AS; ☎071/222 9251; write to Valerie Wenham, enclose an International Reply Coupon and ask for the free booklet, *Information for Visitors with Disabilities*, also available at all *NT* properties; the *BTA* office in New York keeps a few copies and will probably send a Xerox copy on request) has also adopted the Model Policy Statement, welcoming disabled visitors at most of its properties, and offering several fully accessible cottages in its range of vacation accommodation in England, Wales, and Northern Ireland (brochure, *National Trust Holiday Cottages*, from The National Trust Enterprises Ltd., PO Box 101, Melksham, Wiltshire SN12 8EA; ☎0225/705676).

ENGLAND & WALES TRAVEL NOTES

Country Holidays (Spring Mill, Earby, Colne, Lancs BB8 6RN; Disabled Persons' Helpline, ☎0282/445340; fax 0282/844268) have over forty cottages suitable for wheelchair users, and some 300 with no internal stairs or steps that would be fine for those with limited mobility. The brochure for disabled clients has basic access information, and staff give further advice on the Helpline. Bookings can be made direct or through agents in North America (USA, *Heart of England Cottages*, ☎205/687-9800; Canada, *Condor Vacations*, ☎604/682-0625).

The following accommodation is recommended by our contributors. Vivienne Adcock stayed at *Priory Cottage* (Kington St. Michael, Chippenham, Wiltshire; ☎024975/222). Contact Colin and Priscilla Labouchere for reservations.

Christine Warburton recommends one place (self-catering) in Wales and three in England. The owner of *Hen Ysgol Holiday Homes* (Rhoscolyn, Isle of Anglesey, Gwynned LL65 2RQ; ☎0407/741593), himself disabled, built the two bungalows (six-berth), which are fully accessible, with wheel-in shower, handrails, "monkey bars," bed blocks, wheelchair-height electrical switches and kitchen, and level patio. The views are stunning, the beach is about two miles away, and it's an ideal spot for a quiet break or as a base for touring North Wales.

A country inn and restaurant situated on the A683, the *Fat Lamb Hotel* (Ravenstonedale, Kirkby Stephen, Cumbria; ☎05873/242) has first-floor rooms with access for most wheelchairs, but the bend in the corridor is difficult for chairs with extended leg-rests to negotiate.

For B&B only, *Alexa House Hotel and Stable Cottages* (26 Ripon Road, Harrogate HG2 2JJ; ☎0423/501988) offers accessible, *en suite*, first-floor rooms in converted stables. Breakfast is served in the main house, which has a couple of steep steps. The ramp could not be found on Christine's visit, but help was willingly given.

Again for B&B only, *Leasow House* (Laverton Meadows, Broadway, Worcester WR12 7NA; ☎0386/73526) has a large, comfortable, *en suite*, first-floor room in a converted barn. Breakfast served in main house—no steps at entrance. If necessary, Mrs. Meeking will serve breakfast in guests' own room, which has table, chairs, and facilities for making tea or coffee.

There are a number of religious establishments in Britain, most of them set in beautiful countryside, which offer the sort of vacation described by Jane Nyman on p.129. These are listed in *Away From It All*, by Geoffrey Gerard (Lutterworth Press). Jane stayed at Mount St. Bernard, Coalville, Leicestershire; write to the Guest Master.

Veronica Smith stayed at the *Churchtown Farm Field Studies Centre* (Lanlivery, Bodmin, Cornwall PL30 5BT; ☎0208/872148).

Facilities for disabled **campers** are far from perfect, but better on the newer sites. Contributors generally found that they could cope, perhaps with a folding stool for use in the shower, or with help from a companion. Contact *The Forestry Commission*, the *Camping and Caravanning Club* (Greenfields House, Westwood Way, Coventry CV4 8JH; ☎0203/694995), or *The Caravan Club* (East Grinstead House, East Grinstead, West Sussex RH9 1UA; ☎0342/326944) for details of sites which have accessible rest room and washing facilities.

Many accommodation addresses, with access details, are given in the *RADAR* guide; the *RAC* accommodation guides are another source; there is more skimpy information in the *AA* guides (see *Books*). Use the regional tourist boards and the *Holiday Care Service*.

Access and Facilities

There is great scope for improvement of access at tourist attractions, on transport, and in accommodation, but things are changing—slowly. It is impossible to list all the **new initiatives**: the opening of a new lakeland walk along the shore of Derwentwater by the *National Trust*; the publication of a guide for less mobile bird-watchers in and around Suffolk; the provision of good access to the recently reopened Imperial War Museum, London; the awarding of a *Tourism for All Accessible* symbol to another hotel; the inclusion of access details for arts and entertainment spots in the London telephone directory; the launch of a new *Hoseasons Holidays* (Sunway House, Lowestoft NR32 3LT; ☎0502/500505) narrowboat, fitted with a wheelchair lift and accessible toilet facilities . . . .

ENGLAND & WALES TRAVEL NOTES

To keep up to date with these developments (and other matters of concern to disabled people) it's a good idea to subscribe to publications such as *Disability Now* (published by *The Spastics Society*, 12 Park Crescent, London W1E 3HU; ☎071/636 5020; annual subscription for overseas readers £20 for 12 issues, surface mail, payable by credit card or sterling check); this newspaper also covers vacations outside Britain, and the situation for disabled people in other countries. There are items on access and vacations, as well as mobility, in *The Disabled Driver* and *Magic Carpet* (the magazines of the *Disabled Drivers' Motor Club* and *Disabled Drivers' Assocation*; see Ireland *Travel Notes*).

Several operators in the tourist and travel trade deserve praise for their efforts, but development of better access and facilities is needed in all areas. Perhaps most important, there must be better **communication**—between vacationers and operators, between designers or planners and disabled people, between hotel or tourist attraction management and the market they hope to attract.

Useful Contacts

Holiday Care Service, 2 Old Bank Chambers, Station Road, Horley, Surrey RH6 9HW; ☎0293/774535; fax 0293/784647; Minicom 0293/776943; 24-hr answering service. A national charity providing free advice and information on all aspects of travel. Publishes a series of accommodation guides (see *Sources of Information*) and some 250 information sheets, updated during 1992, covering vacations in Britain and abroad, transport, travel tips for people with specific disabilities, and more. They will send information overseas without payment, but an International Reply Coupon or small donation is always appreciated.

TRIPSCOPE, 63 Esmond Road, London W4 1JE; ☎081/994 9294 (and Minicom). Transport information and advice for people with disabilities planning local, long-distance, or international journeys. It's a free service, but doesn't include making reservations, or recommending accommodation.

RADAR (*The Royal Association for Disability and Rehabilitation*), 25 Mortimer Street,

London W1N 8AB; ☎071/637 5400; Minicom 071/637 5315. Produces and distributes annual vacation guides and other useful publications (see *Books*, below); distributes locally compiled access guides to many towns (ask for publications list); operates the National Key Scheme (see *Transport*, above).

ARTSLINE (5 Crowndale Road, London NW1 1TU; ☎071/388 2227, voice and Minicom) is London's information and advice service for disabled people who wish to visit theaters, movie theaters, galleries, and museums in the Greater London area.

Automobile Association (*AA*), Fanum House, Basingstoke, Hants RG21 2EA (☎0256/20123).

Royal Automobile Club (*RAC*), PO Box 100, RAC House, 7 Brighton Road, South Croydon CR2 6XW (☎081/686 0088; publications department, ☎081/686 2525).

Books

The *RADAR* guides (see *Useful Contacts*) are somewhat overloaded with advertising copy (every other page), and much of their information is supplied by hotel managers and not verified, but they are functional and well-established reference works, and at least provide a good starting point. All prices quoted below include transatlantic postage by airmail, but you can avoid this extra cost by arranging to have the books sent to your vacation accommodation address, for collection on arrival in Britain. *Holidays in the British Isles. A Guide for Disabled People* (£5.51) is published annually, at the beginning of each year, and available by mail order (sterling checks, VISA or Mastercard accepted) or from WH Smith or Dillons bookshops in the UK. It covers all types of accommodation (including campgrounds), transport, and access at tourist attractions.

Other *RADAR* publications, available by mail order, or direct from the *RADAR* office, include *Historic Buildings of England* (1992; £3.43), which gives access details, opening times and charges, location, and list of other attractions, as well as a few historical notes about each building; it's easy to read (no symbols) and phone numbers are given so that visitors can find out more if necessary. *A Guide to British*

ENGLAND & WALES TRAVEL NOTES

Rail for Disabled People (1991; £3.91) lists access details of the 540 principal stations that have at least some accessible features (there are some 2500 BR stations) and describes facilities on trains. *The Countryside and Wildlife for Disabled People* (1990; £6.95) lists facilities at nature reserves, picnic sites, adventure centers, and conservation areas all over Britain.

Access in London, produced by the *Pauline Hephaistos Survey Projects* (*PHSP*, 39 Bradley Gardens, West Ealing, London W13 8HE), is recommended. It is detailed, comprehensive, and written with a sense of humor, and the access symbols used in the guide are explained in French and German—quite a departure from the normal assumption that everyone speaks English. A complete resurvey of the accommodation was carried out in order to compile a 1992–1993 supplement, which will be sent out with the 1989 edition of the guide. In principle it is free of charge but *PHSP* ask for a donation toward the costs of the survey and the postage; they suggest that North Americans should send $15 cash (checks are expensive to process), or pay less and pick it up in Britain.

AA Guide for the Disabled Traveler (from UK bookshops) is designed to be used in conjunction with other *AA* publications (see *Useful Contacts*). It contains some useful information but not enough detail on access to accommodation and places of interest.

The *RAC* (see *Useful Contacts*) guide for disabled motorists, *On the Move* (new edition November 1992, £3.99), was first published in conjunction with the *RAC*'s special breakdown service for disabled motorists, and is compiled in consultation with the *Disabled Drivers' Association*. It covers access at accommodation, including campgrounds, and tourist attractions. The *RAC* accommodation guides (*Hotel Guide*, £12.99; *Small Hotels, Guesthouse, Inns and Farmhouses*, £6.99; *Farm Holiday Guide*, £5.99; *Camping and Caravanning*, £7.99; all guides cover Britain and Ireland) use the wheelchair symbol. In the main hotel guide some 600 hotels are listed, with an indication of those with reserved parking spaces, level or ramped entrance, level access to public areas, accessible rooms with adjacent or *en suite* adapted bathrooms. The guides can be obtained from UK bookstores.

Places that Care (1991, £4.99, from bookshops, tourist information centers, *National Trust* shops and *RADAR*) is a 254-page guide—with an unfortunate title—to places of interest in Britain, including stately homes, *National Trust* and *English Heritage* properties, RSPB (Royal Society for the Protection of Birds) reserves, zoos, and gardens. Facilities such as wheelchair accessibility (terrain, steps, accessible rest rooms), seat availability, wheelchairs, or batricars for those with limited mobility, special routes and cassette or Braille guides for disabled visitors, and the location of places that display the "sympathetic hearing scheme" sticker, are indicated via a battery of symbols.

Access Holiday Guide (1991, £4 for overseas orders, equivalent dollar checks accepted) is available from Access Publishing, 7 Roundberry Drive, Salcombe, South Devon TQ8 8LY (☎0548/ 843551). Researched and compiled by wheelchair user Ian McKnight, the guide is a small booklet, listing a selection of accessible accommodation (self-catering, hotels, inns, guesthouses, farmhouses, activity vacation centers, and youth hostels), mainly in England, but some in Scotland, a few in Wales, and a couple in Ireland.

TELEPHONE CODE:

From the US and Canada dial 011 (international code) and then 44 for England or Wales.

France

Je Vais Chercher un Parachute

As a result of polio in 1953, Pete Kendall is unable to stand or walk, or sit without support. She travels on her own every year by taxi to London's Gatwick airport and thence by air to Lancashire and Scotland. Less often, she makes the journey to France, and in 1988 she stayed in the Cévennes with her sister, who is married to a Frenchman.

It was time I visited France again: my last trip was over ten years ago. I couldn't conduct a single-handed poll, but I wanted to know what at least some French people were thinking. I wanted to explore, to visit new places, and, above all, to see my sister and her husband, as well as assorted nephews and nieces and their families, some French, some English, all living in France.

Having made my usual preparations for traveling, I sat in the taxi bound for Gatwick, thinking gleefully of the letters accumulating on the mat and the phone ringing in vain. I had packed my belongings into one suitcase and one zip-bag with pockets; checks and credit cards were in my money belt; passport and tickets were in a pocket of the bag. My shoes were taped on to prevent them from dropping off during lifting, and I carried spare tape and scissors. Bright orange labels adorned my luggage: one on the wheelchair was marked, "Please do not unload wheel-

chair with luggage, but leave by aircraft for use of passenger." It is best to mention this to the cabin crew as well; otherwise, the wheelchair may be left, reduced to its component parts, circulating with the baggage, while you are obliged to use an airport chair—cushionless and possibly lacking footrests.

At Gatwick I rang the appropriate airline using a special phone for disabled travelers. This time, a helper came quickly but no porters or trolleys were free, so we managed with my bag on my knees and my suitcase perched across the arms of my chair. Once I'd parted with the suitcase and been issued with a boarding card, I had only my bag to keep an eye on while it went through the X-rays and I received my body check. Then came the only part of a journey that I dislike—being lifted up the steps into the plane in a carry-chair.

My knees fall apart, my feet fall off the narrow footrest, and sometimes there is no safety-belt. Scotch tape for feet and knees can help. (Some airports do provide carry-chairs with safety-belts and wide footrests.) However, the ordeal was soon over and I was deposited in my seat.

"Seven liters of mussels were barbecued and consumed with garlic butter, saffron rice, salad, and wine"

In no time, it seemed, we were landing at Montpellier. Only one man, with no carry-chair, awaited me. He looked at me quizzically.

"Il faut que je tombe?" I asked.

"Mais non," he replied, "Je vais chercher un parachute!" Luckily, I am light and flexible, and he carried me down the steps to my chair. He said that I was fortunate with the weather; this was the first fine day for a week.

My sister and brother-in-law were there to meet me, Bertha slowed down by Parkinson's disease, Jean-Pierre diminutive, sprightly, very bald, unable to lift as a result of an accident years ago. It was lovely to see them, and soon we were on our way to Aumessas, a village in the Cévennes, in the southeast corner of the Massif Central. The route is beautiful, through the spectacular scenery of the Causses—great limestone plateaux deeply dissected by gorges, full of underground streams and caverns, and sparsely covered with vegetation. We followed the gorge of the Hérault river, which rises among the older rocks (schists and granites) on Mont Aigoual in the Cévennes. We passed through small villages and the town of Ganges, which from the time of Louis XIV was famous for the manufacture of silk stockings, replaced more recently with rayon and then nylon.

Presently, we turned west along the valley of the Arre (from the Latin *aurum*, gold, which was panned in many valleys hereabouts). To the north are the old hard rocks of the Cévennes, to the south the abrupt limestones of the Causses. Dizzily perched at the summit of a hill is the tiny village of Esparon, so named because it is on a spur (*éperon*) of the Causses. The valley of the Rivière d'Aumessas runs southward through the Cévennes to join the Arre, and the village of Aumessas huddles in the valley. The lower parts of the Cévennes are clothed in sweet chestnuts, the waysides yellow with broom. Sometimes the rocks are bare, sinuously folded and glistening with mica flakes.

We passed through Aumessas, with its viaduct, Catholic church, and Protestant temple, then darted suddenly up a steep track full of potholes and mini-cliffs. There at last was the house, surrounded by cherry trees and conifers. Lower down on the long strip of garden was the "chalet"—a smaller house still occupied by Bertha and Jean-Pierre because the new one, after endless problems with builders, was incomplete. I was given a finished room in the house, and a cordless phone for communicating with the chalet.

"I could do nothing but stare through my camera and think hard about f-stops"

After lunch, we sat on the balcony of the house, with a fine view over the valley to the mountains. Large, pale swallowtail butterflies were moving with a beautiful gliding flight among the trees, and lizards sunbathed on the stones. We could hear the sound of sheep-bells mingling with the call of the cuckoo. A gnarled old lady greeted us. I didn't understand a word she said. "I don't either," said Bertha. "She's the shepherdess, and every day she takes her flocks to a different pasture. She's of Italian origin but speaks the local dialect."

The next day, members of the family, young and old, converged from all parts of France. Seven liters of mussels were barbecued and consumed with garlic butter, saffron rice, salad, and wine; Bertha produced her brandied cherries. Some of the family gossiped, some swam in the little pool by the chalet, some went out and caught fish for supper. We talked far into the twilight.

In the following days I was taken on too many excursions to count. One day after lunch we crammed into two cars and set out to explore the upper part of the Aumessas valley. There were fine views from the sharply bending road, and the roadside was bright with flowers—a small, vividly mauve cranesbill, broom, orchids, vetch, periwinkles, sainfoin, and many others unknown to me. We passed a waterfall making its way down a steep hillside to a stream bridged by the road, and so came to the hamlet of Le Travers, where the houses were of stone with red pan-tiled roofs. Some were deserted, testimony to rural depopulation.

"Sometimes the hippies come down here from the mountains"

We left the cars and followed the road above the village for a view down the valley, marveling at its extent and at the variations from green to blue as cloud shadows passed over the waves of trees in its depths, or slightly darkened the paler heights where grass and bare rock prevailed. In the distance, tiny blocks of color indicated the buildings of Aumessas. The ground sloped steeply away below the road and a few trees grew along its margin. From time to time a shaft of light would illuminate their branches, revealing every leaf and twig against the slate blue of the hills behind. Then, all would be reversed; dark trees would be silhouetted against the pale wall of the valley, across which, improbably suspended, ran a tiny thread of red-roofed houses—the hamlet of Le Caladon.

On another excursion we viewed this hamlet from above. We drove down a track through chestnut woods to an open space with a precipice on one side and, set at the cliff edge, a rambling house where until the twelfth century there had been a castle; this was Le Haut Caladon. My nephew, Pierre, pushed me to the top of the cliff to look down the valley and see the rooftops of Le Caladon immediately below. "Just fifty centimeters farther," he said, while Bertha hung on to the back of my chair. Pierre pushed aside a broom tree so that I could look down past my feet at the hamlet. I could do nothing but stare through my camera and think hard about f-stops.

Several times I joined shopping parties to Le Vigan, a small town at the confluence of two tributaries with the Arre. It is at the heart of a fertile agricultural area and was the center for silk thread manufacturing. There are parks, a great avenue of chestnut trees, memorials to military heroes, houses of character, and a lovely stone bridge, the single semicircular arch of which meets its reflection to form a perfect circle.

Through the bustle of the marketplace we would push our way to buy long sausages, vegetables, organically produced honey-cake, spices, or meat. "Sometimes the hippies come down here from the mountains," said Pierre. After shopping we would stop for coffee or cassis under the trees in the main square, comparing notes about our lives or discussing stories in the newspapers of varying political hue, bought by Pierre in a nearby shop.

We visited the Cirque de Navacelles, a natural amphitheater formed by a deeply incised "abandoned meander" of the Vis river in Causse country. On our way there, we stopped for a fine peasant lunch at a farm, where the dining room was reached by a long, outside flight of stone steps. Sundry nephews and strangers hauled my chair to the top and made way for me to sit near a welcome log fire.

The Cirque is a spectacular bowl some 275m deep, approached by a series of hairpin bends. Nephews and nieces carried me, chair and all, over a steep humpbacked bridge and up a rocky path for a better view. They also pushed me out onto a slab of rock jutting terrifyingly over the river, so that I could take a photograph. "Je sais que Pete aime des précipices!" said Pierre. (I don't!)

"There were many places from which one could fall right out of Esparon with no trouble at all!"

Another expedition took us to the little village of Esparon, which I'd seen during the drive from Montpellier. The streets are extremely narrow and punctuated by flights of steps, up or down which Pierre and his wife, Marie-Noëlle, pushed me, at the same time carrying their seven-month-old baby, Juliette. There were views of the Causses to the south, the Cévennes to the north. At the village fountain we met an old lady using elbow crutches, but carrying a pail of water. She told us that during the last nine years of her husband's life he had been in a wheelchair, and she'd found it difficult to manage in the steep streets. To me, it looked impossible—there were many places from which one could fall right out of Esparon with no trouble at all!

We visited La Couvertoirade, too, a tiny walled town with turrets, built in the heart of Causse country, begun by the Knights Templar and completed by the Knights Hospitaller of St. John. Once again, nephews and nieces humped my chair along narrow cobbled streets and up flights of stony steps, but not, I'm glad to say, up onto the town wall, which was topped by an unfenced path only three feet wide!

In Aumessas itself I was shown *clèdes*, small buildings in which chestnuts used to be dried before treading or beating off their shells. The best nuts were for human consumption, the inferior ones for pigs and other animals. Silk production later superseded chestnut growing, after a cold winter killed many of the trees, which were then replaced by mulberry trees. The eggs of the silk moths were hatched in incubators, or sometimes in little bags kept warm between women's breasts! There were special buildings for rearing the silkworms and for processing the silk.

Crowds of us would go for walks in and around Aumessas. Sometimes the children would stop to play on swings and slides in a grassy area near the old train station, where games of *pétanque* were in progress. On July 14, dancing takes place here—"the only time Maman has ever been known to dance!" One walk took us along a steep, rocky path above the river valley. We looked down over gardens and roofs to the valley bottom, where beehives were set out in rows. Among the butterflies we saw a few black-veined whites, extinct now in Britain. Afterward, we walked up the valley. The sun was hot. I saw ivy-leaved toadflax, white campions, red clover and white, hop trefoil, and cleavers. *Robinia* trees were white with their heavy-scented blossom and the hawthorn bushes were strewn with hammock-like cobweb shelters, full of caterpillars.

One night, Jean-Pierre, with all the younger members of the family, took off to help a radio ham in difficulties with his computers. (Jean-Pierre is unofficial consultant to innumerable computer users—the district nurse, the baker, and many others make detours during working hours to seek his advice!) They were away until the small hours, helping Bernard solve his problems. A few days later, Bernard and his "radio widow," accompanied by a similar couple, turned up bearing an enormous *gâteau* and a bottle of champagne, as a gesture of thanks. Elections were in progress, and Bernard expressed some fairly racist views. I was cheered, and a little surprised, to hear Jean-Pierre contesting these vigorously. One of the radio widows spoke out against Monsieur Le Pen and his followers.

Another day, the valley echoed to the roars of high-powered cars taking part in a rally. I felt it wrong to disrupt the peace and put animals and people at risk on the roads, but found no support for my opinion. "It's the great event of the year in Aumessas. All the old women love it; they gather by the cemetery to watch. If you look through the binoculars you'll see them!" Sure enough, there they were, and I retreated in the face of the evidence.

When the baker stop at the village he would honk his horn, and people would congregate to buy bread and exchange news. After one such occasion, when Bertha returned with the loaves, she said that an old man who had gone out looking for mushrooms had failed to return. Villagers and police formed search parties, but so far in vain.

Not long before my departure, I developed an annoying cough and the doctor came to prescribe something to suppress it during my journey. He was young, informally dressed, full of laughter. He told us that his wife was English, and that he often visited her home county of Cornwall. I wished that I could have stayed longer in the microcosm of Aumessas. I had come to know some of my family better, with their problems and their pleasures. I had also begun to know a little about the surrounding community and to feel at home there.

A year later, I am sad to learn that the old man, lost while seeking mushrooms, was never found, and I am sharply grieved to learn that the young doctor has died of cancer. Holidays are not necessarily an escape.

Savoie Fare

Now 59, Ian Marshall has been confined to a wheelchair with paraplegia since the age of 31, and a visual disability makes it impossible for him to drive. He visited the Savoie in 1988 with his wife, Judith.

Lying in the east of France on the slopes of the Alps, just below the southwest corner of Switzerland, the Savoie is an area of mountain scenery and lakes. It is familiar to the winter sports enthusiast, but it has much to offer the summer visitor, too, as has the journey there.

The region now comprises two departments—Savoie and Haute Savoie—but it is a shadow of its former self, for in its heyday it covered parts of modern Italy and Switzerland as well as France, spreading from Nice to Berne, and from Turin to Lyons. As it only became part of France in 1860, its towns look and feel quite different from those in other parts of the country. In July 1988 we visited the spa town Aix-les-Bains, stopping on the way at Vichy—another spa town but also infamous for its World War II role as the seat of Marshall Pétain's government.

We took the night ferry (*Brittany Ferries*) from England to Caen and had a good night's sleep in the specially adapted cabin which was easily accessible for a wheelchair user, though the "up-and-over" entrance to the *en suite* facilities was not easy to negotiate. Arriving early in the morning, we took the opportunity to visit Bayeux, a few miles along the coast.

The famous tapestry is now housed in a specially designed building (the Centre Guillaume le Conquérant), which is accessible to wheelchairs via a back entrance (some of the staff do not appear to be aware of this fact and you may have to be persistent, but it's well worth the effort). As the hour was still early, even after our first French breakfast of the trip, we had time to kill before we could get in to see the tapestry. We gingerly tried the door of the cathedral, half expecting it to be locked, only to find a tourbusful of Germans sitting in the pews, being lectured even at that hour of the morning.

This early activity gave us a full day for traveling, and we set off, picking our way through the area of Suisse Normande, promising ourselves a more leisurely visit one day. The town of Vichy was disappointing but its setting, in a natural bowl in the foothills of the Massif Central, was not. The River Allier has been used to form a lake, flanked by the Parc d'Allier and the Parc des Sources, which make up the spa's social center. Wandering beneath the plane and chestnut trees along wheelchair-friendly asphalt paths, some protected from hot sun or rain by ornamental roofing, we realized just how seriously the French view spa treatments—the park was filled with people carrying small lidded baskets which held their cups for "taking the waters."

Each spa specializes in alleviating a particular malady—digestive disorders in the case of Vichy. The four main springs are housed in the Pavillon des Sources, a splendid nineteenth-century edifice, now joined by a modern hotel to the Grand Etablissement Thermal—the largest treatment center of its kind in Europe—and the Bains Caillou not far away. The whole place has an atmosphere evoking the *belle époque*, with horse-drawn carriages for hire, a bandstand still used in the evenings, and small cafés serving English afternoon tea and cake to groups of devotees sitting on the innumerable chairs scattered throughout the park. I could

imagine some of the more famous *curistes* from the past—Louis XV's daughters, Napoleon's mother—enjoying the balmy air.

> *"I just wondered if the comparatively plain fare offered by the hotel restaurant had any connection with the nature of the spa's specialty"*

Perhaps incongruous in this setting, the air conditioning in our modern hotel (the *Thermalia Novotel*) afforded welcome relief from the more than balmy temperature on our arrival in the late afternoon. There is flat access to the hotel and environs, and one of the two elevators is large enough for a wheelchair. I've stayed in different rooms and the bathrooms have always been accessible. I just wondered if the comparatively plain fare offered by the hotel restaurant had any connection with the nature of the spa's specialty.

Leaving Vichy, we traveled mainly east to Roanne, enjoying the drive through forests flanking the upper reaches of the Saône, to Villefranche in Beaujolais country, where we should have paused to taste and perhaps buy. Instead we pressed on through Nantua to our destination, the small town of Rumilly. We had chosen to stay in a quiet, family-run hotel (the *Relais du Clergeon*) outside the town. Situated on the side of a hill, the first floor of the hotel housed the public rooms and some bedrooms; the rest were built below as the ground sloped away at the back, giving a wonderful view over the valley from the balconies. The hotel was not adapted in any way (there were no hand-rails, for example) but it was just what we wanted because each of the places that interested us could be visited in a day—even Chamonix, at the foot of Mont Blanc.

We preferred to take the slower, more scenic route to Chamonix, via Chambéry, Albertville, Ugine, Mégève, and St. Gervais, saving the more direct route for the journey back. The first tourists arrived in Chamonix in 1741 and they were English, but the first ascent of Mont Blanc (15,978 feet) was made by two Frenchmen—Balmat and Picard—in 1786. Depending on the weather, time available, your pocket, your mobility, and your nerves, many walks and excursions can be made from the town. The Mont Blanc Carousel takes you over the mountain range by the highest cable car and back through the new 7-mile tunnel. Other cable cars go up to the belvederes at Brevent and Flégère.

"My undoing was the specialty of the house—vacherin—full of calories and cholesterol"

Most people's favorite town hereabouts is Annecy, and there is much to see and do there, but Aix-les-Bains, on the neighboring Lac du Bourget, is ours. The lake is the greatest expanse of water in France, some ten miles by two and up to 100m deep. There is plenty of room to park under the trees and from there we strolled by the side of the lake, watching the hilarious antics of the children learning to sail in fleets of dinghies, supervised by frantic instructors shouting, whistling, and tearing about in motorboats. There is a swimming area in the lake, and opportunities to sail or windsurf. We crossed the lake by launch to the Abbaye Hautecombe, where the royal princes of the House of Savoie are buried and services are still sung in Gregorian chant.

The town has many fine buildings, including two casinos, one incorporating the opera house, and gardens, in which I was surprised to find a bust of Queen Victoria, who spent a summer here. There are museums housing a range of exhibits, from Roman remains to works by Rodin. The spa specialty is rheumatism. There are two sulfur springs used in therapy, and two sources used for mineral water.

Before returning to base that day we climbed the 12-mile winding road up Mont Revard (4900 feet) and parked at the summit to admire the panoramic view laid out before us—including the Mont Blanc range. We ate lunch late in the summit restaurant, where the *patron* joined us and chatted in English about his time in Bristol.

We returned to Chambéry to explore this one-time capital of the sovereign state, still the capital of the department of Savoie and seat of the Archbishop. With few other tourists about we enjoyed wandering down the old city center's narrow streets, and the wide boulevards where the city walls once stood. About a quarter of the city buildings, toward the station, were lost in World War II, but these have mostly been replaced or restored. The castle was the ancient residence of the Counts and Dukes, and occasionally the Kings of Sardinia.

We found more tourists on our visit to Annecy, only 27 miles away from Geneva, where we enjoyed Sunday lunch at one of the many outdoor restaurants, choosing one which served good live jazz with good Savoie fare. We finished off our visit with a leisurely drive around the lake.

It was time to return home. Knowing that I had eaten too much, as usual in France (my undoing was the specialty of the house—*vacherin*—full of calories and cholesterol), I wondered if I could afford a visit to the treatment rooms at Vichy.

The Dordogne

In 1989, for the first time, Ian (who is paraplegic) and Judith Marshall were able to go abroad in May—Ian's favorite month. They had the use of a cottage in the Dordogne designed and built, not simply adapted, for wheelchair users.

We'd both recently retired, so with more time to spare we decided to spend a night en route, rather than tear down there in about seven hours of non-stop driving from the north coast. We chose to stay at Laval, where there is a modern hotel with at least one of its first-floor rooms fitted with an adapted *en suite* bathroom. This had been confirmed the previous year, when we inspected the hotel, having learned by experience that the wheelchair symbol in guidebooks cannot always be relied on.

Next morning we traveled south through Château-Gontier, following the valley of the Mayenne to cross the Loire at Angers. The wide and almost empty road system carried us speedily across the Loire, avoiding the city, into the vineyards of Saumur and on to Poitiers. Again a bypass took us on our way to Angoulême along another *route nationale* which offered three picnic areas; the one we happened to choose sported a disabled rest room. Angoulême has not the luxury of a bypass but a one-way system, which is hardly a substitute. As this is the gateway to the Dordogne, and the French respect parking places for the disabled, we returned later to give the place our full sightseeing attention.

From Angoulême we traveled through Cognac country by minor roads, which are well maintained these days and wide enough to take large pieces of agricultural equipment; they are a joy to use as they carry very little traffic. The countryside is sparsely populated because the young people are leaving to find work in the cities and farther north. Our hamlet (Gresignac) consisted of a few farms, a ruined church, and cottages—some empty—spread over a large area but with not a single shop. It is still rated as a commune (the smallest unit of local government), with a mayor and elected council, despite the electorate having fallen to barely more than a hundred.

It was a pleasure to move into accommodation which had been so thoughtfully designed and actually built by a young English couple in the old farmhouse next door. Our spare bedroom (the only upstairs room) was soon in use when our daughter and son-in-law arrived later that evening. They used the fly-drive service from Heathrow to Bordeaux (both *Air France* and *British Airways* operate this service); if your time is limited, or you do not want the long drive, this method is worth considering—the airport is a two-hour drive away and wheelchair users are regularly carried.

"Wherever we went, I could indulge my romantic notions of the past and my love of wine"

The next day was Sunday and Judith's birthday—what better excuse for trying the excellent food of the region? We turned to the visitors' book in the cottage, in which previous occupants had made recommendations, and chose Brantôme, which nestles in a curve of the Dronne, a tributary of the Isle. We entered the town by a peculiarly angled old bridge and found it bustling with activity—kayak racing on the river, a traveling fair in full swing, and the fire brigade turning out. There was a choice of restaurants and we did justice to the occasion. Returning home should have been a simple matter but in attempting to take a short cut across a river on a pontoon-type bridge we acquired a flat tire. If you have to change a tire of a foreign rented car in the dark, start feeling for the tools under the hood.

The region is compact enough to make it unnecessary to travel far to places of interest. If you like prehistory there are the caves at Lascaux and Les Eyzies (the Lascaux cave has been closed since 1963 because of the deterioration resulting from the heat and humidity generated by armies of visitors; you have to be satisfied with a replica and a museum). If you are more interested in the French meaning of *cave*, some of the finest wine tasting can be had between Périgueux and Bordeaux.

Wherever we went, I could indulge my romantic notions of the past and my love of wine. Bergerac lies on the Dordogne at the point where the ancient route from Lyons to Bordeaux crosses that from Paris to Lourdes. The town was captured by the Earl of Derby in 1345 at the start of the Hundred Years' War; the war ended in 1453, downstream from Bergerac at Castillon-la-Bataille. Near Castillon you can see the study—all that remains of the château—where Montaigne wrote his essays (which caused me to give up French at school).

"It seemed that the tourists had not yet arrived, but we met a few of the ex-pats"

The center of Bergerac is pedestrianized, so that getting around in the wheelchair and viewing all the sights was relatively simple. The town is surrounded by vineyards, including the famous Château de Monbazillac, 4 miles to the south. The old wharfs in Bergerac are still intact, and it was from here that the wine went downstream to be loaded onto ocean-going vessels at Libourne. There is a small wine and boating museum at place de la Myrpe.

I used to believe that châteaux had to mean the Loire, but the Dordogne is

estimated to contain over a thousand, many of them lived in and some open to visitors. A village near the cottage boasted a beautiful example, and I asked the owner of the local bar how the tiny village came to have such an edifice. He explained that up to the revolution the local vineyard (long since gone) supplied much of the wine to the royal court. He seemed in a sad mood sitting on the curb outside in the dark. Women and children, he said, had started to come with their menfolk for their aperitifs, and he couldn't stand the noise!

Days of outings were interspersed with days of exploring the immediate locality—perfect for bird-watching or trying to recognize wild flowers. We were shown a small valley full of unusual orchids, one variety of which not even a professional Dutch grower could identify. The weather was dry for the time of year, but cold at night—one day a farmer near Thiviers told me that there had been a frost the night before which damaged his strawberries and some of his vines.

One cannot think about France, and particularly this area, without mentioning food. Perigord is famous for the quality of its goose fare (*confit d'oie, pâté de foie gras*) and its truffles, not to mention 101 things that they do with the walnut. New to us was eating at a *ferme auberge*, where we booked in advance and where the half-dozen diners had the undivided attention of the young farmer and his wife as we slowly ate our way through six courses of home produce from the grapefruit or walnut aperitifs to the liqueurs.

It seemed that the tourists had not yet arrived, but we met a few of the expatriates, one a retired architect living in a 200-year-old farmhouse which had been empty for fourteen years. I asked him why so many buildings incorporated turrets in their design. It seems these were dovecotes, the birds being kept for their droppings, which provided the only form of fertilizer at one time. We found a teacher from our local school who had taken over a ten-bedroom hotel, and in his bar met an ex-Spitfire pilot living in the vicinity.

I enjoyed the vacation more than I expected and I am not sure why. Perhaps because there is more than appears on the surface and I enjoy probing gently.

A Strange Phenomenon

Since developing rheumatoid arthritis in 1982, Alison Walsh has matched the progression of her disease with various modes of transport, starting with a bicycle, moving on to a moped when her knees complained, and retreating to the relative safety, warmth, and comfort of a car when a few months of moped riding in central London ended in a crash. The effects of constant gear changing on arthritic ankles dictated the purchase of another vehicle, and she now relies heavily on a car with automatic transmission. She took it to Paris in December 1989 and May 1990.

Driving in Paris is a cinch (and that includes parking)—good news for people who are unable to use buses or the Métro. If you cannot grapple with high steps and impatient bus drivers, or endless underground corridors, awkward doors, and yawning gaps between train and platform, try exploring Paris by car. This is not to say that I feel good about adding to the four million noisy, noxious cars which already threaten to swamp a beautiful city: if my feet were what they used to be I'd tramp the streets all day—the best way to discover any city—but those of us who are incapable of that must look for an alternative. In the

absence of accessible public transit, this has to be the private car; we can only hope for a cleaner, quieter version in the future.

Driving *to* Paris from Britain is also easy. Based on the recognition that for people with mobility problems their car is a necessity rather than a luxury, some car ferry companies carry disabled drivers' cars free of charge or at reduced rates (contact the *Disabled Drivers' Motor Club*). I have a personal preference for *P&O* boats, and always receive polite and efficient service from their staff. In December our ferry was delayed because of fog, but in May we left on time and sat in brilliant sunshine, eating bacon sandwiches in a sheltered corner of the nearly deserted deck.

The route from Calais to Paris couldn't be simpler; it's well marked and the road is fast—you'll be there in three to four hours . . . unless you choose a foggy day. Spinning along under a scorching sun in May, with the windshield steadily collecting a splattering of dead flies, windows down, and the roar of wind and trucks preventing conversation, I found it difficult to recall the tortuous journey in December, when maximum speed was 20 or 30mph and all that broke the white monotony was the sudden looming of red brake-lights ahead.

The fog had cleared by the time we reached Paris, and the next day we were able to sit on the open top-deck of a *Bateau-Mouche*, enjoying the sun, ignoring the multilingual commentary which is punctuated by irritating electronic chimes, and instead listening to my brother's latest gossip and his own commentary on the sights. My visits are a mixture of catching up with Steve, discovering Paris—slowly—and meeting designers and fabric buyers in the fashion houses (my traveling companion sells silk to the likes of Yves Saint Laurent and Agnés b).

Bateaux-Mouches run from the Right Bank, between the Pont de l'Alma and the Pont des Invalides. There is parking at the point of embarkation and accompanied wheelchair users should have no problems boarding and sitting on the lower (enclosed) deck; the upper deck on our boat was reached by a spiral staircase. It's a touristy thing to do, and the boats are unbelievably ugly, but you can chat for an hour or so while drifting past such landmarks as the floating, eighteenth-century Deligny swimming pool, the Obélisque in the place de la Concorde, the twin clock towers of the Musée d'Orsay, the Jardin des Tuileries and the Louvre. Rounding the Ile de la Cité and the Ile St. Louis, you catch the best view of Notre-Dame and, at the other end of the island, slip under the oldest Parisian bridge, Pont Neuf.

"A common excuse for bad access to museums (and other buildings for that matter) is the age of the building"

Although the December days were bright and sunny, there was a nip in the air and it was a good time of year for museums. Paris has a mind-boggling choice, and many are accessible: consult your copy of *Touristes quand même!* (Tourists just the same), be prepared to nose around for the wheelchair entrance, and if you want to leave nothing to chance phone ahead to double check.

Forget the Louvre: it's vast, confusing, and intimidating; we spent a lot of time shuttling up and down in elevators which wouldn't stop at the floors we wanted (or thought we wanted) and I couldn't help thinking that it was all part of a nightmarish school trip, in which I had to view every one of the more than 300,000 works of art before I was allowed to see the few I'd set out to see.

The Musée d'Orsay, on the other hand, is a delight and worth more than one visit. It is accessible (rest rooms, too), well laid out, well lit, with plenty of space, and a manageable collection. There are fine views through the clock faces, across the Seine and up toward Sacré-Coeur. If you can negotiate a flight of eleven steps at the entrance, and squeeze into a slimline elevator, the Musée Marmottan (rue Louis-Boilly, 16e) will reward you with a sumptuous basement selection of Monets. The few people there spoke in reverential whispers, the carpet deadened their footsteps, and there is comfortable seating for those who wish to ponder, admire, and catch their breath. I found the *Nymphéas* (Waterlilies) here more pleasing than those in the oval rooms at the Orangerie des Tuileries (place de la Concorde) which does, however, house some much loved works by other Impressionists. The Orangerie is accessible to accompanied wheelchair users.

A common excuse for bad access to museums (and other buildings for that matter) is the age of the building. The Institut du Monde Arabe (23 quai St.-Bernard) doesn't have this problem: it's new and accessible, a mass of glass and polished metal. The "winking wall" on the south side is made up of thousands of contracting and expanding light filters, and is supposed to resemble the lattice-like pierced screens so common in Arab architecture. Inside, every aspect of Arab life is covered, with special exhibitions as well as the permanent displays. We saw a fascinating presentation of the art of carpet making, *Tapis present de l'Orient à l'Orient*, and many superb examples of this painstaking craft.

At the Petit Palais (entrance for wheelchairs on av Dutuit) we happened on an exhibition entitled *L'art de Cartier*—a dazzling array of jewelry and clocks, beautifully lit and accompanied by the design sketches, with a few bejeweled ceremonial swords thrown in. There were many famous pieces, mostly made for the famous, including the panther brooch—diamonds and sapphires on platinum—made in 1949 for the Duchess of Windsor. From a wheelchair it was a struggle to see many of the exhibits, mounted on pedestals in glass cases, but half the fun of it was in listening to the excited exclamations of the well-heeled *Parisiennes* as they pored over each work of art.

"The Jardin du Luxembourg is the ideal resting place for weary explorers of St.-Germain"

In the May 1990 heatwave we were more interested in outdoor activities. Sunday May 6 was Paris Marathon day, and we watched the gasping stragglers weave along the av. du President Kennedy. In search of less energetic pursuits, we wandered in the dense shade of blossom-laden chestnut trees on the Allée des Cygnes, a sliver of land connecting two bridges across the Seine. At the Pont de Bir-Hakeim you can gaze up at the Tour Eiffel, and at the other tip of the sliver, just past Pont de Grenelle, is the Statue de la Liberté and good sunbathing territory. There are steps down to the Allée from both bridges, but there are plenty of seats and it's a peaceful spot, away from the more famous islands upstream.

For greenery and flowers, the visitor to Paris is again spoiled for choice, with a life-saving range of *parcs*, *jardins*, and *squares* in which to walk off a triple-scoop sorbet, or to sit and eat it. The majority of these carefully tended areas are fully accessible and perfect for picnics.

With the marathon out of the way, we risked venturing into the Bois de Boulogne, for a late lunch in the Parc de Bagatelle (accessible rest rooms here, plus wheelchairs for visitors' use) among a multicolored display of tulips, irises, and peacocks. There are wilder parts to the Bois, and lakes to sit beside or boat on, and parking is easy.

Just beyond the southeastern tip of the Bois are the *Serres* (glasshouses) *de la Ville de Paris*, workshops of the municipal florist, with an accessible entrance and parking on av. Gordon Bennett. Quite apart from the almost iridescent white tulips, the sea of blue pansies, and a beautiful deep pink rose named Ulrich Brunner, the glasshouses themselves made an interesting sight, clearly places of great industry but also built to look good.

Back in the center of things, the Jardin du Luxembourg is the ideal resting place for weary explorers of Saint-Germain, on the Left Bank. You can rest under the chestnut trees, eavesdrop on informal college classes, and potter among the blackcurrant bushes and pear trees growing against the wall in the southwest corner. These *parcs* and *jardins* provide exercise areas for many of the city's children, and their games are an established act in the world of park entertainment. In the Jardin du Ranelagh (16e) we stopped to watch an old-fashioned merry-go-round, cranked by a substantial, no-nonsense nanny, carrying a serious cargo of boys and girls. Foreheads furrowed in concentration, they aimed small batons through rings arranged just outside the sweep of the merry-go-round.

"Some of the Christmas window displays are pure fairytale fodder"

Light years away from this is the hi-tech scientific playground, Parc de la Villette (19e). There is underground parking here, or you can leave your car on the quai de l'Oise, cross the bridge over the Canal de l'Ourco, and sit in the park for a while before tackling the Cité des Sciences et de l'Industrie—a vast steel and glass laboratory for "hands-on" experience of the wonders of science. Kids, of course, love it, and the Géode—a giant steel ball housing the largest projection screen in the world. It was all too exciting for us; we escaped to the Parc des Buttes-Chaumont and sprawled on the grass which grows over what was, until the 1860s, an old quarry site used as a garbage dump.

"You will be financially penalized for needing a large room"

What's called the Jardin du Forum des Halles is not really a garden, but underneath is one of life's necessities for me—not the shops, which are unexciting here, but the swimming pool (*Piscine Suzanne Berlioz*, place de la Rotonde), which is fully accessible (with hoist), large, and well organized so that swimmers don't tangle with splashers. Take the elevator from Parking Berger; there are accessible rest rooms in the Forum.

Early December is ideal for the shopper, window or the real thing, and some of the Christmas window displays are pure fairytale fodder. Go to Galeries Lafayette or Printemps (both on bd. Haussmann) for a huge range of designer clothes and perfumes (and *Galeries Lafayette* for money changing on Saturdays); just trying on a few way-out hats on the first floor is great fun, but the elevators are big enough for wheelchairs if you want to investigate farther. There are many shops which are tricky for the less agile shopper, such as *Tati* (rock-bottom prices, pickpockets, and soccer-fan crowds) or some of the smaller boutiques, but there is still plenty of scope for consuming.

If eating is the type of consuming you're after, head for the markets. The stalls heave with a luxuriant array of goodies—fruit and vegetables, fish, meat, cheese, flowers, chocolates. Self-catering is a pleasure in Paris, but eating out won't break the bank. Likewise staying in a hotel: the vacationer on a budget is pretty well catered for in Paris.

However, if that vacationer on a budget is in a wheelchair, things are less easy. In general, you will be financially penalized for needing a large room for maneuvering, an accessible bathroom, and a wheelchair-sized elevator. The hotels at the cheaper end of the range more than likely have no elevator and no first-floor bedrooms, tiny rest rooms and bathrooms, and steps up to the entrance. Beware of wheelchair symbols in the guides: they often ignore steps up to elevators, split-level reception areas, narrow doors or steps at the entrance. The only way to be sure is to inspect it yourself: book your first night in a known accessible hotel, blow the expense; then select a few cheaper possibilities, hop into the car and research them; we had no problems booking rooms on the day.

Arm yourself with a good map for this exercise. The *Michelin Paris Plan No. 10, Sens uniques*, with street directory, shows the one-way systems and is indispensable. Buy it in Paris for half the price that the *AA* shop at Dover docks charges. Baron Haussmann completely restructured the capital in the second half of the nineteenth century, and as a self-navigating driver in a foreign city I am eternally grateful. The wide boulevards are a joy to travel along, the side streets can be used with relative ease to skip past trouble spots, and the sheer logic of the layout makes getting lost almost impossible. As for the supposedly volatile French drivers, I like them! What riles them is dithering—don't do it and you'll be spared the barrage of horns. After all, it doesn't matter if you take a wrong turn, or find yourself in the wrong lane—you're on vacation, and can take time to correct your route.

Perhaps I've been lucky, but I've never been thwarted in my search for a parking space; be prepared to take a couple of turns around the block, or the *place* (square), and keep your eyes peeled. Disabled badge holders are exempt from street parking charges (areas marked *PAYANT* in the road) and obtain a 75 percent reduction in parking lots. The traffic wardens and police are tolerant of sensible, unobtrusive parking.

We always managed to park within easy walking distance of our target. Just as well when visiting the fashion houses, dragging a suitcase full of silk samples. At one big-shot's studio we were met by an elf called Sophy, in green and brown spotted shirt, brown mini, and black and white striped leggings; she toned in with the decor, which was muddy green and cream, steel and glass again, with bolts and rivets and pipes—we could have been on board a ship. Club music played in the background, there was much chattering among the workers, and far from feeling intimidated by these dictators of fashion I was pleased to see many pairs of feet in Doc Marten's boots. I have two pairs—standard black ones, and for summer a pair of green "leisure boots"—and I recommend them to anyone with walking difficulties; as important to me as my painkillers, they give adequate ankle support, they are light and flexible, and unlike some well-known brands of running shoes they do not require you to take out a second mortgage.

The phenomenon of two confirmed country bumpkins returning again and again to a city, not simply on business but also for pleasure, takes some explaining. My hairdresser says that I "like a bit of *chic* now and then, darling" but it's more than that. Everything about central Paris appeals to me: the architecture, the coffee, the pleasing vistas at every turn, the museums, the trees, the wrought-iron balconies; all this is mine with only a trace of the horrors of big cities, and with a luxurious freedom of movement. On each visit we are struck above all by the *élégance*—retained in the face of all the usual pressures on a modern capital. We'll be going back soon for another fix.

Independent Living in Nancy

In 1985 Sian Williams began studying French and European literature at university. She soon realized that she must spend some time in France, although as a wheelchair user the problems she envisioned seemed insurmountable. Toward the end of 1986 Sian started writing letters, with the aim of tracking down a suitable place in which to spend a year in France. By March 1987 her initial enthusiasm and optimism had turned to disillusionment, but then the letter she'd been waiting for arrived.

Back in the Sixties a group of physically disabled students in France recognized that great social change was necessary if they were ever to lead an independent life and realize their academic and social potential. Their determination to bring about this change led to the creation of *Groupement pour l'Insertion des Handicapés Physiques* (GIHP), whose aim was to improve integration of people with disabilities in all spheres of society and increase their independence.

GIHP has grown into a national organization, with regional branches throughout the country. *GIHP Lorraine* is at Vandoeuvre, near Nancy, and it provides several services for disabled people in the area. There is an architectural bureau which aims to increase accessibility in the region, and an agency through which care attendants can be employed by those needing daily attention. There are ten adapted minivans with twelve drivers; and although at certain times it is quite expensive and delays do occur, it is on the whole an efficient service and gives a considerable degree of independence to many people living in Nancy. On any given day you can be sure of seeing a *GIHP* minivan on the horizon!

To enable students with disabilities to go to college, *GIHP* has created an accessible and well-adapted residential center (the *foyer*) in Vandoeuvre. Each student has an individual bedroom and meals are provided, as well as physiotherapy and transport to and from the campus. When I received details about this center I knew it was just what I'd been looking for. I made an application and in October 1987, loaded with far too much luggage, I arrived in Nancy.

"Meeting them was an experience that I'll never forget"

Living in a French-speaking environment was initially an exhausting experience. Despite having studied the language for nearly ten years, it came as a shock to hear the speed at which conversations were conducted. And, not content with speaking quickly, everyone also used argot—French slang which never appeared in our school textbooks! However, as a result of total immersion in the French language, both my ability to speak it and my understanding of it improved dramatically.

I enrolled on French courses for foreign students. The subjects varied from geography to literature, from French grammar to history of art. Difficulties that I encountered, such as note taking, were overcome with the help of students and staff, and my efforts were rewarded with two diplomas in French Studies. It was a stimulating experience to mix with people from many different cultures. I met some wonderful people, but the problems of getting about meant that I was unable to socialize with them as much as I'd have liked.

During my stay, *GIHP Lorraine* launched a regional campaign to set up the first *Agence Pour Une Vie Autonome* in France. This campaign was inspired by the American *CILs* (*Centers for Independent Living*).

As a means of gaining publicity for their campaign, *GIHP Lorraine* invited Ed Roberts, President of the American organization, World Institute on Disability, to Nancy. Ed was severely disabled at the age of fourteen by polio but this has not prevented him from becoming a leading figure in the movement for disabled people in the USA. Not only was he the first severely disabled American to get a college degree, but he also went on to help create the first *CIL* in Berkeley. He showed an incredible warmth toward everyone living at the *foyer* and his successes were an inspiration to us all. Judith Heumann, his partner at the World Institute on Disability, came to Nancy a few months later to continue the work that Ed had begun; her positive outlook and encouragement in the fight to improve facilities at the university were greatly missed when she left. Meeting them was an experience that I'll never forget.

Luck was on my side because, as an English speaker living at the *foyer*, I was soon invited to help out with interpretation during Ed's stay. The week included filming for TV, and interviews with the press, with the aim of publicizing *GIHP* and attracting financial support for the *Agence* from local industry. There were many lively debates on subjects such as the *CIL*'s role in the USA. Ed explained that the *CIL* network sees disability-related issues in a social and political context, rather than a medical one, believing that it is society, not the disability, which hinders an individual from achieving an independent lifestyle and fulfilling his or her potential.

"The family's hospitality knew no bounds—who says the French are cold?"

In many countries the improvement of facilities in order to cater to the needs of people with disabilities is something which is generally accepted as desirable but is rarely compulsory. Ed emphasized that legislation is the way forward. After our own difficulties regarding accessibility at the local university, we were amazed to hear, for example, that in certain American states not only is it illegal for a college student to be prevented on the grounds of disability from taking the courses of his or her own choice, but it is also illegal for any class to be held in a room that is inaccessible for a student taking that course.

As this was my first long stay in a foreign country, the race was on to visit as many different places as possible before I left. Although parts of Nancy (the capital of Lorraine) are less picturesque than neighboring cities Metz and Strasbourg, what remains of the original town (*la vieille ville*) is particularly attractive. Its narrow cobblestone streets have been made into pedestrian zones, lined with small restaurants and antique shops. The city is dominated by place Stanislas, a spectacular square dating from the eighteenth century, its gilded wrought-iron gates and railings an impressive sight, especially when illuminated at night. The Museum of Fine Arts (Musée des Beaux Arts) is

here, and there are a number of other museums worth seeing, including the Ducal Palace (Musée Lorrain), which now displays the history of the region, and the Musée de l'Ecole de Nancy, with an interesting Art Nouveau collection.

Just behind place Stanislas is the Parc de la Pépinière, where the annual jazz festival takes place in the autumn. If you're not afraid of heights, you can enjoy wonderful aerial views of the city when the fair pays its yearly visit to place Carnot. Every two years in spring the World Theater Festival is held in Nancy. There are several movie theaters and theaters in the city but access is sometimes a problem. However, Saint-Sébastien is a huge shopping center which does cater to the wheelchair user (rest rooms excepted!).

I spent several long weekends at a friend's home in a tiny village of about a hundred inhabitants, near the small town of Mirecourt. In the past, while Lorraine played a leading role in the steel industry of France, Mirecourt was famous for its violin-making. It was like entering a different world as we drove over narrow stony tracks, collecting the milk on the way, to an old house built of sand-colored stone. The family's hospitality knew no bounds—who says the French are cold?

My visits to the village coincided with some special events. In December we watched the Saint Nicolas celebrations: processions through the streets of Mirecourt, throwing candy to the crowds, while in the village some children acted out Snow White and the Seven Dwarfs and then waited eagerly for Saint Nicolas to distribute his presents! Several months later, the atmosphere was rather more serious, with the presidential elections in full swing. We watched as the mayor of the village counted the votes and that evening, when Mitterand's success was announced, my friend's Dad showed his approval by firing three rifle shots into the air—some of the neighbors were not amused!

I stayed with another French family high up in the Vosges mountains. Their home is even more isolated, surrounded by pine forests and with its own fresh water source. It's not surprising that the Vosges attract many tourists. Gérardmer is very scenic, situated beside a lake and encircled by mountains. Farther up, there are two more lakes, Retournemer and Longemer, and higher still, there are ski resorts that supply snow even in April. Like most regions in France, Lorraine is renowned for its cuisine and the specialties that I enjoyed here included *quiche lorraine, madeleines* (small cakes), and *tarte aux mirabelles* (a tart filled with sweet plums, produced in the region).

Strasbourg is not far from Nancy, in the neighboring region of Alsace. From the train the Germanic influence is evident, gradually creeping into the style of housing. Saverne, situated between these two cities, deserves a visit. It has a beautiful town center, with an eighteenth-century château and very ornate buildings, such as the Maison Katz, which dates back to 1605 and has an intricately decorated wooden facade. As well as being an important center for European politics, Strasbourg has an old quarter called La Petite France, which is full of exquisitely designed sixteenth- and seventeenth-century houses.

I also visited Paris, and traveled by train to Brussels several times. (Although I found the French train system very reliable, this particular route was rather hair-raising: at Luxembourg the train divides in two, one half going to Belgium while the other shoots off to Holland. Need I say more? On one of my journeys a very quick dash was called for!) After nearly a year of planning and organizing, then finding myself alone in a country whose language I could barely converse in, the ensuing nine months were packed with valuable experiences which more than compensated for the months of preparation. In this case, perseverance paid off!

Half a Loaf

Mairene Gordon has suffered from rheumatoid arthritis for over fifty years. She used crutches for fifteen years but now has artificial knees and hips. Of her travels in Italy, Spain, France, Greece, and the UK, Mairene reckons that her vacation in the Dordogne caused most difficulties.

Foolhardy, I suppose, one could call my decision to take a tourbus to visit the Dordogne. Lacking a companion, I thought that travel with a small group was the answer. The biggest snag was that I couldn't manage to board the bus unaided, but I was promised help by the tour operator (*Francophiles*).

I traveled by sleeper from Fife down to London, where, with the help of a beaming porter (who refused a tip), I had a buffet breakfast and found a taxi. The pick-up point was by Waterloo Bridge in the midst of London's ceaseless traffic. The bus was late, having tangled with the Chelsea Flower Show traffic, but eventually I was comfortably ensconced and speeding toward the coast. The Channel crossing was smooth and the bus was parked close to an elevator which whisked me to the upper decks.

After a couple of hours' driving in northern France, we stopped for the night at a pleasant hotel in Beuvry. Dinner was good, and I began to get to know some of my traveling companions. The oldest was 88, a spry retired doctor who was accompanied by an elegant cousin a few years younger. Professional couples and retired teachers made up the bulk of the group.

Next day, we left for Tours, stopping for lunch at Chartres, where we were given time for sightseeing. The Cathédrale Notre Dame stands high above the old town and can be seen from miles away, floating above the roofs and trees like a vision between heaven and earth. The original Romanesque cathedral was burned down in 1194 and only one of the great towers at the west end (Le Clocher Vieux) survived intact. In 1506 the other tower was rebuilt in ornate Gothic by Jehan de Beauce, and is slightly higher than the old one.

As I entered from the bright sunlight, the cathedral seemed very dark, but this made it easier to study the glowing stained glass windows with their vibrant blues and reds. A series of thirteenth-century windows present a panorama of medieval life: kings, princes, and great ladies in ermine and gold cloth mingle with knights and priests; peasants work in their seasonal occupations; artisans sculpt stone, fashion wood, and weave. Other windows depict biblical scenes from the Old and New Testaments: early Church leaders, saints, and martyrs. How keen they were on the suffering and death of saints.

But what impressed me most were the stone sculptures in the choir screen, begun by de Beauce in 1514 and worked on until his death in 1529. There are forty-one scenes—the work of various artists—which took two centuries to complete. They begin and end with the life of Mary, and in between are scenes from the life of Christ. The strength, delicacy, and grace of these works held me spellbound. One which I found particularly charming was of a youthful Mary, in an embroidered robe, sitting sewing. Of course, many hours or even days could be spent viewing this magnificent cathedral, but I felt thrilled by what I had been able to see. At least in a cathedral or church there is always somewhere to sit and rest and meditate.

"I would walk as far as I could, then literally collapse at a convenient café"

At Tours, the bed in my room was too low, so an additional mattress had to be conjured up. Then I discovered that I'd left my "helping hand" (light tongs, essential for picking things up and assisting me when dressing) at the first hotel. However, my long-handled shoe-lift had a curved, hook-like end, so I wasn't altogether stuck. When I sat down to a meal of asparagus in butter, followed by trout with almonds, my difficulties receded into the background, but an injudicious bite at a chunk of French bread dislodged a crowned front tooth. After the initial dismay, I decided to put up with the gap until I returned home.

Toward the evening on the third day, we arrived at Saint-Céré, where we were to spend a week. The hotel was charming, with a terrace bright with flowers and greenery, and a resident mole-colored cat with gorgeous green eyes. Alas, the short flight of stairs which I'd said I could cope with turned out to be a spiral staircase. However, the staff was very good at assisting me whenever anyone saw me making for the stairs. My room was French provincial, with an old-fashioned bed, slightly on the low side, which meant a struggle to get out every morning. The shower taps were too stiff for me to turn on, and the toilet was too low, but I am used to that. Otherwise, everything was fine. The dining room had family tables, so that I did not feel isolated but had a chance to make friends with my traveling companions.

Most days, we were taken by bus to surrounding places of interest. The countryside was lush and verdant, with old stone farmhouses, fields of sunflowers, vineyards, rivers, woods, and deep gorges. One morning was spent exploring interesting villages along the banks of the Dordogne, including La Roque-Gageac, a picturesque place on the curve of the river. The old stone houses are squeezed between the water and the great cliffs behind. It seemed as though the cliff could topple at any moment—in fact, a few years ago a huge slab of rock did crash down on the houses beneath. But, as with people living beneath volcanoes, the villagers cling to their homes.

> *"I was simply too tired to enter and view the interior, knowing that I had to walk back to the bus"*

Another trip was to Domme, an enchanting hill-top town opposite La Roque-Gageac. We entered by one of the original gateways. An inscription on the oldest house (now the *Hôtel de la Monnaie*) told us that the town was built around 1280 on the orders of Philip the Bold. A steep narrow main street, flanked by lovely old houses of warm-colored stone, climbs to an upper square with a church on one corner and the Maison du Gouverneur on the other. On the north side, beyond a fringe of umbrella-shaped pines, a stone parapet guards a sheer drop of hundreds of feet to the valley floor. The view is spectacular: the Dordogne snakes leisurely between fields of corn and tobacco, and beyond are the wooded hills of the Périgord Noir, broken here and there by ochre cliffs.

We visited Rocamadour, strung out along, and built into, sheer cliff, with shops and cafés at street level and, above, churches and chapels reached by a pilgrims' stairway of 216 steps. Pilgrims used to make the climb on their knees to reach the chapel of Our Lady of Rocamadour (Chapelle Miraculeuse) with its Black Madonna, but I could only gaze up from street level.

We spent some hours in Sarlat, the capital of the Périgord Noir. Beyond the main streets with their smart shops lies an entrancing medieval quarter, with cobblestone streets and narrow alleyways, and fine stone buildings dating from the twelfth to the seventeenth centuries. The cathedral was built on the site of a twelfth-century Benedictine abbey church and the town grew up around it. A rather Italianate Episcopal Palace adjoins the cathedral, and opposite stands a beautiful Renaissance house with intricate stone carvings—the Maison de La Béotie. This was the birthplace of La Béotie, renowned poet and friend of Montaigne. In 1563, when La Béotie died, Montaigne was at his bedside, and afterward wrote the famous essay *On Friendship* in his memory.

My strategy was everywhere the same: I would walk as far as I could, then literally collapse at a convenient café, order coffee or lemon tea, and watch the world go by. What I was able to see was always dependent on where the tourbus parked. I did not attempt to see the prehistoric paintings at Font de Gaume, or join the descent at Padirac to take the underground river trip through the caverns. I bought postcards instead.

I did manage to see the first floor of a Renaissance château at Montal, but on our journey back I saw only the facade of Fontainebleau. The grand entrance drive had to be negotiated and I was simply too tired to enter and view the interior, knowing that I had to walk back to the bus. I did at least see the "Horseshoe" staircase, down which, on April 20, 1814, Napoleon walked to bid farewell to the Old Guard as he was taken off to exile on Elba. With an able-bodied companion and a light, collapsible wheelchair, I could have seen much more and in greater comfort. But then, my considered philosophy is simple: "half a loaf is better than none."

Wintering in Roussillon

During the summer of 1981, Enid Fisher celebrated her seventieth birthday and to mark the occasion decided to follow it up by driving alone to the South of France, staying there from the New Year until Easter, to avoid the worst of the English winter.

Overweight and physically disabled by multiple arthritis, I was able to walk only a very short distance, even with the aid of a cane, and I relied heavily on my electric wheelchair and my little car for mobility and independence. By way of preparation, I formulated a program to reduce my weight, which might improve movement in my stiffening joints. I also had to acquire the necessary funds, part of which were raised by the sale of a few household treasures. I purchased a small trailer with ramps, so that I could load my wheelchair and tow it behind the car. This enabled me to see a little more of the countryside than would have been possible from behind the wheel of my car. On the positive side, I had an adequate knowledge of French and past experience of driving on the right.

I traveled overnight on the Portsmouth–St. Malo car ferry. Informed by the office that there was an elevator from the car deck to the cabins, I found on arrival that the way to the elevator was blocked by heavy chains securing trucks to the deck. Help came from a large sailor who carried both my overnight bag and my handbag while I struggled up the stairs. My cabin was very comfortable and I persuaded a kindly attendant to bring me coffee and a sandwich as the restaurant was up a further flight of stairs. The sea was choppy and I slept little, slipping and sliding on my couchette.

We arrived at St. Malo in the early hours; I could find no one to help me,

so I sat and waited, occasionally asking a passing crew member to send me an attendant. Then I heard my car number being called over the loudspeakers. It was obstructing the trucks and they wanted it moved. No use! I could not carry my bags or get downstairs without help, so I stayed where I was. Eventually help arrived and I descended to find my car and trailer alone on the car deck.

I drove out into total darkness and, after losing my way in a maze of one-way streets, enlisted a schoolboy on a bicycle to lead me to the road to Rennes. This turned out to be a nightmare: miles of massive repairs, red triangles, detours, traffic lights, mud, and potholes. But at last dawn came. I was thrilled to see the sky becoming lighter and stopped at a bar for coffee. No croissants, no bread, but "would Madame like a madeleine?" Yes, please.

Two mailmen having their morning glass of beer at the counter were joined by another man who remarked that St. Brieuc was snowbound. In the increasing daylight I found that my trailer had acquired some dents and scratches, also that its electrical connection to the car was detached. I had driven along that busy and obstructed road with no rear or indicator lights on my trailer. However, I managed to attach it and everything worked.

"I began to ponder how to ask for a bed at the nearest house"

At Rennes it began to snow, lightly at first and blowing clear of the road, then more heavily, with deep ruts forming. The rivers were in flood; I crossed a wide stone bridge below which the water was only about a foot lower than the parapet. I began to ponder how to ask for a bed at the nearest house. But I reached Ancenis, and the *Hôtel de la Val de Loire*, without further problems.

Ancenis is an ancient frontier market town between Anjou and Brittany. The hotel was excellent and I thoroughly recommend it to any disabled person. I stayed for three days in a first-floor bedroom with *en suite* bathroom; there were no steps to negotiate, and the food was delicious. The snow disappeared by the morning after my arrival, but the floods remained and the Loire and surrounding inundated countryside were an awe-inspiring sight. One of my outings was to the church of St. Florent le Vieil, on the south bank of the Loire. Full of tombs and memorials, one inscription caught my eye—that of a Royalist leader who, on his deathbed, ordered the release of Republicans imprisoned in the church. His black marble sepulcher had been carved and erected by a Republican sculptor.

> *"I slept in a bed with carved head- and foot-boards upholstered in yellow velvet"*

Soon after I left the hotel, on a Monday morning, disaster struck: the trailer became detached on the outskirts of a town, flew off and buried itself in a heap of litter on the roadside. I tried to move it but had to give up and drive into town in search of a garage. A mechanic, who must have been afraid to venture in a car with such a crazed elderly lady, followed me and easily hitched up the trailer. Monday turned out to be a bad day for driving—heavy vehicles are not allowed on French roads at the weekend, so Monday is busy. It was tiring to follow these trucks—it is always difficult to pass with right-hand drive and no passenger, and my trailer problems had made me apprehensive.

I traveled south to Roussillon in easy stages. Freezing weather prevented exploration of Châtelaillon-Plage, where I stayed for two nights in a comfortable, warm room in the *Hôtel St. Victor* with a wide view of the rocky coastline. At Montguyon I stayed at the *Hôtel de la Poste*, in the town center, with an elevator and level parking.

At Agen (famous for its plums), on the main Bordeaux–Toulouse road, I left behind the traffic, gas stations and garish advertising, and turned off along a country road to Astaffort, where I found the *Hôtel de la Tour*—an old house, with many outbuildings full of antiques and interesting *objets*. There were magnificent views from the two windows in my bedroom, and I slept in a bed with carved head- and foot-boards upholstered in yellow velvet. On the walls were watercolors of Naples, where Madame's uncle had spent his winter months, as well as a painting of the boats on the Seine in Paris that were used as wash-houses in the nine-teenth century. A level garden was full of tiny cyclamen.

While staying at the *Hôtel de la Tour* I visited the thirteenth-century Prieuré de Moirax. A mimosa tree was in full bloom near the doorway. A notice on the collecting box said "Be honest, you may deceive M. le Curé but you will not deceive the Good Lord." On my depar-ture, Monsieur, who was the chef, presented me with a bottle of his own *Prunes d'Agen*, plus an enormous picnic lunch for the journey.

> *"Mimosa bloomed abundantly and when I opened my shutters in the morning the fresh scented air of the garrigue was invigorating"*

After a stopover at Salies de Salat I continued through mountain scenery until I arrived in Quillan, a picturesque and ancient town on the Aude river. *Hôtel Pierre Lys* is on level ground and I stayed in a second-floor bedroom for a few days. This is Cathar country, scene of the fighting that led eventually to the annihilation of this religious sect which was persecuted by the established Church. I visited the ruined abbey at Alet-les-Bains, which was destroyed by the Cathars. The village looked deserted and decrepit.

From Quillan I set off along the narrow Defilé de Pierre-Lys, a rocky gorge with astounding views, but I had to concentrate on keeping the car on the road. I descended through vines and olives into sunshine and lunch at Thuir, in a large restaurant with an all-male clientele. Everyone sat at long tables with bottles of wine from which they helped themselves. No one took the slightest notice of me and the meal was good and cheap.

Eventually I reached the valley of the Tech, which spreads out in a wide plain to the north of the Eastern Pyrenees. Here the weather is dry and sunny even in winter, although it is cold at night and often very windy. When I reached Argelès-sur-Mer, the *tramon-taine* was blowing like a hurricane and there were olive branches scattered on the roads.

I was lucky enough to find a centrally heated apartment belonging to a French couple from the north who had built a house (Les Sorbiers) divided into two apartments as a retirement home. It is situated on the lower slopes of the Pyrenees about 4 miles inland from the Mediterranean. No one could have been more kind and helpful, and we quickly became friends. The owners live upstairs and I had the first floor, which was completely separate with its own front door. Two acres of level garden gave me as much exercise as I could manage, and it was often warm enough to sit out in the sunshine. Mimosa bloomed abundantly and when I opened my shutters in the morning the fresh scented air of the garrigue was invigorating.

I used my car to shop in the mountain village about a mile inland. I joined the local library, did a little sightseeing, visited the Golden Age Club and made quite a few friends. Mostly I cooked my own meals, as two weeks in French hotels had added several kilos to my weight. But how pleased I felt that I had made it, especially when I saw my home town on French TV in a blizzard of snow—I had escaped a hard winter.

The months passed in a manner similar to my life in England but with the added bonus of new and stimulating surroundings, fresh acquaintances, and lots of sunshine. I returned to the same apartment for the two subsequent winters, but a slight stroke, with the attendant problem of being sent home by air, leaving my car with friends in Roussillon, put an end to my voyages south.

FRANCE: TRAVEL NOTES

Sources of Information

French Government Tourist Office, 610 Fifth Avenue, New York, NY 10020 (☎800/990-0040); 1 Dundas Street West, Box 8, Toronto, ON N5G 1Z3 (☎416/593-4723). Many regional hotel guides use the wheelchair symbol to indicate accessibility (no criteria stated), but if the Paris guide is anything to go by (see *Accommodation*) this symbol cannot be relied upon. Apart from a page of notes produced in 1988 the tourist office supplies no information for disabled visitors, and tends to refer inquir-

ers to other sources, in France. On the whole, you'll need to understand French in order to make full use of the following organizations and their literature.

Association des Paralysés de France (*APF*), 17–21 boulevard Auguste Blanqui, 75013 Paris; ☎1/45.80.82.40. A national organization, with many regional branches, set up to deal with the welfare of disabled people in France and not really concerned with visitors. *APF* publishes a guide to accessible accommodation all over France called *Où ferons-nous étape?* (latest

FRANCE: TRAVEL NOTES

edition 1990) but this is of limited value, with too much white space and heavy use of symbols. Regional branches (list of addresses from head office) may be more helpful.

Groupement pour l'Insertion des Handicapés Physiques (*GIHP*), 98 rue de la Porte Jaune, 92210 St. Cloud. The Ile de France section of a national organization runs an accessible transport service in Paris, which must be booked in advance (☎1/47.71.74.90). Several regional *GIHP*s organize a similar service, and it's always worth inquiring at the Mairie (town hall) because many towns in France operate some form of specialist transport for disabled people.

Ligue Française pour les Auberges de la Jeunesse, 38 boulevard Raspail, 75007 Paris; ☎1/45.48.69.84. The *French Youth Hostel Association* will respond to requests in English and send a free guide, in French, English, and German, indicating those hostels (around 25 in France, one on Corsica, one in Guadeloupe) which—in theory—are accessible. Addresses and phone numbers are supplied so further inquiries are possible.

Centre d'Information et de Documentation Jeunesse (*CIDJ*), 101 quai Branly, 75740 Paris Cedex 15. Helpful and will respond to requests in English but all information is in French. Provides an information service for young disabled people and can supply details of courses offered at French universities. Information for disabled people includes fact sheets on vacations and sporting facilities.

Tour Operators

Most of our contributors made their own travel arrangements, but there are hundreds of operators to choose from if you want a package deal, and a wide range of activities—city breaks, wine tours, art appreciation, language courses, camping, boating, sun and sea, and many others.

A number of companies, although not specialists, claim to cater to disabled clients but be skeptical, obtain confirmation in writing that special requests will be granted, and ask lots of specific questions (see *Practicalities*). Mairene Gordon was promised help by

Francophiles, and she did indeed receive advice about her hotels, but it was not absolutely accurate—a short flight of stairs is not the same as a spiral staircase, and the two present very different problems to someone with impaired mobility.

Another British tourbus operator, *Shearings*, (Miry Lane, Wigan WN3 4AG; ☎0942/44246; fax 0942/824978) was praised by a deaf contributor, John Myall, who noted that a blind lady on the tour (in 1990) was also well catered for, that the company will advise which tours stop at hotels with easy access for wheelchair users, and that the booking form has a slot for stating any disabilities and special requirements; there is also a "Help Desk" offering advice to disabled clients.

For specialist treatment and a range of vacations in France (and many other countries) try the *Access Tourisme Service* (8 rue St. Loup, Charsonville, 45130 Meung sur Loire; ☎38.74.28.40 or 38.74.23.17), which is run by disabled traveler Dominique Dupuis. Plans for 1993 include an adapted cruiser with eighteen cabins, six accessible to wheelchair users, which will tour the Atlantic coast of France in summer, and the French West Indies (Guadeloupe and Martinique) in winter. This company also has adapted vehicles for hire (see *Transport*). Agents in North America are *Voyages Goliger* (☎514/849-3571), *Evergreen Travel Services* (☎206/776-1184), *Flying Wheels Travel* (☎507/451-5005), and *Gata Tours* (☎516/944-3025).

Getting There

Paris is one of the cheapest "gateway" cities in Europe. *Air France* has the greatest number of routes, out of several US cities including New York, Chicago, and Washington DC, as well as Montréal and Toronto; an on-board wheelchair—called a "spacemobile"!—is carried on all long-haul flights (no need to request it). The influence of Québec's community has resulted in some good deals on the Montréal–Paris and Toronto–Paris routes; *Air Canada* is the safe option here for disabled travelers, and this airline also flies to Nice (via London) and nonstop to Lyon; *Canadian Airlines* also flies to Paris. The best deals from eastern and central

FRANCE: TRAVEL NOTES

USA are out of New York and Chicago, safest bet probably *United*, from San Francisco, Los Angeles, Chicago, or Washington, or *Delta* from New York, Atlanta, or Cincinnati; *Northwest Airlines* flies from Boston; *Continental* flies nonstop from New York (Newark); *American Airlines* flies from several hub cities. For the best fares from the West Coast aim to flies from Los Angeles, San Francisco, or Seattle.

For those spending time in Britain first, onward travel by air to France is straightforward; shop around about a month in advance for the best deals. Facilities at British airports are described in the England and Wales *Travel Notes*. Facilities at the major French airports are good, but be aware that boarding/disembarking procedures may be fairly primitive at regional airports (see p.177).

Travel **by ferry from Britain** is easiest for wheelchair users if they are taking a car—although assistance can in theory be arranged at the ports if you arrive by train, it's not unheard of for wheelchair users to emerge from their journey in the baggage car on the train to find no waiting porter and a long hike to the ferry. It can be done, but be prepared to manage on your own or ask for help from other passengers—then at least you'll be pleasantly surprised when it all goes smoothly.

P&O European Ferries (Channel House, Channel View Road, Dover, Kent CT18 9TJ; ☎0304/203388), *Sealink Stena Line* (Charter House, Park Street, Ashford, Kent TN24 8EX; ☎0233/647047), *Sally Line* (Argyle Centre, York Street, Ramsgate, Kent CT11 9DS; ☎0843/595522), and *Brittany Ferries* (Millbay Docks, Plymouth PL1 3EW; ☎0752/221321) offer accessible facilities on board their ships. *P&O* recommends the Calais and Le Havre crossings for passengers with limited mobility. *Sealink Stena Line*'s new vessels, *Fiesta* and *Fantasia*, are highly accessible—no storm sills on the main passenger deck, spacious rest rooms with grab-rails, plenty of room in the restaurant area. For information and reservations on **motorail** services, contact *French Railroads* (*SNCF*, through the offices of the French tourist board). Blind travelers can take a companion free of charge. If traveling by rail without a car, contact

British Rail International (1500 Broadway, New York, NY 10036, ☎212/575-2667); 94 Cumberland Street, Toronto, ON M5R 1A3, ☎416/929-3333) for information; but to arrange assistance as far as the French coast phone your departure station on arrival in Britain. *SNCF* are responsible for the rest of the trip and can be contacted via the French tourist board. The completion of the **Channel Tunnel**, scheduled for 1993 but beset with delays and unlikely to be fully operational before mid-1994, will make rail travel between Britain and continental Europe smoother and quicker, and many disabled passengers will appreciate the lack of train changes and transfers to and from ferries.

Transport

Sian Williams judged the French **railroad** system (*SNCF*) to be overall superior to *British Rail*, but similar in terms of accessibility. One marked difference, however, is the steep clamber (at least two large steps) required to board and disembark many French trains—this is true of many continental trains; in general British train doors sit nearer to the platform. Sian found that some stations had ramps to enable wheelchairs to board and descend from the trains, but often it was up to the conductors to carry the chairs. That said, facilities have improved since Sian's trip and most major stations are now accessible, with facilities to assist disabled passengers when boarding or disembarking. There are spaces for wheelchairs and on-board accessible rest rooms on TGVs (high-speed trains). Free copies of a guide for disabled passengers (*Supplément au guide pratique du voyageur, à l'intention des personnes à mobilité réduite*), can be picked up from the bigger stations.

Facilities have also improved on city **metro** systems, the newer ones being designed to be accessible. Grenoble even has a fully accessible **tram** (streetcar) service—accessible stations, level access to trams, wheelchair spaces close to the doors—but, like the rest of Europe, the French still await concerted action on making public **buses** accessible.

The easiest way to get about France is by **car**; facilities at highway service stations are generally excellent (see *Guide des Autoroutes*

FRANCE: TRAVEL NOTES

à l'usage des Personnes à Mobilité Réduite) but finding accessible rest rooms off the auto-routes is sometimes difficult. Parking is not a problem, even in Paris where there are generous concessions to disabled drivers (p.189). Cars with hand controls can be rented from *Hertz* at Paris, Lyon, Marseille, and Nice airports. Lift-equipped vans can be rented from *Wheelchair Travel* (see England and Wales Travel Notes) in England and taken across the Channel by prior arrangement (but costs are high—around £200—as reduced ferry fares for disabled motorists apply only to owner-drivers). The *Access Tourisme Service* (see *Tour operators*) has a Peugeot 309 Automatic with hand controls for rent, and in 1993 plans to make self-drive adapted vans available for the summer season—at present they only offer an adapted minibus with driver for airport transfers (eg Orly–Paris and back, $170; Roissy–Paris and back, $180; Paris–Eurodisney and back, $150) or for sightseeing (eg one day Paris, $270; one day Loire Valley, $330 plus driver's lunch).

Accommodation

Ian Marshall stayed at the following hotels: *Thermalia Novotel* (1 av. Thermale, 03200 Vichy; ☎70.31.04.39); *Hotel Ibis* (Route de Mayenne, 53000 Laval; ☎43.53.81.82)—ask for room 13. He also recommends two campgrounds, which he used when exploring the canals around Decize and Clamecy. There were no special facilities but the shower/toilet blocks were accessible and the entrance to each site was level: *Pont Picot* (*Office de Tourisme*, rue Grand-Marche, Clamecy, 58500 Nievre); *Camping Municipal des Halles* (*Office de Tourisme*, Hotel de Ville, Decize, 58300 Nievre).

The first-floor flat which Enid Fisher stayed in can be rented from M. and Mme. Fissier (*Les Sorbiers*, Route de Sorède, 66700 Argelès-sur-Mer; ☎68.81.13.34, no English spoken). On her way down to Roussillon, Enid asked her hosts at the various stopovers to phone ahead and book her next accommodation, which they were happy to do.

Enquiries and reservations for the accessible cottage in the Dordogne should be addressed to David Marsden (Gresignac, 24320 Verteillac; ☎53.91.04.41). Polly Higgins describes the layout:

"The kitchen was small and compact, so that one could stand or sit at the work surface and reach everything; the living and dining area was spacious and light, and easily heated by a wood stove. French windows opened from this room onto the walled patio with its barbecue and attractive greenery.

"The first-floor bedroom with its handsome limestone fireplace overlooked the walled garden still dotted with pansies in November. This bedroom gave onto the bathroom, designed so that wheelchair users have easy access to sink, toilet, and shower. Upstairs was another double bedroom with views over fields and hills and the graceful ruins of an ancient chapel. Everywhere I looked, both in and around the cottage, there was something to delight the eye and I loved it all immediately."

Of the **hotel chains** that offer wheelchair-accessible rooms and *en suite* facilities, those that present the lowest bills include the following: *Hotels Arcade* (two-star, 60 hotels said to provide at least one bedroom and shower room designed for disabled guests; 12 rue Portalis, 75008 Paris; ☎1/47.59.44.00; reservations ☎1/42.68.23:45); *Les Balladins* (over 100 modern one-star hotels, most on main roads leading into towns, all with at least one bedroom for disabled guests (with wheel-in shower) and accessible public areas; 20 rue du Pont des Halles, 94656 Rungis; ☎1/49.78.24.00); *Campanile* (over 200 hotels in France, all claimed to have first floor rooms specially equipped for disabled guests, but directory is vague and details need checking; 31 av. Jean Moulin, Marne-La-Vallée, 77200 Torcy; ☎1/64.62.46.62); *Climat de France* (160 two-star hotels, many said to have rooms suitable for disabled guests; *Tours Chanteclerc*, 65 rue de Brésoles, Montréal, Quebec H2Y 1V7, ☎514/845-1236); *Fimotel* (70 two-star hotels with at least one room for disabled guests; 5 av. de la Porte de Clichy, 75017 Paris; ☎1/40.25.50.50); *Ibis/Urbis* (240 two-star hotels, many of which have facilities for disabled guests; *Resinter*, USA and Canada, ☎914/472-0370 or 800/221-4542); disabled delegates at a recent *Mobility*

FRANCE: TRAVEL NOTES

International seminar in Paris recommend the *Hotel Ibis Montmartre* (5 rue Caulaincourt, 75018 Paris; ☎1/42.94.18.18)—there are rooms with large *en suite* bathrooms and sliding doors, and all public areas are level or accessible by elevator (1991 price for twin room, with breakfast, was 415F per person per night).

The above addresses or phone numbers provide a central reservation service; if you wish to confirm the suitability of the accommodation you (or your travel agent) should ask the reservations staff to contact the hotel direct. Consult the *RADAR* guide, *Holidays and Travel Abroad* (see *Books*, p.591), and the *Holiday Care Service* (see England and Wales *Travel Notes*) for more ideas, but remember that much of their hotel information is provided by hoteliers and not verified.

The *Primotel Arles*, in **Provence**, has been highly recommended by the *Project Phoenix Trust* (see Italy *Travel Notes*), who stayed there in 1992. It is the first in a small chain of six three-star hotels to be made accessible for disabled guests. There are four large adapted rooms, three large elevators, and an additional elevator installed to overcome the six steps at the entrance to the hotel; the manager, M. Mané, is extremely helpful. Reservations for this chain should be made direct with individual hotels; the Directory is available from *Primotel*, 40 promenade du Grand-Large, F-13008 Marseille; ☎91.72.20.72.

For those staying in **Paris**, *Access in Paris* (see *Books*) is up to date and accommodation has been inspected by an experienced research team, including disabled people, who found that the wheelchair symbol used in the official Paris tourist board hotel guide is unreliable.

Access and Facilities

The minister appointed by President Mitterand in 1988 to oversee disability issues, Michel Gillibert, is disabled (quadriplegic) and has secured some fairly impressive measures to achieve good levels of state benefits, and integration of disabled people into French society. Disabled people travel free by air or rail, and citizens who do not want to do National Service may choose to act as traveling helpers/enablers. Of the money allocated to disabled people, 1000 million francs is raised by setting minimum quotas (six percent) for employers and allowing them to pay 10,000F for each disabled employee they choose not to employ. However, the French Employers Association is pressing for a reduction in these taxes. Sian Williams found that the employment quotas are not adhered to, and the benefits that disabled people can claim are not sufficient for those who require a considerable amount of care; they are forced to rely on family and friends to help out. And, as Mitterand's government comes under pressure to reduce spending, there is a chance that M. Gillibert will be one of the casualties when staff is cut.

Some parts of Paris and many of the small provincial towns are old and do not cater to wheelchairs. In Nancy, although an architectural bureau monitors all new buildings to ensure that they are accessible, there are still breaches of the regulations. Modern shopping centers and *hypermarchés* have good access, but restaurants, theaters, and movie theaters often pose problems.

Entrance to a **university** in France is open to anyone with the *baccalauréat*, whatever grade. There are several independent residential centers for students with disabilities, and those cities with such centers (for example, Nancy, Bordeaux, Montpellier) attract all the disabled students. At Nancy the accommodation is not equipped for severely disabled students. Access to the campus buildings there is variable: an elevator has been recently installed in the arts faculty to enable access to certain lecture rooms, but even the library for one faculty is not accessible. As ever, lack of finance is blamed.

Books

Access in Paris, written by Gordon Couch and compiled by the *Pauline Hephaistos Survey Projects* (*PHSP*, 39 Bradley Gardens, London W13 8HE), was published in 1985 but a new edition is scheduled for publication in spring 1993. Order from *PHSP* (see England and Wales *Travel Notes: Books*).

FRANCE: TRAVEL NOTES

French Farm and Holiday Guide (FHG Publications, £6.99; distributed to US bookstores by Hunter Publishing, 300 Raritan Center Parkway, CN94, Edison, NJ 08818) contains an illustrated selection of over a thousand *gîtes* (reasonably priced, rural self-catering accommodation—small cottage, village house, apartment, perhaps part of a farm), with a description of nine *gîtes* (submitted by the French tourist authorities) which are said to be accessible to disabled guests.

French Federation of Camping and Caravanning Guide (*Le guide officiel Camping-Caravaning*, published annually by the Fédération Française de Camping-Caravanning, 78 rue de Rivoli, 75004 Paris; ☎1/42.72.48.08) details 11,300 sites for camping and trailers and indicates which have special facilities for disabled people.

The Michelin Green Guide—Camping/ Caravanning France (from bookshops) indicates sites with facilities for disabled people but you'll have to check exact details with the site.

The RAC European Hotel Guide, published annually (1992, £7.99), is recommended by several British wheelchair users. The wheelchair symbol indicates hotels with (1) no steps at entrance, (2) restaurant on first floor, and (3) suitable bedrooms with adjacent rest room and bath facilities on the first floor or accessible by elevator (information obtained from hotel managers). The clear layout and ease of cross-referencing to the *RAC Motoring Atlas Europe* (£7.95) makes this guide ideal for use when touring and it is widely available in UK bookshops. Other European *RAC* guides that use the wheelchair symbol and have a good reputation

among disabled travelers are *European Camping and Caravanning Guide* (1992, £7.95) and *French Hotel and Holiday Guide* (1992, £8.99; includes maps). For more details contact the *RAC* (see England and Wales *Travel Notes*).

Touristes quand même!, two volumes, one for France, one for Paris, are available, free of charge, at the Paris Tourist Office (Office du Tourisme, 127 avenue des Champs-Elysés, 75008 Paris). Although long overdue for an update (France published 1986, Paris 1987), they are clearly laid out and contain notes on transport, access to practically everything you are likely to visit—monuments, museums, galleries, theaters, markets, shops, churches, swimming pools, movie theaters, parks, banks, hospitals, wheelchair repair shops; make use of the phone numbers to check details in advance. Symbols are explained in English and the text is easy to understand for anyone with basic French.

Guide des Autoroutes à l'usage des Personnes à Mobilité Réduite can also be obtained from *CNFLRH*, and lists facilities on French highways. Again, symbols are explained in English. The *AA Guide for the Disabled Traveler* uses this information in its section on "The Disabled Traveler Abroad."

Plainpied (10 rue Georges de Porto-Riche, 75014 Paris; ☎1/45.41.40.43) is not a book but the quarterly magazine (20F) of *GIHP* (see *Sources of Information*), worth getting hold of if you can read French and are interested in finding out more about "disability issues" in France.

TELEPHONE CODE:

From the US and Canada dial 011 (international code) and then 33 for France.

Switzerland

Riding the Alpine Rails

In 1951, a mother of two very young children, Janice Perkins contracted polio and has been a full-time wheelchair user ever since. Two more children and nine grandchildren later, Janice and her husband, Jerry, spent two weeks in Switzerland, with excursions into Germany and Italy.

My introduction to Switzerland came as a small child when I read "Heidi," the story of a young orphan girl who lived with her grandfather high in the Swiss Alps. Perhaps because my family spent summers in the Colorado Rockies, I was enchanted with descriptions of mountain meadows on the other side of the world.

Fifty years later, the enchantment was still there, even though forty years in a wheelchair had taught me that level terrain is safer and easier. My husband is a strong, determined helper, undaunted by hills, cobblestones, rain, sleet, or high winds, so we planned a two-week adventure touring on the Swiss Railroad. We were assured that handling a wheelchair would be "no problem" for train personnel, leaving us to enjoy first class comfort without the need to pore over maps or watch out for reckless speeders on switchbacks.

Our *American Airlines* flight nonstop Chicago to Zurich was pleasantly uneventful, and being seated close to the lavatory meant that I could indulge in at least small sips of liquid refreshment. Zurich airport is a model of accessibility for disabled travelers, with unisex lavatories large enough for a wheelchair and luggage cart, and complete with hot water, soap, and towels. The attendant pointed out the roll-in shower next door, but Lake Zurich was waiting, and we were anxious to validate our Eurail Passes for the ride to the city center.

After whisking us into the elevator and up to the train platform, the young *American Airlines* escort began to look worried. Apparently no one had shown him the correct method of boarding a wheelchair-bound lady. As the first cars pulled into view, we looked in vain for a helpful conductor pointing the way to the nearest ramp, but all we saw were narrow, steep steps, and doors automatically timed to snap shut regardless of a foot or wheel left dangling. Fortunately the city center trains depart every ten minutes, and Jerry had his strategy all mapped out for the next one. He and the visibly relieved escort quickly threw our luggage into the vestibule and hoisted me up the steps, managing to get everything tucked away before the train moved.

We reversed the process in Zurich's main stations and went off to talk to the experts at the Information office, asking how to arrange assistance on our extensive itinerary. Here, too, there seemed to be a complete lack of knowledge of the best way to get us on and off the Swiss trains. Finally, after much thought, the perplexed but very kind lady said, "Oh yes, you need to talk to the missionaries, just downstairs, around the corner and behind the fruit stand. And they speak English!"

"Although no one had studied our itinerary, two young men magically appeared wherever our car stopped"

We did, and they did, and all we had to do was arrive at the station just a bit early for our next departure and much help would be given. "No problem!," but we never did learn why they were called missionaries. We connected through Zurich five times, and although no one had studied our itinerary, two young men magically appeared wherever our car stopped. With many smiling gestures, they lifted me as a queen on a throne, or maybe like a load of luggage, to their forklift truck. We bounced through the station at a fast pace with Jerry running behind, while passers-by smiled politely, guffawed out loud, or averted their eyes altogether.

Homework paid off on one very important issue. We knew in advance that we could check luggage through to our next destination. This was helpful when making several connections, but we learned the hard way to carry night necessities with us, as our bags did not always arrive the same day.

At the *Bellerive au Lac Hotel* in Zurich we were shown to a comfortable room overlooking the Promenade, and although only the bathtub had assistance bars, both bedroom and bathroom were large enough for easy transfers. Although Zurich is a cosmopolitan city of finance, the lake gives it a perpetual holiday air, and sunlight dancing on the brilliant blue water was an instant antidote to overnight flight blahs and railroad mishaps. Ramped entrances and plenty of deck space made the lake steamers a good choice for sightseeing, so we joined housewives, schoolchildren, and early commuters on their way home to charming villages. Lakeshore real estate is at a premium, and private dock permits are jealously guarded, passed down from one generation to the next.

Next morning an early wake-up call sent us back to the Bahnhof to catch our train to Oberammergau, Germany. A mini excursion to the Bavarian Alps had been a last-minute decision, to seek the town where twelfth-century villagers had prayed for deliverance from the Plague, promising a Passion Play to the glory of God. Since this was not the year of a performance, we asked to join a group of German visitors in a tour, but the theater manager surprised us by arranging for an English-speaking guide. Next thing I knew, I was lifted in my wheelchair by four young men and carried up three flights to the top row of seats. They wanted us to see how perfectly the building had been designed so that each person could see from any seat in the theater. Although the audience is under a roof, the immense stage is open to the sky, lending authenticity to the outdoor scenes. Our backstage tour showed the simplicity of the sets as well as the richness of costumes being prepared for next year's play.

We chose to stay at the *Alois Lang Hotel*, a country inn on the outskirts of town, away from the main road bustle yet only a short walk to the town center. The terrace overlooking beautiful gardens was a restful spot for mid-afternoon Bavarian cakes and coffee.

There were three steps at the hotel entrance, but someone was always on hand to assist in pulling the wheelchair up to the door. As in many European countries, the elevator was miniscule, so we used the freight elevator just next to it, exactly the right size to accommodate my wheelchair without an inch to spare. We were given a lovely corner room with a bathroom large enough for easy turns, and an interesting view of the oddly shaped Kofel mountain.

Oberammergau is an easy town to explore on foot, and we spent hours strolling the curving streets, gazing in shop windows filled with Christmas decorations, beautifully embroidered linens, and exquisite woodcarvings. Following the path along a stream close to our hotel, we came upon an imposing building which housed a school for apprentice woodcarvers, and rejoiced to see that the love of fine craftmanship lives on. Whenever we turned a corner we saw the well-known painted public buildings and homes, depicting larger-than-life biblical scenes and fairy tales.

"We could hardly contain ourselves when his helpers sent him sprawling on his backside"

Regretfully leaving Oberammergau, Jerry once more pulled me up the train steps, enlisting the help of the conductor and a baggage handler. Each time he performed this maneuver, he would try to explain that if the two men lifting the front of the wheelchair would please wait for him to get his footing as he went backward up the train steps, all would be well. More often than not, their zeal in trying to be helpful ended with a hefty push which sent Jerry scrambling to keep from going over backward. On one occasion, an officious trainman insisted that Jerry stand back and allow him to take the back of my chair, and we could hardly contain ourselves when his helpers sent him sprawling on his backside.

"I was ceremoniously forklifted aboard the local train to Lucerne"

Actually, German trains are a model of efficiency, always departing exactly to the minute of the announced time. Consequently, whenever we heard "Achtung," we sprang to attention and prepared to move quickly. Whenever train personnel did not materialize to give help, other passengers did, and we will be eternally grateful to a lady who saved the day in Murnau. She had been a delightful companion from Oberammergau, telling us of her walking tours each spring in the Bavarian Alps, and lamenting the preponderance of hardy dandelions where alpine flowers once grew, all because of industrial pollution.

As we alighted to connect to our train for Innsbruck, we discovered the way was blocked by another train, necessitating a quick trip down the stairs and through the underground tunnel. As we contemplated this dilemma, the conductor just shrugged his shoulders, but our friend ran to the stationmaster, ordered him to hold our connecting train, escorted us half a block to the road crossing, ran with us back up the platform to the waiting train, then commandeered several young men to get us on board. The feather in her hat was still bobbing in triumph as she waved good-bye.

Our next compartment was shared with a couple returning from Vienna, straining our limited French and German, and their even more limited English. We did a lot of smiling while passing through tiny Leichtenstein, where the border crossing not only brought on board the customary soldiers checking passports but also entailed a change of locomotive.

Galloping through the Zurich station once again, I was ceremoniously forklifted aboard the local train to Lucerne. Traveling most of the day was tiring, but the changing scenery kept us from napping, and we were eager to see the picturesque city on the Reusse river. Our first impression was a bit sour because our taxi driver conveniently got lost during the five-block ride to our hotel. Never mind, having greatly overcharged us, the cabbie missed out on a generous tip. Our next jolt came when we saw the long flight of steps at our hotel entrance, but while Jerry checked in a reception clerk rushed out to take me around to a level entrance through the riverfront terrace café.

Des Balances is a charming hotel, occupying a twelfth-century building with walls a good eighteen inches thick, and an excellent location in the old city. Above the terrace, the second-floor public rooms are elegantly furnished, while around the corner from Reception a private hallway leads to two rooms especially designed for guests in wheelchairs. Not only was there a roll-in shower and assistance bars in all the strategic places, but, wonder of wonders, I could go through the French windows and sit on the balcony.

"Flower-strewn meadows, woodlands, and the occasional hamlet where small chalets were surrounded by spring blossoms"

Church bells and calling swans were the first sounds of morning. On their way to St. Peter and St. Paul Church, parishioners threw breadcrumbs to the large assortment of waterfowl. Jerry sat on the river steps with his watercolors, and small girls and boys sidled up to watch him as he sketched and painted the Lucerne Town Hall.

Just a bit farther on, we joined other tourists in strolling across the medieval wooden bridge, famous for its frescoes. Lucerne is a city where one constantly bumps along cobblestones, and cranes the neck to see ancient towers, but it is all worth the effort. Even Jerry huffed and puffed a bit, after insisting that we go all the way up to the top of the city walls, a neighborhood where homes and schools nonchalantly rubbed shoulders with history. We American Midwesterners wondered if we would ever become blasé about centuries-old monuments.

My favorite was the Great Sleeping Lion, cut out of a rock wall from a model by Danish sculptor Bertel Thorvaldsen, commemorating the courageous Swiss Guards killed while defending the Tuileries Palace during the French Revolution. The lion reclines above a pool in a small park, a quiet place in the early evening, away from traffic and fellow tourists.

Contrasting with city sights, Lake Lucerne is quite simply a perfect picture of deep blue water surrounded by snow-capped peaks. We had made up our minds to see a view from the top so we left the lake steamer at Vitznau to climb aboard the cogwheel railcar which, by the way, is tilting upward even when waiting at the small station. Much help was given and I was transferred to a level seat for the journey to the top of Rigi Kuhn mountain. At last I was in Heidi's country, and I could scarcely contain my excitement as we were pulled up and up, through flower-strewn meadows, woodlands, and the occasional hamlet where small chalets were surrounded by spring blossoms. The pansies were particularly eye-catching, three times the size of any in our garden at home.

The railcar stopped short of the small, level plateau where a resort hotel perched amid other snow-covered peaks, and while everyone else trudged up the steep hill, Jerry pushed me through a tunnel leading to an elevator. Mounds of snow clung to the hotel terrace where we devoured marvelous vegetable soup and fresh rolls, lifting our faces to the sun and laughing at the resident Saint Bernard wearing the traditional cask of brandy. The first floor women's room was not accessible, so we were escorted to one on an upper floor by the manager, who told us that his yearly guests include a group of young people with cerebral palsy. What a fabulous place to spend a week away from the world!

"We felt like experienced world travelers as we boarded the steamer"

Only the thought of balmy breezes could lure us away from Lucerne. We wanted to sample the Italian region of Switzerland, so again we braved the Zurich connection on our way south to Lugano, where the air is softer and the pace slower. The *Hotel Meister*, two blocks from the Promenade, has the look and feel of an Agatha Christie novel—a small hotel where everyone dresses up for dinner, the event of the day. Northern Europeans spend several weeks here, recuperating from their long, cold winters, taking morning walks, afternoon naps, and enjoying card games or reading in the lounge. And yes, the bookshelves do hold many Agatha Christie novels in several languages.

The family management of the *Meister* was apologetic because the other hotel nearby offered up-to-date accessibility but was already booked. We took a look at it and decided the charm of the *Meister* was worth a little inconvenience. The few steps at the entrance were low and wide, and we loved the wheelbarrow overflowing with hydrangeas just outside the door.

This was our third Swiss lake region, and we felt like experienced world travelers as we boarded the steamer to Morcote, a pretty village, but much too perpendicular for me to wander far from the shore. Jerry climbed many flights of stairs to the schoolyard high above the water but did not go all the way to the church. Perhaps the villagers feel that the arduous climb brings them closer to heaven.

Lake Lugano spreads in several fingers, and our last day trip was to Porlezza, Italy, where several tourists disembarked on their way to St. Moritz or Como. We had thought of going on over to Lake Como, but the route involved a bus with steps too high for an easy lift. Our luck with constant sunshine had ended that day, a light mist cast a mysterious veil over the shoreline, and we were happy to return to hot baths and our final gourmet dinner.

Three days in each town we visited had given us a feel for the region, and time to rest between the adventures of rail travel. As the beautiful mountains receded from view, our memories were like the changing patterns of a kaleidoscope—onion-domed churches, their interiors rich with gold leaf; choosing chocolates from local patisseries; distant cow bells and train whistles; and the grinning faces of two young men on a forklift baggage truck.

A Long Love Affair

Ian Marshall first fell in love with Switzerland in 1947. Apart from a sight problem, he was not disabled, but a "grubby school boy" of fifteen. The school trip made such a lasting impression that Ian was determined to return. By the time he achieved this,

he was married with two small girls, and paraplegic to boot.

For our first vacation we chose to take a rented apartment in the canton of Wallis. I asked a Swiss friend, who had recommended the area, to have a look at the apartment on our behalf to check for accessibility. Things are much better these days in this respect and I feel more confident when booking. It is well worth shopping around as prices vary enormously. Accommodation is spotlessly clean and well appointed (even down to the atomic shelter).

My favorite route across the Channel is by hovercraft because it is quick and easy, although not cheap. If you choose a ferry crossing, then the shorter the better: anything over four hours, I think, requires reserving a cabin, and that can present its own problems. Modern vessels have elevators up from the car deck, and a good loading officer will place you exactly opposite the elevator door. Without an elevator it is necessary to muster four crew members and persuade them to carry you up several flights of stairs. Trying to explain in French that I should be carried up backward, and the chair should be tilted back rather than forward, needed a little preparation and practice before boarding a French boat.

We decided to make journeying across France part of the vacation, rather than tearing along highways. Each time we go we choose a slightly different route, and when we later took to camping and towing a trailer we took even longer as there is so much to discover and there are hundreds of sites to choose from. When not camping, two of our favorite hotel stops are Dijon, if entering Switzerland via Pontalier, and Gérardmer in the Vosges if making for Basel to join the Swiss highway system. Payment of a flat fee (SFr30) allows you to use this network for the whole year and is well worth the expense. The disabled rest rooms in highway service stations are some of the finest I have found anywhere. The ordinary roads are determined by topography, so that they are twisting and time-consuming, but the best way to see the country if time permits.

We have found camping in Switzerland most enjoyable but the sites are more crowded than those in France, and it is essential to reserve in peak season. As the Swiss keep their trailers on sites, rather than at home, you may find unoccupied trailers taking up valuable space. The provision of facilities for disabled campers is increasing all the time.

> *"The Swiss sometimes have difficulty in reconciling the interests of disabled people with their national traits of tidiness and conformity"*

One simple piece of luggage, with which I equip myself whether using a trailer, hotel, or rented accommodation, is a sturdy wooden stool, of the type found in a hospital gym. With the seat padded and universal castors attached to the legs, it enables me to move around inside a trailer and in other tight spots where a wheelchair would be far too large.

It is wise to carry warm and waterproof clothing because at high altitude the hottest day can give way to a cold night, and spectacular thunderstorms, a feature of late summer, can drench you in seconds. I find that struggling into a two-piece plastic rain suit will keep me bone dry, and this act alone often keeps the rain at bay! To find the warmest weather, try the Italian-speaking canton of Tessin, south of the Alps, with its famous lakes. Otherwise, Interlaken in the Bernese Oberland, with its many sites and attractions, is hard to beat as a tourist center.

Nearby, overlooking the Thunnersee, I found almost the ideal hotel for wheelchair users. From parking in the village square, or the rear hotel yard, there is not a single curb or step to negotiate to enter the hotel. An elevator gives access to all floors. I say "almost" because the bathroom door was narrow and I would have been in trouble without my stool. But now there is an excellent publication, obtainable from the Swiss National Tourist Office (SNTO), entitled *Swiss Hotel Guide for the Disabled*, which not only makes sure of bathroom door widths but also details elevator accessibility and provides other essential information which enables the disabled person to travel with confidence. This is not always the case with guidebooks displaying the wheelchair symbol, as I have found to my cost.

Where a wheelchair can be a positive asset is on the waterborne part of the integrated transport network. The lake steamers run like clockwork up, down and across the lakes, and provide an ideal means of visiting many of the lakeside towns and villages. Or, as the aforementioned guidebook puts it, "The boats on the lakes invite to discover lovely shores."

Boarding is by a simple gangway from the landing-stage. Waiting passengers hang about nonchalantly, but do not be fooled. At the last moment, panic sets in and they all insist on embarking first. The chair affords good protection as the crowd, six or eight abreast, squeezes onto a gangway designed for two. If you are lucky enough to have three companions, form up in good time with the two brawniest as vanguard, the third as pusher behind, and be ready to surge forward like a cohort of the Swiss Guard when the "off" is given.

For some of the excursions by road our camper was not the ideal vehicle because of its width. In many of the smaller valleys, special passing places are necessary. Even so, we twice nearly came to grief, once when edging around a huge parked timber low-loader, when our wheels just clung to the crumbling edge of the mountain road, and again when squeezing past an on-coming postbus, which naturally had right of way.

To give the driver a rest, and relief from potential heart attacks, there are many tourbus excursions from the main tourist centers. If you cannot manage bus travel, there is usually a local taxi which will offer an excellent full day's outing at a cost per head of little more than that charged by the tour operator. We made a memorable trip to the Rhone glacier by this means. Zurich and some other major towns run specially adapted taxis which take wheelchairs. Trains are an easier option, particularly the intercity services, which even have disabled rest rooms on board and are geared up to help. Ask at the station for the travelers' help service, and look for the SOS logo.

Despite all this, I believe that the Swiss sometimes have difficulty in reconciling the interests of disabled people with their national traits of tidiness and conformity. Such conflict may account for the problems that we experienced as pedestrians in one of their largest cities, where there was no provision made for wheelchairs to cross the road at a busy intersection. Pedestrians were forbidden to cross except by foot tunnel—useless to me because it had steps at both ends. Drivers seemed to accelerate on seeing us making a dash for it. In the event, all that was dented was their reputation. Perhaps this was an exceptional example: in general, "walking" is both possible and rewarding—in cities, towns, and villages on well-maintained sidewalks and roads, and even in rural areas and high valleys.

"With its almost unbelievable landscapes, Switzerland may seem a most unsuitable country for the disabled visitor, but most of it can be reached and experienced"

Some of the Swiss I've met have difficulty also in reconciling a sense of pride in their modern technological nation and a collective conscience about their environment plus a folksy peasant image of the past. In the tourist areas they make full use of the latter, especially on their national day, August 1. If you are drawn to yodeling, flag-throwing, shooting, alpenhorn blowing, or fireworks, not to mention the village band playing their version of "Tiger Rag," August 1 is your day.

With its almost unbelievable landscapes, Switzerland may seem a most unsuitable country for the disabled visitor, but most of it can be reached and experienced. I am constantly drawn back to the place by the magical spell which fell upon me more than forty years ago, and crossing its frontier always feels like going home.

The Eiger on my Doorstep

At the age of 68, Beryl Bristow made her fifth trip to Grindelwald in the Swiss Alps. She was partially sighted and in need of a new knee and pair of hips.

My three passions are photography, painting, and studying Alpine flowers. This may sound somewhat bizarre, considering my poor vision, but I am able to enjoy these hobbies with the help of a close-up lens and strong magnifying glasses. I originally chose to stay in Grindelwald to be near the Alpine flowers. I wrote to the local information bureau and received not only a mass of leaflets, but also a well-written letter in English enclosing a pressed cowslip! In Grindelwald I had what I needed most—good transport in every direction—and I found a delightful hotel, the *Gydisdorf*, whose owners looked after every guest with great care. I felt happy and safe there, so in June 1987 returned for another stay.

I was taken to Torquay station in a Red Cross ambulance and my escorts saw me into my reserved seat—one for disabled passengers—with extra leg room and luggage racks nearby. *Swiss Travel* is the best operator for Switzerland, but I now travel independently, finding it cheaper. The journey is straightforward, providing I travel at weekends, which avoids a change of train at Basel. I already had a railcard, so I bought a Eurocard which gave me half fare on the Swiss main lines and Interlaken lake steamers, as well as concessions on most of the other lines. I booked lower bunk couchettes, reserved seats where possible, and asked for a wheelchair at Dover.

A Red Cross escort met me at London's Paddington station and I was soon speeding across town to catch the boat train. A porter heaved my cart and shoulder bag aboard and I looked for my seat. There were hoots of laughter as I quoted the seat number—I was the sixth person to lay claim to it. However, another seat was empty and its rightful owner, standing behind me, let me take it and settled himself farther down the train.

Finding it difficult to get up and down for my ground-level close-up photography on this vacation, I concentrated on my painting. This was evident from my cart! The pointed feet of my easel stuck out menacingly; my folding chair was tied onto the handle; my oil paints, bottles of medium, brushes, and cloths were in a plastic box at the bottom, with a shopping bag of spare clothes and painting boards stuffed in at the top; every spare corner was filled. My shoulder bag held a large Thermos of hot water and tea bags—a necessity as the train would have no refreshments on board and it was a twelve-hour journey from Calais to Interlaken. Cameras, tape recorder, and a selection from my medicine chest were crammed into the bag's pockets. I had only a small amount of money in my pocketbook, but under my sweater I wore a child's satchel, in which I carried my keys, large bills, check and credit cards and, most important, the numbers of my Swiss travelers' checks. Men wear a money belt but the satchel is better for ladies, particularly if they are plump like me!

"A full moon, rising behind a forest, was reflected in a wide river running alongside the track"

Helping hands at Dover soon had me and my luggage off the train, and I sailed in my wheelchair through the passport office, along the dock, and up the gangway onto the *Sealink* ferry. I found myself a seat next to the Purser's office and went to the cafeteria while the ship was stationary. After an excellent meal I asked the Purser to radio Calais and request a *chaise roulande* for me.

At Calais I was lowered into a huge old wheelchair with copious blankets tucked around me. Piled on my lap was everything except the cart—heavy shoulder bag, duty frees rattling in their shopping bags, a bag of yoghurts and milk shakes, and my pocketbook slung round my neck. We formed a small procession, an old man pushing me and a younger one following with my cart. The station platform was full of small craters and we had to cross a number of train tracks; the younger man assisted my porter in heaving me over these, and at last we reached the right train and my compartment.

I woke in the night and pushed up the blind: a full moon, rising behind a forest, was reflected in a wide river running alongside the track. Soon the river widened into a large lake and the moon cleared the trees, its silvery beam shining brightly on the water—a beautiful sight. Soon after 4am, the train slowed and stopped at Metz. I love this stop. I pushed the window right

down, delighting in the fresh air after a night in the small compartment. There was little activity on the platform but I listened intently and was soon rewarded with the dawn chorus, right on cue!

From then on my excitement grew with every mile we traveled. After stops at Basel, Berne, and Spitz, we approached Interlaken, and I could see that spring had arrived. There were bushes of purple lilac and pinky white clouds of apple blossom everywhere. As we neared the town I spotted the Jungfrau with its snowy crest.

Fellow travelers helped me to transfer to the local train. It's a 25-minute journey to Grindelwald and interesting all the way. Waterfalls of melting snow cascaded down the rocky cliffs to join the river rushing through the fields. The first hay was being cut and stacked on spiky sticks. The Eiger towered above us, then the valley widened out and we drew into the station. The taxi was waiting, as arranged, and we drove up into the village. After a couple of minutes we turned sharp left and I saw the Wetterhorn and then *Hotel Gydisdorf*—the lovely 100-year-old chalet which is the home of two sisters, Hanni and Marie Zimmermann. Their guests share the chalet, and Marie's flower-filled garden.

"In spring the flowers grow knee high and as thick as grass"

My room by the garden door was ready, and breakfast was brought into the lounge so that I could enjoy my favorite view of the Wetterhorn with my coffee, black cherry jelly, and rolls. The chalet is built on three levels: the lower floor has double rooms with facilities, the living rooms are on the main central floor where there are also some single rooms and a double. Upstairs are the remaining bedrooms. The kitchen is Hanni's territory and her cooking is superb. The sisters and their staff obviously enjoy looking after their guests, and many return year after year. It wasn't long before I recognized a voice and saw a familiar face. Hanni and Marie take guests through *Swiss Travel*, whose rep calls regularly, or one can book privately.

Grindelwald lies at the head of a valley, at 3350ft, and the swollen river which flows toward the lakes at Interlaken is fed by two glaciers and numerous waterfalls. The lower meadows are therefore lush, and in spring the flowers grow knee high and as thick as grass. The village became popular as a climbing center in the mid-nineteenth century, and is famous for its guides and mountaineers: a more recent addition is a sports center with large indoor pool and skating rink, tennis courts, and gym.

"The mountains were now coated with thick new snow and the tops shone golden"

I woke at 4:30am the next morning, opened my window and grabbed my cameras. I crept into the living room and looked out at the Eiger in the pink glow of sunrise. Opening the window wide, I leaned out and framed the peak with a branch of apple blossom from the old tree below. At last I had the early-morning shots I wanted! Sunday itself began as it should, the church bells ringing with that resonant tone peculiar to the Alps, and the resident blackbird singing near her nest. I put my tape recorder on the window-sill and switched on; I start each vacation tape with that music. In the same morning, in between sketching in the crevices and filling in the vivid blue sky for a painting of the Wetterhorn, I also recorded cow bells echoing loudly in the narrow street below, and then six hundred young brass band players marching in a village competition.

I had dreaded my first ride in the chair lift, but on my fifth visit it was irresistable. From the *Gydisdorf* the lift (called the "First" because it takes you

up to the Grindelwald "First," at 7115ft) is only a couple of yards and a few steps to climb. The attendant sees you into one of the two-seaters and fastens you in, wrapping you in a vast waterproof if he thinks it wise. I recommend getting off at the second stop, Bort, where I found many varieties of orchid on my first trip. One year the slopes dazzled with a mass of bright yellow hawkweed, the following year there were sweeps of white Alpine buttercups and patches of purple cranesbill among the yellow. I have not seen the orchids again, but I always find gentians and bright-eyed primroses, pale mauve and shades of pink. In 1987 spring was later than usual, so I saw new vistas of color—golden marsh marigolds on the higher slopes, cowslips on the lower— and I spotted my favorite flowers, *Sol danella* (snowbells).

The chair lift stops beside the restaurant and the views are breathtaking. I walked up my favorite path to the waterfall and crossed over a new bridge, which I was glad to see. I took some close-ups of a fine gentian, and a portrait of a silky white goat who disturbed me from behind as I focused, bent double over the flower. It began to rain so I made my way to the restaurant and found a seat with three Japanese and four Swiss, who tried to persuade me to share their sausages and French fries.

The clouds were closing in and I decided to return. Soon the clatter of the chair lift approached and I was amazed to see a lady sat on one seat with a large German Shepherd on the seat next to her. When I told Hanni about it she replied, "Oh yes, it's a neighbor. She always takes him on the chair lift when they go for a walk." As I floated down, the rain turned to snow and the fir trees were sprinkled with a fine coating, like powdered sugar.

It continued damp until after dinner the next evening, when the clouds suddenly parted and cleared over the Wetterhorn and the whole valley.

Everywhere the mountains were now coated with thick new snow and the tops shone golden, then pink in the sunset glow.

I had never seen the glacier sparkle so brightly. I took the bus up to the *Wetterhorn Hotel* and walked down the path through the woods. It is an easy walk, and folk of all ages go as far as the bridge across the river of melting ice. It is an awesome sight, all the more so through a zoom lens. I saw that it was different this year—much wider and bigger than before. Although beautiful, the glacier is really a moving monster, traveling at the rate of one foot a year. The ground was too slippery for me to venture farther than the bridge. It was clear that I couldn't reach the higher paths, so the other guests brought back some flowers for me and we spent a few happy hours in the evenings trying to identify specimens.

Because of avalanches I was unable to make my usual trip on the Pfingstegg cable car. On previous visits I found dozens of Alpines that were new to me. The first time I'd been advised to "take the path to the hut and the goats, and carry on to the glacier." I later had to admit that I'd seen neither hut nor goats, not even the glacier. What I did see was a great variety of flowers—I used two 36 exposure rolls of film in about a hundred yards. This was heaven on earth for me, much better than the Alpine Flower Garden at Schynige Platte (6800ft), near Wilderswil, which was too formal for my taste.

I used my Eurocard for some rail trips. Numerous excursions can be planned with the help of the information bureau booking clerks at Grindelwald station. It's wise to plan in advance, using the freely available timetables, and to take a taxi, if not for the outward journey then for the trip back up the hill from the station after a long day out. Mürren, Wengen, or Kleine Scheidegg are easily reached for spectacular views of the Jungfrau. The

views between Kleine Scheidegg and Wengen are the best you'll ever see.

I went to Alpiglen on the side of the Eiger—just a few buildings, a hotel, and marvelous panoramic views. I loved the place. It had an atmosphere, an aura about it. Later, I read in *The White Spider* (by Heinrich Harper) that climbers had stayed in those buildings before attempting the North Face . . . no wonder it felt like hallowed ground.

"You don't have to be agile to sit in a café and simply take in the views"

The outings requiring the least exertion must be on the lake steamers and the "gondola" (mini cable car) to the Mannlichen (7580ft). The steamers start from a spot near one of the train stations in Interlaken. I like to get off at Brienz for a while and sit on the seats under the trees by the lakeside. This is the birthplace of the woodcarving industry and there are wonderful old pieces to be seen here, such as The Last Supper, carved from one piece of wood in the fifteenth to sixteenth century.

The gondola station is a short walk from Grund train station. If you can manage to climb into the gondola this is a relaxing way to admire the scenery as you glide upward for about half an hour. With binoculars you may see the delightful marmots put on a friendly boxing bout, or perhaps some other examples of the elusive Alpine wildlife.

Grindelwald was one of the first Swiss villages to be developed as a winter resort, but there are many summer attractions which can be enjoyed by the less mobile tourist. The excellent transport network and the well-maintained paths enable those of us who are physically disabled to reach at least some of the dizzy heights that are conquered by the knee briches-clad hiker and the climber with his crampons. And you don't have to be agile to sit in a café and simply take in the views.

SWITZERLAND: TRAVEL NOTES

Sources of Information

Swiss National Tourist Office (*SNTO*), 608 Fifth Avenue, New York, NY 10020 (☎212/757-5944);154 University Avenue, Suite 610, Toronto, ON M5H 3Y9 (☎416/971-9734). A mine of beautiful brochures and maps, the SNTO also distributes the *Swiss Hotel Guide for the Disabled*. Their head office (*Schweizerische Verkehrszentrale*, Bellariastrasse 38, 8027 Zurich; ☎1/288 1111) produces many publications, among them the *Swiss Youth Hostel Federation Guide*, giving accessible hostels and travel information including details of reduced fares.

The twelve **regional tourist offices** (list of addresses in the *Swiss Hotel Guide for the Disabled*) and the local information bureaux are recommended by Beryl Bristow as the best source of information: they will supply hotel and town guides in English, some with reference to disabled people. She also also wrote to *Pro Infirmis* (Hohlstrasse 52, 8000 Zurich; ☎1/241 4411) which was obliging, if slow to respond, but this organization is more than likely to refer inquiries to *MI Schweiz* (see below).

According to *Pro Infirmis*, the Swiss have been slow to provide facilities, perhaps because there has been no war there for 200 years and there are no victims of war to cater to. In addition, each of the 3000 communities in the different cantons is a law unto itself, and some are progressive in their approach to providing for disabled people, others less so. *MI Schweiz* judges Basle to be the most progressive canton in terms of accessibility.

Mobility International Switzerland (*MI Schweiz*), Hard 4, 8408 Winterthur; ☎52/256825; fax 52/256838. This organization is active in many areas, including mobility, travel, vacations, and exchange visits, the gathering of data, the distribution of information, and the recruitment and training of volunteer helpers for camps and vacations involving disabled people. Working with *TAMAM Travel Ltd.*, they are building a complete service center in Winterthur which aims to "eliminate all mobility problems of disabled people in Switzerland." An Infotek computerized information service is being developed and will include details of accessible resorts, hotels, apartments, and other accommodation, all types of transport, travel agencies which offer vacations for disabled people, and other material, focusing on foreign as well as Swiss destinations. A "Travel and Holiday Guide" to Switzerland, covering accommodation, restaurants, tourist attractions, transport, parking permits, and dialysis centers, is planned and will be available in German, French, and English.

In the meantime, *MI Schweiz* distributes about twenty Swiss city access guides (many are old—Basle, 1989, is the most recent—but new editions are planned for Geneva, Fribourg, Jura and St. Gallen; there is a charge of SFr.5 for these guides), free brochures about access to walkways and mountain railroads, a list of accessible restaurants, and a hotel guide, *Swiss Hotels for Disabled People* (1988, SFr.5). The *MI Schweiz Newsletter* contains tips and information for disabled travelers.

Getting There

Flight times to Switzerland are approximately seven hours from the East Coast, eleven hours from the West. On the way you'll have the comfort of knowing that Zurich airport boasts some of the most luxurious accessible rest rooms in the world—with adjustable seats and padded armrests. There are also good facilities at Geneva and Basle.

You'll probably have a smooth journey with *Swissair*: one aisle wheelchair is carried on every transatlantic flight (no need to make a special request), and cabin crews are well trained to assist passengers with any type of disability. Other airlines that operate scheduled nonstop services to Zurich and are generally well spoken of by disabled passengers include *Air Canada*, *Delta*, and *United Airlines*. Janice Perkins had a trouble-free flight from Chicago to Zurich with *American Airlines*; this airline has carried aisle wheelchairs on these flights since April 1992.

Traveling into Switzerland **by train** from elsewhere in Europe can be a comfortable and relaxing way to get there, particularly if you can pick up a TGV or a German EuroCity train (see below), but remember that if you cross the English Channel before the Channel Tunnel is

SWITZERLAND: TRAVEL NOTES

completed, facilities for rail users are not yet perfect at the ports (see France *Travel Notes*), although the promised assistance materialized and things worked out well for Beryl Bristow on her trip. Assistance at stations has to be arranged in Europe—nothing can be fixed from North America.

Transport

From the *SNTO* obtain details of the *Swiss Travel System*. The **Swiss Pass**: allows unlimited travel (for 8, 15, or 28 days) by rail, boat, and postbus, plus trams and buses in thirty cities, as well as discounts on many mountain railroads (list of facilities on mountain railroads available, in German only, from *MI Schweiz*) and aerial cableways. In addition you can take advantage of the Swiss Flexipass, Swiss Card, or the Family Plan. Janice Perkins found that many of the **lake steamers** were accessible, making travel by boat a good way to get around.

Chairlifts and other ski lifts can be hazardous, but many have special facilities or can be slowed down as you board and disembark. It's always worth asking before attempt you attempt to clamber on.

MI Schweiz can supply leaflets (in German, French, and Italian, but symbols are clear enough for non-linguists) about the facilities for disabled travelers on **Swiss Federal Railroads** (known as *SBB*, *CFF*, or *FFS*, according to your choice of language) and at stations; assistance is in theory available at over fifty stations. Only twenty minutes' notice is required at the booking office when asking for assistance on a train journey. Ian Marshall reports good wheelchair accessibility on trains, but Janice Perkins had some problems with boarding, disembarking, and making connections; even a strong companion is unlikely to manage hauling a wheelchair up and down the train steps without help. All intercity services, marked in the timetable by the letters "IC," carry wheelchair users in a compartment in second class. An increasing number of regional trains have space for passengers in wheelchairs, but on older trains you may have to travel in the baggage car if you wish to remain in your wheelchair.

On international routes, French high-speed trains (TGVs) have space for a wheelchair in the first-class compartment (at second-class prices, but must be reserved at least two days in advance), and accessible rest rooms for disabled passengers—TGVs are due to commence services to Switzerland soon. Other *SNCF* trains coming into Switzerland (for example on the Paris–Basle–Zurich route) have space for a wheelchair in the first-class car (passenger pays second-class price). *Deutsche Bundesbahn* (German Railroads) trains (for example on routes from Dortmund, Frankfurt, Hamburg, or Hanover) have two spaces for wheelchairs per second-class car, with accessible rest rooms on newer trains.

Travel **by road** can be exhilarating, if demanding, and **adapted vehicles** can be rented from the following: cars from *Verein Behinderten Reisen Zurich* (VBRZ), Gasometerstrasse 7, Postfach 3343, 8031 Zurich (☎1/272 4030, voice or fax); one minibus from *Hertz AG*, Lagerstrasse 33, 8021 Zurich (☎1/241 8077). The *Swiss Paraplegic Association* (Schweizerische Paraplegiker Vereinigung, Langsagestrasse 2, 6010 Kriens/LU; ☎41/421107) has one adapted car, capacity five including driver.

If you want the freedom to set your own itinerary but without the rigors of mountain driving, daily hire of a standard **taxi** is a good alternative to excursions by tourbus, and comparable in price, if you can transfer to a car seat but cannot cope with the steps on a bus. If you need wheelchair-accessible transport, ask *MI Schweiz* for their list (1990, in German and French) of special taxi services using adapted vehicles, which are available in several cities.

Parking regulations for disabled drivers vary from canton to canton; there is no national scheme. Foreign visitors should take their parking permit and full identification to the local police authority and ask for more information.

Accommodation

Although Ian Marshall recommends the *Swiss Hotel Guide for the Disabled* mentioned earlier, a cautionary note is sounded by Percy Biggs, who is confined to a wheelchair and traveled to Locarno in 1989:

SWITZERLAND: TRAVEL NOTES

"The guide listed the *Hotel Muralto* (four star) as a Category A hotel—accessible to wheelchair users. I booked two weeks in September, with *Kuoni* (a Swiss company), requesting a "superior" room with balcony and lake view. As a precaution I added that the entrance to the bedroom, bathroom, and elevator needed to be adequate to take a wheelchair approximately 30in wide. We then discovered (thanks to the travel agency, *Travel Care*) that the hotel had only one room suitable for a wheelchair user, on the fifth floor at the back of the hotel—no view of lake—and the charge was the same as for a superior room. No other rooms in the hotel were suitable. I complained to both the *SNTO* and the hotel owners (then *Best Western*, but no longer listed in their brochure) and received apologies; the tourist board promised in the future to give a more precise description of hotels in Category A."

Percy then tried the *Esplanade Hotel* in Locarno, also listed as Category A. On arrival at the hotel he discovered that it had absolutely no facilities for wheelchair users and no access to swimming pool, garden, or bar. The manager did make an effort to provide access to the pool, by having two steep ramps installed. Percy lodged a complaint with *Kuoni*, whose services, from booking the vacation through to the journey home, "left much to be desired." *Kuoni* disclaimed all responsibility.

The most recent edition of the guide at the time of writing was published in 1987, so take note of the following, printed under the explanation of the hotel categories: "It is advisable to have the indications certified, regarding the accessibility for wheelchairs, when making the reservation." Also worth noting is the fact that Category A is well qualified, with a list of "less favorably accessible installations," including door widths of bathrooms between 25 and 29in, any of which may make your Category A choice unsuitable—study the guide carefully *and* double check through your travel agent or direct with the hotel.

Janice Perkins is a travel agent and she used her *Travel Planner Hotel and Motel Red Book*, but the "Handicapped" symbol is unreliable so she sent telexes to the hotels; she still received some inaccurate information, and says that it is necessary to travel with a strong companion to overcome unforeseen obstacles.

The *RAC European Hotel Guide* (see France *Travel Notes*) is another source of ideas, though again it is wise to check with hotels direct if you need exact access details before booking.

If you can manage a few steps and a short slope up to the entrance, *Hotel Gydisdorf* (3818 Grindelwald; ☎36/531303) is recommended. Children are made very welcome.

Facilities on **campgrounds** are generally good, with provision for disabled people becoming ever more widespread; consult the *RAC European Camping and Caravanning Guide* (see France *Travel Notes*). It's advisable to reserve ahead in high season.

MI Schweiz recommends the following accessible hotels: *Hotel Christal*, Bahnhofstrasse 36, 7310 Bad Ragaz (☎85/92877); *Elite Hotel Thun*, Bernstrasse. 1, 3600 Thun (☎33/232823); *Albergo Garni*, Esplanade 66, Casella postale, 6648 Minusio (☎93/3313913); *Hotel Olten*, Bahnhofstrasse 5, Postfach, 4600 Olten (☎62/263030); *Hotel Senator*, Heinrichstrasse 254/256, 8005 Zurich (☎1/272 2021); *Hotel Alpenland*, 3782 Lauenen (☎30/53434).

Access and Facilities

Switzerland is primarily a country to enjoy **outdoors**, so the main requirements of disabled tourists are likely to be some good surfaces for walking/wheeling along in the mountains as well as the cities, and reasonable access to some of the local modes of transport—lake steamers, cable cars, chair lifts—and to the best viewpoints.

On the whole, these requirements are met, with well-maintained roads, sidewalks, and walking trails, even in remote villages. The spectacular scenery can be easily admired from a wheelchair at most vantage points, and where a restaurant or café is provided access is usually good. Rest rooms are generally adequate, and those at highway service stations excellent.

Of course there are exceptions (see p.209), and variations in provision for disabled people

SWITZERLAND: TRAVEL NOTES

between cantons, as pointed out by *Pro Infirmis*, but there is much scope for enjoyable vacationing in Switzerland.

Health and Insurance

Check the **altitude** of your destination and the places you want to visit, and confirm with your doctor that it's safe for you to go. The **sun** is very strong at high altitudes; you should take a hat, high-protection suntan lotion, and a sun block for nose and lips. An *alpenstock* is ideal on hills for those unsteady on their feet, and a shooting-stick is useful.

There is an excellent but expensive **health service**: it is essential to have good insurance cover (see *Practicalities*).

There are over twenty different mineral springs in Switzerland for treatment of various conditions. A guide to Swiss **spas**, including hotels, is available from the *SNTO*. There is also a brochure giving details of homes and hotels specializing in convalescence.

TELEPHONE CODE:

From the US and Canada dial 011 (international code) and then 41 for Switzerland.

Austria

Setting out for Mars

Eric Leary, a physiotherapist in private practice, traveled to Austria on the Orient Express, returning by Concorde. Eric is blind, but wrote his account with the help of his wife, Geraldine, who described everything to him throughout the trip.

When mulling over the things we would love to do, trips on Concorde and the Orient Express seemed to come top of the list, although we believed that cost would probably rule them out. I asked a travel agent for further information and received details of vacations entitled "Flights of Fantasy," in which our desiderata were included in one package. This was quite irresistible. We gasped at the cost, but it was quite evident to each of us that the other had made a decision.

Departure was a month ahead. Excitement seized us, and we talked it over from all angles. Who else would be likely to indulge in such a venture? What would the other passengers be like? A thousand such questions. We felt young again, and our tread became lighter.

At last the great day arrived, and we assembled in the *Grosvenor Hotel* at Victoria Station, London, on a Sunday morning in May 1989. We all had coffee together, stiff and polite. Our heavy luggage was taken from us, not to be seen again until we reached Salzburg, and we made our way through several tunnels to the train.

There it stood, elegant, shining, and inviting. Immaculate waiters were at the doors to receive us, relieve us of any small packages and hand luggage, and show us to our tables. The thrill of the occasion gripped us and we reveled in our surroundings: the table and wall lights of beautiful brass (brass is my passion), glorious matching tableware, spacious armchairs, and luxurious drapes. Champagne was served, closely followed by a fine hot lunch, served with care and attention to detail.

At Folkestone we embarked on the ferry, well directed by our couriers, who offered discreet assistance where required. Two passengers in wheelchairs had no difficulty in reaching the private saloon reserved for our party. (However, anyone totally confined to a wheelchair would not be able to cope on the trains, as wheelchairs cannot be used in either the English or the Continental cars.)

We walked a short distance at Boulogne to join the train for the next leg of the journey. We were allowed to cross the rails and inspect the train from all angles, cameras at the ready. I touched the polished brass of the doorhandles and the raised brass numbers and names of the cars—ours was *Perseus*; it had formed part of Sir Winston Churchill's funeral train and was used to carry royalty and visiting heads of state.

Climbing aboard, we were greeted in perfect English by our personal attendant, a young man named Albert. He showed us to our compartment and furnished us with all the details necessary for our comfort. Dinner would be served in one hour, allowing time to settle in and tidy up. We were expected to dress for dinner. It was at this point that Geraldine was desolate to find that she had forgotten to pack my dress shirts! A short depression followed, until she realized that the shirt I was already wearing would just about pass. A strong gin and tonic, which I had remembered to pack, soon put things right.

"At 7:30am, Albert appeared with a large pot of steaming coffee, copious fruit juices, and some delicious croissants and rolls"

Having dressed, we had time to examine our compartment in more detail. There was a comfortable long seat to the left, which converted to two bunks. Below the window was a small table, secured to the wall and covered with literature. To the right of the door was a semicircular closet containing a sink and all the necessary toiletries, including soaps, toothbrushes, and towels. The walls of the compartment were of the most beautiful woods, paneled throughout and illuminated by subdued lighting. Pleasant music was piped throughout the train, emanating, we discovered later, from a live pianist at the bar.

We made our way to the restaurant car, where Geraldine—in a reverie—did her best to describe the glittering china, crisp white cloths, noble silverware and glasses, shaded brass lamps,

perfectly turned-out waiters, and the walls which were decorated with exotic woods and Lalique glass panels. Most passengers were in evening dress, and several ladies wore elegant creations from the Twenties and Thirties.

I could devote the rest of this account to the meal. In addition to the appropriate wines, there were innumerable delicacies, including zucchini flowers with scampi filling, lamb filled with truffle sauce, vanilla and bitter chocolate mousse—this was the *nouvelle cuisine* I'd dreamt of, five courses leaving us utterly content, as opposed to penniless and famished, which is often the case in England. We shared a table with a charming couple; the lady sitting next to me quickly observed the way Geraldine assisted me with certain dishes (such as the plaited potatoes) and immediately, without embarrassment, helped me throughout the meal. She took to the task as though she'd been a friend for years.

We returned to our cabin to find that Albert had made it ready for sleep. He suggested that breakfast should be taken early, as lunch would be served at 11:30am in order to disembark at 1pm. The train rumbled on into the night, along the edge of Lake Konstanz and into the mountains, past silent wayside stations.

Next morning, at 7:30am, Albert appeared with a large pot of steaming coffee, copious fruit juices, and some delicious croissants and rolls. We were still proceeding through beautiful mountain country, which compensated for what we'd missed in the darkness. We packed and moved about a lot, endeavoring to work up an appetite for lunch, another delicious meal.

Leaving many passengers to continue the journey to Venice, we left the train at Innsbruck, where the chefs and attendants lined up beside the train to be photographed. Tourbuses awaited us outside the station and we enjoyed a panoramic drive to Salzburg, listening to our guide and to the strains of what was to become the theme of our stay— "The Sound of Music."

"Prices in Salzburg are in keeping with the surrounding mountains"

Reaching Salzburg at 4pm we were immediately taken to the suburb of Leopoldskron, to see the film's eighteenth-century von Trapp family villa. The next stop was our hotel, a five-star *Sheraton* and most grand. We were left to ourselves that evening, so we had a walk and a light meal before bed.

Amply breakfasted the following morning, we were taken to the Old Town by bus and conducted on a tour by a very well-informed guide. Salzburg certainly deserves its reputation as one of the most beautiful cities in the world, and the views of the Alps from the city are spectacular. The wheelchair users in our party found the Old Town reasonably flat, and easy to explore in spite of the cobblestone streets. We moved through many gracious squares, were shown splendid churches and municipal buildings, and paid homage in front of Number 9, Getreidegasse—Mozart's birthplace and now a museum. We visited the seventeenth-century Schloss Hellbrunn, famed for its *trompe-l'oeil* ceiling, its fountains, and the joke played by its original owner on his guests with the aid of clever engineering and some hidden water jets in the grounds. This is a very tactile experience for the visually disabled.

We returned by bus for lunch at the hotel, but not before our guide had conducted Geraldine and me to a reasonably priced shop where we could remedy my lack of an evening shirt. This gesture was much appreciated, as prices in Salzburg are in keeping with the surrounding mountains.

In the afternoon we walked through the Mirabell Gardens, a lovely parkland area behind the hotel, beyond which lay glorious mountains. We reached the Old Town and searched the squares. The market stands were most fascinating, their glistening white cloths garlanded with flowers, and the doors of the houses behind them surrounded by posies. The bakery stands pleased us most, with their great variety of breads, cakes, and desserts, including *Mozart Kugel* and *Salzburger Nockerl*.

The Salzburg churches are magnificent, with solid marble altars and figures covered with gold leaf, gorgeous stained glass windows and intricate woodcarvings. Marble is everywhere, partly because of the proximity of Italy, but also because a pink marble is quarried in the nearby mountains. Even the pathways are frequently made of marble chips, so plentiful is the supply. We sought out the small church and cemetery where the von Trapp children are said to have hidden. The cemetery is remarkable for the intricately carved monuments above most of the graves.

We visited the Mozardeum—the famous academy of music—and the Hohensalzburg castle which is the largest medieval fortress in Central Europe. We were particularly impressed by the townspeople's friendly attitude toward tourists, and one of our wheelchair users commented on the kind help she had received. Salzburg is far lovelier than we had expected, and we promised ourselves a longer visit there.

"A string of ponies and traps awaited"

That evening we went to the Residenz Palace for a banquet and a classical concert. Mounting the imposing staircase on a red carpet, we were greeted by three horn-players from the Mozardeum playing a specially composed piece to welcome us. More players from the Mozardeum were assembled in the large hall and they performed a Mozart symphony. It was a stimulating performance, with youthful enthusiasm shining through, and at the end the hall rang with loud and prolonged applause.

In another elegant room we were given a champagne reception, after which a meal of the usual high standard was presented, the only difference being that there were six instead of five courses. We were entertained by a mountain band, composed of members of a farming family, who gave us a continuous selection of lively Austrian music. At the end of the evening we were shown down to the square where a string of ponies and traps awaited; thus we clip-clopped our way back to the hotel in the warm night air.

After a free morning and then lunch, we were due to leave. During the last few days the Austrian authorities had announced that Concorde produced noise above their newly prescribed level, so hurried international negotiations took place, resulting in our having to fly home from Linz instead of Salzburg.

As we approached the airport the traffic grew heavier and heavier—the word had got around that Concorde was to fly from Linz for the first time, and the crowds had gathered. Police had been called to enable our bus to get through. There were people everywhere, on roofs, up trees, crowding the perimeter fence, all waving and cheering, obviously thrilled.

Leaving the bus we broke all the rules and circulated around the wonderful machine, taking photographs, until finally we were ushered on board. There was provision for the less mobile here: those in wheelchairs were transferred to a carrying chair and taken up the double flight of steps to the door of the plane. The crowds cheered and clapped as we taxied down the runway, and we, caught up in the excitement, responded with shouts and applause. On the last run, the pilot dropped the nose of the plane in salute and then, when just about everything went mad, we took off!

Champagne and lunch were served almost immediately, and for about thirty minutes we learned of Concorde's achievements from one of the crew. The fact which amazed me most was that when it goes supersonic, the plane expands by about 20cm, so that what was a continuous surface on the flight deck opens up to form a gulley on each side. On the aircraft's bulkheads were mounted several meters, providing such statistics as external temperature, speed, and altitude. The external temperature was well below zero but friction against the side of the plane made the windows quite warm to the touch.

"We had to shout, and we felt our systems rocking with the thrill of it all"

The captain invited us to the flight deck, pointing out that as the trip was so short and there were over a hundred of us, we would have to come up in pairs and spend only a minute or so with him. We all went, however, and I had to bend double—the plane is quite narrow and the flight deck even narrower, with the three crew members cramped together, allowing two of us just to squeeze into the entrance. I was advised by the captain to keep my arms well to my sides—just in case.

Since we could not go supersonic over land, we crossed the coast at Rotterdam, went for a short flip up to Edinburgh and then down to Clacton. At the point of crossing the coast, the burners were switched on. There was a powerful thrust; one sensed the forces operating. Concorde assumed a new dimension: up went the nose, and we had the feeling of setting out for Mars, as the aircraft was lying at a very steep angle. We had to shout, and we felt our systems rocking with the thrill of it all.

This cloud of elation lasted for about twenty minutes and then we leveled off, the burners subsiding. The excitement was exhausting, and we gasped a sigh of relief. We were down to a mere 600mph. In no time we were at London Heathrow and making a faultless landing. We bade each other farewell, still somewhat numb and overawed. Would we do it again? Most assuredly, if we could find a sponsor!

An Improbable Ski Party

Ron Cottrell participated in the Uphill Ski Club (USC) trip to Kirchdorf, Austria, in January 1989. In his account he offers both praise and criticism of the organization and the vacation.

I first heard of the *USC* on a BBC documentary in 1988. The idea of disabled people on skis seemed interesting and I decided to find out more about this little-known charity. Some months later I received the brochures for their 1989 trips and set about raising the necessary funds (by commercial sponsorship).

Having secured a place on the January vacation for beginners, I traveled from my home in Rochester, Kent, to The Spastics Society Assessment Center in Fitzroy Square, London. I found myself in a group which included people with cerebral palsy (CP), Down's syndrome, spina bifida, and disabilities resulting from head injuries: a wide range of abilities, both physical and intellectual.

We traveled in a very large, six-wheeled tourbus, fitted luxuriously with rest room, video, and hot and cold drinks supplies. The seats were quite comfortable and each had an overhead reading lamp.

After struggling through Friday evening rush-hour traffic we headed for Dover and the 7:30pm *P&O* ferry to Calais. The *P&O* staff certainly knew their business with regard to handling disabled passengers: our bus was parked adjacent to the elevators, which took us straight up to the restaurant where we were served immediately with a meal.

At Calais it was the same efficient service and with minimal fuss we started on the overnight trip through France and Germany. There was a brief stop at Baden-Baden for continental breakfast at a roadside service station, and another one later for lunch. And so into Austria and the mountains, finally arriving at our destination at about 2:30pm on Saturday. I was absolutely exhausted and very anxious to retreat to my room and sort myself out.

Rooms and helpers allocated (one helper to each two disabled—a very good ratio), we set about unpacking and arranging our equipment for the week. Dinner that evening was served early, followed by a short lecture from the chief ski instructor on the activities for the week. On a *USC* trip you are obviously expected to ski, and this rule is rigidly enforced; only if "grounded" by the party doctor are you excused from classes.

We were expected to be ready to leave for classes almost immediately after breakfast (8am), in order to be on the slopes by 9am at the latest. Help was constantly on hand and each participant was given equal tuition time by the instructors (three of whom came with us on the bus). However, those who needed extra help were given it, and those who simply couldn't physically cope on skis were given a sled to use instead. No one was pushed beyond his or her capabilities, and as a total beginner I was given plenty of encouragement and a very fair proportion of my instructor's time. Skiers who made progress throughout the week were shifted to different groups farther up the slopes.

"On no occasion did I experience help in a patronizing way"

Although morning sessions were compulsory, most afternoons a choice of activities was available, including shopping, swimming, and more skiing. From a purely personal point of view, the skiing was not entirely successful. After two days I had developed a severe blister on my left foot which made walking extremely painful. Daily medication was required, in the form of dressings and padding, but in spite of this, by Thursday I was unable to wear ski boots. My sincere thanks go to my helper (Jasper) for his kindness in lending me his soft Moon Boots for outside wear. I was by no means excused from classes, and on the final day I took part in the sled race, which turned out well, as I won it!

In some ways the social activities outshone the skiing. They included a sleigh ride, a fondue evening, ski films and tobogganing, all of which I joined in except for the tobogganing. I felt that this was too dangerous for someone with a back problem (apart from my CP), a view that was reinforced by the previous evening's activity.

Simon, our chief instructor, told everyone after our evening meal to dress in ski clothing, excluding boots, for a "surprise" activity on the slopes. My instructor, Moky, assisted me in the long trek across the snow in the fading light, and I quipped that perhaps the *USC* had decided to perform a reconstruction of the "Malmedy Massacre," as seen in the Sixties film, *Battle of the Bulge*. We dissolved in laughter as an imaginary headline came to mind: "Twenty Spastics Massacred in Austria."

On arriving at the scene of our "surprise" activity, we were handed a small paper cup of the local "fire water," not really my thing as I don't drink alcohol. Then came the Activity: we were given some kind of plastic tray to slide under our rear ends and skate down the slope on. Rather than be a spoilsport, I gave it a try, but one slide was enough and I retired with a sore back.

I also had reservations about the fondue evening. The food was good, but I felt that placing a pot of boiling oil in the middle of the table, and expecting people with coordination problems to cope with spearing pieces of meat on forks and immersing them in the oil, was a somewhat risky form of entertainment. Indeed a few near misses did ensue.

These reservations aside, I liked the *après-ski* atmosphere. It was fun, and although I didn't actually take part I was aware that a few "late-night binges" were being enjoyed by some of the party.

On no occasion did I experience help in a patronizing way. Out on the slopes, anyone who fell over and was able to get up again without assistance was left to do so. Jasper definitely had the right attitude: if I needed help he was there; if I could cope on my own he didn't interfere.

Each helper was given a half-day to spend as he or she wanted. I saw this as good organization, allowing the helpers time to themselves which was well deserved, especially since they had not only given up their own time for this vacation, but also mostly paid their own way.

The journey home was very tiring, but went smoothly, with a high standard of service again from *P&O*. Despite the fact that I did not achieve as much as I would have liked to achieve on the ski slopes, the vacation was an enjoyable and worthwhile venture. The organization and assistance throughout the trip were superb and I found very little fault with either.

One point about which I do feel strongly is the mixing of mentally and physically disabled people in one group. In my opinion this simply did not work, and I know that if I were to join another *USC* group I would not wish mentally disabled people to be in the party. Of course, I am aware that some may feel likewise about me . . .

And for the Non-skier

Joy Without Skis is reprinted with permission of The Sunday Times. Margaret Hides was given the brief to find out if a complete non-skier could enjoy a vacation in a ski resort.

At the ski jump I soar fearlessly into the void, body correctly angled, almost lying against my skis, landing a world record away. In international slalom I hold back; it seems churlish to relegate great champions to second place. If ever I take up ice-dance, Olympic title holders will have to look out: my soul dances the pairs competitions single-handed.

Only the fact that disability—congenital, not the result of a flamboyant skiing accident—leaves me with no hip movement and canes to walk with, prevents the flesh joining in. But, like thousands of people who do not participate in winter sports, I love the vitality and the visual impact of the sun-and-snow scene brought to our TV screens.

Well, hallelujah, there has been dawning awareness of the existence of non-skiers as a revenue source over recent years. Much of the attention we have been getting so far, however, misses the point. We are not in the market for left-overs when the day's

skiing is finished. All too often the amenities that are said to have the non-skier in mind are the *après-ski* kind—the disco, the fondue party, the wood-choppers' ball.

The genuine non-skier is not like the vacationer who has gone intending to ski and after a couple of days become fed up with the exertion and dropped out—although a surprisingly high proportion do just that. We are the people who for some reason cannot join in all the athletic pursuits, people who nevertheless value the invigorating winter life and perhaps would like to accompany family members on a winter sports vacation. The ambulatory disabled may be prepared to take gentle country walks. All of us enjoy something to watch: children practicing on nursery slopes, curling, a skating rink. Everyone appreciates a café, and a bright inn with unrestricted access.

Touring Austria, Leichtenstein, and Italy, looking at resorts and hotels in winter, I discovered that the answer to these needs is not simply to be found in taking advantage of a skiers' package deal, especially of the lower-priced kind which usually take vacationers to one unsophisticated little village centered almost entirely on skiing.

For us to choose a resort geared to one activity and go with the intention of opting out is bad economics. You get charming guesthouses, looking like cigarette boxes, run on the assumption that people will be out all day on the slopes, returning only for *après-ski*. No one there finds need to provide a comfortable chair to put on your wooden balcony overlooking the fun of the snow scene. A compact living room is frequently part of a general complex of bar, pocket-hankerchief dance floor, and disco—not a place to relax with a book.

"Better to sacrifice romantic dreams of a beautiful tucked-away valley"

But persevere. There is unexpected enchantment for those of us new to this world. There is the sight of a frozen waterfall looking like pale blue wax congealed on the sides of a candlestick. There are deep crisscrossed ski tracks glittering in the sun on empty white slopes between avenues of gray-green firs. The clean icy touch of mountain air brushes your cheeks, and the smell of hot spiced *gluhwein* welcomes you in from the cold. There is the caress of featherdown as you snuggle, naked and glowing, under a comforter, with the windows thrown open in night temperatures below zero.

Better to sacrifice romantic dreams (I had them) of a beautiful tucked-away valley. It will be full of happy skiers with nowhere for you to go. Choose the bigger, popular resorts; the main objec-

tion to vacationing in a town (traffic noise) is hardly valid because most people go about on foot, skis slung over their shoulders. Do not choose a hotel up a side street, and if necessary be prepared to pay a little extra for a well-positioned room from which you can watch all that is going on. Make sure that there is somewhere to sit in your room other than a hard, high-backed chair.

Seefeld, the largest place I visited, was the one which gave me most pleasure. While companions were out on the slopes I was browsing among the bookshops, or sipping lemon tea, or carrying out exhaustive research into Austrian cakes *mit schlag*. A town like this is big enough to have a little of everything going on around the center, and to offer rides in horse-drawn sleighs. Snug under a great weight of furs, feeling like a princess from a Russian fairy tale, I went over the snows into still, deep forests of tall conifers . . . sleigh-bells jingling . . . the pungent smell of horse . . . our breath visibly hanging on the frost . . . walkers saying "Grüss Gott" as I passed by. (But note: there is a limit to this costly pastime.)

Perhaps I have not yet found the ultimate in resorts and hotels, but I do believe that the Tyrol offers outstanding choices. If I have set you looking, and if you discover answers before I do, let me know!

AUSTRIA: TRAVEL NOTES

Sources of Information

Austrian National Tourist Office, 2343 Massachusetts Avenue, NW Washington DC 20008 (☎202/483-4474); 445 Wilbrod Street, Ottawa, ON K1N 6M7 (☎613/563-1444). The tourist office produces a few notes for the disabled traveler, a rather basic leaflet (*Mobil Spezial*) on accessibility of the sights in Vienna, and a list of hotels and pensions in Vienna which was compiled by the Austrian Round Table and requires great concentration from the non-German speaker. However, the main *Hotel Guide* and most regional or city hotel lists use the wheelchair symbol (no details of

AUSTRIA: TRAVEL NOTES

facilities given), and the *ANTO* will attempt to help with specific inquiries concerning accommodation.

Tour Operators

If a "Flight of Fantasy," or the full round trip on the Orient Express to Budapest, is out of your price range, you might be able to experience the *British Pullman* cars (which take passengers to Folkestone on the first leg) by joining a day excursion in Britain (to Salisbury, Bristol, Bath, or Kent) or one of the special journeys that run throughout the year (to the races, or to celebrate Valentine's Day, Midsummer Night, and other such occasions). For the full range of possibilities, contact *Venice Simplon-Orient-Express Ltd.* (VSOE Reservations, 30th Floor, 1155 Avenue of the Americas, New York, NY 10036; ☎800/237-1236).

The *Uphill Ski Club* (*USC*, 12 Park Crescent, London W1N 4EQ; ☎071/636 1989) is a charity committed to offering participation in winter sports to disabled people. Every year the club takes over 130 disabled people on winter sports vacations. It is also in the process of establishing local groups in Britain for year-round dry skiing.

In answer to Ron Cottrell's criticism, the *USC* brochure clearly states that a mix of physically and mentally disabled skiers are among their membership, and all skiers are invited to a pre-trip meeting so that they can get to know their party and discuss any problems. Furthermore, the organizers feel that one of the advantages of a mixed group is that people with different disabilities can help each other: for example, a person with a learning disability might carry a physically disabled member's skis. This does appear to be more in the spirit of "integration," that much sought-after goal, and since there is a waiting list to join these trips it seems to be a successful formula.

The *ANTO* recommends contacting two Austrian organizations for details of sports courses and facilities for disabled people: *Österreichische Arbeitsgemeinschaft für Rehabilitation*, Brigittenauer Lände 42, 1200 Wien (☎1/336101); *Club Handicap*, Wattgasse 96–98, 1170 Wien (1/467 1045).

Getting There

Austrian Airlines **flies** from New York to Vienna but its staff flounders when asked about the availability of aisle wheelchairs; more switched-on airlines offering direct flights to Vienna include *Air Canada* and *Delta*.

Travel by **train** from Germany should be relatively straightforward; there are reserved spaces for wheelchairs and accessible rest rooms (on newer stock) on board EuroCity trains, and assistance can be arranged at Austrian stations (see below).

Transport

Domestic flights should present few problems; facilities at airports are generally accessible. There are accessible rest rooms, restaurant, and coffee shop at Vienna airport.

Austrian Federal Railroads (*OBB*) uses light-weight wheelchairs to lift disabled passengers onto the **train** and these are narrow enough to be used inside the cars. This facility must be booked three days in advance, at any Austrian station or by phoning the disabled services unit (☎1/5800 35800).

We have not heard of any sources of rental **vehicles with hand controls** so the only option is to rent elsewhere (cars from France or Switzerland; or, for those who can afford the Channel crossing and have plenty of time, a lift-equipped van from *Wheelchair Travel* in England) and bring their vehicles into Austria.

Accommodation

The *ANTO* will supply a selective hotel list for a particular province or major vacation resort, giving addresses of hotels in that area deemed suitable for disabled people. The cities of Vienna, Salzburg, Innsbruck, and Graz publish their own guidebooks, containing access information and special hotel lists for the disabled visitor; these are distributed by the local city tourist boards (Kinderspitalgasse 5, 1095 Vienna; Auerspergstrasse 7, 5024 Salzburg; Bruggraben 3, 6021 Innsbruck; Kaiserfeldgasse 25, 8010 Graz) and the use of symbols makes them useful to non-German speakers.

The *Hotel Ibis Innsbruck* (Schützenstrasse 43, 6020 Innsbruck; ☎512/65544) has one room

AUSTRIA: TRAVEL NOTES

suitable for disabled guests and *Hotel Ibis Wien* (Mariahilfer Gürtel 22–24, 1060 Vienna; ☎1/565626) has four; reservations direct or through *Resinter* (☎914/472-0370 or 800/221-4542).

The *USC* highly recommends the *Hotel Mitteregger* (☎6547/8412) which is centrally situated in the village of Kaprun, approximately four minutes' walk from the ski slopes. The Club has taken mixed-ability groups to this hotel several times and reports excellent facilities.

Nearly twenty Austrian members of the hotel consortium, *Transeurope Hotels* (central reservations: HTR Hotels, Ulmenstrasse 17, A-6064 Rum/Innsbruck; ☎5222/65825), indicate that they have facilities for disabled guests.

It's also worth consulting the *RAC European Hotel Guide* and *European Camping and Caravanning Guide* (see France *Travel Notes*).

Access and Facilities

Contributors with limited mobility, including those using wheelchairs and crutches, report that Salzburg, Vienna, and Innsbruck are relatively easy to explore, in spite of the cobblestone streets. The well-maintained roads and sidewalks are appreciated by the "pushers" and, in the countryside, walks are often clearly marked with an indication of distance, time, and difficulty.

It is encouraging to see that people with all sorts of disabilities can enjoy the facilities for winter sports, and that there is scope in the winter resorts for the non-skier as well as the skier.

More information from the *ANTO* office—a stock of the access guides that are available, and an explanation of the criteria used to award the wheelchair symbol to hotels in the accommodation guides, along with some information on transport accessibility—would be appreciated.

TELEPHONE CODE:

From the US and Canada dial 011 (international code) and then 43 for Austria.

Belgium

There is Nothing like a Nun

Jane Nyman uses a scooter wheelchair and has no qualms about traveling alone unless she is entrusted to British Rail, which despite warnings in advance, always leaves her stranded. For many years Jane has visited the city of Bruges, staying as a guest in the English Convent, and she is probably their only guest to have been banned from the chapel, not on account of bad behavior but for her own safety. She had a bad fall on the stone floor; she did not know at the time that she was developing Parkinson's disease.

Some of my most hilarious vacations have been spent in convents; I have always found them to be full of laughter, perhaps because a good sense of humor is essential in order to cope with community life! The English Convent in Bruges was founded by a relative of Sir Thomas More, and at one time was a school. The nuns now run a guesthouse and have successfully converted the building to accommodate both disabled and able-bodied guests. The accommodation is plain but pleasant, with both single and double rooms. There is a spacious elevator, and rest rooms and shower which are accessible to wheelchairs. Portable ramps allow access to every part of the guesthouse.

The nuns accept groups of disabled people, such as those organized by *The*

Across Trust who bring their own helpers (and their "Jumbulance"), or individual guests provided that they are independent, or with someone who will help them. The food is plain but good, and the very reasonable prices include morning and afternoon coffee, so that it is possible to avoid spending money on snacks. On Sundays or feast days the nuns produce delicious flaky pastries and wine. Light Belgian beer is served with the main meals—I was faintly shocked to see respectable elderly ladies drinking beer, but tried it myself and found it very enjoyable.

The convent has a lovely garden; the guests can take chairs outside and it is very peaceful. I used to be puzzled in the early days to notice that when bad weather threatened, the Guest Mistress, normally a dignified soul, would run through the cloisters, plastic bag clutched in her hand. I later discovered that the nuns had planted a young magnolia, and the Guest Mistress was dashing out to put a plastic hat over its blossom to protect it from the rain!

There is a carillon in the city center, and if you are energetic and can cope with a steep and slippery staircase you can climb up to see the bells, each bearing the name of the man who cast it and the date. This is a city of bells, and from a seat in the convent garden you can hear not only the carillon but also many other church bells; there is a continual background murmur of soft chimes.

One of the sisters is always on duty at the reception desk, ready to sell postcards and deal with any queries. I have learned over the years that there is no finer "fixer" than a Roman Catholic nun. They beat the Mafia any time, and if they do not know the answers they'll find someone who does. I once traveled back to England with a 92-year-old nun, and I wanted to do some last-minute shopping on the way at the airport. She insisted on writing down all the prices, in case she needed the information at a later date!

What to buy? Every time I go to Bruges I buy chocolate. The Belgians make a delicious dark chocolate in bars which are reasonable in price. However, if you want something really special, ask for *fruits de mer* and you will receive beautiful green, white, and brown chocolates in the shape of seashells.

Bruges, or Brugge, to give it its Flemish name, is one of the loveliest cities in Europe. It was built by the Count of Flanders in the ninth century as a defense against the Norse invaders. Standing on the Reie river, the city rapidly established itself as a center for trade. In the thirteenth century it became very prosperous, and was famous for its weaving and manufacture of cloth. Its annual fair was the most important in Flanders. The banking community thrived and import businesses flourished: fabrics from the East, furs from Russia and the Balkans, metals from Hungary, Poland, and Bohemia, wool, coal, and cheese from Britain, fruit from Spain and Egypt, Arabian spices, and Rhenish wines.

The city attracted famous artists, such as Jan Memling and Jan van Eyck, and produced fabulous tapestries. The canny burghers invested their money in buildings and solidly built houses, which they decorated with beautiful paintings. Zoning regulations are very strict in Bruges, and the buildings have been preserved or reconstructed perfectly. No modern buildings or industries exist within the boundaries of the city. The inhabitants are rightly proud of their city, and it is a common experience to see householders scrubbing the sidewalks outside their houses. Each house has immaculate white lace curtains, drawn slightly back to display some treasure or potted plant. There are flowers everywhere.

Bruges is also renowned for its lace, and some of the houses carry small glass plaques depicting a woman making lace, to show that the craft is still practiced there. In the area called the Béguinage, which is a collection of old almshouses, where respectable spinsters received sheltered accommodation in the past, there is a cluster of shops selling lace. When the weather is fine you can watch the lacemakers sitting outside, with their bobbins flying at breakneck speed.

"The important thing is that everybody tries to communicate"

Within 200m of the convent is an interesting lace school, the Kantcentrum, where there are superb examples of lace designs from the past and where the techniques of both traditional and modern lacemaking are taught. Still within the same radius is my favorite church, St. Annekirche. Most of the churches in Bruges contain great paintings or other works of art, but their architecture is a hotchpotch of styles. The St. Annekirche is the second church to be built on its site—

the first was destroyed by fire. The result is a perfect example of the Baroque style, which contains the most beautiful woodcarvings.

Other museums farther afield include the Groeninge (Museum of Fine Arts), Memling, and Brangwijn museums. The Groeninge and Memling museums are wheelchair accessible. The Gruuthusemuseum does not have access for disabled visitors—no wheelchairs in the fifteenth century! It is a burgher's palace containing a display of lace, woodcarving, old furniture, and tapestry, as well as collections of musical instruments and flat and goffering irons, used to produce the perfectly starched lace collars and frills seen in the paintings of this period.

"The cobblestones, though picturesque, make it hard to push wheelchairs"

If your taste is for sitting and watching the world go by, there are plenty of seats on the canal towpath, also very close to the convent. The main canal is used for the transport of commercial goods, and the barges occasionally tie up to the bank, offering a fascinating glimpse of life for the family on board. There are lines of washing fluttering in the breeze and often a row of potted geraniums; the household pets are given an outing, and the children let loose to play.

For a different perspective of Bruges, take one of the canal trips from the center, starting off with half an hour on the quiet backwaters before joining up with the main canal which encircles the city (if you are susceptible to mosquito bites, arm yourself with plenty of repellent). It is unlikely that you'll be able to take a wheelchair on board because the boats have to be very small in order to pass under some of the bridges in the backwaters. I recommend abandoning the chair and requesting help with boarding. The Belgians are an eminently practical race, and never miss a chance to earn some money!

The city center is called the Markt, and once a week there is a large, busy market, selling everything from food to clothes. Just a few yards away are the traditional and very colorful fish and flower markets, and down by the Béguinage a weekly market selling china, books, brass, and bric-à-brac. Markets have been part of the way of life for the inhabitants of Bruges for centuries. Also in the Markt is a tourist office, where they speak a number of languages and dish out brochures and information on every conceivable subject with typical Belgian efficiency.

Although Catholic, the English Convent accepts guests of any faith. Flemish is spoken in this area of Belgium, but the nuns are trilingual and speak English, French, and Flemish. Because visitors come from all over Europe, some from outside Europe, the Masses are said in more than one language. It is not in the least unusual to find the priest preaching a sermon which begins in one language and ends in another. The Easter Vigil Mass—when I became a Catholic—was in French, Flemish, and English, and I was so bemused that I forgot that my responses were supposed to be in English, and dried up. In typically practical fashion, an English nun came to my rescue. As I had not been able to decide who should be my sponsor from the many nuns I knew, it was agreed that one nun should represent the whole community, so I ended up with 36 godmothers, which beats the royal family!

At the dining table you are likely to hear at least four languages being spoken, but the important thing is that everybody tries to communicate, and even if you can only manage a "good morning" in French your efforts will be applauded. The nuns are of various nationalities and will always translate if you are having difficulty. It is sad that the same tolerance for language does not exist outside the convent.

How to get there? I have tried a number of routes. You can take a train from London Victoria (always very crowded) which connects with the Channel ferry to Ostend. If you tire easily, book a cabin. The station is only yards away from the dock in Ostend, there are frequent trains to Bruges, and the complete journey takes about four hours. The station in Bruges is outside the city, so you will need a taxi. Other possibilities are to fly from London Gatwick to Ostend, then take a taxi to Bruges, or to fly to Brussels and continue by train from there.

When traveling alone you can arrange for the Red Cross to meet you and put you on the right boat, train, or plane (helpful, but I find them pricey); you must arrange this well in advance, stating the exact nature of your disability and what kind of help you require.

My experience of the Belgian Red Cross was that they were very pleasant and efficient, and I would use them again. If you travel by car, remember that Belgium did not introduce compulsory driving tests until quite recently, and driving can be hair-raising!

Bruges is a compact city: with the aid of a map you can cross it within an hour. It was not designed with the disabled person in mind—the cobblestones, though picturesque, make it hard to push wheelchairs—but there is an easy path following the main canal around the city, past windmills and the historic city gates. It is advisable to visit in the spring or early summer, when the blossom is out. Later in the season the city becomes very crowded, particularly in the center, as tourbuses decant tourists from all over Europe, and the schools make it a focus for educational trips.

BELGIUM: TRAVEL NOTES

Sources of Information

Belgian Tourist Office, 745 Fifth Avenue, New York, NY 10151; ☎212/758-8130. The hotel guide uses the wheelchair symbol to denote those suitable for disabled guests, and a fact sheet for disabled visitors explains the criteria for awarding the symbol: level entrance, or maximum incline six percent; minimum door width 80cm (31in), minimum corridor width 130cm (51in); some bedrooms and rest rooms must be on the first floor or accessible by elevator; the elevator must be 31in by 51in or larger. The **provincial and city tourist offices** also use the wheelchair symbol in their brochures, so it's worth making these your first port of call. The *City Tourist Office* in Bruges (*Dienst voor Toerisme*, Burg 11, B-8000 Brugge; ☎50/44 86 86), for example, indicates accessible hotels and restaurants, in its brochure, *Brugge*; and rest rooms for the disabled are marked on the city map. The art gallery and museum guide for the West Flanders region (in four languages, including English) classifies buildings as inaccessible, partially accessible, and fully accessible to wheelchair users.

Belgian Red Cross (*Croix Rouge de Belgique*), rue Joseph Stallaert 1—Bte 8, B-1060 Brussels; ☎2/645 46 28. Gives general advice, gleaned from a number of access guides, can help with rental of aids and equipment as well as accessible transport (see below), and offers the usual escort service.

Mobility International Flanders (*MI Vlaanderen*), Douglaslaan 20, B-2190 Essen; ☎3/667 40 25. Reported to be in the process of building up a databank of information on accessible vacations in Belgium and the rest of Europe which should be a useful source; they would be pleased to receive access information for the databank.

BELGIUM: TRAVEL NOTES

Getting There

Belgium's national **airline**, *Sabena*, flies from Boston, New York, and Montréal into Brussels; according to *Sabena Special Assistance Service* at Zaventem National airport, Brussels (located on the left of the departure hall; ☎2/723 6381), aisle chairs are available on transatlantic routes; when leaving Brussels, if you need help, you are advised to phone this number to make sure ground staff are on hand to assist you until you board the plane. *United* operates flights from the East and West coasts into Brussels. Other options include *Delta* (nonstop) and *Air Canada* (to Brussels via Manchester, UK).

For those traveling **by ferry from Britain**, *North Sea Ferries* (King George Dock, Hedon Road, Hull HU9 5QA; ☎0482/795141) operates from Hull into Zeebrugge and has adapted cabins on each of its ships. *P&O European Ferries* (Channel House, Channel View Road, Dover, Kent CT18 9TJ; ☎0304/203388), generally well equipped for wheelchair passengers, operates Dover–Ostend (on the fully accessible *Prince Philip*), Dover–Zeebrugge (facilities vary on ships sailing this route; the *Pride of Bruges* is recommended), and Felixstowe–Zeebrugge (elevators to all decks, adapted cabins and accessible rest rooms on all ships); there are accessible toilet facilities at all ports.

Of course, if things go according to plan and the **Channel Tunnel** opens in 1993 (full service not expected until mid-1994), rail travelers will be able to make the journey from London to Brussels, via Paris, in six hours, without changing trains. Meanwhile, the train journey **from London to Bruges**, via Dover and Ostend, doesn't take much longer and is not too arduous: assistance at ports or stations can in theory be arranged; most people with reduced mobility will require help with boarding and disembarking. Assistance in Belgium must be arranged by phoning the stations in advance (see below); ask the tourist board for a list of stations. At the time of writing there are no TGV services into Belgium **from France**, but there are accessible rest rooms on newer trains and spaces reserved for wheelchairs (two in second-class cars) on *Deutsche Bundesbahn* (*DB*) EuroCity trains operating into Belgium **from Germany**.

Transport

Airport facilities are generally accessible, and domestic flights should present few problems.

Intercity **trains** do not have wheelchair spaces, accessible rest rooms, or lowered steps at the entrances; the only space available for wheelchairs is near the entrance to compartments, outside in the vestibule. Disabled people are advised to phone the departure station 24 hours in advance to make sure a railroad officer is available at destination stations. There are no public elevators on stations, but disabled travelers can use service paths and elevators if accompanied by a railroad officer. Most major stations have mobile ramps and staff to assist with boarding or disembarking. The central station of Brussels does not have these facilities, but they are available at the other main stations, Bruxelles Midi and Bruxelles Nord. There is a brochure, in Dutch and French, listing facilities at stations; facilities are also indicated in the regular timetable. Contact the *Belgian Railroads Bureau* (50.122, rue Ravenstein 60/24, B-1000 Brussels; ☎2/525 3601) for more information.

The cities of Bruges and Brussels have low-floor **buses** on a few lines but these are not wheelchair-accessible. Only Liège has two lines of lift-equipped buses.

Parking places for disabled drivers are indicated by the usual blue and white "P" sign with additional wheelchair symbol. Usually you won't have to pay at meters. Contact the *RAC de Belgique* (rue d'Arlon 53, B-1040 Brussels; ☎2/230 08 10) for more information about driving in Belgium.

There are no rental **cars with hand controls** in Belgium, but they can be rented from *Hertz* at French airport locations (Paris, Lyon, Marseille, Nice). The *Belgian Red Cross* has two adapted vehicles, available at reasonable cost, to suit both groups and the individual traveler. The "Time-off Coach" (*Car de l'Evasion*) is suitable for groups and is equipped with lifts, wheelchair fastenings, and chemical toilet; the interior can be modified according to the needs of the group. The "Run-off" (*Escapade*) is a van, similarly equipped but on a family scale. Contact *Croix-Rouge de Belgique*, Service "Car de l'Evasion," rue de l'Industrie

BELGIUM: TRAVEL NOTES

124, 5002 Saint Servais (Namur); ☎81/73 02 24. Another possibility, for those who can afford the time and money for the ferry crossing, is a lift-equipped van from *Wheelchair Travel* (see England and Wales *Travel Notes*).

Accommodation

As a starting point try the tourist office publications, and the *RAC* guides, *European Hotel Guide* and *European Camping and Caravanning Guide* (see France *Travel Notes*); *The Michelin Guide to Benelux* uses the wheelchair symbol to indicate accessible accommodation in Belgium, Luxembourg, and the Netherlands; as always, details of facilities can only be obtained direct from the hotel or—the only foolproof way—on the spot.

Jane Nyman recommends The English Convent (Carmersstraat 85, B-8000 Brugge; ☎50/33 24 24): write to the Guest Mistress for information and reservations.

Hotels at the cheaper end of the scale that claim to offer accessible rooms include: *Arcade Hotels*—in Antwerp (☎3/231 8830), Brussels (*Hotel Sainte-Catherine*, ☎2/513 7620), Ghent (☎91/25 07 07), Hasselt (☎11/24 19 48), and Leuven (☎16/29 31 11); *Hotel Ibis Brugge Centrum* (☎50/33 75 75), *Hotel Ibis Brussels Airport* (☎2/725 4321), *Hotel Ibis Brussels Center* (☎2/514 4040), *Hotel Ibis Gent Centrum* (☎91/33 00 00), *Hotel Urbis Liège Opera* (☎41/23 60 85); and four *Campanile* hotels—in Bruges (☎50/38 13 60), Brussels (☎2/720 9862), Ghent (☎91/20 02 22), and Liège (☎41/24 02 72). For reservation details see France *Travel Notes*.

Access and Facilities

There seems to be a lively access movement in Belgium, but similar problems to those that are still to be overcome in the many other parts of Europe: limited access to public transit, narrow choice of accessible accommodation in the lower price brackets, room for improvement in provision of access in eating places.

Access to tourist attractions is reasonably good, and although there is an air of defeatism where older buildings are concerned (if it was built in the fifteenth century it's not wheelchair accessible and that's that), it's heartening to see the use of the wheelchair symbol in so many tourist brochures, and to see the release of a new, free guide (see *Books*), produced with input from the *Action Group for Better Accessibility for Handicapped People*.

Books

Guide Touristique et des Loisirs à l'Usage des personnes à Mobilité Réduite (free from Ministère de la Communauté Française, Direction Générale des Affaires Sociales, Manhattan Center, rue des Croisades, 3-1210 Brussels) lists hotels, restaurants, sports facilities, and tourist attractions in the provinces of Brussels, Brabant Wallon, Hainaut, Liège, Luxembourg, and Namur (ignoring the Flemish North of the country) and uses symbols to indicate accessibility. It classifies properties as accessible to wheelchair users with or without assistance, or to those who can walk but with difficulty; it also covers parking, access to elevators and rest rooms, and facilities for visually disabled and hearing-impaired visitors.

The Michelin Guide to Benelux indicates accessible accommodation in Belgium, the Netherlands, and Luxembourg, but, as always, details of facilities can only be obtained direct or—the only foolproof way—on the spot.

The Real Guide: Holland, Belgium, and Luxembourg. Best of the general guides.

TELEPHONE CODE:

From the US and Canada dial 011 (international code) and then 32 for Belgium.

The Netherlands

Put your Money on a Good Hotel

Philippa Thomas uses a wheelchair, although she can manage on crutches for short distances. She also has a less visible disability— epilepsy. In February 1989 she took her first break, a long weekend in Amsterdam.

She's on the phone—Tamsin, my daughter—cheering me up as usual, encouraging me to come out into the world after this long time imprisoned by my immobile body (well, immobile legs). In fact, since November 1988 I've been peripatetic—I borrowed the money and bought a bike, a "booster-type scooter wheelchair."

"Nice to see you out and about: it must be lovely to do your own shopping; glad you're feeling better."

Bloody liars, I think, smiling: don't they realize I'm not, and not going to be better. Smile again, Philippa, you might need their help. "I know, it's absolutely wonderful to be able to do my shopping." May the ground open and swallow me up.

So, she's on the phone again: "Mother, book the tickets, Amsterdam, half term" (she's a teacher), "write it down, February 16th to 19th, home Monday, *book the tickets*." Money and Larkin come to mind:

> *Quarterly, is it, money reproaches me:*
> *Why do you let me lie here wastefully?*
> *I am all you never had ...*
> (Philip Larkin: "Money")

It's a major feat arriving at *Lewes Travel*, perched as it is at the top of Station Street, not to mention negotiating my way on crutches to the counter. Never booked a vacation in my life: we used to get in the car and go somewhere, before the illness, before the divorce. Leave the bike where the girl can see it, good for the image.

First decision: don't mention the epilepsy. "Amsterdam, long weekend, cheap as possible, me and my daughter." She looks at me—a pretty girl, with youth in her eyes—and smiles and selects some leaflets. "Put all your money on a good hotel," she advises. "If it's central you'll save, be able to walk everywhere ... well, ride, I mean ... and there's the fire risk you know ... wheelchair symbol." She smiles again and looks down, then picks up the phone.

Back home, safe and warm; Christ, what am I doing, how the hell do I get to London, let alone Amsterdam? Slowly the pieces fit together: bike to the station, ramp to the train, Carelink from Victoria to Liverpool Street, Tamsin will meet me . . .

And there she is, smiling, and here I am on the bike, knapsack and battery charger in the basket, mohair rug strapped behind me—off to Harwich surrounded by rush-hour London. We've booked second-class seats, but *British Rail* put us in first class so that I can transfer easily from luggage car to seat. The train gains speed and the journey begins.

"I transfer to my seat: it's going to be bloody uncomfortable despite the reclining positions"

Sealink meets us at Harwich—takes a bit of time because naturally they were looking for us where we'd booked and not where we'd been put. Suddenly Tamsin's gone, and strange men guide me across the wharf to the boat. It's so huge, and in the dark the smell of diesel oil and the black glistening ropes are a magic world. The air is wet and windy and I feel like a child again— "Little Tim and the Brave Sea Captain," and images of herrings and the northern sea. I drive on board where the trucks are loaded and an elevator takes me to the deck. Our reclining seats are booked and through the window I can see shining stars. Above the bustle of the ship I hear the sound of waves.

Tamsin arrives with our passports, and checks emergency exits. I transfer to my seat: it's going to be bloody uncomfortable despite the reclining positions. I realize that somehow I am going to have to sleep on the floor, the problem being how to get there. Eventually, after pain-killers and sleeping tablets, I manage.

In the morning, the *Sealink* staff arrive to collect us and the ramp, to be loaded on the Dutch train heading for Amsterdam. The train, similar to our subways, is crowded and the bike takes up a lot of room. Still, everyone smiles and is nice, but I'm glad I've got my money belt and passport well hidden. I should have mugged up basic Dutch "Help" words and written them on cards. The train rest rooms look pretty impossible, too.

We arrive in Amsterdam just after 9am. It's raining, Lewes is somewhere in the past and Amsterdam is not what I'd expected; it's small, and there are trams and canals everywhere. We stroll the short distance to the hotel and pass through automatic plate glass doors onto the smartest, plushest carpets, in a foyer spangled with jewelry display cases containing diamonds, exotic plants, and an amazing clock showing the time in London, Zurich, San Francisco, and here. On the reception desk is a gigantic brandy glass filled with squares of chocolate for the taking, and no one, absolutely no one, minds me.

We are shown immediately to the elevator and to our room, which is soft silvery blue and white with a veritable wall of louvred closets, a secret mini-bar and fridge, comfortable chairs, TV, and writing desk. Then the bathroom: a wall of mirrored dressing table, piles of fluffy white towels, and the goodies—shower cap, bath gel, soap, mending kit. You name it, they've got it, and room service can supply anything else. Prefer a comforter? Naturally. Non-slip bath mat? In an instant, and with everything delightful squares of chocolate.

We plug the bike in to recharge, have hot showers and a rapid sleep, after which I am strong enough to face the rain and a canal trip. It is *so* pretty—the tall narrow houses, the shape of the gabled roofs against the skyline, and the soft romantic colors. Negotiating my way onto the covered barge was difficult, admittedly, and the thought that I cannot swim did cross my mind, but the trip is lovely. My daughter, who teaches art, is already sketching details of bridges and waterways; it *is* romantic.

That night we slept well, and after a traditional Dutch breakfast we visited the Rijksmuseum. The early Flemish paintings are enchanting, but best of all, among the fourteenth-century majolica, I find a plate depicting an absolutely furious Madonna scowling at the Christ Child who holds an apple in his hand.

On the way home we discover the flower market, just a street by a canal. The stands contained not the boxed hot-house flowers I had imagined, but interesting structural forms: huge bunches of magnolia in bud, and branches of alder and birch. Because it is Amsterdam and February, we fill the basket of the bike with white tulips to bring home—plastic but very traditional!

On Sunday it's raining and we are going to meet Gary, Tamsin's boyfriend. The itinerary is Van Gogh, with the added bonus of a special Millet exhibition. I focus on Van Gogh's use of color and see the reflection of his growing madness. Gary and his students join us, with terrible tales of their hotel: burst pipes, double reservations, and inadequate heating. We were obviously well advised. Soon we are back in our hotel in time to pack, recharge the bike and rest before leaving.

On the spur of the moment, we both say "Diamonds!" and the porter arranges a taxi to one of the diamond factories where we can see them cut and polished. On the way we see the Jewish synagogue and a page of a diary with spidery writing in blue-black ink,

indecipherable—Anne Frank—a pressed flower, a violet, floats into my mind. I look at my daughter: "We shall have to come back again." She smiles, knows my identifications, and we go on to the factory, which is full of wealthy Japanese tourists.

We are treated as if we too are wealthy. In a locked room we are shown diamonds of incredible value and taught the difference between carat and colors. Shut in the strongroom with only the jeweler, watching him talk to my daughter of stones and settings and gems, I think of that other daughter and her writing, glimpsed and remembered, and how she and I would have shared a star, though of different colors.

Time to go home, time to go home, and the boat looms out of the darkness. *Sealink* is there to meet us, me on my bike and loaded with tulips. Tamsin goes through customs, then the man from *Sealink* smiles and shows us to a cabin: "Compliments of the Captain." My heart is warmed by the kindness.

Harwich, Liverpool Street, Victoria, Lewes, and home. The castle is still here, the cats have been fed, and the papers are waiting; no chocolate though. Next day, I meet someone I haven't seen for ages. "This is wonderful," she says, looking at my bike. "It must be lovely to do your own shopping again."

"Super," I say, with a ring of sincerity, "couldn't be without it."

Falling for the Countryside

Barry Atkinson has been to the Netherlands three times, the visits spanning a time of coping with a relentlessly progressive disease. In 1983, although using a wheelchair a lot, he was able to walk a little with crutches; by 1990 he was wheelchair-bound and, although able to transfer to toilet, bed and car, his balance had become very bad.

I first went to the Kingdom of Netherlands simply because it was there, close at hand, and an unknown quantity. There was no burning ambition to visit the country, just a mild interest. Yet now I have been three times and expect to go again. I remain undecided as to the exact nature of its appeal, and find myself confused by a conflict of good and bad points.

The Netherlands are busy, full of life and color, often beautiful in an unadventurous sort of way. The people are refreshingly matter-of-fact and extremely hospitable. But, at the same time, I find that their affluence leads to an unattractive smugness. There is also a disconcerting air of insularity which, although understandable in a small land, is not always easy to tolerate.

My introduction to the lowlands was in 1983, on a brief trip with my mother to see the tulip fields. Then, in July 1985, I spent three weeks under canvas at Ockenburgh in Den Haag with a Dutch work-camp. I went through the International Voluntary Service and was the only disabled participant. We traveled each day through Den Haag by bus and tram to Scheveningen, where we worked at Sparring, a day center for disabled people. My return during the heatwave of 1990 was to revisit Sparring and to stay with friends.

I can only claim to have any knowledge of the Netherlands south of Amsterdam, mainly Den Haag, Rijswijk and the seaside resort of Scheveningen. It is the industry and commerce of the small, overpopulated country (over 14,300,000 in little more than 13,000 square miles) that has usually surrounded me, but this was least apparent when with Erik and Tonny at Rijswijk. The town is situated on the southeast of Den Haag and their apartment is on the southern edge. When I had a night free of the work-camp in 1985 I stayed with them; at that time their balcony overlooked peaceful, flat fields where horses grazed. By 1990 another line of houses had been built;

the fields are still behind these, but my friends' balcony now stares at a busy road and at other people trying to lead private lives. It's a common enough story today, but none the easier to cope with for that.

"Even the disabled often thought they were receiving too much"

Erik suffers from multiple sclerosis. The well-adapted apartment made life much easier for me and, together with facts gleaned at Sparring, gave me an insight into the benefits available to disabled people in the Netherlands. In 1990 I noticed a change: 1985 was rich bonanza time—even the disabled often thought they were receiving too much! Monetary benefits were high and relatively easy to procure. Adapted cars were free and readily available. But by 1990, with much of the world finding finance tighter, I found the Dutch disabled less happy. They are "feeling the pinch," like everyone else.

However, unlike the English, they are given powered wheelchairs for outdoor use, usually of the most expensive type and extremely comfortable. That said, bureaucracy causes problems in the Netherlands as everywhere else: an aquaintance of mine had moved house, and the much-needed work on his necessary power-chair was not being done because the paperwork was not right.

Erik and I went into the fields at Rijswijk, he often pushing my self-propelled chair (I have a motorized wheelchair but it's not so easy to transport on the plane) from his sleek power-chair. There are bicycle paths (*fietspaden*) beside the roads in any busy area, and of course the country is mostly flat, so the going is relatively easy.

We left the houses and took a quiet, brick lane past the crematorium to a little bridge, crossing the gentle waterway which runs to nearby Delft. Cyclists rattled across the timbers of the bridge, heading up and down the lane which passed through the flat, open meadows and between glass-houses full of tomato plants. We could see the church of Wateringen between lines of poplars. We sat there for a while. The sun was warm and a herd of fly-bothered cows stood under the bridge. A soft breeze swayed the reeds and willow-herb. The water was still, with patches of duckweed and white flowering water lilies. We followed the waterway towpath for a while, passing a renovated windmill. It was the Netherlands at their best, pleasing to the eye and the opposite side of the coin to the world of modern business.

"The towns and villages are too clean and perfect for my taste"

About this time, I was also taken to Friesland, the northern part of the country which, rather like Scotland, sees itself as individual and independent, with some justification. From Amsterdam we drove into West Friesland and took the road across IJsselmeer to the main body of Friesland. The crossing of the waterway is spectacular. To our left, hidden by the rise of the dike, lay the North Sea (more exactly, the Waddenzee, which stands between the mainland and the Frisian Islands). To the right was the broad expanse of the freshwater *meer*. Wildfowl swam at the edge, hard to identify from a speeding car but I saw mute swan, coot, and grebe aplenty, and thought I saw pochard and scaup. Small boats sailed and fishing nets stretched across poles. At the end of the dike was a busy canal for the boats to pass between salt and fresh water.

We came to Sneek, in its lush agricultural setting, the countryside far less built up than the south and with even more waterways. With its perhaps too studied atmosphere of gaiety, Sneek is justly famed as a boating center. It is also well known for its sports facilities for disabled people. We visited the house of my companion's friend to drink coffee. Like all the Dutch houses I have been in, it was compact, pristine, and overflowing with plants, cut flowers, and great cacti. It is as though everyone agrees that the country will be extended by a national effort of nurture! But, attractive and original though they undoubtedly are, the towns and villages are too clean and perfect for my taste. It was the exposed, uncluttered landscape which appealed to me.

Our return to the south was via the reclaimed fields of the Noord-Oost Polder and Flevoland. A livid sunset bordered the black clouds of an approaching storm. We drove through Amsterdam in torrential rain, the normally busy Dam cowed and deserted. The built-up south was decidedly unwelcoming.

I spent ten days of my 1990 stay alone in a Den Haag apartment. A worker at Sparring had offered me the use of his home while he was away. Pleased to avoid the expense of a hotel, and preferring to be alone anyway, I gladly accepted. It was, however, not all easy. There were no steps, but lips at every doorway forced me to enter every room backwards. The owner had thoughtfully placed little ramps on the steeper lips, but it was the narrow corridors, just wide enough for a wheelchair, that almost defeated me. These ran from the front door to the living room and from there to the bedroom. I had to travel the latter corridor backwards, and I was not entirely successful in my efforts to avoid scraping the walls. I could not get into the shower, and the toilet was difficult.

There were, of course, good points. On four days I was collected by the Sparring transport and taken to spend the day with them. Erik and Tonny came to see me. Ans (from Sparring) took me shopping and generally kept in touch to see that all was well. She also watered the many plants! The apartment was situated on the fairly gentle Loosduinsekade which, despite the passing of trams and traffic, and a motorcycle shop next door, had many a quiet lull. I used to sit on the wide sidewalk in front of the *fietspad*, or in the tiny back garden in the shade of a sycamore tree. It would not have been possible for too long, nor without the help around me (more truthfully, it would not have been worth the effort), but I decided to stay put. I either showered at Sparring or washed at the kitchen sink.

On my next visit I hope to stay at the fully adapted *Hotel Restaurant Vredebest*, 200yd from the sea at Wemeldinge (listed in the *RADAR* guide). The uniform flatness of the terrain, together with slightly better facilities and greater awareness than in England, make the Netherlands one of the easiest countries in Europe for a disabled visitor.

THE NETHERLANDS: TRAVEL NOTES

Much of the information included here was supplied by Jeanette Huber, who offers this opinion: "Because of its almost fanatical nationwide organization, its outstanding facilities for the disabled, and the generally good-natured and caring people, the Netherlands must be the most welcoming country for the disabled visitor." Another contributor, James Franey, says of Amsterdam, "Very civilized. Where else could one find a disabled driver's parking space unoccupied even in Damrak—Amsterdam's version of Oxford Street."

Sources of Information

Netherlands Board of Tourism, 355 Lexington Avenue, New York, NY 10017 (☎212/370-7367); 25 Adelaide Street East, Suite 710, Toronto, ON M5C 1Y2 (☎416/363-1577). As well as using the wheelchair symbol in their main hotel guide, the tourist board publishes a booklet, *The Handicapped*, listing accessible accommodation (including campgrounds and RVs), restaurants, gas stations, tourist attractions, animal parks, museums, and pleasure boats. Many of these have been awarded the wheelchair symbol by *De Gehandicaptenraad* (The Handicapped Organization, Postbus 169, St. Jacobstraat 14, 3500 AD Utrecht; ☎30/313454, holds no information for disabled travelers but does have a list of Dutch disability organizations), indicating that they are accessible to unaccompanied wheelchair users with reasonably good arm function; those without the symbol have adapted rest rooms, elevators, or other facilities which render them suitable for accompanied wheelchair users or slightly more mobile travelers. There is, as ever, the rider that visitors are advised to confirm that facilities meet their own specific requirements by letter or phone call. But the booklet is nicely laid out, easy to use, updated annually, and free.

Mobility International Nederland, Postbus 165, 6560 AD Groesbeek; ☎8891/71744 (Wednesday, 9am–4pm). Primarily concerned with international tours and exchanges for individuals and groups of people with disabilities, as well as projects that encourage integration, but may be worth contacting well in advance of your trip for specific information or advice.

Getting There

KLM Royal Dutch Airlines carries aisle wheelchairs on transatlantic flights (747s and DC10s) and flies to Amsterdam out of nine US cities, including New York, Chicago, and LA, and six Canadian cities, including Toronto, Montréal, and Vancouver. *United* flies direct from Washington DC to Amsterdam, and from New York via London. *Continental* flies to Amsterdam via London from Denver, Houston, and Newark. *Northwest* (*KLM*'s American partner) flies to Amsterdam from Boston. Amsterdam is one of the cheapest "gateway" cities into Europe, and Schiphol airport has a

THE NETHERLANDS: TRAVEL NOTES

good reputation for accessibility and facilities for disabled passengers; the international assistance service, *IHD* (International Hulpdiensten), has a desk at the airport, open 24 hours a day in summer, from 6am to midnight in the winter, and offering all kinds of assistance to disabled travelers: IHD Schiphol Service, Postbus 75559, 1118 ZP Luchthaven Schiphol; ☎20/648 0093; fax 20/648 0293.

Flying from London, Barry Atkinson also recommends Rotterdam airport which is small and ideal for a wheelchair user. He took a forty-minute flight from Heathrow to Rotterdam (paying £89 round trip), preferring it to the seven-hour *Sealink Stena Line* (Charter House, Park Street, Ashford, Kent TN24 8EX; ☎0233/647047) **ferry crossing** from Harwich to The Hook (£26 each way for a stay of more than five days), even though he could have booked a fully adapted double cabin, with *en suite* rest room, for £15. According to Philippa Thomas (who received charming service from *Sealink*), a cabin is pretty well essential for any degree of comfort on the ferry. The *Koningen Beatrix* has adapted cabins and rest rooms, and elevator access to most decks.

Olau-Line (Sheerness, Kent ME12 1SN; ☎0795/580010; reservations, ☎0795/666666) sails from Sheerness to Vlissingen (Flushing) in eight hours; *North Sea Ferries* (King George Dock, Hedon Road, Hull HU9 5QA; ☎0482/795141) takes ten hours from Hull to Rotterdam. Both offer fully accessible ships and specially adapted cabins (on *North Sea Ferries* that includes drop-down seat in the shower, low-level sink and alarm button as well as the usual wide doors and adapted rest room) which should be reserved well in advance. There are wheelchair-accessible rest rooms at Harwich, Hull, Sheerness, Rotterdam, and Vlissingen, but not The Hook.

Travel **by train from Germany** should be comfortable enough, with assistance arranged a stations; there are reserved spaces for wheelchairs and accessible rest rooms on the newer EuroCity (EC) trains on the Keulen (Cologne)–Amsterdam route, and on EC 3/2 Rembrandt (Chur–Basle–Keulen–Amsterdam) and EC 105/104 Berner Oberland (Interlaken Ost–Basle–Keulen–Amsterdam).

Transport

By using the **bike paths** a motorized wheelchair user could, if well protected from the weather, travel all over the country, preferably accompanied by a friend on a bike (or in another wheelchair). But check with the *ANWB* (see below) for local restrictions. You should always be prepared for dour weather: most of the bike paths are tree-lined or in some way protected from crosswinds, but winter winds can be very cold; check the weather forecast before venturing far from town. Six train stations rent out **tandem bicycles** for use by the disabled traveler with escort: Beilen (☎5930/22260); Eindhoven (☎40/436617); Haarlem (☎23/317066); Naarden-Bussum (☎2159/45530); Roosendaal (☎1650/37228); Venlo (☎77/511487). Rental costs Hfl 7.50 per day.

If you can use **public transit** it is efficient, clean, and cheap; a taxi will only be necessary in truly remote areas. In Barry Atkinson's experience, taxi drivers and staff on public transit are extremely helpful. *Nederlandse Spoorwegen* (*Dutch Railroads*) publishes a timetable in Braille, and special booklets for the disabled traveler (*Gehandicapten op reis met de trein* and *Fiets en Trein*—in Dutch only) which are available from *Nederlandse Spoorwegen* (Dienst van Exploitatie, Afdeling Service en Verkoop, Postbus 2025, 3500 HA Utrecht; ☎30/354603). Assistance at train stations is made available if notice is given before noon on the day before traveling (*NS Bureau Assistentieverlening Gehandicapten*, ☎030/331253, Mon–Fri 8am–4pm). There are accessible rest rooms at over eighty stations; facilities for blind passengers include Braille menus in station restaurants and Braille buttons in elevators. On new intercity trains serving the following routes there are spaces for wheelchairs in the compartments: Rotterdam/Den Haag–Enschede/Groningen; Zandvoort aan Zee–Heerlen/Maastricht; Den Haag CS–Venlo; Hoofddorp–Enschede/Bad Bentheim; Hoofddorp–Leeuwarden/Groningen.

John Bignell describes his attempt to travel by train from Schiphol airport to the center of Amsterdam in 1988:

"There is an elevator from ground level down to the platform. The train had sliding

THE NETHERLANDS: TRAVEL NOTES

doors but with a central pillar. This meant that my chair had to be collapsed to get it onto the train. The other passengers were most helpful but they had great problems with the chair. It is much easier to show people how to deal with the chair and then to get on the train, rather than get on first and then give instructions!

There is a steep ramp at the Dam Square exit, Centraal Station. Here I discovered the significance of my chair's tendency to turn to the right despite an even application of power to both wheels. Every time I took a run at the ramp, I got halfway up, then the chair slewed to the right. The incline took over and I swung right around to point downhill. After a couple of attempts I gave up. I hailed the first fit-looking person I saw and, with a cheery grin, he soon had me at the top."

The tourist board booklet, *The Handicapped*, states that the Amsterdam metro is accessible to wheelchair users with normal arm function, but since most of the metro stations are in the suburbs this is not much help for exploring central Amsterdam. The trams and buses are inaccessible, so the alternatives are motorized chair, taxi, boat trips on the canals, or rented car.

The **ANWB** (*Algemene Nederlandse Wielrijdersbond*) is the *Royal Dutch Touring Association* (Postbus 93200, 2509 BA Den Haag; ☎70/3147147), similar to the American *AAA*, and offers not only mechanical assistance to members of foreign automobile organizations (nationwide number ☎06/0888) but also parking permits and a wealth of information and maps. (Disabled drivers with the appropriate permit may **park** indefinitely in blue zones or places with time restrictions, in special reserved spaces, and for two hours in no-waiting zones if there are no parking facilities nearby.) For the disabled traveler there are booklets and fact sheets—all in Dutch, but the ones covering accommodation and restaurants use the wheelchair symbol and can be followed. These can be bought by non-members at the *Stichting Informatievoorziening Gehandicapten Nederland*, PO Box 70, 3500 AB Utrecht (☎30/316437). The *ANWB* is an essential contact for anyone traveling by car (or using the cycle routes). Help is also offered for trips

to neighboring countries. Every town of any size has an *ANWB* office, but the larger offices in Amsterdam, Den Haag, Rotterdam, Utrecht, or Maastricht carry information on the surrounding areas. You will find the listing in the telephone book under *ANWB*.

The Vakantie en Handicap Foundation (Marconistraat 3, 6716 AK Ede; ☎8380/36558) has an **adapted camper van** for rent, suitable for five people including a wheelchair user, and four trailers, one folding, with wheelchair lift and adapted toilet (reservations ☎8380/34441)

Accommodation

Hotels may pose problems. Many Dutch inns and hotels are old, narrow, town houses without elevators. However, every village in the Netherlands is represented by an information office, or **VVV** (pronounced "vey, vey, vey"—which stands for *Vereniging voor Vreemdelingenverkeer*), and most of these have hotel lists and should be able to help you find (and reserve) accessible accommodation. You will find telephone numbers of these offices in all local telephone books: look for *VVV*. Most offices have English-speaking helpers. They will cheerfully give you all kinds of information—maps, museum guides, opening times, restaurant guides, where to get a wheel repaired, anything! *VVV* offices in Amsterdam are outside Centraal Station and at Leidsestraat 106; both are accessible.

The information supplied by the *ANWB* (see above) on accessible accommodation is worth getting hold of—it covers the complete range (hotels, motels, pensions, apartments, RVs, campgrounds) and is well up to date. The *RAC* European hotel and camping guides (see France *Travel Notes*) might provide more ideas, and the *Michelin Guide to Benelux* uses the wheelchair symbol to indicate accessible accommodation in the Netherlands, Belgium, and Luxembourg; as always, details can only be obtained with certainty on the spot.

Philippa Thomas recommends the peaceful *Ascot Hotel* (Damstraat 95–98, 1012 LP Amsterdam; ☎20/260066). There is a disabled person's room with wheelchair-accessible shower room and adjoining single room suitable for carer (or parents plus child). The staff

THE NETHERLANDS: TRAVEL NOTES

were extremely courteous, and there were no problems with elevator access or with leaving the scooter wheelchair in the breakfast room!

Moderately priced hotels that claim to offer rooms suitable for disabled guests include the following: *Hotel Ibis*—Rotterdam/Vlaardingen (☎2968/94377), Tilburg (☎13/636465), Utrecht (30/910366), and Veenendaal (☎8385/22222); *Hotel Urbis* Den Haag Scheveningen (☎70/354 3300); *Campanile* hotels—in twelve locations. For reservation details see France *Travel Notes*. There are also fifteen *Transeurope Hotels* (central reservations: Holland Hotels, Postbus 432, 1400 AK Bussum; ☎2159/49845) listed as offering facilities for disabled guests.

Several **youth hostels** have special features to tempt the *rolstoelgebruiker* (wheelchair user). Two are purpose-built: NBAS-Bondshuis, Oldebroek (facilities include 98 beds on the first floor, wide doors, adapted bathrooms, and wheelchair-accessible walkways in the surrounding woodlands); Oer 't Hout, Grou (8 rooms on the first floor with wide doors and adapted bathrooms; accessible landing stage for boating). Around ten other hostels can accommodate guests in wheelchairs, at least part of their buildings being adapted. Further information, including the youth hostel *Handbook 92/93*, in Dutch and English, can be obtained from *Stichting Nederlandse Jeugdherberg Centrale* (NJHC, Prof Tulpplein 4, 118 GX Amsterdam; ☎20/551 3133).

Access and Facilities

Jeanette Huber found that only the interiors of windmills and some castles were inaccessible. Most museums welcome and do not charge for visitors in wheelchairs, and some museums and castles have separate entrances and special routes inside for wheelchairs. In the northeastern province of Drenthe lies a perfect example of the accessible tourist attraction. The **museum village of Orvelte** (run by the Orvelte Foundation, Dorpsstraat 3, 9441 PD Orvelte; ☎5934/335), won the *European Year of Tourism 1990* award for providing the best tourism facilities for disabled people in Europe. The village shows rural life in the 1800s, and there are demonstrations of old trades and customs throughout the year. The buildings include a working mill, candy shop, smithy, clog workshop, sawmills, and cheese factory: all are wheelchair-accessible, and stairlifts have been installed in the few buildings that need them. There are wheelchairs available at the entrance, and a cassette tape, plus signs with raised numbers in Braille marking for visitors with visual disabilities. Orvelte gives employment to many disabled people, including those with learning difficulties.

Theaters make arrangements when notified in advance; for example, if requested a day ahead, or when tickets are booked, the Muziektheater in Amsterdam offers free use of a wheelchair which will be brought by an attendant to the parking lot on your arrival.

Books

The Time Out Guide to Amsterdam (Penguin, US$14.95, Can$22.99) describes wheelchair access at accommodation, restaurants, and tourist attractions such as museums and galleries.

A Travelers' Handbook for Persons with Epilepsy is available from the International Bureau for Epilepsy (PO Box 21, 2100 AA Heemstede; ☎23/339 060).

TELEPHONE CODE:

From the US and Canada dial 011 (international code) and then 31 for the Netherlands.

Scandinavia

Sweden under Scrutiny

Charlotte Billington, who has cerebral palsy, took part in a Project Phoenix Trust Study Tour, a fact-finding trip to Sweden, in August 1984. The group set out to observe the country's much admired state welfare system, particularly in relation to its services for the disabled population, and to tackle a self-catering vacation in a specially adapted chalet-style farmhouse.

Our group was made up of thirteen able-bodied and ten disabled people, all confined to wheelchairs, with various disabilities including multiple sclerosis, cerebral palsy, and spina bifida. Nearly all members provided their own funding but *Project Phoenix* does supply a small donation in cases of extreme hardship.

I chose to travel this way because, having been on a couple of these tours in the past, I knew that I would end up with more than just a collection of blurred snapshots and I would enjoy sharing and discussing our experiences with the rest of the group. Disadvantages are that you cannot expect to have much time to yourself, and that a grueling timetable has to be maintained if all the goals of the vacation are to be achieved. A fair degree of physical stamina is required, as the general rule is demanding: very late to bed and up very early the next morning. Anyone requiring a great deal of nursing, or injections on a regular basis, would not find these trips suitable.

However, great care is taken to ensure that the people chosen for the trip are fit enough to cope with the strains of traveling. The Trust's board of directors also does its utmost to avoid personality clashes in each group, but everyone is expected to take the rough with the smooth. However well planned and streamlined things may look on paper, no one can predict the minor hiccups which inevitably occur.

We traveled from London to Sweden in a "Jumbulance," loaned to us by *The Across Trust.* It had eight berths, sixteen seats, a small galley where simple drinks and meals were prepared, and a chemical toilet. A rota was worked out to ensure that all the disabled members of the group had a six-hour rest period while the helpers had three hours wherever possible, but inevitably plans do go awry. None of us got much sleep on that 26-hour journey, so we were all shattered by the time we arrived outside the farmhouse near Falkenberg, a small fishing port on the southwest coast of Sweden.

Sunday, our first full day, brought the local media out. They wrote up the piece with great enthusiasm—it seemed that taking groups of disabled people abroad on vacation was new to them. We were local celebrities, and Falkenberg even ran up the Union Jack in our honor. We were taken on a guided tour of the town, with its tiny cobblestone streets and quaint fishermen's cottages. The most interesting aspect was the Lutheran church, which was very plain and simple but had a fishing boat suspended from the middle of the ceiling.

"A spectacular four-hour lunch which included cold fresh salmon among its many courses"

We ended the day with a visit to an example of *Fokus* (cluster housing), which aims to enable disabled people in the area to live an independent life within the community. It was very impressive, with all the latest facilities, and the residents had their own apartments and were free to come and go as they pleased. But we detected overtones of a "ghetto" mentality in both residents and staff, which we came across again later in our stay, at another residential center on the outskirts of Lund and at the largest leisure and vacation resort in Sweden, in Malmö. Although admirable in many ways, the resort appeared to be no more than a luxurious ghetto for the disabled, and the thought of a vacation there made most of us shudder.

In the light of these visits, I felt that the Swedes, for all their talk of freedom and rights for everyone, only want integration on the able-bodied majority's terms. We saw another example of their "caring" policy being dished out a little too efficiently for comfort when our Swedish hosts presented a slide

show of a young girl called Maria. She was ten years old, very severely disabled by cerebral palsy, and had to rely on 24-hour care. A photographic record was being kept of her progress throughout her life. Every conceivable picture had been taken from every possible angle to chronicle her life from infancy to early puberty, including school and leisure activities. As we watched, the images blurred and the poor girl was reduced to the level of a performing animal in a cage. All this was to demonstrate the thorough workings of the welfare system.

On the plus side, a powerful political lobby of disabled people ensures that disability issues are not ignored in the Swedish parliament. A disabled child is sent to the local public school if he or she can manage it, and is provided with all the necessary aids. Otherwise, the special schools supply first-class education and exercise routines, as well as training in social skills for adult life. No employer is allowed to discriminate on the basis of disability, so that everyone gets a fair crack of the whip when applying for a job. The average able-bodied Swede treats his or her disabled counterpart as just another member of society and we encountered no prejudice during our stay.

We visited the equipment center in Halmstad, Falkenberg's nearest large town, and spoke to the therapists and technicians about the aids and facilities that they provide for disabled clients in the area. We were so impressed by the fantastic electric wheelchairs and the bathroom and kitchen gadgetry (all supplied free) that we stayed longer than we had anticipated. After a picnic lunch and some shopping we drove to Hyltbruk for a barbecue laid on by one of the Swedish organizers of the trip at her lakeside farm. In the middle of a clearing in a pine forest stood a palatial chalet; a private beach, fishing boat, and well-stocked lake were part of the estate. While some of the non-swimmers stayed at the chalet to help prepare the food for the barbecue, most of the group trundled down in their wheelchairs through the thicket to the edge of the lake, where some dabbled their toes and those who could walk went wading in the cool, clear water.

"He treated us like visiting heads of state"

Southeast Småland is known locally as *Glasriket* (Glass Kingdom), and we were up early in order to reach the Kosta Boda glassworks by midday. Venetian craftsmen came to Sweden in the sixteenth century, but the glass industry was established by German immigrants in the eighteenth century. Surrounded by thick forests (providing fuel), the glassworks attract thousands of visitors each year. We watched the craftsmen at work and then picked up some remarkable bargains among the "seconds" in the large shops nearby.

In Gothenberg we inspected another well-equipped center for the disabled, then visited the famous Liseburg Park—the biggest amusement park in Scandinavia. Here, among the beautifully kept gardens, you can find all the fun of the fair if that is your wish. It wasn't mine, so my helper and I went in search of a reasonably priced meal in one of the numerous cafés dotted about the fairground.

The longest and perhaps most tiring day of the trip began with breakfast on the Jumbulance at 8am, the beautiful scenery of Skåne rushing by as we munched our cornflakes. We arrived at an old monastery in time for a spectacular four-hour lunch which included cold fresh salmon among its many courses. There were speeches from our hosts and from various members of our group, after which there was just time for a quick stroll around the grounds, taking in a magnificent view of the nearby lake, before driving to our next port of call—a millionaire's stud farm.

Our host for this next stop was a jolly man in his seventies who has donated a substantial part of his fortune to cancer research, and used another sizable chunk to purchase some of the finest Arab stallions in the world of which he was justifiably proud. He treated us like visiting heads of state: a row of chairs had been set out in front of the yard, and while we watched these superb creatures being put through their paces we were served ice cream and Campari and sodas by a band of waiters who silently materialized at our sides. Now we know what it must be like for royalty—heaven! Our host insisted that we see the latest new-born foals, which meant some nifty maneuvering of the Jumbulance down a narrow lane to another part of the estate, but it was worth the hassle—they were adorable!

From the stud farm we traveled to Lund, a medieval cathedral and university town, for dinner at the residential center for the disabled. We were running an hour late, and our hosts had become a little agitated by our lack of punctuality (Swedes are sticklers for protocol and thoroughness). Although they were eager to get us into the dining room, a couple of people in our group managed to take advantage of the center's swimming pool before dinner. Soon we were all seated around the pool, chatting about the day's events, and we arrived back at our farmhouse well after midnight.

"The fact that we had to clean up, pack and leave on the next day did not stop us carrying on into the small hours"

Our last day in Sweden gave us the opportunity for shopping in Halmstad, but before we were let loose to buy souvenirs and food for our Last Night Party, we visited the ambulance depot, and a few of us went on to visit the local hospital. Shopping spree over, we returned to the farmhouse to prepare our farewell feast, a token of thanks to our hosts for their generosity and kindness in making our first self-catering vacation so successful. There was enough food to feed the population of southern Sweden and much of it unfortunately went to waste, but apart from that everyone seemed to have a good time. The outside of the farmhouse was decked with colored streamers and flags, making a festive backdrop for the folk dancers who came to entertain us. The fact that we had to clean up, pack, and leave on the next day did not stop us carrying on into the small hours.

The aims of the trip were achieved with only a few minor hitches—mainly timing; an overnight stay would be incorporated on the next visit, as the journeys there and back proved too tiring to be completed in a day. Both sides were given food for thought: the Swedes might think more positively about organizing group vacations abroad; we would take home some of their general attitudes towards disabled people, concerning education and employment. And we all learned a little more about integration.

The Earth beneath your Wheels

In October 1990, Alison Walsh, who has rheumatoid arthritis and limited mobility, traveled to Sweden at the invitation of the Swedish Tourist Board, to investigate facilities for disabled visitors.

Wheeling and strolling gently under the pine trees, faintly conscious of superfluous padding on hips and waistlines, we stand aside to watch another corps of lean, blond roller-skiers thunder past. These are members of Sundsvall Biathlon and Timra SOK, at Skonviksberget, northern Sweden, a training and competition paradise for sports enthusiasts—on snow skis or roller skis, in running shoes, or in wheelchairs. As well as a shooting range, there are 8530 feet of illuminated, fine-grained asphalt, used solely for roller skiing and wheelchair racing; this is just one of a long list of indoor and outdoor sporting facilities that disabled Swedes can enjoy.

Sweden is essentially a squeaky-clean, fresh air, and exercise vacation destination. There is water everywhere—thousands of lakes, great rivers such as the Ljungan and Indalsalven, and many miles of ragged coastline. There are beautiful beaches, endless forests, and rocky wilderness. The view from the country's midpoint, at Flataklocken, is a magnificent panorama of freshwater blue and pine-needle green, as far as the eye can see.

For the disabled visitor to Flataklocken there is a wooden boardwalk from parking lot to viewing point and picnic area, and a chalet-style rest room with wide door and ramped entrance. The boardwalk peters out at the edge of the picnic area, and it turns out that this is not attributable to lack of funds or bad planning: the ground beyond is rough but passable, and wheelchair users can feel the earth beneath their wheels; the boardwalk takes them smoothly over the impossible section—steep and rocky—but then leaves them to enjoy the twists and turns through the trees, rising and dipping over their roots, and gazing between them to take in glorious views.

We saw the forests in the fall, when the turning leaves of birch, sycamore, lime, mountain ash, and oak splash brilliant orange and yellow across the landscape. The weather is unpredictable, there's a sharp chill in the air, but when the skies suddenly clear and we happen on a trio of grazing elk or a charming huddle of wooden houses in an isolated fishing village, the odd downpour seems insignificant and a small price to pay for the rewards of avoiding the busy high season (July). The best time to visit, though, is probably late May to early June, or September, when temperatures are kinder and sunshine hours longer.

> "It's an easy task to wheel across the rocks to the sea's edge, and feel the soft salt spray"

Vasternorrland is the most densely forested county, and nowhere is nature conservation—almost a religion in Sweden—more in evidence. The aim is simple, to preserve wild areas in their natural state so that flora and fauna can develop freely. To that end, all visitors, whether scientists, day trippers, or tourists, are given access and basic facilities (marked footpaths, shelter, rest rooms, safe sites for lighting fires, picnic tables) with minimum disturbance to the environment.

In Rotsidan, a small nature reserve of forest and seashore between the two fishing hamlets of Barsta and Fallvikshamn, the trails look natural but have been carefully prepared, using packed asphalt and asphalt grains which become harder when it rains; they fit quietly into the surroundings and enable wheelchair explorers to fit in, too. Meandering along them, listening to the trees whispering overhead, it's possible to lean out and pick berries—blueberries, cloudberries, crowberries, red whortleberries—or examine yellow, rubbery finger mushrooms and any number of delicate mosses, lichens, orchids, and heathers.

The trail emerges on the coast, windswept and bleak in October but perfect for sunbathing in summer with its flat slabs of polished, greenish rocks. There's a barbecue area, with chopped up tree trunks to sit on, and it's an easy task to wheel across the rocks to the sea's edge, and feel the soft salt spray on your face. A short way inland a few log-cabin rest rooms are provided, clean and wheelchair-accessible.

North of Rotsidan, along the deeply indented Hoga Kusten (the High Coast, which stretches from the Angerman river in the south to Skagsudde in the north), is Norrfallsviken, where a fishing community has lived since the 1500s. The boiling houses and boathouses remain but the village is now a vacation center, set in a woodland nature reserve on a peninsula of red granite.

Described in the brochure as a "recreation village," the widely scattered chalets are beautifully fitted out in pine, spacious and comfortable. Each four-room chalet is equipped with wheelchair-accessible toilet and shower facilities, and entrances can be ramped. In a country renowned for high prices, this is affordable accommodation, worth considering for families or small groups. There is a central, airy restaurant (with nearby accessible rest room), plus swimming pool, tennis courts, and sauna. Other activities include trips to the sandy Nordingra-Storsand beach, orienteering, windsurfing, horse-riding, fishing, and sailing.

> "The Swedes look after their heritage in the same spirit with which they approach environmental conservation"

If all this sounds a little too strenuous, there's some consolation for those in search of cultural stimulation. The extraordinary light, colors, and shapes of the High Coast have attracted many artists to the area. Barbro and Anders Aberg have created a complex, known as Vardshuset Mannaminne, which includes a museum, art gallery, artists' workshop, and student cafe. Visitors can wander around art exhibitions, inspect fishing boats and tackle in various stages of restoration, listen to live bands, drink coffee, and eat delicious home-made chocolate cake. Most of the buildings are accessible.

The Swedes look after their heritage in the same spirit with which they approach environmental conservation. In rural areas there are well-preserved churches, old timbered buildings, homestead museums, displays of ancient crafts and trades, and each city has its carefully restored Old Town. Of course, there is greatest scope for culture vultures and nightlifers in the towns, most of all in Stockholm, where the jewel in the crown of accessible tourist attractions is perhaps the Vasa Museum.

"This welcome for visitors in wheelchairs extends to many of the restaurants, shops, museums, and galleries in Stockholm"

Opened in June 1990, this houses the richly ornamented warship *Vasa*, which sank in Stockholm harbor on her maiden voyage in 1628. Preserved in mud for over 300 years, the ship was raised along with 12,000 objects in 1961 and now forms the centerpiece of a startling hall on the water's edge. As if the ship itself, shimmering damply in the semidarkness, wasn't impressive enough, the museum also offers illustrated historical accounts of her construction and the inquiry into the reasons for her sinking, and fascinating exhibitions of salvaged objects. There is even a reconstructed section of the stern (accessible of course) so that visitors can get the feel of the ship below deck without tramping over the delicate original.

The main entrance to the museum is through very heavy, double-swing doors (to preserve humidity and temperature inside) but wheelchair users can go through the adjacent automatic doors. From here, all levels and parts of the museum, including rest rooms, shop, restaurant, and theater, have excellent wheelchair access.

This welcome for visitors in wheelchairs extends to many of the restaurants, shops, museums, and galleries in Stockholm, although Gamla Stan (the Old Town) is tricky in places, with narrow sidewalks and doorways, and cobblestoned streets. Wheelchairs are a fact of life, accepted without fuss by waiters, shop and hotel staff, tour guides, taxi drivers, and the Swede in the street. It's a relaxed city, almost rural, green and uncrowded, with manageable traffic (none in Gamla Stan), uncluttered sidewalks and, of course, water at every turn.

It would be a pity to travel to Sweden and never take to the water. As well as special hoists and adapted canoes at several locations, there are rafts and hand-operated pedal-boats for hire, and facilities for virtually every form of boating, from white-water rafting to game fishing. Access to the larger vessels—steamships, pleasure boats, ferries, and hydrofoils—is generally good and crew are happy to assist with boarding.

We left Stockholm in the newly built *M/S Kungsholm*, for a trip to see the oldest portrait collection in the world at Gripsholm Castle, in Mariefred. Boarding was straightforward, there was plenty of space forward, on the lower deck, to park a couple of wheelchairs, and it was a smooth journey, just over an hour long, with comfortable seats and friendly snack bar service. The big shock came when attempting to visit the restroom, marked with the wheelchair symbol: it was in the stern, up two large steps, and it was impossible to maneuver a wheelchair (28 inches wide) down the aisle between the seats from bow to stern. By this time we had come to expect high standards of accessibility in Sweden, and it was surprising to find that designers make mistakes here as in other parts of the world.

There was another surprise waiting at Gripsholm, which is an attractive, red brick and stone castle, originally built around 1540, but added to and changed in the sixteenth, eighteenth, and nineteenth centuries. Since 1822 it has been the home of the Swedish State Portrait Collection and there are many paintings to linger over, including some modern works, as well as Gustav III's perfectly preserved round theater.

"Proof that ancient buildings can be made accessible without major structural alterations"

The guided tour is interesting, conducted at a gentle pace, and—the surprise—a stair-climbing wheelchair is provided. It was purchased at a cost of about $6000, much cheaper than installing chairlifts on winding staircases, or elevator shafts that would damage the fabric of the building. It means that full-time wheelchair users can see every room on the tour, and is proof that ancient buildings can be made accessible without major structural alterations.

Of course, on a trip like this we were taken at breathless pace around the high points in terms of access (with one hiccup on the *M/S Kungsholm*), and it was not enough to make an accurate assessment of facilities throughout Sweden. But is was cheering to see a tourist board approaching the subject with such enthusiasm, when so many others fail to show a flicker of interest, either in providing information for disabled visitors or in updating it. It was also interesting to discover something which perhaps sets Sweden apart from much of the rest of Europe—a determination to make the natural environment accessible to all, Swedes and foreigners alike, whatever their abilities.

High Mountains, High Prices

Confined to a wheelchair for the last seven years as a result of multiple sclerosis, Dorothea Boulton travels regularly. In 1986 she and her husband accepted an invitation to visit friends in Oslo, Norway, and combined this with a trip to the west coast. Traveling in their own car cut down the expense and enabled them to take both electric and self-propelled wheelchairs.

After consultation with our Norwegian friends and with the Norwegian Tourist Board, we chose to travel with *Fred Olsen Lines* from Harwich, in eastern England, to Oslo. Their Goat Trail Tour provided us with vouchers for ten nights in hotels, to be used as we wished. Information supplied included suggested tours and details of hotels, as well as an excellent book, *Motoring in Norway*. The crossing took two nights—a mini-cruise—and was an experience in itself.

We reserved a specially adapted cabin with shower and toilet *en suite* (fine as long as your companion is fit and able to climb onto the top bunk!) and we found that we could reach most parts of the ship with my wheelchair. We enjoyed the entertainment provided, we sat on the deck in the sunshine, and when the ferry called at Hirtshals in northern Denmark we saw the most memorable sunset.

At rush hour on a Monday morning, with a public transit strike, Oslo was hair-raising. Fortunately we were heading west, out of the city, guided by our friends who accompanied us to our first hotel, high in the mountains at Geilo. Midway between Oslo and Bergen, Geilo is predominantly a winter sports resort. In early June most of the skiing had finished, though we could still see the ski runs. The town was quiet as the summer walkers and anglers had not yet arrived.

Early next morning we waved good-bye to our friends. We were on our own. The road became narrower and more winding as we headed still higher into the mountains. We passed a sign saying that the pass up ahead had been opened only the day before, and the weather was deteriorating! We had left Geilo in beautiful sunshine but now the mist was descending.

After the first day we soon adapted to the differing climatic conditions as we dropped from the mountains to sheltered green valleys, and then climbed up again. Driving between walls of snow ten feet high was no exception. Most of the driving was exciting but the most heart-stopping section was a descent through dense fog on route 7 to Hardangerfjord. We had expected to see the Voringfossen, Norway's most admired waterfall with a drop of 450 feet, but instead experienced the eerie sensation of hearing the tremendous roar but seeing nothing from the observation platform.

"We had coffee and Norwegian pastries beside a roaring log fire"

Our base for exploring the Hardangerfjord was the *Kinsarvikfjord Hotel* in the village of Kinsarvik. My most abiding memory of this area is the apple blossom around Lofthus. Norwegians travel for miles to see the blossom, enhanced as it is by the exceptionally beautiful setting—the blue water of the fjord backed by snow-capped mountains that seem to rise directly from the water, numerous waterfalls tumbling down their steep sides, and all bathed in glorious spring sunshine.

We traveled from Hardangerfjord to Sognefjord along routes 68 and 13 from Kvanndal and Voss. The road climbing into the Vikafjell range appeared vertical as we approached, and we could make out the four switchbacks which have a road width of 16 feet and a gradient of 1 in 12. It was a relief to arrive safely at the top, where we stopped for coffee and admired the views of Lake Myrkdalsratn and its delta, home to nearly eighty species of bird. Our destination in the Sognefjord region was Balestrand, a small resort which we reached by ferry. We enjoyed three restful days at *Kvikne's Hotel*, situated on the side of the fjord, and explored the village and surrounding mountains.

To do the fjords justice it is necessary to use the ferries, which add a new perspective to the vacation. We never had difficulty in boarding them and they always ran on time. Only one of our journeys was made in bad weather (rain and low mist); otherwise we had marvelous views.

We left Balestrand on what promised to be the most spectacular of our ferry trips. Unfortunately this was the day it rained! While staying in Balestrand we learned that a new road tunnel under the Jostedalsbreen glacier had been opened the previous week. This meant that we could travel by ferry up Fjaerlandfjord to Fjaerland and then by road to Skei, thus avoiding a long drive with a detour to see the glacier. Despite the rain the scenery was dramatic and we were able to drive to an arm of the glacier called Supphellebreen, where we had coffee and Norwegian pastries beside a roaring log fire. From this café my husband went on to examine the edge of the glacier—I stayed by the fire! The drive under the glacier, with the ice shining blue-green, was out of this world.

This was our last day by the fjords and we headed northeast, eventually working our way south to Oslo. Again our route took us across snow-covered mountain plateaux and through warm green valleys, one of which (Skjak) is the driest part of Norway, with a rainfall similar to that in the Sahara desert. We stayed at the ski hotels in Grotli and Beitostolen, and although it was June we caught the atmosphere of winter sports at Grotli where the Finnish national ski team was practicing. We stopped many times to view waterfalls and to eat at isolated log-cabin cafés which invariably commanded the most exciting views. We saw many old houses with grass growing on the roofs for warmth, and examples of the stave churches found in most villages.

"We arrived at the hotel to find that 'one step' was in fact 'one flight' of twelve steps"

Our return to Oslo completed the circle and our trip. We spent two days visiting some of the many tourist attractions, including the Holmenkollen ski jump which stands high above the city and gives excellent views across it. The jump was built for the 1952 Olympic Games and attracts visitors all the year round. In summer the ski basin is a lake on which floodlit concerts are held, the orchestra playing on a floating platform.

The Vigeland Sculpture Park should not be missed. In beautiful landscaped parkland all the works of Gastar Vigeland are displayed. His sculptures cover all aspects of human life from birth to old age, the centerpiece being composed of 121 intertwined human figures—a humbling sight.

Oslo has many museums: I found the Norwegian Folk Museum, the Viking Ship Museum, and the Kon-Tiki Museum most fascinating. The first reconstructs the interiors of town and country homes from recent centuries, and brings together over 150 buildings from all over Norway in an outdoor exhibition, arranged to demonstrate regional variations in rural architecture. The Viking Ship Museum houses three

restored Viking ships, built for the ship burials practiced by the Vikings. The decorative items carried on board and now on display include jewelry, cloth, and ceremonial sleighs for use in the afterlife. The Kon-Tiki Museum commemorates the voyages of the Norwegian adventurer, Thor Heyerdahl: the first on a balsawood raft (_Kon-Tiki_) from Peru to Polynesia; the second on a papyrus raft (_Ra II_) across the Atlantic.

We found the Norwegians kind and welcoming wherever we went. They seem to be generally very much aware of the needs of disabled people. Communication was reasonably easy as most Norwegians speak English (they are taught it in school from the age of six). Even so, we had the occasional hitch as a result of translation difficulties. When booking our hotel at Grotli, my husband inquired about access and was told that there was one step—fine, we could cope with that. We arrived at the hotel to find that "one step" was in fact "one flight" of twelve steps.

Throughout our vacation we enjoyed the Norwegian cold table (_koldtbord_) and other typical food. Breakfast was always a very large meal—smoked salmon and scrambled eggs, cold meats and cheese. In the larger hotels, hot breakfasts were also available. For touring it is wise to be equipped for lunchtime picnics, as cafés are few and far between. Hotels will fill Thermoses —but at a price. When eating out you will be reminded that Norway is an expensive country. The state has a monopoly on the supply of alcohol; wine, beer, and spirits for private consumption can only be bought at state stores, and that which is served in restaurants and hotels is far from cheap. Wine with our evening meal was our luxury treat—but one bottle of a modest rosé at $30 had to last us three evenings!

Despite the expense we fell in love with Norway, and jumped at the chance to go again in 1989, this time to a wedding. It came as an unpleasant shock to find that prices were even higher than we'd remembered. But a visit to this beautiful country is well worth saving for. Probably one of the cheaper ways to do it is to shop around for an inclusive package deal, preferably including hotel vouchers or giving discount rates at hotels of your choice so that you can plan your own itinerary. We paid about $450 per person in 1986, for ferry and hotel vouchers (including breakfast); this did not include other meals or any meals on the ferry. It was possible to reclaim the cost of any unused hotel vouchers on return to England.

SCANDINAVIA: TRAVEL NOTES

Sources of Information

Norwegian Tourist Board, 655 Third Avenue, New York, NY 10017; ☎212/949-2333. Produces an accommodation guide that uses the wheelchair symbol and may still have a few copies of the *Travel Guide for the Disabled*, which was compiled in 1982 by the Norwegian Association of the Disabled and covers accommodation, transport, and tourist attractions. The intention to update every two years is stated in the Preface, but this doesn't seem to have come off—a shame because it's difficult to rely on ten-year-old information.

Swedish Tourist Board, 665 Third Avenue, New York, NY 10017; ☎212/949-2333. In 1990, the European Year of Tourism, Sweden launched a major campaign to improve the lot of the disabled tourist, concentrating on transport, accommodation, and facilities at tourist sights. As part of the campaign the tourist board launched a new edition of the excellent *Holiday Guide for the Disabled* in English and German. It is a sizable book, free, and packed with information for tourists with mobility problems; allergy sufferers, people with visual or hearing disabilities, and those who require dialysis are also catered for. There are details of a wide range of accommodation, advice on transport, and brief notes on all manner of activities and sights.

The bad news is that in June 1992 the Swedish government shut down the tourist board, and declared that its work could be carried out by private trade organizations under the control of the Swedish Travel and Tourism Council (Chairman Leif Forsberg, Avenska Penninglottereit AB, 02180 Visby); at the time of writing there are no plans to update the guide, but until the end of August 1993 the 1990 edition can be obtained from the New York office, and in the directives for the new organization the government specifically states that funds should be made available for projects concerning people with disabilities—it is the firm opinion of the Chairman that the 1990 handbook will be updated in some way.

Danish Tourist Board, 655 Third Avenue, New York, NY 10017 (☎212/949-2333); PO Box 115, Station N, Toronto, ON M8V 3S4 (☎416/823-9620). In conjunction with the Committee for Housing, Transportation, and Technical Aids, and with plenty of input from organizatons of disabled people, the Danish Tourist Board publishes a refreshingly honest guide for disabled visitors, *Access in Denmark—A Tourist Guide for the Disabled*, with information on accommodation, transport, rest rooms, restaurants, and places of interest. The latest edition was printed in January 1989 and stocks ran out by the middle of 1990, but the tourist board will send you a clear photocopy of all 100 pages.

Finnish Tourist Office, 655 Third Avenue, New York, NY 10017 (☎212/949-2333); PO Box 246, Station Q, Toronto, ON M4T 2M1 (☎800/346-4636). Its booklet, *Tourist Services for the Disabled* (1991), lists accommodation for groups of disabled people, hotels with facilities for disabled guests, and transport facilities for disabled travelers to and within Finland.

SCANDINAVIA: TRAVEL NOTES

Tour Operators

Since Dorothy Boulton's trip *Fred Olsen Lines'* North Sea routes have been taken over by *Color Line* (c/o Bergen Line Inc., 505 Fifth Ave., New York, NY 10017-4983; ☎212/986-2711). *M/S Venus* sails from Newcastle in northern England to Bergen and Stavanger, and the brochure offers a selection of cruises, mini-cruises (see p.528), chalet stays, escorted tours and "go as you please" driving vacations.

Getting There

Alison Walsh flew from London Heathrow to Stockholm with *SAS*. The seating was a little cramped but bearable for two to three hours; passengers with unbendable legs would have problems—they might squeeze in on the front row aisle seat, but more likely would have to reserve two seats. The wheelchair service at both airports was excellent; Stockholm's Arlanda airport is small and friendly. Passengers in their own chairs can remain in them until they board the plane and be reunited with them at the door of the aircraft on arrival.

SAS flies from New York to Stockholm/Copenhagen, from Los Angeles/Seattle to Copenhagen, connecting to Stockholm (hourly flights connect the two cities, luggage is checked through), and from Chicago to Copenhagen, connecting to Stockholm, using *Austrian Airlines* aircraft on this route. Wide body aircraft carry an aisle wheelchair. *Delta* flies to Stockholm, Oslo, Copenhagen, and Helsinki. Other possibilities include *American Airlines* to Stockholm, Oslo, or Copenhagen.

There are good facilities for disabled passengers aboard many of the **ferries** operating in the waters around Scandinavia. On 24-hour crossings to Gothenburg from Britain, *Scandinavian Seaways* (Central Reservations Office, Scandinavia House, Parkeston Quay, Harwich, Essex CO12 4QG, UK; ☎0255/241234) offers adapted four- and two-berth cabins (level entrance, 20.5in-wide doors, wheel-in shower with fold-down stool and grab-rails, space and grab-rails around the toilet).

If you're planning a grand European tour it's worth noting that *Color Line* (see *Tour operators*) sails to Norway from the Netherlands, Germany, and Denmark as well as Newcastle. *Sealink Stena Line* (Charter House, Park Street, Ashford, Kent TN24 8EX, UK; ☎0233/647047) offers several routes between the Netherlands, Germany, Denmark, Norway, and Sweden. The *Finnish Tourist Board* lists three ferry companies, sailing from Germany or Sweden to Finland, that offer ships equipped with special cabins for disabled passengers: *Silja Line* (fare concessions for disabled passengers with identification: US agent: Bergen Line Inc., 505 Fifth Ave., New York, NY 10017; ☎212/986-2711. Canadian agent: Group Systems International, 102 Bloor Street West, Suite 460, Toronto, ON M5S 1M8; ☎416/968-9064); *Wasa Line* and *Viking Line* (Scantours Inc., Suite 209, 1535 Sixth Street, Santa Monica, CA 90401; ☎213/451-0911).

Transport

In general, it seems that **air travel** within the Scandinavian countries is the best bet for wheelchair users without their own cars. Certainly in Sweden it is surprisingly inexpensive, and even at the smaller airports the staff is smooth and efficient in its handling of passengers with disabilities. Swedish airports allow disabled passengers their independence before boarding: check in your baggage, spend a minute registering at the service desk, then do as you please until about ten minutes before the other passengers are due to board when you report back to the service desk for pre-boarding. Facilities at major airports in Denmark are described in detail in the tourist board access guide. The Norway guide covers air travel but is out of date. The Finnish guide contains some basic information but for more detail consult the national airline, *Finnair*.

Rail travel is, on the whole, difficult, with adapted trains still in the experimental stage and only on major routes. Denmark's trial trains and Sweden's new type of second-class cars enable passengers to remain in their wheelchairs throughout some intercity journeys. Full details are given in the tourist board guides for disabled visitors. Some of the intercity trains in Norway are equipped with a special car which has a hydraulic lifting platform and an adapted compartment for wheelchair users.

SCANDINAVIA: TRAVEL NOTES

The information on rail travel in Finland is sketchy—there are only a handful of cars equipped to carry wheelchair users, assistance is available at stations, and blind travelers take a companion free of charge—but it is heartening to know that Helsinki now has an accessible subway system as a result of a blockade by disabled inhabitants of the city. In Stockholm, most T-banan (subway) stations have elevators, and these are indicated on the timetable; there are specialist minivans and taxis for hire, but the standard buses are inaccessible to wheelchair passengers. Disabled Swedes receive generous mobility allowances to cover taxi fares if they are unable to use public transit, but for disabled visitors taxis are expensive.

Accessible vehicles for groups are readily available in Sweden: Alison Walsh traveled in a small (14-seater) bus with hydraulic lift and tie-down space for four wheelchairs, which cost about $125 per day, not including gas. There are numerous bus companies that rent adapted vehicles all over the country. The situation for groups wanting adapted buses is also good in Finland—details in the tourist board guide, as well as a list of four operators of adapted taxicabs for individuals.

Rental of adapted **cars** is difficult, if not impossible, but you could rent one from *Hertz* in Britain or France, or an adapted van in England, or adapted camper van in the Netherlands (see relevant *Travel Notes*), and take it across to Scandinavia by ferry; driving in these generally underpopulated countries, on well-maintained roads, is easy. In Sweden the provision of adapted toilet facilities at rest areas is becoming more widespread; the incidence of adapted rest rooms at gas stations, motels, and hotels is reasonably high and those along main roads are listed in the *Swedish Tourist Board* vacation guide. The Danish guide lists facilities on highways and main roads. This is an unfortunate omission in the Norway guide.

Holders of badges bearing the international wheelchair symbol should apply to local police stations to discuss **parking** arrangements in Sweden, Denmark, Finland, and Norway; there are concessions although no formal agreements exist with North America.

Accommodation

The *Swedish Tourist Board* vacation guide includes listings of suitable accommodation in hotels, chalet villages, and campgrounds. There is also a separate listing of campgrounds (and chalets) with facilities for disabled people, and the wheelchair symbol is used in the brochure, *Camping in Sweden*, available from the tourist office; or try *Sveriges Campingvärdars Riksförbund*, Box 255, S-45117 Uddevalla (☎522/39345). The general hotel guide also uses the "H" symbol but no details are given.

Accommodation is listed in the Danish access guide, and the general hotel guide uses two symbols to indicate accessibility for unaccompanied and accompanied wheelchair users (access criteria are explained in full).

Both the Finland guide for disabled visitors and the general hotel guide indicate accessible accommodation, but there are no details of facilities in bedrooms or bathrooms.

The Norway guide covers accommodation but is rather out of date—access details need checking; the general annual accommodation brochure uses the wheelchair symbol but this also needs checking. Dorothea Boulton comments on the hotels she used (the hotel guide referred to is the *Norwegian Tourist Board* accommodation guide):

Geilo Hotel, Geilo. Wheelchair symbol in the hotel guide but step at entrance and four steps to first-floor bedroom corridor. Neither bedroom nor bathroom specially adapted.

Kinsarvikfjord Hotel, Kinsarvik. No wheelchair symbol in guide but access good. Level entrance with no steps; elevator; adequate bedroom but bathroom only accessible with help.

Kvikne's Hotel, Balestrand. Wheelchair symbol in guide. Extensive range of facilities; specially adapted bedroom and bathroom; elevators; easy access at entrance (no steps).

Grotli Hoyfjells Hotel, Grotli. No wheelchair symbol in guide. Entrance difficult (impossible without strong assistant); bedrooms not adapted and bathroom difficult.

Beito Hoyfjells Hotel, Beitostolen. Wheelchair symbol in guide. No steps at entrance; adapted first-floor room; elevators; large indoor swimming pool but no hoist or ramp.

SCANDINAVIA: TRAVEL NOTES

Nye Helsfyr Hotel, Oslo (just outside the city center). Wheelchair symbol in guide. Good access, level entrance; elevators; excellent adapted bathroom; large twin-bedded room. Business hotel prices but some good deals.

It may be worth consulting the *RAC European Hotel Guide* and the *Camping and Caravanning Guide* (see France *Travel Notes*), particularly for Norway.

Access and Facilities

As noted in Charlotte Billington's account, **Sweden** has been held up as an example to all of us regarding provision of facilities for its own disabled people, and not without good reason—the Swedes enjoy generous disability benefits and pensions, free aids and appliances, grants for housing alterations and car purchase, employment quotas and more. **Denmark** has a similar reputation.

But of course it's not all roses. Employment quotas sound good, but in Denmark disabled people live comfortably on their benefits; there are mutterings among employers that it is impossible to employ disabled people because they do not apply for jobs—they have no incentive to work. This level of aid for disabled people is extremely expensive; the Danish government is attempting to reduce personal taxation rates and a large balance of payments deficit by taking the responsibility for funding and administering social services from central to local government and by moves toward privatization. Residential centers are out of favor and the trend now is toward individual, adapted apartments or shared houses.

Similarly, in Sweden there is a move away from the cluster housing (*Fokus*) of the Sixties toward *Boendeservice* (housing with service) apartments, in which residents do not share common bathing, laundry, kitchen, and dining facilities. During the last few years some residents have negotiated for their own personal attendants to manage the entire morning routine, after which they rely on workers from the central *Boendeservice* staff (see *Independent Lving and Attendant Care in Sweden: A Consumer Perspective*, by Adolf Ratzka; *World Rehabilitation Fund*, New York).

The attitudes encountered in 1984 by the *Phoenix Trust* study group have changed enormously. There is decisive rejection of "resorts" or "centers" for disabled people; the emphasis has shifted to integration in the true sense of the word. In spite of these developments, it's interesting to note that both Danish and Swedish finalists in the European Year of Tourism competition to find the best facilities for disabled tourists in Europe were owned and run by disability organizations: the *Hotel Årevidden* in central Sweden is part of a group of four hotels owned by the *Swedish Federation of Disabled Persons* (*DHR*). Dronningens Ferieby holiday village, near Grenaa in Jutland, was built by the *Danish Multiple Sclerosis Society* (*Scleroseforeningen*).

There is clearly some way to go before commercial operators learn from these beautifully designed and fully accessible—both inside and out—properties, and act on the principles of tourism for all. But it is good to see that such accommodation is open to disabled tourists and their families or friends. The Swedes and Danes are keen to make the facilities which they have long provided for their compatriot available to, and known to, disabled tourists.

Useful Addresses

Danish Multiple Sclerosis Society (*Scleroseforeningen*), 15 Mosedalvej, DK-2500 Valby, Denmark; ☎31 17 04 66.

Swedish Federation of Disabled Persons (*DHR*), Katrinebergsvägen 6, S-117 43 Stockholm, Sweden; ☎8/18 91 00.

Rullaten ry, Mr. Jens Gellin, Vartiokyläntie 9, 00950 Helsinki, Finland; ☎0/322 069; fax 0/326 887. A Finnish organization "specializing in assisting the disabled in planning their travel and leisure time activities."

Invalidiliitto ry (Association of the Disabled), Kumpulantie 1 A, 00520 Helsinki, Finland; ☎0/146 3466. General information.

TELEPHONE CODES:

From the US and Canada dial 011 (international code) and then 45 for Denmark, 46 for Sweden, 47 for Norway, 358 for Finland.

Germany

The End of East and West in Berlin

James Franey contracted poliomyelitis some years ago, and as a result uses crutches all the time. He visited Berlin before the Wall came down.

The Berlin Wall was erected in 1961, when East Berlin was pronounced the capital of the new German Democratic Republic. West Berlin became an island of capitalism and democracy inside East Germany. Only designated roads through East Germany could be used to reach Berlin, and there were three air corridors, all barred to *Lufthansa*, the German national airline.

In West Berlin, Kurfürstendamm (or Ku'damm, as it is colloquially called) became the main shopping street, full of glossy department stores and BMW showrooms. Prior to dismantling of the Wall, Ku'damm carried many tourists but little traffic for such a major city center. At the top is the ruin of the Kaiser Wilhelm church, left as a monument after World War II, and beside it a modern bell tower.

At night Ku'damm comes to life, with tourists and locals alike sitting at street cafés, and street musicians or bands playing impromptu concerts in the road. The atmosphere is laid back and friendly. Nightlife elsewhere in West Berlin, however, ranges from the extraordinary to the downright dubious.

Away from the bright lights and glitter is the area of Kreuzberg, which the

guidebooks generally point out as being full of the black flags of anarchy and alternative lifestyles. Because of its special status and position in the midst of East Germany, the West German government gave tax concessions to people willing to live in West Berlin and exempted potential conscripts from service if they chose to live there. As a result, many radicals and fringe groups came to West Berlin and most settled in Kreuzberg. But with the demise of radicalism in the mid-Seventies it seems to have lost some of its gloss—visitors now find a run down, inner city area.

The general picture, though, is one of a well-kept, wealthy city with parks, art galleries, theaters, museums, excellent food, and good public transit. Most people speak English and are friendly. The Dahlem-Dorf Museum contains many fine paintings, including works by Rembrandt and Rubens. It is in the suburbs and easy to reach on the efficient, clean and accessible U'bahn (subway system). Also worth a look is the Charlottenberg Palace which lies to the north of the city.

But there is another side to Berlin and, before the Wall came down, there was another city to travel to. Entry to East Berlin from West Berlin was, for Western tourists, by one of two means—either by train through Friedrichstrasse Station, or by sightseeing bus.

I first took the S'bahn (the suburban train) from Zoo Station, near Ku'damm, to Friedrichstrasse. The train was old, with wooden bench-seats, and it was crowded with West Berliners taking much-needed provisions to relatives and friends in East Berlin. The journey took only a few minutes and we passed through the Wall and No-Man's Land.

At Friedrichstrasse passengers left the train and made their way to the transit hall, which was straight out of a spy novel. Shabby, with beige paint peeling in places, it was heavily guarded by East German militia. As always, there was a great line to the booths where parcels were examined and day visas (a sheet of paper with a map of East Berlin on the reverse side) were issued.

The attitude of the East German authorities varied widely. Once, while I was standing at the back of a long line, a militia man came over to me, looked at my crutches and said, "Ein tag?," to which I replied with almost the only German word I knew, "Ja." I was quickly escorted to the front of the line, which saved me a wait of 45 minutes. This act of consideration was not matched by the militia man's counterpart in the glass booth. I was instructed to put my hair behind my ears to reflect my image in my passport. After much glancing between the passport photograph and myself, the man in the booth gave me a visa and I walked to the currency counter where I exchanged the mandatory 25DM for 25 Ost Marks.

Leaving the building and entering Friedrichstrasse itself, I was met by nuns in full habit collecting money for the church, and by East Berlin policemen escorting a large group of soccer fans away from the train station. It was only a short walk, past a house where Engels once stayed, down to Unter den Linden, the famous road which leads down to the Brandenberg Gate and the Wall.

Most of the main buildings in East Berlin lie in Unter den Linden, including the Arsenal Museum, St. Hedwig's cathedral, and the Humboldt University. Nearby, at the Tomb of the Unknown Warrior, the East German Guard was changed in goose-stepping style reminiscent of a pre-1939 newsreel.

In the Arsenal Museum, which had no passenger elevator, I was escorted (without asking) to the service elevator by an official. He told me in broken English that I would be most interested in exhibits on the second floor which covered World War II. The service elevator was obviously used for taking away the garbage.

"Here was the heart of East Berlin, and it was akin to Allentown on a bad day"

On arrival at the second floor I was told to ask one of the other attendants to lead me back to the elevator when I had finished. However, during my inspection of the exhibits I became aware of being followed—one of the attendants had decided to ensure that I wouldn't miss the return elevator. As for the exhibits, there was a strong Soviet bias—which has been changed since the events of November 1989.

When I was ready to leave, my escort took me back to the elevator and out through the main doors. I thanked him for his kindness and complimented him on his English. He told me that he spoke Russian better than he spoke English, and then added, mordantly, "the chiefs are American, the chiefs are Russian."

On leaving the Arsenal Museum I went by bus to Alexander Platz. Everyone was very kind on the buses and trains in Berlin, and I always received many offers of a seat. After getting off the bus I became aware that here was the heart of East Berlin, and it was akin to Allentown on a bad day. The architecture was of the Stalinist variety—heavy, designed by someone who trained using kindergarten blocks, and poorly built. In the center of Alexander Platz was what the guide-books proudly called "the world clock." Why anyone would want to know the time in Caracas while standing in the middle of Berlin was beyond me.

"It is possible to detect just a tinge of regret"

The food, too, was of amazingly poor quality. In the snack bars it was bad cold cuts or ghastly sausage, served on stale bread. In contrast, the beer was excellent. A short walk to an ice cream vendor supplied me with ice cream which tasted like Crisco and had to be thrown away. A box of chocolates also had to be discarded.

In short, there was nothing on which to spend my 25 Ost Marks. A visit to the *Zentrum* department store was also disappointing. The goods on sale were shoddy, but cheap. I saw the wives of British servicemen buying lampshades; the sight of British servicemen in full uniform in East Berlin was even more bizarre.

People on the whole looked poor and badly fed. Rather incongruous, then, were the expensive hotels near Friedrichstrasse Station, all serving drinks at exorbitant prices and clearly not aiming for a local clientele.

The vehicles in East Berlin were all Trabants and Wartburgs. Road signs indicated Warsaw, Prague, and all

points east. For me, exit back to the West was on the U'bahn. The train slowed down as we passed through lit but unused stations, staffed only by East German guards, before we arrived in West Berlin.

For my second trip into East Berlin I joined a sightseeing tourbus. We went through Checkpoint Charlie and an East German tourist guide came onto the bus once we had crossed the border. It was worth traveling this way not only to reduce the amount of walk-ing and for the convenience, but also to witness the sight of young East Berliners making rude gestures at rela-tively wealthy Western tourists.

Our bus took the party (largely consisting of Americans and Japanese) to the Soviet War Memorial, a number of sarcophagi commemorating those who died in World War II. Again, it was a reflection of the Soviet influence and their view of the war. As a party from the Soviet Union was standing to have its photograph taken, the younger Japanese in my group cavorted over the stones, laughing and giggling.

On board the bus we were told how rich East Germany was in all fields, and how such was the shortage of labor that a number of "guest workers"— from Mozambique, Vietnam, and all over Eastern Europe—had come to swell the workforce. Nowadays, accounts of racism in East Germany are commonplace, and the "guest work-ers" find themselves strangers in a strange land.

We visited the Pergamon Museum, which stands on Museum Island and is a wonderful example of classical archi-tecture. The ancient Pergamon altar stands proudly aloft inside.

On the way back an East German border guard searched the tourbus for dissident East Germans trying to flee to the West. He checked the rest room and used mirrors to scan the chassis. The journey back to the West struck home the differences between the two sides of Berlin. The cars were invariably

Volkswagens, Mercedes, and BMWs; the people were sleek and well dressed.

Of course, what split the city was the Wall. Near Checkpoint Charlie there were viewing platforms, from which it was possible to read the graffiti. There was a heavy covering of slogans such as "the Wall must fall," as well as the usual obscenities. I went to inspect the Wall near Schlesisches Tor in Kreuzberg. On leaving the U'bahn station I walked down the road for about half a mile, until my way was blocked by concrete, stark and unmarked, running across a major thoroughfare and splitting families, streets, and communities. The buses had to do a U-turn in order to retrace their route.

Now the Wall is no more and Berlin is again the capital of a united Germany. Already there is an architectural competition for the redevelopment of Potsdammer Platz (once No-Man's Land), which was effectively the crossroads of Europe. Trabant has been taken over by Volkswagen, and massive aid will go to the East.

In West Berlin, the sense of being an island has gone. Ironically, West Berliners complain about the worsening traffic conditions and crowding on the subway system. It is possible to detect just a tinge of regret concerning the passage of East and West Berlin into history.

GERMANY: TRAVEL NOTES

Sources of Information

German National Tourist Office, 747 Third Avenue, 33rd Floor, New York, NY 10017 (☎212/308-3300); 175 Bloor Street East, North Tower, 6th Floor, Toronto, ON M4W 3R8 (☎416/968-1570). Several German towns and cities publish access guides, and the tourist office can supply the addresses from which to order these. The office also provides a free leaflet, *Disabled Visitors to Germany*, which lists a number of sources of accommodation guides in Germany, plus addresses to write to for information on transport. An information request coupon is attached to the leaflet, and intending visitors can send it (with SAE and International Reply Coupon) to an organization in Germany (*BAG der Clubs Behinderter und ihrer Freunde e.v.*, Eupener Strasse 5, D-6500 Mainz; ☎6131/225514) that has a database containing over 6000 accommodation (all types) addresses worldwide. There is very little information available on what was East Germany.

Touristik Union International (TUI), Postfach 610280, 3000 Hannover 61 (☎0511/ 5670) has a centralized information bank on many German hotels and pensions that cater to the needs of disabled travelers or those with specific dietary requirements—not in specially designed and separate establishments, but within the mainstream of tourist facilities. The *TUI* can book you onto a package tour or organize rooms according to individual itineraries, taking into account each customer's needs, which are gauged from a questionnaire filled out before booking arrangements commence. Their services also include such details as providing suitable wheelchairs for train travel, the transportation of travelers' own wheelchairs, and the provision of transport at airports and stations.

Deutscher Paritätischer Wohlfahrtsverband, Brandenburgische Strasse 80, 1/41, Berlin (☎30/86 00 10). Local advice on choosing hotels and wheelchair rental.

Landesbeauftragter für Behinderte, An der Urania 12, D-1000 Berlin 30 (☎30/21 22 0). Local umbrella group of disabled and self-help organizations, useful for finding addresses of more specific groups.

GERMANY: TRAVEL NOTES

Tour Operators

Madge Davidson and her husband joined a *KD German Rhine Line* (170 Hamilton Ave., White Plains, NY 10601; ☎914/948-3600) cruise on the Rhine in May 1988. She uses a wheelchair and was particularly impressed with the crew, who were extremely helpful: "they never made me feel any different to the other passengers." One of the *KD* boats, the *Italia*, is equipped with a stairlift for wheelchairs; otherwise, you'll have to manage a flight of steps between decks. There are no special cabins or wheelchair-accessible bathrooms, but disabled passengers are frequently carried on these cruises. *KD* will organize a wheelchair at the airports on outward and return journeys.

Getting There

Lufthansa German Airlines has been recommended by some seasoned wheelchair travelers and they fly direct to Germany out of many US cities, and from Montréal, Toronto, Calgary, and Vancouver (Canadians may find it cheaper to fly via New York or London, however). There are several other possibilities—*Delta*, *United*, *Northwest*, *Continental*, *American*, *Air Canada*, and *Canadian*.

If **driving from Britain**, it's probably better to avoid the long Harwich–Hamburg crossing on the none-too-accessible *Scandinavian Seaways* ferry, *MS Hamburg*. Go for a shorter one, such as Harwich–Hook of Holland with *Sealink* (see p.234) and drive east through the Netherlands.

Transport

Deutsche Bundesbahn (**German Rail**) publishes a booklet, *Reiseführer für unsere behinderten Fahrgäste*, mostly in German but with a useful section of text in English and all symbols explained, listing services and facilities at stations; it's available at most ticket counters in Germany and from the tourist board offices. *German Rail* will arrange assistance at stations. Assistance is provided by the "welfare center" at each station; they must be notified a few days in advance. EuroCity and Intercity trains have reserved spaces for wheelchairs in the second-class compartments, with adapted restrooms on the newer rolling stock.

Facilities at German **airports** are generally very good. Somewhat dated information in German—a booklet published in 1986—can be obtained from *Arbeitsgemeinschaft Deutscher Verkehrsflughäfen* (ADV), 7000 Stuttgart 23 (☎711/79011). Frankfurt airport publishes a guide (*Frankfurt Airport Guide for the Handicapped*, 1990) in English for disabled passengers; ask the tourist board to send you a copy.

There is a list of **highway service stations** with facilities for disabled people, *Autobahn Service für Behinderte*, available in German only, from the tourist board or from *Gesellschaft für Nebenbetriebe der Bundesautobahnen* (Poppelsdorfer Allee 24, D-5300 Bonn); send an International Reply Coupon. Many Autobahn rest areas are now equipped with designated parking spaces, wheelchair-accessible telephones and restrooms. **Parking** spaces reserved for disabled drivers in towns may be used if a "Disabled" badge or sticker is clearly displayed. The *Frankfurt Airport Guide for the Handicapped* claims that "several rental car companies provide vehicles equipped with **hand control** devices"—their counters are located on the arrivals level in terminal section A—but this should be confirmed by International Reservations Offices in North America and reservations made well in advance.

Accommodation

There are several regional **hotel lists**, available from addresses in Germany (see tourist board leaflet), that use the wheelchair symbol. The **German Hotel Guide DEHOGA** (*Deutscher Hotelführer*) is published annually, obtainable from the tourist board (there is a small charge to cover mailing), and contains hotels that claim to have facilities for disabled guests, but the criteria for awarding the wheelchair symbol are not described. If you're passing through Britain first it's also worth picking up the *RAC* guides to European hotels and campgrounds (see France Travel Notes). As a general rule in Germany the large, modern hotels are mostly accessible.

The *German Automobile Club* (*ADAC*, Am Westpark 8, D-8000 München) publishes a **camping** guide (*ADAC Campingführer I + II*)

GERMANY: TRAVEL NOTES

which lists nearly 300 sites that are declared suitable for disabled people. The small number of contributors with experience of camping in Germany seem to bear out this optimism: Michael Turner, for example, comments favorably on German sites (p.517), and Jean Dyke, who is a full-time wheelchair user and travels around Europe in an adapted camper van, found the "best campground" in southern Germany, near Berchtesgarden—fully accessible facilities, with shower for the disabled in the same private room as the lavatory.

In Berlin, one **hostel** has been specially adapted for the handicapped: **Gästehaus der Fürst-Donnersmarck-Stiftung**, Wildkanelweg 28, 1/28 (☎30/40 20 12). It's essential to reserve well in advance.

Access and Facilities

The profusion of access and accommodation guides covering what used to be West Germany suggests that general awareness is good and that provision of information for disabled travelers is taken seriously. (At least for German-speaking disabled travelers—many of the publications are available only in German.) Tourists exploring the country by car and making as much use of these guides as their linguistic abilities allow are unlikely to encounter insurmountable difficulties.

In Berlin, facilities in the western area are better than those in the east. Most of the major western museums have wheelchair access, as do many other public buildings. The full color U- and S-Bahn map also indicates which stations are accessible by wheelchair.

But all the familiar problems—of only partially accessible public transit and public buildings, of high unemployment among disabled citizens (in spite of employment quotas and fines for employers who discriminate), of only half-hearted commitment to true integration of disabled persons into the community—are alive and well in Germany, and positively flourishing in the old East German territory.

The hope for improvement in these areas lies in large part with the independent living centers, which are located in a number of German towns. These organizations not only provide support, information, and advice to local disabled people, but also act as a mouthpiece, pressing for change.

Books

According to James Franey, the best book on East Berlin is *Zoo Station*, by Ian Walker (Abacus); *Berlin: Coming in from the Cold* by Ken Smith (Hamish Hamilton) is also good and the best guidebook is *The Real Guide: Berlin*.

TELEPHONE CODE:

From the US and Canada dial 011 (international code) and then 49 for Germany.

Poland

A Survival Guide for Poland

A sharp contrast to Annie Delin's Irish vacation (see p.130) was her trip to Poland in December 1989. Annie is just over three feet tall, and uses a child's stroller when traveling.

On the list of places suitable for vacations for disabled people, Poland should come a long way down. This is not to imply that there are countries of the world where disabled people mustn't venture, but it's worth knowing that if you decide to sample the culture, history, and political upheaval of this particular Eastern Bloc destination you should be ready for a hard time.

We traveled to Poland when the euphoria of a new democracy was sweeping Eastern Europe. The Berlin Wall had fallen, Czechoslovakia was swept by the fervor of revolution, Poland had elected Solidarity representatives to government.

Yet there was no party atmosphere in Poland—far from it. The Poles were grappling with forty percent per month inflation, food shortages and gluts, galloping pollution from the iron and steel works in Silesia . . . and no repressive regime to blame any of the problems on. These, added to the historical problems—the after-effects of Nazi occupation and wartime devastation, and insufficient investment in development since the war—make Poland one of the more depressed and depressing countries of Europe.

Two immediate difficulties face travelers with disabilities. One is that people in service positions (waiters, hotel staff, station porters, travel agents) are demoralized, undermotivated, and completely without any desire to do their jobs properly. Try, for example, booking a train ticket or requesting room service in scanty Polish—you are very unlikely to receive a sympathetic response.

The second problem is a purely logistical one. The condition of the roads and sidewalks does not make life easy for anyone in a wheelchair. On one occasion, when trying to cross a road at a crossing, we came up against chasms up to 8in across where the tram tracks had dislodged huge areas of cobblestone road and they had never been repaired. Lucky for us that the driver of the oncoming tram decided to stop and wait for us to finish struggling across.

Against all of this, twelve days spent in Poland at this particular crossroads in history made up probably the most educational trip I'd ever undertaken. I learned about the impact of great political upheaval on ordinary people, the realities of food and money shortages on a grand scale—even, on a trivial level, what it's like to be *really* cold.

I could not have absorbed the significance of the events plastered all over our papers during the past few months, as Eastern Europe changed its political structure, if I had not had the chance to meet people from both Poland and Czechoslovakia, with their very different accounts of what the changes meant.

"It was hard to imagine how things could be made harder than they already were for the Polish people"

For the Czechs, this was an exciting time. Strikes organized by students were actually having an impact, not just on people in the street but on the shape of government. Some of those I spoke to gave accounts of the spirit of cooperation and order within the university buildings during the strikes and sit-ins. There was a general feeling that we stood on the brink of a brave new era of freedom and enlightenment.

In Poland, without the safety net of government restrictions, food supply, working conditions, and money had gone haywire. Just days after we left the country, the new government announced that Poles would have to put up with a cut in wages of twenty percent in real terms. It was hard to imagine how things could be made harder than they already were for the Polish people.

The word "inflation" took on a new meaning. When you've been in a country in which you are completely unable to spend all your money while those around you desperately save for the things you ignore, a couple of cents on the price of a pint of milk at home seems pretty insignificant. (In most of

the hotels we stayed in, milk was unobtainable.)

When we arrived in Kraków, at an airport the size of some people's living rooms, we had our first "experience." Our plane was due to fly on to Warsaw and so, we discovered in the nick of time, was our luggage. Thanks to *British Airways*, our bags had been labeled "Warsaw" in spite of the fact that our tickets said "Kraków." As a result, my sister was required to climb into the hold of the plane and search out her own bags, while, below her, soldiers stood around smoking cigarettes.

Our three-night, off-season package gave us no choice of hotel but, in fact, the *Hotel Wanda* came well up to scratch. It couldn't have been much less central—well out in the seedy suburbs—but with taxi fares generally less than $1 we could have sailed in and out of town all day without making much of a dent in our spending money.

Kraków city center was once a gracious hub composed of medieval churches, a fine old market square, university buildings, monasteries, and the magnificent Wawel castle, where for ten years a certain Karol Wojtyła was bishop before moving on to better things in the Vatican. The graciousness which was Kraków, however, is now faded and scarred by decay. Acid rain is washing the faces off the stone saints; smog removes the painted facades of old buildings; the bugle call which traditionally greets visitors every hour from St. Mary's cathedral floats across a market square caked in grime.

In Kraków, we sampled for the first time the quality of service of *Orbis*— "Europe's oldest and most experienced travel agents, with sixty years' experience of service." There are *Orbis* offices everywhere, and they supply not only tourists but also Polish residents with train, bus, and airline tickets.

The first *Orbis* office we called at told us that they didn't sell train tickets, and directed us to a main office which was closed all day Saturday and Sunday. (We had to travel on Monday, and train tickets must be reserved 24 hours in advance.) Not daunted, we actually went to the train station and managed to buy our own tickets at the third office we lined up in. Later experiences of *Orbis* service included a 45-minute line, incorrect information about a suitable hotel, inability to provide any map of the city center, and being sent around the corner to a TV and radio store when we tried to change money at the exchange desk.

The central part of our vacation in Poland was attendance at a conference hosted by the University of Silesia in Szczyrk—a tiny mountain village close to the border with Czechoslovakia. This was our second visit to the Tatra mountains. Our first had been a day trip from Kraków to the little wooden town of Zakopane, where we were charmed by the intricate carvings on the houses, took a ride on a one-horse open sleigh, and envied the kids with their sled-runner "prams"—so much more practical than wheels when the snow is 18in deep and all the roads are ice-runs!

> *"We religiously followed wheelchair signs with arrows which plunged us into a dank, subterranean maze of urine-scented passages under the station"*

In Szczyrk we stayed in a triangular lodge built and run by the state for the miners of Katowice, for their relaxation and health—just as well when you consider the disgusting air of Katowice. Szczyrk is a truly beautiful location for a ski trip, not commercialized or noisy, still a home for wildlife, and intersected by paths cut out of the snow, along which you can ski, sled, or walk with ease. Once again, fitting runners to the wheels of your wheelchair would make life a lot smoother, but our hotel reception staff did lend us a sled!

From Szczyrk I spent one day visiting the Museum of Martyrdom at Auschwitz (Oświęcim on the Polish map). From Katowice, Kraków, or Szczyrk it is sensible for a group to take a taxi, even though there are trains and buses. The taxi cost $80 between four of us; for this we received door-to-door service on a visit which included two hours' travel and nearly six hours in the museum. Auschwitz is, for some people, an important feature of a trip to Silesia—certainly for me it was something of a pilgrimage. On the practical side, the guides are well used to helping people with disabilities, although nothing can overcome the fundamental discomforts of the buildings where the many exhibitions are housed. You will get cold and tired at practically any time of year.

When we returned to Katowice after the conference, we had to travel on to Wrocław by train. A very switched-on taxi driver took us to the disabled persons and baggage entrance to the station. We religiously followed wheelchair signs with arrows which plunged us into a dank, subterranean maze of urine-scented passages under the station. There were no directions of any kind, and were it not for the appearance of a baggage handler on an electric truck we would be there still. Charitably, we must suppose that the sign we couldn't read in Polish said "Disabled people should be accompanied by a member of the station staff."

A little more cautious about signs with wheelchairs on them, we found our own way out of Wrocław station—using the stairs. Our hotel, however, greeted us with a reassuring sign: "Hotel attends to inmates physically not fully proficient."

It seemed in general that Poland does make an effort to accommodate the needs of disabled people, with reserved parking spaces, a ramped route into some of the museums we visited, and station access routes. Still, we couldn't help noticing the reluctance of taxi drivers approached by my sister pushing me in a wheelchair, and the evident relief when I sprang out of the chair and it folded away to almost nothing before their eyes. We also asked ourselves what use it might be getting into an art gallery by ramps and then finding that only the scanty first-floor gallery was accessible because of internal staircases. Then again, is it always so much better at home?

On our last day we had reached Warsaw, where we fell into the arms of an unofficial mafia of station porters, taxi drivers, and hotel staff, all demanding tips in dollars or sterling. Our taxi driver attempted to charge twenty times the metered rate for the journey to the hotel (I am taking into account the fact that the fare for any trip should have been fifty times what the meter read, because of inflation).

A survival guide to any such visit to Poland should advise as follows. Do not expect your polite attempts to speak Polish to open any doors—a firm demand and a cool "thank you" will stand you in equally good stead. Accept the help of any member of the public, while resorting to station porters and the like only if you have to—they expect substantial financial reward. If you have vegetarian dietary requirements, get someone to write down the Polish for "I do not eat meat" before you travel, and place it in front of every waiter. Learn some German before you go—it is more widely spoken and understood than English. Take small bars of soap, chocolate, and coffee sachets—for yourself and to give to receptionists and cleaners in hotels.

And when you meet someone who wants to make friends and have a conversation, fall upon them with cries of joy. They will give you an insight into the country that you cannot get as a tourist, and they'll defend you against the waiters, the taxi drivers, the porters.

Czechoslovakia

A Seminar in Prague

Kent Kloepping, a wheelchair user, visited Prague in November 1991, before nationalist differences between Czechs and Slovaks came to a head in 1992. He describes his trip, which lasted only one week, as an experience he will never forget.

In the early summer of 1991, I had the good fortune and great pleasure of meeting a rather extraordinary gentleman from Prague, one Dr. Jan Halousek. Jan, who is Director of Foreign Operations for the Czechoslovakian Blind and Partially Sighted Union, was in America visiting a colleague of his in California, and had come to the University of Arizona to tour its program and facilities for students with disabilities.

During the course of his two-day visit, he asked me if I would be willing to attend a seminar in Prague late in the year and present a professional paper (it turned out to be two) even though they could offer no financial support for the trip. I had almost given up on the idea, but with encouragement from my wife (to get me out of the house for a week), our New Zealand and British traveling companions, and my brother's offer to go along to assist me (and serve as a drinking buddy), I left Tuscon, Arizona, on November 22, 1991, for Czechoslovakia, home of the duke of Bohemia, Good King Wenceslas.

I spent no time investigating accessible hotel/motel accommodations, transportation, or tourist attractions as, first, I wouldn't have known who to ask (the tourist board has no such information) and, second, Jan told me not to worry: "We'll see that you are taken care of!"

Indeed, that was the case. Accessible transportation is a key factor in traveling for wheelchair users, and, while public transit is available in abundance—taxis, buses, trains, streetcars—none of these systems, to my knowledge, is accessible for the wheelchair traveler. I was told that in the city of Prague there were only three wheelchair-accessible vans. Jan had one of the three vans for part of each of the six days that I was in Prague. I'm not sure how he managed it, but I assume he was given access to this precious resource because he was hosting an international meeting, and the availability of a lift-equipped van for tourists would be practically nil. The one "private" service that was provided to me on several occasions was a Volkswagen van with portable ramps—it worked fine as long as there was a "strong body" to push me up the steep incline into the bus. There may be other privately operated vehicles that would accommodate wheelchair users, but that remains for the next visitor to investigate.

"That single instance came to typify the helpfulness and courtesy that was the rule throughout my week in Prague"

The *Hotel Cristal*, our conference center and accommodation for the week, when first seen from the outside was an attractive sixteen-story, concrete and steel building. However, upon closer inspection it was in fact a very shoddily built, drab testimony to poor workmanship! We were told that it took eight years to build and had been a government headquarters "show-place." Two flights of stairs at the main entrance presented themselves, and I soon learned that this was the *only way* into the building! There was a very brief discussion (in Czech) among the group and then, unexpectedly, the van driver took charge! he tilted my manual chair back (front wheels up) and proceeded to hoist me unaided up some twenty steps. He wasn't even breathing heavy and, with a quick smile, he lit a cigarette, shook hands, and bounded back down the steps to his van on the way to his next pick-up. I had offered him a small tip which he adamantly refused; that single instance came to typify the helpfulness and courtesy that was the rule throughout my week in Prague.

In that brief encounter I caught a glimpse of the quality and character of the Czech people—their seriousness, sense of purpose, and willingness to take charge of the situation. These are a people who have endured a long history of oppression. With the conclusion of the Battle of White Mountain they lived under Habsburg domination from 1620 to 1918. The birth of the Czechoslovakian Republic in 1918 was to provide only a brief respite as, after only twenty-one years of freedom, the six-year reign of terror by the Nazis ensued. That was followed by another forty odd years of suffocation of the human spirit by the communist regime. While the country faces overwhelming economic challenges, and has massive rebuilding and modernization needs, the people seem to possess an indomitable spirit which has seen them through a history of confronting problems head-on—and solving them.

Back to the *Hotel Cristal*, and matters of wheelchair accessibility. Once up the two flights of stairs, access to a small restaurant, elevators to our eighth-floor room and other facilities was assured (I thought). The room was not very usable, and I had to transfer from wheelchair to straight-backed chair to use the lavatory and also to a separate room housing the sink and a shallow tub/shower combination.

The first evening in Prague, our hosts had arranged for a brief sightseeing trip to the center of the city and the Charles Bridge, so named after the country's most famous monarch, Charles IV (1316–1378), King of Bohemia, who was elected Holy Roman Emperor in 1346. It was a bitterly cold late afternoon but we trekked across the entire length of the bridge. Although closed to vehicles, large crowds stroll back and forth, stopping to inspect the wares of the innumerable entrepreneurs offering a variety of trinkets, jewelry, Russian hats, prints, food, and beverages. When I went sightseeing I did not eat or drink; Prague is a medieval city and many of the buildings are literally hundreds of years old. I had asked Martin, one of our guides, about the availability of public rest room facilities that would accommodate a wheelchair, and he replied, "I think there are none." He was right, there were none!

We spent one afternoon and evening on a planned tour of Prague. Most of the conference participants were taken by bus from one location to another, and although our hosts offered to have someone carry me on and off the bus at each stop (so I would be part of the group), I declined and rode instead in the comfort of one of Prague's lift-equipped vans. We spent considerable time in the Old City Central, a large plaza area that has received a good bit of renovation to buildings and streets; to my amazement, there were even a few curb-cuts. On reflection, it wasn't so surprising, considering that the Czechs are so energetic and forward thinking—facing massive reconstruction of their cities and transportation systems, they have made a start toward achieving accessibility.

> *"The elevator jerked and bounced and groaned to the next level, which was backstage and adjacent to the concert hall"*

Our tour guide pointed out the birthplace of Franz Kafka, just one door in a building facade of dozens of doors. We visited the oldest synagogue in Central Europe, dating back to the thirteenth century—I had to be lifted down four steps, but there were many willing helpers. Prague Castle, called Hradcany Castle, means something between a castle and a fortress—"a little of both," said the wife of our host. We didn't go into any of the buildings—many of them are Federal buildings as the seat of government is located within the complex. Accessibility throughout the exterior areas was level and paved. We visited the castle area very late in the afternoon and despite the cold, the fog, and the gloomy atmosphere there were large numbers of people in the area—I imagine the grounds are a priority visit for locals as well as tourists.

Part of the agenda for the conference participants during the week was attendance at a concert in one of Prague's magnificent old theaters. Although badly in need of major refurbishment, the grandeur and ornateness of the triple-balconied main concert hall was spectacular. The Czechoslovakian people love music; the tradition is strong throughout the country and state-supported schools of music flourished during the communist regime. Once again, gaining access to the theater required a major initiative to overcome the obstacles: first, locate someone with a key to unlock a huge wrought-iron door at the side of the building; next, drag the wheelchair over and around an accumulation of junk (old theater chairs, worn-out curtains, broken stage railings, light fixtures, ceiling tiles, and more), and negotiate six or eight steps to a tiny landing with a door to, I think, the first elevator ever built in Prague. Well, the elevator jerked and bounced and groaned to the next level, which was backstage and adjacent to the concert hall. What an experience! The concert was wonderful!

Our week in Prague was quite inexpensive. The hotel bill for my brother and I (six days) was 3100 *koruna* (Czech crowns), about $110 in November 1991. However, the *Hotel Cristal* is owned by the conference organizers, hence the very low bill. Rates for the more modern hotels tend to be high and can range from $100 to $300 per night. In general the food is good value; pork, beef, noodles, and soups are prevalent, and very nice meals, including drinks, were available for around $10. Czech beer is great: the name Pilsner, now applied to an entire class of light ales, originated in the Bohemian town of Pilsen. We encountered a good number of German tourists who validated the high quality of the Czech brews.

For the wheelchair traveler contemplating a visit to Czechoslovakia and adjoining countries, I suggest they think seriously about setting up transport arrangements through a service such as *Wheelchair Travel* (see England and Wales *Travel Notes*) and taking the vehicle across the Channel from England to the Continent. The other option would be to use a standard van with seats removed and portable ramps.

Notwithstanding all the unknowns, I would encourage anyone to visit this storied country and its competent, hospitable people. The countryside—as seen in a picture album I bought, and reported by Dr. Halousek—is lovely. Prague alone is worth the trip if you venture no further. Best time to travel is spring or summer as winters can be cold, damp, and foggy.

As a final thought, I believe it would be prudent to follow the unfolding of political events in Czechoslovakia. At the time of writing (1992) the news headlines speak of "regionalism" and the increasing impetus for dissolution of the Czechoslovakian state as the province of Slovakia seeks autonomy. My hope for the people of these historic lands—Bohemia, Moravia, and Slovakia—is that they can resolve their regional differences and direct their collective energies toward restoration of this beautiful country to its rightful place as a leader among the nations of the world.

The CIS

Art Appreciation in Moscow and Leningrad

In December 1988, Joy Schwabe traveled with three friends to Russia for a five-day tour. She is a "little person," just three feet tall, a coeliac, and at the time of the vacation had cataracts in both eyes.

The gluten-free diet was comparatively easy to cope with. Food is not of prime importance to me and, besides, the range of foods that I am allowed is quite comprehensive and I took special cookies with me. I can walk only a limited distance, so I travel with a child's stroller. I can manage a few steps if they are shallow. My friends knew of and understood my limitations; it required two people to overcome some of these, such as carrying me and my "pusher" up flights of steps.

We flew from Gatwick airport, a group of 29 plus tour manager and guest lecturer—the prime reason for the trip was to see art and architectural treasures. No special provisions had been asked for at the airport, and they proved unnecessary. I found the flight rather uncomfortable as I have a respiratory difficulty which worsens when I am sitting in a restricted position. But the cabin attendant was kind and attentive, providing two extra pillows which were a great help.

The passage through Moscow airport was slow. There were few carts and no porters, and we had no offers of help. However, no complaints—we had not asked for any special treatment. Our bus was waiting for us at the airport, and we were taken on a brief tour of Moscow before going to a hotel for a meal, prior to taking the overnight train to Leningrad.

First-class sleeping compartments had been booked for us and with two to a compartment we were very comfortable. A fully made-up bed was provided, together with tea and piped music. The heating was very efficient so we thoroughly enjoyed this part of the journey.

The view from the train was enchanting. It was almost unreal, straight out of *Doctor Zhivago*—brilliant moonlight sparkling on the snow, the silver birches and larches making wonderful groupings and patterns. I suppose it is a rare sight that absolutely matches up to one's preconceived ideas, but this scenery certainly did.

Our hotel in Leningrad was comfortable, with an elavator to all floors. I could not operate this by myself, so I was obliged to go about with one or other of my friends. I had to share a room because I am unable to manage most light switches and some door handles; if there is no stool or chair available I cannot even use the sink. We took a golf ball with us, as we'd been told that sometimes there are no plugs; in the event, our bath had a plug but the sink did not.

The hotel was well heated, as indeed were all the buildings we visited. In the public buildings, including museums and theaters, it is customary to leave one's outer clothes in the cloakroom. In the cloakroom of the Hermitage Museum I obviously brought out the attendant's motherly, or even grand-motherly, instincts—she gave me a piece of candy and patted me on the head (I am over seventy years old).

I am very interested in art, and had for many years wanted to visit the Hermitage. It was built by Catherine the Great as a private palace where she could go to escape the formality of court life. A very acquisitive lady, she began to collect works of art of many kinds. When she really got going, and was buying up as many European art collections as she could afford (of course, she had enormous wealth), the palace was enlarged.

The pictures which Catherine bought from the Walpole collection were of particular interest to me because the Walpole family house, Houghton Hall, is in Norfolk, not far from where I live. Among more than a hundred pictures purchased at that time from the Walpoles were two Rubens, four Van Dycks, and no fewer than nine Rembrandts. I do not know if the removal of any of these was responsible for the especially large silhouette of darker wallpaper in one of the Houghton rooms, but that's the sort of thing which fires my imagination. If I couldn't see the picture back at home, I'd have to travel to Russia.

The Hermitage not only houses pictures from earlier centuries but also offers a huge collection of modern art, with some of the very best works of the artists represented. Some of Matisse's most famous pictures are on show, as well as a comprehensive Picasso collection, Monet, Gaugin, Van Gogh, and many, many more—no wonder I couldn't wait to get there.

"I found myself hoisted aloft in my "pusher" and solemnly carried upstairs by two large men"

We were allowed to take my "pusher" into the building, but this was because it was a comparatively quiet time, out of season. What the ruling is about wheel-chairs I don't know. There were no wheelchair users there when we visited, and no chairs on view at the entrance, awaiting the casual visitor as one might expect in our museums or galleries. There are no elevators in the Hermitage, and it is a strange sight to see enormous and priceless works of art being manhandled all over the build-ing by the museum attendants; their experience worked in my favor, however, because when it came to nego-tiating the imposing staircase I found myself hoisted aloft in my "pusher" and solemnly carried upstairs by two large men.

The pictures were beautifully hung and the lighting was good. Of course, I was at a disadvantage, viewing from my peculiar angle and with cataracts, but if anyone had tried to describe the pictures to me I'd have bitten their ankles. It was somewhat unnerving for the person who was pushing me about, as I did occasionally stand on the seat of my stroller without warning.

We decided to have lunch and continue viewing later. There is a choice of cafeteria or restaurant. The stools were too high for me in the cafe-teria but we were allowed to eat our cafeteria meal in the restaurant. There are no packaged foods; fruit juices came in glasses and food was served straight onto plates, which we returned at the end of the meal; not a chip packet in sight.

> *"We only scratched the surface, and I think we all felt some sadness when we considered all the things left unseen"*

Among my lasting impressions of the former Soviet Union is the monstrous scale of the place—more noticeable than usual, for me! Red Square is huge, the colors of its buildings made more vibrant by the contrast with dazzling white snow. After seeing that we passed through vast, snowy wastes on our train journey, and then came Leningrad, the great Winter Palace and the Hermitage Museum. When visiting the Winter Palace we had to wear giant felt boots to protect the beautiful marble and marquetry floors. As these are made to fit over the largest size of boots, you can imagine what I looked like!

Although there was always a solution to the problems we encountered, such as the staircase and high stools in the Hermitage, we saw no wheelchairs and no facilities for wheelchair users—no adapted rest rooms, for example. We couldn't see the curbs for snow, so I don't know if these are lowered anywhere. The deep snow was no deterrent to us, as we were taken to our various destinations by bus. The entrance porch of one building was wet ice, so to prevent me falling (I was walking at the time) one of my friends put her bright woollen gloves on my feet.

We visited the Kirov ballet while in Leningrad and saw an evening performance of *The Nutcracker* by what seemed to be a young company. The colors of the interior of the theater are glorious—pale turquoise, gilt, and cream, like a scene from *Sleeping Beauty*. The Imperial Box is still there, no doubt used by state and visiting dignitaries. The theater has kept one tradition, that of promenading in the corridor during the interval—all miraculously going the same way round.

Of course, we only scratched the surface, and I think we all felt some sadness when we considered all the things left unseen. On the other hand we were well satisfied with what we had experienced, and not one of the sights was a disappointment to me.

Our return to Moscow was by plane, not nearly as romantic as the train journey. At Moscow airport we had a rather distressing wait in near darkness on some stairs, and the flight behind us was called first, with the result that we were badly jostled. The flight to London was comfortable enough and at Gatwick one of my friends and I were picked up by a buggy. We sailed past the other passengers, including our two friends, leaving them to battle with the luggage. There have to be *some* advantages to being "different."

EASTERN EUROPE AND THE CIS: TRAVEL NOTES

Sources of Information

IBUSZ, 1 Parker Plaza, Suite 1104, Fort Lee, NJ 07024; ☎201/592 8585 or 800/367-7878; and M/C79/50 5000 Airport Plaza Drive, Long Beach, Los Angeles, CA; ☎213/593-2952. The agents for the *Hungarian National Tourist Office* provides the only official literature for the countries of Eastern Europe in which any wheelchair symbols can be seen.

Tourist offices for **Poland** (342 Madison Ave., New York, NY 10173; ☎212/867-5011), **Czechoslovakia** (10 East 40th Street, New York, NY 10016; ☎212/689-9720) and the independent states that were the Soviet Union supply no specific information for disabled tourists.

Reliable information concerning transport, accommodation, and other facilities is difficult to obtain, and will only emerge as more disabled tourists explore these countries.

Tour Operators

The choice of package operators is narrower than for the rest of Europe, but there are enough ideas to tempt intrepid travelers. Approach travel agents confidently, state your abilities as well as your disabilities, and persuade them to work on the possibilities rather than concentrate on the obstacles. Independent travel is not impossible, and probably more rewarding, but most full-time wheelchair users will need help so take along some muscle.

For information on an operator offering tours for small groups to Hungarian lakes, national parks, and conservation areas (facilities for disabled people include adapted accommodation) contact *Rodata Rehabtours*, 1028 Budapest, Princeszer u. 14-26, Hungary; ☎1/176 5101 or 176 5555; fax 1/176 5755.

Getting There

United Airlines is probably your best bet for flights to Warsaw, Prague, Moscow, Budapest, or Bucharest; some route through German cities. *American* flies direct to Budapest. Wheelchairs are now available at Moscow, also at major Polish, Hungarian, and Czechoslovakian airports.

Transport

As Kent Kloepping points out, adapted transport is very difficult to get hold of in these countries. One alternative is to travel with a driver who doesn't need hand controls; *Hertz* has franchisees in Czechoslovakia, Poland, Bulgaria, Hungary, Romania, Estonia, and Russia, and in 1992 was negotiating agreements with representatives in Ukraine, Latvia, and Lithuania. Another option is to rent a standard van and make some basic modifications (seat removal, use of a portable ramp). It may also be possible to take adapted vehicles from other European countries across the borders (see *Travel Notes* of specific countries and contact the relevant operators). *Wheelchair Travel* (see England and Wales *Travel Notes*) has no objections to the use of their lift-equipped vehicles in Eastern Europe in principle, but they are not unnaturally concerned at the lack of facilities in case of a breakdown—travelers must be aware that there is not the same network of gas stations and services as in other parts of Europe, and anyone considering such a trip should contact the manager, Trevor Pollitt, well in advance to discuss their plans. In the end, the extra insurance costs, not to mention the cross-Channel fares, may prove prohibitive for many.

Accommodation

The *RAC European Hotel Guide* (see France *Travel Notes*) lists a few possibilities: in Bulgaria, the *Sheraton Sofia Balkan* (Sofija, ☎2/876541); in Czechoslovakia, the *Kyjev* (Bratislavia, ☎7/52041), the *Slovan* (Brno, ☎5/745455), and the *Panorama* (Prague, ☎2/416111); in Poland, the *Holiday Inn* (Warsaw, ☎22/200341). The *RADAR* guide (see England and Wales *Travel Notes*), *Holidays and Travel Abroad* (see *Books*, p.590), has a few more offerings in Poland, Hungary, and Czechoslovakia. The *RAC Camping and Caravanning Guide* lists only one campground in Eastern Europe with facilities for disabled people—*Yacht Camping*, in Balatonalmádi, Hungary (☎80/38906).

Mobility International News (spring 1992) reports that an accessible house is available to rent in a small Hungarian town called Gárdony,

EASTERN EUROPE AND THE CIS: TRAVEL NOTES

on Lake Valence, less than a mile from the hot springs. It has five double rooms (two of which are wheelchair-accessible), one single room, four bathrooms, and a fully fitted kitchen; there's a small yard and a large terrace. Prices are 120DM (around $80) per day, or 100DM per day plus holiday tax if there are at least two disabled persons in the group; minimum period of rental is one week. Contact Mozgássérültek Fejér Megyei Egyesülete, Székesfehérvár, Pf 55, H-8003 Hungary (fax 22/55253).

Access and Facilities

Although there are a few showpiece medical centers at the forefront of treatment of certain disabilities (such as the Peto Institute in Hungary), and a few reports of good accessibility (for example from a blind traveler who found public transit in Budapest easier to use than London's buses and trains), the general picture is pretty grim for the disabled Eastern European: scant regard to access by architects of public buildings; tortuous procedures for acquiring special aids and appliances—most have to be imported; wheelchairs and work very hard to come by; general preference for segregation rather than integration of disabled people into the community; in Romania the treatment of disabled citizens has only recently come to light, and is summed up by one word—neglect.

In **Czechoslovakia** under communism, private charities were banned, with the intention that the state would provide for any ill or disabled citizens. But the state had neither the funds nor the drive to do this. Disabled people became social outcasts, the facilities in their institutions inadequate and antiquated. Much has changed in the wake of the recent political upheavals. In 1990 Olga Havel, the wife of Vaclav Havel, set up a "Goodwill Committee," whose aims included the revival of charities and the eradication of the fear and ignorance that resulted in society's rejection of people with disabilities. With the help of TV programs and public meetings the committee raised awareness, put disabled groups in touch with each other, and initiated fund-raising projects. In 1991 the *Federation of Disabled Persons in Czechoslovakia* was set up and is reported to

work from large, accessible offices in Prague (Karlínské namestí 12, CS 186 03 Prague 8; ☎2/235 6592); areas of concern include social rehabilitation projects, international relations with other disability organizations, and maintenance of a database of information for disabled people; there is also an accessible room above the offices, for anyone on a short visit to the city (contact Dr. Miroslav Luczka, Secretary General, at the above address).

In the Soviet Union, disabled people were kept under wraps for years. There is a chronic shortage of wheelchairs and other basic equipment in the newly formed **Commonwealth of Independent States**. Disabled people receive tiny allowances and pensions and most cannot find employment. With Mikhail Gorbachev's arrival on the scene, charities were allowed to operate and all disabled people allowed to form societies (in the past, only blind and deaf people could do this). The president of *APPAREL* (*Association of Young Disabled People KMO*, 7/8 Bogdan Khmelnitsky Street, 101846 Moscow; ☎095/2068 542), Alexei Kupriyanov, has become a new committee member of *Mobility International*, and in 1992 there were exciting plans for youth exchanges with Armenia, Belorussia, Georgia, Russia, and Ukraine. But conditions for disabled people living there remain harsh.

Life is no easier in **Poland**. Annie Delin's account gives some hints for surviving as a disabled visitor, but Poles with disabilities need more than a survival guide. Again, state benefits are low and work hard to find; medicines and appliances are scarce; the list goes on.

To keep up with developments in Eastern Europe (as well as other parts of the world), subscribe to *Mobility International News* (228 Borough High Street, London SE1 1JX; ☎071/403 5688) and *Disability Now* (see England and Wales *Travel Notes*). See also Susan Sygall's account, in *Travel, Tours, and Cruises*, for another perspective on travel in these parts.

TELEPHONE CODES:

From the US and Canada dial 011 (international code) and then 7 for anywhere in the former USSR, 42 for Czechoslovakia, 48 for Poland.

PART FOUR

MEDITERRANEAN EUROPE

Introduction

The kindness of both **climate** and **people** is a strong theme in these reports of vacations in Mediterranean countries. In almost every account there is acknowledgement of friendly, unpatronizing hospitality, advice, or physical help from the locals. The lure of guaranteed sun is strong, but those who find extreme heat intolerable can also be satisfied, either by heading for higher ground or by traveling out of season. The benefits—of spending all day out in the fresh air without feeling chilled, of exercising rarely used limbs in warm and buoyant sea water, of slowing down mentally to the pace of life in warmer climes—are obvious.

Another big draw for European vacationers, or for those who stop over in northern Europe, is the low cost and speed of **travel to the south**—no expensive long-haul flights to different time zones, less outlandish travel insurance premiums to pay, and for many people the freedom and independence of using their own transport, adapted to their needs. For those who fly, of course, the journey may be lengthened by delays at airports at peak times, but this is an occupational hazard for all travelers.

For **North American visitors** to Mediterranean Europe the options have increased considerably in recent years, with more direct charters and scheduled services to choose from. In some cases, particularly for Canadians, savings can be made by flying to London and picking up a cheap charter flight from there. The majority of European airlines handle disabled passengers smoothly, and facilities at most major Mediterranean airports are adequate, with full assistance given where required, even if methods sometimes seem a little primitive.

The most competitve **airfares** can be searched out via the Sunday newspaper travel sections, good travel agents, discount flight specialists, discount travel clubs, or airline ticket consolidators. And there are numerous package deals for those who decide against independent travel—again, refer to *Practicalities* (p.558) for advice on getting the best out of tour operators, travel agents, and airlines.

Weighing against the relative ease of getting there is the high cost of **getting about** once there. Public transportation in these countries is generally for the fit and agile—there are few concessions to the disabled traveler, although some people do manage, with help which is usually cheerfully given. Car rental is expensive and hand controls are rarely available; *Hertz* is again the shining exception to this, with adapted cars available at all corporate locations in mainland Spain. Although taxi rates in most places are relatively low, fares soon mount up.

What you lose on transport, however, may be made up on the food and drink budget; the cost of eating and drinking well is still low in many areas, particularly away from the tourist honeypots. **Food**—fresh, simple, and delicious—features often as a highlight of the vacation in these accounts; even those on restricted diets find no difficulties in countries where eating is a pleasure, to be drawn out, and every meal an occasion. Being able to eat outside adds to this pleasure, especially for the wheelchair user accustomed to maneuvering in crowded restaurants and coping with steps at the entrances.

Another attraction for visitors is **variety**: there is more to Mediterranean Europe than sun and sand. Nightlife can consist of tranquil meals under the stars, or all-night partying in bars and nightclubs. Lazing on the beach can be combined with escapes into remote rural villages, or visits to ancient sites and historic buildings: in Spain the magnificent Moorish palaces; in Italy the feast of buildings from almost every architectural era; in Greece the historic sites spanning four millennia of civilization. Access to many of these places is difficult and rest rooms for the disabled visitor are few and far between, but this is not a problem peculiar to Mediterranean Europe, and with the best will in the world it would be impossible to make a craggy Greek island into a paradise for wheelchair users.

It's probably fair to say that the countries covered in this section are behind those of northern Europe in terms of provision for disabled tourists; indeed, there is widespread ignorance of the fact that people with disabilities *do* travel, particularly in the more remote areas. Attitudes to disability vary from friendly indifference in Rome to muttered prayers in Cyprus, but always there is kindness, always an offer of help without embarrassment to either party. And there *are* hopeful signs, such as the accessibility project in Venice and an increasing number of new hotels offering rooms for disabled clients. At the time of writing, there are certainly grounds for optimism in Spain, where facilities for disabled visitors were incorporated at the two big events of 1992—the Paralympic and Olympic Games in Barcelona, and Expo in Seville— although there were glaring gaps in the provision of accessible transport, and accessible hotel rooms showed signs of being specially designed *for*, rather than *by* (or at least in consultation with) people with disabilities.

All things considered, the barriers that prove too much for the disabled traveler in Mediterranean Europe are surprisingly few. If disabled vacationers continue to be undeterred by these and their numbers increase, then it's probably not hopelessly unrealistic to expect a gradual growth of facilities, in the same way that earlier waves of tourists have been adapted to and provided for.

Spain

Poppies in Spain

Peter and Jill Rann took their two small children to the Costa Brava in 1983. Peter has an unremitting form of multiple sclerosis and is completely wheelchair-bound.

If it hadn't been for an attack of pneumonia we might never have gone abroad again. Young children and multiple sclerosis put a stop to any thoughts of travel outside Britain. But after a long dark winter and three weeks in hospital for Peter with pneumonia, we wanted some fun and sunshine.

So in May the four of us set off for three weeks in a Costa Brava that not everyone sees. The fields were awash with wild flowers, including the scarlet poppies of my childhood; now almost disappeared from Britain, they were everywhere in northern Spain. There were few tourists then, so we were greeted like the first swallows of summer. The beaches were clean and empty, and the shopfronts smelled of fresh paint. And if the sea was a bit cold for the adults, that made Peter— too disabled even to want to swim— equal.

But back in March we looked at our restrictions. Peter was unable to walk or stand, and his arm weakness meant that he needed help to cut his food and sometimes feeding at the end of a meal. The children were aged three and six. Beyond everything, there were the finances: after three years on income support our savings were gone, so we

did something terribly rash—we paid for as much as we could by credit card.

We planned the trip around our car, though it did not honor the trust we placed in it, and for four days each way it became our little world. It was small and we were packed tight. The children lived in the back with buckets of building blocks and potato chips, wedged in by "Green Hippo" and "Blue Blanket." There they fought (mostly), played, and slept, and learned to say "Yes, lovely" without looking up as we passed spectacular snow-tipped mountains or golden eagles on the high plains stretch between the Atlantic and the Mediterranean. We had our tapes in the front, though the sound of that vacation will always be an old recording of "Mr. Men" stories, "Silly old Wizard. . .."

The car, bought through the UK's *Motability* scheme and still under warranty, broke down two days before our departure date. The garage we were contracted to specialized in splendid apologies and poor repairs. Collecting it the day before leaving, we sat open-mouthed as the manager cheerfully explained that due to some hitch at the factory we would have to drive without keys, stopping and starting with a screwdriver. This was to cause dark looks at Spanish gas stations, which are all full service only.

We just about made it home before all the electrics blacked out. A desperate telephone call caught the departing manager who, kinder than he was proficient, gave up his evening to finding the fault—a mysteriously unlisted fuse. Nothing was going to stop us now, we'd remembered to pack the wheelchair pump and Peter's drugs, plus all those extra odds and ends which you need if disabled.

We set off the next day but by the time we had crossed town the car was faltering and within 100 miles the engine died, with luck as we passed a highway service station. We ground to a halt outside a repair shed and a mechanic coming off duty saw our desperate faces and the Orange Badge. He poked and scraped under the hood, talked of distributors, refused payment, and said "Get high-octane gas, but that'll see you to Plymouth." And so it did, plus a couple of thousand miles and back to our front door, admittedly with a top speed of 58mph but at least we got to look at the scenery. Apart from an earth-mover knocking us off the road on our way to buy fresh Spanish bread one morning, there was no more trouble with the car.

After an overnight stay in a family room at the *Holiday Inn*, which was one of the few hotels in Plymouth to cater to wheelchair users, we used a *Brittany Ferries* 24-hour crossing to northwest Spain to save us the long drive through France. Traveling in May gave us the advantage of out-of-season prices and a special offer—two free nights in a *parador*, the state-run Spanish hotels in fabulous historic buildings.

The ferry was marvelous and the staff were exceptionally helpful. I'd forgotten that I get seasick and couldn't leave the cabin, reserving my energy for Peter's needs—meals, assistance to the toilet, and physiotherapy. The crew knew our situation and looked after Amy and Tom, who ran free and happy all over the ship. The ship's movie theater had well-designed seating and Peter was able to enjoy films in comfort for the first time in years. (Sadly, the *Bretagne*, which has since taken over the Plymouth–Santander route, has two movie theaters only accessible by steep stairs; but there are elevators to all decks, accessible rest rooms, and special cabins for disabled passengers.)

I was nervous about driving in Spain; before our trip I had never driven at night, on a highway, or on the "wrong side of the road," and I'd passed my test only two months ago. Peter had lost all use of his legs and had limited arm movement. In fact, my inexperience gave him the chance to drive again: although I turned the wheel, he talked me through the entire journey, including his bad driving habits such as passing by slipping through the L-shape of a truck tortuously negotiating a tight bend near Santander.

> *"Arriving at our destination . . . at nearly midnight, we found that I'd left the address of our villa in London"*

We'll never forget the luxury of arriving that first evening at our *parador*, a rosy brick building in gardens with fine views. The children, released from the back seat, ran to the playground. The hotel had no special thoughts for the disabled, but apart from two steps at the front and an inaccessible lounge it proved perfect because of the large scale on which it was built. It had elevators and a huge bathroom with great fluffy towels. For me the floor would not stop moving, a strange aftereffect of the ferry crossing, but we slept like logs and awoke in the morning to geese cackling in a small yard across the road. Breakfast was extraordinary (we were last, of course, after the long process of getting Peter ready for the day): the table was arranged with rings of cakes and brioches, and the children were given something like hot chocolate Juncket to drink. It was all both very comforting and very foreign, after a journey more fraught than expected.

Out of season, the Spanish highway across the country is almost deserted, with the trucks taking alternative routes to avoid the tolls. We trundled at 58mph past the foothills of the Pyrenees to the north and saw Zaragoza—half medieval turrets, half highrises—shimmering on the distant plain. Arriving at our destination, Estartit, in the dark at nearly midnight, we found that I'd left the address of our villa in London.

"We were led with blue lights blazing, through red traffic lights, right across Santander"

By sheer luck the owner of the first bar we went into knew our landlady, who was also a singer in the summer season, and left his bar to lead us to the villa. On our journey home, I'd unforgivably done the same thing with our overnight *parador* in Santander. There we asked at the fire station (Peter thought they'd know all the hotels because of fire checks) and were led with blue lights blazing, through red traffic lights, right across Santander. Disability can bring some rather special experiences as well as the more dreary quests for rest rooms.

The villa, which we'd seen advertised in our local newspaper, had some drawbacks. It was small and furnished with awful mattresses and excruciating armchairs. But the personality of the owner, who lived upstairs, made up for this. She was a retired English actress, whose magnificent bosom had caused car crashes in her youth. She threw mats on the old enemy gravel, enter-

tained the children while we slept late in the morning, took us out to dinner and quietly spooned the regional sheep's milk pudding into Peter's mouth when he became tired. Amy and Tom loved the villa so much that they sometimes refused the beach, preferring to play with our landlady's collection of pets—many dogs, a monkey, and a parrot—or to net butterflies in the lane at the back.

The local beach was wide and sandy but a little breezy; we drove miles through the pretty countryside exploring hilly towns and finding new bays and fishing villages. If a beach was inaccessible people would always help if asked, though they were often too shy to volunteer. At first we were uncomfortable at the locals' tendency to stare at us but we later learned that the Spanish don't have a tradition of vacationing away (who needs it with their wonderful climate?) and they thought us mad to travel with small children, never mind disabilities.

We found the climate in May just warm enough and the sun strong enough to burn quickly if we weren't careful. We ate out cheaply some evenings in an uncrowded restaurant overlooking the harbor. Simple fish, paella, roast pork, and salad, escalopes, or pasta did not unnerve the children. We visited a local potter and sculptor, a small farmer who lived in a series of cement forms which he'd created—his car was garaged in a large concrete dinosaur.

We had to cope with difficulties. Peter wouldn't drink during part of the day to avoid searching for rest rooms and we carried a bottle for emergencies. If disabled you have to plan harder than most; you are not allowed the indulgence of forgetting vital equipment or leaving things to the last minute, at least in theory. But disasters fuel one of the best parts of any vacation—recounting it afterward. After all, no one really wants to hear what a wonderful time you had.

In fact, we are left not with a catalogue of woes, nor with a credit card debt (help is available from many sources, in this case mainly a charity, but the government can also help, relatives may chip in, or try auctioning something that you can live without) but with very rosy memories—and the photos don't betray them.

Lessons in Communication

Julie Smethurst's first experience of vacationing abroad alone, in July 1989, was arranged by ONCE, the Spanish National Organization of the Blind, a care foundation dedicated to improving the quality of life for all disabled people.*

I have found that one of the greatest pleasures of traveling alone is that I almost always get into conversation with the most interesting people. From its very beginning my first solo trip abroad proved to be no exception: by the time I reached Birmingham airport I had already met a West Indian who was spending three months in England studying agriculture, and a Liverpudlian whose sister lives within a stone's throw of my parents back in Yorkshire. These encounters, plus a straightforward journey to the airport, augured well, and my spirits were high as we soared through the sunshine, bound for Barcelona.

There I was met by Esther, one of the ten "hostesses" whose job it would be for the next ten days to help the visually handicapped members of our party in any situation where sighted assistance

Julie has also written about her travels with sighted companions in the Greek Islands (p.320), and the two pieces make an interesting contrast.

was necessary. I was next introduced to Juan Jesus Torres, like myself totally blind, and the organizer of the whole project. As we drove down the coast to Segur de Calafell, I tried to convey to Juan and Esther how excited I was about the trip and how happy I felt about this my second visit to Spain. Luckily their English was far superior to my Spanish, so they were able to come to my rescue when vital but unfamiliar words eluded me.

"I encountered no other English people until I returned to Barcelona airport"

Although this vacation, about which I was waxing so enthusiastic, was primarily geared to the needs of visually disabled people, a number of fully sighted friends and relatives were also present. The party was international, with visitors coming from as far away as Japan and Norway. I was somewhat daunted to discover that I was the only English participant; indeed, I encountered no other English people until I returned to Barcelona airport on my homeward journey.

Juan's perfect understanding of what might present difficulties for a blind person meant that practical concerns had been well thought out in advance, thus minimizing our anxiety about them. He had chosen a small hotel whose layout was easy to assimilate, and the first activity on my arrival was a conducted tour with Esther. This included not only learning the way around the interior of the hotel, but also such minute yet important details as the location of light switches, elevator buttons, and those eminently breakable tooth-glasses, which often balance precariously on the end of a glass shelf and are the bane of my life when exploring a hotel room without sighted help.

> **"As with many other aspects of life, the Spaniards seem to treat blindness in a much more relaxed, laidback manner than do the English"**

Even at this early stage I was greatly impressed by the hostesses' attitude: while offering us the most thorough and constructive help they never for a moment patronized or underestimated our capabilities. They and the hotel staff demonstrated clearly what I am coming to regard as the "Mediterranean" approach to visually impaired visitors: very helpful, very thoughtful, but absolutely matter-of-fact. As with many other aspects of life, the Spaniards seem to treat blindness in a much more relaxed, laid-back manner than do the English. This produces—in me, at any rate—a reciprocal feeling, so that I am more at ease and less inhibited than when among strangers at home.

Naturally enough, Juan had not underestimated our collective independence either, and the program was structured so as to give us the maximum amount of freedom—including freedom from anxiety. The main responsibility for achieving this marvelously Utopian aim fell to the hostesses, who worked very hard as guides, interpreters, and troubleshooters. They were always there and on the lookout in case they were needed, yet they also managed to integrate and become our friends, too. It would have been so easy for them to band together, and for an "us and them" situation to develop—the carers and the cared-for. But their warm and spontaneous manner, and the fact that they seemed to be enjoying themselves and having just as good a time as we were having, set us all at our ease.

Notwithstanding all this, I don't think my first night in Segur was exactly what the organizers had intended. After a dinner over which I made the acquaintance of Wolfgang, Lydia, and Meike from Germany, we were all asked to introduce ourselves to the party in our own language. In the ensuing hubbub of conversation two of the hostesses approached me: there was a problem, they said; would I mind changing rooms for one night only? Inwardly a little reluctant—I'd just got nicely unpacked—I nevertheless complied, and with their help moved my things across the landing to a room already occupied by Nabuko (from Japan) and Meike. I then retired to the bar.

It was quite late when I returned to find my two roommates asleep. The room was stiflingly hot, and examination of the window revealed that the outside metal shutter had been lowered to within six inches of the floor. I didn't relish trying to raise it—the noise would probably disturb the others and anyway I wasn't sure how the thing worked. I lay in my folding bed, trying not to toss, for with every movement it let out groans and squeaks of protest. Finally, in desperation, I took to the floor and spent the remainder of the night there. It was cool to the touch and made no noise, however much I wriggled and fidgeted. I placed my pillow as close to the few inches of fresh air as possible, and slept intermittently. Not quite what the hotel management had in mind for its guests, I imagine, but I've slept in and through much worse conditions, and it was a good ice-breaking story to tell at breakfast!

It was at mealtimes that the international dimension of the vacation really asserted itself. In the early days the hostesses did their best to find us tablemates who had at least one language in common. But as time went by and we all knew each other better they linked us up with friends. For example, it became known that I wanted to improve my Spanish, and increasingly I found myself sharing a table with some of the Spanish visitors. One particular lunchtime stands out in my memory as a perfect example of the meeting of nations: besides myself at our table there was my roommate Ana Maria (Argentinian but now living in Sweden), Nathalie (French), and Elisa (Italian). Under such circumstances it was hard to know which language to adopt and we found ourselves conversing in a curious fragmentary mixture!

Vacationing began in earnest on the first morning, with most of us eager to go to the beach. Relays of hostesses made it possible for us to come and go more or less as and when we wanted to, and a large area of beach had been cordoned off for our exclusive use. I took a long swim in the delightfully warm sea and discovered that a rope extended far out into it, acting literally as a "landmark" when we wanted to relocate our party. Then, with the help of one of our attentive hostesses, I found my things and settled to the pleasurable business of drying off in the sunshine.

"Where music is concerned language barriers cease to be important"

It was at this point that I met Pilar and Tere, and immediately embarked on what became my daily impromptu Spanish lesson. From then on Pilar always sought me out after the morning swim and we ensconced ourselves in the shade to study idioms and for me to copy down quantities of irregular verbs. I'd tell her in English what I wanted to say and we'd then translate into Spanish. Sometimes, however, our conversations became so involved and interesting that we hadn't the patience to wait while I laboriously attempted the translation; on these occasions we

simply relied on Pilar's excellent command of English.

Juan had made every effort to overcome the problems presented by language barriers. All the hostesses spoke at least one language in addition to Spanish, and several spoke two or three. During a quite formal discussion about employment they actually worked as interpreters, while we listened in on the Simultaneous Translation Facility provided by the *ONCE* Educational Resource Center. Many of the participants themselves spoke more than one language and it is surprising how many tactile signals can be devised. We found that for some—the Japanese, for example—who were using a second language (English) as their main communication medium, English spoken with a non-English accent could be quite difficult to understand. I was amused and somewhat intrigued to find myself translating for them from quite complex English spoken with, say, a Spanish accent, to quite simple English spoken with an English one.

Where music is concerned, however, language barriers cease to be important. There were several excellent singers, guitarists, and pianists among the participants and many an evening ended with a group on the terrace—or once on the beach—making music into the small hours. On other evenings there was live music for dancing; one particular musical highlight was the visit of a well-known student group, who played and sang for us during dinner and then stayed on to share a few more beers with us while we all continued the singing late into the night.

One of the most delightful evening events was the so-called "Dinner on the Beach," which took place behind the Yacht Club on a large terrace overlooking the sea. We feasted on fresh sardines barbecued over the fire, fresh mussels, huge hunks of bread, potato salad, and as much *sangría* as we wanted. This was followed by enormous slices of watermelon and a typical

Catalan drink called *ron cremat*—a sort of rum punch *flambé*. A Catalan folk group played and sang for us during the meal then afterward for dancing, and, as we were leaving, the Yacht Club presented each of us with a *poron* of Muscatelle wine.

Juan had tried hard to include some "new experiences" in the program and one of these was the opportunity for us to learn flamenco dancing. The spot was a club at Villanova—about fifteen minutes' drive from Segur—and after some champagne, dry sherry (billed as "typical Andalucian wine"), and splendid entertainment, the professionals and hostesses took us in hand and did their best to teach us the rudiments of the dance. I can now say that I have rarely tackled anything so energetic or exhausting as ten minutes of flamenco!

Segur de Calafell is a typical Spanish "summer village," where Spaniards go to spend their vacations and where the wealthier ones keep summer houses. The town of Calafell itself lies some miles inland, and one evening Ana Maria and I, together with Esther and some other Spanish friends, made an abortive attempt to visit the Roman remains there. After a lengthy wait for the bus, we gave up and went for a walk in the smart area of Segur, with its imposing houses, large gardens, and parkland. As an inveterate seeker after authenticity, I was particularly thrilled by the experience which followed.

> **"It is amazing how close a bond of friendship can be forged in ten short days"**

On our walk we met Marie-Carmen—one of our party—and her friend Jaime, both exercising their guide dogs. The upshot was an invitation for us all to go to Jaime's summer house for drinks. Via Esther I explained what a special pleasure it was for an English person to visit a Spanish home. After that, Jaime's wife gave me a thorough conducted tour of this palatial establishment: I explored every room, I examined all the fruit ripening in the garden, and I inspected the soccer and basketball areas, where the children of this large family were playing noisily.

All too soon the final-night party was upon us. I was one of the last to leave Segur, which was nice because it meant I could enjoy the pleasures (and share the sorrows) of this last social get-together without having to worry about my packing or the catching of an early-morning flight. Many addresses, gifts, and promises to keep in touch were exchanged; many warm farewells were said, and not a few tears shed. It is amazing how close a bond of friendship can be forged in ten short days. As the various parties left, the hotel became quiet. Meals took on a calm gentility distinctly absent from our riotous lunches and dinners. It was as if all concerned were drawing a deep breath after the onslaught of a whirlwind.

Reflecting on a vacation which offered me many new sensations, I have now discovered another advantage of solo travel: when one is alone among a group of strangers one *has* to make the effort to form new friendships, thus extending one's circle in new and potentially interesting directions. There is nothing better than sharing a vacation's rich harvest of experience with a trusted and like-minded friend, but sharing experiences with a whole new set of friends is just as exciting and rewarding. It is important that disabled people, like non-disabled people, should have the choice of traveling and vacationing independently if that is what they wish to do. Juan and *ONCE* have taken a major step toward making this possible for visually impaired people, and I very much hope that others will follow their lead and provide more such opportunities. If there was one Spanish word which we all learned and remembered during our vacation, it was *Vamos!* (Let's go!)—need I say more?

The Au Pair Network

In 1970, at the age of 37, Jean Dyke was told she had multiple sclerosis (MS). Over the next ten years her mobility became progressively restricted and she is now confined to a motorized wheelchair which she operates with her chin. In 1988 Jean and her husband Stanley traveled in an adapted VW bus to the Navarra region of northern Spain.

Over the years we've had a number of au pairs from many different countries helping in our house; although I'm able to move around the house in my wheelchair, I rely on others for almost everything else. Since there is such close contact between the girls and myself, most have become part of the family and many keep in regular contact with us. When Stanley retired we accepted invitations to stay with two of our recent au pairs, Isabel and Fernanda, in Spain.

We discovered that campers and motor homes could be purchased free of tax by disabled people; servicing and extra fitments are also exempt. After a few months we decided on a VW and had the vehicle fitted with a permanent ramp for the wheelchair and clamps inside to secure the chair when we were mobile. A number of other features made the bus ideal: a swivel passenger seat, central heating, and a portable toilet. This last was to prove invaluable during the drive through France—although all the campgrounds we stayed on were well maintained, they rarely had special facilities for wheelchairs.

So that our visit coincided with the annual festivals, we planned our trip for August–September and took the less busy ferry route from Poole to Cherbourg—the channel ports are often congested in the summer.

After an unhurried journey through France and across the magnificent Pyrenees, we descended into Pamplona, the capital of the Basque territory of Navarra.

The city has retained much of its original charm, so that it has the feel of a much smaller place. Many of the old streets are very narrow, with most of the older buildings formed around attractive courtyards. The skyline is also relatively uninterrupted, unlike many other Spanish cities.

There are many churches, the typical bullring, and a beautiful Gothic cathedral to admire, as well as one of Hemingway's old haunts—*Marceliano*. The bar is full of character, a "spit and sawdust" place in one of the oldest parts of the city center. It was a bit of a struggle with the wheelchair, because of cobblestones and uneven steps, but with Stanley's expert handling and maneuvering we managed.

> *"The phrase Invito yo, roughly translated as "I'll get it," invariably beats you to the bar"*

Just outside of Pamplona there are some excellent sights, in particular the spectacularly set Monasterio de San Salvador de Leyre, which overlooks the artificial lake, Embalse de Yesa. A few miles south is the castle of Javier, birthplace of Saint Francisco Xavier. It is of the fairytale kind and intact, but steps have to be tackled!

The real charm of Pamplona, however, is supplied by the people, who display admirable patience toward "interested" foreigners, not to mention great generosity. The phrase *Invito yo*, roughly translated as "I'll get it," invariably beats you to the bar. It is unusual to find so many people proud to offer better than professional explanations of their traditions, culture, sights, and cuisine.

Isabel's parents gave us their wooden summerhouse for the duration of our stay. This was ideal as it was close to the city center but secluded and with a small attractive garden. From here Stanley could easily take me in the wheelchair to all the sights of the town, as well as to our evening entertainments with our hosts and other friends. The climate was perfect at that time of year—constant sunshine but not insufferably hot because of the altitude.

After a week in Pamplona we traveled on to the sleepy village of Cortes, which is set in a beautiful valley just beyond Tudela, halfway between Pamplona and Zaragoza. The cluster of picturesque white houses with terracotta tiling lies dormant for most of the year, but comes to life when the September festival begins.

> **"The fiesta, a tribute to the village patrón (patron saint), is the perfect excuse for the villagers to enjoy themselves"**

We were put up by Fernanda's family, who had taken great trouble to convert one of their first-floor rooms into a bedroom for Stanley and myself. There was also a first-floor bathroom, which made life much easier. We were the only foreigners in the village and in such a small place news travels fast; soon everyone knew who we were and where we were from.

The *fiesta*, a tribute to the village *patrón* (patron saint), is the perfect excuse for the villagers to enjoy themselves. The men gather in the bars before entering into one of the major events—the "bull-run." This is not a bloodcurdling affair but a display of male bravado, with men running in front of the young bulls and darting aside at the last minute. The spectators cheer from safe vantage points and the balcony of the town hall is reserved for those with some form of disability. I watched some of the day's events from here while Stanley dressed in red and joined the men diving from one bar to the next. In the evening there was a free party, with a simple and delicious meal of beef stew (*not* the bulls that appeared earlier!), bread, beer, and soft drinks, finishing off with fireworks in one of the village squares.

Leaving Fernanda, family, and friends behind, we moved farther into the hills to the spa resort of Fitero, which lies along the Pamplona–Soria road. The thermal baths (Baños de Fitero) are well known throughout northern Spain and are particularly popular with Basques from the industrial towns of San Sebastián and Bilbao. The resort is a couple of miles from the village of Fitero and is state-run, consisting of two hotels, the *Spa Hotel Bequer* and the *Spa Hotel Palafox*. We were now in for a period of inexpensive luxury, staying in a double room with en suite facilities (even the toilets are flushed with thermal water!) and all meals included in the price (around $45), dinner being a six-course affair inclusive of wine. There are elevators to all levels in both hotels.

Fitero advertises itself as a center for thermal treatment for the relief of rheumatism, arthritis, and circulatory, nervous, digestive, urinary, and respiratory system disorders. The resort doctor prescribes the temperature and length of immersion in the waters.

Our consultation with the doctor was an interesting experience since he spoke no English and our Spanish is minimal. We muddled along with the help of the receptionist who was the only person in the hotel to speak a little English.

Stanley took me to the baths and two assistants lifted me from the wheelchair to the large walk-in bath where I soaked for nearly an hour. As well as being a pleasurable activity, the thermal bath is particularly helpful to MS sufferers because it encourages some degree of muscle relaxation. (For severe MS sufferers like myself, limbs are "locked" because of muscle tautness, so the warmth and buoyancy of a hot bath assist in limb movement.)

We spent four days in the resort; there is a range of activities to enjoy, including swimming in the heated outdoor pools and playing tennis. The village of Fitero provides an ideal base for exploring the hills of Sierra de Alcarama to the west and the mountains of Sierra del Moncayo to the south.

Our first trip in the camper was a great success, enabling us to see some out-of-the-way parts of Spain and to visit good friends. But that was just the beginning: it was southern Austria in 1989 and Portugal in 1990—our European au pair network continues to serve us well!

Hell on Wheels

Joan Cooper is a regular volunteer with charities that organize vacations for the disabled. Her trip to Spain in 1989 was arranged by Winged Fellowship.

"Torremolinos for two weeks in a group of eighteen people, with nine confined to wheelchairs. Sounds like hell on wheels, and this is your Easter vacation from teaching. You must be mad."

With these cheering words from a colleague ringing in my ears, I arrived at London's Gatwick airport two hours before departure to Málaga and met, for the first time, the rest of the group. The ratio was one voluntary helper to one severely physically disabled "guest," and the eighteen members of the group came from all over Britain. Everyone makes their own way to the airport, although a list of names and addresses is sent out in advance, in case it is possible for people to share transport.

My experience of group travel from Gatwick is good, with priority loading onto the aircraft and paramedical help to carry the disabled passengers to their seats. However, foreign airports vary enormously in size and facilities: passengers at Málaga disembark down a flight of steps and those who are disabled must be carried down by companions and reluctant Spanish paramedics.

On the plane the helpers sit intermingled with guests to assist with meals, drinks, and trips to the rest room; by now polite conversation is over and the ice well and truly broken. The disabled travelers are always last off the plane—once the wheelchairs are waiting on the ground (they travel in the hold) the helpers have their work cut out identifying which wheelchair, cushions, and footrests belong to each guest, but they learn quickly! The *Winged Fellowship* driver is waiting with a specially adapted luxury Mercedes tourbus to take us to our hotel.

The *Don Pedro* has elevators and ramps, accessible public rooms, and a buffet-style dining room. Three steps to the swimming pool and sunbathing terrace aren't a problem for a group. The staff are accustomed to looking after wheelchair users, those traveling in family groups as well as in groups like ours, and they are amenable even when they find that a bathroom door has been lifted off its hinges.

Torremolinos is a large, commercial resort, frequented by most European nationalities: a quiet and restful vacation isn't really what you come here for. However, there are hotels at all ratings and all the amenities of any large vacation center, including numerous "free" discos, with drinks at exorbitant prices. There is plenty to do but help is needed for the disabled visitor. Attractions include Tivoli World (a theme park), where disabled people are welcomed on rides, but the place is set on the side of a hill. The Aquapark, with open-air jacuzzi, is popular and good fun, a welcome relief for bodies aching after too many rides on cobblestones.

Torremolinos makes an ideal base from which to tour the Costa del Sol. And talk about tour—you name it, we saw it, visited it, ate it, drank it, and had a go on or at it! For two weeks our party covered more of Andalucía than the average single traveler or package deal family would ever see. With good transport, an experienced driver, and plenty of help, everyone had their money's worth.

> *"There are plenty of experienced people to carry wheelchairs in situations where one helper would have no chance"*

There are obvious drawbacks to group travel but it does have its advantages. As the vacation is booked and organized by an experienced charity, paying great attention to wheelchair access, much of the worry of quizzing travel agents (often inexperienced in handling disabled clients) is removed. Insurance is arranged and an itinerary drawn up—all you need to do is supply medical details, pay up (help is often available for those on very low incomes), and turn up with luggage, money, and passport. There are plenty of experienced people to carry wheelchairs in situations where one helper would have no chance.

On *Winged Fellowship* vacations, helper and guest share a hotel room and private bathroom. The helper provides any personal care needed, as well as assistance with meals. While the matching up of guests and helpers can be a bit of a hit-and-miss affair, it is surprising how often it works out well. People seldom change "partners"

during the vacation, although this is possible if there are difficulties on either side, whether in care given or as a result of personality clashes. The courier assigns roommates, using medical notes, any available knowledge of personalities, and a lot of "gut feeling."

Apart from sharing accommodation, roommates do not have to stick together as a couple. The best fun is had if guests choose a different helper every day; this means a change of conversation and viewpoint and the arrangement is less demanding for any one helper. Undoubtedly this sort of vacation is physically hard work and can be mentally and emotionally demanding—just when you feel like a rest, it's time to be up and off again. And there are not only your own post-cards to write and suitcases to pack, there are your roommate's, too!

Ideally, the group is located in a block of rooms, rather than scattered throughout the hotel, so that helpers can move easily between rooms to help with lifting. One of the volunteers is a registered nurse, providing daily medical care—a luxury denied to the individual traveler.

It is made clear in the literature that as it is a group vacation, everyone is expected to fit in with the planned activities and general wishes of the group, which some might find a deterrent. However, it is possible to opt out of a particular activity if desired, and something which you wouldn't normally choose may turn out to be an enjoyable experience. In Torremolinos, 79-year-old Bob revelled in his first ever nightclub and revisited it twice!

One of the best parts of the Costa del Sol, probably never seen by many of its tourists, is reached by spectacular drives, leaving behind the busy coastal road and climbing high above the crowded beaches to the mountain villages. Casares is one much-photographed example, its whitewashed houses with orange-tiled roofs built haphazardly on the rocks.

The narrow streets are hard to negotiate in a vehicle and wheelchair pushing is impossible, but the views from the restaurant terraces are well worth the effort of carrying nine wheelchairs and their occupants in the baking heat of the midday sun. We enjoyed the welcome breeze as we lingered for two or three hours over our lunch, in true continental style, eating delicious ice-cream desserts to build up our strength for carrying the wheelchairs back down to the bus. I have to admit to creeping off on my own for ten minutes for a quick look at the village. Two old men sat weighing fish in a balance scale and a woman was making lace—if I'd seen it on a travel program I'd have dismissed it as a set-up.

Another mountain village worth a visit is Mijas, usually combined with a wander around Fuengirola market, which is a large weekly affair, very crowded and hot. Pushing a wheelchair in a busy market has its advantages— you can "ankle bash" a few folk to reach the front of a stall—but pocketbooks slung on the backs of wheelchairs provide easy pickings for thieves. Not that we gave anyone a chance to steal our money—what better place to keep it safe than under your bottom!

Probably the best and most hilarious way to see the winding streets of Mijas is by donkey-taxi. This is a typical tourist trap and quite expensive, but good fun and just another obstacle course for the helpers. The buggy has a canopy overhead and seating for two adults, and the owner walks alongside, leading the donkey. Try maneuvering stiff legs between the shafts of the cart and the donkey's backside! I spent the tour of Mijas keeping Margaret's legs out of the way of the donkey's. But Margaret enjoyed the adventure—it's not something she does every day. I did panic a bit when the donkey slipped on a steep hill but the owner didn't bat an eyelid. He was probably sleepwalking—it was siesta time.

There is a magnificent vantage point over the Mediterranean at Mijas. A ramp is thoughtfully provided next to the steps, but be warned that it's slippery; we worked as a team and took the wheelchairs up the steps.

"Even the most enthusiastic helper would find the going tough with the temperature touching 100°F"

Another fascinating day was spent in Ronda, one of the most ancient cities in Spain, where Celts, Phoenicians, Romans, and Arabs have left their mark. They obviously didn't plan for wheelchairs—the cobblestones proved a challenge for the helpers, while guests tried to "grin and bear it." The usual way to tackle cobblestones is to tilt the chair onto its back wheels but even the most enthusiastic helper would find the going tough with the temperature touching 100°F and a passenger wearing a huge sombrero— try looking around the side of that!

A day trip to Gibraltar is possible from Torremolinos, about three hours' drive through Marbella, Puerto Banús (where the other half lives, with their palatial apartments, yachts, and fast cars), and Estepona. The journey is one long traffic jam, but fascinating nonetheless. Crossing over the border from Spain is a culture shock—British "bobbies" (cops), cars, gas stations, and red telephone booths.

Gibraltar is busy, crowded, and dirty, but extraordinary. The highlight is definitely the view from the top of the rock, accessible by cable car. Wheelchairs can be loaded straight onto the cable car, which is like an elevator with windows. This is fine except for the long, narrow flight of concrete steps up to the boarding stage. There is no way that anyone with only a single helper could negotiate them, and no chance of asking the public to help—it's far too difficult. Our group managed it, though it was hot work. The café, bar, shop, and rest rooms at the viewing area are all inaccessible, reached via a staircase. Never mind, our disabled group members all agreed that the views were marvelous, and helpers get their exercise that way—fetching drinks, ice cream, and souvenirs.

The main street in Gibraltar, popular for duty free purchases, is narrow with deep curbs, but the locals are friendly and helpful. Alcohol, perfume, jewelry, and electrical goods are on sale everywhere. Pushing a wheelchair with bottles hanging off the back is no joke! But we were only in training for the biggest assault course yet—Granada.

The skyline at Granada is dominated by the Alhambra, palace of the Nasrid Sultans, rulers of the last Spanish Moorish kingdom. It is defended by a series of towers and walls—and cobblestones and steps. The Alhambra is an architectural marvel: the ornate stonework and the lattice windows, the symmetry of the courtyards and the reflecting pools are magnificent, but it is hot, dry, and dusty, and exploration is a real test of strength. Everyone cooled off by wetting T-shirts and hats with water from the drinking fountain; this time the usual splashing and waterplay was serious business, not just a silly prank.

It *is* possible to achieve more on a group vacation and in spite of the disadvantages it is a great way to travel and meet people from a wide social range. The problems of group dynamics may develop as people relax, as personalities unwind and friendships grow. Two weeks among people who were originally strangers can be a long time, particularly as it is almost 24 hours a day intensive interaction—probably more than most of us see our loved ones! Yet there are surprisingly few problems. I don't see the helper as a self-denying citizen, a martyr to the cause of the disabled. Able-bodied and disabled on vacation together help each other to enjoy themselves; they simply make different contributions. And that's what vacations are about, isn't it?

Feeling Square in Mallorca

For someone with renal failure secondary to diabetes the real problem in traveling is not mobility but the availability of dialysis. The British Kidney Patient Association (BKPA) runs a dialysis center in Cala Mayor, Mallorca, and Judy Page made this her base for her first venture abroad as a person on haemodialysis.

Mallorca would not have been my natural choice for a vacation, partly because I'd already been there and I like to explore new territory, but also because I favor uncrowded, uncommercialized areas. Cala Mayor, described in the brochures as a lively spot for funseekers, with a nightclub on every corner, ranked pretty near the bottom of my choice of resorts, but it was where the *BKPA* dialysis center was situated and at least it promised to satiate my desire for hot sun and warm sea.

The island does have its unspoiled areas and if I were to return I'd make my base in San Augustin (within walking distance of Cala Mayor) or perhaps Illetas, or even farther away if I was traveling with a driver. The ideal way to explore the island is by car on the very good roads, but there are also alternative, quieter resorts on the bus route. It is worth checking thoroughly what kind of resort you are committing yourself to before booking.

For such a small island, Mallorca has a surprisingly colorful history. It has center-staged in several disputes, being conquered in turn by the Phoenicians, Romans, Vandals, and Moors before falling to the Spanish Aragonese in 1229. They created the Balearics as a territory in their own right but resumed sovereignty in 1349, only to cede the islands to the British in 1713. However, they were restored to the Spanish monarchy in 1802 and the royal family maintains a vacation home there to this day. There is a degree of animosity in some parts between Mallorcans and Spanish, which is noticeable on the altered road signs: the Mallorcans have a language of their own which differs from Spanish and causes a clash over spellings—hence the red paintbrush corrections.

Although the traditional industries are farming (fruit and vines), fishing, and quarrying, tourism has largely taken over. The island caters to all tastes, with the natural beauty of its coastline and mountains, the historic buildings, museums, crafts, and untouched villages, in addition to the purpose-built tourist attractions— Marineland, El Dorado (a Western town, Hollywood-style), Aquapark and Aquacity (giant water complexes), and endless nightclubs, including *BM's* at Magaluf, reputedly the biggest in the world. The area around Palma is built up and commercial, but it's easy to find places where life plods on as it did a hundred years ago and locals regard you with a complacent curiosity that says "Well, the wind didn't blow anything very exciting our way today, then."

Lorraine and I arrived in Cala Mayor in the heat of August. It was about 2am and appeared to be rush hour. Between dawn and midday, I later discovered, all was quiet—people slept late in Mallorca. Unlike some of our keen fellow travelers, who instantly hit the local nightspots, Lorraine and I went tamely to bed.

At the Welcome Party the next morning (a small gathering of young women) we could not have felt more square had we been wearing cardigans and pearls and doing our knitting. What was with these people, complaining that Cala Mayor was dead by daybreak? Hadn't they heard of sleep? We exchanged nervous glances and sipped our "champagne" dubiously, wondering whether our loud shorts and tops would disguise the secret of our inward fuddy-duddiness. Sleep was going to feature on our itinerary, and not in precious sunshine hours.

"I probably appeared quite ordinary next to the hordes of permanently tipsy vacationers"

We had chosen self-catering accommodation because hotel food and mealtimes don't suit me and I wanted a fridge for drugs and drinks. What we unwittingly selected was an apartment in a pair of characterless high-rise towers largely occupied by the deservedly notorious Club 18–30. One imagines tales of such riotous singles vacations to be greatly exaggerated. They are not. To be fair, they seemed generally good-natured, if somewhat antisocial and definitely not my scene, and there would be a lull around six or seven in the morning when an uneasy peace descended during the hooligan recuperation period.

We encountered a universal friendliness among our fellow British, an eagerness to chat and relate experiences. With regard to my "disability" we met only enthusiastic support, but I should point out that I am fully mobile and the only visible sign of not being totally "normal" is the scarring on my arm from the access graft. However, I also have peculiarly limited sight (as a result of diabetic retinopathy), and I found the number of steps around Cala Mayor slightly alarming. It's not ideal for wheelchairs, although some people were coping admirably in them. As I made my precarious way around I probably appeared quite ordinary next to the hordes of permanently tipsy vacationers. The beach at least was quite hazard-free and there I was in my element. There were times, moreover, when my inability to alter my focus quickly was an advantage—while my fellow passengers clung nervously to their seats during some of the more hair-raising mountain journeys, I was quite unperturbed, gazing at the distant crags.

> "I sat too close to an obnoxious little boy who would rather have gone to Disney World"

The bus service from Palma and Cala Mayor proved both efficient and economical, enabling us to sightsee at far less extortionate prices than the organized tours. The drivers are used to linguistic incompetents and have a level of patience and a mastery of English that would win over the most cynical or cautious traveler. The buses are spacious enough to take wheelchairs on board but a strong helper is required to lift it up the steps.

Palma, the bustling capital which nestles around a busy harbor, was one place we visited by bus. The rain could not disguise totally the appeal of this city, with its mixture of modern apartment buildings, tall grandiose structures, elegant marble-floored squares and fountains, and the intriguing warren of dark, narrow backstreets where the filthy, tightly shuttered houses almost meet overhead.

We accidentally toured the old palace—built by the Moors, once the official royal residence and now a military headquarters—because, like most people standing in line, we thought we were going into the cathedral. At the top of the steps from the harbor path the cathedral is on the right, the palace on the left. The simple, austere palace, though sparsely furnished, will give a fair insight into the island's history.

Having located the correct line, we made our last destination in Palma the cathedral. For many people this is the highlight of Mallorca. I found the magnificent and very ornate monument somewhat dark but Lorraine assured me that it was quite special! Even I could appreciate the stunning stained-glass windows and the cool tranquillity of the hushed atmosphere. A word of warning: like so many of the sights, the cathedral is closed from midday to 4pm; during this period there is little to do but eat and sleep, so you might as well resign yourself and adapt your lifestyle accordingly.

Although the Caves of Drach are highly publicized and said to be very beautiful, we were recommended those at Genoa, less than two miles up the road from Cala Mayor. We set off, only to encounter the usual problem of prolonged siesta closing. We wandered around the village and sat in a café but the caves proved well worth the wait. The tour group was small and informal and conducted in a charmingly amateurish way. The caves were amazing, a hidden treasure trove lurking behind a shabby door and a sign on the wall marked *CUEVAS*. Genoa also had some genuine Mallorcan restaurants within a reasonable taxi fare of the resort and this made a pleasant change from the fast-food atmosphere of Cala Mayor.

There are various boat trips available, offering the two basic alternatives of viewing the coast (monotonous but relaxing) or getting drunk (I hate being seasick and have a 16oz a day fluid restriction, even if Spanish wine were allowable; dry white wine and certain spirits are permitted in moderation but most alcohol is too high in potassium for someone on a renal diet). We went on a cruise to a "genuine fishing village": I spotted no fishing boats at all and sat too close to an obnoxious little boy who would rather have gone to Disney World. By the end of the three-hour cruise I wished he *had* gone to

Disney World. What I enjoyed most was the hunk of Mallorcan cake that comes in a flat hexagonal box and tastes like a cross between a croissant and Danish pastry.

Most of the postcards sold in our hotel would have deterred all but the strangest type from visiting Mallorca, but there was one exception—an inspirational view of a place called Torrente de Pareis. Lorraine and I spent some time locating it on the map and pondering how to get there. It happened to be the destination chosen by two affable Welshmen with a car, who offered to take us us out for a day. The drive through the barren beauty of the island's mountains took some time but we were rewarded as we dropped into the valley above the dazzling coves of Torrente de Pareis. The cliffs fell steeply into the turbulent blue sea and to reach the secluded pebble beach we had to grope through a narrow, dimly lit cave. I was content to relax to the hypnotic sound of the sea while my companions battled with the waves.

Two factors contributed greatly to my enjoyment of this vacation: the first was the dialysis center, with its excellent staff. The Senior Nurse was very proficient and managed to create an atmosphere such that I felt like a person, not a patient. It is hard to express the significance of that and how much I gained from stress-free dialysis, thanks to his attitude and approach. The dialysis room itself helped, too—overlooking the sea, light and airy, with up-to-date facilities, pictures on the wall, and pleasant furniture. It's not surprising that some people come back year after year.

The other highlight was my air-bed. I was content to drift for hours. The air-bed was my escape from people—out there on the scarcely undulating water I could retreat into a world of undisturbed daydreams. These times of relaxation alone would have justified the vacation in terms of the psychological benefits, but to find in addition that Mallorca is a fascinating and enchanting island was an unexpected bonus.

SPAIN: TRAVEL NOTES

Sources of Information

Spanish National Tourist Office (*SNTO*), 665 Fifth Avenue, New York, NY 10022 (☎212/759-8822); 102 Bloor Street West, Suite 1400, Toronto, ON M5S 1M8 (☎416/961-3131). Produces excellent pamphlets (including good maps) on the all the major Spanish towns and a fact sheet (1990) for disabled tourists which lists useful addresses and includes some notes on transport, city guides, and wheelchair rental.

Organización Nacional de Ciegos de España (*ONCE*), Calle de Prada 24, Madrid; ☎1/4311900. Julie Smethurst's trip was through the Delegación Territorial de Cataluña, Calabria 66–76, Barcelona 08015. Write for details.

The BKPA **dialysis center** at Cala Mayor, Mallorca, closed down in 1991, but dialysis is available at Policlinica Miramar, Avda Son Serra s/n, Palma de Mallorca 07011 (☎71/450212 or 71/455212, fax 71/456688). This center is included in **THE LIST** (of more than 2500 dialysis centers worldwide accepting transient patients), which is updated annually and published each July by Creative Age Publications. Copies can be obtained, priced $10 ($8.50 each for three or more), from the Circulation Department, THE LIST, 7628 Densmore Ave., Van Nuys, CA 91406-2088 (☎818/782-7328).

SPAIN: TRAVEL NOTES

Tour Operators

Joan Cooper joined a vacation organized by **Winged Fellowship Trust**, Angel House, Pentonville Road, London N1 9XD, UK; ☎071/833 2594. Write for details of their vacation program, or for a Volunteer Application Form.

Those who travel to London and book a package from there should consider contacting *Blue Riband Holidays* (Birmingham; ☎021/355 1184). This company set up *Accessible Travels*, a joint venture with *Viajes 2000* in Spain, in 1990, to offer a range of accessible hotels and apartments in mainland Spain, Mallorca, and the Canary Islands for disabled vacationers and their families or friends. A detailed fact sheet was prepared for each property, and transfers and sightseeing trips were to be by adapted vehicles. The venture failed, partly because the price of this "special treatment" was around £100 more than a comparable vacation from a mainstream tour operator, and partly because potential clients were put off by the mistaken belief that they would be traveling with groups of disabled people. The accessible hotels can still be booked through *Blue Riband Holidays* (or through UK travel agents, who can obtain the access data on properties in the *Blue Riband* brochure), and there are still some adapted transfer vehicles in place—one was used for clients visiting the Paralympics.

Getting There

Iberia Airlines of Spain has been criticized by a couple of our contributors, both seasoned travelers, wheelchair users well used to traveling alone—one was told that unaccompanied disabled passengers are not accepted, the other says the airline simply made a fuss about his wheelchair. You may be lucky and receive better treatment—if you want to give it the benefit of the doubt *Iberia* fly nonstop from New York, Miami, Los Angeles, and Montréal into Madrid. Safer nonstop options might be *Delta* (Atlanta–Madrid and on to Barcelona), *United* (Washington–Madrid), or *American* (Dallas or Miami to Madrid).

For those who fly to **London** first the charter flights to Spain are cheap and plentiful all year round; although charter flights are cramped, the flight times to Spain are short enough for most people to endure (see also Stephen Hunt's accounts of Italy, Egypt, and Tunisia); tickets can be picked up from the larger London travel agents, or via the ads in *Time Out*, the weekly London listings magazine.

For those who **drive** from Britain (see *Transport*, below), the 24-hour **ferry** crossing from Plymouth to Santander with *Brittany Ferries* (Millbay Docks, Plymouth PL1 3EW, UK; ☎0752/221321) aboard the *Bretagne*, is a relaxing way to start a driving vacation, and there are facilities on board for disabled passengers. There are no fare concessions for disabled drivers on this route. *Brittany Ferries* also operates routes to France (Plymouth–Roscoff, Portsmouth–Caen/St. Malo, Poole–Cherbourg); see France *Travel Notes* for details of other ferry crossings.

Transport

The major Spanish **airports** are reasonably accessible, and in recent years facilities have been adapted for wheelchair users. The *Holiday Care Service* (see England and Wales *Travel Notes*) has a fact sheet on access at Spanish airports.

Facilities on **trains** are not ideal, but wheelchairs are available at major Spanish stations, and even wheelchair spaces in some cars. Overall, though, there are few facilities and no evidence of a long-term policy to make the service fully accessible to passengers with any type of disability.

It is possible to **rent cars** with hand controls, from *Hertz* corporate locations throughout mainland Spain. Those who can spare the time and money to cross the Channel from England could drive down through France in the comfort of a lift-equipped van rented from *Wheelchair Travel* (see England and Wales *Travel Notes*), or they could take it aboard the Plymouth–Santander ferry. Remember that road surfaces in rural areas are rough, and the coastal roads in high season dangerous. Toilet facilities for disabled drivers are a rare sight.

Buses are generally difficult for those with mobility problems, but **taxi** drivers are usually helpful and the odd day excursion or short ride

SPAIN: TRAVEL NOTES

to the airport won't break the bank. One contributor has discovered an English-speaking taxi driver with an **adapted vehicle** that can carry one person in a wheelchair and three other passengers: Carlos Noqueras Rivera, C/ Diferente No. 6, Carric Fuente Alegre, Puerte de la Torre, Malaga. Carlos is only licensed to carry passengers in the Fuengirola area, so this service cannot be used for airport transfers from Malaga airport, but he is planning to purchase a larger vehicle and try to expand his operation.

Accommodation

Although hotel owners are waking up to the idea of providing for disabled guests, the choice of well-known, fully accessible **accommodation** in Spain is fairly limited and tends to be in the busiest areas. The *Holiday Care Service* has inspected hotels in the popular resorts; ask for their fact sheet. The *RADAR* holiday guide offers more ideas (see *Books*, p.590), and the *RAC European Hotel Guide* (see France *Travel Notes*) also has a few possibilities.

The situation off the beaten track—whether in hotels, pensions, rented villas, or *paradores*—is far from hopeless, and accommodation can often be rendered suitable with some minor modifications. This is on the whole more satisfactory than staying in a hotel in the "concrete jungle" which purports to be accessible but is blighted by elevators that don't work and noise that makes sleep impossible.

A list and map of Spanish *paradores*, many of which are converted from castles, palaces, and monasteries, is available from the *SNTO*. Although not converted with the disabled guest in mind, these properties tend to be on a grand scale, with plenty of room to maneuver a wheelchair inside. *Paradores* are not cheap, but there are special rates for a minimum of two nights out of season. Malby Goodman, a regular visitor to Spain, recommends a *parador* a few miles southeast of Teruel, in southern Aragón, for drivers: *Euro-Ruta Restaurante y Hostal* (La Puebla de Valverde, 44450 Teruel; ☎74/670136); the bar, restaurant, and bedrooms are all on the first floor.

There are numerous **spa resorts** in Spain. Jean and Stanley Dyke stayed at *Baños de Fitero* (31594 Fitero, Navarra, Spain; ☎48/776100, 776275). Opening dates are, for *Hotel Becquer*, June 15 to October 14, and for *Hotel Palafox*, July 1 to September 30.

Maxine Smith recommends the *Hotel Poseidon* in Benidorm (☎6/5852355) for good accessibility, and on Mallorca the *Hotel Santa Lucia*, Palma Nova (☎71/681358).

Access and Facilities

Ramps are not unheard of in these parts, but exploration of many tourist attractions involves considerable muscle power—Joan Cooper describes a visit to the Alhambra at Granada as a "test of strength"—and a number of sights are simply inaccessible without a team of helpers. Public transportation is not wheelchair friendly and, apart from the new stretches of highway (920 miles built to link Expo '92, Seville, with the rest of Europe), roads are not particularly well maintained. Uneven sidewalks, cobblestones, and steps make walking/wheeling heavy going, particularly in the high-season heat of southern and inland Spain. As well as opening up more of the tourist attractions and widening the choice of accessible accommodation and transport, more guides for disabled visitors and more printed information would be a great help.

That said, Spain and its islands are popular destinations among our contributors—there must be some compensations, perhaps the *tapas* or *sangría*, the beauty of the Moorish architecture (which can be admired in spite of sometimes tricky access), the scenery, the charms of the people. Active and forceful groups of disabled people, especially *ONCE*, offer hope for improvement.

The staging of the 1992 **Olympic and Paralympic Games** in Barcelona, and **Expo** in Seville, provided added impetus. Every Olympic stadium was built with full wheelchair access; the tourist board accommodation guide for Barcelona (*Hoteles, Campings, Apartamentos: Barcelona, Cataluña*) uses the wheelchair symbol, and there's a city access guide available from *ECOM* (Federation of Spanish Private Organizations of Disabled People), Balmes 311,

SPAIN: TRAVEL NOTES

Entresuelo, 08008 Barcelona; ☎3/200 1980 or 3/209 5925. However, the provision of accessible public transit links was poor. Standard taxis were the only advertised means of getting from hotel to stadium for those who could not use trains or buses during the Games.

Facilities were better at Expo. Wheelchair user Stephen Hunt visited the site and found it crisscrossed with level walkways; overhead cable cars could be reached by elevator; an accessible monorail system circled the site; wheelchairs and electric buggies were laid on for those who need them; and an induction loop audio system was provided in the arena. The new train station at the Expo site was designed for easy access. The only negative report from Stephen concerned his room in an otherwise fully accessible and thoughtfully equipped hotel in Seville (*Hotel Melia Sevilla*; ☎54/422611) which bore the hallmarks of design by the able-bodied with the disabled in mind—some night maneuvering of bedroom furniture was required before he could get into bed.

Books

The Real Guide: Spain is the best general guide. Try also *The Real Guide: Barcelona*, for that city and the surrounding area.

TELEPHONE CODE:

From the US and Canada dial 011 (international code) and then 34 for Spain.

The Canaries

December Cocktails

At the age of 39 and with multiple sclerosis (MS), Peter Stone had been using a wheelchair for three years when he first arranged a vacation in Lanzarote, in the Spanish Canary Islands. He has since been back twice, and this account is compiled from tape recordings of his thoughts on the island.

Lanzarote is the most easterly of the Canary Islands and lies about 100 miles off the west coast of Africa. Less than 40 miles long and only 16 miles across, the island is the result of enormous volcanic eruptions from the Atlantic sea bed. The majority of the landscape is barren and in parts more akin to a moonscape. Nevertheless, the land is farmed and there are successful crops of grapes, lemons, melons, and tomatoes.

Strict regulations mean that there is no high-rise building, and all housing is painted white, with the woodwork left natural or painted green or blue. Lanzarote seems to be the least commercial of the three main Canary Islands, and it was because of this, and the fact that it offered the warmest winter temperatures in my price range, that I chose the island for a vacation.

The native tongue is Spanish, despite the distance from mainland Spain, its governing country. I found that the local people serving in the shops, banks, and restaurants spoke some English but treated my attempts at basic Spanish (memorized from a crash course of cassettes from my local library) with a mixture of delight, amusement, and encouragement.

Puerto del Carmen, the major resort, stretches for about three miles along a huge sandy beach and there is a great variety of shops, bars, and restaurants along the roadside. (Resist the duty free shops at airports and on the plane; much better value can be found in the shops on the island.) Nightlife centers around Puerto del Carmen and ranges from a quiet drink or meal to a lively bar or disco. Not my scene anyway, the three discos are all inaccessible to wheelchair users. Another problem in this town is that the curbs are generally very high, but I've found that there's always someone to lend a hand when an extra push is required.

For those, like me, who prefer a quieter seaside resort, there is Playa Blanca, an ex-fishing village on the southern coast of Lanzarote. There have been building developments nearby but Playa Blanca remains unspoiled. In the center of the village there's a small sandy beach and an attractive promenade. I particularly relished sitting in the sun outside one of the two seafront bars, drinking a spectacular-looking cocktail in the middle of December!

On the coast between Playa Blanca and Puerto del Carmen is *Las Salinas*—the salt works. This is a large bay containing desalination beds, from which the island obtains its domestic water, profiting from the resulting salt. If you can't see drinking desalinated water, bottled mineral water is readily available in the shops.

I visited Lanzarote for the second time in December 1988, accompanied by a female care-assistant friend. As I wanted to taste the local restaurant food and not be restricted to hotel eating times, I booked seven days in an apartment in Puerto del Carmen. I asked for a first-floor apartment and taxi transfer from the airport. Most of the taxi-drivers I've had dealings with on Lanzarote have been helpful and patient, but you may encounter the odd impatient misery. We got him! Never mind. We arrived safely at our apartment, which stood in a complex of about thirty buildings, surrounded by beautiful flowers—bougainvillaea, hibiscus, and poinsettia.

> *"The heat from the mountain is used to cook, barbecue-style, in the large, circular restaurant"*

Taxi fares and car rental are very reasonable. Since my companion had past experience of driving on the right we chose to rent a car for three days, at a cost of about $20 per day. During our stay only one day was cloudy, and even then the temperature reached 65°F; we chose this day to drive to Fire Mountain, at Timanfaya. This is a National Park, reached by traveling inland through miles of barren volcanic terrain, interrupted occasionally by a small village or hamlet, the houses distinctive with their white paint and Moorish design.

There was much activity in the parking lot, caused by a long line of camels that were taking the tourists for twenty-minute rides across the hillside. Although I'm sure I'd have been given all the help I needed to mount the camel and climb into the chair on its back, there were no restraining straps, and as it looked like a bumpy ride I gave this one a miss. It turned out, however, that riding a camel was one of my companion's unfulfilled ambitions, so for just under $8 she was helped on, and I watched her bounce off into the distance. I spent a very entertaining half-hour sitting in the car, watching groups of people loading onto the kneeling camels, hooting with laughter as the camel jerked to its feet, and clinging on to their seats as they wobbled off.

We traveled on to Fire Mountain which, as its name implies, is a volcano, albeit dormant. The summit can be reached by road and when we showed the parking lot attendant my wheelchair we were waved on to the top of the slope. The heat from the mountain is used to cook, barbecue-style, in the large, circular restaurant standing on the summit. Further demonstrations of the heat beneath us were given at regular intervals by a guide who poured water into a hole in the ground and shouted, "Ready with your cameras!"—at which point a powerful jet of steam shot into the air.

We returned via the village of Yaiza, where we stumbled on a wonderful old restaurant set among orange and palm trees. As with other restaurants that I've experienced on the island, the waiter was very friendly and I particularly enjoyed the feeling of not being hurried through my meal. On another occasion we went to a restaurant in Puerto del Carmen which I'd visited twice on my previous trip, and I was greeted by the waiters like a long-lost friend, with much shoulder-slapping and shaking of hands.

We spent most of our remaining days relaxing in the warm sunshine, although we did enjoy the colorful Sunday market at Teguise. The cobblestone marketplace was a little rough on wheelchair pusher and occupant but it was well worth it for the fun of haggling over prices in the busy, cosmopolitan atmosphere. On our return to England we were delayed for an hour at Lanzarote airport. The facilities were quite adequate and the disabled persons' rest rooms were larger, better equipped, and cleaner than those back home. By the time I arrived for my third vacation, in October 1989, the airport had an adapted van to ferry disabled passengers between the aircraft and terminal, even though this is only a distance of a hundred yards or so.

We rented a car for a few days to explore the northern half of the island, taking the easterly coast road to the northern tip and returning by the mountainous westerly route. Our first impression of the north was that it is greener than the rest of the island; this is mainly because large areas are being used to grow prickly pears. Twenty minutes into our journey we reached the large resort of Costa Teguise, which has been highly developed for the tourism. Despite the lack of rain there is a golf course here with nine highly watered greens, standing out in shiny contrast to the surrounding landscape.

Preferring to get away from it all, we left behind the complex of luxury hotels and apartments and drove to Arrieta on the northeast coast. As we entered the village we spotted a beautiful sandy beach and turned off the main road toward it. The road petered out at the edge of the village and after a few yards of bumpy track we parked on a fairly flat surface, virtually on the sand. We had the beach to ourselves, apart from a few local children swimming and surfing in the sea. My companion

went in for a swim and we sunned ourselves for an hour or so before driving back into the village and parking on the dock.

There were two cafés on the dockside and we lunched at one of them, a new culinary experience for both of us—limpets with garlic dressing. After a cool drink we set off northward again. There are three tourist attractions in the area, only one of which is wheelchair accessible. The two inaccessible spots are the Grotto Jameos del Agua and the nearby Green Caves.

"Lanzarote is a perfect place for doing very little: a bit of drinking, sampling the local cuisine"

The accessible attraction is *Mirador del Rio*, situated on the northernmost point of the island. The journey from Arrieta took us past what I consider to be the most attractive coastline on Lanzarote. For one or two miles there are white sand dunes and several beaches accessible by car. The area is quiet, with no facilities, but ideal for relaxing beside the turquoise sea.

Mirador del Rio used to be a fortification, commanding the most magnificent views of the island of La Graciosa. This has been tastefully converted into a belvedere from which to admire the breathtaking scene. There is a snack bar and a good parking area, with totally flat access throughout.

Our journey back took us through the more familiar volcanic landscape of the western and central areas. We passed many vineyards (easily identifiable by the semicircular walls which protect them from the northeasterly winds), where vines are cultivated in a unique way. Small holes are dug, deep in the soil. The vines are then planted inside and covered in layers of black lava granules. Being porous, the granules absorb the dew at night and dripfeed it down to the roots below. They also screen the vines from the harsh rays of the sun. That evening we enjoyed the fruits of these labors—a good bottle of local red wine!

Lanzarote is a perfect place for doing very little: a bit of drinking, sampling the local cuisine, lounging in the sun, some unhurried exploration of the island. Bearing in mind the time of year of my visits, it was very satisfying to be able to wear T-shirt and shorts; the temperatures were in the mid-seventies and humidity was low—an exhilarating climate for someone with MS.

Still Searching for the Perfect Vacation

Maxine Smith developed Still's disease (childhood rheumatoid arthritis) at the age of seven, and has been confined to a wheelchair for 36 years, although she can hobble a few steps with a crutch and someone to help her. Accompanied by her mother, Maxine has traveled extensively and tried several travel agents and tour operators, including a "specialist" company for disabled travelers, none of which has been completely satisfactory. In January 1987 she spent three weeks in Puerto de la Cruz, Tenerife.

The shriek of the engines reached a crescendo, then slowly faded as the plane taxied to a halt. Now I could relax and begin to enjoy our vacation on Tenerife. I developed a fear of flying after only my second flight, which was particularly turbulent, throwing meal trays all over the floor. My mother and I had just wedged ourselves into the tiny toilet when the stewardess cried, "I'll have to leave you, we're landing!" and dashed away. I looked at my watch, realized that we couldn't possibly have reached our destination yet and became hysterical, convinced we were crash-landing into the sea. Unbeknown to us, a heavy tail wind had cut forty minutes off the flight time. There we were, locked in the rest room until the plane landed and all the other passengers had disembarked.

My traveling companions for Tenerife were Bill and Dorrie, my parents. We try to have a vacation abroad every year and for the last six years we've taken winter breaks to avoid disrupting my studies. We have experienced a nightmare car journey in blizzards across the Pennines to reach Manchester airport, and endured a long train–Carelink–Airbus journey to London's Heathrow, so we prefer to fly from one of our two more local airports. Both are convenient for a relative or friend to drive us there and back, but unfortunately the choice of resorts you can fly to is very limited, particularly in winter.

As public transportation is usually impossible for me, we generally choose fairly flat resorts with plenty of shops, nightlife, and interesting places to visit within walking distance of a suitable hotel. We'd already run through the list of resorts recommended by friends or travel agents as suitable for me— Benidorm, Lloret, and Mallorca in Spain, Rimini in Italy, Budva and Sliema in Yugoslavia—so we decided on Tenerife. Travel agents advised against the more hilly resorts in the north of the island, and suggested Los Cristianos or Playa de las Americas— flat, with better beaches, in the sunnier south. Neither appealed to us, however—the former appeared to be a small, quiet village and the latter a concrete jungle, specially built for tourists and with no chance of getting a wheelchair on the beach.

A few months later friends returned from a vacation in Puerto de la Cruz with the names of three hotels which they assured us were suitable and in a flat area. Once again we studied the brochures, discovered which company used these hotels, checked with the company for the most accessible hotel, and booked three weeks at the *Hotel Las Vegas*. Normally we take four or five weeks in winter, as the cost per week reduces as the length of stay increases, but each extra week in Tenerife cost $250, so three weeks it had to be.

At last we'd arrived! Patiently waiting for the airport porters to lift me off, while the cleaners worked around me, I had visions of the plane returning to England with me still on board. One of these days it will happen. Eventually I was reunited with my wheelchair. The staff at all the airports we've used have been very helpful, escorting me and my companions to the baggage carousels and straight through customs.

As the taxi drove us along the main road from south to north Tenerife the scenery changed dramatically. At first the landscape was bleak and barren, no trees or greenery, only parched earth, interspersed with steep gray cliffs dotted with caves—some apparently inhabited, as laundry was draped across the entrances. My parents and I became apprehensive and wondered if we'd made a mistake in coming to Tenerife. Our holiday spirits returned, however, as the scenery became more colorful the farther north we traveled: tropical trees, vineyards, fruit plantations, exotic flowers, all able to flourish in the kinder, more humid climate of the north.

Our anger and dismay at seeing several steps at the hotel entrance quickly evaporated when we were directed to a side door with only one step. Although there were three elevators, only one was large enough to accommodate my four-foot-long wheelchair; needless to say, this was the one which broke down several times a day. During the first four days we became increasingly frustrated and tired at hearing "Sorry, elevator kaput, only five minutes please"; which in Spanish time meant one to two hours. However, once our request to change to a bedroom on the second floor (the same floor as the dining room, thus reducing the number of times we used the elevator) had been granted, we found the hotel very pleasant and convenient. The staff were friendly and helpful, and one of them even repaired a flat tire on my wheelchair. Why does that always happen on vacation and never at home?

"The old town was only a few minutes away from our hotel—for walkers"

We'd booked half-board, but the self-service breakfast and evening buffets offered such a huge and tempting variety of delicious dishes that we wanted only a cake or ice cream (every flavor under the sun and a meal in itself) during the day. The hotel provided two types of entertainment: a resident musical trio for nightly dancing in the bar-café, while in the salon a compère organized "do-it-yourself" entertainment, which entailed hotel guests entering competitions or playing silly games—actually, some were quite funny. Professional artists appeared three times a week, including flamenco dancers, an excellent group playing South American music, and local folk singing and dancing (a cross between British folk dancing and Austrian thigh-and-bum smacking).

Puerto de la Cruz is V-shaped: one side is the old town, very hilly, and the other side, where our hotel was situated, is flatter and has gradually developed to cater to the tourists—hotels, apartments, bars, restaurants, cafés, and shops lie along gently sloping side-streets leading from the long, level boardwalk, or Playa, as the locals call it.

That may sound like a typical resort, but it is the other side of the Playa, the seaward side, that makes Puerto such a popular resort. At one end of the Playa steep hills provide natural shelter for the small area of beach, which is not golden sand but black volcanic ash, dirty and unpleasant for children to play on. However, to compensate for the poor beach and the fact that the very strong tides and numerous rocks make swimming dangerous, a huge swimming area (the lido) has been constructed on the lower level of the seafront boardwalk.

"During twenty years of travel we've noticed little improvement in facilities for disabled people"

The Lido contains several swimming pools, sunbathing areas, fountains, pretty gardens, and areas for evening entertainment. The developers have managed to provide what tourists want in an attractive way that harmonizes perfectly with the natural beauty of the area. You can spend all day there for less than two dollars. Although the Lido is not very accessible to disabled tourists, some might think it worthwhile to accept the offers of help and be carried down the few steps at the entrance, and see how far they can get.

In the Lido and along the Playa there are numerous groups of seats, facing different ways, some with small thatched canopies, and everywhere an abundance of trees, flowers, and exotic purple birds of paradise. Plants, boulders, seats, and trees are artistically and strategically placed to provide color, beauty, and a feeling of privacy.

The old town was only a few minutes away from our hotel—for walkers. Down a flight of stone steps, across a level path, then up another flight of steps—impossible for wheelchairs. A bridge linking "our side" to the old town would be ideal. Dorrie and I tried several detours, unsuccessfully, but Bill discovered a way through an alley and

up a steep road (strong pusher required). Although many of the streets in the old town are hilly, with narrow, bumpy sidewalks and high curbs, it's well worth the effort to view the highly decorative architecture, the market, and the bazaar, and simply to see where the locals live.

We intended to visit the volcano, Mount Teide, but were warned that it is cold and the air is very thin up there, not advisable for people with breathing problems. The trip involves a bus or taxi ride through spectacular scenery, then a cable car that almost reaches the top. Those disabled tourists who can manage buses might enjoy some of the "free" bus trips available—to a fashion show or leather factory, banana plantation or parrot park—but be warned, some require passengers to pay an entrance fee or purchase something once they get there. One couple in our hotel decided to save on taxi fares by using a "free" bus to a time-share complex, in a village where their friend lived. They were left stranded when the bus driver refused to take them back to Puerto because they hadn't looked around the time-share complex.

As Tenerife is part of the Canary Islands, which are governed by Spain, we expected the people and customs of Puerto to be Spanish. We've noticed over the years that many Spanish resorts have become increasingly commercial: muggings and bag snatching have multiplied, making us nervous when walking at night, and shopkeepers are quite rude if tourists walk out of their shops without buying anything. We were, therefore, surprised to find Tenerife different; in fact, the islanders detest being referred to as Spanish. They are extremely polite and courteous, and we were able to browse without buying, or sit all day over a cup of coffee in a crowded café. We enjoyed many late-night strolls, feeling completely safe. The only unpleasantness that we encountered was the exploitation of tiger cubs, monkeys, and parrots, doped and hawked around by photographers who harassed the tourists, urging them to have their pictures taken with these poor animals.

Puerto is not ideal for wheelchairs, but we enjoyed a very pleasant and relaxing vacation and encountered no more difficulties there than anywhere else. Special facilities for wheelchairs are virtually non-existent in Europe—at most, small ramps—and Puerto is no exception. We've not found one special rest room for the disabled in any of the eighteen resorts in ten different countries that we've visited.

During twenty years of travel we've noticed little improvement in facilities for disabled people. A few travel agents and tour companies are slowly becoming aware of the needs of disabled people on vacation but their definitions of accessibility are inadequate. No matter how much preparation we make,

problems always occur. Airlines rarely inform cabin staff about my unbending legs and some argue that I should book two or three seats. Quite rightly, I'm not allowed to sit near the exits, but airlines have not made any alternative arrangements. Until travel agents, tour operators, and airlines realize that disabled people have a right to a vacation, too, travel will not become any easier. We have yet to find a foolproof method, but so far we've always managed to overcome the difficulties without too much suffering. Looking back, it's the disasters that make a vacation memorable—such as arriving in Rimini at 4am to be locked out by the hotel manager as soon as he saw my wheelchair.

My advice is, if you are adventurous, have a sense of humor, are prepared to put up with inconveniences and the occasional disaster, *and* have a good helper, go and pester your nearest travel agent tomorrow!

CANARY ISLANDS: TRAVEL NOTES

For general sources of information, see the Spain *Travel Notes*, p.293.

Allan Green booked a vacation with *Thomson* (Greater London House, Hampstead Road, London NW1 7SD, UK; ☎071/387 9321); recommended by several of our contributors, this is one of the few British tour operators to make a concerted effort to gather basic access data (in a system called **Factfile**) for their disabled clients—ask for the **Client Welfare Department**, which deals with some 2000 requests per month from disabled tourists. *Thomson* vacations can be booked through

around 7000 British travel agents (who can access Factfile via the computerized Thomson Booking System).

Allan stayed in the *Hotel Vulcano*, Playa de las Americas (☎22/792035). It has some special rooms for disabled guests—large, with spacious bathrooms and wide doorways—and can cope with large groups of disabled people.

TELEPHONE CODE:

From the US and Canada dial 011 (international code) and then 34 (the international code for Spain) for the Canary Islands.

Portugal

An Ideal Hobby

Theodora Hampton has rheumatoid arthritis and has had both hips and knees replaced in the last ten years. In 1988 she went wine tasting in Portugal.

As a hobby for a disabled person—drugs, doctor, and transport permitting—wine tasting has a lot to offer. It can be enjoyed from a wheelchair, does not involve much walking, and enables one to meet a wide variety of people. I've been wine tasting for years but it was not until recently that I considered going with a friend on an organized wine tour abroad.

The tour base was a large hotel in Ofir, a resort on the Costa Verde. Transport was by tourbus and only one night was spent away from the base hotel. Two "rest days" were written in to the tour and this appealed to me—I felt that two days beside a swimming pool with a good book would enable me to cope with bus travel on the remaining five days. I also hoped to swim but unfortunately the pool turned out to be very cold, so I had to make do with a deck chair in the sunshine.

The prospect of bus travel was rather daunting for two reasons: I was worried about the steps and I was not sure how stiff I'd become sitting in one position for longish stretches. In the event both worries proved unfounded. The driver was somehow always present when we were getting in or out of the bus and unobtrusively gave me a helping hand. The other tourists on the trip—mainly

older but not disabled—were quick to realize that I needed more time than most to negotiate the steps. As for stiffening up, the trips all included frequent stops to stretch legs and, since the tourbus was by no means full, for much of the time I had a double seat to myself. For anyone who can manage a few steps—with a cane, perhaps—this means of transport should not be automatically rejected.

The first wine visit was to Brejoeira Palace in the *Vinho Verde* area. The owner escorted us on a tour of the estate, much of which was wooded, with grottoes, artificial streams, small fountains, and occasional rustic bridges. After about ten minutes we reached the edge of the woods and ahead lay the vineyards, stretching away into the distance.

I found the walk back a bit of a struggle and while the rest of the party was shown around the state rooms of the palace I sat outside in the shade of a large tree. There was no time to get bored, however, as very shortly a procession of servants emerged from the palace and began preparations for our buffet lunch. Long trestle tables were spread with shining white tablecloths, chairs were set up, and then came the food—tray after tray of small edibles to be eaten with the fingers. Just as the rest of the party began to wander back, the wine was brought out.

Vinho verde is a light white wine, with almost a touch of green to it (as its name suggests). It is slightly sparkling and, like many light white wines, is best drunk on its home ground. Somehow back home it seems to lose some of its sparkle and become just another slightly fizzy wine, enjoyable but hardly memorable. The *vinho verde* produced at Brejoeira Palace, however, is the famous Alvarinho, acknowledged to be one of the best, if not *the* best, of the *vinho verde* wines. Set out on the lawns of the estate, the long green bottles in their ice buckets looked very welcoming indeed. The wine made an excellent accompaniment to the food—smokey bacon with dates, fish and meat balls, cheese and, when we tired of these, some delicious almond cream tarts.

Our second expedition was a moderately grueling two-day trip, stopping first at the Quinta de Avalida at Peñafiel. Again we started with a stroll through the grounds. We inspected the goat enclosure—rather like an enormous dovecote, with small brown and white goats trotting up and down the rickety wooden steps and looking down at us out of their strange pale eyes. Nearer the house, the woods gave way to gardens, with large colorful flowerbeds, masses of red and pink geraniums, petunias, and great swathes of purple bougainvillaea on the walls of the house itself.

We tasted the *vinho verde* standing on the verandah which ran along the back of the house, overlooking the rose bushes and, behind them, the vines, shimmering in the midday sun. At Avalida we had what was without doubt the best meal of the trip. Vegetable soup, roast pork, and crème brulée were expertly served on fine china, in a large, airy dining room. We were very impressed and later discovered that the *patrona* provides meals only two or three times a year; this was the first time *Blackheath Wine Trails* had qualified for the full treatment!

Our visit to Avalida preceded the drive to Lamego, where we were to spend our one night away from Ofir. It was a long day, finishing with a tasting and tour of the production lines of a sparkling wine estate. Made by the *méthode champenoise*, the samples were excellent but I think we were all a little too tired to give them the appreciation they deserved.

"The Douro is one of the few regions in which some of the estates carry on the practice of trampling the grapes by foot"

The *Hotel de Parque* at Lamego is set in the grounds of the Sanctuary dos Remedios, high above the small town. We could see the lights twinkling below as we waited for dinner. I seem to recall an excellent trout but by that stage I was more interested in my bed.

The following morning, most of the party was keen to walk down to Lamego, which could be reached down more than a hundred steps through a series of terraced gardens. I decided that this would have to be a "miss" for me, but when the hotel porter realized that my friend and I were thinking of taking a taxi he offered to take us down in his car. We were happy to accept and although he had hardly more English than we had Portuguese (none!) he chatted away cheerfully, pointing out the sights as he drove, and enjoying the short trip as much as we did.

From Lamego our tourbus took us up the winding roads above the Douro valley, each bend revealing a fresh panorama of steep terraced slopes covered with vines. We were heading for Quinta do Noval, one of the best-known producers of port and for many the highlight of the tour.

The grape harvest in the Douro is in September. When we finally reached Quinta do Noval we found that the grapes had already been gathered and were in the process of being crushed in large granite *lagars*. The Douro is one of the few regions in which some estates carry on the practice of trampling the grapes by foot. The human foot is considered the ideal "crusher." It releases the color from the grape skin and frees the juice from the grapes without piercing the pips, whose bitter flavor would ruin the wine. It is thought that the warmth of the human body helps the fermentation of the grapes. The men wade knee-deep in grapes and "trample" in four-hour shifts.

"We were given more port to taste"

When the juice reaches the right color and about halfway through the fermentation process, it is drawn off into barrels, called *toneles*, in which a quantity of grape spirit (similar to cheap brandy) has been placed. This arrests the fermentation and the wine is then left to mature. The short period of fermentation accounts for both the rich color and the sweetness of the port.

We tasted both red and white port at Quinta do Noval, standing outside the estate house and overlooking the vines which covered the hillside in every direction. The meal here was again a buffet and we finished with some fine green figs.

Later in the afternoon the bus took us down to the town of Regua, where we joined the local train to Oporto. The train was fun, rather old-fashioned, with hard seats and a shrill whistle. We meandered along the side of the Douro valley, following the river all the way to Oporto. Another of my worries proved groundless as the train, unlike many continental trains, had doors that opened level with the platform—no steep steps to climb.

Between the early eighteenth century and the beginning of the twentieth more port was drunk in England than any other wine, and the British influence remains strong in Portugal, where many of the Port Lodges are British owned or part-owned. *The Factory House* in Oporto, a club and business premises combined, was established by the British merchants. We were given an informed tour by Signor Delaforce, the current president of the club and the senior member of one of the oldest port firms. One of the most interesting rooms to me was the kitchen, a relic of the Victorian era and situated on the top floor but one! A more modern kitchen has been installed in the last few years—within easy walking distance of the dining room.

In Vila Nova de Gaia, on the banks of the Douro, we saw a line of *rabelos* at anchor, the square sail on each bearing the name of a Port Lodge. These ancient river boats used to carry the new wine from the Quintas downstream to Vila Nova de Gaia, where the wine was stored. However, the river is now dammed in several places for the generation of hydroelectric power and the voyage, always hazardous because of the rapids, is no longer possible. Now the pipes of wine are brought down by truck and, sadly, the boats are mainly decorative.

In Vila Nova we went first to Sandeman and watched the process of storing and bottling port, starting with the cooperage sheds, where the oak barrels are still made by hand, and finishing at the bottling plant. At Calém, another long-established firm, we were given more port to taste and an unexpectedly enjoyable lunch. I say "unexpectedly" as the dish provided was a local specialty, the basic ingredient of which was tripe—after a hesitant start our party cleared the lot!

We made this tour during the first week of October and were lucky to have sunny weather throughout. It was never too hot, just right for a vacation of this kind, and the scenery in this part of Portugal is particularly pleasing.

Apart from the plunging slopes of the Douro valley, with thousands of vines clinging to the narrow man-made terraces, the countryside is scattered with farms and small villages, cattle grazing peacefully, the occasional pig, some hens, and heavily laden apple trees. With luck the area may remain unchanged a little longer—it is relatively undeveloped as a tourist area, and away from the coast much of the land is a protected nature reserve. In October the trees made a bright splash of fall colors; a month later and everything might look a little bleak.

PORTUGAL: TRAVEL NOTES

Sources of Information

Portuguese National Tourist Office, 590 Fifth Avenue, New York, NY 10036 (☎212/354-4403); 4120 Yonge Street, Suite 414, Toronto, ON M2P 2B8 (☎416/250-7575). General tourist information and details of *Portuguese Railroads* services are supplied, but the only reference to disabled visitors is a contact list of three disability organizations and some hotel recommendations (see below). On the spot you'll find tourist offices, *Turismo*, in almost every town of any size—these can be very helpful.

National Rehabilitation Secretariat (*Secretariado Nacional de Reabilitacão*), Av. Conde Valbom 63, 1000 Lisbon; ☎1/761081. Publishes a guide to transport facilities and a Lisbon access guide, both in Portuguese but symbols explained in English in the Lisbon guide.

Getting There

TAP Air Portugal flies to Lisbon from New York, Boston, Toronto, and Montréal, but does not carry aisle wheelchairs. A more wheelchair-friendly airline, *Delta*, flies New York–Lisbon. There are good-value charter fares for flights out of New York, San Francisco, and Los Angeles, and savings can also be made by flying via Madrid, or—a smart move for Canadians, in particular those west of the Rockies—picking up a cheap British charter (frequent flights to Lisbon, Porto, or Faro) from London.

Transport

The major **airports** are reasonably accessible, and getting better; there are adapted rest rooms at Lisbon. Facilities on **trains** are not ideal, although one contributor found that access from the platform to train, on her route at least, was level; ask the tourist office for advice on selecting the most accessible lines; assistance can in theory be arranged at stations where necessary. There are accessible rest rooms on some Portuguese stations, and on-board toilets have been adapted on international trains, but there's room for improvement in access to and on domestic trains. **Buses** are inaccessible, but **taxis** are relatively cheap, and their drivers generally helpful.

For **rental cars** with hand controls, your best bet would probably be to drive in from Spain: *Hertz* offers adapted cars at all corporate locations in mainland Spain. In both Spain and Portugal, road surfaces in rural areas can be tough going, and toilet facilities for disabled

PORTUGAL: TRAVEL NOTES

drivers are rare. Another way to get around inaccessible public transit—if you have plenty of time and money—is to rent a lift-equipped van from *Wheelchair Travel* (see England and Wales *Travel Notes*), take it across the Channel and drive down through France and Spain, or sail direct to Spain and drive from Santander.

Accommodation

Accessible accommodation is scarce and tends to be in the busiest areas. The *Holiday Care Service* (see England and Wales *Travel Notes*) and the *RADAR* guide, *Holidays and Travel Abroad* (see *Books*, p.590 have some suggestions. As in Spain, though, places off the beaten track are often more adaptable.

Portuguese *pousadas*, the local version of the Spanish *parador*, are again often former castles and palaces, and again fairly pricey and fairly inaccessible, though some will be manageable with help or some minor adaptations. The network covers the country and rates are reduced out of season. A list and map may be obtained from the tourist office.

The *Institute for the Promotion of Tourism* (*IPT*, Rua Alexandre Herculano 51, 1200 Lisbon; ☎1/681174) and the *National Rehabilitation Secretariat* (see *Sources of Information*) have produced a list of hotels (mainly four-star and a sprinkling of three-star) that are rather vaguely

classified as being "without barriers or with few obstacles" to wheelchair users. It can be obtained from the *Portuguese National Tourist Office*, or by consulting the *RADAR* holiday guide. The Ibis hotel chain (see France *Travel Notes*) has five properties with at least one room suitable for disabled guests, in Lisbon, Porto (2), Faro, and Setubal.

Spas abound in Portugal: again you can get details from the tourist office in London, or locally.

Books

As an introduction to her passion, Theodora Hampton recommends the *Pocket Guide to Wine Tasting*, by Michael Broadbent (Christies Wine Publications). *Hugh Johnson's Wine Companion* and the *World Atlas of Wine* (both by Hugh Johnson and published by Mitchell Beazley) and *The New Wine Companion* by David Burroughs and Norman Bezzant (Heinemann) contain detailed accounts of the various wine regions, including those in Portugal.

The Real Guide: Portugal is the best all-around guide.

TELEPHONE CODE:

From the US and Canada dial 011 (international code) and then 351 for Portugal.

Italy

Roman Style

Stephen Hunt, who sees his wheelchair as a tool for travel, took a City Break in Rome with friend and helper, Tim.

The plane banks steeply and the Eternal City slides briefly past the window opposite my customary aisle seat. For most of the two-hour flight I've been resting forward with a cushion on my meal table in a pleasant doze of anticipation; a packed charter flight is cheap and cheerful and the seats don't recline. The cost of only four nights off-peak B&B for myself and Tim in a central hotel would have taken me halfway around the world in my hitchhiking days. Looking at freedom in those terms, though, wouldn't have taken me across the road to the travel agent.

We land at Ciampino and passengers slowly struggle out to a waiting bus. Some have enough luggage to spend their entire City Break indoors, changing clothes. I sweep past them with our two small bags on my lap and Tim pushing; better mobility than gentility.

The airbrakes release with a hiss and we pull out, into the sunburnt Italian countryside. At last I'm getting away from it all—the four walls, the familiar streets, the routines, and regimes. Soon we're entering Rome and heads are swiveling faster than a tennis umpires' convention.

The interior of the hotel that Tim and I have chosen is in the grandiose "palazzo" style but with monetarist innovations: we glide across the marble floor to what had once been a single generous elevator but is now two miserly cost-effective elevators, which my wheelchair won't fit into. The plan, then, is for me to wedge myself upright just inside while Tim belts upstairs and calls the elevator from our floor, luckily the second, quickly unfolding the wheelchair in time for my arrival. Unfortunately we forget the vital role of the "HOLD" button in such a plan. Tim has hardly installed me before the door slides shut. I ascend rapidly to the fourth floor, where I'm confronted by a group of camera-festooned Japanese. Thinking that I'm trying to get out, the men enthusiastically rush forward while their wives and mothers bow encouragingly in the background. I fend them off, struggling to keep my balance until at last the door closes and the elevator descends to the second floor. But Tim isn't there. Within seconds the door has closed again and the elevator is reascending, this time to the sixth floor. Here, more Japanese await me and rush forward, helpful as ever. Holding them at bay, I call out for Tim. Before the door closes his answering voice comes from below, rising past me as the elevator starts descending again. I arrive back in the lobby just as Japanese reinforcements are checking in. Tim and I are now at opposite poles of the building, my legs are starting to give way, and I am wondering if we will ever come back together again. But the gods are with me, in their own way, and the elevator mercifully ascends to the second floor, where a disheveled Tim is waiting for me to collapse into the wheelchair.

Our room is of course palatial, though in the vertical rather than the horizontal sense, so we get down to some urgent furniture rearrangement. In the bathroom, the lavatory prevents access to the sink, but at least it's not the other way around.

By now the afternoon is closing fast and Rome still lies undiscovered outside. Hurrying back to the elevator we put Plan B into operation and I meet Tim almost instantly in the lobby. In front of a classical fresco a giant electronic guide-map shows us that the famous Trevi fountain is hardly a coin's throw away. We set off into Rome's burgeoning evening rush and arrive three hours later. I'd imagined straight roads. They are, but so enmeshed in a maze of narrow streets and alleys that in the end it's impossible to know which way up to hold the street guide. Not that it matters. There's so much to see that we even pass through one little piazza three times from different directions and only realize later. The Trevi fountain is also a surprise. This is no municipal park goldfish-squirter. It is said that Rome's numerous fountains provided ideal places for plots and intrigues to be discussed discreetly. Conspirators at the Trevi fountain

would have needed ear trumpets to hear anything against the background deluge, gushing and cascading triumphantly from every orifice of this half-human granite mountain.

Back at the hotel, while Tim is trying to reach his wife on the phone before she goes to bed, I watch an old movie on TV. It's a dubbed Hollywood World War II drama: gum-chewing Italian soldiers fearlessly charge a Nazi stronghold. Things are definitely not as I've been led to believe.

"The Vatican's answer to Disneyland: a vast indoor theme park of the spirit"

Going up the wide Via della Conciliazione toward St. Peter's, it's impossible not to feel self-conscious. How many wheelchairs have flowed in prayerful hope along this Pilgrim's Way before me? I even feel a strange tremor of anticipation myself, although I hardly qualify for a new set of tires. In St. Peter's Square our eyes automatically go up to The Balcony—focus of the hopes and fears of a quarter of civilization.

The interior of the basilica is the Vatican's answer to Disneyland: a vast indoor theme park of the spirit, designed to fill the soul rather than empty the pocket. Emerging disoriented, back into the mortal world, we head for the Papal post office to buy "Sunset over St. Peter's" postcards and are accosted by women and children selling newspapers or begging. Suddenly I feel prying hands fumbling in the folds of my jacket. At first they have the advantage: my reaction has to change from sympathy to disbelief to outrage before I lash out. Rob a poor defenseless invalid and his harassed attendant, would they! In fact they try it twice more before we leave Rome. But forewarned is forearmed, and they don't know that I'm already trained to a peak of fitness by the street hustlers of Morocco.

So we continue unmolested on our way across the river in the vague direction of the Villa Borghese. Although most of Rome would fit onto two pages of my London A to Z map book, our constant rambling makes the Eternal City go on and on. Again we wander into Piazza Navona, once Domitian's athletic stadium, where exuberant Bernini fountains now sport against a background of mellow ochre-washed houses, all chariot-free thanks to the City Council. The Villa Borghese is another haven for the fugitive pedestrian: originally a Goth campground, now Rome's largest public park, it houses fine collections of paintings and sculptures.

Back at the hotel that night, while Tim is trying again to get through to his wife, I stretch out and unpleat after a day on the cobblestones. To relax me on TV a soap opera that—even with my meagre Italian—makes "Search for Tomorrow" look like a towering intellectual achievement.

Next morning we risk our one and only taxi ride, as far as the high-rises of the suburbs. The careful and friendly assistance we receive when getting into and out of the car somehow doesn't relate to the homicidal maniac at the wheel. The guidebook mistakenly lists Porto Portese as an antique flea market but at similar sites all over Britain the same milling Sunday morning crowd is shuffling past the same stalls of second-rate domestic clutter and mass-produced fashion.

Yet Porto Portese is a must for the dedicated tourist. Just over the street lies the sort of contrast that guidebook clichés are made of. Crossing into Trastevere is truly "a step back in time." The faithful are now at lunch, the tourists still at St. Peter's. We trundle through peaceful medieval streets, vine-hung and flower-scented. Dappled by the warm October sunshine, the stonework has the faded opulence of old Persian carpets. Here is Santa Maria in Trastevere, said to be the oldest Christian church in Rome.

Nearby, from a pair of open doors, comes the soft rasp of a saw. In the gloom among the cobwebs a man is working on an ornamental balustrade; around him are stacked chairs, gilt picture frames, and other antique furniture and fittings. In Rome there must be as many restorers as cabbies.

From Trastevere on to the island in the Tiber to rest and eat, as usual resisting the pasta blowout. To wallow like stranded whales at the hour when Rome is most free of traffic would be a waste. Instead we end up later for another snack at a sidewalk café in the Piazza della Rotunda (the Pantheon). Built under Hadrian, it's one of the most impressive and best-preserved relics of Imperial Rome. The interior of the great building is hollow, almost featureless, its encircling walls rising up to the dome from where the only light appears. Visitors seem subdued and expectant in the strangely empty space.

"Here, as elsewhere in Rome, I'm regarded with the same friendly indifference as any other tourist"

That night, while Tim is trying to get through to his wife, I watch "Culpo Grosso," a deregulated TV strip-quiz, during which car mechanics and receptionists lose their clothes and win money.

It could be a seriously vandalized indoor parking lot. But, next morning, as we approach from the Piazza Venezia, the emotions are already stirred by an air of melancholy glory. As we slowly circumnavigate the Colosseum's battered walls I'm almost sad that the days of bread and circuses are over.

On our way to the Forum the clouds thicken; it looks like rain and there's barely time to see the sights before it starts. We find a sidestreet bar, just an ordinary place for ordinary Romans. Yet its style makes my local bar look like a bus shelter, and the barman and the guys arguing soccer tactics exude that sophisticated panache which TV commercials labor after. Among strangers I'm used to being stared at rudely, ignored politely, or smiled on sympathetically. But here, as elsewhere in Rome, I'm regarded with the same friendly indifference as any other tourist. It's relaxing for me and must be how the inhabitants survive the year-round invasions: Italy is the most visited country in the world, I'm told.

After consulting our wallets, our last evening is spent window-shopping around the nightlife of Rome. Back at the hotel, Tim finally connects with his wife and tells her that we've arrived safely and will return the next day.

We have only the morning left for the Sistine Chapel. "No one can leave Rome without seeing the Sistine Chapel" say the brochures. Well, I can. On the coach going up the Appian Way to the airport I no longer feel the pang of disappointment. After all, if I'd wanted somewhere with ramps and walkways I could have stayed at home. A vacation for the disabled person is about possibilities and Roma has more than enough to offer the independent traveler. Imagine your local grocery store in a lofty temple, the post office a stately palazzo, the church a Renaissance art gallery . . . and that's just one street!

The Italian Cure

Anna Thomson is 52 and has had rheumatoid arthritis for about twelve years. In June 1989 she traveled alone to Abano Terme, a spa in northeast Italy.

After years of trial and error, I know that a vacation on my own suits me. I'm better able to relax and appreciate my surroundings while alone; only in the evenings do I occasionally feel lonely. My ideal companion would be someone with whom I was madly in love, or a loner like myself who would disappear until supper time; in the absence of both I go it alone.

I have loved Italy since my first visit there when I was a healthy eighteen-year-old, and I have long been aware of the existence of spas, where vast numbers of Italians take the "cure" for just about every ailment under the sun, but for arthritis in particular. Information from the Italian State Tourist Office helped me to decide on Abano Terme, which has a worldwide reputation, has been a center for hot thermal mud and water treatments since Roman times, and is approximately 25 miles from Venice.

Although a few tour operators do feature vacations to Abano and other spas, none offered flights from Edinburgh, and I couldn't find a two-center vacation incorporating Venice, so I booked a flight only and reserved the hotels by telephone. This turned out to be surprisingly easy—but I do speak some Italian.

Over the years I have been taking less and less luggage on vacation: while assistance with luggage at airports is generally very good, sometimes it is not forthcoming or is begrudged, and on two occasions my suitcase has disappeared altogether. Taking only absolute basics, I can dispense with the suitcase and swing a travel bag, weighing only about ten pounds, over my shoulder. The sense of freedom is marvelous—there are no long, drawn out inner conflicts over what to wear, nor are there any agonizing waits at airport carousels.

It was in such a carefree state that I stepped off the Edinburgh–Venice flight early in June to be confronted by a torrential downpour, but at least the air was warm after the frozen north. I knew there was a bus service to Abano but no one seemed to have any information on it until I asked a friendly road-sweeper, who had all the time in the world to give me directions.

"I had a feeling that a special healing power was present in this place"

By the time we reached Abano, the sun's rays were penetrating the last of the storm clouds, bathing the town in a mysterious golden light. I had a feeling, the first of many, that a special healing power was present in this place. The bus stopped very close to my hotel, where I received a warm welcome. As lunch had just started, I was soon enjoying delicious pasta with local red wine and reflecting that the early rise in Edinburgh had been well worth the effort.

Abano, with its relaxing ambience and beautiful gardens, appealed to me immediately, so there was no "settling in" period: I arrived, I relaxed—it was as simple as that. More than anything, I was looking forward to swimming in the warm thermal pool. Swimming eases my arthritis but it is never easy to find warm water in the UK. The hotel had two swimming pools, one outside in an attractive garden and one inside on the fourth floor, with a view of the surrounding hills. As I descended the shallow steps of the still, blue indoor pool, the soft touch of the slightly oily water soothed me immediately, and memories of swimming movements gradually returned to my stiff joints. At first I felt very weak, so I tried not to push myself too hard, taking breaks from swimming to float or do simple exercises. As the vacation progressed, my swimming became decidedly stronger and I was able to swim underwater for the first time in years. Many of the pool users were non-swimmers

and some were quite severely disabled; all seemed to benefit from the thermal water, which was kept at a temperature of 86°F.

Before too long I realized that I was the only British person at the hotel, although I did see the occasional compatriot in the cafés and shops. Most of the guests were Italian, some German and a few Swiss, Belgian, and Austrian. Not everyone was disabled—I'd say around fifty percent—but Abano Terme is certainly an ideal place for disabled people. The town is very flat, the sidewalks are in excellent repair, with no high curbs, and there are no steps or bridges. In the evenings many streets are closed to traffic. There are gardens everywhere and plenty of seats for resting. Naturally the hotels are very much oriented to the needs of disabled guests, and the staff is kind and sympathetic. There are many attractive cafés and the Italian custom of sitting with a cup of coffee or a glass of wine, simply to watch the world go by, can very easily become an addiction. At night there is a program of entertainment, often at open-air spots, including street parades and folk dancing. There is a marked absence of discos and wild young people, but the Italians do tend to be boisterous and I found a pair of earplugs invaluable when getting off to sleep.

Before commencing the hot thermal mud treatment, I had to be examined by the hotel doctor, who was very charming but with not a word of English. However, arthritic joints are fairly obvious things and I remembered the Italian for some parts of the body, so we were able to communicate fairly well. The treatments take place in the morning and I was given a choice of times, the earliest being 4am! I settled for the last one, at 9am.

The chambermaid gave me a white terry towel with a hood to wear before and after the treatment. Even in the elevator, on the way down to the treatment center, I could smell the hot mud; somehow it felt comforting. The center reminded me of a hospital clinic. I was shown to a small, tiled room with bed, chair, sunken bath, and shower. Two large buckets of steaming mud lay on the bed. They call the mud *fango*, and the attendant who gives the treatment is a *fangina*. My *fangina*—Leonora— was young, strong, cheerful, and over-weight. As she prepared my "bed" of thick, gray mud, I couldn't help think-ing that it looked terribly hot.

My bathrobe had been threatening to slip off since I put it on (it was large and long and I am small and thin), so I let it go and stepped bravely forward. Leonora asked me to sit on the edge of the bed first, while she rubbed hand-fuls of *fango* into my back, giving me a chance to judge the temperature. Finding it just bearable, I reckoned it could only get cooler, so I eased my body into the oozing mass. Leonora wrapped me tightly in the strong linen sheets which had been under the mud, put a wool blanket on top, and disappeared.

"The pool was my constant delight"

With only my head sticking out and my arms imprisoned in the sheets, I felt like an Egyptian mummy. The heat was actually very pleasant and the mud was soft and soothing against my body. As I had no idea how long I was supposed to lie there, the first treatment was slightly unnerving but I did hear a clock ticking away in the background, and Leonora appeared occasionally to wipe the sweat from my face with a rough towel (the Italians are wonderful people but their towels have the texture of rye crackers).

The alarm went off after twenty minutes and I was freed from my cocoon. After removing some excess mud from my body with her strong hands, Leonora led me to the shower where I was given a good hosing down. The sunken bath had been filled with

thermal water and I was led down the steps to relax in the warmth and to enjoy the free movement of my limbs in the water—this was a lovely part of the treatment.

After the bath I felt pretty good. Leonora helped me to dry off and wrapped me up in my bathrobe, making sure the hood was over my head to conserve the heat. As I walked to the elevator I could feel new strength in my limbs. I was told to return to my room to await yet more treatment—a massage. I immediately warmed to my masseuse, Adriana, and we were soon chatting like old friends as she put my reluctant joints through their paces. She called me *uccelino*, which means "little bird."

Each morning followed the same pattern, except on Sunday when there was no treatment. The pool was my constant delight and I'd be in the water for about an hour before lunch and again before dinner. All were equal in the pool and people talked freely about themselves and their lives. I learned that many Italians enjoy spa vacations, all expenses paid, through state health benefits or through their companies. They were astonished to hear that I had to pay for everything. Some were regu-lars who had been coming for twenty years or more. Everyone said the same thing—it's best to have the treatment every year to maintain the benefit.

Although Abano is an excellent center for touring, and the surrounding countryside is very beautiful, I was content to have a mostly lazy vacation, enjoying the sunshine and the wonder-ful food and wine, or taking little walks through parks and gardens. I did try the local bus service, which reminded me of the buses back home—not designed with the disabled passenger in mind. But there were usually plenty of people willing to assist.

Toward the end of my stay, I took a bus close to the foot of a wooded hill with a monastery on top, which I had admired every day from the breakfast terrace and which at first looked unattainable but, as the treatment began to take effect, presented both a possibility and a challenge. I'll never forget my joy as I climbed the winding road to the top with the sun shining and the birds singing. The views were superb and my body felt healed and strengthened. I knew then that the treatment had worked for me and that I would return.

Venice for All

While spending nine months in Nancy, France, studying for her degree in French and European literature, Sian Williams (a wheelchair user) was one of a party of about twenty people who took an Easter break in 1987. They traveled in convoy—two cars and two minivans—to Lido di Jesolo, a resort not far from Venice.

The idea was originally dreamed up by some workers for the regional branch of *APF* (*Association des Paralyzés de France*), an organization which aims to promote and improve the integration of people with disabilities into the community. Not surprisingly, we jumped at the chance to explore Venice—a city that I expect many disabled people would steer well clear of. The party included about ten people with different types of disabilities; the others were the "enablers"—some who worked for *APF*, others who also had experience of living and working with disabled people, and a few students for whom this trip would be their first contact with the likes of us!

The gray skies and drizzle that accompanied us through France and Germany in the early hours of the morning were soon forgotten when, emerging from one of Switzerland's many tunnels, we were met by brilliant sunshine which stayed with us throughout our week in Italy. Arriving at the hotel in the evening, our surprise at seeing steps outside was nothing compared with our surprise when we saw the size of the elevator. With a bit of quick thinking, however, the problem of where some of us were to spend the night was solved . . . .Those whose wheelchairs were too big to fit in the elevator spent the night with the Space Invaders and one-armed bandits in a makeshift dorm on the first floor. The following day, after calling a good proportion of the local property owners, we tracked down a villa with an accessible first floor. Those whose vital statistics were bigger than those of the elevator packed their bags and moved four hundred yards around the corner.

In spite of this initial inconvenience, which arose from being misinformed, for most of us the facilities in the hotel were adequate and the staff proved to be some of the friendliest and warmest people we had ever met. They were always ready to help and they showed exceptional openness toward the disabled members of our party. We encountered similar attitudes among the locals: when asked by one of us to change a rather large bank note, the owner of a pizzeria didn't hesitate—on seeing us all outside, eagerly awaiting our Italian currency, he invited us in and gave us a round of drinks on the house.

We had our own means of transport—the minivans were adapted to take wheelchairs—so that on the mainland we didn't have to rely on public transit and could come and go as we pleased. One day we drove to Aquileia to visit the basilica, which dates from

1031. From the outside it is not particularly impressive but inside the architecture is breathtaking. Huge stone pillars are surrounded by brightly colored mosaics with elaborate designs, such as peacocks and fishing scenes. There is a tape-recorded account, in many different languages, of the historical origins and architectural design of the basilica; this is especially useful for blind or partially sighted visitors. At the far end of the basilica there is a crypt containing Carolingian pillars and its walls and ceiling are covered in well-preserved frescoes. In common with many ancient buildings, though, this one provided considerable access difficulties and some of us could not enter it. I wonder whether total accessibility could be achieved without damaging the looks of such buildings.

In Venice we expected 160 canals and 118 islands, connected by 411 bridges, to present insurmountable barriers, but we successfully visited sights that had once been mere pictures in books or images on TV: the Bridge of Sighs and St. Mark's Square, with its cathedral and Doges' Palace—and its pigeons. Venice is often swamped with tourists; wandering through its streets full of expensive restaurants and shops selling leather goods, jewelry, and glassware, it is easy to forget that the city is also home to many people, but we had only to glance upward at the rows of laundry strung across the streets to remind us.

Whenever we had to travel across stretches of water, we made use of the *vaporetto*, or water-bus. This form of public transit is suitable for those with mobility difficulties because the deck of the water-bus is at the same level as the dock, so that wheelchairs can board and disembark quite easily. It was the sights themselves which posed the access problems, but these were usually overcome with the help of our enablers.

In future, however, disabled visitors may be able to manage without the muscle-power of their companions. An architectural establishment has recognized the need to improve the accessibility of Venice and has launched a project called *VENEZIAPERTUTTI* (Venice For All). A city map and guide have been produced, indicating those islands which are accessible and giving details of facilities in the accommodation on each of these islands. The aims of the project include construction of retractable ramps between those islands which can only be reached on foot, and production of a detailed map showing places of historical and cultural interest with descriptions in Braille. Fingers crossed that there are also plans to build some accessible rest rooms! This was the nightmare during our stay—we sometimes spent over an hour looking for a suitable spot!

"Venice and its surroundings do present problems for the disabled tourist"

We took the opportunity to visit two other islands in the region: Burano and Murano. The former is famous for its lace goods and many islanders rely on this trade for their livelihood. Fishing is another important source of income and the canals throughout Burano were lined with fishing boats as brightly colored as rows of beach cabanas. There were far fewer tourists on this island than in Venice; it was quiet and clean, with the atmosphere of a close-knit community.

Murano is renowned for its production of glassware and I was amazed at the variety of styles and colors of the samples that decorated the shop windows. We visited one of the workshops and were able to see some of the glassblowers at work. Although some of us were unable to negotiate the steps of most of the craft shops on these islands, the salespeople willingly allowed their merchandise to be taken outside for inspection.

Venice and its surroundings do present problems for the disabled tourist but on the whole our week's vacation was an enjoyable experience. The Italians were very friendly, facilities *are* improving, and our enablers eliminated many of the difficulties that we encountered. It was interesting to see the changes in attitude that occurred in the enablers who had had little previous contact with disabled people. At the start of our vacation, there were those who presumed that we enjoyed waiting on sidewalks while everyone else went into a bank or souvenir shop; some did not hesitate to decide what time some-

one with a speech difficulty should go to bed; others were surprised to hear that one of us who uses a wheelchair has two children! By the end of the week, however, there was much greater awareness not only of our personal needs, since some members of the group require help for daily activities such as dressing and eating, but also of those attitudes and barriers which hinder the integration of people with disabilities. Our companions came to realize that even if some of us cannot eat spaghetti without assistance we are nevertheless capable of leading fulfilling and independent lives!

ITALY: TRAVEL NOTES

Sources of Information

Italian Government Travel Office, 630 Fifth Avenue, New York, NY 10111 (☎212/245-4822); 1 place Ville-Marie, Suite 1914, Montréal, PQ H3B 3M9 (☎514/866-7667). No brochures for disabled tourists; some regional accommodation guides use the wheelchair symbol but these cannot be totally relied upon. There is a list of addresses to write to for copies of access guides (*Guide di Accessibilità*), which have been published by some fifteen Italian cities.

Progetto VENEZIAPERTUTTI, Unitá Locale Socio Sanitaria (ULSS), Piazzale Roma, Dorsoduro 3493, 16 Venezia. Go in person, or write to Settore Sociale at this address, for a free copy of the city map and guide (listing accessible hotels and rest rooms, and tourist attractions that can be reached by water bus) that have been produced for the *VENEZIAPERTUTTI* project. A two-volume guide for people with visual disabilities can be borrowed during their visit; arrange to pick up the guide by phoning Marco Polo airport (☎041/541.5017), Sta Lucia rail station (☎041/715.016), or the municipal parking garage in Piazzale Roma (☎041/522.8640).

Ufficio Informazioni API (*Azienda Promozione Turistica*), San Marco, Calle dell'Ascensione 71c, Venezia. Write and ask for their magazine *Un' Ospite di Venezia* (A Guest in Venice). Published weekly in summer and monthly in winter by the local tourist board, this includes much useful information, although it's not aimed specifically at tourists who are disabled. It can also be picked up in Venice at the *EPT* (*Ente Provinciale per il Turismo*) offices or in the receptions of the larger hotels.

Tour Operators

Project Phoenix Trust (Overseas Study Tours for the Disabled, 56 Burnaby Road, Southend-on-Sea, Essex SS1 2TL; ☎0702/466412) is a non profit-making organization with an excellent record for providing special interest vacations for adults who need some physical assistance. It arranges accommodation, transport, and helpers; although all tours leave from the UK, disabled people from overseas can apply— Americans and Canadians, both able-bodied and disabled, have joined these tours in the past. Send large envelope and International Reply Coupon for details. Overseas travelers can also contact the Trust for specific advice on

ITALY: TRAVEL NOTES

places it has visited, including reliable information on accessible hotels: it has organized numerous trips to Italy. Destinations for 1992 were Provence and Egypt, for August 1993 it's art history in Belgium.

Getting There

Milan and Rome are two of the cheaper "gateway" cities in Europe; *Alitalia* flies from Los Angeles to Milan, for example, for around $1000 in summer. Bad reports of *Alitalia*'s service to disabled passengers, however, include one from an unaccompanied wheelchair user (an experienced traveler with full use of his arms) who was refused a ticket unless he took a companion. Safer options for wheelchair travelers might include *Delta*, *United*, *American*, and *Canadian*. Full assistance, with wheelchairs if required, is available at the major **airports**.

Transport

Italian State Railroads (*FS*) provides no special facilities for disabled passengers, although there is an assistance center for disabled passengers at Rome station, open from 7am to 10:30pm. Buses are out of the question for lone wheelchair users, and the **car** is probably the best form of transport within Italy; the nearest source of rental cars with hand controls is *Hertz* in France, at airport locations—Paris, Lyon, Nice, Marseille. In town centers the private car comes a poor second to public transit but local authorities are required to make some arrangements for disabled drivers to **park**, and reserved parking spaces are marked with the international wheelchair symbol.

Accommodation

Wheelchair-accessible hotels are few and far between, especially in cities such as Rome, Venice, and Florence, where steps, both inside and out, are features of most buildings. But Sian Williams found that the warmth of the hotel staff more than compensated, and her group quickly tracked down alternative, more suitable accommodation by telephone. It's definitely worth looking into villa accommodation—large, airy, first-floor rooms with smooth marble floors shouldn't be too difficult to come by.

Anna Thomson stayed at *The Aurora Hotel* (Via Pietro d'Abano, Abano Terme; ☎49/669.081). She returned in 1990 and paid around $65 per night for full board and use of the swimming pool; there was a supplement for the mud treatment.

Project Phoenix Trust recommends the *Hotel Cavour* (☎55/282.461) on the via del Proconsolo in Florence—there are four adapted rooms and a large elevator.

Try the *RAC European Hotel Guide* (see France *Travel Notes*) and the *RADAR* guide, *Holidays and Travel Abroad* (see *Books*, p.590) for more ideas, but your best assessment of facilities will be gained on arrival—reliable information is difficult to get in advance.

Access and facilities

If asked which city in Italy might present most barriers to a visitor in a wheelchair, most people would think of Venice, with its hordes of visitors, waterborne transport, bridges, narrow streets, old buildings, and steps. But the *vaporetti* were accessible, and Sian Williams reports some good initiatives from the *VENEZIAPERTUTTI* project; with strong helpers, the wheelchair users in her group were able to see most of the sights. Their main difficulty was the lack of toilet facilities for disabled people, and this is not a problem confined to Venice.

In Rome, Stephen Hunt was thwarted only by the Sistine Chapel, but again he had a fit companion to help with busy narrow streets, steps, and cobblestones (not to mention an inaccessible hotel elevator). It seems that visitors in wheelchairs must be tough if they are to explore these cities without companions, not only to cope with the difficult surfaces and awkward access to buildings, but also to face Italian drivers when struggling across the wider streets.

In more peaceful Abano Terme, Anna Thomson found the terrain ideal for wheelchairs—the town is flat, the sidewalks well maintained, and there are many resting places for those with limited stamina for walking.

In general terms, there is room for many more *VENEZIAPERTUTTI*-type projects and great scope for improvement in the provision of better access (to buildings, transport, and jobs), aids, equipment, and financial assistance to Italians

ITALY: TRAVEL NOTES

with disabilities, many of whom are unable to obtain even simple car adaptations to enable them to drive. But, as far as the tourist is concerned, general attitudes toward people with disabilities appear to be excellent—a relaxing blend of disinterested acceptance and cheerful readiness to offer assistance.

Books

Access in Rome and *Access in Florence* are published by the *Project Phoenix Trust* (see *Tour Operators*). The guides are updated each time the Trust groups visit the cities—for Rome 1989, Florence 1991—and cost £2.25 plus postage. Stephen Hunt used the Rome guide, which was helpful "even though they don't supply the team of body-builders pictured lugging wheelchairs up and down the steps."

The *Real Guide: Italy* is the most complete general guide.

TELEPHONE CODE:

From the US and Canada dial 011 (international code) and then 39 for Italy.

Greece

Welcomed in Greece

Julie Smethurst is totally blind and an enthusiastic Greek island-hopper. Three of her favorites—Sími, Tílos, and Kárpathos—are in the Dodecanese, southeast of mainland Greece. Here she travels with sighted friends; her account of visiting Spain alone appears on p.281.

SÍMI

Sími announced herself to me by means of an overwhelmingly powerful aroma of herbs: after a hot day, the mingled fragrances of wild thyme, sage, and oregano rose from the hills in great waves and were carried to us on the evening breeze. In the gathering dusk the *Sími I*, which plies daily between Sími and Rhodes, left Turkey astern—we had come within yards of the coastline—and rounded the headland into Sími harbor.

Sími lies closer to Turkey than to any part of the Greek mainland. The island is very small and very hilly—probably not the ideal place for someone with walking difficulties, as reaching anywhere beyond the two main centers of population involves a long walk, a rough climb, a boat journey, or a combination of all three. For example, the tiny community of Nimborios, where we once spent a whole day on the beach and saw only two other people, can be visited by boat or on foot along a rough track which follows the coastline. But the most interesting route is via a tough climb over the headland, where carpets of wild flowers

blossom in their season and you might meet a goatherd minding his animals, their bells gently tonking as they move.

During my first two visits to the island we lived in the *Villa Katerína*, one hundred and nine steep and irregular steps up from the harbor. What was once a quite grand Simiote house, in the wealthy days of the nineteenth century, has been converted into a villa and a studio, both with perfect views over the whole harbor area. From the balcony we could watch all its varied comings and goings: the arrival of the VIPs' launch on a festival day; the daily tripper boats from Rhodes; the inter-island ferries and the Rhodes "waterboat," rising higher and higher as its vital cargo was discharged into the Sími water system. There is now a desalination plant near Emborió but the still-limited supply of water is probably the very factor which has protected Sími from over-rapid growth as a tourist center.

The main thoroughfare around the harbor is horseshoe-shaped, following the dockside, and a walk along it takes you past all the boat moorings plus many shops, cafés, and tavernas. One of my companions had been to Sími before and his return not only meant several warm reunions but also kept us in free drinks for most of the vacation. My first encounter with this particular brand of Greek hospitality was in a dockside café—with our order of coffee and cakes came three enormous brandies ("a present from Sotíris") and from then on we rarely left his café without something in the way of a "present": free coffee, lemonade to take to the beach, the loan of a bottle-opener. We passed many a blissfully idle hour at our favorite table on the edge of the dock.

I rediscovered an old but neglected love of swimming as a result of another reunion, with another Sotíris, who owned a boat in which he would take visitors for day trips to different parts of the island. To leap from the boat into unknown depths of clear, invigorating water was sheer delight. The Aegean is very salty and therefore extremely buoyant, so that there is little or no danger for a confident swimmer—if you become tired it is easy to float until rested. Swimming from this boat is one of the most "independent" experiences I've ever had, for Sotíris generally had some loud music playing on board, so that I could swim freely and alone, using the sound as a beacon for my return.

I found the Greeks very willing to accept my independence and very matter-of-fact about the presence of a blind person. At the same time they were thoughtful when helping, so that the help was practical rather than "fussy" as it often is back home. In a

supermarket which I used regularly on Sími the manager was always careful to sort out my change so that it was easy for me to handle and know which notes and coins I'd received. When I scrambled in and out of boats the Greeks were very quick and adept at conveying where I should place a foot or hand in order to be safe and manage in the easiest way. On the whole, I found their assistance less clumsy than that proffered by my fellow tourists.

TÍLOS

We used the Sími travel agency to reserve a few days on the island of Tílos, about two hours' journey on the inter-island ferry. So it was that we found ourselves aboard the *Panormitis*, the tiny ship which visits all the smaller islands of the Dodecanese at least once a week throughout the year, sailing across a misty sea. There are always interesting people on such ferries if one is inclined to chat: on this one we made the acquaintance of a cab driver on his way home to Kálimnos. He corrected my halting Greek and told us that we must visit his beautiful island one day!

> *"Music poured out of the dockside taverna and it seemed that everyone had turned out to meet the ferry"*

Our arrival at Livádhia, the port of Tílos, was like something out of a romantic novel. The late afternoon sun shone on white houses and little boats, music poured out of the dockside taverna and it seemed that everyone had turned out to meet the ferry. As we stepped ashore we were greeted by our hotel manager, Panagiótis, who loaded our bags into his truck and said "Have a drink here, and come whenever you are ready."

Sími is not exactly noisy but Tílos seemed almost silent. We discovered a beach taverna (the *Irína*) at which we had supper and breakfast within a few yards of the rippling sea. When we told the owner that we should like to visit Megálo Horió (Big Village) and the beach at Éristos Bay, he simply called his friend who owned a truck.

Our driver was something of a raconteur and, like most Greeks, was proud and pleased to show off his island to interested visitors. He had been in the merchant navy and, besides Greek, could speak English, Italian, and Turkish. Now he had settled to look after his farm, whose ripening oranges he pointed out as we passed. He also showed us one of the ruined crusader castles and an archaeological site which he graphically described as a "cemetery of elephants"—a cave where the fossilized remains of dwarf mammoths have been found. Reaching Megálo Horió he showed us a good place to eat and then dropped us off at the beach with a promise to pick us up at the taverna later.

The beaches on Tílos are more extensive than those on Sími but, perhaps because of the time of year, we were badly plagued by flies, which lurked in ominous swarms at the edge of the sea and started biting the moment we emerged. After a swim and lunch in the shade of the recommended taverna's orange trees, we returned to the beach to find a strong wind swirling the sand about in stinging showers. So we contented ourselves with a walk and were back at the taverna in time to meet our truck driver.

Waiting for inter-island ferries can be a very relaxed and pleasant occupation. We ate a late lunch of red mullet and sat out the heat of the day under the awning of a dockside taverna, then strolled around the harbor as the people of Tílos gathered for the arrival of the ferry. She slid into place exactly on time and our new friends waved us off—our truck man, and Panagiótis and his crusty old uncle from the hotel. Two hours later we were once again disembarking in front of Sotíris' café, glad to be back and receiving the "welcome" treatment all over again.

KÁRPATHOS

I arrived on Kárpathos—one of the larger Dodecanese islands—in a tiny, nineteen-seater *Olympic Airways* skyvan. It taxied to a halt and spilled its handful of passengers onto the sliver of ground which until very recently served as the only runway. A short minibus ride brought us to some huts—the airport buildings—and a hearty welcome from George Philippides, the island's "Mr. Tourism."

It was our good fortune to be allocated by George to Minás' taxi for the half-hour journey to our apartment, which was just outside Pigádhia, the main village on Kárpathos. When I complimented him on his music his face immediately lit up (so my friend Sandra told me later). From then on the conversation proceeded happily in a mixture of our two languages. As he said goodbye, after helping with our bags, he gave us his card: "If you want to go anywhere, just give me a call!"

First, though, we explored on foot. As we returned from a long walk, George's hitherto clear instructions seemed to run out about a mile short of home. At what appeared to be a dead end, we were hailed by a friendly man who we assumed would set us on our way. So he did, but only after he'd invited us onto his neighbors' verandah for coffee and a chat. I was reminded, not for the first time, that in Greek "stranger," "guest," and "traveler" are the same word (*xenós*).

Northern Kárpathos is rugged and mountainous, characterized for me by a blustery wind which the villagers of Ólimbos assured us "blows all the time." We visited Ólimbos on one of George Philippides' tourbus trips via a precipitous coastal road which was closed the following week due to fear of landslips! Luckily there is an alternative route by sea via Dhiafáni. The old windmill in the village still grinds flour, and we tasted the distinctive bread which is made from it—so rock hard that it has to be soaked in water before it can be eaten. The wind, the rocky terrain, and the absolute remoteness led me to feel that life in Ólimbos must be tough. Yet the house into which we were invited for cakes gleamed with cleanliness, the people were as friendly and hospitable as ever, and the well-cared-for condition of the churches bore testimony to much love and attention.

"When told that we were visitors she presented each of us with a beautiful fresh artichoke"

It is helpful, and altogether much more relaxing, if one can adopt a flexible approach when participating in Greek island life. A day dawned when the boat trip we had planned proved not to be running. Everyone (except us) knew that the boat was not going to Dhiafáni but no one seemed able to say quite why. The islands can be like that—it usually has something to do with the state of the sea, or the fact that the Greeks do not consider it summer until the beginning of June. If you visit the islands in May—which is not too hot and is the best time to see and smell the flowers—it is likely that some places will not be open and some excursions will not be running yet.

Faced with a suddenly empty Sunday we found Minás and drove from Pigádhia on the east coast of Kárpathos to Arkássa on the west. On the way we frequently drew up to greet Minás' friends—he appeared to know everyone. One of them, an old lady carrying a large basket of vegetables, was given a ride. When told that we were visitors she presented each of us with a beautiful fresh artichoke.

As we arrived, about an hour later, Minás drew our attention to the priest, quietly drinking coffee outside one of the cafés in the village square: "If you ask him, he will show you the museum—he has the key." The priest did indeed show us the museum. Not only must I handle all the objects which defied his or Sandra's description—

various measuring devices and articles used in the Greek Orthodox liturgy— but I must also be shown how all the farming and domestic implements worked. From a jumble of Greek, German, and English we learned that our guide's daughter had attended college in England and that there was a magnificent mosaic which we must not miss seeing on our way to the beach. This was in fact a section of the floor of the Byzantine church of Saint Anastasia, of which it is the only remaining part. Finally, he picked us a bunch of wild flowers and delightedly we repeated after him the Greek names for moon-daisy (*margaríta*) and carnation (*garifalló*).

Before leaving us, Minás had pointed out a track through some rough land which led to the most exquisite sandy beach—long, totally deserted, and bordered by a sparkling sea of exciting rolling waves—in which it was impossible to swim but delightful to play. A major practical advantage of being befriended by an islander with a car is that one can reach places such as this, not normally on the tourist trails. Prices are generally reasonable (a full day out with Minás cost us about $75) and many cab drivers are enthusiastic guides, pointing out interesting features and giving information about their island.

"The workers gathered around, pressing us to eat"

For our last day Minás took us to the three remaining principal villages which we had not so far seen. First, Apéri, said to be one of the richest villages in Greece, populated by Greeks who, once or twice a year, bestir themselves from their olive or lemon groves to travel west and inspect their New York stores.

Next came Mesohóri (Middle Village), remote and primitive, where the women were busy washing clothes in the spring. Greek courtesy being what it is, they immediately removed their bowls of blankets and packets of detergent, inviting us to drink from the spring, which we did. No one spoke any language but Greek, except for the schoolteacher, who could manage French. As we paused to watch some workers laying paving stones, a man appeared with a tray of hot, freshly cooked *loukoumades*—something like a hot doughnut. The workers gathered around, pressing us to eat. Soon my stumbling Greek and Sandra's sign language were being severely tested under a barrage of friendly questions. When they were certain that we could manage no more cakes we headed back to the car, meeting a traffic jam of donkeys blocking the narrow streets on the way. The streets were all made up of steps, so that the donkey is the only "vehicle" which can successfully negotiate them.

We spent the rest of that perfect day in the tiny village of Léfkos—just a few houses and tavernas strung out along the edge of a bay which is almost a lagoon. A swim, a delicious lunch of sea bream at Maria's taverna, siesta under a large tree, and another long swim brought our stay on Kárpathos to an end.

I've heard it said that if you've seen one Greek island you've seen them all, but with more than two thousand islands scattered over an area of ten thousand square miles this has to be untrue. Every one has its own individual color and personality, and I hope to have the privilege of getting to know many more of them, as well as revisiting old friends. For there is no sensation in the world quite comparable with being welcomed as a "guest" by the Greek islanders.

A Rough Ride in Crete

Jo Austen is spastic, severely disabled, wheelchair-bound and has no speech. In September 1989 she went with her able-bodied husband to northwestern Crete.

We flew from London's Gatwick airport, where the hand-luggage checkers were baffled by my light pen, which I wear on my head to point to letters on a card—that's how I communicate. With its plastic casing, long wire, and battery charger it was bound to arouse the curiosity of the security men!

At Haniá airport a taxi driver managed to cram four people's luggage plus my wheelchair into his trunk and we set off for Plataniás, 6 miles west along the coast. We had a choice of

two available apartments in the *Villa Dora*; we chose the one up seven steps, not from sheer cussedness but because in the other one it was impossible to get my chair anywhere near the toilet.

Our first few days were spent being thoroughly lazy. We used a technique we had perfected on other Mediterranean vacations for getting me in and out of the sea: John would put our air-bed at the sea's edge, pull me in my chair backward across the sand and then dump me on the air-bed. Next he walked backward into the sea, pulling the air-bed behind him (fortunately I am fairly light!) until he could stand waist deep; then he'd tip me off the air-bed and hold my head while I swam for five or ten minutes using my peculiar doggy-paddle. When I'd had enough he'd dump me back on the bed, where I'd warm up in the sun while he had a swim. He'd tip me off for another swim as many times as I wanted before towing me back to the shore to sunbathe. Using this method I could have four or five swims a morning without John having to work too hard. This was ideal except for the day when a well-meaning gentleman, with whom we didn't share a common language, approached while John was tipping me off the air-bed and assiduously tried to put me back on!

We rented a car for a week; it's awfully expensive but that or taxis (much cheaper) are essential to us for sightseeing—on the organized bus tours we wouldn't have had time to get around with the wheelchair. On our first day out, we went to the lovely sheltered bay at Falasarna, in the far west of Crete. This part of the island is for the moment unspoiled by tourism: the villages are isolated and roads often no more than rough tracks.

Another day we drove past Haniá to a hilltop called Aptera, where there are ruins dating from the fifth century BC and from early Christian times. Like many ancient sites in Greece, it was almost deserted and virtually inaccessible to wheelchairs. But John tipped the chair up on its big back wheels and we charged off down a precipitous track—my question was whether I was more likely to fall out of the chair sideways or forward! Our reward was to see a vast Roman edifice which looked like three arches of a vast train station and whose use remains a mystery.

Luckily, two other tourists arrived, and they were dragooned into helping us back up the path. After that we swam at Kalíves, where we were able to park on the sand three feet from the water's edge. We decided to have an early supper before driving back, so John pushed me along the main road, looking for a taverna. The road was quiet at this time and it was clear that none of the villagers who watched us from their doors had seen a wheelchair in Kalíves. This didn't surprise me, but I was embarrassed later on when an old man approached me, muttering in Greek and making the sign of the cross—I couldn't tell whether he was praying for me or warding off the evil eye!

The ancient site I'd always wanted to visit was Knossós, but since it was 95 miles away we decided to make our visit a two-day event, renting a room for the night. We took the best road in Crete, to Réthimno and Iráklio; Knossós is just 3 miles southeast of Iráklio. The site is vast, much bigger than the modern village in which we found a suitable room—three steps up to the entrance and no way of squeezing my chair into the bathroom but we coped for a night.

"Royal Road, probably the oldest road in Europe and definitely not built for wheelchairs"

The palace of Knossós is a relic of the Minoan civilization that thrived over 3500 years ago. It was excavated by Sir Arthur Evans, who made some dubious reconstructions that at least provide fuel for the imagination and give some idea of how the palace might have looked. It is certainly like the legendary labyrinth (built by Daedalus to contain the Minotaur: half-bull, half-man) and I can only describe things as I remember them, between being hauled up and down flights of steps by more or less willing tourists (Knossós is not recommended for wheelchairs, especially if you or your pusher is shy of asking for help, but with determination you can go anywhere).

I remember looking down from the reconstructed second floor onto a row of storerooms with giant *pithoi* (jars) which would have held grain, wine, or oil—they were certainly bigger than me! I liked the Throne Room, which has a reconstructed fresco of two griffins just visible on the far wall and a tiny throne complete with footstool, whether for a ruler or a priestess is unsure. The Queen's Suite is luxurious, leading off the Hall of the Colonnades and with a dolphin fresco along one wall of the main living room. Down a short passage is the Queen's bathroom, with its clay tub protected behind a low wall. My last memory is of the Hall of the Double Axes, where this symbol is carved into every block of masonry. We came out to the theater, with its two tiers of seats, and I sat on the podium which is thought to be the site of the royal box. From there we walked along what remains of the Royal Road, probably the oldest road in Europe and definitely not built for wheelchairs.

The Archaeological Museum in Iráklio houses treasures from Knossós and the other ancient sites of Crete. There were tiny models of goddesses with serpents climbing their arms, long swords with handles inlaid with gold, and many small Minoan clay coffins. But the most interesting collections for me were upstairs, so we pounced on a passing tourist (no elevator, of course) and struggled up. It was the Hall of Frescoes that I wanted to see—carefully reconstructed wall paintings from Knossós and other sites. My favorite was the depiction of bull-leaping, in which acrobatic young men and women leapt and somersaulted over the backs of the sacred bulls.

Heading south from Iráklio through fields of drying grapes we drove over the mountains to Festos, a ruined palace much smaller than Knossós and surrounded by hills. Here, reconstructions were kept to a bare minimum but plenty remains, including most of the storerooms. The central court is huge and, now that the two-story buildings on each side have crumbled, the views across the plain of Messará are spectacular. The north corridor leads to the spot where you can look down on the royal apartments; the Festos disc, which we had seen in the museum, was found nearby. Made of clay, it is marked with hieroglyphic characters that are still undeciphered. Before we left Festos, I downed two mugs of the deliciously cool drinking water which is provided free at the main sites.

The sea was rough for our last two days in Plataniás—that can be a problem on Crete—but we found a small harbor where the water was always calm enough to swim. On our last day John packed while I lay in the sun, and at midday, which was really too early for the taverna, we had our last meal, served by our favorite waiter.

Crete is not for the unadventurous, but if you have a strong companion and are willing to ask others for assistance it is a wonderful experience.

Somewhere Warm and Somewhere New

As the result of an operation, Allan Green has the symptoms of a stroke victim: he is unable to walk or use his right arm and his speech and vision are also affected; in addition he suffers from polymyositis. Allan and his wife, Lorna, went to Greece in 1988.

As a comparative newcomer to the ranks of the disabled, I didn't know what a wheelchair user could expect when traveling by air. So for the first trip after I came out of hospital, Lorna and I chose the short flight from Bournemouth, England, to Guernsey, one of the Channel Islands off France, which took only half an hour. The aircraft was small and it was my first experience of being carried aboard, in one of the airline's narrow, portable seats. The journey and the staff, both on board and at the airports, were very pleasant and we had no difficulty at all, so we thought we'd venture a little farther afield.

Since Lorna has taken premature retirement to look after me, we can go on vacation when it suits us. We wanted to avoid the busiest time of year, to fly from a local airport, to go somewhere warm and, preferably, somewhere new. It didn't take us long to decide on the Greek island of Rhodes (Ródhos) in September. The travel agent knew of my condition and we took a hotel recommended by the tour operator (*Thomson*). We were told that the travel agent would see to everything but we rang the airline a few days before departure to explain our requirements and book a front seat.

"We sat in the shade where, we are told, Hippocrates taught medicine in the fifth century BC"

When the day came, we were helped through the few formalities at each airport and helped when we were on the plane, so we arrived without any trouble. As I cannot board a bus we had to take a cab to our hotel—a pleasant, unhurried ride of about twenty minutes. The *Hotel Metropolitan Capsis* is large, with several elevators, no steps at the front or inside, ramps to the two pools and to the restaurant in the grounds, and even a rest room for disabled guests on the same level as the pools. As in many hotels, the beds were low and it would have been difficult for Lorna to lift me from mine. We asked for an extra mattress and it was supplied immediately.

The hotel is in Ixia, a short distance from Ródhos town; anyone feeling energetic could walk in half an hour, but we were on vacation and there was no sidewalk along one section of the road, so we went by taxi for a couple of dollars each way. Ródhos town has two distinct parts, the old and well-preserved medieval town, and the spreading new town

with its hotels, bars, casinos, discos, restaurants, shops, and banks. We particularly liked the old town, and its narrow cobblestone streets did not defeat my wife and the wheelchair. It's true that the shops in the main street of the old town (Odhós Sokrátous) were of the type seen in most vacation resorts, but they don't destroy the charm completely and there is much to see away from the shops, and much pleasure to be gotten from simply wandering the attractive lanes.

Two or three times we enjoyed strolling around the smaller of the two harbors (Mandhráki), where small boats and ferries were moored. The temperature was in the eighties and after walking for a while in that heat we'd accept the hospitality of one of the many bars, and watch the world go by. Here, too, we booked ferries to other islands; we could have arranged these in advance but we wanted to check the boats for access.

Our first trip was to Kós, which is smaller than Ródhos but has a similar relaxed and friendly atmosphere and a similar Knights of St. John castle overlooking the harbor. The ferry took three and a half hours (hydrofoil is quicker) so we had only a few hours on the island and saw only Kós town. There are many Greek and Roman remains here, and a very old plane tree at the entrance to the castle. We sat in the shade where, we are told, Hippocrates taught medicine in the fifth century BC. (The tree is not *that* old, but certainly one of the oldest in Europe.) The gangway of the ferry to Kós was wide enough to take my wheelchair, but on the *Sími I* it wasn't. This was easily overcome, though, by two crew members who carried me (in the wheelchair) on and off. Sími is even smaller, and something of a contrast to Ródhos and Kós. The houses seemed to scramble up the steep slopes rising from the harbor. I saw Sími town described in a travel book as "like a film set" and that's how it appeared to me.

There were stands along the dockside, some selling sponges, for which the island is famous. It also had a reputation for boat-building at one time, but is now just home to several old seafarers.

Being unable to board a bus, we missed out on the organized tours on our own island, so we hired a taxi for the day. It cost about $90, or the equivalent of two bus tours each. Most tourists on Ródhos pay a visit to Líndhos, about 30 miles south of Ródhos town, and this was our first stop. It is a picturesque, whitewashed town, with winding pebble streets. Lorna managed to maneuver my chair around the town, but I stayed chatting to our driver in the shade of a café while she climbed higher to the ancient acropolis, with its Doric Temple of Athena (sixth century BC).

We crossed to the other side of the island, passing through one or two small villages, and after a delicious fish lunch headed back toward Ródhos town. On the way we stopped at the "Valley of the Butterflies" (*Petaloúdhes*), which was well wooded with a stream running through it. In fact it is the valley of the Jersey tiger moths—orange and black striped, well camouflaged when stationary on a tree.

"It brought home to us the advantages of hiring a cab"

Our last stop was the Filérimos monastery, about 3 miles inland from Triánda, among the pines on Filérimos hill. There were a number of steps here, so I was unable to go in, but Lorna looked around. We came across a party from a cruise liner being unceremoniously herded onto their tour-buses and told to board without delay; it brought home to us the advantages of hiring a cab—we could go where we liked and linger as long as we chose to.

Most evenings we ate at our hotel, for the food was good. There was always a selection of cold dishes to start with, all sorts of salads and perhaps stuffed vine leaves and squid.

The main dishes were rather international but always included a fish dish, presumably local and usually tasty. Dessert could be anything from fresh fruit to sticky *baclavá*. There was a vast choice at breakfast, hot and cold; my favorite was peaches with Greek yoghurt, followed by salami with feta cheese. We usually finished the night off in our favorite bar, appropriately called *The Sea House* as it's almost on the beach, where we met up with some of the friends we'd made.

Talking of people, throughout our stay everyone, including hotel staff, taxi drivers, boat crews, and bar staff, was very helpful. In addition, though I find British people at home very kind, if anything they were even better on vacation. For example, there were some public rest rooms in Ródhos town, not specially for disabled people, but whenever I wanted to use them there was no shortage of willing helpers.

When the time came to fly home, we arrived at the airport early, checked in, and made ourselves known to our rep. Passport control and departure gates are on the second floor, up a flight of stairs, and there is no elevator. The rep took our passports, had them stamped and asked us to wait on the first floor until someone came to collect us. We'd be the last on the aircraft, so we were not to worry about the other passengers boarding. Lorna asked a few questions and was assured that we'd not be forgotten as all the important people knew about the arrangement.

I suppose we waited about an hour until our flight began boarding. We assumed that someone would collect us shortly but we waited and waited and no one came. Then we heard an announcement: "Will the last two passengers for Cardiff please report to Gate Five." We knew the message was for us but what could we do? There was no way of getting me up to the second floor. We couldn't find a rep, from *Thomson* or any other tour company, so we approached a desk and tried to communicate with the Greek member of staff behind it. Another announcement blared out: "This is the last call for the two passengers for Cardiff. Please report immediately to Gate Five." We were speaking, gesticulating, pointing to the speakers and, somehow, our Greek friend must have realized our predicament. He wandered off, in no particular hurry, and came back two or three minutes later with a colleague.

This one did hurry. Taking a firm hold of the handles of my wheelchair, he shouted for a way through the milling crowd, and raced me in and out of a baggage handling section, through passport control for arriving passengers, and out onto the runway, with my wife running behind. I was quickly transferred to an airline chair, carried up the steps, and installed in my seat. Almost immediately we taxied away and I could imagine the other passengers wondering what on earth we'd been up to. Lorna explained what had happened to one of the cabin staff who was very sympathetic—we were supplied with free drinks all the way. So the plane didn't leave us behind, which was a pity in a way because we wouldn't have minded a little longer on Ródhos.

GREECE: TRAVEL NOTES

Sources of Information

National Tourist Organization of Greece (*Ellinikós Organizmós Tourismóu*, or *EOT*), Olympic Tower, 645 Fifth Avenue, New York, NY 10022 (☎212/421-5777); Upper Level, 1300 Bay Street, Toronto, ON M5R 3K8 (☎416/968-2220). Supplies maps and general information, but little on disability—a short list of hotels said to have facilities for disabled guests (at least the facilities are listed). The *Travel Agent's Manual* has a paragraph on "Travel for the Handicapped"—dated and of limited value.

Mobility International Hellas, 101 Egnatia Street, 8th Floor, Thessaloniki GR-54635; ☎31/234489, 206667. *MI Hellas* grew from a specialist travel agency called *Lavinia Tours*, managed by wheelchair-user Eugenia Stavropoulou, and is involved in disability issues in Greece and at an international level through the *MI* program of meetings, leisure weeks, and exchanges.

Tour Operators

Grecofile (Sourdock Hill, Barkisland, Halifax, West Yorkshire HX4 0AG, UK; ☎0422/375999) acts as a consultancy for Greek vacations and as a travel agency (*Abakos Worldwide*) for trips to other parts of the world. It does its best to suggest suitable destinations but stresses that it is bound by what the tour operators have to offer and by the physical restrictions of Greece itself.

Julie Smethurst obtained advice from *Grecofile* on which tour operators cover the small islands. *Laskarina Holidays* (St. Mary's Gate, Wirksworth, Derbyshire DE4 4DQ, UK; ☎062982/2203) and *Twelve Islands* (Angel Way, Romford, Essex RM1 1AB, UK; ☎0708/752653) were most efficient in making her travel arrangements, particularly for the transfers within Greece itself.

Jo Austen explained her needs to *Grecofile* and asked for accommodation very near the beach, close to a village and tavernas, and fairly accessible. *Grecofile* recommended a set of apartments available through *Sunvil Travel* (7–8 Upper Square, Isleworth, Middlesex TW7 7BJ, UK; ☎081/568 4499), which points out in its brochure that most of their vacations are unsuitable for wheelchair users—they are often built on sloping ground, with many steps to negotiate. But it will try to help, if consulted well before reservations are made.

GREECE: TRAVEL NOTES

In a country of craggy islands with villages clinging to cliffsides, there must be give and take between tour operator and disabled client. If both parties are honest, and all efforts are made to find manageable accommodation, there should be no recriminations. Jo was satisfied with both *Grecofile* and *Sunvil*. The *Sunvil* rep in Haniá was very helpful, and Jo feels that this company is one of the more caring small tour operators.

Allan Green was given good advice on accommodation by *Thomson*, and with the introduction of *Thomson's Factfile* (see The Canaries *Travel Notes*) it should be possible to obtain some access details on properties in all *Thomson* group brochures.

Getting There

Several tour operators run charter flights to Greece from the USA and Canada, but comfort levels on charter flights of this duration may be too low for some. *Olympic Airways* flies from New York, Boston, and Chicago to Athens; flights from Montréal and Toronto are via New York; aisle chairs are not carried. *Delta* operates daily flights via Frankfurt, *United* via Paris.

Most European airlines connect North America with Greece, via major European cities: those with good reputations among disabled travelers include *British Airways*, *KLM*, *Lufthansa*, *Air France*, and *Swissair*. The flight to Greece **from London** is short enough to bear even a charter flight, and most airlines should provide adequate service. Take the cheapest deal you can find. If you encounter any problems on a flight to Greece, they'll be at **Athens airport**, where a few travelers have reported less than friendly handling, and where if you are flying onward from the domestic terminal you may be taken along subterranean passages or have to fight for a taxi outside the international terminal (if you are changing planes in Athens, flying in with *Olympic* saves a long trek from the East Air Terminal, used by all international flights except *Olympic*, to the West Air Terminal, for *Olympic* and all domestic flights). For some islands, if traveling from Europe, you can avoid flying to Athens altogether: there are direct flights to Rhodes, Crete, Corfu, Lesvos, and more; Kárpathos is reached via Rhodes.

Driving to Greece is feasible and enjoyable if you have the time, perhaps passing through France and Switzerland, aiming for ferry ports in Italy or—if the fighting stops—Yugoslavia (consult *The Real Guide: Greece* for suggested routes and details of ferry services). Taking an adapted car (eg from *Hertz*, France) or van (eg from *Wheelchair Travel*, England) will solve potential accessible transport difficulties, but don't expect to find a network of highways, and be aware that driving in Greece can be hazardous (see below).

Transport

Olympic Airways operates all **internal flights**, using small aircraft. Be prepared to be carried up and down the steps from the plane. The island airports are tiny, with no special facilities, but they can be negotiated, even if passport control and departure gates are upstairs.

The width of gangways varies but **ferry** travel is always possible for wheelchair users with help from the crew, and it's an important part of many vacations in the Greek islands. A blind person can obtain a free ticket for a companion on Greek ferries run nationally.

Buses are inaccessible and often overloaded. **Taxis**, though, are cheap, especially when shared, and they tend to be Mercedes with plenty of room for luggage and wheelchair in the trunk. The roads are terrible in many areas so don't expect a smooth ride. Cars can be rented, without hand controls, but it's no fun driving on Greek roads and better to befriend a local taxi driver.

Accommodation

On the larger, more developed islands some of the modern hotels may have suitable facilities. The *Hotel Metropolitan Capsis* (Ixia, Rhodes; ☎241/25015), recommended by Allan Green, has elevators, no steps, ramps to the swimming pools, and even a public rest room for disabled guests.

But staying in village rooms, villas, or small hotels will require compromise—taking a room in a house with several steps at the entrance because you can get into the rest room, using chair-to-chair transfer to get through the bath-

GREECE: TRAVEL NOTES

room doorway—and some assistance. That said, there has been one report from a paraplegic who arrived on a rugged, sparsely populated island, with no accommodation booked in advance, and found a fully accessible village room only minutes from the beach—if you're prepared to risk it, there's a fair chance you'll strike lucky.

Access and Facilities

Jo Austen's account proves that some of the roughest ground to be found in Greece can be covered in a wheelchair, but not without strong helpers and a pioneering spirit. Remember to take a puncture repair kit. (There are a few hints on coping with rough ground in the *Tours and Cruises* section.)

Those who are not wheelchair-users but are unsteady on their feet or have limited stamina for walking should study the terrain of their chosen destination with care. If your island is hilly and you need good ankle support, don't plan to wear flimsy sandals simply because you expect hot weather: steep and winding streets, composed of large, uneven stone slabs or cobblestones, put great stress on arthritic joints, for example. Feet, ankles, knees, and hips will take a pounding, so pack hiking boots.

Of course, Greece isn't all rocky outcrops and ruins, and there are accessible pastimes, including pottering around the docksides and eating outside one of the numerous restaurants. You won't find too many public rest rooms, let alone accessible ones, but Greek hospitality is justly renowned, and our contributors report a practical, unpatronizing approach to their disabilities. It's one of those countries in which the charms of the people make light of the physical obstacles.

Although there are no signs of government recognition of access as a right for disabled people, there is a thriving disability "movement," typified by *Mobility International Hellas*.

Health and Insurance

State-run outpatient clinics, found in rural areas and attached to public hospitals, are fine for most problems that cannot be sorted out with the pharmacist. But get there early to avoid the lines. This report is from a paraplegic, Nic Fleming: "In 1987 I suffered a severe burn on my left heel, by stupidly letting my bare foot rest on the floor of the car whilst I was driving in very hot weather. The blister was bigger than a golf ball, and the whole heel went black after a few days. The head of a local medical clinic treated it brilliantly."

For complaints that require hospitalization it is wise to use private hospitals because nursing care is not adequate in state hospitals. So make sure that your insurance policy will cover the costs of private medical treatment.

Take a copy of the prescription for your drugs, using the generic name. This will not only enable you to obtain fresh supplies, but also smooth the way with customs officials, who may wish to confirm that none of the drugs contains codeine—it's recently been banned in Greece.

Books

The Real Guide: Greece is the most complete and practical guide.

TELEPHONE CODE:

From the US and Canada dial 011 (international code) and then 30 for Greece.

PART FIVE

NEAR AND MIDDLE EAST

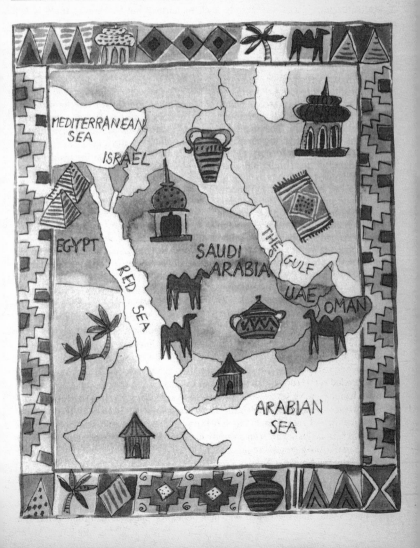

MEDITERRANEAN SEA

ISRAEL

EGYPT

RED SEA

THE GULF

SAUDI ARABIA

UAE

OMAN

ARABIAN SEA

Introduction

A t the time of writing, nearly two years after the **war in the Gulf**, tension in the Middle East continues to cast a shadow over any travel plans. During the war, most flights were canceled or diverted; tour companies shuffled resorts and temporarily suspended their operations; hotel chains pulled out; cruise ships were requisitioned as troop carriers. Since then the airlines have reinstated most of their flights, and many places are entirely back to normal, but the tourist trade is still recovering. Anti-Western demonstrations rumble on, reaching fever pitch in some areas. Ancient sites have been destroyed, wildlife and habitats remain devastated; many inhabitants of the region have become disabled as a direct result of recent wars and ongoing squabbles.

It's difficult to see beyond all this and envision any sort of long-term recovery and stability, given the long list of failed peace conferences, the rigid stances adopted by the major players, the violent oppression of minority groups, and the interference from outsiders mainly concerned with losing control of their oil supply. But, assuming eventual return to some semblance of normality, this part of the world will continue to attract many tourists: to visit sites of religious significance or the remains of early civilizations; to learn something of the feuds and struggles that punctuate the history of the Arab Emirates; to experience the stunning landscapes of the desert and the famed hospitality of the desert peoples; to float down the Nile in a felucca or shop in the souks.

For the disabled tourist the main problems are finding accessible accommodation at less than four-star prices, gaining access to sights, making do (almost everywhere) without any form of accessible transportation, and tracking down a lavatory that doesn't require either the removal of the rest room door or a delicate balancing act in order to use it. These are not insurmountable problems, but it would be cheering to see more widespread efforts to remove them.

The scarcity of accessible transportation does not prevent tourists in wheelchairs from joining **organized tours**, given a tour company with the right approach—three of our contributors found local companies happy to assist. Guides are usually helpful and willing to push chairs or assist with boarding and disembarking; taxi drivers are also helpful. In Egypt there is a company that specializes in tours for disabled people, using an accessible, albeit basically equipped, vehicle. But the introduction of hydraulic lifts on at least half of tour buses would be a great step forward, as would the availability of hand-controlled rental cars and minivans with tail-lifts.

Israel has seen most progress in all these areas, probably as a result of the organizations of disabled people, such as the *Israel Rehabilitation Society* (18 David Elazar Street, Hakirya, Tel Aviv 61909; ☎3/217043) which, through conferences and meetings, attempts to make changes on a variety of fronts, including access to buildings and awareness of disabled people's requirements. Many of the improvements in access and facilities have been brought about as a result of pressure from war veterans.

Some **legislation** has been pushed through concerning hotel facilities (see Israel *Travel Notes*), but either this has failed to make an impact at the cheaper end of the market, or there has been a failure in communication. Perhaps some of the smaller hotels have made improvements, widened doorways, adapted bathrooms, but the promotion of this new-found accessibility has not been effective—there is certainly nothing in the tourist board brochures.

Increasing **awareness** of the (often minor) modifications needed to make accommodation and sights accessible to people with disabilities is of prime importance in countries where a wheelchair is a rare sight and there is an alarming lack of understanding of the problems of those with limited mobility, vision, or hearing. Barry Atkinson comments on being directed to impossible places by a customs official on the border between Israel and Egypt; the officer clearly had no experience of wheelchairs. This is an area of the world where, in general, people with disabilities are kept at home or in institutions. Even in Israel, where the concept of independent living appears to be more widely accepted, researchers gathering information for the guide, *Access in Israel*, reported in 1988 that although they met many people who were concerned they "often encountered complete incomprehension concerning the needs of disabled people or the shrug of the shoulder, indicating indifference."

Attitudes might have changed over the past five years or so, but it's difficult to be optimistic when the response of the Israeli tourist board to a request for information for disabled travelers is to send not only a copy of *Access in Israel* but also a package of leaflets on health resorts and medical treatments for psoriasis—equating disability with sickness and "cures" is a sure sign that the idea of a disabled person as a tourist like anyone else has not yet sunk in. A better response would be a copy of the access guide, with an insert updating any addresses and phone numbers that have changed, plus the standard set of brochures, all of which should contain some mention of facilities for visitors with disabilities—at accommodations, on transport, at tourist attractions, with local tour companies.

That said, Israel is ahead of its neighbors on this issue, and this is the real world—there isn't a country in it that deals adequately with provision of access information in its tourist literature—but in the 1990s, in countries that have devoted considerable energies and funds to arming themselves, there is really no excuse for failing to provide basic physcial access for their own war veterans (and other disabled people), and failing to grasp that just as their own people need to travel freely, without barriers, within their countries, foreign visitors could also use the accessible facilities supplied—and will pay to do so.

In many countries the money is there, the ritzy hotels, the shops, the hospitals, the highways, the modern airports. But the forces that fired the independent living movements, the pressures that brought about the necessary environmental changes in other parts of the world are largely absent or only just beginning—or, in a few countries, they are established but engaged in a long battle with governments which have placed access and equal rights for disabled people way down the list of priorities.

Israel

The View from Masada

Barry Atkinson spent three weeks in Israel, in January 1989, including a trip into Egypt's Sinai desert. He is virtually confined to a wheelchair but has strong arms and is well used to traveling alone.

It was not the entry to the country that I had imagined. I was alone and in a wheelchair, riding an Airbus to Ovda, instead of tramping wearily to some kibbutz near Jerusalem. But, let's face it, I was extremely lucky to be where I was. The tight security at London's Gatwick airport, the two-hour delay when customs officers refused a couple entry, the five-hour flight, all added to my anticipation.

Rather against my natural inclinations, I had chosen a hotel in the tourist area of Eilat, on the Red Sea, and a package agent, *Intasun*. The usual bank loan had paved my way; the hotel had the wheelchair symbol in the *Best Western* guide (which I had always found very satisfactory); I had a pocket full of travelers' checks and felt safe. True, because of media coverage and the possibility of terrorist attacks on planes, many people had advised me not to go, but I had quite a bit of travel experience, and my interest in the conflicts between Islam and Christianity, plus the aura of desert lands, held sway. It was one of the best decisions I have ever made.

The Airbus landed in the dark at Ovda, in the Negev desert. I was carried

off the plane (there is no high-lift vehicle at present) and the *Intasun* bus drove to Eilat along the Egyptian border. My hotel, although living up to the luxury of its four-star status, did not, to my mind, deserve the wheelchair symbol. The steps to the dining room were soon overcome because I was given special service in an accessible coffee room. But, even with the door taken off, I could not get my wheelchair from the bedroom into the bathroom.

The *Intasun* rep advised me to move to the *Sport Hotel*, which has adapted rooms, but I liked where I was and did not want to pay the extra money to stay at the *Sport*. Instead, I obtained a second wheelchair from the local hospital and left it in the bathroom; I could then transfer from my own chair to that one when I wanted to use the bathroom. Problem solved! But I had to pay $350 returnable deposit to the hospital, which meant money tied up that I could ill afford (I used the credit card instead). This incident illustrates the advantage of having a tour company rep on the spot—she arranged the wheelchair loan for me. (I have since complained to *Best Western*, which sent a standard "sorry" reply and said that they had sent my letter to their branch in Israel. I have heard nothing more.)

My first trip was a two-day tour to Jerusalem, Bethlehem, the Dead Sea, and Jericho—biblical names to conjure with! Via the *Intasun* rep, I had explained the position to the tour company and they had agreed to cope with the wheelchair and my lack of mobility. Later, after a marvelous two days, I paid the guide and driver a big tip. The same tour company refused to take me, unless accompanied, on a five-day trip to Cairo. Fair enough! I was in no position to argue and, judging by comments from those that went, perhaps they were right. I wheeled myself to a local restaurant and had a red-hot meal and bottle of wine instead.

One of the aspects of disability that I find difficult is coping with an early start. When traveling, especially alone, this is unavoidable and has to be accepted; often it is the only way to achieve anything. The trip to Jerusalem meant rising at 4am, but it was worth it. During the day, Eilat, although windy, was basking in hot sunshine at 75–80°F. It was early when we started but as we drove north amid the scree and rocky wastes of the Negev desert, the temperatures dropped. Forlorn acacia trees clung everywhere to the loose, gritty surface. As the sun rose, a collection of strange shadows appeared on either side of the road.

As the light grew we became aware of unexpected green areas, as kibbutzim broke from the desolate landscape. Israel has watered itself from north to south by a National Water Carrier pipe which keeps even the deep south of Eilat (with an average annual rainfall of less than an inch) fertile. The Sea of Galilee, fed by the River Jordan, is its main reservoir. The water-line, together with the intensive agriculture of the kibbutzim, are vital to Israel's survival.

When we came to the Dead Sea (actually two shrinking lakes) the sky was blue but the temperature cool, so few floated in the mineral waters. Instead we watched the rapidly changing salt deposits, which bloom across the sea like eaten mushrooms or lines of battered coral. The factory complex which is built on the site of ancient Sodom bursts with economic vitality 24 hours a day, using the minerals formed here.

"'Jerusalem has no heavy industry—only religion.' The immediate impression is one of graves"

Next we went to Masada where, in 73 AD, the Jews made a last desperate stand against the Romans, eventually committing a grisly mass suicide. Today the Zealots' action is revered, and I have seen pictures which show that the archaeological site is both carefully preserved and deeply interesting. But there was no way that my wheelchair could reach it. Masada rises 1300 gaunt feet from the Dead Sea, and the ruins are on a plateau at the top. A cable car takes you halfway up, from where the view is magnificent, but a multitude of steps continue.

Sitting on the cable car platform, staring across the miniaturized desert and Dead Sea, I tried to put my frustration into perspective. There was a lot of life in front of me: the Jordanian border running through the center of the Dead Sea, and nearby Qumran, now an unearthed Essene settlement, where the priceless Dead Sea Scrolls were discovered; and there was the Judean desert, barely disturbed by humankind.

In the manner of bus tours, Jericho—a peaceful city of date palms to the northeast of Jerusalem—was a rushed visit which left me with a feeling of attraction that only a repeat visit can confirm. Like Bethlehem, Jericho is an Arab town. Throughout the ages the city, which has been rebuilt many times, has remained close to Elisha's Spring. A site known as Tel es-Sultan has been excavated at intervals since 1868, and evidence of a colony as early as 8000 BC has been found. The falling of the city walls to Joshua's famed trumpets, whatever the real cause, happened about 1250 BC. We listened to the tour guide's patter, bought citrus fruit at a local market, and drove on to Jerusalem.

There was no disputing the guide's next statement: "Jerusalem has no heavy industry—only religion." The immediate impression is one of graves. The tombs lie on all the slopes of the walled, ancient city because the Jews are still awaiting the arrival of the Messiah, who will enter the Temple Courts through the now blocked Golden Gate. The dead buried here will be the first to rise.

"I was humbled at simply feeling the mortar, ancient and pitted, beneath my fingers"

Israel has a total population of over four million: over three million are Jews, 525,000 Muslims, 95,000 Christians, and 53,000 Druze. Jerusalem is a holy city for all; despite the external conflict, the atmosphere is one of religious freedom. The followers of Christ move along the Via Dolorosa, with its fourteen stations of the cross, and worship in the Church of the Holy Sepulchre. Muslims visit their third holy city after the hadj (pilgrimage to Mecca; their second holy city is Medina).

A portion of the Koran speaks of a night journey made by Muhammed, accompanied by an angel. This journey is believed to have ended at Solomon's Temple, where the Dome of the Rock was built. Muslims visit this and the nearby Al-Aqsa mosque. To the Jews, the Temple Mount—home to Islam's Dome of the Rock—is Mount Moriah, where Abraham bound his son Isaac for sacrifice. The hillcrest was also the site of David's altar, over which Solomon built the Temple, eventually replaced by Herod's edifice.

Today, only Herod's western wall (the famous "Wailing Wall") remains, and it has become a symbol of the unwavering faith and devotion of Judaism. After being vetted by the armed guards, we arrived at the Wailing Wall and found it very much alive, constantly visited by Jews who pray and rock in anguish before it. I rolled up to the men's section in my wheelchair and put my hand on the rough surface. Beside me a young orthodox Jew, black suited and with plaited hair falling beneath his dark, wide-brimmed hat, seemed to play out his nation's grief, his hand clutching the Torah. On my other side a rabbi talked with the male members of the family of a bar mitzvah boy; out of my sight the women gave vent to the poignant trill of Eastern, female emotion. I was humbled at simply feeling the mortar, ancient and pitted, beneath my fingers.

Perhaps Jewish hotel bathrooms are all the same because, once again, I could not get my wheelchair through the door. Luckily, I could just get to the toilet and sinks by using the sinks as grab rails and swinging around. It was only for one night, and somehow the sinks took my weight, but it was not the best of situations!

The morning saw us leave for Bethlehem and the Church of the Nativity, which is shared by the Armenians, the Greek Orthodox Church, and the Latins. We passed the little synagogue built on the spot of Jacob's burial of his young wife, Rachel. Bethlehem was disappointing in that, unlike much of the Holy Land, it has a totally commercial, "tripperish" feel.

The gaudy tourist shops in the square by the church disperse all reverence. My wheelchair kept me out of the Grotto of the Nativity, and perhaps actually being in the place of Jesus' birth would have restored some of the emotion, but I was happy to leave and return to the Mount of Olives with its fantastic view of old Jerusalem. Here, despite the Arabs offering rides on their stolid, gaily bedecked camels, or pestering us to buy trinkets, there was no distraction. Below us was the ancient, walled city in all its splendor, fronted by the bright gold of the Dome of the Rock and the silvered rotunda of Al-Aqsa mosque.

We returned to warmer Eilat, some 186 miles away, where, knowing my illness and aware of the need to pace myself, I spent a few quiet days sunbathing by the pool or slowly wheeling myself along the boardwalk. With friends I had made on the Jerusalem trip, I went to Coral World, nearby on the Red Sea. The underwater observatory was inaccessible to me but there was a marvelous aquarium. Red Sea marine life is unbelievably varied and colorful; the fish make a brilliant display, swimming amid the delicate lacework of the coral. Apart from the observatory, Coral World is ramped and access easy; I paid reduced admission because of the observatory. For those who are able, the Red Sea is justly renowned for sub-aqua diving.

After some lazy days I decided on another trip. As before, I arranged this with the *Intasun* rep and a local company. I was to go into Egypt, to St. Catherine's Monastery in the Sinai desert. I already had a visa, although I learned when booking the trip that you can visit the monastery without one. As usual, the start was early; indeed, the dawn did not break until we were in Egypt, waiting outside the wretched frontier huts for a second tour bus to pick us up.

An Israeli bus had brought us to Taba (a tiny stretch of land then in dispute,

now handed over to Egypt), and we had walked across the border. The guide pushed me and helped happily throughout. My experience of traveling in Arab lands has been that the ways of dealing with a wheelchair are often simply not understood, the problems of steps not considered. Here, the lethargic customs officials ushered me to impossible places, and were nonplussed when I could not go; only the common sense of the guide saved an awkward situation. But my excitement at being on the edge of such a famed desert could not be dampened, even if, watched by the tired eyes of the customs officers, we had to wait for ninety minutes for our second bus.

"My shouts of pain and panic were ignored; my legs trailed beneath the chair, waiting to break"

The early cloud departed and our transport arrived. At first we drove past hills of red and green rocks, alternating with regions of flat scree. Then came the higher ground, and layers of sand that hinted at Africa's Sahara, now so near. Sometimes a lone camel wandered past, sometimes a bedouin, protected and hidden beneath his robes. Where was he going? To the coast? To an isolated nomadic camp?

St. Catherine's Monastery is run by Greek Orthodoxy, not by the Coptic Church as is wrongly stated in the tourist brochure. Named after the finding of St. Catherine nearby, it still maintains the (disappointing) burning bush, and it overlooks Mount Moses. Not so long ago the only entry into the monastery was by basket, hauled up the walls. Today there is a door, but so narrow that a wheelchair has no chance. Besides, I could glimpse flights of steps inside, so I decided to wait outside with the sleepy bedouin "servants" to the monks.

However, two Egyptian guides were now in charge of us and, ignoring my protests, they carried me through the door, deposited me awkwardly on the ground and returned for the folded wheelchair. Somehow I clambered aboard and, panting, was inside the monastery. In fact there was little to see except the ornate grandeur of the incense-soaked church, and the burning bush which is almost hidden behind thick walls.

Trouble came, as I had foreseen, with the steps. The Egyptian happily pushed me along but when we came to the steps he simply carried on as though they did not exist. My shouts of pain and panic were ignored; my legs trailed beneath the chair, waiting to break, while I clutched uselessly at the armrests. Luckily, a member of the party saw what was happening and forced the bewildered guide to stop. Highly relieved, I was carried the rest of the way down.

Once outside, we visited the piles of bones of all the dead monks in the charnel house, then boarded the bus again. The mishaps in the monastery were soon forgotten amid the evocative spaces of the desert. A desert landscape is not only different, it is special. One's mind, attempting to deal with the empty spaces, is forced into strange, almost spiritual regions. If I ever get to the Sahara it surely cannot affect me as much as this, my first time in Sinai.

ISRAEL: TRAVEL NOTES

Sources of Information

Israel Government Tourist Office, 350 Fifth Avenue, New York, NY 10118 (☎212/560-0650); 180 Bloor Street West, Suite 700, Toronto, ON M5S 2V6 (☎416/964-3784). By far the best equipped in the region to deal with inquiries from disabled travelers, with copies of *Access in Israel* (see *Books*) to distribute. In addition, it's good to see a mention of "Facilities for the Handicapped" in the general booklet, *Israel: A Visitor's Companion*; two useful contacts are supplied—*MILBAT* (The Advisory Center for the Disabled), which should be able to help with visitors' inquiries and is located at Sheba Medical Center in Tel Aviv (☎3/5303739), and the *Yad Sarah* organization, which has branches all over Israel (main office in Jerusalem, ☎2/244242) and can provide wheelchairs, crutches, and other appliances on loan, free of cost (small deposit requested), as well as an adapted vehicle for airport transfers (see *Transport*, below).

Tour Operators

Although he usually travels independently, Barry Atkinson booked an *Intasun* package in Israel and was glad to have a rep on the spot to deal with such matters as arranging wheelchair rental from a local hospital, and explaining his mobility limitations to the guide when fixing up trips with Israeli tour companies. It's reasonable to expect this service from any mainstream tour company—no specialized knowledge of travel for people with disabilities is required.

For the independent traveler Israel presents fewer problems than most Near and Middle Eastern countries because there is a reliable guidebook (*Access in Israel*) for tourists with disabilities, and a number of helpful organizations within Israel (see above).

Getting There

El Al has no flights from North America at the time of writing, so it's necessary to take another carrier to London first, or fly direct to Tel Aviv from New York with *Delta*, or from Montréal with *Air Canada*. The choice widens if you travel via Europe; several airlines fly from major European cities.

International flights land at Ben Gurion **airport**, where there are adapted rest rooms,

ISRAEL: TRAVEL NOTES

low tables in the cafeteria, and low-level public telephones. The "ELALIFT" will disembark or board up to ten wheelchair users at a time, and passengers with other disabilities may also use this service. Allow plenty of time if making a connecting flight because other airlines make use of the lift and there may be some delay before disembarking.

If you are flying on from here you may have to transfer to Sde Dov airport—it's about a thirty-minute taxi ride. There are unlikely to be lifting vehicles at the regional airports, but check with *Arkia Israel Airlines* (Sde Dov Airport, P.O.B. 39301, Tel Aviv 61392; ☎3/422777), the domestic operator. Barry Atkinson flew direct to Ovda on a charter flight, and was carried off the plane.

There are regular **ferry** sailings from Greece, Cyprus, and Italy to the Israeli ports of Haifa and Ashdod.

Transport

Internal flights are straightforward, with basic manual lifting services at airports, but most people will find that the distances involved do not merit the expense of air travel. Although road conditions are pretty good, self-drive is not recommended in the desert—put yourself in the hands of an experienced guide and driver, either as part of a group or by renting a taxi by the day (negotiate the price before setting off). Taxis are usually large and probably the best mode of transport in the region, certainly for individual sightseeing or for getting about the cities.

Cars with hand controls can be rented from *All Tours Ltd.* (14 Gaza Street, P.O.B. 4249, Jerusalem; ☎2/667676), and an adapted vehicle with tail-lift can be rented for transfers from *Yad Sarah* (Society for Loaning Medical Equipment, 43 Hanevieim Street, P.O.B. 6992, Jerusalem 91069; ☎2/244242).

Buses and trains are generally difficult—high steps, narrow doorways, and a stampede when the time comes to board. Don't plan to use them without a companion or two. On tour buses the guides are usually helpful, but be sure to discuss your capabilities before booking and don't be surprised if some tours are simply not practical unless you are accompanied.

Accommodation

The law requiring all new hotels to provide facilities for guests in wheelchairs, before they are given an operating license, has not been strictly enforced, and although the *Access in Israel* team set out to find three-star or cheaper hotels with good access, they found that there were nearly always some obstacles—mainly steps and narrow doorways. As ever, the more expensive hotels are more likely to comply. Nevertheless, there are some active disability organizations, and with pressure from disabled war veterans it may be that the situation has improved since this research was carried out.

There are some alternatives to the luxury hotels—*Access in Israel* lists a few accessible Christian hospices (up-to-date list from the tourist office or the Israel Pilgrimage Committee, P.O.B. 1018, Jerusalem 91009) and one youth hostel; kibbutz hotels are mostly three-star establishments and some of these have sympathetic owners, adapted rooms, and good access.

A problem reported by our contributors, as well as by the researchers for *Access in Israel* and the *RADAR* guide (*Holidays and Travel Abroad*; see Books, p.590), is the prevalence of narrow doorways, particularly *en suite* facilities, and lack of turning and sideways-transfer space in rooms. The Israeli tourist board guide to Eilat states that the *Neptune* has ten rooms for disabled guests, but this hotel was visited by a *RADAR* inspector who found no turning space and no room for lateral transfer in the bathrooms. Barry Atkinson was unable to get his wheelchair through to the bathroom, even after taking the door off, at the *Caesar Hotel* in Eilat. The *Sport Hotel* (North Beach, P.O.B. 82, Eilat; ☎59/33333) does have adapted rooms but Barry found it too expensive.

Best Western no longer has properties in Israel but in 1991 they listed five hotels as having "facilities for disabled persons": *Red Rock Hotel* (Eilat sea shore, Eilat 88107; ☎59/73171); *Sea View Hotel* (P.O.B. 27, Rosh Pina 12000, North Galilee; ☎6/937013); *Ganei Hamat Hotel* (Habanim Street, Tiberias 14100; ☎6/792890); *Grand Beach Hotel* (250 Hayarkon Street, Tel Aviv 63113; ☎3/5466555); and *Kfar Maccabiah Hotel* (Bernstein Street, Ramat Gan 52109; ☎3/715715).

ISRAEL: TRAVEL NOTES

Camping is also a possibility—for site locations, and some idea of the facilities, contact the tourist office and the *Israel Camping Union* (P.O.B. 53, Nahariyya 22100); organized sites are well equipped and offer accommodation in cabins, chalets, or static house trailers as well as space for private tents.

Access and Facilities

Travelers with mobility problems are likely to need help in Israel, whether it comes from a companion, guide, or taxi driver. More often than not, two pairs of hands will be required. Barry Atkinson's experiences suggest that willing hands sometimes need guidance, simply because the ways of the wheelchair are not understood. But if ancient sites, tombs, and churches are not always the easiest places to get to, at least local attitudes are in the main positive.

Away from the resorts and hotels, finding **accessible rest rooms** can be a problem, especially as regulating fluid intake is not an option—it's essential to drink plenty of water in these **temperatures**. If your disability prevents normal sweating, you'll need a different cooling system, such as liberal use of a spray-gun. Remember your limitations if joining organized tours: very early starts and stifling heat can be exhausting.

Books

Access in Israel (1988), written by Gordon Couch and researched by *Pauline Hephaistos Survey Projects* (PHSP, 39 Bradley Gardens, West Ealing, London W13 8HE, UK), is a little old now but still valuable, readable, comprehensive, and up to the same high standard as the other *Access* guides—London and Paris. The symbols used in the guide are explained in some detail in English, French, and German. Obtain your free copy from the *Israel Government Tourist Office*. This small series of access guides is distributed free and produced by an independent investigative group mainly composed of boys and old boys (able-bodied and disabled) from the Hephaistos School, Reading, and St. Paul's School, London. Anyone who uses and appreciates the guides should be aware that the surveys and research are expensive to carry out, and *PHSP* relies entirely on donations and sponsorship. They have managed to produce updated supplements for the London and Paris guides, but cannot update the Israel guide unless they can obtain funding; donations of any size are always welcomed.

TELEPHONE CODE:

From the US and Canada dial 011 (international code) and then 972 for Israel or the Occupied Terrirories.

Egypt

Ups and Downs

Stephen Hunt's muscles have been progressively wasting since childhood, but getting a wheelchair rekindled his love of travel. In 1989 he went to Egypt.

I'd long dreamed of going to Egypt but the cost and logistics of the usual tour seemed beyond me, until I heard that Luxor had opened up to direct charter flights from Britain. This meant that I could just afford a two-week, "stay-put" package for myself and a friend/helper, and also be within my comfort limit for air travel. Luxor, once Thebes, lies between Cairo and Aswan, accessible to most of Egypt's ancient history.

My preparations are minimal. Too much anticipation and I'll start worrying if it'll work out. After all, a three- or four-star hotel is bound to have a lift and decent-sized bedrooms, with bathrooms a wheelchair can more or less get in and out of. No point in letting the hotel anticipate too much either; that's a superstition of mine.

Anyway, we get the best room in the place, our balcony overlooking the Nile toward the distant mountains guarding the Valley of the Kings. At least, that's how I see it. All day and for most of the night, the street and river life was not far below our balcony. For me, a city dweller, this was just added atmosphere, but the constant tooting, blaring, and shouting coming through the open window was an assault on John's untrained ears. Our nights turned into a constant lottery of either an airless room with no noise or a ventilated one with sound effects. Then the lift broke down, and we were offered temporary accommodation at the back of the hotel. John went to inspect it, and came back with a glowing report, which immediately put me on my guard. Sure enough, when he trundled me into our new home, our nice spacious suite had shrunk to a room of less hospitable proportions, but John had eyes only for what lay beyond.

Outside, a tree covered with gently fluttering leaves filled most of the view within an encircling courtyard wall, above which the elegant tower of a minaret rose into a serene sunset. That night I lay forlornly in my bed as John snored rapturously from the other side of the room—until daybreak, that is, when the fluttering leaves suddenly turned into roosting sparrows and a thousand piercing referees' whistles burst into life, immediately joined by the huge loudspeaker atop the minaret, exhorting the faithful to prayer: "Allah akbar!" John rose in acknowledgement, and nearly hit the ceiling . . . .

The friendly *Etap Luxor* is in the center of town, five minutes' walk from the magical Temple of Luxor. A short taxi ride in the other direction is mighty Karnak, Temple of Amun, featuring a history-and-histrionics light show where I keep banging into things and nearly end up in the sacrificial lake.

"In the vast, gloomy emptiness of the temple we're alone with the ghost of Hathor, and a squeaky wheelchair"

I've never liked being with organized groups; independence is best. With some bedtime reading before going site-seeing, I can let my imagination be my guide. Traveling around by car is much more convenient than a bus tour, often cheaper, and, for me, always more sociable. It gives me a stronger sense of place—driving along in Gemal's dusty Peugeot, Egyptian music on his cassette player, stopping at the kind of cafés he likes.

Gemal is our regular driver. We find him on the taxi rank outside the hotel among the other rogues. "I give you reasonable price!" means an exorbitant fare which you must finally reduce to about a third and then walk away, waiting to be called back. Unlike most, though, Gemal seems to realize that we could be a regular earner over the following two weeks, and so resists the temptation to go for the jackpot straight off and blow his chances. I also like his style—the fancy stitching on his jellaba, the car-phone cigarette lighter, the jaunty Santa Claus bobbing in the windshield. "They're only after your money," cynics say. But it's just a game, a survival game, and I can appreciate that. Besides, I've always got along well with the people on this side of the Mediterranean. They accept me, it is the will of God. Gemal takes us to everywhere that's reachable on both sides of the Nile.

We start at Dendera, less than 40 miles away, a short day's excursion. The temple is one of the more recent, only a couple of thousand years old. It's a real blockbuster, a Hollywood epic of a place, complete with extras—wearing white running shoes and sunhats and carrying their own cameras. The problem isn't the crevassed stone floor, the sand, or the boulders; it's keeping the tourists from under my wheels. I detour briefly to irrigate the desert and, on return, they've all gone, the last tourbus just leaving the parking lot in a cloud of dust. In the vast, gloomy emptiness of the temple we're alone with the ghost of Hathor, and a squeaky wheelchair.

Next, to Edfu and Esna, going south, a more ambitious day out, provisioned with bread, cheese, and fruit from the *Etap*'s resplendent breakfast table. To economize further we share the ride with a couple we've met in the bar. The temple is dedicated to the god Horus, the just avenger, a fierce-looking falcon wearing a sort of clerical hat. It's a huge, rococo building, breathing dignity and power. The man who owns the papyrus shop in Luxor, where we drink tea every day, used to be the station master at Edfu train station. Now that's what I call kudos!

"I've got nothing to prove; I already know how wonderful I am, and how marvelous it is, the way I get around"

Esna, for some reason, is not on. Gemal, for the first and only time, dissents. "It's down, down," he repeats emphatically. Does that mean down-river? But Edfu was all right. "Edfu is up, up!" I don't understand. I insist he takes us to Esna. We just drive around the town, nice in its way, ramshackle, lively, and I eventually realize that the temple has a lot of steps—down. It's getting late, so we all agree not to press the matter. He was only trying to help.

We make several trips across to the left bank of Luxor on the car ferry. Unlike most tourists, on their "Wonders of Egypt" all-inclusive packages, we have time to explore the Valleys of the Kings and Queens at our own pace. We buy a comprehensive ticket and take pot luck. Some of the nobles' tombs will be too "up" and some of the kings' too "down." Tutankhamen's, for instance, is like a garden shed at the bottom of a fire escape, and crowded, too. I've taken on improbabilities before, but not if the disruption I'd cause would spoil the pleasure of others. After all, I've got nothing to prove; I already know how wonderful I am, and how marvelous it is, the way I get around. Of course, everyone takes John for granted. He's just the friend who's been heaving and hauling me around the temples and tombs, dumping me in and out of bed, handing me my toothbrush, and the rest of it; that's all.

Anyway, there are more than enough attractions on the west bank. The ultimate is Queen Hatshepsut's Temple, a massive terrace of honey-colored stone set into the face of a granite cliff. It's approached along a noble avenue of sphinxes and souvenir stands leading to a sloping causeway where, according to the "God was an astronaut" theory, Pharaohs launched their rocket planes. Finally, that glorious colonnade filled with picture-walls, and crowds of jostling rubbernecks. So powerful is the ancient ambience, though, that I effortlessly feel it as it really was.

Our shortest ride is to the airport, for the 400-mile flight to Cairo. "No trip to Egypt is complete without seeing the pyramids," the brochure says; that's what has been foolishly nagging me. So, by noon, we've bargained our way to Giza where I perambulate among the awesome trio for an hour and a half. Then it's a dash to the *Nile Hilton* for a quick browse around the bargain buffet, a romp through the Egyptian Museum, where I catch up with Tutankhamen, and we just make it back to the airport for the last flight to Luxor. That night I'm tossed in a tangled web of impressions and wake up feeling hung-over on adrenalin, wondering if it was all worth it. Well, at least we covered the same itinerary as the organized group at about half the cost.

We deserve a rest, a relaxing note to finish on. How delightful, then, the prospect of cruising in a felucca down the Nile! It's Gemal's cousin, of course, who owns one of these traditional sailing boats. He and his toothless crewman get helpfully in the way as the wheelchair plonks down on the deck. Then we're away, gliding smoothly downstream, past the crumbling glory of the Temple of Luxor, the brash, rising *Club Med*, and on between fields tilled in the same way since before any of it.

"A furious altercation breaks out, trigger fingers twitch, they grapple with our boat"

Our destination, it turns out, is Banana Island, a well-known stopoff for tourists and, while John goes ashore to be exploited, I stretch out luxuriously on embroidered cushions. The Nile slaps softly around me, clumps of water lily drifting by. The sky is clear, azure blue fading into the far haze of the mountains. From the stern of the boat come the musical mutterings of the old boatman's afternoon prayers. Is it a dream? Is it really me here? John comes back, stamping his feet. He gave some baksheesh to an old beggar poised arthritically at the roadside and, on returning to the café to buy me a can of 7-Up, found him fully reclined under a tree having a cigarette! What's more, he had the nerve to put out his hand again. I almost fall off the cushions laughing.

On our way back, the river police make us pull into the shore as some big VIP boat is due to pass. But time means money in tourists' pockets for our sharp young Captain Moussa in his brightly painted Nile felucca. As soon as they've gone, recklessly urged on by us, he hoists the sail again. All goes well; we're beating along, hugging the shore, almost opposite the point where we left when, out of the blue, the police inflatable roars back around the bend and catches us in the act.

A furious altercation breaks out, trigger fingers twitch, they grapple with our boat. Suddenly I get a flash of inspiration and start waving my arms around and groaning loudly. As if on cue, with barely a pause, Moussa turns and gestures dramatically toward me: "This man is sick! I must take him to a doctor!" he's telling them. Whatever, it has just the right effect and the police veer off, muttering, leaving us to continue on our way. My old friend on Banana Island would have been proud of me; maybe I'll come back and do a summer season with him next year.

Sand, Flies, and Holes in the Ground

Apart from hobbling a few steps with the aid of a crutch and helper, Maxine Smith is wheelchair-bound and cannot bend her legs. With her mother, Dorrie, she spent six days in Egypt, in November 1988; it was an expensive disaster.

Dorrie and I have vacationed abroad annually for twenty years. We have used several different travel agents, tour companies, and airlines, but no matter how much preparation is made we have yet to experience a trouble-free vacation. We thought we'd found it when we discovered a company specializing in vacations for disabled people, set up by a travel agent after he became wheelchair-bound. Attracted by the brochure's claims of "hand-picked hotels, helpful staff, spacious bedrooms, assistance at airports, trouble-free vacations," Dorrie and I eagerly booked for a group tour of Egypt, seven nights half-board for £790 each (about $1500). Father declined to join us, grunting, "I had enough of sand, flies, and hole-in-the-ground toilets when I was stationed there during the war."

Suspicions that it was not going to be as "carefree" as the brochure claimed surfaced three weeks before departure, when the travel company (*Threshold Travel*, Manchester) informed us that they had changed the Egyptian hotel and we would be unescorted as the group leader was ill. Four days before departure we were anxiously calling them for flight tickets.

We have always used local airports to avoid arduous train or cab journeys, but on this trip we had no choice but to travel via London, so arranged to stay overnight in the *Skyways Hotel* at the airport. Crossing London to the airport was a nightmare—we had spent weeks trying to get information on the best routes, but in the end the bus drivers were the only people who knew what really went on. They at least were extremely helpful. The courtesy limo driver refused to transport me to the hotel but the driver of the bus that had brought us to the airport kindly did so when he saw our predicament. The hotel was accessible in that the entrance was level and had automatic doors, the corridors were spacious, restaurant, bars, and some rooms were on the first floor, and we were allocated a large, first-floor bedroom and bathroom, so no elevators to worry about. However, I think it was accessible by chance rather than by design—there was no wheelchair symbol beside this hotel in the brochure.

"More trouble at Cairo airport: our luggage was missing"

The following morning we took a taxi to the airport, waited in the coffee lounge while the *Threshold* rep checked our luggage in and booked our seats. And we waited. Thirty minutes before take-off, no sign of the rep, so Dorrie had her paged while I anxiously watched people going through to the departure lounge. The rep appeared with our tickets ten minutes before take-off, by which time the other passengers had already boarded, some not too happy at being knocked as I was carried in, or at having to change seats. Although I had given explicit instructions several times to *Threshold* and to the rep, we were allocated unsuitable seats—no space for my stiff legs, not near a toilet, in the non-smoking section—and, as usual, the cabin attendants had not been informed of my requirements.

More trouble at Cairo airport: our luggage was missing. We arrived at the *Siag Pyramids Hotel* late at night, shattered after two grueling days, but at least there was no unpacking—only the warm winter clothes we were wearing and a spare pair of panties from the previous day. The hotel was ramped at the entrance and had two large elevators, but small bedrooms and we could not get the wheelchair into the bathroom without taking the door off. It was manageable, but I would not recommend it.

An excellent Egyptian company (*ETAMS Tours*) provided the trips and transport, but not for us the luxury of a hydraulic lift on the tourbus, only a simple, two-piece, portable wooden ramp, so long that it often obstructed the sidewalk or road and required two men to run a wheelchair up it. No clamps or safety straps, so the three

wheelchairs in the group occasionally collided together on bumpy roads. On all the tours we were accompanied by a courier and a guide, both Egyptian, friendly, and very helpful. The guide made the tours extremely interesting by giving running commentaries explaining the history of ancient Egypt, the lives of the Pharaohs and goddesses, and some of the local customs.

These trips were superb, the saving grace of an otherwise dreadful vacation, and some we could never have managed on our own. One in particular stands out vividly in my memory, the one most people would associate with Egypt—our excursion to the pyramids. Only a few miles away from bustling Cairo the bus began to snake through the vast Lybian desert. It is difficult to describe the feeling of isolation and tranquillity—no noise, no movement, except when a Bedouin occasionally galloped by, kicking up clouds of dust.

"Cairo is a beautiful city but it's not very accessible"

After a short stop for camel rides, which I politely declined after watching one brave disabled lady almost topple off a spitting, mangy-looking beast, we drove around Sakkara and Giza. I was amazed at the size of the pyramids— 443ft high, 738ft along each side—and at their state of preservation. The courier and guide helped to drag and lift each wheelchair over sand and rough stony paths around King Zoser's pyramid, through a walled temple and courtyard which were in the process of painstaking renovation.

Next we were helped into Princess Idut's tomb, the walls covered with hieroglyphs depicting ancient rituals and everyday life, painted in 2000 BC, but the colors still bright. They were simplistic, as though drawn by small children—figures all faced front, no perspective, background objects painted above rather than behind the foreground objects. Hand-painted copies can be purchased in the papyrus factory, which we visited another day. The cheaper versions for sale in Cairo are not on genuine papyrus, but as the difference is imperceptible unless side-by-side they make ideal presents.

Egypt was not as barren as we had imagined. We were surprised to see exotic flowers and trees flourishing in Cairo, along the banks of canals, and in the desert at the El Fayuum oasis there are fields of fruit and vegetables. The population has increased rapidly over the last few years, resulting in mass unemployment, poverty, and homelessness. We were sad to see people living among the mausoleums in Cairo's "City of the Dead," and families squatting by the roadside, their only possessions a couple of pans.

The Egyptians are very enterprising in the face of these hardships, and they charge tourists wherever they can—to take a camera into the Egyptian Museum, for cloth "booties" to put over your shoes before entering the mosques, for the loan of a blanket at the Sound and Light Spectacle at the pyramids (very cold, so wrap up well; Dorrie was too concerned about the strange creatures scampering about in the darkness to enjoy it).

"We looked like idiots with our wool pants rolled up to the knees"

Cairo is a beautiful city, with its colorful flowers and trees, and many ornate mosques, but it's not very accessible. There are high ridges on the edges of sidewalks and down the center of roads—difficult for wheelchairs; parts of the city are quite hilly, and all of it is thronged with people and very noisy. Many roads have six lanes, but consideration and signaling are unheard of. During a hair-raising car ride we jokingly asked the courier if Egyptians take a driving test. "Yes, I passed first time," he proudly replied. "I had to drive straight for five minutes and then turn left!"

Important buildings were pointed out by the guide as we drove around Cairo, being deposited at places of interest. The Egyptian Museum displays statues and artifacts excavated from the tombs; those from Tutankhamen's tomb cover a whole floor (there is an elevator). At the Khan-el-Khalili bazaar we were escorted through a maze of dark, narrow, bumpy alleys, every few yards engulfed by an overpowering aroma of spices and perfumes. Colorfully robed storekeepers, all men, squatted outside tiny stores among piles of exotic souvenirs and other goods, cheerfully encouraging the tourists to buy.

In spite of the fascinating trips and guided tours, by the fourth day we were thoroughly unhappy. The hotel was awful (unhelpful staff, inefficient waiters, monotonous food, no choice, lounge in a drafty foyer so nowhere to sit in the evenings, bedroom and bathroom too small, disco too crowded) and our suitcase was still missing. All that preparation to squeeze everything into one bag had been a waste of time and effort; it contained lovely cool clothes, sandals, half my painkillers, incontinence pads and underpants bought specially, knowing there might be few accessible rest rooms.

With temperatures in the eighties we were hot, sticky, and smelly, still wearing the warm clothes we'd traveled in: we looked like idiots with our wool pants rolled up to the knees, and the only things we'd managed to buy so far—cheap, gaudy T-shirts emblazoned with camels and Pharaohs' heads. Dorrie's heavy walking shoes were killing her; we both had "Pharaoh's curse"; I was in pain, eking out my painkillers (refused the guide's offer of substitutes after swallowing suppositories by mistake on earlier vacations). And, of course, I was desperate as usual—the only opportunity for rest rooms on tour days was at the lunch stop.

Some rest room visits were traumatic, although we can laugh about them now. At the first stop we were relieved in more ways than one to find a "proper" toilet, but it was a painful experience: we hadn't noticed a large "meat hook" sticking up inside the bowl (perhaps to prevent long Egyptian garments falling in the water?). I tipped a small girl who'd helped us; suddenly a gang of children appeared from nowhere, rubbed their tummies, pointed at their mouths and tried to grab my handbag—very distressing and frightening.

> *"On their own the problems we experienced might sound trivial, but together they turned our dream vacation into a nightmare"*

At one café the guide said the rest rooms were dirty, so she directed us to "more hygienic ones." Yes, a hole in the ground and what a performance! With my feet on what looked like a cattle-grid, Dorrie gripped me tightly, stood me up and leaned me back so that I wouldn't wet my pants but my feet kept sliding. After several attempts we gave up, and remained desperate for an hour.

More problems on the journey home. Our missing suitcase reappeared at Heathrow airport, and Dorrie had great difficulty pushing me and carrying two bags (we bought one in Cairo for essential clothes and toiletries). We had no assistance from the *Threshold* rep—we were outside at the Airbus stop when she eventually arrived. Traveling north to Cleveland we encountered more mishaps: the train stopped briefly at our local station, then carried on, with us still on board! The waiting porters had looked in the reserved compartment and found it empty—we'd been put in the wrong one at King's Cross in London. We arrived back an hour later, expecting to find my sister waiting to drive us home; instead there was a taxi, meter ticking away, as my sister was ill.

On their own the problems we experienced might sound trivial, but together they turned our dream vacation into a nightmare from beginning to end. One expects a few difficulties on package vacations but at least they are cheap. This "carefree" vacation was worse than a package but twice the price, which we had willingly paid on the understanding that we would enjoy the specialized services advertised in the brochure. Admittedly, some of the problems were not the fault of the travel company, but we sought an apology for those that were. Receiving nothing but excuses over a four-month period, I was determined that others should not suffer the same ordeal; I reported them to the Association of British Travel Agencies, only to be told that *Threshold Travel* had ceased trading. We are not surprised.

EGYPT: TRAVEL NOTES

Sources of Information

Egyptian Tourist Authority, 630 Fifth Ave, New York, NY 10111 (☎212/246-6960); 323 Geary Street, San Francisco, CA 94102 (☎415/781-7676); Place Bonaventure, Frontenac 40, PO Box 304, Montréal, Québec H5A 1B4 (☎514/861-4420). This office provides no information for tourists with disabilities.

Tour Operators

After some conflict with *Sovereign* over a penalty payment (due to an unavoidable change of helper), Stephen Hunt commented that he would choose *Thomson*, a British mainstream operator with plenty of experience of accommodating disabled travelers on their programs (see The Canaries *Travel Notes*) and

EGYPT: TRAVEL NOTES

offering a number of packages in Egypt (see *Worldwide* and *Winter Sun* brochures). If you travel via London (see *Getting There*) you could consider taking a package deal offered by British tour companies; as well as *Thomson*, those operators that have a fairly positive and flexible attitude to handling requests from clients with disabilities include *Hayes & Jarvis* (152 King Street, London W6 0QU, UK; ☎081/748-5050) which has a range of stay-put vacations, tours, and cruises, and *Kuoni* (Deepdene House, Dorking, Surrey RH5 4AY, UK; ☎0306/740888) which offers flight-only deals as well as other packages.

There are a number of Egypt specialists in the USA (see *The Real Guide: Egypt*) and it's worth seeing if these can accommodate your particular needs. You are likely to be told that stay-put vacations are best if you use a wheelchair, escorted tours are difficult, and cruises are suitable if you have limited mobility but can manage steps and walk a little (the pace is slow on Nile cruises, and crew members generally willing to assist, but the boats aren't wheelchair-accessible). For most travelers this is sensible advice; remember that if you opt for a one- or two-center stay you can hire a taxi by the day and sightsee at your own pace.

Maxine Smith was badly let down by a company purporting to specialize in arranging travel for disabled people. She suggests booking your own flight and letting *ETAMS Tours* (*Egyptian Tourism and Medical Services*, 99 Ramsis Street, Cairo; ☎2/745721 or 752462) arrange the rest. Their programs include accommodation, and a wheelchair-accessible vehicle is used for transfers to and from Cairo airport, as well as for sightseeing trips. Their guides and couriers are friendly and very helpful. But be prepared for a bumpy ride, with no tie-down facilities for securing the wheelchairs, and rather primitive boarding via a couple of planks.

It is also perfectly feasible to reserve your own flight and accommodation, and to explore on your own, if you can transfer happily from wheelchair to car, or if you can persuade local tour operators to take you on guided tours (generally not too difficult); if you have a companion or two you may even be able to brave the buses and trains.

Getting There

The only direct **flights** to Egypt from North America are with *EgyptAir*, from New York to Cairo four times a week; this airline does not carry on-board wheelchairs. If looking for an airline offering on-board wheelchair and rest rooms that have some adaptations, your best bet is to go via Europe or Israel—all the following airlines should give good service to passengers with disabilities. *Air Canada* flies from Montréal and Toronto to Cairo via Paris; *British Airways* flies to London from several North American cities, then on to Cairo; *United* flies from most US cities into Paris or Frankfurt, linking with other airlines to complete the journey to Cairo; *Lufthansa* flies via Munich or Frankfurt, *KLM* via Amsterdam; you could also fly via Israel.

There are regular **ferries** from Greece, Cyprus, and Italy to the Egyptian ports of Alexandria, Port Said, and Suez. Details can be obtained from the national tourist offices, and information plus advice from *The Real Guide: Egypt*.

Transport

EgyptAir operates internal flights to all parts of Egypt, and *Sinai Air* flies into north and south Sinai. There are accessible rest rooms and fork-lift (or similar) facilities at Cairo and Luxor airports.

Ground and water transport are not easy but not impossible. Driving in the desert is potentially hazardous if you don't know what you're doing, buses and trains extremely crowded with high steps and narrow doorways. You're better off entrusting yourself to an experienced guide and driver, either as part of a tour group (especially one using the "converted" bus operated by *ETAMS*) or by hiring a taxi by the day. Taxis are usually large and reasonably priced (negotiate the price before setting off), ideal for individual sightseeing or for getting about the cities. Feluccas are manageable with help, and worth the effort of getting aboard; there are no facilities for disabled passengers on the cruise boats and paddle steamers but, again, these should not be ruled out if you have strong companions.

EGYPT: TRAVEL NOTES

Accommodation

Hotels that offer rooms for disabled guests in Egypt are usually of four- or five-star standard (eg *Hilton* and *Sheraton*), and these are located in all the major tourist destinations; there may also be accessible possibilities at the "tourist villages" of the Sinai and Red Sea resorts, where accommodation is in one- or two-story units. Try the *Holiday Care Service* (see England and Wales *Travel Notes*) fact sheet on Egypt for more ideas.

Maxine Smith was able to have her bathroom door removed at the five-star *Siag Pyramids* (59 Marriouteya, Sakkara Road, El Haram, Giza; ☎2/856022) but there was little room for maneuver, in bedroom or bathroom; on top of that, Maxine was unimpressed by food, service, and other facilities. Stephen Hunt stayed at his four-star hotel, the *Etap Luxor* (Corniche El Nil, El Bahr Street, Luxor; ☎95/382011)—and liked it.

Access and Facilities

The things that draw the crowds in this part of the world—pyramids, tombs, monasteries, forts, ruined cities, excavations—are, to say the least, difficult to reach in a wheelchair. A perfect example is Stephen Hunt's description of Tutankhamen's tomb—viewed from a wheelchair, it's a "garden shed at the bottom of a fire escape." The only course of action is to enjoy what can be reached, and adopt a philosophical attitude to the rest.

To see anything much, you're likely to need help, whether it comes from a companion, guide, or taxi driver—preferably more than one. But Stephen Hunt found that attitudes to his disability this side of the Mediterranean were easy to live with—the will of God and to be accepted without comment or discrimination.

Toilet facilities outside the big hotels are minimal, and holes in the ground require agility; those who are unable to support themselves on their legs may be in for a miserable time, particularly if planning to join sightseeing tours, visiting desert villages and so on. Until more wheelchair-accessible rest rooms are provided, disabled tourists who cannot cope with squatting over a hole must use incontinence pads, condom and drainage bags, or indwelling catheter, or—the least exciting prospect—never stray far from a hotel. Regulating fluid intake is not an option—it's essential to drink plenty of water in these temperatures. (If your disability prevents normal sweating, you'll need a different cooling system, such as liberal use of a spray-gun.) Remember your limitations if joining organized tours: very early starts and stifling heat will exhaust most people, so take plenty of rest days. Sightseeing by taxi allows you to set the pace.

TELEPHONE CODE:

From the US and Canada dial 011 (international code) and then 20 for Egypt.

Oman & The UAE

Boiling Oil and Velcro

Betty and John Layton visited the United Arab Emirates and Oman in February 1989. Betty is an amputee.

We flew to Dubai overnight by *British Airways* from Gatwick: as usual the wheelchair service and pre-boarding were excellent, with John dashing alongside carrying the hand-baggage—including the spare leg! *Kuoni*, which organized our tour, used *Orient Tours* of Sharjah as their agents and a rep took us from the airport to the *Dubai Inter-Continental*. Our room (near the elevator as previously requested) was ready, although it was only 7am. We used *Inter-Continental* hotels throughout our travels and we were pleased with all of them; the staff was most friendly and helpful.

There are seven Arab Emirates and we only had time to visit three—Dubai, Abu Dhabi, and Sharjah. Their histories are fascinating, with troubles and family feuds only a few years (and in some cases, months!) in the past. Our first walk along the creek which divides Dubai transported us to another world. The huge wooden dhows were lined three or four deep along the creek, advertising their sailing times and ports of call, and offering transport to all manner of cargo. *Abras* (water-taxis) dash across the creek, loaded with passengers going to work in the shops and offices of the new town. Near the

end of our tour, Theresa treated us to a ride in an *abra* so that we could see the hustle and bustle of the town and dockside from the creek. The crewman (and others) helped me on board.

The morning our tour itself was to start, we gathered in the hotel foyer, luggage at the ready. There were twelve of us, plus driver (an Omani called Sultan) and guide (Theresa, a German woman from *Orient Tours* who had lived and worked in Sharjah for eight years). Theresa knew the Emirates and Oman and their history well—no question defeated her, and her English was excellent. We twelve were a mixed bag: a group of three women; a pharmacist and his wife; a retired professor; a lone woman, much traveled; a banker and his wife; and a well-known retired newsreader.

We had an air-conditioned bus for the trip. The luggage was stowed away in the back and there were plenty of spare seats; I was able to select one where my artificial leg would be most comfortable. Setting off south to Abu Dhabi, we obtained our first glimpse of real desert from well-maintained highways. There was high wire fencing to keep the camels from wandering on to the roads and, in some places, camel tunnels have been built for their safe crossing. Photo stops were made where the winds had blown the sands into spectacular ridges. I found it very uncomfortable, plunging unevenly into the hot, dry sand, and had to be content to watch my companions scramble about.

"Both mother and baby seemed amazed at what had happened"

Abu Dhabi, like Dubai, is a clean, bright, modern city which has risen from the desert in just 25 years. A drive along the corniche by day or night is quite splendid, with views of the sea, beautiful gardens, and magnificent fountains to admire. The desert has truly been made to "bloom," and we were shown films of the Arabs' achievements in the oil industry and in agriculture. Some native crafts are still practiced in Abu Dhabi; at the boatyard in Bateen we watched dhows being built and renovated exactly as they have been for hundreds of years.

Farther from the city limits the women are usually veiled and not many are seen on the streets. When we asked Theresa if the women were still treated as chattels she was highly amused and told us that they have a marvelous life: the men do all the work, bring the money home and do all the shopping for provisions while the women rule the house with a rod of iron—with help from the servants! They would not have life any other way, she assured us.

Most of Theresa's "lectures" were delivered in the comfort of the bus, thus avoiding the need to stand around too long—something I appreciated. All the public rest rooms on the tour were holes in the ground; with an artificial leg one adapts, of necessity, to the required balancing act.

We drove inland through arid desert to the city of Al Ain, from which the Omani mountains can be seen in the distance. We visited a camel market where the sellers and buyers were doing their bargaining under the few scrubby trees, with the camels tethered and hobbled, well fed on green leaves and branches. We missed witnessing a birth by a few minutes; both mother and baby seemed amazed at what had happened!

In each area we went to the local souks—selling vegetables, fruit (dates!), fish, and meat—and were impressed with how clean and neat they were. The "litter laws" are frighteningly strict and it shows. In addition, any dogs found wandering around loose are shot; the only ones which seem to be kept are guard dogs.

The Buraimi oasis gave us a welcome cool walk through palm-shaded groves. This town has a turbulent history—it has been fought over by Oman, Saudi Arabia, and Abu Dhabi, conflicts which have only recently been resolved. Even now the inhabitants are suspicious of foreigners and keep their doors, with huge iron studs and bolts, firmly shut against prying eyes.

"Wind towers with sea breezes coming through open windows from the Indian Ocean"

Our entry to Oman was through the border post a few miles from Al Ain in the Hajar mountains. Our cases were hauled from the bus and each one opened and searched thoroughly. Any bottles were carefully sniffed at in case we were smuggling in hard liquor which, we had been warned, was absolutely forbidden (although alcohol is readily available to tourists in the hotels in Oman). Our "No Objection" certificates, passports, and luggage were in order and we were waved on our way after over an hour in the hot sun. According to Theresa that was a quick and uneventful entry!

We went straight to Suhar, the main port of the Batinah which is the long, sweeping coastal plain, stretching from the Emirates border down to Muscat. The fish market beside the beach afforded a little shade—a roof over waist-high concrete slabs, on which cross-legged sellers sat, furiously bargaining with the buyers. On to a splendid fortress in Suhar, for which we needed permission to enter from the Wali's office across the road. The fort proved to be another cool haven, with thick mud and sand walls, and wind towers with sea breezes coming through open windows from the Indian Ocean. I seldom climbed to the highest level in the forts, but even the mid-level views were spectacular.

"A lush, green coastal plain, with coconut groves and banana plantations"

We drove down the coast, calling at Sahm where we saw shallow reed boats still used for fishing. After a long day we finally arrived at Muscat's magnificent *Al Bustan Palace Hotel*, built within the last five years for a meeting of the Gulf Cooperation Council. A fishing village was demolished and rocks blasted from the mountains behind the beach to make way for the hotel. The villagers were simply moved two miles down the coast and new houses built. In our bedraggled, travel-weary state we felt somewhat overawed by the hotel's opulence, the vast entrance hall with fountains playing—"a spacious atrium reflecting the colors of its aqua blue tile and gold trim," says the brochure.

When Sultan Qaboos Bin Said, who was educated in England, finally managed to oust his father in 1970, he began to spend Oman's enormous oil wealth on housing, schools, clinics, hospitals, universities, roads, and industrial investment. Before this change of ruler there had been no education for girls, only three boys' schools in Muscat, and only tent schools (again for boys) in the interior. Now everyone is given an education and in the evenings the mothers, too, can go to school. Women are encouraged to enter the professions, and at the airports we were greeted by women security officers.

Tourism is being cautiously encouraged but the rules are strict and until recently only visitors who were married and over 35 were allowed the "No Objection" certificate essential for obtaining a visa. We had some wonderful tours in Muscat, exploring the old town, a natural history museum, an aquarium, and the harbor where generations of British sailors have scrambled ashore to paint the names of their ships in large white letters on the encircling rocks.

Westward from Muscat is Matrah, with its grand harbor and rambling souk of dark, shady alleys. Stalls selling clothing, spices, coffee, gold, and silver are guarded by fierce-looking Arabs in traditional dress, with large daggers at their waists which one imagines are not only for decoration.

Late one afternoon, we flew 500 miles south to Salalah on the Arabian Sea. There was no wheelchair service or pre-boarding on internal flights in Oman, but the walks to the aircraft were quite short and at Salalah a tour-bus took us to the airport building. Salalah is situated on a lush, green coastal plain, with coconut groves and banana plantations sprawling along a glorious sandy beach, the Dhufar mountains providing a backdrop.

From Salalah we drove east to Taqah, a fishing village where camels roam down to the beach. We saw the remains of old, wooden, "stitched" boats, their planks stitched together with leather thongs and the gaps and cracks filled with camel dung. While we were watching a group of fishermen selling their catch, a man from a small shop across the road begged us to have a cool drink from his large refrigerator. He wouldn't let us pay, so some of us picked up a few items from his store to buy, in recompense, whereupon he insisted that they also were gifts! The renowned hospitality of the Omani Arabs is undiminished by the encroachment of modern ways.

On to Khor Ruri and Sumhurum Bay, the old frankincense port and the remains of one of the legendary palaces of the Queen of Sheba. Here I felt daunted by the terrain—the prospect of clambering among the steep ruins did not appeal. But Theresa insisted, "You *can* do it!" and she hauled me through gaps and over walls, determined to get me to see the superb views and the wall inscriptions. It was well worth it.

The other way along the coast, westward from Salalah, took us to Mughsayl, within about 20 miles of the Yemeni border. The mountains are high and in some places sheer cliff drops down to the ocean. Inland, we went to Nabi Ayoub—Job's tomb— which is set in an elaborate garden and well guarded (no photographs!); we had to take shoes off to enter, which is impossible for me—I just looked through the doorway.

Back in Muscat our party divided, six to remain in the luxury of the *Al Bustan Palace Hotel* before flying home, and six to continue our travels— even more room in the bus! We went to the interior of Oman, through the Sumail gap in the Hajar mountains, to Nazwa, one of Oman's ancient capitals and now the economic and provincial center of the interior. Here the women are in purdah; tethered goats and camels are traded under a large tree in the town center, and the souk is a dimly lit jumble of shops with the merchants sitting around in disorder.

"We were on the outskirts of Dubai just in time to see the start of a camel race"

After leaving Nazwa we visited an eerie ruined village, then stopped at Jabrin to examine a castle which is being restored. The ceiling paintings and decorations were very fine. The joy of our visits to the many forts and castles was their peace and quiet and cooling breezes. Of course there were also the grim reminders of their original purpose, that of repelling enemies—secret rooms and staircases, dungeons, spy-holes, and the openings to the outside through which the defending forces poured the traditional boiling oil!

We arrived at the border at Jebel Hafit for our re-entry to the Emirates, and stopped overnight at Al Ain before driving back to Dubai through the desert. We were on the outskirts of Dubai just in time to see the start of a camel race. It took quite a while to get the forty or so camels lined up with their tiny jockeys (nine- or ten-year-old boys) firmly attached to their saddles with Velcro! They were finally off, some camels going the wrong way and being thoroughly whipped for doing so. We didn't stay to the finish as the course is about 6 miles long, but it was an exhilarating last memory of a wonderful and exciting vacation.

OMAN AND THE UAE: TRAVEL NOTES

Sources of Information

United Arab Emirates Embassy, 600 New Hampshire Avenue, NW, #470, Washington DC 20037; ☎202/338-6500. The information unit may be able to help with specific inquiries, or they may refer you to the **Dubai Commerce and Tourism Promotion Board**, PO Box 594, Dubai; ☎4/511600.

Emirates, PO Box 686, Dubai; ☎4/228151. The Dubai office of the national airline will be able to help with questions about airport facilities.

Oman Directorate of Tourism, c/o Ministry of Trade and Industry, PO Box 550, Muscat; ☎794206). Tourism is a relatively new business in Oman and there is no tourist office in North America, but the head office may have some useful information, and you could also try the **Embassy of the Sultanate of Oman**, 2342 Massachusetts Avenue, NW, Washington DC 20008, USA; ☎202/387-1980.

Tour Operators

Betty Layton was pleased with *Kuoni*'s arrangements, and this British operator has become more flexible in its approach to disabled clients in recent years. *Orient Tours* (PO Box 772, Sharjah, UAE; ☎6/549333) did a good job: as well as offering encouragement and assistance, the guide ensured that Betty sat in her preferred seat on the bus and that "lectures" were given while sitting in the bus. As in Egypt and Israel, escorted tours are hard going if you have limited mobility, but with the right tour company this doesn't have to be a problem. If you book flights and accommodation yourself it will be a fairly simple matter to sightsee independently, and to join short local guided tours.

Getting There

Although *Saudia* (*Saudi Arabian Airlines*) has direct flights from New York or Washington to Jeddah and Ryadh, and connecting flights to Dubai and Muscat (*Saudia* does carry on-board wheelchairs), getting there usually involves travel via Europe. Most major carriers will be able to offer flights that connect with other airlines in European cities for the onward journey to the Middle East. *Emirates* carries aisle chairs on its A310 and A300 aircraft (which are used on all London routes)—these will just fit into the specially adapted rest rooms for disabled passengers. The major *Emirates* service from Britain is London Gatwick to Dubai, but it also flies from Manchester, and to Egypt and Saudi Arabia; other European departure cities are Paris and Frankfurt. Wheelchair passengers are disembarked by high-lift at Dubai, and there are accessible rest rooms in the terminal; wheelchairs are available. *Gulf Air* flies out of London Heathrow, Paris, and Amsterdam; most flights are to Bahrain but there are also direct flights to Abu Dhabi and Doha in the UAE, and to Muscat in Oman; there's an on-board wheelchair but rest rooms are not accessible. *British Airways* flies to most Middle Eastern countries, and has a good reputation for services to disabled passengers. Other possibilities include joining a long-haul flight from Europe to India or the Far East and leaving it at the Dubai stopover.

Transport

In general there are few concessions to passengers with disabilities, but there are adapted rest rooms and fork-lift (or similar) facilities at the major UAE **airports**. Betty Layton found no wheelchair service or pre-boarding procedures for disabled passengers at Oman's airports; she either walked the short distance to the terminal or was taken by bus.

You are likely to take **tours** for long-distance sightseeing: driving in the desert requires preparation, and distances are vast, though the roads are well maintained. In the cities, taxis are easily available and usually spacious.

Accommodation

In this part of the world you have little alternative to luxury hotels. Betty Layton used *Inter-Continental* hotels: *Dubai Inter-Continental* (Bin Yass Street, PO Box 476, Dubai, UAE; ☎4/227171); *Abu Dhabi Inter-Continental* (PO Box 4171, Abu Dhabi, UAE; ☎2/666888); *Al Ain Inter-Continental* (PO Box 16031, Al Ain, Abu Dhabi, UAE; ☎3/654654); *Al Bustan Palace Hotel* (PO Box 8998, Muttrah, Muscat, Oman; ☎740200). All gave friendly and efficient

OMAN AND THE UAE: TRAVEL NOTES

service but, as with Israel and Egypt, this is accessible accommodation at the top of the price range.

More moderately priced rooms can be found at a couple of Mid-East *Holiday Inns* which advertise "wheelchair accommodations": *Al Jubail* (Tareeg 101, Madinat Al Jubail Al Sinaiyah, PO Box 10167, Jubail, Saudi Arabia; ☎3/3417000); and *Jeddah* (PO Box 10924, Jeddah, Saudi Arabia; ☎2/6611000).

Access and Facilities

As in Egypt and Israel, the problem of high temperatures, which means drinking plenty of fluids, combined with lack of rest room facilities, has to be faced, as do the physical barriers at tourist attractions, the generally difficult terrain, and a certain amount of incomprehension and/or indifference regarding mobility problems. Attitudes will only change and more facilities be provided as more visitors with disabilities explore this region, and as tourism develops.

TELEPHONE CODES:
Dial 011 (International Code), then 972 for Israel, 20 for Egypt, 971 for UAE, and 968 for Oman.

PART SIX

AFRICA

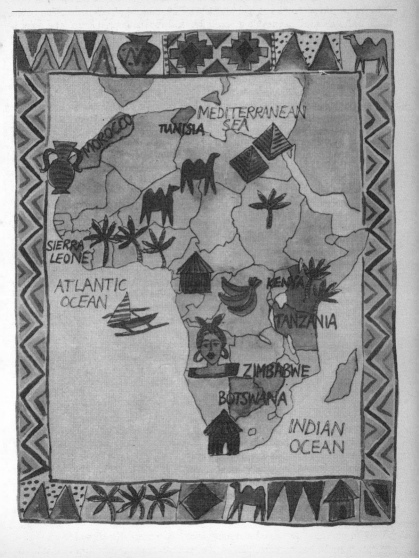

Introduction

S o long as famine, widespread malnourishment, and indescribable poverty exist in the African continent, and wheelchairs are unheard of, talk of installing ramps and walkways, or providing accessible rest rooms, is premature. The point is brought home by John Bignell when he describes sitting in his NHS (British National Health Service) chair, gazing down from his hotel window at a demonstration of the local design of wheelchair—a plank on four castors.

In Sierra Leone, one of the world's poorest countries, and neighbor to some of the world's most appalling violence in Liberia, disabled people have no hope of owning a wheelchair, or any other aid—they must, in Kate Margrie's words, "make the best use of what mobility they have," with no prospect of any physiotherapy or other essential medical treatment. Government money is too often swallowed up in civil wars or by corrupt leaders, instead of being used to finance public health and welfare programs.

Even with a wheelchair, the chance of greater independence and freedom of movement for people in the poorer countries would be remote. The infrastructure is non-existent, or creaking under the strain of age and lack of maintenance. The terrain is as rough as you'll find anywhere. Public transit is overcrowded and dangerous as well as uncomfortable—decrepit buses or trucks overflowing with people and animals. A smooth ride is impossible, even in the safari Land Rovers and Volkswagen buses.

For the visitor, whether disabled or not, the major obstacle is **getting around**—in comfort and without too many delays. Internal strife in several African countries presents another negative image to the tourist, and these and the Gulf conflict have taken their toll on the industry, as Stephen Hunt discovered when he traveled to Morocco in February 1991—the echoing halls of the airport terminals, vacant taxi ranks, and closed hotels gave a new meaning to the term "getting away from it all."

Although the situation has improved since then, most tourist boards and operators continue to report that they receive very few inquiries from disabled people hoping to travel to Africa. As Stephen Hunt says, this could be due to lack of spending power, but is more likely the result of overemphasis on the potential obstacles on the part of the travel operators, and lack of means to spread the word among other disabled travelers that, with improvisation, travel in this part of the world is possible for disabled tourists. Perhaps the accounts in this section will go some way toward reassuring those who have yet to explore these countries.

For those who have experienced travel in Africa, the attractions far outweigh the challenges. The excitement of **wildlife** observation seems to make a more lasting impression than the hazards of travel in safari vehicles. One contributor delights in the opportunity to get to know people who could almost be living on another planet, their outlook and way of life are so utterly different to her own; another finds the locals mysterious and impenetrable. The beauty of the scenery, the seediness of some of the cities, the thrill simply of being in Africa—all have an appeal, and can be experienced with a little preparation.

Outside the more developed and more aware countries—Kenya and South Africa, perhaps also Morocco and Tunisia, the Gambia and Togo—Africa should be approached with caution; but it can be approached, whatever the more pessimistic tour operators have to say. Be honest and don't gloss over the less appetizing aspects: the

climate can drain the energy from a strong, fit, able body; insect bites can bring a range of nasty diseases; food and water may carry other diseases; a simple journey can take hours longer than planned; medical facilities will be few and basic.

The only concessions made to disabled travelers will come from the people you meet—but, with luck and if you take good advice before leaving, this may be all you need. When Stephen Hunt traveled on the overnight train from Nairobi to Mombasa, he found no ramps for boarding, and standing room only in his tiny couchette. But he was bombarded with offers of assistance on the platform, and reports that for the equivalent of $2 you can rent an extra holiday helper: "people will always lend a hand with a smile, if you smile, and there's nothing demeaning about a small payment made in the right spirit." This applies not only at stations, but also at airports, hotels, tourist attractions—wherever there are steps, awkward entrances, or potholes.

It is important that travelers (not tour operators) make the final decision on whether or not Africa is a suitable destination; if disabled travelers who have their eyes open to the problems find it a desirable destination then every effort should be made to accommodate them within mainstream tourist operations, and independent travelers should be given every assistance from the tourist boards when researching their trip, whether to find accessible accommodation or to ascertain facilities at airports. Then, as the numbers of disabled visitors grow, we might expect a few more ramps, some more wheelchairs at airports, the odd grab-rail or two in hotel bathrooms, and better provision for wheelchair users who wish to join standard scheduled safari tours.

Because the information is patchy, because we received information on countries not covered by specific accounts, and because much of the general advice can be applied throughout the continent, the *Travel Notes* for this part of the book have been combined into a single section at the end. Hopefully future editions of this book will have a lot more to say.

Morocco

Berber Doctor

Trevor had never been farther than the twenty-something miles across the Channel from England to France before traveling, as companion and care assistant, with Stephen Hunt to Marrakesh. On their first evening, Trevor injured his back, lifting Stephen from the bath into his wheelchair.

Now Trevor lies flat on his bed, firmly clamped down by Walkman headphones and virtually useless, while I gaze up at the ceiling from my pillow, able only to contemplate the illusion of my independence.

Next morning he manages to reach the local hospital just around the corner from the hotel, but the verdict is grim. Our balcony view of the distant snow-peaked Atlas seems likely to be his only souvenir of my favorite Moroccan city. At least, though, we can take a taxi and visit my friend Hassan in the kasbah.

Hassan is an archetypal Marrakchi, laid back yet tuned up, of no fixed commercial enterprise, seeming to hover permanently on the brink of extreme wealth and abject poverty. One look at Trevor, whimpering in his doorway, is enough: "He must see the Docteur Berbere immediately!" But first we must share a meal with the usual lively menage of family and friends that fill the little house.

When we emerge, over two hours later, Hassan goes ahead by moped to his "boutique," a new one to me, leaving Aziz to take over my helm. Trevor trails along in our wake—through the

exotic alleys of the kasbah, past the walls of the ruined Palace El-Badi ("The Incomparable"), the beautiful Saadian tombs, the noble Koutoubia mosque—oblivious to it all. Urged on by yet another "just a bit farther" from Aziz, he stumbles through mounds of donkey droppings and down potholes amid the swirling street life of the Medina. The flow takes us across the Djemaa El Fna (the guides call it the "big square"), eddying around the acrobats, musicians, snake charmers, story tellers, tooth pullers, and food stands. Finally, we're sucked down a narrow alleyway into the glittering maze of the souks, from which few tourists escape without paying high prices.

By the time we reach Hassan's "boutique," Trevor is almost on his knees. Aziz helps us both inside where we're introduced to a sallow young man with a droopy moustache who sits hunched over a glass of tea. He's not even one of the crusty old quacks from the square.

"His father is a doctor, and his father before him," Hassan murmurs reassuringly as the young man dons a greasy white coat and begins prodding and scowling at Trevor, who registers a glimmer of apprehension on his haggard countenance.

"Mush mush killa," the young man mutters—"No problem"! What sort of diagnosis is that? I'd call a halt now, while Trevor is being stretched out on a kilim on the floor, if it wasn't for my curiosity. Too late—they're already rolling up his Status Quo T-shirt and the "doctor" is rubbing yellow stuff all over his back. Besides, why worry if it's just a massage?

The hands are hardly those of a flesh-kneader or joint-cracker, though. They're long and slender, almost delicate, like a musician's. The fingers and thumbs are double-jointed and can overlap each other, applying varying degrees of pressure in different places at the same time. I watch, mesmerized, as they slide smoothly over Trevor's skin, creating shifting patterns of force around every nuance of his somewhat spotty back. It's extraordinary—an impression of immense yet completely controlled power being subtly orchestrated, slowly becoming more complex, and growing in intensity until it even seems to be reaching out to me.

Minutes pass, it could be hours, before I become aware of Trevor again. In fact he is yelling blue murder as Aziz bends his arms and legs, according to instruction. Poor old Trev—when they finally roll him over it looks as if he's just gone ten rounds of tag wrestling. The scowling young man merely walks away, wiping off his hands on the white coat and muttering something to Hassan.

"You can get up and walk now," Hassan informs Trevor. This should be interesting.

For a while, there's no sign of movement. Then, unbelievably, Trevor slowly sits up. He looks confused. Swaying slightly, he rises to his feet and stands, cautiously flexing his muscles, as if unsure that his body still belongs to him. Reassured, he takes one or two tentative steps forward, as if treading on egg shells. Then a few more, firmer this time. A smile gradually begins to form on his lips. He walks faster, the smile broadens. Round and round he goes, windmilling his arms faster and faster, with little leaps in the air, beaming, until the tiny shop can no longer contain him. Then, with a great whoop of joy, he bounds through the open doorway into the street.

Hassan wheels me out to watch Trevor cavorting, and leans over, chuckling smugly, "Docteur Berbeeerrrre!"

"I was carried upstairs to sit on a tassled banquette in the guest salon"

So Marrakesh, with its unique energy and atmosphere, turns up another surprise. The lure of this city has remained through the ages and, quite apart from supplying one of the world's greatest perpetual sideshows in the square, as well as glittering souks of labyrinthine proportions, for me it's always been wheelchair-friendly and disabled-people-friendly, and the frequency of pot-holes, donkey droppings and high curbs is no more than the North African average.

In fact, I've found that a few well-placed obstacles can serve to break down social and cultural barriers: steps and pot-holes can lead to anything from guided tours to restaurant invitations. In Marrakesh it gave us a privileged look behind one of those anonymous and mysterious doors set into the blank walls of the lanes in the Medina. We were ushered into a spacious house, a cool oasis of exquisite mosaic tiles slowly drowning in the shadow cast by the sunlight that poured into the well of its single, central room through the rolled back roof. I was carried upstairs to sit on a tassled banquette in the guest salon and eat from a steaming *tajine* of lamb and vegetables with our fingers—another world, and an experience to take home and recall as required, it's just what the doctor ordered.

"The jagged peaks of the Atlas pile higher and higher into the distance, cloud-streaked and snow-plumed"

Tourists who stay a little longer than the day's excursion from Agadir will find more surprises across the plain beyond the ancient city walls. A fine spring day is just the right time to rent a car and set off to visit the distant snow-capped Atlas mountains. Trevor is driving, and sharing the car are Hassan and another old friend, Abdel. Hassan has closed his little shop for our day out. Abdel, more reserved since becoming a civil servant, is on official holiday. It's he who wants to take us to Oukaimeden, about 50 miles away, up in the mountains. Just the sort of place we'd like, he says. Yes, even more than Imlil, where we had a picnic last year and the café owner walked half a mile up a track and waded across a stream to bring us our pot of mint tea.

First, though, we make a routine diversion to a Berber market in the foothills, this one in the village of Dar Caid Ouriki. Expecting the usual open-air jumble sale, I'm unprepared for a sight that leaps out at me straight from the pages of the Arabian Nights. On the banks of a rocky river, hundreds of gray, nodding donkeys in decorated wooden saddles are tethered, brought here for sale or barter. Behind them squats the familiar huddle of tents and stands, slightly hazed by cooking smoke. Helping hands reach out to guide me over the ruts and stones to a refreshment stand. Merely to stop here for a cup of coffee is against all my inclinations, but the morning sun is already high and Abdel is insistent.

Driving on, we make our way steadily upward, ears popping. Only occasional traffic passes us. At switchbacks,

stands display pottery and carpets and curling fossils the size of hubcaps, while children hold out huge lumps of glittering quartz. Maybe these children come from the Berber village that clings to the mountainside across the valley like an outcrop of rocks.

Just below the snowline, we park the car on a narrow roadside ledge and, while the others get out to take care of the photos, I stay and admire the view from where I sit. Stretching before me the jagged peaks of the Atlas pile higher and higher into the distance, cloud-streaked and snow-plumed, defying belief that the Sahara desert is beyond. When the car starts rolling backward my panic is slow to come: sensing already that I am a helpless captive with timeless moments left to contemplate fate behind me, I am hardly even aware of the slight backward lurch of the car. Only when I realize it is rolling does the truth, and panic, hit me.

Never—before or since—have I seen a Moroccan move so quickly. In a flash of leather jacket, Hassan is diving at full stretch through the car door, grappling with the brake, just in time. A second later, Trevor appears, shaking from head to foot and minus suntan. Abdel giggles and curses, peering over the sheer precipice that drops a few feet behind the car.

Still subdued by the shock we continue, and in such intoxicating surroundings happiness soon breaks through again. Cradled in a valley of snowy peaks, and bathed in warm sunshine from a crystal-blue sky, we've almost reached Oukaimeden, our Moroccan Shangri La. One more bend to go, and Trevor and I stare ahead, transfixed.

We are looking at the tail of one of the worst traffic jams I've seen this side of London. Radiators gently steaming, cars and coaches shake through the slush, cajoled by whistle-blowing, baton-waving traffic cops. We pass several gross, prefabricated parodies of alpine chalets, summed up finally by a crude, Hiltonesque hotel, its picture windows glaring blindly at the distant crowded ski slopes. Skiers trudge merrily past us, red-faced and brightly clothed. I spot a *Club Med* badge, and hear a blast of Status Quo. Just ahead, après-skiers throng shops, boutiques, and restaurant terraces. For the first time in Morocco, Trevor and I are refused drinks because we don't also want to order a meal.

In our rapid departure from Oukaimeden we leave behind a puzzled Abdel, surely not the same Abdel who sang for us—those strange and undulating Moroccan songs accompanied by his small *tan-tan* drums—when we picnicked last year at Imlil. He's spotted some friends, here for the day. Like him, they wear designer sweaters, smart sweat pants, and squeaky-clean, hi-tech running shoes—the uniform of the new Euro-African. He was so sure

that Oukaimedem would be our sort of place.

Hassan shrugs his shoulders and guides us down the mountain, to a valley in the foothills where spring has suddenly burst through, splashing trees with blossom and covering riverside pastures with a patchwork of fresh green grass through which run pebble-strewn rivulets. On either side the rocky slopes of the mountain rise up, honey-colored in the benign afternoon sunshine.

In the little village of Setti Fatma, Hassan and the café owner carry a table across the road to a nice-view meadow where I can stretch out on the grass, wafted by a warm breeze that carries all the aromas of spring, along with a hint of the spicy Moroccan *tajine* that is being prepared for us. We are in a place called Ourika, known as Paradise Valley. That comes as no surprise.

A Meeting in the Desert

Ivy Geach is in her late seventies, has arthritic knees, and walks with the aid of two canes. In January 1988 she traveled, with a friend, to Morocco for a week's vacation.

Evelyn, though a few years younger than me, suffers from a painful back, so neither of us is very mobile. But that hadn't stopped us having a good time in Tangier in 1987; we enjoyed North Africa so much that we decided to pay another visit, this time to Marrakesh.

We had to make carrying our luggage as easy as possible, so we each bought a medium-sized suitcase, light-weight and with four wheels and a handy strap to pull it along. (One drawback was that in a hurry it tended to fall sideways.)

An electric buggy was available at London's Gatwick airport to transport us and our luggage to a van, the driver of which helped us onto the plane. The charter flight was smooth and we found no fault with the service. At Agadir a bus was waiting to take us to Marrakesh. The airport is small, so a porter is unnecessary if you can manage a short distance with your luggage to the bus which waits outside the arrival hall.

The four-hour drive to Marrakesh was tiring but so full of interest that it didn't seem too long. To someone used to desert scenery it might have been monotonous, but I found the changing light on the sand dunes hypnotic. I occasionally glimpsed a long-robed, hooded figure walking across the barren wastes; there was no sign of habitation—where had he come from and where was he going? I asked the courier about the mysterious figures but he smiled, shook his head and shrugged as if to say, "If I told you, you wouldn't understand." He was probably right. We stopped at a wayside café for coffee or mint tea and a visit to the rest room—a square hole in a tiled floor. Avoiding splashes was difficult but it was warm so we dried quickly!

"There was a peace and rightness about this scene which is hard to convey"

Hotel Kenza was splendid, exactly as described in the brochure, the bedrooms *en suite* with elevators to each floor and everywhere immaculate. There was one drawback for anyone using a wheelchair—three steps leading to the dining room—but that could be easily overcome with the willing help of some strong-armed staff. The other guests were mostly French or Spanish, so the few Britons tended to stay together. We ranged in age from teenagers to a lively eighty-year-old gentleman who wore shorts and a tartan bobble-cap, and we all got on splendidly. The teenagers couldn't have been more helpful, offering to fetch and carry for us and lending us their somewhat lurid novels.

Moroccan food is delicious and there is such a variety of dishes that any special diet shouldn't be a problem. The waiters were always polite and smiling, even when my heavy metal walking cane slipped from the back of my chair onto their feet—a not infrequent occurrence.

Marrakesh, much loved by Winston Churchill, is fascinating. According to legend, a date-carrying tribe from beyond the Atlas mountains besieged the early settlement, which was a crossroads for caravan trails going south. Date stones fell to the ground, germinated, and so produced the famous palm grove, today the largest in the world. Under Ali Ben Youssef, Marrakesh became a fortified city, with underground irrigation canals to provide water for the palmery; these are still used to supply water to the beautiful gardens in the city. The old quarter, the Medina, is enclosed by a ten-mile wall. Outside is Gueliz, the modern part, well laid out, with buildings of a delightful pink ochre color.

Marrakesh is a strange mix of the sophisticated and the primitive. The contrast between wealth and heartbreaking poverty is shocking. Expensive cars next to shabby carts, pulled by even shabbier donkeys, fill the roads, which have no traffic lights or pedestrian crossings. But the wide, tree-lined avenues are flat, so it's easy walking for disabled pedestrians, although the litter on the sidewalks can be a hazard.

Drinking coffee or tea outside one of the many cafés was quite an experience. We took to heart the words inscribed in Arabic on one of the many fountains: translated, they mean "Drink and contemplate." One morning I remember in particular. The sun was hot, the jacaranda trees in bloom, and we were sitting beneath an ornamental orange tree, watching the world go by. A haunting voice rang out from the minaret calling people to prayer. A jellaba-clad gentleman passing by suddenly stopped, unrolled the little prayer mat he was carrying, and laid it on the sidewalk. Unmindful of us, he removed his shoes and knelt in prayer. A donkey trotted by, carrying, a woman enveloped in long, dark robes, only her eyes exposed. There was a peace and rightness about this scene which is hard to convey.

The next day we visited the Djemaa El Fna—the famous square of Marrakesh, and entertainment in itself. The centerpiece of the town, it has everything: shops, fast food, snake charmers, fortune tellers—and beggars. The thronging crowds make it a riot of color but the beggars, mostly children, tend to be a nuisance. It is impossible to give to all, so a friendly smile and a shake of the head will send them darting off to other tourists.

Around the square are shops and beyond the shops to the north are the souks, a maze of alleyways and open-fronted shops selling wares of every description. A helpful Frenchman joined us and showed us how to bargain, for bargain you must, even if it goes against the grain. We asked the price of some lovely caftans, looked aghast, offered a third, then ended up paying half the asking price. The beaming shopkeeper not only shook our hands but also gave each of us a small silk scarf to show that we were worthy opponents! He raised his hands in blessing as we left and we felt we'd made a friend for life. If you don't buy, there is no hard feeling on the side of the seller; if there is nothing that pleases you and he cannot make a sale, no matter—it is the will of Allah.

The spice shops were a joy: every conceivable spice displayed in big glass jars; powdered saffron sold by weight, an ounce of saffron for about fifty pence. For a couple of pence we bought small, roughly made clay dishes, which when dampened and rubbed produce a scarlet dye used by Berber women as a cosmetic.

"I wandered up and down the labyrinth of streets, eyed by hooded men"

The teenagers went with Evelyn and Mr. Bobble-Cap up one alley looking for leather and jewelry. Being so slow, I lagged behind and got lost. I wandered up and down the labyrinth of streets, eyed by hooded men who sat cross-legged and motionless outside their shops. (The Moroccans are great ones for sitting: they sit beneath trees, against walls, and on the edge of sidewalks.) I was about to ask, in my atrocious French, the way to the square, when a smiling little Arab boy came to

the rescue. Without a word he took my hand and led me through the maze to the waiting bus. A cheer went up as I limped along with my ragged escort, who went away ecstatic, clutching a bar of chocolate and a handful of candy.

One day we went on a bus tour to the Valley of Ourika, a complete contrast to the sandy roads we'd traveled to reach it. The valley is long, lush, and green, cutting deep into the High Atlas. The steep sides are studded with trees and slashed by waterfalls, and streams snake across the valley floor. It's a perfect place to escape the oppressive heat of Marrakesh, and many people camp and hike in the area.

On the way back we passed a Berber village of beige, flat-roofed, clay dwellings, set far back from the road and enclosed by a high wall. Hassan, the guide, told us that the women were only allowed out of the compound on one day a week. That was to take their laundry to a nearby river where they could meet and chat to other Berber women also on their day out.

"Big deal!" I heard one teenager murmur to her friend, a remark fortunately not heard by Hassan. Morocco is very much male dominated. Although we experienced only polite, helpful men, we could not escape the feeling that they don't approve of female freedom. I tried several times to have a conversation with some of the Berber women, without success. They simply covered their faces more fully, smiled with their eyes, and walked gracefully away—and how I admired that walk!

It was so hot the next day that I stayed alone in the the hotel while the others traveled to see the olive groves of Menara. I wished I had a sunhat, so I strolled along to a nearby café, hoping to buy one there as it stocked a variety of goods. No luck, but knowing there were more shops farther on I asked whether or not they sold hats, thinking I'd save myself a walk in the heat. The café owner didn't understand English, even though I patted the top of my head to illustrate my request, so I tried French. He shook his head, looking more mystified than ever. He must have wondered why an elderly foreign woman, evidently a tourist, wanted to buy a horse. Well, it's not easy to recall schoolgirl French, and *cheval* and *chapeau* aren't too dissimilar.

"For just over $2 I bought a chunk of roughly hewn amethyst weighing about 6oz"

The next bus tour was to a donkey market and to the Valley of Asni, famous for its minerals and semi-precious stones. The weekly donkey market was not only a place for selling or exchanging, it was also a lively get-together for the Berbers who came in from the desert to sell their wares and meet their friends. The sellers spread their goods in any available space between pits and boulders, and we had some difficulty weaving our way around tethered animals and squatting figures, some selling beautifully hand-embroidered caps. Long-robed Berbers blocked the way as they chatted excitedly to each other; as usual, no women were to be seen.

I think we were all glad to leave the smells and the obstacle course, and travel to the Valley of Asni, which was beautiful. We stopped at a village—just a café, a few clay houses, and a shop—and the view from there was spectacu-lar, the snow-covered Atlas mountains in the distance looking so unreal in the shimmering heat that they could have been a backdrop in an old film. The shop had a variety of minerals and semiprecious stones on display, all excellent value. For just over $2 I bought a chunk of roughly hewn amethyst weighing about 6oz, a treasured reminder of the Atlas mountains.

On our final day we set off before dawn for Agadir, stopping again at the little café we'd visited before. I left the others there while I walked down the lonely road. It was cold but the sun was beginning to show, bathing everything in a pinkish, misty glow. Not thinking of anything in particular, I suddenly became aware of a dark figure standing motionless at the foot of a sandhill.

She was some way back from the road and I wondered what she was doing there. Except for the café there was no sign of any habitation. Had she come in from the desert? We stared at each other, and I felt a surge of empathy toward the still figure. What she felt I don't know, but she slowly nodded her head and raised a hand. Before I could respond she disappeared into the mist.

They were calling me from the bus and as I was helped in I looked back down the road, searching for the mystery figure. There was only the empty landscape. It was one more strange memory of a remarkable vacation.

Just a Hint of Pathos

In February 1991, Stephen Hunt escaped the English winter and the Gulf War media circus, traveling with helper Dave to the former Spanish Sahara, sometimes referred to as the Western Sahara, in Morocco. Reports of anti-Bush/Thatcher demonstrations in North Africa had taken their toll on the tourist industry, and Stephen found deserted hotels, empty swimming pools, and puzzled, friendly locals, deprived of their usual form of income and longing to swing into action in their taxis, shops, and hotels.

It takes two changes of aircraft to reach our destination on the northwest coast of Africa. By the time the baggage handlers have bundled me onto the third one, a small propeller plane, I'm more than ever convinced that every disabled air ticket should carry a government health warning.

My helper and I are heading for the territory of Western Sahara. Annexed from Spain in 1976 by 300,000 unarmed civilian Moroccans in a remarkable coup known as the Green March (*La Marche Verte*), it's only recently (1988) been made accessible to anyone, let alone me in my wheelchair. Before that the area was under military control as the Moroccan authorities countered attempts by Algerian-backed Polisario (*Frente Popular para la Liberación de Saguia el-Hamra y Rio de Oro*) guerrillas fighting for independence for the Saharans, or Sahrawis.

At Tan Tan the plane duly releases its contingent of soldiers who keep the conflict with the Polisarios fizzling gently along the Algerian border, although it is all but burned out and an agreement between Morocco and the Sahrawis is increasingly likely, particularly in the light of better relations with Algeria. Now, at last, we are flying over real desert: it lies below us, a drab brown tundra joined to the blue Atlantic by a seam of surf. Despite my present confinement, a feeling of space is already liberating me and it adds another dimension to getting away from it all.

In the brochure the old Al Ayounne has been transformed into Laayounne, "Pearl of the South," the new administrative center for the region's bright future in mining, agriculture, and tourism. When we land, the empty, marble halls of Hassan II airport seem to mock this promise—as does the vacant taxi rank. But improvisation is the art of disabled travel, and soon I have done a deal with the owner of a battered pickup truck, parked nearby.

So we make our triumphant entry into Laayounne seated on high, me enthroned in my wheelchair, Dave on a piece of old carpet, the wind parting our hair—only to find that our hotel is closed.

It's only after a long, painful conversation in broken Arabic and French with the soldier/doorman that I learn the hotel down the street (*Hôtel Parador*) is going to honor our booking. As if in a dream, our travel-worn caravan, trailing cabbage stalks and bits of cement bag, is welcomed in a palace by an Ali Baba lookalike. Drifting after him, we wander through air-conditioned corridors lined with antiquities, past palm-shaded mosaic courtyards sparkling with fountains, to our luxury suite.

"A little girl hides in her mother's skirts, screaming in terror, until I have passed safely by"

Of course, I don't mind concertinaing the wheelchair and breathing in hard to get through the narrow bathroom door. It's only later that we discover the cascade of steps down to the restaurant and sun-bed area. But the well-tried formula of firmness, politeness, and (dare I say it?) just a hint of pathos, has worked wonders with hotel managers worldwide. By siesta time we are relaxing in our courtyard on sun-beds with mint tea and a sandwich, delivered by room service, looking forward to what Laayounne will have to offer.

If Dave toils up the hill from our hotel, we arrive at the new town, two rows of nondescript trade facing each other on a pot-holed divided highway. If we roll downhill, we are in the old town, a friendly jumble of streets and street life. It's here that a little girl hides in her mother's skirts, screaming in terror, until I have passed safely by. Hardened disabled traveler I may be, but it's a moment of terror for me, too, in a different way.

We take a solitary tour around the empty ceremonial spaces of the Place du Mechouar, and its Great Hall, which celebrates the Green March in a series of large photographs. And for more lively entertainment we join the week-end throng of townspeople who help us stroll with them up and down the terraces on the Colline aux Oiseaux—the Hill of Birds—an aviary built on landscaped natural rock and concrete terraces. Hundreds of brightly colored budgerigars are color-separated in ornate aviaries, wooden pagodas complete with little shutters to protect delicate feathers against the blast of sandstorms.

"Nomads' tents sprout like groups of magic mushrooms"

These attractions are easily fitted in around our foraging for ingredients for our lunchtime picnics, or searching for somewhere to eat in the evening, usually a café-restaurant that struck a balance between the gastronomic menu prices of the *Parador* and the area's staple beans-and-bread diet. We expected no more of Laayounne which is, after all, a basic, easygoing desert town where the sun always shines. Under a warm blue sky our days slow to a relaxed, pleasingly humdrum rhythm. No care rotas to work out, no social services to chase, no social security forms to fill in, no funding letters to write, no emergency phone calls to make, not even the chains of winter to imprison me indoors.

For me, though, it is the desert that represents the ultimate freedom—or would do if my wheelchair had been fitted with half-tracks. As it is, we make do with a rental car and a local guide, called Sammy, who offers us his own experience and a variety of itineraries. It's an art, knowing where to leave the main road and weave across patches of hard sand to reach a rift valley, an old fort, or an oasis, to keep concentrating on those long stretches of straight road, to read obscure signs, and to slip quickly through the police checkpoints that ring Laayounne.

We start off with an introductory, budget-price, three-deserts-in-a-day excursion. We see them all—rocks, rolling dunes, tundra. Another day, we visit Laayounne's beach, 12 miles from town and marked only by a somnolent *Club Med* complex and a forlorn, half-finished villa-village. Pristine golden sand studded with seashells stretches away in both directions, sloping down to meet the creamy wash of the ocean. There's not a soul in sight, and the only sounds are the cry of the sea birds and the slow beat of the waves under a serene sky.

Our last trip is to Tarfaya, a fishing village about 75 miles north of Laayounne, across the *hammada*—bleak desert that is scarred with stone and wind-blown scrub. It is starkly dramatic, and for the occasion Sammy wears his flowing "sons of the desert" jellaba, looking like a displaced biblical figure as he sits at the wheel and commentates.

As if stage-managed, a camel train dances through the heat haze, and nomads' tents sprout like groups of magic mushrooms. Farther along comes a reverential pause at a monument built by King Hassan II to mark the opening of this territory, and beyond that a mirage materializes into a village, full of people, seemingly with nothing to do. After a short, bumpy interlude across rocky terrain to the shores of a huge salt lake, Sabkhat Tazghal, I leave the photos to Dave and do my routine stretch on the ground to ease the body-corrugating effects of off-road driving.

The curtain finally comes down at Tarfaya, a desolate huddle of houses half-buried by sand on one side, half-inundated by sea on the other. The nearby Khmiss Lagoon is probably North Africa's greatest stop-off for migratory birds. Staying only long enough to wash down fried fish, beans, and bread with the inevitable bottle of Fanta, we set off for Laayounne.

The *hammada* seems unending. A straight road leads away ahead and behind us, disappearing into the horizon. Overhead, the graying sky has flattened into a vast mirror of emptiness. Sammy half-dozes in his best armchair-driving style. Dave is slumped over his Walkman. I gaze out of the window as we slide down to Laayounne between heaven and earth, savoring the knowledge that I have had at least a taste of "getting away from it all."

Tunisia

Tunisian Package Tour

Traveling with an able-bodied companion, essential for Stephen Hunt, doubles the cost of the vacation. So when looking for winter sun he was keen to take advantage of package prices. Two weeks, flying from London Gatwick to Monastir, on the east coast of Tunisia, cost around $500 for a double room in an accessible hotel next to the beach.

Jim and I sit drinking mint tea at our favorite sidewalk café in the center of town, watching the clamorous North African world go by. Rising beyond, palm-fringed, are the ancient walls of the Arab Medina. To pass through the gates is to enter a different world of tangled, jostling alleys echoing with the cries of street traders: "Come on down, the price is right!"; "I give you special discount for handicap!" Yes, this is Sousse.

It was almost inevitable that I would land here. Winter was coming and I needed to stock up on sunshine. The obvious answer was a package tour. Where else could I have obtained so cheap a break, so far away, and one which I and a helpful companion could comfortably enjoy?

A quick flip through the brochures drew me to the coast of Tunisia and then everything could be left to my friendly travel agent and the tour operator (most major operators have Tunisian packages).

Good news: I have the most comfortable seat on the plane. Bad news: it's the usual packed charter flight. Still, I'll travel strapped down to the wingtip if it means breaking free from the restricted routine that disability so easily imposes, especially in winter. Escaping to different places, people and experiences, new sights and sounds and smells, is what keeps me going. I'd only fill their little sick bag if I kept thinking about our age of advanced technology, with its automatic pilots and supersonic aircraft with droopy noses, while I'm obliged to pay what amounts to a double fare without even being allowed a comfortable seat or a civilized pee.

I am able to stretch only when we arrive and, thankfully, transfer to the car, specially laid on by the tour operator. We are booked in to the *El Hana*

Hotel. Once you've stayed in one four-star resort hotel, you've stayed in them all. As far as I'm concerned, that's what's good about them. The only problem with this one is the pizza bar atop an impassable winding staircase. Still, who needs pizza?

When our first golden day dawns I'm already switched into holiday mode. A leisurely breakfast and we're strolling along the corniche, breathing in deeply the soft sea breezes. Then it's down just a few steps onto the beach. Lacking four-wheel drive, my wheelchair has to be heaved backward through the loose sand to a nice spot. Then all it takes is some quick sand sculpture and I'm down on my contoured sun-bed—bliss.

Sousse has its own charms for inquisitive wanderers like Jim and myself. But the Medina is the constant magnet, even though it's bumpier to get around. There's a gem of a museum and garden, and stunning mosaics hinting at the area's rich history. The intriguing maze of the kasbah and souk culminates in the Grand Mosque, where only the squeak of my wheelchair disturbs the peace of the cobblestone courtyard.

We can go farther, though. For me, renting a car for a few days is an expensive must. Most major rental companies have an office in Sousse and it's best to arrange this before departure. Driving south down the coast we reach Mahdia, which makes Sousse look like Coney Island. Here the souk is quieter, with the subdued atmosphere of a church, ringing with the bell-like tones of silversmiths' hammers.

Across the broad, fertile plain of olive groves laced with prickly pear lies the town of El Djem, the remains of a Colosseum-sized Roman amphitheater rising bizarrely out of its center. I do as I did in Rome and find a handy young tourist who helps Jim carry the wheelchair down the entrance steps.

Next comes Kairouan, Tunisia's answer to Mecca. We arrive late and most of the attractions are closed, leaving me prey to the den of thieves occupying the bazzaar. We part with little, but it leaves the only bad taste of this trip.

"A jagged layer of powdered sugar decorating the marzipan shore that sweeps around to Sousse"

On our last day with the car we wind northward to Hammamet and visit the house on the hill built in the 1920s by an eccentric Romanian millionaire. Here it all started, and below it continues: international luxury hotels jostle each other as rudely as on any Las Vegas boulevard, soon giving way to a lower order of gleaming white tourist palaces—a jagged layer of powdered sugar decorating the marzipan shore that sweeps around to Sousse.

Love it or loathe it, the package tour has opened a doorway onto the world for many. Why, then, did I see only one other noticeably disabled person during my two-week stay? It could, of course, be lack of spending power. Or is the travel industry not doing much to reassure a large potential market that the door *is* wide enough for wheelchairs? And are the mainstream operators using the specialists in "vacations for the disabled" as a cop out, passing the "problem" on rather than making all clients their concern, so that disabled people are left to pay inflated prices to the specialists and lose out on the benefits of the package deal?

Sierra Leone

Nor Touch Arata

In spring 1989 Kate Margrie, who is paraplegic, traveled to Sierra Leone, attracted by a Health Education Project. She spent two months working with youngsters in the Eastern Province.

The four-month sabbatical which I took from work left me with two months' preparation time. I got my visa, my shots, my travelers' checks, and my air ticket (via Moscow with *Aeroflot*). I had thought sanitation would be a problem, so paid a visit to my urologist; I didn't want to be carting around loads of catheters and pads. In the event there was always somewhere to go to the toilet, even if it was just a hole in the ground, and supplied with washable pads I ended up being healthier during my two months away than I ever am in England.

A friend, Cath, had set up a youth workshop attached to the Lassa Fever and AIDS Research Project based in Segbwema, in the Eastern Province. This project was the brainchild of an American doctor, Jo McKormac, who established it in the Seventies in an attempt to control and understand the disease. It is now funded by the Centers for Disease Control in Atlanta. For this reason an American is always appointed director of the project. This causes its own problems—coming in from the outside, the director may not be familiar with or understand local working methods, customs, or needs—but does mean that the Lassa team

receives a higher than average wage by Sierra Leone standards.

The Lassa Project has a laboratory, where tests are carried out on the blood of affected people, and their own ward in the Nixon Memorial Methodist Hospital, where—unlike all other treatment—patients are treated free of charge. Education has always been a high priority for the project as Lassa fever is preventable. This gave rise to the post of Youth Workshop Coordinator funded by Volunteer Service Overseas, which is where Cath came in. She spent a year in Segbwema, initiating some spectacular events, culminating in the grand LASSARAMA which drew together nationally and locally known musicians who composed songs especially for it. The resulting tape is now played in every nightclub in the land, and people still talk about that wild night. However, since Cath's departure nothing really happened on the youth education side.

Nine months later, I arrived. I had already decided that I wanted to be based in one place and that I wanted to share my skills in community drama. I did a lot of research on youth education and AIDS, I tried learning some Krio and Mende (the two languages spoken in the Eastern Province), and I made a video with one of our Youth Theaters to begin an exchange with young people in Sierra Leone.

I arrived at Heathrow with a home-made rucksack, designed to hang off the back of my chair, my concertina, and a car-load of friends to see me on my way. Then the trouble began. *Aeroflot* wouldn't let me on the plane without an escort, for "insurance purposes." Of course I could travel on that flight but only if I paid for an extra seat (£500) to allow one of their staff to accompany me! They claimed to have had no information from the travel agent, despite my insistence when booking that it be made clear to the airline.

"Moscow airport at night is not a very welcoming place"

There was no way that I was going to miss that flight, so I lied. "Yes, I can walk up steps. No, I won't ask for any assistance. Well, of course I could get out quickly in the event of an emergency" (as if it would make any difference!). I knew that once I was on the runway they'd simply have to help me on. It worked, but it did mean being carried by a cabin attendant whenever I wanted to leave my seat, causing many eyes to turn. And that was only the beginning.

Moscow airport at night is not a very welcoming place. There is no elevator to the restaurant, where I had to wait for eight hours, nor were any of the airport officials prepared to carry me down again. In the end, I asked some friendly passengers to help; I'd gotten this far and would never forgive myself if I missed the connecting flight! Many

hours and a beautiful sunrise later we touched down at Lungi airport, Sierra Leone. Getting through customs could have been a very harrowing experience if Abdul had not been there to whisk me through. (Abdul is the cousin of a friend and just happens to be the Chief Security Officer.) I had arrived, disoriented by the hustle and bustle, and hypnotized by the brilliant colors all around me. I had no idea what the next two months would hold.

My first night was spent in Abdul's house on the airport compound. We sat on the porch as the sun went down and the electric lights came on in the military compound opposite. I learned something of the corruption, the links between the President and the army, and the rocketing inflation (which tripled while I was there). Sierra Leone is considered one of the poorest countries in the world; the majority of the people hover between survival and starvation. Yet its land is agriculturally fertile and holds many minerals, including diamonds, and its waters hold a rich stock of fish. So what went wrong?

From 1961 to 1971 a very shaky, multi-party democracy operated, following on from British rule. But in 1971 Doctor Siaka Stevens became Executive President and from then on Sierra Leone has been a one-party republic. While I was there, an Asterix-style cartoon book was on sale, following Stevens' rise to power, expounding his virtues, and providing an easy-to-read, colorful piece of propaganda. In 1985 Major General Joseph Momoh took over as President, after an "election" riddled with ballot rigging and petty bribery. Momoh was the only candidate. He was previously head of the armed forces, and while everyone expected him to reform the oppressive sanctions practiced by his predecessor, nothing changed.

Soldiers now receive even greater privileges, such as very cheap rice and electricity in their compounds. The people living in the country are becoming increasingly disillusioned as the economy goes haywire and Momoh has to honor his deal with the IMF by floating the leone (le). People are depressed and becoming more willing to speak out against the regime. Every single person I met wanted to leave Sierra Leone and never come back.

"I spent many an evening out on the porch trying to dispel a few myths about England"

No one really mentioned my disability, which I thought strange at first, particularly in comparison with the fuss made at the European end, until I realized what was going on. As a white woman (*poumie*) I was odd enough anyway, so the fact that I was sitting down, wheeling myself around, didn't make a lot of difference. Sierra Leone is not an easy place to trundle about—the terrain is very rough—so I relied on people pushing, which practically at least was no problem. But there was a fine line between what I saw as my needs as a disabled woman, and what they saw as the needs of a white colonial, there to be served. Sierra Leone only gained its independence from Britain in 1961, and the "white is good" ethos remains. I spent many an evening out on the porch trying to dispel a few myths about England.

The Lassa Project is based in the Methodist hospital and nearby are a few ex-colonial houses. I was lodged in the bungalow; spacious, flat, and an ideal site for nurseries, parties, and rehearsing puppet shows. There was a mango tree outside and at 5am we collected the fallen mangoes to take for the kids in the education workshop. Every child I worked with was malnourished, and when the mangoes are ripe that's all they eat. Who can afford rice at 3000-le a sack, when the average monthly wage is between 500 and 1000-le.

With a few ramps installed, my base was accessible. But I'm not that skilled at oil-lamp maintenance, at building and cooking on fires, or drawing water from the well. I needed help, and the only way I could attempt to even this out was by giving in other ways . . . every morning at 8am Soloman picked me up in one of the Lassa Project trucks to go down to the workshop. All along the red-dust track, women make their way to the town to sell their produce from laden baskets balanced skillfully on their heads. The Limba men—palm wine collectors—pass by with a gourd in one hand and a long, sharp knife in the other; using a rope they scale the never-ending heights of the palm trees to gather the alcoholic juice amassed in yesterday's gourd.

At the workshop several boys would be waiting, eager to sweep the floor, open the shutters, or play on the drums. Word spread fast and soon dozens of kids were passing through our tiny workshop each day. I made badges with them, belts, hats, headbands, and, once we'd got used to each other, puppets. I wanted to introduce something that they could spend time making and use, even after I had left.

With brown paper, local fabrics, and many hours of posting and sewing (girls and boys alike), the characters for our puppet show, *Nor Touch Arata* (Don't Touch Rats), were born. Lassa is spread by a certain type of rat, and our story told of a young boy who caught the fever from eating food already touched by rats. The puppets were loosely based on several local characters, including the Lassa doctor, and there was always banter between the fascinated audience and the puppets. The response was amazing wherever we went: we piled into the truck, drove for hours to a tiny village where we were met by adults and children keen to watch, listen, ask questions, and hopefully learn a little, too.

As might be expected, several of the people I worked with had physical disabilities. One boy with no speech was picked on by his peers as mercilessly as he would have been back home. One of the teachers in the local high school had his own wheelchair, which amazed me at first, then he told me that a doctor had sent it from England in 1988. During my stay I also visited a residential home for children with disabilities in Freetown, the capital. It is supposed to be a *Cheshire Home* but receives no financial assistance from the UK based charity. Established in another ex-colonial house, the atmosphere is wonderful but the buildings are in a terrible state of disrepair. The girls' dorm is upstairs and only a few lucky children have braces.

With no training facilities for physiotherapists in Sierra Leone, disabled people just have to make the best use of what mobility they have, without much hope of ever acquiring aids such as wheelchairs. Nobody I came across owned a car, and public transit is a case of squeezing as many people as possible into a van. Mr. Koli, the schoolteacher, had to pay extra to take his wheelchair on board. It was not unusual to pass an overturned truck on the highway, with all its passengers trying to flag down the next one to come along.

"I ended up staying in a Catholic convent due to lack of cheap, accessible accommodation"

The workers on the Lassa team are lucky: they have two well-used, never-reliable trucks which are continually taken to bits by the four drivers; traveling in them was a lot of fun, our journeys always ending in laughter. Apart from my daily trip to the workshop and excursions to surrounding villages, I actually traveled very little. But Wednesday nights are for nightclubbing and even during Ramadan (the drivers are Muslim) we piled into one of the trucks, ready to boogie!

The nightclub reopened the day I arrived (good timing!). From the outside it looks like a wooden ranch hut, with a few tables and chairs on the balcony. Inside it's a different story. All around the walls are crudely painted portraits of Madonna, Michael Jackson, Stevie Wonder, and Bob Marley. In the middle is the checked dance floor and the inevitable disco lights which flash in time to the music. The DJ hides away in a room no bigger than a box and turns up the decibels to make everyone from miles around think it's all happening at the club. It was good to see men dancing with men, and women dancing with women, and to hear every now and then the familiar heavy bass of "Lassa Fever No Gud-o," one of the project songs.

Perhaps I have made it all sound easy. It wasn't. Many times I felt very frustrated, for example on my visit to Freetown, where I ended up staying in a Catholic convent due to lack of cheap, accessible accommodation. The hotels are extremely expensive and very international, so if you're looking for somewhere to stay, the YMCA is cheap, clean, and wheelchair accessible, but you do have to reserve in advance. Freetown is an incongruous mixture of solid office buildings, enormous hotels, banks with tinted windows, and foreign embassies, rubbing shoulders with one-room shacks squashed together next to open sewers. Laundry hangs between the shacks and the women cook as the children play.

The capital got its name from the freedmen (emancipated slaves) who were shipped over from America. The huge cotton tree, so-called because its fruit looks like cotton balls, remains in the center of the city as a reminder of those not-so-far-off days when slaves were bought and sold here. Sierra Leone was an unexplored land at that time, so someone had the idea of using it as a dumping ground for unwanted, "free" black men, women, and children, many of whom had never been to Africa before. This naturally caused friction between tribes and even now many Creoles (descendants of the freedmen) consider themselves one up from the indigenous tribal people. It's a colonial history we should be ashamed of.

"A tiny shack with an enormous sound system which seemed to be holding up the walls"

One of the songs which was played on every radio, in every bar, was "King Jimmy Bonga" and I wanted a tape of it as a memento. So we made our way through bumpy back streets, dodging kids, hens, and garbage, to a tiny shack with an enormous sound system which seemed to be holding up the walls. With a bit of cash, a nudge, and a wink, we struck a deal and next day the transaction was completed. Another day the Lassa truck needed some spare parts so we drove out to what can only be described as the district of the second-hand car dealers. Bamboo structures house hub caps, alternators, wheel exhausts . . . every imaginable part piled high behind their seller, who sits patiently listening to a small transistor. "King Jimmy Bonga" keeps him company.

There is another side to Freetown. On its outskirts are the luxury apartments and vast, foliaged compounds with lush green plants and swimming pools. This is where the expats and bank managers live, in bright white buildings to match the bright white bodies. These places are "protected" by a high white wall, decorated threateningly with pieces of jagged glass. The Sierra Leonian watchman is on duty day and night, and earns less in a month than the occupants spend in a day. There's a harshness about Freetown, and the glimpse I had of its other side was enough to make me yearn for the mango trees I'd left behind in Segbwema.

Being dependent on others was quite hard work, in sharp contrast with the lifestyle I'm used to. It meant that I didn't get to see the sights of Sierra Leone, but that wasn't what I was particularly interested in. On the other hand, it was wonderful to have more time than I've ever had to talk with people, to listen, and to learn those essential Mende words for "star," "moon," and "How many scorpions have you killed?"—these were the good times, whiling away the evening with old Pa Bocharie (the night watchman) and his wife, Matu, drinking palm wine by their fire under the stars.

"Do you have a moon in London?" Pa Bocharie asked me one night toward the end of my stay. How many moons apart our two worlds appeared then. And so I waved goodbye to newly made friends and all their warmth, to the rich soil, the corruption, and the sunshine. Another tourist passing through. I will always remember the first showing of "Nor Touch Arata," performed in the middle of Segbwema with hundreds of people gathered around—the good times. But people are still dying of Lassa fever; despite all the research in America there is still no antidote; there is even doubt as to whether, once discovered, the inoculation will be made available to the Sierra Leonians because it will be so expensive.

Kenya

Independence on Safari

In April 1991 wheelchair user Sue Kelley, husband Tony, and friend Sharon, a double amputee, traveled to Kenya. They experienced surprisingly good levels of comfort and access, and observed a wide variety of wildlife.

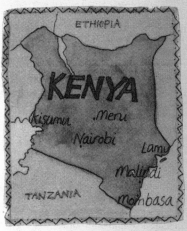

We had booked our flight through *Kuoni* but did not book any safaris before arriving in Kenya as we wished to make independent arrangements to suit our own needs. Our outward, nonstop, *Kenya Airways* flight left London Heathrow at 5pm. *Kenya Airways* staff gave us excellent treatment. We used our own wheelchairs to the entrance of the plane and were taken by aisle wheelchair to our seats. The aisle chair was not carried on board, so although I was able to make the short distance to the rest room with the aid of my cane and Tony's arm, Sharon is a full-time wheelchair user and had to be carried by Tony. The service on board was good and we were given assistance down the aircraft steps when we arrived at Moi International airport, Mombasa, at 6am the next morning.

After completing immigration and customs facilities we boarded (with help) a minivan for our hotel, a journey of just under an hour. We crossed from Mombasa to the southern mainland coast on the Lokoni car ferry.

We had chosen the five-star *Diani Reef Grand Hotel* as our base, not knowing in advance whether or not there were facilities for wheelchair users; we felt we could always look for an alternative hotel if necessary. After being helped from the van into our wheelchairs and pushed by the staff down a short, steep ramp into reception, we were shown our rooms, which were large and even the balconies overlooking the sea were accessible.

Despite being built on a coral cliff, the hotel was ramped throughout, although the ramp down to the beach and pools was extremely steep and treacherous when wet. There was a goods lift down to this level but we did not use it. The beach was a long stretch of white sand. Lounge chairs were available and there was plenty of shade from umbrellas or coconut palms. The two pools were large and accessible.

Seven out of the eight hotel restaurants, which were based on different themes and cultures, were accessible. The French restaurant was not ramped and access to the disco was via numerous steps, but Sharon found several willing people to assist her.

We found another wheelchair-accessible hotel in the area, the *Safari Beach Hotel*, where accommodation was in double-storied circular "huts." There was a very small step down onto the beach, but otherwise access was probably better than at the *Diani Reef*. There were fewer choices of restaurant but drinks were cheaper.

Both hotels offered watersports facilities and lessons in windsurfing, waterskiing, and scuba diving. Sharon opted for scuba diving and, once the hotel doctor had pronounced her fit, she spent the first two lessons in the swimming pool learning diving techniques and safety procedures. On the third day she went on her first sea dive to a depth of about 60 feet. The cost of the two lessons plus one dive was £150 (approximately $270; they prefer payment in pounds or dollars). Sharon undertook two more dives and her log book is one her proudest possessions.

"A chorus of frogs filled the air and the sky was alight with fireflies"

The drive to the game parks and reserves was some 4–5 hours, along very rough roads, so Tony and I joined an air safari to Amboseli, Taita, and Salt Lick, costing 9800 Kenyan shillings (about $515) per person and including meals and one night's accommodation. We booked with the *United Touring Company*, which had a desk in the hotel. We set off in a seven-seater plane from Ukunda airport at 6:30am. I was helped into the rear seat while the others had to climb over the wings into their seats. The flight was noisy but the scenery spectacular, especially snow-capped Mt. Kilimanjaro. Amboseli airport was just an asphalt runway, beside which was parked our safari Land Rover.

Unable to stand up in the rear, I sat in the front seat beside the driver and had a good all-around view. Within minutes of leaving the airstrip we had seen elephant, wildebeest, impala, Thomson's gazelle, and a giraffe. We drank coffee and watched zebra and wildebeest from the verandah of *Ambolesi Serena Lodge*, which overlooks the game park and, being a single-story building with ramps, is very suitable for wheelchair users.

After coffee, we left on our first game drive. We saw large herds of elephant, two types of zebra, three types of giraffe, Grant's and Thomson's gazelles, wildebeest, baboons, and ostrich, as well as many beautiful birds—the blacksmith plover, the carmine bee-eater, the lilac-breasted roller, the secretary bird, and the paradise flycatcher. After another game drive in the afternoon, we reboarded our plane for the one-hour flight to Taita Hills. As we were about to take off, a vast number of pink flamingoes landed on the lake, an amazing spectacle.

The plane landed on the dirt runway at Taita Hills, then taxied into the parking lot outside the reception area of the *Taita Hills Lodge*, a smart hotel but impractical for wheelchair users. The restaurants, bars, and shops are on the first floor and the rooms are on the upper level. There were no elevators, but the staff was very willing to assist. When in bed I was able to look out over the water hole and, by arrangement, guests could be woken if any large game visited it during the night. A chorus of frogs filled the air and the sky was alight with fireflies.

Within minutes of leaving the hotel at 6am we saw six lionesses sprawled in the grass and another stalking an impala. After collecting the other four in our party from the *Salt Lick Lodge*, where they had stayed overnight, we continued our drive, sighting impala, bushbuck, buffalo, giraffes, zebra, warthogs, and many birds, including vultures, eagles, herons, storks, and crowned plovers.

We returned to the *Salt Lick Lodge* for breakfast. The lodge was raised on stilts and the restaurant was on the second floor but, once again, there was obliging staff to get us up there and the breakfast was well worth the effort. By 9:30am we were back on the game drive. Our driver spotted a male lion in the distance, dragging along its kill. We followed this lion and were only a couple of feet away from him as he devoured his catch, a large impala. The noise of tearing flesh and crunching bone brought home the reality that the lion is a powerful predator and potentially dangerous animal.

We encountered wild dogs and a pair of dik-diks, members of the antelope family and not much bigger than a rabbit. Dik-diks feed on leaves, short roots, and tubers, and can go without water indefinitely.

After lunch at the *Taita Hills Lodge* we were taken on our final drive and saw enormous ant hills—major feats of engineering that contain a network of passages producing a flow of air and serving the same function as an air-conditioning unit. There were two lions stretched out in the sun where we had left the lion devouring its prey that morning, but no sign of any remains of the kill.

Although a somewhat sanitized safari, we thoroughly enjoyed it and were delighted with both the variety of birds and animals sighted and their proximity to our safari vehicle.

Sharon had managed well on her own at the *Diani Reef Hotel* in our absence, and had booked a three-day trip to the Masai Mara, staying for two nights in a tented camp, the *Intrepids Club*. All the tents were equipped with a toilet and shower and were well furnished. Sharon was allocated a personal assistant and was glad of the extra help as the pathway to her tent was gravel, as were the paths to the dining areas and bar. The rest room in the dining area was up six steps.

Like myself, Sharon sat in front with the driver during her safari, and saw a great variety of wildlife. She encountered no insurmountable difficulties and made several friends among her German and Swiss traveling companions. The fact that Sharon was able to join the safari as an independent, unaccompanied member of the group made the trip very special for her. On her return she said it had been one of the best experiences of her life.

Tanzania

I Felt like a King

John Bignell has multiple sclerosis, diagnosed in 1983, and is now unable to walk more than a few steps out of doors. He uses a standard-issue, hand-propelled wheelchair, which he regards not as a prison but as his passport to the world. In June 1988 he was invited to present a paper to a workshop on phosphates, organized by the Commonwealth Science Council at Arusha in northern Tanzania.

When I booked my flights—Heathrow to Kilimanjaro via Amsterdam and back—I informed the airline (*KLM*) of my disabilities and that I would be unaccompanied. I requested wheelchair assistance at all airports: no problem, I was assured. I packed all my luggage in a small suitcase which I could suspend over the handles of my wheelchair with two elastic grips, so that I could move myself and all my gear about quite easily.

I arrived at London's Heathrow airport one Saturday evening to learn that the Amsterdam flight was on time but the Tanzania flight was delayed by technical trouble for eighteen hours! I transferred to an airport chair and was wheeled rapidly, by a very pleasant gentleman, through the customs and security checks and eventually to the aircraft door.

At Schiphol, Amsterdam's airport, I was met at the door by one of the cabin crew with my own chair, and wheeled straight through the formalities to the airport *Hilton* for my enforced overnight stop. The design of my chair was much admired by the *KLM* staff. After a Sunday morning spent traveling by train in and out of the city center and trying to discover where the disabled could embark for a canal trip (by the time I had established this, there was no time for the trip!), I was taken in the hotel courtesy limo back to the airport.

I checked my luggage and wheelchair in and was transferred to an airport chair. I then began to understand why my chair had been so much admired. The airport chair had four small wheels, making it virtually impossible for the occupant to move it, and with no cushion it was very uncomfortable.

Because of the delay, instead of a magnificent midday view of Kilimanjaro to welcome me to Tanzania, I arrived at 4am, bleary-eyed and in the dark. At the foot of the aircraft steps I was met by a wheelchair with very flat tires. For once I had to wait my turn to be processed by immigration, health, and currency officials, but at least I was sitting down! In the baggage hall I reclaimed my chair but not my case. At the missing bags counter I met some colleagues also attending the workshop who, unbeknown to me, had traveled on the same flight. Out of four of us, three had lost their bags.

"He drove like the proverbial bat out of hell"

We were taken to the hotel where I could unpack my camera bag, and then on to the Arusha International Conference Center. The center had not been designed with the disabled in mind. The nearest car-parking spot was some way from the door with a curb to negotiate. Even on the first floor there were steps all over the place. Fortunately, whenever I approached any steps, without being asked, four pairs of hands would grab the chair and hoist it and me into the air and up or down.

My presentation was in the afternoon, and the following morning we all left on a two-day field trip, giving no one time to buy new clothes. So, in clothes borrowed from other members of our group, I set off to visit the local geological sights. Out of the city, the roads, where they existed, were not well maintained. The driver of the Land Rover was very skillful but he drove like the proverbial bat out of hell. This resulted in a fast and bumpy ride. So bumpy that I managed to put my shoulder through the Land Rover's side window toward the end of day one. I spent the rest of the trip trying to hold my chair cushion

between myself and the broken window to avoid being cut to ribbons.

We drove from the lush green of the Arusha area, pleasantly cool at about 4000ft, down to the hot, arid, and dusty surrounds of Lakes Manyara and Natron. Like many sufferers from multiple sclerosis my disabilities get worse when the temperature rises, so I relied on helpers to push me in my chair when I wanted to move more than a few feet from the car. I have a most unflattering photograph of me in my chair perched on the lip of a spectacular extinct volcano crater, to illustrate the sort of places I was taken to. This was reached after several hours of hard, dusty driving through an apparently deserted wilderness of powdery volcanic ash. The dust had barely settled when two Masai ladies appeared from nowhere to sell their colorful bead necklaces. When we stopped a few miles farther on, we were surrounded by children, and the bartering currency of the moment was ballpoint pens.

The one thing missing was wildlife. We saw only a few baboons, giraffe, and zebra at close quarters. In the distance we did see a pink coloration on Lake Manyara, which, we were assured, was produced by thousands upon thousands of flamingoes. We also spotted a few vultures, hideous at close range but magnificent in flight.

"I had only to trundle through the restaurant door for food to arrive"

The *Novotel Mount Meru* (Arusha) was simple but clean and comfortable. It was three stories high and had one small elevator which could just accommodate me in my chair, but there was no room to turn. As the doors closed automatically after only a few seconds, as soon as I reached my floor I had to back out fast and hope all was clear behind me. Breakfast was always a buffet, mostly fresh fruit. As I cannot carry food and move, the hotel staff plied me with food at the table. They quickly cottoned on to what I liked, so I had only to trundle through the restaurant door for food to arrive.

The workshop talks continued to the end of the week, and on Friday at noon our suitcases arrived (via Brussels) and borrowed clothes could at last be returned. It was a good thing the hotel had an efficient and fast laundry service.

One morning, when I looked out of the hotel window, I saw how the local disabled fared. A man was seated on a wooden plank, fitted with what looked at a distance like chair castors. He propeled himself by pushing on the ground with his hands. Seated in my National Health Service chair, I felt like a king.

I was taken by one of the workshop participants, a Dutchman on secondment to Tanzania from a Canadian university, to see Kilimanjaro. Or, rather, to see a bit of it. The top was always hidden by cloud. Ballpoint pens were acceptable in this part of the country, too.

Sunday was the final day in Tanzania. The hotel desk was sure that there was a suitable service at the cathedral at 10:30am. They were wrong. I arrived by taxi at 10:15am, part way through a eucharist being taken by the bishop—in Swahili. Although I arrived late, knew no one, and didn't understand a word, I felt very welcome and part of the congregation. At the end of the service I was greeted by the bishop and his fellow clergy like a long-lost brother. A charming young American woman appeared and gaily announced that taxis were hard to get in this part of town but she would try to fix me up with a lift back to the hotel. She disappeared and reappeared a couple of minutes later at the wheel of a car—the bishop's car. Incidentally, she was the only person I met on my trip who knew how to collapse my chair without first being told.

I returned to the hotel to find it in the midst of a power outage, so the elevator was out of action. The current had not been restored some four hours later, when it was time to leave. One of the staff retrieved my case, which fortunately I had packed before I went to church. I went to the airport with the Dutchman; on the way, the clouds parted a little to reveal the snow-capped summit of Kilimanjaro, but at a range of about 30 miles it was not spectacularly clear—I had to inspect my photographs closely to convince myself that I really had seen the summit.

The airport was in chaos: they had also been affected by the power outage. With the help of some local knowledge and the chutzpa of my Dutch friend I soon found myself sitting in the departure lounge in the airport chair, still with the very flat tires. Because the control tower had been without power our plane had been rerouted and our departure was delayed by four hours. This meant that a meal was served, upstairs of course. As there was no elevator, my meal was brought down.

"A man was seated on a wooden plank, fitted with what looked like chair castors"

At Amsterdam I was asked, as is customary, to sit in my seat until all the other passengers had disembarked. After everyone else had gone, the crew looked outside for the expected wheelchair. It wasn't there. Hasty recourse to the radio, followed by "Just a minute, sir, it will be here soon." After a few minutes there were more inquiries by radio, and the cabin crew was beginning to get agitated.

"Could I walk along the ramps to waiting trolley?"

"No."

"You may have to wait twenty minutes."

I had nothing better to do, as long as I made my connection. The ground-crew arrived to clean out the cabin, but the chair didn't. The only member of the cabin crew left on board was going frantic, talking into his radio. After about half an hour something had to be done or I would miss the connecting flight. On the arm of a well-built and charming ground staff member, I walked along a seemingly endless ramp and through the arrival lounge to a waiting trolley. I was then driven to the departure lounge and had to struggle along another ramp to the next plane.

Back at Heathrow, I was met at the cabin door by another friendly face who sympathized over my experience at Schiphol. "You should have gone by *BA*." (He worked for *British Airways* and had only been loaned to *KLM* for my benefit.) I was whipped through immigration, one of the few advantages of traveling in a wheelchair, and into the baggage hall. My case was quickly found but my wheelchair was eventually located in Amsterdam. I was loaned an airport chair to see me home, and my chair was specially delivered to my house later the same day.

I wrote to *KLM*, complaining of my experiences, particularly the lack of wheelchair at Schiphol. After six weeks I had received no reply so I wrote again, asking specific questions about wheelchair availability at Schiphol. Their reply crossed in the post. It apologized for the misplacements and blamed a new baggage handling system. The reason for the delay in replying was that they were awaiting the results of an investigation. No find-ings were disclosed but they hoped that the "generous" gift of a *KLM* marked ballpoint pen would compensate for the inconvenience. (It might have been of some use in Tanzania.) The second letter elicited nothing more than that *KLM* were surprised that I was not satisfied by their response. Still no explanations.

I tried contacting the Dutch Embassy in London, asking whom I could write to. They suggested their Ombudsman. His office replied that it was not their responsibility; they added that the embassy should have known better than to involve them. I also wrote to the Dutch Multiple Sclerosis Society. Their reply, far from being helpful, suggested to me that they were rather pained at me for querying the efficiency of their national airport and airline.

Finally, *KLM* admitted that they were having trouble with their new baggage handling system and that all available staff had been sidetracked to try to sort things out, thus no wheelchair help could be provided at Schiphol. This was hardly news, but surely prior commitments should be honored, particularly since *KLM* staff had to be on hand anyway—all that was missing was the chair!

The attitude of *KLM* leaves something to be desired, although the staff I met was all splendid and as frustrated as I was by the problems encountered on my trip.

Zimbabwe

Silent Zimbabwe

For fourteen years John Myall has suffered from Ménière's disease, a condition that can cause severe attacks of giddiness and nausea, often without warning and lasting for several hours; at the same time it destroys the hearing. John's attacks have now lessened, enabling him to enjoy his passion for wildlife and wilderness areas, but the deafness remains. In June 1989 he traveled alone to Zimbabwe, to stay with friends and photograph wildlife.

The Land Rover edged its way along the track which was still unrepaired after the previous season's rains. The sun was well up and we were able to start shedding sweaters. It was mid-winter in Zimbabwe, an ideal time for travel in this part of the world. Although the nights are distinctly chilly, the day temperatures are more akin to those of a pleasant English summer, and—the biggest blessing—the insect life is mostly inactive.

We were hoping for a sight of a black rhinoceros; his tracks had been spotted the day before and he was the first one to wander into this area for many years. As our Land Rover reached the brow of the hill, the driver stopped. Some 900ft ahead lay a thicker area of bush and, above, vultures were circling. Something was either dead or dying, and we had to investigate.

The Land Rover was parked off the track and four of us proceeded on foot.

At our approach the birds reluctantly withdrew; they had started to feast on three dead impala, each one with a wire snare cutting into its neck. The snares had been wired to trees, so that the harder these graceful antelope had struggled, the more quickly they had strangled themselves.

Sten (the guide) and I stayed put, not wishing to disturb anything as the two Shona trackers cast about for any evidence of the identity of the poachers. Only one set of tracks was found, made by well-worn soles with a distinctive chip out of the left heel. The man was almost certainly a local herdsman from the nearby village, out to obtain some meat to sell. He must have been delayed in checking his snares as the giveaway birds were making good use of his handiwork.

We checked out the remaining area and retrieved another ten wires, then the Shona pointed to a movement in the dry grass about 225ft away—yet another impala with the deadly choking wire. He had struggled hard and the branch which the wire was attached to had snapped off. Although still alive he was beyond saving. As Sten went off to collect the Land Rover, so that we could load up and take away the carcasses, he handed me his rifle. He knew that I had had plenty of experience of African wildlife and firearms. Moving into close range, I worked the bolt to feed a cartridge from the magazine into the breech, aimed, and fired. The impala jerked and then lay still. I barely heard the shot as I am now almost completely deaf.

The 140-square miles cattle ranch (not particularly large by Zimbabwean standards) is situated along the banks of the Crentedzi river, which is home for a fair number of crocodiles and hippos. George and Madeleine, friends of long standing, had invited me some time back to pay them a visit as soon as I felt up to traveling. In addition to ranching, they arrange photographic and hunting safaris. As a result of well-managed conservation policies, there is a good surplus of game which can be hunted without fear of endangering any species.

"A family of warthogs, led by an old fellow with some very impressive tusks, broke cover and took off"

Accommodation for clients is the typical African safari camp, with roomy sleeping tents (all fitted with insect screens and snake-proof zippers), camp toilets, showers, mess tent, and, of course, the traditional log fire to sit around in the evening, drinking, exchanging stories, and—for those who can—listening to the sounds of the animals in the bush. Dotted around the perimeter are the bits that make the whole thing work: cookhouse, stores, vehicle servicing area, and tents for the camp workers.

The flight from London to Harare caused me no major problems, although airport check-ins (like hotel receptions) can be a bit tedious if questions have to be written down for me. I was met at Harare by an air charter pilot who ferried me through customs at great speed, after which it was a short hop in a light plane to the ranch's private airstrip. This spared me an arduous nine-hour road journey.

Wherever I go, I make a point on arrival of putting the news about that I am deaf and a hopeless lip-reader, indicating my ever-present pencil and notebook (for those who can write in English). However, on the first day out with Sten and his two trackers, after a lengthy hike without seeing much, the party stopped suddenly and ducked down. Sten pointed and whispered to me. I saw and heard nothing, and was bewildered as to what I was supposed to be looking for. To my confusion, he whispered again, no doubt louder, when a family of warthogs, led by an old fellow with some very impressive tusks, broke cover and took off. They had heard the voice. It was here that we stopped to refine our system of communication.

A pencil and paper is not always ideal for bush use, and Sten was a slow writer, so it had to be a series of hand signals to identify the various animals. The most graphic was undoubtedly the scratching of the armpit to represent the baboon! In fact, Sten was quite an expert, as he had done all this before. As a professional hunter he had led many of the big safaris in Tanganika (now Tanzania) and Kenya, as well as working with the lions for the film, "Born Free." Some of his clients did not speak English (or his native Swedish), so hand signals became the common language when out on the hunt where quietness is absolutely necessary. Although I was armed with nothing heavier than a selection of cameras, the same rules apply; game must be stalked silently for a good shot.

A deaf person moving through the bush is presented with another problem. It is easy to presume that because you hear yourself making little or no noise, you are moving quietly. Not so! You may well only feel the dry twig snap, or your boot scuff on a rock, or the numerous thorns raking across your clothing, but the noise will be clearly audible to the nearby animal life. One morning I thought I had done particularly well as we approached a mixed herd of wildebeest and zebra. This was in spite of the fact that Sten had given me several reproachful looks. Idly thinking that all my old skills from years back had not deserted me, I had been lulled into a false sense of security—in fact, my hearing aid battery had gone flat.

> **"Behind a clump of bushes a mere 130ft away—my planned destination—lay a lioness with the remains of her dinner"**

A trip farther afield, well clear of the main ranching area, hammered home the need for careful observation to make up for my lack of hearing. I had a dose of the "East African Quickstep" and signaled for the Land Rover to stop and let me run for it. A pair of strong hands grasped my shoulders and kept me firmly in my seat. Behind a clump of bushes a mere 130ft away—my planned destination—lay a lioness with the remains of her dinner. She had roared, which had alerted the others; when I knew where to look and what to look for I could make out her outline. We moved on and I found another bush; after all, she was there first.

The other clients at the camp were an American honeymoon couple and a German hunter; six is about the maximum number of clients at any one time. Each person or small group can go out by day or night to do their own thing. The Americans spent several nights waiting up in a blind to watch the leopard feed. A blind is a ready-prepared hiding place, made of bushes and

grass, for two or three people. It provides a clear view of the feeding animal while the watchers remain unseen. But the leopard's sense of hearing is acute, so any "unnatural" noise alerts him instantly and he disappears in one blurred movement. I tend to fidget, then fall asleep under such circumstances, so I gave the blind a miss. Gone is the boundless energy of my youth!

The odd afternoon sitting in the sun on the "beach" is a little more in my line these days. Just a small clearing on the river bank, the beach was about 230ft from our tents. Small, brightly colored birds darted about and monkeys chattered in the trees. One afternoon I got through three chapters of my book while being watched by a curious hippo who remained motionless in mid-river, with only the top of his head above the surface. I learned that he was a regular visitor, known as Fred. Although not renowned as a vicious animal, the hippo's huge mouth does inspire a sense of awe. Several species of African animal are capable of biting a human in half, but only the hippo can bite one into three! Fred and I made a pact: he stayed in the river and I stayed on the beach.

It was a vacation I am sure to repeat, and the photos (some at least!) were almost professional. Before leaving, I photographed as many of the African camp staff as I could with my Polaroid camera and gave them the prints. On the last evening we had a farewell party around the campfire. Apart from the fact that it was time to say goodbye, I felt a tinge of sadness for another reason: the party emphasized the handicaps that deafness causes. In the flickering light of the fire any form of lipreading is next to impossible, likewise writing things down; even sign language gets lost in the dancing shadows.

AFRICA: TRAVEL NOTES

Sources of Information

Most African tourism organizations supply no relevant information and have no plans to produce it, but some will make efforts to answer specific questions from individual inquirers, usually by referring to their head offices.

Morocco National Tourist Office, 20 East 46th Street, #303, New York, NY 10017 (☎212/557-2520); 421 North Rodeo Drive, Beverly Hills, CA 90210 (☎213/271-8939); 2001 Rue Université, Suite 1460, Montréal, PQ H3A 2A6 (☎514/842-8111).

Tunisia Tourist Office, 1 ave Mohamed V, Tunis, Tunisia; ☎1/341077.

Embassy of Sierra Leone, 1701 19th Street, NW, Washington DC 20009; ☎202/939-9261.

Kenya Tourist Office, 424 Madison Avenue, New York, NY 10017 (☎212/486-1300); 9100 Wilshire Boulevard, Doheny Plaza #111, Beverly Hills, CA 90121 (☎213/274-6634).

Tanzania Tourist Corporation, 205 East 42nd Street, 8th Floor, New York, NY 10017 (☎212/972-9160); PO Box 2485, Dar es Salaam, Tanzania (☎51/27671).

Zimbabwe Tourist Development Corporation, 1270 Avenue of the Americas, New York, NY 10020 (☎212/332-1090); Tourism House, Fourth Street and Stanley Ave, PO Box 8952, Causeway, Harare, Zimbabwe (☎4/793666).

Travel to **South Africa** will remain controversial until apartheid is unambiguously abolished, but the combination of the country's relative wealth and its desire to promote tourism in the face of the travel boycott means that its infrastructure for disabled travelers is the best on the continent.

South African Tourist Board, 747 Third Avenue, 20th Floor, New York NY 10017; ☎212/838-8841 or 800/822-5368. Will obtain answers to specific inquiries from their head office in Pretoria and will contact hotel chains to ascertain the accessibility of particular hotels. The Pretoria office has compiled some basic information, including hotels that have facilities for disabled guests, which should now be available from the US office.

Tour Operators

Although there are several companies in the US offering inclusive vacation and safari packages to Africa, many quote prices for the land arrangements only, and the choice is much wider and the deals much better with British operators. One company worth highlighting, **Abercrombie and Kent**, has offices in the UK and the US (1420 Kensington Road, Oak Brook, IL 605211; ☎800/323-7308) and is an experienced and flexible mainstream operator offering customized tours; it does not specialize in travel for disabled people but has taken clients in wheelchairs on safari in Tanzania and Kenya, either lifting them manually into the safari vehicle or making a few basic adaptations to the vehicle so that it can accommodate a wheelchair; it's good to hear a travel company point out the plus side for wheelchair users—everyone on a safari is vehicle-bound, so there is no risk of slowing down the rest of the group.

Sue Kelley reports that the ranger on her Kenyan safari provided a good service and is willing to undertake and arrange safaris to suit disabled clients. John Mutero can be contacted at Oletuala, PO Box 18, Namanga, Amboseli, Kenya.

Ian Piercy, of *Zambesi Hunters Ltd.* (PO Box 139, Ruwa, Zimbabwe; ☎73/2567) handles reservations for George and Madeleine's ranch. *Zambesi Hunters* uses several areas for its safari camps, depending on what type of scenery and animals the clients are interested in.

The number of mainstream package operators featuring Zimbabwe in their programs has increased over the last year or two, partly as a result of overcrowding and overdevelopment in Kenya, but tourism is not yet the smooth operation that it is in Kenya, and awareness of disabled tourists' needs is low.

Morocco Bound (Suite 603, Triumph House, 189 Regent Street, London W1, UK; ☎071/734-5307) handled arrangements for Stephen Hunt in its "impeccably sympathetic style," but this company does not arrange connecting flights from North America. Another specialist, *CLM* (Creative Leisure Management, 4a William Street, London SW1, UK; ☎071/235-2110), is a flexible and reliable agency who will arrange flights (including US/Canada–London transfers)

AFRICA: TRAVEL NOTES

and personally planned tours and accommodation; most of the Marrakesh hotels used have large elevators, and *CLM* suggests that the *Hotel Essaadi* would be suitable for most wheelchair users. Of the British package operators, Stephen recommends *Thomson*—its *Winter Sun* brochure offers vacations in Morocco, Tunisia, Kenya, and the Gambia; the *Worldwide* brochure features Kenya; all the resorts are covered by *Factfile* (see Canary Islands *Travel Notes*). *Horizon* is also plugged into *Factfile* and its African destinations include Tunisia and Kenya.

Roger Elliott visited **South Africa**, and was delighted with the itinerary and arrangements made by *Tempo Travel* (Brunswick House, 91 Brunswick Crescent, London N11 1DG, UK; ☎081/361 1131). Its ground handling agents, *Welcome Tours* (PO Box 306, Hout Bay 7872, Cape Province, South Africa; ☎21/434-3890), organized all tours and transfers within South Africa and gave "excellent service." It is worth bearing in mind, though, that any tour arranged in South Africa is likely studiously to avoid exposing travelers to those parts of the country where the agony of apartheid is still in evidence (as Roger's tour did).

Evette Johnson of *Titch Travel* (15 Banksia Road, Rosebank, Cape Town 770, South Africa; ☎73/2567) specializes in tailor-made tours for deaf or blind travelers, and can arrange tours for wheelchair users given sufficient time.

Getting There

Most **flights** to Africa from North America are indirect, routed through various European capitals. This can be used to advantage if stopping over in London, for example, from where it is possible to obtain exceptionally good-value package tours from British tour operators. It is also feasible to piece together a good deal for flights by finding a cheap round-trip to London and adding on a flight to the African city of your choice. The cheapest way to reach Africa from London, on the Russian airline *Aeroflot*'s flight via Moscow, with a long stopover in a none-too-accessible airport, is not recommended for wheelchair users.

There should be few problems on the other major **airlines** that operate services to African countries—apart from the usual uncomfortable seating and cramped rest rooms. Roger Elliott reports good service from *South African Airways* which carries aisle chairs (with one "accessible" rest room per aircraft) and provides "passenger aid units" at all major airports. A *British Airways* flight from London is the safe option for disabled passengers traveling to Tanzania, Sierra Leone, or Zimbabwe: the aircraft are equipped with aisle chairs which can squeeze into two of the rest rooms.

Royal Air Maroc (☎800/344-6726) operates direct flights to Casablanca from New York and Montréal; these can be bought in conjunction with add-on flights to other Moroccan airports or with flights east to Tunisia or Egypt. *British Airways, Air France, KLM,* and *Iberia* fly to a number of Moroccan destinations—Tangier, Casablanca, Marrakesh, and Agadir are most common—through London, Paris, Amsterdam, and Madrid. *Iberia*'s attitude to unaccompanied wheelchair users has come in for criticism from some travelers.

Kenya Airways does not operate transatlantic flights but maintains a New York office (6th Floor, 424 Madison Avenue, NY 10017; ☎212/832-8810) and offers a year-round fare to Nairobi of $1499, using other airlines for the transatlantic leg (for this, call ☎800/343-2506). *Kenya Airways* is the only airline to offer a direct flight to Mombasa; it's more expensive than flying to Nairobi, facilities at Mombasa airport are basic (see below), and the train journey from Nairobi to Mombasa is feasible for wheelchair users (see *Transport*, below). On other scheduled airlines there are very few good fares all the way through from North America to Kenya, and since from the States they are all routed through New York and then stop over in Europe—usually London or Frankfurt—it makes sense to stay overnight and shop around for a cheap onward ticket the next day. Most Canadian travel agents send their customers to Britain first anyway, although *Air Canada* has flights operated by *Swissair* to Nairobi via Zurich from Montréal and Toronto. London tends to be the cheapest departure point, and good airlines for disabled passengers include *Air France, British Airways, KLM, Lufthansa,* and *Swissair*.

AFRICA: TRAVEL NOTES

It is at the African **airports** that difficulties may arise; often their only good point is a relatively small terminal building, so that the distance from aircraft to taxi rank (or bus pick-up point) is short—as at Agadir, Morocco. Facilities vary enormously. In South Africa there are rest rooms and lifts and passenger aid units at major airports. In Tanzania (Kilimanjaro airport) John Bignell was transferred in a wheelchair with flat tires, and the terminal building had no elevator, with restaurant facilities on the second floor. Freetown's Lungi airport is a disaster, and getting into town can take as long as three hours, depending on the state of the ferry across the Sierra Leone river; the alternative is a five-hour taxi ride.

On her flight to Kenya in 1988, Jean Hamilton twice asked the crew to radio ahead for a wheelchair but on arrival at Nairobi there was no chair waiting for her. One hour after the other passengers had disembarked, a chair (plus irate attendant) appeared. Jean was taken around the back of the terminal and dumped at the lost and found. Also in Nairobi, the parts of Stephen Hunt's wheelchair arrived at ten-minute intervals on the luggage carousel—standards of baggage handling leave something to be desired, although this is certainly not a problem confined to Africa.

Sue Kelley experienced some problems on her flight home from Mombasa in 1991. Despite requesting that the *Kuoni* rep inform the airport of their need for assistance three days in advance, and being assured that this had been done and there would be someone there to meet them, Sue arrived to find no one to help and at check-in they were told to sit anywhere on the plane until they reached Nairobi, where passengers would disembark for two hours and seats would be allocated. The departure lounge was chaotic—no signs, no information, no preboarding for disabled passengers. They eventually realized that their plane was boarding, at which point the promised helper from *Kuoni* appeared. He took over Sharon's chair but showed reluctance to help her up the steps to the aircraft. Sue slowly crawled up, Tony carrying all the hand luggage and wheelchair cushions. When Tony gave the

young man some money he agreed to carry Sharon up the steps. Once inside the plane, the cabin attendant cleared the second row for them, and they managed to retain these seats after the reshuffle at Nairobi, where they remained on board (although there is a boarding satellite at this airport, there are a couple of flights of stairs to negotiate on the way to the transit lounge).

For travelers from Europe with no time constraints, aiming for northern parts such as Morocco and Tunisia (or even farther—see p.504), the **drive** through France and Spain makes an interesting alternative to flying. Ferries or hydrofoils from Spain to Morocco should be booked well in advance in high season (see *The Real Guide: Morocco* for details).

Transport

Most Moroccan towns are small enough to explore by foot (or wheel), especially if you manage to find a central hotel. For getting about larger towns, such as Arusha in Tanzania and Nairobi in Kenya, **taxis** are generally cheap and drivers helpful. For journeys out of town, and independent sightseeing at your own pace, **car rental with a guide** is not too expensive: it works out at between $60 and $90 per day in Morocco. Travel by **self-drive car** is—in many parts of Africa—only for the adventurous and mechanically minded. The only country in which hand-controlled rental cars are available (from *Avis*) is South Africa. Local **buses** come in a variety of shapes and forms; most are overloaded and all inaccessible without assistance.

For cross-country journeys, **trains** may be usable with a companion, although the cars are definitely not designed for passengers in wheelchairs. When Stephen Hunt took a two-berth couchette on the overnight train from Nairobi to Mombasa (costing about $35 round trip), he found no widened doorways and no extra space for wheelchairs; in fact there was barely room to stand (supported from behind) at the sink, and regular bouts of exercise and massage were necessary throughout the night to prevent cramp. But there is plenty of help available at stations.

AFRICA: TRAVEL NOTES

Air travel is a (rather expensive) possibility if you can shrug off the poor facilities at many airports. In South Africa, efficient passenger aid units at airports make domestic flights a good way to get around.

If booking a place on a **safari**, or on tours using rented minivans or Land Rovers, be warned that the road surfaces are usually appalling, and passenger comfort is not a priority when drivers are working to tight schedules—traveling at speed over rough ground is no joke. On custom tours the pace can be more leisurely but the ride will still be bumpy.

Accommodation

There is accessible accommodation in many African countries: in the cities of the poorer ones it is restricted to a few, often overpriced, big-name hotels; in wealthier countries there are more possibilities in the moderate price bracket. Off the beaten track and in rural areas you'll find more single-story buildings, with better prospects to the wheelchair user. You'll also be swamped with willing assistants, all ready to improvise—with ramps and other aids to accessibility—in buildings which at first glance seem devoid of facilities and totally unsuited to anyone in a wheelchair.

Bearing this in mind, it's probably not essential to go to great lengths to determine facilities, door widths, or other details before departure. Accommodation is likely to present the smallest problems in Africa—terrain and transport are the main stumbling blocks. That said, some research is a good idea, the amount depending on the country to be visited.

Kenyan hotels with some facilities for the disabled include the *Nairobi Hilton* (PO Box 30624, Nairobi; ☎2/334000), the *New Stanley Hotel* (PO Box 30680, Nairobi; ☎2/333233), the *680 Hotel* (PO Box 43436, Nairobi; ☎2/332680), the *Hotel Inter-Continental* (PO Box 30353, Nairobi; ☎2/335550), the *Nairobi Serena Hotel* (PO Box 46302; ☎2/725111), the *Safari Park Hotel* (PO Box 45038, Nairobi; ☎2/802493), the *Castle Hotel* (PO Box 84231, Mombasa; ☎11/23403), the *Jadini Beach Hotel* (PO Box 84616, Mombasa; ☎01261/2021), and the *Diani Reef Grand Hotel* (PO Box 35, Ukunda; ☎01261/2062), most of which are expensive.

Refer to *The Real Guide: Kenya* for less expensive places to stay—cheap does not always mean inaccessible. While staying at the *Castle Hotel* for $80 a night for a double room, Stephen Hunt discovered similar amenities a short walk down Msanifu Kombo Street at the *Hotel Splendid* (PO Box 84851, Nairobi; ☎11/20967), for less than half the price.

Accessibility at Kenyan safari lodges is getting better; indeed, *Abercrombie and Kent* (see *Tour Operators*) says that most of the lodges it uses would be accessible to most disabled guests. But Sue Kelley found that the lodges she stayed at were generally inaccessible, although she coped with help from staff and her husband. Her companion found suitable facilities, including shower and lavatory, at her safari camp, although gravel paths made movement between tented areas difficult. *Kilimanjaro Safari Lodge,* in Amboseli Reserve, and *Lake Nakuru Lodge* are reported accessible by travel writer Nancy Bear after her visit to Kenya with a friend who is a full-time wheelchair user.

Information on **Zimbabwean hotels and safari lodges** is difficult to obtain. *Spurwing Island Safari Lodge* (Private Bag 101, Kariba, Zimbabwe; ☎61/2466) is reported to be reasonably accessible to most disabled people. *Zimbabwe Sun Hotels* (86 East Lane, Wembley, Middlesex, UK; ☎081/908 3348) have about fifteen properties, some of which are accessible to wheelchair users. *Sikumi Tree Lodge* (Hwange National Park, Private Bag 5779, Dete; ☎18/2105) has one chalet designed for disabled guests, built closer to the ground with a ramped entrance. The *Hwange Safari Lodge* (Private Bag DT 5792, Dete; ☎18/331) has two modified rooms with wider doorways and grab-rails around toilet and bath; ramps are used throughout the hotel. The *Victoria Falls Hotel* (PO Box 10, Victoria Falls; ☎13/4203) has several ramps and all doors and rooms are large enough for wheelchairs. The *Monomatapa* (54 Park Lane, PO Box 12245, Harare; ☎4/704501) would also be manageable with prior notification.

In **Morocco**, the *Hôtel Kenza* (Marrakesh; ☎4/448330) is recommended for ambulant disabled guests; wheelchair users would have to find a way around the three steps to the

AFRICA: TRAVEL NOTES

dining room. Stephen Hunt stayed at the *Hôtel Parador* (Rue Okba Ben Nafia; ☎8/38-29) in Laayounne, although he had originally booked the *Al Massira*; both are owned by *Club Med*. In Marrakesh he stayed at the *Hôtel Chems* (☎4/444-814) which is wheelchair friendly.

In **Tunisia**, Stephen Hunt stayed at the *El Hana Hotel* (☎3/26900) in Sousse, next to the beach and five minutes' walk/wheel from town; two weeks in early November, flying from London Gatwick to Monastir, cost around $500 for a double room with bathroom/shower and balcony including breakfast and dinner. The *Tunisian National Tourist Office* says that the "ideal hotel for a tourist with disabilities" is *Hotel Lido*, in Nabeul.

If booking a **package tour** in Morocco or Tunisia from London use the *Thomson Factfile* (see *Tour operators*) to assist with selection of accessible hotels in the *Thomson* or *Horizon* brochures. Also in the UK, the *Holiday Care Service* (see England and Wales *Travel Notes*) publishes a fact sheet on Morocco and Tunisia.

Reasonably priced, accessible accommodation is hard to find in Freetown, **Sierra Leone**. Kate Margrie recommends the *YMCA* (Fort Street, PO Box 243; ☎22/23608) which is clean, accessible, and inexpensive but often full: book in advance.

In **Tanzania**, John Bignell stayed at the *Novotel Mount Meru* (Moshi Road, PO Box 877, Arusha; ☎57/2711) which although not advertised as suitable for guests with disabilities in the *Novotel* directory, was wheelchair accessible in spite of the small elevator. He found that the *Arusha International Conference Center* (PO Box 3081, Arusha; ☎57/3181) was poorly designed in terms of access for disabled people. *Abercrombie and Kent* (see *Tour Operators*) suggests that the *Arusha Mount Meru Game Lodge* and the *Ngorongoro Crater Lodge* would be accessible to most people. Some of their tours in Tanzania feature nights under canvas and this would also be feasible, with minor adaptations to make the lavatories usable.

The *Holiday Inn* directory indicates that there are special rooms for handicapped guests at five African hotels: in **Morocco**, the *Holiday Inn Crowne Plaza Casablanca* (Int'l Ave Abdelmoumen and Ave Hassan II, Casablanca;

☎2294949); in **Zimbabwe**, the *Holiday Inn Harare* (Samora Machel Ave, Corner 5th Street, PO Box 7; ☎4/795611); in **South Africa**, the *Holiday Inn Bloemfontein* (1 Union Ave, PO Box 1851, Bloemfontein 9300; ☎51/30-1111), the *Holiday Inn Durban* (167 Marine Parade, PO Box 10809, Durban 4056; ☎31/37-3341), and the *Holiday Inn Sandton*, Johannesburg (Rivonia Road and North Street, PO Box 781743, Sandton 2146; ☎11/783-5262).

When booking hotels that are known to possess special accommodation for disabled guests in **South Africa**, request the "paraplegic room" and insist on written confirmation of the booking—take the letter with you.

The most satisfactory accommodation on Roger Elliott's South African tour was the fully accessible *Hazyview Protea Hotel* (PO Box 105, Hazyview, Eastern Transvaal; ☎13/1242, then ask operator for 51 or 115). *Protea Hotels*, however, say that in general their properties are not particularly well suited for disabled guests. Roger was told that there are some accessible huts at one of the rest camps inside the park. His experiences were less good at the *De Waal Sun* (PO Box 2793, Cape Town 8000; ☎21/45-1311), but this hotel, part of the *Southern Sun* chain, does in theory have a well-equipped room for disabled guests (31.5in bathroom door width, about 36in either side of the toilet, 6ft next to the bath but no "drive-in" shower).

The following *Novotel* hotels advertise rooms for disabled guests: the *Bujumbura* (BP 1015, Bujumbura, **Burundi**; ☎2/22600); the *Accra* (PO Box 12720, Accra North, **Ghana**; ☎21/667546); the *Abidjan* (BP 3718, Abidjan, **Côte d'Ivoire**; ☎320457); the *Dar el Barka* (BP 1366, Nouakchott, **Mauritania**; ☎253526).

Access and Facilities

Having found an accessible hotel, wheelchair users traveling alone will probably find that they are imprisoned within its grounds—high sidewalks, pot-holes, ruts, and boulders make many African streets impassable without help. As Stephen Hunt points out, help is always readily available, but travelers must be prepared for some loss of independence: Kate

AFRICA: TRAVEL NOTES

Margrie describes how the terrain made her totally dependent on others for mobility, in sharp contrast to her life at home.

The picture is not all gloom. General awareness is probably best in Kenya (host to the 17th World Congress of Rehabilitation International in September 1992) and South Africa, although general attitudes toward disability, in terms of acceptance of it as a fact of life, are probably equally good in other countries, such as Morocco and Tunisia. Sue Kelley's hotel in Mombasa was ramped throughout, and she found ramped ramparts and wheelchairs at the entrance of Fort Jesus in Mombasa—disabled tourists are expected in some places. Roger Elliott found several facilities for disabled visitors at the Kirstenbosch Botanical Gardens in South Africa, and he was impressed to find most of the attractions of Gold Reef City accessible. And all contributors report that whenever they struggled, passers-by came forward without prompting.

Health and Insurance

It is important to take **medical advice** on inoculations and other precautionary measures such as anti-malaria medication. Depending on your destination and the type of vacation, you should carry insect repellant, mosquito net, anti-diarrheals, suntan cream, hat, water-purifying tablets, and/or first-aid kit (see *Practicalities*, p.569); wheelchair users should carry a small emergency repair kit, although in towns you'll probably find someone to help.

Consult Richard Dawood's *Travelers' Health* (see "Books," p.591) as well as a reliable travel guide, and carry a first-aid/medical handbook with you. Although it's not good to pore over details of gruesome symptoms every time you feel a little off-color, a brief check may enable you to take speedy action if you have the early signs of something unpleasant.

Check out the flying doctor service in the country you plan to visit; if there is none, make sure your **medical insurance** covers the cost of being taken by light aircraft to the nearest major hospital. For example, in Kenya the service is good and reasonably priced; patients are flown to Nairobi for treatment or repatriation. In Zimbabwe at the time of writing there is no such service (although there is a talk of setting one up), and to rent a small plane costs a fortune; you could be stuck at Victoria Falls, or at your safari camp, for 24 hours before being airlifted to Harare.

Books

Real Guides are available for Kenya, Zimbabwe & Botswana, Morocco, and Tunisia. *Africa on a Shoestring* is the only book to cover the entire continent, though parts can be very outdated.

TELEPHONE CODES

Dial 011 (International Code), then 212 for Morocco, 216 for Tunisia, 232 for Sierra Leone, 254 for Kenya, 255 for Tanzania, and 263 for Zimbabwe.

PART SEVEN

ASIA

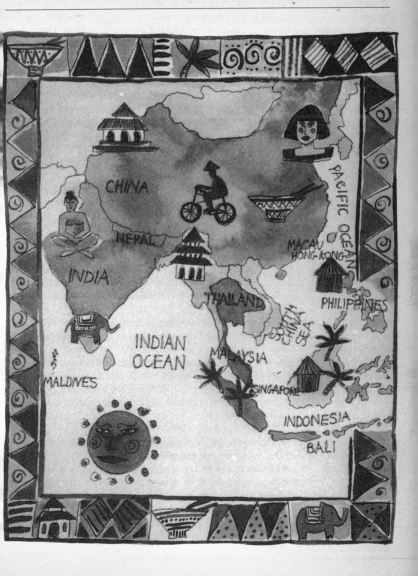

Introduction

I t is perhaps unjust to lump countries as diverse as China and the Maldives into one section, but one feature of travel to this area is the popularity of two- or multi-center holidays—it is a long way to fly, and many travelers feel that to make it worthwhile they should take in more than one country, hopping from Singapore to Thailand, or covering Hong Kong, Macau, and China in one trip. Attitudes toward providing facilities for disabled people vary both within and between countries, and this can only be a brief survey of the countries visited by our contributors.

Enormous sums are poured into the promotion of tourism. Visit India, Visit Thailand, designated "Visit" years, with their heavy advertising campaigns and free trips for the press and travel trade, attract millions, often to the detriment of **local populations**, whose homes, health, cultural mores, and livelihoods are trampled in the rush to develop luxury resorts. The brochure pictures of gleaming white hotels in Goa, or of smiling Thai women, sit uneasily with the facts of life for Goan villagers who have their water supply turned off for most of the day and night, or for the Thais who are caught up in the AIDS epidemic sweeping Thailand's sex trade.

These are, of course, dilemmas familiar to many other parts of the world: perhaps it is the gloss of tourism promotion, the overuse of the words "luxury" and "paradise," that heighten awareness here more than anywhere else. But it seems more likely that it has something to with **traveling in the East**. Vacations in these parts are an assault on all the senses, at times an enormous culture shock, and no amount of reading or research will prepare you for the sights, smells, and sounds of the East. The observations of some contributors—the poverty, the lack of basic amenities and infrastructure in many areas, the contrast between fancy hotels and makeshift roadside shelters, the clear lack of freedom or individual choice for the inhabitants of some countries—bring forcefully home the dilemmas of tourism.

Almost inevitably the countries whose tourism promotion machines make most noise are the ones that ignore the provision of information for visitors with disabilities. The **Singapore** and **Hong Kong** tourist offices are the only two to publish regularly updated access guides for visitors. In both these countries the authorities, urged on by voluntary organizations, are making some progress in their efforts to improve access to public buildings and spaces, although progress is slower on the transportation scene.

In **Singapore**, the authors of *Access Singapore* admit that legislation is needed to reach the goal of a barrier-free environment, but there are encouraging signs, including increasing provision of ramps and wheelchair-accessible public rest rooms. The Singapore government announced in its 1989 budget that it will allow tax deductions to businesses for expenditure on features that improve accessibility.

Hong Kong's obvious disadvantage for the disabled visitor is the **lack of space**— tall buildings, crammed together, many with steps at the entrance. Nonetheless the 1990 edition of *A Guide for Physically Handicapped Visitors to Hong Kong* found that the proportion of hotels with accessible public rest rooms and bathrooms had roughly doubled in three years. The Hong Kong government has brought in building regulations that require all new buildings used by the public to be accessible and include facilities for disabled people.

In **China**, disability activists have an uphill struggle. Although there have been some achievements, including tax incentives for employers who take on disabled workers, there is a long way to go, not only in terms of physical access and basic aids and equipment for people with disabilities, but also in the areas of education and rehabilitation; there is also a great deal of work to be done to remove prejudice and lack of belief in the capabilities of disabled people—to study, to work, to travel. This last is a worldwide problem, but attitudes that have, at least on the surface, been largely swept aside in many Western countries remain entrenched, both at government level and among ordinary people. Infanticide and abandonment of disabled children are still commonplace in China, a situation not helped by the one-child law.

There are important changes taking place—new laws, new rehabilitation centers, better opportunities in education—many of which are due to the efforts of Deng Xiao Ping's son, Deng Pufang, who has used a wheelchair since breaking his back while fleeing from the Red Guard during the Cultural Revolution—but the scale of the challenge is mindblowing. There are more than fifty million disabled people in China.

Given the lack of facilities, and the lack of information provided by the tourist board, it comes as a pleasant surprise to find an excellent **guide**, *You Want To Go Where? A Guide to China for Travelers With Disabilities and Anyone Interested in Disability Issues* (see p.454), describing the experiences of disabled travelers on three trips organized by *Mobility International USA*. It's an illuminating source of information on the situation in China. *MIUSA*'s continuing program of educational trips to China offers a chance to keep up with the developing disability movement as well as see the sights.

The physical barriers in the **Philippines** were many when Alfred Azzopardi visited the country in 1984. But he found that some of the sights were accessible, and the introduction of the **Accessibility Law** in 1987 was a step in the right direction. This, requiring owners and operators to install facilities such as ramps, wide entrances, railings, large elevators, accessible public transit, low-level public telephones, and reserved parking spaces, may not be rigidly enforced, but it's at least a start.

There is little to report on facilities for disabled nationals or visitors in **India**, the **Maldives**, **Bali**, **Thailand**, or **Macau**, although there is some impressive work going on with disabled people in institutions, such as the schools run by the *Indian Spastics Society*. Where access is gained it is more often by accident than by design.

Many contributors report warm welcomes and cheerful assistance: Alfred Azzopardi was treated like royalty in the Philippines; Hong Kong salespeople hurried forward to open doors for Sue Kelley; the people of Bangkok rushed to help with Barbara Horrocks' chair; Susan Preston was impressed by the Thai readiness to assist; Daphne Pagnamenta was rescued from a crowded street by a young Indian boy. If there is one area in the world where you are guaranteed a helping hand this is it. In some places a tip might be expected, but this is hardly surprising where wealthy tourists are often the only source of income.

As in Africa and Latin America, the fact that you can rely on an army of assistants, either paid or voluntary, means that if travel companies are reluctant to accept you on organized tours, there is an alternative. If you have the time and the patience, and do your homework, **independent travel** in Asia is ultimately possible. The problems encountered in some countries result not so much from the lack of facilities for disabled visitors, as from lack of tourist infrastructure, good communications, and fair, reliable booking procedures.

The *Travel Notes* in this section have been arranged in two parts: India and the Maldives, and the Far East.

India

India at Last

Daphne Pagnamenta was involved with the Riding for the Disabled Association for many years, responsible for their vacation organization, and in 1978 was awarded a Churchill Fellowship to study outdoor facilities for disabled people in North America. In February 1989, coping with an artificial leg and a new hip, she spent ten days in India.

From the age of ten I had wanted to go to India, probably because for two years I was at school with a group of children whose fathers were all in the Indian Army and Civil Service. I studied their faded photographs of "Daddy's polo ponies" and "my ayah with her family," and listened with envy to their descriptions of colonial life and voyages home by *P&O* through the Suez Canal, impressed by their certainty that when school was over they would be going back.

I lost touch with my school friends, but my interest in India continued. I buried myself in the *Jungle Books* and *Kim*. I tried to understand the troubles of the Thirties, and was electrified by an enlightened history teacher who announced, "Mr. Gandhi is not all bad, whatever your parents may say." World War II made it all more distant and after that I was fully occupied with a busy life and bringing up a family. During middle age a good deal of travel came my way, but India remained a distant dream.

In 1965 I lost a leg, but learned to live on good terms with my artificial one, which did not slow me down too badly. However, arthritis in the other hip gradually worsened, difficulties increased and I returned to crutches and wheelchair, with the future looking black. In 1988, after several disappointments, the doctors managed a complete hip replacement. The immediate pain relief was like a miracle; I could expect to have one reasonably good leg again to help the tin one along. Two days after the operation I sat up in bed and said firmly, "Next year I am going to India."

I started off with ambitious plans: I must see the Himalayas and something of the south, as well as the more obvious Taj Mahal and the Ganges. I wanted to get to a game reserve in search of tigers, and wondered if I could fit in Calcutta and Mother Theresa. Very soon I realized that neither my stamina nor my bank account would stand all this, and I must cut my plans down to size. I had to face up to my disability and my age. At seventy, my staying power was not as good as it used to be, and a very new hip, tin leg, and rather doubtful back would pose problems. It was no good overestimating my ability, and I must be content with just a bit of India instead of the grand tour. The obvious bit is Moghul India—the "Golden Triangle" of Delhi, Agra, and Jaipur—which is well served by package tours. Unless you are young and robust, or have reliable local contacts who know the ropes, it would be rash to try to do it alone.

I contacted the Government of India Tourist Office and a great many tour operators and studied a vast amount of literature. I found enormous variation in prices, according to whether private cars and luxury hotels, or buses and tourist hotels, were used. When I mentioned my walking limitations, operators immediately became cautious. One who appeared to run a suitable tour refused even to consider me, saying that they found the disabled a "worry."

Eventually, I landed with *Bales*—an established family firm—and discussed my problem with their overseas manager who was extremely helpful. Having convinced her that I was unlikely to be a liability and produced the requested doctor's certificate, I was booked in and promised all possible assistance. They gave excellent value and I never regretted my choice.

Before reaching this point I had had to solve the problem of a traveling companion. At first I insisted that in an escorted party I could manage on my own, but in my heart I knew that I needed someone with me. Any troubles would be more difficult to cope with than in a Western country, and it is not fair to trade on the kindness of strangers. To my delight a daughter proved willing to abandon job and family, provided that we would not be away for more than ten days, so ten days it had to be. When I looked at it realistically, ten days for two, in comfort but not luxury, was just about what I could afford. The grandchildren cooperated and were tickled pink at the idea of Mom taking Grandma to India in a bus. Mom was to discover a wanderlust that she didn't know she had.

"We dozed through an uncomfortable night and landed in the pink glow of a Delhi dawn"

I had four months for preparation, none too long. I went into training to get my new hip working as well as possible, plugging away at the physiotherapist's exercises and systematically increasing my walking distance by a few yards each day. I wanted to get the best out of my tour and my reading list was formidable: I learned a little about India's many ancient civilizations and caught up with her modern history; I became intimate with the great Moghul emperors and tried to sort out what Hinduism is all about.

The great day of departure came at the end of February—a good time for northern India, when temperatures are 70–80°F and the chance of rain is remote. Security was high at the airport where, as usual, the metal detector was excited by my tin leg. *British Airways* looked after me well while boarding, but the flight was an endurance test—a Jumbo packed with Indian family parties, wandering children, and mountains of cabin luggage.

We dozed through an uncomfortable night and landed in the pink glow of a Delhi dawn. A surly carousel eventually spat out our suitcases (how glad I was not to be on my own) and we sat in a corner of the airport arrivals hall waiting for the *Bales* party to assemble. I could hardly believe I was in India at last. My daughter ventured through a door marked "Toilets," only to return hastily after finding herself in a narrow alley where the door to the women's room was blocked by a row of elderly beggars sitting on the ground. We were certainly in India, and any further doubts were dispelled by the cows and swarming crowds in the streets, even at this early hour, on the way to the *Oberoi Maidens* hotel.

"How can you refuse to give in the face of such poverty?"

The hotel was a surprise and delight—a gracious, white, colonial building, sheltered from the busy street by a belt of trees, with a colonial atmosphere and a lovely garden full of handsome bougainvillaea and green parakeets. After a very necessary rest and grilled cheese sandwiches (less good value than the inexpensive Indian vegetarian dishes, we discovered later) we felt ready to face Delhi. The hotels we were to use at Agra and Jaipur were less special but perfectly adequate, medium grade, and built with Indian touches—peacock feathers on the walls, plus some eccentricities in the electricity and plumbing. Always there was kindly and willing service.

Our bus, to which we became absurdly attached, was a robust vehicle, as it needed to be. *Bales* had warned apologetically that Indian buses were different from Western buses, perhaps hoping to discourage unsuitable travelers at an early stage. In fact I found it more comfortable than expected, and I suffered no hardship, even on long journeys. The steps were a bit steep, but the splendid small boy who traveled with us as bus guard and general gofer always made it his business to help me up and down, and I was grateful to be allocated a seat near the front with good legroom. I took care

not to hold others up on entry and exit—I wanted to avoid being a nuisance in a party with an able-bodied majority. Most important, our driver was excellent and it says a lot for him that in often chaotic traffic conditions he never gave us a bad moment.

Firmly in charge of our pleasant party of 27 was our young Indian tour manager. He had an endless fund of information, as well as knowing the tricks of every trade. He assessed me and my limited walking ability very quickly and we came to an understanding. Where an extra long walk or an obstacle such as steep stairs lay ahead, he would warn me and suggest that I stay in an appointed place to be picked up by the party on its way back, leaving the final decision to me. In this way I ran no risk of holding everyone else up or of reaching a disastrous point of no return.

I had to miss a few things I should like to have seen, but managed about ninety percent of the sightseeing. I was glad I had not attempted to take a wheelchair with me: there would have been no room for it in the bus locker, and it would have been of little use on uneven and potholed sidewalks. I used two canes and had crutches in reserve, although I never needed them. What was invaluable was a light, folding camp stool—a must for anyone of limited walking or standing power. I used this while guides talked and while waiting on my own, and quite enjoyed my solitary sojourns, watching the life of India go by. Only once was I anxious, in the teeming Red Fort at Delhi, before I had become acclimatized, when our party seemed to take a long time returning and I wondered how on earth I should find a taxi to take me to the hotel if I had indeed been abandoned.

Travelers in India must be prepared for hassle at the tourist sites, which can be alarming at first. As soon as you climb down from the bus you will be pursued by pedlars selling junk of every kind, some of it attractive. It takes ruthless determination to get past them to the sanctuary of the site itself. They are waiting for you when you emerge, even more persistent, and the best course of action is to return to the bus, the door of which is well guarded by the boy, and conduct any bargaining through the window. If you have hands fully occupied by canes it is very difficult to ward off the items pressed on you and to struggle with cash, and there is extra persecution in the form of offers to "help you."

The sight of beggars in various stages of decay, of disabled children pulled on crude carts, and of lepers holding out stumps of hands, shocks and distresses. How can you refuse to give in the face of such poverty? Begging is officially very much discouraged, but if you cannot resist some pitiable figure give your small sum from the safety of the bus as it leaves; news travels fast and otherwise you will soon be surrounded. It is perhaps better to soothe your conscience by sending a donation to one of the overseas aid charities as soon as you get home. I also found the animal suffering very upsetting, and had to screw myself up to face the sight of overladen, worn out, ancient horses on the roads, and miserable sick cows that may not be put out of their misery.

"In India, splendor and poverty lie close together"

The sightseeing was very concentrated—this was not a take-it-easy tour. In Old Delhi we struggled shoeless, as required, up the many steps to India's largest mosque, the Jama Masjid, and looked down on the maze of streets below. We were charmed by a modern cream and pink Hindu temple, full of flowers, and sensed the reverence at Gandhi's cremation place. We drove around the elegant avenues of government buildings in New Delhi and wondered at Qutb Minar Tower, built in the twelfth century "to spread the shadow of God over East and West."

Approaching Agra we visited the great Emperor Akbar's tomb, later seeing the memorial to his favorite elephant at Fatehpur Sikri, the great city which he built in the sixteenth century. Of course, the Taj Mahal was the high spot of the circuit and even more magnificent than expected. We were given plenty of time to take in its ethereal beauty. I had to summon up all my staying power for the long walk through the gardens, but am so thankful that I just managed it and could see the marvelous inlaid work; a wheelchair would have been an asset there.

Jaipur held many treasures, especially in the City Palace complex, now a museum but built as a home for Jai Singh II. Elaborate blue and green gateways contrast with the pink walls, and within the complex is the Hawa Mahal (Palace of the Winds) where the royal ladies in purdah were able to look out on the wide streets from behind screened windows. But, as always in India, splendor and poverty lie close together: in a back street we visited a workshop where fine carpets were woven by hand; they made an impressive display as they hung in the sun to dry after washing. Among the workers were little girls of six or seven years old who were paid a few rupees for a full day's work, winding the wool and knotting the fringes with their tiny fingers.

At Amber, the fortress city and old capital of Rajasthan, a few miles to the northeast of Jaipur, we rode elephants up the steep approach. Yet another exquisite palace stretched along the crest of the hill, but the walking distance defeated me and I had to content myself with soaking up the view of the rugged Rajasthan ranges and watching the steady procession of elephants into the courtyard. I had a mild confrontation with one of the resident monkeys, who told me in no uncertain terms that I had usurped his favorite spot on the ramparts. He had already snatched someone's pocket-book so I did not argue with him.

It was not all buildings and works of art. From the windows of our bus we had an ever-changing view of the rural scene between cities. We saw the amazing difference between irrigated and arid land, the women working in the fields in their bright saris, droves of donkeys carrying fodder and bricks in panniers, and camels as we entered Rajasthan; the long journeys were never boring. We spent several hours at Bharatpur, once the scene of the Maharajah's great duck shoots but now one of India's most important bird sanctuaries.

> **"Although I delighted in seeing marvelous buildings and craftmanship, it was in the end the people who were most important"**

There was one more excitement for me on the long road back to Delhi, in the form of a camel ride. I met the camel sitting in the garden of a rest house where we stopped for tea, and I could not resist the temptation. The mounting system is so simple: a dignified step on board, two violent heaves, and you are up and away—another test for the new hip and good for Grandma's morale.

We had the final day in Delhi to ourselves and spent about £5 on a splendid taxi which took us all over the place and waited at each stop. Most important was the President's Garden where, under conditions of strict security, we joined hundreds of Indians in best clothes and on best behavior in procession around the magnificent garden, Moghul in design but full of English flowers. We felt that with them we were paying homage to their country, and it was a fitting end to a memorable trip.

It only remained to get to the airport at 3am for an even more exhausting flight home, with a long delay in Kuwait. Some people continued on tours to Madras and Nepal, and of course I had regrets that circumstances did not allow us to go on, making the most of the long-distance air fare, but I had stretched myself and was very tired and battered; I doubt that I could have managed more traveling without a week's rest first.

India for the disabled? It is a developing country with organized tourism still comparatively new, so expect no concessions or special arrangements. I never saw a wheelchair, a ramp, or an adapted rest room, and anyone who walks with difficulty is very vulnerable. Crossing the street is a hazard; sidewalks disappear into potholes and piles of rubble; crowds jostle; and "Delhi belly" is apt to strike even those who eat and drink carefully. You need to be well prepared and robust enough in body and spirit to survive and to enjoy, and not feel threatened by the tremendous impact of a totally different culture.

When I look back I realize that although I delighted in seeing marvelous buildings and craftmanship, it was in the end the people who were most important. Amid poverty and squalor that makes our own urban deprivation seem trivial, a zest for living and a capacity for enjoyment shines through and defies definition. There is a welcome and a warmth, and much kindness which is very moving.

I cherish in particular the memory of a packed market where things went wrong for us. I failed to keep up with the party and the police had forced the bus to move on. The two of us could not find a square yard on which to plant my camp stool except by an open sewer where the smell was unbearable. A boy of about sixteen saw our plight and gently offered his help in rather formal English. He took us back to his brother's shop to rest and drink slightly curious tea until our bus reappeared, while a smaller boy gave us crumpled, faded rosebuds from a market stand. We bought spices, the least we could do, but there was no sales pressure and it was a bit of real hospitality.

Getting around India

Robin Reeley has multiple sclerosis (MS), diagnosed in 1985, and for many years had wanted to travel in India. When he sought advice from his GP and neurologist he was told, "We don't advise people with MS to visit hot countries and your mild condition could be affected by the heat. However, your condition is such that we would not insist that you cancel your plans. Your decision will be your own . . ."

Ashley and Jane Butterfield charter a "second-class tourist car" every fall and run a number of four-week train tours covering all of India. The "Bogie" is home, traveling between towns in a series of overnight trains. Two living/ sleeping rooms for up to 26 passengers, dining room/library, rest rooms, and showers are provided in this car. Most breakfasts and some evening meals are prepared by Jane and Ashley in the on-board kitchen, other meals being eaten out. Hotels are used for some parts of the tour.

I reserved a place on a tour starting in February 1987, and booked a round-trip flight to Delhi (this is not arranged with the railroad tour but left to the choice of individual passengers). Wheelchairs were provided for me at both Heathrow and Delhi airports, saving me from the fatigue of standing in lines, and easing the effects of the high temperature in Delhi.

A bus tour of Delhi was laid on, and we stayed two nights in a hotel before proceeding to New Delhi station and boarding the Bogie. As we headed south, the daytime temperature exceeded 90°F and I became steadily more tired, more often. I thought the increase in my disability was slight until one evening in a movie theater I

tried to stand up and stumbled. I was alarmed to find that I could not stand. Two friends carried me, shoulder high, back to the hotel, where I had an uncomfortable night and wondered, is this it? Have I pushed myself too far, goodbye India and future travel plans?

The next day I readied myself for the worst. Carefully, I climbed out of bed. I could stand—just—and was able to walk slowly to breakfast. I shared an "auto" (motor tricycle rickshaw) to the bus station, from where a crowded vehicle took us to Mysore. I was beginning to feel better; we stayed in a hotel and were free to tour alone.

The widespread availability of rickshaws—combined with reasonably comprehensive information supplied by Ashley and Jane—gave me confidence to tour towns by myself. This fits in with the idiosyncrasies of my medical condition: at some times during the day I walk faster than most people, but I often have to walk more slowly. I carried my walking stick, not only for support but also to say "I'm ill, not drunk."

"Overnight bus travel in India is not very comfortable"

When we reached Cochin, only 130 miles from the southernmost tip of India, we were allotted six days of individual travel to reach Madras, some 375 miles distant. My chosen route covered about 700 miles and went via the peaceful "canals" of Kerala, the beautiful forests of Tamil Nadu, then Kanniyakumari, Madurai, and Kodaikanal. The "canals" are actually coastal lagoons, used for transport of freight (in traditional motorboats) and passengers (on ferries). The boats ply between larger towns, calling at many halts en route. Alleppey and Changanacheri are small towns with both railroad and backwater connections, a morning being sufficient for the tranquil backwater journey between the two. The waterways are surrounded by pine forests and fields.

Kanniyakumari is the Land's End of India, where the Bay of Bengal meets the Indian Ocean: you can watch the sun rise over one and set over the other. The town is a popular pilgrimage destination for Hindus and center for Indian vacationers, but the beaches are not very good. There are many comfortable, inexpensive hotels. A regular ferry service operates from the mainland to the Sri Vivekanada Memorial, located on two rocky islands about 200 yards from the shore. Built in 1970, the memorial commemorates a visit by the crusading Indian philosopher, Swami Vivekananda, in 1892.

Kodaikanal is acclaimed as the most beautiful hill station in the south of India. On the southern crest of the Palani hills, the town lies 75 miles northwest of Madurai. The altitude is 7000 feet and the views are spectacular, over thickly wooded slopes and precipitous rocky outcrops. The bus from Madurai follows a beautifully scenic route and takes about four hours. I was very happy to meet a variety of travelers at the youth hostel in Kodaikanal, including a mountaineer from the USA, a young Australian couple, and an Israeli girl who helped me down the steps to the hostel and persuaded the warden to let me stay, although there were no beds left that night.

I returned by bus to Madurai and had intended to take an overnight train to Madras. I was told that there were no seats—trains had been canceled. I could not find out why, so I booked a seat on the overnight bus which was more than full on departure. Overnight bus travel in India is not very comfortable, but I arrived safely the next morning, having slept fairly well on my seat; some people had to sleep on the floor. I learned the reason for "no trains"—a terrorist bombing at Tiruchchirappalli had killed nearly thirty Indians and destroyed a bridge.

Madras is India's fourth largest city and the capital of Tamil Nadu. The city is relaxed and public transit efficient: buses are not overcrowded and urban commuter trains provide a convenient service. A long seafront on the Bay of Bengal ensures a supply of fresh sea air and a pleasant location for walks. There are several fine churches and temples.

The village of Mahabalipuram (Seven Pagodas) is a short bus ride from Madras: here there are fine beaches but the tide is very strong. Mahabalipuram is famous for its shore temples, which date from the seventh to eighth centuries. These temples have an appealing freshness and simplicity, in contrast with the more grandiose monuments seen later on the tour, in Agra.

In Madras I met up with the other Bogie passengers for a long train journey—one night and one day—to Bombay, some 630 miles away. Then on to Agra, Delhi and the flight home.

In March 1988 I was back again, this time on a tour of northern and eastern India.

Our chartered car left Delhi for the 900-mile journey to Howrah Station, Calcutta, a two-day trip with many short stops. We were sustained by plenty of *chai* (tea plus milk plus sugar, boiled together) from platform stands, and Western-style meals cooked by Jane and Ashley. We arrived in Calcutta and were directed toward the trams, which travel through some of the oldest and narrowest streets in the city.

"I was walking with difficulty—heat and exhaustion had taken their toll"

Calcutta is the largest city in India, the capital of West Bengal, with an enormous population of very poor people. The slums at Anand Nagar (made famous in *City of Joy*, by Dominique Lapierre) have been razed to make way for the Underground (metro), which runs between the city center and the business area of Tollygung. Often described as an ugly and desperate place, Calcutta to many people sums up the worst of India, yet it is also one of the more fascinating cities and has some scenes of rare beauty—flower sellers beside the misty, ethereal Hoogly river, the superb collection exhibited in the Indian Museum.

Partition affected Calcutta more than any other Indian city. The jute-producing and export center of India, Calcutta became a city without a hinterland, while across the border in East Pakistan (now Bangladesh) jute was grown without anywhere to process or export it. West Bengal and Calcutta were disrupted by tens of thousands of refugees fleeing from East Bengal, although without the communal violence and bloodshed that Partition brought to the Punjab. Calcutta has been a troubled city, but it is a city with a soul.

I traveled on the Underground, and later in the day I sought directions from a helpful Indian man who both directed and supported me, since I was walking with difficulty—heat and exhaustion had taken their toll. We went a short distance in a rickshaw pulled by a man. There are many thousands of these in Calcutta, and a corresponding number of very poor people depending on them as a source of income. My return to Howrah and the Bogie was by local bus—an adventure, since I had to stand out in the street to catch it.

We continued from Calcutta to several towns of interest farther south (thus hotter). I could get around OK by day, walking short distances and using cycle rickshaws. The majority decision of other passengers on the Bogie was to shut the wooden blinds at night, in order to keep out the mosquitoes. Mosquitoes don't like me, so no risk of being bitten at night for me, but it was very hot with the blinds shut. I woke one night and tried to turn over. My legs didn't respond and I fell to the

floor. Not only were my legs as good as paralyzed, but also my voice was not fully operative. I was able to utter a few garbled noises, but could not make my cries for help understood. In the end, arm strength, driven by determination, got me back on the bench, there to sleep without moving.

"Never mind an illness having affected your handwriting, sir, the signatures don't match"

India is a dusty country, and I developed a cough. I asked a cycle rickshaw driver if he could take me to a pharmacy for some cough drops, but he didn't speak any English. Sign language was of no avail, so I forced a cough and the driver seemed to understand. I climbed into the rickshaw, and off we went to the local hospital! Eventually I found a doctor who spoke good English and I was able to explain my quest. He noticed that I was staggering and I explained why. MS is a very rare illnes in hot places like India; the doctor had read of the condition but had never seen a real live MS person. Investigations of my balance, sensitivity, reflexes, and arm strength followed before at last the doctor gave me some cough syrup and lozenges.

We returned via Rajasthan to Delhi, where I visited the *Indian Airlines* office to pay for my domestic air tickets. The problem came when I signed a travelers' check to make payment: "Never mind an illness having affected your handwriting, sir, the signatures don't match—you'll have to go to the bank." Over a mile and two hours later, I returned with a fistful of rupees and paid for my tickets. That evening we went for a group meal in a Tibetan restaurant, leaving Old Delhi station on the night train for Kalka.

At Kalka we left the Bogie to travel on the narrow-gauge railroad to Simla, the most important hill station in the days of British rule—in the hot season it was the "summer capital" of India.

The former Viceroy's palace (Rashtrapti Bhawan) is now a school for higher education. For many years Simla (at 7000 feet) was isolated from the lowlands except by mountain trail. The railroad was constructed in 1903, and roads came later. Today the town of Simla is anything but restful, being visited by many people, but the mountainous landscape is beautiful and the air fresh and cool.

"Kashmiri chicken, with a good selection of spices and plenty of rice"

From Simla I traveled alone by bus to Chandigarh for my first *Indian Airlines* flight to Srinagar, the capital of the state of Jammu and Kashmir, famous for its canals, houseboats, and Moghul gardens. Now what? Four days' relaxing on a sumptuous houseboat on Nagin or Dal lake? Not me. I wanted to go trekking: there are numerous beautiful treks in and around the Kashmir valley, varying from short day walks using the hill stations as starting points, through longer walks in the valley and across the surrounding ranges, to hard treks out of the Kashmir region to Zanskar or Ladakh. My illness would not permit me to walk very far, so when I visited the tourist information center I asked, "How about pony trekking?"

My guide, Siddiq, asked me whether I would prefer to visit mountains or rivers and lakes: I chose the mountains. We gathered food, blankets, stove, and fuel before making our way by autorickshaw toward the Srinagar bus depot. The roads in Srinagar are narrow and the drivers pushy: a local bus going the other way crunched one side of the rickshaw, forcing it back a short way and removing the turn light.

The rickshaw driver stopped to assess the damage to his vehicle; the bus driver did not stop. Siddiq and I picked up our things and walked to the bus depot. The bus for the hill resort of

Pahalgam was just leaving: in desperation I stood on the rear ladder and prepared to climb up to the roof box, only to be dissuaded by Siddiq.

We caught a bus to Anantnag, a small town known chiefly for the curative properties of its sulfur springs, and from there went by tonga to visit Siddiq's friend in the village of Kaymu. Siddiq bought some chickens for supper; they were alive—just—to keep them fresh in the absence of refrigerators. Kashmiri chicken, with a good selection of spices and plenty of rice, made a delicious meal and I felt honored to be eating in a village home. We watched some Indian and some Pakistani TV, keeping candles at the ready—three brief power outages occurred during the evening.

Siddiq and I returned to Anantnag the next day, continuing by bus to Pahalgam. Two ponies and a ponyman were hired—one pony for me, one to carry the food (including a chicken) and other items. We walked together down the main street and along the mountain track toward Aru, which lies on a grassy plateau, surrounded by pine forests and mountains.

The seven and a half mile journey took about three hours. The mountain valley trail is a road in summer but covered by snow in winter. There was no snow in Pahalgam but an increasing amount as we trekked nearer Aru. My pony walked very close to the outside of the path. "He is a good walker," Siddiq assured me—just as well, since there would have been nothing to stop us sliding twenty yards down a steep hillside into the river if the pony had stumbled. We kept mostly to the path, taking one shortcut across a field where the snow was about a foot deep, and fording several streams. Ponies don't like crossing streams, especially when the water cascades down a rockface nearby; my pony was reluctant but obedient.

We met Siddiq's young friend, Fayaz, in Aru and stayed in his "tourist bungalow"; the ponies and ponyman returned to Pahalgam. The power line had collapsed several months previously, so no electric light. There were no washing or toilet facilities and little furniture, but it suited me fine. There was plenty of water, and cardamom or cinnamon *chai* to drink, and the chicken—cooked by Siddiq and Fayaz—tasted nearly as good as the one in Kaymu.

Fayaz and his father joined Siddiq and me for the trek back to Pahalgam, after which I traveled with Siddiq by bus to Srinagar and then by plane to the mountain town of Leh, the capital of Ladakh. There were many soldiers and no other Europeans on the *Indian Airlines* flight to Leh. My water bottle caused suspicion at the check-in desk: "*Pani*" (water), I explained, and drank some to prove it.

The road between Srinagar and Leh is closed by snow for most of the year, so flying is the only way in before June. The runway at Leh is short and the surrounding mountains loom very close. The town stands at 11,500 feet and the area is largely barren with little grass and few trees. The air is rarefied and visitors should spend time at an intermediate altitude (Srinagar, for example) rather than fly direct from Delhi or other low-lying areas.

The old town of Leh is clustered at the bottom of a hill beneath the old palace of the kings. Few Western travelers visit this Buddhist center, which is culturally closer to Tibet than to India. Along the banks of the Indus, close to Leh, lie several interesting buildings, including Shey—once the summer palace of the kings of Ladakh—and, farther south, the Tikse Gompa, a 500-year-old monastery currently used by the largest contingent of monks in Ladakh. The most important word in the Ladakh language is *jullar* (hello); people are very friendly and the children are especially inquisitive toward Western visitors.

I spent two days in and near Leh before flying back to Delhi. The railroad tour had been good and Leh interesting, but pony trekking was, for me, the most wonderful experience. This is an ideal activity for disabled people who can walk, but not very far. I kept in touch with Fayaz and in October 1988 I made another pony trek in Kashmir with him and his Uncle Hassan. My inspiration is Dame Freya Stark, a remarkable traveler who used riding and pack animals to reach distant parts of the subcontinent when she could not walk by herself—a perfect example for the less mobile adventurer!

Visit India

Alison Walsh has rheumatoid arthritis. In January 1990 she traveled to India for the first time, with a companion who has visited the country six times in ten years and covered everything from tigers in the jungle to film stars in Bombay. The trip turned out to be a five-week endurance test.

Not expecting much in the way of facilities for disabled people in India, I landed in Delhi on a cold morning in January and was pleased to find a wheelchair waiting. My surprise at spotting a door marked "HANDICAP" next to the women's room at the airport quickly turned to disgust when I finally managed to heave the door open: plenty of room to maneuver a wheelchair inside, grab-rails, too, but the bowl overflowed with excrement.

Hoping to see more of the countryside than aerial views, we purchased Indrail passes—around $200 each (first-class, non air-conditioned), valid for thirty days. These must be paid for in foreign currency and the story is that they give you priority when booking seats on the hopelessly overcrowded trains. Not so: priority is given to those who pay back-handers at the ticket office, and even this much-loved system falters under the sheer weight of numbers clamoring for seats.

Train travel is ludicrously cheap and is used by millions, not only to get to work but also to attend every family event including births, deaths, and marriages, not to mention all the religious festivals. You would have to spend the whole thirty days on the train to notch up the equivalent of two hundred dollars' worth of journeys: better to reserve well ahead, just for the journeys you want to make; better still, avoid the trains altogether.

In Jodhpur, no amount of persuasion could find us a seat on the train to Udaipur and we finally agreed to take a "deluxe" bus, setting off at 5:30am (necessitating a 4:30am wake-up). I realized then that my idea of deluxe and the Indian understanding of the word were poles apart. The road was, from beginning to end, appalling—a bumpy, narrow strip of paving, full of pot-holes and in many places deteriorating into a gravel track. The bus rattled—every joint and every window shook violently until our heads seemed filled with the noise. None of the windows shut properly (it's very cold in the desert at night).

A combination of vibration and cold is not the best therapy for arthritic joints. The final straw was having to tie my legs in knots after the first stop, when a crowd of pushy Indian men filled the front of the bus, squatting, standing, and slouching, covering every inch of space including my leg room. At every subsequent stop we were jostled and shoved, by men and women, when getting on and off the bus. This apparent lack of courtesy was in fact nothing of the sort—it's just the way it's done on Indian buses (trains, too), and our fellow travelers were not to know I have sensitive wrist and ankle joints (one of the joys of invisible disability). But the discomfort, combined with lack of sleep and a festering sinus infection, made it difficult to reason this out at the time.

After two *chai* stops, when the hot sweet tea brought temporary relief, we honked our way through a busy market, scraping stands stacked high with produce, and shuddered to a halt outside a workshop. Much hammering and welding in the region of the front axle, then more swaying down narrow streets until we left the town and headed toward the Aravalli mountains, gears crashing in anticipation of the struggle to come. We did make it to Udaipur, but in no state to appreciate anything except a long sleep and a dose of antibiotics from the hotel doctor—we were both, by this stage, groggy with sinus infections.

"An astonishing medley of farts, belches, snores, incessant high-pitched chatter, reverberating nasal snorts, throat clearing, and spitting"

After we had checked out of our hotel in Udaipur and arrived at the station at 5:30pm we were met by our man from *TCI* (*Travel Corporation India*) who told us that he could not get us a seat in first class; would we be prepared to pay our way into the second-class sleeper car? We had no choice—we had arranged to meet someone in Jaipur at 6am the next day, he was to meet us on the train. Never mind, smiled the *TCI* man, at the first major stop the guard will move you into a first-class sleeper.

When we eventually found the guard during the Chittaugarh stop he was drunk and abusive. We returned to second class and lay down on the narrow three-tier bunks and shivered through the next nine hours, surrounded by an astonishing medley of farts, belches, snores, incessant high-pitched chatter, reverberating nasal snorts, throat clearing, and spitting.

This tale is not a reflection of *TCI*'s incompetence: we used the agency to reserve all our accommodation and train journeys, and valiant efforts were made on our behalf at their Delhi, Agra, Jaipur, Jodhpur, and Udaipur offices. But at each office we gleaned something of the difficulties they face: the struggle to obtain one telephone (can you imagine a travel agent working without a telephone?), the lack of a coherent policy on tourism, the lack of funds for preservation of the sights. The manager of one office said despairingly, "India is crumbling."

It did not surprise me to discover that none of our Indian hosts used the railroads. They fly the state-owned *Indian Airlines*, which has a monopoly and is universally criticized by Indians and foreigners alike. Internal flights are a nightmare, known for their excruciating delays, blatantly rude staff, heavy overbooking, and frequent disruption of reservations by traveling "VIPs" (government officials or army officers).

How *should* one travel then? Rent a car and driver? Expensive and not worth the hassle with drivers who want a tip every time they change gear. Nor did the Indian idea of a "deluxe" car (like the "deluxe" bus) coincide with mine—good suspension is a high priority in this country (particularly for a disabled person), and it is quickly destroyed by the crippling road surfaces. An old college friend, a journalist in Bombay, told me that she never moved from Bombay unless absolutely necessary and that I was *mad* to travel in her country!

The joys of domestic travel made a ten-day tour from Delhi a trial of strength, both mental and physical.

The physical hardships are easy to imagine, the mental stresses difficult to convey. First, of course, the human and animal suffering leaves you reeling, however well prepared for it. Tiny children with rampant diarrhea drag their red-raw bottoms along the side of the road; a mean-eyed man hurls bricks at a donkey's head because it has sunk to the ground, unable to carry its load up a steep slope.

Next to that, your constant battles to carry out the simplest task, from booking a train ticket to buying a box of tampons, are hardly worth mentioning. But when your resistance is lowered by unrelenting noise and pressing crowds, you cannot fail to be rattled by bureaucratic time-wasting, or by the fifth argument of the day with a rickshaw driver who insists on taking you to look at his brother-in-law's cousin's carpets when you want to go somewhere else— *anywhere* else as long as it's quiet.

One of our problems was that we were two women traveling without male accompaniment—an arrangement which didn't seem to go down well; another was that we are British, and we encountered some hostility for the part our ancestors played in the occupation of India during the Raj. But probably the main cause of my aggravation was a simple culture difference, not so noticeable for my companion, with her Slav roots. For me it was a clash of British reserve and desire for orderliness with the Indian fear of silence or of being alone, and the apparent chaos of Indian streets and public transit.

Our family of friends in New Delhi did much to soothe these differences by providing a haven of hospitality to which we could return, exhausted, from each of our sightseeing trips. The girls, Rohina and Poonam, hooted with laughter over our mishaps and adventures, showed us Delhi, and introduced us to *TCI*; their father, Deep, played generous host and gave us good advice; their mother, Pammi, saw to it that we ate well, a manageable blend of the familiar and the exotic, all beautifully prepared by the real head of the family—and cook—Prem Singh.

The Taj Mahal was first on our agenda and although the Taj itself is breathtaking, its setting produced mixed feelings. Agra struck me as a dirty, grasping little town. Agra Fort is reached across a deep moat that has become an open sewer. The buildings are neglected and overrun by monkeys; every darkened room we explored stank of urine. Fatehpur Sikri, 23 miles from Agra, was full of hawkers and persistent little men and boys constantly hovering and offering their services as "official guides."

"Open sewers and piles of rotting garbage combine with the fumes to produce a clinging, sickly smell all over the city"

Jaipur, next on our itinerary, appeared to be no longer "The Pink City," more a grubby orange-brown, choked by hordes of ancient vehicles churning out noxious black fumes, their engines clattering and exploding, horns blaring. Open sewers and piles of rotting garbage combine with the fumes to produce a clinging, sickly smell all over the city; after a sightseeing trip by autorickshaw we would return to the hotel with blackened faces, stinging throats, and clogged nostrils.

By maintaining a safe distance from the city center we found Jodhpur more bearable: the views from the fort are spectacular and the museum well laid out, the guides informed and efficient. A tour of desert villages (arranged from the guesthouse *Ajit Bawan*) is a blessed relief from city squalor—you can eat lunch with the villagers in spotless huts built from cow dung and urine. The Maharaj will insist that as well as doing the standard camel ride you inspect the male camel's backward pointing penis and work out how he achieves copulation in spite of this

apparent handicap (they do it sitting down). The bone-shaking jeep ride might be difficult for a disabled person and the desert presents problems for a wheelchair, but the silence is like manna from heaven.

"Monstrous old trucks driven by maniacs who would sooner squash you than alter their route or use their brakes"

None of the cities on this route could be easily negotiated in a wheelchair. Where there are sidewalks, for example in New Delhi, the curbs are impossibly high, built for the monsoons; you would have to stick to the road, keeping a wary eye on the traffic. Although there are many human-drawn carts, bullock carts, and cycle rickshaws, which travel slowly, the "Public Carriers" are monstrous old trucks driven by maniacs who would sooner squash you than alter their route or use their brakes. In the older parts of the cities the streets are rough, edged by open sewers and crammed with animals, people, and vehicles. There will be heaps of garbage to steer around, as well as spreading puddles when the sewers overflow.

It *is* possible to find accessible hotels because of the tendency to ramp flights of steps for the movement of luggage and equipment, but it is by accident rather than by design and you will have to stick to the luxury variety. The old palaces have bathrooms the size of tennis courts (no baths in the non-Westernized hotels, often no shower, simply a tap, a large bucket, and a pitcher) but they may well have a step or two at the entrance—and wet stone or marble is *very* slippery, even for nimble feet. I found an accessible swimming pool at the *Shivniwas Palace* in Udaipur—some decorative marble steps to shuffle down—but usually there were steep ladders to negotiate, or else the pools were empty—it was winter, we were told.

The stunning architecture and air of past opulence in these hotels that were once palaces is something to savor, if you can afford to stay in them; it's a great shame that some are badly managed and the buildings poorly maintained. The *Narain Niwas Palace Hotel* in Jaipur is an example of both: cracked and disused swimming pool in neglected grounds, rooms dirty, staff unconcerned except when given a blast by our *TCI* man, food soon abandoned in favor of instant packet soups and dry cookies.

Leaving aside the deservedly admired Moghul architecture, I was unimpressed by more recent designs. I was directed to Chandigarh in the Punjab as an example of a "beautiful" modern city. Designed by Le Corbusier because the Punjab government convinced Nehru that no suitable Indian architect could be found, Chandigarh is a uniformly ugly series of concrete "sectors." Nek Chand's famous "Rock Garden" (sculptures made from everyday trash) provides the only relief from the monotony.

The tragedy is that Chandigarh is not an isolated case: the Indian architects of the post-1947 period were carried away by Le Corbusier's concrete mania and duplicated his work all over the country. India's architects are just beginning to look to their own culture for inspiration, and to design more "people-friendly" buildings. Perhaps the next stage will be to plan accessible as well as habitable structures.

Toward the end of our trip, I visited Meena Verma, who has muscular dystrophy, is a full-time wheelchair user, and lives in Ghaziabad, about twelve miles northeast of Delhi. Her mother explained that when she could no longer lift Meena (tiny though she is), an English friend had sent them a hoist. It took nine months to clear this essential piece of equipment through Indian customs.

This is bureaucracy at its most absurd and an illustration of an attitude present at all levels in Indian society: in a population of more than 810 million, disability, both mental and physical, is common. It may be the result of deliberate disfigurement at birth, so that the child grows up as a money earner (through begging). It may be the result of disease, or genetic defect, in which case it is seen as punishment for evil committed in a past life or by one's ancestors. Disabled people must accept their lot and remain at home, cared for by their family, or they should get down to the station on their chariots and demand their benefits from the train passengers.

Meena said she would love to travel and see something of her own country but she has been no farther than Delhi because she cannot rely on receiving help along the way. She attracts a crowd of onlookers but her mother is left to struggle alone while lifting her out of the car and into her wheelchair. Then the problems multiply—unpaved roads, lack of sidewalks, very limited access to buildings, and scarcity of accessible public rest rooms.

"Those who do not fall under India's spell will suffer every time they leave their five-star hotel"

In spite of the obstacles, Meena has chosen to remain in India—she runs a kindergarten for twenty children in her house, she writes Urdu poetry, and has a circle of good friends whom she will not leave. For the disabled visitor who falls in love with India, who delights in the noise, the colors, and the smells, the problems will also be insignificant. But those who do not fall under India's spell will suffer every time they leave their five-star hotel.

India is a developing country in which the money for the building and maintenance of basic amenities too often simply does not reach the right department—it is siphoned off along the way by corrupt civil servants. The money for conservation of the Moghul masterpieces and other historic monuments has clearly gone astray. Yet the Indian government planned to attract over two million foreign tourists in 1991, designated "Visit India" year.

Those involved with "Visit India," including tour operators, might consider whether the country can cope with the numbers already visiting before attempting to attract more. They might consider taking steps to safeguard the Indian population (and

the wildlife) from the harsher effects of mass tourism—villagers around Goa have their water supply cut off for 23 hours out of 24 so that the beachside hotels receive a constant supply.

There is an urgent need to return to basics, to make improvements to the transport networks, the sewage systems, the hospitals, the public buildings, the standards of hygiene in restaurant kitchens—and a few public rest rooms outside the luxury hotels wouldn't go amiss, particularly if they were wheelchair accessible.

The Valley of the Gods

In 1933, as a young and agile soldier serving in India, Hugh Chetwynd-Talbot visited the Kulu Valley, a hundred miles north of Simla in the Himalayas. In his diary he recorded that it was as near heaven as one could get, and in 1977, paralyzed by polio from the hips down, he took his wife to see it.

Since the second century and probably earlier, the Kulu Valley has been one of the main routes between India and Central Asia. Manali, a village at the northern end of the valley, is at 5900 feet, and from there a track goes over the Rohtang Pass (13,300 feet) into Lahoul and on to Leh, near the Tibetan border. From the top of the Rohtang Pass there is a fantastic panoramic view over massive peaks.

I saw it at dawn in 1933, and it had been my hope, until I became disabled, that my wife would see it, too.

In 1976 we saw an advertisement for a package tour under the patronage of

the *RSPB* (*Royal Society for the Protection of Birds*) and the *RHS* (*Royal Horticultural Society*), a birdwatching and botanical visit to Kashmir and the Kulu Valley. The itinerary involved a stay of six days on a houseboat on the Dal Lake near Srinagar, two days in a hotel in the mountain resort of Gulmarg, and eight days in the Kulu Valley based at Manali. I learned that since the Indo-Chinese War the Indian government had built strategic roads in the Himalayas so that, where I had walked along precarious mule tracks, a car could now be driven. Houseboat living might present difficulties, as might a grueling itinerary and my braced and bandaged legs in the heat, but there seemed no insurmountable obstacles. We decided to take the plunge.

At the end of May 1977, in a party of eighteen, we flew from London to Bombay where, after a hot wait of two hours, we flew on in an *Indian Airlines* plane to Delhi; another change took us to Srinagar. That final leg of the journey was hot but dramatic. The line of the Himalayas appeared low on our right soon after taking off, and the snow-covered peaks came closer as we flew almost parallel to them.

Srinagar is a military air base, and our arrival coincided with that of the Indian Minister of Health and the Commander-in-Chief of Kashmir. At that time India maintained a large garrison there against the threat of Pakistani invasion (a situation which has not changed). The drive from the airport took us through Srinagar and was stifling and bumpy, an exhausting end to some thirty hours of traveling during which we had had little sleep and the temperatures had been in the eighties and nineties.

"Embarkation was a bit of a scramble for me, done mainly on my behind"

We came to a stop on the shore of Dal Lake where *shikaras* (gondola-type boats) were waiting for us. Embarkation was a bit of a scramble for me, done mainly on my behind, but the cool, smooth progress across the still water of the lake, in its lovely setting surrounded by mountains, was a blessed relief. The houseboats are ranged along the far side of the lake; there are scores of them and they constitute one of the main attractions for visitors. Many of them have been in the ownership of the same Indian family for years, and some talk nostalgically of the good old days when British families spent the hot weather there.

The houseboats are mostly moored close to the shore and are boarded by a rather makeshift plank structure which I found perilous—the water below is far from pure! Each houseboat has three or four bedrooms, a living room, dining room, kitchen, shower, and toilet; the plumbing is inclined to be erratic, as is the electricity. Nabis and Bashir, the houseboat servants, gave us superb service and always seemed to be on hand when I needed help.

On the morning after our arrival we were woken about 5am by a cuckoo, and got up in time to see the sun light up the peaks, turning everything a pale

rose with marvelous reflections in the lake. Later, during breakfast on the after-deck, we were interrupted by the arrival of a flower-seller, his *shikara* piled high with roses, syringa, and all sorts of sweet-smelling, exotic flowers. He was closely followed by others, peddling carpets, carved trinkets, and embroidered cloth, all very attractive but at prices which, we were warned, were exorbitant.

At about 10:30am we set off, a fleet of four *shikaras*, downriver to Srinagar. Two locks regulate the flow from Dal Lake into the rapidly flowing River Jehlum, and going downstream is easy. But the very strong current makes it hard work coming back and it takes two men, paddling with all their strength, to do so. The banks are lined with a native houseboat community, living an odd sort of semi-static life on the water. The conditions are incredibly squalid: sewers, which all but made us ill as we passed them, run into the river just upstream of women washing clothes or cooking utensils; they in turn are just upstream of children bathing or women drawing water for cooking; the sequence repeats itself, with additional pollution from cattle that are stabled in many of the houseboats. Surprisingly, the river itself does not smell, and the scene is an artist's dreamland.

During the next day or two, nearly all our party succumbed to gut trouble of varying intensity. The heat, the altitude, the diet, and some fatigue no doubt contributed, but visitors can reduce the risks by ensuring that they drink water which has been boiled or purified, and by taking the usual precautions with food, in particular fruit and vegetables.

Getting about once ashore is not easy for a disabled person because of ditches and steps which have to be negotiated. I was lucky to be looked after by Nabis and Bashir. One evening they helped me all the way to a meeting in Ray's houseboat (Ray was the party leader), and they were waiting for me after the meeting ended at about 10pm. We had just completed the return journey when John (*RSPB* expert) came over and asked us to go back for a drink. We did, and when we left again, at 11:30pm, there were Nabis and Bashir waiting to see that I got back on board our houseboat without falling into the water on the way. I had told them not to wait.

"A gallant chap lifted me off my steed and humped me, like a sack of coal, up the path to the hotel"

The following days were spent by the rest of the party visiting the bird sanctuary, and various gardens and temples. I could take little part in that, so I explored the labyrinth of backwaters which surround Srinagar, and took a ninety-minute *shikara* trip, part of it through Kashmir's famous floating gardens, to the lovely Lake Nagin.

Soon the time came to say farewell to the faithful Nabis and Bashir, and to drive the fifty miles to Gulmarg, some 4000 feet higher than Srinagar. We passed through paddy fields and silkworm farms, then, as we climbed higher, through deodar (Himalayan cedar) forests. We emerged into a large, open, bowl-shaped area, around which are the houses and hotels of Gulmarg, and we came to a halt amid a crowd of porters and ponies. Our driver explained that no cars are permitted beyond that point; otherwise, the porters and pony-wallahs would be out of a job!

"Where's the hotel?" I asked, with a sinking feeling. He pointed to one on the far side of the bowl, standing at the top of a steep hillock and quite inaccessible to me. I explained this to the driver and an animated discussion ensued, involving about fifty Indians. They were fascinated by my braces. Two of them advanced on me as I stood by the car and, before I knew what was happening, I found myself astride a pony, my stiffened braces wedging me firmly, if uncomfortably, in the saddle.

We made good going and I felt almost regal as I saw the crowd escorting me. But the feeling did not last long. Within a short distance of the hotel but at the foot of the hillock, we came to a narrow gate. It was too narrow for my jutting-out legs to pass through and the procession came to a halt. An even larger crowd had gathered by then, and an even louder debate followed as to what should be done with me. Eventually it was settled by a gallant chap who lifted me off my steed and humped me, like a sack of potatoes, up the path to the hotel. He was pleased and tickled when I paid him double for being both a porter and a horse.

The main attraction of Gulmarg is the profusion of alpine plants on the mountain slopes in the spring (*gul* means flower; *marg*, meadow) and, in winter, the excellent skiing. It now bears little resemblance to the flourishing resort it used to be, a large part of it having been, to use the Indian expression, "taken away for burning by the Pakistanis on the day of separation." While the rest of the party went up the mountains, botanizing, I enjoyed a pleasant day admiring the lovely view from the hotel verandah and being chatted up by Indian fellow-guests.

"Our bus cannot have been more than six inches from the edge of a thousand-foot drop"

Our flight back to Delhi was delayed for two days by low cloud over Srinagar, which prevented our plane from taking off. Delhi was very hot indeed, in the region of 100°F, with high humidity. We were only there for a few hours before going on by bus to Chandigarh, in the Punjab, where we spent a rather hot and uncomfortable night. We left next morning at dawn on the 190-mile drive to Manali, traveling this time in a local bus with little in the way of springs and very hard seats.

The climb up from the plains was spectacular and we were soon some 3000 feet up and in deliciously cool air. The road was new and well graded but tortuous. Indian drivers blast their way everywhere with their horns, which we found somewhat trying, but that soon changed to a sense of relief when we outblasted the oncoming vehicles. Nevertheless, the twisting and turning and climbing, only to lose height again, made the journey most exhausting.

At noon we reached a mountain village called Mandi and it was decided that we should stop for a rest and lunch. I was delighted because it was there that, in 1933, on my journey back from Kulu, the road had been carried away by heavy rain, taking my bus with it, and I had been stranded for a week. I was finally able to walk out with my baggage on mules. It was interesting to see the place again after so many years.

The road onward from Mandi is now much changed, running through the sheer, deep gorges at a higher level; we could see the old one far below. The new road is still narrow and twisting, and hair-raising episodes are common. There are few passing places, and drivers do not like reversing; they prefer to try to pass each other. At one such crisis, when we met an army truck, the wheels of our bus cannot have been more than six inches from the edge of a thousand-foot drop to the River Beas. One of the party was heard to ask if she could get out and walk!

In the late afternoon we emerged with relief into the Kulu Valley, a widening expanse of green with the rushing, gray waters of the Beas running through it. Above the fields and the orchards there were heavily wooded hillsides and, ahead, snowcapped mountains. The valley is dotted with prosperous homesteads, each with its orchards of every imaginable fruit and its fields of grain. The villages of Kulu, Katrain, Nagar, and Manali have developed into small tourist centers, and everywhere there are ancient Buddhist temples. No wonder it is called "The Valley of the Gods."

"As we lay on our backs in the sun we watched a pair of golden eagles"

Since the Indo-Chinese War there has been a considerable military presence in the valley, as well as camps of Tibetan refugees. Where, in 1933, I camped in isolation beside the river where I could catch my breakfast trout, there are houses and cultivated fields. Yet it remains idyllic, and although we had taken a grueling ten hours to cover 185 miles the fatigue and discomfort seemed entirely worthwhile. The morning after our arrival in Manali, I looked out of the windows of John Baynon's Guest House, through an orchard of cherries and plums, down the valley to high peaks which looked like heaps of powdered sugar in the morning sun.

A couple of days after our arrival, our companions left for a four-day bird-watching and botanizing trek, which was out of the question for me. My wife and I rented a car and driver, and took on a cheerful lad called Preem who could cook for us. We set off in an attempt to get over the Rohtang Pass, staying nights in dak bungalows—travelers' rest-houses, which are spaced at intervals along main routes throughout India and are a legacy of the British Raj.

The road from Manali deteriorated to a single-track affair, hewn out of the mountainside. Climbing steadily, we soon left the green valley and the roaring river below us and were above the tree line. The only vegetation was coarse grass and scrub. We arrived at the *Khoti Dak Bungalow* (12,300 feet) at 12:30pm. The *gusselkhanas* (rest rooms) were arranged Indian-style, that is at ground level, which presented problems, but we were welcomed by an efficient *chowkidar* (caretaker) and the place was clean and well kept.

The bungalow had five bedrooms, each with its own *gusselkhana*, and a kitchen and servants' room at the rear. It was perched dramatically on a small, level area facing across the valley. As we lay on our backs in the sun we watched a pair of golden eagles working the mountainsides opposite us; the air was so clear that we felt we could almost reach out and touch them.

The next day we stopped just over two miles short of the top of the Rohtang Pass, thwarted by a twelve-foot-high snowdrift. It had been a hair-raising drive as the road was officially closed and we were the first car to venture that far since the last snowfall. When the car came to a halt my wife insisted on continuing on foot. It was a stiff climb, especially at that altitude, and I was very pleased when both Preem and the driver decided to go with her.

My wife's diary describes the culmination of the climb: "At times we crossed what must have been the road but mostly it was snowfield to be traversed, falling now and then into water-holes invisible under the snow. The height and the steep ascent reduced my pace to forty steps forward and then a pause. The summit at last and a tremendous feeling of achievement overcame that of exhaustion. We sat in the brilliant sunshine, chewed cookies, and watched through binoculars the magnificent snow peaks around us, and the endless panorama of range after range of the Himalayas."

They were gone for more than four hours and I was considerably relieved when I saw them returning. It only gradually emerged what a heroic climb my wife had performed and she did it, of course, largely for my benefit as I sat, frustrated, by the side of the road. It was no game for a grandmother and she did wonders to reach the top and add her flag to those on the Prayer Post which marks the summit. Thank goodness the weather was clear and she was rewarded by that wonderful view; apparently it came up to expectations.

The Maldives

Stuck in the Sand

In August 1989, despite misgivings from the tour operator over the suitability of the Maldives for a full-time wheelchair user, Sue Kelley, her husband Tony, and their daughter Joanne took advantage of an offer for a three-for-the-price-of-two vacation in the islands.

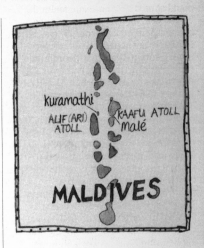

Tony has often enthused about the Maldives, a group of coral islands off the southern tip of India. He had visited the island of Gan with the navy, and he painted a picture of real tropical islands, complete with swaying palm trees, white sandy beaches, and crystal-clear lagoons. As we had traveled to a number of exotic destinations using the same tour operator (*Kuoni*), and we had overcome most problems on these trips, it was eventually agreed that as long as Tony and Joanne helped lift me on and off the boats, we should be able to manage a vacation in the Maldives.

The islands, covering an area of some 54,000 square miles, vary in size and character from mere sandbanks to lush tropical islands; they lie outside the cyclone belt and enjoy a warm, tropical climate throughout the year. It is thought that the first settlers were either South Indian travelers or Sri Lankans. The position of the Maldives on the sea routes from the Middle East to Malacca and China attracted the attention of Arab traders, whose contact converted the Maldivians to Islam in the twelfth century.

We were advised when packing to include umbrellas or waterproofs as it can rain heavily in the Maldives. Essential items included sunglasses, plastic shoes for swimming (to prevent nasty cuts from the coral), and an old T-shirt or pyjama top to wear while snorkeling. A basic first-aid kit, plus medicines for upset stomachs, sunburn, and seasickness are advisable, as is a course of anti-malaria drugs.

We rented a car to take us to London's Gatwick airport, arriving well before *Air Europe* opened their check-in desks. Finally we got our boarding passes and our luggage was taken. I was allowed to stay in my wheelchair until transferred to my seat on the plane, after which my chair was stowed in the hold. There wasn't much legroom, considering it was a long-haul flight.

We were delayed for an hour at Dubai because of an unaccounted-for passenger, but some four hours later we were descending over the Maldives. We could see large, green rings and horseshoe shapes, glinting like emeralds in the sun, and we could pick out those islands which were inhabited. We touched down on the runway at Malé airport with water either side, and I was assisted off, Tony and two others carrying me down the steps of the 757. In less than an hour we had cleared immigration, met the courier, and were seated on the boat destined for our island, Kuramathi, a four-hour journey.

Getting onto the boat was easy: the stern was brought in tight to the dock and we rolled the wheelchair straight on. To begin with I stayed in the wheelchair in the aisle between the seats, but as we left the protection of the coral reefs the sea became quite rough, so I transferred to a seat. Several of the passengers were seasick. Despite a sea breeze it was extremely hot.

Kuramathi looked quite large from the sea. It is the largest of a group of islands which form Ari atoll; the next two are Rasdhu (occupied by the fishing fleet and their families) and Treasure Island (uninhabited). Disembarking was as easy as boarding. A large number of men was waiting to carry our luggage, but at the end of the dock there was a drop of about nine inches onto the sand—there were no paths, just sand! There was only one way of reaching the hotel: I had to be dragged, in my wheelchair, backward across the beach.

We were met by the hotel manager and given the keys to our bungalows. The English contingent was accommodated in bungalows numbered in the eighties and nineties; because of the wheelchair we were allocated bungalow 26, amidst the Germans, situated near the sea, restaurant, and coffee shop. Other facilities included a bar, disco, and a small shop in the Kuramathi village.

From the outside the bungalow looked very much as expected—round, with a thatched roof which overhung at the front to form a shady porch. Inside was very basic, with one double bed, one single, an electric fan, a small table, a bottle of questionable drinking water, and an alcove with a rail for our clothes. The bathroom was only just wide enough for my wheelchair (which is small, only a 14in seat width); it was tiled from ceiling to floor with white ceramic tiles, many of which were badly cracked.

"Our staple diet for two weeks was fish"

The courier had given us time to unpack and freshen up before meeting her in the bar. On entering the bathroom we found that there was no water, and our neighbors informed us that there was a fault and the supply should be back on later. I unpacked our clothes and Joanne hung them up; this proved to be a mistake, as the high humidity made everything feel very damp within hours—including our beds.

At the meeting we were told that it takes approximately thirty minutes to walk from end to end of the island, and that there are three resorts—ours, an Italian Village, and the Blue Lagoon. Money was not required on a daily basis in any of the resorts: instead we signed for whatever we required and paid in full at the end of the week in US dollars. It is sensible to make a note of what you sign for, as many of us found that we were charged for facilities that we didn't use.

There was a diving school on the island; snorkeling and windsurfing lessons were also available, as well as fishing and island-hopping excursions. When visiting islands that are inhabited by the Maldivians, we had to observe rules on dress—no shorts or bare shoulders for women, no bare chests or short shorts for men. We were not allowed to take alcohol onto the islands (the islanders are Muslims), but it is for sale in the bars in the tourist resorts.

Kuramathi tourist resort is staffed by Maldivians, Indians, and Sri Lankans. Their families are not permitted onto the island and the men were housed in dormitories. A mosque was provided amidst their living quarters and they were encouraged to participate in soccer, cricket, and volleyball. Many didn't see their families for six months or more.

We were on half-board and our staple diet for two weeks was fish. Everything else is shipped in from India, Sri Lanka, or Singapore; fruit and vegetables were few and far between, and meat was a rarity. The fish was well presented, in various forms: curried, fried, baked, and barbecued. The Maldivians made their own bread and cakes, so those were fresh and plentiful. Joanne is a vegetarian and she was provided with cheese instead of fish when it was available.

Eventually the water came back on in our bungalow, and it turned out to be sea water. When it rained it was not unusual to see people standing outside washing their hair, in order to remove the salt deposits. Bottled water, like everything else on the island, was rather expensive.

The beach was covered with small pieces of coral. (It is forbidden to take home any coral, and your luggage will be searched to ensure that you don't.) Hermit crabs and small sand crabs were also in abundance; I found them very amusing to watch. The fish were another source of entertainment: I had only to place a piece of bread in the water and they came racing for it, even taking it from my fingers. They were all colors, from grays and browns to rainbow stripes, pink spots, blues and greens, yellow angel fish, and small reef sharks.

Joanne and Tony can swim and snorkel well and they spent a lot of time in the water. I am not able to move in water, so Tony procured a large rubber ring, over the top of which I lay, wearing snorkel and mask. Tony pushed me out over the coral reef which encircles the island, where I could observe the beautiful underwater garden. The colors and shapes of the corals were breathtaking, as were the fish, which ranged in size from those smaller than my little finger to some as large as my lower arm. The most fascinating were the clown fish, diving in and out of the anemones. These daily trips were the highlight of my vacation.

As well as fish and crabs, the island played host to two herons and one of these birds became very crafty. When I fed the fish from the jetty, the heron walked down the steps and waited there patiently for the right fish to come and take the bread; then he dipped in his beak and made his catch without getting his feet wet! At about 4pm the fruit bats started to leave their roosts in the trees, and later they formed silhouettes against the moon— it was like the opening shots of a horror film.

"No paths or roads suitable for a wheelchair, and dragging one through sand puts a considerable strain on the puller and pusher"

Tony and Joanne took a couple of boat trips to the neighboring island of Rasdhu, where they saw many coral and turtle-shell goods for sale despite the laws against export and import of these items. They purchased several T-shirts and brightly painted, wooden Indian masks. I didn't go with them because the terrain was similar to that on Kuramathi—no paths or roads suitable for a wheelchair, and dragging one through sand puts a considerable strain on the puller and pusher.

For anyone confined to a wheelchair, with limited or weak arm movement like myself, it is impossible to move anywhere on Kuramathi under one's own steam. When Tony and Joanne wandered off somewhere we made sure that I had everything I required and that I was placed where I would be in the shade for the duration of their absence; the sun was very hot and burned very quickly. I also kept my raincover handy as the showers appeared suddenly and were often accompanied by an increase in windforce. The ground was soon inches deep in water after such showers, but it disappeared almost as quickly as the rain came.

> **"The helicopter arrived at 9:30am, kicking up an immense cloud of dust as it approached"**

Joanne made plenty of friends of her own age, and they usually got together with a picnic lunch supplied from the restaurant, retreating to the far end of the island where they swam, listened to their Walkmans, and played card games. They also did a lot of reading and exchanged books between themselves. Tony and I found many people to talk to, and we also got through several books. Resort workers and fellow tourists on the island were helpful and polite; we encountered no hostility regarding my disability.

Toward the end of our stay we were informed of the start of a new service: some British helicopter pilots had purchased a helicopter and were trying to persuade people to charter it for flights from islands like ours to Hulhule island, where the capital, Malé, is situated. We inquired about using it for the transfer to Malé airport, to avoid the four-hour boat trip. If we could muster twenty people at $94 each, we were told we could fly from Rasdhu (our island didn't have a clear area large enough on which to land the helicopter).

On the day of departure our suitcases were loaded onto the boat at 6:30am, along with those passengers not going by helicopter. We were taken to Rasdhu at 8:30am by boat; the sea was calm and the crew boarded and disembarked the wheelchair, with me in it, without problem. We were

escorted by the villagers, who appeared to have taken time off from their duties to observe the helicopter make its first landing on the island's soccer field.

The helicopter arrived at 9:30am, kicking up an immense cloud of dust as it approached the ground; luckily, we were safely assembled under the shade of a tree, away from this dust-bath. After a safety talk, Tony and the pilot carried me on board and then loaded the wheelchair once everyone was seated. The flight was probably the best way to see the islands and the atolls.

On alighting from the helicopter and paying our dues we were escorted to the terminal building to await the arrival of the boat with our baggage on board. After a cursory search by the customs officers we proceeded with boarding the plane. Getting on was a problem! The three of us were led away separately from the others by a young Maldivian, who then abandoned us at the bottom of the steps to the plane. I eventually had to climb them on my backside—a very tiring procedure. When I was almost at the top a flight engineer arrived and gave Tony a hand to lift me into my seat. The crew apologized and then complained to the airport staff for not providing assistance or informing them that I required help.

The four-hour flight to Dubai was interesting—so clear that we could make out the atolls and reefs; then the desert in Oman, with its dunes, rock formations, and small settlements. Dubai was very hot and I stayed on board while everyone else went shopping.

I'm glad to have had the opportunity to see the Maldives (especially as they are destined to be the first land masses to disappear if the theories about the greenhouse effect are correct). It was a restful vacation, but marred slightly by the sand, which effectively made my wheelchair nothing more than an armchair. I don't suppose we'll ever see the equal of the marine life we observed there, but I suspect it's not a vacation I'll repeat in the future. That said, there were many satisfied customers among our fellow travelers, particularly those who joined the diving school's expeditions.

INDIA AND THE MALDIVES: TRAVEL NOTES

Sources of Information

Government of India Tourist Office, 30 Rockefeller Plaza, Room 15, New York, NY 10020 (☎212/586-4901); 3550 Wilshire Boulevard, #204, Los Angeles, CA 90010 (☎213/380-8855); 60 Bloor Street West, Suite 1003, Toronto, ON M4W 3B8 (☎416/962-3787). Plenty of leaflets, but nothing with any mention of disabled tourists.

Maldive Travel, 3 Esher House, 11 Edith Terrace, London SW10 0TH, UK; ☎071/352 2246. Known among the islanders as "The Maldive Lady," Toni de Laroque of *Maldive Travel* is the British representative of the Maldives Ministry of Tourism (F/2 Ghazee Building, Ameer Ahmed Magu Malé 20-05; ☎32/3224; there is no representative in the USA or Canada). She does receive some reservations from North America, and has a refreshingly positive approach to disabled travelers (see *Tour Operators*).

The American **Consular Agent** in the islands is at Mandhu-edhuruge, Violet Magu, Malé; ☎32/2581.

Tour Operators

Many escorted tour operators are wary of taking a wheelchair user—or even someone with walking difficulties—to India, fearing that the progress of the group will be slowed and schedules disrupted. However, if that's how you wish to travel it's worth persevering to find a company that will accept your booking. The trick is to sound knowledgeable about your proposed destination, and determined to go.

Sue Kelley is a seasoned traveler and, accompanied by her husband and daughter, she has booked with *Kuoni* (Deepdene House, Dorking, Surrey RH5 4AY, UK; ☎0306/740888) on a number of trips—to Hong Kong, Macau, and China and, most recently, to Kenya, as well as to the Maldives and India. The tour company therefore knows her well and will usually make the arrangements she asks for, although there was some hesitation over India and the Maldives. (Sue knows what she is capable of doing and is quick to explain her abilities to any operator who expresses doubts as to the suitability of the destination she chooses to visit; if necessary, she points out that she prefers not to be discriminated against on grounds of her disability.)

While recognizing that the soft sand is a major poblem for wheelchair users, Toni de la Roque of *Maldive Travel* insists that disabled people should not be discouraged from visiting the islands, particularly if the vacation is intended to be restful: each island is tiny; there is not much scope for walking and the Maldives are essentially for lazy swims and lying in the sun, neither of which requires great agility. She suggests aiming for resorts close to the capital, Malé. This avoids the need for long, uncomfortable journeys by boat to the more far-flung atolls. Kurumba and Laguna Beach, where there are at least some concrete walkways between rooms (usually "bungalows" or cabins), are ideal; room number five at Laguna is virtually on the beach. She also points out that the warm water of the lagoons is perfect for swimming, and the experience of feeding the fish while in the water, feeling them brushing against you, is not to be missed—something a blind person could perhaps also appreciate. *Maldive Travel* also offers programs in Sri Lanka, the Laccadive Islands, and south India.

INDIA AND THE MALDIVES: TRAVEL NOTES

Robin Reeley enjoyed a combination of organized and independent travel, using *Butterfield's Indian Railroad Tours* (Burton Fleming, Driffield, East Yorkshire YO24 0PQ, UK; ☎02620/87230) and, for pony trekking (riding ponies, pack ponies, meals, tents, and bedding provided as required), Fayaz Ahmad Milik (s/o Assdull Milik, r/o Aru, p/o Pahalgam, p/n no. 192126, Kashmir, India).

Independent travel enables greater freedom and is often more rewarding (and cheaper) than either group tours or customized packages. Searching out your own style of hotel and using local drivers and guides means that you make arrangements that suit you rather than the tour operator. But the aggravations—of making train or bus reservations, of negotiating with drivers and obtaining firm reservations with hotels—can be overwhelming for some; in which case arrangements should be managed by *Travel Corporation India* (*TCI*) (N-49 Connaught Circus, New Delhi 110 001, India; ☎11/45181); the Delhi office is up two flights of steps but the Agra, Jaipur, and Jodhpur offices are accessible. If possible, write in advance and tell them where you want to travel.

Getting There

Flights from North America to **India** go via Europe or Asia. *Air India* flies from New York to Bombay or Delhi via London every day, and the journey takes around 22 hours. However, *Air India* did not respond to our requests for information regarding services and facilities for disabled passengers, they will not accept groups of disabled passengers, and their flights tend to be full to bursting point: on her return from India Alison Walsh found movement along the aisles difficult, with bulging bags protruding from beneath seats—every passenger seemed to have the equivalent in hand luggage of what most people send to the hold. In contrast, Alison's outward flight with *Air France* was smooth and comfortable.

The best course of action for disabled travelers from North America is to shop around among their own favorite carriers to Europe or Asia, select the one offering the best fare and reasonable timing for the onward connection to India. Most direct flights out of London are operated by *British Airways* or *Air India*, but numerous other airlines, including *Air France*, *KLM*, *Lufthansa*, *Emirates*, and *Thai Airways*, stop over in India on their way to the Far East or Australia, and there are plenty of flights to choose from out of other European cities, too. Airlines offering flights to **the Maldives** include *Air Lanka* (from Columbo, Sri Lanka), *Emirates* (from Dubai and Columbo), *Singapore Airlines* (from Brussels, Paris, Zurich, and Singapore).

Airport facilities at Delhi and Bombay are not too bad: the rest rooms should be given a wide berth, but wheelchairs are available, even if at Bombay you may be given a choice of a chair with flat tires or one without footplates, and the airport attendants who push the chairs will ask for a tip before they have covered more than half a corridor; if they don't get it they'll abandon you. Malé in the Maldives is basic, but effective—you'll probably be carried off the plane.

Transport

In India, accessible **public transportation** is virtually non-existent, and any method of travel is likely to be slow or uncomfortable or both; this applies even to the vehicles used on expensive escorted tours—beware the word "luxury," it is used often and has a different meaning in India. Where roads are more than tracks they are poorly maintained. Buses and cars are usually pretty spartan; trains are difficult to get into and the rest rooms impossible. Domestic **flights** probably offer the best level of comfort and cut down journey times, but *Indian Airlines* is notoriously inefficient, with few facilities for boarding and disembarking, often no wheelchair service, and endless bureaucracy to cut through when booking a ticket—and you'll see nothing of the countryside.

Accommodation

In India the top-rate hotels are reasonably accessible—and reasonably priced by European standards—many of them have

INDIA AND THE MALDIVES: TRAVEL NOTES

ramps and good-sized elevators. In the older buildings the style of the bathrooms lends itself to wheelchair-accessible showers—sloping floors, no lips or sills around the shower/tap, stool or chair readily supplied.

Robin Reeley recommends the *Hotel Ashok Yatri Niwas* (19 Ashok Road, New Delhi 110 001; ☎11/344511), Daphne Pagnamenta the *Oberoi Maidens* (7 Sham Nath Marg, Delhi 110 054; ☎11/2525464). Some of the rooms in the *Shivniwas Palace* (Udaipur 313 001; ☎294/28239) are accessible; the pool and courtyard provide a quiet haven but the food was poor. *Ajit Bhawan* (Near Circuit House, Jodhpur 342 006; ☎291/20409) has the songs-around-the-campfire atmosphere of an upmarket youth hostel, and its own cult following—guests return year after year for the desert trips. The food is delicious, the gardens restful; steps to the central courtyard (where meals are eaten) and in reception could be ramped.

Access and Facilities

In the cities, high curbs, narrow, crowded sidewalks and dripping heat make getting around something of a trial; a companion is almost essential. The traffic can be heart-stopping, and litter—in the form of mounds of rotting garbage—is often another obstacle. In rural areas the terrain can be formidable, with soft sand, rocky paths, and dirt tracks to negotiate. Robin Reeley got around this in Kashmir by pony trekking, but for many the only way to see the countryside is from a vehicle: bus, train, taxi, or even helicopter.

Access to sights even when you get there is too often only partial, which means that wheelchair users must sit and view the monument from outside, or be content with the exhibits on the museum's first floor, and those with limited walking powers must see only half a Moghul palace.

Apart from problems with physical access, disabled travelers may come across a frustrating tendency, wherever there are rules laid down and procedures to follow, to place bureaucratic niceties above the needs of a disabled person. This is a common experience for Indians with disabilities, but can also affect those on vacation. In 1990 *Air India* sent Sue Kelley's wheelchair to Bombay while she went to Delhi. Sue was kept waiting nearly two hours before they acknowledged that the chair had gone missing, but the next day the wheelchair was ready for collection at Delhi; Sue's husband then wasted most of the day retrieving it.

But foreigners with a visible disability, such as those in wheelchairs or using canes or crutches, are likely to be cheerfully assisted whenever they need help. And unprompted and unexpected offers of help from passers-by, as well as generous hospitality, are reported by many travelers.

Health and Insurance

The main threats to good health in this part of the world come from contaminated food and water and, in some areas, disease-carrying mosquitoes. The effects of high temperatures and humidity should not be underestimated, and remember also that nights can be cold. There is bad air pollution in several areas—most cities, and around industrial complexes such as the one near the Taj that is responsible for erosion of the marble by acid rain—and it's a good idea to take antibiotics, cold remedies, nasal decongestant medication or spray. But don't *over*estimate the dangers: with some simple precautions and common sense, plus advice from a good guidebook or from Richard Dawood's *Travelers' Health* (see "Books," *Practicalities*), you are unlikely to suffer more than a couple of days of "Delhi Belly."

If you don't have a strong stomach, it's worth taking a small travel kettle and some granola bars, or other foods that you know and love—when recovering from a bout of diarrhea and faced with strange and spicy food, the comforting thought of familiar food helps restore interest in the world around you.

Books

India: A Million Mutinies Now, by VS Naipaul (William Heinemann, 1990; Minerva, 1991). As Paul Theroux says, "literally the last word on India today." The country is brought alive by a series of interviews with Indians from all walks

INDIA AND THE MALDIVES: TRAVEL NOTES

of life—some of their stories will make your hair stand on end, some will make you laugh or cry, but mostly they'll simply explain all of what you'll see on vacation and more.

The Great Moghuls, by Bamber Gascoigne (Dorset Press, New York). Beautifully illustrated and entertaining account of Indian history from Babur to Aurangzeb.

TELEPHONE CODES

Dial 011 (International Code), followed by 91 for India, and 961 for the Maldives.

Singapore

Looking for Excellence

Susan Preston has muscular dystrophy and uses a wheelchair outdoors; inside, she can walk a little, using a wall for support. In August 1987 Susan spent three weeks in Singapore, visiting a friend from her college days. The trip included a few days on Phuket Island, Thailand.

The ideal place to be in steamy Singapore is sitting in a wheelchair! The jungle of the island has gone and the tigers no longer roam wild, but the tropical climate remains, tempered by sea breezes that fan the warm air. I had just to sit back and think of all things oriental; my companions (my mother and Mary, a family friend) had to push, pull, and tip my chair in the perspiring heat.

The reason for my trip was a friendship which began several years ago. Ah Mei studied with me at a British university, and after graduating had to return home to Singapore. Ah Mei is a conscientious organizer: her third-story flat was inaccessible, so she trekked around the city-center hotels to find one of reasonable cost with suitable facilities for me.

We were slightly surprised when she wrote to say that she had booked us into the YMCA! But she assured us that it was a hotel, not a male youth hostel. It proved to be excellent value for money, centrally situated at the beginning of Orchard Road, the mile-long shopping belt of the city.

On reflection, it was perhaps unwise for me to stay in an eighth-floor room—in the event of fire—but we had a splendid view of a small, green park below, the terraced, pastel-colored Chinese houses, and the towering buildings of the modern city beyond. And from that height the flow of cars on the multi-laned, one-way system moved silently.

For my three weeks in Singapore, I was lazy: I barely had to walk at all. I had a bit of clambering to do, though, mainly in and out of taxis, but those taxis were a boon—there were droves of them! One guidebook estimated 10,000 in a city with a population of 2,500,000. Because they were so plentiful, inexpensive, and anxious for custom, sightseeing was not a burden. All the taxis were large four-door sedans, and my chair fitted easily into the trunk. Normally there was a dollar charge for each item of luggage, but window stickers in each taxi indicated that wheelchairs were carried free of charge. The reactions from the drivers were generally delightful, especially when they learned where we came from: "Scot-lend! Cel-teek!"; "Scot-lend!

Whis-kee!"; "Scot-lend! So far! I think you very brave!"

Singapore was in the middle of its National Day celebrations while we were there, commemorating its emergence as an independent republic in 1965. The pop song "We are Singapore" resounded from every loudspeaker; a giant rainbow, with the motto "Together . . . Excellence for Singapore," was constructed in the heart of Orchard Road; the TV propagandized the virtues of the nation and the unity of its people. From our lofty bedroom window we watched the annual parade of brightly lit floats, military contingents, and dragon dancers, while jets soared overhead against the night sky. A percentage of the GDP is spent on this spectacle: during the recession of the early 1980s the floats had been few; this year, people told us, the celebration had regained its former glory.

"For our first few days there, part of me wanted to believe in the dream"

I had expected excellence from Singapore—an efficient, clean, tightly run, competitive society, a prosperous place. My first experiences confirmed this: Changi airport was beautiful, all brown, cream, and chrome, with moving corridors and a fountain falling through three floors. A porter pushed me, and guided us through all the procedures (another advantage of being in a wheelchair—you bypass lines!). Our "caretaker" was Malaysian, wore a brown uniform to match the decor, and was kind but took his responsibility very seriously: "Sit right back in the chair, please." Yes, sir.

The cleanness of the City of Singapore was immediately evident on the broad sidewalks of Orchard Road. Fines for dropping litter are enforced. As it is the shopping and hotel belt, you need money to be there, so the first people I saw were predominantly young, healthy, and stylish. The TV, the radio, the posters, all told us that Singapore strives for perfection and looks after its people. Given our first impressions of the island, we could not argue with the media.

I was physically shaken, then, as I waited to cross Orchard Road, to see a thin, unshaven man in his early fifties open the bin on the lamppost next to me, lift out a juice carton and suck up the dregs. I noticed that one of the letters strung out across the Orchard Road rainbow had fallen off. I saw bent, shrunken, old Chinese ladies sweeping the shop floors. And I heard a disturbed man shouting at no one in particular across the café tables.

Of course, all of these things I can see, probably to a greater extent, on British streets. But our TV and newspapers reflect this sadder side of life. In the midst of National Day celebrations the state-controlled Singaporean media projected a Utopian society and, for our first few days there, part of me wanted to believe in the dream. The broken rainbow over Orchard Road seemed symbolic of the reality.

What concern is there for the less able in Singapore? What of the "less perfect" members of society? Since my trip in 1987, I have been encouraged to learn from Ah Mei that the government has established a committee to improve provision and access for the disabled. While there, I noticed that the newest shopping complex had special rest room facilities; one or two public buildings we visited had ramped entrances. The high-rise shopping centers which line both sides of Orchard Road are wheelchair friendly because of the large public elevators between floors. I met a group of young disabled people in one store: they spotted me first and came whizzing over in fashionable sports chairs to say hello. Their English was not good, but I gathered that they lived in a purpose-built complex.

Basic wheelchairs can be bought in the drugstore departments; I saw one Singaporean gentleman being pushed in one by his wife. Deaf teenagers eagerly communicating in sign language were quite a common sight on Orchard Road. Pavement curbs are by necessity very high because of the floods in the monsoon season; they are too great an obstacle for the lone wheelchair user.

"I learned to avoid the gristly fish balls, and wasn't tempted by the pig's brain soup"

The government's liking for orderliness has its disappointing aspects. A picture of Singapore, circulated worldwide in the brochures, depicts the Chinese junks crowding Singapore river, enclosed by the old and new buildings of the city. I arrived at the spot with my camera, only to find the water bare. And the clutter of market stands in the old town has also been tidied up: they are now unimaginatively contained within specially constructed concrete arcades.

But traditional ways of life are irrepressible. Singapore has its "Little India," its Chinatown, its Arab Quarter—the natural groupings of its people. Smells and cultures mingle: the stench of open sewers in the Chinese street with a colonial name, Clyde Street; a tri-cart piled high with pineapple; the old Chinese man with his bare, concave chest, waiting to cross the road with me. A magnificent sultan mosque dominates Arab Street, where the cracked facades of the shuttered dwellings revealed warmth and homeliness inside. Fear of intrusion made me resist the temptation to photograph an old Arab in his blue jacket and white skirt, standing and eating from his bowl outside his pink and white house, a light burning within.

Ah Mei was keen that we sample authenticity, and with her we ate at the hawker centers. Originally, all kinds of food-sellers trundled their carts through the streets of Singapore. Today they are still called "hawkers" but are established at permanent centers throughout the island. The one on Ah Mei's development was typical— a large, covered, outdoor café area with competing small food kitchens forming the perimeter and serving freshly cooked, inexpensive Chinese food. This is where the "ordinary people" congregate. I don't recommend bean cake, a violently colored sweetmeat, green or pink on the outside, white, pasty, and sickly on the inside. I learned to avoid the gristly fish balls, too, and wasn't tempted by the pig's brain soup. But the other new tastes were sensational.

"I read and I forget. I see and I remember. I do and I understand." That is the philosophy of Singapore's Science Center, built in 1977. It was the forerunner of a new breed of science and technology museums, concentrating on the "hands-on" learning experience for visitors of all ages. There are over 400 exhibits to push, pull, crank, and pedal. All aim to explain the world around us and what it is to be human. It is one of the liveliest museums I have ever visited; we spent hours there and had great fun.

Aerial photographs of the island show the skyscrapers but hide the leafiness of the city. As well as the generous sprinkling of rich green trees and flowering shrubs around the streets, there are several large, cultivated parks, usually outside the city center. The oldest are the superb Botanic Gardens, founded in 1859. The gardens are famous for their collection of palm trees and for the Orchid Enclosure, but something new and more exciting for me was a walk through the designated Jungle Area—several acres left to grow wild. This was Singapore in its natural state, with strange, unknown bird and insect sounds emanating from the towering trees. The air was dank and heavy. It was a wonderful experience.

The Zoological Gardens are world class, with the emphasis on establishing natural habitats for the creatures, and Jurong Bird Park is said to be the finest in Asia. Tiger Balm Gardens have their own, horrible fascination, with larger-than-life, colorful, fibre glass models of mythical Chinese creatures in a hilly, open-air setting—a kind of Chinese Disneyland without the fun-rides!

"In this unlikely setting was a rest room for the disabled, albeit used as a broom closet"

Visitors to Singapore are not confined to the island. There are day-long bus tours across the border to Malaysia, and boat trips to the several small islands off Singapore's shore. The farther away the island, the less developed and "touristy" it is. These islets with their sandy beaches are very popular with Singaporean families at weekends. Sentosa is the nearest (only five minutes by ferry or cable car) and the most commercialized, with monorail, musical fountain, and roller-skating rink among the attractions. In contrast, on Kusu island, 45 minutes by ferry, there are only two small temples (one Chinese, one Muslim), palm trees, and a tortoise sanctuary. Some of the islands are totally uninhabited. Lifting the wheelchair on and off the ferry posed no problems for the crew.

We also went farther afield, to Phuket, an island off the western coast of Thailand. Our taxi driver to Changi airport was friendly, with firm views: as all roads lead to the airport, all faiths lead to God; he is a Singaporean—he does not need to sing the new song, he does not need the message of unity; he is loyal, this is his homeland. We flew *Thai Airways*, which coped smoothly with me and my chair. The cabin attendants were dressed in long, richly colored silk national dress, and each female passenger was given an orchid. The flight was scheduled to take ninety minutes, but a monsoon was raging

over Phuket. We circled the bumpy skies for forty minutes. I began to hope that we might be diverted to Bangkok, and we were.

In all, I boarded and disembarked from seven planes during the vacation, by a variety of means. Of course, in Bangkok, they had no advance warning of my arrival, but when we landed I was assigned a porter as before. This time, however, the poor fellow had to carry me down the steep flight of steps from the plane. He was trembling, I said a prayer, but Ah Mei's first words when we reached terra firma were, "Oh, I wish I had had my camera!"

We were guided through the empty, glittering new airport building to the original passenger lounge—rather old-fashioned, with its dark wood. In this unlikely setting was a rest room for the disabled, albeit used as a broom closet. For the first time on our trip to the East, we experienced the isolation of not being able to communicate with those around us; a feeling heightened by uncertainty over where we would be taken next. Our porter unexpectedly produced sandwiches and Coke for us, then without a word we were "portered" via a transit bus to the luxurious *Airport Hotel*, where we had a meal and spent the night courtesy of the airline. In the murky light of the next morning's dawn, on the way to the airport, we glimpsed the shanty dwellings on the fringes of Bangkok.

"We went to bed in clammy darkness, but awoke to a transformed scene"

A nylon transit seat, or carrying chair, was a wise investment prior to our vacation. It has no rigid structure and rolls up when not in use. We did not have it "at the ready" when we were unexpectedly diverted to Bangkok, but we were better prepared when we landed at Phuket's small airstrip. And it was nice to see my own wheelchair waiting for me at the foot of the steps!

The monsoon had abated sufficiently for the plane to land, but I have never seen such heavy rain. The driven air was very warm. Our dinner that evening was eaten by the light of a small candle: a fallen coconut tree had brought down the power line and the hotel's emergency generator had simultaneously exploded! We went to bed in clammy darkness, but awoke to a transformed scene. The waves were still quite high but the Indian Ocean glimmered a deep turquoise, crested with surf, and the white sand dazzled.

Singaporeans have a Western air of sophistication, an aloofness; the Thai were more open. None were kinder than the driver of the hotel minivan and the young lad who came along to help lift me, on our day trip around the island. By chance we had the bus to ourselves. I strapped myself into my transit seat and we soon established a quick procedure for transferring from bus to wheelchair, and vice versa.

From my vantage point I saw the islanders living their lives: an old man in a sarong hoed his garden; two young boys boxed with red gloves; a young woman threw a pail of water over herself in the heat of the day; a middle-aged woman beat the dust out of her bed; and a young man sat on his doorstep, just watching. The landscape was detailed with wild, large-leafed banana trees and papaya, rubber plantations, ochre fields, and green hills, bison-like cows, black and tan goats, white or pink Buddhist temples, and the occasional arched gateway leading nowhere. Corrugated iron, stone, and palm-leaf dwellings were strewn along the wayside, with a few houses on stilts. Motorbikes were the means of transport for everyone: we saw an old lady on hers; schoolgirls in blue uniform rode three astride; one man carried his dog perfectly balanced behind him on the passenger seat!

Before leaving Phuket, one balmy evening, we stumbled into a private party on the raised poolside area at our hotel, an event in honor of the Thai national soccer team who had reached the finals of the ASEAN games. Myriad colored lights were reflected in the pool and lit the young Thai dancers—girls of nine or ten in silk and gold traditional costume.

People applauded as the girls finished their routine and two of the troupe tripped daintily around the side of the pool to where the guests were seated. We watched admiringly, too, then it dawned on us that they were coming in our direction. They bowed sweetly, took off their beautiful garlands of mauve orchids and slipped them over our heads! A brilliant spotlight dazzled us; glancing toward it, we noticed a TV camera recording the incident! The applause continued. We blushed with embarrassment but were utterly thrilled.

I haven't mentioned the sixteen-hour flights to and from Singapore, perhaps because next to the thrills and new experiences they fade into insignificance. If I have one plea to make, it is that the specially adapted toilets on board *British Airways* aircraft be made wide enough to accommodate the aisle wheelchair. A pamphlet of hints for the disabled traveler, which I read prior to the vacation, advised drinking only the minimum necessary to avoid dehydration—too true! But I'd do it again, and gradually I hope to become a seasoned traveler, able to fall asleep at will and let time fly by.

Thailand

A Prayer to the Emerald Buddha

After spending eight weeks in Australia (see p.461) Barbara Horrocks and her husband Bill flew on to Thailand. Barbara has a congenital disease of the spine, of which she was not aware until well into her forties, when walking became very difficult and the pain unbearable. After two operations she is able to get about the house but has to use a wheelchair outside.

Bangkok is reputed to be the hottest city in the world. It must also rank as one of the most crowded and traffic congested. Despite these drawbacks it is a magical place, fascinating in its complexity, the mean hovels and magnificent temples jostling for position with hotels and shopping plazas.

We were caught up in a strike at Sydney airport, and consequently arrived in "The Land of Smiles" at 2:30am, expecting consolation by way of a rapid and traffic-free ride through a deserted city. How wrong can you be! The taxi ground to a halt in an enormous traffic jam, the sidewalks were thronged with people, and the mobile food vendors were doing a roaring trade.

A frantic traffic cop sorted out the jam and before long our cab turned under an arch into a deserted back street. Although I am well past the first flush of youth and never go anywhere without my wheelchair, I was

convinced that I was about to be kidnapped! On better acquaintance I realized that many of Bangkok's best hotels are reached via this network of narrow streets, but for the moment I was relieved to see ours, every bit as ritzy as the brochures had pictured it. Our room was waiting, air-conditioned and welcoming with a basket of tropical fruit, and orchids on the pillows.

The following morning we breakfasted on what was surely the most sumptuous spread of our travels so far. Not the least of its attractions were the made-to-order-before-your-very-eyes pancakes with unlimited maple syrup. The memory still makes me drool and I have yet to lose their legacy from my waistline.

Our hotel, like so many in Bangkok, stood on the banks of the River Chao Phya (the River of Kings) and we were content to spend the next few hours on the terrace, watching the world sail by. The river is the lifeblood of Bangkok: many of her people live on it, and it teems with boats—ferries, shuttle boats (provided free by many of the hotels for their guests), fishing boats, private rental boats, floating food vendors, and enormous barges consisting of one leading boat with maybe eight or ten others in tow, all loaded to the gunwales. To add to the congestion, great swathes of water hyacinth float downstream and threaten to clog the navigation channels.

A network of canals spreads out from the river in both directions; these, too, are crowded, lined with humble dwellings—I hesitate to call them houses, although I was assured that they have all utilities, including electricity. Judging by the profusion of TV aerials sprouting from the roofs, it must be true. The Thai people use the waterways for bathing and doing the laundry, laughing and waving at passers-by.

Later in the day we used the shuttle boat—helped on and off with a smile—to visit River City, one of the many shopping plazas in Bangkok. They are cool and air-conditioned, with smooth marble floors that wheelchair users (and pushers) love, and they sell almost anything. But made-to-measure clothes, ready in 24 hours, are their specialty. The windows overflow with handmade Thai silk, in exotic patterns and colors to tempt the most reluctant purchaser. Bill was easily tempted, succumbing to the luxury of made-to-measure shirts in no time at all, but it was several days before I took the plunge.

That night we dined out of doors, sampling the delicious Thai food, a sort of cross between Indian and Chinese, very spicy, with lots of noodles laced with red-hot chillies which the Thais eat with impunity. The wine was expensive, so we stuck to the local beer, which was ideal in the hot, steamy climate.

The next day, recovered from our tiring journey, we joined an organized tour of the Grand Palace and the Emerald Buddha. The former is really a collection of palaces and temples, each more fabulous than the last—a world of mythical beasts, covered with layers of gold leaf which glitters in the sun, to guard against evil spirits. The Chapel Royal contains the Emerald Buddha, the most sacred of all images. Unfortunately, a short flight of steps leads into the chapel, and wheelchairs are not allowed inside (I think they equate the tires with shoes, which have to be removed). But if, like me, you are able to manage a few steps, it is impossible not to be overawed, or to say a prayer, whatever your religion.

"Coconuts served with the top sliced off and a spoon for scooping out the soft, sweet flesh"

After the tour we took the shuttle boat to River City again, so that Bill could have a fitting. We ate a delicious lunch in the plaza's restaurant for less than $3 each, and watched an exhibition of Thai dancing in the flower-decked foyer before returning to the hotel to laze away the rest of the day.

Bangkok is not an easy city for the disabled. Like all cities on the monsoon trail, the curbs are very high and we found no ramps. The sidewalks are crowded and often in a state of disrepair. The traffic makes London seem like a haven of peace and quiet.

Nevertheless, we were determined to see as much as possible, so the next morning we rose before it was light and joined a tour to the legendary bridge on the River Kwai. Although the tour included a ride on The Death Railroad and a visit to the beautifully maintained military cemetery, the day was not all gloom and doom. It was good to see rural Thailand. We lunched on board a floating restaurant on the River Kwai and stopped at a fruit market for an afternoon break. Here we bought juicy pomelos (huge grapefruit) which have a rich, refreshing taste, and the local coconuts which are served with the top sliced off and a spoon for scooping out the soft, sweet flesh.

Bill is a Normandy veteran, and one of our fellow passengers was an American lawyer who had been injured in Vietnam. They got on like a house on fire, assisted by great quantities of the local beer, and I will always remember the lawyer's soft, southern drawl, his politeness and his quiet way of offering assistance without making me feel in any way inadequate: "Let me help you, ma'am."

"The hot wind caught the spray from the fountains and showered us with cool water"

Needless to say, we had to keep asking the driver to stop, so that the men could rid themselves of one lot of beer, and buy more to counteract the heat. At every stop, curious, smiling children gathered around, just able to speak enough English to ask where we hailed from. When we told them (Liverpool) their smiles grew bigger and one of them invariably produced a soccer ball. Bill, who hasn't played for longer than he'd care to remember, was prevailed upon to do a bit of coaching, in dusty gas-stations and narrow strips of land beside the road.

The next day we stayed closer to home, taking a ride in a *tuk-tuk*, a sort of motorized rickshaw, powered by a two-stroke engine and driven erratically and at great speed in and out of minute gaps in the Bangkok traffic. *Tuk-tuks* have a roof but no sides, so they are very cool, although it's impossible to avoid breathing in lungfuls of exhaust fumes. This kind of taxi is very cheap, while conventional taxis are not; you can cover quite long distances in a *tuk-tuk* for $2—less if you are adept at bargaining! We found them convenient, with room to store the wheelchair, and great fun.

Very few *tuk-tuk* drivers speak English, but we were lucky and found one with slightly more than most. We agreed a price for a couple of hours' sightseeing, and our first stop was the Gold Buddha—five and a half tons of solid gold, and quite a sight. Our driver took us in and out of narrow streets and back alleys, finding ways to avoid the more congested routes, stopping at temples, gem factories, and silk emporiums, with a visit to Chinatown thrown in. We parted company at the gates to Lumpini Park, an oasis of greenery and peace laid out around a large lake, where we hired a boat, complete with shady canopy.

Despite the language difficulties, we were able to persuade the attendant at the ticket stand to look after my wheelchair, and while on the lake we had an interesting conversation in sign language with some Chinese tourists, swapping cameras to take photographs of each other and laughing in unison as the hot wind caught the spray from the fountains and showered us with cool water.

We felt able to face another early start the next day, and left the hotel in a private hired boat at 7am for a tour of the canals. It included a visit to a snake show, which I thought was repulsive, in a fascinating sort of way, but which Bill actually enjoyed, and one to the floating market. Here, women in straw peasant hats paddle their tiny sampans, filled with fruit, flowers, and vegetables. The sight is a photographer's paradise, and if you can only manage one waterborne trip, this is the one to choose. Ensure that you are taken to the market at Damern Saduak; it is a long trip but worth it. The nearer floating market of Wat Sai is not much in use any more, but unscrupulous tour operators may try to palm you off with it. If your disability precludes boats it is possible to go by bus.

Our stay in Bangkok was flying past, and there was still so much to see: should it be another temple, a Thai boxing match, a trip to Khao Yai National Park? We settled for a tour to the Rose Gardens, a large park about 20 miles west of Bangkok, beautifully landscaped with roses and tropical plants. There are demonstrations of Thai crafts, plus a show including Thai boxing, a Thai wedding, the ordination of a monk, and traditional dancing.

We also saw a demonstration of elephants working logs. One of them became very curious about me, waving his trunk at my lap. Everyone except me was highly amused. Then Bill cottoned on, asking, "What have you got in your bag?" I realized that it wasn't me the elephant fancied, but the bananas intended for our lunch! Nervously I held them out. The elephant took them from me, as gentle as a kitten, and devoured them with relish.

The crowds were milling around, waiting for the show to begin. I was just wondering if we'd have to give it a miss, when I was tapped on the shoulder by a smiling Thai. He gestured for us to follow him, and we were guided around the back, through the stage door, and given good seats on the front row. My only complaint about the Rose Garden is that we'd booked a half-day tour, and realized too late that we needed a whole day to do it justice.

Bangkok *can* be explored by the disabled person; it takes a bit of spirit but is well worth the effort. Before we went, our travel agent said that everyone always wishes they'd had longer there. When we heard that we changed our plans and booked for eight days instead of four; even so, I wish we'd had longer. The Thai people may be diminutive (at five foot four I felt like a giant) but their smiles are enormous and ever present. They always helped with my chair, beaming from ear to ear when it was folded up, and positively splitting their sides when my folding walking stick disappeared into the depths of my pocketbook.

I'd like to see much more of Thailand, visit the beach resorts and the mountains, perhaps taking a trip into neighboring Burma, political unrest permitting. Leaving aside (as we did) the red light district, the transvestite theater, the bars, and discos, there's a great deal of Bangkok still waiting to be explored. I hope the Emerald Buddha heard my prayer and that one day I'll get my chance to visit him again.

Bali

A Taste of Bali

Veronica Smith is 37 years old and confined to a wheelchair as a result of degeneration of the spine with neurological impairment. In March 1989 she traveled as a member of the Great Britain team to the World Rowing Championships for the Disabled in Perth, Australia. The championships had to be abandoned as they were hit by the tail-end of "Cyclone Dan," but Veronica went on to enjoy two weeks' vacation, spending a short time in Bali.

The Indonesian island of Bali is a place that I should dearly like to return to for a longer stay, not only for the climate and beaches, which are excellent, but for the atmosphere, the character of the countryside, the fascinatingly different culture, and the natural charm and friendliness of the Balinese people. We stayed in the very comfortable, traditional chalet-style *Ramayana Hotel*, surrounded by tropical gardens, in Kuta which is one of the main tourist areas. It is on the coast, a couple of miles from the airport and six miles from the capital city of Denpasar.

The accommodation at the *Ramayana* is easily accessible, provided that one can cope with the occasional step in the gardens and on the paths leading to the chalets. The main entrance to the cottages is up three or four steps, so the wheelchair user needs someone to help with registering in the reception area. The easiest way to reach the chalets and gardens is via the side entrance, which is on the level although rather rough. The chalets themselves are on one level and just big enough to maneuver a wheelchair inside. Each chalet has its own rest room and bathroom with level access. The spacious bar and restaurant are adjacent to the swimming pool and accessible via one small step.

Some visitors feel that Kuta is too "touristy" and too full of Australians. This didn't bother me and, even if it had, a short walk would have been enough to leave the majority of tourists behind. Kuta was vibrant from early in the morning, when the ground was strewn with individual, luncheonplate-sized offerings to the gods, made from palm leaves, petals, and incense sticks, until late at night, when the street market and food stands were still doing a brisk, noisy trade. I found it an intriguing place that should be explored early or late in the day when it was cooler and rather less crowded.

The large street market in Kuta is well worth a visit, even if you are staying elsewhere. It runs the length of the main street and onto a wider, traffic-free area which leads to the beach. The market is obviously aimed at tourists but it is easy to find inexpensive, good-quality gifts and souvenirs. The best bargains are hand-tooled leather goods, beautiful batiks, and hand-carved and painted wooden items such as traditional masks. It is often possible to watch the artists at work.

As well as these traditional-style gifts there are more evidently "touristy" ones; they do a particularly good line in astonishingly cheap T-shirts, shorts, and pants known as Jakpacs which are cool and comfortable. The ones I bought cost about $6 and are still going strong after 18 months of regular use. All market traders expect their customers to bargain with them and they clearly enjoy the process; once I overcame my initial diffidence, so did I.

"Locally distilled arak resembles a lethal brew of turps and methyl alcohol"

The most unhappy and thought-provoking aspect of the market is its beggar population. Bali is a poor country and many of its people live below the poverty line. The majority of the beggars are women with young children and babies: some may be out to exploit the tourists but many are in genuine need. I found it difficult to know how to cope with this: if I gave money to one I was at once swamped by others and pestered continually; on the other hand it seemed heartless to give nothing.

The market had the most atmosphere from about 7pm onward and it was fun to wander around and mingle with the crowd. For serious shopping, rather than just looking, the evening was too crowded for a wheelchair user to shop easily. I found the best time was early morning, before breakfast, when there were only a few tourists about and bargaining could be carried out in a pleasantly unhurried manner, amid the scent wafting from the incense sticks on the morning offerings to the gods.

"The simplicity of the setting has left a vivid memory"

Eating out in Kuta was a delight: the local Indonesian food was very good and reasonably priced; I especially enjoyed a Balinese dish of baked lobster. For the less adventurous there is plenty of familiar food, including the ubiquitous "fish and chippies!" Water from the faucet should be avoided, but bottled water is cheap and plentiful. The freshly squeezed fruit juices, particularly lemon, are delicious and refreshing, a glass of mixed fruit juice being a meal in itself and thick enough to support a straw upright. The same cannot be said of the locally distilled arak, which is made from the juice of the coconut palm or rice and molasses; it resembles a lethal brew of turps and methyl alcohol.

All the restaurants and bars I saw in Kuta were on one level with room inside for a wheelchair. As a precaution against flooding in the wet season, most buildings have one or sometimes two sizable steps at the entrance. These would be a problem for an electric chair but are perfectly manageable in a manual chair if one has a friend to help when necessary; if not, the Balinese seemed quite happy to help.

On our first evening we rented a minivan and driver and were driven inland to Bone (pronounced Bona), a village near Gianyar where we watched an enthralling display of traditional dancing. The majority of Balinese people are followers of the Hindu Dharma religion, in which dancing plays an important part.

The first dance was a *kecak*, a unique Balinese dance which is accompanied not by a gamelan (orchestra) but by a choir of a hundred men. The *kecak* has its origins in an old ritual *sanghyang*, or trance dance, in which the dancer, in a state of trance, communicates with the deities or ancestors. Using the dancers as a medium, the deities or ancestors make their wishes known to the people. In the 1930s the ancient Indian epic, *Ramayana*, was incorporated into the dance. The atmosphere created by the sometimes restful, sometimes exciting rhythms chanted by the choir was powerful and compelling, unlike anything I have previously experienced. The sound complemented the dancing perfectly, alternately dreamy and dynamic.

The next two dances were also forms of *sanchyang* which developed from the religious function of maintaining a healthy and prosperous village by the driving away of evil spirits. The final performance was a fire dance, involving a man in a trance dancing repeatedly through and on burning coconut husks. The dignity and grace of the dancers, combined with the magnificence of the costumes and the simplicity of the setting—a dirt-floor, barn-like building of bamboo and palm—has left a vivid memory.

Bali is not the easiest of places for wheelchair users to travel around. Many of the roads are rutted dirt tracks; even the paved ones tend to be full of potholes and badly driven motor scooters, bikes, and minivans (cars are rare). Many locals (and tourists) rely on "*bemos*," which are battered, canvas-topped jeeps, providing a very cheap, frequent public transportation service. They are generally packed tight with locals, tourists, and, sometimes, livestock! It is not unusual to see the Balinese hanging off the sides and back of the *bemo* if the inside is full. Great fun for the able-bodied but definitely inaccessible to wheelchairs!

Despite these difficulties, transport was not the problem I anticipated as minivan rental is cheap and efficient. It is possible to rent an air-conditioned van and driver for a whole day for a very moderate sum (about $20–30). Keith and I decided to do this for our second day; the other two members of our group were more interested in soaking up the sun, so we left them by the hotel swimming pool.

We asked the driver to avoid the main tourist attractions and drive through the less well-known areas. It was an excellent day: we traveled along narrow roads lined with bright, vigorous poinsettias five or six feet tall, passing villagers—even tiny children—carrying huge loads on their heads. We went through terraced rice fields, palm groves, and villages, past ornately carved temples, and away into the mountains with their live volcanoes and vast, still lakes.

As we drove through the villages we frequently heard the distinctive music of the local gamelan. Many dances, festivals, and ceremonies are accompanied by this orchestra, which consists of a two-string violin, a flute, gongs, drums, and various combinations of unusual metal keyboard instruments suspended over bamboo resonating tubes, rather like organ pipes. The music produced is strikingly beautiful, but difficult at first for ears accustomed to Western music.

The Balinese are artistic and creative people, fond of poetry, music, dancing, and festivals; they are highly gifted in arts and crafts, especially woodcarving and silverwork. We drove slowly past numerous open-fronted workshops made of bamboo and palm, where men carved stone or wood and painted the finished sculptures. We saw women and girls constructing elaborate, tall temple offerings which were carried on the head to be placed in the temple courtyard.

So far, the Balinese have managed to retain a dignified individuality and maintain their unique culture. It would be a great loss if increased tourism, which is essential to the Balinese economy, were to erode these attributes. I hope that when I return I will find them intact.

The Philippines

No Concessions, no Prejudice

Alfred Azzopardi lives in northern Queensland, Australia, and has been quadriplegic since a road accident in 1965. On his first trip to the Philippines, in 1980, he wound up marrying his penpal, Gina; they returned to the islands in 1984 with their first child.

The hustle and bustle of the vibrant marketplace, somewhere in Manila, capital city of the Philippines, is almost overwhelming. Countless stands display almost every conceivable commodity, from antiques and wood-carvings to poultry and fish (dead or alive). A Filipino man sells pieces of pork, impaled and freshly roasted on bamboo sticks; another tows a cart selling ice creams. Vendors occasionally cool themselves with straw fans, and chase flies away with feather dusters. Shoppers stream everywhere and sounds of bargaining fill the air.

Children play, watch wide-eyed and sometimes tag along, fascinated and delighted by the sight of a foreigner in a chrome wheelchair. The heat is intense, the humidity stifling, and the sweet scent of Oriental incense mingles with pungent wafts from market refuse. I move steadily onwards in my wheelchair, with my wife and the small group of my Filipino in-laws. I might be an unusual sight but I can tell that I am welcome here. An in-law usher leads the way, waving his hand for people to move aside, making me feel like some kind of dignitary.

We soon find what I am looking for—abundant tropical and exotic fruits, of astonishing variety (my hobby back home is rare-fruit growing). There are bright yellow, ripe mangoes, spiky, pungent durians, smooth, shiny, purple or green star-apples, enormous, knobbly jackfruit, and hairy rambutans. I tell Gina and my in-laws which ones I want, and leave them to do the buying, not because I am in a wheelchair but because they are better at bargaining than a foreign *turista*.

When I arrived in Manila, the first thing which struck me was the cascade of color and noise. The endless traffic, making its way through congested intersections, without traffic lights, has to be seen to be believed. The horns, sirens, and shrills are incessant. Security guards, in starched uniforms with shining badges, seem to stand at every corner. Street workers in red shirts wear handkerchiefs tied over their faces to protect them from the traffic fumes.

The colorful "jeepneys" are a tourist attraction in themselves. Vivid graffiti, in keeping with the latest fads and fashions, decorate these vehicles, and their blaring stereo systems belt out the latest hit songs. Jeepneys are descendants of leftover US army jeeps, converted by imaginative Filipinos into flamboyant buses, carrying a dozen or so passengers. My standard-size wheelchair just fits between the two bench seats, and I have to bend my neck to avoid the ceiling, but the experience of riding in a jeepney, wheelchair and all, is worth any discomfort.

The best way for the traveler in a wheelchair to get around Philippine cities is by taxi, but taxi drivers are apt to forget to switch meters on for foreign visitors, disabled or not! Foreigners are very popular—and so are their dollars. In a country of low wages, high unemployment, and no unemployment benefits or welfare system, money really does talk. Tourists will naturally be charged more than locals, but travelers from the richer countries can, nevertheless, vacation in the Philippines at much lower cost than in most other parts of the world.

As darkness falls, closed doors on ordinary downtown streets explode into an orgy of color, music, and entertainment—and, of course, there are girls. In a beer house, bar girls dance to music on a mirrored stage which confuses the tired eye. Foreigners and Filipinos alike drink San Miguel beer and inexpensive drinks at wooden tables, and the cigarette smoke is too much for the air conditioners to handle.

We retire to a quiet restaurant with fine service, very cheap by Australian standards. The menu is mind-blowing. Philippine cuisine is an exotic, spicy blend of native, Southeast Asian, Chinese, and Spanish influences. Dishes are elaborate, spiced with tangy flavors, and tempered with rice. Traditional *lechon*, pig roasted on a spit

over hot charcoal, is popular. *Halu-halo* is a favorite dessert—a rich concoction of several Philippine fruits, sweetened beans, and other ingredients, piled in a glass, topped by crushed ice, and laced with milk.

"Strawberries thrive in the mountain climate, and a dollar will buy a basketful"

Manila is very twentieth-century, with modern skyscrapers, fine tourist accommodation, hurried pace, fashionably dressed youth, and, unfortunately, slum districts and pollution. Lunetta Park, on Manila Bay, offers some escape. A path runs beside a neat line of young coconut trees, stretching for over a mile along the bay, and often paced by joggers. People picnic on the thin lawns under the trees, overflowing in places into the burning sunshine.

In the ruins of Fort Santiago, hundreds of years of Spanish rule come to mind. The stone walls, eroded now, are surrounded by well-kept gardens. People walk silently and respectfully through the relics, noticing the plaque, painting, and tributes to national hero, José Risal, whose writings and subsequent execution by the Spanish in 1896 fostered the cause of Philippine nationalism and independence.

To escape the clatter of the city we make the trip up the mountains to Baguio, the former summer capital and "city of pines." It is about six hours' drive from Manila. The transition from urban to rural scene is almost instantaneous: behind us the city is hazy, blurred and distorted by the smog and oily heat. Along bumpy roads we meet modern Japanese cars, old rusting buses, overloaded trucks, tricycles, bicycles, carts, and jeepneys. I'm happy not to be driving.

We pass multitudes of roadside stands and ramshackle *sari-sari* stores. The checkered pattern of green rice fields predominates, with patches of sugar cane, tobacco, corn, and other vegetables reflecting the fertility of the densely settled lowlands. Bananas and sweet potato vines seem to grow everywhere in the Philippine countryside. Occasionally there's a *carabao* (water buffalo) at work in the fields.

The road becomes narrow and hazardous as it winds upward into the cool mountains, skirting picturesque gorges and streams. Craggy mountains glare yellow and green-brown in the sun. Around a corner we meet a huge, weathered lion's head, carved out of rock and perched alone by the roadside, high above a tree-clad ravine. Recently painted eyes, as large as archery targets, and fangs the size of a child, must have required quite a climbing feat. Later we stop at a park with ornamental and pine trees, and lunch on preboiled rice, sweet bread, pork, chicken, vegetables, corn on the cob, boiled peanuts, pineapple, and soft drinks.

In the Baguio markets, fine craftwork sells at much lower prices than in Manila. Strawberries thrive in the mountain climate, and a dollar will buy a basketful. Jams are dirt cheap and we load up with them. We buy necklaces of the exquisitely perfumed sampagita national flower from a young Igorot (mountain people) girl with a charming smile.

As we journey back to Manila the sticky heat greets us; it seems to get hotter every few miles. We cannot wait to get out of it again, to explore other rural areas. Our travels take us to Laguna province, with its large, freshwater lake where we watch a man walking out along rickety planks to feed his fish, farmed in cages of bamboo sticks, nets, and wire.

If nothing else makes an impact on the visitor to Laguna, or indeed to most other provinces, the vast coconut plantations should. The land around the lake is covered with a forest of coconut trees, almost as far as the eye can see. Everything else seems secondary, huts and dwellings blending into the green-yellow environment. We stop and buy a drink at a roadside stand; a grinning boy slices the tops off each green coconut with one or two nimble strokes of his *bolo* (a type of machete). Nearby, in the shade (not of a coconut tree—people have been killed by falling nuts), two young men study their chess game.

Not only is the coconut a source of food and drink, but it also provides income-producing copra (dried kernels) and coconut oil. Stacks of stripped and plaited leaves are used for thatch, craftware, hats, mats, fans . . . the possibilities are endless. Souvenirs and utensils are made from the shells. The fibrous husks are turned into rope and matting or used for fuel. Even the tree sap is used, fermented into a powerful liquor.

Beaches, within a few hours' drive from Manila, are idyllic: sun-bleached, creamy sand and inviting, turquoise sea against an evergreen, tropical backdrop where butterflies chase one another among the gold or pink and white, sweet-scented frangipani blooms. I am only slightly taken aback when we have to stop and pay for these privileges at a toll-gate along the road leading to the beach.

"I suddenly realize that this is dangerous—I cannot move because of the crowd and confusion around me"

Almost everywhere outside the commercial areas I see poultry, in particular slim roosters which look like hens because their red combs and wattles have been removed, streamlining the birds for the notorious *sabong* (cockfighting). The gamecocks are secured in safe, shady spots by string attached to a leg, or are held, stroked, and fussed over, by their masters. Cockfighting, though the brochures won't mention it, is the most popular indigenous sport.

One Sunday morning I am taken to a cockpit arena somewhere in the hills near Quezon City. In a large, grassy clearing among towering trees and dilapidated sheds, the cocks and their owners gather. The stench of droppings is overpowering and the crowing continuous. I am carried, wheelchair and all, by several men (they are all men here) eager to lend a hand, and placed within yards of two speckled cocks which are held back by their owners. A razor-sharp gaff, an inch or more long, is tied to a leg of each cock. Hundreds of boisterous onlookers clamor for action.

The cocks, fighting with beak and spur, come my way, and I suddenly realize that this is dangerous—I cannot move because of the crowd and confusion around me. For seconds that seem like eternity the cocks deliver their death-blows right beside my chair. I am out of the arena before the next fight.

"Be prepared to see some sights which the tourist board won't advertise"

Access can be difficult for people with substantial physical disabilities in the Philippines, mainly as a result of the sheer weight of numbers of other human beings, but also because of the lack of smoothly paved footpaths and the absence of any special concessions—no special buses or taxis, no specially designed rest rooms. The lot of disabled Philippine people is a tough one: there are no disability benefits, and aids such as wheelchairs are expensive and hard to come by. Poor beggars in rags with obvious disabilities are sure to be encountered—be prepared to see some sights which the tourist board won't advertise.

But the disabled tourist's problems are not insurmountable; I saw and experienced as much as the average able-bodied visitor to the Philippines. I had the advantage of living with a Filipino family, although this was important more for learning about the country than for overcoming obstacles as a severely disabled person. Foreigners, including disabled ones, are inexplicably given film-star status, so you can forget problems of disability-induced prejudice. Philippine people told me: "We look at what a person is like inside rather than outside." Disability never seemed so irrelevant. I was received everywhere with unselfish hospitality, smiles, genuine concern, and a courteous desire to please which helped me to forget any aches and pains, and to feel comfortably free of self-consciousness.

Hong Kong & Macau

The Pied Piper of Fushan

Sue Kelley is disabled by an MS-type virus, and uses a wheelchair. She has traveled a good deal, with the help of her husband, Tony, and daughter, Joanne. In 1988 they booked places on Kuoni's "Asian Adventure Holiday," and here Sue describes their experiences in Hong Kong, Macau, and China.

Descending into Hong Kong airport was quite a nerve-racking experience. The plane sank down amidst the rooftops of Kowloon, past laundry hung on poles protruding from windows, and landed on a runway built on reclaimed land which projects into the harbor (Hong Kong is Chinese for "Fragrant Harbor"). The airport itself held no problems for the wheelchair: once we had been whisked through customs and immigration the *Kuoni* courier escorted us to a waiting bus for the journey to our hotel.

An array of shops flashed by the bus windows, their neon signs coming alive as darkness drew in. Much of Hong Kong is vertical, so the few areas of flat land are crammed with buildings which seem to reach endlessly into the sky. Our hotel was in the busy Kowloon peninsula, surrounded by other hotels, nightclubs, bars, and shops. The room allocated to us was large and accommodated the three of us adequately.

Beyond Kowloon are the New Territories which extend to the frontiers of mainland China; here the colony changes character from industrial complexes and new suburbs to duck farms and banana plantations. By far the best-known region, and containing a quarter of the total population, is Hong Kong Island.

The most interesting and cheapest way to get from Kowloon to Hong Kong Island is by *Star Ferry*, which has excellent, clearly marked access for wheelchairs on the second-class deck. The mass of buildings as we approached the Island made a spectacular urban vista, and the cacophony of the busy harbor was thrilling.

Our main aim in Hong Kong was to enjoy the hustle and bustle of shopping. Taxis were very cheap and the drivers most courteous; they never objected to putting the wheelchair in the trunk. In the shops, sales staff rushed to open doors, which saved a lot of trapped fingers when maneuvering through the entrance. Ramps were frequently provided and we often gained access via dropped curbs, designed to allow easy movement of goods in and out of the shops.

We did try public transit on one occasion, boarding a free bus to the *Peak Tram* funicular railroad which climbs straight up the mountainside to Victoria Peak (on Hong Kong Island). The driver assisted us on and off the bus, and at the funicular station we were boarded in a special compartment equipped to carry wheelchair-bound passengers. The train ride was rapid and at the summit we alighted into a shopping area from which elevators took us up to the viewing platform. We could see all over Hong Kong. It was very windy on the platform, so we descended to the shops, bought ourselves sweaters and then returned to watch darkness fall and the neon lights spring into action on the skyline.

We took the hydrofoil from Hong Kong to Macau, the last bastion of Portugal's sixteenth-century empire. Access to the hydrofoil was ramped, and once aboard I was able to sit with Tony and Joanne while my chair was stowed beside the seats. The journey took about an hour; we were met by a courier and taken by bus to our hotel for lunch before a tour of the island.

Macau is famous for its casinos, open 24 hours a day, and handily surrounded by pawn shops. As the bus wound through the streets we could not help being impressed by the elegance of the houses we passed. On Macau's highest point is the Penha Roman Catholic church, and from this vantage point we looked down over the island, the harbor, and the bridge— about a mile-and-a-half long—which connects Macau with the island of Taipa. In the harbor an ornate dragon boat lies alongside the maritime museum; access for wheelchairs is limited to the first floor in the museum but it's well worth a visit.

We were taken to view the Buddhist temple in the harbor known as "Matock the Goddess of Ama," where we learned the origins of the name Macau: Ama is the goddess of fisherfolk, and *cau* means "bay" in Portuguese; the island

was originally called Amacau. This mixture of Eastern and Western culture, epitomized by the ruins of St. Paul's church, with its facade of saints, Chinese dragons, and Portuguese *caravela,* can be observed throughout the island.

We returned to the hotel for our evening meal, after which the three of us decided to take a stroll around the town center. The streets are cobblestoned and quite steep, so it was hard work for Tony who was pushing the wheelchair, but we did find some ramps. Tourist shops mingled with the local hardware, herbalist, and noodle stands.

Seventeen fellow tourists joined us in the hotel foyer the next day for our trip into China. The bus took us to the Barrier Gate, erected more than a century ago, which separates Macau from the People's Republic of China. We had to get off with all our luggage and we were each given a numbered badge; these numbers were stuck on the fronts of our passports. Particular attention was paid to the number of cameras carried by each tourist and on return they made sure that we brought out the same number.

"I got out and sat on the floor while the children took turns to sit in the chair"

After passing through the gate we were met by three Chinese: Yen and Kathy—our guides—and the bus driver. The bus was large and comfortable, with two refrigerators which we could use to keep drinks or edibles cool. Tony helped me into the front seat of the bus alongside Joanne, while the driver placed the wheelchair in front of the seat opposite for easy access. Everyone was helpful to us on entering and leaving the bus—not once were we left to struggle on our own.

Despite the fact that there are no privately owned motor vehicles in China (all belong to the state or to arge corporations), the roads were quite congested. We passed through a countryside of duck farms, paddy fields, and fruit plantations, stopping in the village of Yongmai to see how the people live and work in a farming commune. The home of one of the farm leaders was spartan compared to Western homes, stone-built with a tiled roof, and no washing machine or other labor-saving appliances. Cooking was on an open fire and the lounge contained wooden benches along one wall. I was unable to go upstairs but those who did reported clean but bare rooms.

We saw the workers in the fields, one woman with a baby strapped to her back as she hoed. Moving on to the village school for children aged three to seven years, we were surprised to see that they did not wear a school uniform. They were playing games in the playground but stopped to stare at us, regarding me in particular as though I had arrived from outer space. Kathy told me that I was the first wheelchair-bound person she had brought on this tour and that the children were not used to seeing disabled people out and about. I got out and sat on the floor while the children took turns to sit in the chair, but they would not be pushed in it.

Our next stop was the memorial house of Doctor Sun Yat-Sen, the founder of the Chinese Republic. Referred to by the Chinese as the "Father of China," he is credited with freeing the people from feudalism. Photographs and documents tell the story of this physician who trained in the USA and became a revolutionary statesman. It was interesting to learn that his medical knowledge helped to change traditional practices such as the binding of girls' feet. Once again I was restricted to the first floor but as most of the information was here I didn't miss much.

Lunch was served in the *Zongshan International Hotel*. The dining room was elegantly furnished and the meal consisted of seven courses accompanied by beer or orange juice, followed by Chinese tea. Fushan—a city famous for its silk and porcelain—was to be our next stop for the night, and here the dinner consisted of yet another seven courses. The food is not my best memory of this vacation—I often wished I'd brought some supplies with me, along with some silverware, as my limited hand movements turned eating with chopsticks into a major feat.

"On looking up from my writing I was astonished to find myself surrounded by a sea of smiling faces"

After dinner Yen and Kathy took us on a walk to the village store where they sold food on the first floor, trinkets upstairs. The stairs were very steep, so I opted to stay put among some floral displays and write my postcards while the others went to browse. On looking up from my writing I was astonished to find myself surrounded by a sea of smiling faces.

My first thought was that I must look very odd writing with a pen stuffed inside a foam bicycle-handle grip, but once joined by Kathy and Yen I learned that it was the wheelchair again attracting attention. The crowd numbered well over a hundred, and as the store closed and I was reunited with the rest of the group we were amazed to find these Chinese people falling in behind us, more adding to their number as we walked back to the hotel. Several of our group took photographs of the scene, which must have resembled the Pied Piper in a wheelchair.

After leaving the hotel around 9am we stopped at Fushan's art and craft workshop, where we observed the workers making lanterns and paper sculptures, and painting scrolls; the finished products were available for purchase. The silk factory was next, its antiquated appearance and work methods reminiscent of conditions in English mills in the late 1800s. The silk was on sale for approximately $3.50 a yard.

"In China the drive to separate the visitor from his foreign currency was much in evidence"

We arrived in Canton, or Guangzhou as it's locally known, in time for lunch. The biggest city in Southern China, Canton straddles the Pearl river and teems with people and bicycles. At peak times the cyclists sit in silent traffic jams that make the jams in our cities look like minor hold-ups. After eating at the *Guangzhou Restaurant* we walked to the local market which sold fish for ornamental ponds, as well as food in the form of livestock (live being the operative word), including snakes, frogs, chickens, cats, dogs, ducks, and what looked like maggots! Many of these items had featured on our tables at previous meals, and the more sentimental among us were pleased to clamber back on board our bus, heading for the zoo.

We had hoped to see the pandas at the zoo, but only one emerged briefly from his house. As compensation we did see some beautiful white peacocks. The zoo is situated on a hillside, which makes hard work for wheelchair pushers. Tony was fortunate that Yen took turns with him, enabling me to see more than might have been possible on our own.

It was late afternoon when we arrived at our hotel, *The White Swan*, which is a world showpiece. As we entered, a waterfall cascaded from the fourth floor down into an ornamental pool surrounded by jade statues and pagodas; a jade tree, about six feet tall with large peaches hanging from its branches, graced one side. After our evening meal Kathy and Yen walked us

to a local park for a cultural show, a form of opera with colorful costumes. On the way back to the hotel we watched the activity on the busy Pearl river.

The next morning our bus deposited us at the train station, where checking of passports and baggage was slow but we eventually found ourselves aboard the train bound for Hong Kong. I was transferred to a reclining seat beside Tony and Joanne; the wheelchair was stowed behind us. The compartment was clean and smart, complete with a TV set.

The journey back to Kowloon gave us a final glimpse of China, and time for reflection on the diversities that we had observed during this brief visit. In China the drive to separate the visitor from his foreign currency was much in evidence and almost certainly accounts for the many stops in shops and factories on our tour, although the sales methods used were more subtle than the high-pressure techniques used in Hong Kong. We wondered whether the takeover in 1997 would affect the huge gulf between rich and poor in Hong Kong—our impression was that in China everyone shared life's basics, and while they were materially poor in our eyes we saw no evidence of abject poverty or starvation. Admittedly, however, the tour was designed so that we had little free time to wander, and those who did found that one of the couriers followed them and guided them back to the fold.

On re-entering high-tech Hong Kong we felt we had passed through a time-warp, leaving China's utilitarian state behind us. Our visit left us with much to ponder, and a desire to return and perhaps consider the gains or losses made on either side—in terms of wealth, lifestyle, and individual liberty—when the dust settles after 1997.

China

Fame at Last

For Betty Layton and her husband, John, the festive season of 1987 was a Christmas with a difference: no slaving over a hot stove or mountains of dirty dishes; instead they went to China on a three-week *Kuoni* tour, from Peking (Beijing) in the freezing north to Canton (Guangzhou) in the subtropical south, with suitable clothing packed for the extremes of weather and Betty's spare artificial leg in the hand baggage.

We set off on a *British Airways* flight from Heathrow on December 19, leaving behind a bewildered family. The wheelchair service and pre-boarding were excellent as usual, and we enjoyed every moment of the flight. During our waking time we were visited by Julia, the young *Kuoni* rep who was kept busy seeking out and introducing herself to all 21 members of our group. Julia was superb—helpful, diplomatic, wise beyond her years, and calm whenever disaster threatened.

Next day at noon, we arrived in Hong Kong where we stretched our leg(s) before taking off for Peking. Getting into China is a slow process. We all had a number stuck to the cover of our passports and had to line up strictly in order at immigration; this was the only identification recognizable by the very young soldiers who stared at our passports and at us, trying to match both with their visa lists. My

wheelchair had been sent to meet the wrong plane and there was—with a shrug of resigned shoulders—nothing to be done about it. I had to walk every inch of the way, and very long it was, too, up and down stairs and slopes to the luggage carousel. John and I were numbers 3 and 4 in the group, so the immigration line did not move until we arrived!

The drive from the airport to the hotel kept us awake. It was fascinating—bicycles by the thousand, most cyclists and pedestrians wearing mouth and nose masks. We arrived exhausted at our hotel at 5pm, only to be told to meet at 6pm for dinner. From this moment we were conditioned to early meals, early starts, and not a minute wasted. We were met in the foyer and taken by bus to the *Sun Park Restaurant*. By this time it was dark and the bikes were still weaving about—no lights!

Our first dinner in Peking taught us that if hungry we had better learn the art of using chopsticks (take your own chopsticks, by the way—some wooden ones are very dubious). The Chinese called us the "Group of 21" and we always had two large tables, with a turntable in the center. The food whizzed around and if we were lucky we managed to grab a passing morsel with our chopsticks. Small dishes of appetizers were ready on the turntable as we sat down; then the main meat, fish, shellfish, and vegetable dishes arrived, followed by rice and then soup! Fruit or sweet cakes came next, and throughout the meal tea, soft drinks, or beer were served. Each course was served and whipped away quite quickly, and a great pile of hot face cloths were usually brought to the table for a clean-up half way through the meal.

"The tombs, regalia, and artifacts were well worth the effort of climbing 91 steps"

On most tours, hotels are not known until arrival in a particular town. All ours were Westernized, with *en suite* facilities, and the only advice I can give is to ask for a room near an elevator (some corridors seem very long at the end of a day's sightseeing). Perhaps fortunately, we did not stay in ordinary Chinese hotels or lodging houses. Apart from breakfast we rarely ate in our hotels; it seemed that we were to be shown as much as possible by having lunches and dinners in different places each day. We were often given a separate room in restaurants, which was a pity. There were large Thermoses of hot water and tea bags in our rooms, so we could make tea at all times. Drinking water could also be provided.

The *CITS* (*China International Travel Service*) agents met us and took charge in each location, settling our program with Julia. In Peking, two young girls, one of whom was a student guide practicing her English, took us to the Ming Tombs. We approached them through the Sacred Way and the Avenue of the Animals, lined with massive statues of real and mythical beasts, along which the Ming Emperors were carried to their tombs. The visit was well within my capabilities, and the tombs, regalia, and artifacts were well worth the effort of climbing 91 steps.

On to the Great Wall, special parts of whose enormous length are easily accessible. From here you can walk for miles in either direction, with extensive views over the hills. The slopes were difficult for me, and it was cold and windy, but I managed to get to the famous section where Queen Elizabeth had had her photograph taken in the fall of 1987.

Back in Peking, the Forbidden City was the site of a splendid tour which took two hours, yet we did not see all the temples, palaces, and museums. The exhibitions of clothes, carriages, and furniture were well set out and we were left to view at our own pace, then met and taken to the next sight. After this came the now-infamous Tiananmen Square, with the Great Hall of the People on one side. As we walked around, astonished at its vastness, we were being stared at, long and hard. We got used to this in time, but it was quite disconcerting at first. Many Chinese, especially those from the country districts, had never seen Westerners before and they think we are so ugly—large noses, protruding eyes, and queer-shaped faces!

After a Peking Duck Banquet on our last night, we left very early the next day for Xian. We were to go by military plane but the fog came down and we were stranded in the spartan surroundings of the military airfield buildings. The authorities certainly did not lose face—they sent us to a brand new hotel nearby (it seemed to be for the exclusive use of the high-ranking army and airforce personnel) and we were given the best meal of our stay in China.

The fog eventually lifted and we took off for Xian. Airport wheelchair service does not exist for internal flights in

China, nor does pre-boarding. However, we always managed to get to the plane before it left! On the flight we were given tea, orange juice, chocolate cookies, a half-pound packet of wafers, a model airplane, and a souvenir bag! We decided that the military personnel were trying to outdo the civilian airlines. On our journeys throughout China we were inundated with gifts—key-rings, brooches, postcards by the packet—and fruit, drinks, cookies, and chocolates were always available on boats, trains, and aircraft.

The tour of the Terracotta Army site was the high spot of our visit to Xian. Once again we were left to wander around the huge building (about the size of a football field) which has been erected over the "army." One end is set out with the repaired army figures and horses in rows; across the middle are the sections they are working on—with a leg, an arm, and the odd hand being painstakingly excavated from the mounds of soil and rock.

"Gin and tonic has never tasted so good out of plastic film cartons"

From Xian we were scheduled to fly to Nanjing, but the Chinese had "forgotten" to tell *Kuoni* that the flights did not operate in winter. The alternative was to travel overnight and most of the next day by train. The *CITS* agent vanished into thin air, leaving Julia to sort this out—no mean feat as they hadn't booked enough sleepers for us. There was quite a fight, with Julia holding her own against a barrage of objections from the sleeping car guardian, the cook, guards, and all manner of officials. A delightful, English-speaking Chinese wife of a professor came to Julia's rescue and it was finally sorted out with Julia paying excess for the sleepers and for the meals that they "forgot" to book.

As it was Christmas Eve, the Group of 21 celebrated in the appropriate style once the battle was won. Glasses were

at a premium, and gin and tonic has never tasted so good out of plastic film cartons. We were determined to make the cook work for the extra payment he had received, so we bravely faced his wobbly eggs and toast on Christmas morning. Getting on and off trains could be a problem, but there is always a "mounting block" and plenty of hand-rails and helping hands.

In Nanjing we went to Sun Yat-Sen's Mausoleum which I viewed from a distance (392 steps). The founder and first president of the Chinese Communist Republic, Doctor Sun Yat-Sen lived in several different cities and each *CITS* agent gave us a potted history of his life, showing us the houses he lived in and offering us a number of different dates for his death. We saw the two-tier road and rail bridge over the Yangtze and went up by elevator to look down on the river's busy traffic. We took a short train trip to Wuxi, a delightful town.

While waiting for our trains we always found ourselves in the first-class waiting rooms with high ranking Chinese but no "ordinary travelers," of which there were hundreds. We were ushered out of the waiting room as the train approached and settled in a special car. When we moved from place to place we put our luggage outside our hotel rooms and it appeared as if by magic at the next hotel. It received quite rough treatment, but nothing was lost apart from a few straps and handles.

In Wuxi, on Sunday morning, we were taken to a student college where the teenage students and their families were taking part in a song, dance, and magic performance on a makeshift stage. The Chinese laugh hysterically and enjoy any performing act; they shuffled along the benches to make room for us to join in the fun. They all wanted to practice their English, and Julia was persuaded to ask us up onto the stage where we sang "Jingle Bells"—they were very polite and clapped enthusiastically. As we were leaving, they crowded around, eager to hear about Western housing, shopping, work, school—every conceivable aspect of life, in fact.

In the afternoon we embarked on a journey along the Grand Canal to Soochow. I worry about leaping aboard boats with my artificial leg, but from sampans to hovercraft the crews have always made light of my problems and been most helpful. From the canal we saw a real slice of Chinese life: old houses line the canal and the dwellers wash their clothes and fish in it; the barges, piled high with vegetables, reeds, bricks, and other commodities, are skillfully steered in long "trains," missing bridges and other boats by inches. They simply push each other out of the way with long poles—us, too, when we were in their way.

"Very young children walking in single file pointed at us in the bus and exploded with laughter"

Soochow is another fascinating town. We visited landscaped classical gardens, all beautifully kept, with courtyards, little bridges, pools, and gazebos; lovely trees, flowers, and bonsai trees. They are very peaceful and have attractive names—The Humble Administrator's Garden, the Lingering Garden, the Fishermen's Garden. We went on to a sandalwood fan factory and to the Institute of Embroidery where we saw exquisite work in progress, using minute stitches. No wonder nearly all the workers in the dimly lit rooms needed glasses—or soon will.

Another train journey took us to Shanghai, a very different city, packed with twelve million people. A bus trip of two miles took us at least an hour, sometimes more, and the congestion on sidewalks, streets, and bike lanes was accepted as normal by the Chinese. The traffic was either stationary or just creeping along, and this gave us wonderful opportunities to observe life in the city.

Laundry was hanging from lines stretched from upper windows to trees on the roadside. The bicycles and carts (drawn by men and women) groaned under mountains of goods. The only people with cars are high-ranking officials; there are lots of taxis and the government owns them too. Very young children walking in single file pointed at us in the bus and exploded with laughter; our progress was so slow that they passed us again and again, with renewed laughter each time.

We were taken to the Zhing Zua commune, just outside Shanghai, which has its own shops, schools, smallholdings, and hospital. We were astonished to be shown the treatment rooms in the hospital—heaving with patients, lying head to toe on benches around the room, with needles in various parts of their anatomy. The camera fiends among us really got going! Doctors, nurses, and patients all took our visit with bland equanimity. In the pharmacy small quantities of dried herbs, bugs, and caterpillars were being weighed into brown paper packets, to be boiled up by patients into a sort of infusion—a truly different world.

From Shanghai we flew to Guilin, where Julia was delighted to find an old *CITS* friend and, unusually, another official from Canton. She never knew who was meeting us at each destination; they seemed to vary the agents for each tour—some were most cooperative, some a little awkward! It was New Year's Eve and we were handed invitations to a special dinner and official entertainment that evening in Guilin.

The day was spent on the Li river, admiring its extraordinary scenery—conical hills and mountains, riverside villages, bamboo rafts, water buffalo, and cormorant fishermen. Lunch on board was Mongolian hotpot, which was quite hard work: we had to cook everything ourselves in a large dish of boiling water kept hot over charcoal—one pot to every half-dozen people. We cooked bits of chicken, fish, meat, vegetables, and beans, and at the end drank the broth—it was a challenge and a change. (Which reminds me, some public rest rooms in the East are only holes in the ground, and balancing can be very tricky with an artificial leg, but hotels, restaurants, and, surprisingly, boats and many trains have Western-style toilets.)

"We were on TV, in the newspapers and were wined and dined until we were giddy"

We flew from Guilin to Canton on New Year's Day and began to realize why the Canton *CITS* agent had been dogging our steps. We were given numbered envelopes on the flight and told to remain on the plane until all the other passengers had left, then disembark in number order. Looking through the plane windows we could see a troupe of dancing girls with feather fans, a band, and a group of officials. A large banner proclaimed that we were the "First Group to Arrive in Canton on New Year's Day in the Most Auspicious Year of the Dragon—1988!"

On leaving the plane we felt like royalty. The band played, the girls danced, the TV cameras whirred, and we were introduced one by one (in number order) to the city officials. Our envelopes contained invitations to various celebrations which went on during our two-day stay. We were on TV, in the newspapers (they presented us with copies and photographs to take home), and were wined and dined until we were giddy.

We also found time for some interesting visits in Canton: a jade factory; the 5000-seat Sun Yat-Sen Memorial Hall; a granite sculpture of five goats, the city emblem of Canton (quite a climb); the Temple of the Six Banyan Trees which is the seat of the Buddhist Society of Canton; and the truly beautiful Chen Clan Classical Learning Academy gardens and temples, desecrated during the Cultural Revolution but now being restored.

Our last dinner was preceded by a cocktail party given by *Kuoni* in the Songbird Room (real birds) of the *White Swan Hotel*. The next day we boarded the train to Hong Kong and after a few days to recover from some 3000 miles of travel in China, flew home to London. Christmas and New Year will never be the same again.

THE FAR EAST: TRAVEL NOTES

Sources of Information

Hong Kong Tourist Association, 548 Fifth Avenue, New York, NY 10036-5092; ☎212/869-5008. It's good to find a tourist office that distributes, free of charge, a regularly updated booklet for disabled travelers. *A Guide for Physically Handicapped Visitors to Hong Kong*, the latest edition of which was published in May 1991, covers 273 sites, including banks, shops, hotels, restaurants, movie theaters and performing arts centers, museums, leisure and recreational facilities, and has a useful section on transportation. The research was undertaken by a working group set up by the *Joint Council for the Physically and Mentally Disabled*, and the criteria for determining accessibility are explained in full. As well as the wheelchair symbol there are notes giving additional access information.

Singapore Tourist Promotion Board, 590 Fifth Avenue, 12th Floor, New York, NY 10036 (☎212/302-4861); 8484 Wilshire Boulevard, Suite 510, Beverly Hills, CA 90211 (☎213/852-1901); 175 Bloor Street East, Suite 1112, North Tower, Toronto ON M4W 3R8 (☎416/323-9139). Another tourist office with current information for disabled visitors. The third edition (1991) of *Access Singapore*, a project of the *Singapore Council of Social Service* (11 Penang Lane, Singapore 0923; ☎336-1544), is pretty much the same as the 1989 edition, apart from the short list of new buildings such as Changi airport Terminal 2 (fully accessible) and some name changes for hotels that have come under different management. It is similar in layout to the Hong Kong guide and covers hotels, hospitals, places of interest, shops, libraries, movie theaters—every sort of building you are likely to visit; the one important omission is that there's nothing on transport.

National Tourist Office of the Philippines, 556 Fifth Avenue, New York, NY 10036; ☎212/575-7915. No information for disabled visitors, except that all luxury hotels in Manila are equipped with ramped front and back entrances, public rest rooms designed for disabled persons, grab handles in bath tubs, wider doors to bedrooms and bathrooms, and designated rooms with key controls such as light and air-conditioning switches at wheelchair height—great if you can afford luxury prices. The *National Council for the Welfare of Disabled Persons* (2nd Floor, Philippine Sugar Center Annex Building, North Avenue, Diliman, Quezon City; ☎73/961165) may be able to help with specific inquiries.

China National Tourist Office, 60 East 42nd Street, New York, NY 10165 (☎212/867-0271); 333 West Broadway, Suite 201, Glendale, CA 91204 (☎818/545-7505). The effect of Tiananmen Square has been reversed, and tourist numbers are on the increase again, but there is no information for disabled visitors; tourist office staff advises that travel in China is very difficult for disabled people and there are no facilities for them.

Macau Tourist Information Bureau, 608 Fifth Avenue, Suite 309, New York, NY 10020 (☎212/581-7465); 3133 Lake Hollywood Drive, Los Angeles, CA 90068 (☎213/851-3402); 1530 West 8th Avenue, #305, Vancouver BC V6J 1T5 (☎604/736-1095). General brochures only but staff is helpful, and will attempt to obtain answers to specific inquiries from head office (*Macau Government Tourist Office*, PO Box 3006, Macau; ☎77218 or 375156). The Director says frankly that "Macau is short of proper facilities for the needs of the disabled, either concerning buildings or thoroughfares, or social integration." But he is hopeful that things will get better: there are some accessible hotels, and new ones are supposed to be built to comply with a law that governs "suppression of architectural hindrances"; The Forum—where the main festivals and conventions take place—is equipped with ramps at the entrance, accessible rest rooms, and good access throughout the building.

Tourism Authority of Thailand (TAT), 5 World Trade Center, Suite 2449, New York, NY 10048 (☎212/432-0433); 3440 Wilshire Boulevard, Suite 1101, Los Angeles, CA 90010 (☎213/382-2353); Eastern Canada rep, 250 Clair Avenue West, #307, Toronto ON M4V 1R6 (☎416/925-9329). Thailand's tourism industry has suffered two setbacks in the last few years: first, the AIDS epidemic took off in 1988—

THE FAR EAST: TRAVEL NOTES

cause unacknowledged, but fear of frightening off the tourists probably accounted for the government's failure to devote resources and personnel to a consistent campaign to raise public awareness of the threat of AIDS, particularly during 1987, "Visit Thailand Year"—and then the media coverage of the massacre of unarmed demonstrators by government troops in Bangkok in May 1992. A few months later, the tourism promotion machine was in full swing, with *TAT* working overtime to restore Thailand's image, but visitors with disabilities are apparently not being targeted—there are no glossy brochures for them.

Indonesian Tourist Promotion Office, 3457 Wilshire Boulevard, Los Angeles, CA 90010; ☎213/387-2078. As with Thailand, media coverage of bloodshed and repression has damaged the tourist industry, and the provision of information for disabled visitors is an unlikely event for the forseeable future.

Tour Operators

Depending on the destination (Singapore, Hong Kong, and Bangkok cause least consternation), operators may balk at the prospect of accepting a wheelchair user, or even someone with limited walking capacity, into their tour group—they consider the obstacles too great, particularly for an elderly, inexperienced, or unaccompanied traveler. But, with a bit of persuasion, some will take the plunge.

Betty Layton has had previous experience of traveling with *Kuoni*, and was delighted with their very capable rep on her Chinese tour. It seems that although first-time inquirers may receive a polite refusal from *Kuoni* for certain destinations, if you persist and build up experience you might be treated to a more positive response.

The greater freedom of **independent travel**, however, can be more rewarding (and cheaper) than either group tours or tailor-made packages. Searching out your own style of hotel, using local drivers and guides means that you make arrangements that suit you rather than the tour operator. Whether the headaches outweigh the rewards is very much a matter of individual taste.

Getting There

It's well worth shopping around for the best **air fares**; most of the major carriers flying routes to Asia from North America can cope smoothly with wheelchair users or other disabled passengers, so it's a matter of choosing something to suit your schedule and your bank account. Whoever you fly with, however, journey times from North America are long (*Cathay Pacific* flies Los Angeles to Hong Kong in nearly sixteen hours, from Vancouver in thirteen), economy-class seating is cramped, and even specially adapted rest rooms are not big enough for comfort. Prepare to wake up on your first morning in the Far East feeling stiff and very tired.

The major **US and Canadian airlines** that fly to Asia and should give good service include *United* (most flights are out of San Francisco, one goes direct to Hong Kong but most are routed through Tokyo, Japan; there are also direct flights to Tokyo from Chicago and New York; from Tokyo you can fly on to Beijing, Shanghai, Bangkok, and Singapore, or via Taiwan to Manila; you can also fly to Manila via Seoul from San Francisco); *Delta* (from Los Angeles to Hong Kong via Anchorage, Alaska; from Portland to Bangkok via Seoul and Taiwan; a few flights to Japan from Portland or Los Angeles); *Northwest* (direct from Seattle to Beijing, and on to Shanghai; to Hong Kong from New York, Los Angeles, or Seattle with one stop, and from Memphis with two stops; from Detroit to Singapore with one stop; to Bangkok from San Francisco or Los Angeles with one stop, from Memphis with two; to Manila from Chicago or Seattle with one stop, from Boston or Memphis with two stops); *Continental* (one direct flight from Seattle to Tokyo, but otherwise their Pacific route system radiates from three main hubs—Honolulu, and the islands of Guam and Saipan in the Marianas; there are flights into Honolulu from Houston, Denver, Los Angeles, San Francisco, and Vancouver; from Honolulu you can travel on direct to Manila, or via Guam to several destinations, including Denpasar, Bali); *Canadian* (Vancouver direct to Hong Kong, and on to Bangkok; direct to Tokyo from Toronto, Edmonton, or Vancouver); *Air Canada* (from Vancouver, direct to Hong Kong

THE FAR EAST: TRAVEL NOTES

and Seoul, to Bangkok with two stops, to Singapore with one stop; from Toronto there are one- or two-stop flights to Bangkok, Hong Kong, and Kuala Lumpur.

You can also expect good service from several of the **national airlines** of the region, including *Air Lanka, Cathay Pacific, Singapore Airlines*, and *Thai Airways International*; remember also that *British Airways*, another safe choice for disabled passengers, flies from Hong Kong to Beijing and Shanghai. It might be wise to avoid *Garuda (Indonesian) Airlines*, which assured Veronica Smith that aisle carry-chairs would be available on all flights, that seats had been reserved near the rest rooms, and that arrangements had been made to transfer her safely from one plane to the next. There were no carry-chairs, and Veronica and her companions had great difficulty obtaining seats near the rest rooms. Getting on and off the planes involved shuffling up flights of steps, being carried without a carry-chair or, on one occasion, entering the plane via a food conveyor belt which deposited them on the wet floor of a refrigerated food truck, where they waited until the truck was raised to the level of the aircraft door. The Indonesian staff were polite, cheerful and well meaning, but that was the only positive comment made in Veronica's subsequent letter of complaint to Garuda's head office in Jakarta. After a lengthy correspondence with Jakarta, the matter was dealt with more efficiently by the London office, and each member of Veronica's group received £100 in compensation. A better way to reach Bali would be to fly with *Cathay Pacific* from Hong Kong (nonstop, about five hours), or *Continental* (see above).

Airport facilities vary from basic but adequate (as in Bali) to good, with wheelchair-accessible rest rooms, elevators, ramps, and reserved parking (as at Hong Kong International, Changi Singapore, and Narita International Tokyo). At Seoul, in South Korea, scene of the 1988 Paralympics, the elevators are provided with buttons and information panels at wheelchair height and coded in Braille.

Disembarking from international flights is usually by air-bridge or lifting vehicle, but be prepared to be carried off in Bali and if flying shorter hops such as Singapore to Bangkok.

Transport

Facilities for disabled passengers are confined to parts of the Hong Kong and Japanese **public transit** networks: a Dial-a-Ride service during off-peak hours and at weekends in Hong Kong; boarding and toilet facilities for disabled travelers on the Kowloon–Canton railroad; special compartment for wheelchair passengers on the funicular train to Victoria Peak (Hong Kong Island); accessible second-class (lower) deck on the Hong Kong Island–Kowloon *Star Ferry*; ramped access to the Hong Kong–Macau hydrofoil; some facilities for disabled passengers on parts of Japan's train network—including the installation of tiny cubicles for passengers in wheelchairs in several cars of the Japan Bullet Train, as one British traveler puts it, "so that wheelchair users can sit in solitary depression, isolated from the general run of humanity."

In general, however, contributors have made excellent use of the available, **non-adapted transport**. Taxis are fine for exploring Singapore and Hong Kong, their drivers helpful. *Tuk-tuks* (if you can clamber in) or shuttle boats and ferries (with help from the crew) are the thing in Bangkok. It's even possible to ride a Philippine jeepney, wheelchair squashed between the two bench seats, head touching the roof. In Bali, an air-conditioned van can be rented quite cheaply for a day's sightseeing—with a roll-up transit chair and a couple of friends, getting in and out of the bus is an easy operation.

For cross-country journeys, any method of travel is likely to be slow or uncomfortable or both. Where roads are more than tracks they are poorly maintained. Buses and cars are often pretty spartan; trains are difficult to get into, the seating less than luxurious and the rest rooms impossible. Domestic **flights** probably offer the best level of comfort and cut down journey times, but expect no automated facilities for boarding and disembarking, no accessible rest rooms at the minor airports, often no wheelchair service, and endless bureaucracy to cut through when booking a ticket—and you'll see nothing of the countryside.

THE FAR EAST: TRAVEL NOTES

Accommodation

As in so many other parts of the world, the more **expensive hotels** tend to be the ones with wheelchair access. Barbara Horrocks stayed in two of the very luxurious *Shangri-la* hotels (89 Soi Wat Suan Plu, New Road, Bangkok, ☎2/236-7777; 22 Orange Grove Road, Singapore 1025, ☎737-3644), both fully accessible, 1991 prices started at $160 a night.

If the *Access Singapore* guide is to be believed, the city of Singapore offers a wide choice of hotels with good facilities for disabled guests, including full acccess to bathrooms. Susan Preston stayed at the **central YMCA hotel** (1 Orchard Road, Singapore 0923; ☎336-6000). She joined the YMCA for the purposes of her vacation, and paid a nightly rate of $14 per person, room only (1991 rates were about $40; book at least five weeks ahead). Sue's air-conditioned room contained three beds, color TV, refrigerator, telephone, and tea-making facilities, and the *en suite* shower room with lavatory had plenty of space for maneuver in the wheelchair. The hotel has its own cafeteria and a *McDonald's* on the first floor.

In **Hong Kong** there are wheelchair-accessible facilities at several hotels, and the 1991 edition of the guide for disabled visitors indicates that the problem of narrow bathroom doorways is less frequently encountered than in 1987, when the previous edition was published, but it's still a good idea to check when making a reservation. Sue Kelley stayed in spacious accommodation at the *Park Hotel* (61/65 Chatham Road, Kowloon; ☎3661371), with easy access to the *en suite* facilities.

In **Macau**, Sue stayed at the accessible, five-star *Mandarin Oriental* (Avenida de Amizade; ☎567888). There are cheaper options among the *pousadas* and guesthouses, but you'd have to contact them direct to ascertain facilities for wheelchair guests. The *pousadas* are generally converted Portuguese churches, so access to these may be difficult.

In **Bali**, Veronica Smith stayed at the *Ramayana Hotel* (Jalan Bakungsari, Kuta, PO Box 333, Denpasar 80001; ☎361/88429), which was accessible apart odd steps in the gardens.

The **Philippine** tourist office recommends the *Philippine Village Hotel* (Naia Avenue, Pasay City; ☎2/8338081), the *Manila Hotel* (Risal Park, Manila; ☎2/470011), and the *Manila Peninsula Hotel* (Ayala/Makati Avenue, Makati, Manila; ☎2/8193456); the first two are reported to offer adapted transport.

Access and Facilities

There are plenty of ramps in Hong Kong and an increasing number in the City of Singapore, as well as facilities for disabled people in many Japanese cities; in Nagoya, for example, all the sidewalks, curbs, and subways are marked with coded, ribbed strips to guide blind people.

But outside the air-conditioned, marble-floored shopping plazas that have become a feature of some Asian cities, the going gets tough for wheelchair users. High curbs, narrow, crowded sidewalks, and heat make getting around something of a trial; a companion is almost essential. Traffic and litter provide an added obstacle in a number of cities. Singapore, with its heavy and enforced fines for littering, is the shining exception to this.

The terrain in rural areas can be formidable, with soft sand, rocky paths, and rough dirt tracks to negotiate: for many the only way to see the countryside is from the seat of a vehicle. Susan Preston explored Phuket island by minivan, Veronica Smith saw Bali the same way; others used buses, trains, jeeps, boats—none of them adapted for disabled passengers but all manageable with help.

Access to sights, however, is too often only partial: without the usually plentiful offers of assistance from passers-by, wheelchair users must sit and view monuments from outside or be content with the exhibits on a museum's first floor. That said, there is much that *can* be explored, and there is good access to some outdoor attractions such as the Rose Gardens in Bangkok, or the Singapore Zoological Gardens, but the scope for introduction of ramps, elevators, and wide doorways, not to mention some accessible public rest rooms, is enormous.

Health and Insurance

The main threats to good health in this part of the world come from contaminated food and water and, in some areas, disease-carrying

THE FAR EAST: TRAVEL NOTES

mosquitoes. *MIUSA* reports (see *Books*, below) that air pollution in China causes respiratory problems for most travelers, and recommends taking along cold medications or antibiotics; water pollution is also so bad that not even the Chinese drink the water without boiling it first. The effects of high temperatures and humidity should not be underestimated, and remember also that nights can be cold. But, as a general rule, don't *over*estimate the dangers: with some simple precautions and common sense, plus advice from a good guidebook or from Richard Dawood's *Travelers' Health* (see "Books," *Practicalities*) you are unlikely to suffer more than a couple of days of "Delhi Belly."

If you don't have a strong stomach, it's a good idea to take a small travel kettle and some packet soups, or granola bars for emergencies.

If you are traveling outside major cities or in some of the poorer countries, it's worth using a reliable guidebook to check out the medical and hospital facilities in the region you intend to visit, as there's some variation in standards. Travelers in China may like to investigate some of the 5000-year-old Chinese healing techniques, which include acupuncture, herbalism, breathing exercises, and masage therapy; these can be used to treat minor complaints as well as a number of disabling conditions. The Chinese may have a way to go before they catch up with the West's rehabilitation and technical aids for people with disabilities but they have a massive head start as far as drug-free treatments are concerned.

Books

You Want to go Where? A Guide to China for Travelers With Disabilities and Anyone Interested in Disability Issues, by Evelyn Anderton and Susan Sygall (Mobility International USA, 1990). This is essential reading for anyone going to China, written with humor and insight. There's something on every aspect of travel in China—what to take with you, how to make even the cheaper hotels accessible, how to get around by "hitching" a wheelchair to a bike ("probably not legal...but it's great fun and a wonderful way to tour this fascinating country"), accessible (and not so accessible) sights, Chinese customs explained, alternative medicine Chinese style, lists of useful contacts, and an interview with a disability activist. To obtain a copy send $9.95 (plus $5 postage outside the US; discounts for members) to MIUSA, PO Box 3551, Eugene, OR 97403; ☎503/343-1284 (voice or TDD).

Real Guides are available for Thailand and Hong Kong & Macau. For other areas both Moon Publications, with their *Handbooks*, and Lonely Planet's *Travel Survival Kits* are reliable.

TELEPHONE CODES

Dial 011 (International Code), followed by 65 for Singapore, 66 for Thailand, 62 for Indonesia (Bali), 63 for the Philippines, 852 for Hong Kong, 853 for Macau, and 86 for China.

PART EIGHT

AUSTRALIA AND NEW ZEALAND

Introduction

here are wedding bells in more than one of the accounts in this section, and only one trip which does not involve visiting relatives or old friends. But even without the cushioning effect of contacts down under, Australia and New Zealand are two of the world's more civilized destinations for the disabled traveler. The message of these accounts is that disabled people are expected and welcome visitors, rather than surprise guests, in accommodation, public buildings, and at tourist attractions. Perhaps the exception is public transit—most types are inaccessible to lone wheelchair users.

General attitudes toward disability are good, Donald Crowther (p.469) being the only contributor to experience any unpleasantness. Most people report widespread friendliness and unfussy assistance whenever required. It is particularly refreshing to read of bus drivers and tour guides who are cheerfully willing to lift tourists in wheelchairs, in marked contrast to the more usual attitude that if you cannot manage yourself then you must be accompanied.

When considering a vacation in Australia or New Zealand, one of the biggest hurdles for the inexperienced traveler is probably **getting there**. US or Canadian travelers can stop over in Honolulu or Fiji but it's still a long haul—eleven to thirteen hours to New Zealand from the West Coast. For those who cannot manage on these flights by controlling fluid intake prior to take-off, the problem of visiting the aircraft rest rooms is not necessarily solved by airlines that claim to offer accessible facilities: the "adapted" rest room may be only marginally bigger than the standard broom closets that pass for rest rooms in the economy section. Even if the on-board wheelchair fits into the cubicle, the physical contortions required to transfer to the toilet seat will defeat many travelers.

The best way to cover long distances within Australia and New Zealand is probably by air. *East West* is the cheapest **domestic airline** in Australia; *Australian* produces a comprehensive brochure for its disabled passengers; *Ansett* scores highly as travel agents as well as for good service in general on domestic flights in Australia. *Air New Zealand*, *Mount Cook Line*, and *Ansett New Zealand* cope well with disabled travelers within New Zealand.

Access on Australian **interstate trains** and on New Zealand's *InterCity* services is generally poor: it's impossible to get a wheelchair along the corridor, much less into the rest room. Train travel is not out of the question—major stations have collapsible wheelchairs (these are available for use on board the *Indian Pacific* from Sydney to Perth)—but full-time wheelchair users will have to arrange assistance.

For overland travel a **rental car** or RV (camper van) allows greater independence, and cars with hand controls are available in both countries, but we have received no reports of rental firms offering camper vans with hoists or lifts. Carrying your own set of hand controls, or renting a set there, will open up a wider range of options. Roger Elliott experienced great kindness from other road users when he ran into trouble on a couple of occasions in remote areas.

Getting around the cities presents few problems, although Roger had to grapple with high curbs and difficult access to shops and banks in northern Queensland. Sydney is equipped with the fully accessible Monorail, and taxi drivers are helpful everywhere. **Wheelchair-accessible taxis** can be booked in advance in almost every

Australian state capital. In New Zealand, the *Total Mobility* project, set up and coordinated by the *Disabled Persons Assembly*, provides an accessible, discounted taxi service for some New Zealanders and visitors with mobility problems. Visitors can take advantage of this form of transport by simply contacting the DPA on arrival.

All types of **accommodation** are covered in these accounts, from prebooked, luxury hotels, through cheap motels found along the way, to basic campgrounds. If facilities were not always perfect, they were always adaptable to suit individual needs, and the general awareness of the requirements of disabled people is said to be good in both countries. Perhaps the biggest plus is that travelers who need wheelchair access are not confined to the luxury hotels—there is a good spread of accessible options across the price range.

No single source lists all the accessible accommodation in Australia, but the numerous disabled support organizations in each state can help with inquiries and the experiences of our contributors suggests that it is not difficult to find suitable rooms en route. The scarcity of accommodation allowing independent access noted by David Gray in New Zealand in 1984 seems to have been improved upon, according to Kent Kloepping who had more problems with overbooking than with access during his 1992 trip.

Few **tourist attractions** or **recreational activities** are out of bounds for disabled visitors: both David and Kent found that it wasn't necessary to hike the mountain trails to appreciate the scenery in New Zealand; and you don't have to be able to walk to enjoy swimming and diving among brilliant coral fish on the Great Barrier Reef. A practical and positive approach from the crew makes small boats and light aircraft accessible. Boardwalks and sealed-surface or compact-chip tracks enable wheelchair users to wander through rainforests and national parks. Barbara Horrocks' worries about access at Ayers Rock were swept away by a cheerful tour guide, and Sheila Murray found few problems in Perth, taking her severely physically and developmentally disabled daughter everywhere—to the beach, the dolphinarium, the shops, even to dinner at the Yacht Club.

Easy access cannot be taken for granted: there is room for improvement in many areas, but overall the levels of awareness and the provision of facilities for disabled people are better than average. John Moore found that in some places rest rooms for disabled people were not indicated by the usual wheelchair sign because it is assumed that accessible rest rooms are incorporated everywhere. And help is always at hand: the friendliness of both Aussies and Kiwis, their readiness to assist, is perhaps the strongest theme of these accounts. To find the two together—generally good access *and* willing helpers—is rare indeed.

Australia

Wheeling around Queensland

Andrew Healey is a Navy-trained heli-copter pilot who broke his back in a flying accident in 1985. Now paraple-gic, he is a public relations consultant and freelance aviation writer. As a result of the crash, Andrew was unable to attend his brother Nick's wedding in Queensland, but made it for his first anniversary, in January 1987, traveling with his wife, Linda.

We found a good deal on the tickets, applied for the visas, organized hotels, packed braces and crutches into my ski bag and set off just after Christmas, flying first to Singapore for two days, then overnight to Brisbane for the meat of the trip and finally home from Sydney after four weeks away.

For the longer legs of the trip we booked with *British Airways*, mainly because at the time they were adapting their Boeing 747s to make one of the rest rooms accessible to the aisle wheelchair. I am sure they have completed the conversions by now, but we flew to Singapore in an aircraft "yet to be modified."

If it happens to you, don't panic—your body dehydrates during a long flight and although I drank plenty of fluids like a sensible traveler should, I didn't need to empty the leg bag once. If you can manage a long-ish transfer from the aisle wheelchair you should be OK. I also stood up at times by haul-ing myself up on the headrest of the

seat in front (I recommend you intro-duce yourself to the occupant first).

At Brisbane airport we had to take a ten-minute taxi ride from the interna-tional to the domestic terminal. We flew north to Rocky (Rockhampton) in a very smart *Ansett Australia* Boeing, after which the airport at Rocky was a surprise—very small and utilitarian. I had to suffer the indignity of being fork-lifted down from the aircraft—hated that. Nick met us there, though, and we could start the serious vacationing.

We had only the weekend to get over the jet lag, acclimatize, and meet up with my uncle and aunt in Yeppoon (a small town on the "Capricorn Coast," to the east of Rocky) before Nick and his wife Jane drove north with us toward Cairns and the Barrier Reef. Nick had a Volkswagen camper van and the idea was to use the campgrounds along the coast, then find a chalet or something in Cairns.

The sites we came across during the four-day trip were surprisingly easy to deal with from a wheelchair. I could use the rest rooms in each one, and because we took along a collapsible plastic stool I could shower every evening. We soft-bellied Poms were initially a little nervous of using the rest rooms after dark: every time the toilet was flushed it set off a cacophony of croaks from the tree frogs living in the cistern above. And the possums are fearless—so accustomed to people that they wander arrogantly all over the campgrounds. One evening I heard a scrabbling noise and wheeled around with the flashlight. If someone had done that to me I'd have jumped a mile, but the possum—for it was he—just stared. We got used to all this wildlife as time went by.

After one leg of the journey we stopped for the night at a campground at Eungela (inland a bit from Mackay), with spectacular views from the top of a ridge and one lovely hotel complete with pool—and launch ramp for hanggliders! At the campground there were signs inviting visitors to take a woodland trail through the tropical rainforest, so we set off. That was a mistake. What started off quite innocuously as a clear, swept path ended up as an assault course, from which we finally emerged, sweating and swearing (them sweating, me swearing) as night was falling. As a diversion, Nick then assured me that a nearby stream and pool were full of platypus, so I set up post with my camera and tripod. I have some great shots of bubbles and ripples if you're interested: good ploy, Nick.

Farther up the coast, we caught a ferry from Townsville to Magnetic Island, rented a Moke (a kind of miniature jeep), and found a beach for the day. There was room for us all in the Moke if we each carried a bit of the wheelchair—thank God for lightweight chairs. The beach was delightful, straight out of the brochures and practically deserted, except for flocks of brightly colored lorikeets and a bar and grill in the shade of the trees. They served Cokes and stubbies (bottles of beer—I was beginning to talk Strine by then), as well as toasted sandwiches—what more could a chap ask for?

"We left in a hurry after ten days, before the scratched and scored skirting boards were discovered"

On the beach we made rather imaginative (I thought) use of a sturdy airbed we had bought in Yeppoon. Any time I felt like a swim, I left the wheelchair with the rest of the stuff, sat on the air-bed and went for a drag down to the water's edge. We felt quite smug after that. Our day on Magnetic was great fun, so much so that we repeated the exercise on the way back south.

By the time we reached Cairns, the novelty of living out of suitcases in a camper van was beginning to wear thin for Linda and me, so we were keen to find somewhere a bit more permanent. We moved into a campground chalet, while Nick and Jane—hardier types—pitched their tent nearby. Linda was so relieved at finally being able to unpack that she prowled around our new home like an expectant lioness.

The chalets were all raised above the ground with two steps up, so once inside I was there for the night. There wasn't a great deal of room for the wheelchair, but I managed. We shifted the bed against the wall so that I could maneuver the chair from the bed to the bathroom, and that was all that was required. The room wouldn't have suited me if I'd been alone, but it was only a place to sleep, after all—we spent all day every day outside, either exploring or loafing around the pool. We left in a hurry after ten days, before the scratched and scored baseboards were discovered.

The high point of the whole journey was, of course, the Great Barrier Reef. We took a day trip out there on a big catamaran and had a wonderful time. The boat from Cairns was no problem (the rest room was, but then with the heat . . .) and if getting into the water meant a little bum-shuffling it was more than worth it to be able to snorkel around and take it all in. I could make it to the stern in my chair and shuffle onto the diving platform (almost at deck level) which was then lowered to the water.

"On the odd occasion when we needed outside help we encountered nothing but good-humored willingness"

I saw plenty, most of which I couldn't identify. There were thousands of brilliantly colored reef fish, like you see in the pictures, but I particularly remember enormous groupers and giant clams. Through my diving mask the groupers seemed to be between two and four feet long and almost as broad. They looked fearsome but were quite harmless, I was assured. The clams were dotted about the sea bed and we swam down to take a closer look. In reality they close up very slowly, so that the old myth of divers getting their feet caught is just that—a myth.

The only slight disappointment was my inability to scuba dive. Nick could, and he rented a tank to go exploring a bit lower down the reef. He saw a great deal more as a result, and I envied him that. But the inability was nothing to do with the disability: there was a piece in the local paper while we were there about a young American paraplegic who was doing the diving course. I could have done it, too, but I didn't want to commit myself to the same place for most of our stay in Cairns. For the same reason we only went to the reef once; as a diver I could have done a proper exploration, so learning to dive is now a priority.

One of the tours offered on the reef was to Green Island, where I was unable to get to the underwater observatory.

Together with a rock pool at Josephine Falls on the journey up, these were the only two things I couldn't take part in during the entire trip.

We did one other beach day while we were in Cairns, to the Northern Beaches. We had become thoroughly spoiled by then, so the idea of sharing a beach with over a dozen more people didn't impress, but we went for a drag and a swim, splashing around for a good half-hour. There were marked and netted areas for swimming because it was "stinger" season—enormous box jellyfish are found along the Queensland coast from late October to early May, and they have a reputation for injuring and sometimes killing those who brush against them. While swimming, we noticed a couple of guys sticking notices in the sand, but since the wording was facing away from the sea we ignored them. It was only after we got back to our towels that we read, *Danger: no swimming allowed—netted areas infested with box jellyfish.* Thanks, guys.

Northern Queensland is very hot in January. We made two trips inland to escape the heat, to an area called the Atherton Tablelands. It was still hot here, but less sticky. It's dairy country and, if you don't look too closely at the vegetation, not unlike England. We visited a marvelous freshwater lake called Lake Eacham. Although I have always been a little wary of swimming in "fresh" water (because it is usually anything but), I think this was the best swimming I had in Australia (barring the reef, perhaps). There were picnic tables in the shade of gum trees, a disabled rest room (it's a shame to have to use the design of public toilets as a yardstick for a good day out), and to get into the water all I had to do was fall off the dock! It was only about a two-foot drop, so getting a lift out was not too difficult. The water was cool and crystal clear, a pleasant change from the sea, which was so warm it often wasn't refreshing at all.

Cairns is a fast-growing town with its own international airport and several swish hotels. It has lots of smart clothes shops, and restaurants of varying standards. I ate an interesting "Dundee Platter" (water buffalo, crocodile, and venison filet, I am now embarrassed to relate) in one, and a pretty tasteless Mexican meal in another.

After ten days in Cairns we made our way south again. From Rocky we flew to Sydney (upgraded to first class, which was nice) and after weeks of slumming it in camper van, tents, and campground chalets, we booked into the *Southern Cross*, a smart hotel in the city center. They have some adapted rooms and I thoroughly recommend it, as long as you don't want to use the rooftop pool, which is inaccessible.

Sydney is a nice city (usually a contradiction in terms as far as I am concerned): airy, cosmopolitan, and dead easy to get around. We caught the harbor ferry (all sloped access) across to Manly and also went to the top of Centerpoint tower. We ate in Chinatown and drank in some smart bars; I'd like to go back some day.

We flew straight home from Sydney, on a modified 747 this time, to the worst snowfall for years. I wouldn't fly direct again, but that is nothing to do with being disabled—it's just a boring flight. I also wouldn't dream of suggesting that the whole trip was a breeze: there were times when obstacles did present themselves, but with a little planning (plastic stool for showers, airbed for sand-dragging sort of planning), most of them can be overcome without the frustration that would spoil any trip. We were with friends, but on the odd occasion when we needed outside help we encountered nothing but good-humored willingness—"She'll be right, mate." I wouldn't do a trip like that on my own, but then I wouldn't anyway (tried it once, years ago, and had a rotten time).

What would we do differently next time? Steer clear of the meat pies—still the Australian national dish and to be viewed with suspicion—and make sure the mosquito spray is in a different shaped tin to the athlete's foot spray. I covered myself liberally with the latter one sultry night at the Cairns drive-in.

Old Haunts, New Thrills

Barbara and Bill Horrocks used to live in Australia, and in November 1988 they returned for a vacation—a sentimental journey, a reunion with friends and relatives, and an exploration of places not seen the first time around. Barbara is a wheelchair user but can walk a little.

Our *Qantas* plane touched down at Sydney and passengers had to disembark even if Melbourne was their final destination. Because I am disabled we were allowed to stay on board and we took the opportunity to freshen and brush up. From Melbourne we were booked on a domestic flight to Launceston, Tasmania, where Bill's brother and his Australian wife were waiting to meet us.

At Melbourne we were escorted by a friendly Aussie, who chatted twenty to the dozen. "No worries," he kept repeating, in the broadest Strine, as we made our way through customs and immigration and down miles of corridors to the luggage collection point, where I was reunited with my wheelchair. Unfortunately, the same could not be said of my suitcase. It had been off-loaded at Sydney. This proved to be only a minor hiccup, as my medication was in my hand luggage, and the suitcase turned up the next day.

Tasmania is a lovely island, about the size of England but with only a fraction of the population (less than 500,000)—ideal, then, for those who seek peace and quiet. Like England it has four distinct seasons and a temperate, though warmer and more settled, climate. The scenery is beautiful, with a great deal of variation.

We spent some time recovering from jet lag, discovering Launceston, and meeting friends and relations before renting a car and driving south to Hobart, the island's capital. The "highway" between the two cities turned out to be nothing more than a two-lane road, but the traffic was very light.

Hobart is small, with a pleasant, "solid" feel to it. We visited Battery Point, reckoned to be the most complete colonial village in Australia. Many of the houses, all of which are lived in, are still as they were in the 1830s and 1840s, with picturesque wrought-iron railings on their verandahs, yet the high-rise casino (without which no self-respecting Australian city is complete) is within walking—and wheeling—distance. Nearby Salamanca Place is a restored dockland area, jam-packed with craft shops and restaurants.

No worries with access to the revolving restaurant on the top floor of the casino: it is reached by an elevator which goes from the first floor and opens directly into it. My memories of that evening are of good food and excellent service, complemented by ever-changing views of majestic Mount Wellington, the pretty harbor, and the city nestling close against it, the magnificent Tasman Bridge, and the vast, blue Southern Ocean which stretches without interruption from Tasmania to the South Pole. We were particularly lucky to be there for the end of the Sydney to Hobart yacht race, and to witness the winner drop her sails and come gracefully to rest.

"But for the efforts of a friendly Ansett travel agent, who managed to find us a serviced apartment, we would have tasted the joys of sleeping in the park"

The next day we drove to the old convict settlement of Port Arthur, situated on a long, narrow peninsula and joined to the mainland by an even narrower neck of land. The terrain is rugged, with deep inlets reminiscent of Scottish lochs, and densely wooded mountains. The convicts were not intended to escape, and none who tried were successful. Closed in 1877, after a decline in the number of convicts, Port Arthur lay derelict for many years, but it has been beautifully restored.

We stayed two days in Hobart before driving back to Launceston up the east coast, passing through little seaside towns with familiar names—Swansea, Falmouth, and Beaumaris—and others more exotic, like Triabunna, Bicheno, and Binalong Bay, where we picnicked on fresh crayfish, purchased from a roadside stand.

By this time, having passed through Singapore and Bangkok on the way to Australia, we were old hands at airport procedures: when the staff at the Launceston check-in desk tried to transfer me into yet another airport wheelchair, we declined the offer. We pointed out that my own chair was more comfortable, easily folded, and light to handle. After a little persuasion, they agreed, and I was not separated from my chair until we were at the door of the aircraft. After that I was never parted from my own wheelchair one minute sooner than necessary, and by the time our holiday ended we had flown in eighteen different airplanes and been loaded aboard in every conceivable way.

(Once, when we flew out to the Barrier Reef in a battered eight-seater, I was heaved into the aircraft by the pilot himself! Aussies have no delusions of grandeur, and will turn a hand to anything—or anybody! My slimline wheelchair came into its own on this occasion because the "hold" was the space behind the back seat, and a conventional wheelchair would have caused problems.)

Our plans included a three-day visit to Canberra, and that's where we headed next. I thought Canberra a stunning city, with its purpose-built Courthouse, Library, and superb Parliament Building, which has a garden on the roof where you may walk, or be pushed, because the architect believed that the people should be above parliament. All the public buildings have easy access for wheelchairs and the city is flat as a pancake, so "no worries" if you fancy going walkabout. Once on the move, however, it is difficult to pick up a cab, so make sure that your pusher is up to the task.

There's much to see in Canberra, and most of it is worth the seeing (including Australia's War Museum, although that might put a damper on the holiday spirit), but in the end it all seemed a bit sterile—soulless, somehow—and I was quite ready for Sydney, the next stop on our itinerary.

As we soon discovered, Sydney is anything but soulless; bustling and vibrant, it was the one place where we almost came unstuck. Not wishing to be tied to time, we hadn't booked ahead, and soon realized that neither love nor money would buy us a hotel bed for the night. But for the efforts of a friendly *Ansett* travel agent, who managed to find us a serviced apartment, we would have tasted the joys of sleeping in the park.

But, as so often happens, our lack of foresight turned out for the best. We thoroughly enjoyed the apartment, which was luxurious and very centrally situated. We sallied forth each morning to explore, and never needed to use buses or trains, although we did resort to the odd taxi. All the fresh air gave us a healthy tan, and Bill developed some fine leg muscles.

We stayed five days, taking in the shops, Darling Harbor, Circular Quay, and the adjacent Rocks—yet another resurrected dockland area, full of atmosphere. I was wheeled through Chinatown, and we took a cab (a touch of extravagance there) out to the famous, but rather seedy, Bondi Beach. We rode the Monorail and enjoyed a fascinating tour of the Opera House, both of which have special facilities for the disabled. We also took a Captain Cook tour of the harbor, and the ferry boat crew, like the Monorail and Opera House staff, was more than helpful. We ate out each night—Italian, Chinese, Spanish, even Korean—and once at an open-air restaurant on the Rocks, built to resemble a sailing ship, complete with masts and sails. Of course, we had to find places that had easy access, but that was no real problem.

"We rented a car for the week so that we could do the sentimental journey bit"

Our next stop was Brisbane, where we once lived for three years. I was younger then, and not in any way disabled; in my eagerness to pick up the threads, I had forgotten what a hilly place it is. *The Summit Central Apartments*, though within normal walking distance of the center, are situated high above the city. Bill's arm muscles grew to match those in his legs as he struggled to stop me running away from him, and the uphill homeward journey was no joke in the humid heat.

We rented a car for the week so that we could do the sentimental journey bit. The suburbs had grown a lot in twenty years, but otherwise they were much as we remembered: a jumble of pastel-colored wooden houses, resembling a fading patchwork quilt, with many of them built on stilts to catch the breeze and allow the floodwaters to run away. Lush gardens, bright with bougainvillaea, poinsettia, and jacaranda, sweep down to the river where the well-to-do have their own private docks. Altogether it is a pleasant, easygoing, subtropical city, but for the disabled tourist, without old haunts and old friends to look up, I reckon two or three days would be enough, especially taking those hills into consideration.

Our last evening in Brisbane we dined al fresco at a riverside restaurant, on lobster, crayfish, and gigantic shrimp, accompanied by a salad which was a work of art to look at and a delight to eat. After saying our sentimental farewells the next morning, we set off in the rented car for Mackay, nearly 650 miles to the north, well and truly in the tropics, and the gateway to the Barrier Reef.

> **"I was a little worried that I would be out of place among so many bronzed, athletic specimens of humanity'"**

If you like fruit you will never starve in this part of Queensland. Mangoes, pineapples, melons, bananas, pawpaws, and more, grow in profusion. Huge self-service fruit stores abound, and at farm gateways carts piled high with produce tempt the traveler to stop and buy. The owner is usually asleep under a large umbrella, or else there is a notice inviting customers to help themselves and throw their money in a bucket!

Driving makes one aware of the size of Australia: mile after mile of unremarkable scenery goes by, punctuated by one-horse towns; we were struck by the sameness of the gum trees and the fruit plantations, by the relentless dust, and the "highway" which in reality is a narrow, rather bumpy paved strip. The fruit plantations gave way to sugar cane

and, as evening fell, we reached Mackay, a pleasant little town which is part resort, part sugar terminal. We stayed one night; I'd have liked to have stayed longer, but our flight to the Barrier Reef was already booked.

Our little jaunt to the Barrier Reef, and a later one to Ayers Rock, were the only bits of our holiday which were in any way "packaged." There are dozens of islands and as many choices of accommodation. You pays your money and takes your choices. We chose South Molle, under the impression that it was less commercialized than some. Even so, I was a little worried that I would be out of place among so many bronzed, athletic specimens of humanity. As a wheelchair user I was in the minority, but in fact it didn't matter a bit.

We were slightly disconcerted to be greeted at South Molle Island by a uniformed hostess, and we soon realized that our island was more developed than we had been led to believe. However, after the initial introduction, we were left to our own devices.

We had a lovely cabin right on the beach, with palm trees that rustled in the evening breezes and the lapping of the Coral Sea to lull us to sleep. During the day I sunbathed and wallowed in the warm sea water, while Bill went for walks around the island, collecting coconuts and bits of coral from the beach. We breakfasted each morning by the Olympic-sized pool, where we could have had snorkeling lessons and played water polo if we'd been so inclined, and later we watched the brightly colored reef fish from the wooden dock, as they came in search of leftover rolls. Our evenings were spent just enjoying the balmy temperatures and gazing at the stars. Faint strains of music reached us from the bar-lounge, but these only served to heighten the romantic atmosphere.

After three days we were well rested and ready to resume our travels. Water-taxi and plane took us to ─

Townsville, where we collected another rental car and drove to Cairns. If I had to choose one place out of all Australia in which to spend a vacation, it would be Cairns. A town of wide, shady boulevards on the Queensland coast, with the Atherton Tablelands at its back, Cairns is renowned for its big game fishing. The boats belong on a movie set—we simply looked and dreamed.

From Cairns we toured the Tablelands, both by car and by bus. It is an area of rushing waterfalls and dense, hardwood forests which open out into rich dairy farming country, dotted with towns which appear to be locked in a 1920s time-warp. At the opposite end of the scale, we visited Port Douglas, with its ultra luxurious *Sheraton Mirage* holiday complex and what is reputed to be the biggest free-form swimming pool in the world. We rode on the Kuranda scenic train, sipping champagne as we marveled both at the breathtaking scenery and at the ingenuity and bravery of the men who constructed the railroad during the gold rush. (Access to the train is difficult if you cannot walk at all.) We pottered about the villages that lie along this stretch of coast, buying souvenirs and gifts, and we had fun devising a way of cracking open a coconut which we found lying on the beach.

Eight days were too few, and it was with mixed feelings that we relinquished the rental car and flew to Alice Springs, the jumping-off point for our tour of Ayers Rock and The Olgas. Transfer from the airport to the town was by bus and the driver greeted us cheerfully: "Good afternoon, folks; welcome to Alice Springs. You're very lucky—it's cooler today, only 104 degrees. Yesterday was a scorcher (did he mean 104 wasn't?) and tomorrow the forecast is 110 degrees."

No wonder I almost burned a tender part of my anatomy when I sank into my wheelchair, for it had been standing in the sun, and I was scantily clad! A cool beer was called for, but we were dismayed to realize that we had been foolish enough to arrive in Alice at 4pm on a Sunday and the town is dry until 7pm on Sundays. They were the longest three hours!

"We had spent five weeks on the move and it wasn't long enough"

The next morning the luxury bus arrived at 6:45am to take us to Ayers Rock, a five-hour journey with a stop for morning tea and a short break at a camel station, where the more adventurous members of our party could ride on one of the beasts.

Nothing—movie, book, or TV program—had prepared me for the impact of Ayers Rock. Despite the proliferation of Aborigine souvenirs and the busloads of tourists, the Rock maintains its air of mystery, and I came away deeply moved and impressed by the dignified Aborigines and by the sincerity of their beliefs concerning Uluru, the name by which they know Ayers Rock.

I went prepared to remain on the bus while the more able-bodied visitors explored, and I was more than a little concerned about the whole thing. In the event, I saw as much of Ayers Rock as most. With the help of the *Pioneer Trailways* guide, a burly, cheery individual, and other willing tourists, I was wheeled, somewhat bumpily, around the base of the rock, and lifted into the caves to see the paintings. And I certainly wasn't the only one not to attempt the steep climb to the summit—you have to be very fit for that. There's nothing wrong with my eyesight, and I was able to enjoy the changing face of the rock as the sun went down, camera clicking frantically, the same as everyone else.

Our tour-about was almost over. The next day we flew to Melbourne, en route for Tasmania and a last visit with our relations. We had spent five weeks on the move and it wasn't long enough.

Australia is a vast continent, pretty well adapted to the needs of the disabled. We covered many thousands of miles by land and air, but we still had to miss a great deal.

Our path was smoothed before we went by *Travelbag* agents of Alton, England, experts in their field who made all our initial reservations, and within Australia by *Ansett*, which produces beautiful brochures and through which we were able to obtain not only plane tickets, but also hotel rooms and our tours to the Barrier Reef and Ayers Rock. I am grateful to the members of staff of *Qantas* and *Ansett*, who were unfailingly courteous, and to all the Aussies who helped me on my way.

Honeymoon First

As a result of a gunshot wound sustained whilst serving with the British army in Northern Ireland in 1981, John Moore is disabled and uses a wheelchair most of the time. In 1989 he and his fiancée, Stephanie, spent five-weeks in Queensland.

We arrived in Brisbane, Queensland's capital, to be greeted by my aunt and uncle, with whom we were to stay for much of our holiday. The sky that evening was dark and cloudless, studded with bright stars. By day or night, the sky is an impressive feature in the southern hemisphere, more vivid and colorful than England's dull shades of gray.

The southern Queensland climate is subtropical, with warm or hot days in the summer, and sunny, cool days in the winter. In January and February, heavy showers develop and the temperature can reach 85°F or so. In March, while we were there, it rained heavily for three days but then the clouds gave way to perfect blue skies and the occasional clump of pure white cloud. In the winter months (June to August), the weather is ideal, with very little rain and plenty of warm sunshine, temperatures averaging 72°F. Many Australians living in the cooler states take a vacation in Queensland at this time of year.

Some of our time was spent with my relatives, visiting their favorite haunts. The Sunshine Coast, named for obvious reasons, is only a thirty-minute drive from their home in Burpengary, near Brisbane. At the southern end of the Sunshine Coast are the mysterious Glasshouse Mountains, the result of volcanic activity millions of years ago. The mountains, with their trachyte peaks, present weird and wonderful shapes, especially at dusk and dawn.

The mountains are surrounded by well-wooded pastures and plantations of tropical fruit, stretching toward the coast. Mooloolaba, Calundra, and Noosa Heads are small towns on the Sunshine Coast offering miles of unspoiled beaches and total serenity. Poised on the edge of Laguna Bay is the resort of Noosa Heads, with its 1062-acre national park containing a network of walking tracks that wind through the rainforest and command wonderful ocean views. The park also houses an animal sanctuary, and coastal lakes which are inhabited by elegant black swans, pelicans, and cranes.

Everywhere we traveled along the Sunshine Coast we noticed the provision for disabled people; most places were accessible to wheelchairs. One outstanding example, often billed as one of the world's tackiest tourist attractions, was "The Big Pineapple," some 65 miles north of Brisbane. This large fruit plantation is among the most popular sights in Queensland: the 52-foot-high, plastic pineapple has a top-floor observation deck overlooking the tropical fruit trees.

Access is excellent, allowing disabled people to all levels, and we were particularly impressed with the audio-visual displays, telling the story of the pineapple. We managed a short ride on a sugar-cane train through acres of mangoes, pineapples, sugar cane, nuts, and spices. Toilet facilities and parking spaces for disabled people were provided everywhere, making me feel very welcome.

My aunt had kindly pre-booked a hand-controlled car from *Budget*, outlining my disability so that they could provide suitable controls. We used *Budget* because we had been pleased with its service on our previous trip in Australia. It is advisable to reserve a vehicle well in advance and confirm it in writing.

"The whole area alive with wild creatures, including possums, cockatoos, frogs, and lizards"

Driving regulations in Australia are virtually the same as in the UK—drive on the left, don't drink and drive, and don't exceed the speed limit which is 100kph (65mph). We were made aware of the Queensland police force's tough stand on speeding one hot and humid day, when we were caught traveling at 114kph and fined A$40 on the spot.

The car we rented had ample room to store my wheelchair in the trunk. As well as automatic transmission (standard on most cars), it had the essential air conditioning—an absolute must in this climate. In all we traveled nearly 2000 miles in three weeks, including a memorable trip to Mackay, some 600 miles north of Brisbane, at the south-

ern end of the Great Barrier Reef.

On the map, the distance to Mackay seemed quite short, and there appeared to be only a few places worth visiting on the way. How wrong we were. The Bruce Highway follows the coastline of Queensland from Brisbane to Cairns. Only 50 miles north of Brisbane the four-lane highway peters out, and the farther north one travels the more remote and lonely the road becomes, although it is well maintained, with no potholes and very few tight bends.

The surrounding countryside is magnificent, with tall gum trees scattered about and the whole area alive with wild creatures, including possums, cockatoos, frogs, and lizards. Unfortunately, we did not see many live kangaroos—most were lying at the roadside, victims of fast-moving cars and trucks. Kangaroos rest in the shade during daylight hours and move about at dusk and dawn, often crossing roads to reach new pastures; this is when most fatalities occur. Some vehicles have "roo-bars" fitted on the front to prevent damage from large kangaroos.

After a full day on the road, we stayed at the *Gladstone Country Club Motor Inn* which had a small number of rooms for disabled people, with flat access, wide doors, level shower, and, of course, air conditioning. The next day we arrived in Mackay, a lovely town boasting modern shopping facilities and fantastic beaches which were completely empty. During our four-day stay at the *Miners Lodge Motel* (again, well equipped to accommodate disabled guests) we achieved our ambition of seeing the Great Barrier Reef—or at least a small part of it.

Our first glimpse of a reef was from the air. We hired a small aircraft and pilot from the airport nearby and planned a short flight over the Whitsunday Islands, landing at a remote island called Brampton for lunch and a quick swim. What an adventure! We spent nearly an hour in the tiny airplane, gazing at the beauty below—the clear greens and blues of the tropical sea, dotted with small islands and darkened in places by banks of reefs—and nearly three hours on Brampton Island which is a perfect setting for its luxury hotel with two fine swimming pools and a miniature airstrip. Our brief stay (too brief) allowed us to take a cool dip in the sea and enjoy a wonderful fresh salad on the patio outside the hotel, admiring a view of the sort only usually seen on postcards: a calm bay, surrounded by lanky palm trees and lush vegetation, with a pale blue sea washing gently along a narrow white sandy beach—paradise!

"An entrepreneur with a spray-gun treating lines of bronzed sunbathers with suntan oil"

The following day we boarded a large sea cruiser with about a hundred other people for a trip to Credlin Reef. At first we were unimpressed by what we saw—just endless sea and sky. But as soon as we were persuaded to try snorkeling our mood changed dramatically. Although I am only an average swimmer, without much use of my legs, I found snorkeling quite easy. Stephanie, too, was eventually coaxed into the water, and she enjoyed every minute.

The warm sea with the strong sun filtering through it, and the vibrant colors of fish and coral, made our two-hour swim an unforgettable pleasure. The coral makes an incredibly beautiful picture, a dazzling mixture of purple, pink, yellow, white, and red, sculpted into spectacular shapes. There are over 340 varieties of identified coral; the most common ones we saw were the staghorns and mushroom corals. Spread among these were waving fields of soft coral, colorful anemones, sea urchins, and sea slugs. Shellfish clung to the reef while schools of fish, including red emperors, coral trout, and demoiselles, darted around us. Finally,

with the tide going out and threatening to strand us all, we returned to Mackay.

Back in Burpengary, we visited Brisbane's new Botanical Gardens which are in the foothills of Mount Coot-tha. The tropical house, in the form of a futuristic dome, has a superb display of plants and full wheelchair access. The gardens also contain a lagoon and pond, a demonstration garden, ornamental trees and shrubs, and a large collection of Australian native plants. While in the area we called in at the Lone Pine Koala Sanctuary by the Brisbane river. There is good access and the keepers allow visitors to "cuddle" a koala and have their photograph taken, for a small fee. The sanctuary houses about a hundred koalas, some tame kangaroos, lizards, and native birds.

Possibly one of the best-known parts of Australia is the Gold Coast, where the Aussies go for their vacations. Only an hour's drive south of Brisbane, it has a reputation for possessing all the glitz and glamor of an international resort but at about half the pace. The "Coast" is a stunning stretch of white, sandy beach, washed by white-capped waves and lined by modern apartment buildings, hotels, and restaurants. This is a sun- and fun-lovers' paradise, and for those who can resist the enormous temptation to lie on the beach all day there is a great deal of entertainment on offer.

Dreamworld is a Disney-type fantasy for all the family; Sea World is Australia's largest marine park, with dolphins, whales, and sea-lions on display. We chose Surfers' Paradise, a resort known for its large waves, and we found ourselves a small spot on the beach as soon as we'd checked in to a comfortable and reasonably priced motel (*Earls Court Motor Inn*). We watched an entrepreneur with a spray-gun treating lines of bronzed sunbathers with suntan oil—the Australians have a healthy respect for the power of the sun and the risk of skin cancer.

After a few hot hours on the beach
e returned to the motel to use the
vimming pool there (the sea was far
o rough for me). Toward evening we
ok a two-hour trip on a river cruiser
ound the man-made waterways to see
e magnificent homes of some of
ustralia's richest people—impressive,
it a bit too perfect!

During our short stay on the Gold
past we spent a day in the hinterland
ound the Tambourine mountains and
e stunning areas of rainforest which
e only a forty-minute drive from the
aches. The day we chose to go the
eather was poor, with low cloud and
casional showers, but even that could
ot mar the beauty of the towering
ountains, luxuriant rainforest, and
delicate orchids. Stephanie even
managed to push me along a rough
track beneath giant trees and staghorn
ferns to a cascading waterfall. The fast-
flowing waters, though, were extremely
cold and we didn't feel brave enough to
take a dip.

Our final visit to Brisbane, two days
before we returned to the UK, was for
an important event—our marriage! We
had fallen in love with Australia on our
first trip there and decided to marry in
Queensland. So in our case the honeymoon came first! Whether it's
marriage, a honeymoon, or a holiday
you're after, I recommend Australia,
especially for disabled people—you'll
be surprised at the excellent facilities
and easy access to most places.

asmania to the ropics

onald Crowther lives in Hobart,
asmania, separated from mainland
ustralia by Bass Strait. As a result of
rachnoid cysts in his spine, Donald is
araplegic and confined to a
vheelchair. In July 1988 he traveled
vith his wife to Cairns, North
ueensland.

Ve booked our round-trip flight from
lobart straight through to Cairns with
ast West Airlines about ten weeks
efore we intended to travel. There
ere two reasons for choosing this
irline: it was the only one which
llowed us to make the journey without
hanging planes, and it was cheaper
nan the larger operators, *Australian
irlines* and *Ansett Australia*.

A week before we were due to leave,
ur travel agent called to say that our
homeward flight with *East West* had
been canceled, and arrangements
made for an alternative flight with
Ansett, leaving Cairns at 6am, changing
at Brisbane and Sydney where there
would be an hour's wait, then flying to
Melbourne for a three-hour stopover
before flying on to Hobart. We were not
at all pleased with this development, so
after much negotiation we were booked
on a flight leaving Cairns around noon,
with a change at Brisbane, then direct
to Melbourne and only a short wait
there for the flight to Hobart.

A couple of days before our departure my doctor called and fitted a catheter. This allowed me some time to get
used to it before flying. At Hobart
airport my wheelchair and I were put
on a fork-lift truck and driven to the
small Fokker where we were lifted to
the aircraft door. I was carried to my
seat while my chair was stowed in the
hold.

During the six-hour flight the airline
staff was very helpful; we landed at
Devonport, Sydney, Coolangatta,

Brisbane, Townsville, and, finally, Cairns. My wheelchair was waiting on the ground when the fork-lift lowered me from the aircraft, and I was wheeled to the reception lounge where our daughter, Jill, was waiting.

> **"The manager was very hostile, and said that she would refuse to take disabled people in wheelchairs in future"**

Jill had booked us into a self-catering unit at *City Gardens Hotel/Motel*. This consisted of a large living room, bedroom with two single beds, toilet and shower, a kitchen with stove, dishwasher, and refrigerator, and a laundry with washing machine and dryer. Like most modern beds, ours were too low—OK to get into but too low to get out of—and this was the cause of the only unpleasantness we encountered on our trip.

My wife went to the reception desk and explained the problem, suggesting as a solution a brick placed under each leg. The manager was very hostile, and said that she would refuse to take disabled people in wheelchairs in future. A young Swedish student, working as a general porter, overheard this and came around to our room to apologize for the rudeness of the receptionist. He found two wooden beams which he placed under the bed, and this did the job to perfection.

Cairns is very flat and ideal for a wheelchair. It's in the tropics but all the buildings are air-conditioned. On our first day we booked a Calm Water Lunch Cruise, which started at the pier. I was pushed up the gangway onto the enclosed upper deck of the catamaran, *Terri-Two*.

We cast off and sailed into the harbor, with a running commentary from the skipper on the various vessels that we passed, including Jacques Cousteau's floating observatory with rotary paravane sails. Also pointed out were the old Customs House, now converted into a modern shopping arcade, the naval dockyard, and the seaplane base where the Americans used to operate Catalinas in World War II.

A little farther on we entered the mangroves, where we spotted blue cranes, white egrets, and a giant sea eagle. Usually it's possible to see the odd crocodile sunning itself in the heat of the day, but not that day. We pulled into one of the little inlets for lunch, a pre-packed meal of chicken and shrimp salad and various tropical fruits.

Starting back after lunch along another stream, we passed an old hull, the story of which was related by our skipper. In the 1950s a man called Moodie came to Cairns. He was believed to be a Canadian and his intention was to build a boat out of mangrove wood. Everyone laughed at this, as it is well known that mangrove timber doesn't float. Moodie's reply was that steel doesn't float, but they build ships out of it and they float!

After a spell in town, Moodie disappeared into the swamp, appearing at times to buy supplies and fittings for what became known as "Moodie's Ark." When several weeks went by without his customary trips to Cairns for supplies, the police were called in. They went to Moodie's camp and found him dead. He died of a heart attack, and rumor has it that there is a fortune in a Cairns bank, waiting to be claimed by Moodie's next of kin. So far, despite inquiries in Canada and Ireland, no one has been found.

Another way to explore the mangrove swamp is the Board Walk, which is close to Cairns airport and accessible to wheelchairs. The walk is raised about six feet above the swamp and there is a choice of routes, one taking about twenty minutes, the other about an hour. A notice at the entrance advises visitors to smear themselves liberally with insect repellent, but we did not take this precaution and suffered no bites. The advantage of the

Board Walk is that it enables visitors to view the various types of mangrove growth at close quarters and, by remaining quiet for a short time, to see many of the swamp's inhabitants, including crabs and mud skippers, birds, and butterflies.

Our next cruise was a full-day outing to Green Island, a coral outcrop of the Great Barrier Reef about 12 miles east of Cairns. It's a real "Robinson Crusoe" tropical island, with a good selection of white coral beaches, swaying coconut palms, and thatched huts.

Once again the journey was by fast catamaran. To board it I went up the gangway to the top deck but at the island I was carried to the lower deck for unloading. The island is totally accessible and there is a large outdoor café/bar where you can eat under palm-thatched shelters. Among the many attractions on Green Island is the aquarium—with crocodile pens—and an exhibition of Aboriginal arts and Melanesian culture.

My special interest is agriculture, so the most fascinating visit of our vacation for me was on the mainland, to a fruit farm northwest of Mossman. The proprietors have planted an array of tropical fruit trees and shrubs, and a guide takes parties of about ten people around the trees, explaining where each one came from and describing the taste and use of the the fruit. Back in the reception area we were able to sample some of the dried fruits as well as those fresh fruits that were in season.

Innisfail, to the south of Cairns, is the heart of the sugar industry and on the Bruce Highway is the CSR Sugar Museum, very well laid out and readily accessible to the wheelchair-bound visitor. Displays chart the development of the early sugar plantations and describe how the Kanaks (South Sea Islanders) were brought in to work the fields. Later, the Italians started to dominate the industry in north Queensland. We saw the old locomotives and trucks, as well as the equipment used in the harvesting and processing of cane sugar, and finished our visit with an interesting film.

Some 12 miles or so from Innisfail, on the Palmeston river, is the legendary Babinda. The story goes that two Aborigines fell in love but they were from different tribes so their love was forbidden. They ran away together but the elders of the tribes chased them. When cornered, the two lovers jumped into the deep waters of the gorge at Babinda and were drowned. The spirit of the girl remains and lures single young men to their death: every year there is some tragedy, when young men slip off the rocks into the freezing water. There are strong undercurrents, and the men are gone in moments. A plaque at the entrance reads "In loving memory of our beloved son, who came for a visit and stayed for ever."

"I would make the trip for this view alone"

We took a number of day trips during the remainder of our two-week vacation, including a few to some of the beautiful beaches in the area—Holloway Beach, Yorkeys Knob, and Trinity Beach—and a spectacular train trip to Kuranda. Unfortunately, the wheelchair and occupant have to be lifted manually both onto and out of the train, but the journey is well worth the trouble.

The train follows the coastal plain, through fields of sugar cane, and then starts to climb the mountains. The track hugs the mountainside and crosses chasms on trestle bridges to pass in front of the breathtaking Barron Falls—I would make the trip for this view alone. There are steps out of the station at Kuranda, so we were unable to visit the town and its market, but we had a cup of tea and admired the station gardens before returning.

We drove to the Tablelands, following the zigzag road from the coastal plain, up through dense rainforest to fertile plateau and the small town of Atherton, center of a thriving tobacco and peanut industry. Our next stop was Lake Tinaroo, where the North Queensland Electricity Authority has built a dam and developed the lake into a recreational area, with café, boating, and walks. We had lunch and went for a short stroll, meeting a cassowary along the way. One of Australia's comic birds, the cassowary is rather like an ostrich but with bright blue legs. Some visitors were feeding it but this bird can be dangerous and should be given a wide berth.

On the way to Mossman we stopped for a light lunch at the expensive *Sheraton Mirage Port Douglas*. It is completely accessible and its golf course, acres of tropical gardens, and swimming pools are worth seeing, but only the very affluent will consider staying. We were disappointed that we could not travel to Cooktown—the roads are not good and the boats not accessible to wheelchair users.

But we did not miss very much, and finished our vacation with a slap-up dinner at the *Cairns Hilton* to celebrate Jill's birthday. The town is so level that we were able to walk—and wheel—to the hotel and back. In spite of the confusion over our flight home to Hobart, it went off without a hitch.

In my experience, travel for paraplegics in Australia is generally easy. I carry a fold-up toilet, which is accepted by airlines and takes up very little space in the car. If traveling by car it is advisable to stop at about 3:30pm and book your accommodation, especially in popular areas. Australian country motels are usually one story and accessible. If booking a hotel in advance state the width of your wheelchair, as some bathroom doors are too narrow. One thing is certain: nothing is perfect for everyone. Beds may be too low, or even too high, and rest rooms may lack rails or grab-bars, or be tucked behind doors, but most facilities are usable or adaptable.

A Spirit of Adventure

Operation Raleigh takes young people all over the world to give them the opportunity to develop their self-confidence and leadership skills. The venturers come from a variety of countries and the projects they undertake involve scientific research, community tasks, and adventure. In the summer of 1989, after a demanding selection process and hectic months of fund-raising to cover the cost of his place, Roger Elliott, who has spina bifida and is confined to a wheelchair, joined an expedition to Queensland as a member of staff.

On arrival in Cairns I found the temperature very warm and the airport staff very helpful, quickly taking me through all the formalities. Although Cairns is the newest international airport in Australia, there was only one disabled parking bay, which was hard to find; the door of the disabled rest room was difficult to open and the layout poor. I hope that the new terminal building, which was under construction, will provide better facilities.

The drive to Operation Raleigh's base at Herberton, southwest of Cairns, was eventful as we took the road which runs around the Gillies Range—there are 186 switchbacks! It's a distance of not much over sixty miles but the drive takes about one and a half hours, especially at night when you have to watch ut for cattle, kangaroos, and other wildlife on the road. The area around Herberton is known as the Atherton Tablelands and comprises volcanic lakes set in virgin rainforest, rolling outback plains, and rich red farmlands.

Our headquarters was a disused vehicle workshop which by its very nature had limited facilities. It became known as "Laurel's Shed," Laurel being the owner of the property. She lived nearby and became a good friend. Our living conditions were very basic: two electric burners for cooking (I never want to see pasta again!); the water was often cold and clothes had to be hand washed or taken to the laundromat in Atherton. In October we had to call the fire service to burn off the undergrowth around Laurel's Shed because of an influx of poisonous snakes and ticks which had hospitalized a local person and killed one of Laurel's cats.

My first job was to telephone the manager of the bank to be used by the expedition, as part of my duties related to the finances of the project. I found that access was going to be difficult as there was a flight of steps at the entrance to the bank. After some discussion it was agreed that we should meet in the staff room at the rear of the bank which would be accessible with some help.

I discovered that both Herberton and Atherton had access problems. In order to enter many of the shops I required assistance and because of the hilly nature of the area and the high summer rainfall, high curbs and storm drains are needed to deal with the volume of water. However, I always found the locals ready and willing to assist me.

After two days in Australia I was driven to Cairns to collect my rental car from *Budget*, which had fitted hand controls to a four-door, two-liter automatic with power steering and air-conditioning. A couple of slow trips around the block were enough to get used to it. I tried the wheelchair in vari-ous positions in the back of the car, but finally had the front passenger seat removed, which provided a better storage area.

"I had been told in London that the expedition would be hard work and not a holiday"

Because of the distances between the towns and cities in Australia, it is necessary to plan journeys carefully, checking the types of road you will encounter, and to take a map, noting the names of the towns you will pass through. You must check oil, water, gas, brakes, and tire pressures, and look under the vehicle for any leaks or loose parts. Spare cans of water and gas should be carried, also chewing gum in case of damage to the fuel tank. You should take some food and drinking water, and stop regularly while on the road to refill the gas tank and to drink.

The monotony of driving through mile after mile of outback is relieved by the sight of wheeling kites and eagles on the lookout for food and swooping on unsuspecting small mammals, birds, and snakes. Other wildlife to be spotted include kangaroos, wallabies, emus, budgerigars, and colorful parrots.

If you have a breakdown, you should stay with your vehicle, and if it is very hot get into the shade underneath the car. However, when I had a flat tire at night, while returning from a visit to some newly made friends, I waited for thirty minutes for a passing car without success. I got out my wheelchair and made my way back to a small town, where I found that the home of the garage proprietor was only accessible up a flight of steps. Having managed to attract attention, I was invited in to wait while the garage owner took my car keys and sorted out my problem, for which he made no charge.

I had been told in London that the expedition would be hard work and not a holiday. This certainly proved to be the case—no eight-hour days and five-day weeks! Apart from work on the accounts, I helped with public relations, talking to schools and other groups about the work of *Operation Raleigh*. The radio was attended by a staff member in order to keep in touch with the project sites, and I did this from time to time.

"There was so much to see, hear, and smell that I simply let my senses take over"

There were two disabled people among the forty members of staff, and one disabled (deaf) venturer out of 109 youngsters from Australia, Italy, Japan, the UK, and USA. The venturers were divided into groups and moved from site to site in order to involve them in as many projects as possible. Only six or eight staff remained at base at any one time; most were out on the sites, supervising the projects. Considering the range of ages and backgrounds among staff and venturers, the atmosphere was generally harmonious and a spirit of adventure and enthusiasm always evident.

I was able to visit some of the sites, most notably that at Cape Tribulation, where Captain Cook's ship, *Endeavour*, went aground in 1770. Here, where the rainforest literally meets the reef, the venturers assisted the Parks Service with the construction of a walking trail, incorporating signage, displays, and viewing points. The only access to the national park is via the Daintree river ferry and a four-wheel drive vehicle, and it was a relief to find a level parking lot on arrival in the national park.

The trail included a 400-yard boardwalk which I was invited to try out in my wheelchair. Walking or pushing was easy, and there was so much to see, hear, and smell that I simply let my senses take over. There are some eighty different types of trees towering above, creating a canopy through which shafts of sunlight pick up the hues of the multicolored birds and

butterflies. Below the lush undergrowth, insects scurry about, collecting and consuming fallen vegetation, and the brush-turkey and flightless southern cassowary peck busily at the ground. I found it all very exciting, and it's good to know that the new boardwalk will enable disabled Australians and tourists to enjoy this experience.

I went to the Undarra lava tubes, a huge radial pattern of tunnels nearly sixty miles in length, formed by the movement of lava outward from a series of now-extinct volcanoes. It is hoped that the area can be opened up to tourists; an airstrip has already been constructed and hotel accommodation is planned. The venturers checked to ensure that all existing caves were plotted accurately, numbered, and tagged. They did a thorough survey of each cave and the vegetation around the entrances, finding some rare and unrecorded species of insects. The lumps of volcanic rock strewn over the area prevented access in my wheelchair, but with the help of the venturers I was carried up to the entrance of a couple of the caves. The trees and ferns are greener here because most of the caves contain water. An unpleasant smell greeted me, resulting from the bat droppings and the damp.

"The rains came and with them an invasion of cane toads, croaking in chorus"

I also visited the canoeing and rafting project on the Gregory river where, with some difficulty, I was able to do some canoeing. I saw the restoration work being carried out by the venturers on the old jailhouse and the train station in Normanton and, because some of our other projects were delayed by a hold-up of equipment in the Melbourne dock strike, I arranged for the Bishop of Carpentaria's church at Forsayth to be completely refurbished. Due to the condition of the church, services were being held in the local pub but on November 23 the church was re-consecrated.

I joined in some of the activities of the area, attending the Tin Miners' Festival Ball, the Atherton Flower Show, theatrical performances, and viewings of work by local artists. I was contacted by the Chairperson of the Atherton Disabled Group and invited to meet them and talk about access and facilities for the disabled in the Greater London area. I helped them to start a survey for presentation to the local authority.

As summer started, the rains came, and with them an invasion of cane toads, croaking in chorus. The smaller ones came in under the door of the shed to join the large spiders and a range of other insects that kept us company. Clothes had to be shaken and shoes checked every morning. More friendly, if noisy, visitors were the kookaburras who came to the shed daily in the hope of being fed. Their usual diet is insects, reptiles, and small mammals but they eagerly accepted sausages and burgers, and some became so tame that they could be hand fed.

Although life was tough and the work hard, I did make the most of my free time. I did an 1800-mile drive, starting down the coast road which leads from Cairns to Townsville. I stopped at Cardwell, in sugar cane territory, where I stayed on the waterfront, in a guesthouse run by a very pleasant Australian family who provided excellent room-service meals. There are superb views over the Great Barrier Reef and Hinchinbrook Island, the world's largest island national park, with towering mountains, sometimes shrouded in cloud, waterfalls, and thick vegetation. It is possible to take a boat trip around the clear waters of the Hinchinbrook Channel—35 miles of enclosed waterways—to view some of the 400 species of coral, 1500 varieties of tropical fish, and many unique forms of marine bird life.

"At small airstrips it is not at all unusual to find cows or kangaroos creating a hazard"

From Townsville I took the main road which follows the line of the railroad to Mount Isa. The capital of northwest Queensland, Mount Isa is built around a huge copper, silver, lead, and zinc mine, attracting miners from all over the world. Underground excavations exceed 230 miles and there are 75 miles of underground railroad lines. Tours of the mine, both below and above ground, are available and I was able to go a mile underground and watch the trains and special mining vehicles at work. I also went to the mining exhibition which opened in 1988 and is the only one of its kind in Australia.

Other stops on my journey were Pentland, Hughenden, Julia Creek, and Cloncurry (home of the first flying doctor base). One night, having not found anywhere to stay, I pulled off the road and prepared to sleep in the car. This was fine for a while, but I was soon disturbed by kangaroos grazing nearby and passing road trains, so I decided to drive on. I was horrified to discover that the wheels were bogged down in loose gravel and I could not move the car.

I waited until a truck approached in the opposite direction and flashed him down with my headlights. He stopped, climbed down from his cab, and I explained the problem. He fished out a tow rope and in minutes had me back on the road. His parting gesture was to hand me a copy of a map showing all the truck parks on the Flinders Highway, a kind thought and typical of the help I so often received in Australia.

In addition to a great deal of driving, I did some flying. Tourists can join the mail planes on their flights and I went to Normanton as well as several cattle stations. When landing at small airstrips it is not at all unusual to find cows or kangaroos creating a hazard.

The pilot has to perform a low over-pass, or sometimes two, to frighten them off.

I obviously wanted to see the Great Barrier Reef, so I took a flight on one of the seaplanes that fly over it. I chose the 43-year-old Grumman Widgeon with the apt registration VH-WET, and flew over the reef to Princess Charlotte Bay, home of the main shrimp fishing fleet. I was also lucky to be invited to join privately chartered aircraft for a number of trips, including one to a tin mine at Kangaroo Creek and another to the biggest gold mine in Australia at Kidston (no samples allowed!). I even tried rounding up cattle in a helicopter (a Bell 47). We flew very low among the trees, rapidly changing direction and catching the branches with the helicopter's landing skis. I love flying but have never felt so vulnerable, and I was sure that we would crash. It was an experience I do not wish to repeat!

While taking a look at Mareeba airport, I accepted an invitation from a helicopter pilot to join him on a flight to check bush fires in the area. I was surprised by the loud retorts of explod-ing tree trunks, and the pungent smell of burning eucalyptus. By day, all one sees are large areas of smoke, but by night the red ribbon of fire is a dramatic sight. The fires can be started by electrical storms, careless picnick-ers, or landowners clearing the area to encourage new growth of grass for cattle. Normally left to burn themselves out, the fires can get out of hand if a strong wind develops. Then the small fire fighters are joined by the local community to create fire-breaks in an attempt to stop the fire spreading.

I flew home to England in November, leaving behind a tempera-ture of 85°F and arriving at a very chilly London airport. At Christmas I exchanged greeting cards and letters with some of the Operation Raleigh staff and venturers as well as some of the Australians I met. It is good to keep in touch and perhaps meet again some-time. I only saw a very small part of Australia and I hope to return. In the meantime I have had some interesting experiences, and retain many great memories and *hundreds* of photographs!

Family Matters in Sydney and Perth

Lorna Hooper has multiple sclerosis (MS), diagnosed in 1980, and she is now confined to a wheelchair. She traveled to Australia at the end of July 1989.

I was both excited and alarmed when my second son David brought his Australian fiancée home to meet the family and wanted us all to attend their wedding in Mudgee, northwest of Sydney. One of my problems is that I cannot stand heat and I know that Australia can be very hot. After my first reaction, which was to say, "Yes, we'll go," I got cold feet. But David and Raeleen decided that their wedding would take place in August, which is of course winter in the southern hemi-sphere, and remembering my son's words ("think positive, Mum") I resolved to make the trip, come what may.

It is absolutely vital for anybody as disabled as I am to undertake such a journey with a companion of the same sex. My daughter Catherine agreed to accompany me and to share with my husband Brian the problems involved in taking me to the rest room. I suffer incontinence and my bowels frequently take me by surprise. In private places Brian could cope, but not all public conveniences have facilities for the disabled, and in these situations Catherine took over.

"If we had known then what we know now, we would have faced the trip with confidence"

A secretary in London and well used to making travel arrangements for her boss, Catherine undertook all the reservations. She found that by traveling with *Qantas* we could have a free internal flight; this proved useful as my brother and his family live in Perth and we wished to spend some time with them in Western Australia.

We chose to break the journey at Singapore to give me time to adjust to jet lag. Besides, the thought of such a long flight appalled me: I am restricted to sitting most of the time but it is vital that I exercise my limbs and move around a little as I would otherwise seize up. There is not much room in airline seats and there are no special seats for disabled passengers. Brian worried about the effect of the heat in Singapore on me but his fears were largely dispelled by the facts that I survived the hot English summer of 1989 better than expected, and that our hotel in Singapore would be fully air-conditioned.

I was at first refused a visa on medical grounds, but a report from my doctor, who said that I was fit to undertake the journey, soon did the trick. As the day of our departure approached we were filled with a mixture of excitement and apprehension. On reflection, if we had known then what we know now, we would have faced the trip with confidence. Our fears were mainly figments of our imaginations—visions of embarrassing ordeals and insurmountable barriers. As it turned out, all were unfounded.

When we arrived at the aircraft door the cabin crew brought a small aisle wheelchair, to which I was transferred. I was wheeled to my seat and lifted into it by my husband and one of the cabin attendants. My own chair was loaded in the hold and transported free of charge. One of our worries was that it would be lost, or even parts of it lost, because it disassembles into five parts. But we labeled every part and suffered no losses.

One minor setback in all the aircraft was the lack of space in the rest rooms for somebody like me who requires the assistance of a helper. Most of the aircraft we boarded had no special rest rooms for disabled passengers; the ones we did see had grab-rails either side of the seat but were only slightly larger. Brian and Catherine found it quicker and easier to manhandle me to the nearest rest room, where with some difficulty my daughter provided the necessary assistance.

The journey to Singapore consisted of a flight to Athens, a one-hour wait there, and another eleven and a half hours to Changi airport, Singapore. I managed to get away with only two visits to the rest room on the second leg. Catherine explained my predicament to passengers lining up for the toilets and they gave me priority. I found people very kind and considerate, willingly allowing me to move to the front of the line.

I did of course go equipped with incontinence pants and pads, and these frequently needed changing. However, to avoid real embarrassment we had prepared ourselves well: my doctor had arranged for me to have a supply of enemas, which could be self-administered, and I had one before each flight.

At two of the airports on our itinerary (Changi and Sydney) disabled passengers were boarded by "high lift"—a vehicle which operates hydraulically and looks rather like a large moving van but has a platform at the rear and over the front cabin. Its only drawback is the time it takes. When we arrived at Sydney the three of us in wheelchairs were last to disembark. By the time we claimed our luggage and were free to leave, all the other passengers had gone. Fortunately, David and Raeleen had the fortitude to hang on and we eventually met up—great relief all around. On the other hand, we saw parts of airports that one is not normally permitted to see, and I greatly appreciated the efforts made by *Qantas* to accommodate me—I cannot praise them enough.

Although we loved the hustle and bustle of the City of Singapore, we found it to be a paradise for shoppers and gourmets rather than for wheelchairs and disabled people. The hotel staff was helpful and the taxi drivers very considerate, but being pushed around on the uneven sidewalks was most uncomfortable. Sydney, however, is a different world, where disabled people are well catered for.

Australian hotels and motels are required by law to provide facilities for disabled guests. There were plenty of adapted rest rooms and these were always spotless. (The first thing we noticed about Australia was the lack of litter.) When we visited attractions such as zoos, gardens, and marine parks I was allowed in free and my "pusher" at half price.

Our first few days in Sydney involved champagne breakfast at a beach café in Manly, a suburb of Sydney where David played most of his rugby. We toured the beach and promenade, and I bought a handmade stone replica of a duck-billed platypus. We sunbathed on Palm Beach and visited the zoo, which is known for its spectacular view over the city. A ride on a monorail also gave us a bird's-eye view of part of the city and the harbor.

After about a week we left Sydney and crossed the Blue Mountains, climbing well over 3000 feet and then dropping down to the inland plateau where the town of Mudgee is situated, some 1500 feet above sea level. The drive took four and a half hours—Australians always measure journeys in time rather than distance.

"I was above the guard rail, looking straight down—I've never been so scared in my life"

Mudgee is a renowned vineyard area and we stayed among the vines at a motel built and run by David's new parents-in-law. The motel (*Hithergreen Lodge*) had one room for disabled persons, with a large *en suite* bathroom, toilet, and shower complete with grabrails. We were the first guests to test it out and I am pleased to say the room passed with flying colors.

The wedding was to take place in the Mudgee church and the reception at the motel. The day before the wedding my husband was taken fossicking (panning for gold), admittedly in a worked-out creek but he thoroughly enjoyed the experience. Meanwhile, I had a facial, my first ever, and I felt wonderful afterward. I was also taken out by a lady friend of the family to look around Mudgee. I saw some beautiful, old colonial-style bungalows and some very fashionable new ones, with a multitude of different colored roof tiles, so that no two streets looked alike. I was taken a few miles into the bush, where my guide's husband had grown up during the Depression in a little cottage made from mud and wattle. The earthen floors were kept damp in the hot weather to keep it cool and lay the dust.

After the wedding, which went off very well, we all felt rather flat, so decided to go hot-air ballooning. I was lifted in by my other son Richard and placed on a stool, so that I could see over the top of the basket. David held on to me and then Richard got in, the idea being that two strapping helpers would be better than one. However, when the pilot got in, the balloon would not take off, so Richard had to get out and Raeleen took his place.

What a wonderful trip it was, so quiet and peaceful, and of course a completely different view of the landscape. I saw the Blue mountains in the distance, giving off the deep blue haze from which they derive their name—this results from the scattering of light by dust and droplets of oil exuded from the leaves of the eucalyptus trees, a phenomenon found nowhere else in the world. The pilot gave me a perfect landing, but everyone else a bumpy one—I think he wanted to shock all the others but took pity on me.

In the evening we went out looking for kangaroos and saw about eight. They are very shy creatures and we were lucky to come upon them so close to the town. We were treated to another memorable glimpse of Australian wildlife the next day, in the Blue mountains, where we saw some beautiful birds, mainly galahs (cockatoos), their plumage bright with lovely colors. We also saw and heard the famous kookaburra. The viewing points in the mountains were accessible to wheelchairs, a ramp being provided next to any steps.

One viewpoint we stopped at had a vertical drop of several hundred feet immediately below. I was sitting on a bench farther back when Richard came over and said, "Mom, this you must see." He picked me up and carried me over to the edge; with him being so tall and me at chest level, I was above the guard rail, looking straight down—I've never been so scared in my life.

Back in Sydney, on one of our last days, we rented a launch, both families joining for a final celebration. No sooner were we under way than out came the champagne. Raeleen's father had been attached to the harbor police earlier in his career and was able to point out all the landmarks—the famous "coathanger" bridge, the Opera House, and Darling Harbor where all the tall ships moored during the bicentenary celebrations—and also the best place to buy fresh shrimp and oysters for lunch.

The men took turns steering the launch and my husband was delighted that during his turn he piloted the boat back under the bridge—not many people can claim to have done that. We wound up a perfect day with dinner at the top of the Centerpoint tower, which has a revolving restaurant over a thousand feet above the city. The views over the city lights were magnificent.

"The wild flowers were just beginning to come out. I brought a few home, pressed them, and put them among our photographs"

All good things come to an end, and we had to move on to the second part of our trip, visiting my brother, his wife, and son in Perth. We hadn't met for 26 years and after all that time wondered how we would get on. We needn't have worried; in no time at all we were chattering like monkeys, recalling events from our early days and bringing each other up to date with our lives. He took a week off work and showed us around the city.

We liked Perth, with its old-style city center, pedestrian precincts, and raised shopping galleries. It was all so clean, and unspoiled by new blocks set among the old buildings. We wandered in Kings Park and gazed down at the Swan river. My husband, once a keen cricketer, insisted on visiting the WACA ground (for the uninitiated, this means West Australian Cricket Association) where he touched the sacred turf.

While in Perth we met old school friends who had retired to the area; it certainly seemed to be a popular place for people who had lived abroad most of their lives and did not relish returning to the cold, damp UK. None of our friends had experienced any difficulty integrating into Australian society. We had heard before our trip that the British were not too popular in Australia but we found everybody most amicable and pleasant.

The temperature was considerably warmer than in Sydney, and the wild flowers were just beginning to come out. I brought a few home, pressed them, and put them among our photographs in the album. They set it off beautifully. It was a memorable first visit to Australia and although I do not suppose we will ever go again I like to think that I could. Who knows? We might have to return to see our first grandchild.

An Outdoor Life

Sheila Murray is a single parent with a severely mentally and physically disabled daughter, Thea. In November 1987, just before Thea's third birthday, Sheila took her to Australia for a vacation.

"And if you ever get the money together, do come and visit." I have friends, both nurses, who emigrated to Australia in 1981 and now live in semi-luxury in a suburb of Perth. How could I resist? We had the money—my savings from when I last worked—and we had the time. After making a few telephone calls, taking advice from friends and the medical world, the project seemed more and more attractive.

Thea is severely brain damaged as a result of meningitis. She cannot walk or talk but is a bright, happy child and a joy to be around. I owe it to her and myself to give her the best possible quality of life and that includes a taste of adventure! We finally boarded the jumbo jet after months of planning, careful checking of dates to ensure that we lost no social security payments, and obtaining letters from doctors declaring her fitness to travel.

The flight was better than I expected, although Thea was awake for nearly twelve hours with excitement, and she lived on a diet of porridge and bananas for twice as long. We changed flights at Singapore, where we were shown great kindness by the Chinese airport staff; I doubt if any of them will forget the sight of me squatting in the crowded lounge in oppressive heat, trying to get some liquid into Thea.

After an ecstatic reunion, over a champagne and croissant breakfast, my friends and I began to plan the next four weeks. The feeling of freedom from doctors' appointments, physiotherapy, and hospital visits was worth every penny—I was finally alone with my child. The most immediate problems were practical, and a trip to the shops for supplies was necessary that afternoon; forget jet lag—I wasn't going to miss a minute!

> *"She was in the swimming pool every day with the local children whether she was in agreement or not"*

The Sunday markets in Australia are a treat—no restrictions, so a whole week's shopping can be done, including exotic vegetables, fruits, seafood, meat, even clothes. Suitable diapers proved difficult—I could not find my favorite brand, and many were tried before I eventually settled on a satisfactory alternative. A small slip-mat for the shower and a potty were the other basic essentials.

Staying with friends was a bonus as they had all the required sun blocks and fly repellents for Thea. She was lathered up each morning, and since we all spent so much time keeping her out of the sun it was a surprise to watch her turn a honey brown. Although visiting British passport holders can be treated in public hospitals under the reciprocal agreement with Australian Medicare, my hosts had provided for us temporarily on their private health insurance policy. To be absolutely safe I had also taken out insurance to cover any medical expenses that might be incurred.

The two teenage daughters of the house readily and eagerly took over much of the physical caring for Thea—she was in the swimming pool every day with the local children whether she was in agreement or not. Thea loved the stimulation of a happy, noisy household. The hot climate seemed to encourage visiting, and the pool was always full of laughter.

A small capsule on the West Coast, Perth is an exciting, vibrant, skyscraper city with the emphasis on a modern experience rather than culture. There were few problems with wheelchair access, elevators in all stores, and ramps in air-conditioned shopping malls. I am used to the stares of the general public when out with Thea but this was not much in evidence down under. In fact, people were friendly and more than once I was stopped by passers-by: "My sister's boy has cerebral palsy—his name is Tom, what's your little girl called?" Few inhibitions and a refreshing openness made shopping trips less of an ordeal and more of a day out (no problems with the language either).

Australia is mostly a hedonistic society, with fancy cocktails, excellent restaurants, expensive designer clothes, and a great deal of time spent on outdoor pursuits. They have the climate and amenities to convert restless energy into surfing, sailing, and beach activities. The disabled are welcome and I had no difficulties in taking Thea to the beach (except on very hot days), the sailing marina, the dolphinarium . . . we even dined at the exclusive Perth Yacht Club.

One of Thea's favorite outings was to the Dolphinarium and Aquatic Center, just a few miles from Perth. Her face lit up as she listened to the barking sealion being fed, the splashing aquatic show with seals jumping through hoops, and a spectacular finale with my friend's daughter—"Princess for the day"—swimming with the dolphins in the pool as part of the Aztec theme show. It was wonderful.

"Eating in Australia was a revelation"

Eating in Australia was a revelation. I had anticipated burgers, pizza, and barbecues, but I was pleasantly surprised to find a gastronomic experience which could hold its own anywhere in the world. I tasted some of the best Chinese food outside the Orient: butterfly shrimp in honey and sesame seed, fresh fruit cup with textures and tastes I could not guess at. Cooking with fruit is an Australian specialty—triangles of rainbow trout gently fried and served on a bed of mango purée, wafer-thin escalope of pork in a hot plum sauce, and delicate baby chicken baked in lemon. Each day brought new takeout delights—cheese sausage with crisp french fries, and irresistible flavors of ice cream. The weight piled on in leaps and bounds but it was worth it!

Set in the beauty of the Australian bush, 40 miles from Perth, is a Spanish villa complex with a wide range of activities for the whole family. The excitement of a chair lift was tempered by coping with a wriggling child, but with the view of Mount Bodeguero and the surrounding countryside as prize I was glad to have made the attempt. The highlight of the day was provided by the performing Andalusian horses which are trained for seven years before appearing in the ring. We all enjoyed a smorgasbord lunch (an

Aussie favorite) before watching the horses in a memorable show set to Spanish marching music and involving difficult maneuvers such as the capriole, Spanish walk, passage, and levarde.

I had expected Australia to be similar to the USA, but I could not have been more wrong. Although both countries are vast in comparison to most European nations, their people's concept of travel differs widely. Internal flights in Australia are not as cheap as I had anticipated—the cost of a round-trip fare from Perth to Sydney was the same as to Hong Kong or Singapore. A trip to Melbourne, Darwin, or Canberra is what I had mentally planned before leaving England, but unlimited funds or time are necessary for this sort of traveling. There is a regular train service from Sydney to Perth which, I was reliably informed, would be an interesting journey and ideally suited to a disabled passenger who could see the countryside at a leisurely pace in the comfort of an air-conditioned car. However, as we had only four weeks, this was out of the question for us.

"Snakes, crocodiles, and poisonous spiders are not found in every garden"

We found that whereas in parts of America people think nothing of driving up to a hundred miles for a meal, this is not the case in Australia. Any venture outside the major towns or cities has to be treated with respect and caution; the bush is not a place to get lost or even to go for a stroll on a Sunday afternoon. Miles of featureless landscape have confused the best equipped explorers, the survival rate being lowest in high summer when temperatures exceed 105°F. We took our holiday from early November to December, when the average temperatures are between 74 and 96°F— comfortable for an adult and bearable for a small child in a wheelchair. The

months of January, February, or March are best avoided by the disabled traveler.

Contrary to popular myth, snakes, crocodiles, and poisonous spiders are not found in every garden, but the wildlife, especially the birds, is rich. Parrots are constant visitors and the sound of the kookaburra is a delight. Pure white cockatoos cross the main highway and we even heard of a kangaroo in a nearby suburb, nonchalantly hopping down a busy street. Household pets are big business and most families have at least one cat or dog; many have more unusual animals. It was very amusing to hear the sound of two cats, a parrot screeching, guinea pigs squeaking, a canary singing, and Thea shouting, in unison, with the kookaburra chipping in from outside, all wanting their breakfast at the same time.

But color, rather than sound, is my most abiding memory of Perth, from the dazzling reds, pinks, yellows, and greens of the young people's clothes in the city center, through the many shades of the plants and foliage in the suburban gardens, to the deep blue ocean and creamy sand of the beach.

A visit to Perth would not be complete without experiencing Rottnest, a small island off the coast in the Indian Ocean. A short boat ride transported us to a tropical paradise used mainly by the locals as an escape from the city. No cars are allowed and it was a joy to be able to push the wheelchair around undisturbed by traffic. The beaches, although crowded, were clean, the rock pools warm (yes, Thea was in again!), and the seafood was delicious.

Gentle kwokkas—small, furry animals unique to the island—roam about in safety, completely tame and loved by the visitors. I felt satisfyingly relaxed and could scarcely believe that a bustling city lay on the horizon. Apart from lazing on the beaches, voyages around the island are popular with the tourists. Seated in armchair comfort, passengers can view schools of brilliantly colored fish, as well as hundred-year-old wrecks lying trapped by coral formations, from the glass-bottomed boats.

"As I enjoyed the warm sunshine for the last time I felt a supreme sense of achievement, even peace"

It would be easy to think of Australia as England with sunshine, but the differences emerge after a few weeks. Cultural stimulation is thin, and even the Australians admit that their TV schedules are probably the worst in the world! However, the outdoor life beckons and is enjoyed by all. When the time came for our departure I must admit to a sense of sadness, not only for leaving dear friends, but for saying goodbye to a nation whose main catchphrase is "G'day." We had encountered a level of friendliness which will be hard to forget, and I should love to return.

On the morning of our departure the house was in chaos with last-minute packing, so I slipped away quietly for a final dip in the pool. The sun shimmered on the water as I swam and there was hardly a sound—unusual for an Aussie morning. I know what the future holds, caring for a handicapped child, but as I enjoyed the warm sunshine for the last time I felt a supreme sense of achievement, even peace, knowing that I had been capable of looking after my child without the backup of a well-meaning but occasionally intrusive medical service. At that point, I was ready to face anything or anyone.

We returned to a cold, wet December evening and Thea laughed and sparkled. Both our lives have been greatly enriched by experiences which colored our activities for many months. There is still sand from the Indian Ocean at the bottom of the wheelchair—somehow I can't bear to brush it away.

New Zealand

Racing Around New Zealand

Kent Kloepping is Director of the Center for Disability Related Resources at the University of Arizona. In February 1992 he and his wife—both wheelchair users—traveled with two friends (both "walkies") to Hawaii for three days, Australia for twelve, and, finishing off their trip, spent fourteen days touring New Zealand.

Planning, planning, and planning is the key to a hassle-free holiday! Mapping out the two basics—transportation and accommodation—provides the building blocks of a successful trip. Of course, pinpointing rest rooms, or "loos," represents another vital chore for the traveler in a wheelchair.

We flew *Qantas* to Hawaii: while the crew was helpful, there was no access to the rest room; an on-board wheelchair will get you to the door of the lavatory, but then you are on your own. Our solution to this problem in the past has been to carefully monitor liquid intake before take-off (12–24 hours prior); this time neither of us had any discomfort or need to use the facilities, then or on the later eleven-hour Auckland to Los Angeles homeward journey.

We found no organization in Hawaii or New Zealand that could rent us a self-drive vehicle (van) with a wheelchair lift, so we decided to purchase a set of telescopic, portable ramps

(weighing some fourteen pounds), took them with us, and rented a standard six- to eight-passenger van. We had one seat removed and it worked out fine.

March 12, we arrived in New Zealand, "the land of the long white cloud." *Adventure Vans* (see *Travel Notes*) told us they were very interested in serving persons with disabilities, and you should contact them to inquire about options. Another very accommodating twosome are Eddie Fessler and his wife, Vivian, at the *Airport Harbor Views Motor Lodge*, Auckland. Not the greatest views in the world, but the room was excellent, with stainless steel roll-in shower.

From Auckland we drove south through Hamilton, heading for the Lake Taupo area. There is easy access and beautiful sapphire-blue water at

Huka Falls, but before that we ate lunch at the Timber Museum, where the rest rooms were very accessible. Do not order a hamburger there! You'll be served cabbage, beets, and other unusual items accompanying a wafer-thin patty of meat (I think). Meat pies and other items are fine. We stayed in Turangi, on the south edge of Lake Taupo, but due to overbooking we missed the *Anglers Paradise Resort Motel*, which is fully accessible for wheelchairs.

Heading south, sightseeing, through the Tongariro National Forest, we stopped for a late morning brunch at the lovely *Chateau Tongariro*, a beautiful old hotel built in 1929 in the French chateau style; the furnishings inside are elegant, the food and service excellent, and the setting, in the shadow of Mount Ruapehu, is majestic. Check out the Maori legends concerning the mountains Tongariro and Taranaki (the guys) and Pihanga (the girl). The chateau has steps to the front entrance, but staff members were very eager and adept at hoisting chairs up about six to eight steps. It's worth it, so go!

On toward Wellington, our stop for the evening. Anyone with some knowledge of geography will have figured out that we are on a much too rapid pace through New Zealand. We'll go slower next time, but on this trip we wanted to see the "whole forest and less of the trees." The countryside is breathtaking: every curve in the road brings a new vista of deep valleys and high, sweeping, grass-covered hillsides; seemingly endless panoramas are dotted with sheep stations, picturesque homes, winding roads, sheep, cattle, deer, and turkeys; and we saw it all in a blaze of fall colors. We arrived late in Wellington, and stayed at the *Sharella Motor Inn*, in an excellent room with roll-in shower, lowered clothes closet, kitchen, and cooking facilities—no complaints there.

We crossed over to the South Island on a ferry with a fully accessible lounge, rest rooms, and dining area; unfortunately, access to the outside decks is over a six- to eight-inch sill, designed to keep out the water in rough seas—you'll need a big boost over that. After the ferry ride (which took 3hr 30min) we landed at Picton and drove south through Blenheim toward the eastern coast, which reminded me of Oregon. We stopped to watch sea lions at Kaikoura and one of our traveling companions walked to within five feet of a huge bull!

"We saw seals, bottle-nose dolphins, and breathtaking scenery the entire boat trip"

Christchurch is said to be the most English city outside of England, and it's lovely—the river (Avon), the cathedral, quaint homes, beautiful flowers, and great shops. The *Belmont Motor Inn* was very good for wheelchairs and the owners very obliging, though they need to change some electrical outlets for easier reach from a wheelchair, and the "ramp" to our room was "stee-eep"! *Cobbs* was a good place to eat; there are *Cobbs* restaurants all over New Zealand and they have a pleasant family atmosphere.

The day we headed for Mt. Cook and the Southern Alps terrible winds blew in a major rain and snow storm, and for several days the weather deteriorated badly. We didn't see Mt. Cook, but Lake Tekapo is beautiful—the color of the water is aquamarine, says my wife—and we stayed at Twizel, a small village, in an excellent hotel motel, *McKenzie County Inn*. There were no showers (bathtub only), but otherwise the rooms were fine, with superb views of the Alps.

We arrived in Queenstown in the rain. The *Earnslaw Lodge* on beautiful Lake Wakatipu was very accessible, but our room faced the street! We usually ate our morning meal in our rooms, and the "cooked breakfasts" are especially good. It's rare to find places to stop and eat breakfast, as we do in

America, so eat before you leave your motel or hotel.

It was still raining when we arrived at the *Te Anau Downs Motor Inn*, the jumping off point for Milford Sound. They had overbooked, but the Australian chap who had "our room" said it was great. Ha! We made it to Milford and took the boat ride through the spectacular nine-mile-long fiord. We needed help to board the boat but the crew is used to handling wheelchairs. The fiord is flanked by sheer walls of solid rock; center stage is Mitre Peak, 4633 feet above the water; Cliff House Rock rises vertically over 2000 feet above the sound and drops 2000 feet below the surface. There are six permanent waterfalls, Palisades and Bowen originating over 5000 feet above the sound. We saw seals, bottle-nose dolphins, and breathtaking scenery the entire boat trip.

"Haast Pass was spectacular, with literally hundreds of waterfalls"

We retraced our route north to Queenstown, stayed at the *Earnslaw Lodge* for one night, and then took off for the western coast and the Franz Josef and Fox glaciers. It rained nonstop the entire drive to Franz Josef. Haast Pass was spectacular, with literally hundreds of waterfalls, but we made only one "pit stop" and lunch break in Haast. The Mount Aspiring National Park Headquarters had fascinating exhibits, focusing on the native Maori people and their use of the land—flax for clothing, harvesting seafood from the Tasman Sea, searching for *pounamu* (green stone)—as well as on the flora and geologic features of the area; the park center has very accessible rest rooms. The rain continued throughout the evening at the *Glacier Gateway Motor Lodge* (excellent room with roll-in shower), and into the next day on our drive to Hokitika, where we stopped and bought some greenstone (New Zealand jade).

The final leg of our journey on the South Island, to Picton, seemed endless, and we arrived late at the *Anchorage Lodge*. We had a large, beautiful room, but the shower was unusable because of a door, and the lavatory only just usable. At 5am the next day we crossed the Cook Straits and drove all the way to Rotorua. We were all feeling the effects of too much driving: 375 miles that day, and the day before.

Ledwich Lodge Motel, in Rotorua, has good access for wheelchairs and is situated in a wonderfully diverse region. It is the center of the northern Maori culture, a unique thermal area of hot mineral pools, geysers, craters, and boiling mud, and has many neat tourist attractions, not the least of which is the Agrodome Leisure Park (an agricultural theme park with two daily stage shows featuring New Zealand's 19 breeds of sheep, sheep shearing, and sheepdog demonstrations; there are some 10 acres of kiwi fruit orchards, and other activities include horseriding and helicopter trips). Plan to spend several days in the area and do participate in a traditional Maori feast, a *hangi*, and visit Ohinemutu Village, a Maori community, and the Maori Arts and Crafts Institute. The Whakawerawera Thermal Reserve (geysers and hot springs), the Rainbow Springs wildlife park, and Te Wairo, the village buried by the 1886 eruption of Mt. Tarawera, are among the other attractions.

That's it: we drove to Auckland via Te Puke and again stayed with Eddie and Vivian Fessler at the *Airport Harbor Views Motor Lodge*. We spent our last day trying to recover from the previous thirty days of traveling at a breakneck pace! We packed at a more leisurely pace and checked in early at the *Air New Zealand* desk for a 9pm flight. We eventually arrived home in Tucson, Arizona, at 8pm on the same day—an hour before we left!

On boarding the *Air New Zealand* plane in Auckland, we were told by the flight attendant that he would assist

ther my wife or I to the rest room, if
eeded: this is the first time we have
ad that offer. Although we didn't use
e facilities, the attendant told us that
e on-board wheelchair did fit inside
e rear rest room of the plane.

I would not recommend the pace we
et for New Zealand. It's such a beauti-
l country that you must allow time to
et in and out of the vehicle frequently,
"see things"; of course, there will be
esignated stopovers on your itinerary,
ut the natural scenery is awesome and
ere will be innumerable unscheduled
ops to admire it. Next trip, we'll take
more time to sniff the daisies—or the
kiwi blossoms.

That said, I don't regret a single
moment. The most difficult aspect of
traveling internationally for most
disabled persons is making the
decision to go, but with good planning
and homework it's really a breeze. One
final piece of advice: write for and
request every brochure, access guide,
and publication that you can find; fifty
percent or more of the material will be
of no help, but the other fifty percent
will provide what you need. You can
even write to me. I answer my mail!

Going for the Big One

**hirteen years ago David Gray broke
is neck playing rugby. Although tech-
ically a quadriplegic, he did regain
ubstantial power and control in his
ands and arms. In 1984, not keen to
ush from college to an office job, he
urchased a round-the-world air
cket. David's account concentrates
n his experiences in Australia and
ew Zealand.**

was reluctant to ask any but my clos-
st friends if they'd like to come with
e, for fear they might think I wanted
nd needed a carer (pig-headed inde-
endence is one of my faults). No one
n the approachable list had the time,
e money, *and* the inclination to come
long, so my choice was made for me—
would go alone.

Once the money was paid there was
o backing out. Preparations were
ade months in advance: extensive
xercise to get myself to peak fitness (a
elative term), reading every guidebook with even a shred of information
on access (for all my research, most
such information related to the USA),
fitting solid tires to my wheelchair (the
outback is not the place to get a flat),
and arranging supplies of every medication I might need. I even practiced
balancing my suitcase and travel bag
on my lap, a skill which was to get
plenty of use.

Finally, armed with an address book
listing some relatives and "friends of
friends," I set off to London one
January morning. My trip did not get
quite the flying start I had hoped for. At
my first stopover, Singapore, the cabin
crew, and airport staff contrived
between them to overlook the fact that
I needed assistance to disembark, and I
eventually left the plane in an undignified manner with my arms hooked
around the shoulders of two of the stur-
diest stewards.

Jet lag did not encourage exploring,
but the really intimidating fact was that
I was *on my own*! If I was to see
anything beyond the streets around my
hotel, I had first to get in and out of a
taxi (assuming one would stop for me)
and next to take the risk that my destination would prove impractical for me

in my wheelchair. Add potential language problems and it all seemed very daunting.

Nevertheless, I did make it to a few places, including *Raffles Hotel*, where some passing strangers were press-ganged into assisting me up the flight of steps at the entrance. Over one of the hotel's famous gin slings I made the acquaintance of an Australian businessman who has since become a regular pen pal and assured me of knowing at least one person in Australia.

The flight to Sydney was uneventful, although being sprayed on arrival (to prevent import of insect pests) was a novel experience. My wheelchair appeared without one footplate, which turned up later considerably bent, but several blows with a hammer provided an adequate repair job.

"For an angler like myself, the first stop had to be the Bay of Islands"

Arrival time was before 7am, so I had booked no accommodation, assuming it would be easier to locate when I wasn't several thousand miles away. The tourist information desk suggested a downtown hotel but I discovered that "flat access" actually meant five steps in the lobby, and "suitable rooms" meant that the bathroom doors were too narrow for my chair. After several fruitless telephone calls, I remembered the name of a brand new hotel, mentioned by my neighbor on the flight. My hunch turned out to be correct: the *Southern Cross* offered state-of-the-art accessible accommodation. The only drawback was the de luxe price, leaving me no alternative but to find another hotel as soon as possible.

A visit to the downtown tourist office (only twelve steps to negotiate) supplied the answer. They helped me to locate a great hotel with reasonable prices in the rather tame "red light" district. The *Crest*, used by *P&O* for its staff, subsequently became my base and provided a room with a stunning

view of the Opera House and harbor bridge. There was flat access from the street to the lobby.

Early January in my home town of Belfast is more often than not wet, cold and windy; in Sydney the sun shone every day and the temperature was delightful. The Opera House was high on my list of places to visit and more than lived up to expectations. It has its critics but to my eye is an outstanding piece of architecture, complementing beautifully its setting in Sydney harbor. Nearby is the ferry terminal where there are numerous boats to be boarded (without difficulty) for sightseeing or travel to other parts of the city. Ever seen a sail-board marathon? I did, and the sight of three thousand sails remains fixed in my memory.

The first floor of my hotel contained a number of shops, including a travel agency where discussions with the owner led to a trip to a local winery. He arranged for a few willing hands to lift me to the front seat of the bus when it stopped at the hotel, and similar help at each place of interest. The main attraction was the wine tasting and steak barbecue, preceded by demonstrations of sheep-dog handling, sheep shearing and boomerang throwing.

During my month in Australia I sampled life thousands of miles to the west, in Perth, where on several days the temperature reached 100°F but the relatively low humidity made this tolerable. Introductions from friends to some locals opened doors for me, and I was able to share the pleasures of more wine tasting, a cruise on the Swan river and a night at the races before heading back to Sydney and then eastward again to Auckland, New Zealand.

I had arranged for a rental car and, as promised, *Avis* provided one with hand controls. The steering knob I had specified was missing but fortunately I had taken the precaution of bringing one with me. The car proved invaluable over the following two weeks, as I wandered around the North Island,

lthough it took some getting used to
he hand controls were of an unfamil-
ir type) and was quite exhausting to
rive since it was very large, had no
ower steering, and its four-door
esign required me to devise a totally
ew means of getting myself and, more
nportantly, my chair into the car
naided.

*"I gave a lift to a hitchhiker, who in
return helped me along a forest
path to see the biggest kauri of
them all"*

For an angler like myself, the first
top had to be the Bay of Islands in the
ir north of North Island—the El
'orado for big-game fishermen. I
eaded over the Auckland harbor
ridge (widened by the addition on
ach side of an extra prefabricated lane,
onstructed by the Japanese and
nown locally as the "Nippon clip-ons")
nd on to Paihia. On the journey my
nthusiasm was whetted by radio bulle-
ns reporting the progress of a strug-
le between a giant marlin and a
sherman who had hooked it the previ-
us day! Victory went to the fish after
2 hours, when the line had to be cut as
storm threatened the boat.

I checked in to the modern *Paihia
ands Motel* which had a ramp to one of
s apartments. Surprisingly, the archi-
:ct had then spoiled his good work by
istalling a cabinet which blocked free
ccess to the bathroom. However, I
und I could manage by using an ordi-
ary chair, placed immediately inside
ne doorway, and the friendly motel
wners (Bill and Wanda) made up for
ny problems. They cheerfully cooked
ly catches and even took me out to
inner one evening.

Bill arranged for a bus tour to the
lorth Cape and helped me get aboard.
'his turned out to be a day well spent:
ne driver's commentary was interest-
ng; the area was rich in history and
ights, including the Cape itself (where
ne Pacific Ocean and Tasman Sea

meet); and we had a thrilling drive
through the surf for part of the Ninety
Mile Beach (actually only fifty miles
long).

The old whaling town of Russell, on
the other side of the Bay of Islands, is
also well worth seeing, and a cruise on
the bay is a must, even for non-anglers.
At Waitangi there is a Maori meeting
house, complete with war canoe, at the
site of the signing of the Waitangi
Treaty between the Maoris and *pakehas*
(white men) in 1840. My car developed
a flat on the way to Waitangi, on a fairly
deserted road, but my luck held—while
I sat and considered how to tackle it, a
car drew up and two Dutch tourists had
the situation sized up and the tire
changed in no time at all.

On the journey back to Auckland I
chose the west side of the northern
peninsula, famous for its forests of
kauri, immense trees with straight
trunks which live for centuries, if given
the chance. I gave a lift to a hitchhiker,
who in return helped me along a forest
path to see the biggest kauri of them
all, named "Tanemahuta," in the
Waipoua Forest Sanctuary.

Some distance southeast of
Auckland is Rotorua, the center of the
active thermal springs area of New
Zealand (complete with power station
driven by naturally produced steam)
and also an important stronghold of the
Maori people. Combined with the fascinating geologic sights in the area,
these springs make Rotorua one of the
most popular holiday resorts in New
Zealand, despite the sulfurous fumes
from the many geysers.

While most geysers are difficult to
approach closely, there is little problem
in finding a viewpoint. A nearby cultural center at Whakarewarewa gives
exhibits on New Zealand's history, as
well as talks and demonstrations of the
Maoris' traditional skills, such as woodcarving; there is a reconstructed Maori
village to examine at your leisure. The
Agrodome makes an entertaining show
out of educating visitors about every-

thing to do with the country's major industry—sheep farming—and there are examples of most important breeds, plus displays of shearing and sheep-dog handling.

Next stop was for more fishing, this time for the legendary trout in Lake Taupo. Question was, where to try my hand? I spotted a boat being drawn out of the water by three men and decided to ask their advice. They showed me their catch—thirteen *huge* trout which were apparently considered only average in size! The fishermen confessed to being unsure where I could gain access to the lake shore, and asked me back to the boat owner's farm for a cup of tea while they discussed the problem.

Despite having guests staying with them they then insisted that I stayed the night. Once that was arrranged, they towed the boat back to the lake, launched it, arranged my licence, and took me out for a few hours, during which I hooked and landed my prize trout. Dinner that evening was a grand affair, and the next day I ate trout before heading on my way.

"We enjoyed a celebration meal with fellow "survivors" in the park visitors' center, while we waited for earth-moving vehicles to free our cars"

My route took me southward through Tongariro National Park, a spectacular area with several volcanoes which simmer for most of the time, and occasionally erupt. A fairly good road leads up to the permanent snow line, where there are chalets for winter skiers. Driving is at a leisurely pace since the main highway passes next through the Paraparas, a scenic area of hills which cause winding bends for some 30 miles before the road reaches the coast at Wanganui, where I stopped with relatives for a while and where financial constraints dictated the return of the rental car.

A local festival gave me an opportunity to meet people and savor the "Kiwi" lifestyle. The importance of farming was again apparent, with contests of both sheep shearing and log cutting. Food was produced from a *hangi*, a traditional oven created by putting embers in a hole in the ground over which food is steamed in baskets. The results were edible, but it is definitely not a case of "the old ways are best!"

Wanganui offers pleasant parks, a good regional museum, and jet-boat trips on New Zealand's second longest river, but it wasn't long before I was off again, this time sharing a trip around the South Island with two cousins. We caught the ferry from Wellington on one of the days when the elements were living up to the local name for the town—"Windy Wellington." After an uncomfortable crossing of the Cook Strait (during which some enterprising schoolboys collected up all the bags provided for those feeling seasick, and then sold them to the desperate passengers!), we sailed into the calm waters of beautiful Queen Charlotte Sound and docked at Picton. A short drive in the waiting rental car brought us to Nelson for an overnight stop with friends.

For the next few days we traveled down the west coast, calling at the odd-looking Pancake Rocks at Punakaiki, a natural glow-worm dell at Hokitika, and a seal colony at the unfairly named Cape Foulwind. The Southern Alps rise only a few miles inland, and with the moist air coming off the sea torrential rain is not uncommon in this area, but the sun shone for us the whole time. Before long, we reached Westland National Park, which features superb views of Mt. Cook and the park's two glaciers, the Franz Josef and the Fox. It was here that the most dramatic incident of our trip occurred.

A narrow road wound along a steep-sided valley, providing the only access to the Fox Glacier. A rare thunderclap sent everyone dashing for their cars,

t before we could leave, the valley's
wollen streams brought rock slides
ashing down across the road, block-
g it to depths of about 6m and strand-
g nine cars. By sheer good fortune no
e was hurt. While we assessed our
sition the forest rangers arrived and
cided that a speedy withdrawal was
led for. Several tourists helped to
ist me, in my wheelchair, over lots of
ud and rock, after which we enjoyed
celebration meal with fellow "survi-
rs" in the park visitors' center, while
waited for earth-moving vehicles to
e our cars.

"I succeeded in spinning the car off the road in a flurry of gravel"

Once reunited with our car, we
ove through more and more breath-
king scenery—the Haast Pass,
keland, Queenstown, the
emarkables (a range of mountains),
Anau, and Fiordland National Park.
e views of Milford Sound from one
the regular cruise boats are out of
is world and not to be missed by any
sitor to the area. Undoubtedly, the
any hikers and walkers who head for
e famous trails among the mountains
in most from this natural paradise
t there is plenty to see from accessi-
e sites, too.

In contrast, accommodation
signed for wheelchairs was quite
arce in 1984—to tour without book-
g ahead required flexibility and will-
gness to rely on help, at least to get in
d out of the usual cabin-type motel
oms. The situation has improved
nsiderably since then, but if finding
commodation as you go isn't your
yle, some research will be needed in
der to organize an itinerary around
itable stopping points. The tourist
ard guide, *New Zealand—Where to
ay*, uses the wheelchair symbol, and
ere is now a separate, annually
dated access guide listing a good
nge of accessible accommodation—
e *Travel Notes*.

Back on North Island I stayed for a
few days at Palmerston North, with a
family I had met in Paihia. After only a
brief acquaintance they had invited me
to visit them and they were most generous with their hospitality—another
example of the friendly attitude I found
to be the norm among New Zealanders.
Perhaps it is a legacy from the days
when the early European pioneers
relied on each other as they struggled
to make a living in a new land, or
maybe it stems from the fact that so
many Kiwis have themselves been travelers, either as students or when
emigrating from other parts of the
world.

My ten-week stay was rounded off
with another trip in an adapted rental
car, this time to the Coromandel
peninsula where I succeeded in
spinning the car off the road in a flurry
of gravel (unsealed roads are quite
common), fortunately without causing
too much damage. Again, the
mountains, coastline, and forests made
marvelous scenery, and a couple of
wild dolphin put on a show in
Whitianga harbor.

A drink at a nearby bar reminded me
that so far the really monster fish had
eluded me, for above the door was the
preserved head of a giant marlin,
landed in Mercury Bay. So back I went
to the Bay of Islands, stopping again
with Bill and Wanda. One of their
friends kindly took me fishing in his
boat free of charge (professional boats
can charge up to $500 per day). Despite
my efforts nothing big came my way,
but any sense of disappointment was
minor given the beautiful weather and
views.

Having stayed longer than intended
in New Zealand, I skipped my planned
visit to Fiji and flew on to Hawaii. From
there I continued to the States, stopping off in San Francisco, San Antonio,
and New Orleans. Florida was to have
been my final destination but, in truth,
homesickness suddenly took hold and,
combined with a dwindling supply of

travelers' checks, sent me flying home from Miami only a few hours after I arrived. I hadn't seen or done absolutely everything I had dreamed of, yet I'd savored more than most people ever get the chance to experience. Many a time I'd received help, sometimes vital help, but for all that, my original concerns and fears disappeared in Singapore, to be replaced by a confidence which is perhaps one of the greatest rewards of travel.

AUSTRALIA & NEW ZEALAND: TRAVEL NOTES

Sources of Information

Australian Tourist Commission, 2121 Avenue of the Stars, Suite 1200, Los Angeles, CA 90067 (☎310/552-1988); 2 Bloor Street West, Suite 1730, Toronto ON M4W 3E2 (☎416/925-9575). The *Australian Tourist Commission* can provide copies of *Travel in Australia for People with Disabilities* (July 1990), a useful twenty-page Xeroxed guide produced by the commission after consultation with various Australian disability organizations. Copies are also available from the Senior Information Officer, Information Section, Australian Tourist Commission, 80 William Street, Woolloomooloo, NSW 2011 (☎2/360-1111). The text is concise and frank, with sections on getting there, getting around, equipment rental, where to stay, and what to see. Publications, support organizations, specialized services, tourist bureaux, and tour operators are listed state by state; the only gripe here is that for many organizations only the phone number is supplied—the address would be useful. The intention was to update every two years, and in mid-1992 updating was under way, publication of the new edition expected by the end of the year.

ACROD (*The Australian Council for the Rehabilitation of the Disabled*), PO Box 60, Curtin, ACT 2605, Canberra; ☎62/824333; fax 62/813488. *ACROD* has a library and information service, holds copies of a large list of access guides, and can tell inquirers where to obtain these.

New Zealand Tourism Office (NZTO), 501 Santa Monica Boulevard #300, Santa Monica, Los Angeles, CA 90401 (☎213/395-7480 or 800/388-5494); in Canada, call or visit Suite 1260, IBM Tower, 701 West Georgia Street, Vancouver, BC (☎604/684-2117); write or fax NZTO, PO Box 10071, Pacific Center, Vancouver, BC V7Y 1B6 (fax 604/684-1265). Almost unique among tourist boards in its demonstration of a commitment to update and improve its information for disabled visitors on a regular basis (every year), the *NZTO* distributes *Access: A Guide for the Less Mobile Traveler*, a clear, glossy brochure produced in Wellington by the *New Zealand Tourism Department* (PO Box 95, Wellington; ☎4/472-8860). It lists accessible accommodation, restaurants, and sightseeing attractions, and advice on transport covers rental vehicles, air travel, ferries, trains, buses, and taxis. The criteria for acceptance in the guide were supplied by the **New Zealand CCS** (formerly known as the *NZ Crippled Children Society*, 86–90 Vivian Street, PO Box 6349, Te Aro, Wellington; ☎4/384-5677; fax 4/382-9353), another useful contact organization with an extremely helpful Information Manager, Michelle Hill. The general tourist board guide, *Where to Stay*, also specifies suitable accommodation ("paraplegic units") for disabled people, again using the *New Zealand CCS* specifications.

New Zealand Disabilities Resource Center (NZDRC), 840 Tremaine Avenue, Palmerston North; ☎6/356-2311; fax 6/355-5459. One of nearly twenty members of the *NZ Federation of Disability Information Centres* (list of addresses available from *NZDRC*), this center gathers and updates information on travel and recreational opportunities for disa-

AUSTRALIA & NEW ZEALAND: TRAVEL NOTES

led people—transportation, tour companies
fering vacations for people with disabilities
ncluding escorted tours, skiing, camping,
ding, and other outdoor pursuits), contact
ddresses. Sheena Taylor, Information
onsultant at the *NZDRC*, contributed much of
e information on New Zealand in these
ravel Notes.

**isabled Persons Assembly (New
ealand) Inc.** (*DPA*), PO Box 10-138, The
errace, Wellington; ☎4/472-2626, voice or
ax. The *DPA* is involved in a number of differ-
nt activities relating to their aim of "Full
articipation and equal opportunities for all
eople with disabilities in all aspects of New
ealand society"; these include setting up the
otal Mobility project (see *Transport*), and
ursuing issues such as building access, equal
mployment opportunities, and anti-
scrimination legislation. There are 35
egional *DPA* assemblies, and it's worth
ontacting them for local information; for exam-
e the Christchurch and Districts *DPA* has
ecently (1990) published an excellent 300-
age book about the Canterbury region (price
Z$5, from *Disabled Persons Centre*, 314
Vorcester Street, Linwood, PO Box 32074,
hristchurch; ☎3/795636). Although the
egional *DPA*s may not be able to answer all
avel inquiries they'll put you in touch with
omeone who can.

Tour Operators

ndependent travel in Australia or New
ealand is easy to organize, not least because
f the helpful publications from the tourist
ffices and the wealth of advice and informa-
on available from organizations within these
ountries. General access is relatively good and
ccessible accommodation can often be found
ong the way without prebooking, although
uring high season it's advisable to reserve in
dvance in many areas; accessible transporta-
on can be arranged but this usually requires
ome advance planning.

There are a number of specialist **tour oper-
tors for disabled travelers** in **Australia**,
ome of which act as information agencies;
etails are given in the tourist commission

guide. *Barrier-Free Travel* (57 Albyn Road,
Strathfield, NSW 2135; ☎2/742-5918) is a
recent arrival, set up by a group of disabled
travelers who offer information on accessible
accommodation, access to attractions, specialized transport, personal care needs, and wheelchair repairs in cities around the world as well
as in Australia. A one-off A$50 fee is charged
for as many consultations as it takes to arm
prospective travelers with the information they
require.

Some of the **US-based specialist opera-
tors** (see *Practicalities*, p.597) include Australia
and/or New Zealand in their programs, for
example *Nautilus Tours, Dvořák's Expeditions*,
and *New Directions*.

In **New Zealand**, *Disabled Kiwi Tours* (East
Coast Highway, PO Box 550, Opotiki; ☎7/315-
7867; fax 7/315-5056) was recently set up by
Allan and Shona Armstrong and offers escorted
customized tours in wheelchair-accessible
motor homes which provide all essentials (lavatory, stove, refrigerator, mobile phone) during
the day, while overnight accommodation is in
accessible hotels or motels. Maximum group
size is four, with no more than two disabled
travelers. Costs per person for a group of four
would be around $145 per day; if there are only
two people this goes up to around $200.
Travelers can choose their own itinerary, with
the proviso that accessible accommodation is
scarce in some areas, mainly in the South
Island. Those who simply want to rent the vehicle plus driver and arrange their own accommodation pay $440 per day total. Be warned that
the Armstrongs are aiming to provide a service
for those with "severe disabilities," so they
attempt to cover all eventualities by asking
detailed questions about medical, dietary, and
toileting requirements in their application form,
and clients must obtain a statement of fitness
to travel from their doctor. If you don't like to
be fussed over, choose another operator.

For most travelers with disabilities, the
services of a specialist in travel for disabled
people will be unnecessary. There are
hundreds of **mainstream vacation packages**
to choose from, with something to suit every
taste and pocket; whether you travel with a
general tour company or one specializing in

AUSTRALIA & NEW ZEALAND: TRAVEL NOTES

Australia or New Zealand, the chances of finding a company that can match a vacation to all your requirements (including disability-related ones) are high. The national airlines offer a range of generally good-value package deals: have a look at the *Qantas* South Pacific book, *Qantas Vacations Australia, New Zealand, Fiji and Tahiti*, and the *Air New Zealand Go As You Please* brochures for Australia, New Zealand, or the Pacific Islands. New Zealand's domestic carrier, *Mount Cook Line*, also offers several packages from air travel only to wilderness expeditions. Barbara Horrocks was pleased with *Ansett Travel Service* (offices all over Australia) which made flight, accommodation, and tour reservations while she was in Australia.

Atlantic and Pacific Tours (USA office at Suite 308, 230 North Mayland, Glendale, CA 91206; ☎818/240-0538) is now offering bus tours for groups through *Southern World Vacations* in Auckland (☎9/309-8273); it has one wheelchair-accessible and lift-equipped bus for group tours of New Zealand, with extensions to Australia and Fiji (10 wheelchair lock-downs, plus seating for 16 other passengers); it also runs *Horizon Holidays* and *Newmans*. Margaret Whitta (*Whitta Tours*, 57 Ridge Road, Howick, Auckland; ☎9/537-3300) organizes vacations for people with disabilities in association with *Atlantic and Pacific Holiday Shoppe*, Howick.

The organizers of Roger Elliott's expedition—not a tour company, of course—are at **Operation Raleigh** Headquarters (Alpha Place, Flood Street, London SW3 5SZ, UK; ☎071/351 7541). Operation Raleigh is an international charity which aims to develop the potential of young people. There are around eight to ten expeditions a year, each lasting about ten weeks; an expedition may consist of 120 young people, split into groups of between 5 and 15 to tackle individual projects that may be concerned with conservation, community work, or pure adventure such as jungle treks, desert crossings, mountaineering, white-water rafting, and canoeing. Anyone aged 17 to 25 who can swim 500 meters and speak some English can apply. Selection procedures are tough—the expeditions are usually in harsh environments where

conditions are basic and the work can be arduous. Staff is hand-picked for specialized knowledge and experience, and may include explorers, scientists, doctors, nurses, youth leaders, or service personnel. In principle people of all nationalities, backgrounds, and abilities are actively encouraged to become Venturers (or members of staff), but disability may preclude some people from joining in some activities and expeditions, depending on individual capabilities (a primary health survey in a remote area, for example, might involve a 60 mile trek). There are special programs to encourage young people with disabilities.

Outward Bound Australia (PO Box 4213, Sydney, NSW 2001; ☎2/261-2200) organizes adventure holidays along similar lines. Their "Mixed Ability" programs are designed to "bring disabled and able-bodied people together in a wilderness setting to participate in outdoor adventure holidays." *Outward Bound Trust of New Zealand* (PO Box 3158, Wellington; ☎4/472-3440) runs special courses for people with disabilities at the Cobham Outward Bound School, Anakiwa, in the Marlborough Sounds near Picton (☎3/574 2016).

The *Spirit of Adventure Trust* (Operations Office, PO Box 2276, Auckland, New Zealand; ☎9/373-2060; fax 9/379-5620) offers special voyages (duration ranging from a half day to four days; no age limit) on the sail training ships *Spirit of Adventure* and *Spirit of New Zealand* about twice a year. People with a slight physical impairment may also be eligible to join a standard youth (15 to 18 years) voyage.

The *Outdoor Pursuits Centre* (Private Bag, Turangi, New Zealand; ☎74/65511) runs two courses each year for people with physical disabilities, and may be willing to organize some activities for groups if arranged in advance. Outdoor acitivities can include snow caving, climbing, ropes courses, skiing, tramping, camping, kayaking, canoeing, and white-water rafting.

The *NZ Paraplegic and Physically Disabled Association*, Inc. (PO Box 610, Hamilton, New Zealand) should be able to provide information on sporting activities available throughout New Zealand.

AUSTRALIA & NEW ZEALAND: TRAVEL NOTES

Getting There

Qantas produces a whole series of passenger care leaflets, the relevant one for disabled passengers being *Travel Care—Air Travel for People with Disabilities or Special Medical Conditions*. The Australian airline comes highly recommended, by several contributors, for efficient service, good facilities, and willingness to treat each passenger as an individual. *Qantas* flies daily nonstop from Los Angeles to Sydney, with connecting flights to Perth, Adelaide, Melbourne, Brisbane, and Cairns (also to Auckland, Christchurch, and Wellington in New Zealand); flights from Chicago, New York, Boston, and Washington DC are routed through Los Angeles; flights from San Francisco go via Honolulu. From Vancouver there are flights to Brisbane, Cairns, Melbourne, and Sydney via Honolulu; flights from Toronto also route through Honolulu.

Roger Elliott asked *Qantas* staff at the Heathrow check-in desk if his lightweight wheelchair could be stored on the flight deck rather than in the hold—no problem. He was transferred to the on-board wheelchair at the door of the aircraft and taken, without fuss, in this chair to the rest rooms whenever necessary during the flight. Roger comments that although the on-board chair was suitable for him (he is quite small, weighing only 125 pounds), larger passengers might have a struggle.

Air New Zealand has a Newton Skychair for use on board its aircraft. The footplates are reported to be somewhat high, which might be tricky for people with stiff hips or knees, but otherwise it's comfortable, with soft vinyl seat and removable armrests. Disabled passengers are given seats behind the crew rest, where there is adequate legroom but no fear of blocking the exits. According to Kent Kloepping, assistance may be offered to wheelchair users wishing to visit the on-board rest rooms; we have also received reports that passengers may be taken to the first-class facilities if more space is needed. This airline, like *Qantas*, has a good reputation for handling passengers with disabilities as people rather than medical cases.

Air New Zealand operates two nonstop flights a week from Vancouver to Auckland, with connections to Wellington, Christchurch, and other New Zealand cities. From Los Angeles there are nonstop flights to Auckland (*Qantas* also flies direct from LA to Auckland); stopovers are available in Hawaii, Tahiti, Cook Islands, Fiji, and Australia.

Major **US and Canadian carriers** that operate flights to Australia and New Zealand and should cope smoothly with disabled passengers include *Canadian* (from Vancouver or Toronto via Honolulu to Auckland or Sydney, connecting to Melbourne) and *United* (from Los Angeles direct to Sydney or Auckland, connections to Melbourne or Brisbane; from Chicago, Denver, Los Angeles, San Francisco, or Seattle via Honolulu to Auckland, connecting to Sydney or Melbourne). As always, shop around for the best deal.

Andrew Healey used *British Airways* and flew back on a modified Boeing 747 with one aircraft rest room just accessible to the aisle chair. He suggests avoiding direct flights, not because of difficulties with disability but because of the boredom factor. Most people traveling from Britain seem to stop over in Singapore or Bangkok, and are glad of the break. This is less of a problem for travelers from North America as flight times are generally shorter—flying time from the West Coast to New Zealand is about 12 hours—but crossing the International Date Line can throw your "body clock," so it's still advisable to take a rest day at the start of your trip.

Transport

The leading **domestic airlines** in Australia and New Zealand seem pretty well geared up for disabled passengers. Reservations are generally made through international carriers or travel agents, and special requirements should be stated at this time. Although internal flights may seem expensive there are a number of discounts available to overseas visitors, details of which can be obtained from a travel agent or your international airline.

Australian Airlines publishes a brochure for disabled passengers which contains ground plans of the major domestic airports; there is a frequent flyer program which avoids the need

AUSTRALIA & NEW ZEALAND: TRAVEL NOTES

for repeated handling advice. *Ansett Australia*'s brochure is only available from its Melbourne office; this airline also has a frequent flyers program, *Ansacare*, a club for regular disabled travelers—their details are kept on file and handling advice is unnecessary. *East West Airlines* offers a fifty-percent reduction on the economy fare to a disabled passenger who has to travel with an escort (a letter from a disability organization must be produced when tickets are purchased).

New Zealand's three main domestic carriers are *Air New Zealand*, *Ansett New Zealand*, and *Mount Cook Line*. Reservations on *Mount Cook Line* are made through *Air New Zealand*. Passenger care leaflets are available from *Air New Zealand* (Head Office, Private Bag, Auckland; ☎9/797515) and *Ansett New Zealand* (Head Office, PO Box 4168, Auckland; ☎9/396235) travel centers throughout New Zealand. The handling of disabled passengers is smooth, with the full range of services: wheelchairs at airports, folding aisle chairs, seat-belt extensions, quadriplegic harness, leg rests, oxygen equipment, incubators, carriage of guide dogs and electric wheelchairs, safety briefings for passengers with impaired hearing or vision.

Facilities at **airports** are usually adequate. Roger Elliott had problems with rest rooms and parking at Cairns before completion of the new terminal building, but most airports throughout Australia and New Zealand offer parking close to the terminal, accessible rest rooms and cafeterias, ramps, elevators, and, in some cases, phones fitted with inductive couplers. Airbridges are used only at Sydney, Melbourne, and Cairns; boarding is by fork-lift at other Australian airports. In New Zealand, disabled passengers board and disembark along with everyone else by air-bridge at Wellington, Auckland, Christchurch, and Dunedin. At other airports or if traveling by small aircraft you'll probably be carried on and off.

Roger Elliott made a number of flights in **light aircraft** with private charter companies such as *Hinterland Aviation* (☎70/559831). *Coral Wings* (☎70/518042) arranged his trip on the Grumman Widgeon flying boat over the Great Barrier Reef; *Cape York Air Service* (☎70/359399) runs post office charter flights that take fare-paying passengers; *Sunbird Airlines* (☎70/359999) runs charter and regular services all over Queensland. All these companies are based at Cairns airport.

Rail travel is possible with advance warning in both countries, but facilities are far from perfect. *Railroads of Australia* (4–85 Queen Street, Melbourne, Vic 3000; ☎3/608-0811) and *New Zealand Rail Ltd.* (Wellington Railroad Station, Bunny Street, Wellington; ☎4/498-3413 or 0800/802802, toll free) can supply more information.

Ramps and special folding chairs are required to transfer full-time wheelchair users from platform to a seat on the train—a standard chair cannot be used on board. Perhaps for that reason, there are no wheelchair-accessible rest rooms on the trains. But there's good news for visually impaired travelers on New Zealand's *Intercity* train services—a fifty-percent discount on all fares—and for wheelchair users in Sydney, where a relatively new overhead train system (Monorail) is fully accessible, with ramps and elevators at stations, and a special car for wheelchair passengers at the front of the train.

New Zealand Rail Ltd. (Cook Strait Timetables, Bunny Street, Wellington; ☎4/498-3949; after hours use the toll-free number, ☎0800/658-999) also controls the **Interislander ferry services** that run between Picton (South Island) and Wellington (North Island). Two ferries, *Arahura* and *Aratika*, are wheelchair accessible, equipped with rest rooms for disabled passengers, and carry motor vehicles; crew will assist where necessary. As facilities vary on different ships, it's probably a good idea to check the availability of elevators between decks by calling in advance, and the best method of boarding—via passenger walkways or by elevator from the vehicle deck—with shore staff.

Travel on the launches, catamarans, and other **passenger boats** that ply between the island resorts and mainland Queensland, may involve some manhandling by the crew, either between decks or when boarding and disembarking; accessible rest rooms are rarely, if ever, provided on board.

AUSTRALIA & NEW ZEALAND: TRAVEL NOTES

A few wheelchair-accessible **buses** are available for group rental in Australia (contact ACROD) and New Zealand (see *New Zealand Access* and consult disability organizations). There are no bus companies in either country that fit hydraulic lifts to their vehicles for general use, but on standard tours the drivers will assist with boarding, ensure disabled passengers sit nearest the door, and store wheelchairs or other equipment in the luggage compartment. Barbara Horrocks was pleased with the assistance given by her *Pioneer* tour guide; *Pioneer*, along with *Greyhound*, is now part of one of Australia's largest express bus companies, *Australian Coachlines*. Urban buses are generally inaccessible if you cannot manage the steps.

Avis and *Budget* were used by our contributors for **adapted car rental** in New Zealand and Australia respectively, but cars with hand controls are no longer available from *Avis* in either country.

Hertz now offers hand controls at its airport locations in Australia—Adelaide, Brisbane, Melbourne, and Sydney. Also in Australia, *Budget* has a few vehicles equipped with hand controls (Roger Elliott rented his from *Budget Rent a Car*, Lake Street, Cairns, Qld; ☎70/319222); another option is to take your own set of controls with you and have them fitted to a standard rental car on arrival—that way you can shop around for a good deal with a local firm. The *Paraplegic and Quadriplegic Association* (phone numbers of regional branches listed in the tourist commission guide) can help with the fitting of controls.

In New Zealand, *Budget Rent a Car* (Head Office, 83 Beach Road, Auckland; ☎9/309-6739) has hand controls fitted to a Ford Falcon in Auckland for the North Island, and a Holden Commodore in Christchurch for the South Island; they must be reserved well ahead of your trip.

New Zealand Disabilities Resource Centre (see *Sources of Information*) is scheduled to have a Toyota automatic four-door hatchback with power-steering and hand controls (and a range of other options to suit most people with disabilities) available for rental from December 1992.

Portable vehicle hand controls can be rented from *Serco Services* (29–35 Latimer Square, Christchurch; ☎3/343-0809; contact Richard Abernathy or Trevor Satherley) or from the *Disability Resource Centre* Waikato, 20 Palmerston Street, PO Box 146, Hamilton; ☎7/839-5506; fax 7/834-9982.

At the time of writing there was hope that Bernard O'Neill (*O'Neill Rentals*, 4A Watts Street, Sockburn, Christchurch; ☎3/343-3199; fax 3/343-3211), who has been approached by the *NZ Paraplegic Association*, might install a hoist or ramp on the back of one of his vans, and also that *Adventure Vans* (142 Robertson Road, Mangere, PO Box 43235, Auckland; ☎9/256-0255) may soon be able to offer a two-berth van with ramp and floor clamps.

The major highways are mostly well maintained but be prepared for some rugged surfaces in wilder parts, and remember that distances on the map are deceptive; carry a fold-up toilet if the journey spans many hours between towns. Treat long drives as minor expeditions rather than Sunday jaunts.

Visitors to New Zealand can join the *Operation Mobility* **parking** concession scheme by presenting a doctor's certificate and filling out a short application form (from any branch of the *New Zealand CCS*) and obtaining a temporary Mobility Card; there is a fee of NZ$28. This allows a vehicle carrying a disabled driver or passenger to use any of the reserved parking spaces; it allows time concessions on metered spaces and restricted areas, as well as stopping to unload or pick up in restricted areas. The Operation Mobility Directory, updated in 1992, includes accessible parking facilities throughout New Zealand. There are specified parking spots for disabled drivers in Australian cities; see access guides or ask city councils for details.

Availability of **wheelchair-accessible taxis** is good but advance notice is required (at least 24 hours) in Australia, and prebooking is advised in New Zealand, particularly around school beginning and ending times. *Qantas* can arrange for one to meet you at the airport on your arrival in Australia. There is a fleet in every Australian provincial capital except Hobart, and phone numbers for booking are supplied in the tourist commission guide.

AUSTRALIA & NEW ZEALAND: TRAVEL NOTES

In New Zealand, the *Total Mobility* scheme, a project of the *DPA* (see *Sources of Information*), enables people who are unable to use public transit to use taxis and Maxi Taxis (vans with wheelchair ramps or hoists) at subsidized rates. Organizations working with people who have disabilities issue vouchers that entitle the holder to a discount, 50 percent in all participating regions except Hawkes Bay, where the discount is 25 percent, on the standard fare. A list of the participating areas and taxi companies is available from the *DPA*. Visitors should contact the *DPA* (5th Floor, Central House, 26 Brandon Street, Wellington; ☎04/472-2626) on arrival, and they will arrange for vouchers to be issued.

Accommodation

You should be able to find some kind of **accommodation** to suit any budget or access requirements, from campgrounds to five-star hotels, particularly those built after 1980. Motels and motor inns seem to provide the most accessible low-cost accommodation. If you travel without booking ahead, stop by mid-afternoon to allow plenty of time to look around. It's probably a good idea to prebook if planning to stay in cities during high season. The following accommodation is recommended by our contributors.

If money's no object, the *Regent of Melbourne* (25 Collins Street, Melbourne, Vic 3000; ☎3/653-0000) is, according to Barbara Horrocks, magnificent, the only glitch being that breakfast is served in a mezzanine restaurant (if not in your room), access to which is via a service elevator.

The *Southern Cross* (Cnr Elizabeth & Goulburn streets, Sydney, NSW 2000; ☎2/20987) is centrally situated and in the de luxe (five-star) price bracket. It has adapted rooms but the rooftop pool is inaccessible. David Gray suggests the *Crest* (111 Darlinghurst Road, Kings Cross, Sydney, NSW 2011; 2/3582755) as a much cheaper alternative, with flat access from street to lobby, and rooms with stunning views of the Opera House and harbor bridge.

Hithergreen Lodge (Henry Lawson Drive, PO Box 169, Mudgee, NSW 2850; ☎63/721022)—"your home away from home in the vineyards"—is run by Peter and Robyn Burgess and

has one well-equipped room for disabled guests, with spacious *en suite* bathroom.

Australian contributor Cathy O'Reilly, who is quadriplegic and lives in Adelaide, recommends *The Wheel Resort* (Lot 1, Broken Head Road, Byron Bay, NSW 2481; ☎66/856139), a small group of comfortable self-contained cabins, all specifically designed to accommodate wheelchair users and set in over 6 acres of natural coastal bushland and established gardens. There is a 50-foot, solar-heated pool with ramp and PVC wheelchair, and wide pathways through the bush. Byron Bay's beaches and facilities, for a range of activities including scuba-diving, windsurfing, horse-riding, and fishing, are within easy reach. Disabled and able-bodied guests are equally welcome and rates are very reasonable.

SATH (see USA *Travel Notes*) reports that there are self-contained, barrier-free units on a five-acre site overlooking D'Entrecasteaux Channel, an hour south of Hobart airport in Tasmania. Features include roll-in shower, bed with overhead hoist (plus additional single bed and sofa bed that sleeps two), open-plan living room, and specially equipped kitchen. *The Melaleucas* (Woodbridge, PO Box 35, Kingston Beach 7050, Tas; ☎02/674877; fax 02/674878) is within easy reach of popular tourist attractions and the owner, herself a wheelchair user, helps guests plan accessible outings.

Wrest Point Hotel Casino (410 Sandy Bay Road, Hobart, Tas 7000; ☎02/250112), also de luxe, has easy access and an elevator to all floors; it's advisable to reserve ahead because this is a very popular hotel.

Sheraton Hobart (1 Davey Street, Hobart, Tas 7000; ☎02/354535) and *Sheraton Ayers Rock* (Yulara Drive, Yulara, NT 0872; ☎89/562200) are typical *Sheratons*—comfortable, good access, five-star prices. The *Sheraton Mirage Port Douglas* (Davidson Street, Port Douglas, Qld 4871; ☎70/995888) is fully accessible and worth visiting just for a drink if the room rates are out of your range.

The *Lakeside International Hotel* (London Circuit, Canberra, ACT 2601; ☎62/476244) is four star, within walking distance of Lake Burley Griffin (ask for a room overlooking the lake), and easily accessible.

AUSTRALIA & NEW ZEALAND: TRAVEL NOTES

The Summit Central Apartments (Cnr Leichhardt and Allenby streets, Brisbane, Qld 4000; ☎7/8397000) are accessible, with pleasant staff, but a steep climb from the city center.

The four-star *Ramada Reef Resort* (Cnr Vievers Road and Williams Esplanade, Palm Cove, Qld 4879; ☎70/553999) is a low-set development with easy access, right on the beach and designed around a grove of ancient melaleuca and palm trees; the staff are helpful and there is a free shuttle bus into Cairns.

There is a variety of accommodation available on South Molle Island resort, which is reached by plane from Townsville to Hamilton Island, then water-taxi to South Molle—a bit awkward for wheelchair users, but Barbara Horrocks found everyone helpful. She stayed in a comfortable, chalet-style room on the first floor of a "Whitsunday Unit," with views over the Whitsunday Passage. The price includes all food, and to feel that you've had your money's worth you'll need a huge appetite.

Consult the *Queensland Tourist and Travel Corporation* (Queensland House, 392 The Strand, London WC2R 0LZ, UK; ☎071/836 7242) for a comparison of all the islands and resorts along the Great Barrier Reef; their brochure tells you how to get there, what you can do on each island, what's included in the cost. There's even a mention of facilities for disabled visitors, with an address to write to for more information.

John Moore stayed at the *Gladstone Country Club Motor Inn* (Cnr Far Street and Dawson Highway, Gladstone, Qld 4680; ☎79/724322), the *Miners Lodge Motor Inn* (60–62 Nebo Road, Mackay, Qld 4740; ☎79/511944), and the *Earls Court Motor Inn* (131–133 Nerang Street, Southport, Qld 4215; ☎75/914144), all of which are wheelchair accessible.

Roger Elliott recommends the budget *G'Day Tropical Village* (7–27 MacLachlan Street, Manunda, Cairns, Qld 4870; ☎70/537555).

The annually updated *NRMA Accommodation Directory* (National Roads Motorists Association, 151 Clarence Street, Sydney, NSW 2000; ☎2/2609222) indicates establishments with "independent access" and "access with assistance," but facilities do not have to satisfy any standard criteria and are not verified, so it can only act as a starting point.

By the end of 1991, the *Australian Automobile Association* (*AAA*) in each state (addresses in the tourist commission brochure, *Australia: A Traveler's Guide*) hoped to have completed a new survey of accommodation throughout Australia, using questionnaires supplied by *ACROD* (see *Sources of Information*). The aim was that access information should be consistent and reliable, and be incorporated in the *AAA*'s mainstream national tour books, using symbols to denote "independent access" and "partially accessible—inquire further." According to *ACROD* in August 1992, the *AAA* has begun listing accessible hotels and motels but the system is not yet foolproof as only some states are participating.

In NZ, David Gray stayed at the *Paihia Sands Motel* (Paihia, Northland; ☎9/4027707), where he gained access to the bathroom using a chair placed just inside the doorway, but the friendly owners more than compensated for this design fault.

The *NZTD* guide, *Access: A Guide for the Less Mobile Traveler*, lists a wide selection of accessible accommodation; all the motels or hotels used by Kent Kloepping are listed in this publication, except for the *Sharella Motor Inn* (20 Glenmore Street, Wellington; ☎4/723823) which was included in the 1990/91 edition but not in the 1991/92 edition, and the relatively inaccessible *Anchorage Lodge* (4 Rutland Street, Picton; ☎3/5736192) which was listed in *South Island Guide: Accommodation & Camping*, published by the *New Zealand Automobile Association*.

Several youth hostels have been recently upgraded and made accessible; for details of these contact the *Youth Hostels Association of New Zealand* (PO Box 436, Christchurch; ☎3/379-9970; fax 3/365-4476).

Access and Facilities

The overall picture is fairly rosy, and the tourist boards seem to work well with disability organizations to ensure accuracy of information; *NZTD* has the advantage in terms of updating, with its *Access* guide, but it's also pleasing to see some reference to disabled visitors in at

AUSTRALIA & NEW ZEALAND: TRAVEL NOTES

least two general brochures from the Australians(*Australia: A Traveler's Guide* and *Queensland*); the logical conclusion would be the incorporation of access information throughout all brochures.

Access and facilities at tourist attractions are, by all accounts, good. High curbs may be a problem in the tropical and subtropical regions, but most cities are relatively easy to explore in a wheelchair (prepare for some tough gradients in Brisbane). Special facilities—ramps, wide entrances, elevators, and so on—are generally provided at museums, zoos, theaters, and public buildings, and accessible restaurants and rest rooms are widely available. And for the visitor there are plenty of access guides, "mobility maps," "loo" (rest room) guides, and lists of reserved parking spaces to consult.

But to get the best out of Australia and New Zealand, the great outdoors must be sampled, whether that means lying on the beach, donning a wet suit, wheeling through the rainforest, or floating above the scenery in a hot-air balloon. Most contributors report that they were excluded from very few activities on their holidays, although even the Aussies have yet to come up with a solution to the problem of getting a wheelchair down the beach to the sea—perhaps more boardwalks?

Again, access guides have been produced, detailing the opportunities open to wheelchair users; some, such as the guide to accessible walks and picnic areas in New Zealand (*Out and About*, 1988), are out of date or out of print, but there are some that are still current; for example the NSW National Parks and Wildlife Service publication, *Outdoor Access for Everybody*, which lists 193 places across New South Wales where access is easy for everyone—a staff member in a wheelchair checked out the sites in 1989, and since many are natural attractions such as walking tracks, waterfalls, and lookouts, it is unlikely that access information will have changed a great deal since then, apart from the addition of a few accessible rest rooms, or the opening up of another accessible nature trail. There are also a number of sources of up-to-the-minute local information: regional departments of sport and recreation, environment and planning, conser-

vation and land management, woods and forests (ask tourist offices for addresses), as well as the disability organizations and resource centers.

This is not to say that Australia and New Zealand are "barrier-free." Disability groups are actively involved in encouraging greater public awareness of the need to remove architectural barriers, to provide much greater access to public transit, to achieve equal employment opportunities and legal redress where discrimination occurs. All the familiar battles are going on, but for the visitor with disabilities both countries provide enough facilities to make them very accessible vacation destinations.

Health and Insurance

No worries about standards of health care, and pharmacists will supply most drugs (you'll probably need a prescription from a resident doctor). Take a letter from your doctor or clearly written prescription for your usual drugs, particularly if you are carrying a large supply.

In Australia, insect repellents, sun blocks, and a light folding wheelchair are likely to make the biggest contribution to comfort. Mosquitoes will be a nuisance in many areas; it can be very hot and very humid—if excessive heat worsens your disability try to travel in November or December, avoiding January, February, and March; a slimline wheelchair is invaluable for trips in light aircraft, small boats, or overloaded cars and camper vans.

Apart from the dreaded jellyfish, the unfamiliar Australian wildlife is more likely to startle than injure—sharks, crocs, and poisonous spiders do exist, but your chances of an encounter are extremely slim. The bush should be treated with respect but it can be explored, and, as Sheila Murray observes, the gardens are not *all* crawling with snakes and redbacks.

The only poisonous creature in New Zealand is the very rare katipo spider, and maximum summer temperatures are nothing more than pleasantly warm.

TELEPHONE CODES

Dial 011 (International Code), then 61 for Australia and 64 for New Zealand.

PART NINE

TRAVEL, TOURS, AND CRUISES

Introduction

On most of these trips the journey constitutes the vacation: in effect this is one big section on "Getting There," and these are, perhaps, experiences of travel in its purest form. For Jack Davidson the journey was a race along mountain roads; for David Bonnett it entailed crossing the Sahara; for some a cruise, for others a European tour. In nearly every case the traveler sets out to achieve a goal—to win the race, to arrive at the other side of the desert, to reach the polar icecap, to take the helm of a large sailing vessel—and most of these goals would be a revelation to those in the travel industry who seek to keep disabled travelers in their place, traveling to the "safe" destinations, easy access guaranteed. Perhaps the most important message in this final section of the book comes from Tracy Schmitt, who was born a four-way amputee, has done everything from Operation Raleigh to trekking in Nepal (see *Travel Notes*, p.548), and was too busy at an *Ontario March of Dimes* summer recreation camp to write a full account for us: "Just because I don't have legs doesn't mean I don't want to climb the Himalayas."

The following accounts are, on the whole, success stories, usually as a result of a little bit of help along the way—some extra hands to put up the tent (p.517), some local knowledge of accessible hotels (p.512), protection from man-eating tigers (p.510), assistance from able-bodied crew members (p.520)—combined with a few strokes of good luck and an attitude best described by Roderick MacDonald—"we didn't go looking for things to go wrong, nor did we worry if they did."

Careful **planning** also plays a part: it can be fun, and is essential for expeditions in remote areas, but there is a lot to be said for leaving some things to chance; you should start a long trip fresh and full of energy—unlikely if you become mired in documentation and research. This applies in particular to the task of finding accessible accommodation, which can be arduous and only partially successful if attempted before departure (p.550).

From a luxurious cabin on a cruise ship to a homemade tent in the desert, our contributors report no disasters with **accommodation**, although at times a change of itinerary was necessary because no suitable hotel could be found at the planned stopping point. But the advantage of touring is that stays of one or two nights are the norm, and most people can manage most access problems on a short-term basis.

Another bonus is that apparently rugged conditions can not only be survived but also prove far more memorable than a suite in an accessible *Hilton*: a night under a mosquito net in Australia's Northern Territory seemed almost magical to Frankie Armstrong (p.534); a trip to an uninhabited island, armed only with bedroll, notebooks, and first-aid kit, formed a lasting impression on Nic Fleming (p.551); an evening with Arab guests in David Bonnett's thornbush encampment was a highlight of his Saharan expedition (p.506).

Of the many forms of transport used when covering long distances, the car and the ship seem popular; they offer the easiest access and the most comfortable ride (barring seasickness) for wheelchair users. **Cars** can be altered to suit individual requirements with a range of adaptations, from hand controls and hoists to lumbar support cushions and swiveling seats. Large, modern **cruise ships** are increasingly equipped with spacious elevators to all amenities, ramped storm-sills, cabins for disabled passengers, accessible rest rooms and showers; although this generally applies to the more luxurious and expensive cruise liners, clever travelers can sometimes find similar facilities (or at least usable ones) for a fraction of the price on state-run ferry systems or other less flashy vessels (see "Transport," Travel Notes, p.549). A small number of vessels are specially designed and built to accommodate physically disabled people: the *Jubilee Sailing Trust*'s sail training ship is a leader in this field.

Long-haul tours by **train or bus** are possible with a companion or two, but probably not the easiest options for wheelchair travelers. Dee Hopkins managed a journey on *Greyhound* buses across North America (p.62), but found the going pretty tough and had to stop short of her goal for an enforced rest. If you have no helper and have to rely on assistance at stations, the prospect of arranging it all before departure, which is what most train companies demand, will be unappealing. Even after meticulous planning and advance warnings, the promised assistance may well fail to materialize.

For travelers with visual impairment an **aircraft** feels safer than a train—it's impossible to step out on the wrong side, and airlines in general are more geared up to handling disabled passengers. But a ship is probably ideal, even for unaccompanied visually disabled passengers—there's space to wander, and crew members or fellow passengers are on hand to look out for obstacles.

The traveler who covers a lot of ground, crosses many frontiers, and passes through remote areas, cannot expect to find good standards of accessibility and facilities for disabled people everywhere. But, according to the following accounts, it somehow doesn't seem to matter in the way that it might on a two-week vacation spent in one resort.

Drawn on by the sense of rising to a challenge, perhaps hoping to achieve their "Personal Everest," some of these writers took on long and difficult journeys. In describing them they talk mostly of the thrill of extraordinary experiences, of total departure from their normal lives, of adventures that would be dismissed by the majority of tour operators as "unsuitable" for disabled people. The rewards are obvious.

Expeditions

Sand in my Braces

The idea came in 1969, when David Bonnett, who is disabled by polio, and some student friends coaxed an ancient, disintegrating Ford across the Atlas mountains in Morocco. From the mountains they saw the desert and they resolved to drive across the Sahara one day . . ..

Seven years later, poring over my school atlas, so old that it still has the British Empire marked in pink, we planned a route passing through France, Spain, Morocco, and on to Algeria, from there across the desert to Niger and finally to Lagos in Nigeria. Whether then to turn right or left would depend upon the location of the most recent military coup, but from Lagos we would loop north, homeward bound.

My three fellow armchair dreamers were old student friends, wiser now and conscious of being drawn into an unwelcome world of careers and mortgages; this was to be a last petulant kick before settling down. We had traveled together as a group before and were reasonably aware of our respective strengths and weaknesses. As the only disabled member of the group I was fairly confident of support in difficult moments.

We found a thirteen-year-old, long-wheelbase Land Rover, and an inspection confirmed our feeling that this was a sound vehicle. The next problem was the selection of hand controls. I had decided that a bellows-type vacuum clutch unit was essential in order to avoid the effects of sand on moving

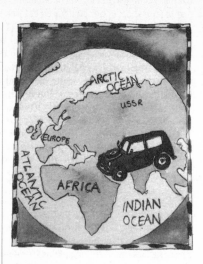

parts. Quotes from specialist firms proved numbingly expensive, and inept attempts at attracting sponsorship were politely rebuffed. Fortunately, Terry Willett of the *Paraplegic Olympic Committee* came to the rescue and the conversion was carried out with servo-assisted brakes and spares for everything. He will remember my test drive with horror; I remember his pale face with some amusement. But here was a lesson for the future: the controls were installed down to a price and subsequently proved unreliable and a major source of frustration to me.

Preparations continued with what seemed like endless detail; no one should underestimate the amount of work involved, including calculations of distances, journey times, fuel consumption and capacity, and—most difficult of all—obtaining visas. Medical and other insurances were mostly arranged through the *Automobile Association*, as were the various driving documents; the *AA* was consistently helpful and practical with its advice.

There were regular deletions and additions to our huge list of requirements, but shopping finally began: canned foods, dried foods, camping gear, motor parts, binoculars, compasses, maps, and water containers, not forgetting two thousand tea bags and eighty rolls of toilet paper (yes, we used all of them). Using *Disabled Drivers' Motor Club* concessionary ferry tickets, *Townsend-Thoresen* patiently altered their paperwork to suit my panic calls, swapping dates and times. But, at last, travelers' checks and passports in hands, we sailed for France.

Being October, the time of the wine harvest in Charente, southern France, I had rashly agreed to earn extra money with the others by picking grapes for two weeks. Adopting the motto of the three Musketeers—all for one and one for all—somehow seemed appropriate, but two weeks in rain-soaked French furrows almost broke my spirit. I still wince at the memory of my rusting braces and sodden surgical boots.

Nevertheless, this time did allow us to work together under some pressure and survive with a good deal of humor. Another week remained in our rented cottage, enabling us to complete sewing our mosquito-proof tents (don't be fooled, no such thing exists), a vehicle service (my job), and carefully planned loading of the Land Rover. Reeking of oil, French cigarettes, and garlic, we set off for Spain. The fall weather showed no mercy for our trial run at camping, and three damp, cold days later we arrived at Algeciras.

Ferry tickets were cheap and, clutching our picnic lunches and bottles of beer, we happily settled into our deck chairs like all good English holidaymakers. The juddering boat skirted Gibraltar and about an hour later we bumped gently into our African

berth. Jostled by cloaked men and veiled women along palm-shaded streets, we purchased cheap wines and spirits in anticipation of scarcity farther south. Loaded thus, we drove through Moroccan customs conveniently oblivious of the fact that these should have been declared.

We detoured first to Chechaouen, where we and our illicit alcohol were warmly received by an old friend. The presence of a band of European travelers quickly came to the notice of both pedlars of "heaven" and the local police. Our subtle interrogation by a detective inspector wearing a fez made us unwilling celebrities; the scene had all the charm of a film clip from *Casablanca* but, unlike Bogy, we didn't stay. Instead we packed our bags and fled over the Rif mountains, back to the coastal scenery we had left just a week before. Despite the southern latitude, our climb to 3000 feet took us through a blizzard all the way to Ketama; thank goodness I had taken my thickest sweater.

"I realized with a sinking feeling that we were lost"

After a few days in Algiers, we headed south to the desert. The 800 miles from the coast to In Salah were straightforward for us in our reliable Land Rover; even the steep and twisting route across the Atlas mountains to Laghouat was not too difficult. Climate changed slowly but topography dramatically, from the lofty peaks to the seemingly endless plateaux. The distant horizon, shimmering in the heat, was at times flat in every direction, and the unerringly straight road became almost hypnotic. Pulling over to the side to allow the occasional oncoming truck to pass was the only relief. Confusing mirages frequently played tricks on us under the increasingly hot sun, and we arrived at In Salah desperate for some shade but feeling that we were at last getting somewhere—this was where the road ended.

In Salah was breathtaking and came up to all my picture-book expectations of an oasis town. Its ancient walls rose straight out of the sand; they had resisted intrusion for centuries but the town opened its gates casually to the modern, motorized traveler. Inside was the welcome shade of fig trees, sculptured mud houses, and narrow alleys in deep shade. It was hot and silent; the market would not open again until after dark.

Several other expeditions were in the central area of the town; they, too, were preparing for the drive south. After hand-pumping 50 gallons of gas into our tanks and our ten jerrycans, and taking on 20 gallons of water, we scurried off alone. This was not bravado, but to avoid the embarrassment of an audience when we surely got stuck in all that sand. Within just a few miles calamity struck and our hitherto unused shovels were brought into action as the rear wheels sank into the soft desert sand—a regular feature of the ensuing 1400 miles. In such situations the benefits of being a disabled driver became clear—at least I was spared all that dreadful digging and pushing. My contribution was to remain at the wheel.

"Out of the impenetrable blackness, two cloaked Arabs appeared, perhaps guided by our fire"

The liberal sprinkling of abandoned wrecks across the desert sometimes took the humorous edge off our struggles. At one point, while following the piste (the broad track formed by heavy desert trucks), I was bewildered by the route passing either side of a large dune. The guiding oil drums, weighted with sand and made more visible with a tall pole, were suddenly no longer to be seen. After traveling along what seemed to be the obvious route for some time, I realized with a sinking feeling that we were lost. In tense silence and feeling very alone, we

backtracked, a difficult process with little to mark our way. With someone posted on the roof rack, desperately straining eyes through binoculars, an oil drum was finally spotted. Allah, for the moment at least, was still smiling on us.

The Sahara is unrelentingly hot and emphatically silent, the tranquillity disturbed only by us or a greedy gerbil foraging around the campfire. Choosing a campground was sometimes impossible; the beautiful sunsets quickly gave way to total darkness, after which we simply had to stop where we were. In the light there was a compelling need to identify something—a large rock or a thorn bush, anything, as a reason for stopping precisely "there." Shelter from the wind could be another deciding factor, for although our tent was attached to the Land Rover it felt frail in a strong desert wind. Even long tent pegs are of little use in sand, and we usually collected rocks as anchors.

Camping in the marginal shelter of a solitary thorn bush one night, we had some surprising visitors. Out of the impenetrable blackness, two cloaked Arabs appeared, perhaps guided by our fire. How they later returned from whence they came still puzzles me. An amusing evening was spent with our guests, attempting to converse in sign language while sipping sweet coffee. This was what we had come for, and we were not disappointed.

The last Algerian town that we visited was Tamanarasset, a dusty collecting ground for travelers and those who feed off them. It was an obligatory stopping place where papers and passports were checked. Once in, we were warned that it would take several days to get out, and the town was full of anxious people, kicking their heels until they could move on. We decided to accept the delay: after submitting our papers we drove back north for a short distance to the beautiful Hoggar mountains where we camped for a few days. We found a deep pool of water in the mountainside, fed from the 9000-foot-high peaks, and here we swam and rested in our private paradise until our papers were finally cleared.

"Camping for a few days on silver beaches where coconut trees drape their leaves in the water"

Some days later we crossed an invisible border at Assamaka into Niger. From the sands to the savannah, passing busy water holes and grass-hut villages, the fierce sun barely glimmered through a dust haze which extended for several hundred miles. At Dannet we were more than usually grateful to find cold beer available; this was our first stopping place in Niger. Camped in our homemade tent, we were lulled to sleep by throbbing drums and chorus singing from a village nearby. The following evening we ventured into the village to see a play which took place in an open school playground. Despite our difficulties with the language, and the lack of props or backdrops, the story was clear, compelling, and witty. The subject? The risks of adultery!

Halfway across Niger is Agadez, an orderly town with wide spaces and a large market, dominated by its mosque. Unlike Tamanarasset, here we felt like travelers, not tourists, and the people, while as curious about us as we were about them, just went on with their business. After a couple of days, loaded with some fresh vegetables, fuel, and water, we pushed on, to the grasslands where the tracks were occasionally as tricky as anything we had experienced in the desert. Dried-up river beds of fine silt had to be crossed, and we seemed to be constantly in four-wheel drive. The local solution to these problems appeared to be to hurtle at great speed toward the obstacle, hoping that momentum would see the vehicle through. It did not always work.

Three days' driving brought us to Zinder, where we encountered paved road after 1400 miles of bone-shaking tracks and soft sand. As the roads became better, so the driving became worse, judging by the number of wrecked and overturned trucks that marked the route to Lagos. On one occasion I had to administer first aid to a stricken driver who beamed at me while I cleaned his open wound with neat antiseptic.

When we reached Lagos, our southernmost destination, I swore never to curse a London rush hour again. The bustle and intensity of the West African coastal cities was an unwelcome contrast to the solitude of the desert. Problems with obtaining papers from the Sudanese consulate in Lagos forced a decision to drive west along the Atlantic coast rather than east toward Ethiopia. We drove through the corridor of Benin to Togo, camping for a few days on silver beaches where coconut trees drape their leaves in the water, another African paradise.

But all was not well in our paradise. The frustration of creeping indecision had generated a tension between us. The hand controls on the Land Rover were playing up again, and dry leather brace straps kept tearing. I was having to tack rubber sheeting to the soles of my boots in a clumsy attempt to repair them, and I had run out of walking-stick rubber caps. We were travel weary, a situation not to be underestimated, and I was beginning to feel ill. We had been away from home for about four months, most nights spent in our tent for four. We were all yearning for privacy and the chance to make independent decisions.

That chance came sooner than expected. I had felt increasingly lethargic, and looking at myself in a wing-mirror one morning I saw that my eyes were yellow. Thumbing through my well-worn first-aid book, I remember my sick feeling of unwelcome comprehension—I had yellow jaundice. Ten days later, after hospital quarantine in Accra and, for some reason, a diet of poached eggs, I was ignominiously flown home. London airport had just been released from the clutches of a porters' strike and was engulfed in a January snowstorm. It was nice to be back.

Perhaps next time I'll take two vehicles and several friends, and try to get the balance right between pressing on and remaining in romantic places, between the value of being together as a group and the importance of occasional independence. Did I say next time? Quick, back to the armchair.

Personal Everest

Jack Davidson had polio as a child; Mike Jackson lost his arm in a car accident when a teenager. This is the story of their participation in the Eighth and Ninth Himalayan Rallies in India, in 1987 and 1988.

My biggest problem is my height (just under five foot). The seats in most rally cars are bolted down or welded to the floor, and my feet often don't reach the pedals. I need to be relatively close to the steering wheel, as do most rally drivers, to gain leverage, but I also need to have my shoulders hard against the seat to help me operate the clutch with my left foot, the one affected by polio.

I grew up with my disability, and it hasn't hindered me too much, but for Mike, losing a limb while still a teenager was a shattering blow. However, after a rehabilitation period he once again took up the sport he had just begun to enjoy. Mike began co-driving on navigational road rallies, but it wasn't long before he felt he could do better behind the wheel. In fact, he proved that not only could he control the car with his left hand, using his artificial right arm to steady the wheel, he could also win championships.

In 1985, the engine of Mike's Ford Escort blew up in spectacular fashion and destroyed the steering. With the car approaching something like 100 miles per hour, an accident was inevitable; two spectators were injured and this was the start, basically, of the problems with "disabled" drivers competing in motor sport. Despite the fact that Mike had nearly 25 years of experience, the *Royal Automobile Club Motor Sports Association*, the sport's governing body in the UK, banned him, and others like him, from participating in special stage rallies from January 1, 1987.

Although permission was given for Mike to enter road events, he wanted the thrill and excitement that only special stage rallying can bring. In 1987 he expanded his horizons and saw the Himalayan mountain range. With the help of the *Himalayan Rally Association*, Mike secured a sponsored flight on an *Air India* 747. He and co-driver, Howard Patterson, with their Opel Manta in the hold, flew to New Delhi via Geneva and Rome. I accompanied them as a sponsored photo-journalist.

Apart from the obvious problems in freighting the rally car—all the paperwork had to be completed in quadruplicate, individually signed, and bonds posted (to ensure that what you take into the country you take out, even if it's in hundreds of little pieces in dozens of plastic bags)—Mike's main difficulty, with his artificial arm, was in setting off the security alarms in each and every airport. Caused all sorts of panic, that did.

My problem was the length of the corridors between check-in desk and aircraft. I always get the farthest-away room in the hotel, too. I am slightly asthmatic, and often guilty of carrying too many cameras, lenses, film, as well as granola bars and glucose tablets, a tape recorder, pads and pencils, a bottle of Scotch (a gift, you understand), so it got pretty tiring for my left leg.

It was around 90° F when we arrived in New Delhi, to be greeted (not personally, thank goodness) by two fakirs dressed only in a couple of loin cloths and holding hands. Our next introduction was to the roads and driving standards of the taxi drivers and the *Delhi Transportation Corporation* bus drivers.

Most of the time the drivers tend to keep to the left side of the road, but their vehicles have never been tested for road-worthiness. Our taxi was a fairly modern Hindustan Ambassador (based on a 1958 British design), with three operational cylinders and a matching number of shock absorbers. Somehow, with one hand continually pressing the horn, the other on the gear shift, our driver found his way to the *Lodhi*, a grand looking but lizard-infested hotel. (Actually the lizards keep the mosquitoes at bay, so it wasn't that bad.)

Inside, the plumbing, which dates back to the early 1900s and hasn't changed since, is something else. When I turned on the bath faucet, the lights went out; when I tried the shower the water seeped out of the pipes instead. And trying to write under one of those enormous helicopter rotor blades (they call them fans) required a great deal of self-discipline and paperweights . . . .

After about three days, and a few hundred rupees, Mike managed to extract his Manta from the airport customs buildings in time for the rally. (That in itself was a miracle.) Mike was seeded at 17, just ahead of world championship drivers Andrea Zanussi and

Per Eklund. The Eighth Himalayan Rally started from the Jawaharlal Nehru Stadium in New Delhi, and ahead lay a course of 2000 miles, across hot, dusty plains, through dried-up river beds and the jungle of the Jim Corbett Tiger Reserve before a magical first glimpse of the Himalayan mountain range. At first, all we saw was a faint outline through the haze, and we wondered how anything could be so high. I'm used to British hills, so this lot looked gigantic.

Mike set off in his Manta; I was in a rented Ambassador with photographer Gavin Lodge, guide Vikram, and turban-charged driver Palsingh. We had two flats on one of our old (and bald) cross-plies early on day one. "What have I let myself in for?" thought I. I'd already been sick after eating an omelette near the Taj Mahal; I had what is known as "Delhi-belly" and a stack of granola bars and glucose tablets to keep me going. And a supply of cement pills to stop me going!

"I lived on my granola bars, glucose tablets, and porridge for two whole weeks"

At the end of the first day we had climbed to 6500 feet in the mountains, to the old British army resort of Nainital, nestling beside a tranquil lake. It looked good, but smelled awful. Only the rhododendrons gave the place a bit of color and scent. One thing that did surprise me was the porridge—it really was good, almost as good as back home in Scotland. I lived on my granola bars, glucose tablets, and porridge for two whole weeks; I came back slimmer and fitter, and awfully glad to see a plate of my mother-in-law's meatloaf.

From Nainital to Ranikhet we traveled up one mountain, down the other side, up another mountain, down the other side. The scenery was certainly spectacular, perhaps not as beautiful as the mountains and fiords of Norway, or indeed the west coast of Scotland—the deforestation of the Himalayas is quite noticeable—but it had a character all its own. The view of 26,000-foot-high, snowcapped peaks from the _Savoy Hotel_ in Mussoorie was awe-inspiring.

Mike, by this time, had climbed to almost 10,000 feet without oxygen and was in seventh place overall. But the rear axle threatened to break away from the bodywork, and only his vast experience kept him in the rally. He managed to tie it together with wire and rope, but the damage had been done and Mike was forced to retire at three-quarters distance. His first attempt at scaling the heights was over.

In 1988, Mike decided to have another go, with the same car, but converted to Group A specification and fuel injection, and with a new co-driver, Chris Fewlass. My good friend, Geoff Stone, and I rented a Group N Maruti Gypsy (an Indian-built Suzuki Jeep). Like Mike, we had delays upon delays in getting our vehicles out of customs; Gavin had summed it up nicely in 1987 when he said that the Indians make the Spaniards look quick!

"The old man lit a fire by the car to ward off the wild animals"

That said, the Indians were always extremely courteous, helpful, and never said no. Unfortunately they said what they thought we wanted to hear, not what might actually be. They nod their heads from side to side: a severe nod means you've got a good chance of getting what you want; a mild shake means you haven't got a hope; something between the two could loosely be termed the norm. As if anything in India was the norm. I vividly remember seeing a man cutting the presidential lawns near India Gate—the lawn mower was being pulled by a sacred cow.

Other lasting memories of India are the passengers hanging from the roof, the doors, the windows of anything that moved; wall to wall people; ear to ear noise; dawn to dusk sunshine. I made a trip to the Taj Mahal in an air-conditioned bus (that is, the windows were open), complete with a very noisy video; whenever you see a TV screen or hear a radio in India you are subjected to either a blinding headache or a cricket match.

At the start of the Ninth Himalayan Rally, Mike and Chris were at number 9, Geoff and I were at 24. Right away, Mike struck trouble. He stopped on the opening stage with fuel injector problems and fell to last place overall. We plodded on and finished the first leg in an amazing 18th place overall. From then on, as the route went uphill, we slipped back down the field. With rocky, unsurfaced mountain passes, full of switchbacks and 10,000 feet up, our knuckles turned a delicate shade of yellow through the sheer grip on the steering wheel.

On the second day Mike began to climb through the field, passing the elephants and the Marutis as though they were standing still. The twisty, paved road up to Nainital, however, caused a repeat of the problems encountered in 1987, when the rear axle failed, and he retired on the spot. Chris thumbed a lift to summon help and Mike stayed with the car. Things happen slowly in India (as you may have gathered) and it was getting dark when an old Hindu appeared on the scene. He muttered away in Hindi, but Mike, of course, couldn't understand much—except the words "man-eating tiger." Mike leapt inside the car, closed the windows and locked the door, while the old man lit a fire by the car to ward off the wild animals. By morning, Chris had returned with help and eventually they got the car back to Nainital, where they found that Mike's bottle of Scotch had leaked all over his clothes. He went to bed that night smelling happy, but perfectly sober!

Geoff and I were not without our problems: we had bounced off a tree in

Corbett Reserve and someone had thrown a stone which smashed our non-laminated windscreen just prior to crossing the Ganges. If only the *Lodhi Hotel* could provide a shower like that. We also suffered a flat but we battled on until the sixth and last day with our dreadfully slow Maruti. It got slower and slower, until the complete throttle pedal assembly fell off on the last, 15-mile, competitive section.

> *"Geoff changed gear for me as I steered with my left hand and operated the throttle with my right"*

With political extremists throwing gas bombs and stones, an immobile Jeep was the last thing we wanted. Geoff jumped out and rigged up a temporary throttle cable, a vinyl-coated wire, from the carburettor linkage back through the driver's window (which was jammed after our earlier escapade with the tree), whereupon I managed to pull it and speed off down the track. The harder I pulled, the faster the Jeep went. In fact, it had never gone faster in the five previous days due to a faulty location on the bulkhead. Perhaps that was just as well, considering the white-knuckle country we'd driven through. Anyway, Geoff changed gear for me as I steered with my left hand and operated the throttle with my right.

With our Jeep well and truly wound up, we caught up on a Nissan Patrol Jongo (Jeep) before having a sideways "moment" and sensibly slacking off to ensure a finish on what must be the toughest road rally in the world. Geoff managed to effect repairs after the competitive section and only the run-in to New Delhi was left. Following a Jongo, with the crew hanging out of every window and waving aside all oncoming traffic, was very exciting. They waved off the road the overcrowded buses; they waved aside the overloaded trucks, the aged Royal Enfield motorycles, scooters, the cyclists, the bullocks, the camels, and the odd sacred cow. But they missed one Ambassador, on the outskirts of Delhi, heading straight for us. It was Geoff's turn behind the wheel, and somehow he succeeded in squeezing the Maruti between the insane Indian and the bridge parapet, while I managed to push the co-driver's horn button right through the dashboard!

We finished the rally in 42nd place overall, my best ever result on a big event and Geoff's first attempt at a rally. Mike deserved better. After all, to participate and to be competitive, negotiating all those switchbacks, river crossings, and sacred cows, took some doing. India isn't the easiest of places to get around; the facilities leave a lot to be desired, but it is a challenge. I hope that readers will take from this story a share of Mike Jackson's courage, and in return give him their good wishes for a third and successful attempt at his "Personal Everest" when he finds the funds and eventually returns.

Touring

A Giant Buffet

Roderick MacDonald is disabled by a form of muscular dystrophy which confines him to a wheelchair. In June 1984, accompanied by a friend, Neil, and Neil's son, Scott, he traveled by car through eight European countries.

A brilliant sun dazzled our eyes on the morning we headed eastward from Zeebrugge. The fatigue of a 400-mile journey from Scotland and a late night on the ferry soon evaporated on the drive through Belgium. The Datsun's trunk was crammed with luggage and the wheelchair had to go on a roof rack. This proved to be an advantage when stops were made; it was quicker and easier to take the chair from the roof rather than shift everything around in the trunk.

Saarbrücken in Germany was the intended destination that day, and we reached it following a long delay in Luxembourg, where armed police stopped all traffic to search for bank robbers. We couldn't find accessible accommodation in Saarbrücken and had to go on to Strasbourg.

After driving around the city in a fruitless search for a suitable hotel, Neil (a policeman) stopped at a police station. He explained our situation, showing his International Police Federation card. The French police led us through the busy streets of Strasbourg in a police car, lights flashing, stopping other cars as we sped toward a hotel a couple of miles away. They booked us in, made sure we left

nothing of value in the car, and departed with best wishes for a successful trip.

Neil was in the act of fixing up the wheelchair when a small man, perhaps in his late forties, emerged from the hotel. He lifted me out of the passenger seat, regardless of my 167lb weight, and plonked me in the wheelchair. Before we could gather our senses, he proceeded to pull me up a flight of stairs.

It transpired that this hotel was populated by ex-Foreign Legionnaires, mostly of German origin, who spent a few months of each year in France to fulfil a residential regulation for their pension. The rooms were inexpensive (about $10 per night each) but everything was clean and adequate.

After a short rest and a wash, we met the small man again. In a combination of English, French, and a little German we learned that his name was Jean and he'd retired from the Legion in 1969. He was as hard as nails but very amicable, showing us photos of places he'd visited in the South Pacific, and introducing us to Heinz, who'd been shot in the head when parachuting in French Cameroon. Though paralyzed down his left side, Heinz had fought back to remarkable fitness. He insisted on taking us to a restaurant and despite his disabilities we found it difficult to keep up his marching pace.

Surrounded by more Legionnaires we enjoyed an excellent meal with wine and it was quite late when we arrived back at the hotel. Nobody seemed to take any notice of my wheelchair, except when offering help. Our duty-free Scotch appeared and with Heinz and Jean, and later *le patron*, who couldn't sleep because of our noise, we drank until the early hours of the morning.

The showers did not supply hot water—cold was the Legionnaires' preference and it did have the effect of waking us up. Neil and I envied twelve-year-old Scott, bright and cheerful, who was of course too young to have developed bad habits. After breakfast, Heinz took us on a tour of the old part of Strasbourg. As you'd expect from a city housing the European Community Parliament, Strasbourg is modern and cosmopolitan, but it is dominated by the medieval Cathédrale de Notre-Dame and still retains its historical atmosphere.

By noon we were making our way through scorching heat into Germany, toward the Black Forest. Afer visiting the picturesque Rhine Falls, where we encountered a wedding and were showered with candy, we spent the night in *Hotel Kirschen*, Lottsletten, in a small peninsula of Germany which juts into Switzerland. On through Zürich and along the southern shore of two lakes, Zürich See and Walen See, stopping for coffee in Vaduz, capital of

Liechtenstein. We decided to make Innsbruck by nightfall and made good speed until we reached the Arlberg pass. Ignoring the tunnel, we took the high road over the top. The road twisted and turned at acute angles with precipitous drops into rocky ravines only a mistake away. From a parking place at 6000 feet we got out to take a few photos and the cold wind took our breath away.

In Innsbruck, finding an accessible hotel was difficult but we finally secured rooms at the *Wilder Mann Hotel*, which was all but full of British senior citizens. We headed straight for the bar, where a large glass of beer went down very well after a long day traveling. Walking along Innsbruck's tidy streets late that night, after a magnificent dinner, breathing in the refreshing air, I was struck by the proximity of the mountains. When looking up at the jagged peaks silhouetted against the sky my neck was bent right back; when leaving the confines of the restaurant, or peering into shop windows, a glance upward would transport me into another world.

"I insisted on frequent stops at the many beer gardens to avoid dehydration"

From Innsbruck we drove north, passing majestic mountains and crystal-clear lakes, to Munich. In Bavaria we saw the Wagneresque castles which the mad king, Ludwig II, had built at his country's expense. With a multitude of tourists swamping the area the castles were frankly a disappointment, and we pressed on to Munich, where we booked into a hotel opposite a brewery. Our unanimous decision after our two-day stay was that the beer in Munich was good—very good! Feeling sorry for Neil, who had to push me around the city under a cloudless sky, I insisted on frequent stops at the many beer gardens to avoid dehydration and exhaustion.

Munich is a twin city of my native Edinburgh, has excellent facilities, and seemed to be full of friendly people (perhaps the beer had something to do with that). We walked the pedestrian precinct, beginning at the station and progressing through the fourteenth-century Karlstor gate (one of the three remaining gates of the original medieval city) which is situated beside a spectacular fountain—a tempting sight on a hot June day.

The precinct continues along Neuhauser, with its many and varied shops, then opens out into the Marienplatz, the square in the heart of the city. Here we rested in an outdoor café, looking up at the carillon on the New Town Hall (Rathaus), unfortunately fifteen minutes after the 11am performance. The Rathaus is not really new, built in 1909, but much newer than the nearby fifteenth-century Altes Rathaus which today houses a toy museum. To the left, towering over everything else, stands the twin-domed Frauenkirche, the symbol of Munich, dominating the city's skyline.

Using a wheelchair in Munich was very easy, and where help was required there was no shortage of volunteers. Time was not on our side on this vacation, and it is difficult to obtain an objective view of a land and its population during a brief visit, but the Bavarians did seem to me a pleasant and relaxed lot, out to live life rather than simply survive it. In the Englischer Garten, where we anticipated drinking beer, we encountered hundreds of people sunbathing naked—even if our climate was better, I somehow cannot imagine this going on in Edinburgh or Birmingham! Situated to the west of the River Isar, the Englischer Garten dates from the eighteenth century and is one of Europe's largest city parks. The leafy avenues by the river gave us welcome relief from the sun, and the whole effect is one of natural countryside rather than landscaped parkland.

We didn't use our cameras in the Englischer Garten, but many rolls of film were exposed during the tour. Using a medium-format camera I captured some shots in the Olympic Stadium which I was able to sell to a photographic agency back home; from a wheelchair it is easy to obtain steady images without using a tripod, simply by resting the camera on your lap. The view from the top of the 500-foot Olympic tower was startling. The weather was clear, enabling us to see the entire city, with its domes and spires reflecting the light of the morning sun. Also visible was the pool where Mark Spitz won his seven gold medals, and the terraced buildings of the Olympic village where Arab terrorists stormed the Israeli quarters in 1972.

"As I rolled out of the chair I was conscious of the barrier at the bottom of the steps and the 5000-foot drop"

Of course, in Munich we had to visit a traditional Bavarian restaurant: mountains of food and gallons of beer consumed in a vast hall, ringing to the sounds of music and dancing. We had difficulty moving from the table after our weisswurst, a tasty recipe of veal served with baked potatoes and salad. I again felt sorry for Neil when he had to haul himself and me out of the restaurant and back to the hotel. I was OK, sitting in the wheelchair! Neil never complained, and every obstacle was brushed aside with "No problem!," but he did collapse when we got back to the hotel that night.

Leaving Munich it was a relatively short drive, by our standards so far, across the Austrian border to Salzburg. We found an excellent hotel, *Gasthof Grunauer Hof*, in a village called Wals, a few miles from town. Our room had a balcony with a view of the Untersberg; this is "Sound of Music" country and though not great fans of the film we had to admit to spectacular scenery.

In the bar, watching the European Championship soccer match between Spain and West Germany, we were surprised to hear local Austrians cheer loudly for the Spanish. As far as sport was concerned, they explained, they would support anybody except their overbearing neighbors. Thinking of our own situation in Scotland, we recognized a similarity: we also take great delight at the defeat of England. A kind of empathy existed between the Austrians and ourselves, both having neighbors who hogged the limelight.

That evening we sat on the balcony drinking wine and smoking cigars. The air was exceptionally still and warm. A blazing bonfire cast moving shadows of revelers celebrating Midsummer Night. It was just possible to see the outline of the Untersberg against a dark sky, and we decided to go there the next day.

Getting into the cable car involved the ascent of two flights of stairs. With help I was maneuvered into the cable car and I didn't feel too bad, even as it swayed about at a great height over rugged rocks. Getting out at the top was tricky because I had to alight in the wheelchair at right angles to descending steps. A helpful tourist pulled me out but tipped me over; as I rolled out of the chair I was conscious of the barrier at the bottom of the steps and the 5000-foot drop to Salzburg. However, I was assisted back into the chair and managed to bear the incident with equanimity in spite of the laughter from some who should have known better.

The mountain air was chilly, a stark contrast to the heat below, but it was fresh and invigorating. The view over the surrounding mountains was worth the effort, and after a brief lunch of soup, bread, and coffee we were ready for an afternoon touring.

The city of Salzburg is a nice size, and the pedestrian precinct—really a collection of *plätze* or squares—imparts a feeling of space and concise geome-try. The older part of the city, especially around the Getreidegasse, is more crowded, with narrow, cobblestone streets, quaint shopfronts, and ornate signs. Some houses, dating from the fifteenth century, back onto the sheer rockface leading up to the castle. We found the most relaxing parts of the city along the banks of the Salzach river. Late in the afternoon, before returning to the hotel in Wals, it was pleasant to sit and watch the world pass by while Scott fed the swans.

"The official shook his head ruefully when we told him how long we were spending in Vienna"

The fine weather broke and we left for Vienna in a torrential downpour. But it had brightened considerably by the time we reached *Hotel Zur Post*, 25 miles west of the city in the Vienna woods and not far from a small brewery (again!). A fine meal of venison set us up for the expedition the following day to the old capital of the Austrian Empire, the city of culture, music, science, and spies. This was the farthest point east on our grand tour, and I had a special reason for including it: my great-grandfather came from Vienna to Scotland sometime in the last century—I was going back to my roots.

With a map supplied by the helpful Austrian National Tourist Office in London, Neil managed to drive precisely through the city and park beside the brown Danube. There we left the car and began our exploration on foot. Near the giant ferris wheel (featured in *The Third Man*) we were almost run down by thirty Hell's Angels. Undaunted, we reached the Stadtpark and stopped for refreshments; Germany is the land of the beer garden, but here the wine garden ruled and we adopted the local custom.

With so many attractions in the city the choice was difficult. We elected to visit the Natural History Museum, avoiding a multitude of steps with the help of an official who took us to an elevator at the rear of the building. This was no ordinary museum. The spacious entrance hall was built more like a cathedral. While Neil and Scott examined the wildlife displays, I was more interested in the remains of Bronze-Age settlements found to the south of Vienna. The official shook his head ruefully when we told him how long we were spending in Vienna. By the time we had surveyed the Imperial Palace of the Habsburgs it was getting late, and we returned to the car by taxi. One day was not enough.

We drove west along the Danube, then followed the Neckar river to Heidelberg, on the Rhine. Leaving Heidelberg the next morning brought us into the vast jungle of concrete and steel that is Mannheim/Ludwigshafen (on opposite banks of the Rhine). We got lost. For a couple of hours we drove round and round, looking for a way out to the northward. Eventually we escaped and made 40 miles or so before we broke down.

Neil contacted the rescue service and after a few hours hanging about, during which we had a chat with the locals, a transporter arrived to take us back to Mannheim. I couldn't get into the high cab up front, but this enabled me to enjoy a good view of the countryside from inside the car on the back of the transporter. Passing over the Rhine at Worms and through the industrial complexes around Mannheim and Ludwigshafen, I was impressed by the sheer size and spread of it all, especially the BASF works.

Little was amiss with the car. A Polish mechanic, after deriding me for buying a Japanese car, took the carburettor to bits and reassembled it. The engine started first try! It was getting late by then but the garage directed us to local accommodation, where we obtained a welcome dinner and a glass or two of beer.

The following day we reached Brussels by mid-afternoon and had sufficient time to go up the Atomium, a massive construction of aluminum spheres in the shape of an atomic nucleus, built for the World Fair in 1958. A rapidly ascending elevator took us to the top for a view of the city, but this was marred by badly scratched transparent panels; the cathedral was seen through somebody's initials carved on Plexiglass. On this, my third visit, Brussels still seemed a charmless place, unlike many other areas of Belgium.

Our ferry from Zeebrugge left at 11pm and the crossing was uneventful. We made it back to Scotland by early evening, with only an assortment of foreign coins left in our pockets. Altogether we spent twelve nights in Europe and covered 3200 miles. It had been a giant buffet and we'd sampled each main dish. It was an adventure which we may never repeat, but we enjoyed every minute. I haven't mentioned a great deal about the problems of traveling with a disability; the truth of the matter is that there were none that warranted real concern, and minor difficulties were easily overcome. For this I have the people of eight countries, who helped in various ways, to thank, not to mention my companions. But perhaps most important was our attitude: we didn't go looking for things to go wrong, nor did we worry if they did.

Coming Home

Michael Turner and his wife Julie are both 27 years old and both have cerebral palsy. In 1985 they set off on a six-week trip, camping in five European countries.

As the patter of rain developed into what sounded like an avalanche, and lightning lit up the inside of the tent more brightly than our gas-lamp, I began to wonder, "What the hell are we doing here?" Home seemed like a million miles away, and at that moment I'd have given a million pounds to have been there.

This was our first night under canvas. Julie and I were both at college and we had been impressed by our friends' tales of travels in various parts of the world. Many of them had been around Europe by train, and while we felt that we wouldn't get very far on trains and with backpacks, we were confident that we could manage camping with a car.

We left home with a roughly circular route planned that would take us through Belgium (for a short visit to relatives in Brussels), West Germany, Austria, Switzerland, and France. Our tastes were for the scenic aspects of central Europe, particularly the Alps, rather than the heat of the south. However, part of the attraction of camping is being able to plan things as you go along. This proved its worth when we became fed up with being rained on in Switzerland, and decided that the hot south might not be such a bad idea after all; we packed up and went to Antibes in the south of France.

Freedom has its price. Camping was undoubtedly very hard work. We had a small, three-person ridge tent (though where the third person was meant to go remains a mystery) which we'd only previously put up in a soggy back yard in spring. The dry ground of summer (except in Switzerland) proved a fair bit harder. This caused us some difficulty in a number of places, although people nearly always appeared and gave us a hand.

The only time we got into real trouble was the night we arrived in Antibes. We'd driven virtually non-stop for two days to get away from the Swiss rain, and we arrived quite late. By the time we'd eaten it was after 11pm. A combination of rocky and sandy ground meant that some of the tent pegs just would not go in, and others slid out as soon as they did. By 1am we had reached the point where it would probably stay up, and we just had to hope it wouldn't rain (much of the work in putting up a tent is to make it sure it stays waterproof).

As well as the actual putting up and taking down of the tents, camping involves a lot of lugging things around—gas stove, chairs and table, pots and pans—and all have to be put away as soon as you've finished with them. The combination of this and the fresh air certainly made us sleep very soundly.

"I'm sure that our disabilities were actually an advantage on this trip"

Campgrounds are not the best equipped places for disabled people. We found only one site on the whole journey with any specific facilities—a wheelchair-accessible shower and toilet. At many sites there were steps into rest rooms, and shower cubicles were cramped. They were also, with a couple of exceptions, segregated according to sex.

We both walk (with difficulty), so we didn't worry too much about physical barriers, but we had wondered about language barriers. We're rather typically British in that we speak only our own language, but we also have speech impairments and were concerned about the potential for problems with communication. Our fears were unfounded. We are well used to having difficulty making ourselves understood, which meant that a language barrier wasn't anything new to us, and we are also used to backing up what we say with gestures and expressions. More often than not, pointing to the appropriate line of the phrasebook worked perfectly well.

There was one occasion when we were defeated. We were in a restaurant in France and Julie was eating an omelette with french fries, which arrived on separate plates, while my order was held up for reasons unknown. The Frenchman on the table next to us decided that the fries were mine and that I was unable to feed myself; without a word he proceeded to attempt to feed me Julie's fries. It took the timely arrival of my order to convince him that the fries were not mine and I was a dab hand with a spoon and fork!

Apart from this incident, I'm sure that our disabilities were actually an advantage on this trip, since we were not just more English tourists who couldn't speak the language; people were more willing to take the time to understand us.

"Mile after mile of breathtaking scenery and air that remained cool and fresh even in the hottest weather"

One of the very interesting things we were able to experience by traveling through several countries was the varying attitudes and understanding of disability. Obviously it is impossible to draw any firm conclusions, since we saw only a small part of each country and we were mainly in rural areas, but there were some clear differences.

Austria was a curious mixture: while virtually every shop in Innsbruck had a "happy to help" sign in four different languages, this was undoubtedly the country where our disabilities drew the most attention. On one occasion we went into a bar/restaurant in a village

and literally every head in the bar turned to look at us—it was like a scene from a Western. Judging by the amount of staring that people did, it seems that unaccompanied disabled people are far less common on the continent than they are in Britain.

Traveling from Austria into Switzerland was quite remarkable. Suddenly the staring stopped, there were better facilities and we even spotted some disabled people around. In the areas that we visited, the Swiss appeared to be very much more aware of, and more comfortable with, disability. But for the rain, we would have stayed longer, as we thoroughly enjoyed what we did see of the country, in between the low clouds. Lucerne was one of the most pleasant places we stopped at, with its situation on the lake, the many old buildings along the banks of the river, and the intricately decorated old bridge across the river. It was quite touristy, but maintained its charm and atmosphere in spite of the hordes.

Our other favorite country was Germany. We found a marvelous campground on the banks of the Rhine, a little south of Coblenz, where the river runs through a high-sided, tree-covered valley (spoiled only by the noise of military jets and helicopters). There was level access to the showers and to the site shop, and only one or two steps to the rest rooms. The Black Forest was another high point on our tour, with mile after mile of breathtaking scenery and air that remained cool and fresh even in the hottest weather.

It was in Obersdorf, a town in southern Germany on the edge of the Alps, that we had our strangest experience. We'd decided to have a couple of nights' break from the rigors of camping and indulge in a guesthouse or hotel. It was early August, and everywhere we tried was fully booked. Driving out of Obersdorf, toward a campground we'd passed earlier, we saw a small hotel by the road and decided to have one last try. To our amazement there were rooms available, it was very cheap, and there was a marvelous view of the mountains.

In time it became apparent that we were the only people staying there, although there were many members of the family who lived in and ran the hotel. It also became apparent why we were the only guests. During the night the family rowed and shouted, babies cried, and there were crashes and bangs. The following morning we were told that the rest room on our floor was not working. We presumed this was something to do with the plumbing, but found that the toilet had been smashed with a hammer! While this was all very strange, we didn't feel at all threatened, so we made the most of our break from camping.

France was at the end of our circular route, the warmth of Antibes a pleasant relief from the Swiss rain. It was, however, very busy with lots of English tourists, which encouraged us to move on quickly. Making our way up through France we spent time in Avignon, which has a medieval feel despite the onslaught of cars and buses. This is an old, walled town and quite difficult to get around—finding a parking place was only the first hurdle.

From Avignon we moved on to Le Puy, a small town in a dramatic setting among the hills and lava pinnacles of the Auvergne. The town is dominated by a massive, hill-top statue of the Madonna. Having trudged up the hill we found that it is possible to climb up inside the statue to a viewing platform in its crown, but the steep steps and my lack of head for heights got the better of us and we had to make do with the views from the hill.

We indulged ourselves with a hotel for our last night on the continent. It was chosen very carefully as we were getting short of funds—so short that we didn't have wine with our evening meal and didn't even dare to order water for fear of getting expensive mineral water!

After six weeks on the road, the return home to comfortable beds, hot baths, and just knowing where we were was very welcome, and an important part of the journey. Much of the value of traveling, for us, was to arrive home and see it in the light of what we had seen and experienced while touring.

Cruises

A Dose of Romantic Escapism

In May 1988 Terence Wilson made his third attempt at a trip on the sail training ship *Lord Nelson* (the voyages are very popular and it can be difficult to obtain a place at the right time, at the right price, and for the required duration). Although he'd been sailing for about 25 years in smaller craft, he wasn't sure how he'd manage with the problems of multiple sclerosis in a larger vessel, even if the ship was designed for disabled crew members, so he booked a berth on the two-day, Antwerp to Lowestoft voyage, accompanied by his daughter, Sarah, and her husband, Timothy.

The bus let us off at the ferry terminal in Dover, and after a short wait in reception while the party assembled we set off for customs and the departure lounge. This was my first mistake. Thinking that it was just a short distance, I started to walk, but it turned out to be several hundred yards of corridor which I only just managed to negotiate before collapsing into an armchair. Fortunately we had quite a long wait here while our ferry was serviced. Next, a bus transported us across the docks to the ferry and we were on our way.

Around 8:30pm we disembarked at Ostend and a friendly Belgian bus driver shepherded us onto another bus. It was a good job he did! The others had to walk miles to the customs hall with their bags, while we were whisked in and out and back to the waiting bus before you could say "Jaques Robinson." One of our fellow passengers, John, was raised on a special wheelchair lift into the back of the bus and our luggage was piled into the trailer towed behind.

When we left England it was a pleasant, sunny spring day; now it was 76°F, humid, and after fourteen hours of traveling I was beginning to wilt. Bumping over the cobblestone wharfs in Antwerp, the bus pulled into a small lane between two brick buildings and there she was—the *Lord Nelson*. The 400-ton barque shone in the bright lights around the harbor, the sails brailed up to the yards which towered above the dockside. We climbed out of the bus, grabbed our bags, and descended a long, steep gangway to the river level and the waiting reception. A short wait while the crew signed ship's articles in the best seafaring tradition, and we were allotted our berths and watches below.

Sarah and I were Starb'd Aft Watch, while Tim was in a foc'sle berth on Port For'd Watch. Sarah and I shared a wheelchair-berth, with me on the lower bunk and she as my "buddy" on the pipe-cot above me. (Everyone in the crew has a buddy, someone to keep a weather eye on you, to make sure you are wearing your safety line, and to clip you on if things look bad.) We assembled in the lower mess deck where we met the professional crew. Watch leaders were assigned to each watch, then we were given the bad news. First watch on duty was Starb'd Aft Watch, from midnight to 4am, the Middle or "Graveyard" Watch. I came here to discover my limit and this was it! I went to see the Medical Purser and told her my problem.

"That's all right. Go and tell your watch leader and then go and get your head down." What a relief!

Next morning, things looked decidedly better. I awoke to the strum of diesel engines and the PA system calling all hands off watch to the lower mess deck for breakfast. Here we met all the shadowy figures of last night and introduced ourselves properly. Each day—in our case, on this short voyage, at every meal—two or three crew members are given mess duties, setting the tables, handing out the food from the galley connecting us to the galley, and clearing away afterward.

When we were not "on watch" we were lectured on safety at sea, man-overboard drill, and "learning the ropes." We were also introduced to that *Lord Nelson* institution, delightfully misnamed "Happy Hour": dusters, buckets, scrubbing brushes, and cleaning materials were handed out and everybody was assigned to clean something. There were very few occasions when disabled and able-bodied crew were segregated but this was one of

them. Disabled crew were relieved of the more onerous duties, such as cleaning out the "heads," but we were all encouraged to help out with any small job during Happy Hour and at mealtimes. I polished the brass.

"I had no problem getting around, either below or on deck, with my elbow-stick, Long John Silver style"

Soon the *Lord Nelson* was well down the Westerschelde and on her way to the North Sea. Volunteers were called to climb the rat-lines onto the yards to prepare the large sails for sea. Tim was among a small party up aloft and they were joined by several others eager to try their hand. I went below for a well-earned siesta after lunch and when I came on deck again we were heading for the open sea, a strong breeze drawing the main and fore courses, tops'ls and t'gallants. The fore and aft stays'ls, jibs, and spanker were also set and the *Lord Nelson* came alive.

I had no problem getting around, either below or on deck, with my elbow-stick, Long John Silver style. There were two wheelchair lifts up the main companionways, and a single chair lift for crew members like myself who had difficulty walking upstairs. Along the sides of the cabins there were small tie-up seats to perch on, and convenient bollards and machine-housing to squat on, with hand-holds everywhere.

The next watch for Sarah and me was 4am to 8am—the Morning Watch—so after a pleasant drink in the duty-free bar we turned in. I woke several times in the night and secured my lee cloth to stop me falling out of my bunk. When we were woken to stand watch we came on deck to find a gray dawn over the North Sea, with a Force 6 northeaster blowing straight down from the Arctic Circle and the *Lord Nelson* pitching and rolling over the spume-blown waves. I was very glad I had brought my long johns.

The first job, according to Paul (First Mate), was to reduce canvas. Our watch consisted of ten crew members, of which only one (myself) was disabled. It was logical for me to take the helm while the others shortened sail. Starb'd Aft Watch disappeared forward to start with the jib and I felt very much alone—like the Flying Dutchman, at the helm of a 400-ton square rigger bound God-knows-where. Because of complications, the task of taking in some of the sails took longer than anticipated, and I found myself at the helm for the entire watch. Every few minutes Paul's head would pop up over the edge of the bridge with a new course and bearing as we careered into the maze of offshore sandbanks lying west of the Norfolk coast. I wouldn't have changed those four hours for anything.

"We met in the bar and sang sea shanties until we were all too tired to stay awake"

When I went off watch to breakfast that morning, I sat watching the crew tumbling downstairs to the mess deck. Many had succumbed to the dreaded *mal-de-mer*, but instead of the group of tourists and travelers we met at Dover, here were a bunch of hardened seafarers, with oilies and life jackets, their faces red from windburn and saltspray, hair disheveled by the nor'easter, and ready for their kippers and boiled eggs. What a transformation!

As a result of the strong favorable wind, our crossing was so fast that we arrived outside Lowestoft harbor far too early to get in. The anchor was let go just beyond the North Pier while we waited for the tide. That night, tied up to the dock, we met in the bar and sang sea shanties until we were all too tired to stay awake: old songs about Australia and the great Southern Ocean, about girls of easy virtue preying on young sailor lads fresh from the sea—a rollicking end to a sea voyage.

Of course I would do it again. The feeling of achievement, the sense of adventure, the comradeship will stay with me for many years to come. For once, disability did not matter, yet—unlike many everyday-life situations—it was not entirely overlooked. At all times there was a friendly helping hand ready to assist when asked, and disabled sailors were simply part of the crew. Each person's contribution depends on their knowledge of the sea, not their degree of physical ability. For example, watch leaders are the only crew members with any real responsibility (apart from the professional crew) and they must hold the RYA Yachtmaster Offshore Certificate or equivalent practical sailing experience. On this voyage one of the watch leaders was paraplegic: what he couldn't do in a wheelchair isn't worth mentioning. More important, he knew the names of the hundreds of ropes and could give orders for them to be handled by the rest of us. That's what's meant by responsibility.

There is a saying in the Navy, "First turn of the screw pays all debts." Once you are on board the *Lord Nelson*, all debts are paid, the life you lead ashore is behind you, and you can look forward to a few days of romantic escapism and nautical nostalgia, serving before the mast.

To the Edge of the Polar Icecap

For the last four years, Betty Parkin has been partially sighted (registered blind). Initially thinking that this must restrict her choice of vacation to two weeks on a seaside hotel balcony, she now takes a yearly cruise— "expensive, but worth making a few sacrifices for." In July 1989 she joined the *Canberra* for a cruise to Norway.

I had always regarded cruising as a vacation for stick-in-the-muds or bridge fans—no adventures, no visits to unknown or extraordinary places. But a short trip to the Canaries then two weeks in the Mediterranean and I was hooked. The third cruise took me up the coast of Norway to the island of Spitsbergen, in the Arctic Ocean.

Cruising requires as much planning as any other vacation. Studying the prices, the dates, and destinations may be enough for some, but not for me. I need the same cabin—or one very similar—in the same part of the same ship. As far as accommodation is concerned, mostly you get what you pay for; after many years of travel I go for the very best I can afford. There seems no sense in scrimping and saving all year only to end in a month of discomfort—better to lower your sights, cut down the number of days and enjoy a little luxury.

Of course, this is the view of an older person; cabins for three or four occupants are adequate for the young and idealistic, but most disabled people need space. I travel alone and indulge myself with a single cabin so that if I knock anything over, spill my tea, or grovel around on the carpet, looking for my pen or an earring, I am not being a nuisance to anyone else.

Wanting the same cabin for another trip means booking it very early. On the *Canberra* an official comes on board for the last day of the cruise to take reservations for the next year, and many people take advantage of this. As one elderly lady said to me, "If I am spared I shall enjoy the cruise, and if I am not I shan't worry over the loss of my deposit!"

If I was more confident about my sight I might be tempted by the "Take a Chance" offer to those who can take their vacation at any time with only three weeks' notice of a vacancy and at a much-reduced price. My problem is that although I should get a single cabin it might be in a different part of the ship to that which I have grown accustomed to. But it is worth considering if this is not your problem.

Most shipping companies require passengers traveling alone to walk unaided, or with canes, up the gangway of the ship. Wheelchair passengers (the chair must conform to their regulations) must be accompanied by an escort who can push their chair up the gangway. Totally blind persons must also have an escort. My tour agent states on the booking form, "Partially sighted but has previously had this cabin without any problems."

"Traveling from my village home to Southampton is one of the worst problems"

Having accepted the deposit, *P&O* sends out a medical form, three months prior to embarkation, to all who are over seventy years of age (75 with some cruise companies) and to any disabled passengers. This must be completed by your own doctor and it ensures that the ship's surgeon knows of your condition and any medications used, should you require his or her help during the cruise.

Traveling from my village home in northern England to the port at Southampton is one of the worst problems: should I go by train to London and take a taxi across to another station for the special boat train? Or should I risk the once-a-day train from a nearby station which, if delayed, could miss the boat, to say nothing of having to spend the night in a hotel on my return in order to catch the early morning train home? It is all very worrying, but on this trip I was lucky—the cruise I had booked was chosen by the district newspaper for a special tour and this meant bus travel to and from my local town. All my problems were solved.

For the *Canberra* cruise there is a special embarkation time for anyone requiring assistance with wheelchairs, or a chair from train or bus to the ship, or in my case a porter—hand baggage and a white cane leave no hand free for gangways, ticket collection, or passport control. It is essential to carry a valise as luggage may not appear in your cabin until long after the ship has sailed.

Ask for assistance when making the final payment, so that help can be organized and you are not left stranded on the dockside. And some of your usual medication should be packed in your valise so that you are not waiting for that belated luggage to arrive in your cabin. There are large supplies of medications carried in the ship's pharmacy, but neither those nor treatment is covered by any health benefits, so they are very expensive. Insurance may be included in the fare, but usually the first $30–50 has to be paid and the insurance covers only accidents and new medical problems.

When at last I am aboard I take my time, look around and tread carefully, remembering that most doorways have high sills. (The nursing staff tell me that before they leave the home port there are usually shins to be stitched or bandaged, mostly eager, excited, young passengers, rarely the more careful disabled ones.) Doors must be tried with caution as those opening onto decks often require a very strong arm to open and shut them.

I tell the cabin steward who comes to greet me that I am partially sighted but manage fairly well. Would he tell those who vacuum the corridor carpets to keep an eye out for me? I see their machines but the long, snaking cords remain invisible. With the steward's permission I put some bright stickers on glass edges and such, then I stroll around, remind myself of the number of steps in the nearby staircase, refresh my memory about the elevator buttons, and I am ready for the cruise to begin.

There are no Indian temples to explore on the *Canberra*, no Greek ruins to climb, but there is plenty to do and see—classical concerts, cabarets, discos, and dancing, as well as entertainment from stage, TV, and radio stars. The movie theater shows recent films and a lecturer gives excellent illustrated talks on the ports to be visited on the cruise. Special places are reserved in the theater for wheelchairs and their escorts, and the library has a goodly supply of large-print books. Tournaments are held for bridge fanatics, and there are classes covering everything from keep fit to soft-toy making. And the Chaplain takes regular services. For many passengers a long chair on deck suffices.

"The majesty of the mountain-ringed fiords and the tremendous force of the waterfalls overwhelmed me"

Tours are arranged, several of them in each port. They may be expensive but are good value for money and are accompanied by local guides. When *Canberra* cannot berth she anchors nearby and passengers are conveyed to shore by launches, which then keep up a regular service. If the town is any distance away a free shuttle service by bus is provided. Most disabled passengers on our trip were able to manage the gangway from the ship to the launches.

I had visited Norway twice before but the majesty of the mountain-ringed fiords and the tremendous force of the waterfalls still overwhelmed me as we cruised past villages perched high above the zigzag roads. The air was clean and bright, as I had remembered. At Narvik I chose the day trip, which included a visit to a war cemetery and the Chapel of Peace. The Krigsminne War Museum, run by the Red Cross, is an emotive documentation of the German bombing of the town and the sea and air battles which raged around it.

We next took the ore trail into Sweden, traveling along the railroad track used by the wagons that carry millions of tons of iron ore yearly from Sweden for export via Narvik's docks. We passed into the land of reindeer, uninhabited by humans, a strange terrain of lakes, marshes, and rivers; deep valleys lay between snow-wreathed mountains. We lunched on reindeer meat at the Arisko National Park, but most of the animals had moved on to summer pastures and the main attraction of the park at that time of year was its wealth of wild flowers.

My day in Trondheim was spent visiting the cathedral, a very fine one with a beautiful rose window. At 1pm the doors are closed and the organist plays a short program of Norwegian music—a lovely rest period from your shopping. I walked alone here and found it quite easy as Norway has such clearly marked crossings and the traffic always stops at them. Traffic laws are very strictly enforced. There are many good shops, knitwear and silver jewelry being the favorite buys, but the prices were prohibitive for most of us. Even the fruit and flowers seemed expensive.

In Bergen, which was familiar ground, I went to the fish market at Torget where fish of all shapes and sizes are sold, including smoked salmon in packets, ideal for bringing home. There was every type of pot plant in the flower market—in Norway no window is complete without its pot plant. Facing the harbor are the famous old wooden warehouses of Bryggen, the site of the original settlement of Bergen. After a morning spent exploring on my own (thanks again to those crossings), I joined the ship's tour which took me to the Aquarium and to the Bryggens Museum, where a collection of old boathouses and warehouses have been reconstructed.

"Mountains with sides polished bare by glaciers that spill huge chunks of brilliant blue ice into the sea"

The highlight of the cruise was our final destination, Spitsbergen, which is icebound for all but two months of the year. Here are mountains with sides polished bare by glaciers that spill huge chunks of brilliant blue ice into the sea to float like the bubbles in a bath alongside the ship. Reindeer graze on sparse vegetation at the water's edge, and sea birds, geese, and puffins fly overhead.

A lecturer from Bergen had joined our ship for two days and had given a course of four talks about glaciers, which greatly enhanced our understanding of the area. The Captain took the ship to the very edge of the polar icecap which stands high and proud from the ocean like the cut white icing on a wedding cake. It was a worrying time for the crew, with lookouts posted all around the ship, but an unforgettable sight for the passengers. I was delighted to be able to make out most of the scenery through my monocular glass.

During my stay on the *Canberra* I received every help from the ship's company, and while shopping ashore I found no problems to deter moderately disabled, unaccompanied people. Many salespeople speak fluent English and nearly everyone can manage a few useful sentences. In one street where the sidewalk was being repaired, strangers crossed the road to tell me of the hazard and on realizing that I was a tourist and might not understand their instructions they accompanied me past the cavities and over the ramps. Many elderly and disabled folk were using different walking frames from those I'd seen before—obviously adapted for use in icy places.

Before the end of the cruise I visited the ship's hospital (I am a retired nurse) to ask the doctors and nursing staff if they had any advice to offer prospective disabled passengers. One nurse said, "If you are independent in your own home you will be able to manage aboard, but if you require daily nursing care, or cannot cook or do routine tasks, this sort of assistance cannot be provided." Anything that makes life more comfortable can be brought on board, for example a tripod instead of a cane if your balance is poor, a high seat for the lavatory, special pillows, even a hoist to transfer from chair to bed.

Children generally have a wonderful time on a cruise ship, with their own program of events, their own staff of nursery workers and aides, and a club for teenagers. Few of the passengers on the Norway cruise will forget the delightful picture made by a young girl as she sat in her decorated wheelchair joining in the fun of Ascot night, with her pink parasol and matching crepe-paper hat.

Disembarkation of the walking wounded (as I think of us from my service days) was made easy. Our specially labeled baggage was stacked on the shore with waiting porters who escorted us through customs and to the trains, cars, or buses, where we sat and waited in comfort while the rest of the passengers lined up. It was good to be in the bus, sipping hot coffee supplied by the driver, and remember the glory of the mountains and fiords, the sparkling waterfalls, and the blue ice floating past the ship which carried us close to the top of the world.

Caribbean Cruise

Since 1952, when an airplane crash left him in a wheelchair as a paraplegic, Douglass Annand has traveled extensively and is well known as the author of The Wheelchair Traveler, the first edition of which was published in 1962 (see USA Travel Notes). In February 1991, Douglass and his wife Charlie joined a cruise on the Nieuw Amsterdam, of the Holland-America Line, sailing out of Tampa, Florida.

Salt air, blue sky, balmy sunshine, and a good ship to sail—nowadays, even if you use a wheelchair, it's all available to you. We arrived a day early, to meet some friends from California, and stayed at the *Sheraton Grand Hotel* on Kennedy Boulevard. The room was accessible, with enough space to get around and a bed that was on a frame. The bathrooms was a little small, but a 29-inch doorway and support bars made it quite usable.

The next day we all gathered in the lounge to enjoy cool drinks and share excited talk about the coming week as well as sea stories about previous cruises. The cruise line provided transportation from the hotel to the point of departure. We traveled in a station wagon taxicab, the able-bodied passengers in an air-conditioned bus.

After an hour or so of waiting, we were assisted by members of the crew and were finally aboard. The first thing I wanted to do, of course, was to check out our cabin D101. The interior of the ship is quite accessible, and the elevators are large enough for a standard 26-inch wheelchair plus spouse or traveling companion. The cabin was excellent, with a 31-inch-wide cabin door and one of the nicest bathrooms I have seen anyplace. The door was 36 inches wide with a short, steep, no-help-needed ramp. In the left corner was the sink, with plenty of space for my knees, and a low mirror; in the right corner was the toilet with support bars, and in between was a roll-in shower with gently sloping floor to a corner drain; all this was in a six-by-six-foot bathroom.

"The nights were balmy, the days warm and sunny, and we had a great time"

The cabin had a queen-size bed with plenty of space on two sides, two windows looking forward over the bow, also a telephone and color TV. We decided to freshen up so we could watch the ship cast off and be ready for dinner straight afterward. Thoughtfully, the cruise line stipulates casual dress for the first-night dinner; other nights, dressing up is part of the pleasure.

We sailed slowly down the channel past several other ships, including a Russian fishing boat, then under the Sunshine Bridge and out into the Gulf of Mexico, headed for our first port of call, Key West, Florida. After a good night's sleep we pulled into Key West about 9am, docked right up to the pier so all we had to do was go down a medium steep ramp and roll right on into town.

First stop was Mel Fisher's Pieces of Eight Museum, which houses much of the treasure from the Spanish galleon, *Atocha*. The ramp to enter is on the right side of the building; it's a little too long and a little too steep to use without help. Inside are tons of silver bars and gold chains nicely exhibited through the old building.

Next we were off to see some of the old houses. The day we visited, there was a big craft and painting show, with lots of artists showing and selling their wares in booths in front of the houses—all very interesting, but we couldn't see the houses for the booths. We moved off to get a cool drink and go window shopping and looking around all the small shops. There were curb cuts and ramps at street corners, and liquid refreshment available at every turn. A little after noon we came upon the Pier House—as the name implies, not far from where the ships tie up—with crowded tables outside and a good view of the beach with many sailboats bobbing around. Inside we found good food and a table with a fan giving us a gentle breeze.

After a leisurely lunch we wandered over to the dock, listened to a bagpiper, checked out the original oil paintings that were for sale, and watched the magicians doing their thing; the band played, we boarded, and were off to the Western Caribbean.

The nights were balmy, the days warm and sunny, and we had a great time. One of the ports of call was Georgetown, Grand Cayman Islands. The ship was too large to pull up to the pier so we tendered in. Tendering is the fine art of coming down about thirty steps on a stairway on the outside of the ship to a little floating dock that does a certain amount of bobbing up and down while you are being pulled into the tender's 25-inch doorway. (A tender is a boat that is about 50 feet long and holds some 40 or 50 people.)

In Georgetown we rented a car-type taxi for an hour's sightseeing and a half-hour stop at the Turtle Farm. This is an interesting, wheelchair-accessible attraction where you can observe sea turtles ranging from ten inches to three feet in diameter.

Another port of call was Ocho Rios, Jamaica, an easy-off, easy-on stop because the ship pulled right up to the pier. We managed to get rained on while shopping. Ocho Rios is not an easy place for a wheelchair: during our visit the streets were being repaired, and there were curbs 10 to 15 inches high as well as steep driveways to negotiate.

The general schedule of cruising is to sail all night and arrive in a port about 8am, leaving again around 5pm. We arrived in Cozumel, Mexico, at 8am and the passengers who were going to the Chichén Itzá ruins disembarked first to take a van-type taxi to the airport. There they boarded an old airplane right out of an Indiana Jones movie, for the 30-minute flight over the rainforests, followed by another taxi to the ruins. The grounds around the ruins are hard-packed, grassy, and bumpy, and the ruins are not wheelchair-accessible, with steps everywhere, inside and out. So we gave that one a miss, and explored Cozumel, which is a bustling place, with a large open plaza surrounded by stores with good sidewalks, although most of the stores and restaurants had a step at least six inches high at the entrance.

The shore stops presented some problems with access, but nothing that spoiled our vacation, and I cannot say enough to praise the overall accessibility of the ship and the attitude of the crew. The ship has several elevators, the smallest being large enough for at least one wheelchair, and there are at least two ramped exits to each deck. The crew was always most courteous and helpful. Will I go on another cruise? Yes indeed.

And the Sun was Shining!

Betty Airlie's husband John has had two major heart operations and has arthritis in his spine. This means using a wheelchair whenever they leave home. In spring 1989 they joined a mini-cruise to Bergen from Newcastle.

Although I had never been to Norway, John had been there on a climbing trip in his youth. Inspired by the stories of his visit, we studied the *Norway Line* (now *Colour Line*) brochure. The mini-cruise sounded ideal: four days afloat, accommodation in a two-berth cabin with its own shower and toilet, and—most important—the ship had a passenger elevator between decks. All we had to do now was call *Norway Line* and ensure that the wheelchair was acceptable.

As it is difficult to handle a wheelchair and suitcases, we tend to travel light, and because this was to be such a short vacation it was easy to select just a few casual clothes; these and our toiletries fitted into a large valise. A travel bag held tickets, binoculars, camera, and medications. We also carried bottles of mineral water for use in the cabin. All these bits and pieces rested on John's knees, leaving my hands free to push the wheelchair.

As with many disabled people, our car is our main means of transport. At Newcastle a local garage owner arranges, for a fee, to collect your car at the terminal and park it securely while you are on your cruise; he then has it restored to the terminal for your return. We found this a very happy arrangement, with no worries about the car while we were away. Details of the service are included in the *Colour Line* brochure.

Car disposed of, we were ready to start our vacation in earnest. The terminal is spacious, with adequate toilet facilities for the disabled. My dear husband suggested that I had earned a gin and tonic, so off I headed for the cafeteria. Sad to say, it did not serve alcohol, but we did have coffee, John's fortified with brandy from his hip flask.

"Meals were a delightful experience, and we took full advantage"

It is quite a distance to travel by foot from the Newcastle terminal to the ship, but there is a courtesy wheelchair available for anyone with walking difficulties. A wheelchair is carried on board and could be used in Bergen. We had our own wheelchair, and I left John in the hands of two strong crewmen, who intended lifting him, in his wheelchair, up the gangway. Now John is quite a big man, and this feat proved too much for the two men. Instead, they pushed John, a very uncomfortable journey for him on account of the struts across the gangway (which are necessary for the safety of foot passengers). He was glad to be aboard at last.

Soon after we arrived on board, we were quickly taken in the passenger elevator to our comfortable cabin, which was to be home for four days. Throughout that time, we were very well looked after by our charming, attentive Portuguese cabin attendant who kept the cabin spotlessly clean and supplied extra pillows for John without any fuss. We sailed on *MS Jupiter*, but from 1991 *MS Venus* will be making the Newcastle–Bergen run; *MS Venus* has two cabins specially reserved for disabled passengers.

The passenger elevator was easy to operate, and large enough to take the wheelchair without removing the footrests, but it was out of order twice during the cruise. On both occasions, crew members quickly and willingly

came to our assistance, apologizing for the breakdown, and taking us to the desired deck by the service elevator.

Meals were a delightful experience, and we took full advantage of the wide choice and high quality of foods. Evening meals were buffet-style—smorgasbord—and beautifully presented. I took John around the food table on our introduction to the dining room, so that he had an idea of all the goodies he could choose—hot and cold dishes of meats, fish, and vegetables, tempting salads and gorgeous desserts. Choice was always difficult, but as we could return to the table as often as we wished we decided to opt for small and many courses. We never left the dining room hungry! We were given a table where John could use his wheelchair yet not be in the way of other diners. Apart from the dining room, there was a well-supplied cafeteria, and coffee, tea, and alcoholic drinks were always available in the two lounges.

There was plenty to keep us entertained while at sea. We usually used the larger lounge, where there was dancing in the evening, ample seating and tables, and rest rooms nearby. A talented group of musicians played plenty of dance music, and even though not dancing we enjoyed the lively atmosphere; it was good to chat, over drinks and coffee, to our fellow vacationers. During the day this lounge, with its many windows, was an ideal place for John to watch the spectacular Norwegian coastline when we came in sight of land. For those with more mobility, the outside decks were the places to take in the scenery.

The sea was dotted with islands and the coastline pitted with inlets and small jetties. Our first port of call was Stavanger, where we stopped for thirty minutes on both outward and homeward journeys. The harbor is very close to the town, so we were able to admire the picturesque wooden houses from the ship. It looked very quaint, but I suspect too hilly for a wheelchair.

We found Bergen an interesting but expensive city. There was an early-morning bus tour laid on, but we opted to have a leisurely breakfast, then later, with the much-appreciated help of two fellow passengers, we ambled around at our own pace. John seldom lacked someone to talk to when I occasionally dashed off to scan the surrounding territory and find out where it was possible to take the wheelchair. As the ship was berthed very near the center of Bergen, it was a pleasant stroll into town. The tall, ancient buildings of Bryggen—wooden, with very pointed gables—form the heart of the old town. We spent some time at the flower and fish markets on the docks; we were given generous samples of the most delicious smoked salmon and we could not resist bringing a sealed pack home.

"Although we still love to travel, every vacation has to be carefully planned"

Although Bergen is set between seven hills, it is an easy place to wander around as the city center is reasonably flat and there is a pleasant park nearby. There is a funicular up Mount Fløyen which takes you to 1000 feet above sea level; the view of the city is reported to be magnificent. We didn't attempt it with the wheelchair, as a fine view could be gotten, both by day and by night, from the deck of our ship. We were especially fascinated with the harbor area—so many different boats to see. And, to cap it all, instead of the customary persistent rain—for which

Bergen is renowned, even in summer—the sun was shining. Indeed, we were fortunate that the weather was good and the sea calm throughout the cruise.

We were disappointed not to have time to visit some of the grand fiords. Many operators offer boat trips in the fiords in late spring and summer, and we look forward to taking a few of these on a longer cruise, when there is more time for excursions in port. Apart from this minor disappointment, the main problem we had on this cruise was using the gangway to get on and off the ship, especially if there were no crew members around to help. After our visit to Bergen we asked to be permitted to board via the car deck, which is reached by a ramp. Although the gangway in Bergen is on one level and covered (an improvement on Newcastle), it still has struts for passenger safety. Anyone with a wheelchair should arrange access by the car deck when booking their cruise. It means a longer walk but is definitely the easier and more comfortable way.

When our children left home, and we were both fit and healthy, John and I traveled to many countries in Europe. Now, although we still love to travel, every vacation has to be carefully planned: not only do I want John, who has to use a wheelchair most of the time, to enjoy it, but also I hope to make it a holiday for myself as well. Any break should be a holiday for both of us. The mini-cruise fulfilled all requirements, and we'd love to repeat this very pleasant and inexpensive break.

Working

Memories and Magic

Frankie Armstrong sings and runs voice workshops around the world, and occasionally tours with a theater company. Her sight has been very gradually dwindling since 1957; at the time of writing she has little residual vision and uses a long cane to get about on her own. Frankie's work gives her great joy and satisfaction, so that her travels seem like one long, working vacation.

My traveling days began in 1973; before this I had vacationed with friends in Europe, but never traveled abroad on my own. It was not until my sight had reached the point that I needed help to cross busy streets, or to find my way around the subway or train stations, that I realized it no longer mattered whether the traffic came from right or left, whether it was New York, San Francisco, London, or Paris—it was no more or less difficult to get myself around.

I was invited to sing at the Philadelphia Folk Festival, one of the largest in North America, and I was lucky enough to be awarded a Ford Foundation grant to visit drug agencies around the United States: at the time I was the Coordinator of a day center for drug addicts in south London, and there was great mutual interest in the different approaches to addiction and rehabilitation in the two countries. I arranged for several months' leave from the center, and began the now-routine process of learning what can be packed in one rucksack to meet most, if not all, contingencies of weather and occasion.

Early one evening, in August 1973, I sat in the departure lounge at Heathrow, waiting for my plane for New York. Now I come to recall this event, I am amazed that eighteen years later I still entrust myself to airlines. I had been sat down in the lounge by a staff member but when, as far as I could make out, I was the only person left and take-off was less than five minutes away, my anxiety led me to find someone from the airline. She gave a little shriek of horror and immediately phoned through to the plane, which had closed its doors and, to my chagrin, obviously not missed me. This was my first valuable lesson: when in doubt, double check.

So I made my first solo flight with minutes to spare; I had to be put up in a hotel in Madrid overnight because of mechanical difficulties during the flight; I arrived in New York to find no one there to meet me and to witness a stand-up fight at the taxi rank at Kennedy airport. I've never had such a string of bad luck since, so I'm grateful I weathered the worst on my first trip and, while traveling has been far from trouble free, at least I am now better prepared.

In the end I spent nearly four months in the States on that visit. I crossed the country twice from coast to coast, and I did things that, looking back on them, seem courageous or crazy. I remember arriving in downtown Los Angeles at midnight off a *Greyhound* bus: I didn't know a soul; I asked the friendly bus driver to take me to a taxi; I asked the friendly cab driver to take me to a not-too-expensive hotel, and by 12:30am I was happily ensconced in the Mexican quarter in a hotel that I stayed in for a week, loving every minute of it.

"The sight of five colorfully dressed 'cripples' caused amazement and curiosity"

I realize that something about my style of traveling has changed. I can recall talking to every person who sat next to me: on planes I met returned Vietnam vets, businessmen and women, children of five or six traveling on their own from coast to coast from parent to parent; on *Greyhound* buses there were lost young souls hoping to find themselves in a new life on the West Coast. I talked to strangers in cafés and absorbed at least some of the contradictions that make up America.

Now when I travel I look upon time in trains and planes as retreat time—no phones, no doorbell—and if I need to I can get down to some concentrated work or reading (using library cassette tapes). This is partly a function of age and the amount of time I spend traveling. But I'm also aware of another factor: in any public space, alone with a white cane, one is very public. In some ways I'm grateful for this; I was brought up in the country, and I'm sure I'd have found London quite impossible had it not been for needing contact and help from people as I get around. However, as anyone with a visible handicap knows, it also means that you are "public property" and can be invaded by well-meaning (and sometimes not so well-meaning) strangers. I now feel the need to be more in control of these public encounters. I have learned the art of assertively, not aggressively, presenting a "do not disturb" message to traveling companions when I want to create my own space.

During that first trip to the States I made friends with some wonderful people, including Ethel Raim who was to be the inspiration for beginning my own voice workshops. Initially, I ran workshops for friends and friends of friends, simply for the enjoyment and the fascination of experimenting with my own and others' voices. Soon I received invitations from Sweden, Denmark, Germany, and Belgium, to run workshops for theater companies, community arts festivals, folk song societies, and schools.

I must admit to feeling less comfortable traveling on my own on trains in countries where my knowledge of the language extends to little more than asking for a cup of coffee or the way to the rest room.. Train travel, even in the UK, is often more anxiety provoking than air travel. After all, in a plane you cannot step out of the door on the wrong side, or pass your station because the guard failed to announce your destination. These are real fears, and when in addition I was not able to speak the language or see whether my eloquent sign language had borne fruit, I was always highly relieved to find myself at my destination, met by the organizer of the concert or workshop.

One of my most extraordinary trips was a tour of India with the *Graeae Theater Company* in 1983. *Graeae* was set up as a professional company for actors with disabilities. I was asked to join a group of five actors to work with a very talented young theater director to devise and perform a play around the issue of disability and societal attitudes toward disability, suited to an Indian audience. Nigel, the director, had spent many months traveling and studying in India, so with his help we improvised, wrote, and rehearsed a piece which called on our personal experiences and which used song, movement, and magic as well as some more realistic scenes.

Two of the actors were completely wheelchair-bound; one was very small but only needed to use a wheelchair for long journeys; Jag (Indian by birth), who has CP, used crutches to walk; I made up the fifth member of the group. On the streets of Calcutta, Bombay, and Delhi we created a greater theatrical impact than we ever could on stage. Most disabled people in India are either hidden away in institutions or are very visible—begging on the streets, where the aim is to make the disability as debilitating and pathos-creating as possible. The sight of five colorfully dressed "cripples" caused amazement and curiosity. We attracted crowds of Indians who had no sense of embarrassment about touching and staring at us at very close quarters. In a way it was wonderfully refreshing to experience this overt curiosity, rather than the pretence at politeness which may cover pity or even hostility in the West.

In addition to the performances in major theaters in the three cities we visited, we did a number of excerpts, workshops, and mini-concerts in schools, day centers, and employment centers for disabled people. Some of these I found quite distressing as they seemed antediluvian and even exploitative of the disabled, but I'm aware that as an outsider I may have formed the wrong impression. What I am sure about is the quality of some of the schools we visited, especially those run by the *Indian Spastics Society*. I have never before or since experienced such unsentimental love and creativity, or been filled with such hope and joy in an educational institute. The children had little in the way of materials or technological equipment, but the inventiveness with which they used simple wooden sledges and scooters, and the physical freedom and energy with which they moved themselves around was both inspiring and moving.

"Through my cataract fog I could see the crimson sunset reflecting off the plain"

Nigel, Jag, Nabs, and Jim all did conjuring tricks, often involving the children. Their delight and laughter is something I'll never forget. The children's energy of involvement in the little theatrical sketches which they had prepared for us leaves many a Broadway cast looking unexciting and unimaginative. They sang us songs, and I taught them all a Malvina Reynolds song (with actions), entitled "I've got a song." I have taught this song hundreds of times, but I doubt it will ever capture the warmth and vitality of those three or four occasions.

When I started my voice workshops I little imagined that one day I would receive a phone call from Australia, inviting me to run workshops there for several months. I must confess that I held a not altogether undeserved prejudice against Australian men; all those whom I had encountered in Europe seemed loud, crude, male chauvinist, and generally fulfilled my stereotype of macho man. All the more ironic that I finished up marrying an Australian!

Since that first invitation I have become a regular visitor, and with resident status feel it to be my second home. I have enjoyed all the work I have done there but one of my most cherished memories is of a few days' real vacation spent in and around Kakadu, an area in the Northern Territory with many ancient Aboriginal sites. In the wet season, much of Kakadu lies under water, providing a glorious habitat for water birds and crocodiles. An Australian friend, Linsey, and I visited in October, before the build-up of the wet season was fully under way. Even then it was incredibly hot and humid; it reached over a hundred degrees by mid-morning, and I experienced prickly heat for the first and only time.

We left Darwin before sunrise and drove south through bush, eucalyptus, and palm trees, stopping off at Jabaru, a uranium-mining town, for a cooling swim. The water was already the temperature of a warm bath, so, refreshing as it was, it was hardly cooling. We drove on, into the National Park, and found a perfect spot near the flood plains to set up camp and have a picnic. The flood plains make up the area where the water has not totally receded, despite five months of drought.

The sounds were extraordinary: sea eagles and ibis were apparently among the throng, along with many that Linsey couldn't identify immediately; I heard the gentle whir of pelican wings as a flock flew overhead, the chattering of parrots, kingfishers squawking, and the evocative call of literally thousands of water birds, shimmering white in the sunlight so that even I could catch a glimmer of the sun glinting on their outstretched wings.

After lunch we went to one of the bizarre rock formations that are ancient sacred sites for the Aborigines. Happily, there are some signs that the criminal attitudes which have dominated white Australia's treatment of the original black inhabitants are

changing; in Kakadu the Aboriginal elders decide which of their sites can be visited.

It's an awesome feeling, standing in the caves in front of rock paintings that reach back thousands of years, many thousands more than most European cultural sites. These paintings and carvings may go back 40,000 years, and until the invaders settled 200 years ago the Aboriginal cultures had flourished uninterrupted. Out there, hundreds of miles from any sizable town, it was salutory to recall our alienation from our connection and interdependence with Nature. Here was a stillness, a sense of honoring what was and still is truly important for our physical and spiritual survival.

We saw hardly another soul all day and at dusk we were back at our campground. Through my cataract fog I could see the crimson sunset reflecting off the plain. The bird sounds became more vociferous and insistent, as they do everywhere at dusk. Our fire lit up the pendulous peeling bark of the paper bark trees and, as darkness fell, with our meal completed and the fire dying down, there was a near-full moon glowing overhead. I am often asked how far I can see: "Over four hundred and eighty thousand miles, on a clear night lit by a full moon, but while looking at the moon I can easily walk into someone or something a foot in front of me."

That night was one of the most magical I have ever spent. We slept under a mosquito net, tents being unnecessary in the balmy temperatures. We could hear the snuffling of a wild buffalo from across the waters and, nearer at hand, smaller creatures, maybe wallabies. The moon danced through the trees, and I can recall falling asleep with a sense of gratitude. I hope this feeling, along with all the memories I've stored, will never desert me.

The Last Word

Welcome to Where?

In 1988 Dena Taylor was involved in a car accident which resulted in a closed head injury. During her recovery she encountered many survivors of brain injury in need of support, information, and direction; she found communications breakdowns between survivors and their families, professionals in the many interdisciplinary fields related to brain injury, and the community at large. In an attempt to rectify this situation Dena founded The Perspectives Network (see Travel Notes) in August 1990. Here she describes the effect of her injury on her travel experiences.

After my accident it took me roughly a year to reach the point physically where I had all the technical aspects of speech and gaiting down pat. I still had to be careful and take my time but I could finally manage to get down a hall without falling over and knocking a lump on my head, and I could get a sentence out in one breath and with few stutters. Unfortunately, what I said didn't necessarily make sense and the value of having feet that knew how to walk was greatly reduced by a brain that didn't know where it was going.

I certainly didn't like leaving my house so the thought of ever traveling again was yet another reason for me to sink deeper into the pit. A trip to the local shopping center was an exercise in frustration for my husband and me. The fear of running into old acquain-

tances and seeing the look in their eyes when they met the "new" Dena was bad enough, but trying to filter out all the sounds and movement, remembering how to keep my balance and my feet going in the same direction, and attempting not to fall apart emotionally when my brain simply shut down after becoming overloaded on all the stimulation was too much. It overwhelmed me and more doors closed.

Roughly one year after my injury I decided it was time to try a little "sink or swim" therapy. Managing to convince my husband that I could travel without problems, I set off to visit friends in New York. What was supposed to be a nonstop flight turned out to involve a plane change at O'Hare Airport. My nervousness grew to fear when my requests for assistance were dismissed by the flight crew with a quick "Really, anyone can handle a plane change—it's so simple."

My cognitive disabilities and I walked off the plane into a state of total confusion. As I became more stressed, the cognitive problems increased; as they increased, my brain's ability to keep the physical impairments in check decreased. What is so easily performed by the person without cognitive disabilities was impossible for me. My disorientation kept me from knowing where I was. I knew I was in an airport but what airport was anyone's guess. My aphasia kept me from being able to go to the display screens and read where I was supposed to be, where I was supposed to go. My impaired problem-solving abilities kept me from thinking through the problem logically and moving step by step to a solution. I'm sure I made a pretty picture—a grown woman standing in the corner crying because she didn't know where she was, where she was going, or how she was going to get there.

"It took me two years to gather up the courage to make another attempt"

With the help of passers-by, I finally got on the correct plane but I certainly didn't want to face the trip home. It somehow seemed very appropriate that I returned home in the middle of a hurricane. In the past I had been an avid traveler, exploring much of the US and Europe on vacation and even living and working abroad, and I desperately missed the possibilities that travel opened to me—new faces, new cultures, new sights, new adventures—but it wasn't enough to lure me back onto a plane. I sat mired in a world both isolated and lonely.

It took me two years to gather up the courage to make another attempt. In those two years I learned a lot about my brain injury and about my new needs. The injury itself did not change or evolve, but I knew better how to live

with it. When an opportunity arose to step out of my world and into someone else's I said yes without thinking—before I could change my mind. As soon as the excitement of heading off to adventure wore off, the doubts came back, all the "what-if"s imaginable. I forgot all my coping strategies, my tools for living out in the world; I forgot everything except my fear. But I did remember the fun and excitement of seeing things I'd never seen before and meeting new people.

I contacted the airlines and explained it all to them—my brain injury, my disabilities, *and* my abilities. I wanted them to know what my needs were and how they could help me meet them. I didn't need to be cared for, I needed to be worked with. And we planned my flights accordingly. No plane changes; flight crews who knew that I might become disorientated in flight, and knew how to help me get things straightened out; someone to meet me when we landed and walk me through the unfamiliar until I connected with the people waiting for me; someone to count on if there were any unplanned events such as delays.

Before I knew it, I was in Calgary, Alberta, being hugged and greeted. For the first time in years, I drew the breath of an adventurer. I survived not just the travel to Calgary, but checking into a hotel on my own, and waking up that first night confused and scared. And I felt my independence begin to return when I looked at the note I had written to myself before going to bed that night: "Hello Dena, you're at the Westgate Hotel in Calgary, Alberta, and you're going to do just fine. If you need to, call Audrey, but it better be before 11pm or else *really important!*"

I have refined my traveling techniques since that trip in 1991. I know what I can expect from myself and I know that I can count on the unexpected. I just returned from another trip to Canada, this time to Winnipeg, for a brain injury conference. I faced a new challenge on this trip—a scheduled plane change, not an earth-shaking event, but full of unpleasant possibilities. While I'm somewhat improved in handling my cognitive impairments, they are still there and fully capable of tripping me up. So I created a new aid, a traveling letter. It introduces me, gives a very brief rundown on my brain injury, and then gives some specific examples of the problems I might face. I also explain how I can be assisted should those problems occur, and stapled to the letter is my itinerary.

"A new door which had been tentatively cracked by an earlier trip was now thrown wide open"

I expected the traveling letter to work by giving it to the ground crew who would preboard me and pass the letter on to the flight crew who would—well, you get the picture. I didn't count on the fact that everyone found the letter so interesting that they kept it! Fortunately, I made extra copies. And, with few exceptions, the trip went off without a hitch. There were all sorts of new challenges to face at the conference and, of course, I didn't rest like I should have, didn't eat like I should have, didn't do a number of things like I should have. But I did learn, and, more importantly, a new door which had been tentatively pushed ajar by an earlier trip was now thrown wide open.

I'd like to say that the challenges presented by brain injury occur only during travel, but they don't. The cognitive aspects of brain injury can include problems with memory, ability to express yourself, ability to understand what's being said to you, and ability to reason things out. I must deal with these when I'm home and must take them with me when I travel. Conferences only take up so many hours in the day, and I must choose to leave my hotel room during my free

time and venture out into the surrounding city, so I try to take out much of the uncertainty by contacting tourist boards (even when I'm traveling in America) and getting hold of city maps and transportation schedules. I even try to find travel guides that include detailed information about the city and its sights. I try to do this far enough in advance so that I can lay out a general plan. There are always surprises and I cannot say I handle them with grace and ease, but I do handle them, and ask for help when I need it. I never leave my hotel without writing down its name and location. If I'm going to a meeting, I write all the pertinent information down as well. Then, if I get into a situation that I cannot handle, I simply hand over my survivor idenfication card and ask for assistance; that works for taxicabs, city buses, even when I'm walking—I just need someone to point me in the right direction.

"With the right planning, and the right support systems in place, I can travel anywhere"

I'm sure the hotel maids don't understand the note written to myself giving me all the orienting information I might need. They cannot know how valuable that information is when I become disoriented. They probably don't understand why I bring a night-light with me. It can make all the difference when I wake up in the middle of the night physically incapable of moving until I have familiarized myself with the room. All my aids, while appearing trivial to some, do work for me. I not only survived my latest trip to Canada, I enjoyed it. If I had had more free time I would have taken on more than the underground shopping center that I wandered into by accident. I have every intention of returning some day and seeing all the sights of Winnipeg.

With the right planning, and the right support systems in place, I can travel anywhere. I have come to realize that my traveling had always been based less on abilities than on attitudes, and that the doors had closed to me because I lost the most important piece of baggage a traveler can carry—an attitude of mind which says "plan as well as you can and then enjoy the surprises." It hasn't been easy to regain that, and there remain many barriers to traveling with disabilities, but the barriers will not come down without our help. If we keep to our rooms it will be assumed it's because we *can't* do it rather than because we don't *wish* to do it. If we don't tell them what we need to be independent, they will continue our dependency by assuming we are unable to cope on our own. There's an international conference on the brain in London next year—a trip overseas, think of the hazards, and the possibilities—and I've already started work on the trickiest part—the funding.

Free from the Ordinary

As co-founder and director of Mobility International USA, Susan Sygall has spent the last ten years arranging educational programs that enable disabled persons from around the world to live with families in foreign countries, share friendship, and learn about disability rights. Here she describes a few of her own travel experiences—in Central America, New Zealand, Australia, and Europe, ending with an account of her most recent trip, to Bulgaria.

Some people dread airports, I feel at home in them. The excitement, the constant movement, the many faces of the people passing through them—crying as they leave loved ones, or bursting with joy when they see the ones they have waited to see for months, maybe years. That intensity of emotions experienced through travel, and, yes, even the risks involved in travel, make me feel vulnerable but at the same time remind me that life is to be lived today for we know not what tomorrow brings.

Perhaps I was born with my love for travel—my father sailed the seas for fifteen years and speaks eight languages—but when at the age of eighteen I was in a car accident that left me a paraplegic and in a wheelchair, I thought my travels were over. Later, I decided that I was going to try anyway, and I was determined to do it in the manner I had dreamed I'd do it—with a backpack, looking for adventure.

My first trip was to Mexico for four weeks with backpack on my wheelchair and with a fellow paraplegic who was also exploring this new mode of travel. I learned to jump curbs in my wheelchair, and climb onto inaccessible buses on my butt. We traveled on local buses to Guatemala where our wheelchairs rode on top with live chickens and crates of bananas. We learned survival tactics like boarding buses where they originate since an overcrowded bus in Latin America is difficult to board under any circumstances.

With backpacks on our chairs we later spent four months in Europe visiting sports and recreation programs for disabled persons. We learned that having a disability can mean having an extended family of disabled people around the world, and we stayed in the homes of many disabled friends we made on the way.

We also learned not to believe the advice of others when in your heart you know what you are capable of. We climbed to the top of Masada in Israel and the Acropolis in Greece with the help of Canadian friends met on our journey. Everyone said it was impossible. We sledded down a six-mile hill in Switzerland, leaving our wheelchairs behind. Everyone said it was impossible. And we argued with the management of the National Theater in London when they said that two "unchaperoned" persons in wheelchairs constituted a fire hazard.

"I thought this incident was about climbing Ayers Rock, but years later I realized it was about life"

Later we traveled to Australia and New Zealand. My friend Rod and I hitch-hiked throughout New Zealand for six weeks—yes, with two wheelchairs. At first, people didn't realize we were hitch-hiking—perhaps it seemed too absurd—so we separated, and once I got a ride I told them about my friend who was around the corner and was also in a wheelchair; by then the drivers were laughing, and so surprised that they said "oh why not?," and off we went. We were invited to people's homes and stayed in youth hostels only two nights during our entire six-week trip. As I write this almost fifteen years later I am still receiving letters from many of the families I met on that trip.

Women in general are not usually thought of as independent world travelers; though this is rapidly changing, the thought of a woman in a wheelchair traveling on her own is still often met with surprise and shock. To me there is nothing so liberating as setting off on a trip in my wheelchair with a small bag under my chair and my backpack hanging off the back. I have learned to travel light, and the freedom of traveling alone can be both hard and exhilarating.

While I was in Australia, I joined a month-long camping trip with about twenty Australians. After traveling for almost three days to reach the great Ayers Rock, I was told by the bus driver (who wasn't thrilled that someone in a wheelchair was on his trip) that I shouldn't bother leaving the bus as I couldn't climb the Rock. To hell with him, I thought, he really doesn't expect me to just sit here, does he. I returned the dirty look he gave me and proceeded to climb Ayers Rock on my bum, using my arms to inch me up. After almost an hour I was half-way up the rock, with an incredible view of the desert. The bus below me looked like an inch-long car, and people looked like ants crawling around. I didn't make it to the top but I didn't need to. I felt great. I had decided for myself what is possible and what goals I wanted to achieve. At the time I thought this incident was about climbing Ayers Rock, but years later I realized it was about life.

After Australia, I traveled with another woman by local bus through Thailand, Malaysia, and Indonesia. I learned to deal with inaccessible bathrooms, and not to be afraid to pee anywhere—by the Eiffel tower, on a glacier, in a park if that's what I needed to do. And I learned always to carry an extra pair of pants with me because some people with spinal cord injuries have weak bladders, and losing control shouldn't be allowed to ruin a once-in-a-lifetime experience.

"I was happy, I was lonely, I was stared at, I was marveled at"

I traveled through Spain and France for four weeks with a Eurail pass and almost no plans, taking spur-of-the-moment decisions to hop (so to speak) onto any train to any destination—every day was an unplanned adventure. I was happy, I was lonely, I was stared at, I was marveled at. Most important, I was having my dreams come true. As I watched the scenery pass by from the train, it was like watching a movie of castles and green meadows, of flowing rivers and foreign lands, but it wasn't someone else's movie, it was mine.

I write this article very close to the anniversary of the date that my car accident took place in 1971. Whenever I try to think about that day I find it hard to feel sad or resentful. Instead I think of all the places I've traveled to: bicycling through little villages in China (well, my friend had the bike and I hung on in my wheelchair to the back of her bike rack); marching at a peace rally with 2000 women in Gorky Park in Moscow; meeting with a group of disabled people in Bulgaria.

"When he heard where we were attempting to go he laughed"

My experiences in Bulgaria were about broken dreams and open hearts. As my plane slowly descended over Sofia I was reminded how little I knew of this country. I asked the young Bulgarian woman next to me to share some insights with me, and we began to talk. By the time the plane landed, she had invited me to visit her family in Plovdif, and I had agreed to help her when she comes to New York on a scholarship program.

At the airport I was met by Daniella, of the *Union of Disabled Persons of Bulgaria*. My visit was to learn about this organization and to plan their educational exchange organized by *MIUSA*. Daniella greeted me and we set off with their official driver to my hotel. Sofia seemed dreary and bleak to me, although there are some parks where people seem to go for green trees and relaxation. The hotels reminded me of the massive, dark structures found in the former Soviet Union. There were no colors, and the faces of passers-by seemed blank and unhappy.

I took the local bus to Plovdif, which is about one and a half hours from Sofia. I was glad to leave the city, the noise and pollution, and in some ways the sad and sullen atmosphere. I boarded the bus and the driver put my wheelchair in the luggage compartment without any fuss. The other passengers were serious, and only the student from India and I were talking. As we left the city the beautiful countryside surrounded us, the occasional sheep herder with his staff coming as a surprise after the sprawling Soviet-style housing complexes.

My new-found friend was waiting at the bus stop. I felt like I was meeting an old lost friend. It's an intensity I love and I think we both felt it, knowing our time was so short together, as we grabbed a cab in pouring rain and went to her home. Albena lives with her family in a small upstairs apartment and I was soon struggling with three flights of stairs on my canes; her mom helped drag up my wheelchair. I was their first guest from the USA and we had lots to talk about.

Later we walked to the city which has many trees, a river, and large pedestrian walkways. It has a more European flavor than Sofia, with sidewalk cafés and numerous small kiosks selling items such as cigarettes, liquor, clothes, detergents, and bananas, which are all new for Bulgaria as they begin to experience capitalism. The atmosphere is lighter here, with more people laughing and relaxed—the sign of a smaller, more rural city.

Albena wanted to show me the Roman ruins high up on a hill. She paused to think of the easiest path for my wheelchair but there isn't one. We went up and down some steps and then faced a huge cobblestone hill. After we had struggled for a while I finally asked a young man to assist us. When he heard where we were attempting to go he laughed and said, "Only someone born in a free country could have the determination to do this." I think he was referring to the fact that there were so few disabled people on the streets, and I contemplated the notion of being orn "free" as we all broke into sweat climbing the hill.

It was worth it. The amphitheater nd Roman ruins are spectacular against the background of a modern highway, and the air was cool and crisp. We celebrated in a quaint café which my companions would usually never enter because of the expense. We talked about the changes in Bulgaria; it seems that's what people are always discussing, with growing sadness and disillusionment.

"Many disabled persons are still in institutions that are said to be terrible"

Back in Sofia, at a friend's house, I met a film director who has made an award-winning film on the deteriorating environment of Bulgaria and the rest of the world. I discover that most of the Black Sea is too polluted to swim in, and that the people of Bulgaria did not learn about Chernobyl until two years after it had happened. The only exceptions were the high-ranking officials who warned their children not to play in the contaminated sand or drink milk immediately following the incident, but did not share this warning with the rest of the population. The film-maker talked about himself as part of the lost generation; he is in his late 40s and has lived under communism his whole life. Now the situation is worse, and he believes it will take another ten years for the country to gain the benefits of a democracy. For him it will be too late; for his seven-year-old daughter there will be a future. "There had to be a sacrificial generation and I am it," he explained philosophically.

I met many different types of people. A sculptor immersed in his art said little about the change of government. His wife, a communist, had a good life under communism; now she says they have barely enough to live on—there is unemployment, prostitution, pornography. "It was better before," she

asserted. She thinks that Gorbachev is to blame and thinks he might have been working for the US. Her daughter was a radical protesting student, fighting for the "change" and is happy to see it, but the hard times it has brought have made people confused and disillusioned: "We thought it would be a better life. So far, it is only worse. People are greedy and trying to get money fast. There are no values."

The transition government, both democratic and authoritarian, is faced with a severe economic crisis, and there are unemployment problems for everyone. When broaching the subject of employment for disabled persons, I encountered little interest and some fear that if they complain too much they may lose the small pension that they receive. The new president of the *Union of Disabled Persons* is disabled himself and understands the complex issue of disability from the sociological, economic, political, and psychological viewpoints. Politically, he agrees that disabled people need to develop a cross-disability power base. National legislation on access and other issues needs to be declared and enforced. He also spoke of the need to encourage programs that embrace self-help— disabled people have been looked after in a paternalistic manner by the government and need to redefine themselves and take responsibility for their lives.

This mentality of being cared for, which makes people apathetic, is something that is mentioned not only in terms of disability but also in relation to the entire population. "It is a mentality that was drilled into us for many years—you need to understand that it was part of the system—you can't blame the people." Many disabled persons are still in institutions that are said to be terrible, causing psychological problems in addition to physical disabilities.

In the former Soviet Union, groups of persons who are blind and deaf were allowed to organize before persons with mobility-related disabilities. The *Union of Physically Disabled Persons* was illegal and there was no mention of any person with physical disabilities for many years. It was only after the physically disabled organization in the USSR became legal that Bulgaria was given permission to have a similar organization which was formed around 1989. The *Union of Disabled Persons* is now supported by the government but would like to be more independent financially.

"I can't wait twenty years for change. I can't wait ten"

Up about ten steps and in a small, dark elevator, I am on my way to visit the local group for disabled persons in Sofia. Marina, who uses a wheelchair, is head of this group which consists of over 100 members. She has invited some of them to her apartment where she lives with her mother, so I can hear what life is really like for disabled people. Marina feels strongly that disabled people must take action themselves, but she is so overwhelmed by the problems she does not know where to begin.

"I tried to talk to politicians, but disabled persons aren't even allowed in the national assembly where their offices are. Politicians in the past who have promised to work with us have just forgotten all these promises once they are elected. No one will give us jobs—no matter what your disability is. Our pensions are not enough to live on. I am supported by my mother and if something happens to her, what will happen to me? The institutions are inhumane and once you go there you are psychologically damaged for life. Everything is so inaccessible it is hard to move around at all. If I want to go out, I have to wait for a neighbor who is home to help me down the stairs—sometimes this can mean waiting for two or three hours. I tried to put a ramp just on the last step to make it easier, but my neighbor complained she didn't like it."

"Why did you listen to her?" I ask.

"Because I depend on her to help me when my mother isn't around and I can't have her angry with me."

Marina has ideas of encouraging disabled persons to run their own businesses, but there is no money to start these projects. "How do you do it in the States? Tell me where to begin." I search for an easy answer but there is none. I tell her about the disability movement in the US, but to have a movement we also have resources to lean on.

"If the government is angry at us they could take away our small pension—they could send us to an institution," Marina replies. I know that Bulgarians cannot use the strategy of another country with a different system and culture—they need to decide what to do in Bulgaria. The US disability movement took more than twenty years.

Marina has tears in her eyes. "I can't wait twenty years for change. I can't wait ten. People say wait until tomorrow, things will take time, but I'm young—I want to start living today. I have not had any opportunity my whole life. Now there are supposed to be big changes here. Why are they importing all these Western ideas on capitalism? Will they also be importing ideas on disability rights and accessibility?"

"Their greatest gift was to teach me the meaning of hospitality"

I begin to wonder. Will US funds, both public and private, be used to build inaccessible buildings and businesses? Will persons with disabilities be part of the economic growth or will they be left with new programs and buildings full of steps because government and business people will not be forced to make things accessible? Can we in the US stop this from happening? Will any of the millions in aid go to organizations run by persons with disabilities? We talk about these issues, and many more. I wish I could be more helpful. When we go downstairs we exchange hugs and hopes. It begins raining on us but we don't care.

I am in my own room now, back in Oregon, looking at my pictures. Although during my trip I had wonderful experiences in Luxembourg and Germany, my thoughts always come back to Bulgaria. As I look at the faces of my Bulgarian friends in my photographs, I am again moved by their generosity, their open hearts. I stayed with two different families who treated me to everything they had. They took me to dinner (which cost almost half a month's salary), made special meals for me, drove me to the beautiful mountains outside Sofia, and made me part of the family. They did all this without reservation, yet I knew how difficult financially this was for them. They absolutely refused any financial help, as I was their guest. At the airport, they gave me lovely records and tapes of Bulgarian folk music, but their greatest gift was to teach me the meaning of hospitality. I couldn't help but think that those of us with more resources are usually not nearly as generous. We all have much to learn from each other. As I put my pictures away I know that I will return to Bulgaria despite all the difficulties it poses to a traveler who uses a wheelchair.

My involvement with *Mobility International USA* has brought me many of my travel experiences. As the world grows smaller and disabled persons assert their rights to travel I believe that more and more of us will share these types of life-changing travel experiences. The world must make its hotels, transportations services, and communications systems accessible to persons of all disabilities, not because it's the nice thing to do but because travel is a *right* of every person with a disability throughout the world.

Maybe it's the intensity of travel that I crave—those friendships that are born within a few minutes, the exhausting times, the disappointments, the exhilarations, the feeling I have when I am flying down the road in France in my wheelchair, breeze in my hair, the stares on the street, and the knowledge that no one knows what I can do, nor what I can dream:

So much inside to sing
Caged by limited perceptions,
Free your wings from the ordinary
Soar to the boundaries of your
  dreams.

Sources of Information

American Automobile Association (*AAA*, 1000 AAA Drive, Heathrow, FL 32746-5063; ☎407/444-7000) offers general advice for drivers, plus help with route-planning and obtaining the necessary documents for foreign travel, via its World Wide Travel Agency, which can help with air, land, and sea arrangements. The *AAA* is the official outlet for obtaining an International Driving Permit (IDP), which can be obtained at any *AAA* office by anyone aged 18 or more (two passport-size photos required); the permit costs $10 and is valid for one year. More than 160 countries recognize the IDP as a valid form of identification—your driver's license is translated into eight languages. Some countries, such as Spain and Greece, require all foreign drivers to have IDPs, and others, including Germany and Italy, require a translation of a US driver's license. IDPs eliminate a lot of confusion and frustration and prove helpful to non-English-speaking officials and police officers. The *AAA* maintains reciprocal agreements with automobile clubs in around 20 foreign countries, so that members traveling in these countries can take advantage of any services offered by the foreign association to its own members; a complete country listing is available from any *AAA* office. The British **Automobile Association Travel Services** (Fanum House, Basingstoke, Hants RG21 2EA, UK; ☎0256/492004; plus a nationwide network of *AA* shops) is recommended by David Bonnett for similar facilities in Europe and beyond.

Canadian Automobile Association (1775 Courtwood Crescent, Ottawa, ON K2C 3J2; ☎613/226-7631). Also gives comprehensive route-planning guidance and assistance for international trips, distributes IDPs, and has reciprocal arrangements with foreign automobile associations.

The Perspectives Network. For information contact Dena Taylor at 9919 Orangevale Drive, Spring, TX 77379-5103; ☎713/251-7005, voice or fax. Some of the services the Network offers are: a quarterly magazine written by brain injury survivors and professionals; brain injury identification cards; communication and support networks for survivors, families, and friends; information and educational material.

Mobility International (*MI*), a non-profit, non-governmental youth organization, was set up in London in 1974 to offer travel experiences which promote the integration of disabled and non-disabled people. The emphasis has shifted slightly, to include the "empowerment" of disabled people, with integration optional. *MI* members include umbrella regional or disability-specific organizations in Europe, the USA, the states of the former Soviet Union, Africa, and India, and some of these are useful contacts when planning a trip or when in difficulty abroad; where relevant they are mentioned in the *Travel Notes* of the appropriate country. *MI News* is the quarterly newsletter, and it will keep you up to date with some of the new developments on the travel scene.

Mobility International USA, PO Box 3551, Eugene, OR 97403; ☎503/343-1248, voice or TDD. Set up in 1981 by Susan Sygall and Linda Phelps, the US office of *Mobility International* is a national, not-for-profit organization whose purpose is to promote and facilitate opportunities for people with disabilities to participate in international educational exchange and travel. In addition to coordinating exchange programs, *MIUSA* publishes some valuable resource books (see p.590), produces videos, and a quarterly newsletter, *Over the Rainbow*, helps individuals to apply to international workcamps and exchange programs, and provides a travel information and referral service to members. Individual membership is $20 for a year, and members can use the information and referral services, receive the newsletter, and obtain discounts on publications, videos, and *MIUSA*-sponsored exchange programs.

Tour Operators

The aim of the **Jubilee Sailing Trust** (Test Road, Eastern Docks, Southampton SO1 1GG, UK; ☎0703/631388, reservations 631395) is "for physically handicapped and able-bodied people to share the challenge of crewing a ship at sea." During the *STS Lord Nelson*'s first two seasons she carried 2000 crew members, half

TRAVEL, TOURS, AND CRUISES: TRAVEL NOTES

of whom were disabled people and, of those, 400 wheelchair users; some North Americans have joined voyages in the past. The main season is March to October, and the 1993 program includes cruising off the French coast, along the Irish coast, among the Scottish isles, and two gatherings of tall ships in July and August. For more information, and details of winter seasons in the Canary Islands, write to the Voyage Administrator.

An organization with similar aims in the US is the **National Ocean Access Project** (*NAOP*, PO Box 33141, Farragut Station, Washington DC 20033; ☎301/217-9843), which provides learn-to-sail experiences, training of volunteers and experienced sailors in adaptive teaching methods, and competitions enabling disabled sailors to reach their highest levels of athletic achievement. Aims include the development of new chapters and programs, particularly in areas of the country where organized programs for disabled sailors do not exist. In developing its national and international programs, *NAOP* will work closely with *National Handicapped Sports*, the US representative on the *International Sports Organization for the Disabled*. *NAOP* has been selected to host the 1993 World Championships in Boston; training camps are being planned with the Courageous Sailing Center.

Princess Cruises (10100 Santa Monica Boulevard, Los Angeles, CA 90067; ☎213/553-1770), operates four *Princess* ships with a total of nearly 40 cabins for disabled passengers—*Star*, *Sky*, *Crown*, and *Regal Princess*—offering a range of cruises in the Caribbean and Atlantic Oceans, and the Mediterranean, Baltic, Black, and Red Seas. Contact *P&O Cruises* (77 New Oxford Street, London W1A 1PP, UK; ☎071/831 1234; reservations, ☎071/831 1331) for details of the same company's *P&O Cruises* and *Swan Hellenic* tours and cruises, which sail from Britain. *P&O* appears to have well-established procedures for accommodating disabled passengers, as well as for assisting them on and off the ship; there are some cabins with wide doors (wide enough for standard wheelchairs), low sills, and grab rails around bathtubs, and there are ramps to provide

access to all public rooms and passenger areas on deck.

Holland America Line (300 Elliot Avenue W, Seattle, WA 98119; ☎206/281-3535) cruises the Caribbean, through the Panama Canal, Mexico, the South Pacific, the Mediterranean, and Alaska. Some tours are tricky for wheelchair users, because of the transport used on shore, but otherwise this company seems to have an efficient, no-fuss approach to carrying disabled passengers. The brochure indicates which cabins (there are four on each ship) are wheelchair accessible on the *Westerdam*, *Nieuw Amsterdam*, and *Noordam*; bathroom sills can be ramped in several cabins on the *Rotterdam*; there are around ten accessible cabins on the *Statendam*, which came into service in 1992. Douglass Annand was delighted with his cabin D101 on the *Nieuw Amsterdam*, and with overall levels of accessibility on this ship.

Colour Line (Tyne Commission Quay, North Shields NE29 6EA, UK; ☎091/296 1313) advises that you discuss all your requirements before booking. This is affordable cruising, perhaps something to be built into a vacation in Britain and northern Europe: their mini-cruise, or "4-day breakaway", cost the Airlies around $110 per person (meals extra); departures are in May and June.

In addition to those operators used by our contributors, there are several other cruise companies that are building accessible new ships and even retrofitting accessible features when older vessels are refurbished, although some are more reluctant to do this than others. Two that supplied us with more than usually helpful information are *Cunard* and *Kloster Cruise Limited* (*Royal Viking Line* and *Norwegian Cruise Line*).

Cunard Line (555 Fifth Avenue, New York, NY 10017-2453; ☎212/880-7500 or 800/221-4770) offers a total of 58 "handicapped accessible" cabins aboard three cruise ships—*Queen Elizabeth 2*, *Sagafiord*, and *Vistafiord*. None of these cabins have sills in the entrance doorways, many also have no bathroom sill, all have bathroom grab bars; the majority are within 50 feet of an elevator. Cabin and bathroom door widths are 26 inches on all three

TRAVEL, TOURS, AND CRUISES: TRAVEL NOTES

ships, 26–31 inches on the *QE2*. Elevator widths and depths are as follows: *QE2*, 36 and 45 inches; *Sagafiord*, 29 and 47 inches; *Vistafiord*, 29 and 47 inches. The public areas on all three ships have strategically placed ramps to provide access for passengers in wheelchairs, and all have at least one accessible open-air deck. The *QE2* has for loan a variety of aids such as raised lavatory seats, bath seats, nonslip bath mats, shower stools, canes, crutches, Zimmer frames, and wheelchairs.

Although *Cunard*'s other four vessels are not fully accessible, cruises aboard the *QE2*, *Sagafiord*, and *Vistafiord* offer ample choice of destination, including the Caribbean, Panama Canal, South America, the Amazon, Alaska, the South Pacific, the Mediterranean and Black Seas, Western and Northern Europe, the Atlantic, and North Africa.

Kloster Cruise Limited (95 Merrick Way, Coral Gables, FL 33134; ☎305/447-9660) has cabins for passengers in wheelchairs on four *Norwegian Cruise Line* ships. The *Norway* has ten cabins with minimum door width 27.5 inches, bathroom doors 26 inches; there are five elevators between 30 and 41 inches wide; all except the uppermost deck are accessible, and there are accessible public rest rooms. The *Seaward* has four inside cabins with 38-inch-wide cabin and bathroom doors and roll-in showers; there are three elevators between 34 and 36 inches wide; all decks are accessible, and there are accessible public rest rooms. The *Dreamward* has six cabins with 38-inch-wide cabin and bathroom doors, the largest of which are 8041 and 8240 on Norway Deck; there are seven elevators between 34 and 36 inches wide; all decks and activities are accessible except the Sky Deck; there are no accessible public rest rooms. The *Windward* has six cabins with 38-inch-wide cabin and bathroom doors; there are seven elevators between 34 and 36 inches wide; all decks and activities are accessible except the Sky Deck; there are no accessible public rest rooms.

There are no cabins for wheelchair users on the *Westward*, *Southward*, *Starward*, and *Sunward*—cabin doors are about 23 inches wide, bathroom doors 18 or 19 inches. Cabins

for hearing-impaired passengers are planned for the *Dreamward* and *Westward*. This operator advises that a narrow (22–23 inches) wheelchair is recommended for better maneuverability on all ships. *Norwegian Cruise Line* offers three-, four-, and seven-day cruises to the Caribbean, Bahamas, Bermuda, California, and the Mexican Riviera.

Royal Viking Line has four very spacious (264 sq ft) cabins (category F: #420, 422, 423, 425) with roll-in showers and "wheel-in closets" on board the *Royal Viking Sun*. Cabin and bathroom door width is 35 inches; mattress height on the beds is just under 20 inches; there is TV and VCR with remote control in each cabin. The four elevators are 36 inches wide, and all but the uppermost deck are accessible. There are no accessible public rest rooms. On the *Royal Viking Queen*, scheduled for completion in 1993, all decks will be accessible, including open deck areas, but there will be no accessible public rest rooms. The three elevators will be 32 inches wide. Four suites will have accessible bathroom and shower, grab rails around the toilet, and cabin and bathroom door width 32.5 inches.

The *Royal Viking Line* program for 1993 includes the Americas, Europe, the Pacific Rim, Africa, and a world cruise lasting 102 days.

If you want to get off the standard cruise routes, *Melanesian Tourist Services* (302 West Grand Avenue, Suite 10-B, El Segundo, CA 90245; ☎310/785-0370) seems to have a positive attitude to accommodating clients with disabilities and offers a tempting program of Niugini Exploration Cruises in **Papua New Guinea**, aboard the *Melanesian Discoverer*, a 117-foot deluxe catamaran with a 52-passenger capacity. There are no specific facilities for disabled passengers, and no elevators on board, but Terri Mather (Regional Manager, North America) advises that exploration of this part of the world overland would be very difficult for anyone with a disability because the highland lodges and the road conditions render much of the country inaccessible—he reckons the *Melanesian Discoverer* is "quite frankly the only way to do it." The boat's hallways and staircases are wide, and disabled persons are accommodated in the cabins on the main deck for easy access to dining room and gangway. The crew to passenger ratio is three to one, and staff members will assist with lowering passengers with limited mobility to the tenders and jet boats as required; the on-board dive master is trained to accommodate disabled scuba divers. The ship docks at the *Madang Resort Hotel*, which has ramped access, and Head Office in Madang can supply further details on accessibility on request.

Several of the **tour companies** that specialize in travel for people with disabilities (see *Practicalities*, p.597) offer cruises, including *Evergreen Travel Service*, *Flying Wheels Travel*, *Uniglobe Action Travel*, *New Directions*, and *Sundial Special Vacations*. Two that have become experts in the organization of cruises for travelers with specific medical conditions are *Journeys on Dialysis* (formerly Dialysis at Sea; 65 East India Row 22G, Boston, MA 02110; ☎617/523-0446 or 800/622-0446) and *Life Unlimited/Robbins and Associates* (17101 SW 200 Street, Suite Z28, Miami, FL; ☎305/441-6819 or 232-1908; or call *Caribbean Travel* in Miami on ☎800/327-5540).

According to David Robbins, President/Executive Director of *Life Unlimited*, more than 70,000 individuals in the US are receiving some form of oxygen therapy in their homes and are restricted in their ability to travel far from their local health care provider. The availability of liquid oxygen systems now allows for ventures away from home lasting eight days or so, and other oxygen-conserving devices can extend travel times still further. After some 30 years in the respiratory care field, *Life Unlimited* has combined health care and travel into individualized travel programs, making arrangements for tours in the USA as well as cruises to the Bahamas, Caribbean, Alaska, the Mississippi River, the Mediterranean—almost anywhere else you might wish to travel. Through an affiliation with Eurolung Assistance, *Life Unlimited* can also make travel arrangements to most locations in Europe.

Founded by Linda Byers McGrath, a dialysis patient herself with many years experience of travel and "dialysis travel," *Journeys on Dialysis* is a total package company, making all travel and medical arrangements. Dialysis treatments are scheduled while at sea, allowing plenty of time to explore ports of call. Cruises to the Caribbean, Bermuda/Caribbean, Trans-Canal/Mexico, Alaska, and Europe/Mediterranean are offered aboard ships of the *Holland America Line* (including the inaugural Caribbean cruise of the *Statendam*), *Costa Cruise Lines*, *Crystal Cruises*, *Royal Cruise Line*, and *Royal Viking Line*.

As a result of receiving many inquiries about **land vacations**, *Journeys on Dialysis* searched out and now recommends a European company specializing in dialysis land tours: *Spa and Dialysis Travel* (12 Colbert Road, Newton, MA 02165; ☎617/965-6020 or 800/972-6020), with its main office in Frankfurt, Germany, specializes in complete dialysis vacation arrangements to major cities and resorts in Europe, Israel, and Asia. All dialysis centers are said to have state-of-the-art equipment and no reuse of supplies.

Charities and Expedition Organizers

If you are looking for involvement in an **expedition with a purpose**, there are a number of options, including **Operation Raleigh** (see p.494). Those interested in environmental, scientific research and conservation projects should contact **Earthwatch** (680 Mt. Auburn Street, PO Box 403, Watertown, MA 02272-9104; ☎617/926-8200), a leading international charitable organization that matches paying volunteers with projects that need their help. One of the largest non-governmental funders of field research in the world, *Earthwatch* supports research and conservation projects run by leading scientists, then recruits interested men and women who are willing to lend a hand as staff volunteers. Their attitude regarding disabled volunteers is "anything is possible" but the needs of the research projects always come first and abilities/disabilities must fit in with the tasks to be carried out. This can mean helping archaeologists excavate the ancient villages of the Asante tribe in Ghana or a Bronze Age village in Spain; it can mean assisting marine ecologists studying tropical fish in the Canary

TRAVEL, TOURS, AND CRUISES: TRAVEL NOTES

Islands or humpback whales in Hawaii; it can mean digging for mammoths in South Dakota or dinosaurs in Australia.

Volunteers with disabilities have joined projects in the past: a man with one leg was able to work high up in the canopy of the rainforest, people in wheelchairs have worked as radio operators, or logging data on computers, or sorting archaeological finds. Costs of joining these projects range from around $800 to over $2000, exclusive of travel. If you're unsure of taking part, you can simply become a member of *Earthwatch*, receive the magazine and a catalog listing projects for the coming year, and follow the projects at home; for those who feel powerless to "do" anything about the destruction of the environment, this organization gives an opportunity to get involved.

In October 1992 **Mobility International USA** hosted a group of young disabled persons from Bulgaria in Eugene, Oregon, and in the summer of 1993 *MIUSA* will be recruiting young persons with and without disabilities (ages approximately 16–22) to spend **three weeks in Bulgaria** learning about environmental issues, disability issues, Bulgarian language and culture. Also in the summer of 1993, *MIUSA* will be sending a group of young persons (16–22) to the **Commonwealth of Independent States** (former Soviet Union) for four weeks. Both programs will involve living with host families. In Oregon, MIUSA will host a leadership program for five weeks, for which they are recruiting persons with disabilities from the US (ages 18–26). For information on any of these programs contact Exchange Programs, MIUSA, PO Box 3551, Eugene, OR 97403; ☎503/343-1284, voice and TDD. The *MIUSA* publication, **A World of Options for the 90s** (see *Books*, p.590), gives information on international voluntary workcamps and community service projects, as well as valuable advice on how to obtain help with funding your travels.

The **Ontario March of Dimes** (60 Overlea Boulevard, Toronto, ON M4H 1B6, Canada; ☎416/425-0501) is an organization committed to the integration of disabled people into the mainstream of community life. Their program of

Summer Camps ("Each ten-day vacation will provide a healthy change of pace from your day to day routine. Take time to soak in the sun, sand, serenity, and more!"), **Mainstream Adventures** ("The list of outdoor experiences is limited only by your imagination!"), and **Geneva Park Holidays** ("for disabled adults who need attendant care, on the shores of Lake Couchiching—an ideal spot to enjoy the company of family and friends") is geared toward offering disabled adults the opportunity to experience new activities and challenges.

A recent expedition, the first-ever integrated Canadian party to **trek in Nepal**, was the brainchild of Cathy Smart (Camping and Recreation Co-Ordinator for the *Ontario March of Dimes*) and Maureen and Marc Langlois of the **HeartWood Institute for Health, Learning, and Leisure** (RR #1 Rose Bay, Lunenburg County, Nova Scotia B0J 2X0; ☎902/766-4351). The 1991 trek was undertaken by a team of fourteen Canadians, including four with disabilities, four Nepalese students, their teacher, and nine porters. When participants with disabilities became tired they were ferried by the porters in specially designed aluminum carrying chairs, called "dandies." Tracy Schmitt, a four-way amputee since birth, remembers getting out of the dandy to continue walking, while the porters took a rest:

"A Nepalese farmer, who surprised me by carrying a hay bale three times his size on his back, came up to the porters and said in Nepalese, 'If she looks like that, what do the rest of them look like?' (There I was, walking along with half an arm, legs only to the knees, and a hand missing.) The porters replied, jokingly, 'One of them doesn't have a head!' If only acceptance could be so freely expressed in Canada."

Stephen Couchman, writing in *Abilities* magazine (spring 1992; see Canada *Travel Notes*), sums up the spirit of this sort of travel:

"Though the *Community Travels-Nepal* team did not make any summit attempts, or traverse mountain ranges, or attempt new routes in winter without oxygen, they did accomplish the main goal of any major expedition—they pushed the limits of human ability.

TRAVEL, TOURS, AND CRUISES: TRAVEL NOTES

"During their time in the mountains, each member of the group found time to reflect on their own limitations. Whether their personal challenge was to climb a difficult set of steps or to walk a few yards more without assistance, or to accept that great accomplishments are not always measured in miles and feet, each team member became a better person for their participation. When the last person arrived at the evening's lodgings, a great cheer would rise up from the group. Another successful day! Another Everest conquered!

"On the final night of the expedition, the team gathered for the last time. Over ginger tea, by candle light, they shared the excitement of their personal accomplishments and their hopes that the expedition would have wider ramifications.

"'Maybe if people see us working together and enjoying each other's company, they will re-think the way they relate to people with disabilities,' reflected Tracy Schmitt."

The November/December 1992 trek was at the time of writing scheduled to involve ten days of trekking in the beautiful Annapurna and Dhaulagiri ranges, with evenings spent in family-run guest homes in quiet hillside villages. The focus of the trip is community, cultural sensitivity, and environmental appreciation. Rather than rushing through the mountains, the program encourages side day trips, village exploration, visiting with villagers or schools, and perhaps assisting with local harvests. "The program is open to any individual 18 years or older prepared to undertake a moderate physical challenge. There have been special provisions made for individuals with physical or perceptual disabilities." The total cost to participants was set at just under Can\$3000. Contact HeartWood's Community Travels Program at the above address for more information.

Transport

For long journeys, involving many hours at a stretch on the move, the self-drive vehicle and the cruise ship with at least some accessible facilities probably offer the highest comfort levels. **Cars** can be fitted with hand controls, the seats adjusted, and equipment and luggage arranged for easy access. On the luxury **cruise ships**, larger ferries, and specially adapted sailing vessels such as the *Lord Nelson*, there are few problems in moving between decks, using the rest rooms, or settling into a comfortable seat. Intending cruise-goers should remember, however, that disembarking for shore excursions may be tricky and that rough seas can do more than just induce seasickness—anyone who is unsteady on their feet or uses a wheelchair will need to take extra care when moving about the ship in these conditions. Some travelers may also be deterred by the fact that on cruise liners it is often the more expensive, larger cabins or suites that are allocated as suitable for disabled passengers; and it seems to be standard policy to request that passengers with disabilities produce a medical certificate, or evidence of fitness to travel, and to insist that travelers in wheelchairs are accompanied.

Storm sills and steps make it difficult for wheelchair users to move rapidly around the less accessible ships—the smaller, older cruise ships, the more basic ferries, and fishing boats—but portable ramps are increasingly being made available and there are usually plenty of fit sailors to lend a hand, and at least the prices are usually more accessible on these vessels. For example, Peg Smith recommends traveling on the state-run ferry system, instead of the cruise ships, to explore Alaska's Inside Passage—it's cheap and reasonably accessible, and cars can be transported, although cabins are small. Contact *Alaska Marine Highway* (☎800/642-0066) for schedule or reservations. A two-year "Handicapped Person Pass" is available for a \$10 fee from Alaska Marine Highway (Attn: Pass Desk), PO Box R, Juneau, Alaska 99811-2505; applications take up to six weeks to process. The inter-island ferries in Greece provide another example of "cruising" with reasonably good access at affordable prices. In general, even on the so-called accessible ships, the narrower your wheelchair the easier the access—there are often tight corners to negotiate, space in cabins and bathrooms is usually at a premium, and doorways are only just wide enough.

TRAVEL, TOURS, AND CRUISES: TRAVEL NOTES

Aircraft, large or small, provide a good service on short trips but seating is usually cramped and rest rooms are too small to make long hauls enjoyable. Getting on and off **trains and buses** is difficult for the majority of travelers with limited mobility, and impossible for most without help, except on a few accessible networks.

Nic Fleming, a paraplegic government scientist with many years' experience of mainly work-related travel, has used almost every form of transport imaginable, from helicopters to submarines. He finds it preferable to get out of his chair in a road vehicle, or a train for that matter, and sit in a big, comfortable seat with padded cushions, armrests, and high back-rest:

"Such seats are made to support and restrain the passenger during corners, bumps, and normal swaying or juddering. A wheelchair does not support you in this way, and is much more tiring. Transport authorities should understand that for many (although I am sure not all) disabled passengers it is better to get out of their chairs. Passengers should be given the choice, but often they are not."

Accommodation

It is impractical to set rigid itineraries on long tours—there are too many unknowns—and the task of ascertaining in advance the accessibility of likely stopping places, particularly when you plan to spend only a night or two in each, will probably seem too much like hard work. Of course, if every hotel directory and every tourist accommodation brochure contained reliable access information, this task would be simple. Instead, it is time-consuming and frustrating. Nic Fleming, in common with many of our contributors, does not even attempt it:

"On trips across Europe I have just stopped at **hotels** with few problems. The hotel staff are almost always completely untroubled by the arrival of a customer in a wheelchair. I assure them that any potential problems are easily solvable, and they are happy to believe it. The porter or other staff are usually pleased to help with the odd step. Elevators are sometimes too narrow, but Madame the

concierge will find a small chair, onto which I can transfer and pull my folded wheelchair in beside me. Bathroom doors are often too narrow, but these can also be negotiated by transferring to a small, straight-backed kitchen or desk chair.

"It may seem cavalier not to research visits to hotels more thoroughly. People who do not have strong arms could not use the chair-transfer, and would have to make more careful preparations. My reasoning is that all obstacles can be overcome on the spot in a matter of minutes. Once staff see that solutions are easily found, they stop worrying.

"If you try to sort out all potential problems in advance, the time and worry is much greater for everyone. The staff have to count steps and measure doors, elevators, and bathroom dimensions, then report back by phone or letter. Are there two steps or three to the dining room? Does it matter? Are there steps at the hotel entrance, and a revolving door? Does it matter? By the time these points have been checked, everyone is jittery and anxious, and you still find that the parking lot is 50 yards away, down ten steps, which nobody thought of.

"If you are stopping in a different hotel every night, and passing through four countries in ten days, the labor of investigating all these access details for each hotel for one night would be ludicrous. In my experience, every hotel from Stavanger to Suva, from Pammukkale to Palermo, can cheerfully accommodate a wheelchair traveler after two minutes' thought on the spot. The biggest and most expensive hotels have wide doors, big bathrooms, smooth marble floors, and huge elevators; the smallest hotels in remote mountain villages or tropical islands have strong friendly staff who will carry you upstairs. It all works out.

"On serious business travel, or if you are passing through a city at fiesta time, it is essential to reserve in advance to ensure that you have accommodation close to your place of work, or to ensure that you have a room at all. I never warn the hotel staff that I am disabled. It is more important to have a good, efficient hotel, at the right price, a few minutes from where you are working in a foreign city (or from the sights you want to explore) than a hotel with no steps at the entrance half an hour away by taxi. In more than twenty years of travel I have never been completely stumped, although on occasion I have had to look at two or three rooms before finding a convenient one."

For those who can manage chair-to-floor transfers, and cope with the physical demands of erecting the tent or lugging equipment around, **camping** provides the cheapest form of accommodation and for a long trip this is an important consideration. Lists of accessible sites in Britain, France, Germany, and Switzerland are available to members of *Camping for the Disabled* (20 Burton Close, Dawley, Telford, Shropshire TF4 2BX, UK); there's advice on suitable sites in other countries, too. Other sources include tourist board guides (such as Sweden's *Holiday Guide for the Disabled*) and *Michelin* guides.

An RV or trailor make life easier, but all forms of camping, from sleeping on the ground under the stars to towing a luxury house trailor, can be made accessible—by vehicle adaptations, by carrying a small folding camp-stool for use in the showers, by using a stool on castors for maneuvering inside a trailor.

Nic Fleming advises that a light, army cot, or a foam-rubber mattress, provides ample padding for the somewhat sensitive skin of a paraplegic. The biggest problem when camping is lavatory equipment—you need some sort of stool or chair to sit on in private. It is not difficult to adapt a folding camp-chair, with a light metal frame.

Nic finds the greatest pleasure in keeping equipment to a minimum: "Field projects involving dives close to the coast in remote areas require teams who are prepared to sleep out for weeks at a time. In Crete we had been living out for a month or more when the opportunity came to visit the uninhabited island of Kuphonisi, where I wanted to see an ancient Phoenician city. The fishermen at Ierapetra said that they were not officially allowed to carry passengers, but if we went to a rocky headland a few miles along the coast, they would pick us up and take us to Kuphonisi where they would be fishing all night.

We waited on the rocks in the evening light, and I took on board just my foam rubber bedroll, my notebooks, and a travel kit containing the essential medical bits and pieces. There was an incredible feeling of lightness. Leaving the world behind. We slept on the beach of Kuphonisi, explored the city the next day, and returned. It was a liberation."

Access and Facilities

The more conventional trips—by car or train or large ship—posed no insurmountable problems. Two travelers were able to drive around Europe without booking accommodation in advance, although a little patience and persistence were necessary at times. Access to the tourist sights was obtained—sometimes with difficulty, aided by fellow travelers, and occasionally via the back door, but nothing was out of bounds.

The contributors who took to the sea were pleased with the facilities on board their vessels. There is room for improvement in the arrangements for including disabled passengers in plans for shore excursions, and in making all amenities on board easily accessible, but good progress has been made by some shipping companies.

When contemplating tours which are more accurately described as "expeditions," over rough terrain, perhaps in remote areas and with inhospitable climate, it is easy to make assumptions about accessibility and rule out ideas which are, in reality, possible. More advice from Nic Fleming, who has encountered fairly rugged conditions on oceanographic projects:

"Much of my work is in rough terrain, away from roads, and on rocks or sandy beaches. Sometimes we have to ford rivers, traverse mountain paths, or get through thick scrub. Backwheel balance (see *Practicalities*, "Health and Comfort") gives the basic mobility in rough terrain and on steep slopes or irregular rocky surfaces. This can be handled solo. Deep sand and gravel almost always require help. It can be OK going down a beach on backwheel balance, but coming up again is almost impossible. River beds and cobblestones need assis-

TRAVEL, TOURS, AND CRUISES: TRAVEL NOTES

tance; it is better to turn the chair backward and have one or, preferably, two people simply tow you through the rough spots.

"Steep mountain paths can only be traversed safely with assistance. Sometimes a track is navigable for a while, and then gets narrow just for a few yards, and you would certainly tumble sideways down the hillside if you tried it alone. Impassable ground can be dealt with by climbing onto a man's shoulders: in Crete I reached some important archaeological cuttings on the edge of a cliff after being carried along the cliff edge on a friend's shoulders, while another man carried the chair; in Cuba I was able to explore some stalactitic caves for an hour or more, carried aloft on the shoulders of a man of colossal strength.

"Another invaluable maneuver for the paraplegic traveling rough is the chair-to-floor transfer (see *Practicalities*, "Health and Comfort"). You can use it to get down onto the deck of a small boat in which you would be unstable if you remained sitting high in your chair. You can use it get down onto the dock or bank, and then into a canoe, or to sleep on the ground when camping."

Health and Insurance

Remember that as you travel farther from "civilization"—hospitals, pharmacists, and so on—your first-aid kit must become more substantial and there are some extra precautions to be taken before you leave (see *Practicalities*, "Health and Comfort"). If your expedition involves any activity that could be classed as dangerous by the insurance companies, make sure your policy covers you. Check also that your 24-hour emergency medical service will cope with all eventualities. You may want to consider joining organizations such as *International SOS Assistance* (One Neshaminy Interplex, Suite 310, Trevose, PA 19053; ☎215/244-1500 or 800/523-8930; in Canada, ☎514/874-7674 or 800/363-0263) or *Prepaid Air Rescue* (National Travelers Corporation, 5000 Quorum Drive, Suite 620, Dallas, TX 75240; ☎214/788-1257 or 800/338-4919) in order to guarantee medical evacuation. Contact them for more information concerning geographic

coverage as well as other services such as medical referral and emergency medication.

Membership in the *International Association for Medical Assistance to Travelers* (IAMAT: in the USA, 417 Center Street, Lewiston, NY 14092; ☎716/754-4883; in Canada, 40 Regal Road, Guelph, ON N1K 1B5; ☎519/836-0102; and 1287 St. Clair Avenue W, Toronto, ON M6E 1B8; ☎416/652-0137) gives access to a world directory of English-speaking doctors who have agreed a set scale of fees for their services, and a clinical record which is completed by the traveler's own physician before departure and will provide a foreign doctor with a quick reference to the traveler's complete medical history. In addition *IAMAT* members can obtain a world immunization chart, world malaria risk chart and protection guide, and world schistosomiasis risk chart and information brochure. *IAMAT* membership and directory are free.

Books

The US State Department (Bureau of Consular Affairs, Department of State, Washington DC 20402) issues a number of publications which may be of interest. These are available from passport offices or from the Superintendent of Documents (US Govt. Printing Office, Washington DC 20402) and include: *Background Notes; Country Information Notices; Travel Advisory Memoranda; Tips for Travelers; A Safe Trip Abroad; Travel Warning on Drugs Abroad; Key Officers of Foreign Service Posts* (names of key US officers abroad with addresses of all US embassies and consulates). Travelers can also call the Citizens Emergency Center (☎202/647-5225) and listen to pre-recorded Travel Advisories; these have been criticized by some, particularly the travel industry, for inaccuracy and political bias but others, such as Martin B. Deutsch, Editor and Publisher of *Frequent Flyer*, say they are worth monitoring—forewarned is forearmed.

Richard Dawood's *Travelers' Health* (Oxford University Press, 3rd edition 1992) is not only invaluable in itself, but also includes some useful titles for expedition organizers and members in the Further Reading list.

The World Health Organization, Geneva, publishes *International Travel and Health:*

TRAVEL, TOURS, AND CRUISES: TRAVEL NOTES

Vaccination Requirements and Health Advice every year, in the spring, and it's available from the UN Bookshop, New York.

The Real Guide: Europe is the best guide for independent travelers in Europe and *The Real Guide: Morocco* includes some thoughts on crossing the Sahara.

A Book of Travelers' Tales, by Eric Newby (Picador) contains some inspirational, if rather short, accounts from travelers great and small.

And to take with you, *Into the Heart of Borneo*, by Redmond O'Hanlon (Penguin)— better to laugh at someone else's misfortunes than get bogged down in your own.

PART TEN

PRACTICALITIES

Planning

The preceding accounts show that worldwide travel for people with disabilities is certainly possible, if not always trouble free. Perhaps the biggest issue for the 1990s is to achieve genuine **integration** of travelers with disabilities into the mainstream travel scene. There is still a widespread desire to segregate, to siphon disabled travelers off into "special programs," to lump us together in groups, to direct us to specialist travel agents or tour companies which shower us with offers of special services that should really be part of any conscientious operator's job. Like any other traveler, we simply want to flick through the brochures and choose a vacation.

Currently, there are very few operators who bother to provide useful information for disabled clients in their brochures. So another challenge for the 1990s is to ensure that **access information**—on all aspects of travel, provided by tourism offices, travel companies, transportation operators, accommodation operators, etc—is not only available but also current and accurate. There is a long way to go before we achieve this goal: despite enormous sums spent on the production of glossy tour guides and accommodation brochures, the gathering of access information is mostly left to volunteer, non-profit, or charity organizations, with limited resources. It is a daunting task to keep this information up to date, so be prepared to verify details yourself.

The **addresses** of organizations listed in the following sections are, where not given, listed in the Directory, starting on p.592.

RESEARCH

Government tourism offices vary widely in what they have to offer the disabled traveler. The *New Zealand Tourism Department* produces a well-researched, regularly updated, clearly presented guide. The Swedes produced a fine guide in 1990, but at the time of writing there were great upheavals at the tourist board and no sign of an update. The *Israeli Tourist Board* freely distributes the excellent *Access in Israel*. Some (Austria, Denmark, Finland, the Netherlands, Switzerland, Hong Kong, Singapore) use the wheelchair symbol in their accommodation guides and/or offer a small booklet or fact sheet for disabled visitors. Some (Australia, Britain, Canada, France, Germany, USA) rely heavily either on organizations for the disabled within their own country or on regional tourist offices to supply information. Many produce no literature at all, and staff members look (or sound) blank when asked.

It is important to be **persistent** when contacting tourism offices: if you know there is a brochure for disabled visitors, insist that it is available (quote your source); it is not uncommon to be told at first that there is no such publication. You may also be assured that there is only one copy left—so ask them to Xerox it for you. They rarely run out of the general brochures; why should disabled inquirers be deprived of literature aimed at them? Ask when the brochure was published; if it's out of date, express disappointment and ask when it will be updated.

As an example of the prevailing attitude among tourist boards, at the **1991 World Travel Market**, Olympia, London, only the *New Zealand Tourism Office* exhibited its access guide along with the glossy brochures. Staff on most of the stands were bewildered, apologetic, or angry when questioned; they offered the standard information packs, determined that no one should go away empty-handed. Similar reactions came from representatives of tour operators, travel agents, airlines, hotel chains, car rental companies, bus operators, and train companies. Some notable exceptions are mentioned below, but too many people in the travel trade remain ignorant of—or perhaps indifferent to—the needs of a large, potentially lucrative group of travelers.

The standard **brochures** do have some use, in that they are usually lavishly illustrated. Pictures can provide clues about the terrain if your destination is unfamiliar. A visit to the travel section of your local **library** will serve the same purpose: pre-vacation reading not only means that costly (and sometimes overcrowded) sightseeing tours can be avoided, it also gives you a preview of the area to be visited.

Many **specific disability groups** gather and distribute information on travel and transport, as well as organizing vacations or managing accommodation. Although not comprehensive, these sources are well worth investigating, not least because the information gathered will be pertinent to your own disability.

There are also **organizations covering a wide range of disabilities** and disability-related issues, and many of these can help with most aspects of planning an international trip; the major ones that have information on destinations all over the world are listed in the *Travel Notes*—*Mobility International USA*, *Travelin' Talk*, and *SATH* under the USA; *Kéroul* and *CPA* in Canada; the *Holiday Care Service* and *RADAR* in England and Wales. Other more country-specific organizations are listed in the appropriate *Travel Notes*: see also the **Directory** (p.592) for complete listings.

FINANCIAL HELP

The cost of travel is prohibitive to many people, but it should be possible for those with disabilities to travel on a tight budget, in spite of the fact that facilities are often best on the more expensive types of transportation and in the more luxurious hotels. Many in the travel industry fuel the myth that services and facilities can only be offered to disabled clients at inflated prices, but the writers in this book support the argument that what we need is not expensive "special" services but a flexible approach, a little extra pre-trip research and planning, and perhaps a few minor changes to transportation or accommodation arrangements.

Several of our contributors suggest a variety of **cost-cutting exercises** (traveling out of season, putting up with the discomfort and using charter flights, taking a cheap package deal, booking six months in advance, sharing taxis for sightseeing, eating out at lunchtime rather than in the evening, looking at budget or self-catering accommodation with an eye to "putting up," rather than believing that only five-star hotels are accessible) that enable them to take part in ordinary mainstream vacations; some offer thoughts on **saving or raising the money** once you've pared down the overall price.

On **group tours and travel programs** run by charities or non-profit organizations there is often some provision made for those who are unable to meet the full cost of the trip. They may also be able to help with looking for other sources of finance.

Those whose travel plans are ambitious, long term, and perhaps involve work which will benefit others (for example, Roger Elliott's participation in Operation Raleigh, p.472), may consider seeking **sponsorship**. This requires a bit of lateral thinking—to find a link between some aspect of your trip and the sponsor, and an opening for the sponsor to promote his or her services or products. Mention the trip to everyone you know, use every available contact, and gather as many ideas as possible. Consult the *MIUSA* publication, **A World of Options in the 90s** (see *Books*, p.590), which has a useful section on financial aid resources. Write *brief* applications, describe your project with enthusiasm, and be specific about what you need—equipment, fares, supplies.

Booking

Whether you go to a travel agent or book through the tour operator, you will probably find that you need to take the initiative in stating your needs and making sure that they are met: most are non-specialists, who deal with disabled clients only as and when they appear. Few companies give staff any training for basic skills such as communication with deaf or speech-impaired people, passing on clients' requirements to airlines or hotels, and understanding the mysteries of airline medical forms—which clients need to give only handling advice, which must supply medical details. This doesn't mean that they all fail to make adequate arrangements—many contributors report faultless service—but some certainly do.

NON-SPECIALIST TRAVEL AGENTS

Several local **non-specialist travel agents** were praised by contributors, so perhaps the best general advice is to experiment in your own area until you find one who is efficient, sympathetic to your needs, willing to help with researching such things as the nature of the terrain and accessibility of hotels, and meticulous about informing all who *should* be informed of your travel plans. Try to establish a working relationship along the following lines:

The basis of all travel arrangements should be that **no destination is "unsuitable"** for a disabled person. Both traveler and travel agent must discuss the choice of vacation with an open mind, giving equal weight to the positive and negative aspects. Too many travel agents dwell on the potential obstacles, and some travelers are put off by barriers that could be overcome.

Only the traveler knows his or her capabilities. First-time travelers may seek more advice than seasoned travelers, but all must be forceful in stating their abilities as well as their disabilities, remembering that travel can be both physically and mentally demanding, and that there's a fine line between challenging yourself and punishing yourself.

Travelers who need to be satisfied in advance that their **individual access criteria** are met must demand more of their travel agents, and they must give more detailed information about themselves and their requirements (minimum door widths for entry to hotel rooms and bathrooms, bed height, etc). Only those travelers who have absolute faith in their agents can skip the next chore, which is to double-check that transport operators, tour company reps, ground handling agents, hotel staff, and tour guides have been informed of any requests for assistance or "special" facilities.

NON-SPECIALIST TOUR OPERATORS

The majority of contributors either traveled independently or booked vacations with non-specialist operators. There are a number of possible explanations for this but it is probably largely the reflection of a general desire to **participate in mainstream tourism**, to be catered for there rather than be segregated, forced to make "special arrangements" and—to cap it all—pay through the nose for the privilege. Antipathy toward the "wrapped in cotton treatment" has been expressed by many disabled travelers who feel that an accessible transfer vehicle should be part of the service, not a luxury item for which they must pay a supplement.

The number of non-specialist tour operators that claim to cater to disabled travelers is increasing but it is difficult to single out any for unqualified praise. It is becoming much more common to see some mention of clients with "special needs" in the brochure, usually with a request that these people call for more information about the resorts and accommodation, and

discuss their requirements when booking. There are also some wheelchair symbols creeping onto the glossy pages.

This is a welcome beginning, but we are still a long way from widespread availability of *reliable* **information**. There are too many stories of fruitless phone calls, being passed from one department to another until satisfactory answers are obtained. Even then, disappointment may follow, and assurances that accommodation is accessible evaporate on arrival at the hotel entrance. Against this background of broken promises it is refreshing (though sad, in the light of recent events in Yugoslavia) to see in the *Yugotours* (summer 1991) brochure the statement, "There are unfortunately no hotels suitable for clients in wheelchairs, only some hotels which are less unsuitable!"

Many tour operators make what can only be described as a **token effort** to accommodate disabled clients: staff are floored when asked the simplest questions about resorts in their brochures, although the standard paragraph for less mobile vacationers assures us that help is only a phone call away. What is needed is to research, verify, store, and update details of resort and accommodation facilities and access, to consider the accessibility of transfer vehicles from airport to hotel—in short, to anticipate the needs of all travelers.

Ideally, this information should be included in the main brochure; if limited space is the excuse, then a supplement for disabled clients should be available. *Country Holidays* (see England and Wales *Travel Notes*) is a model example in Britain: in addition to their main brochure, they produce a second brochure, *Holidays for Disabled People*, which contains a selection of cottages suitable for people with disabilities. There is a detailed description of each property and if you cannot find one which meets all your requirements you are invited to call the "Disabled Person's Helpline" (☎0282/445340); by asking a lot of questions the staff will endeavor to find the perfect cottage for you.

Relying exclusively on endless phone calls when trying to find a suitable holiday is both unsatisfactory and expensive for the client. We have received no reports of American or Canadian companies that have attempted to respond to this. In Britain, *Thomson Tour Operations* (Greater London House, Hampstead Road, London NW1 7SD; ☎071/387 9321) has introduced **Factfile** which is a computerized information service accessible to some 7000 travel agents who can book with *Thomson* companies (*Thomson Holidays, Horizon, Skytours, Wings, HCI,* and *OSL*). The service is used by non-disabled clients, too, if they require more detail than that provided in the brochure.

There are four pages of information on every hotel and apartment in the brochure, one of which is aimed at "less mobile" clients. The information is gathered via a questionnaire (covering general suitability, surrounding area including access to beach and town center, steps at entrance and within the hotel, approximate door widths to entrance, elevator, bedroom, bathroom, and balcony, and details of any other relevant facilities, such as grab-rails and availability of first-floor rooms) which is sent out to the *Thomson* reps in the resorts. The main cause for concern is that the questionnaire may be filled in by hotelier or rep—hoteliers are not renowned for their accuracy in these matters, so it would be more reassuring if reps were given training and took responsibility for completing the questionnaire themselves; in addition, the term "less mobile" is too vague and there is no mention of facilities for blind or deaf clients. However, Factfile is backed up by experienced staff in the **Client Welfare Department**, through which extra information can be obtained, assistance arranged at airports, special meals be requested, and so on.

Another way of tackling the problem is for a non-specialist tour company to **team up with a specialist operator** or travel agent. Many of the US and Canadian specialists listed in the *Directory* (p.592) act essentially as travel agents and offer group packages set up with mainstream tour or cruise companies. In Britain, there is a more formal arrangement between *Virgin Holidays* and the specialist tour company for disabled people, *Threshold Travel* (80 Newry Street, Banbridge, County Down BT32 3HA, Northern Ireland; ☎08206/62267; see Ireland *Travel Notes*, and below). Using a small selection of accommodation in the existing *Virgin* brochures, a "fly-drive" program has been drawn up specifically for disabled clients, using adapted rental cars. These vacations are no more expensive than the standard *Virgin* packages, and the flight is non-stop on a Boeing 747 with aisle wheelchair. *Virgin Holidays* was one of the first operators to adopt the *Tourism for All* Model Policy Statement (see p.167) and it must have done something right—

by November 1990 *Virgin/Threshold* had surpassed its 1990 reservations figure even before the 1991 brochure was published. Fully accessible "Fly Cruises" and "Two Center Cruises," a result of teaming up with *Norwegian Cruise Line*, were added to the program in 1991.

In the end, though, these are **stop-gap measures**, cop-outs by operators which should be directing their efforts toward making the majority of their tour programs accessible to all travelers, disabled or not. It's time to see an end to the attitude that says, "I'm not a specialist, so I can't help you." This is particularly prevalent among **budget and discount operators**, but it does not necessarily make them out of bounds to disabled travelers, many of whom are simply looking for a good deal and either have no special requests or are prepared to handle these direct with the airline or hotel—generally safer than going through a third party anyway.

CRUISES

A few **cruise operators** seem to be responding to the needs of mobility-impaired travelers (see *Travel, Tours, and Cruises*), with new ships being built to higher standards of accessibility. *Holland-America Line* even marks cabins for disabled passengers on the deck plans in its brochure. However, what the cruise line deems accessible may be a long way from meeting your requirements. As with hotels, then, if you want to be sure of accessibility before setting off, you must ask lots of questions, not forgetting height of storm-sills. This throws up all the problems mentioned above (whom do you ask, can you rely on the accuracy of the answers, and why has no one thought of including in the brochure a small plan of the cabin(s) for disabled passengers, with all relevant measurements clearly marked?). As a last resort, some travelers make the journey to inspect the ship before their cruise.

As a safety precaution, most operators insist that passengers who are unable to walk unaided up the gangway are accompanied by an able-bodied companion. Thoughts of disabled passengers seem to stop at the gangway, however, so that, again for safety reasons, if the ship cannot berth (as happens in small ports) wheelchair users may not be allowed to attempt the transfer from cruise ship to launch—usually by ladder or steps. Sometimes, crew members will carry disabled passengers down to the waiting launch—again, more questions necessary.

Shore excursions will be tricky for some, usually because of the transportation used; it's probably best to be independent once off the ship. Then there are the on-board activities to consider: can you reach all the public rooms? What about the movie theaters? Can you use the swimming pool? It seems crazy to provide cabins for disabled passengers and then allow access to only some of the entertainment and leisure facilities, but it happens.

SPECIALIST TRAVEL AGENTS AND TOUR OPERATORS

While those involved in mainstream tourism are being persuaded to work toward the goal of integration, the specialist travel agent or tour operator may be the answer for some—perhaps those who have not traveled before, or those who are unwilling to ask for special treatment on a vacation not designed for disabled people, or those who prefer to feel confident that all their requests will be understood and taken care of.

Of course, this confidence may be misplaced, in which case it is galling to have paid over the odds, as Maxine Smith discovered when she traveled, disastrously, to Egypt (p.346). The main specialist operators are listed in the *Directory*, p.597.

VOLUNTARY/NON-PROFIT ORGANIZATIONS

The **specialist voluntary or non-profit organizations** (see the *Directory*, p.600) get a better rating than the commercial operators from our correspondents. Several contributors (traveling companions or escorts as well as disabled travelers) booked very successful vacations with these organizations, all of which have developed interesting programs and well-thought-out facilities; in addition they seem to put the traveler first and his or her wallet last, keeping the costs down as well as subsidizing in cases of hardship. Most of these organizations offer something more than simple sun and sea vacations, taking the opportunity to combine travel with adventure and some sort of learning experience, whether this is a strenuous outdoor activity or a language course.

This is just as well because although some commercial **adventure/activity vacation** operators accept people with disabilities, not many have the imagination, resources, *and* the will to say yes; only a few operators have woken up to the fact that disabled people might like a challenge, too. (If you do try to reserve with a mainstream operator, since broken promises might be worse than inconvenient when struggling up the Amazon, it's probably best to select a company with some experience of taking disabled clients, or one which is keen to try—waste no time on negative thinkers.)

The non-profit organizations that have made serious attempts to accommodate people with disabilities usually set up special programs, such as the **Access to Adventure Courses** at the *Canadian Outward Bound Wilderness School* (PO Box 116, Station S, Toronto, ON M5M 4L6; ☎416/787-1721 or 800/268-7329), but some also accept applicants on standard courses or expeditions according to their abilities (for example, *Earthwatch*, p.547; *Operation Raleigh*, p.494).

On some trips you are on your own in a **group of persons with disabilities** (plus able-bodied escorts/enablers/helpers); this may not suit everyone but there are advantages, not least to severely disabled people who may otherwise be unable to travel. The British charity *Winged Fellowship* (p.287) packs an astonishing amount into its trips, enabling quite severely physically disabled people to reach places that would probably be inaccessible without the *Winged Fellowship* team of helpers. *Project Phoenix Trust* (p.243) provides some fascinating study tours for anyone who needs some sort of physical assistance. The *Uphill Ski Club* trips are physically challenging and their program is unusual in that it includes mixed groups of mentally and physically disabled skiers (p.222).

Many other organizations take disabled person plus family or friends, or a **mixture of able-bodied and disabled**. *Disaway* vacations (p.146) are for groups of physically disabled people and volunteer helpers are supplied, but group members may take their own helper/friend if they wish. The *Jubilee Sailing Trust* accepts disabled and able-bodied crew members on its voyages, so you can apply with friends or members of your own family (p.520).

Mobility International USA (p.544) has an excellent **exchange program** for young persons with and without disabilities, providing affordable opportunities for travelers to stay with host families and explore new cultures and languages, discuss environmental and disability issues, as well as enjoying leisure and sightseeing activities, in a number of continents including Latin

America, the Commonwealth of Independent States, and Europe.

The **Ontario March of Dimes** (p.548) is another organization committed to the integration of disabled people into the mainstream of community life, offering camps and recreational opportunities including a recent expedition to Nepal, organized with Maureen and Marc Langlois of the **HeartWood Institute for Health, Learning, and Leisure** (RR #1 Rose Bay, Lunenburg County, Nova Scotia B0J 2X0; ☎902/766-4351).

GOING IT ALONE

Choice of **independent or package** and **group or solo** travel is very much a personal thing. The attractions and disadvantages of each are discussed throughout the accounts and there is no clear winner as far as providing the formula for a successful vacation is concerned. Perhaps the only guideline is that the travel plans should first fit in with your interests, tastes, and budget, then if necessary be adapted to suit your accessibility requirements, rather than the alternative scenario in which you may be directed to "suitable" destinations or packages, or told to use a specialist in travel for disabled people, or forced to compromise to suit the tour company's rules and regulations.

Of course there are times when compromise is appropriate: the flexibility necessary when taking part in a **group vacation for disabled people** is best described by Joan Cooper (p.287) and Charlotte Billington (p.243). Having to go along with group decisions, keeping up with a tough schedule, and getting on with complete strangers for two weeks might cause problems, but the advantages of these vacations are also clear—plenty of helpers to negotiate steps and difficult terrain, often the opportunity to learn something more than the average tourist, and the chance to make new friends.

The joys of the **organized tour group** (with no special arrangements for disabled people) are expounded by Betty Layton (pp.352, 445), the compromises by Daphne Pagnamenta (p.398). Christine Panton (p.28), and Robin Reeley (p.403) successfully combined organized tour with some individual travel. If you accept that you may not be able to participate in every activity on the tour, it is generally possible to join these groups, although some operators may be wary, especially of older travelers, if conditions are rough in the countries to be visited. For example, Daphne

Pagnamenta was refused by several companies when looking for an escorted tour in India.

One big advantage of the inclusive tour is that the use of charter flights, contracts with local guides and transfer vehicle companies, and group discounts at hotels, enables the tour operator to offer **competitive prices**. The advantage will be lost if you cannot find a tour that suits you in every respect, and this is not unlikely if you have some form of disability. If you want to alter the itinerary or make changes to any part of the package you will have to pay for it—customized vacations cost more than ready-made ones.

If you require some assistance but don't want a group tour, you should be able to find a helper (see *Travel Escorts*, below), though it will usually involve a bit of asking around—there are several organizations that emphasize the "nursing" and "care" aspects of acting as an escort, not so many that simply match up an able-bodied volunteer willing to act as companion and "pusher," or "enabler" (p.569). Peter Stone (p.297) and Stephen Hunt (p.309, 362) **traveled solo** this way; you may also prefer to do your own reading about the sights and see them at your own pace by taxi, rather than be herded along on organized tours. If you'd rather see the sights on a guided tour, lack of mobility doesn't have to be a barrier, but discuss your abilities with the tour leader first.

A number of contributors booked standard **package deals** without experiencing insurmountable problems. Philippa Thomas (p.234), Eric Leary (p.218), Theodora Hampton (p.304), Stephen Hunt (p.343), and Ivy Geach (p.365) were well satisfied with their trips; Mairene Gordon (p.192) less so with hers.

Many contributors **made their own travel arrangements**: some used a travel agent to reserve flights only, finding accommodation (David Gray, p.487; Arthur Goldthorpe, p.17; Andrew Healey, p.458) or taking part in organized projects (Roger Elliott, p.472; Kate Margrie, p.374) on arrival; some made direct reservations with hotels (Beryl Bristow, p.210); some took off in their car and found hotels or campgrounds along the way (Roderick MacDonald, p.512; Michael Turner, p.517; Enid Fisher, p.195).

These are only a few examples. The immense satisfaction to be had from **masterminding your own trip** is a major theme of this book. And if ready-made vacations cost less than tailor-made packages, it can be even cheaper to do it yourself.

Insurance

It is essential to be adequately insured, not only to cover the cost of medical treatment, but also because being in a wheelchair, or having some other visible disability, is no protection against petty thieving (p.29,310) or simple loss of your luggage.

Your private or group health insurance may cover out-of-country medical expenses, and bank Gold Cards or other credit cards may also offer some protection, but you should check restrictions. Some houseowners' policies already cover items such as wheelchairs or other essential equipment, and this can be extended to include vacation use; some property insurance companies also offer travel insurance plans. If you purchase a package vacation from a tour company insurance cover is often included, but you must check that the plan meets your requirements. If these options do not provide sufficient cover, you can purchase individual travel insurance.

Travelers with disabilities should, like all travelers, obtain answers (from the insurance company issuing the policy) to a few key questions concerning their travel insurance plan before paying up and heading for the airport:
1. Is cover affected by any pre-existing medical condition, ongoing medical treatment, current medication, age of traveler, destinations on the itinerary, participation in sporting activities? If so, what are the limits and exclusions?
2. Is there a toll-free or collect telephone number that can be reached from anywhere on your travels and will give access to emergency assistance?
3. Are you covered in the event of baggage loss, trip cancellation, visits to foreign hospitals or clinics, and emergency repatriation?
4. In the event of a claim, what is the procedure, what documents are required, what are the maximum sums payable, and are there any deductions? Who pays the bills on the spot, for example if you need medical treatment overseas?

The majority of travelers with disabilities will find that cover supplied by most general travel insurance plans will be adequate, and it is a question of looking around to find the best value from a reliable company. Those who might experience unpredictable flare-ups of a disease, such as asthma attacks, may have more difficulty finding an appropriate policy and have to pay extra.

The **Canadian Life and Health Insurance Association Inc.** (The Information Center, CLHIA Inc., 1 Queen Street East, Suite 1700, Toronto, ON M5C 2X9; ☎416/777-2344 or 800/268-8099) publishes a helpful brochure, *Health Insurance for Travelers*, and issues a list of insurance companies that offer individual health insurance for Canadians traveling out of Canada, all members of the CLHIA and the Canadian Life and Health Insurance Compensation Corporation (CompCorp)—the industry's Consumer Protection Plan:

Commercial Union Life Assurance Company of Canada (contact the *John Ingle Agency*; ☎416/961-0666 or 800/387-4770).

Cooperators Life Insurance Company (☎519/824-4400, or 800/265-2662 for area codes 416, 519, 705 only).

Mutual of Omaha Insurance Company (☎416/598-4083, or listing in local city).

Reliable Life Insurance Company (contact *Travel Wise Company*, ☎800/661-0330; available through travel agents).

Voyageur Insurance Company (☎416/791-8700; available through travel agents).

The following property and casualty companies, all members of CompCorp, also offer travel insurance plans:

Laurentian P & C Insurance Company Inc. (contact *Medicare International*, ☎800/461-2100 or, in Ontario only, ☎416/759-4113; or *21st Century*, ☎800/461-2100).

The Sovereign General Insurance Company (contact *Travel Insurance Co-ordinators*, ☎604/926-7779 or 800/663-4494).

Zurich Indemnity Company of Canada (contact *TRAVELRITE Travel Insurance*, ☎416/777-1690 or 800/563-8615 English, 800/663-1788 French; available through travel agents).

In the **USA**, the same rules apply—shop around and ask the necessary questions, and don't leave home without your travel insurance documents and the emergency assistance telephone number. **SATH** (see USA *Travel Notes*) has published a list of companies that offer health insurance and/or assistance for overseas travelers:

Access America (☎212/490-5345 or 800/284-8300).

American Express (☎800/824-3916).

Arm Carefree (☎516/294-0220 or 800/645-2424).

Global Assistance (☎800/523-8930).

International Airline Passengers Association (☎800/527-5888).

International Association for Medical Assistance to Travelers (*IAMAT*; ☎716/754-4883; see p.552).

International SOS Assistance (☎215/244-1500 or 800/523-8930; in Canada, ☎514/874-7674 or 800/363-0263; see p.552).

Mutual of Omaha (☎800/228-9792).

Travel Assistance International (☎800/821-2828).

Travel Guard International (☎800/826-1300).

The Travelers Companies (☎800/243-4174).

Worldcare Travel Assistance (☎800/521-4822).

Health and Comfort

PREPARATIONS

When traveling, especially if you have any allergies or sensitivities (eg aspirin, penicillin, insect stings), or have a medical condition that could be made worse by treatment given in ignorance of your drug regimen (eg diabetes, bleeding disorder, renal failure), it's wise to carry a doctor's letter (translated into the appropriate language) explaining your medical condition and the treatment you are receiving. An alternative is to wear a **Medic Alert** bracelet or necklace (from *Medic Alert Foundation International*, 2323 Colorado Ave., Turlock, CA 95381-1009; ☎800/ID-ALERT; regional offices in Chicago, ☎312/280-6366, and New York, ☎212/213-4510). One-time membership in *Medic Alert* is $30, and membership includes an engraved, stainless steel emblem in the form of a bracelet or neckchain, annually issued wallet card copy of the member's medical record, and lifetime emergency 24-hour hotline service (number is engraved on the emblem so that medical personnel anywhere in the world can gain immediate access to your medical details).

There are other medical identification jewelry and medical alert cards on the market (a leading manufacturer in the US is **Health Enterprises**, 15 Spruce Street, North Attleboro, MA 02670; ☎508/695-0727 or 800/633-4243), with space for basic medical details and phone numbers of your doctor/hospital. There is no emergency hotline number, but this may not be necessary, particularly if you also have a 24-hour emergency medical assistance number with your insurance policy

and you carry a note of this number along with your medical details.

It's also worth contacting the local branch of the national association for your own disability—several organizations have designed their own emergency ID cards, some including helpline numbers (though not a 24-hour service), and will distribute these free to members; the spring 1992 issue of *Access-Able* (see *Books*, p.590) carries a survey of the types of card available from muscular dystrophy (and allied disorders) groups around the world. These cards serve another purpose for travelers with conditions that might cause misunderstandings both at home and overseas: for example, swaying, slurred speech, or inability to walk in a straight line might be construed as the symptoms of someone under the influence of drink or drugs, and policemen or women may take some persuading that they are actually the result of disability—an official-looking card might help.

If you have to see a doctor and you are unsure—perhaps because of language difficulties—of his or her knowledge of your disability, how it is affected by other conditions, and how your drugs interact with other medicines, then you should attempt to find another doctor. Membership of *IAMAT* (see p.552) might help you locate an **English-speaking doctor**. Disability organizations and information centers within the country (there is usually at least one) can be contacted for help in finding a doctor or hospital with experience of your particular disability. You can also try your emergency medical service, part of most good insurance policies, or your own physician in the US. On the other hand, many complaints will be totally unrelated to your disability, and you may have a hard time persuading a doctor to concentrate on the cough rather than the multiple sclerosis (p.405)!

If traveling to sparsely populated or less developed regions, make a few extra preparations. Nic Fleming, a paraplegic, offers this advice: "If you are going on a really rugged trip in arduous and remote conditions, it pays to get medical advice in advance, have a good check-up, and know the addresses of hospitals with expertise in treating your particular disability in the country you are going to. The remoter you get, and the longer the possible delay before reaching a hospital, the more medical equipment you should carry (this is a general rule, whether you are disabled or not)."

Several contributors emphasize the value of **getting into training** before a trip. David Gray, for example, practiced balancing his suitcase and travel bag on his lap (p.487). Enid Fisher lost weight in order to be fit for her journey (p.195). Nic Fleming recommends that paraplegics devote some energy to perfecting three maneuvers: "**Backwheel balance**, if you can do it, solves hundreds of problems—curbs, steps, rough ground, steep slopes, long grass. It can also be used to get your chair onto and off escalators when there is no convenient elevator. If you enjoy living rough and getting off the beaten track, backwheel balance makes all the difference.

"Paraplegics use **chair-to-chair transfers** repeatedly to get in and out of bed, onto the lavatory, into a car—but it has much wider implications. Airlines may provide you with small aisle chairs, and you can quickly get onto the aisle chair and into your seat. You can transfer to comfortable, supportive seats in a train or a taxi. When faced with narrow doors in hotels (to bathroom or elevator, for example) you can transfer onto any old kitchen chair placed just the other side of the opening, and the doorway is no longer an obstacle. You no longer have to worry whether or not a hotel is 'suitable for wheelchairs'.

"**Chair-to-floor transfers** are routinely taught in paraplegic rehabilitation training, but the point is the way you use the maneuver. You can get down onto the deck of a small boat which would be unstable if you remained sitting high up in your chair. You can transfer to the dock or bank and then into a canoe or kayak. You can sleep on the ground when camping, or sit on the ground while you repair your wheelchair."

This last point applies to any disability— whatever maneuvers and tricks you have mastered, use them imaginatively and they will get you out of all sorts of difficulties.

EQUIPMENT

Most potential causes of discomfort can be foreseen: if you take time to find out about the conditions you are likely to encounter, you'll be better able to equip yourself to survive them. Probably the ultimate sources of information on every imaginable aid for people with disabilities are the **Resource Directory for the Disabled** and **The Complete Directory for People with Disabilities** (see *Books*, p.591); the former provides more detail on each product, and it even comes up with an answer for wheelchair users looking for help on sandy beaches, although it still relies on the presence of a companion—from Commonwealth Inc. (☎804/746-4088), the Sand-Rik, a cross between a rickshaw and lounge chair, has two large back tires, no front ones, and a shaft to permit someone to pull you across the sand; it's rustproof, and it floats!

There are also numerous tips to be gleaned from our contributors, and many helpful suggestions in the *MIUSA* publication, *A World of Options for the 90s* (see *Books*, p.590); you can also pick up useful ideas at *Centers for Independent Living*, traveling aids/new technology exhibitions, local disability resource centers, and from organizations such as *MIUSA*, *Travelin' Talk*, the *Canadian Paraplegic Association*, and other associations of disabled people.

Blind or partially sighted travelers may want to refer to the *International Guide to Aids and Appliances for Blind and Visually Impaired Persons*, published annually by the *American Foundation for the Blind* (15 West 16th Street, New York, NY 10011; ☎212/620-2000 or 800/AFBLIND; regional offices in Atlanta, ☎404/525-2303; Chicago, ☎312/269-0095; Dallas, ☎214/352-7222; San Francisco, ☎510/392-4845; Washington DC, ☎202/457-1487).

Those who need to travel with a ventilator or other **respiratory** equipment can obtain advice and information from *The Rehabilitation Gazette* (4502 Maryland Avenue, St. Louis, MO 63108; ☎314/361-0475), and from LIFECARE, a company specializing in respiratory apparatus and able to provide service, equipment, and information for anyone wishing to travel throughout North America (head office, 655 Aspen Ridge Drive,

Lafayette, CO 80026, USA; ☎303/6669234; in Canada, there are three distributors—Raxon Medi-Tech, ☎514/326-7780; Medi-Gaas, ☎204/786-4719; ARS, ☎403/453-6166).

If you are relying on any electrical equipment, such as a ventilator, remember to check the voltage of the electricity supply in the countries you plan to visit, and ensure that you have the appropriate adaptor, transformer, or battery charger for use with that supply.

Whether it's a roll-up carry-chair, a folding stool, a spray gun which can be used to cool the skin, a portable fold-up lavatory ("portapotty") for the car, an ultra-lightweight wheelchair or a wheelchair-narrowing device, there is a piece of equipment to deal with most situations. But don't get carried away: keep luggage to a minimum, and remember there will be situations that you cannot plan for (see p.578). One contributor packed her "helping hand" (light tongs for picking things up and assisting when dressing) to make life easier on her bus tour, and then left it at the first hotel (p.193); but improvisation will solve any problem—in this case, making do with a long-handled shoe-lift.

Many wheelchair users carry an **emergency repairs** kit: small puncture repair outfit (unless you have solid tires fitted to your chair—a good idea if you are traveling in remote areas across rough ground), two tire levers, lightweight tire inflator with connectors for both sizes of valve, spare nuts, wrench, perhaps a spare inner tube. The repairs kit and the spares, of course, are carried in your hand luggage.

According to your destination you can obtain help when equipment breaks down from a variety of sources: garages, bike shops, hospital supply companies, hospitals or clinics, disability organizations; this can be researched before departure, and it's always a good idea to take phone numbers of any contacts you have, but in general repair sources are easily discovered when the breakdown occurs. Travelers usually find local people eager to assist, and if you are with a good tour company the rep will sort out most problems.

EQUIPMENT FOR TRAVELERS WITH HEARING LOSS

Norris Blackburn, a freelance "outdoors" writer in Tennessee, has contributed this section. He lost interest in travel after an auto accident resulted in a broken neck and almost total deafness, but regained his enthusiasm after learning about **Assistive Listening Device Systems** (ALDS):

"These helpful gadgets come in several sizes. Large ALDS have been installed in churches, theaters, and auditoriums. At the opposite end of the spectrum there are small personal ALDS, consisting of a microphone, a small amplifier which fits in the pocket of a shirt or coat, and an ear plug like those used with small transistor radios. The microphone may be aimed at a speaker or other sound source to improve communications.

"Many hearing aids can be equipped with a **telecoil**, or **T-switch**. When the switch is in the normal position, all sounds are amplified by the internal microphone in the aid. Trying to call from a roadside phone booth or one in a noisy restaurant is impossible due to amplified background noise. When the switch is moved to the "T" position, only the signal from the telephone is amplified, improving one's ability to communicate.

"When hearing aids equipped with a telecoil are combined with a personal ALDS, there are many more situations where hearing is enhanced. Hearing aids are molded to fit the user's ear, and the snug fit of the aid prevents much unwanted noise from entering the ear. With an ALDS device, you can replace the ear plug with a neck loop. In operation, the effect is similar to using the T-switch for telephone conversations: voices and other signals are picked up by the ALDS microphone or other source, amplified, then sent to the neck loop. The loop is similar to a necklace and may be worn under clothing if desired. It acts much like a radio station's transmitter and sends the sound signal to the hearing aid by inductance. At a lecture or on a tour bus, the ALDS microphone may be pointed at the speaker or a public address system speaker to reduce much of the background noise.

"The **advantages gained when traveling** are numerous. In personal or public transportation, an ALDS improves your ability to hear fellow passengers or a tour director by reducing engine and road noise. In your hotel room, you can hear the TV without disturbing guests in adjacent rooms: many TV sets, radios, and stereos have external jacks for headphones or auxiliary speakers; by substituting an audio patch cord for the ALDS microphone cord, thus connecting the ALDS to the sound source, you can adjust the volume levels of your ALDS and hearing aid to meet your needs without disturbing others. When your tour group stops for dinner, you can participate in close conversations with little interference from outside background noises.

"A personal ALDS can be used when your hearing aid does not have a telecoil and even if your hearing has not deteriorated to the point of requiring a hearing aid. Many people with only moderate hearing loss find an ALDS extremely beneficial. But maximum efficiency comes from combining an ALDS with hearing aids equipped with a telecoil.

"Modern technology has provided many other helpful devices. There are small, **portable telephone amplifiers** which fit over the phone's receiver and are held in place by an elastic band. With one of these, I could have avoided a situation that occurred shortly after my accident: a few hundred miles from home my car broke down, steam pouring from beneath the hood, the result of a burst radiator hose. I walked back to a store which was not open but did have a public phone outside. Due to noise from passing traffic, I was unable to hear the person at the service station I had called. I began trying to flag down another driver to make the call. Americans have become hesitant about stopping to assist other motorists in distress due to crime, but a driver finally stopped and made the call for me. A service truck arrived some time later and I was soon on my way, approximately three hours after stopping. With my portable amplifier I could have made the call on my own. Likewise, in a hotel room without an amplified handset, I can make any necessary calls without help.

"The key to my discovery of ALDS and other devices was an organization called **Self Help for Hard of Hearing People** (*SHHH*, 7800 Wisconsin Avenue, Bethesda, MD 20814; ☎301/657-2248, voice; ☎301/657-2249, TDD) which is actively involved in promoting communicatively accessible travel, bringing the needs of hearing-impaired people to the attention of lodging owners and other public facilities. There are local *SHHH* chapters in cities throughout the world where members meet to see new products demonstrated, learn of the latest surgical procedures, and simply to socialize. Members traveling to unfamiliar cities can contact a local *SHHH* member who might be able to provide information about accommodation, theaters, etc.

"After hearing loss occurs, according to *SHHH*, a normal tendency is to become somewhat reclusive. I followed the pattern. It was less frustrating to stay at home than to travel, even across town to a restaurant or party. Today, as thousands of others do, I go where I please and

enjoy the outing to the limit of my abilities—but not without my assortment of gadgets. On a trip they are as much a part of my luggage as my socks, and add no more than a pound of weight. Do not expect ALDS to remedy all problems in all environments, but they will minimize or eliminate many.

"If your hearing loss affects your desire to travel, see an ear specialist first, then a certified audiologist for a hearing evaluation and recommendation of the type of aids to best meet your needs. Depending on the type and severity of your loss, a 'behind-the-ear' model may offer maximum efficiency for you, rather than the 'almost-invisible' style; since these devices will be with you for many years and can constitute a major investment in terms of money and peace of mind, heed the advice of a professional, rather than yielding to vanity. Be sure to ask if the aid has a telecoil and is compatible with personal ALDS."

For more information about ALDS and other products to assist the traveler with hearing loss, contact *SHHH* (publications include *ABCs of Hearing Aids*, $2; *A Consumer's Guide for Purchasing a Hearing Aid*, $1.25; *Beyond the Hearing Aid with Assistive Listening Devices*, $1.50; *Travel for Hard of Hearing People*, $1.50) and any of the following companies: Harris Communications, 6541 City West Parkway, Eden Prairie, MN 55344 (☎612/946-0921); Quest Electronics, 510 South Worthington Street, Oconomowoc, WI 53066 (☎800/558-9526); Audex, 713 North Fourth Street, Longview, TX 75601 (☎800/237-0716); JL Pachner Ltd., 13 Via Dinola, Laguna Niguel, CA 92677 (☎714/363-9831).

The **National Information Center on Deafness** (Gallaudet University, 800 Florida Avenue, NE, Washington DC 20002-3625; ☎202/651-5051, voice; ☎202/651-5052, TDD) publishes numerous brochures, mostly free, including *Hearing Aids and Other Assistive Devices: Where to Get Assistance*; *Hearing Aids: What Are They?*; *Devices for the Hearing Impaired*; and *Travel Resources for Deaf People*.

DIALYSIS WHEN TRAVELING

Travelers who need to dialyze face one major problem: that of finding a reliable medical center, in which the risks of AIDS and hepatitis B transmission are minimized, conveniently situated on their travels. There are a number of publications and organizations that can help to locate a dialysis facility in the area to be visited, and with the correct advance planning thousands of dialysis users are able to travel widely.

THE LIST of Dialysis Centers Accepting Transient Patients is updated annually and published each July by Creative Age Publications. The 1992 list contains more than 2500 centers worldwide, most in the US but centers in many other countries are included. There are also some basic guidelines on arranging transient treatments, written by Barbara Shaw, Patient Travel Co-ordinator for National Medical Care (see below); these will be useful to renal social workers or patient-care providers who are often asked to assist with scheduling transient dialysis. Copies of *THE LIST* can be obtained from Circulation Department, THE LIST, 7628 Densmore Avenue, Van Nuys, CA 91406-2088 (☎818/782-7328). Prices are $10 (or $8.50 each for three or more copies) for orders in the US; $13 ($11.50 for three or more) for foreign orders; Mastercard, VISA, and checks are accepted; payment must be in US dollars.

The **National Medical Care Patient Travel Service** (National Medical Care, Inc., Reservoir Place, 1601 Trapelo Road, Waltham, MA 02154; ☎617/466-9850; Patient Travel Service, ☎800/634-6254, Mon–Fri, 9am to 5pm EST) can help locate dialysis facilities in any area, and make arrangements (with four weeks' notice) for treatments at their own dialysis centers (over 400 locations) in the US, Spain, or Portugal. Patient Travel Co-ordinators are knowledgeable in many areas, including insurance, treatment modality, and medical record requirements. They can also advise on travel agencies and tour companies that specialize in travel for people who need to dialyze. There are two agencies that handle individual travel arrangements: *Adventure Travel Service* (28 West Adams Avenue, Detroit, MI 48226; ☎313/961-6114) and *Al Miller Travel* (602 Essex Street, Lynn, MA 01901; ☎617/599-5113); see also the Travel, Tours, and Cruises *Travel Notes*.

The **National Listing of Providers Furnishing Kidney Dialysis and Transplant Services** can be obtained from the Superintendent of Documents, Government Printing Office, Washington DC 20402; ☎202/783-3238.

The **American Association of Kidney Patients** (1 Davis Boulevard, Suite LL1, Tampa, FL 33606; ☎813/251-0725) has copies of *EURODIAL* (see below) but otherwise does not publish anything for travelers.

For travelers to Europe, there is a list of dialysis centers accepting transient patients throughout Europe, called **EURODIAL**, available from Elisabeth Simon, International Dialysis Organization, 153 rue du Pont, 69390 Vernaison, France (☎72.30.12.30; fax 78.46.27.81). This non-profit organization supplies information and advice to travelers looking for transient dialysis facilities all over the world. In addition, the *National Federation of Kidney Patients Associations* (*NFKPA*, Laurentian House, Stanley Street, Worksop S81 1EE, UK; ☎071/736-6267) produces a quarterly magazine, an advisory leaflet, and a booklet, **Dialyse Europa**, which lists European dialysis centers. The *NFKPA* stresses that it is impossible to recommend any because they don't have the resources to check each one. However, travelers have successfully used many of the dialysis facilities listed. Some UK units provide a portable dialysis machine for vacation use. Given sufficient warning, most of the major airlines will carry mobile dialysis equipment.

Those who are on CAPD (continuous ambulatory peritoneal dialysis) find travel much easier. CAPD supplies can be delivered to a vacation address in the US, Canada, or abroad, but suppliers like at least three months' notice.

TRAVELERS WITH HEMOPHILIA

The *World Federation of Hemophilia* (4616 St Catherine Street West, Montréal, PQ H3Z 1S3; ☎514/933-7944) publishes *PASSPORT: A Guide for Travelers with Hemophilia*, which gives advice to intending travelers and lists national member organizations and treatment centers in more than seventy countries. Other publications include medical papers, proceedings of the WFH congresses, *WFH Bulletin*, and *Life Paths*, a quarterly magazine for members. The Federation's objective is to advance and stimulate services for hemophilia and other related disorders worldwide; individual membership is US$40, Can$46.

MEDICINES

Probably the best known law of travel is to carry *in your hand luggage* enough of your **regular drugs** to last the duration of your trip—and never let this bag out of your sight. Carry additional supplies in the suitcase. The inconvenience of becoming separated from your vacation wardrobe is described by more than one contributor, but losing essential medicines is much more than an inconvenience. With clearly written prescriptions (using the chemical or generic names), you'll probably be able to obtain fresh supplies, but searching out doctors and pharmacists is not an exciting way to start a vacation.

Think also **beyond your usual drugs**, particularly in relation to the country you will be visiting. Advice on precautions with food and water, insect repellants, and local health problems can be found in any *Real Guide*, or other reputable travel guide. A good reference work, covering all sorts of medical matters for travelers—from sunstroke to snake bites—including a section on the disabled and the diabetic traveler, is Richard Dawood's *Travelers' Health* (see *Books*).

Dr. Dawood suggests which medical supplies to take with you, although of course this varies according to your destination and your own preferred treatments. Nic Fleming again: "The minimal **first-aid kit** contains Band-aids, antiseptic, scissors, small bandage, and a foam rubber patch which can be cut and fitted over a pressure point. In tropical climates you should carry your favorite remedy for control of dysentery and stomach upsets; I prefer the non-antibiotic remedies based on kaolin, but everybody has a system which works for them. As you travel farther and farther from help, the medical kit expands to include items such as disinfectants, sterile gauze, splints, antibiotics, morphine, equipment for stitching wounds, aids to artificial respiration, and so on."

You'll also be able to make some plans based on your own health history. For example, if you are prone to sinus infections and you are traveling to an area which is dusty or suffers from air pollution, it's a good idea not only to use a decongestant spray on the flight (to ease the effects of pressure changes) but also to carry a course of broad-spectrum antibiotics, or at least a note of the one you usually take.

There is no need to take a separate suitcase for your first-aid kit, but equally it's foolish to assume when reading about the problems likely to be encountered that "it won't happen to me." And seemingly minor irritations like insect bites, sunburn, and diarrhea can ruin a vacation if not effectively treated.

CLIMATE, ALTITUDE, AND FATIGUE

Perhaps the most overlooked potential problem is **fatigue**. Many types of disability cause people to tire more readily, and in the excitement of traveling to new countries it's easy to forget the need to pace yourself. If you try to do too much you'll end up enjoying nothing.

Travelers may suffer long waiting periods in uncomfortable conditions, loss of sleep, jet lag, and stress-related tiredness if things don't go according to plan, or simple fatigue caused by attempting to be more active than they are in their home lives. A bit of yawning isn't serious, but a tired person with impaired balance and mobility is very likely to trip over a step, to misjudge distances, to crash into things. It's not worth risking an accident by racing around that one last museum.

Tourist offices and guidebooks give plenty of information on **climate** so travelers can judge the best time of year to suit them. Sensible clothes, footwear, and drinking and eating patterns will make most temperatures bearable; paralyzed skin requires a bit more than average protection from the sun. Nic Fleming survived fierce frosts, well below freezing, in Moscow by wearing fur-lined flying boots, an old, heavy fur coat, wool hat, and industrial rubber or plastic gloves worn over woollen mittens (fancy ski gloves last only a few days before wearing through and letting in the damp snow). For more advice on coping with extremes of heat and cold, wind, and humidity, including some comments on sunscreens, consult Colonel James Adam in *Travelers' Health*.

Anyone with disease of the heart, lungs, or blood should consult their physician before traveling to **high altitudes**. There may be increased risk of attacks for epilepsy and migraine sufferers. Cold and exertion may induce an attack in asthmatics, but high altitude alone will not. Mountain sickness may occur at heights over 2000m—people vary in their susceptibility—and the secret of prevention is to acclimatize. Dr. John Dickinson, writing in *Travelers' Health*, recommends "rest days" every 900m above 2700m for fit walkers.

TRAVEL ESCORTS

Caryl Lloyd (p.154) recommends spending some time, preferably at least 24 hours, with a prospective helper to allow both parties to assess the likelihood of hitting it off while on vacation. It's also important to agree money matters before departure. Problems that arise after careful consideration at this first meeting can usually be overcome with a little tolerance and a sense of humor. Caryl and other contributors who traveled with volunteer helpers report easy relationships, and Stephen Hunt, who always traveled this way, considered his companion's contribution to be an important and enriching part of his travel experiences (p.343), valuing the friendship as much as the muscle power.

Some **specialist travel companies** listed in the *Directory* (p.592) provide companions and escorts, including *Accessible Journeys, Friends of the Family,* and *Tomorrow's Level of Care.*

MedEscort International, Inc., ABE International Airport, PO Box 8766, Allentown, PA 18105-8766 (☎215/791-3111—call collect outside the USA—or 800/255-7182) can provide escorts for ill, frail, or disabled clients, everything from meet-and-greet at airports (for example, helping someone make a transfer from an international to a domestic flight; this service would cost about $100), to medically trained escorts for trav-

elers who must be flown home for treatment. The company recruits regularly employed doctors, nurses, and respiratory therapists to serve as MedEscorts on their off-duty days. Other services include pre-trip preparations, door-to-door services, worldwide travel coordination and travel agency services, and ground transportation.

If you require an escort, adapted taxi, or private ambulance service in order **to reach your point of departure**, whether it be airport, train or bus station, or sea port, consult the Yellow Pages, local public transit operators, and local disability resource centers. In some areas, such as Vancouver (see Canada *Travel Notes*, p.85), there are taxicab companies offering wheelchair-accessible vehicles.

It's also worth contacting organizations such as the **Travelin' Talk** network (see USA *Travel Notes*); *Travelin' Talk* has compiled extensive listings and may also be able to help with finding a vacation traveling companion or medical escort. In Canada, provincial *CPA* offices can probably assist (see Canada *Travel Notes*).

Red Tape

Overcoming bureaucratic obstacles can be an infuriating way to start a vacation—but not half as bad as not being allowed to fly because you've failed to fill in a form. Other forms, such as applications for parking permits, are worth the effort of completing. Below are some problems you're likely to come across, and how to handle them.

MEDICAL CLEARANCE AND HANDLING ADVICE

The majority of disabled travelers should not need medical clearance before flying. The *MEDIF* (*Medical Information Form*) was introduced primarily to detect passengers with heart conditions who should not really be flying. If presented with a form, *MEDIF* will make up the second part and may usually be ignored. The important bit is part one, *INCAD*, the *Incapacitated Passengers Handling Advice* form which gives the airline details of your requirements—what assistance you need and where.

Travelers with stable medical conditions should obtain a *FREMEC* card (*Frequent Travelers*

Medical Card), which is accepted by most major airlines and issued free by them. This is preferable to repeated form filling and can be produced when asked to complete *MEDIF* by a zealous travel agent or airline official who hears the word "disabled" or "wheelchair" and immediately assumes that medical clearance is required.

Very occasionally, there may be a problem with visa applications such as Lorna Hooper experienced (p.476). If this happens, the best advice is to be forceful: produce medical evidence of fitness to travel if absolutely necessary but otherwise remember that you are dealing with bureaucrats (see p.574) and explain patiently and firmly that your disability should not even have to figure in your application for a visa.

BOOKING FORMS

A large number of disabled people have found that they can travel quite happily without giving advance warning of their disability, making no "special requests" and dealing with any obstales as and when they arise. In view of the fact that special requests stated on the booking form are often ignored anyway, this seems sensible. It is also the goal that all operators and travelers should be aiming for—the day when the arrival of a client in a wheelchair gives no more cause for concern than the arrival of a client without a wheelchair, and doesn't necessitate major upheavals, extra expenditure, specialized equipment, or special staff.

There are many tour operators, transport operators, and hoteliers who will make every effort to accommodate clients with disabilities. But a significant proportion of them—in particular the tour and transport operators—insist on advance warning. And there are many disabled travelers who prefer to make their requests for facilities or assistance in writing, and who prefer not to arrive unannounced.

If you do get involved in outlining your disability and asking for help, perhaps in boarding the bus or carrying your luggage, or for a high bed or accessible bathroom, then keep it brief, but include all relevant facts and measurements—typed or in very clear handwriting. In return, you should expect promises of facilities or assistance in writing, so that you can wave the evidence in front of the operator's nose when he or she denies all knowledge of the request. If you do make arrangements over the phone, be sure to get the employee's name and position, and make a note of the time, date, and content of your conversation.

PERMITS AND KEYS

The *Travel Notes* for each country mention the validity of US or Canadian parking permits, as well as the availability of temporary permits, registration cards for Dial-a-Ride and similar adapted transport systems, procedures or vouchers for obtaining fare concessions on public transit, and keys for adapted rest rooms. These can often be sorted out in person, at the start of your vacation, but some might view this as a waste of valuable sunbathing or sightseeing hours, and it may be necessary to make applications in advance; if so, allow several weeks for an exchange of letters—initial inquiry (sometimes two, if unsure of the correct address), dispatch of application form, return of completed form, processing of permit, and more.

DOCUMENTS FOR GUIDE DOGS

Travelers with guide dogs have to cut through more red tape than most when traveling outside North America, but the value of obtaining the correct documents cannot be overstated. They are essential if foreign Departments of Agriculture are to be satisfied and entry regulations met, but will also come in handy whenever customs officials, airline staff, hotel management, or restaurant owners appear to have problems with accepting your animal as a *guide*, as essential as a wheelchair to someone who cannot walk, rather than as a pet. Procedures for traveling to different countries vary, and of course some are out of bounds because of quarantine regulations (eg Britain, and several Caribbean destinations with British colonial pasts, including Antigua, Barbados, Grenada, Jamaica, St. Lucia, and Trinidad and Tobago); the tourism offices should be able to tell you how to proceed. Sometimes you must contact the agriculture department in the destination country and obtain a form, sometimes all the official stamps can be obtained in the US or Canada; you'll have to pay a fee, usually small; and you'll have to visit the vet and obtain an International Animal Health Certificate, usually within a certain period before you depart.

As well as the official documentation, two blind travelers writing in the *Abilities* magazine (Fall 1991; see Canada *Travel Notes*), Marie Laporte-Stark and Chris Stark, suggest that it's a good idea to draw up a letter, preferably with an offical stamp or on government letterheaded paper, explaining the function of your guide dog in the language of the country you will be visiting. If you cannot manage this, make back-to-back copies of guide dog information that comes with the entry permit. Marie and Chris also recommend that you insist that reference to your guide dog appears on *all* travel documents that contain your name, including booking forms and travel insurance papers—this means that if there are any problems, for example with hotels accepting your dog, you can prove that the presence of the guide dog was known and accepted at the time of booking your vacation.

Getting There by Air

Despite the length of the section below, and the apparent complications, flying is overall one of the best organized means of transport for disabled travelers. Certainly, airports and airlines have put more action into provision of facilities than most land transportation operators.

AIRLINES

For independent travelers, **choosing an airline** is usually all about comparing prices and selecting a convenient flight, with minimum number of stopovers, preferably from a nearby airport. On the face of it, independent travelers with disabilities can do the same: the air travel industry would have us believe that procedures and facilities for transporting disabled passengers are well worked out and cope smoothly with any eventuality. In fact, there are differences in approach and facilities that are worth considering along with the fare. Unfortunately, it is extremely difficult to ascertain exactly what each airline does offer the traveler with a disability—few airlines bother to produce comprehensive and regularly updated disabled passenger information brochures, and staff at reservations offices, airport desks, and customer services departments frequently give imprecise and conflicting answers regarding facilities and procedures.

During the research for the British edition of this book, a simple questionnaire was sent out to around forty airlines. Only twelve (*Aer Lingus, Aeroflot, Air Canada, Air New Zealand, Air Malta, Canadian Airlines, El Al, Japan Airlines, Olympic Airways, SAS, Thai Airways, Virgin*) responded in full to every question; five (*Cathay Pacific, KLM, Lufthansa, Qantas, Swissair*) dispatched their passenger care leaflets, only one of which (*Qantas' Travel Care* series—clear and up to date) gave sufficient information; over fifty percent of airlines, including *Air France, Air India, Alitalia, American Airlines, British Airways, Iberia, Singapore Airlines* and many more, did not bother to reply. The Gulf airlines, *Emirates* and *Gulf Air*, made brave attempts to respond but their head offices were busy with more pressing matters; *Emirates* staff at the airport desk were particularly helpful and filled in the gaps.

During updating and research for this edition, full responses were obtained from the following North American airlines: *Air Canada, Canadian Delta, Northwest, United,* and *Continental*.

Some of the airlines that ignored the questionnaires make all the usual arrangements for disabled passengers—indeed, *British Airways'* facilities and service are praised throughout this book—but too many of their front-line staff, dealing directly with the general public, are ignorant of both facilities and procedures for passengers with disabilities, and shrug off questions with impatience.

That said, most major airlines have their act together as far as passenger **handling at the airport** is concerned, provided that they are given instructions at the time of reservation. If you don't have absolute faith in your travel agent, phone the airline desk at the airport a few days before departure and ensure that your details have been entered on the computer.

First-time travelers, or travelers new to a particular airline or airport, may want more advance information than that provided in the passenger information leaflets, many of which are out of date and lacking in detail. If this is the case, and you are concerned about parking arrangements, being met off your train, being allowed to remain in your own chair, under your own steam, as far as the aircraft door, or about boarding procedures (wheeled straight on, lifted manually, or carried aloft on a lifting vehicle?) then quiz the airline, and the airport if necessary, when booking.

These details would be swiftly established, or even swept aside, if every airport and airline provided flawless printed information and if all airport and airline staff relaxed and treated each individual as a customer with a mind of his/her own rather than an object to be molded by company policy.

THE BASICS: SEATING ARRANGEMENTS AND ACCESS TO REST ROOMS

Once airborne, most disabled passengers have two major concerns: **seating and rest room facilities**. Although several airlines provide onboard wheelchairs and some designate one or two rest rooms as accessible, visits to the rest room still require superhuman contortions and economy seating is usually nothing less than an endurance test—we are a long way off flying in aircraft that have been designed for *independent* travel by disabled passengers.

As Stephen Hunt says, "Comfort in the air is the biggest pain of all. On long-haul flights I try to travel out of season and/or on slack days, when I can lie down on empty seats. On charters, many with bolted, upright seats, I rest forward on the meal table. I'm carried onto planes that have steps. There are no seats specially for disabled people. Even the seats by the exits have to be taken by non-disabled. Using the plane toilet with a walking frame is like doing aerobics in a closet, which is why I wear a leg-bag. All I'm asking for is a decent seat and a dignified pee—for every economy class to have one special reclining seat and one reasonable rest room."

Comfortable seats and adequate legroom, especially on long-haul flights, are unlikely in economy class. No airline has a policy of upgrading a disabled passenger if there is space in business or first class and if disability (an unbendable leg, for example) and build will make life unpleasant in economy seats. *Air Canada* showed a flexible approach and arranged this for Steve Veness (p.69), and on *Virgin* charter flights, seats with greater angle of recline can be purchased for a small supplement; on *Thai Airways* flights the captain may sanction moving a severely disabled passenger to first class if there's room.

But, in general, aircraft seating leaves much to be desired: one contributor, only five feet tall, with unbendable legs, was given a front seat on a 767 and had to remove her shoes in order to wedge herself into the seat. A significant number of disabled travelers, including many wheelchair users and many who travel with guide dogs, find that a bulkhead seat is the only one that allows sufficient space for comfort, so it is important to select an airline that gives **advance seat allocation**. Strangely, there is no reference to this in the Air Carrier Access Act (ACAA; see USA *Travel Notes*), only guidelines on the circumstances under which a disabled passenger may be denied certain seats. Although in theory most major airlines will preassign seats, there is great variation regarding when this can be done: some will only allocate seats at check-in, some at the time of reservation (eg *Air Canada*), and some specify a certain period (up to 60 days prior to departure for *Delta*; up to 90 days for *Northwest*). We have had some reports of difficulties with two US airlines:

When Stephen Fuller (see p.37) flew with *Continental* to Hawaii he was told that they wouldn't preassign seats, and was also boarded last. The plane was over an hour late departing, and the airline then blamed Stephen for the delay. The situation may have improved: when asked in 1992 about seat preassignment *Continental* said, "Advance seats are available for all customers on all flights, however advanced seats are limited. Continental does not have specific seat allocation for disabled customers, however every attempt will be made to assign a specific seat when requested."

Angela Deakin flew *USAir* on all her internal flights during a vacation in the USA in August 1989. This is her report: "We had problems with USAir. They issued boarding cards with seat numbers but changed the seats around by the time we reached the aircraft. This is particularly upsetting for disabled passengers who need someone with them. Our three seats together in non-smoking became three separated seats in the smoking section on two of the flights we undertook. For the first time in our lives, Robin and I stood in the middle of a crowded aircraft, having a blazing row with the cabin crew. They saw no reason why our physically disabled, blind, and non-speaking child could not manage among total strangers in the smoking section. Eventually, we got three seats as designated on the boarding cards, but by this time the plane was late and no one was happy." *USAir* did not respond to our inquiries so we are unable to comment on their procedures in 1992.

The policy of refusing to allow disabled passengers to sit in comfort by **emergency exits** has not been satisfactorily explained—we all know about the FAA Exit Row Seating rule, but why not send one able-bodied passenger down first to handle the bottom of the emergency chute, and then throw the disabled passenger down the chute, clearing the exit area for other passengers? The familiar cry, "It's against safety regulations" has been used too often to deny disabled passengers the seats they want, as well as restricting them in other ways. This is a symptom of the air travel industry's greatest problem—**inflexibility**. The mindless enforcement of regulations, as well as the abuse and incorrect application of regulations, is reported at all levels, from baggage handler to Captain. One well-traveled paraplegic, Nic Fleming, puts it this way:

"In my experience there is only one serious problem for disabled travelers, and that is bureaucrats and officials. Individuals all over the world seem to be almost universally kind, and the existence of kind people means that no physical obstacle is actually an obstacle at all. It may be a nuisance, but it can always be overcome. By contrast, the bureaucrat who says 'You can't do that. It's against company policy/the law/fire regulations. It's more than my job's worth' can be an insuperable barrier.

"For example, I was told, 'You can't go in there alone, Sir, you are a security risk' by an armed guard at the entrance to the *BA* departure lounge at J.F. Kennedy airport, New York (1990). I demanded to be let in, and all the other passengers standing in line supported me, refusing to go past me. The guard called two other armed guards by radio and put his foot in front of my wheel. I rolled over his foot (not seeing it) just as the manager arrived. He seemed nonplussed that anyone in a wheelchair should travel unescorted. *BA* subsequently promised to change practices at the terminal.

"Arriving in Sydney (1981), I was informed by the immigration authorities that I would need a full medical examination before I could leave the arrivals area and meet the friends waiting for me. I asked if the rule would apply if I could walk, and said that I had entered Australia several times previously without this indignity and delay. The officer pointed to the door of the lounge and said if I could walk through it I did not need a medical. I put on my braces, wheeled up to the door, walked through it, pulled the chair after me, and sat back in the chair. Bureaucracy satisfied.

"Brussels airport has a wonderful system: disabled passengers are directed to a special service desk, where you find a remote telephone. You dial a distant office and say which flight you want to catch. You then wait indefinitely until someone feels that they have time to come and help you. This is typical of bureaucratic systems that devise 'special services for the benefit of our disabled customers', and then put you firmly in the slow track. Officials never seem to expect that wheelchair passengers have to meet deadlines and get jobs done on time like everybody else.

"Of course, these are the exceptions, and most airlines and airports provide a magnificent service, but a reminder of the most perfect welcoming phrase won't hurt: 'Hi, Sir, do you need any help, or would you like to go through to the aircraft on your own?' Then everything falls into place—honor is satisfied, efficiency maximized, and the airline saves money."

A number of airlines carry **aisle wheelchairs**, and the majority of aircraft have some seats with movable armrests to ease the transfer from aisle chair to aisle seat. All US airlines are required to provide an on-board wheelchair on aircraft with more than 60 seats if there is an accessible lavatory or if a passenger provides advance notice that he or she can use an inaccessible lavatory but needs an on-board chair to reach it (see USA *Travel Notes*). Many other airlines either carry aisle chairs as standard procedure or will provide one on request; the national airlines that do are mentioned in the *Travel Notes*, under "Getting There."

The provision of aisle wheelchairs is only half a solution if none of the **rest rooms** are enlarged to allow some room to maneuver inside; squeezing through the doorway is one thing, transferring to the toilet seat quite another. Some airlines, including *Air Canada*, *Canadian*, *United*, retrofitted *Delta* aircraft, and *Aer Lingus*, provide screens so the rest room can be used with the door open; on *Air Canada*'s 767, 727, and A320 aircraft at least one rest room has this facility as well as fold-down or fixed grab-rail, low-level lever door-handles, and a switch to turn the light on without closing the door. *Air New Zealand* cabin crew have been known to take disabled passengers to more spacious first-class rest rooms, and were ready to offer assistance to Kent Kloepping on his recent trip (p.484).

The enactment of the ACAA should result in improvements in this area on US airlines over the next few years (see USA *Travel Notes*). Meanwhile, faced with less than adequate access to rest rooms, most travelers with mobility-related disabilities improvise. Some manage with assistance from a companion; others stagger down the aisle with the aid of braces or leaning on seat backs or food carts; those who must remain in their seats survive with some preparation—limiting liquid intake, using medication, indwelling catheter, protective pads, condoms and drainage bags. In spite of the inconveniences, most travelers report that their initial fears concerning this aspect of flying were unfounded or exaggerated—after the flight, the excitement of arriving in a new country, or seeing family or old friends, takes over.

OTHER CONSIDERATIONS

Other factors that might influence the choice of airline include the requirement to fill out medical forms, the carriage of power-chairs, dialysis equipment, and guide dogs, the acceptance of groups of disabled passengers and unaccompanied disabled passengers, and general attitudes among airline staff.

Most disabled travelers should be able to fly without completing complicated **medical forms**: unless there is a special health problem or special equipment is required (such as respirator or stretcher) the airline needs handling advice, not medical details (see *Red Tape*, p.570). US airlines (since the enforcement of the ACAA; see USA *Travel Notes*), Aer Lingus, Air New Zealand, British Airways, Lufthansa, SAS, Virgin, and Olympic Airways are reported to have a particularly relaxed attitude.

But some airlines insist on medical notes and evidence of fitness to travel. *Canadian Airlines*, for example, asks for a physician's letter to certify fitness to travel and capability of self-care if traveling alone. *Air Canada* asks passengers with disabilities to complete a medical form; in some instances this may lead to a request for clearance from the traveler's physician. When making a reservation with *Thai Airways*, a disabled passenger is invited to complete a medical form which is then forwarded to the "Sales Procedure Department" whose job it is to consider whether or not the passenger will be allowed to board the plane! Medical forms are issued by other airlines, and the best way around this is to use a *FREMEC* card (p.570).

Carriage of power-chairs, dialysis equipment, and guide dogs is usually free, and guide dogs can accompany passengers in the cabin. The potential problem with power-chairs is the size of the hold: on a 737, for example, it is 42in deep and the door is only 41in high; large chairs have to be tipped, so batteries can be removed or tightly secured to the chair; small chairs may be loaded upright and stowed without removing the batteries. The dry-cell battery must be disconnected, the terminals insulated; the wet-cell battery must be drained of acid.

Most airlines will carry power-chairs (wet- or dry-cell). There are clear guidelines for US airlines under the ACAA (see USA *Travel Notes*). *Air Canada* and *Canadian Airlines* have special containers for wet-cell batteries; on wide-body planes *Canadian* gives passengers the option of having the terminals disconnected and taped, and the caps replaced with special spill-proof ones— the battery can then remain in the chair and the chair can be loaded and kept upright in the hold. Remember that if you are traveling in a power-chair you'll need to arrive at the airport in plenty of time to allow for disassembly and packaging of your chair (see below, p.578).

It's advisable to ask the airline for written notification of their procedures for carriage of **guide dogs**, as these vary and airline employees encountered at the airport and on the plane may not be aware of them. As with the provision of general information for passengers with disabilities, this is an area where confusion and ignorance reign. If you can provide written evidence of the identification required, the procedure for seating your guide dog, whether or not the animal is required to wear a muzzle, and so forth, there will be no arguments, unnecessary delays, or other aggravations on your day of departure.

Several carriers can make provision for passengers needing **oxygen** during their flight, but you must give advance warning, usually at least 48 hours; arrangements for carrying your own oxygen and respiratory equipment in the hold must also be made ahead of time as there may be special packaging procedures to follow for apparatus powered by wet-cell batteries. Most airlines insist that only their own oxygen supply is used; some (eg *Continental*) do not accept passengers requiring oxygen. *Air Canada* can supply Medipaks of oxygen at a small charge but these must be requested at least 72 hours in advance. *Canadian Airlines* also makes a nominal charge for oxygen at flow rates of 2 or 4 liters per minute; passengers with their own oxygen supply may fly on *Canadian*'s Boeing 737 aircraft if the supply is gaseous, the container is not larger than 22 inches, and the flow rate is not greater than 4 liters per minute. Oxygen is available on all *Northwest* flights with 48 hours' notice, plus a medical certificate outlining flow rate, and whether mask or nose cannula is required. *Delta* supplies oxygen via the Puritan Bennett Aero Med which has an adjustable flow rate of between 2 and 8 liters per minute; the charge is $50 per flight coupon. *United* supplies therapeutic oxygen using different assemblies according to the flow rate required; reservoir masks are available on special order.

Airlines with considerable experience of carrying **groups of disabled passengers** include *Air*

New Zealand (used by several US travel agents which specializes in disabled travel) and *Aer Lingus* (which operates many charters to Lourdes). *Air Canada* offers special arrangements and fares to teams of disabled athletes and similar groups. *El Al* places no limit on the number of disabled passengers taken aboard any one flight. *Air India* does not accept groups of disabled people.

In general, airlines insist that passengers who cannot attend to their personal needs travel with **a companion**. Airlines offering a discount to companions of disabled passengers who are unable to travel alone include *Air Canada* (for travel within North America), *Canadian Airlines* (within Canada, and to and from the USA), and *America West*. Some carriers, including *Alitalia*, *Iberia*, and *Japan Airlines*, do not accept unaccompanied disabled passengers (*Iberia* does not, according to a couple of contributors, cope smoothly with wheelchair users). No one expects cabin crew to act as nurses, but if the rest rooms were fully accessible and the aisles wide enough to pass along on crutches, braces, or the on-board wheelchair, many passengers who do not normally need help to visit the rest room would be able to travel alone. Besides, many travelers make alternative arrangements on aircraft with inaccessible rest rooms, and are therefore able to travel without assistance.

The ACAA does not adequately deal with the question of when to interfere with a traveler's assertion that he or she can travel alone. It partially addresses this issue from the point of view of safety and emergency procedures, by stating that a carrier may only require a passenger to be accompanied under certain circumstances (see USA *Travel Notes*), and if these run contrary to the passenger's assurances that he or she can travel alone, the carrier cannot charge for the transportation of the attendant, though the carrier may designate an individual to act as the attendant—purely to assist in evacuation, not to help with personal needs such as getting to the rest rooms or emptying a bag.

Problems with the **transportation of wheelchairs** are probably statistically rare but occur too often in view of the fact that most wheelchair users see their chairs as an extension of their bodies, not just a piece of luggage (pp.385, 578); in fact, damage to wheelchairs is the most frequent problem reported to *TIDE* (see USA *Travel Notes*) by disabled air travelers. Apart from the role of the baggage handlers, mentioned

earlier, the airline has a responsibility to ensure that such a vital piece of equipment, once separated from its owner, is loaded and labeled correctly, transferred smoothly from one plane to another en route, deposited at the same destination as the owner, and reassembled correctly. One contributor, making a connection at Belgrade, insisted on locating his chair and found it abandoned in the corner of a lounge, despite all assurances from cabin crew that it had already been transferred to the new aircraft. The same traveler has arrived in Darwin with his wheelchair in Sydney, and in Glasgow with his chair in Edinburgh.

Users of power-chairs experience problems with ramp services personnel who fail to hook up their batteries correctly. Airlines argue that there are so many sophisticated models on the market it's impossible to keep their employees trained to deal with all of them, but this is not really valid—the basics are the same for most chairs, and with proper training the disassembly/packing/reassembly processes should be quick and uncomplicated; this was demonstrated at the 7th Access to the Skies Conference, in 1992, when Michael Collins showed a video of his own chair being disassembled and packaged for transport.

The majority of contributors, using a variety of airlines, report courteous and attentive **service from airline staff**, at the check-in counter, in the terminal, and on board the aircraft. Whether by standard training procedures or special training in communication (including sign language, direct eye contact, good enunciation) and lifting techniques, many airlines seem to be producing the right results with most of their staff, and the check-in clerk who insists on speaking to the wheelchair pusher rather than the occupant, the flight attendant who refuses to ensure that a disabled passenger is seated in his or her preassigned seat, the ramp staff who break the wires while reassembling a power-chair, or the passenger rep who ignores a disabled man struggling to transfer from airport wheelchair to his own chair (p.78), though annoying, are rare exceptions.

A few North American airlines have made a point of stressing their **training initatives and customer service** regarding handling of disabled passengers. *Northwest Airlines* pronounced 1992 "Year of the Customer/Passenger" and their president said, "We value the business of our disabled customers and want to be their airline of preference. We are strongly committed to

nvenient access to our aircraft for all people
th disabilities." At the time of writing this
rline was producing a brochure detailing all its
ervices to disabled passengers. *America West* is
oud to have conducted a Sensitivity Program for
ustomer service personnel two years before the
w required such training. *Delta* took action in
992 with their Passenger Service Initiative.
nited's philosophy is simple, and ideal if it is
anslated into action: "not to make assumptions
s to what services a disabled traveler needs but
ather to ask if assistance is needed and then
nform what assistance United is able to
rovide." *Air Canada*, *Canadian*, *Northwest*, and
Continental say that all public contact staff
eceive appropriate training.

It's cheering to hear many reports of **cabin
crew** responding to the needs of individual travelers, by shuffling passengers about, allocating
better seats, making use of spare seats, and,
when the need arose, carrying a disabled passenger to the rest room—good cabin crew make the
best of a bad job in aircraft that are still essentially designed to pack in the maximum number of
slim, short, agile passengers.

The way forward must be to **build on this
flexibility**, extending it to more check-in and
ground staff so that disabled passengers are
given a choice and are in control from the moment
they enter the terminal, and then to see acceptance of unaccompanied disabled travelers and
groups by every airline; to make training in
communication with sight-, hearing-, or speech-
impaired passengers more widespread, and to
improve and update all passenger information
leaflets.

AIRPORTS

Three factors should influence your choice of
departure airport: the journey to and from the
airport, which should be as brief and as relaxing
as possible; facilities at the airport; and the
airline you are to fly with. Responsibility for
handling of disabled passengers is usually with
the airline (or their customer service agent), so
ask what the arrangements are when booking.

PARKING AND ACCOMMODATION

If you drive yourself, parking charges and accessibility of courtesy vehicles from long-term parking
lot to terminal building will be important considerations. **Flying from a local airport** has several
advantages: the journey to the airport will proba-

bly be short and simple; there will be fewer
people and a less frenetic atmosphere at the
airport; parking lots tend to be closer to the terminal buildings, and parking charges are not
astronomical.

Your vacation package, however, may leave
you with no choice but to fly from an airport a
long way from home. If this is the case, and even
though it eats into your vacation, it may be worth
considering finding **accommodation near the
airport** for the night before you fly. There is
scant attention paid to listing any accessible
accommodation, let alone a selection to cover all
budgets, in the airport information publications.
You can consult local tourism information offices
as well as the directories of some hotel chains
and publications such as *The Wheelchair Traveler*
(see USA and Canada *Travel Notes*). If you plan
to leave your car at the hotel, find out about
transport from hotel to airport.

FACILITIES

Apart from accessible public transportation
connections and designated, reasonably priced
parking near the terminal buildings (or courtesy
buses on which wheelchair accessibility is a
standard feature), **facilities** at airports should, in
an ideal world, include the following: ramps,
walkways, and elevators for easy movement
within the terminal and for access from train
platforms or bus stops; textured surfaces, guide
rails, and clear signs; a good supply of
wheelchairs or electric carts; lowered telephones
(preferably fitted with amplifiers); clear
announcements, both visible and audible;
induction loop audio points; fully accessible rest
rooms, bars, restaurants, and shops; lowered
counters at bank, check-in, and post office;
adequate methods of boarding the aircraft.

Staff should be well trained to deal with all
possible situations involving disabled passengers, particularly in the field of communicating;
some should be trained in the use of sign
language; anyone who has to lift disabled
passengers must be proficient. Last but not least,
easily obtained, reliable information for disabled
passengers—including details of a range of
accessible accommodation near the airport—
should be available.

In reality, airports have many but not all of
these facilities. It's impossible to describe facilities at even the major US and Canadian airports in
the space available here, but a copy of **Access**

Travel: Airports (free from Consumer Information Center, Pueblo, CO 81009) should provide most of the information needed, and *SATH News* (see *Books*) keeps travelers up to date with new developments and facilities. Further details can be obtained by calling the airport direct or by consulting passenger information material (some airports, Edmonton and Seattle-Tacoma for example, have separate access guides for disabled travelers). The ADA and Canada's five-year National Strategy (see *Travel Notes*) should help break down some of the remaining barriers, and there is at least a growing awareness of the problems caused by communications barriers which in the past have been eclipsed by the more obvious physical impediments.

On the whole, facilities and procedures for handling disabled air passengers are not bad; with due attention to the rules of giving advance warning and allowing plenty of time on the day, you should have a smooth passage—described by some contributors as "VIP treatment"—from check-in to boarding.

Areas that need attention include staff training, the supply and effective communication of accurate information, and treatment of wheelchairs by baggage handlers.

PASSENGER RESPONSIBILITIES

Passengers can make life easier for airport staff by turning up on time: delays in departure of aircraft caused by late arrivals at the boarding gate are increasing, and since it is usually more convenient (and better for the disabled person) to board disabled passengers first, it is unhelpful to arrive at the last minute. As a rough guide, you should arrive between one and two hours before departure, allowing extra time if it's an international flight. A cautionary tale from Bjo Ashwill, who traveled with *Mobility International USA* to Europe from Eugene, Oregon, in 1988:

"I planned my trip with an eye for all the possible disasters that could happen. As a result, it took several relatives and a neighbor to get my suitcases shut. Mistake number one. Someone should have forced me to shut and carry it myself. I would have jettisoned two thirds of it right then, rather than spend the next four weeks wishing I had. The library of books I might wish to read was unnecessary. I never used the emergency sewing kit. The spare wheelchair electronics board was a real nuisance. So, you see, I was

ready. I had read all the travel books. I ha[d] ordered my special adaptor for the batte[ry] recharger for my wheelchair (100 and som[e] dollars). I had extra plugs, extra parts, and th[e] special transformer that was sent up fro[m] California seconds before I had to leave. I wa[s] ready! The first exciting event, which of course I had not planned for, was missing my plane. [I] neglected to understand the importance of leav[ing] more time to board the plane because I'm in [a] power wheelchair. In addition, it was an interna[t]ional flight. So, I went home and took a nap."

Bjo's experience also illustrates the perils o[f] thinking you can plan for every eventuality: thi[s] applies to all aspects of travel of course, bu[t] long-haul flights can be a particularly dauntin[g] prospect for travelers with disabilities, and it'[s] important to realize that although a bit of prepar[-] ation and research is necessary in order t[o] choose a suitable airline and a convenient route after that you might as well relax and go with th[e] flow—there's nothing you can do to avoi[d] delays, unscheduled stop-overs, or mishaps with luggage, all of which happened on Bjo's trip:

"The second exciting event occurred afte[r] getting on my flight. It had several unexpected stop-overs, one overnight in London, England. [I] loved that. Of course, all I got to see was inside the airport, which looked like all the other airports, and the inside of an ambulance (yes! a[n] ambulance!—after all, I am physically disabled and therefore could need medical care and they were taking no chances). I would have taken offense at this except I'd already been awake for many many hours and was unable to produce that much energy, and, secondly, they were so charmingly British that I forgave them on the spot. They tucked me into the *Sheraton Hotel*, fed me, and woke me early the next morning to finish my trip to Germany. I was also given the jolting news that the *Pan Am* people had managed to destroy my wheelchair somewhere over the Atlantic Ocean.

"I arrived in Germany and borrowed a manual chair, not such a good idea since I have rheumatoid arthritis and hurt too much trying to propel myself around. So the group I was traveling with helped me rent a power wheelchair. Its joystick set-up, size, and speed were different from what I was used to, it would die in the middle of heavy traffic at an intersection, it stuck me in an elevator, and it ran over many people's toes, but there I was, in Germany, the Rhineland wine country, the dream of a lifetime, and I was thrilled."

Getting There by Land and Sea

If you're not flying to your destination, you'll be traveling on trains, buses, or in your own vehicle; and maybe taking a ferry, too. Longer journeys—to Europe or Asia, for example—may involve a combination of several modes of transport; most possibilities are covered in this section, in the *Travel Notes* following each country section, and in *Getting Around* (p.585).

CARS, TRAINS, AND BUSES

Perhaps the least traumatic mode of transport of all is your own **car or RV**: accessible, comfortable, and adapted to suit you; few worries about coping with heavy luggage; room for portable aids and equipment that will make life easier at your destination or save the day when an accessible rest room cannot be found; freedom to fix your own schedule and the means to get off the beaten track.

An increasing number of rest areas or service stations cater to disabled travelers, with adapted rest rooms, flat access, room to maneuver in shops and cafeterias, and low-level telephones. A few state tourism offices supply information on the availability of these facilities along major routes by marking road maps with the wheelchair symbol. A less helpful trend is the increase in self-service gas stations: although Conoco has initiated moves to provide full service for disabled customers in Colorado, and the state of California has changed its laws to require most service stations to do the same, these are exceptions; it may be a good idea to carry a "Help" pennant if traveling alone.

Possible difficulties include mechanical breakdown and tiredness. **Touring** (see p.512) usually involves covering very long distances, so driver fatigue is not unlikely. To avoid it, don't be too ambitious, make frequent stops, and, if possible, share the driving. Take advice from the *AAA* or *CAA* on driving—route planning, repair and recovery service, what spares to carry, and so on (see Travel, Tours, and Cruises *Travel Notes*).

Those who are unable to walk short distances or manage a few steps will require boarding assistance if they are to travel by **train**, and if stopping at intermediate stations this may mean traveling with a companion who can help. Facilities on *Amtrak* and *VIA Rail* networks are described in the USA and Canada *Travel Notes*.

If you can get through the planning stage, if the promised assistance materializes, and if you are traveling on routes served by trains with accessible rest rooms—best of all, if you have some degree of mobility—train travel can be a relaxing way to see the countryside, and there are many reasonably priced passes and "rover" tickets for travelers on a tight budget. *Amtrak* gives discounts to disabled passengers, and *VIA Rail* offers two-for-one fares for disabled passengers who must travel with an escort.

If planning to **fly first and then explore by train**, you'll generally find that any assistance with getting on and off trains or transferring between platforms, as well as wheelchair service at stations, must be arranged after arrival in the country—sometimes by phoning a helpline in advance of your train trip, sometimes by simply turning up early at the station of departure and arranging things from there, sometimes by contacting the head office of the national railroad. As a rule, nothing can be arranged in North America, and staff in the US or Canadian offices of the rail networks seem to hold little information on the subject of facilities for disabled travelers.

Traveling by **intercity bus or charter bus** in both the USA and Canada is tricky for wheelchair users and those who have difficulty with steps. This situation is unlikely to change for several years as operators in the US fight for more time to make their vehicles accessible, and those in Canada are only in the planning and experimental stages of introducing features such as hydraulic lifts, funded in part by the government under its National Strategy for the Integration of Persons with Disabilities (see USA and Canada *Travel Notes*). In the meantime, the ADA at least ensures that passengers with disabilities using inaccessible vehicles are given assistance by the operator.

A few charter bus companies offer wheelchair-accessible vehicles for rental to groups. These provide a useful service, but do nothing to meet the needs of disabled individuals who want to join **mainstream escorted bus tours**. Some tour operators carry a folding chair on their buses, so that passengers with limited walking powers can reach all the sights on the itinerary, but such passengers must be accompanied. Most drivers and guides on bus tours with tight schedules stick rigidly to their job descriptions—no indulging in spontaneous wheelchair pushing.

It would be a great step forward to see buses used on these tours equipped with hydraulic lifts and a few tie-down spaces for wheelchair users. This would cause no inconvenience to other passengers, other than a few minutes' delay while the wheelchair passengers were loaded or unloaded at each stopping place. In addition, some information on accessibility of accommodation en route would be simple to acquire. This type of vacation is popular and usually good value for money: it should be opened up to people with disabilities, along with the possibility of traveling independently by intercity bus.

FERRIES

The facilities on *BC Ferries*, *Marine Atlantic* ferries, and the *Alaska Marine Highway System* are briefly described elsewhere in the book (Canada *Travel Notes*, Travel, Tours, and Cruises *Travel Notes*). In general, most **ferry terminals** in the Atlantic provinces and on the west coast of Canada are reasonably wheelchair accessible, and the newer boats are fully accessible, with elevators between vehicle and passenger decks, accessible rest rooms, and a few accessible cabins; older vessels are gradually being retrofitted with at least some adaptations to improve access.

If you book one of the **longer crossings**, and you want to get some rest, you'll need to reserve a cabin—lounge seating, even if reclining, allows only hardened travelers to sleep comfortably (see p.234). Remaining in your wheelchair is unwise if it's a rough crossing—a sudden lurch may send you flying, with or without the brakes on. And if you require an adapted cabin, reserve it well in advance—most ships have no more than a few wheelchair-accessible cabins.

The **cross-Channel and North Sea ferries**, from Britain to continental Europe, are fairly widely used by our contributors. They are mentioned in the relevant *Travel Notes* (France, Belgium, the Netherlands, Scandinavia), but here's an at-a-glance guide. The choice of **accessible ships** is wide, with only a few older vessels lacking facilities for wheelchair passengers:

Brittany Ferries offers good access (except t the movie theaters) and adapted cabins aboar the *Bretagne*, which sails from Plymouth England, to Santander, Spain. *British Channe Island Ferries* provides wheelchair-accessible cabins and rest rooms aboard its ships which leave from Poole. The *Truck Line* ferry from Cherbourg (France) to Poole is also owned b Brittany Ferries, and is reported to be comfortabl and equipped with elevators.

Color Line (formerly *Norway Line* and *Jahre Line*, and now incorporating the *Fred Olsen Line* North Sea routes) operates from Newcastle ir northern England to Bergen/Stavanger in Norwa as well as sailings from Germany, Denmark, and the Netherlands. The *M/S Venus*, which sails from Newcastle, has adapted (three-berth cabins, with handrails around the lavatory and ir the shower. There are accessible rest rooms and elevators to all decks. Storm-sills must be nego tiated to get out on the decks.

North Sea Ferries provides elevators between all decks and specially adapted cabins on its ships. There are wide doors to the cabins and er suite facilities, a drop-down seat in the shower, low-level sink, and alarm button. Three adapted cabins are provided on each of the vessels sailing from Hull to Rotterdam, and one on each of the Hull–Zeebrugge ferries. This company will offer advice on suitable hotels to passengers booking inclusive vacations.

Olau-Line sails two jumbo ferries, *Olau Hollandia* and *Olau Britannia*, between Sheerness, England, and Vlissingen (Flushing), Holland. Each ship has elevators to all decks and a few cabins with no sills or steps, plus specially adapted rest rooms and handrails for visually disabled passengers.

P&O's "Superferries," *Pride of Dover* and *Pride of Calais*, sail the short Dover–Calais route between England and France and are fully accessible, with elevators to all amenities and adapted rest rooms. On the Dover–Boulogne route, the *Pride of Canterbury* and *Pride of Hythe* have accessible rest rooms and an elevator to the passenger deck, but no wheelchair access to the Club Class facilities. The *Pride of Bruges* is the recommended ship for Dover–Zeebrugge (in Belgium) crossings. All ships have accessible rest rooms on the longer England to France Portsmouth–Le Havre/Cherbourg crossings. *P&O's* Belgian partner, *RMT*, operates the Dover–Ostend crossing; *RMT* introduced a new luxury ferry, the

Prince Philip, to this route during 1991, as well as refurbishing the existing fleet. In addition to elevators and accessible rest rooms, there are adapted cabins on the *Nordic Ferry* and *Baltic Ferry* (Felixstowe–Zeebrugge), on the *Pride of Winchester* and *Pride of Cherbourg* (Portsmouth–Cherbourg), and on the *Pride of Le Havre* and *Pride of Hampshire* (Portsmouth–Le Havre). On all vessels the elevator from car deck to main passenger deck is a service elevator, so advance warning is necessary so that crew can be on hand to operate it.

Sally Line's two ships, *Sally Star* and *Sally Sky*, sail from Ramsgate to Dunkirk (both ports fully accessible, with rest rooms) and have the rare distinction of carrying Braille menus in the restaurant. The *Sally Star* has a wheelchair-accessible elevator from car deck to all decks and one accessible rest room on the main deck. Adapted cabins have two-foot-wide doors and a small (two-inch) ridge in the doorway; *en suite* lavatory and shower are accessible. The *Sally Sky* has an elevator only to the main corridor, where all dining facilities are situated, so there is no access to the duty free or the top-deck Sky Bar.

Scandinavian Seaways ships have good general access, and three—the *Dan Anglia*, *Tor Brittania*, and *Tor Scandinavia*—have adapted two- and four-berth cabins (30-inch-wide doors and level entrance) with wheelchair-accessible bathrooms (wheel-in shower with fold-down stool and grab-rails; space and grab-rails around the lavatory). The routes covered are Harwich or Newcastle to Gothenburg or Ejsberg in Sweden, Newcastle–Bergen, Norway, and Harwich–Hamburg, Germany.

Sealink Stena Line's older ferries are only partially accessible but facilities are excellent on the *Fantasia*, *Fiesta*, *Côte d'Azur* (operating between Dover and Calais; accessible rest rooms, elevators, easy access around the ships), and good on the *Koningen Beatrix* (Harwich to The Hook of Holland; adapted cabins and rest rooms, elevators to most decks) and *Stena Normandy* (Southampton–Cherbourg; adapted cabins and rest rooms, elevators to all decks). The *Stena Line* Group offers more route options to Scandinavia than any other operator via its three companies, *Sealink Stena Line*, *Stena Line*, and *Lion Ferry*, and accessible ships on all routes.

There are no wheelchair-accessible rest rooms on board *Hoverspeed*'s Dover–Calais hovercraft, and boarding requires some assistance, but there's a unisex rest room in the departure lounge and the speed of crossing (if not the fares) must be popular with some.

Contributors generally report very good service from ferry company staff, in particular *Sealink* (p.235) and *P&O* (p.185).

In general, **facilities at ports** are reasonably accessible, and there are accessible rest rooms at most terminals. Boarding the ships is more difficult for foot passengers than for those in vehicles (drivers simply ask to be parked next to the elevator), but with advance notice most ferry companies can offer assistance.

Sleeping

Destination and type of vacation, availability of information, and your own requirements and approach to traveling will determine whether you try to locate a suitable **place to stay** before departure or on arrival. Making special requests regarding diet or asking for a room with a refrigerator for the storage of insulin or special foods for travelers with diabetes should in theory present few problems, though even these simple requests have been known to go astray between travel agent and hotel. For those who like to have some idea in advance of the layout of rooms, door width measurements, numbers and size of steps, availability of grab-rails, and so on, the pre-trip planning can involve a considerable degree of frustration.

Of course, you can get around this by **traveling with an organization** such as *Mobility International USA* (see Travel, Tours, and Cruises Travel Notes), run by people who know the ropes and research their trips thoroughly; or (not always foolproof, but generally safe, if expensive) with a travel agent or tour company that specializes in travel for disabled people and has plenty of experience to draw on (see *Directory*, p.597). An increasingly popular option is to take part in home stay or **home exchange**, and *Mobility International* can advise here. *Intervac* (organizers in the US are Lori Horne and Paula Jaffe, 30 Corte San Fernando, Tiburon, CA 94920; in Canada, Suzanne Cassin, 606 Alexander Crescent, NW, Calgary, AL T2M 4T3) is a long-established home exchange service with some disabled members; they give plenty of guidance on setting up an exchange; you can also consult *The Vacation Home Exchange and Hospitality Guide* (see Books, p.591).

Those who want to **travel independently** or with mainstream **tour operators** on standard vacation packages might find the following **guidelines** helpful.

In many countries of the world (particularly in some parts of **Mediterranean Europe**, **Africa**, **Asia**, the **Middle East**, and **Latin America**) disabled travelers have to rely on a combination of good luck, good will, and their own resources in order to make the best of the available (and affordable) accommodation. However, disasters seem remarkably rare; lack of choice, inconvenience, and enforced dependence on others are more common experiences.

In the **USA**, **Canada**, **Australia**, and **New Zealand** it should be possible to find accessible accommodation in all price brackets without booking in advance; some state/provincial tourism offices indicate accessible properties in their brochures; the New Zealand Tourism Office and a few state tourism boards produce separate access guides for visitors with disabilities. In **Europe**, a good deal of information is provided by the *Holiday Care Service* and *RADAR* (see England and Wales *Travel Notes*), but accurate and verified accommodation listings are produced by only a handful of tourist boards, of which the Swedes stand out with their *Holiday Guide for the Disabled* (p.252), available in English and German. The English Tourist Board's involvement with the *Holiday Care Service* and the *Tourism for All* project, and in the USA the enforcement of the ADA, should result in more widespread use of symbols that can be relied on within the next few years.

For **touring** it is usually impractical to reserve ahead; advice on this sort of traveling is given on p.550. For **long-stay vacations** or if visiting popular places in high season, reservation is advisable. The *Travel Notes* sections offer a range of accommodation recommended by our contributors, and list any guides produced by tourist boards or disability organizations in each country. Other sources include disability newsletters and magazines (see *Books*, p.589).

Although most central reservations staff will contact specific hotels direct to establish more precise **access information**, depressingly few directories and publicity leaflets produced by the hotel chains contain more than a few vaguely defined symbols: a wheelchair symbol is not enough, and "facilities for the handicapped" could mean anything from a grab-rail in the bathroom to a fully accessible bedroom and bathroom, with tactile/Braille room number, visual alert, low-level light switches—the complete range of facilities. Criteria for deeming the hotel accessible must be stated if the information is to be of any use.

The provision of information regarding facilities for travelers with **visual or hearing disabilities** is generally inadequate, and these travelers must usually rely on publications such as *The Voice* and *SATH News* (see *Books*, p.591), organizations such as *SHHH* (see p.567), *MIUSA*, *Travelin' Talk* (see USA *Travel Notes*), and other travelers for advice. Deaf traveler Norris Blackburn reports that *SHHH* has been actively involved in bringing the needs of hearing-impaired guests to the attention of lodging owners in the USA, and many motel chains now have amplified telephone handsets; many chains have introduced TDD numbers for reservations, and there is also increasing awareness among staff, especially registration clerks, of the need to face the hearing-impaired guest when speaking, in order to communicate effectively. The ADA should bring about more rapid improvements in communicative accessibility at accommodation establishments in the USA, but worldwide there is much to be done in terms of facilities for deaf and blind travelers.

Marie Laporte-Stark and Chris Stark (see *Red tape*, p.571) recommend that blind people traveling with **guide dogs** insist that the tour operator sends an explanation of the dog and its function in the language of the country concerned *along with the request for a reservation*. Some hotels will refuse, some may make conditions such as demanding that your dog is muzzled, and it's better to reject these at the booking stage than argue the point when you arrive. Marie and Chris also suggest choosing chain hotel properties, so that although there may be no laws governing access in the country you are visiting, the affiliate hotel is bound by rules made in the parent country.

What to do in the event of **fire** is something that worries many people in wheelchairs who find themselves on the fifth floor and may be faced with elevators that are out of order, unaccompanied blind travelers, and hard of hearing travelers who will not be able to hear a fire alarm. Linda Crabtree has designed "Ability Alert" cards, with red flames surrounding the international access symbol, on which guests can write their name, room number, dates of stay, and any assistance needed; the card is handed over to the registration clerk—it is hoped that the clerk will take more notice of the card than an easily forgotten verbal instruction. Distribution addresses for the cards ($6 for a dozen, in the currency of the country you order from) are CMT International, One Springbank Drive, St. Catharines, ON L2S 2K1, Canada; and Travelin' Talk, PO Box 3534, Clarksville, TN 37043-3534, USA.

If there is no reliable published information, and no central reservations office to assist, facilities and accessibility may be **researched** via travel agents or tour operators, or direct from the hotel itself. But this is not always successful and often more trouble than it's worth: travel agents and tour operators may be more concerned with taking a booking than ensuring that the accommodation is suitable; inquiries by letter to hoteliers may take weeks, inquiries by phone will be expensive, and in either case there may be language difficulties.

If you do book through a travel agent, and you need to establish facilities in advance, it's important to **be specific about your requirements**—ask for exact door widths rather than simply, "is the door wide enough for a wheelchair?"—and take your business elsewhere if you are not satisfied with the answers. There is a general reluctance among tour companies to guarantee provision of almost any aspect of a vacation package, so you might find that if you ask a tour operator about accessible accommodation you'll be given advice about the suitability of the hotels used but not guaranteed a particular room. This is true even of the few mainstream tour companies that make concerted efforts to assist disabled clients.

Operators argue that it's extremely rare that hotels are unable to offer the requested room, and they cannot accept responsibility and be liable for compensation in those few cases that do occur. Most travelers are able to take the risk, knowing that they can adapt and manage in any room in a basically accessible hotel; but there will be some, for example lone wheelchair users who need certain accessible features in order to be able to travel alone, who cannot afford to pay for a vacation knowing that there's a chance, however small, that they'll arrive to find the one specially adapted room in the hotel is already occupied. The options for these travelers are: to reduce the chances of disappointment still further by choosing a hotel with more than one accessible room; find another operator which will guarantee a specified room; or travel independently, and make your own arrangements with the hotel—obtain written confirmation of the reservation and room number.

In the end, many travelers find it unnecessary and even detrimental to give advance warning of their disabilities (see pp.343, 550). The best assessment of accessibility is carried out on the spot—calm, confident appraisal of any difficulties usually meets with a positive response from the hotel staff (pp.120, 550) and there is something to be said for the belief that too many requests for information will throw the hotelier into a panic. If your main concern is finding **inexpensive accommodation** this is certainly the best approach: in many countries the hotel chains that provide facilities for disabled guests are in the top half of the price range, and if you are looking at smaller, independent hotels or guesthouses in far-flung places, the problems of determining numbers of steps and doorway widths in advance will probably prove too much.

Although luxury four- and five-star hotels can generally be assumed to be reasonably accessible because they can afford to think big and provide spacious elevators and bathrooms, economy lodgings shouldn't be ruled out, particularly in rural areas where there's plenty of space to build, and single-story accommodation is often accessible with minor modifications and the help of friendly staff. Wherever possible in the *Travel Notes* after each country we have tried to point out some more moderately priced accommodations that are reported to be accessible.

There are a number of lightweight pieces of equipment that can be carried (see p.565) in case of obstacles, and several items that can be provided by the hotel (blocks to raise beds, stool for the shower, extra chair to enable transfer through a narrow doorway, etc) but your most effective weapon is the attitude that anything can be solved with a little improvisation, and if the situation really is unworkable then there's always another motel, B&B, or campground around the corner. Owners of inaccessible properties will often point you toward something more suitable in the area, and local tourist information offices are usually very helpful—you're unlikely to find yourself on the street.

Eating and Drinking

It's possible to find **wheelchair-accessible** eating and drinking places in most parts of the world. Awareness is good in North America, Australia, New Zealand, and some northern/western European and Asian countries; access to restaurants is described in several publications produced by disability organizations or tourist boards, and the wheelchair symbol is used in a few restaurant and pub guides. *McDonald's* and *Burger King* score well for accessible rest rooms.

But choice is still limited in many parts of the world: restaurants are often sited at the bottom of a steep flight of stairs; the small neighborhood restaurant is usually more concerned to pack in the tables than allow space for maneuver of wheelchairs. Tables are too low, bars are too high, and provision of low-level and TDD-equipped phones, or Braille menus, is rare; acceptance of guide dogs is often grudging and even where restaurateurs have the right attitude the atmosphere may be ruined by thoughtless or ignorant diners who do not understand the function of a guide animal.

Where temperatures allow, as in Mediterranean Europe, Africa, Latin America, Asia, and the Middle East, eating and drinking outdoors makes access easier. It doesn't solve the problem of accessible rest rooms, but there may be facilities nearby, in five-star hotels, modern shopping malls, or fast-food restaurants.

Coping with **special diets** should be straightforward if you are prepared for the sort of foods and drinks likely to be encountered; a good guidebook will supply the necessary information. Contributors who report dietary experiences include vegetarian Annie Delin in Poland (p.262), celiac Joy Schwabe in the Commonwealth of Independent States (p.270) and Christine Pantor and her diabetic husband in the USA (p.28). Travelers with diabetes who need to maintain their normal eating routine should make use of a reliable guidebook or the tourist board to find out about eating times in the country they are planning to visit (for example, in Mediterranean countries the evening meal is usually eaten a couple of hours or more later than is customary in North America); they should also inquire about frequency of stops on an escorted tour so that they can plan to carry their own snacks and food supply if necessary; crossing time zones may affect diet and medication regimens.

With advance notice most airlines can satisfy a wide range of dietary requirements, and hotels will usually make at least a token effort to produce food that you can eat, but vegetarians have a hard time in several areas of the world, wherever a meal isn't a meal without meat (West African and Eastern European countries, the CIS, to name a few). In these parts vegetarianism could almost be classed a disability.

Getting Around

Almost all forms of transport are accessible with help, and there are reports throughout this book of traveling in dugouts, helicopters, Jeeps, and cable cars, as well as the more conventional ferry, bus, train, plane, taxicab, and rental car. In some countries the public transportation authorities are improving access to their existing vehicles and designing more accessible rolling stock for the future: a few of the systems singled out for praise by our contributors are the USA's *Amtrak* rail network, Canada's *VIA Rail*, San Francisco's *BART* and *MUNI* buses and trains, Metrorail in Washington DC, *BC Transit's* SeaBus and SkyTrain in Vancouver.

But getting around independently is difficult in many countries for many disabled travelers, including those with visual or hearing impairment. Aircraft, ferries, rental cars, and taxis present the smallest access problems. Aircraft are probably easiest for blind or deaf people. Trains are usually more tricky, and buses a real problem for anyone with limited mobility.

BY AIR

Like international flights, **domestic air travel** involves cramped seating and inaccessible rest rooms, but the shorter journey times make these much more bearable. For exploring large countries, such as Australia or North and South America, flying is the only way to pack a lot of sightseeing into a short vacation. It may be expensive, but there are often special discounts and passes, and a common deal offered by national carriers is a free internal flight included in the price of the international flight.

One potential disadvantage is that there may be free-for-all boarding rather than pre-boarding of disabled passengers. This means that disabled person and companion may be separated, which is disorienting for blind or deaf passengers relying on seeing or hearing escorts, or for a severely disabled person who needs help with eating or communicating with the cabin crew. In addition, a personal safety briefing before other passengers board is impossible. In some countries there are only basic facilities at the smaller, regional airports—with boarding by fork-lift or manual lifting, and perhaps no wheelchair service, accessible rest rooms, or eating place.

BY SEA

Ships and boats vary enormously in accessibility. On the one hand is the modern car ferry (p.580) or hydrofoil (p.441), with facilities such as spacious passenger elevators, ramps over the storm-sills (or no sills at all), adapted rest rooms, space for maneuver in the restaurants and bars, Braille menus, and larger cabins equipped for wheelchair users. Our contributors report a number of journeys by ferry in different parts of the world (including the English Channel, Greek islands, Hong Kong to Macau, and Canada's west coast); most found facilities adequate, and some were impressed with standards of access.

If there is one area where most ferry companies fall down, it is the publication of basic access information, updated each year along with all the other details in their general brochures. The glaring omission in the heap of glossy brochures published by the ferry companies is a *full* description of facilities for disabled passengers: details of cabin layout, height and location of storm-sills, accessibility of bathrooms and lavatories, are often difficult to extract. This is not good enough for travelers wishing to compare prices/concessions, facilities in the cabins, and access on board ship or at the terminals. If they could study the brochures and make an informed decision like everyone else, life would be simple; instead they must consult guides produced by disability organizations, which may or may not be up to date, and for door widths and bed heights they must write letters that are passed from one department to another, or make expensive and often fruitless phone calls,

Next on the scale after the large car ferries are the smaller, inter-island cruisers and catamarans (p.461), with no special adaptations—and no rest rooms—but hefty crewmen to see you aboard, short journey times, and maybe some hot sun to dehydrate you.

And at the other end of the scale there are the small boats—the jet-boats (p.74), sailing boats (p.164), and canoes (p.113)—for which the big problem is boarding or disembarking. If this can be overcome, the disabled person's lack of mobility no longer matters—you can't walk far in a sailboat. Here some lessons could be learned from Sweden and Cornwall, England: the Swedes have installed simple hoists and adapted canoes at a number of locations so that disabled people can enjoy some of their country's lakes; and the *Churchtown Farm* center in Cornwall has a flat-bottomed cruiser at Fowey which allows wheelchair boarding of their canoes and adapted sailing dinghies (p.165).

BY ROAD AND RAIL

Self-drive rental cars offer the disabled traveler the greatest freedom and flexibility but the availability of hand controls on a worldwide basis is not good, and the price of car rental is often prohibitive. Even where hand controls are supposed to be available, promises of adapted cars waiting at the airport are not always honored (pp.23, 69). Smaller companies often say that they are unable to bear the cost of having controls fitted for one client, then removed for the next.

There are a number of ways to avoid inconvenience and disappointment. If you are traveling alone or with a non-driver in the USA, Canada, Australia, Britain, France, or Spain, *Hertz* should be a reliable supplier of cars with hand controls (see USA *Travel Notes*); *Hertz* can supply cars without hand controls in every other country covered in this book apart from Sierra Leone, China, Macau, the Maldives, and Bali. When visiting other countries beyond the reach of your own car, take a set of controls and find a local company which will fit them; disability organizations within the country you are visiting may be able to recommend someone. If accompanied by a driver, forget the hand controls unless you are planning to cover a lot of ground and want to share the driving. The cost per person will be lower for a group, particularly when compared with rail or air fares. You can also save money by shopping around for a local company.

On the whole there have been surprisingly few reports of problems with finding **parking** spaces close to hotels, shops, or sights, and they are confined to big cities such as London, England (seen by many as the worst culprit), or small villages such as the hill villages of Provence in France, where steep winding streets and lack of space leave little scope for building parking lots. Some British contributors found abuse of reserved spaces by able-bodied drivers to be far less common outside the UK.

Although there are few official reciprocal parking arrangements for holders of US or Canadian disabled driver's permits in Europe, such permits may well be recognized in practice or can be used to obtain temporary permits in many countries. There are concessions and reserved spaces in other parts of the world, including Australia, New Zealand, Singapore, and Hong Kong, and where there are no rules laid down the authorities will often show tolerance of visiting disabled drivers who park without causing obstruction.

Taxicabs are used extensively by our contributors both for getting around cities and for longer sightseeing trips. They make an easily accessible alternative to buses and organized bus tours, and cab drivers are generally reported helpful. For travelers with sight or hearing difficulties, and for those who need to set their own pace, this one-to-one service is ideal. In most countries the vehicles used are large, if sometimes ancient, so that there is plenty of room for transferring to the car seat and storing the wheelchair in the trunk. Even the smaller, more colorful variations, such as Bangkok's *tuk-tuks* (p.430) and Manila's jeepneys (p.437), can be used with some assistance.

Adapted taxis are available in various parts of the world, their only failings being expense and the need to reserve well ahead. New Zealand's *Total Mobility* taxi service (p.498) appears to have overcome at least one of these, acting as an affordable alternative to inaccessible buses and trains; advance booking is not always necessary, but advisable at peak times.

The matter of choice is equally important on **trains**. Some well-intentioned and costly alterations have been made to cars without keeping this in mind. So wheelchair passengers are ushered into special compartments (p.452) or told that they must remain in the vestibule or baggage compartment (p.151) instead of wheeling themselves onto the train and electing either to sit in the wheelchair space, with tie-down facility, or to transfer to a seat and stow the folded chair between the seats.

This is not to denigrate the great efforts that have been and are being made by some networks, but rather to encourage the use of adaptations that allow maximum flexibility and avoid putting disabled passengers in the slow lane—if you have to wait for assistance to get from parking lot to ticket office, then wait for a station porter to accompany you via special elevators to the departure platform, and wait again for someone else to help you board the train, it's all time wasted that could be more enjoyably spent settling into your train seat and reading a book or getting to know your fellow passengers.

Boarding is made difficult by narrow doors (often with awkward handles), steps, and a gap between platform and train. These obstacles are being slowly removed in parts of northern Europe, the USA, Canada, and Asia, but with emphasis on the "slowly," and in other countries there is no hint of change. The situation on the newer **subway** networks is slightly better: the trains more often come in flush with the platform and there are wide sliding doors—but even these doorways are sometimes spoiled by a vertical bar placed in the center of the entrance (p.241).

Standard wheelchairs are useless on older trains with narrow corridors or aisles; in these cases it would be helpful if more rail companies supplied narrow, folding chairs (rather like airline aisle chairs) that could be used throughout the journey. On long-distance routes, trains should be equipped with at least one rest room accessible to these chairs.

There are growing attempts to make route planning and **ticket purchase** easier for blind and deaf travelers, with the use of induction loops at ticket office windows, TDD numbers for reservations, and Braille timetables. Tactile markers on the edge of platforms, large lettering on signs, and clear announcements make the journey easier on several overland networks and subway systems—but not nearly enough.

In short, there's much to be done on the world's railroads if we are to achieve independent and spontaneous travel for disabled passengers. Too often, assistance has to be requested in advance and communications fail somewhere along the line, so that the expected porter with wheelchair is not there. In view of the fact that most disabled passengers will need assistance, it seems only fair that some enlightened rail companies, including *Amtrak* (USA), *VIA Rail* (Canada), *British Rail*, *SNCF* (France), and *NS* (Netherlands), give substantial discounts to disabled passengers and/or to those who are unable to travel without a companion.

The sorry state of the world's **buses** is mentioned in many accounts. Usually the cheapest form of city transport, buses cannot be used by the majority of mobility-impaired people because of near-vertical steps at the entrance. Modern vehicles are now designed to be more low slung, with fewer, shallower steps, big bright handrails and easily spotted "stop" buttons, and with front seats "reserved for disabled passengers."

But, except for a growing number of US cities, the adaptations stop short of a wheelchair lift, and even where this is installed the wheelchair passenger may be thwarted by drivers who cannot be bothered to get out and operate it (p.56). The alternative is to shuffle up the steps on your backside (p.109), or ask two strong passengers to lift you aboard—Nic Fleming reports that he has never been refused help in this way, traveling solo on buses in Malta, Israel, Paris, and the USA, as well as on airport buses in a number of countries. In some countries drivers on organized sightseeing tours will cheerfully provide this lifting service. However, Nic says, "Buses are a bore. I probably use them two or three times a year, less if possible."

Neither method of boarding is ideal, and the introduction of special minivans for disabled travelers is not a solution—as with adapted taxis, using them invariably involves booking at least 24 hours (sometimes more) in advance, and they often operate on restricted routes. The answer must lie in designing totally accessible vehicles that do not require a long stop in order to board a wheelchair passenger, and proper training of staff so that *all* passengers are welcomed aboard.

Work and Study, Sports and Activities

Most people with disabilities will be able to participate in a wide range of projects and courses abroad, but research will be necessary in some cases. Sian Williams, for example, almost gave up hope when looking for a college campus that was both accessible and offered an appropriate course (p189). In many countries, access for disabled students is the goal of hard-fought battles, and limited opportunities for education and training contribute to poor levels of employment among the disabled population. For the time being the US leads in accessible educational facilities: if your ambitions lie elsewhere, persistent letter writing is, in Sian's experience, the key.

If you need help with the research, consult *Mobility International USA* and the *MIUSA* publication *A World of Options for the 90s* (see *Books*, p.590). The *Mobility International* program (see Travel, Tours, and Cruises *Travel Notes*) consists of a series of **educational and leisure projects**—cultural, activity-based, language courses, discussions, seminars. These are open to young disabled people (usually 18–30 years, but sometimes no upper age limit) of different nationalities and abilities. The 1992 program included European Creativity Week in Germany, Deaf-Blind Arts and Activity Week in Italy, outdoor adventure activities in the Ardennes (Belgium) for people with learning difficulties, Discover Slovakia week, and the Russian Youth Festival in Moscow.

For **conservation work**, there are several options open, including Operation Raleigh (see p.494) and *Earthwatch* (see p.547). Teams of *Earthwatch* volunteers work on environmental projects all over the world, from preserving sea turtles in the Yucatán peninsula to pinpointing coastal wildlands in need of protection along Britain's coastline. Disabled volunteers have joined projects in the past, and the organizers have a very positive approach to placing people with disabilities, subject to the physical constraints of the project (all volunteers have to produce a medical certificate, giving a doctor's assurance that they can cope physically with the work involved).

Other contributors who traveled with more serious missions than pure vacationing include Charlotte Billington, who joined a *Project Phoenix Trust* Study Tour of Sweden (p.243); Julie Smethurst improved her Spanish on a group vacation (p.281); Joy Schwabe studied art and architecture in Russia, on a five-day tour organized by the Royal Academy, London (p.270); Kate Margrie shared her skills on a Health Education Project in Sierra Leone (p.374); Carolyn

Lucas was funded by the *Winston Churchill Memorial Trust* in her investigation of training and employment of actors with disabilities in the USA (p.4).

Participation in **sports or activity vacations** is a popular way to combine an interest in sport with a love of travel. Ron Cottrell learned to ski in Austria with the *Uphill Ski Club* (p.222), and Terence Wilson joined the crew of a sail training ship (p.520). Information on sports clubs and training for disabled people can be obtained from many disability organizations (extensive listings in the *Resource Directory for the Disabled*), including *National Handicapped Sports* (451 Hungerford Drive, Suite 100, Rockville, MD 20850; ☎301/217-0960) and the *Canadian Wheelchair Sports Association* (212–1600 James Naismith Drive, Gloucester, ON K1B 5N4; ☎613/748-5685). The *Paralyzed Veterans of America* (PVA, Sports and Recreation Department, 801 Eighteenth Street, NW, Washington DC 20006; ☎800/424-8200) has published a free 32-page booklet, *Wheelchair Sports and Recreation*, which lists equipment suppliers, recreation organizations, and recreational and competitive sports opportunities for wheelchair users in the USA. Competition often involves travel to events abroad—see Jack Davidson's account of taking part in the Himalayan Rally (p.508).

John Bignell (p.382), Nic Fleming (pp.550, 574) and Frankie Armstrong (p.531) describe **work-related travel** experiences. It seems that the disabled business traveler remains an unexpected arrival at conferences and on planes. Many operators are put off their stride by a wheelchair user in a hurry to get to a meeting, rather than the more common, passive variety who's on vacation and sits patiently waiting for the airport wheelchair to be delivered to the aircraft door when all the other passengers have long gone.

After Your Trip

At the end of your stay it's important to make the operator aware of both good and bad aspects of his or her services or facilities. If you are delighted with everything, or only one thing, say so. If the grab-rail is in the wrong place, or transfer to the lavatory is awkward, if no stool is provided in the shower, mention this to the hotel management. In addition to giving the operator some sort of feedback, it is helpful to **share access information** with other disabled travelers.

One of the most frequently voiced requests is for reliable information. Only a handful of tourist boards attempt to meet this need; few tourism operators research facilities and incorporate access details in their brochures. There are fact sheets, newsletters, and guides produced by organizations such as *Mobility International USA, Travelin' Talk, SATH, TIDE, Kéroul*, the *Holiday Care Service*, and *RADAR*, but they cannot hope to cover every resort, hotel, campground, tourist attraction, and transport network, and lack of staffing and financial resources prevents them from verifying each entry in their publications. Likewise, this book is no access guide to the world, but a contribution to the information pool.

The best way to update and correct this information is for travelers to report their experiences, to recommend the accessible places and point out the defects in other cases. If you are using a guide or fact sheet and you come across inaccuracies, send your comments to the publisher. Accounts will (we hope) be required for a second edition of *Able to Travel*; meanwhile, any additions, criticisms, or amendments concerning information given in this first edition should be sent to Alison Walsh, c/o The Real Guides, Prentice Hall, 15 Columbus Circle, New York, NY 10023.

If you are unfortunate enough to experience bad service, broken promises, or inadequate facilities, you may feel bound to end your vacation with the tedious process of **making a complaint**. Angela Deakin has the following advice to offer.

"Make a written note of the complaint when disaster strikes—do not wait until you get home. Take photographs (garbage in a swimming pool or a flooded apartment are more convincing six months later if you have a set of photographs). Ensure that a tour rep fills out the appropriate form and signs it; ask for a copy.

"On return, call the company and make a formal complaint; note the name of the person to whom you complain. Then set out clearly in writing the exact nature of your complaint and what you expect the company to do about it. Keep a Xerox of this letter and send it to the highest official in the company—it's easier to start at the top.

"Do not send any evidence with the initial complaint. Study any reply carefully: if the matter is settled immediately, be very thankful—most settlements are reached after many months or even years. More correspondence may result in an amicable settlement, but the threat of legal action is often effective. Complicated claims will require the help of a good lawyer—in any case a lawyer's letter often brings a more realistic response from the company.

"Ask yourself whether or not your claim justifies the possible legal costs, but remember that if you go ahead and win, the settlement should cover these."

Books

The following books, magazines, or newsletters have been recommended at some stage in *Able to Travel*, and only those that relate to world travel—or at least cover several countries—are listed here; country-specific publications are mentioned in the relevant *Travel Notes*.

Probably the largest **collection of guides for disabled travelers**, started in 1979 by medical librarian Irene Shanefield and still growing, exists at the *Jewish Rehabilitation Hospital* (3205 Place Alton Goldbloom, Chomedy, Laval, PQ H7V 1R2, Canada (☎514/688-9550). You can request information on almost any country, and relevant guide(s) will be Xeroxed for a small fee; if treatment such as dialysis is required while traveling,

details of where this can be obtained will be included. The *National Library Service for the Blind and Physically Handicapped* (The Library of Congress, Washington DC 20542) can supply a list of travel books that are available on cassette or in Braille editions.

Abilities (Canada's Lifestyle Magazine for People with Disabilities). This quarterly full-color magazine is professionally put together, and articles are informative, entertaining, and cover a huge range of topics, coming under the following general headings: Perspectives (disability rights); Sports, Activities, Fitness; Education; Travel; Health; Employment; Housing and Technology; Profile; Lifestyle. Subscription rates in summer

1992 were Can$12 for four issues (one year), Can$18 for eight issues (two years).

Access-Able Information is mailed quarterly as an insert in the *SMDI International Newsletter* and contains some travel items. The Society for Muscular Dystrophy Information International is at PO Box 479, Bridgewater, NS B4V 2X6, Canada (☎902/682-3086). Suggested donation to receive the newsletter is Can$25 annually for individuals, but any amount is gratefully received.

Access Travel Airports (Sixth Edition, 1991). Free from the Consumer Information Center, Pueblo, CO 81009. A summary of facilities at airports worldwide and toll-free and TDD numbers for airlines, car rental, and hotel chains.

A Travelers' Handbook for Persons with Epilepsy, from the *International Bureau for Epilepsy* (PO Box 21, 2100 AA Heemstede, The Netherlands; ☎23/339 060).

A World of Options for the 90s: A Guide to International Educational Exchange, Community Service, and Travel for Persons with Disabilities, by Susan Sygall and Cindy Lewis (1990, *Mobility International USA*; $16 non-members, $14 members). Fine writing by people who know all the wrinkles. Covers the world and contains useful sections on: international educational exchange programs (study, volunteer, and/or live with a host family) and community service projects; travel by air, train, bus, car, and cruise ship; listings of specialized tour and travel agents, organizations that assist travelers with disabilities, resource materials, hotels; and some entertaining personal travel experiences.

Directory of Travel Agencies for the Disabled, by Helen Hecker (1992, $19.95; from Twin Peaks Press, PO Box 129, Vancouver, WA 98666-0129, USA; ☎206/694-2462; toll-free orders, ☎800/637-2256, US and Canada; also available on audiocassette). A listing of nearly 400 travel agencies and tour operators that specialize in travel for deaf, blind, developmentally or physically disabled persons. Entries may need checking, as parts are out of date.

Disabled Traveler's International Phrasebook, specialist vocabulary for European travel (£1.50, plus postage, from *RADAR* or the publisher, *Disability Press*, 17 Union Street, Kingston upon Thames KT1 1RP, UK; ☎081/549 6399).

Disability Now (published by *The Spastics Society*, 12 Park Crescent, London W1N 4EQ, UK; ☎071/383-4575; fax 071/436-2601). Monthly news-sheet covering developments on the British scene but also featuring articles on the situation for disabled people in other countries, as well as travel items and an annual "Holidays" guide. Annual subscription (1992 rate) for single copies overseas is £20, payable by check in pounds sterling to *The Spastics Society*, quoting DN.

Handicapped Travel Newsletter (HTN; Editor Dr. Michael Quigley; PO Drawer 269, Athens, TX 75751, USA; ☎903/677-1260, voice and fax). Bimonthly covering all aspects of travel, articles contributed by some highly experienced disabled travelers; particularly hot on cruise ship accessibility. Subscription is $10 annually.

Handi-Travel: A Resource Book for Disabled and Elderly Travelers, by Cinnie Noble (1987, but updated supplements available in 1992). Comprehensive travel guide for people with disabilities affecting mobility, hearing, or sight. Send $12.95 plus $2.50 shipping to Abilities, Box 257, Station P, Toronto, ON M5S 2T1.

Mobility International News (quarterly newsletter of *Mobility International*) is produced in Brussels and available on subscription for £8 per year from MI's London office: 228 Borough High Street, London SE1 1JX, UK (☎071/403 5688). It includes articles by MI members, many on European issues and events, personal experiences, worldwide vacation and travel information, publications reviews, and MI news and comment.

Over the Rainbow (quarterly newsletter of *Mobility International USA*). Includes personal worldwide travel experiences, current travel information, and *MIUSA* news. Individual membership in *MIUSA* is $20 annually; subscription for the newsletter only is $10; add $2 for postage outside the USA. The newsletter is available on four-track cassette.

RADAR publications: (see England and Wales Travel Notes for full list) *Holidays and Travel Abroad* (1992/93 edition £4.50 plus postage). Most of the accommodation information is not verified, and the copious pages of advertising and the contents list stuck somewhere around page 60 make it difficult to use, but most travelers will gain something useful from this guide; there are lots of contact addresses, and it's updated regularly, more countries being added every year (about 100 in the 1991/92 edition).

Real Guides: Forty titles, from bookshops. One of the few mainstream travel guide series to make any attempt to include (brief) advice for disabled travelers.

Resource Directory for the Disabled, by Richard Neil Shrout (1991, $45; Facts on File, Inc., 460 Park Avenue South, New York, NY 10016). Nearly 400 pages, hardbound, divided into four sections—General Resources, and Resources for Mobility Impaired, Visually Impaired, and Hearing Impaired. Each lists Travel Helps; Appliances, Devices, and Aids; Recreation, Sports, and Social Opportunities; Organizations; Associations and Support Groups; Employment/Training Opportunities; Education; Publications—with both US and Canadian entries. There are full descriptions of most entries, a sensible layout makes it easy to use, and it's reasonably priced for its size. Not worth buying for the travel information alone (the Travel Helps sections for mobility-impaired and visually-impaired people are very brief, though there is a big entry for those with hearing disabilities), but there are reams of addresses of useful organizations, companies, and suppliers of every imaginable type of equipment.

SATH News (quarterly newsletter of the *Society for the Advancement of Travel for the Handicapped*; see USA *Travel Notes*). Reports on access developments in the travel industry. Reprints 1987–1992 have been bound. Annual membership $45.

The Complete Directory for People with Disabilities, edited by Leslie Mackenzie (1991, $69.95; Grey House Publishing, Pocket Knife Square, Lakeville, CT 06039; ☎203/435-0868). Nearly 600 pages, paperbound, containing 6000 entries divided into: Institutions, Media, Products, and Programs. Not worth buying for the Travel and Transportation section alone, which certainly isn't "complete," but a useful general reference work.

The Disabled Traveler: A Guide for Travel Counselors, by Cinnie Noble (1991, Canadian Institute of Travel Counselors of Ontario). Packed with information on all aspects of travel for people with all types of disability, useful for travelers as well as counselors.

The Vacation Home Exchange and Hospitality Guide, by John Kimborough (1991, $14.95; from Kimco Communications, 4242 West Drayton, Fresno, CA 93772, USA, or from The Disability Bookshop, see *Travelers' Health*, below). How to locate and arrange a home exchange or hospitality stay in the US or overseas. *Mobility International* members are listed as contacts for accessible homes worldwide.

The Voice (PO Box 2663, Corpus Christi, TX 78403; ☎512/884-8388). Bimonthly magazine for hearing-impaired people. Annual subscriptions (for six issues) are $14 (US) and $20 (Canada).

The World Wheelchair Traveler (1990, £3.95 plus postage), from the *Spinal Injuries Association* (76 St. James's Lane, London N10 3DF, UK; ☎081/444-2121); a small booklet, limited in its coverage of worldwide facilities, but including some useful tips from spinal-injured travelers.

TIDE'S IN (quarterly newsletter of *Travel Industry and Disabled Exchange*; see USA *Travel Notes*). Useful information for those in the travel industry and for travelers with disabilities, including some hard-hitting articles fighting the travelers' corner. Annual dues $15.

Travelin' Talk is the name of the network, the Directory, and the newsletter (see USA *Travel Notes*). Valuable source of travel advice and information put together by and for the members of this growing international network of people with disabilities. There's a one-time registration fee: $10 for individuals, $5 for SSDI recipients, $1 for SSI recipients.

Travelers' Health: How to Stay Healthy Abroad by Dr. Richard Dawood (1992, £7.99; Oxford University Press, Walton Street, Oxford OX2 6DP, UK; ☎0865/56767; fax 0865/56646). The third edition of this guide is not distributed in North America, but listed because it has been recommended throughout this book. It's current, highly readable, and thorough. Equivalent American publications include: **Traveler's Medical Resource: A Guide to Health and Safety Worldwide** ($19.95) and **The Traveler's Self-Care Manual** ($6.95), both by William W. Forgey (available plus postage from The Disability Bookshop, PO Box 129, Vancouver, WA 98666-0129; ☎206/694-2462; 24-hour toll-free orders, ☎800/637-2256, US or Canada), and **Traveling Well**, by Scott Harkonen (Dodd, New York), described by *MIUSA* as the complete travelers' health guide.

Directory

AIRLINES

Air Canada, Air Canada Center, PO Box 14000, St. Laurent, PQ H4Y 1H4 (☎514/422-5000 or 800/361-8620; different 800 number for each province, and each state in the US; TDD ☎800/361-8071).

Air India, 345 Park Ave., New York, NY 10154-0139 (☎212/407-1300 or 800/223-7776); 1801 McGill College Ave., Suite 530, Montréal, PQ H3A 2N4 (☎514/842-1805).

Aer Lingus, 122 E. 42nd St., New York, NY 10166 (☎212/557-1110 or 800/223-6537).

Air France, 888 Seventh Ave., New York, NY 10106 (☎212/830-4000 or 800/237-2747); 875 N Michigan Ave., Chicago, IL 60611 (☎312/440-7922); 2000 rue Mansfield, Montréal, PQ H3A 3A3 (☎514/284-2825); 151 Bloor St. W., Suite 600, Toronto, ON M5S 1S4 (☎416/922-5024).

Air Jamaica, 444 Brickell Ave., Suite P55, Miami, FL 33151 (☎800/523-5585); 55 St. Clair Ave W., Toronto, ON M4V 1K6 (☎800/523-5585).

Air Lanka, 767 Fifth Ave., New York, NY 10153 (☎800/421-9898); 789 Don Mills Road, Suite 700, Don Mills, ON M3C 3L6 (☎800/668-5224).

Air New Zealand, 1960 E. Grand Ave., Suite 900, El Segundo, CA 90245-5055 (☎310/648-7000 or 800/262-1234); Pacific Center #1201, 701 W. Georgia St., Box 10110, Vancouver, BC V7X 1C6 (☎800/663-5494).

Alitalia, 666 Fifth Ave., New York, NY 10103 (☎212/582-8900 or 800/223-5730); 2055 Peel St., Montréal, PQ H3A 1V8 (☎514/842-5201); 120 Adelaide St. W., Toronto, ON M5H 2E1 (☎416/363-2001).

America West, 4000 E. Sky Harbor Blvd., Phoenix, AZ 85034 (☎800/247-5692; TDD ☎800/526-8077).

American Airlines, PO Box 619616, Dallas/Fort Worth International Airport, Dallas, TX 75261 (☎817/267-1151 or 800/433-7300; TDD ☎800/543-1586 in continental US, except Ohio, ☎800/582-1573; for flights to Latin America call ☎800/624-6262).

Austrian Airlines, 608 Fifth Ave., New York, NY 10020 (☎800/843-0002 or 800/843-0002); 444 N. Michigan Ave., Chicago, IL 60611 (☎312/527-2727); 2 Bloor St. E., Toronto, ON M4Q 1A8 (☎416/964-3558).

British Airways, 530 Fifth Ave., New York, NY 10017 (☎800/2479297); 1021 bd. de Maisonneuve Ouest, Montréal, PQ H3A 3C8 (☎800/668-1055); 60 Bloor St. W., Toronto, ON M5G 2B2 (☎416/250-0880); 4120 Yonge St., Suite 100, North York, ON M2P 2BB (☎416/250-0250 or 800/668-1080).

Canadian Airlines International, Suite 330, 2912 Memorial Dr. SE, Calgary, AL T2A 6R1 (☎403/294-2000 or 800/363-7530; TDD ☎800/465-3611; for reservations in the USA, ☎800/426-7000).

Cathay Pacific, 300 N. Continental Blvd., Suite 500, El Segundo, CA 90245 (☎800/233-2742); 650 W. Georgia St., Vancouver, BC V6B 4N8 (☎604/682-9747 or 800/663-0318 in BC and Alberta, 800/633-1338 in rest of Canada)

Continental Airlines, 2929 Allen Parkway, Houston, TX 77019 (☎713/821-2100 or 800/231-0856; TDD ☎800/343-9195).

ČSA Czechoslovak Airlines, 545 Fifth Ave., New York, NY 10017 (☎212/682-5833 or 800/223-2365); 2020 University St., Montréal, PQ H3A 2A5 (☎514/844-4200); 401 Bay St., Toronto, ON M5H 2Y4 (☎416/363-3174).

Delta Air Lines, Hartsfield Atlanta International Airport, Atlanta, GA 30320 (☎404/765-5000; TDD ☎800/831-4488).

Ecuatoriana Airlines, 590 Fifth Ave., 10th Floor, New York, NY 10036 (☎212/354-1850; reservations☎800/328-2367).

Egyptair, 720 Fifth Ave., New York, NY 10019-4168 (☎212/581-5600 or 800/334-6787).

EL AL Israel Airlines, 120 W. 45th St., New York, NY 10036-4003 (☎212/852-0625 or 800/223-6700); 555 Rene Levesque Blvd. W., Montréal, PQ H2Z 1B1 (☎800/361-6174 or 800/268-7175).

Emirates, General Sales Agent: Emirates Travel, Inc., GM Plaza, 767 Fifth Ave., New York, NY 10153 (☎800/247-8480).

Finnair, 10 E. 40th St., New York, NY 10016 (☎212/889-7070 or 800/950-5000); 130 Bloor St. W., Toronto, ON M5S 1N5 (☎416/927-7400).

Garuda Indonesian Airways, 3457 Wilshire Blvd., Suite 201, Los Angeles, CA 90010-2203

(☎213/387-3323 or 800/342-7832); 1040 W. Georgia St., Vancouver, BC V6E 4H1 (☎604/681-3699).

Gulf Air, 420 Lexington Ave., Suite 2626, New York, NY 10170-0002 (☎212/986-3950 or 800/223-1740).

Iberia, 655 Madison Ave., 20th Floor, New York, NY 10021 (☎212/644-8841); 6300 Wilshire Blvd., Los Angeles, CA 90048 (☎800/772-4642); 2020 University St., Suite 1310, Montréal, PQ H3A 2A5 (☎514/985-5201 or 800/423-7421).

Icelandair, 360 W. 31st St., New York, NY 10001 (☎212/967-8888 or 800/223-5500).

JAT Yugoslav Airlines, 630 Fifth Ave., New York, NY 10111 (☎212/246-6401 or 800/752-6528); 180 N. Michigan Ave., Chicago, IL 60601 (☎312/782-1942); 1130 Sherbrooke St. W., Montréal, PQ H3A 2M8 (☎514/286-9074).

Kenya Airways, 424 Madison Ave., New York, NY 10017-1142 (☎212/832-8810).

KLM, 565 Taxter Rd., Elmsford, NY 10523 (☎212/759-3600 or 800/777-5553); 225 N. Michigan Ave., Chicago, IL 60601 (☎212/861-9292); 1255 Green Ave., Westmount, Québec, PQ H3Z 2A4 (☎514/933-1314 or 800/361-1887).

LOT Polish Airlines, 500 Fifth Ave., New York, NY 10110 (☎212/869-1074); 333 N. Michigan Ave., Chicago, IL 60601 (☎312/236-3388); 2000 Peel, Room 680, Montréal, PQ H3A 2W5 (☎514/844-2674).

Lacsa - The Airline of Costa Rica, 1600 NW LeJeune Rd., Suite 200, Miami, FL 33126 (☎800/225-2272); 512 Duplex Ave., Tauris House, Toronto, ON M4R 2E3 (☎416/440-0212).

Lufthansa, 1640 Hempstead Turnpike, East Meadow, NY 11554 (☎718/895-1277 or 800/645-3880); 875 N. Michigan Ave., Chicago, IL 60611 (☎312/751-0111); 55 Yonge St., Toronto, ON M5E 1J4 (☎416/360-3600 or 800/665-2282); 2020 University St., Montréal, PQ H3A 2A5 (☎514/288-2227).

Malev Hungarian Airlines, 630 Fifth Ave., New York, NY 10111 (☎212/757-6446 or 800/223-6884); 175 Bloor St. E., Toronto, ON M4W 3R8 (☎800/334-1284).

Northwest Airlines, 5101 Northwest Drive, St. Paul, MN 55111-3034 (domestic ☎800/225-2525; international ☎800/447-4747; French language reservations ☎800/345-7458; TDD ☎800/328-2298).

Olympic Airways, 647 Fifth Ave., New York, NY 10022 (☎212/838-3600 or 800/223-1226); 168 N. Michigan Ave., Chicago, IL 60601 (☎312/329-0400 or 800/223 1226); 500 S. Grand St., Suite 1500, Los Angeles, CA 90014 (☎212/624-6441); 80 Bloor St. W., Suite 502, Toronto, ON M5S 2V1 (☎416/920-2452).

Qantas Airways, 360 Port St., San Francisco, CA 94108-4995 (☎510/445-1400 or 800/227-4500); PO Box 49288, Four Bental Center, Suite 1714, 1055 Dunsmuir St., Vancouver, BC V7X 1L3 (☎604/684-8231 or 800/663-3423).

Royal Air Maroc, 55 E. 59th St., Suite 17-B, New York, NY 10022-1112 (☎212/750-5115 or 800/344-6726); 1001 bd de Maisonneuve Ouest, Suite 440, Montréal, PQ H7A 3C8 (☎514/285-1435 or 800/361-7508).

Sabena, 720 Fifth Ave., New York, NY 10022 (☎800/955-2000); 5959 W. Century Blvd., Los Angeles, CA 90045 (☎213/642-7735); 1001 bd. de Maisonneuve Ouest, Montréal, PQ H3A 3C8 (☎514/845-0215).

SAS, 9 Toledo Ave., Lyndhurst, NJ 07071 (☎800/221-2350); 205 Airport Rd., Suite 205, Mississauga, ON L4V 1E1 (☎416/672-5600 or 800/465-0569).

Saudia, Saudi Arabian Airlines, 747 Third Ave., New York, NY 10017-2881 (☎212/758-4727 or 800/472-8342).

Singapore Airlines, 8350 Wilshire Blvd., Beverly Hills, CA 90211-2387 (☎310/655-9270 or 800/742-3333); 1111–1030 W. Georgia St., Vancouver, BC V6E 2Y3 (☎604/689-1065 or 800/663-3046).

South African Airways, 900 Third Ave., New York, NY 10022-4771 (☎212/826-0995 or 800/722-9675); 5255 Yonge St., Suite 1500, North York, ON O2N 6P4 (☎416/512-8880 or 800/387-4629).

Swissair, 608 Fifth Ave., New York, NY 10020 (☎718/995-8400 or 800/221-7370); 1253 McGill College Ave., Suite 950, Montréal, PQ H3B 2X5 (☎514/954-5600 or 800/267-9477).

Taca (Honduran Airways), 5885 NW 18th St., Bldg. C2200, Miami, FL 33122 (☎305/526-8238); 1200 Shepard Ave E., Suite 104, Willowdale, ON M2K 2S5 (☎416/756-3356).

TAP Air Portugal, 399 Market St., Newark, NJ 07105 (☎201/344-4490 or 800/221-7370); 1010 Sherbrooke St. W., Montréal, PQ H3A 2R7 (☎514/849-4217).

Thai Airways International, 720 Olive Way, Suite 1400, Seattle, WA 98101-3898 (☎202/467-9898 or 800/426-5205); 250-666 Berard St., Vancouver, BC V6C 2X8 (☎604/687-1412 or 800/426-5204).

THY Turkish Airlines, 821 United Nations Plaza, 4th Floor, New York, NY 10017 (☎212/986-5050).

Trans World Airlines, 100 South Bedford Rd., Mount Kisco, NY 10549 (☎914/242-3000; domestic ☎800/221-2000; international ☎800/892-4141; TDD ☎800/421-8480, except California, ☎800/252-0622).

United Airlines, PO Box 66100, Chicago, IL 60666 (☎708/952-4000 or 800/241-6522; TDD ☎800/323-0170, from US, Canada, and Mexico).

US Air, Crystal Park Four, 2345 Crystal Drive, Arlington, VA 22227 (☎703/418-7000 or 800/428-4322; TDD ☎800/245-2966).

Viasa Venezuelan International Airways, 1101 Brickell Ave., Suite 600, Miami, FL 33131-3147 (☎800/221-2150); 102 Bloor St. W, Suite 1530, Toronto, ON M5S 1M8 (☎800/268-3783).

Virgin Atlantic Airways, 96 Morton St., New York, NY 10014 (☎212/206-6612 or 800/862-8621).

USEFUL RAIL ADDRESSES

Amtrak, National Railroad Passenger Corporation, 60 Massachusetts Ave., NE, Washington DC 20002 (☎202/906-3000 or 800/USA-RAIL or 800/872-7245; TDD ☎800/523-6590, except Pennsylvania, ☎800/562-6960; in Canada, ☎800/4AM-TRAK).

VIA Rail, PO Box 8116, Station A, Montréal, PQ H3C 3N3 (☎514/871-1331; 800 numbers and reservations numbers differ across the country— see booklet, *Services for Passengers with Special Needs*; TDD ☎800/268-9503, except in Toronto, ☎368-6406).

British Rail International, 1500 Broadway, New York, NY 10036 (☎212/575-2667); 94 Cumberland St., Toronto, ON M5R 1A3 (☎416/929-3333). Holds copies of *A Guide to British Rail for Disabled People* (see England & Wales *Travel Notes*).

Rail Europe , 226–230 Westchester Ave., White Plains, NY 10604 (☎914/682-2999 or 800/848-7254); and branches in Santa Monica, San Francisco, Fort Lauderdale, Chicago, Dallas, Vancouver, and Montréal. Perhaps the best place to reserve European rail tickets, including eastern

Europe. They have some copies of guides for disabled travelers on European networks but stress that arrangements for assistance must be made in the country you are traveling in.

CAR RENTAL COMPANIES OFFERING HAND CONTROLS

Avis, ☎800/331-1212 (USA), ☎800/879-2847 (Canada), voice; ☎800/331-2323, TDD.

Budget, ☎800/527-0700, USA.

Hertz, for USA reservations ☎800/654-3131, international reservations ☎800/654-3001, AAA members ☎800/654-9080; in Canada, for reservations worldwide, ☎800/263-0600, from Québec ☎800/263-0678, from Toronto ☎620-9620.

National, ☎800/328-4567, voice; ☎800/328-6323, TDD.

Tilden Rent A Car: ☎800/387-4747.

INTERNATIONAL HOTEL CHAINS

Unless otherwise noted, these 800 numbers are good in the USA and Canada.

Best Western, PO Box 10203, Phoenix, AZ 85064-0203 (☎602/957-4200 or 800/528-1234; for hearing-impaired customers in contiguous 48-states only, ☎800/528-2222, TDD and answering machine). Worldwide.

Campanile, 31 av. Jean Moulin, Marne-La-Vallée, 77200 Torcy, France (☎1/64.62.46.62). Europe, mainly France.

Canadian Pacific, 1 University Ave., Suite 400, Toronto, ON M5J 2P1; ☎416/367-7197; reservations, ☎800/268-9411. **(Doubletree** in the US: New York National Sales, 555 Madison Ave., Suite 815, New York, NY 10022; ☎212/754-7800 or 800/528-0444, voice ☎800/528-9898, TDD). Canada and USA.

Choice Hotels International (Clarion Hotels, Quality Inns, Comfort Inns, Sleep Inns, Roadway Inns, Friendship Inns, Econolodges), 10750 Columbia Pike, Silver Spring, MD 20901 (☎301/593-5600; reservations ☎800/221-2222, voice ☎800/228-3323, TDD, except Maryland, ☎301/681-8040). North America, Europe, the Pacific, India.

Consort Hotels and Transeurope Hotels, Selective Hotel Reservations, 9 Boston St., Suite 10, Lynn, MA 01904 (☎617/581-0844 or 800/223-6764). UK and rest of Europe.

Days Inns of America, Inc., 2751 Buford way., NE, Atlanta, GA 30324-3276 (☎404/325-0000 or 800/325-2525, voice; ☎800/222-3297, TDD, except California, ☎800/325-3297). USA, Canada, Mexico.

Flag International, 1 Newport Place, 1301 Dove St., Suite 880, Newport Beach, CA 92660 (☎714/63-1244 or 800/624-3524). Australia, New Zealand, the Pacific, Thailand, USA including Hawaii, UK.

Golden Tulip Hotels, 437 Madison Ave., 25th floor, New York, NY 10022 (☎212/838-5022 or 800/344-1212). Europe, Africa, Middle East, Canada, USA, Latin America and the Caribbean, Asia.

Hilton Hotels, PO Box 5567, Beverly Hills, CA 90209 (☎213/205-4545 or 800/445-8667, voice; ☎ 800/368-1133, TDD). Worldwide

Holiday Inns, Corporate Headquarters, Three Ravinia Drive, Suite 2000, Atlanta, GA 30346-2149 (☎404/604-2000 or 800/465-4329 (☎800/HOLIDAY), voice; ☎800/238-5544, TDD). Worldwide

Howard Johnson, Corporate Headquarters, 339 Jefferson Rd., PO Box 278, Parsippany, NJ 07054-0728 (☎201/428-9700 or 800/446-4656 (☎800/I-GO-HOJO), voice; ☎800/654-8442, TDD). USA, Canada, Mexico.

Hyatt International Corporation, 200 W. Madison St., Chicago, IL 60606 (☎312/750-1234 or 800/233-1234). Worldwide.

Inter-Continental Hotels, 1120 Avenue of the Americas, New York, NY 10036 (☎212/852-6400; reservations ☎800/327-0200). Worldwide

La Quinta Motor Inns, Inc., PO Box 790064, San Antonio, TX 78279-0064 (☎512/366-6000 or ☎800/531-5900, voice; ☎800/426-3101, TDD). USA, Canada, Mexico.

Marriott Hotels, 1700 Broadway, 4th Floor, New York, NY 10019 (☎212/704-8797; reservations ☎800/228-9290, voice; ☎800/228-7014, TDD). Worldwide.

Oberoi Hotels, 820 Second Ave., Suite 1302, New York, NY 10017 (☎752-6565, New York City only; ☎800/5-OBEROI): India, Nepal, Sri Lanka, Indonesia, Australia, Egypt, Saudi Arabia.

Ramada, Worldwide Sales Offices for International Properties and US Renaissance Hotels, 625 N. Michigan Ave., Suite 500, Chicago, IL 60611 (☎312/751-4256); 1600 Broadway, Suite 609, New York, NY 10019 (☎212/956-0753); 9620 Airport Blvd., Suite 253, Los Angeles, CA 90045 (☎310/216-6667); 999 Ninth St., NW, Washington DC 20001 (☎202/898-9000); 2300 Yonge St., Suite 1701, Toronto, ON M4P 1E4 (☎416/485-2692; 1133 W. Hastings, Vancouver, BC V6E 3T3 (☎604/688-6678). Reservations, from the US: for inns and hotels, 800/2-RAMADA (272-6232); for Renaissance and non-US hotels, ☎800/228-9898; TDD, ☎800/228-3232. Reservations, from Canada: in Toronto area, ☎485-2610; French-speaking, ☎800/544-9778; all other areas, ☎800/268-8998.

Resinter (Lucien Barriere, Pullman, Sofitel, Altea, Mercure, Novotel, Ibis, Urbis, Arcade), 2 Overhill Rd., Scarsdale, New York, NY 10583 (☎800/221-4542). Worldwide.

Shangri-La International Hotels and Resorts, 5777 W. Century Blvd., Suite 1105, Los Angeles, CA 90045 (☎310/417-3483 or 800/942-5050). The Far East, Canada, Fiji.

Sheraton, 60 State St., Boston, MA 02109 (☎617/367-3600 or 800/325-3535, voice; ☎800/325-1717, TDD). Worldwide.

Travelodge, Forte Hotels, Inc., 35 E. 64th St., Suite 3B, New York, NY 10021 (☎212/249-5300 or 800/255-3050, voice; ☎800/255-9523, TDD). North America and Europe. For worldwide (Europe, North America, Caribbean/Atlantic, Middle East, Pacific) Forte Hotel reservations ☎800/225-5843).

TOUR OPERATORS AND TRAVEL AGENTS

DISCOUNT FLIGHT AGENTS, TRAVEL CLUBS, CONSOLIDATORS

The following agents can be used by travelers who are prepared to make any special requests themselves, dealing direct with carriers—these outfits are run on tight budgets and in order to offer discount tickets most have an agreement with carriers that they will not pass on any requests from travelers with "special needs." So if you need to keep costs down and want to buy tickets this way, don't mention anything to do with disability—they'll probably hang up on you! Bearing in mind that many travelers cannot rely on their travel agents to pass on requests for on-board wheelchairs, arrangements for carriage of power-chairs, or procuring seating with space for a guide dog, and other simple instructions, this is not such a big deal—most travelers double-check for themselves anyway.

Access International, 101 W. 31st St., Suite 104, New York, NY 10001 (☎800/TAKE-OFF). Consolidator with good East Coast and central US deals.

Council Travel, 205 E. 42nd St., New York, NY 10017 (☎212/661-1450). Head office of the nationwide US student travel organization. Branches in San Francisco, LA, Washington, New Orleans, Chicago, Seattle, Portland, Minneapolis, Boston, Atlanta, and Dallas, to name only the larger ones.

Discount Travel International, Ives Bldg., 114 Forrest Ave., Suite 205, Narbeth, PA 19072 (☎215/668-2182 or 800/221-8139). Good deals from the East Coast.

Encore Short Notice, 4501 Forbes Blvd., Lanham, MD 20706 (☎301/459-8020 or 800/852-6900). East Coast travel club.

Interworld, 3400 Coral Way, Miami, FL 33145 (☎305/443-4929). Southeastern US consolidator.

Last-Minute Travel Club, 132 Brookline Ave., Boston, MA 02215 (☎617/267-9800 or 800/LAST-MIN).

Moment's Notice, 425 Madison Ave., New York, NY 10017 (☎212/486-0503). Travel club that's good for last-minute deals.

Nouvelles Frontières, 12 E. 33rd St., New York, NY 10016 (☎212/779-0600); 800 bd. de Maisonneuve Est, Montréal, PQ H2L 4L8 (☎514/288-9942). Main US and Canadian branches of the French discount travel outfit. Other branches in LA, San Francisco, and Québec.

STA Travel, 17 E. 45th St., Suite 805, New York, NY 10017 (☎212/687-9372 or 800/777-0112); 166 Geary St., Suite 702, San Francisco, CA 94108 (☎510/391-8407). Main US branches of the originally Australian and now worldwide specialist in independent and student travel. Other offices in LA, Boston, and Honolulu.

Travac, 2601 E. Jefferson St., Orlando, FL 32803 (☎800/872-8800). Good consolidator.

Travel Brokers, 50 Broad St., New York, NY 10004 (☎800/999-8748). New York travel club.

Travel Cuts, 187 College St., Toronto, ON M5T 1P7 (☎416/979-2406). Main office of the Canadian student travel organization. Many other offices nationwide.

Travelers Advantage, 49 Music Square, Nashville, TN 37203 (☎800/548-1116). Reliable travel club.

Travel Avenue, 641 W. Lake St., #201 Chicago, IL 60661-1012 (☎312/876-1116 or 800/333-3335). Discount travel agent.

Unitravel, 1177 N. Warson Rd., St. Louis, MO 63132 (☎800/325-2222). Reliable consolidator with 25 years' experience.

Worldwide Discount Travel Club, 1674 Meridian Ave., Miami Beach, FL 33139 (☎305/534-2082).

GENERAL TOUR OPERATORS

American Express, World Financial Center, New York, NY 10285 (☎212/640-2000 or 800/800-8891). Packages, city breaks, all over the world.

Contiki Holidays, 1432 Katela Ave., Anaheim, CA 92805 (☎714/937-0611 or 800/626-0611). Bus tours for under-35-year-olds.

Cosmos/Global Gateway, 92-25 Queens Blvd., Rego Park, NY 11374 (☎800/221-0090). The leading budget tour operators to Europe in the US. Bookable through travel agents only.

Europe Through the Back Door Tours, 109 Fourth Ave North, C-2009, Edmonds, WA 98020 (☎206/771-0833). Excellent travel club which publishes a regular newsletter packed full of travel tales and advice, sells its own guides and travel accessories, *Eurail* passes, and runs good-value bus tours taking in the biggest European cities. Worth joining for the newsletter alone.

Europe Train Tours, 198 Boston Post Rd., Mamaroneck, NY 105431 (☎814/698-9426 or 800/551-2085). What it says.

Jet Vacations, 1775 Broadway, New York, NY 10019 (☎212/247-0999 or 800/JET-0999). Packages to Europe, especially France.

Mountain Travel, 6420 Fairmont Ave., El Cerrito, CA 94530 (☎800/227-2384). Hiking specialist.

Scantours, 1535 6th St., Suite 205, Santa Monica, CA 90401 (☎213/451-0911 or 800/223-SCAN). Scandinavia and eastern Europe specialists.

Trafalgar Tours, 11 E. 26th St., New York, NY 10010 (☎212/689-8977 or 800/854-0103). Bus tours around the world.

Trophy Tours, 1810 Glenville Drive, Suite 1124, Richardson, TX 75081 (☎800/527-2473). Good-value bus tours all over Europe. Good on Britain and Ireland.

Access Adventures, 206 Chestnut Ridge Rd., Rochester, NY 14624; ☎716/889-9096; **Bonaparte Travel**, ☎716/385-6050 or 716/454-3001. Debra Lisena-Tyo founded Access Adventures in 1988 and teamed up with Bonaparte Travel in 1991, offering a full travel agency service for individuals or groups of disabled travelers planning business or vacation trips, as well as organized tours. Destinations include the Canadian Rockies, Tucson and the Southwest, Walt Disney World, and—a four-day cruise—Freeport and Nassau.

Accessible Journeys, 35 W. Sellers Ave., Ridley Park, PA 19078; ☎215/521-0339. America's first Registered Nursing service specializing in recreation programs exclusively for disabled travelers. Services include planning for accessible vacations, escorting groups on vacation, and arranging travel companions for travelers who need assistance away from home. Tours offered include Alaska, the Caribbean, Kenya, India, Nepal, CIS, and China.

Access Tours, Inc., PO Box 2985, Jackson, WY 83001; ☎307/733-6664; or, winter through mid-May, 2440 South Forest, Tucson, AZ 85713; ☎602/791-7977. "Able-bodied or physically challenged, it makes no difference to us." Clint Grosse offers ten-day tours (all $1395 per person, double occupancy, land only) of southern and central Arizona in the winter, Montana with Glacier National Park, or Wyoming with Yellowstone and Grand Teton National Parks, all at a relaxed pace, with small groups, using lift-equipped vans, and making frequent stops. Advisable to reserve two months in advance.

Alaska Heritage Tours/Alaskan Accessible Tours, PO Box 210691, Anchorage, AK 99521; ☎907/696-8687. All tours, including the eight-day Alaska Discovery Tour (around $2000 per person) as well as shorter tours (Columbia Glacier, Seward/Kenai Fiords, marine wildlife cruises), are designed not only for physically challenged travelers but also for the slow walker and anyone who likes to travel in a small group with personalized attention from hosts Glenn and Dee Williams. Recommended by Bob and Bea Huskey (see p.33). Summer tours are usually fully booked by May.

Dialysis in Wonderland, 1130 W. Center, North Salt Lake, UT 84054; ☎801/298-6632 or 800/777-5727. Specialists in travel programs for people on dialysis. The 1992 program included a fully escorted "Wild West—Cactus Blossoms" tour in May, beginning in Phoenix and taking in Tucson, old Tombstone, and the desert.

Dvořák's Kayak and Rafting Expeditions, 17921-B US Highway 285, Nathrop, Colorado 81236; ☎719/539-6851 or 800/824-3795. Whitewater rafting or kayaking through nearly thirty different canyons on ten rivers in Colorado, Wyoming, Utah, Arizona, Idaho, Texas, and New Mexico. International trips are also available to Mexico, Australia (diving and sailing), and New Zealand (rafting and kayaking). A ten-day rafting trip on the Dolores river costs $1040 (adult) or $940 (youth, minimum age 10). There are special rates for families, and a third of trips each season are run for non-profit groups. There are kayak and canoe programs to suit a variety of physical disabilites, and this company has experience of providing trips for special needs groups including those with emotional and behavioral disorders.

Evergreen Travel Service, 4114 198th St. SW, Suite 13, Lynnwood, WA 98036; ☎206/776-1184 or 800/435-2288. An appropriate name for a company into its fourth decade of specializing in travel for people with disabilities. Tours cover a wide range of destinations worldwide, and are designed for travelers with a variety of abilities. *Evergreen* did not respond to our request for information, but *SATH* (see USA *Travel Notes*) tells us that their 1992 Wings on Wheels program included China, Italy, the South Pacific, Florida, Hawaii, and cruises to Alaska; White Cane tours took in Greece, Germany/Switzerland, and Hawaii; there was a selection of "Lazybones" tours and cruises for those who prefer a leisurely pace, an Alaskan tour for deaf/hearing-impaired travelers, and tours (Hawaii and Disneyland/Los Angeles) for "developmentally delayed" travelers.

Flying Wheels Travel, Inc., 143 W. Bridge St., PO Box 382, Owatonna, MN 55060; ☎507/451-5005 or 800/535-6790. Founded in 1970, this full service travel agency and tour operator has plenty of experience of arranging group tours and independent travel for physically disabled clients and their friends or families. The 1992 program (sample prices are based on two persons sharing and do not include air fares) included escorted tours to Walt Disney World (6 nights, $1025), the

Canadian Rockies (11 nights, $2590), England (13 nights, $3900), eastern Europe (Prague, Vienna, Budapest; 14 nights, $4700), China (14 nights, starting at $2895) and Israel (12 nights, $1800); custom itineraries to Africa; cruises to the Panama Canal, the Alaska Inside Passage, the western Caribbean, and the Mediterranean.

Flying-W-Outfitters, PO Box 3, Bighorn, MT 59010; ☎406/342-5695. Specialists in hunts for the disabled sportsperson. Four-wheel drives are used for hunting, and wheelchair users can either shoot from the vehicle or be assisted off and into their chair. One large double bedroom in the cabin has been adapted to accommodate a disabled person. Any special equipment required can be rented or bought from the medical center at Billings, 60 miles from the camp. Scenic tours of the area are also offered.

Friends of the Family, The Travel Enhancement Company, Suite 109, 1727 Orlando Central Parkway, Orlando, FL 32809; ☎407/856-7676 or 800/945-2045. Offers a combination of toll-free advice helpline and fee-based services for vacationers in Florida. By calling the toll-free number travelers with disabilities can do the following: arrange for a tour guide to push a wheelchair user around Walt Disney World, Universal Studios, or any other theme park (guides will offer strategies to avoid waiting in lines, and to obtain best value for money when shopping or eating); find appropriate hotels; find medical equipment companies offering the best value; rent a lift-equipped vehicle or reserve shuttle service; find an accessible restaurant; discuss accessibility of tourist attractions. Information provided is continually updated. Fee-based services include detailed itinerary writing, airport meet-and-greet, and tour escorts. *Friends of the Family* also conducts "Sensitivity and Awareness Sessions" aimed at helping service industry personnel to effectively satisfy the expectations of customers with disabilities, and ADA Workshops aimed at minimizing risk and expense to the travel industry while at the same time promoting provision of appropriate facilities. Other "special projects" include affordable accessibility surveys, and software development for portable closed-caption devices.

Handicapped Freedom Tours, 103, 339–50 Ave., SE, Calgary, AL T2G 2B3; ☎403/299-2888 or 800/661-3516. Offers camping and the great outdoors at Camp Freedom in Alberta. Physically disabled or mentally challenged people can participate in a range of activities, including fishing, hot-air ballooning, sailing, horse-cart riding, use of the ATV Freedom Rider II (all-terrain vehicle with joy-stick control), and hot tubbing. Accommodation is in heated cabins.

Hinsdale Travel Service, 201 E. Ogden Ave. Suite 100, Hinsdale, IL 60521; ☎708/325-1335. Wheelchair traveler Janice Perkins (see Switzerland, p.203) works from home for this professional travel agency, and about a third of her clients are wheelchair users; she provides an expert liaison between disabled clients and travel suppliers, and complete understanding of special needs and services.

Hospitality Tours, PO Box 2186, 20 Willow Ave., Hyannis, MA 02601; ☎508/771-1331 or 800/966-1331. This operator does not handle individuals or transportation; the groups received number from 10 to 45 and travel in their own vehicle or bus. All tours are customized, covering all of the New England states, and packages can include hotels, restaurants, attractions, and guides; Cape Cod and Boston are the most popular destinations.

Journeys on Dialysis. See Travel, Tours, and Cruises *Travel Notes*, p.547.

Life Unlimited/Robbins and Associates. See Travel, Tours, and Cruises *Travel Notes*, p.547.

Multi Travel, Department for the Disabled Traveler, 2 W. 47th St., New York, NY 10036; ☎212/382-3370 or 800/234-7172. Arranges package tours for travelers with disabilities. Wheelchair-accessible offerings in 1992 included two weeks in Israel, and one week in Puerto Rico.

Nautilus Tours, 5435 Donna Ave., Tarzana, CA 91356; ☎818/343-6339; or All About Travel, 11225 Tampa Ave., Northridge, CA 91326; ☎818/368-5648; see also TIDE, above. Can arrange a 16-day accessible tour of New Zealand (both islands), and is reported to offer a wheelchair-accessible Amazonian cruise from Manaus, Brazil, and accessible accommodation and lift-equipped tour bus on European tours—Germany and Austria ($2700, land only) in 1992.

New Directions, Inc., 5276 Hollister Ave., #207, Santa Barbara, CA 93111; ☎805/967-2841. This is a non-profit organization; prices reflect the cost of comprehensive, "chaperoned", customized tours (eg Oahu, 7 days, $1980; Las Vegas Winners Weekend, $610), but some travel grants are available. Programs are open to everyone, with or without disability, and include those who have mild to severe developmental, physical, emotional, or medical disabilities. Major areas of activity are "special travel," taking people with disabilities across America and around the world—campouts, ski trips, cruises, photographic safaris, river rafting, city tours, all kinds of vacational experience; holiday celebrations, hosting traditional family-style holidays—without charge—for people living in residential facilities or who are unable to be with their families at holidaytime; totally integrated social events such as dinner parties, picnics, and dances; international exchange programs.

Oceans Unlimited, 187 Midlawn Close, SE, Calgary, AL T2X 1A7; ☎403/256-7871. Offers an assortment of trips for individuals or groups depending on age and abilities: tandem sky diving; llama treks; dog sledding; heli-hiking in the Rockies; salmon fishing and sightseeing charters on a specially equipped 26-foot yacht in BC's Discovery Passage; group and custom tours by wheelchair-accessible bus with on-board accessible rest room. Individual travel arrangements can also be made using a database containing details of access at many hotels and attractions.

Over the Rainbow, Inc., 186 Mehani Circle, Kihei, Maui, HI 96753; ☎808/879-5521. This on-site travel, tour, and activity agency is the home business of David and Jan McKown; they can fix every aspect of a vacation on Maui—airport arrangements, accessible accommodations and transportation (Over the Rainbow is the Hawaiian agent for Wheelers Accessible Van Rental of Arizona), personal care, recreational activities too numerous to list, even real estate.

Sundial Special Vacations, 600 Broadway, Seaside, OR 97138; ☎503/738-3324 or 800/547-9198. Specialists with eighteen years' experience in organizing vacations for developmentally disabled adults. Tour guide ratio is one to seven, depending on the capabilities of the group. For most tours, travelers must be ambulatory, but wheelchair users can call to discuss requirements. Destinations and sample prices (excluding air fares) include USA (Alaska, 7 days, $1356; Oregon coast, 4 days, $499), Rome and Athens (10 days, $1569), and the Caribbean (7 days, $1105).

The Guided Tour, 613 W. Cheltenham Ave., Suite 200, Melrose Park, PA 19126-2414; ☎215/782-1370. Specialists in travel for developmentally disabled clients, with programs in the USA, the Caribbean, and Europe.

Tailored Tours, Inc., PO Box 797687, Dallas, TX 75379; ☎214/612-1168 or 800/628-5842. Julia Brown's agency specializes in tours for physically disabled travelers; the aim is to provide high quality arrangements at "affordable prices" (this is a difficult term to define: sample price—four nights at the International Hot Air Balloon Fiesta, Albuquerque, NM, $1019 per person double room, land only) and a personalized service. Tours in 1992 included riverboat gambling on the Mississippi river, Yellowstone National Park, Grand Canyon, and Nashville, Tennessee.

Tomorrow's Level of Care (TLC), PO Box 470299, Brooklyn, NY 11247; ☎800/932-2012. For those whose disability or medical condition makes travel difficult, TLC offers a seven-night vacation package in Barbados, including accommodations, nursing services for an hour a day, airport transfers, baggage handling, and taxes, for prices ranging from $465 to $979 per person.

Travel Trends Ltd., #2 Allan Plaza, 4922–51 Ave., PO Box 3581, Leduc, AL T9E 6M3 (☎403/986-9000); or Main Floor, Center 104, 5241 Calgary Trail, Edmonton, AL T6H 5G8 (☎403/435-1010). Specialists in group departures for people with disabilities or those who need a little extra assistance. They work with several mainstream tour suppliers, including *Holland America*, *Royal Caribbean Cruise Lines*, and *Canadian Holidays*, and claim to secure "tremendous" group savings that allow clients to travel at a discount.

Uniglobe Action Travel, 13035 Olive Blvd., Suite 218, St. Louis, MO 63141; ☎314/576-9736 or 800/231-8646; TDD, ☎314/576-5177. Owned and run by experienced travel personnel, *Uniglobe* has been in business ten years and takes particular care over the accessibility details of ground transfers, air, hotel, car, cruise, and bus tours. For the past six years it has offered a "Caribbean Breathe Cruise" for people with respiratory disease and their friends and relatives. Clients who use wheelchairs have successfully joined honeymoon cruises and European trips. Peggy Lang is the specialist in accommodating the needs of travelers with disabilities.

Voyages Goliger Travel, 1130 Sherbrooke St. W., Suite 1310, Montréal, PQ H3A 2M8; ☎514/849-3571; call Soryl Rosenberg, Disabled Traveler Department. Program includes cruises for the active disabled traveler to the Caribbbean, Mexico, Mediterranean, and South America; land tours to Europe, Africa, Egypt, and New Zealand. All trips are with experienced group operators for disabled travelers.

Wheelchair Journeys—a division of **Redmond Travel,** 16979 Redmond Way, Redmond, WA 98052; ☎206/885-2210. This agency provides individual travel arrangements for persons with disabilities and those who travel with them. As an outgrowth of this work, *Access for Travel* (1429 10th St. W., Kirkland, WA 98033; ☎206/828-4220 or 206/488-8297) was founded by Carol Lee Power and Norma Nickols, who give presentations and workshops for travel industry workers; participants will develop a better understanding of the needs of disabled travelers, become aware of the laws, learn how to determine accessibility, and develop communications skills.

Wheelchair Wagon Tours, PO Box 700637, St. Cloud, FL 34742; ☎407/957-2044. Tour company that provides accessible transport by bus. Travelers can be met at the airport, transferred to the hotel of their choice, and offered a tour of Walt Disney World, Epcot Center, Sea World, and the usual attractions of this area; a new Florida tour, to the east coast and Miami, the Keys, and back up the west coast to Orlando was planned at the time of writing.

VOLUNTARY/NON-PROFIT ORGANIZATIONS

There are many more non-profit organizations than we can list here, particularly in the USA, so this is a selection of the major national associations which can direct you to local branches and other contacts; you can also consult the *Resource Directory for the Disabled* and *The Complete Directory for People with Disabilities* (see *Books*). The Yellow Pages (Human, Health, or Disability Services) and main phone books will list more possibilities in your own area.

In the USA

American Foundation for the Blind, 15 W. 16th St., New York, NY 10011 (☎212/620-2000 or 800/AFBLIND). Regional offices in Atlanta (☎404/525-2303), Chicago (☎312/269-0095), Dallas (☎214/352-7222), San Francisco (☎510/392-4845), Washington DC (☎202/457-1487). Useful publications, and ID cards for reduced fares on public transit.

Arthritis Foundation, 1314 Spring St. NW, Atlanta, GA 30309 (☎404/872-7100). Publishes *Travel and Arthritis* plus a quarterly newsletter; local chapters all over America.

Disability Information and Referral Service, 3805 Marshall St., Wheat Ridge, CO 80033 (☎303/420-2942, voice; ☎800/2553477, TDD). Computerized data base containing information from private and government-supported agencies.

The Disabled Outdoors Foundation, 2052 W. 23rd St., Chicago, IL 60608 (☎312/927-6834). Information on recreational facilities and adaptive recreational gear can be found in their quarterly *Disabled Outdoors* magazine.

Earthwatch, 680 Mount Auburn St., PO Box 403, Watertown, MA 02272-9104 (☎617/926-8200). Charity with a mission to study and conserve the environment; positive attitude to disabled volunteers.

Eastern Paralyzed Veterans of America, 75–20 Astoria Blvd., Jackson Heights, NY 11370-1178 (☎718/803-EPVA). Several useful publications.

Mobility International USA, (MIUSA), PO Box 3551, Eugene, OR 97403 (☎503/343-1284, voice and TDD). Major source of advice and information on all types of travel, with own program of exchange travel; see *Travel, Tours, and Cruises*, and USA *Travel Notes* for more information.

The Nantahala Outdoor Center, US 19W, Box 41, Bryson City, NC 28713 (☎704/488-2175). Some programs accommodate people with disabilities.

National Association of the Deaf, 814 Thayer Avenue, Silver Spring, MD 20910 (☎301/587-1788).

The National Audubon Society, Audubon Ecology Camps and Workshops, 613 Riversville Rd., Greenwich, CT 06831 (☎203/869-2017). Reported to be able and willing to accommodate people with disabilities on some of their programs.

National Federation of the Blind, 1800 Johnson St., Baltimore, MD 21230 (☎301/659-9314).

National Handicapped Sports, 451 Hungerford Drive, Suite 100, Rockville, MD 20850 (☎301/217-0960).

National Information Center on Deafness, Gallaudet University, 800 Florida Ave., NE, Washington DC 20002 (☎202/651-5051, voice;

202/651-5052, TDD; ☎800/332-1124, tele-consumer hotline, voice and TDD. Information on TDDs as well as a booklet listing resources for hearing-impaired travelers, *Travel Resources for Deaf and Hard of Hearing People*.

National Ocean Access Project, PO Box 33141, Farragut Station, Washington, DC 20033 (☎301/217-9843). See Travel, Tours, and Cruises *Travel Notes*.

Outward Bound, 384 Field Point Rd., Greenwich, CT 06830 (☎203/661-0797 or 800/243-8520). Accommodates people with disabilities on some of their programs.

Paralyzed Veterans of America (PVA), 801 18th St., NW, Washington DC 20006 (☎202/872-1300 or 800/424-8200). Publishes *Paraplegia News*, *Sports 'n Spokes*, the *Access to the Skies Newsletter*, a booklet called *Wheelchair Sports and Recreation*—and more.

Pathways for the Future PO Box 2114, Sylva, NC 28779 (☎704/586-2471). Promotes barrier-free outdoor recreational programs and activities.

The Opening Door, Inc., Route 2, Box 1805, Woodford, VA 22580 (☎804/633-6752). Family group committed to better awareness of disability and related issues; publishes the Virginia Access Guide and acts as consultant to the Embassy Suites chain (see USA *Travel Notes*).

The Perspectives Network, 9919 Orangevale Drive, Spring, TX 77379-5103 (☎713/251-2005, voice or fax). Support network for survivors of brain injury; see Dena Taylor's account in *Travel, Tours, and Cruises.*

Self Help for Hard of Hearing People (SHHH), 7800 Wisconsin Ave., Bethesda, MD 20814 (☎301/657-2248, voice; ☎301/657-2249, TDD). Advocacy group, promoting communicatively accessible travel, with chapters all over the world; see p.567.

Society for Advancement of Travel for the Handicapped (SATH), 347 Fifth Ave., Suite 610, New York, NY 10016 (☎212/447-7284). Publishes quarterly newsletter, SATH News, full of information for travelers with disabilities; see USA *Travel Notes* for more information.

Travel Industry and Disabled Exchange (TIDE), 5435 Donna Ave., Tarzana, CA 91356 (☎818/343-6339). Newsletter, workshops, and seminars, provide forum for better communication between industry and consumer.

Travelin' Talk, PO Box 3534, Clarksville, TN 37043-3534 (☎615/552-6670). Network of travelers with disabilities; information provided via extensive listings, newsletter, and directory—see USA *Travel Notes*.

In Canada

Canadian Association of the Deaf, 2435 Holly Lane, Suite 205, Ottawa, ON K1V 7P2 (☎613/526-4785). At the same address are the **Canadian Deaf and Hard of Hearing Forum** (☎613/536-4867) and **Canadian Hard of Hearing Association** (☎613/526-1584, voice; ☎613/526-2692, TDD).

Canadian Association of Independent Living Centers, 905–150 Kent St., Ottawa, ON K1P 5P4 (☎613/563-2581).

Canadian Council of the Blind, 405-396 Cooper St., Ottawa, ON K2P 2H7 (☎613/567-0311).

Canadian Disability Rights Council, 926-294 Portage, Winnipeg, Manitoba R3C 0B9 (☎204/943-4787).

Canadian National Institute for the Blind, 320 MacLeod St., Ottawa, ON K2P 1A3 (☎613/563-4021). Around fifty offices in major cities, listed in the phone directory under CNIB.

Canadian Outward Bound Wilderness School, PO Box 116, St.ation S, Toronto, ON M5M 4L6 (☎416/787-1721 or 800/268-7329). Access to Adventure courses.

Canadian Paraplegic Association (CPA), 1500 Don Mills Rd., Don Mills, ON M3B 3K4 (☎416/391-0203). Major source of information for travelers; for provincial head offices and more information, see Canada *Travel Notes*.

Canadian Mental Health Association, 2160 Yonge St., Toronto, ON M4S 2Z3 (☎416/484-7750).

Canadian Rehabilitation Council for the Disabled, 45 Sheppard Ave., Suite 801, Toronto, ON M2N 5W9 (☎416/250-7490).

Canadian Wheelchair Sports Association, 212 James Naismith Drive, Gloucester, ON K1B 5N4 (☎613/748-5685).

Columbia Society of Interdependent Living (SOIL), Box 19, Spillimacheen, BC V0A 1P0 (☎604/346-3257 or 3276). Outdoors work on improving access and encouraging accessible community living in BC's national parks; see Canada *Travel Notes*.

Disabled Peoples' International, 101–107 Evergreen Place, Winnipeg, Manitoba R3L 2T3 (☎204/287-8010).

Disabled Women's Network, 658 Danforth, Suite 203, Toronto, ON M4J 1L1 (☎416/406-1080).

Epilepsy Canada, 2099 Alexandre de Sève, Suite 27, CP 1560, Station C, Montréal, PQ H2L 4K8 (☎514/876-7455). Nearly 60 offices in major cities, listed in the phone book; issues certificate of eligibility for "two for one" fares on *VIA Rail*.

HeartWood Institute for Health, Learning and Leisure, RR #1 Rose Bay, Lunenburg County, NS B0J 2X0 (☎902/766-4351). Community Travels; see Travel, Tours, and Cruises *Travel Notes*.

Jewish Rehabilitation Hospital, Health Sciences Information Center, 3205 Place Alton Goldbloom, Chomedey, Laval, PQ H7V 1R2 (☎514/688-9550). Vast collection of access guides (see *Books*).

Kéroul, 4545 Pierre-de-Coubertin, CP 1000, succ. M, Montréal, PQ H1V 3R2 (☎514/252-3104). Membership organization with many services for travelers; see Canada *Travel Notes* for more information.

Learning Disabilities Association of Canada, 333 Chapel St., Ottawa, ON K1N 7Z2 (☎613/238-5721).

Multiple Sclerosis Society of Canada, 250 Bloor St. E., Suite 820, Toronto, ON M4W 3P9 (☎416/922-6055).

The Ontario March of Dimes, 60 Overlea Blvd., Toronto, ON M4H 1B6 (☎416/425-0501). Summer camps, adventure programs; see Travel, Tours, and Cruises *Travel Notes*.

Walter Dinsdale Center (Disability Information Services of Canada), 839 5th Ave., SW, Suite 610, Calgary, AL T2P 3C8 (☎403/266-0095).

In the UK

Across Trust, 70/72 Bridge Rd., East Molesey, Surrey KT8 9HF (☎081/783 1355). "Jumbulances" for organized European vacations or for rent to other groups.

Arthritis Care, 18 Stephenson Way, Euston, London NW1 2HD (☎071/916 1500). Vacation accommodation in the UK, publishes *Arthritis News* which covers many issues and contains travel items.

Association for Spina Bifida and Hydrocephalus, Asbah House, 42 Park Rd. Peterborough PE1 2UQ (☎0733/555988) Residential activity and leisure courses.

British Deaf Association, 38 Victoria Place, Carlisle, Cumbria CA1 1HU (☎0228/48844 voice; ☎0228/28719 Vistel). Some organized vacations.

British Diabetic Association, 10 Queen Anne St., London W1M 0BD (☎071/323 1531). Activity and study courses.

British Nursing Association, 82 Great North Rd., Hatfield AL9 5BL (☎0707/263544). Also local branches. Trained nurses for escort, residential, or visiting assistance in Britain or abroad.

British Red Cross, 9 Grosvenor Crescent, London SW1X 7EJ (☎071/235 5454). Also local offices. Holidays, escorts, helpers, loan of equipment within the UK.

British Ski Club for the Disabled, Mr H.M. Sturges (Chairman), Spring Mount, Berwick St. John, Shaftesbury, Dorset SP7 0FQ (☎0747/88515). Holidays and instruction abroad.

British Sports Association for the Disabled, 34 Osnaburgh St., London NW1 3ND (☎071/388 7277). Information on sports and training.

Camping for the Disabled, 20 Burton Close, Dawley, Telford, Shropshire TF4 2BX (☎0952/507653 evenings; ☎0743/75889 day). Advice on campground facilities in the UK and abroad, organized weekends in the summer.

The Caravan Club, East Grinstead House, East Grinstead, West Sussex RH9 1UA (☎0342/326944). List of club sites in England, Scotland, and Wales with adapted rest room/showers.

DIAL UK, Park Lodge, St. Catherine's Hospital, Tickhill Rd., Balby, Doncaster DN4 8QN (☎0302/310123). Disability helpline.

Disability Now, monthly newspaper, published by *The Spastics Society*, 12 Park Crescent, London W1N 4EQ (☎071/636 5020).

Disabled Drivers' Association (*DDA*), Ashwellthorpe Hall, Norwich NR16 1EX (☎050841/449). Manage fully accessible *Ashwellthorpe Hall Hotel*, and arrange ferry concessions for members; travel and access reported in magazine, *Magic Carpet*.

Disabled Drivers' Motor Club (*DDMC*), Cottingham Way, Thrapston, Northants. NN14 4PL (☎08012/4724). Information for disabled drivers, ferry concessions, travel and access reported in magazine, *The Disabled Driver*.

Disaway Trust, 2 Charles Rd., Merton Park, London SW19 3BD (☎081/543 3431). Group vacations in the UK and abroad.

Holiday Care Service, 2 Old Bank Chambers, Station Rd., Horley, Surrey RH6 9HW (☎0293/774535). Information on all aspects of travel; see England and Wales *Travel Notes*.

John Grooms Association for the Disabled, 10 Gloucester Drive, London N4 2LP (☎081/800 8695). Accessible hotels and self-catering accommodation throughout the UK; room rate concessions at the *London Tara Hotel*.

Jubilee Sailing Trust, Test Rd., Eastern Docks, Southampton SO1 1GG (☎0703/631388; reservations ☎0703/631395). Voyages on the specially designed *Lord Nelson*.

MENCAP (*Royal Society for Mentally Handicapped Children and Adults*) *Holiday Services Office*, 119 Drake St., Rochdale, Lancashire OL16 1PZ (☎0706/54111). UK vacation program for unaccompanied children and adults; guide listing accommodation where mentally disabled guests are welcome.

Mobility International, 228 Borough High St., London SE1 1JX (☎071/403 5688). Travel information and advice, plus own program of leisure and study.

Multiple Sclerosis Society, 25 Effie Rd., London SW6 1EE (☎071/736 6267). Travel information and UK accommodation.

National Federation of Kidney Patients Associations, Laurentian House, Stanley St., Worksop S81 7HX (☎0909/487795). Travel advice.

Operation Raleigh, Alpha Place, Flood St., London SW3 5SZ (☎071/351 7541). Expeditions worldwide.

Parkinson's Disease Society, 36 Portland Place, London W1N 3DG (☎071/255 2432). Group vacations in the UK and Venice.

Physically Handicapped and Able Bodied (*PHAB*), 12–14 London Rd., Croydon CR0 2TA (☎081/667 9443). Program of vacations, some abroad, for all ages and abilities.

Project Phoenix Trust, Overseas Study Tours for the Disabled, 56 Burnaby Rd., Southend-on-Sea, Essex SS1 2TL (☎0702/466412). Group study tours, travel advice.

RADAR (*The Royal Association for Disability and Rehabilitation*), 25 Mortimer St., London W1N 8AB (☎071/637 5400; TDD ☎071/637 5315). Information on all aspects of travel (as well as many other matters); see England and Wales *Travel Notes* for more information.

Riding for the Disabled Association, Avenue "R," National Agricultural Center, Kenilworth, Warks. CV8 2LY (☎0203/696510). Riding and driving vacations.

Royal National Institute for the Blind (*RNIB*), 224 Great Portland St., London W1N 6AA (☎071/388 1266). Information on their own holiday hotels. Books available on cassette or in Braille can be obtained from Customer Services, PO Box 173, Peterborough PE2 0WS (☎0733/370777).

St. John Ambulance HQ, 1 Grosvenor Crescent, London SW1X 7EF (☎071/235 5231). UK ambulance, escort, nursing or care attendants arranged through local offices (listed in phone book).

Spastics Society, 16 Fitzroy Square, London W1P 5HQ (☎071/387 9571). Runs the *Churchtown Farm Field and Studies Centre*; publishes *Disability Now* (see above).

Spinal Injuries Association, 76 St. James's Lane, London N10 3DF (☎081/444 2121). Fully adapted trailers and narrowboats; Care Attendant Agency; co-production (with the *Automobile Association*) of *The World Wheelchair Traveler* (see *Books*).

Uphill Ski Club, 12 Park Crescent, London W1N 4EQ (☎071/636 1989). Program of winter sports vacations.

Winged Fellowship Trust, Angel House, 20–32 Pentonville Rd., London N1 9XD (☎071/833 2594). Group tours for severely physically disabled adults at adapted UK centers and overseas.

WRVS (*Women's Royal Voluntary Service*), 234–244 Stockwell Rd., London SW9 9SP (☎071/733 3388). Non-medical escort service on public transit or for journeys to and from local stations or airports.

WHEREVER YOU GO, WE'LL BE WAITING.

From Stockholm to Sydney, New York to Beijing, there's a Holiday Inn® hotel that's just right for you.

In more than 1,600 locations in 53 countries around the world, you can choose among Holiday Inn®, Holiday Inn Crowne Plaza®, Holiday Inn Express®, or Holiday Inn Garden Court®* hotels to match your travel needs. You'll always find comfortable rooms and quality service you can depend on.

No matter where your travels take you, it's nice to know that Holiday Inn will be there, waiting for you.

STAY WITH SOMEONE YOU KNOW®

Amtrak®

It's called a train. And on it you'll find yourself settled comfortably, glancing out your window at awe-inspiring landscapes you will only see by crossing America by train. Passing the time with a good book. A good nap.

Think of it as taking a cruise through a desert, some mountains, a forest and the occasional tunnel.

Dining on fine cuisine prepared by our chefs. And being served by a gracious staff. On a train you can travel to any one of over 500 destinations. And see at least that many undiscovered places along the way.

Amtrak offers priority to passengers with disabilities who wish to reserve Special Roomettes and Special Bedrooms. These are private accommodations specially designed for use by passengers with disabilities and offer seating by day and comfortable provisions by night. All of Amtrak's major city stations, and most other staffed stations, are accessible to passengers with disabilities and will offer assistance in boarding and detraining, including wheelchair lifts.

Air Canada are striving to provide accessible transport for everyone. We look forward to welcoming you aboard.

For further information on our services please contact your local Air Canada office.